ISBN 978-0-265-04484-1
PIBN 11035237

English
Français
Deutsche
Italiano
Español
Português

www.forgottenbooks.com

Mythology Photography **Fiction**
Fishing Christianity **Art** Cooking
Essays Buddhism Freemasonry
Medicine **Biology** Music **Ancient**
Egypt Evolution Carpentry Physics
Dance Geology **Mathematics** Fitness
Shakespeare **Folklore** Yoga Marketing
Confidence Immortality Biographies
Poetry **Psychology** Witchcraft
Electronics Chemistry History **Law**
Accounting **Philosophy** Anthropology
Alchemy Drama Quantum Mechanics
Atheism Sexual Health **Ancient History**
Entrepreneurship Languages Sport
Paleontology Needlework Islam
Metaphysics Investment Archaeology
Parenting Statistics Criminology
Motivational

THE PRACTICE

IN

CIVIL ACTIONS AND PROCEEDINGS

IN THE

SUPREME COURT OF PENNSYLVANIA,

IN THE

DISTRICT COURT AND COURT OF COMMON PLEAS

FOR THE

City and County of Philadelphia,

AND IN THE

COURTS OF THE UNITED STATES.

BY FRANCIS J. TROUBAT AND WILLIAM W. HALY.

THIRD EDITION—BY FRANCIS WHARTON.

IN TWO VOLUMES.
VOL. I.

PHILADELPHIA:
JAMES KAY, JUN. & BROTHER, 193 MARKET STREET.
LAW BOOKSELLERS AND PUBLISHERS.
1853.

PHILADELPHIA:

T. K. AND P. G. COLLINS, PRINTERS.

TO

PREFACE TO THIRD EDITION.

UPON the retirement of Mr. TROUBAT from active practice, shortly after the publication of the second edition of this work, the preparation of the present edition devolved upon Mr. HALY, who at the time of his death had collected a great mass of Notes which it was his intention, had he lived, to have at once worked into the text. The materials which thus passed into the hands of the undersigned he has used with but little alteration, confining himself to placing them in what appeared to him their proper position, and adding to them references to the omitted cases, so that the work should present a complete abstract of the practical decisions in the Pennsylvania courts down to the publication of the sixth volume of Mr. HARRIS's Reports. In closing his duties, he has the pleasure to return his acknowledgments to several professional brethren for their aid, and in particular to Mr. TROUBAT for the chapters on Foreign and Domestic Attachment, to Mr. LEX for that on Scire Facias, to Mr. M'MURTRIE for that on Affidavits of Defence, and to Mr. M. P. HENRY for those on the Federal Courts, and on Costs. To one other gentleman, also, it may not be out of place to ascribe a large portion of whatever value the present edition may possess. Judge SHARSWOOD was good enough to place in the editor's hands the manuscript volumes containing his decisions on questions of practice since he entered upon the Presidency of the District Court. They have been introduced at large as notes to the following pages, under their respective heads; and to them the student will turn for a terse elucidation of the law, and the lawyer for an authoritative exposition of the practice. To this edition, also, will be found appended, a Table of Cases, and a Full and Complete Index embracing both volumes under one head.

Mr. HALY died early in the morning of December 27th, 1851. A violent fire was raging a few steps from his home, and when he was last seen he was endeavoring to assist the tenant of a shop on the lower floor of the burning building to remove a portion of his goods. Immediately afterwards the rafters fell in, and when, in a few hours, the ruins were cleared away, the memorials that remained were enough only to justify the belief that his death must have been as instant as it was unwarned. He was a man of excellent professional acquirements, of kindly manners, and of an open and genial temper, which never failed him in life, and which threw around his last melancholy hour a grace which will print his memory the more deeply in the breasts not only of his professional brethren, but of the hundreds who have drawn and may yet draw from this work their first acquaintance with the practice of the Pennsylvania Law. Perhaps the best monument that could be erected to his memory is the volumes which his first labors aided to construct, and his last efforts retouched.

F. W.

PHILADELPHIA, *February*, 1853.

TABLE OF CONTENTS.

VOLUME I.

CHAPTER I.

OF THE COURTS.

CHAPTER II.

OF THE EQUITY JURISDICTION OF THE FOREGOING COURTS.

I.—B

CHAPTER III.

OF THE OFFICERS OF THE COURTS.

CHAPTER IV.

OF THE COURTS OF THE UNITED STATES.

CHAPTER V.

OF ATTORNEYS, AND OF THE PROSECUTION AND DEFENCE OF ACTIONS BY
ATTORNEYS.

CHAPTER VI.

OF THE MODES OF COMMENCING ACTIONS.

CHAPTER VII.

OF THE CAPIAS AD RESPONDENDUM FOR THE COMMENCEMENT OF PERSONAL
ACTIONS.

CHAPTER VIII.

PRIVILEGE FROM ARREST UNDER ACT ABOLISHING IMPRISONMENT FOR DEBT.

CHAPTER IX.

OF THE COMMENCEMENT OF ACTIONS BY THE AGREEMENT OF PARTIES
WITHOUT A WRIT

CHAPTER X.

OF THE ARREST; OF THE BAIL TO BE TAKEN BY THE SHERIFF.

CHAPTER XI.

OF THE RULE TO SHOW CAUSE OF ACTION, AND WHY THE DEFENDANT
SHOULD NOT BE DISCHARGED ON COMMON BAIL

CHAPTER XII.

OF SPECIAL BAIL, AND BAIL UNDER ACT OF 1842.

CHAPTER XIII.

CHAPTER XIV.

OF JUDGMENT BY DEFAULT.

CHAPTER XV.

OF JUDGMENT BY CONFESSION.

CHAPTER XVI.

CHAPTER XVII.

OF PROCEEDINGS BETWEEN THE DECLARATION AND PLEA.

CHAPTER XVIII.

OF PLEAS.

CHAPTER XIX.

OF DISCONTINUANCE AND NOLLE PROSEQUI.

CHAPTER XX.

CHAPTER XXI.

CHAPTER XXII.

CHAPTER XXIII.

OF THE PROCEEDINGS FROM ISSUE TO TRIAL.

CHAPTER XXIV.

OF TRIAL, AND ITS INCIDENTS.

CHAPTER XXV.

OF MOTIONS FOR NEW TRIALS, AND TO TAKE OFF NONSUITS, AND ARREST OF JUDGMENT.

CHAPTER XXVI.

OF JUDGMENT.

CHAPTER XXVII.

PROCEEDINGS IN ERROR.

CHAPTER XXVIII.

OF COSTS.

CHAPTER XXIX.

OF EXECUTION.

CHAPTER XXX.

OF MOTIONS AND AUDITA QUERELA.

CHAPTER I.

OF THE COURTS.

By the Constitution of Pennsylvania(a) the judicial power is vested in a Supreme Court, in Courts of Oyer and Terminer, and General Jail Delivery; in a Court of Common Pleas, Orphans' Court, Register's Court, and a Court of Quarter Sessions of the peace, for each county; in Justices of the Peace, and in such other courts as the legislature may from time to time establish. The legislature has availed itself of the power thus given to it, to establish various *District Courts*, for the trial of *civil pleas*, in various parts of the State, and amongst them, one for the city and county of Philadelphia. The present chapter will present a view of the organization and jurisdiction of the Supreme Court, and also of the District Court, and the Court of Common Pleas, for the city and county of Philadelphia. If it should be inquired why we thus restrict the consideration of the subject, instead of endeavoring to produce a work which should comprehend the course of practice in the District Courts and Common Pleas of the other counties, we reply, in the first place, that a great portion of the following pages will be found applicable by the practitioners in those courts; and in the second place we adopt, as an answer, the language of the revisers of the laws of this State, when detailing the difficulties to be encountered in compiling a satisfactory system of procedure. "Local peculiarities which cannot be melted down; the constitution of our courts which has been often changed, and has rarely been adapted to the suitable exercise of all necessary powers; the jurisdiction of justices of the peace to try civil actions; certain legislative reforms already alluded to, enacted with the benevolent view of lessening the amount of litigation, and enabling all persons to act for themselves in the pursuit and application of remedies, but which, it is believed, have not produced the expected result: all these circumstances must be considered and allowed for, in the revision of the laws relating to the administration of justice. We may be permitted to make another remark in this connection. We have in this commonwealth a Supreme Court, composed of five judges; four District Courts, composed of six judges; fifty-two Courts of Common Pleas, containing eighteen president judges and one hundred and four associates, making altogether, one hundred and thirty-three judges of courts

(a) Art. V. § 1. By an amendment of the Constitution, adopted in 1850, the judiciary of Pennsylvania has been made elective, and other changes effected in the organization of the courts. The provisions of this amendment, as well as those of the act of April 15, 1851 (Pamph. L. 648), passed to put it in practical operation, will be found under the appropriate heads.

of record, not to mention justices of the peace. The District Courts
and Common Pleas are independent of each other, and to a considerable
extent of the Supreme Court. There must always be in those tribunals
a great amount of business and proceedings which is not subject to the
revision of the Supreme Court, by writ of error or appeal. This is
peculiarly true of the method of administering justice, and hence it will
be seen that in calculating any scheme for the administration of justice,
by so many independent tribunals, great allowances must be made for
its irregular or inconsistent operation, and for great varieties in the
understanding and application of it, which cannot be set right by the
ordinary control of the Supreme Court. The local position, too, of the
different courts, is a circumstance not to be lost sight of. The habits
and arrangements of the courts in the cities are widely different from
those of the rural districts, and these latter often differ widely from
each other in those respects. The system of process and pleadings,
which might suit very well the convenience of the city courts, might be
found to work very badly in the country; and that which was adapted
to a thickly settled country, might be very inconvenient in a newly
settled one. The peculiarities in our condition which we have adverted
to, *tend to create varieties of practice, or to interfere with that uniformity
which should characterize the administration of justice throughout the
commonwealth;* and, at all events, embarrass the compilation of a general and comprehensive system, which ought to embrace all quarters and
apply to all courts."

SECTION I.

OF THE SUPREME COURT.

Under this head will be considered:—
    I. Organization of Supreme Court.
    II. Organization of Nisi Prius under act of 1834.
    III. Past History of Supreme Court.
    IV. Present Jurisdiction of Supreme Court.
    V. Present Jurisdiction of Nisi Prius.
    VI. Review by Commissioners.

I. *Organization of Supreme Court.*

There shall be holden and kept at the times and places, and during
the terms hereinafter appointed, a court of record, the name and style
whereof shall be "The Supreme Court of Pennsylvania."

The Supreme Court is hereby declared to consist of a chief justice
and four associate judges; and the said judges, or a majority of them,
when convened for the purpose agreeably to law, shall have power to
hold the said court. § 2.

It shall be the duty of the governor, from time to time, as any
vacancy may occur in the office of chief justice or of a judge of the said
court, to commission, by a distinct patent, under the great seal of the

commonwealth, a person of known integrity and ability, skilled in the laws, to supply such vacancy, distinguishing in such patent, the name of the office to which he may be so appointed.(d) § 3.

For the purpose of holding the said Supreme Court, the commonwealth is hereby declared to be divided into four districts, denominated the Eastern District, the Western District, the Northern District, and the Middle District: the Eastern District consists of the city and county of Philadelphia, and the counties Bucks, Chester, Delaware, Northampton, Montgomery, Lehigh, Pike, and Wayne,(e) [Monroe,(f) Schuylkill,(g) Carbon;(h)] the Northern District, of the counties Northumberland, Luzerne, Lycoming, Bradford, Potter, Tioga, Susquehanna, Columbia, Union, [Wyoming,(i) Sullivan,(j) Montour,(k) M'Kean, Clinton;(l)] the Middle District, of the city and county of Lancaster, the counties Dauphin, Berks, York, Lebanon, Mifflin, Centre, Clearfield, Juniata, Huntingdon, Cumberland, Bedford, Franklin, Adams, Perry, [Blair,(m) Fulton;(n)] the Western District, of the city of Pittsburg, and the counties Alleghany, Somerset, Westmoreland, Fayette, Greene, Washington, Beaver, Butler, Mercer, Crawford, Erie, Warren, Venango, Armstrong, Cambria, Indiana, Jefferson, [Clarion,(o) Elk,(p) Lawrence,(q) Forrest.(r)] § 4.

The judges of the said Supreme Court shall annually hold five terms of the said court, at the places and at and during the terms hereinafter specified, if the business depending in the said court at the respective places of holding the same shall require it, to wit: One term at the city of Philadelphia, to commence on the second Monday in December, and to continue three weeks, for the Eastern District aforesaid; one other term at the said city of Philadelphia, to commence on the third Monday in March, and to continue two weeks, also for the eastern district aforesaid; one term at the borough of Harrisburg, to commence on the second Monday of May, and continue eight weeks, for the Middle District aforesaid; one term at Pittsburg, in the county of Alleghany, to commence on the first Monday of September, and to continue eight weeks, for the Western District aforesaid; one term at Sunbury, in the county of Northumberland, to commence on the second Monday in July, and to continue two weeks, for the said Northern District. § 5.(s)

Provided, That the judges of the said Supreme Court shall continue, by adjournment, the said terms, whenever the business which may be depending before them at any of the places aforesaid shall render it necessary, so always as not to interfere with their duties in any other of the districts aforesaid. § 6.

(d) Altered, *post*, pp. 5, 6.
(e) See Act 1841, Pamph. L. 55, § 9, and Act 1849, Pamph. L. 254, § 1.
(f) Act 1836, Pamph. L. 434, § 11.
(g) Act 1842, Pamph. L. 458, § 1.
(h) Act 1843, Pamph. L. §§ 5, 9.
(i) Act 1842, Pamph. L. 226, § 12.
(j) Act 1847, Pamph. L. 465, § 13.
(k) Act 1850, Pamph. L. 660, § 11.
(l) Act April 2, 1852, § 2.

(m) Act 1846, Pamph. L. 64, § 14.
(n) Act 1850, Pamph. L. 807, § 10.
(o) Act 1839, Pamph. L. 53, § 10.
(p) Act 1843, Pamph. L. 312, § 11.
(q) Act 1849, Pamph. L. 553, § 9.
(r) Res. April 11, 1848, Pamph. L. 1851, App. 745, compared with Act of 1849, Pamph. L. 368, §§ 1, 3.
(s) See *post*, p. 5.

It shall be the duty of the judges of the said Supreme Court, or one of them, to attend on the last Monday in July, at the place appointed by law for holding the said court for the Eastern District aforesaid, to grant rules, make all necessary orders touching any suit, action, writ of error, process, pleadings, or other proceedings, returned to or depending in the said court at the said place, preparatory to the hearing, trial, or decision of such action, writ of error, process, pleading or other proceeding. § 7.

The said Supreme Court shall have, in each of the districts aforesaid, a seal, for the use of the said court, having engraven thereon the arms of this commonwealth, and underneath the arms the figures "1776," and around the edge and near the extremity or margin thereof the words following: "Seal of the Supreme Court of Pennsylvania," and such other words and devices as are inscribed on the seals of the said court now in use; and the said seals may be renewed under the direction of the said court as often as occasion shall require. § 8.

A prothonotary or clerk shall be appointed for the said Supreme Court at each of the places of holding the same as aforesaid; he shall have the custody of the records and seal of the court for the respective district, and keep the same at the place of holding such court, and in the apartments provided by authority of law for that purpose; and he shall faithfully perform, under the direction of the court, all the duties appertaining to his office. § 9.

The prothonotary of the said Supreme Court, and such other discreet persons as the said court may from time to time appoint, shall be, within the districts where they respectively reside, commissioners of bail, having, severally, full power to take and receive recognizances of bail in any suit or action depending in the said court. § 10.

The first day and last day of every term of the said Supreme Court, in every of the said districts, shall be a common day of return of all writs and process, whether original, mesne, or judicial, or other proceeding, issuing from the said court, in the respective districts, at the election of the party suing out the same. § 11.

Provided nevertheless, That judicial process, which shall bear teste on the first day of any term as aforesaid, shall not be made returnable on the last day of the same term, except in such cases and for such purposes only, as the said court by their rules or by special order appoint and direct. § 12.

The last Monday in July, in each and every year, shall be a common day for the teste and return of all writs and process issuing out of the said court, in the Eastern District aforesaid, in the same manner as at the regular terms of the said court. § 13.

The said Supreme Court is authorized also to appoint special return days in the said court, in term time or vacation, in each and every of the districts aforesaid, for the convenience of suitors and the furtherance of justice, and the days and times so appointed, having been entered upon the records of the said court for the respective district, shall thenceforth be deemed legal return days therein. § 14.

The judges of the Supreme Court shall have power to prescribe, by rule of court, certain days within the terms thereof, to be holden as aforesaid, for the return of writs from the several judicial districts comprized within the respective districts of the said Supreme Court, and the causes returned thereon shall be taken up in the order so established. § 15.

By a Resolution of 10th April, 1835,(t) it was provided, That the judges of the Supreme Court of this commonwealth shall have power and authority to hold adjourned courts at the city of Lancaster, in the county of Lancaster, for the argument and decision of writs of error, and other business depending in said court from the county of Lancaster, at any time they may in their discretion think proper.

In 1850, the following amendment of the constitution was adopted. The judges of the Supreme Court, of the several Courts of Common Pleas, and of such other courts of record as are or shall be established by law, shall be elected by the qualified electors of the commonwealth, in the manner following, to wit: The judges of the Supreme Court by the qualified electors of the commonwealth at large; the president judges of the several Courts of Common Pleas, and of such other courts of record as are or shall be established by law, and all other judges required to be learned in the law, by the qualified electors of the respective districts over which they are to preside or act as judges; and the associate judges of the Courts of Common Pleas by the qualified electors of the counties respectively. The judges of the Supreme Court shall hold their offices for the term of fifteen years, if they shall so long behave themselves well (subject to the allotment hereinafter provided for, subsequent to the first election;) the president judges of the several Courts of Common Pleas, and of such other courts of record as are or shall be established by law, and all other judges required to be learned in the law, shall hold their offices for the term of ten years, if they shall so long behave themselves well; the associate judges of the Courts of Common Pleas shall hold their offices for the term of five years, if they shall so long behave themselves well; all of whom shall be commissioned by the governor; but for any reasonable cause, which shall not be sufficient grounds of impeachment, the governor shall remove any of them on the address of two-thirds of each branch of the legislature. The first election shall take place at the general election of this commonwealth next after the adoption of this amendment, and the commissions of all the judges who may be then in office shall expire on the first Monday of December following, when the terms of the new judges shall commence. The persons who shall then be elected judges of the Supreme Court shall hold their offices as follows: One of them for three years, one for six years, one for nine years, one for twelve years, and one for fifteen years, the term of each to be decided by lot by the said judges, as soon

(t) Pamph. L. 435.

after the election as convenient, and the result certified by them to the governor, that the commissions may be issued in accordance thereto. The judge whose commission will first expire shall be chief justice during his term, and thereafter each judge whose commission shall first expire shall in turn be the chief justice; and if two or more commissions shall expire on the same day, the judges holding them shall decide by lot which shall be the chief justice. Any vacancies happening by death, resignation or otherwise in any of the said Courts, shall be filled by appointment by the governor, to continue till the first Monday of December succeeding the next general election. The judges of the Supreme Court and the presidents of the several Courts of Common Pleas shall, at stated times, receive for their services an adequate compensation, to be fixed by law, which shall not be diminished during their continuance in office; but they shall receive no fees or perquisites of office, nor hold any other office of profit under this commonwealth, or under the government of the United States or any other State of this Union. The judges of the Supreme Court, during their continuance in office, shall reside within this commonwealth; and the other judges during their continuance in office shall reside within the district or county for which they were respectively elected.

By the 12th Sect. of the Act of April 15, 1851,(u) adopted in pursuance of the foregoing amendment, it was enacted, That in the event of any vacancy occurring in any judgeship in this commonwealth by death, resignation, removal from office, the failure to elect or otherwise, the governor shall appoint some suitable person to fill such vacancy until the first Monday in December following the next general election; and the qualified electors shall, at the first general election, which shall happen more than three calendar months after the vacancy shall occur, elect in the manner hereinbefore provided, a suitable person to such office for the unexpired term in the case of a judgeship of the Supreme Court, and for the full term of office in case of any other judgeship.

II. *Organization of Nisi Prius under Act of* 1834.

The Supreme Court, in term time, or a majority of the judges thereof in vacation, are empowered and enjoined, when occasion shall require, to direct the holding of Courts of Nisi Prius in the city of Philadelphia, for the city and county of Philadelphia, before the said judges, or some one or more of them, at such days, and during such times, as they shall designate. § 16.

The judges of the Supreme Court shall severally, as often as may be consistent with their other duties, and at least once in every year, at such times and for such periods as they shall appoint, hold Courts of Nisi Prius within the city and county of Philadelphia, and not elsewhere. § 17.

III. *Past History of Supreme Court.*

By a law passed in the year 1722, a Court of Record was established, and styled the Supreme Court of Pennsylvania.

(u) Pamph. L. 648.

This enactment declared that the court should hear and determine all pleas, plaints, and causes, removed or brought there from the various Courts of Common Pleas of the province, by virtue of writs of error, habeas corpus, or certiorari, or other remedial writs or process, and generally should minister justice to all persons, and exercise the jurisdictions and powers thereby granted as fully and amply as the Court of King's Bench, Common Pleas, and Exchequer, at Westminster, or any of them might or could do. The act of 1791, consequent upon the adoption of the constitution framed in convention the previous year, limited the exercise of this jurisdiction so far as to make it consistent with, and subordinate to, that constitution; and many subsequent acts of assembly lessened the powers of the Court still more.(v)

This Court was not a Court of Errors and Appeals *in the last resort*, until 1806. In the charter granted by Charles II. to William Penn, the king reserved to himself and his successors, an appellate jurisdiction touching any judgment which should be given in the Courts of the province. This provision was put in practice until the Revolution. By an act passed in 1780, this reserved jurisdiction was vested in a Court of Errors and Appeals. This act was repealed in 1791, and the court was then organized upon a plan adapted to the changes made by the Constitution of the United States and that of this State. The new Court of Errors and Appeals consisted of the president judges of the several Common Pleas, and of the judges of the Supreme Court, and was held at the seat of government. It reviewed the decisions of the latter court upon appellate process.(w) By the act of 24th February, 1806, this court was abolished, and its powers and jurisdiction were vested in the Supreme Court.

Previously, or at least for a long time prior to the year 1786, this court exercised no original jurisdiction in civil actions, except in cases of fines and common recoveries, which, though actions in form, are in substance no more than conveyances of record.(x) It was not until that year that this jurisdiction was given by act of assembly, which confined it to the county of Philadelphia, where issues in fact were tried, both in bank and at Nisi Prius; and thus the law continued till the year 1806, when this jurisdiction was taken away. It was restored in 1810 to the same county, in actions wherein the matter in controversy was of the value of five hundred dollars and upwards, but the trial of issues in fact by the court in bank was prohibited;(y) and so the law stood until abrogated by the legislature in the year 1825. But it was restored in the succeeding year, and the same jurisdiction still continues.

Between the years 1786 and 1799, assizes or Courts of Nisi Prius in the several counties were held by the justices of this court between the terms, at such times as they thought most convenient for the people. But original writs did not issue from the Supreme Court to the several counties; but writs of *certiorari* and *habeas corpus* only, by virtue of which, actions were removed from the inferior courts, and the issues in fact arising on them were tried at Nisi Prius, after which judgment was rendered in bank.(z) In 1799, Circuit Courts, as they were called,

(v) 2 Rawle, 386.
(w) See Brac. Law Mis. 166, 253.
(x) 4 Binn. 121.

(y) Ibid.
(z) Ibid. 122.

were substituted for Courts of Nisi Prius, so far as respected the counties exclusive of the city and county of Philadelphia. They were of the same nature as the latter courts, except that judgment *could be rendered* at the Circuit Courts, but subject to revision in term by *appeal*, in certain cases.(a) Two judges sat on trials at these courts, as they were wont to do at Nisi Prius, though not required by the act of assembly. But in 1806, the legislature provided that they should be held by one judge only, at least once in every year, in each county, and that no issues in fact should be tried by the court in bank. The circuit courts being found unwieldy and inconvenient, were abolished in 1809, and without a revival of the Nisi Prius courts in the same counties.(b)

The same act that restored the jurisdiction at Nisi Prius, in the county of Philadelphia,(c) also resuscitated the Circuit Courts for the other counties of the State. But the latter, after a faithful trial of them for eight years, were again abolished in 1834.

Prior to the act of 1836, before mentioned, and about to be quoted, the jurisdiction and powers of the Supreme Court were not expressly and conclusively defined or fixed by the Constitution of the State, or by any express enactment. Much of its jurisdiction was derived from statutes passed from time to time, according to exigencies. Part of its jurisdiction rested upon its own decisions. The case of the Commonwealth *v.* M'Closkey,(d) and the authorities in the same court which it confirms, deciding that the court had power to issue a *quo warranto* as a *civil* remedy, furnish an instance of this. Such also is the case of Hagerty,(e) which ruled that this court can send a *certiorari* to the Common Pleas, to remove their proceedings in civil cases for the purpose of inquiring whether they have exceeded their jurisdiction.

Some of its jurisdiction, or rather some jurisdiction that was thought to belong to it, was questioned; had never been exercised, and was left in doubt, until the enactment of 1836; as, for example, the power to issue a *mandamus* to the Common Pleas.(f) As far as regards its territorial extent, the jurisdiction of the Supreme Court is coextensive with the sovereignty and jurisdiction of the State; and it is the only tribunal which has the power to interfere by the writs of mandamus and quo warranto; or, to remove into it for revision and correction, by means of the writs of certiorari and of error, or by other appellate process, the proceedings of all the other inferior civil tribunals of the State. It still retains the powers and jurisdiction coextensively with the three great courts at Westminster, which the old act of assembly, before quoted, invested it with; restricted, however, by the constitution and laws in the manner above mentioned. It also, as will be more particularly seen hereafter, possesses the power under an act of assembly, to devise and frame new writs and forms of proceeding necessary for the complete exercise of the powers and jurisdiction of all the civil courts of the commonwealth.

(a) See Brac. L. Mis. 285, 191. 3 Binn. 90.

(b) Brac. L. Mis. 167, 285.
(c) The act of April 8, 1826.

(d) 2 Rawle, 369.
(e) 4 Watts, 305.
(f) See Kolb's Case, 4 Watts, 154.

IV. *Present Jurisdiction of Supreme Court.*

The act of June 16th, 1836(*g*), declares that the Supreme Court of this commonwealth shall have power to hear and determine all, and all manner of pleas, plaints, and causes which shall be brought, or removed there from any other court of this commonwealth by virtue of any writ or process issued by the said court, or any judge thereof, for that purpose, in the manner now practised and allowed, to examine and correct all, and all manner of errors of the justices, magistrates, and courts of this commonwealth, in the process, proceedings, judgments, and decrees, as well in criminal as in civil pleas or proceedings, and thereupon, to reverse, modify or affirm such judgments and decrees, or proceedings, as the law doth or shall direct; and generally, to minister justice to all persons, in all matters whatsoever, as fully and amply, to all intents and purposes, as the said court has heretofore had power to do, under the constitution and laws of this commonwealth;(*h*) and is required to issue execution or other process for the recovery of costs which have accrued, or may accrue in said Supreme Court, as well as in all cases which have been heretofore decided. § 1. (Derived from the 13th sect. of the act of 1722.(*i*))

The Supreme Court shall have original jurisdiction within the city and county of Philadelphia, in all civil actions, wherein the matter in controversy shall be of the value of five hundred dollars, or more. § 2. (Taken from the 1st sect. of the act of 1810.(*j*))

It shall be the duty of the Supreme Court, at their sessions in bank, from time to time, to devise and establish, by rule of court, such new writs and forms of proceedings, as, in their opinion, shall be necessary or convenient to the full, direct, and uniform execution of the powers and jurisdiction possessed by the said court, or by the Courts of Common Pleas, District Courts, Orphan's Courts, or Register's Courts. § 3. Vide *post*, the end of this section.

Provided, That nothing herein contained, shall be deemed to authorize the said court to enlarge, abridge, or alter the jurisdiction of any of the courts, or to impair the right of trial by jury, or to dispense with or to supply the use of any form of proceeding, which shall be made necessary, by any act of assembly. § 4.

Whenever the said court shall devise and establish any new writ or form, as aforesaid, or make any rule or order relative thereto, they shall cause notice thereof to be given to the courts, or to the president judges of the courts for which such writ, form, or rule shall be made or

---

(*g*) Pamph. Laws, 784.
(*h*) A portion of this section, six or seven lines, has been omitted by us. It gives the judges four dollars per day instead of thirty shillings for travelling expenses. It was evidently introduced in the Legislature after the other parts of the section were composed, as it makes the "Chief Justice and assistant judges" the nominative to the verb "*is*," of the line "is required to issue execution," &c.
(*i*) 1 Sm. Laws, 139.
(*j*) 5 Sm. Laws, 158.

appointed, and also to the governor of the commonwealth, for the information of the legislature at their next session. § 5.

The courts, or the president judges of the courts to which any such rule shall be made known, shall cause the same to be published in open court, and to be recorded with the rules of court, and after the expiration of three months from the recording of such rule, the same shall be deemed to be obligatory, and in full effect.   § 6.

The judges of the Supreme Court shall have full power and authority, when, and as often as there may be occasion, to issue writs of habeas corpus, writs of certiorari, and writs of error, and all remedial and other writs and process, returnable to the said court.   § 7.

All the writs shall be granted of course, and the style thereof shall be " The Commonwealth of Pennsylvania;" they shall bear teste in the name of the chief justice of the said court for the time being, or if he be a party, in the name of one of the other judges of the said court, and they shall be sealed with the judicial seal of the said court. § 8.

These sections (the 7th and 8th) are taken from the act of 1772, §§ 11—16, with such alterations as are necessary to adapt the provisions to our present form of government.

Besides the powers hitherto possessed by the Supreme Court, to issue writs of mandamus, the said court shall have power to issue such writs to any other court or tribunal constituted by the authority of the laws of this commonwealth, in all cases where such interposition shall, in the discretion of the said court, be necessary to the advancement and due administration of justice.   § 10.(k)

As soon as the Supreme Court shall have rendered judgment, or made a final decree or decision, in any cause, action or matter brought into the same by writ of error, certiorari, or appeal, such court shall order the records thereof, with their judgment or decree thereon written, and duly certified, to be remitted to the appropriate court, which judgment, decree, or decision, such court shall duly carry into execution and effect; or the said Supreme Court may, if they see cause, order execution thereof to be done by process, issued out of the same, and thereupon, order the record to be remitted, as aforesaid.(l)   § 11.

The Supreme Court has inherent power to revise the proceedings of all inferior jurisdictions, to correct errors on the face of their proceedings;(m) but this revisory power may constitutionally be taken away or withheld in express terms, or by necessary implication.(n)

(k) See Kolb's case, 4 Watts, 154.
(l) For explanatory remarks on the various heads of this act, see the end of the present section, and for adjudication on powers of Supreme Court, see Wharton's Digest, Courts, viii. The original jurisdiction of the Supreme Court in Equity, will be treated of in chapter II.
(m) Daniels v. Com. 7 Barr, 371. Torrence v. Com. 9 Barr, 184.
(n) Carpenter's case, 2 H. 486.

V. *Present Jurisdiction of Nisi Prius.*

The original jurisdiction of this court, exercised when sitting as a court of *Nisi Prius* in the county of Philadelphia, was, as prescribed by the 2d section of the above act, confined to suits where the matter in controversy shall be of the value of five hundred dollars or more. In actions sounding *purely in tort*, there is no standard for determining its jurisdiction, but the damages laid in the declaration;(*o*) except in *replevin*, where an issue is joined on the plea of no rent in arrear, and the amount of the rent claimed appeared from the indorsement on the writ or otherwise, this amount will alone determine the jurisdiction.(*p*) The Court of Nisi Prius was originally held twice a year in this county, (in the autumn and spring,) by a single justice of the Supreme Court, for the trial by jury of all civil actions, real, personal, and mixed, where the amount in controversy comes within the rate or degree above mentioned.· Unlike the Circuit Courts for the remaining counties, it possessed no other powers and attributes of a court than those necessary for the purpose of trying issues of fact; and in regard to it, the court in bank is in the nature of an appellate tribunal, reviewing its acts, upon motions for a new trial or in arrest of judgment. The following acts, however, give it, as will be seen, entirely a new complexion.

The Act of 26th July, 1842,(*q*) provided that it shall be the duty of one of the judges of the Supreme Court of Pennsylvania, to hold jury trials in all cases now pending or hereafter to be brought in said court in the city and county of Philadelphia, on original process, and for that purpose to hold four sessions per year, commencing on the first Mondays of (September),(*r*) November, January, and March, in each and every year, to continue two months if necessary, with power to direct the issuing of all the necessary precepts and venires, for the drawing, returning, and summoning of juries according to the laws now in force in the said Supreme Court, relating to jurors, to make all such rules of court as may be necessary for the speedy administration of justice within his jurisdiction, to hear and decide all motions relating to said process and cases, and to grant new trials when in his discretion it may be just. § 4.

Each of the said sessions shall be divided into two periods for jury trials, of at least three weeks each or longer, at the discretion of the said judge, and the remainder of the said session shall be appropriated to arguments. And it shall be the duty of the said Supreme Court, and it is hereby required to assign one of their number alternately to hold the said court of Nisi Prius as aforesaid, and the remaining judges of the said Supreme Court are authorized and required to hold courts in bank, in the several districts during the time occupied by one of the judges holding said Nisi Prius court. § 5.

And it shall be lawful for either party to take a bill of exceptions to any opinion or charge of the said judge, as is now practised and allowed

---

(*o*) 5 Binn. 522. 1 Serg. & R. 269.
(*p*) 5 Binn. 552.
(*q*) Pamph. L. 430.
(*r*) By the Act of April 18; 1846,

(Pamph. L. 378), so much of this section as makes it necessary for the Nisi Prius to be held on the first Monday in September, is repealed.

in the Courts of Common Pleas of this State, and whenever the said judge shall refuse to grant a new trial on points of law, or whenever either party shall tender a bill of exceptions as aforesaid, or in any case in said court where a writ of error is now allowed in a like case, to any Court of Common Pleas or District Court, it shall be lawful for the party aggrieved to require the said judge to grant an order to certify the record and bill of exceptions or either, as the case may be, to the judges of the Supreme Court in bank, for a hearing at the next term thereof, upon such party, his agent or attorney, making an affidavit that said order is not sought by him for the purpose of delay, and upon giving absolute security, with two sureties by recognizance for the payment of all damages and costs, in case the proceedings shall not be affirmed in the manner now practised and allowed in cases of writs of error, to the Courts of Common Pleas of this State : *Provided,* That such order shall not be a supersedeas to an execution, unless taken and perfected within twenty-one days after judgment shall be rendered and before said judge: *And Provided,* That nothing herein contained shall be construed to prevent the said judge from granting a new trial in any case as provided in the fourth section. § 6.(*s*)

The return days of all original process and final writs of execution, shall be monthly in the said courts, and the provisions of the second section of an act passed twenty-eighth March, one thousand eight hundred and thirty-five, entitled "An act to establish the District Court for the City and County of Philadelphia," and the provisions of the fourth, fifth, seventh, eleventh, and fourteenth sections of the supplement to the said act, passed eleventh March, one thousand eight hundred and thirty-six, and the provisions of the supplement thereto, passed the twelfth day of March, one thousand eight hundred and forty-two, and the provisions of the first, second, and third sections of the act of the twenty-second March, one thousand eight hundred and twenty-five, entitled "An act to prevent the failure of trusts," and the first, second, third, fourth, and fifth sections of the act, passed fourteenth April, one thousand eight hundred and twenty-eight, entitled "An act to prevent the failure of trusts, to provide for the settlement of accounts of trustees, and for other purposes," and the fifteenth, sixteenth, seventeenth, eighteenth, and nineteenth sections of the act passed the fourteenth June, one thousand eight hundred and thirty-six, entitled "An act relating to assignees for the benefit of creditors and other trustees," and the provisions of the second section of the act of the seventeenth March, one thousand eight hundred and thirty-eight, entitled "An act to empower the Court of Common Pleas of the City and County of Philadelphia, to appoint assignees or trustees in the place of the deceased assignees or trustees of John Vaughn, and for other purposes," shall be and the same are hereby extended to all original actions brought or to be brought in the Supreme Court of Pennsylvania, in the city and county of Philadelphia, and all the cases of trusts therein referred to, shall be and hereby are added to the jurisdiction of the said Nisi Prius judge, and all the powers, jurisdictions, and duties of the several courts therein prescribed and set forth, are hereby vested in the said Nisi Prius judge, in all such original

(*s*) 2 Barr, 406.

actions brought or to be brought in the said Supreme Court, in the said city and county, and to all such cases of trustees and trust estates: *Provided*, That any party who may intend to move for judgment, for want of an affidavit of defence in any original action now pending in said court shall file a copy of the instrument of writing or affidavit of loan, upon which such action was brought, within one month from the passage of this act, and give two weeks' notice thereof to the opposite party, or to his, or her, or to their attorney: *Provided further*, That no such motion for judgment, for want of an affidavit of defence, shall be made until the expiration of one month from the time of filing the copy of the instrument of writing or affidavit of loan. § 7.

The said judge holding courts of Nisi Prius, shall have full power and authority to enter judgment in all cases brought or to be brought in said Supreme Court, on original process, and to make all orders and decrees in such cases as fully as any court of record could or might make, and all trials of contested facts in equity or otherwise, which the Supreme Court in bank may order and direct, shall be tried before the said judge. § 8.

The said Nisi Prius judge shall take cognizance in all cases in equity now pending or hereafter to be instituted in the said Supreme Court, in the city and county of Philadelphia, under all existing and future acts of assembly, vesting equity jurisdiction in the said Supreme Court, in the city and county aforesaid, and shall hear and decide the same, and make all necessary decrees, as fully as the said Supreme Court in bank might or could do, and all subpœnas in equity shall be returnable on monthly return days, and it shall be the duty of the said judge to make and establish rules of court for speedy administration of justice in such cases, and upon any final decree in any case of equity which may be made by the said judge to grant an order to certify the records of such cases to the judges of the said Supreme Court in bank for revision upon the party aggrieved, his agent, solicitor, or attorney making affidavit, and on entering security as required by the second section of this act in cases commenced in said court by original process: *And provided*, That such order to certify the record shall not supersede any attachment or other process to enforce a final decree in equity, unless taken and perfected within twenty-one days after such final decree, and the said Nisi Prius judge shall, in all cases in equity, fix the amount of security to be entered by the aggrieved party, after final decree made by him, and it shall be the duty of the said judge to make and establish a tariff of fees and costs in such equity cases, and in all other cases in the said court, for services not provided for by the existing acts of assembly. § 9.

So much of any law as is altered or supplied by this act is hereby repealed. § 10.

Act of 15th March, 1847:(*t*) It shall and may be lawful hereafter to carry by certificate, judgments rendered in the Court of Nisi Prius, for the city and county of Philadelphia to the Supreme Court for review,

(*t*) Pamph. L. 348.

notwithstanding that the party obtaining such certificate shall not have given absolute security, with two sufficient sureties, by recognizance, for the payment of all damages and costs, in case the proceedings shall be affirmed; and notwithstanding that such party shall not carry the said judgment to the Supreme Court for hearing, at the next term thereof: and such certificate shall be a supersedeas of execution, issued out and executed in those cases, and in those only where the certificates shall have been required and obtained, and security entered, within three weeks from the day on which judgment shall have been rendered: *Provided always*, That the said certificate shall be required and obtained, within seven years after the judgment shall be rendered against the party requiring and obtaining the said certificate, unless the party entitled to the said certificate shall, at the time such title acrued, be within the age of twenty-one years, *covert, non compos mentis*, in prison, or out of the limits of the United States of America, in which case such person, his or her heirs, executors or administrators, (notwithstanding the said seven years be expired,) shall and may carry such judgment, by certificate, to the Supreme Court for review, so as the same be done within five years after his or her full age, discoverture, coming to sound mind, enlargement out of prison or return into some one of the United States of America, but not afterwards nor otherwise: *And provided also*, That the same tax shall be paid to the commonwealth, in those cases, as are now paid in cases of removals on writs of error. § 1.

As will be seen, these acts turn the Court of Nisi Prius into a distinct and independent court, whose duty is to enter judgment whenever a party is entitled to it. It bears very much the same relations to the Supreme Court, as does the District Court.(*u*)

Under the act which makes the Nisi Prius an independent court with power to give judgment, either party may take a bill of exceptions to the opinion of the judge as in the Common Pleas. By it two ways are provided for bringing *the law* of the case before the Supreme Court. 1st. By bill of exceptions to the rulings of the judge at the trial. 2d. By a certificate of his decision on the propriety of those rulings. Either of them may be taken, but not both; one or other must be superfluous. If a motion for a new trial be made and denied, it is conclusive. It is not ground for a writ of error at common law or under this statute. The court of error has no concern with the merits of the case.(*v*)

On appeal from Nisi Prius, where there is a certificate in defendant's favor, the plaintiff appealing must give security for that amount and costs.(*w*) But executors are not bound to give security.(*x*)

VI. *Review by Commissioners.*

The commissioners appointed to revise the civil code, say, that the principal part of this law is taken from the existing acts of assembly,

(*u*) Wharton's Dig., Courts, viii. (i.)
(*v*) Klein *v.* Franklin Ins. Co., 1 H. 249.
Sergeant *v.* Ingersoll, 3 H. 343.
(*w*) Churchman *v.* Parke, 2 B.arr, 406.
(*x*) Maule *v.* Shaffer, Ibid. 404.

and that, upon the subjects embraced in it, they thought it prudent to tread in the footsteps of their predecessors.

The 3d section is new in terms, but the principle is to be found in the old law. The statute of the 13th of Edward I., c. 24, enacted A. D. 1825, declares, " that whensoever, from henceforth, it shall fortune in the Chancery, that in one case a writ is found, and in like case falling under like law, and requiring like remedy, is found none, the clerks of the Chancery shall agree in making the writ ; or the plaintiffs may adjourn it until the next parliament ; and let the cases be written in which they cannot agree ; and let them refer themselves until the next parliament ; by consent of men learned in the law, a writ shall be made, lest it might happen after that, the court should long time fail to minister justice unto complainants." This part of the statute has been declared by the judges of the Supreme Court to be in force in this State. We have no general Chancery, however ; and according to the opinion of the Supreme Court in a recent case (*y*), " it is the duty of the *courts* themselves, so to fashion our remedies, as to administer relief to suitors according to the exigency of their business," &c. To maintain uniformity in legal proceedings among the various tribunals of this commonwealth, and prevent that conflict of practice which is often found inconvenient for the community, it seems to us proper that the Supreme Court should possess the power anciently given to the Chancellor of England,(*z*) of devising such new writs and forms of proceedings, as, in their opinion, shall be necessary or convenient for the due administration of justice. They possess, at present, the power of revising all inferior courts in this and other respects ; but without interfering with their authority as a court of error, it appears to us that much will be gained by giving them power to provide, by general rules, in the first instance, for any deficiency in the remedial law."

" The next three sections relate to the same subject. The 4th forbids any regulation which may interfere with the trial by jury, and the 5th requires notice thereof to be given to the governor, for the information of the legislature, at their next session. These provisions will prevent the possibility of any unconstitutional or unfit regulation being carried into effect."

The 10th section appeared necessary, " for the purpose of removing doubts respecting the power of the Supreme Court to issue writs of *mandamus* to inferior tribunals. This authority, which is sometimes essential to the adequate administration of justice, ought, we think, to be possessed by the Supreme Court—at present the highest judicial tribunal in the commonwealth."(*a*)

The 11th section is adopted from the 4th section of the act of 11th March, 1809,(*b*) with an addition, authorizing the Supreme Court to order execution, if they shall see cause, which may sometimes be expedient."

(*y*) Martzell *v.* Stauffer, 3 Penn. Rep. 402.

(*z*) 3 Black. Comm. 51.

(*a*) See 4 Watts, 154.

(*b*) 5 Sm. L. 15.

SECTION II.

OF THE DISTRICT COURT FOR THE CITY AND COUNTY OF PHILADELPHIA.

A chronological digest of the statutes relating to this court will afford, in the first instance, the best idea of its powers and jurisdiction.

The act of the 30th of March, 1811,(c) passed to provide for the erection of an additional court within the city and county of Philadelphia, after reciting that the Court of Common Pleas of the City and County of Philadelphia, from the various objects of its jurisdiction and the great increase and accumulation of business, was incompetent to the speedy and effectual administration of justice to the citizens of that district: enacts,

That there shall be a court of record established in and for the city and county of Philadelphia, by the name and style of *The District Court for the City and County of Philadelphia,* which shall consist of a president, and two assistant judges, any two of whom, in case of the absence or inability of the other, shall have power to try, hear, and determine all civil pleas and actions, real, personal, and mixed, and for the trial of all such pleas and actions, shall have and exercise the same powers, authorities, and jurisdiction as are now vested by law in the Court of Common Pleas for the City and County of Philadelphia: *Provided,* that the said court shall have no jurisdiction either originally or on appeal, except where the sum in controversy shall exceed one hundred dollars. § 1.

After providing for the transfer of causes from the Common Pleas then pending to this court, the second section continues, and the original jurisdiction of the said Court of Common Pleas of the city and county of Philadelphia, in all civil actions where the sum in controversy exceeds one hundred dollars, shall thenceforth cease and determine. § 2.

No suit shall be removed from the District Court by *certiorari* or *habeas corpus,* but in all cases the final judgment of the said District Court may be examined and affirmed or reversed on a writ of error from the Supreme Court, in a similar manner, and subject to the same limitations and provisions under which writs of error are now issued from the Supreme Court to the Court of Common Pleas of the City and County of Philadelphia. § 3.

The said District Court shall hold four terms in the course of each year, one to begin on the first Monday of June, the second on the first Monday of September, the third on the first Monday of December, and the fourth on the first Monday of March, respectively, and shall have full power and are hereby enjoined to hold adjourned courts whenever

(c) 5 Smith, 223.

the state of the business shall require it, and also make such regulations of practice as may most facilitate the progress of justice: *Provided always*, that if the number of suits before the said court should render it necessary, the judges of the said court shall sit daily (Sundays only excepted), during at least nine months in every year: *And provided also*, that the determination of no cause or action before the said court shall be delayed, beyond the fourth term, including that to which the said action was instituted, if the parties be prepared for trial at the times appointed by the said court; and if the judges of said court should wilfully delay any cause, suit, or action in readiness for trial as aforesaid, it shall constitute a misdemeanor in office. § 4.

The act of the 3d of March, 1812,(*d*) provides in the 2d and 3d sections that this court may direct that one or more panels of general or common jurors, and also one or more panels of special jurors shall be selected, summoned, and returned (according to the laws in force), for any one term of said court; and the process for each and every panel shall be made returnable at such particular day of the term as the said court shall direct and appoint. And every person whose name shall be drawn, and who shall have been legally summoned, but who shall not appear before the court, after being called three times, and due proof made by oath or affirmation, of the sheriff or other credible person, that each person, so making default, had been lawfully summoned, shall forfeit and pay for such default in not appearing, any fine not exceeding thirty dollars, that the court may think proper to inflict; and every juror, including those who shall not have appeared as aforesaid, shall forfeit and pay for every default in not answering when called, during the said term, such fine, not exceeding five dollars, as the court may think proper; which fines the court may direct the sheriff to levy and collect in the usual manner, and the said fines, when collected, shall be paid and applied, agreeably to the 3d section of the act of the 29th of March, 1805: *Provided nevertheless*, that the court, upon reasonable and satisfactory cause being made appear to them, may remit the whole, or any part of such fines.

With regard to these latter sections, it will be seen that the act of 1835, which created the present District Court, refers to and re-enacts them, so that they now constitute a part of the source of its powers and jurisdiction. During the interval of time that elapsed between the making of the acts of 1812 and 1835, six acts of assembly were passed in relation to this court, some of them to reorganize it for an additional term of years; but having expired by the limitation prescribed by the legislature, they are now of no interest, and of no utility to show the present framework or objects of this court.

The act of the 28th March, 1835,(*e*) being that to which the present court owes its organization, provides as follows:—
From and after the 30th day of March, 1835, there shall be a court of record established in and for the city and county of Philadelphia, by the name and style of *The District Court for the City and County of*

(*d*) 5 Smith, 300. (*e*) Pamph. L. 88.
I.—2

Philadelphia, which shall consist of three judges learned in the law, one of whom shall be president, who shall have and exercise the same authority, power, and jurisdiction, and be subject to the same duties and governed by the same provisions, as are enacted by the act, entitled, "an act to provide for the erection of an additional court within the city and county of Philadelphia," passed the 30th day of March, 1811, and the supplement to the said act, passed the 3d day of March, 1812; and so much of the said two last-mentioned acts as are not inconsistent with this act, are hereby revived and continued in force, from and after the said 30th day of March, 1835: *Provided,* That the first Monday in each and every month, shall be a day for the return of writs of summons (except summons in partition), of writs of *capias ad respondendum, scire facias of replevin,* of attachment of vessels under the act of 17th of March, 1784, writs of inquiry of damages and executions issued from said court, and such writs shall be directed to be returned to either of the said monthly return days, which may happen before the next term, or to the first return day of the next term, at the option of the party taking out the same; and in all suits instituted in said court, where returns are directed to be made to a monthly return day, the party may, after such returns of writs of summons, and *capias, scire facias, replevin,* attachment and inquiry, file declarations and other pleadings, put causes to issue and have them tried, and do all other matters and things in the prosecution of suits that might be done if the said writs were returned on the first return day of any term of said court: And *provided also,* That it shall be the duty of the said court to make such rules and regulations respecting proceedings against bail as will prevent bail from being fixed in any case sooner than if the above proviso relative to return days had not been enacted; and provided also that the stay of execution allowed by the seventh section of the act entitled, "an act to regulate arbitrations and proceedings in courts of justice," passed the 21st day of March, 1806, shall count from the return day to which the original process was returnable. § 1.

The next section which relates to the powers and jurisdiction of this court, is the fourth, the intervening ones appertaining to subjects which will be more appropriately treated of in future chapters. The 4th section is as follows:—

From and after the 30th day of March, 1835, all actions, matters, and things depending in the present District Court for the City and County of Philadelphia, and all process issued from and returnable thereto, shall be transferred to and proceeded in by the court established by this act, and shall have the same effect in law as if there had been no limitation to the present court, and the governor shall, on or before the 30th day of March, 1835, appoint and commission three persons learned in the law, to be judges of the court established by this act; and it shall be the duty of the said judges to meet on the 30th day of March, 1835, or as soon thereafter as possible, and proceed in the business of the court, and the judges of the present District Court for the City and County of Philadelphia are hereby enjoined and required to order the arrangement of business for the March term, and direct *venires* to issue for summoning the requisite number of panels of jurors to attend at said term of the court established by this act, agreeably to the provisions of the 2d section of the act entitled " a supplement to an act to provide for the erection of an additional court within the City and County of Philadelphia," passed the 3d day of March, 1812.   § 4.

The fifth·section provides, that any one of the judges of the court hereby established shall have power to try all civil pleas and actions, real, personal, and mixed, and to grant motions; and for these purposes shall have and exercise the same powers, authority, and jurisdiction as are hereby vested in the said court; and it shall be the duty of at least two of the said judges to sit separately at the same time, for the trial of causes, and the prothonotary of the said court shall appoint competent clerks to attend at said trials, when not present in person; and whenever it shall so happen that all of the said judges are not sitting at the same time, either separately or together, questions of bail, and other matters requiring early attention (to the decision of which a single judge is by the foregoing provisions or ordinary practice competent), shall not be permitted to interfere with jury trials, but shall be heard and disposed of by such one or more of the said judges as may not be then sitting for the trial of causes as aforesaid; that it shall be lawful for any one of the said judges, when he thinks expedient, to reserve questions of law which may arise on the trial of causes for the consideration and judgment of all the judges of said court sitting together: *Provided*, That either party shall have the right to a bill of exceptions to the opinion of the court as if the point had been ruled and decided on the trial of the cause.

The third section of the act of 1836,(*f*) passed as a supplement to the law under consideration, provides that each of the judges sitting alone shall have power to render judgment by default under the twentieth section of the prior act, and also in actions of partition.

The ninth section of the act of 1835, also provides, that each of the judges of the court hereby established shall have power to take and receive the acknowledgment or proof of all deeds, conveyances, mortgages, or other instruments of writing, touching or concerning any lands, tenements, or hereditaments, situate, lying, and being in any part of this State, and also power to take and receive the separate examination of any *feme covert*, touching or concerning her right of dower, or the conveyance of her estates, as fully to all intents and purposes whatsoever, as any president of any Court of Common Pleas may or can do.

The following sections, of the above-mentioned act of 1836, provide further as to the constitution of this court, that the said court sitting in bank, shall have power from time to time, by general rules and orders, to make such alterations and regulations in respect to the time and manner of pleading, and the form and effect of pleadings,· and the verification and amendment thereof, and to variances occurring between the cause or causes of action alleged, and the evidence offered in support thereof, in suits brought in the said court; and such rules for

(*f*) Pamph. L. 76.

carrying the same into effect, either by way of staying proceedings in
the action, or by the payment of costs, or otherwise, as shall be conducive to fairness, economy, and dispatch in the trial of such actions:
Provided, That nothing herein contained shall be so construed as in
any way to impair or affect the provisions of the fifth section of the
act passed March 21, 1806, entitled "an act to regulate arbitrations
and proceedings in courts of justice." § 6.

Whenever the defendant, upon the trial of a cause in the said court,
shall offer no evidence, it shall be lawful for the judge presiding at the
trial to order a judgment of nonsuit to be entered, if in his opinion the
plaintiff shall have given no such evidence as in law is sufficient to
maintain the action, with leave, nevertheless, to move the court in bank
to set aside such judgment of nonsuit; and in case the said court in
bank shall refuse to set aside the nonsuit, the plaintiff may remove the
record by a writ of error into the Supreme Court for revision and reversal, in like manner and with like effect as he might remove a judgment
rendered against him upon a demurrer to evidence. § 7.

The judges of the said court, or any two of them, shall have power,
during the periods appropriated for the trial of causes by jury, to meet
in bank, if they deem it necessary or proper, upon the Saturday of each
week of such periods, and dispose of all motions and questions requiring early attention which a single judge is not by law competent to
decide. § 9.

The authority and power given to the District Court for the City and
County of Philadelphia, by an act passed on the 14th day of April,
1828, entitled "an act to prevent the failure of trusts to provide for
the settlement of the accounts of trustees, and for other purposes," are
hereby declared to be vested in the court established by the act to which
this is a supplement, and also to have been vested in the court established by an act passed on the 26th day of March, 1832, entitled "an
act to establish the District Court for the City and County of Philadelphia." § 10.

It shall be the duty of the said court to cause writs of *venire facias* to
issue for summoning the requisite number of jurors, to be drawn in the
manner now prescribed by law(*g*) to attend before each of the said
judges for trial of said causes, and each of the said judges shall have
power to fine the said jurors for non-attendance; and while sitting for
the trial of causes shall have the same power and authority that
is now possessed by the District Court for the City and County of
Philadelphia; and the seal heretofore used by the District Court for the
City and County of Philadelphia shall be the seal of the court established by this act. § 6, act of 1835.(*h*)

The said court shall have power to award writs of *venire* for the
summoning of jurors at any time not less than thirty days before the
day appointed for the return of such writs, notwithstanding the term

---

(*g*) Act of 14th April, 1834.   (*h*) See *ante*, p. 13, 2d and 3d sections
                                              of the act of 1812.

during which the said writs shall be returnable shall have commenced at the time of the issuing thereof.(*i*)

By the 9th section of the act of April 3 1851, the court is continued "until it shall be duly abolished by law."

Having introduced such parts of the text of the various statutes that pertain to the constitution and powers of this court, it will now be proper to consider the decisions that exist in relation to them. The court, as has been seen, was constituted with original jurisdiction in cases "where the sum in controversy shall exceed one hundred dollars," and that of the Common Pleas made to cease and determine at that sum in *all civil* suits. The court is, therefore, a District Court of Common Pleas, superior to the Court of Common Pleas only as to the *sum* in demand; its jurisdiction beginning where that of the latter court terminates, and being without limit. This jurisdiction attaches where the sum *substantially* in controversy exceeds one hundred dollars.(*j*) In torts or trespass, and in all cases savoring, in reality, of damages, and where there is no mode of computation, the demand in the declaration is the criterion.(*k*) But, in replevin of goods distrained for rent, if an issue is joined upon the plea of no rent in arrear, and the amount of the rent claimed appears from the indorsement on the writ or otherwise, this and not the damages laid in the declaration, will determine the jurisdiction.(*l*) If the writ be issued as a means of trying the title to property, it is in the nature of detinue, and the value of the article replevied is the real matter in dispute.(*m*)

In the case of an ejectment, this court would be obliged to receive affidavits as to the value of the controversy; but in most cases it may be ascertained from the nature of the dispute.(*n*) When a sum below the jurisdiction of the court is found by the verdict, the jurisdiction is not affected,(*o*) unless the value of the thing put in demand by the plaintiff's declaration, is under one hundred dollars. Where the declaration states a cause of action founded on a contract wherein the subject matter exceeds one hundred dollars, and the District Court gives judgment, there the jurisdiction is to be sustained, though the recovery be for less than one hundred dollars.(*p*) For if the ultimate recovery were to govern, then, though the sum were reduced by defalcation, this not appearing on the record, the plaintiff could not only not recover costs, but would be thrown out of court; and thus understood, the opinion that the court would judge of the jurisdiction from the evidence in the case would be quite correct. But where on the declaration the whole subject

(*i*) Section 2 of act of 1836.

(*j*) 2 Br. 271. See Kline *v.* Wood, 9 S. & R. 294.

(*k*) 2 Br. 271. See 9 S. & R. 299, 300. Hancock *v.* Barton, 1 S. & R. 269. Bazire *v.* Barry, 3 S. & R. 461.

(*l*) Ancora *v.* Burns, 5 Bin. 522. See *post* Rep.

(*m*) 9 Wheaton, 527.

(*n*) 2 Br. 271. See Kline *v.* Wood, 9 S. & R. 299.—Warfel *v.* Beam, 3 Pa. R. 397, which involved the subject of the jurisdiction of the District Court of Lancaster. The action was trespass *quare clausum fregit*, and it was held, that, as the plaintiff's attorney had not certified in his *præcipe* the amount in controversy, and no declaration had been filed, and an award of arbitrators had been obtained and filed by the plaintiff but for $30, the court had not jurisdiction.

(*o*) Hancock *v.* Barton, 1 S. & R. 269.

(*p*) Kline *v.* Wood, 9 S. & R. 294.

matter of the contract does not exceed one hundred dollars, as it is set out in the declaration, there the want of jurisdiction appears on the record, and the court are bound to reverse. In a matter before justices of the peace, the court in examining the proceeding, may call in the aid of affidavits to see whether they have exceeded their jurisdiction. But an award of arbitrators is different from a trial in court; and where the award is not for more than 100 dollars in the District Court in an action founded on contract, it is different from a judgment of a justice of the peace, and there it is difficult to ascertain what was the real sum in controversy, and what reduced by defalcation.

The value of the thing put in demand is another criterion of jurisdiction, for the demand of the plaintiff is not alone to be regarded. Thus in debt on bond for £100, the principal and interest are put in demand, and the party can recover no more, though he may lay his damages at £10,000. The form of action in that case gives the legal rule. But in an action of trespass, and other torts, where the law prescribes no limitation to the amount to be recovered, the plaintiff has a right to estimate his damages at any sum. The damage stated in the declaration is the thing put in demand. The proposition then is this: where the law gives no rule, the demand of the plaintiff must furnish one; but where the law gives the rule, the legal cause of action, and not the plaintiff's demand, must be regarded in a question of jurisdiction.(q) Therefore, where some of the counts of the declaration in an action of assumpsit, were for damages sustained by the defendant's selling to the plaintiff an unsound horse, for the sum of 80 dollars, and the verdict was for 40 dollars, it was held that the cause of action was not within the jurisdiction of the District Court, though these counts averred that the plaintiff had been put to expense in feeding and keeping the horse to the amount of $150.(r)

Another criterion of the jurisdiction of this court is, where justices of the peace have jurisdiction of the sum in controversy. Wherever the plaintiff could not recover costs if he sued in the Common Pleas, unless he had filed a previous affidavit, before the erection of the District Court, there the District Court have no jurisdiction.(s) It appears, therefore, that a plaintiff cannot secure costs in the latter court by filing a previous affidavit, as in the Courts of Common Pleas, in other counties; he must bring his demand within its jurisdiction to entitle himself to costs. If there be jurisdiction costs will follow. If there be no jurisdiction, there can be a recovery of neither damages nor costs. As then the jurisdiction of this court does not attach but in cases where the plaintiff could have recovered costs if he had sued in the Common Pleas (before the erection of this court), without having filed previously an affidavit that his demand exceeded $100, although his verdict was for a sum less than $100, it becomes necessary to ascertain in what cases such an affidavit was then a prerequisite for the securing of costs on a recovery of less than $100. Such an inquiry necessarily involves the consideration of the effect of a *set-off*, upon the claim of the plaintiff, and it is one of some difficulty, from the latitude allowed in this State

(q) Kline v. Wood, 9 S. & R. 299, 300, 301.

(r) Id. See also Wharton's Digest, Courts, ix.

(s) Kline v. Wood, 9 S. & R. 300, *post*, p. 30.

of making set-offs, not only of liquidated, but of unliquidated, and of what are called *equitable*, demands. There are two decisions upon this subject, which exhibit the whole doctrine involved in it, fully and ably discussed. The first is the case of Sadler *v.* Slobaugh,(*t*) and the second, Grant *v.* Wallace.(*u*) In the former, the plaintiff sued in the Common Pleas, for a debt over $100 for a horse, without filing a previous affidavit: his demand was reduced to less than that sum, by a set-off of an *unliquidated* demand, a breach of the warranty, and he was allowed his costs. And the spirit of the reasoning is, that the plaintiff is bound to elect the proper tribunal at his peril, where due precaution will enable him to proceed with safety. In the latter case, it was decided, that if the demand of the plaintiff is reduced below $100 by *a set-off* (without designating the nature or quality of the set-off), he is entitled to costs. The chief justice dissented, and gave his reasons at length. He was an associate justice of the court at the time of the decision of the former case; and both he and the majority of the court relied on it as an authority, supporting their respective views. It is a defect in the report of the latter case, that it does not state what *kind* of set-off was made, whether for a definite or an unliquidated amount, but it may be generally *inferred* that it was of the former character. If so, the case can hardly be reconciled with that of Sadler *v.* Slobaugh, nor with the general leaning of subsequent adjudications, in which, as will be seen, it is held that direct payment divests jurisdiction; though it still must be considered the law that no matter whether the plaintiff knew of the set-off, either as regards its amount or quality, he is not obliged to make the account, and go into a court having jurisdiction of the *balance* solely. The general principle, it is true, has been frequently asserted that the court has jurisdiction, and costs are carried, even where the sum is reduced by set-off to 100 dollars or less,(*v*) though perhaps, this may be qualified by a very recent case to be noticed more fully hereafter.(*w*) But where there is a plea to the jurisdiction, and the evidence is that the plaintiff's claim is reduced by *direct payment* below one hundred dollars, the court will direct a verdict for the defendant.(*x*) Under the plea of non assumpsit, the practice seems otherwise.(*y*) A plea to the jurisdiction, however, can be interposed at any time.(*z*)

(*t*) Sadler *v.* Slobaugh, 3 S. & R. 388. See, generally, *post*, p. 30.

(*u*) Grant *v.* Wallace, 16 Id. 253.

(*v*) Odell *v.* Culbert, 9 W. & S. 66; Meredith *v.* Pierie, 2 P. L. J. 331. (See Whar. Dig. Courts, ix.)

(*w*) Shoup *v.* Shoup, 3 H. 361, *post*, p. 30.

(*x*) Cahill *v.* Naulty, D. C. Dec. 13, 1851.

(*y*) Meredith *v.* Pierie, 2 P. L. J. 58.

(*z*) The following opinions of Judge Sharswood are important on this point:—

Williams *v.* Beatty, Jan. 20, 1849.— Rule for judgment. *Per curiam.* This case presents a singular difficulty. It is a *sci. fa.* on a mechanic's claim for $115 72. The defendant alleges that certain items in the bill, $21 72, were never furnished to the building. This reduces the claim to $94. The plaintiff is willing to take judgment for this amount, but by doing so he admits the truth of the affidavit, and that he never had any claim for more than $94. How then can the jurisdiction be sustained? If he goes to trial, even though he should fail in the proof of those items, the jurisdiction will still include the case. As the matter stands therefore, we are not prepared to give a judgment on this rule. R. D.

Hanna *v.* Wilson, June 10, 1848.— Why attachment sur judgment should not be dissolved. *Per curiam.* This was a judgment entered upon a bond and warrant, conditioned for the payment of $100 with interest. It was entered on the day of its date, so that, at the time of its entry, no interest was due.

This court has not jurisdiction of an action on a bond, with condition for the payment of a sum less than $100, although the penalty is for an amount greater than $100.(a) Therefore a judgment entered by virtue of a warrant of attorney on a bond, in the penal sum of $120, with condition for the payment of $60, is erroneous, and will be struck off on motion.(b)

The court has not jurisdiction of recognizances forfeited in criminal cases,(c) which by the act of April 22, 1846, are vested in the Court of Quarter Sessions. But it has of the action to recover the penalty given by the act of 1729 to prevent clandestine marriages, that being a civil remedy for a private injury.(d) So, of a proceeding by attachment against a vessel, for work or materials.(e)

The court has not, however, been invested with all the powers of the Common Pleas in civil cases, other than in those under one hundred dollars which are specially exempted from a magistrate's jurisdiction; for the latter court still retains its jurisdiction in cases under particular acts of assembly, and not of a common law character; as, for example, in granting divorces, the citation of assignees, care of lunatics, discharging insolvent debtors, proceedings against aldermen or justices, and in a few particular cases, in which it is made by the constitution to supply the office of a Court of Chancery. But it does not retain its jurisdiction of all these cases in exclusion of that of the District Court; for this

There is a clear defect of jurisdiction, therefore. (Coates v. Cork, 1 Miles, 270.) This motion is on behalf of the garnishee, who is entitled to have the attachment set aside. Attachment set aside.

M'Allister v. Levering, Mar. 24, 1849. Motion for a rule for a new trial. *Per curiam.* The only thing material to be noticed is in regard to the jurisdiction. It was alleged that the plaintiff's claim was reduced to less than $100 by direct payments; and however that may have been in point of fact, the judge decided in conformity to precedent, in this court, that *defect of jurisdiction* on that ground to be taken advantage of must be specially pleaded. Meredith v. Pierie, (2 P. L. J. 58.)

(a) Coates v. Cork, 1 Miles, 270.
(b) Ibid. By the plain language of the act, this court has no jurisdiction. The result would be the same in every case in which the principal and interest, at the date of the judgment, do not altogether amount to the sum exceeding one hundred dollars. In Kline v. Wood, 9 S. & R. 300, the Supreme Court says, that wherever the plaintiff could not recover costs if he had sued in the Court of Common Pleas, before the erection of the District Court, without having filed a previous *affidavit* under the 26th section of the one hundred dollar

law, there the District Court has no jurisdiction. Though, by the operation of the acts relative to the District Court, a plaintiff in the Common Pleas of Philadelphia County cannot secure himself in regard to costs by a previous *affidavit,* yet it is conceded in Kline v. Wood that the jurisdiction of the Common Pleas as to debts and demands not exceeding one hundred dollars is not by any law taken away. Cooper v. Coats, 1 D. 308, and Stewart v. Mitchell's Administrators, 13 S. & R. 287, are authorities to prove that, prior to the establishment of the District Court, a party situated like the present plaintiff could not have recovered costs if he had entered up the judgment in the Court of Common Pleas. Taken in connection with Kline v. Wood, they show that, though the Common Pleas could have entertained jurisdiction of a suit upon this very bond, yet that the plaintiff would not in that court have been entitled to costs. The test then suggested by the Supreme Court is directly applicable. *Per* PETTIT, *Pres't,* delivering the opinion of the court.

(c) Norbury v. Commissioners of Philadelphia County, 8 S. & R. 151.
(d) Ely v. Beaumont, 5 Rawle, 124.
(e) Ship Portland v. Lewis et al., 2 S. & R. 197.

court has now concurrent jurisdiction with the Common Pleas in compelling assignees to settle their accounts.

We have seen that the third section of the act of 1811(*f*) prescribes that no suit shall be *removed* from that court, but that in all cases its final judgment may be examined, and affirmed or reversed, on a writ of error from the Supreme Court. The law is the same with regard to judgments rendered by the Common Pleas, except in a few cases in which an appeal lies to the Supreme Court. As, in actions of debt on forfeited recognizances wherein the judges have a power to moderate and remit according to equity and legal discretion, an appeal lay from their decision to the Supreme Court,(*g*) so, by the act of 1815, § 13,(*h*) either party may, within one year,(*i*) appeal in a suit for divorce, from the final decree of the Common Pleas, though made in pursuance of a verdict, upon entering into the required security. Except, too, in the case of a judgment upon a *certiorari* to a magistrate, the judgment of the Common Pleas being final therein.

Before the act of 1846,(*j*) the District Court for Philadelphia had no jurisdiction in an action of partition, between parties who take by descent from one who died sole seised.(*k*)

The court has jurisdiction of apportioned mechanics' claims filed against several houses, where the aggregate is over one hundred dollars, although the individual claims are under that sum.(*l*)

How far the court is bound by the act of 1722 to order a special court is still an open question; it is settled, however, that no such court will be granted until the case for which it is asked is at issue.(*m*)

SECTION III.

OF THE COURT OF COMMON PLEAS FOR THE CITY AND COUNTY OF PHILADELPHIA.

In the early times of the Province of Pennsylvania, a civil and criminal jurisdiction was vested in the county courts, and they were

---

(*f*) *Ante*, p. 12.
(*g*) Roop *v.* Meek, 6 S. & R. 545.
(*h*) 6 Re. Laws, 286.
(*i*) 7 Re. Laws, 151.
(*j*) See *post*, "Partition." Vol. II.
(*k*) McMichael *v.* Skilton, 1 H. 215; affirming Clawges *v.* Clawges, 2 M. 34.
(*l*) Woodruff *v.* Chambers, 1 H. 132.
(*m*) Murphy *v.* Jarvis. Motion for a special court. Jones *v.* Jarvis. Same motion. D. C. *Per curiam.* This motion is founded upon the 25th sect. of the act of May 22, 1722 (Purd. 254), which provides that "If any defendant or defendants in any suit or action, by reason of his or their sudden departure out of this province, shall require a more speedy termination in such action or suit than can be obtained by the common or ordinary rules of proceedings in any of the Courts

of Common Pleas in this province, the said justices, upon application to them made, shall grant to such defendant or defendants special courts, and shall proceed to hear and determine the premises according to the course and practice of the said Courts of Common Pleas, and for the usual fees therein taken." Without meaning to decide that, in other respects, this act of assembly is applicable to this court or to these cases, we are clearly of the opinion that no order of the kind asked for can be made until the cases are at issue and ready for determination. It is not according to the course and practice to issue a venire in any case until it is first ascertained whether the parties will come to an issue of fact requiring the presence of a jury to decide. Motion refused.

founded on a plan similar to that of the county courts of England, in the days of their pristine greatness. In the year 1722, these jurisdictions were separated; and power was only given to this court to hear and determine all civil pleas and causes, personal, real, and mixed. The criminal jurisdiction was at the same time transferred to a court, then instituted and styled " The General Quarter Sessions of the Peace and Gaol Delivery." At present, a Court of Common Pleas is established for each county under the constitution of this State.(n) That for this county has been reorganzied by recent acts of assembly, and at present consists of three law judges. The Courts of Common Pleas of all the other counties have the same common organization, and consists, each, of a president judge selected from the ranks of the bar, and of two associates, who need not have been qualified by previous legal studies, or admitted to practise the law.

This court, together with the Common Pleas of every other county, owes its organization to the act of the 14th of April, 1834. It will be difficult so to dissect this act as to obtain from it a separate view of the Common Pleas for this county alone. We shall, therefore, introduce it generally, omitting, however, the enumeration of the judicial districts contained in the 24th section, and of the terms, contained in the 29th.

I. *Of the Organization of this Court.*

There shall be holden and kept, in every of the counties of this commonwealth, a court of record, the name and style whereof shall be, " The Court of Common Pleas of the [respective] county." § 18.

The Courts of Common Pleas of the several counties of this commonwealth, except the County of Philadelphia, are hereby declared to consist of a president judge and two associate judges. § 19.

The president and associate judges of the Courts of Common Pleas, or any two of them, or the presiding judge, in the absence of his associates, shall have power to hold the said courts, and to hear and determine all causes, matters, and things cognizable therein, according to the constitution, laws, and usages of this commonwealth. § 20.

The president, or the legal associate judges of the Court of Common Pleas, of the County of Philadelphia, shall have power, from time to time, as may be found requisite, to hold a Court of Common Pleas for the trial of civil issues depending in such court, although two of the judges of the said court should be holding, at the same time, an Orphans' Court, a Court of Quarter Sessions, or a Court of Common Pleas. § 21.

Every Court of Common Pleas shall have a seal for the use of said court, having engraven thereon such words and devices as are inscribed on the seal now in use in the respective court, and such seal may be renewed, under the direction of such court, as often as occasion shall require. § 22.

(n) Art. 5, § 1.

A prothonotary or clerk shall be appointed, and commissioned for each of the said courts; he shall have the custody of the records and seal of the respective court, and keep the same at the place of holding such court, and in the apartments provided, by authority of law, for that purpose. And he shall faithfully perform, under the direction of the court, all the duties appertaining to his office. § 23.

It shall be the duty of the governor, from time to time, as vacancies may occur in the office of a president judge, in any of the said districts, to appoint and commission, under the great seal of this commonwealth, a person of knowledge and integrity, skilled in the laws, to be president and judge of the Courts of Common Pleas, in each of the counties composing the district for which he may be so appointed. § 26.

It shall also be the duty of the governor, from time to time, as any vacancy may occur in the office of judge in any of the said counties, to appoint and commission, in the manner aforesaid, a suitable person to be judge of the Court of Common Pleas of such county. § 27.

Provided, That on the death, resignation, or removal from office of either of the associate judges of the Court of Common Pleas for the City and County of Philadelphia, appointed previously to the eighth day of February, one thousand eight hundred and thirty-three, no appointment shall be made to fill the vacancy; but thereafter the said court shall consist of one president, and (by a subsequent act) two associates, learned in the law. § 28.

The Courts of Common Pleas of every county shall be holden four times in every year, at the court house of the respective county, and at and during the times hereinafter specified for each term, if the business depending in the said courts respectively shall require it. § 29.

It shall be the duty of the president and associate judges of the several Courts of Common Pleas of this commonwealth, to hold adjourned Courts of Common Pleas in their respective counties, in addition to their regular terms, whenever the business of the said courts shall require, so always as not to interfere with their duties, in any of the said counties, at the terms appointed by law. § 30.

The judges of the Courts of Common Pleas, in every county wherein a term of two weeks is appointed, as aforesaid, shall have power to order, at any term thereof, that the said court, at the next term, shall continue during one week only thereof, and such order being entered upon record, such succeeding term shall be abridged accordingly. § 31.

The judges of the Courts of Common Pleas, in every county, shall also have power to order, at any term thereof, that the next succeeding term shall be extended during one or more weeks beyond the time hereinbefore allowed for the continuance of such court, but in such manner, always, as shall not interfere with any term of the courts in any other county of the respective district, and such order being entered upon record, such succeeding term of the court shall be enlarged accordingly. § 32.

The Court of Common Pleas in every county wherein a term of two weeks is appointed as aforesaid, shall have power to order, at any term thereof, that the trial of issues in civil causes depending in the respective courts shall be commenced during the first week of the next succeeding term, at a day fixed; and such order being entered upon record, the court shall award a venire for jurors, and the trial of such issues shall be commenced accordingly, or as soon thereafter as the other business of the judges of the said court will permit.   § 33.

Whenever any term of the Court of Common Pleas of any county shall be abridged by order of the judges to one week; also whenever the said judges shall order that the trial of issues in civil causes shall be commenced during the first week as aforesaid; the said judges shall order the sheriff and commissioners of the respective county to annex and return one and the same panel of names to all venires awarded by them for the summoning of the petit or common jurors returnable during that week.   § 34.

Whenever any term of the Court of Common Pleas shall be enlarged as aforesaid, the said court shall have power to award a venire for jurors, returnable on such day of the term so enlarged as the business of the said court shall require.   § 35.

The Courts of Common Pleas of the several counties shall have power respectively to adjourn the sessions of the court from time to time, as they may think proper, and at such adjourned courts to act upon and decide all matters depending therein, with the same effect as they might or could do at the terms appointed for the holding of such courts as aforesaid.   § 36.

Special Courts of Common Pleas shall be holden in the several counties of this commonwealth, at the respective places appointed by law for holding Courts of Common Pleas, in every of the cases following, to wit:—

I. Whenever the president judge of any of the said courts shall be personally interested in the event of any cause depending in any county of his district.

II. Whenever the title under which the parties, or either of them, claim in any cause depending as aforesaid, shall have been derived from or through such president, or whenever the president shall hold under the same title with either of the parties in the cause.

III. Whenever any near relative of the president judge of any of the said courts shall be a party to any cause depending as aforesaid, or interested in the event thereof.

IV. Whenever the president judge of any of the said courts shall have been concerned as an attorney or counsel for either of the parties in any suit depending as aforesaid, or in any other cause touching the same subject matter, or for any other person under whom the said parties, or either of them, claim.   § 37.

Provided, That the parties to any such cause may, in any of the cases aforesaid, agree, in writing to be filed of record, to a trial before such president, or before him and any one or more of his associates, or before the associates.   § 38.

Whenever any special court shall be necessary for the trial of any cause or causes depending as aforesaid, it shall be the duty of the president of the court in which such cause shall be depending, to give notice thereof to the prothonotary of such court, who shall forthwith make out a list of all such causes, and transmit the same to the president judge who may reside nearest to the place where any such cause is to be tried: on the receipt of such list it shall be the duty of such president to appoint a time for holding a special court in the county where such cause or causes ought to be tried, and at the time so appointed to hold the said court, with one or more of the associate judges of the county; and courts so holden may be adjourned from time to time until all such causes shall be finally determined: *Provided*, That public notice be given of the time of holding such court during sixty days.   § 39.

All proceedings had before any special Court of Common Pleas, held as aforesaid, shall be of the same force and effect, to all intents and purposes, as if the same had occurred before the proper president of the district; and shall in like manner be subject to appeal or writ of error, in due course of law, as in other cases.   § 40.

Provided, That nothing in this act shall be so construed as to interfere with any special provision, heretofore made by law, respecting special courts in any of the counties of this commonwealth.   § 41.

By the act of 4th April, 1843,(*o*) the provisions of the thirty-seventh, thirty-eighth, thirty-ninth, fortieth, and forty-first sections of the act of fourteenth April, one thousand eight hundred and thirty-four, shall be construed to extend to all cases in the Orphans' Court, Registers' Court, Quarter Sessions, or Oyer and Terminer, in which the president judge or associate judges, or either of them, shall be personally interested or otherwise disqualified for the performance of judicial duty, from any of the causes specified in said sections: *Provided*, That in cases affecting the interest of one associate judge only, it shall be discretionary with the president judge of the court where the cause is depending to direct a special court under the provisions of said sections, if he shall deem it essential to a proper administration of justice.   § 8.

The act of 10th April, 1849,(*p*) provides that, whenever it shall be necessary to hold a special court in any county of any judicial district, agreeably to the law in force, an arrangement may be made between the president judge of such district and the president judge of any adjoining district, to hold the court of any regular term for holding the courts in such county, or at any adjourned term of said courts; and the judge of such adjoining district shall take the place of the other, without additional notice or special venire, and all proceedings had before the said court shall be of the same force and effect, and be conducted accord-

(*o*) Pamph. L. 131.   (*p*) Pamph. L. 619.

ing to the same rules and regulations, to all intents and purposes, as if the same had occurred before the proper president of the district. § 1.

If the dispatch of business shall require it, the said judges may so arrange it, that the judge whose place is supplied may take the place of the other judge at any regular term of said court in his district, or at any adjourned court; and all proceedings had before any such court so holden, shall be of the same force and effect, and be conducted according to the same rules and regulations, to all intents and purposes, as if the same had occurred before the proper president of the district, and shall in like manner be subject to appeal or writ of error, in due course of law, as in other cases. § 2.

II. *Of the Jurisdiction and Powers of this Court.*

The Courts of Common Pleas shall have jurisdiction and power within their respective counties, to hear and determine all pleas, actions, and suits, and causes, civil, personal, real, and mixed, according to the constitution and laws of this commonwealth; and the said courts shall have power to grant under their judicial seals, all lawful writs and process necessary for the exercise of such jurisdiction: *Provided,* That the Court of Common Pleas for the City and County of Philadelphia shall not have jurisdiction in any civil plea or action, where the sum or value in controversy shall exceed one hundred dollars, as heretofore.(q)

The jurisdiction of the Common Pleas is limited to the sum of 100 dollars in the county of Philadelphia, which is the amount of that of aldermen and justices of the peace, and appeals from these or writs of certiorari directed to them, make also a copious subject of this court's jurisdiction. For, if an action be brought in the Common Pleas for a demand within the jurisdiction of a justice of the peace, the jury cannot give costs.(r) And if less than 100 dollars be recovered in the Common Pleas of any other county, not having its jurisdiction limited by the establishment of a District Court, without a previous affidavit by the plaintiff, that he believed the defendant owed him more, the former is not entitled to costs,(s) unless his claim were reduced by set-off exceeding 100 dollars, or under the former practice, which perhaps no longer exists, by a cross demand of an unliquidated kind, or indefinite amount.(t) But in cases of trespass, trover, and other actions founded on a *tort*, brought in the Common Pleas of those counties having no District Court, if the plaintiff lay his damages at more than 100 dollars, and recover less than that sum, he may still have his costs.(u)

(q) Sect. 12. Act of 16th June, 1836; Pamph. L. 784, 787–8.

(r) Sneively v. Weidman, 1 S. & R. 417. Clark v. McKisson, 6 S. & R. 87.

(s) Guier v. M'Faden, 2 Bin. 587.

(t) This was decided in Sadler v. Slobaugh, 3 S. & R. 390, where, in an action on a single bill for a horse, a breach of warranty was set up. But this case is overruled in Shoup v. Shoup, 3 H. 361, where it is distinctly held that under the words "damages on assumption," in the 7th section of the act of 1810, unliquidated damages for a breach of contract, being an existing demand, must be set off before a justice. It must be confessed, however, that it is very difficult to understand how a plaintiff is to ascertain beforehand the exact amount of a defendant's cross demand when unliquidated, so as to determine the jurisdiction he is to select.

(u) Clark v. McKisson, 6 S. & R. 87.

It has been determined by the Supreme Court, that the Common Pleas of this county have original jurisdiction in civil actions where the demand is under 100 dollars, but the plaintiff cannot recover costs.(v)

To ascertain the jurisdiction of this court, it will be necessary to consider what cases are, and what are not, within the civil jurisdiction of an alderman or justice of the peace, known by the general name of *magistrates*. In the actions not within the jurisdiction of a magistrate, and which may, therefore, be instituted in this court where the demand does not exceed 100 dollars, it follows that such costs may be recovered by the plaintiff if he have a verdict, as his verdict would carry, if the justice of the peace statutes had never been passed. By acts of assembly, the excepted actions are ejectment—replevin—slander—actions on real contracts for land—actions for breach of promise of marriage—trespass, where the defendant has made affidavit before the magistrate that title to land would come in question—assault and battery—and false imprisonment. By judicial construction of those acts, the excepted actions are trespass on real or personal property, where the damage does not arise by an *actual* or *immediate* injury done to it.(w) But,(x) the trespass or injury need not be permanent or visible to the eye, to bring it within the act; thus, trespass for entering a third person's house to distrain, where no goods were found, is within the jurisdiction of a magistrate.

So, trespass on the case, where the injury is consequential, as a nuisance(y) is excepted from the jurisdiction of magistrates. So, actions to recover damages for a deficiency in quantity, on a contract for the sale of land.(z)

So, also, actions of debt on penal statutes, as, for the penalty imposed by the act of 1791, for not entering satisfaction of a judgment,(a) or, for the penalty for travelling as a peddler without a license, (b) the jurisdiction of a magistrate being confined to contracts express or implied, and a right to a penalty arising out of neither.

Unless it appear on the record that parties appeared and confessed judgment for a sum exceeding 100 dollars, the justice has no jurisdiction.(bb)

So, also, a suit on a sheriff's official bond, with a penalty over 100 dollars, although the plaintiff's claim be less than that sum.(c) But this went on the ground that the statute as to sheriffs' bonds contemplates a trial in a court of record, as it mentions the sum to be found by *verdict*. So an action upon a bond given by a constable, conditioned for the faithful performance of the duties of his office, no matter what the claims.(d) So, likewise, actions against executors for a *devastavit*.(e) So, too, actions against the sheriff for the escape of a party in execution for a sum under 100 dollars;(f) where it is said that "it is not the action, but the nature of the subject matter of it, which must decide the question of jurisdiction." So, likewise, actions of account render.(g)

(v) Kline v. Wood, 9 S. & R. 294. 6 S. & R. 648.

(w) Masteller v. Trimbley, 6 Bin. 33. 1 Br. 331.

(x) Hobbs v. Geiss, 13 S. & R. 417.

(y) Bates v. Shaw, 13 S. & R. 420.

(z) Lee v. Dean, 3 R. 325.

(a) Zeigler v. Gram, 13 S. & R. 102.

(b) Ibid.

(bb) Camp v. Wood, 10 W. 118.

(c) Com. v. Reynolds, 17 S. & R. 367. GIBSON, C. J. and TOD, J. *dissent.*

(d) Blue v. Com., 4 W. 215.

(e) Wilson v. Long, 12 S. & R. 58.

(f) Shaffer v. M'Namee, 13 S. & R. 44.

(g) Wright v. Guy, 10 S. & R. 227.

It may also be stated as a general rule, that a justice of the peace has no jurisdiction, except where his judgment is to be for a sum certain.(h) In giving jurisdiction to justices of the peace, the legislature had only in view those actions in which judgment is for a specific sum, where, if there is no appeal, execution is to issue.(i)   And, for this reason, it has been determined, that a detinue is excepted from that jurisdiction, the judgment in that action being, that the plaintiff do recover the goods detained, or the value of them, if the plaintiff cannot have the goods, and damages for the detention.(j)

A justice has no jurisdiction of an action on a judgment of a justice of the peace in another State.(k)

Actions for the recovery of money due on judgments obtained in the Common Pleas, are also excepted.(l)   And so,actions to recover damages for negligence in the execution of work, employment, trust, or duty, under a contract, are not cognizable before a justice.   The proper remedy is a special action on the case in a court of record.   It is substantially for a *tort*, although a tort deducible from the existence of a contract.(m)

Actions on insolvents' bonds are within the jurisdiction of magistrates,(n) even where the penalty is over 100 dollars, provided the sum demanded do not exceed it.(o)   If a defendant in a suit before a justice, wishes to rely on a tender, so as to avoid costs of a subsequent suit, he should plead it before the justice, having the money there, and at the same time offering it to the plaintiff, and then on his appeal, pay it into court, and plead the tender of the money before suit commenced.(p)

The judgments of aldermen and justices of the peace are reviewed in this court by writs of *certiorari*, where the exceptions are of law; and by appeal where the mistake is alleged to be of fact.   A *certiorari* may issue for any amount.   But no appeal lies, unless the judgment of the magistrate exceeds five dollars and thirty-three cents.(q)   This relates to causes which have been heard and decided by the magistrate himself, under the act of 20th March, 1810.   But if a cause be submitted to reference under that act, if the award do not exceed twenty dollars, there shall be no appeal from the magistrate's judgment upon it.(r) And if the award of the referees be in favor of the defendant, no appeal will lie by the plaintiff from the judgment entered on it,(s) unless the plaintiff's cause of action, or the debt sued for, as set out on the docket of the magistrate, exceeds twenty dollars.(t)   And the same construction obtains where the arbitrators reduce the plaintiff's demand to less than twenty dollars.(u)   Under the act of 22d March, 1814, which extends the jurisdiction of justices to trover and trespass, if the cause be referred under this act, and the judgment on the award is in

(h) Knight v. Wiltberger, 4 Y. 127.
(i) Wright v. Guy, 10 S. & R. 229.
(j) Sprenkle v. Spots, C. P. York County, *R. Demo. Press*, Dec. 6, 1825.
(k) Ellsworth v. Barnton, 7 W. 314.
(l) Eason v. Smith, 8 S. & R. 343; Wilson v. Long, 12 Id. 58.
(m) Zell v. Arnold, 2 Pa. R. 292.
(n) Jones v. Smith, 2 Pa. R. 462.
(o) Sharpless v. Hopkins, C. P. Philad. 1835; MS. See *ante*, p. 19, in n. See

also other cases, 2 Wh. Dig., tit. Justice of the Peace, B.
(p) Siebert v. Kline, 1 Barr, 38.
(q) 1 Br. 161.
(r) M'Kim v. Bryson, 2 S. & R. 463. Ulrick v. Larkey, 6 Id. 285.   *Sed vide* 1 Br. 336.
(s) M'Kim v. Bryson, 2 S. & R. 463.
(t) Stoy v. Yost, 12 S. & R. 385, 387.
(u) Soop v. Coats, Ibid. 388.

favor of the defendant, the plaintiff has the right of appeal, provided his demand exceeded five dollars and a third. A *certiorari* lies in all judicial proceedings in which a writ of error does not lie; and being a substitute for a writ of error, it is governed by the same, or strictly analogous principles; consequently no point can be raised on it which is not apparent exclusively on the proceedings removed by it, and the courts refuse in all such cases to enter into the merits or to decide facts on depositions.(v)

When contested questions of payment on judgments before justices of the peace arise, they must take jurisdiction of them by controlling the execution until the parties agree to an amicable action which would be a subject of appeal, or it may be tried on a *scire facias*. But the Common Pleas cannot, on *certiorari* to such judgment, direct an issue to try disputed facts in relation to such payments (w)

In an action of debt for a penalty for the violation of an ordinance, the magistrate should state on his record not only the substance of the ordinance, but what is alleged against the defendant, as to his acts, or omission of anything to be done, which exposes him to the penalty.(x)

Where there are two penalties imposed by an ordinance, the judgment must be specific, for which penalty it is rendered, and a judgment for too small a sum is as fatal as if for a larger sum than is given by the ordinance.(y)

In certiorari, the court will notice a substantial and fatal error in the proceedings, although the counsel have omitted to make it a special exception, when it is deemed essential for the purposes of justice.(z)

In a summary conviction, the magistrate is bound to set forth the evidence at length on his record, for the proof must appear upon the record, to sustain every material charge. The magistrate must state the whole evidence on both sides, and not merely the result of it.(a)

On a judgment by default before an alderman or justice of the peace, it must appear by the record, that the process was served as required by law, otherwise the judgment will be reversed on certiorari.(b)

Proceedings were reversed where it appeared by the record in a return to a certiorari, that the cause of action was "for a violation of the 1st section of an ordinance of the district aforesaid passed the 1st July, 1820," nothing more being stated.(c)

An appeal by one defendant from a judgment against two by a magistrate, is good, notwithstanding the other comes into court, and dissents.(d) The rule that there can be no severance in a personal action, applies to plaintiffs and not to defendants.(e)

As a general rule it seems that by a stipulation, a maker of a note may give up his right to appeal as a matter of course, under the act of assembly. Still, there are numerous exceptions to the rule.(f)

(v) Philad. and Trenton R. R. Co. 6 Wh. 41.
(w) Pool v. Morgan, 10 W. 53.
(x) Manayunk v. Davis, 2 Par. 289.
(y) Ibid.
(z) Com. v. Cane, 2 Par. 265.
(a) Ibid.

(b) Fraily v. Sparks, 2 Par. 232. Buchanan v. Specht, 8 Leg. Int. 162.
(c) Fraily v. Sparks, 2 Par. 232.
(d) Gallagher v. Jackson, 1 S. & R. 492.
(e) Ibid.
(f) See Pritchard v. Denton, 8 W. 372.

I.—3

After a plaintiff has declared, it is too late to move to dismiss the appeal, because it was not entered within the twenty days, which are to be computed from the final decision by the justice.(g)

Where, on an appeal by defendant, no new count is required so as to cover an additional claim which was not made before the arbitrators, the plaintiff may make and recover such claim before the jury.(h) It is otherwise if a new substantive cause of action be offered requiring an additional count.(i) Where the award is on a note of which a statement has been filed, plaintiff may on the appeal declare on the original debt for which the note was given; or he may declare on the note as an amendment to the statement.(j)

If the justice's judgment be for less than $5 33, no cross demand being set up and no greater sum in dispute, the Common Pleas cannot receive an appeal.(k)

Neither party is bound in an appeal in an action of trover, by the amount of damages stated on the justice's docket. He is confined only to the same cause of action as is there stated.(l)

If, on the appeal, it appear from the transcript, that. the justice has exceeded his jurisdiction, or that he had no jurisdiction at all, that of the Common Pleas does not attach, and the defendant may take advantage of the defect, even after a trial on the merits.(m)

On an appeal from a magistrate, it is a settled rule that the proceedings are *de novo* as to the declaration, pleadings, and evidence, but the cause of action must continue the same,(n) and the plaintiff cannot substitute another and a different claim. Thus, having proceeded in debt before the former, he cannot, in the appellate court, declare in account render.(o) But, the cause of action appearing the same, and the judgment being for a sum within his jurisdiction, if, on the appeal, judgment be given for a sum beyond it, it will yet be good ;(p) though it is undecided what the law would be in case it appeared that the court were of opinion that the cause of action, as it originally stood before the justice, was of an amount more than 100 dollars.(q) The principle upon which this distinction would rest, if it could be supported at all, is, that where it is possible to suppose that the increase was owing to the addition of interest, and of damages for the vexation and expense of the appeal, the judgment above could be supported; for, " it has been determined that when a cause came to trial by jury on an appeal, there was no impropriety in adding interest to the sum recovered before the justice, although the aggregate amount should be more than 100 dollars."(r)

When the appeal is defectively entered, the proper mode is to call on the appellant to perfect it in a given time, or show cause why it should not be quashed. It would be error in the Common Pleas to quash such appeal in the first instance.(s)

(g) Sleck *v.* King, 3 Barr, 213.
(h) M'Connell *v.* Micheltree, 4 Barr, 197.
(i) Ibid. citing 5 W. & S. 33.
(j) Robinson *v.* Taylor, 4 Barr, 242.
(k) Ellis *v.* Brewster, 6 W. 277.
(l) Miller *v.* Criswell, 3 Barr, 449.
(m) Wright *v.* Guy, 10 S. & R. 229.

(n) Owen *v.* Shelhamer, 3 Bin. 45.
(o) Wright *v.* Guy, 10 S. & R. 229. See also Bechtol *v.* Cobaugh, id. 121.
(p) McEntire *v.* McElduff, 1 S. & R. 19.
(q) Id. 21-2.
(r) Id. 21.
(s) Carter *v.* McMichael, 2 Pa. R. 431. Means v. Trout, 16 S. & R. 349, 350.

Upon an appeal from the judgment of a justice of the peace, the de-fendant cannot have oyer of the original writ so as to make it the sub-ject of a plea in abatement.(*t*)

Nor can he plead in abatement on the appeal, if he has neglected his opportunity to do so before the justice.(*u*)

In computing the twenty days allowed for entering an appeal from the judgment of a magistrate, by the act of 1810, the day on which the judgment was entered is excluded.(*v*) Under this act the transcript must be filed on or before the first day of the next term, after entering bail on the appeal.(*w*)

If the appellant neglect to file the appeal, and he has the whole of the first day of the term to do it, the magistrate before whom the judg-ment was entered, may issue execution at the instance of the appellee, or proceed by scire facias against the bail.(*x*)

An affidavit, previous to the issuing of a *certiorari*, must be made ac-cording to the 21st section of the act of March 20, 1810, which must pursue the words of the act *substantially*.(*y*) The *certiorari* may issue in civil cases without a special *allocatur*, that is, an application to the court in term, or to a judge in vacation for an allowance of the writ.(*z*) On *certioraris* to remove the judgments of aldermen and justices, the particular exceptions intended to be insisted on, must be filed on or before argument day, and on default thereof, the judgment below shall be affirmed of course; the assignment of general errors is insufficient and void.(*a*) This rule has been determined to be a valid rule, and proper and necessary for the dispatch of business.(*b*) When the judg-ment of a justice is affirmed on *certiorari*, execution may issue at once out of the superior court, without referring the cause again to the jus-tice.(*c*) There are four terms in the Common Pleas, which commence on the first Mondays in March and June, third in September, and first in December. The first day only of each term of this court was formerly the return day, though recently monthly return days have been esta-blished.(*cc*)

It has been long and definitely settled, that both under the acts of March, 1810 and 1814, it is the amount of the demand adjudicated, and not merely the numerical amount of the judgment rendered by the justice, that regulates the right of appeal.(*d*)

Though the technical judgment entered should not exceed the sum of $5 33, or, where a reference was had, $20, yet if the amount actually passed upon exceeded these respective sums, the right to ap-peal is recognized though perhaps not given by a literal construction of the acts.(*e*)

The act of 12th July, 1842, abolishing imprisonment for debt, abo-

(*t*) Hinckley *v*. Smith, 4 W. 433.
(*u*) Ibid.
(*v*) Browne *v*. Browne, 3 S. & R. 496.
(*w*) See 1 Br. 160. Beale *v*. Dougherty, 3 Bin. 432.
(*x*) Act of April 1, 1823, § 5, Pamph. L. 288.
(*y*) 1 Br. 217.
(*z*) Com. *v*. Turnpike Co., 2 Bin. 257.
(*a*) Rules, 23. C. P. Philad.

(*b*) Snyder *v*. Bauchman, 8 S. & R. 336.
(*c*) 1 D. 410.
(*cc*) Act of June 13, 1836, § 32.
(*d*) Prestly *v*. Ross, 1 J. 411. Bell, J. See Stoy *v*. Yost, 12 S. & R. 385; Soop *v*. Coates, Id. 388; Klinginsmith *v*. Noll, 3 Pa. R. 120; Stewart *v*. Keemle, 4 S. & R. 72; McCloskey *v*. McConnel, 9 W. 17.
(*e*) Ibid.

lished bail in all but the excepted cases mentioned in it; but by the act of March 20, 1845, the bail on appeal must be absolute for costs.(*f*)

A recognizance on appeals since the act of 1842 abolishing imprisonment for debt, "conditioned to prosecute the appeal with effect," is void.(*g*)

The most liberal construction must be given to the act regulating appeals from justices so as to secure the right of a trial by jury.(*h*)

A defective recognizance on appeal from a justice may be amended even after decision of a motion to quash the appeal. It is the appellee's duty to call on the appellant for a good recognizance by a rule. After error brought he may file a new one, *nunc pro tunc*, bearing even date with the previous one: failing which the appeal may be quashed *de novo*.(*i*)

A defendant whose set-off is refused, has an appeal under the acts of 1810 and 1814.(*j*)

By the act of March 20, 1845, the right of appeal from the justice's judgment is extended to the defendant in all cases, where under existing laws the plaintiff would be entitled to an appeal.(*k*)

An appeal from the judgment of a justice, is in time, if filed in the Common Pleas within the twenty days, although a return day has intervened, prior to which the appellant had entered an appeal, and given bail, which he withdrew after the return day, and entered other bail, and though execution has issued.(*l*)

(*f*) Purd. 81. See Beers *v.* West Branch Bank, 7 W. & S. 365.
(*g*) Donley *v.* Brownlee, 7 Barr, 110, citing 2 Pa. R. 475.
(*h*) Potts *v.* Staeger, 2 J. 363.

(*i*) Adams *v.* Null, 5 W. & S. 363.
(*j*) Prestly *v.* Ross, 1 J. 410.
(*k*) Ibid.
(*l*) Potts *v.* Staeger, 2 J. 363.

CHAPTER II.

OF THE EQUITY JURISDICTION OF THE FOREGOING COURTS.

THE first settlers of Pennsylvania brought with them the whole body of the English jurisprudence (applicable to, and requisite for their wants and situations), both that which was administered in the courts of chancery, and that which was the guide of the courts of law. The principles of *equity*, as well as those of *law*, flowed in upon them from the parent source, but in their simple state of society, they found but little occasion for distinguishing the channels. So far as regarded those principles or rules of justice, our jurisprudence was not greatly defective. They were always recognized, and pervaded our system as thoroughly, perhaps, though not in the same manner, as in the English system.(*m*) And the whole *theory* of that equitable jurisprudence became incorporated with our own code, and its principles circulated through all the channels of our judicial system. They were adopted by us as fully as by any of our sister States in which a regular chancery tribunal exists, and became as binding as those of the common law;(*n*) although, up to the time of passing the act of 1836, which will be presently introduced, we had, for the most part, different modes of administering relief.(*o*) *Equity* and *law* became convertible terms;(*p*) and still are. The power of exercising that jurisdiction, in a limited degree, became *blended* with the power to administer law, under the same forms.(*q*) It was in consequence of this mode of administering justice, that the want of separate equitable modes of procedure was sensibly felt. In order to make the common law forms of procedure subservient to the purposes of equitable relief, it became necessary to resort to fictions, and accordingly fictions became, and are still, the substratum of our equity system. Before the Revolution, the means of doing justice for the time being were withheld from the existing tribunals, a state of things occasioned by the conflict of opinion, first, between the legislature of the province and the privy council in England, and afterwards between the proprietary or royal governors and the legislature, upon the expediency of establishing a separate chancery tribunal.(*r*) And though, since the Revolution and the framing of the present constitution, these wants have from time to time been in some measure supplied, yet, notwithstanding

(*m*) Rep. of the Com. on the Civ. Code, 1834–35, p. 5.

(*n*) See The Case of Torr's Estate, 2 R. 252.

(*o*) Report, 15—16.

(*p*) Kuhn *v.* Nixon, 15 S. & R. 125; Hawthorn *v.* Bronson, 16 Id. 278—9.

(*q*) Shoemaker *v.* Meyer, 4 S. & R. 455; Peebles *v.* Reading, 8 Id. 491; Collins *v.* Rush, 7 Id. 155; Ebert *v.* Wood, 1 Bin. 217; Hawthorn *v.* Bronson, 16 S. & R. 278, 9.

(*r*) Rep. of Com. *ubi supra.*

these defects of form were often lamented by our judges, the jurisprudence of the commonwealth continued to labor under the reproach of
inability to do complete and effectual justice, until the promulgation of
the acts of assembly, commencing with that of 1836, by which has been
established an almost entire equity organization.

SECTION I.

OF THE POWERS TO GRANT RELIEF IN EQUITY USUALLY EXERCISED
BY THE COURTS OF PENNSYLVANIA BEFORE THE CONSTITUTION OF
1790.

An examination of the early legislative history of Pennsylvania
proves that equity was for a long time considered a necessary ingredient
in the administration of justice; and repeated efforts appear to have
been made to unite the chancery powers with those of the common law
courts; which were as often frustrated by the paramount authority of
the British government.

It appears from the minutes of the Provincial Council, that in 1684
a court consisting of five judges was constituted " to try all criminals
and titles of land, and to be a *Court of Equity* to decide all differences
upon appeals from the county courts." It is believed that this court
transacted little business.

By an act passed in 1693, the several county courts were empowered
to hear and determine " all matters and causes in equity," where the
subject in controversy was under ten pounds sterling in amount or value.
In 1701, in an act " for establishing courts of judicature in this province and counties annexed," we find a provision, that the judges of the
several Courts of Common Pleas should have full power " to hear and
decree all such matters and causes of equity as shall come before them
in the said courts; wherein the proceedings shall be by bill, and answer
with such other pleadings as are necessary in chancery courts, and
proper in these parts; with power also for the said justices to force
obedience to their decrees in equity, by imprisonment or sequestration
of lands, as the case may require."(s) The Supreme Court had power
by the same act to hear and determine appeals in equity causes, and to
make such decrees thereon as should be agreeable to equity and justice.
This act was repealed by the queen in council, in 1705.

In 1710, another act was passed "for establishing courts of judicature," by which it was provided, that "that there shall be a *Court of
Equity* held by the judges of the said respective County Courts of
Common Pleas four times a year, at the respective places, and near the
said times as the said Courts of Common Pleas are held, in every county
of this province; and that the prothonotary of the Common Pleas shall
be the register of the said Court of Equity in every county; which
said justices, or any three of them, within the limits of their commissions and authorities to them appointed, as is aforesaid, shall have full
power, and are hereby empowered and authorized, to hear and decree
all such matters and causes of equity as shall come before them in the

(s) MS. L.

said courts, where the proceedings shall be, as heretofore, by bill and answer, with such other pleadings as are necessary in chancery courts, and proper in these parts; with power also for the said justices of the respective Courts of Equity to issue forth all manner of subpœnas, and all other process as may be needful, to oblige and force defendants to answer suits there; as also to award commissions for taking answers and examining witnesses; and to grant injunctions for staying suits in law, and stopping wastes, as there may be occasion, observing, as near as may be, the rules and practice of the High Court of Chancery in Great Britain; with power to make orders, and award all manner of process, and do all other things necessary for bringing causes to hearing, and to force obedience to their decrees in equity, which may be by imprisonment of bodies, or sequestration of lands; and admit bills of revivor, as the case may require. And if any defendant or defendants, in any suit which shall be commenced against them in one of the said counties, shall, after he or they are served with a subpœna, or other process, remove into any other county of this province, all process necessary to bring such defendant to answer, and all commissions for taking of their answers, and examining of witnesses, with all other process necessary to bring such causes to a hearing, shall, and may be awarded out of the court where those causes or suits shall be first commenced, into any other county of this province, as the case may require.

" *Provided always*, That no subpœnas, or other process for appearance, shall issue out of any of the said Courts of Equity till the bill is filed with the proper officer, except bills for injunctions to stay wastes, or suits at law.

Provided also, That if any person or persons shall find themselves grieved with any decree or sentence made or given by the said justices in equity, it shall and may be lawful to and for him or them, so grieved, forthwith to appeal, or have recourse to the judges of the Supreme Court, to set forth his or their cause, by petition, bill, or plaint, so as the sum adjudged to be paid by such decree amount to ten pounds or upwards, this country money; and so as he or they, so appealing, first pay down the court charges, and either satisfy the decree or sentence, so given, or deposit with the justices the sum awarded, or give sufficient security to prosecute the said appeal, and pay all costs and damages that shall be awarded against him or them; and then, albeit the party appealing be imprisoned upon that decree or sentence, he shall be enlarged; and that such appeals shall supersede all further process upon the decree or sentence appealed from, till the same be heard, tried, or dismissed, in the said Supreme Court. *Provided also*, That nothing herein contained shall give the said justices any power or authority to hear, decree, or determine in equity, any matter, cause, or thing, wherein sufficient remedy may be had in any other court, or before any other magistrate or judicature in this province, either by the rules of the common law, or according to the tenor and directions of the laws of this province. But that when matters determinable at common law, shall be brought before them in equity, they shall refer or remit the parties to the common law; and when matters of fact shall happen to arise upon their examination, or hearing of the matters and causes to be heard and determined in the said court, then, and in every such case, they shall order the matter of fact to issue and trial at the Court of

Common Pleas for the proper county where the fact ariseth, before they proceed to sentence or decree in the said Court of Equity."(t)

By the third section of the same act, it was provided, that "there shall be a Court of Equity held by the judges of the respective Supreme Courts in every county of the province," for the determination of matters brought before them upon appeal. This act shared the fate of its predecessors, having been annulled in England in 1713. Two years afterwards, another attempt was made, by the passage of an act "for erecting a Supreme or Provincial Court of law and equity in this province," in which it was provided that the judges of the Supreme Court shall have authority "to hold pleas in equity, by bill, appeal, petition, or suit, to be brought or exhibited in the said court, by, for, or against any person or persons whatsoever, for any discovery or other matters relievable in equity, and thereupon to issue out process of subpœna, or distringas, and all other usual process for compelling the parties defendants in such suit to appear, put in their answers, and make their defences to such bills, appeals, petitions, or suits, and for the parties to proceed thereon and thereupon according to such rules or orders, and in such manner and form as the Courts of Chancery and Exchequer in Great Britain have used to proceed by," &c.(u)

This act was annulled in England in 1719. In the succeeding year, in consequence of a resolution of the assembly, Governor Keith established a separate Court of Equity, exercising the functions of chancellor in his own person, assisted by certain members of the council; and this tribunal appears to have existed, nominally at least, until about the year 1736, when, in consequence of the determined opposition of the legislature, it was discontinued, or suppressed.

After that year, no attempt appears to have been made, either to create a District Court of Chancery, or to invest the common law courts with general chancery powers.

The *Orphans' Court* has indeed always been essentially a Court of Equity.

Its jurisdiction is limited, but within its peculiar range it has from the earliest times exercised many of the functions of a Court of Chancery.

The act of 1713, § VIII., gave to this court power to compel obedience by attachment and sequestration "as fully as any Court of Equity may or can do."

By the act of 1722, § XIII., the judges of the Supreme Court were authorized to "minister justice," and exercise the jurisdiction and powers thereby granted concerning the premises "as fully and amply to all intents and purposes whatsoever, as the justices of the Court of King's Bench, Common Pleas, and Exchequer at Westminster, or any of them may or can do."

The Court of Exchequer in England has chancery powers, but this section has never been supposed to confer them upon our Supreme Court.

By the same act, § XXI., the Courts of Common Pleas were authorized to "hear and determine all manner of pleas, actions, suits, and causes, civil, personal, real, and mixed, according to the law and constitution of this province." No express authority to exercise chancery powers, was given by this act to them, nor can any be implied.

(t) Ed. 1714, p. 120.   (u) MS. Laws, quoted in Rep. of Com. *ubi supra.*

In 1772, an act was passed "to oblige the trustees and assignees of insolvent debtors, to execute their trusts.(v)   This act was repealed in 1818.(w)

Commissioners were to be appointed by the court, who had authority to call the trustees before them, and compel them to settle their accounts, and to call before them witnesses, and examine them, &c.   This appears to have been the first attempt to give relief as in equity, in the case of trustees, and is the only instance of the kind, that we have met with previous to the Revolution.

The constitution of 1790 declared, that "the Supreme Court, and the several Courts of Common Pleas of this commonwealth, shall, besides the powers usually exercised by such courts, have the powers of a Court of Chancery, so far as relates to the perpetuating testimony—obtaining evidence from places not within this State, and the care of the persons and estates of those who are *non compotes mentis;* and such other powers as may be found necessary by future general assemblies, not inconsistent with this constitution."

The first grant of equity powers, subsequently to this constitution, appears to have been occasioned by the frequent complaints of the loss of deeds during the Revolution.

By an act passed the 28th March, 1786,(x) power was given to the Supreme Court, upon bill or petition filed, setting forth the loss of deeds, or other writings, to issue a subpœna, requiring the persons named to appear and make answer on oath, &c.—to refer to a master, and, upon his report, to make such order and decree in the premises as to justice and equity shall appertain.   This act was limited to continue in force five years, and consequently expired in 1791.   But in 1791 it was revived, and extended to the respective courts of Common Pleas; and is yet in force.

The next instance of the grant of equity powers was in 1789, when proceedings in the nature of a bill of discovery, were authorized in the case of foreign attachment.

By the act of 28th September, 1789,(y) it was declared that it should be lawful for any plaintiff in a writ of attachment, after judgment obtained against the defendant, to exhibit interrogatories in writing to the garnishees, who were required to file their answers in writing, and under oath.

These are all the powers of relief in equity, that appear to have been granted or exercised previously to the constitution of 1790.

SECTION II.

OF THE POWERS TO GRANT RELIEF IN EQUITY CONFERRED BY THE CONSTITUTION OR GRANTED BY THE LEGISLATURE BETWEEN 1790 AND 1836.

We proceed now to inquire, what powers were conferred by the constitution, or have since been granted.   By express grant in the constitution,(z) the Supreme Court, and the several Courts of Common Pleas, have power to grant relief in equity, so far as relates—

(v) 1 Smith's Laws, 414.
(w) 7 Smith, 33.
(x) 2 Smith, 375.

(y) Ibid. 500.
(z) Art. 5, § 6.

1. To the perpetuation of testimony.
2. To the obtaining evidence from places out of the State.
3. To the care of the persons and estates of those who are *non compos mentis.*
4. Such other powers to grant relief in equity as may be necessary.

1st. The first of these powers has been exercised by the courts directly under the constitution, without any legislative provision respecting it. The proceedings are in accordance with the English chancery practice.

2d. The second is exercised by these courts, and indeed by all the courts of the commonwealth, without any chancery forms in the way of commissions, and by rule of court.

3d. The power of determining upon the alleged insanity of persons is exercised upon petition, and through the medium of commissioners and an inquest, according to the practice of chancery; and the appointment of committees of the person and estate is according to the same rules. The legislature has given authority to the Courts of Common Pleas to allow the sale or mortgage of the real estate of a lunatic, by two acts— one passed in 1814,(a) and the other in 1818,(b) and by the act of June 13, 1836, an entire system for the management and control of lunatics' estates has been established.

Besides the powers expressly given by the constitution, the legislature has from time to time granted authority to the courts to administer relief in equity, in the following cases:—

1. *Specific performance of Contracts.*

The act of 31st March, 1792,(c) provides for the specific performance of written contracts to sell lands, in cases where the vendor has died. The proceedings are by petition to the Supreme Court or Common Pleas, in the chancery form; and the court is authorized to make an order empowering the executors or administrators to execute a deed. The act of 1804,(d) extended the authority to the case of executors of executors and administrators *de bonis non.* The act of 1818,(e) authorized similar proceedings in the case of *parol* contracts; and the act of 1821,(f) applied the remedy to the case of covenants for the release or extinguishment of ground-rents. And now, by the act of 24th February, 1834, it is directed that the proceedings in the case of a contract by a decedent, shall be in the Orphans' Court, who have power to decree the specific performance of the contract.

By the act of 1790,(g) the same proceedings are authorized against the committee of a lunatic.

2. Very important and useful powers have also been granted in cases of trusts and trustees, by several acts of assembly, of which the following is believed to be a correct abstract:—

Power has been given by the act of 1772, to bring actions against executors for the recovery of legacies, which places these actions on the footing of a bill in equity.(h)

(a) 6 Smith, 104.
(b) 7 Smith, 13.
(c) 3 Smith, 66.
(d) 4 Smith, 158.
(e) 7 Smith, 79.

(f) Id. 355.
(g) 3 Smith, 129.
(h) Dunlop *v.* The Executors of Johnston, 2 Pa. R. 307.

Power has been given to compel a settlement of accounts by assignees of debtors,(*i*) and other trustees,(*j*) the proceedings being according to the chancery practice, by citation and answer—interrogatories in place of bill of discovery, &c.

Power to remove assignees who are in failing circumstances, or wasting the estate, or neglecting the trust, or about to remove, and to appoint others in their place.(*k*)

Power to remove trustees, created by conveyance, &c., under similar circumstances, and to appoint others.(*l*)

Power to appoint trustees in all cases, where the duties of the trust cannot be performed, by reason of death, infancy, lunacy, or other inability—or where a trustee named in any deed or will refuses to act, or where one of several is dead.(*m*)

Power to discharge trustees on their own application, after settlement of accounts, &c.(*n*)

Power to compel trustees to convey the legal estate, where the trust has expired.(*o*)

Power to compel trustees in domestic attachment to settle their accounts, and to dismiss or discharge them.(*p*)

Power to dismiss assignees under a voluntary assignment, and appoint others.(*q*)

Power to compel trustees for religious and charitable societies, to account; and to dismiss them and appoint others in their stead.(*r*)

These powers are now vested in the respective Courts of Common Pleas, as well as in the Supreme Court, and in some instances in the District Courts.

3. Besides these general authorities, there are many special acts of assembly, giving powers to the courts to grant relief in equity, in particular cases of trust.

Power has been conferred on the courts, to give relief in certain cases, by compelling answers on oath to interrogatories in the nature of a bill of discovery.

In the case of stock in a body corporate, owned by a debtor, the act of 1819 authorizes interrogatories to be administered to the person in whose name the stock is held, and requires answers on oath.

In the case of assignees' accounts, by the act of 1828, auditors are authorized to examine them on oath touching their account.

In the case of corporations, against whom a judgment may be obtained, with a return of *nulla bona* to an execution, citation may issue to any officer a member, and answers on oath to interrogatories may be required and compelled.(*s*)

In one particular instance the legislature has gone the whole length of creating an equity tribunal, with plenary powers, viz. in the act passed 9th March, 1820, entitled "An act to provide for the settlement of the concerns of the Marietta and Susquehanna Trading Company." The first section declares that the District Court of Lancaster "shall have

(*i*) Act of 24th March, 1818.
(*j*) Act of 1825, act of 1828.
(*k*) Act of 1818.
(*l*) Act of 1828.
(*m*) Acts of 1825 and 1828.
(*n*) Acts of 1825 and 1828.

(*o*) Ibid.
(*p*) Act of 1829.
(*q*) Act of 1831.
(*r*) Act of 17th February, 1818.
(*s*) Act of 1828.

all the authority, powers, and jurisdiction of a Court of Equity, so far as relates to the Marietta and Susquehanna Trading Company, its trustees, debtors, creditors, and stockholders, or any other person or persons interested in the concerns of the said company." The second section provides for the mode of proceeding, which is to be by bill and answer. The decree is to be according to "equity and law." The bill is to be taken *pro confesso*, if the party do not appear and make answer. If money be decreed, execution is to issue as on judgment. If anything is to be done by the party, the decree may be enforced by attachment and sequestration.

Analogous to the proceedings in chancery, though the cases are not within the jurisdiction of the English chancellor, are the proceedings in cases of *divorce*,(t) and *habitual drunkards*.(u)

SECTION III.

OF THE POWERS TO GRANT RELIEF IN EQUITY CONFERRED ON THE COURTS BY THE ACT OF 1836 AND THE SUBSEQUENT ACTS.

1. Act of 1836, and report of commissioners thereon.
2. Equity legislation since 1836.
3. Equity adjudications.

1. *Act of* 1836, *and report of commissioners.*
By the 13th section of this act,(v) the legislature have provided for the cases in which it appeared to them expedient to authorize the courts designated to proceed according to the manner of a Court of Chancery, beginning with the instances mentioned in the constitution.

That section thus provides: The Supreme Court, and the several Courts of Common Pleas, shall have the jurisdiction and powers of a Court of Chancery, so far as relates to—

I. The perpetuation of testimony:
II. The obtaining of evidence from places not within the State:
III. The care of the persons and estates of those who are *non compotes mentis:*
IV. The control, removal and discharge of trustees, and the appointment of trustees, and the settlement of their accounts.
V. The supervision and control of all corporations other than those of a municipal character, and unincorporated societies or associations, and partnerships:
VI. The care of trust moneys and property, and other moneys and property made liable to the control of the said courts.
And in such other cases as the said courts have heretofore possessed such jurisdiction and powers, under the constitution and laws of this commonwealth:
And in every case in which any court as aforesaid, shall exercise any of the powers of a Court of Chancery, the same shall be exercised accord-

(t) Act of 1815.
(u) Acts of 1819, 1822, and 1836.

(v) Pamph. L. 789, 790.

ing to the practice in equity, prescribed or adopted by the Supreme Court of the United States, unless it be otherwise provided by act of assembly, or the same shall be altered by the Supreme Court of this commonwealth, by general rules and regulations, made and published as is hereinbefore provided.

And the Supreme Court, when sitting in bank, in the City of Philadelphia, and the Court of Common Pleas for the said city and county, shall, besides the powers and jurisdiction aforesaid, have the power and jurisdiction of Courts of Chancery, so far as relates to—

I. The supervision and control of partnerships, and corporations other than municipal corporations.

II. The care of trust moneys and property, and other moneys and property made liable to the control of the said courts.

III. The discovery of facts material to a just determination of issues, and other questions arising or depending in the said courts.

IV. The determination of rights to property or money claimed by two or more persons, in the hands or possession of a person claiming no right of property therein.

V. The prevention or restraint of the commission or continuance of acts contrary to law, and prejudicial to the interests of the community, or the rights of individuals.

VI. The affording specific relief, when a recovery in damages would be an inadequate remedy; *Provided*, That in relation to the discovery of facts material to a just determination of issues, and other questions, the District Court for the City and County of Philadelphia, shall have the same power and authority, within its jurisdiction, as is hereby conferred on the Court of Common Pleas for the said city and county: *And provided further*, That no process to be issued by the said courts of the City and County of Philadelphia, or the Supreme Court, sitting therein, under the chancery powers herein specially granted, excepting such as have heretofore been exercised, shall at any time be executed beyond the limits of the city and county aforesaid.

The bill reported by the commissioners embraced the whole State; but the legislature limited it to Philadelphia, and extended the jurisdiction as to *the discovery* of evidence to the District Court.

The jurisdiction of the chancery in England, say the commissioners in their report, is divided by a late writer of authority,(w) into three branches; a division which it is convenient to adopt here to avail ourselves of in another part of this inquiry.

   I. *Exclusive.*

   II. *Assistant.*

   III. *Concurrent.*

   I. The *exclusive* jurisdiction embraces,

      1. Trusts.

      2. Mortgages.

      3. Equities of married women.

      4. Idiots and lunatics.

      5. Infants.

      6. Charities.

      7. Receivers.

(w) Mr. Jeremy in his Treatise on Equity.

II. The *assistant* jurisdiction.
   1. Discovery of facts material at law from *parties*.
   2. Obtaining evidence from persons not parties.
   3. Compelling suppression of facts, &c., not affecting merits.
III. The *concurrent* jurisdiction.
   A. Peculiar means of administering *distributive* justice.
      1. By reference to masters.
      2. By directing trials and issues.
      3. By its mode of executing certain special decrees.
        § 1. In ascertaining boundaries.
        § 2. In making partition.
        § 3. In setting out dower.
   B. Peculiar means of administering *preventive* justice.
      1. By *injunctions*.
        § I. To restrain nuisance.
        § II. To restrain trespass.
        § III. To restrain waste.
        § IV. To restrain proceedings at law.
      2. By decrees upon bills *quia timet*.
   C. General means of administering justice.
      1. In cases of accident.
      2. In cases of mistake.
      3. In cases of fraud.
      4. In cases where the remedies afforded by the courts of law are inappropriate.
        § 1. By compelling specific performance of agreements.
        § 2. By enforcing delivery of specific chattels.
        § 3. By relieving against forfeitures and penalties.
        § 4. By rescinding agreements.
        § 5. By preventing abuses of the rules and practice of the courts of law.
      5. In cases of account.

Taking this enumeration of the powers of chancery to be sufficiently full and comprehensive, let us see to what extent our courts possess these powers, and whether they are exercised as such, and according to the forms of chancery proceedings, or through the common law channels.

I. Of the exclusive jurisdiction of chancery, and herein,
   1. Of *Trusts*.

The principles of our law, upon the subject both of express and implied trusts are believed to be precisely the same as those of chancery, and we are not aware that any difficulty is experienced in the application of those principles to the cases arising in the courts.

It is in the direct and visitatorial power of chancery over trustees, that its superiority over our courts was, until within a few years, very apparent. These powers consist in,
   1. The removal of trustees for misconduct, and other causes which render them unfit to execute the trust.
   2. The discharge of trustees, at their own request.
   3. The appointment of new trustees, in all cases of vacancy or inability, whether by death, removal, or otherwise.

4. To give relief in the cases of infant, idiot, insolvent, or absent trustees, by directing conveyances, &c.

5. To compel conveyance of the legal estate to the *cestui qui trust*, when the trust has expired.

To what extent have these powers been imparted to our courts?

1. The acts of 1823, 1825, and 1828, give power to remove trustees appointed by deed, will, or other instrument, in case of misconduct, incapacity, &c.

Some doubt has been expressed whether the provisions of these acts extend to the case of a trustee, who has in part executed the trust; and the case of implied trusts is not provided for at all.

2 and 3. The discharge of trustees, and the appointment of others, are also fully provided for by the above-mentioned acts.

4. We have no provision precisely of this kind. The object is attained however, by the appointment of a trustee for the purpose.   ·

In England, it appears to be thought that a trustee ought not to be removed, merely by reason of infancy or lunacy, but that the court ought to have the power of directing the infant, or the committee of the lunatic, to convey, in cases where a conveyance by the trustee is required.(*x*)

We think upon the whole, that our law is broad enough for every valuable purpose, and that the authority to appoint a new trustee, which might perhaps be extended to the appointment of temporary trustees, during the minority or absence of the nominal trustee, is sufficient and more convenient in its operation.

5. The acts of 1825 and 1828 give express authority to the courts to compel trustees to convey the legal estate, when the trust has expired.

Little, therefore, seems to be wanted to complete the powers of our courts, to give relief in equity, in this branch of its jurisdiction, excepting the application of them to the case of implied trusts, and the other cases to which we have adverted.

2. In the case of *Mortgages*.

Here we have a system of our own, which possesses advantages of a peculiar kind, and, it appears to us, is preferable in all respects to the artificial and complicated system which has grown up in England. We find no defects in our law upon this point, and have no occasion to borrow any of the powers of the English chancery. The recording acts have relieved us from many embarrassing questions of frequent occurrence in England; and the proceeding by *scire facias*, has rendered obsolete most of the law about foreclosure and equity of redemption.

3. *Equitable Rights of Married Women.*

No doubt is entertained, that the principles of equity upon this subject are the same in our courts as in chancery.

The doctrines respecting the separate estates of married women, their rights and liabilities, have been recognized in this commonwealth from the earliest dates. Upon the subject, however, of the equity of a married woman to a settlement or provision out of property devolving

(*x*) See the acts 7 Anne, c. 19, 4 Geo. 2, c. 10, 1 & 2 Geo. 4, c. 114, 6 Geo. 4, c. 74, &c.

upon her husband, or his assignees, in her right, the case is somewhat different. In *Yohe* v. *Barnet*,(y) C. J. Tilghman said: "It is to be regretted that the courts of this State are not vested with the power exercised by the Court of Chancery in England, of insisting on some provision for the wife, when the husband applies to them for the purpose of getting possession of her personal property. But we have no trace of any such exercise of power by our courts. It must be taken for granted, then, that they possess no such power." So in *Slifer* v. *Beates*,(z) Judge Duncan said: "In our last inquiry, the difficulty arises from the want of adequate chancery powers: and this court have on various occasions been distressed in the distribution of the wife's real estate, converted by the act of the law into personal: for if the husbands of these two feme coverts, who have brought this action, came into a Court of Chancery against the trustees, for the trust-money arising from the sale under the decree of the Orphans' Court, that court, where there was such, would be the only tribunal. Here there is no such authority exercised by the court. Chancery would compel a reasonable settlement on the wives," &c.

By the act of 29th March, 1832, § 48, power has been given to the Orphans' Court, to make provision for the wife in all cases in which money shall be awarded to her by that court, for her share or portion of the estate of an intestate.

It seems to us to be proper, to give similar authority to the common law courts in cases of partition, and in all other cases in which the wife's real estate may be converted into personal—as in the case of the surplus proceeds of a sale of the wife's land under an execution; and we think that so far the legislature is called upon to go, by obvious principles of justice and expediency. But do these principles require us to carry the rule to the extent of compelling the husband to make provision for his wife in every case in which he seeks the aid of the court to recover her money or property? The rule in England is by no means a satisfactory one. If the husband is obliged to go into the Court of Equity to recover his wife's choses in action, that court will require him to make a reasonable settlement upon her. But if he can recover them through the means of the common law courts, chancery will not interfere. With us, however, there is but one species of tribunal for the recovery of property, whether in possession or action. No distinction can therefore be made which can be sustained upon any clear principles.

We incline upon the whole to think that, in such questions, it will be better to let them take their course without interfering between husband and wife, with the exception only of the case in which the wife's real estate has been converted into personal by process or operation of law; when, we think, that she should not stand in a worse situation than if the property had continued to be real; unless, upon a separate examination, she should consent to the appropriation of the fund to her husband.

If, therefore, we extend to the common law courts the power which has been given to the Orphans' Court in this respect, it appears to us

(y) 1 Bin. 365.   (z) 9 S. & R. 182.

that we shall confer as much additional chancery power with regard to this subject, as is desirable at present. We wish to limit this remark, however, to the particular question we have been considering. There are difficulties and hardships arising out of the present law and powers of the courts relating to divorce and insolvency, which require serious consideration; and we have before us some plans upon these subjects which we expect to submit to the legislature, intended to secure to married women a suitable portion of their personal property in the event of a divorce, or of the insolvency of their husbands, without impairing the marital authority, or interfering with the just claims of creditors.

4. The next subject of chancery jurisdiction, is contained under the head of *Idiots and Lunatics.*

Here, as has been already shown, the general jurisdiction is given by the constitution, in express terms, " the care of the persons and estates of those who are *non compos mentis.*" These expressions would seem, from the context, to give the court all the powers usually exercised by the chancellor in England; and such, doubtless, was the intention of the framers of the constitution. It is not necessary, therefore, in reference to our present object, to inquire what were the powers of the Court of Chancery, or rather, of the chancellor in person, in England, in respect to Idiots and Lunatics at the date of the constitution, since they have passed of course to our courts. But since that date, important alterations have been made in the English law, respecting both the method of proceeding upon commissions of lunacy, and the care and treatment of this unfortunate class of persons, some of which deserve to be incorporated with our code. We have prepared a bill on this subject, which, we think, will be found to contain some essential improvements of the law.

5. *Infants.*

The power of the English chancery to appoint and control guardians, and to regulate the maintenance of infants, is vested in its fullest extent in our Orphans' Court; which also possesses authority to allow the sale or mortgage of their real estate, to an extent which it is believed the English chancery does not possess ; but our Orphans' Court has never interfered, on the subject of their marriage, as has been done in England. It does not appear to be expedient to incorporate this part of their equity jurisprudence with ours. Another branch of chancery power, arising from their general jurisdiction over infants, viz.: the control of the parents' custody of them,(a) has been exercised by the Supreme Court on *habeas corpus*,(b) and by the Common Pleas,(c) and probably no additional power is required.

6. *Charities.*

The chancellor in England exercises a general superintendence over charitable corporations and societies, and controls trustees appointed for such purposes, in the same manner as others. One of his most important functions in this capacity, is the direction of such trustees, in the execution of the trust; keeping them in the channel of the donor's

(a) 2 Russell, 1 Wellesly *v.* Duke of Beaufort.

(b) 5 Binn. 520, Commonwealth *v.* Addicks.
(c) 1 Br. 143, Commonwealth *v.* Nutt.

intention, where it is practicable, and where that is not the case, making new channels for them *as near that* as possible, or, in the technical language, *Cy pres*. So far as regards the appointment, removal, or discharge of trustees, our courts have now the same powers as the chancery, and may exercise them in the case of charities, as in other cases.

The act of 17th Feb. 1818, gives express authority to the courts to call to account and remove trustees holding property for religious, literary, or charitable purposes, and the acts of 1825 and 1828 extend the authority of all cases of trusts.

These powers will probably be found sufficient to keep trustees to their duty, and to prevent the trust failing for want of a suitable trustee. But in regard to the other branch of the chancellor's jurisdiction and powers, which we have mentioned, his interference, namely, in relation to the fulfilment of the charitable purposes, the case is different. It is believed that no instance has occurred in this State, of a similar exercise of authority by our courts; and their power to interfere under existing laws may well be questioned. If, for example, a testator should bequeath funds for charitable purposes, generally, without mentioning the particular objects, or, for some charitable purpose which cannot be attained, or the like; and the trustees should be willing and competent to act, has any court in this commonwealth power to direct, *à priori*, the application of the fund to a purpose near to that which may be supposed to have been intended, or to direct it at all? We say *à priori*, because, doubtless, when the executor or trustee, as the case may be, comes to settle his accounts, the court which has jurisdiction of his accounts will determine whether his application of the funds has been in conformity with the directions in the will.

We think that our courts do not possess the power of controlling such trustees, otherwise than as just mentioned, and indirectly, by the power to dismiss them if they shall mismanage the trust funds; and it appears to us, upon the whole, that considering the delicate nature of many questions arising upon trusts for religious and charitable purposes, it is as well to leave the law on its present footing.

7. The Court of Chancery also exercises the power of taking charge of property both real and personal, for the benefit of the parties interested therein, wherever this is necessary, for the due administration of justice: And this is done through the medium of a receiver appointed for the purpose.

The power to interfere in cases of this description has rarely been exercised by our courts. It is nevertheless a most salutary attribute of preventive justice; and if any doubt should exist, respecting the jurisdiction of the courts, we think it ought to be at once removed. We can see no reasonable objection to giving all the courts express authority for this purpose.

There are cases in which it may be absolutely necessary, as in the instance of an insolvent corporation, which will be remarked upon hereafter, and we think that, to prevent abuses, it may be well to provide that security shall be required, in all cases, from receivers.

II. Assistant jurisdiction of the chancery.

   1. Discovery of facts material at law from parties.

It has been already shown, that the power of compelling a discovery from parties has been given by our courts.

1. In the case of garnishees in foreign attachment.

2. In the case of lost deeds.

3. In the case of stock held in a corporate body, in the name of a third person.

4. In the case of the accounts of assignees.

5. In the case of suits against corporations, to discover their property.

To which may be added.

6. The power of compelling the production of books and papers, given by the act of 1798.

7. In the Orphans' Court, the power of compelling answers in the case of executors, administrators, and guardians.

And analogous to this, is the power requiring answers upon oath by persons applying for the benefit of the insolvent laws.

It remains to be considered whether this power ought to be enlarged so as to embrace the whole sphere of litigation; namely, to compel discovery in all cases from parties to a suit, where by the rules of equity, they may be required to answer. We think that there is no substantial reason in the way of our adoption of this practice.

The march of justice is often interrupted and sometimes defeated in our courts for want of this important aid; and although there is alleged to be danger of perjury, we think that the experience of the courts of equity proves that this is very small.

Under the restrictions, and with the exceptions with which it is exercised in the English chancery, we cannot but think that it will be found a very useful addition to the means possessed by our courts of doing justice, and therefore that it is proper to introduce it into our system.

The commissioners appointed by the British government to inquire into the practice of the courts of common law, have proposed to give those courts power to examine the parties in all cases upon interrogatories, as an equivalent to the bill of discovery.

2. Discovery of facts from persons not parties.

The powers exercised by chancery and classed under this head, viz.

    1. Examining witnesses out of the jurisdiction of the courts, by means of commissions, &c.

    2. For the perpetuation of testimony,

Are already possessed and constantly exercised by our courts. The first in the court, whatever it may be, in which the evidence may be required. And the second in the Supreme Court and Common Pleas, in the regular chancery form, by bill and answer.

We propose, in a bill relating to the action of ejectment which accompanies this report, an additional method of securing the perpetuation of testimony in certain cases. Nothing further seems necessary to be suggested upon these points.

3. Another of the powers of chancery is said to be exerted in compelling the suppression of facts and circumstances which do not affect the merits of the question at law.

This is one of the titles into which the head of the assistant jurisdiction of chancery is divided in the treatises upon equity; but it is not perceived that it is in reality a distinct branch. It is connected with the subject of *notice* and *attendant terms*, which have little or no significance or value in our law, and at all events, the power of suppression here alluded to, is sufficiently possessed by our courts on the trial of questions in which they arise.

Thus it is said that if a person entitled to real estate fears that some mere *legal* obstacle will be set up by his opponent, he may file a bill of discovery, and if it shall appear upon the answer and hearing that the plaintiff has greater equity and the defendant a naked legal title, the court will enjoin him against using it to prevent the plaintiff's recovery at law. The principles of law and equity being amalgamated in our jurisprudence, our courts reach the same result by considering the legal title conveyed to the plaintiff, and thus save the expense and trouble of a proceeding in equity. No addition to our law appears to be necessary, therefore, in this respect.

III. Concurrent jurisdiction of the chancery.

A. Peculiar means of administering distributive justice.

1. By reference to masters.

The advantages of a reference to masters are obtained in our courts by the appointment of auditors or commissioners. In the Orphans' Court auditors are as essential a part of the machinery as masters are of the English chancery. In the Supreme Court and Common Pleas they are usually appointed on questions relating to the distribution of money paid into court, and upon the accounts of trustees, and occasionally for other purposes. No addition to the power of the courts in this respect seems necessary.

2. Trials and issues in courts of law.

One mode of administering justice in chancery is by directing trials at law to determine particular facts in litigation. This of course it is not necessary to consider here, since by our system the trial is in the court possessing chancery powers.

3. There are certain special decrees made by chancery in which relief is given in a peculiar manner.

§ 1. By commissions to ascertain *boundaries*.

These are believed to be seldom resorted to, and not of sufficient importance to make their extension to our courts desirable.

§ 2. Commissions to make *partition*.

The proceedings in the *Orphans'* Court to make partition between the heirs of an intestate, are believed to be sufficient to enable the court to do justice to all parties. In the common law courts, however, inconveniences are sometimes experienced, from the difficulty of proving the titles of the parties interested. In chancery, the answer of the defendants sets forth their title, and a reference to the master ascertains it, and upon his report the court dismisses the petition as against those who do not appear entitled. The appointment of commissioners to set out the respective portions, appears to be in some respect better than the proceeding before a jury. We think that some advantages would be gained for the administration of justice by the adoption of the chancery practice upon these points, at least so far as to substitute *commissioners* for an *inquest*, where the parties assent to it.

§ 3. *Commissions to set out dower.*

The same remark may be made upon this point as under the preceding head, viz.: That the commission to set out dower is more convenient in general than the proceeding before an inquest, because the commissioners are fewer in number, and selected with more especial reference to their competency for the task.

B. Peculiar means of administering *preventive justice.*

1. It is here that the powers of the courts of equity appear to possess a decided superiority over those of the courts of common law, and that instances most frequently occur of defects in our administration of justice. The principal cases mentioned in the chancery books in which the court interferes by its writ of injunction to prevent or restrain the commission of acts injurious to others, are

§ 1. In case of *nuisances.*

§ 2. In case of *trespass.*

§ 3. In case of *waste.*

In all these cases the power is most important and valuable. Indeed, no system of justice can be considered to be complete without the means of prevention and restraint. In the case of *waste* our courts have been invested with powers to the fullest extent, and there appears no reason why they should not be extended to the other cases mentioned. It will be seen that, in the bill relating to *estrepement,* we have suggested a method of restraining the commission of trespass upon lands in certain cases.

§ 4. *To restrain proceedings at law.*

The Courts of Chancery interfere by injunctions to restrain proceedings in the courts of common law, whenever the result of such proceedings would be contrary to equity. The objects attained by this method of chancery procedure are effected in many cases in our courts, in the ordinary mode of administering justice on the trial of the action. There are two classes of cases, however, coming under this head, in respect to which our courts are deficient in the means possessed by chancery, in consequence of the inflexibility of the rule of law relating to the parties to suits, viz.: bills of peace and bills of interpleader. In both these cases it is necessary to introduce other persons than those who are parties to the record at law, and in both the right or title is settled in one proceeding, and costs saved and further litigation prevented.

Among the provisions intended to be submitted to the legislature in this connection, we shall suggest some methods of supplying the deficiencies in our practice, and completing the means of doing justice to the extent possessed by the Courts of Chancery.

2. Preventive justice, by means of a bill *quia timet.*

We have nothing of this kind in our jurisprudence, except so far as relates to threatened *waste*, in which case the acts of assembly, as we have seen, authorize the issuing of a writ of *estrepement.* In the case of chattels or funds, of which the party is not entitled to the immediate possession, we have no means of securing his rights except so far as the 40th section of the act of 1834, relating to executors and administrators, has supplied the defect. This is one of the " powers to grant relief in equity," which, it appears to us, ought no longer to be withheld from our courts. We have accordingly made some provisions upon the subject, in some of the bills relating to particular actions, as ejectment and contribution; and we intend to submit to the legislature other suggestions designed to complete the measure of relief.

C. General means of administering justice by decrees better adapted to the case, or administered in a more satisfactory manner than can be obtained in the courts of law.

1. In case of accident, as in the instances of lost deeds, bonds, &c.

In these and similar cases, the principles of equity are recognized by our courts, and satisfactorily enforced through the medium of their ordinary power and practice.

2. In case of *mistake.*

3. In case of *fraud.*

The same remarks may be made of the chancery rules upon these subjects. They require no exercise of power different from those which have been already noticed, and the principles upon which they rest are familiar to our jurisprudence.

4. Means of administering justice where the remedies afforded by the courts of law are inadequate.

§ 1. By compelling the specific performance of agreements.

This is a highly important part of the chancery jurisdiction, one in which its superiority over the common law is most frequently alleged, and in which the exercise of its powers is very frequently invoked. We possess, nevertheless, in our Pennsylvania practice, remedies which some eminent jurists have considered to be quite equal in their results to those of chancery. The value of the chancery proceedings consists in its *compelling* the thing to be done which has been contracted to be done, viz.: the conveyance of land, or the delivery of a chattel. The *method* of compulsion consists in punishment by attachment and sequestration, if the decree of the court is not carried into effect by the defendant. If he should prefer to lie in prison rather than execute a deed, the English Court of Chancery could do no more. With us the proceeding is by *ejectment*, under which actual possession of the premises is recovered: and nothing is wanting but the deed, which may sometimes be obtained from the defendant by the compulsion of damages assessed by a jury. It may be proper, however, to enlarge the existing powers of the courts, so far as to authorize them after judgment in ejectment to make an order upon the defendant for the execution of the necessary conveyance, and to enforce such order in the manner of a Court of Equity. The remedy by ejectment, however, is believed not to be altogether adequate to the purpose of compelling specific performance, and at the same time of compensating the plaintiff for the damages which he may have sustained in consequence of the non-performance of the agreement. To complete the remedial law in this respect, we propose an enlargement of the action of covenant, by giving it in some respects the properties of a bill in equity, and enabling the court to enforce specific execution of the covenant, by a writ of *habere facias possessionem.* By the alteration proposed, it is not intended to dispense with the accustomed proceeding by ejectment, but merely to increase the number of remedies designed to supply the place of the bill for specific performance.

We have thus far considered agreements for the specific execution of contracts, for the conveyance of land, as in *writing*, and therefore within the provisions of the statute of frauds. There are instances, however, in which agreements of this description have been made by *words* only; and in such cases, if there has been a part performance in conformity with the agreement, our courts, as well as most of those administering similar laws, have compelled the execution of them so far as their means admitted. Where the chancery method prevails, no great difficulty exists, because the *facts* are admitted by the defendant's answer to the bill of discovery, and this is taken to be equivalent to an agreement by him in writing; but no similar authority having heretofore been exercised by our courts, cases have occurred of inability to do complete justice in this respect. The addition to the powers of our courts, which we have already mentioned, to compel answers to bills of discovery or interrogatories upon that method, will, we think, remove the only remaining defect in our law relative to the specific performance of agreements for the conveyance of real estate.

§ 2. By enforcing delivery of *specific chattels.*

We arrive at the same result, or rather possess a more certain and speedy remedy by means of the action of *replevin* which has been extended by our practice to all cases in which goods are detained from the rightful owner, though by the modern English practice (at least) this action is confined to the case of goods unlawfully taken by the defendant.

There does not seem to be any necessity, therefore, for incorporating the chancery procedure in this respect with ours.

§ 3. By relieving against *forfeitures* and *penalties.*

The principles of chancery in respect to this subject are adopted in our code, and administered in the courts in which the forfeiture or penalty is sought to be enforced. This is a much more simple and convenient mode of proceeding, the symmetry of which would be impaired by the introduction of the chancery remedies.

§ 4. By *rescinding agreements* where there was no consideration or it would be unconscientious to require the performance of them.

The remarks upon the last head apply to this, with the addition that we are deficient in the chancery method of compelling the delivery up of an agreement to be cancelled. Perhaps this is not of much importance since the possession of the paper containing the agreement would be of little value to the party, if the contract is declared to be void. If the possession of the paper should, however, be deemed to be material, we are not deficient in the means of compulsion, since the action of *detinue*, or *trover*, or perhaps *replevin*, may be brought for the purpose. It may be proper also to confer upon the courts express power to order the delivery up of instruments in all cases in which it would be contrary to equity to enforce them.

§ 5. By preventing abuses of the rules and practice of the courts of law.

Everything which can be procured in a bill of chancery for this purpose, is with us obtained by application to the court in which the proceedings took place.

5. In cases of *Account.*

" The ground upon which chancery has assumed a concurrent jurisdiction, with the courts of law on matters of account, has been said to be, that the remedy which it is capable of affording is much more complete than that which may be obtained by action."(d)

The superiority of the proceeding in chancery, in this respect, has been denied by some writers, who contend that the action of *account-render* is as comprehensive in its nature, as speedy in its operation, and as complete in its results, as the bill in chancery for an account. It is certain, however, that if a defendant in the action of account-render, choose to avail himself of the power which the law gives him, he may involve the plaintiff in considerable expense, procrastinate greatly the decision of the cause, and produce a series of issues of a complicated and difficult character. The chief advantages of the chancery proceeding appear to be; 1st. In the means of obtaining the *answer* of the defendant on oath.

It is true, that by the statute 4 & 5 Anne, c. 16, s. 27, the auditors at law are empowered to interrogate the parties on oath, yet, the chancery proceeding is superior in convenience by reason of its application to the conscience of the defendant in the first stage of the cause. A plaintiff in the action of account-render, may be embarrassed at the outset, and unable to obtain a judgment *quod computet*, for want of evidence which he might obtain from the defendant, if entitled to his answer.

2d. In chancery, the proceedings after an account is ordered, are generally more expeditious and easily managed, than in the action at common law, auditors in account-render being looked upon as mere clerks, and incompetent to determine any question of fact, it frequently becomes necessary to raise a series of issues, by which great delay is occasioned. In a former report, we expressed the belief that this action is susceptible of great improvement. We have now under consideration, a bill in which we have attempted to carry into effect the suggestions there made. We hope to be able to introduce into our practice some of the advantageous methods of the chancery proceeding, either by engrafting them upon the action of account-render, or by establishing them as distinct and substantive modes of proceeding.

There remain to be noticed two important cases in which relief is given in equity, and which have not been enumerated under either of the foregoing heads, viz.:—

1. *Contribution.*—The nature of chancery proceedings renders them peculiarly proper to give a remedy in cases of this kind. Every professional person is acquainted with the difficulties that surround the action for contribution in the common law courts, and knows how entirely inadequate the remedy is, where there are many parties. In Nailor *v.* Stanley,(e) Judge Duncan, speaking of a case of contribution, said : "This is one among some other instances in which our jurisprudence is defective for want of chancery powers."

In the Orphans' Court we have a proceeding similar to that in equity, to obtain contribution between heirs and devisees, which requires only a conformity with the rules of chancery in relation to pleadings and practice, to be equally beneficial.

(d) Jeremy's Equity, p. 504.   (e) 10 S. & R. 454.

In cases not within the jurisdiction of the Orphans' Court, we propose to enlarge the power of the common law tribunals, so as to enable them to mete out an equal measure of justice. We have prepared a bill regulating the method of proceeding in the action of contribution, which, we hope, will be found to remove most of the existing objections.

2. In the case of Gratz v. Bayard,(f) in which questions arose concerning the power of the courts to interfere to restrain a partner from carrying on the business against the consent of the other partner or his representative, Chief Justice Tilghman said: "In the argument of this case several points of great moment were suggested, which must add to the regret we all feel at the want of a chancery jurisdiction. If prospects had so changed after *Carrel's* death as to render it manifestly advisable to relinquish the plan, and *Connell* had refused to relinquish it, contrary to the advice of the administrator of *Carrel*, I know not how he could have been restrained. But chancery, in such case, would interfere without hesitation; and in many other cases it would interfere where there was strong probability that the salvation of the firm and the rights of creditors depended upon such interference. If the surviving partner acted with gross impropriety, his hands would be tied, and an agent appointed to collect the debts and distribute the effects, under the direction of the court. These are powers which, however desirable, are possessed by no court of this commonwealth." The powers which the eminent and lamented magistrate, whose words we have quoted, considered to be wanting in our jurisprudence, are exercised in the equity courts by the means of the writ of *injunction*, and through the agency of *receivers*. Some remarks upon these points have already been made. If the legislature shall see fit to confer upon our courts general authority to give relief in the case of partners in like manner and with like effect as is practised and allowed in courts of equity, they would possess the means of doing substantial and sufficient justice. But the case of *partners*, in the ordinary acceptation of the word, is far from being that in which an enlargement of this kind of power is most needed. There exists in this commonwealth a great number of societies or associations of persons incorporated and unincorporated, for the proper supervision and control over which adequate powers are not to be found at present in our courts. What is wanting for the due administration of justice is authority to restrain their proceedings when the continuance of them would be prejudicial to the interests of the creditors or of the members; to appoint receivers to take charge of the funds, and protect them from misapplication; and to distribute their assets among creditors, according to the rules established in the case of the insolvency of individuals. In most of the States, these powers are believed to exist in the courts, and of late years have been exercised beneficially for the community."

2. *Equity legislation since* 1836.

Act of 13th June, 1840.(g) The equity jurisdiction of the Supreme Court, within the City and County of Philadelphia, and of the Court of Common Pleas for said county, shall be extended to all cases arising in

(f) 11 S. & R. 47, 48.   (g) Pamph. L. 666.

said city and county, over which Courts of Chancery entertain jurisdiction on the grounds of fraud, accident, mistake, or account.(*h*) § 39.

Act of 6th April, 1844.(*i*)   When any bill in equity shall be filed in
any of the courts of this commonwealth, to perpetuate the evidence of
title to lands, tenements, and hereditaments, in which bill the commonwealth is a necessary party, the process may, and shall be served on the
attorney general, or his deputy, for the county where such lands, tenements, or hereditaments may lie, whose duty it shall be to attend to the
interests of the commonwealth, in the premises.   § 1.

Act of 6th May, 1844.(*j*)   No injunctions shall be issued by any
court or judge, until the party applying for the same shall have given
bond with sufficient sureties, to be approved by said court or judge, conditioned to indemnify the other party for all damages that may be sustained by reason of such injunction.   § 1.

Act of 17th March, 1845.(*k*)   Any person or persons, body or bodies
politic or corporate, parties to any suit in equity now pending, or hereafter to be instituted in the Court of Common Pleas of the County of
Philadelphia, who may be affected by any [interlocutory or](*l*) final order
or decree in such suit in equity, hereafter to be made by the said Court
of Common Pleas, shall be entitled to appeal therefrom to the Supreme
Court in and for the Eastern District of Pennsylvania, upon the same
terms, and with the same regulations as are provided by the existing
laws, in regard to appeals from any definite sentence or decree of an
Orphans' Court: *Provided always*, That in addition to a compliance with
the foregoing terms and regulations, it shall be necessary for the party
appellant, in order to secure to himself the advantage of a stay or
supersedeas of execution, to comply with the following further terms
and conditions:—

I. If an appeal be made, from any order or decree of the said Court
of Common Pleas in Equity, directing the payment of money, such
appeal shall not stay the issuing of execution or other process, to enforce
the decree or any proceedings thereon, unless a bond be given by or on
behalf of the appellant, to the adverse party, in a penalty at least double
the sum decreed to be paid, with two sufficient sureties, to be approved by
the said Court of Common Pleas, or one of the judges thereof, conditioned,
that if the appellant shall fail to prosecute his appeal, or if the same
be dismissed or discontinued, or if the decree appealed from, or any
part thereof, be affirmed, then that such appellant will pay and satisfy
the amount directed to be paid by such decree, or the part of such
amount as to which such decree shall be affirmed, if it be affirmed only
in part, and all damages which shall be awarded against the appellant
by the said Supreme Court upon such appeal.

II. If the decree appealed from direct the assignment or delivery of
any securities, evidences of debt, documents, chattels or things in action,

---

(*h*) See *infra*, 8.
(*i*) Pamph. L. 213.
(*j*) Pamph. L. 564.

(*k*) Pamph. L. 158.
(*l*) Words in brackets repealed by act
of 16th April, 1845, § 4, Pamph. L. 543.

the issuing and execution of process to enforce such decree shall not be stayed by such appeal, unless the articles required to be assigned or delivered be brought into court, or placed in the custody of such officers or receivers as the said Court of Common Pleas shall appoint, or unless a bond in a penalty, at least double the value of the articles so directed to be delivered or assigned, be given to the adverse party, with two sufficient sureties, to be approved as hereinbefore directed; conditioned, that the appellant will abide and obey the order of the said Supreme Court, made upon the subject of such appeal.

III. If the decree appealed from direct the execution of any conveyance or other instrument by any party, the issuing and execution of process to enforce such decree shall not be stayed by such appeal, until the appellant shall have executed the conveyance or instrument directed, and deposited the same with such officers or receivers as shall be designated by the said Court of Common Pleas.

IV. If the decree or order appealed from direct the sale or delivery of the possession of any real property, the issuing and execution of process to enforce the same shall not be stayed until a bond be given with sureties as hereinbefore directed, in such penalty as the Court of Common Pleas shall deem sufficient, conditioned, that during the possession of such real property by such appellant, he will not commit or suffer any waste to be committed thereon: and in case such appeal be dismissed or discontinued, or such order or decree be affirmed, such appellant will pay the value of the use and occupation of such property, from the time of such appeal until the delivery of the possession thereof pursuant to such order or decree. § 1.

Whenever, in the foregoing cases, an appeal shall be perfected by bringing into court, or depositing pursuant to its order, any articles required to be so deposited, or any instruments required to be executed, or by the giving a bond as herein prescribed, such appeal shall stay all further proceedings in the said Court of Common Pleas, upon the order or decree appealed from, and upon the subject-matter embraced in such order or decree; but shall not prevent the said Court of Common Pleas from proceeding upon any other matter included in the bill, and not affected by said order or decree: *Provided, however,* That whenever the order or decree appealed from directs the sale of perishable property, notwithstanding any such appeal, and the compliance with the foregoing directions, such property may be sold by the final order of the said Court of Common Pleas, after the making of such appeal, and the proceeds of such sale shall be brought into the said court, to abide the final order and decree of the said Supreme Court. § 2.

The Supreme Court in and for the Eastern District of Pennsylvania, and the Court of Common Pleas for Philadelphia County, shall each have all the power and jurisdiction of a Court of Equity, in all cases of dower and partition, within the City and County of Philadelphia. § 3.

Act of 16th April, 1845.(*n*) Section thirty-nine of the act entitled, " An act regulating election districts, and for other purposes," shall be construed to give jurisdiction to the Court of Common Pleas for the

(*n*) Pamph. L. 542.

County of Philadelphia, ,and the Supreme Court within the City and County of Philadelphia, in all cases where chancery entertains jurisdiction under either of the heads of fraud, accident, mistake, and account, whether such fraud, accident, mistake, or account, be actual or constructive. § 3.

Act of 8th April, 1846.(*o*)   No courts within the City and County of Philadelphia shall exercise the powers of a Court of Chancery in granting or continuing injunctions against the erection or use of any public works of any kind, erected, or in progress of erection, under the authority of an act of the legislature, until the questions of title and damages shall be submitted, and finally decided by a common law court; and, in such cases, the court shall have authority to issue a venire for the summoning of a jury, to the sheriff of an adjoining county.   § 1.

Act of 10th April, 1848.(*p*)   The Court of Common Pleas of the City and County of Lancaster, and County of York, shall have the jurisdiction and powers of a Court of Chancery within the said city and county, so far as the same are by existing laws vested in and exercised by the Supreme Court, sitting in bank in the City of Philadelphia, and by the Court of Common Pleas of the City and County of Philadelphia, and under the like regulations and restrictions as are prescribed by law for the said courts; and in all cases an appeal may be taken to the Supreme Court for the middle district, from the final decrees of the said courts in equity, on the same terms and conditions as are provided in cases of appeal from the decrees of the Court of Common Pleas for the City and County of Philadelphia.   § 3.

The Supreme Court and the Court of Common Pleas, in the City and County of Philadelphia, shall have the same jurisdiction and power in all suits now pending, or hereafter to be brought, for the discovery of facts, that are now possessed by Courts of Chancery.   § 4.

Act of 10th April, 1849.(*q*)   The several Courts of Common Pleas of Huntingdon, Bedford, Somerset, Blair, Cambria, and Mifflin, in addition to the powers heretofore conferred, shall have the same chancery powers and jurisdictions which are by law vested in the Court of Common Pleas for the City and County of Philadelphia.   § 5.

Nothing contained in this act shall be so construed as to preclude proceedings according to the usages and practices heretofore existing in the courts of this commonwealth, or under the provisions of the different acts of assembly; but the remedy provided and conferred by this act, shall be considered and construed as additional or cumulative.(*s*)   § 6.

Act of 25th April, 1850.(*t*)   In all cases in which any coal or iron ore mines or minerals have been or shall be held by two or more persons, as tenants in common, and coal, iron ore, or other mineral, has been or shall be taken from the same, by any one or more of said te-

(*o*) Pamph. L. 272.
(*p*) Pamph. L. 448.
(*q*) Pamph. L. 620.

(*s*) See Biddle *v.* Moore, 3 Barr, 161.
(*t*) Pamph. L. 573.

nants respectively, it shall be lawful for any one of said tenants in common to apply by bill or petition in equity, to the Court of Common Pleas of the county in which the lands lie, praying that an account may be decreed and taken of all coal, iron ore or other mineral, taken by said tenants respectively; and the said court shall thereupon proceed upon such bill or petition, agreeably to the course of a Court of Chancery, and shall have full power and authority to make all orders, appointments and decrees, interlocutory and final, that may appertain to justice and equity in the premises, and may cause to be ascertained the quantity and value of the coal, iron ore or other mineral, so taken respectively by the respective parties, and the sum that may be justly and equitably due, by and from, and to them respectively therefor, according to the respective proportions and interests to which they may be respectively entitled in the lands: *Provided*, That all the tenants in common shall be made parties to such bill or petition, and that if any of them reside out of the county in which such lands lie, or out of this commonwealth, the court may make such order for serving process or notice upon them, by publication, or otherwise, as the said court shall deem fit and proper, and may take the bill or petition *pro confesso*, and proceed to final decree, or proceed by attachment and sequestration, against such of them as shall fail to appear thereupon, or shall neglect or refuse to stand to, obey and abide by the orders and decrees of said court. § 24.

Any party may appeal to the Supreme Court from any final decree made by any Court of Common Pleas under this act: *Provided*, That such appeal be taken within one year after the rendering of such final decree, and that the party appealing, before taking his appeal, shall file and make affidavit that the same is not intended for delay, and shall give such security to prosecute his appeal with effect, as shall be required by the said Court of Common Pleas or the Supreme Court. § 25.

From and immediately after the passage of this act, all the powers and authorities conferred upon the Supreme Court and the several Courts of Common Pleas, by the 13th section of the act relative to the jurisdiction and powers of the courts, passed the 16th day of June, 1836, relating to the "perpetuation of testimony," shall be and the same is hereby extended and made applicable to the perpetuation of testimony in cases of lost or destroyed records of any of the courts of record in this commonwealth, whether such records were lost or destroyed before or after the passing of this act; and the same proceedings, orders, decrees and judgments shall be had therein, *mutatis mutandis*, as in cases now authorized by law, and with the like effect; and when proved, such record shall have the same legal operation as the original record would have had: *Provided*, That in all cases the application to perpetuate testimony shall be made in the same court in which the record may be lost or destroyed. § 26.

Act of 15th May, 1850.(*u*) The Court of Common Pleas of Clearfield County, in addition to the powers heretofore conferred, shall have the same chancery powers and jurisdictions which are now by law vested in the Court of Common Pleas of Philadelphia County.(*v*) § 1.

(*u*) Pamph. L. 1059.   (*v*) *Ante*, pp. 59-60.

Act of 3d April, 1851.(*w*)   The Court of Common Pleas of Schuylkill County shall have and exercise all the like chancery jurisdiction and powers that are conferred upon any other court of this commonwealth; and in all cases, an appeal may be taken to the Supreme Court for the eastern district, from the final decrees of the said court, in suits in equity, on the same terms and conditions as are provided in cases of appeal from the decrees of the Court of Common Pleas of the City and County of Philadelphia.   § 12.

Act of 13th October, 1840.(*x*)   The Supreme Court, the several District Courts and Courts of Common Pleas, within this commonwealth, shall have all the powers and jurisdiction of Courts of Chancery in settling partnership accounts, and such other accounts and claims, as by the common law and usages of this commonwealth have heretofore been settled by the action of account-render; and it shall be in the power of the party desirous to commence such action, to proceed either by bill in chancery, or at common law, but no bill in chancery shall be entertained unless the counsel filing the same shall certify that in his opinion the case is of such a nature that no adequate remedy can be obtained at law, or that the remedy at law will be attended with great additional trouble, inconvenience or delay.   § 19.

Act of April 8th, 1852.   Nothing contained in the thirteenth section of the act of the sixteenth of June, one thousand eight hundred and thirty-six, relative to the jurisdiction and powers of the courts, shall be construed to prevent the Supreme Court from exercising original jurisdiction in equity, in any of the cases enumerated in the said section, within any of the counties of this commonwealth, or to prohibit the process of the said court from running into any other county of this commonwealth; but the said court, when in session in any district, shall exercise original jurisdiction in the cases enumerated in said section, throughout the State, and if not decided before the close of its session in said district, shall cause the same, with all proceedings thereon, to be certified to, and filed for action, with the prothonotary of the Supreme Court, in the district within which said court shall be next in session, and so to be certified from district to district until finally decided upon; and so much of said section as limits the chancery powers and jurisdiction to the Supreme Court, when sitting in bank in the City of Philadelphia, and to the Court of Common Pleas of said city and county, be, and the same is hereby repealed: *Provided*, That the said court shall not have original jurisdiction, by virtue of this act, to supervise any partnerships or unincorporated associations or societies: *Provided also*, That this enactment shall not be construed to repeal the first section of the act of General Assembly, passed May sixth, eighteen hundred and forty-four, entitled "An act further to regulate proceedings in courts of justice, and for other purposes."   § 1.

(*w*) Pamph. L. 871.   (*x*) Purd. 7th ed. 43.

3. *Equity adjudications.*

The decisions of our courts on questions of equity jurisdiction and practice may be classified as follows:—

1. Jurisdiction and General Principles.
2. Account.
3. Specific Performance.
4. Injunction.
   (1). When grantable.
   (2). Practice.
5. Discovery.
   (1). When grantable.
   (2). Practice.
6. Election.
7. Fraud.
8. Perpetuating Testimony.
9. Pleading and Practice generally.

1. *Jurisdiction and General Principles.*

The extension of the remedy by actions at law to cases originally within the jurisdiction of equity, particularly in the system adopted in Pennsylvania, of administering equitable relief through the medium of the common law forms, is no bar to the equitable jurisdiction of courts for the same case.(z)

Whether a case may be brought in the chancery form, is only a question of form and not of jurisdiction; and the objection is waived, if not made in due season.(a)

Whether or no in this State, the legal tribunals ought, in the exercise of the chancery powers recently conferred, to assume cognizance of those cases where the action for money had and received affords a full remedy, there can be no objection where the equitable remedy is the more convenient; as, where an account is incidentally requisite. And where a trustee has duties to perform, other than of mere disbursement, a technical and continuing trust is presented which can be satisfactorily treated only in equity.(b)

"For myself," says Judge Bell, in a late case: "I may be permitted to express my strong inclination to give a liberal construction to the several acts of assembly, conferring equity jurisdiction upon our common law courts, as the exercise of this jurisdiction is found to be necessary to the furtherance of justice in a large variety of instances, in which the principles and practice of the courts of law fail to afford adequate relief."(c) It is not sufficient to oust the jurisdiction of a Court of Equity, that the complainant has a remedy at law, unless that remedy be complete and adequate.(d) The remedy at law must be as practical and efficient to the ends of justice, and its prompt administration, as that in equity.(e)

(z) Wesley Church v. Moore, 10 Barr, 273.

(a) Neel v. Neel, D. C. Alleghany. Lowrie, J.

(b) Kirkpatrick v. McDonald, 1 J. 393. Bell, J.

(c) Yard v. Patton, 1 H. 282.

(d) Skilton v. Webster, Bright. R. 203.

(e) Bank of Ky. v. Schuylkill Bank, 1 Par. 220. King, P. J.

" To induce equity to refuse its aid to a suitor," says Judge King—whose clear head and sound judgment have made the two volumes of equity cases, lately published by one of his brother judges, of great practical value—"it is not sufficient that he may have some remedy at law. An existing remedy at law, to induce equity to decline the exercise of its jurisdiction in favor of a suitor, must be an adequate and complete one. And where, from the nature and complications of a given case, its justice can best be reached by means of the flexible machinery of a Court of Equity—in short, where a full, perfect, and complete remedy cannot be afforded at law, equity extends its jurisdiction in furtherance of justice."(f) "The jurisdiction for compensation or damages," he said, in another case, "does not ordinarily attach in equity, except as ancillary to a specific performance, or some other relief. If it does attach in any other cases, it must be under very special circumstances, and upon peculiar equities; as, for instance, in cases of fraud, or where the party has disabled himself by matters *ex post facto* from a specific performance; or in cases where there is no adequate remedy at law."(g)

A decree in equity produces its effect by controlling the course of the person, not by controlling a court of law, or any part of its machinery. A party may proceed at law, in the face of an injunction, and the court of law will adjudicate, if he will brave the consequences of the contempt.(h)

To induce the court to interfere in causes of action arising in a foreign jurisdiction, it must be competent to administer the appropriate equity required by the case, and capable of giving effect to its decree.(i)

The Court of Common Pleas has no jurisdiction of a suit for an injunction to restrain the defendant from diverting a watercourse in an adjoining county, although the defendant was regularly served with process in the county where the suit was brought, and though the watercourse was regulated by a personal agreement between the parties.(j) Nor can the same court take jurisdiction of a proceeding against a foreign corporation, where the decree asked for requires compulsory process against the officers of the corporation.(k)

Where once a Court of Equity takes cognizance of a litigation, it will dispose of every subject embraced within the circle of contest; and where various chattels, some of which can, and others cannot, be adequately compensated for in damages in a suit at law, are the subjects of the same dispute, and make part of the same transaction, equity will decree the delivery up of the whole.(l)

Ignorance or mistake of law with a full knowledge of the facts, is in no case *per se* a ground of equitable relief; but where there is a mistake of a clear, well-established, and well-known principle of law, whether common or statute law, equity will lay hold of slight circumstances to raise a presumption that there has been some undue influence, imposition, mental imbecility, surprise, or confidence abused.(m)

(f) Bank of Virginia v. Adams, 1 Par. 541.

(g) Bank of Ky. v. Schuylkill Bank, 1 Par. 220.

(h) Stephens v. Forsyth, 2 H. 68. *Per curiam*.

(i) Bank of Virginia v. Adams, 1 Par. 547.

(j) Morris v. Remington, 1 Par. 387.

(k) Bank v. Adams, 1 Par. 534.

(l) McGowan v. Remington, 2 J. 56.

(m) Good v. Herr, 1 W. & S. 253.

Equity will not relieve in consequence of a mistake of law, when both parties have the means of knowing the facts, and there is no fraud.(n)

Equity will grant relief when an act is done or a contract made under a mistake or ignorance of a material fact.(o)

It is a general principle that equity follows the law, and where right does not exist at law, a Court of Chancery will not afford the party equitable relief.(p)

Where one party induces another to expend his money on the faith of an arrangement, by which the first is to give land for the erection of a joint mill, if the other give the water-power, the attempt of the former to disavow the contract, is such a fraud as will induce a chancellor to declare him trustee.(q)

Equity disregards preferences which cannot be enforced at law, wherever it has exclusive control of the fund on which they seem to act; and it respects them only where to do otherwise would merely turn the party around to another tribunal.(r)

Equitable conversion takes place, although the election to purchase rests solely with the purchaser, whose optional right may be transmitted to his vendee; and notice of this right will be imputed to a second purchaser from the original vendor through an actual possession of land agreed to be sold, consistent with the contract.(s)

A party cannot have the aid of a chancellor in executing a contract, when by his own laches rights of the third parties, without notice, have intervened, which will be prejudiced by the action asked for(t).

In equity a written agreement may be rescinded by parol; but in order to do so, the parties must be placed in the same situation that they occupied before the contract was made.(u)

Equity will relieve against a penalty; but not against stipulated damages.(v) "Where the covenant," says Lord Mansfield,(w) "is to pay a particular liquidated sum, a Court of Equity cannot make a new covenant for a man; nor is there any room for compensation or relief."

The cases in which equity jurisdiction in bills for specific performance, is properly exercised, are reducible to one of the four heads of fraud, mistake, turpitude of consideration, and circumstances entitling to relief upon the principle of *quia timet,* and each of these should be established by positive and definite proof.(x)

2. *Account.*

A bill in equity lies for a principal to receive compensation from an agent where the alleged infractions of duty are so multifarious, and the procedure so complicated, as to make the remedy at law inadequate, both from the confusion of the subject-matter, and the necessary multiplicity of suits.(y)

It is not necessary in a bill for an account, it was ruled by Judge

(n) M'Ainch v. Laughlin, 1 H. 371.
(o) Jenks v. Fritz, 7 W. & S. 201.
(p) Rittenhouse v. Levering, 6 W. & S. 190.
(q) Swartz v. Swartz, 4 Barr, 353.
(r) Ins. Co. v. Union Canal Co. Bright. R. 48.
(s) Kerr v. Day, 2 H. 115. BELL, J.
(t) Ins. Co. v. Union Canal Co. 2 P.

L. J. 65; Bright. R. 48. GIBSON, C. J.
(u) Espy v. Anderson, 2 H. 308.
(v) Westerman v. Means, 2 J. 97. Remington v. Irwin, 2 H. 145.
(w) Peers v. Lowe, 4 Bur. 22, 25, cited 2 J. 100.
(x) Yard v. Patton, 1 H. 283.
(y) Bank of Ky. v. Schuylkill Bk. 1 Par. 191.

I.—5

Lowrie, when sitting in the District Court of Alleghany County, to call upon the defendant to set forth in his answer the state of the account. This object is better obtained after decree, before the master.(z)

A bill, it was ruled by Judge King, may be entertained between partners for an account, though no dissolution be prayed.(a) It is not necessary now, it is said by the same judge, that a bill for an account should contain an offer on the part of the plaintiff, to pay the balance if found against him.(b)

Where there are several persons claiming rent in the hands of an assignee of a term, it is said by Judge Lowrie, the controversy may be settled by a bill in equity.(c)

A Pennsylvania tribunal, it is declared by the same judge, having jurisdiction of cases both in the chancery and in the common law forms, the fact that a case is brought in the chancery, instead of the common law form, should be taken advantage of by demurrer, and not by an objection to the jurisdiction of the court.(d)

In a late leading case it appeared that C, having united with S and others for the erection of a church edifice, C, before a charter was obtained, at the request of the association, and for its benefit, borrowed money from P, giving therefor his own bond and mortgage, and receiving from S and two others, members of the association, their mortgage as an indemnity. The society having obtained a charter, the church was conveyed to it as incorporated. The corporation making default in the payment of the interest in the mortgage given by C, after the latter's death, the mortgaged premises were sold, and proving insufficient to pay the debt, other lands devised by C were sold to pay the judgment on the bond. It was held, that a bill in equity lay by the devisees of C, whose land was thus sold, against the corporation for reimbursement,(e) and that the statute of limitation did not begin to run until C's property was sold.(f)

Perhaps, however, in the long litigated case of the Bank of Kentucky against the Schuylkill Bank, the most authoritative statement may be found of the Pennsylvania practice in this species of equity procedure. The directors of the Bank of Kentucky, having by resolution in 1835, authorized the president and cashier to establish transfer agencies in New York and Philadelphia, a negotiation was entered into by the president and cashier with L, the cashier of the Schuylkill Bank in Philadelphia, by which the latter agreed to undertake such agency. In 1839, it was discovered that L had fraudulently issued spurious certificates of stock in the Bank of Kentucky to the amount of a million and a quarter of dollars, and to prevent the discovery of the fraud, had paid regular dividends on the same. In 1842, the bank having been sued by holders of the forged certificates, and having no means of escaping its liability on the same, procured an act of the legislature of Kentucky, authorizing it to enlarge its stock, and to thus issue new certificates in place of those fraudulently uttered to innocent holders. It was held by Judge King,

(z) Porter v. English, D. C. All. 7 Leg. Int. 150.
(a) Hudson v. Barrett, 1 Par. 418.
(b) Ibid.
(c) Adams v. Beach, D. C. All. 7 Leg. Int. 179.
(d) Ibid.
(e) Wesley Church, v. Moore, 10 Barr, 274.
(f) Ibid.

and afterwards affirmed in the Supreme Court, that the Bank of Kentucky was entitled to compensation from the Schuylkill Bank for the damages so accruing.(g)

In a case before the same eminent judge, it appeared that the plaintiff, when in a state of temporary insanity, induced by habits of excessive intoxication, conveyed all his estate to D in trust; 1st, to pay his debts; 2d, to pay him, the plaintiff, during life, out of the net income, a sum not exceeding two-thirds, the balance to be paid to his two minor step-daughters, E and A; and 3d, after his death to pay the principal to E and A as tenants in common. The plaintiff had a wife at the time, the mother of E and A; and, except when under the effects of intoxication, was industrious and prudent. It was ruled that a bill in equity lay by him, to set aside the deed.(h)

In a still more recent case, it appeared that a number of individuals having formed an association for a specified term, to engage in mining for gold in California, one advanced money, and the others agreed to proceed to the mines, and engage in the digging for gold. When they arrived, the capital advanced being exhausted, all abandoned the enterprise as fruitless, and two of them engaged in another and different employment of their labor. The court determined that the associate who advanced the money, had no such specific lien on the profits produced by such labor, as could be enforced in a Court of Equity.(i)

3. *Specific Performance.*

The ordinary power of a chancellor extends no further than the execution of a trust sufficiently formed to put the legal title out of the grantor, or to the execution of an agreement formed for a trust founded upon a valuable consideration; and equity will not execute an assignment for the benefit of creditors as an agreement, where the assignee rejected the assignment, because creditors are only volunteers.(j)

A chancellor may refuse to lend his assistance to consummate an inconscionable bargain accompanied by circumstances of suspicion, though not positively unfair; but it by no means follows that hardship, or even suspicion of unfairness, is always sufficient to move him to action; and a consequence of this distinction is, that though equity will refuse to interfere to execute wherever it would revoke, it may refuse to revoke where it would decline to execute.(k)

Equity will not decree one who has purchased land under a parol agreement to convey a portion thereof to another, to be a trustee, and compel performance, unless there has been a fraud or *mala fides* attending the transaction.(l)

If it appear that a misrepresentation of a vendor was the operative cause to the contract, he will be compelled, when specific performance is sought, to make good the misrepresentation.(m)

Where the law does not afford an adequate redress by compensation in damages for the detention of a personal chattel, as in the cases of

(g) Bank of Ky. v. Schuylkill Bank, 1 Par. 191.
(h) Clifton v. Davis, 1 Par. 31.
(i) Waring v. Cram, 1 Par. 516.
(j) Read v. Robison, 6 W. & S. 329.

(k) Yard v. Patton, 1 H. 283; Delamater's Est. 1 Wh. 374.
(l) M'Culloch v. Cowher, 5 W. & S. 427; Rerick v. Kern, 14 S. & R. 287; Swartz v. Swartz, 4 Barr, 353.
(m) Tyson v. Passmore, 2 Barr, 122.

articles which are objects of attachment or curiosity, or where there is no convenient standard of damages, as in the case of possible injuries from the detention *in futuro*, a Court of Equity will compel a return of the thing itself.(*n*)　Thus where certain maps, plans, and drafts, made by the complainant or copied from private sources, essential to the prosecution of his business as a surveyor, were detained by the defendant in breach of trust, a decree was made for their delivery, and a perpetual injunction granted against their use or from copying them;(*o*) and the former rule applies where some of the articles embraced in the same dispute, are not susceptible of compensation in damages, though others are, equity will decree the return of the whole.(*p*)

Where an article is detained in violation of a trust or confidence, though in itself susceptible of compensation by damages, a bill for its return will be sustained.(*q*)

Where an applicant for specific performance has neglected to perform his own part, without being able to assign a justification or excuse for it, and where there is nothing in the acts and conduct of the other party which amounts to an acquiescence in the delay, the court will not interfere.(*r*)

Where a vendee has performed so much of his part of an agreement for the sale of lands that he cannot be put in *statu quo*, and fails to perform the remainder, without default on his part, or is prevented from completing it by default of the vendor, he will nevertheless be entitled to specific performance.(*s*)

The court will not compel a vendee to receive a title resting on a conveyance to one of several creditors, where there is ground for suspicion that the object of the conveyance was to delay other creditors of the vendor.(*t*)　"A purchaser," said Gibson, C. J., "is not bound to take a doubtful title; and why should the defendant below have been bound to take the property under something more than a suspicion, that the conveyance was tainted with fraud, by the 13 Elizabeth?(*u*)

On bill by the vendor for the specific performance of a contract, the question is not so much whether the vendor's title is good as whether it is so clearly so as to justify the court in directing the vendee to take the estate and pay his money for it.(*v*)　The specific execution of a contract in equity, as will presently be seen, is not of absolute right in the party asking it, but of sound discretion in the court.　Hence, it requires a much less strength of case on the part of the defendant to resist a bill to perform a contract, than it does on the part of the plaintiff to maintain a bill to enforce a specific performance.(*w*)

A recovery in damages in Pennsylvania, is not an adequate remedy for the vendor of land, where the cash payments by the vendee are to be made by instalments, and the property is sold subject to existing incumbrances.(*x*)

(*n*) McGowin *v.* Remington, 2 J. 56.
(*o*) Ibid.
(*p*) Ibid.
(*q*) Ibid.
(*r*) Fisher *v.* Worrell, 5 W. & S. 478; Tyson *v.* Passmore, 2 Barr, 122.
(*s*) Larison *v.* Burt, 4 W. & S. 27.
(*t*) Gans *v.* Renshaw, 2 Barr, 34.
(*u*) Ibid.
(*v*) Bumberger *v.* Clippenger, 5 W. & S. 311.
(*w*) Dalzell *v.* Crawford, 1 Par. 45; *post*, p. 72.
(*x*) Ibid. 42.

The contract admitted by an answer, must not essentially vary from the contract set forth in the bill; unless they correspond, a specific performance will not be decreed.(*y*)

Though an agreement which is to be perfected by the execution of an instrument is among the few exceptions to the rule that equity does not decree specific performance of a contract relating exclusively to a personal chattel, it is nevertheless open to all the objections that could in equal circumstances be made to the execution of a contract for the purchase of lands, and against a bill to enforce such a purchase, a delay of fifteen years would be decisive.(*a*)

Though a petition praying for a decree of specific performance of a contract for the purchase and sale of real estate, should state either that the petitioner has performed the agreement on his part or that he is willing and prepared to perform it, yet an omission to make such statement is a defect in matter of form merely, and may be amended.(*b*)

A father and son purchased jointly a tract of land, each contributing a moiety of the purchase-money, the purchase being followed by an informal partition of the tracts, and a distinct possession of the purparts, the legal title remaining in the father. The son continued for twenty years to improve his portion, when the father died, without executing a deed or transferring the legal title. It was held by the Supreme Court, that this was a case where equity would enforce the trust, by directing a specific execution by conveyance.(*c*)

In a contract for the sale of land, no time was fixed for the execution thereof, nor was there any express stipulation that it should be material. The vendee afterwards' died. No actual tender of a conveyance was made, but there was no laches on the part of the vendor. Specific performance was decreed on a bill filed more than five years after the making of the contract.(*d*) It was thought by Judge Bell not to be an objection to the specific performance of the contract, that the vendee who was to execute on such conveyance a bond and mortgage, payable before a certain day, has died since the agreement. The heirs or devisees of the vendee being made parties to the bill, it was said, may be compelled to perform the contract in this respect.(*e*)

A bill having been filed under such circumstances, after the day on which the bond and mortgage were to be made payable, it was *held*, that the objection, were it otherwise valid, had ceased to exist, as the payment of the purchase-money could be at once decreed.(*f*)

On bill, answer, and proofs, in the Court of Common Pleas for Philadelphia County, it appeared that S, being the owner of an unfinished house, agreed by parol to lease it to the plaintiff for ten years, at a progressively increasing rent; that, in pursuance of this agreement, the plaintiff entered into possession, and made considerable improvements suitable to his business; and that pending this lease, S conveyed the premises in fee to T, who had notice of the parol lease. An injunction was decreed to restrain S and T from disturbing the plaintiff in his possession, and S was ordered to execute, and T to con-

(*y*) Parrish *v.* Koons, 1 Par. 97.
(*a*) Ins. Co. *v.* Union Canal Co., 2 P. L. J. 65.
(*b*) Chess's Appeal, 4 Barr, 52.
(*c*) McFarson's Appeal, 1 J. 503.
(*d*) Tiernan *v.* Roland, 3 H. 429.
(*e*) Id. 440.
(*f*) Tiernan *v.* Roland, 3 H. 429.

firm, a written lease to the plaintiff, on the principles provided for by the parol agreement.(*g*)

Equity will not compel a vendee to take a bad title; but a pecuniary charge against a good title presents no objection, provided the purchaser can be protected against it,(*h*) and, therefore, where a vendor of land under a contract, who had at the time of sale only an equitable title under articles, subsequently acquired the legal title, at the same time giving a mortgage for the purchase-money, but the mortgage was released before bill filed, it was held by the Supreme Court, that specific performance might be decreed in his favor.(*i*)

It was held, also, that notice that the vendee refused to consider the contract binding, and repudiated the same, on account of such incumbrance (given through an affidavit of defence, made by him in a suit on a note given for a part of the purchase-money), before the charge was removed, did not amount to a rescission, no demand having been made for the execution of a conveyance.(*j*)

A purchaser of an estate in fee, said Judge Bell, in the same case, will not be compelled to take a life estate only, nor an estate in which the vendor had no interest as owner at the time of sale.(*k*)

But while a Court of Equity, in short, will not compel a purchaser to accept a doubtful title,(*l*) the cases in which courts have refused their aid to a vendor, where they have considered his title good, though disputable, are cases of real and serious difficulty.(*m*)

The doubts, however, which will operate on a Court of Equity, are not doubts made up for the occasion; not based on captious, frivolous, and astute niceties; but such as produce real *bona fide* hesitation in the mind of the chancellor.(*n*) Omissions in the judicial process through which the title passed, which omissions could be supplied by amendment, by the court in which the proceedings were had, will not be considered as sufficient.(*o*)

If in the progress of a suit for specific performance of a real contract, objections to a title are discovered, never made during the negotiation, the defendant cannot insist on such objections as excusing him from performance, if the plaintiff is able and willing to remove them when first pointed out.(*p*) Adverse opinions of conveyancers and counsel alone, are not sufficient ground for a Court of Equity to refuse a decree for specific performance of a contract, for the purchase of land.(*q*)

While a purchaser is not bound to accept title from any one but him from whom he bought, or his representatives(*r*), the mere transmission of the legal title to another, subject to the equity of the purchaser, creates no impediment to a decree for a specific performance, especially where the parties had the previous sale in view at the time of the transmission.(*s*)

(*g*) Farley *v.* Stokes, 1 Par. 422.
(*h*) Thompson *v.* Carpenter, 4 Barr, 132; Tiernan *v.* Roland, 3 H. 441.
(*i*) Id. 429.
(*j*) Ibid.
(*k*) Id. 436.
(*l*) Wetherill *v.* Mecke, Bright. R. 135.

(*m*) Dalzell *v.* Crawford, 1 Par. 57.— KING, P. J. See *ante*.
(*n*) Id. 46.
(*o*) Id. 37.
(*p*) Id. 56.
(*q*) Id. 37.
(*r*) Tiernan *v.* Roland, 3 H. 436.
(*s*) Id. 437; Le Roy de Chamont *v.* Forsyth, 2 Pa. R. 507.

Where the vendor, though not the owner of the fee, has an equitable estate in the premises, under articles of agreement for its purchase, and the right to acquire the legal title, and actually acquires it after the sale by him, but before laches can be imputed, he may compel specific performance.(t)

"A Court of Equity," to adopt the language of Judge King, "has no power in suits for specific performance, except on the application and consent of all parties, to direct an issue for the determination of a matter of fact; nor can it without such an application or consent, direct a case or an action, for the purpose of satisfying itself on a matter of law."(u)

A vendor, after a contract of sale of certain premises by him, conveyed a moiety of his interest in a larger tract of land, comprehending the premises in question, to a third person; subject to the previous contract of sale, and with an understanding that it was to be carried out by such third person. It was held, that such conveyance was no abandonment of the first contract, on the part of the vendor, and furnished no ground for the purchaser to resist specific performance.(v)

An agent created by parol, cannot bind his principal by a written contract, for the sale of lands; and hence the vendor cannot have specific performance of the contract of sale, even though it were signed by the vendee.(w)

"The ground upon which a chancellor executes an executory contract for the sale of lands," says Judge Bell, "is, that equity looks upon things agreed to be done, as actually performed; consequently, when an agreement is made for the sale of an estate, the vendor is considered as a trustee for the purchaser of the estate sold, and the purchaser as a trustee of the purchase-money for the vendor.(x) As a result of this principle, which seems to be of general application, it is settled, that an estate under contract of sale, is regarded as converted into personalty, from the time of the contract, notwithstanding an election to complete the purchase rests entirely with the purchaser; and if the seller die before the election be exercised, the purchase-money, when paid, will go to his executors as assets."(y)

Although the subject and import of the written contract are clear, so that there is no necessity to resort to evidence for its construction, yet if the defendant can show any circumstances, dehors, independent of the writing, making it inequitable to interpose for the purpose of a specific performance, a Court of Equity having satisfactory information on the subject, will not interpose. This discretion is not, however, arbitrary, but exercised in a judicial manner, according to established rules.(z)

In respect to voluntary contracts *inter vivos*, Courts of Equity will not interfere, but will leave the parties where the law finds them.(a)

Although chancery will withhold its aid to consummate a voluntary agreement, unexecuted, where something remains to be done by the

(t) Tiernan v. Roland, 3 H. 429; Leigh v. Huber, 3 Watts, 367.

(u) Dalzell v. Crawford, 1 Par. 45.— KING, P. J.

(v) Tiernan v. Roland, 3 H. 429.

(w) Parrish v. Koons, 1 Par. 79.

(x) Kerr v. Day, 2 H. 114. BELL, J.

(y) Ibid.

(z) Dalzell v. Crawford, 1 Par. 45.

(a) Yard v. Patton, 1 H. 288. Per BELL, J.

contracting parties, yet where it is executed, equity will give effect, to all its consequences. In such a case a consideration is unnecessary.(b)

If a mistake exist, not in an instrument which is intended to give effect to a preliminary agreement, but in the agreement itself, and it is shown to have been produced by ignorance of a material fact, equity will relieve according to the nature of the case; but if the agreement was not founded on such mistake, equity will not decree another security to be given, different from that which had been agreed upon, or treat the case as if the other security had been actually executed.(c)

The duty of promptness of action, as it was determined by Judge King, does not only rest on the vendor, where the time within the contract must be closed is not fixed by its terms. In such a case, if any unnecessary delay is created by one party, the other has a right to limit a reasonable time within which the contract shall be perfected by the other, by a notice, stating that within such a period that which is required must be done, or otherwise the contract will be considered at an end.(d)

Equity will in no shape lend itself to assist a gambling transaction, or in any way to vindicate a contract of which gaming is the object.(e)

A party cannot have the aid of a chancellor in executing a contract, when by his own laches the rights of third persons, without notice, have intervened, which will be prejudiced by the action asked for.(f)

Specific performance will not be decreed in favor of a party who has slept on his rights. Due diligence is necessary to call the court into action, and where it does not exist, a Court of Equity will not lend its assistance.(g)

A purchaser will not be assisted when he has made frivolous objections to the title, and trifled, or shown backwardness to perform his part of the agreement; especially if circumstances are altered.(h)

A bill for specific performance will not be entertained unless it set forth a contract, where the parties have described and identified the land mentioned intended to be conveyed, or the means of identifying it are mentioned in the contract.(i)

Though a Court of Equity will not in general decree specific execution of contracts, in regard to personal property, this rule is limited to cases where compensation in damages furnishes a complete and satisfactory remedy.(j)

A naked covenant to pay money at a particular day, has never of itself been held to make time essential; for the plain reason that it admits of adequate compensation, ascertained by law, in the payment of interest.(k)

Sound reason, operating through equitable maxims, has relaxed the rigidity of the ancient common law, which insisted upon time as an essential in all cases; and now, he who would object a disregard of it,

(b) Yard v. Patton, 1 H. 285. Per BELL, J. See Delamater's Estate, 1 Wh. 375.

(c) Ins. Co. v. Union Canal Co. Bright. R. 48.

(d) Parrish v. Koons, 1 Par. 93.
(e) Lessig v. Langton, Bright. R. 191.

(f) Ins. Co. v. Union Canal Co. Bright. R. 48.
(g) Parrish v. Koons, 1 Par. 92.
(h) Dalzell v. Crawford, 1 Par. 56.
(i) Parrish v. Koons, 1 Par. 95.
(j) Palmer v. Graham, 1 Par. 476.
(k) Westerman v. Means, 2 J. 97; Remington v. Irwin, 2 H. 145. .

must, generally, do so at the earliest opportunity afforded.(*l*) Even where the time within which certain acts are to be done has been fixed in the contract, a party who is to be benefited by such acts will be considered as waiving them if he does not require their completion within the time fixed.(*m*)

4. *Injunction.*

(1.) When grantable.

The English chancery can by injunction restrain the commission of acts contrary to equity. The limited chancery powers of the courts of Pennsylvania extend only to prevent acts contrary to law.(*n*)

Where the plaintiff's title is doubtful, or, the court is in its conscience satisfied that the case is not one of nuisance, according to the legal acceptation, it will not interfere even to put the question in a course of trial. But in a plain case of public nuisance, the court will interpose and determine the question without a trial by jury.(*o*)

It is no longer necessary that the attorney-general shall be a party to proceedings in equity, in cases of public nuisance.(*p*)

A Court of Equity may not only restrain the erection of a nuisance, but direct its abatement, and give compensation in damages, for injuries resulting therefrom.(*q*)

Where the matter complained of is not *ipso facto* a nuisance, but may be so, according to circumstances, it generally becomes necessary to ascertain those circumstances by verdicts; but where it is in itself a nuisance (if there is satisfactory proof of its existence) the court can, and often will restrain without a verdict first being had.(*r*)

Persons injured have a remedy in a Court of Equity by injunction, against the prosecution of a nuisance, when, from its locality, it is injurious to the health or comfort of those residing in its immediate vicinity.(*s*) The court will enjoin an individual from the use of a slaughter-house, for slaughtering cattle, when erected in a city, if erected contiguous to valuable dwellings which are occupied.(*t*)

The court will interfere, although the existence of the nuisance has not been established by law, where the facts are admitted by answer and the threatened injury is irreparable.(*u*)

Equity will enjoin in cases of purpresture and nuisance, even where an indictment lies; but the court will not interfere where a doubt exists as to the character and illegality of the act complained of.(*v*)

But though it is the practice to enjoin in clear cases of nuisance without a trial to establish the right at law, yet Courts of Equity are exceedingly unwilling so to do, and will not interfere when entire compensation can be obtained as damages.(*w*)

A bill for an injunction is a proceeding adopted to control and regu-

(*l*) Shields *v.* Miltenberger, 2 H. 81. BELL, J.
(*m*) Ibid. Parrish *v.* Koons, 1 Par. 93.
(*n*) Hagner *v.* Heyberger, S. C. N. P. in equity; 3 P. L. J. 310; S. C. 7 W. & S. 104; though see Eckstein's Est., *post*, p. 74.
(*o*) Commis. of Moyamensing *v.* Long, 1 Par. 146.
(*p*) Id. 148.

(*q*) Morris *v.* Remington, 1 Par. 395.
(*r*) Smith *v.* Cummings, 2 Par. 102. PARSONS, J.
(*s*) Ibid.
(*t*) Id. 92.
(*u*) Com. *v.* Rush, 2 H. 186.
(*v*) Moyamensing Comm. *v.* Long, 1 Par. 145.
(*w*) Mayor *v.* Commissioners, 7 Barr, 348.

late officers in the discharge of their functions, when they are confessedly such, rather than to try their right to hold and exercise their offices;(x) and the court will take no jurisdiction with regard to the amotion of public officers.

An injunction may be granted on the application of the commissioners of an incorporated district to restrain the erection of a building which encroaches on the line of a public street.(z)

An injunction may be issued to restrain a creditor, who issues an execution and levies on personal property in the hands of the committee of a lunatic.(a)

In a recent case in Philadelphia, P sold his stock and good-will in a business to G for a specific price on credit, with an agreement that if the property was not paid for within a specified time, it should be returned to him with all the new customers whom G should obtain in the course of his conducting the business; G did return the property, with the names of the old and new customers, when G started the same business on the old route, and supplied the old and new customers thus returned to P. The court awarded an injunction against G to restrain him from such improper acts, in violation of the original agreement, as he had agreed to return the property embracing the good-will in *statu quo.*(b)

An injunction will not be granted against waste when the title of the complainant is denied by the answer; and it is refused before answer, unless the defendant has notice of the motion, so as to enable him to make denials by affidavits.(c)

The jurisdiction of the Courts of Equity in Pennsylvania in granting injunctions, extends only to the prevention of acts contrary to law, not of acts contrary to equity.(d)

A Court of Equity will interfere, and by injunction protect the clear rights of a suitor, derived either from contract or ancient possession, against a nuisance produced by the erection of a building by his neighbor, which darkens his windows or destroys his right of way.(e)

Turnpike roads, it was lately held by Judge Lowrie, are entitled to be protected by injunctions against a continued invasion of their franchise, as where a by-road is made to enable travellers on their road to avoid the toll-gate.(f)

A municipal corporation is a proper party to prosecute a suit in equity, for the abatement of a nuisance, affecting the public, or citizens of the corporation.(g)

An injunction may be granted to restrain a partner from exercising a control over partnership property, where the interests of a deceased partner require it.(h)

(x) Hagner *v.* Heyberger, 7 W. & S. 104.

(z) Moyam. Commiss. *v.* Long, 1 Par. 150.

(a) Eckstein's Estate, 1 Par. 70.
(b) Palmer *v.* Graham, 1 Par. 476.
(c) Morse *v.* O'Reilly, 6 P. L. J. 501.
(d) Hagner *v.* Heyberger, 7 W. & S. 104.

(e) Biddle *v.* Ash, 2 Ash. 221. KING,

Pres. This doctrine has, however, been recently doubted in Philadelphia by the same court, so far as ancient lights are concerned.

(f) Greensburg and Pittsburg T. P. R. Company *v.* Breidenthal, (D. C. All. LOWRIE, J.

(g) Com. of Moy. *v.* Long, 1 Par. 146.
(h) Holden *v.* McMakin, 1 Par. 284.

As will hereafter be more fully seen, partnerships have by particular legislation been brought peculiarly within the control of chancery process. Thus, by the action of account-render, every equitable remedy can be obtained ;(*i*) and even in common law suits many of the same advantages may be had.(*j*)

An injunction will be granted to stay waste by a tenant for years; to restrain such tenant from removing the farm manure, hay, straw, &c.;(*k*) to restrain a defendant from erecting a party-wall on the land of another, without a previous survey by a regulator, or payment of a moiety of the cost.(*l*) But where there has been a decision of the regulator unappealed from, or while an appeal is pending, an injunction will not lie.(*m*)

In a late very curious case in Philadelphia, the Councils of the City of Philadelphia having removed the remains of the late Mr. Girard from the burying-ground of a church in which he had directed them by his will to be placed, and left them temporarily with an undertaker in order to a subsequent removal to a sarcophagus at the Girard College, accompanied by masonic and other ceremonies, the consent of the Board of Health and of the trustees of the church having been previously obtained to the removal, a preliminary injunction asked for by Mr. Girard's relatives was refused.(*n*) It was said, by Judge King, that equity will restrain the removal of a body from a common burial-ground, against the consent of the relatives of the deceased.(*o*) But the court will not interfere where the body has been actually removed under claim of right before final hearing to compel the restoration of the body to its former place of interment.(*p*) If the executors of a deceased decline interfering in such case, it was said the relatives might be parties alone.(*q*)

An injunction will not be granted against public officers acting under the authority of the State, to restrain them from taking private property for a public improvement, until suitable compensation shall be made, where a mode is provided by law for the assessment of the damages sustained.(*r*)

A bank will be enjoined from paying out money which has been deposited with them by the plaintiffs, and to which the plaintiffs have a priority over the stockholders.(*s*)

By the Act of May 4, 1852, the second section of the act entitled "An Act to prevent waste in certain cases within this commonwealth," passed the twenty-ninth day of March, one thousand eight hundred and twenty-two, is hereby extended so as to apply to all cases where the writ of estrepement has issued, or may hereafter issue, and the several Courts of Common Pleas in this commonwealth shall, in all cases of estrepement, have power to hear the parties in a summary manner, and

---

(*i*) See *post*, vol. ii. Account Render.
(*j*) Ibid., Partnership.
(*k*) Jones *v.* Whitehead, 1 Par. 304; Waln *v.* O'Connor, 9 Leg. Int. 67.
(*l*) Sutcliffe *v.* Isaacs, 1 Par. 497. Parsons, J.; Cox *v.* Willetts, C. P. Phil. 9 P. L. J. 327.
(*m*) Sutcliffe *v.* Isaacs, 1 Par. 494.

(*n*) *In re* Stephen Girard, C. P. Phila. 11 P. L. J. 17.
(*o*) Ibid.
(*p*) Ibid.
(*q*) Ibid.
(*r*) Heston *v.* Canal Commissioners, Bright, R. 183.
(*s*) Com. *v.* Bank of Penn. 3 W. & S. 184. See 10 Barr, 176.

dissolve said writ or make such further order therein as may seem just and right."

(2.) Practice.

A Court of Chancery will dissolve an injunction on an affidavit, or answer under oath, by the defendant denying the facts, and the equity in the bill on which it was granted. Nor can the counter affidavit of the plaintiff, sustained by other witnesses, prevent it; nor will such affidavits be received, except in certain cases clearly pointed out by the practice in equity.(t)

While the court granted an injunction on the application of the stockholders of an incorporated company, charging that the officers of the corporation were abusing the trust; yet, when the conduct of the officers was approved by a large majority of the stockholders, at a regular election, the court dissolved the injunction.(u)

In cases of waste to prevent irreparable mischief, of nuisance, and of partnership, affidavits of matter not appearing on the face of the answer, will be received where it is alleged and appears that irreparable damage might ensue, if the answer alone was relied upon.(v)

On a motion for a special injunction, where the defendant's answer is filed before the day of hearing, it is to be considered as an application, after answer to the bill.(w)

If the defendant has filed his answer, no affidavits can be read to contradict it.(x)

The exceptions to this rule are cases of waste and of partnership, where it is made clearly to appear that one partner, by acts of extreme misconduct is bringing the subject of the partnership within the principle of irreparable mischief, and so making the case analogous to waste.(y)

They are permissible only to show fraud, mismanagement, or improper conduct in the acting partner, or to show actual or threatened waste, but never to show title in the plaintiff, or the fact of partnership.(z)

The principle is, where the application is upon affidavit, before answer, upon the ground of apprehended irremediable injury, the court will hear counter affidavits until satisfied with the information offered; and the course is the same where the application is to issue an injunction before answer.(a)

An answer filed after the plaintiff has served his notice of a motion for a special injunction, can only be used as an affidavit in opposition to those used by the plaintiff, and that the defendant cannot insist that, under such circumstances, the plaintiff is confined in his injunction to the equity confessed in the answer.(b)

A special injunction is a process issued before final decision of the cause, and from some reason of necessity shown, requiring such a measure. It has always been considered the strong arm of the court, and like all extraordinary powers in the hands of judicial tribunals, it ought to be used with care and caution. A refusal to award such a prelimi-

(t) Carpenter v. Burden, 2 Par. 24; Holl v. Holl, 11 P. L. J. 224.
(u) Ibid.
(v) Smith v. Cummings, 2 Par. 92.
(w) Lessig v. Langton, Bright. R. 191.
(x) Ibid.
(y) Ibid.
(z) Ibid.
(a) Ibid.
(b) Waring v. Cram, 1 Par. 525. KING, P. J.

nary writ, in no respect decides the controversy; it is the simple assertion on the part of the court, that the case is not one which requires it to move, until the cause is ripe for final adjudication.(c)

Unless in a plain case, where irreparable mischief will be done elsewise, an interlocutory injunction (which is a matter resting in the sound discretion of the court) will be refused.(d)

A preliminary injunction is never awarded, except where the plaintiff shows a clear equity, entitling him to the aid and relief of the court.(e)

Security must be given as required by the act before a preliminary injunction can issue.(f)

5. *Discovery.*

(1.) When grantable.

Where a Court of Equity has jurisdiction for discovery, and the discovery is effectual, that becomes a sufficient ground on which the court may proceed to grant relief.(g)

A bill of discovery will not lie on the part of the defendant, in an action on a note against the plaintiff, the object of which is to show that the latter is trustee for a firm, and that the note was transferred to him, with the understanding that one of the firm was to be a trustee in the case.(h)

A bill of discovery cannot be used for the purpose of discrediting a person who may be a witness in a suit.(i)

A bill for discovery does not lie for matter of which the plaintiff has knowledge and means of proof, or of matter whereof he has the same means of information as the defendant, as from the public records.(j)

Where a corporation is defendant, the plaintiff may have a bill for discovery of effects, and is not confined to the remedy by sequestration.(k)

A plaintiff is entitled to the bill, although he has made a levy on goods alleged by the defendant, if the sheriff has been prevented from proceeding by an allegation that the property has been transferred to another.(l)

A bill for the discovery of the defendant's real estate in aid of a judgment against him will be sustained in all cases where the knowledge of such real estate is contained in the mind alone of the defendant, as where property is held in trust for him, either through conveyance in which he is named as *cestui que trust*, or where the trust is entirely secret and concealed; but where the defendant's property, and every interest belonging to him, is spread out on the public records, so that all necessary information can be obtained there by search made by the complainant, the court will not compel the defendant to exhibit the same in his answer.(n)

It seems it is not the practice to compel a discovery of the defendant's

(c) Langolf v. Seiberlitch, 2 Par. 71. KING, P. J. Weber v. Samuel, 7 Barr, 499.

(d) Hill v. Commissioners, 1 Par. 501.

(e) Waring v. Cram, 1 Par. 526.

(f) Holl v. Holl, C. P. Phil. 11 P. L. J. 224.

(g) Bank U. S. v. Biddle, 2 Par. 31.

(h) Allen v. Kyle, D. C. C. P. 7 Leg. Int. 19.

(i) Ibid.

(j) Baker v. Biddle, 1 Bald. 394.

(k) Large v. Bristol Transportation Co. 2 Ash. 394.

(l) Bevans v. The Turnpike, 10 Barr, 174.

(n) Rose v. Lloyd, 2 P. L. J. 321. KING, P. J.

personal property in aid of an execution at law until a *fi. fa.* has issued, and been returned *nulla bona*, though discovery will be compelled of real estate, without such previous execution.(*o*)

A rule to strike off a bill of discovery was refused, notwithstanding it was not signed by the plaintiff himself, but only by his attorney, and was not sworn to.(*p*)

A party who may be examined as a witness, cannot, in general, be compelled to answer a bill for a mere discovery.(*q*)

The chief officer of a corporation may be made party to a discovery, although no decree is sought or could be made against him. And arbitrators, attorneys, and auctioneers have been made parties to bills, although they might also have been witnesses.(*r*)

Mere fishing bills will not be sustained. Thus, in a late case in Philadelphia, a voluntary assignee filed a bill against A, in which he stated that certain property belonging to the assigned estate, had been put up by him at public auction, and had been bought by A for $10,000; that A was not a person of substance, and had no means of performing his contract; that the purchase-money remained unpaid for ten days, whereupon a deed was tendered by the complainant to A; that the property was then put up again at public sale, and knocked down to B for $3,000; that A, at the first sale, acted as the agent of parties unknown, who were the real purchasers, and who put forward B, so that they might fraudulently, by combination with him, ratify the purchase or not, as they pleased. The bill then charged, that the complainant was anxious to bring an action against these parties unknown, and asked for a discovery by A, of their names, &c., and for leave, when discovered, to make them parties to the bill. On general demurrer, the court dismissed the bill.(*s*)

So when C filed a bill in equity, in which he stated that when a child, more than fifty years back, he had been informed that certain estates which had been let out on long leases, would be his when those leases expired; that he had reason to believe that W, the defendant, had possession or information concerning the papers relating to such estates; but that W, on application to him, refused to give any information touching the same, and the bill asked for a discovery, &c., on general demurrer, the bill was dismissed.(*t*)

It seems that the court will not compel a defendant to answer a bill of discovery in which no cause of action is set forth on which a legal action could be founded.(*u*)

A party is entitled to a discovery of all that is *material* to his case, without showing that it is *necessary*.(*v*)

(2.) Pleading and Practice.

The practice upon a *sci. fa.* for the discovery of a judgment defendant's property, under the act of June 16, 1836, relating to execu-

---

(*o*) Ibid., Siter *v.* Waldron, C. P. Phil. Feb. 7, 1852.

(*p*) Caules *v.* Coolbaugh, D. C. C. C. P. April, 1848.

(*q*) Collom *v.* Francis, 1 Par. 533. KING, P. J. Twells *v.* Costen, 1 Par. 378.

(*r*) Twells *v.* Costen, 3 H. 373.

(*s*) Twells *v.* Costen, 1 Par. 373.

(*t*) Collom *v.* Francis, 1 Par. 527.

(*u*) Washington Ins. Co. *v.* Grant, 4 P. L. J. 88.

(*v*) Peebles *v.* Baggs, (D. C. All. Lowrie, J.) 8 Leg. Int. 30.

tions, is substantially the same as those on a *scire facias* in foreign attachment, and, therefore, where the defendant and garnishee, in a bill of discovery, have waived their privilege of trial by jury, by omitting to plead to the *scire facias*, and have submitted their case upon their answers to the interrogatories, the court may render a joint judgment against them both, for the amount of the plaintiff's debt.(*w*)

A bill of discovery, under act of 16th June, 1836, must allege facts which are material to the determination of the issue at law pending between the parties, and must set forth the facts distinctly, so as to show that if the facts were disclosed a defence could be made under the plea of payment or set-off, &c.(*x*)

The defendant is not bound to answer until ten days from the service of a copy of the bill, and interrogatories.(*y*)

The objection that sufficient time did not intervene, cannot be taken advantage of by demurrer. The proper course is to move to quash.(*z*)

It should appear in the bill, that the discovery is sought "in order that the party may have the benefit thereof on the trial of said action."(*a*)

The proceeding to obtain a discovery should be part of the principal action, and not a separate suit.(*b*)

When a bill of discovery is filed, in a cause pending, it is said by Judge Lowrie, the party should be notified by *rule*, and not by *subpœna*, to answer,(*c*) though in Philadelphia the practice is otherwise.(*cc*)

In a bill of discovery in an action of ejectment, it is proper for the plaintiff to state the defence expected to be set up, and to demand a discovery of all such facts as are material for him in answer to such defence, and he may thus ascertain the ground of defence.(*d*)

The allegation of the pendency of a civil action, lays sufficient foundation for a bill of discovery.(*e*)

The plaintiff may require the defendant in a bill of discovery, to answer as to the circumstances and conditions of the delivery of a deed of the land, alleged by the plaintiff to create a trust for heirs, and that plaintiff is an heir.(*f*)

(*w*) Schaffer *v.* Watkins, 7 W. & S. 219.
(*x*) Dall *v.* Amies, 2 M. 134.
(*y*) Ibid.
(*z*) Ibid.
(*a*) Peebles *v.* Baggs, *supra*, 30.
(*b*) Ibid.
(*c*) Ibid.
(*cc*) D. C, Saturday, June 19, 1852. Tilden *v.* Franklin. Rule to show cause why plaintiff should not answer bill of discovery.
PER CURIAM. We are of opinion that the proper practice on filing a bill of discovery is, in all cases, to issue upon it a *subpœna*. It might be convenient, perhaps, to adopt the course of proceeding by rule, but the act of assembly and the rules adopted by the Supreme Court, which are obligatory upon us, seem to point to the former mode of proceeding alone. Rule dismissed.
(*d*) Peebles *v.* Bangs, *supra*.
(*e*) Ibid.

(*f*) Ibid. The very valuable opinion of Judge LOWRIE in this case, will be found of much practical use :—

The mode of obtaining evidence in all cases, by a bill of discovery, is of recent origin in our practice, and though it may be very effectually used to prevent litigation, and to diminish the number of points in dispute in each case, yet our want of familiarity with its use has very much retarded its introduction.

But its principle is no novelty in our practice. We have always acted upon it in cases of foreign and domestic attachments. We have it in its most simple and direct form, as a means of enforcing the production of books and papers, in the act of 27th February, 1798. (Dunlop, L. 159.) We have it, to some extent, in the rules requiring specific affidavits of defence, in certain cases.

It was not until 1836 that our law, in its cherished intimacy with the principles of chancery, and reluctant fellow-ship with its forms, discovered the merits of that feature of chancery character by which the truth of the case is arrived at, though it be known only to the parties. But now our law considers it no forbidden way of arriving at truth, to permit one party to call one upon the other, to state upon oath the relevant facts of the case.

We have no special rules, as to the form of exercising this jurisdiction; but we have the general equity rule, No. 84, directing us to follow the present practice of the High Court of Chancery in England, so far as the same may reasonably be applied consistently with the local circumstances and local convenience of the district where the court is held, not as positive rules, but as furnishing just analogies to regulate the practice.

In England, a bill of discovery exists in what may be called two forms—to wit: when the discovery and relief are sought in different courts, and when they are sought in the same court. And thus these two modes of proceeding are essentially the same, yet there is necessarily the formal difference that, where the proceedings are in different courts, there must be two or more suits.

If the suit in which the relief is sought be in common law court, that court having no power to compel a party to reveal his knowledge of the case, his opponent can get his testimony or admissions, only by the aid of a Court of Chancery; and for this purpose he files his bill of discovery, requiring a full answer, on oath, as to all matters material to the case of the plaintiff in equity. So the opposite party may file his bill of discovery, and thus the common law suit gives rise to two chancery suits.

But, when the suit for relief is in chancery, the bill of discovery accompanies the charges of the plaintiff and the prayer for relief, and all constitute one suit. And even when the defendant files a cross-bill for discovery and relief, or for discovery alone, both the bill and cross-bill are treated, heard, and decided as one.

Now, it would seem plain that the spirit of our equity rule, No. 84, would require us to follow the analogy of the latter form of proceeding in preference to the former, and file our bills of discovery in the same suit in which the discovery is needed; because, with us, the suit for relief, and the bill of discovery, are in the same court, and the whole procedure, being one in substance, should be one in form.

And there is nothing in the substance of this proceeding that requires the adoption of one form rather than the other. The rules that regulate the extent of the discovery, are in both cases the same. The party is entitled to a discovery of all facts, and the production of all papers, that are in the power and knowledge of his adversary. A court of chancery grants a discovery as fully in aid of case at common law as in cases in chancery.—And though formerly a bill of discovery could not be taken *pro confesso* on a failure to answer it, yet now it is treated in this respect in the same manner as a bill of discovery and relief.

Under our form of proceeding, we necessarily get clear of the awkward and bungling way of administering justice by requiring the parties to go into one court to have the truth elicited, and into another to have the cause tried. And the analogy to which I have referred, would seem, of itself, to require that the discovery and relief should all be parts of one suit.

But, the conclusion is much strengthened, by the analogy of our own practice in other matters. Under the act of 1798, where a party files an affidavit to obtain a discovery of papers, &c., it is done in the suit in which the papers are wanted; and the other party must produce the papers, or file a full denial, on oath, of the matters charged in his adversary's affidavit, or judgment will be entered against him, equivalent to taking a bill *pro confesso*.

Where a suit is brought against a garnishee in an attachment, the plaintiff may proceed throughout in the common law form, or he may, in addition, file interrogatories to be answered by the defendant, a substitute for a bill of discovery; and this is part of the same suit, and a failure to answer subjects the defendant to a judgment *pro confesso*.

But still more to the point. Formerly the evidence of absent witnesses could be obtained only by the aid of a Court of Chancery; but, by the constitution, this power of the Court of Chancery is conferred upon the courts of common law. This power is not exercised by means of a bill to take testimony and separate suit; but by the simple and economical process known to every body.—And this would seem to be an exact and ruling analogy for the present case.

These same analogies lead to another result, that is, that the party shall be called upon to answer the bill of discovery by rule and not by subpœna.

Both parties, after suit brought, are

in court for all the purposes of the suit, and the impropriety of a subpœna to bring either of them in at any subsequent stage of the suit, is evident.

Assuming this as the true practice, the bill or petition for discovery will be much shortened and simplified. The statement of the pendency, and character of the suit, will, of course, be omitted. And where the declaration contains specifically all the allegations necessary to found the interrogatories upon, these will not need to be repeated.

It is a beautiful feature of our practice, that it is susceptible of an infusion of equity forms, and adaptation of equity principles. Adopting our own analogies to guide us in the introduction of this new procedure, we have a form, simple, scientific, and economical, and corresponding with other familiar parts of our practice. Adopting the form of proceeding by a separate equity suit, it appears as a crabbed and ill-placed graft, disfiguring our practice.

If, then, this bill had been demurred to for the special reason that it appears as a separate suit, the demurrer might possibly have been sustained.

But a general demurrer does not reach this point.

Besides, it does no harm to the defendant, for she is entitled to her costs as soon as she answers. In the other form, the costs would stand as part of the costs of the cause.

It has not been sufficiently noticed, that every suit in this court may be equivalent to a bill of discovery and relief, and to a cross-bill besides. So soon as an issue of fact is proved, if not before, either party may file his bill of discovery in the cause, and compel an admission of all the material facts of his case known to his adversary. Thus, there may be an immense saving of trouble, time, and expense to the parties.

There will often be judgments entered on the admission of the parties, or where they refuse to answer, without the expense to the public and the parties, of a jury trial. The real point in dispute can always be distinctly ascertained; and frauds perpetrated in secret will be proclaimed upon the housetop.

Taking the principal and collateral proceedings together, they are equivalent to a bill for discovery and relief, a bill to compel the performance of a trust. In our form of pleading in ejectment, the real point in controversy does not appear, for the plea for all cases is, "not guilty." Whereas, if the pleadings were at length on the title, the declaration

would show that the plaintiffs claim as heir of David Boggs. If the title of Boggs were undisputed, the defendant would be compelled to plead a devise or conveyance from Boggs in avoidance.

Now it is perfectly proper for the plaintiff to state, in such a case, what the real point in dispute is, though it does not appear by the pleadings; otherwise, in very many cases, a bill of discovery would be totally ineffectual. He may suggest the claim or defence to be set up, and frame his interrogatories so as to meet and avoid it. This is often done for the very purpose of obtaining a discovery of the adversary's case (not of his evidence), to learn what is the true point of controversy, and to procure a discovery adapted to it. The bill of particulars, in common law pleadings, bears an analogy to this practice. This discovery is often obtained by suggesting a pretence of defence, and herein it is very like to "giving color" in common law pleadings. If the defendant in this case does not claim under a conveyance as charged in the bill, she can say so in her answer, and there is an end of the bill, for on that charge all the other interrogatories are founded.

We are not called upon to decide whether the discovery sought is necessary, but whether it is material to the plaintiff's case; if there is a controversy between the parties, in which the facts sought to be discovered are relevant, then they are material.

The defendant will not be heard to object that plaintiffs can prove the same facts from other sources.—And it is no hardship that she should be compelled to admit the truth.

The heirship of the plaintiffs, is plainly a relevant fact to the case stated in the bill, and is, therefore, a proper subject of inquiry. So are all these questions, as to the consideration of the conveyance, the defeasance, and other facts which are evidence that the defendant is trustee of the plaintiff, by express agreement or by application. If the deed of conveyance exists, they constitute the plaintiff's means of avoiding it.

Several of the foregoing remarks apply to the general as well as to the special causes of demurrer. In relation to the general demurrer, it is necessary only to add that the act of 1836, relating to courts, and the laws constituting the courts, give to this court the same power that Courts of Chancery have, so far as relates to the discovery of facts material to the just determination of issues; and the allegations in the bill of

Service of the subpœna by the complainant or his agent is sufficient.(g)
The court will compel a party respondent to either fix a date to a
material point, or own his inability to do so.(h)

the pendency of a suit is sufficient, if not
disputed, to lay the foundation of this
proceeding.

On this foundation, the plaintiffs may
demand a discovery from the defendant
from every fact in her knowledge, that
it is material for them to prove in making out their cases or any part of it.

But it is objected that it does not appear what the bill is, and what relief is
sought. It is a bill of discovery merely,
and the purpose of the discovery must
be, that it may be used on the trial of
the case referred to in the bill. But this
is left to be inferred, whereas, in strictness, it should be distinctly alleged.—
(Cordas v. Watkins, 5 Madd. 18.) If the
plaintiffs, after the prayer that the defendant should full answers make to the
promises, had added, in order that the
plaintiff may have the benefit thereof,
on the trial of the action of ejectment
"aforesaid," this objection could not
have been made. But, thus far, the demurrer is sustained, and the plaintiffs
have to amend. As to all other matters
the demurrer is overruled, and the defendant must put in her answer in due
course, after the amendment of the bill.

(g) Megarge v. Bate, Sept. 8, 1849.
D. C. Motion to strike off answer to
plaintiff's bill of discovery. Per curiam.
The ground of this motion is that the
service of the subpœna was not made by
the sheriff. The act of June 16, 1836,
provided (Purd. 251) that, "in every case
in which any court shall exercise any of
the powers of a Court of Chancery, the
same shall be exercised according to the
practice in equity, prescribed or adopted
by the Supreme Court of this commonwealth by general rules and regulations."

The 15th rule of the Supreme Court
of the United States, provides that "the
service of all process, mesne and final,
shall be by the Marshal of the District,
or his Deputy, or by some person specially appointed by the court for that
purpose, and not otherwise; in the
latter case the person serving the process shall make affidavit thereof.

The 13th rule of the Supreme Court
of Pennsylvania provides that "the service of all subpœnas shall be in the same
manner as writs of summons are directed
to be served."

There can be no doubt that a subpœna
in equity is mesne process within the

sense of these rules. The 11th rule of
both courts call it so expressly.

It is to be observed the rules of the
Supreme Court of Pennsylvania were
not a mere alteration in certain particulars of the rules of the Supreme Court
of the United States. This appears from
many of the rules being verbatim from
one system into another, and from the
84th rule of the Supreme Court of Pennsylvania. "In all cases, when the rules
prescribed by this court or by the Court
of Common Pleas do not apply, the practice of the courts shall be regulated by
the present practice of the High Court
of Chancery in England, so far as the
same may reasonably be applied consistently with the local circumstances and
the local conveniences of the district
where the court is held, not as positive
rules, but as furnishing just analogies to
regulate the practice." Now the 15th
rule of the Supreme Court of the United
States is certainly omitted in the rules
of the Supreme Court of Pennsylvania,
and it is not supplied by the 13th, which
answers to the 13th of the Supreme Court
of the United States. "The service of
all subpœnas shall be by a delivery of
copy, &c." Both rules regulate simply
the manner of the service. It follows
that in the absence of any rule we are to
recur to the practice of the High Court
of Chancery in England; it is not disputed but that, according to that system,
service of a subpœna may be made by
the complainant or his agent. Motion
refused.

(h) Barnet v. Darragh, Saturday, Sept.
23, 1848. D. C. Exception to answer
to bill of discovery. Per curiam. Upon
a careful examination of this case, we
dismiss all the exceptions except the
third, which is an exception to the answer to the sixth interrogatory. That
answer does not either fix, or aver the inability of the respondent to fix, the period
in or about which the conversations
therein referred to took place.

The exceptions to the answers to several interrogatories being joined together would have been sustained had
the interrogatories been properly drawn.
The old and well established practice in
equity is to direct each interrogatory to
some particular fact of the case, and to
insert in that interrogatory all the questions deemed necessary to bring it fully
out. Here several distinct interrogato-

The proper practice is to direct each interrogatory to some particular fact of the case, and to insert in that interrogatory all the questions deemed necessary to bring it fully out.(*i*)

The court will not compel the respondents to answer an immaterial interrogatory.(*j*)

Matter that would subject the party to a criminal prosecution need not be answered;(*k*) though that the answer would bring the respondent within the misdemeanor of secreting goods, &c., described in the 22d section of the act of July, 1848, will be no ground for demurrer.(*l*)

A bill of discovery was held regular though signed only by the complainant's solicitor, and accompanied with no affidavit.(*ll*)

ries substantially the same were put as to the same fact, and we cannot say that in this particular case the course adopted by the plaintiff in answering the several interrogatories relating to the same fact is irregular. Third exception sustained and the other exceptions dismissed.

(*i*) Ibid.

(*j*) Allen *v.* Kyle, Dec. 29, 1849. D. C. Exceptions to answer to bill of discovery. *Per curiam.* This is an action brought by the indorsee and holder upon certain promissory notes, and it is a bill of discovery filed by the defendant. The object of the bill is to draw from the plaintiff evidence to show that he is merely a trustee for a certain firm. Whether the bill has been successful in this respect, it is not for us to say at the present stage of the case. The allegation and interrogatory to which it is said the answer is defective in not responding, is that the note was transferred to the plaintiff with the understanding that one of this firm should offer himself and be used as a witness to sustain said suit. We think this entirely immaterial, and that plaintiff is not bound to answer it. If Alva Spear appears by the answer or other evidence to be a *cestui que trust*, he will be an incompetent witness—if, on the contrary, he appears to be disinterested at the time of his examination, he will be competent, no matter what the understanding was. A bill of discovery is not to be used merely to impeach the credibility of witnesses. Exceptions dismissed.

(*k*) Bank *v.* Biddle, 2 Par. 31. See *post*, p. 86.

(*l*) Schott *v.* Bragg, June 30, 1849. D. C. Demurrer to bill of discovery. *Per curiam.* In a feigned issue, under the sheriff's interpleader act, the defendant has filed a bill of discovery, stating that the plaintiff in the issue claims title under a sheriff's sale upon a judgment fraudulently concocted by the defendant in the execution, and the plaintiff, for the purpose of defrauding creditors. To this

bill the plaintiff has demurred, and shows for cause of demurrer, "that he ought not to be compelled to discover or set forth any matter whereby he might impeach or accuse himself of an offence or crime for which he might subject himself to fine or corporal punishment." The written argument of plaintiff does not point out how defendant is liable to fine or corporal punishment. It must be on the ground of conspiracy at common law, or under the provisions of section 20 of the act of 12th July, 1842—"an act to abolish imprisonment for debt and to punish fraudulent debtors." It would clearly be within the latter section, and there the 22d section expressly enacts, that "no person shall be excused from answering any bill seeking a discovery in relation to any fraud prohibited by that act, or from answering as a witness in relation to any such fraud, but no such answer shall be used in evidence in any other suit or prosecution." Full protection is thus secured to the party or witness, while the ends of justice are most beneficially reached by compelling a disclosure: otherwise, from the secrecy with which such frauds are always concocted, the provisions of the law for the punishment of such rogues would enure to their benefit and effectually secure the fruition of their purposes. Demurrer dismissed.

(*ll*) McCanles *v.* Coolbaugh, Saturday, April 29, 1848. D. C. Why bill of discovery should not be dismissed. *Per curiam.* The grounds upon which this decree is asked are—that the bill is not signed by the complainant but only by his solicitor. We have been referred to no rule of the S. C. in Equity which makes this necessary—and to no book to show that it is the present practice of the High Court of Chancery in England. (Walker's Rules, 144.) There is no reason why it should be. By the 23d rule of the S. C., "Every bill shall contain the signature of counsel annexed to it, which shall be consi-

Equity will not compel a party in possession of land to deliver up the title deeds to one claiming title to the land. If he succeeds in the recovery of the land at law, equity will then give him that relief.(m)

An averment that the discovery is sought in aid of some judicial proceeding, commenced or contemplated, is indispensable.(n) Where the object of a bill of discovery is in aid of future contemplated litigation, it must clearly appear on its face that the complainant has a present vested title to discovery; and the allegations and charges of the bill must be precise and specific.(o) Where the bill shows only the probability of a future title or interest, on an event which may never happen, the complainant is not entitled to discovery.(p) If the facts set forth in the bill, admitting their truth, do not show a right of action in any court, the objection may be taken advantage of by demurrer.(q)

Under the act of 16th June, 1836, the defendant in a bill to compel discovery of effects liable to execution is bound to answer, although ten days did not intervene between the service and return of the *scire facias*.(r)

6. *Election.*

An heir to whom a devise is given, and who elects to take an estate in opposition to the will, is bound to make compensation, as a trustee, to the devisee he has disappointed.(s)

The doctrine of election in reference to testamentary dispositions applies to the interest of persons under disabilities, as infants and married women ; nor is it material whether these interests are immediate or remote, contingent, of value, or not of value.(t)

The English rule that a fund appointed by a tenant for life under a general power, to a volunteer, is equitable assets for the creditors of the appointor, may be considered as of doubtful authority in Pennsylvania.(u)

Whether the act of 1836, conferring on the Court of Common Pleas the power of a Court of Equity, so far as relates to "the care of trust moneys and property," &c., enables that court to decree compensation to a devisee disappointed by the adverse election of another devisee, is the subject of doubt.(v)

An acceptance of the provisions of a will estops a party from disputing the right of testator to dispose of property belonging to his devisees.(w)

---

dered as an affirmation on his part, that upon the instructions given to him, and the case laid before him, there is good ground for the suit in the manner in which it is framed." This, which is the only rule upon the subject, has been complied with in the case before us. The other reason assigned is, that there is no affidavit by the complainant, or any one for him. During the pendency of a bill of discovery unanswered, it is the practice of this court to continue the cause. This is in effect what is termed in chancery practice the Common Injunction—and it is the well settled practice in England that no affidavit is necessary to obtain such injunction unless the defendant is abroad. The reason is obvious—the defendant himself can at any moment dissolve the injunction by filing his answer. (1 Newland's Ch. 212, 213.) Rule dismissed.

(m) Mangs v. Guenat, 6 Wh. 141.
(n) Collom v. Francis, 1 Par. 533. KING, P. J.
(o) Id. 531.
(p) Ibid.
(q) Ibid.
(r) Large v. Bristol Transportation Co. 2 Ash. 394. See for practice generally *post*, p. 86.
(s) Lewis v. Lewis, 1 H. 79.
(t) Tiernan v. Blackstone, 3 H. 451.
(u) Com. v. Duffield, 2 J. 277. And see Mitchell v. Stiles, 1 H. 308.
(v) Lewis v. Lewis, 1 H. 79.
(w) Preston v. Jones, 9 Barr, 456. S. P., Hamilton v. Buckwalter, 2 Y. 389.

A man cannot take a bequest under a will, and then object to and set aside the will.(x)   And a child cannot take his portion of an estate sold by Orphans' Court, and then prove the sale unauthorized and take the whole from the person who had purchased and paid for and improved it.(y)

This doctrine has been applied to creditors claiming different debts under the same mortgage,(z) and to parties claiming to take under a voluntary assignment.(a)

7. Fraud.

Where one of two innocent persons must suffer a loss, and à fortiori in cases where one has misled the other, he who is the cause or occasion of that confidence by which the loss has been caused or occasioned, ought to bear it.   A party who enables another to commit a fraud, is answerable for the consequences; so, if a party says nothing, but, by his expressive silence, misleads another party to his injury, he is compellable to make good the loss, and his own title is made subservient to the confiding purchaser.(b)

Fraud charged in a bill, will give jurisdiction in equity.(c)

Fraud on the part of an agent to a bank by which spurious certificates of stock were issued to the damage of the bank, is sufficient to give an equitable remedy by bill against the agent.(d)

The revocation of a license to use land in a particular way, under which an expenditure of labor or money has been made, is a fraud, and to prevent it, a chancellor will turn the owner of the soil into a trustee ex maleficio.(e)

Where money has been obtained mala fide, it may be followed, where it can be distinctly traced, as though it were a chattel.(f)

When a confusion of goods takes place through the design of one party without the consent of the other, the law, to guard against frauds, gives the certain property without any account to him whose original dominion is invaded and endeavored to be rendered uncertain without his, consent.(g)

If in equity, it be proved that one of the documents in a transaction was not intended to be what it purports, it subjects other documents in the same transaction to suspicion.(h)

Equity will not, on the mere ground of silence of another, relieve one who is acquainted with his right, or has the means of becoming so.(i)

8. Perpetuating Testimony.

The rule with respect to bills to perpetuate testimony, is the same here as in England, viz., that a demurrer will lie to a bill if there is no

Cauffman v. Cauffman, 17 S. & R. 16; and Stamp v. Findlay, 2 R. 174.

(x) M'Pherson v. Cunliff, 11 S. & R. 422.   Wilson v. Bigger, 7 W. & S. 125.

(y) M'Pherson v. Cunliff, 11 S. & R. 422.

(z) Irvine v. Tab, Western District, 1828, stated by C. J. Gibson, 1 R. 171.

(a) Adlum v. Yard, 1 R. 171. See Hamilton v. Hamilton, 4 Barr, 195; Hays v. Heidelberg, 9 Barr, 207.

(b) Blight v. Schenck, 10 Barr, 293.

(c) Bank of Ky. v. Schuylkill Bank, 1 Par. 222.

(d) Id. 180.

(e) Rerick v. Kern, 14 S. & R, 267; Swartz v. Swartz, 4 Barr, 358.

(f) Goepp's Appeal, 3 H. 428; Petrie v. Clark, 11 S. & R. 377.

(g) Ashmead v. Borie, 10 Barr, 154.

(h) Morris v. Nixon, 1 How. U. S. 119. (From Penna.)

(i) Knouff v. Thompson, 4 H. 364; Carr v. Wallace, 7 W. 401.

impediment to the plaintiff trying his right at law, unless the witnesses are old and infirm.(j)

9. *Pleading and Practice generally.*

If one of two codefendants in a case in equity, dies, the court can decree as to the survivor, but not as to the deceased, until his representatives are brought in.(k)

A rule to answer cannot be entered until after the return day of a subpoena in equity.(l)

An objection to the court's proceedings because the complainant has an adequate remedy at law, cannot regularly be taken after the defendant has answered on the merits. After a defendant has put in an answer, submitting himself to the jurisdiction of the court without objection, it is too late.(m)

Though a Court of Chancery will permit, in certain cases, usually where the act is a violation of law, as a breach of a public trust, &c., one or more persons to represent in a suit all who have similar interests, this is not to be considered a general rule. In all such cases it must be shown that the relief sought is in its nature beneficial to all whom he represents; and if this does not clearly appear the bill must be dismissed.(n)

If a bill requires an answer which may subject the defendant to any pains or penalties, he is not bound to answer it; and in such a case, if he is not bound to answer the facts, he need not answer the circumstances, though they have not an immediate tendency to criminate.(o)

A chancellor will make no decree where the respondent swears directly in answer, and in opposition to the allegations of the bill. In such cases there must be another witness, or else corroborating circumstances to overbear the defendant's answer. Where it is oath against oath, they stand in equilibrio.(p)

The answer of one defendant in equity is not evidence in behalf of another defendant.(q)

In a bill in equity between H. G., executor of J. W. L. F. and J. A. F. for the reconveyance of land, in which the answer of the latter alleged, that he held in trust for N. F., the court directed an issue to be formed in the nature of an action of ejectment, wherein N. F. should be plaintiff, and H. G. defendant, in which the plaintiff should file her description of and claim to the property in dispute, and the defendant enter the plea of not guilty, to try the question, whether the various pieces of property mentioned in the bill when conveyed to J. A. F. were to be held in trust for the said N., the court ruling that in this issue J. A. F. would be a competent witness, if either party desired to produce him as such.(r)

Where a plaintiff sets down his case for argument on bill and answer, without going into any proofs of his case, the plaintiff admits the answer

(j) Blaine v. Chambers, Supreme Court, stated by Huston, J., in M'Williams v. Hopkins, 1 Wh. 278.

(k) Bank U. S. v. Biddle, 2 Par. 31.

(l) Ingersoll v. Notman, C. C. P. C. P. 9 Leg. Int. 11.

(m) Bank of Ky. v. Schuylkill Bank, 1 Par. 222. King, P. J.

(n) Hill v. Commissioners, 1 Par. 501.

(o) Ibid. See *ante*, p. 83.

(p) Horton's Appeal, 1 H. 71. Coulter, J.

(q) Morris v. Nixon, 1 How. U. S. 119, (from Penna.)

(r) Freeman v. Freeman, 2 Par. 91.

to be true in all points, and no other evidénce is admitted, unless it be matters of record to which the answer refers. Even where the defend‑ ant states he hopes to be able to prove such and such matters, they must be considered as proved.(s)

The effect of ·a plaintiff setting down a cause for hearing on bill and answer, would seem to be analogous to a common law demurrer to evi‑ dence, where the party tendering the demurrer not only concedes the correctness of the testimony as given, but admits every reasonable con‑ clusion a jury might fairly draw from such testimony.(t)

After answer, the plaintiff will be allowed to amend his bill on pay‑ ing the costs occasioned by such amendment.(u)

New matter introduced by way of amendment, instead of supple‑ mental bill, is demurrable.(v)

To enable a complainant in equity to file a supplemental bill, intro‑ ducing matters which have arisen since the filing of the original bill, the original bill must be one on which some valid decree could be made by the court. If wholly defective, it cannot be made the basis of a supplemental bill; for if the complainant had no ground for proceeding originally, he should file a new bill, showing a cause entitling him to relief. But if his original bill was sufficient to entitle him to one kind of relief, and facts subsequently occur which entitle him to other or more extensive relief, he may have such relief by setting out such new matter in the form of a supplemental bill.(w)

In equity proceedings, the distinction seems to be that an answer, if responsive, is evidence of the fact it alleges, requiring testimony to re‑ but it; but if the matter set forth be not responsive, it is not evidence of that matter at all, but must be proved.(x)

A Court of Equity will not allow a plaintiff to read a passage from a defendant's answer, for the purpose of fixing the defendant with an ad‑ mission, without reading the explanations and qualifications by which the admission may be accompanied, even though such explanations and qualifications be contained in a distinct part of the bill.(y)

When plaintiff's amended bill is such as to render a large part of the answer useless, he must pay defendant the costs of drawing the whole answer, and defendant will be allowed to withdraw it from the files, and plead or answer *de novo*.(z)

The court is not restricted, in decreeing costs, to the items of the common law fee bill, but may allow to the party the reasonable cost of preparing his pleadings and evidence.(a) But where a pleading is chargeable with prolixity, the court will allow costs only for such part of it as is proper. For very great prolixity all costs may be dis‑ allowed.(b)

It is contrary to the policy of Pennsylvania to allow to a party, in ordinary cases, any compensation for his expenses in providing counsel to advise upon and try his case.(c)

(s) Lanning *v.* Smith, 1 Par. 17. KING, P. J.

(t) Ibid.

(u) Porter *v.* English, D. C. All. Low‑ RIE, J.

(v) Bank of Ky. *v.* Schuylkill Bank, 1 Par. 222.

(w) Ibid.

(x) Com. *v.* Cullen, 1 H. 143. BELL, J.

(y) Parrish *v.* Koons, 1 Par. 97.

(z) Porter *v.* English, D. C. Alleghany, 7 Leg. Int. 150. LOWRIE, J.

(a) Ibid.

(b) Ibid.

(c) Ibid. See Index, Tit. Damages.

Under a prayer for general relief, a mortgagor is not entitled to a decree for the redemption of the mortgaged premises.(d)

Where a prayer does not cover all the relief to which the plaintiff may be entitled, the bill may be so amended as to include the wanting prayer, provided such amendment be consistent with the original prayer; but this cannot be done where such amendment is incompatible, as is a prayer for restoration to membership in an unincorporated charitable association, with a previous prayer for a dissolution and account.(e)

The rule on the subject is, that although, where the prayer does not extend to embrace all the relief to which the plaintiff may at the hearing show a right, the deficient relief may be supplied under the general prayer: yet such relief must be consistent with that specifically prayed, as well as with the case made by the bill.(f)

A Court of Equity may decree the sale of partnership stock, in all cases of partnerships at will.(g)

A party should not be permitted to lie by with technical objection to the sufficiency of pleading, and to spring it upon his adversary, when the latter has, on the answer meeting the case on the merits, with time, labor, and expense, prepared his case for a final hearing.(h)

To authorize the taking possession by the court of property, the subject of the suit, to preserve it until the final termination of the litigation, when it is in the apparent legal possession of the defendant, the plaintiff must show a clear right thereto, or a *prima facie* right with sufficient facts to induce the court to consider the property in danger, while in its existing custody; where serious collateral results might ensue, and where no real evil seems likely to follow from resting quiescent, the court will not interfere.(i)

A bill was filed by the representatives of a deceased, against a surviving partner, asking for the sale and distribution of the partnership effects, and for an injunction and the appointment of a receiver. Before a hearing on bill and answer, an injunction was granted, and a receiver appointed. It was held that this was not such a final decree as to enable an appeal to be taken.(j)

If a demurrer be too general, it will be overruled; for it cannot be good as to a part which it covers, and bad as to the rest; therefore it must stand or fall altogether.(k)

SECTION IV.

RULES OF EQUITY PRACTICE FOR THE SUPREME COURT, AND THE SEVERAL COURTS OF COMMON PLEAS OF THE STATE OF PENNSYLVANIA. ADOPTED AND PROMULGATED BY THE SUPREME COURT, MARCH TERM, 1844.

Preliminary Regulations.

I. The Equity side of the Supreme Court and Courts of Common Pleas shall be deemed always open for the purpose of filing bills, an-

---

(d) Lanning v. Smith, 1 Par. 13.
(e) Thomas v. Ellmaker, 1 Par. 99.
(f) Id. 115. KING, P. J.
(g) Holden v. McMakin, 1 Par. 278.
(h) Bank of Ky. v. Schuylkill Bank, 1 Par. 218.

(i) Langolf v. Seiberlitch, 2 Par. 80. KING, P. J.
(j) Holden v. McMakin, 1 Par. 270.
(k) Bank U. S. v. Biddle, 2 Par. 32.

swers, and other pleadings, for issuing and returning mesne and final process and commissions, and for making and directing all interlocutory motions, orders, rules, and other proceedings, preparatory to the hearing of all causes upon their merits.

II. The prothonotary's office shall be open, and the prothonotary shall be in attendance therein, on the first Monday of every month, for the purpose of receiving, entering, entertaining, and disposing of all motions, rules, orders, and other proceedings, which are grantable of course and applied for, or had by the parties, or their solicitors, in all causes pending in equity, in pursuance of the rules hereby prescribed.

III. Any judge of the Supreme Court or Courts of Common Pleas, as well in vacation as in term, may, at chambers, or on the rule days, at the prothonotary's office, make and direct all such interlocutory orders, rules, and other proceedings preparatory to the hearing of all causes upon their merits, in the same manner and with the same effect as the court could make and direct the same in term, reasonable notice of the application therefor being first given to the adverse party or his solicitor, to appear and show cause to the contrary at the next rule day thereafter, unless some other time is assigned by the judge for the hearing.

IV. All motions, rules, orders, and other proceedings made and directed at chambers, or on rule days, at the prothonotary's office, whether special or of course, shall be entered by the prothonotary in his Equity Docket, to be kept at the prothonotary's office, on the day when they are made and directed—which book shall be open at all office hours to the free inspection of the parties in any suit in equity and their solicitors. And notice thereof given to the solicitors shall be deemed notice to the parties for whom they appear, and whom they represent, in all cases where personal notice on the parties is not otherwise specially required.

V. All motions and applications in the prothonotary's office for the issuing of mesne process and final process to enforce and execute decrees, for filing bills, answers, pleas, demurrers, and other pleadings; for making amendments to bills and answers; for taking bills *pro confessso;* for filing exceptions, and for other proceedings in the prothonotary's office, which do not, by the rules hereinafter prescribed, require any allowance or order of the court, or of any judge thereof, shall be deemed motions and applications, grantable, of course, by the prothonotary of the court; but the same may be suspended, or altered, or rescinded by any judge of the court, upon cause shown.

VI. All motions for rules or orders, and other proceedings, which are not grantable of course, or without notice, shall, unless a different time be assigned by a judge of the court, be made on a rule day, and entered in the Equity Docket, and shall be heard at the rule day next after that on which the motion is made; and if the adverse party, or his solicitor, shall not then appear, or shall not show good cause against the same, the motion may be heard by any judge of the court, *ex parte,* and granted, as if not objected to, or refused, in his discretion.

VII. The process of subpœna shall constitute the proper mesne process in all suits in equity in the first instance, to require the defendant to appear and answer the exigency of the bill; and unless otherwise provided in these rules, or specially ordered by the court, a writ of attachment, and if the defendant cannot be found, a writ of sequestration, or a writ of assistance to enforce a delivery of possession, as the case may require, shall be the proper process to issue for the purpose of compelling obedience to any interlocutory or final order or decree of the court.

VIII. Final process to execute any decree may, if the decree be solely for the payment of money, be by a writ of execution, in the form used in the same court in suits at common law in actions of assumpsit. If the decree be for the performance of any specific act, as, for example, for the execution of a conveyance of land, or the delivering up of deeds, or other documents, the decree shall, in all cases, prescribe the time within which the act shall be done, of which the defendant shall be bound without further service to take notice ; and upon affidavit of the plaintiff filed in the prothonotary's office, that the same has not been complied with within the prescribed time, the prothonotary shall issue a writ of attachment against the delinquent party, from which, if attached thereon, he shall not be discharged, unless upon a full compliance with the decree, and the payment of all costs, or upon a special order of the court, or of a judge thereof, upon motion and affidavit, enlarging the time for the performance thereof. If the delinquent party cannot be found, a writ of sequestration shall issue against his estate upon the return of *non est inventus*, to compel obedience to the decree.

IX. When any decree or order is for the delivery of possession, upon proof made by affidavit of a demand and refusal to obey the decree or order, the party prosecuting the same shall be entitled to a writ of assistance from the prothonotary of the court.

X. Every person, not being a party in any cause, who has obtained an order, or in whose favor an order shall have been made, shall be enabled to enforce obedience to such order by the same process as if he were a party to the cause ; and every person not being a party in any cause, against whom obedience to any order of the court may be enforced, shall be liable to the same process for enforcing obedience to such order, as if he were a party in the cause.

Service of Process.

XI. No process of subpœna shall issue from the prothonotary's office in any suit in equity, until the bill is filed.

XII. Whenever a bill is filed, the prothonotary shall issue the process of subpœna thereon, as of course, upon the application of the plaintiff, which shall be returnable into the prothonotary's office the next rule day, or the next rule day but one, at the election of the plaintiff, occurring after twenty days from the time of the issuing. At the bottom of the subpœna shall be placed a memorandum, that the defendant is to enter his appearance in the suit in the prothonotary's office, on or before the day at which the writ is returnable, otherwise the bill may be taken *pro confesso*. When there are more defendants than one, a writ of subpœna may, at the election of the plaintiff, be sued out separately for each defendant, except in the case of husband and wife defendants, or a joint subpœna against all the defendants.

XIII. The service of all subpœnas shall be in the same manner as writs of summons are directed by law to be served.(z) In cases where

(z) See *ante*, p. 82.

husband and wife are defendants, service on the husband shall be deemed a sufficient service on both.

XIV. Whenever any subpœna shall be returned not executed as to any defendant, the plaintiff shall be entitled to another subpœna, *toties quoties*, against such defendant, if he shall require it, until due service is made.

XV. Upon issuing the subpœna, the prothonotary shall enter the suit upon his docket as pending in the court, and shall state the time of the entry, and upon the return thereof such return.

Appearance.

XVI. The appearance day of the defendant shall be the rule day to which the subpœna is made returnable, provided he has been served with the process twenty days before that day; otherwise, his appearance day shall be the next rule day succeeding the rule day when the process is returnable. The appearance of the defendant, either personally or by his solicitor, shall be entered in the margin of the Equity Docket, by writing his name opposite the name of the defendant for whom he appears.

Bills taken Pro Confesso.

XVII. The plaintiff shall be entitled, immediately after the defendant's appearance is entered, to a rule on defendant, to be entered of course in the prothonotary's office, to file his plea, demurrer, or answer to the bill on the rule day next succeeding that on which he entered his appearance: Provided, twenty days or more intervene between the service of notice of such rule, and the rule day; in default thereof, the plaintiff may, at his election, enter an order (as of course) in the Equity Docket, that the bill be taken *pro confesso:* and thereupon the cause shall be proceeded in, *ex parte*, and the case may be put upon the next Equity Argument List, and the matter of the bill may be decreed by the court when there reached in its order, if the same can be done without an answer, and is proper to be decreed; or, the plaintiff, if he requires any discovery or answer to enable him to obtain a proper decree, shall be entitled to process of attachment against the defendant, to compel an answer, and the defendant shall not, when arrested upon such process, be discharged therefrom, unless upon filing his answer, or otherwise complying with such order as the court or a judge thereof may direct, as to pleading to, or fully answering the bill, within a period to be fixed by the court or judge, and undertaking to speed the cause; or it shall be in the option of the plaintiff when such rule shall have been served as aforesaid, instead of taking the bill *pro confesso*, to have process of contempt to compel an answer; in the latter case, the rule must be served personally upon defendant.

XVIII. When the bill is taken *pro confesso*, and the court shall have proceeded to a decree as aforesaid, such decree, so rendered, shall be deemed absolute, unless the court shall, within three months after the service of notice of such decree on defendant, set aside the same, and give the defendant time for filing the answer, upon cause shown. And no such motion shall be granted, unless the defendant shall undertake to file his answer within such time as the court shall direct, and submit to such other terms as the court shall direct, for the purpose of speeding the cause.

Frame of Bills.

XIX. Every bill, in the introductory part thereof, shall contain the names of all the parties, plaintiffs and defendants, by and against whom the bill is brought. The form in substance shall be as follows:—

" To the Judges of the Court, &c.
and thereupon your orator complains, and says, that," &c.

XX. The plaintiff in his bill shall be at liberty to omit, at his option, the part which is usually called the common confederacy clause of the bill, averring a confederacy between the defendants to injure or defraud the plaintiff; also what is commonly called the charging part of the bill, setting forth the matters or excuses which the defendant is supposed to intend to set up by way of defence to the bill; also what is commonly called the jurisdiction clause of the bill, that the acts complained of are contrary to equity, and that the defendant is without any remedy at law, and the bill shall not be demurrable therefor. And the plaintiff may, in the narrative or stating part of his bill, state and avoid, by counter averment, at his option, any matter or thing, which he supposes will be insisted upon by the defendant, by way of defence or excuse, to the case made by the plaintiff for relief. The prayer of the bill shall ask the special relief to which the plaintiff supposes himself entitled, and also shall contain a prayer for general relief; and if an injunction, or a writ of *ne exeat*, or any other special order pending the suit, is required, it shall also be specially asked for.

XXI. If any persons, other than those named as defendants in the bill, shall appear to be necessary or proper parties thereto, the bill shall aver the reason why they are not made parties, by showing them to be without the jurisdiction of the court, or that they cannot be joined without ousting the jurisdiction of the court, as to the other parties. And as to persons who are without the jurisdiction, and may properly be made parties, the bill may pray that process may issue to make them parties to the bill, if they should come within the jurisdiction.

XXII. The prayer for process of subpœna in the bill shall contain the names of all the defendants named in the introductory part of the bill, and if any of them are known to be infants, under age, or otherwise under guardianship, shall state the fact, so that the court may take order thereon as justice may require, upon the return of the process. If an injunction, or a writ of *ne exeat*, or any other special order pending the suit, is asked for in the prayer for relief, that shall be sufficient without repeating the same in the prayer for process.

XXIII. Every bill shall contain the signature of counsel annexed to it, which shall be considered as an affirmation on his part, that upon the instructions given to him, and the case laid before him, there is good ground for the suit, in the manner in which it is framed.

Scandal and Impertinence in Bills.

XXIV. Every bill shall be expressed in as brief and succinct terms as it reasonably can be, and shall contain no unnecessary recitals of deeds, documents, contracts, or other instruments, in *hæc verba*, or any other impertinent matter, or any scandalous matter not relevant to the suit. If it do, it may on exceptions be referred to a master by any judge of the court for impertinence or scandal, and if so found by him, the matter shall be expunged at the expense of the plaintiff, and he shall pay to the defendant all his costs in the suit up to that time, unless the court, or a judge thereof, shall otherwise order. If the master shall report that the bill is not scandalous or impertinent, the defendant shall be entitled to all costs occasioned by the reference.

XXV. No order shall be made by any judge for referring any bill, answer, or pleading, or other matter, or proceeding depending before the court for scandal or impertinence, unless exceptions are taken in writing, and signed by counsel, describing the particular passages which are considered to be scandalous or impertinent; nor unless the exceptions shall be filed on or before the next rule day after the process on the bill shall be returnable, or after the answer or pleading is filed. And such order, when obtained, shall be considered as abandoned, unless the party obtaining the order shall, without any unnecessary delay, procure the master to examine and report for the same on or before the next succeeding rule day, or the master shall certify that further time is necessary for him to complete the examination.

Amendments of Bills.

XXVI. The plaintiff shall be at liberty, as a matter of course, to amend his bill in any matters whatsoever, before answer, plea, or demurrer to the bill, but he shall without delay give defendant notice of such amendment, and all rules taken by the plaintiff in the case shall be suspended until such notice is given.

XXVII. After an answer, or plea, or demurrer is put in, and before replication, the defendant may, upon motion or petition, with notice, obtain an order from any judge of the court, to amend his bill on or before the next succeeding rule day. But after replication filed, the plaintiff shall not be permitted to withdraw it and to amend his bill, except upon an order of a judge of the court, upon motion or petition, after due notice to the other party, and upon proof by affidavit that the same is not made for the purpose of vexation or delay, or that the matter of the proposed amendment is material, and could not with reasonable diligence have been sooner introduced into the bill, and upon the plaintiff's submitting to such other terms as may be imposed by the judge for speeding the cause.

XXVIII. If the plaintiff so obtaining any order to amend his bill after answer, or plea, or demurrer, or after replication, shall not file his amendments or amended bill as the case may require, in the prothonotary's office, on or before the next succeeding rule day, he shall be considered to have abandoned the same, and the cause shall proceed as if no application for any amendment had been made.

Demurrers and Pleas.

XXIX. No demurrer or plea shall be allowed to be filed to any bill, unless upon a certificate of counsel, that in his opinion it is well founded in point of law, and supported by the affidavit of the defendant, that it is not interposed for delay; and if a plea, that it is true in point of fact.

XXX. The defendant may, at any time before the bill is taken for confessed, or afterwards, with the leave of the court, demur or plead to the whole bill, or to part of it, and he may demur to part, plead to part, and answer as to the residue; but in every case in which the bill specially charges fraud or combination, a plea to such part must be accompanied with an answer fortifying the plea, and explicitly deny-ing the fraud and combination, and the facts on which the charge is founded.

XXXI. The plaintiff may set down the demurrer or plea to be argued, or he may take issue on the plea. If, upon an issue, the facts stated in the plea be determined for the defendant, they shall avail him as far as in law and equity they ought to avail him.

XXXII. If, upon the hearing, any demurrer or plea is overruled, unless the court shall be satisfied that it was intended for vexation and delay, the defendant shall be assigned to answer the bill, or so much thereof as is covered by the plea or demurrer, the next succeeding rule day, or at such other period as, consistently with justice and the rights of the defendant, the same can, in the judgment of the court, be reason-ably done; in default whereof the bill shall be taken against him, *pro confesso*, and the matter thereof proceeded in and decreed accordingly; and such decree shall also be made when the court deems the plea or demurrer to have been for vexation or delay, and to have been frivolous or unfounded.

XXXIII. If, upon the hearing, any demurrer or plea shall be allowed, the court may, in its discretion, upon motion of the plaintiff, allow him to amend his bill upon such terms as it shall deem reasonable.

XXXIV. No demurrer or plea shall be held bad and overruled upon argument, only because such demurrer or plea shall not cover so much of the bill as it might by law have extended to.

XXXV. No demurrer or plea shall be held bad and overruled upon argument, only because the answer of the defendant may extend to some part of the same matter, as may be covered by such demurrer or plea.

XXXVI. If the plaintiff shall not reply to any plea, or set down any plea or demurrer for argument, on the rule day, when the same is filed, or on the next succeeding rule day, the defendant shall have the power so to set it down if the plaintiff shall fail or neglect so to do after ten days' notice.

Answers.

XXXVII. The rule, that if a defendant submits to answer, he shall answer fully to all the matters of the bill, shall no longer apply in cases where he might, by plea, protect himself from such answer and discovery. And the defendant shall be entitled in all cases, by answer, to insist upon all matters of defence (not being matters of abatement, or to the character of the parties, or of matters of form), in law, of, or to the merits of the bill, of which he may be entitled to avail himself by a plea in bar; and in such answer he shall not be compellable to answer any other matters, than he would be compellable to answer and discover, upon filing a plea in bar, and an answer in support of such plea, touching the matters set forth in the bill to avoid or repel the bar, or defence.—Thus, for example, a *bona fide* purchaser, for a valuable consideration, without notice, may set up the defence by way of answer, instead of plea, and shall be entitled to the same protection, and shall not be compellable to make any further answer or discovery of his title than he would be in any answer in support of such plea.

XXXVIII. A defendant shall not be bound to answer any interrogatory in the bill, except those interrogatories which such defendant is required to answer.

XXXIX. The interrogatories contained in the interrogating part of the bill shall be divided as conveniently as may be from each other, and numbered consecutively 1, 2, 3, &c.,(*a*) and the interrogatories which each defendant is required to answer shall be specified in a note at the foot of the bill, in the form or to the effect following; that is to say: "The defendant (A B) is required to answer the interrogatories numbered respectively, 1, 2, 3," &c.

XL. The note at the foot of the bill, specifying the interrogatories which each defendant is required to answer, shall be considered and treated as part of the bill, and the addition of any such note to the bill, or any alteration in, or addition to such note after the bill is filed, shall be considered and treated as an amendment of the bill.

XLI. Instead of the words of the bill now in use, preceding the interrogating part thereof, and beginning with the words "To the end, therefore," there shall hereafter be used words in the form or to the effect following: "To the end, therefore, that the said defendants may, if they can, show why your orator should not have the relief hereby prayed, and may, upon their several and respective corporal oaths, and according to the best and utmost of their several and respective knowledge, remembrance, information and belief, full, true, direct and perfect answer make to such of the several interrogatories hereinafter numbered and set forth, as by the note hereunder written they are respectively required to answer; that is to say:—

"1. Whether," &c.

"2. Whether," &c.

XLII. A defendant shall be at liberty, by answer, to decline answering any interrogatory, or part of an interrogatory, from answering which he might have protected himself by demurrer; and he shall be at liberty so to decline, notwithstanding he shall answer other parts of the bill, from which he might have protected himself by demurrer.

XLIII. No special replication to any answer shall be filed. But if any matter alleged in the answer shall make it necessary for the plaintiff to amend his bill, he may have leave to amend the same upon motion to the court, or to a judge thereof, in vacation.

XLIV. In every case where an amendment shall be made after answer filed, the defendant shall put in a new or supplemental answer within twenty days after the amendment or amended bill is filed, and notice thereof given to him, unless the time therefor is enlarged or otherwise ordered by a judge of the court; and upon his default the like proceedings may be had as in cases of an omission to put in an answer.

(*a*) See *ante*, p. 82.

Parties to Bills.

XLV. In all cases where it shall appear to the court, that persons who might otherwise be deemed necessary or proper parties to the suit, cannot be made parties by reason of their being out of the jurisdiction of the court, incapable otherwise of being made parties, or because their joinder would oust the jurisdiction, of the court as to the parties before the court, the court may, in their discretion, proceed in the cause without making such persons parties; and in such cases the decree shall be without prejudice to the rights of the absent parties.

XLVI. Where the parties on either side are very numerous, and cannot without manifest inconvenience and oppressive delays in the suit, be all brought before it, the court in its discretion may dispense with making all of them parties, and may proceed in the suit, having sufficient parties before it to represent all the adverse interests of the plaintiffs and the defendants in the suit properly before it. But, in such cases, the decree shall be without prejudice to the rights and claims of all the absent parties.

XLVII. In all suits concerning real estate, which is vested in trustees by devise, and such trustees are competent to sell and give discharges for the proceeds of the sale, and for the rents and profits of the estate, such trustees shall represent the persons beneficially interested in the estate or the proceeds, or the rents and profits, in the same manner, and to the same extent, as the executors or administrators in suits concerning personal estate represent the persons beneficially interested in such personal estate; and in such cases it shall not be necessary to make the persons beneficially interested in such real estate, or rents and profits, parties to the suit; but the court may, upon consideration of the matter on the hearing, if it shall so think fit, order such persons to be made parties.

XLVIII. In suits to execute the trusts of a will, it shall not be necessary to make the heir at law a party; but the plaintiff shall be at liberty to make the heirs at law a party, where he desires to have the will established against them.

XLIX. In all cases in which the plaintiff has a joint and several demand against several persons, either as principals or sureties, it shall not be necessary to bring before the court, as parties to a suit concerning such demand, all the persons liable thereto; but the plaintiff may proceed against one or more of the persons severally liable.

L. Where the defendant shall, by his answer, suggest that the bill is defective for want of parties, the plaintiff shall be at liberty, within fourteen days after answer filed, to set down the cause for argument upon that objection only; and the purpose for which the same is so set down shall be notified by an entry, to be made in the Equity Docket, in the form or to the effect following, that is to say: "Set down upon the defendant's objection for want of parties." And where the plaintiff shall not set down his cause, but shall proceed therewith to a hearing, notwithstanding an objection for want of parties taken by the answer, he shall not at the hearing of the cause, if the defendant's objection shall then be allowed, be entitled as of course to an order for liberty to amend his bill by adding parties. But the court, if it thinks fit, shall be at liberty to dismiss the bill.

LI. If a defendant shall, at the hearing of a case, object that a suit is defective for want of parties, not having by plea or answer taken the objection, and therein specified by name 'or description the parties to whom the objection applies, the court, if it shall think fit, shall be at liberty to make a decree, saving the rights of the absent parties.

Nominal Parties to Bills.

LII. Where no account, payment, conveyance, or other direct relief is sought against a party to a suit not being an infant, the party, upon service of the subpœna upon him, need not appear and answer the bill, unless the plaintiff specially requires him so to do by the prayer of his bill; but he may appear and answer at his option; and if he does not appear and answer, he shall be bound by all the proceedings in the cause. If the plaintiff shall require him to appear and answer, he shall be entitled to the costs of all the proceedings against him, unless the court shall otherwise direct.

LIII. Wherever an injunction is asked for by the bill to stay proceedings at law, if the defendant do not enter his appearance and plead, demur, or answer to the same within the time prescribed therefor by these rules, the plaintiff shall be entitled as of course, upon motion and notice, to such injunction. But special injunctions shall be grantable only upon due notice to the other party by the court in term, or by a judge thereof in vacation, after a hearing, which may be *ex parte*, if the adverse party does not appear at the time and place ordered.

Bills of Revivor and Supplemental Bills.

LIV. Whenever a suit in equity shall become abated by the death of either party, or by any other event, the same may be revived by a bill of revivor, or a bill in the nature of a bill of revivor, as the circumstances of the case may require, filed by the proper parties entitled to revive the same; which bill may be filed in the prothonotary's office at any time; and upon suggestion of the facts, the proper process or subpœna shall, as of course, be issued by the prothonotary, requiring the proper representatives of the other party to appear and show cause, if any they have, why the cause should not be revived. And if no cause shall be shown at the next rule day, which shall occur after fourteen days from the time of the service of the same process, the suit shall stand revived, as of course.

LV. Whenever any suit in equity shall become defective, from any event happening after the filing of the bill (as, for example, by a change of interest in the parties,) or for any other reason, a supplemental bill, or a bill in the nature of a supplemental bill, may be necessary to be filed in the cause, leave to file the same may be granted by any judge of the court upon proper cause shown, and due notice to the other party. And if leave is granted to file such supplemental bill, the defendant shall demur, plead or answer thereto, on the next succeeding rule day after the supplemental bill is filed in the prothonotary's office, unless some other time shall be assigned by a judge of the court.

I.—7

LVI. It shall not be necessary in any bill of revivor, or supplemental bill, to set forth any of the statements in the original suit, unless the special circumstances of the case may require it.

Answers.

LVII. Every defendant may swear to his answers before any justice or judge of the court of the United States, or before any commissioner appointed by any court to take testimony or depositions, or before any master in chancery appointed by any court, or before any judge of any court of a State or Territory, or before any justice of the peace or alderman within this commonwealth.

Amendment of Answers.

LVIII. After an answer is put in, it may be amended as of course, in any matter of form, or by filling up a blank, or correcting a date, or reference to a document or other small matter, and be resworn, at any time before a replication is put in, or the cause is set down for a hearing upon bill and answer. But after replication, or such setting down for a hearing, it shall not be amended in any material matters, as by adding new facts or defences, or qualifying or altering the original statements, except by special leave of the court or a judge thereof, upon motion and cause shown after due notice to the adverse party, supported, if required, by affidavit. And in every case where leave is so granted, the court or the judge granting the same, may, in his discretion, require that the same be separately engrossed and added as a distinct amendment to the original answer, so as to be distinguishable therefrom.

Exceptions to Answers.

LIX. After an answer is filed on any rule day, the plaintiff shall be allowed until the next succeeding rule day to file, in the prothonotary's office, exceptions thereto for insufficiency, and no longer, unless a longer time shall be allowed for the purpose, upon cause shown to the court or a judge thereof; and if no exceptions shall be filed thereto within that period, the answer shall be deemed and taken to be sufficient.

LX. Where exceptions shall be filed to the answer for insufficiency, within the period prescribed by these rules, if the defendant shall not submit to the same, and file an amended answer on the next succeeding rule day, the plaintiff shall forthwith order the prothonotary to set them down for a hearing on the next succeeding rule day thereafter, before a judge of the court; and shall give notice of such order to the opposite party, or his solicitor. And if he shall not so set the same down for a hearing, the exceptions shall be deemed abandoned and the answer shall be deemed insufficient: provided, however, that the court, or any judge thereof, may, for good cause shown, enlarge the time for filing exceptions, or for filing an amended answer, in his discretion, upon such terms as he may deem reasonable.

LXI. If, at the hearing, the exceptions shall be allowed, the defendant shall be bound to put in a full and complete answer thereto, on the next succeeding rule day, unless the time be enlarged by order of the court; otherwise the plaintiff shall, as of course, be entitled to take the bill, so far as the matter of such exceptions is concerned, as confessed, or, at his election, he may have a writ of attachment to compel the defendant to make a better answer to the matter of the exceptions; and the defendant, when he is in custody upon such writ, shall not be discharged therefrom but by an order of the court, or of a judge thereof, upon his putting in such answer and complying with such other terms as the court or judge may direct.

Replication and Issue.

LXII. Whenever the answer of the defendant shall not be excepted to, or shall be adjudged or deemed sufficient, the plaintiff shall file the general replication thereto on or before the next succeeding rule day thereafter, unless he shall put the same down on bill and answer; and in all cases where the general replication is filed, the cause shall be deemed to all intents and purposes at issue, without any rejoinder or other pleading on either side. If the plaintiff shall omit or refuse to file such replication within the prescribed period, the defendant shall be entitled to a rule upon him to reply at the next rule day, under the penalty of having his bill dismissed; and if at the expiration of such rule said plaintiff shall not have filed his replication, and shall have had ten days' notice, the defendant shall be entitled to an order, as of course, for a dismissal of the suit; and the suit shall thereupon stand dismissed, unless the court, or a judge thereof, shall, upon motion for cause shown, allow a replication to be filed, *nunc pro tunc*, the plaintiff submitting to speed the cause, and to such other terms as may be directed.

Testimony, how taken.

LXIII. An order to take the testimony of ancient, infirm, and going witnesses *de bene esse* before any alderman or justice of the peace of the respective county, may be entered by either party in the prothonotary's office, of course at any time after the service of the subpœna stipulating a reasonable notice to the adverse party: so of an order for a commission to any place within the State of Pennsylvania, more than forty miles distant from the county seat of the respective county, or to any other State, or Territory, or to foreign parts. But in case of a commission, the interrogatories must be filed in the prothonotary's office at the time, and written notice of this last order and of the names of the commissioners must be served on the adverse party at least fifteen days before the commission issues, in order that he may file cross interrogatories, or nominate commissioners on his part, if he shall deem it eligible. Provided, that depositions taken before magistrates in the method prescribed by this rule, shall only be allowed to be read in evidence on the hearing of the cause, in case the same facts shall appear before the examiner appointed to take testimony in the cause after it is at issue, and be certified by him to excuse the production of such witnesses before him as are necessary for the introduction of depositions taken *de bene esse* on trials by jury in the same courts, or if taken by the commissioner before the cause is at issue, under this rule, it shall appear by affidavit at the hearing that the witnesses so examined were aged, infirm, or going out of the country, or that any of them was a single witness to a material fact.

LXIV. The method of taking testimony, except in cases provided for in the foregoing rule, shall be as follows: After the cause is at issue the court shall appoint an examiner,(*l*) at the request of either party who may first make application, which examiner shall cause such witnesses as either party may name to him to come before him on a reasonable day or days, to be appointed by him, of which he shall give notice to the parties; for the enforcing the attendance of which witnesses, either party may have subpœna or subpœnas, returnable before such examiner, to be enforced by the usual process of contempt. The examination shall be conducted by the counsel of the parties, *viva voce*, and the answers of the witnesses shall be reduced to writing by the examiner, and the questions also, if necessary to the understanding of the answer; or if it be required by either party, the testimony of both parties shall be taken before the same examiner, and the defendant shall not be compelled to proceed with the taking of his testimony until the plaintiff has finished, or declared he has none to take, nor shall the plaintiff be compelled to proceed with the rebutting testimony until the defendant has completed the testimony on his part; but the court may, upon the special application of either party, upon cause shown, appoint an additional examiner before whom the party making such application may proceed to take his testimony, notwithstanding the pendency of the proceeding of his adversary before the examiner first named.

LXV. Either party may, on application to the court, obtain an order on his adversary to close the taking of his testimony within three months after notice of such order; any testimony taken after three months' notice of such order shall not be read in evidence at the hearing of the cause. But it shall be in the discretion of the court to enlarge the time on the application of the party against whom such order may have been granted; and no such order shall be granted against a party while, by the provisions of the sixty-fourth rule, such party is not bound to begin until his adversary has closed.

LXVI. Upon the return of the commission executed, the same may, at the application of either party, be opened by any one or more of the judges of the court, in term time or vacation, or by the prothonotary, and the prothonotary shall give notice to the parties of the return of any commission, and of the filing of depositions taken before any alderman, justice of the peace, or examiner; and the parties shall, within ten days after service of such notice upon them respectively, enter exceptions in writing, if they have any, to the form of the interrogatories or the manner of the execution of the commission, and the taking of the depositions, or be forever precluded from the benefit of such exceptions, which exceptions when so taken may be put down for hearing by either party at the next rule day, giving notice to his adversary thereof.

(*l*) In the Supreme Court, by commission dated 20th Dec. 1844, the court appointed a standing examiner, JOHN W. WALLACE, Esq.: and an application for an examiner in each case is now dispensed with in that court: The practice there is, for the party desiring to take testimony, to inform the examiner, who, without a special direction from the court, appoints a time, and calls the witnesses and parties before him. This, however, does not apply in the Court of Common Pleas.

Form of the last Interrogatory.

LXVII. The last interrogatory in the written interrogatories to take testimony, now commonly in use, shall in the future be altered and stated in substance thus : " Do you know, or can you set forth any other matter or thing, which may be a benefit or advantage to the parties at issue in this cause, or either of them, or that may be material to the subject of this your examination, or the matters in question in this cause ? If yea, set forth the same fully and at large in your answer."

Equity Argument List.(m)

LXVII½. No case in equity will be put on the argument list unless the party desiring it shall in writing require the prothonotary to do so, three days before the calling of the list ; and to be entitled to have such case argued it shall also be the duty of the party desiring it, to give three days' notice in writing to the opposite party that the case is set down for argument.

Cross Bill.

LXVIII. Where a defendant in equity files a cross bill for recovery only against the plaintiff in the original bill, the defendant to the original bill shall first answer thereto, before the original plaintiff shall be compellable to answer the cross bill. The answer of the original plaintiff to such cross bill may be read and used by the party filing the cross bill at the hearing, in the same manner and under the same restrictions as the answer praying relief may now be read and used.

Reference to, and Proceedings before Masters.

LXIX. Whenever any reference of any matter is made to a master, to examine and report thereon, the party at whose instance, or for whose benefit the reference is made, shall cause the same to be presented to the master for a hearing on or before the next rule day succeeding the time when the reference was made ; if he shall omit to do so, the adverse party shall be at liberty forthwith to cause proceedings to be had before the master, at the costs of the party procuring the reference.

LXX. Upon every such reference it shall be the duty of the master, as soon as he reasonably can, after the same is brought before him, to assign a time and place for proceedings in the same, and to give due notice thereof to each of the parties or their solicitors ; and if either party shall fail to appear at the time and place appointed, the master shall be at liberty to proceed *ex parte,* or in his discretion to adjourn the examination and proceedings to a future day, giving notice to the absent party or his solicitor of such adjournment ; and it shall be the duty of the master to proceed with all reasonable diligence in every such reference, and with the least practicable delay ; and either party shall be at liberty to apply to the court, or a judge thereof, for an order

(m) This rule applies only to the Court of Common Pleas.

to the master to speed the proceedings, and to make his report, and to certify to the court or judge the reasons for any delay.

LXXI. The master shall regulate all the proceedings in every hearing before him, upon every such reference; and he shall have full authority to examine the parties in the cause, upon oath, touching all matters contained in the reference; and also, to require the production of all books, papers, writings, vouchers, and other documents applicable thereto; where, by the principles of Courts of Chancery, the production of them may be compelled, and also, to examine on oath, *viva voce*, all witnesses produced by the parties before him, and to order the examination of other witnesses to be taken, under a commission to be issued upon his certificate by the prothonotary; and also, to direct the mode in which the matters requiring evidence shall be proved before him; and generally to do all other acts, and direct all other inquiries and proceedings in the matters before him, which he may deem necessary and proper to the justice and merits thereof, and the rights of the parties.

LXXII. All parties accounting before a master shall bring in their respective accounts in the form of debtor and creditor; and any of the other parties, who shall not be satisfied with the account so brought in, shall be at liberty to examine the accounting party, *viva voce*, or upon interrogatories before the master, or by deposition, as the master shall direct.

LXXIII. All affidavits, depositions, and documents, which have been previously made, read, or used in the court, upon any proceeding in any cause or matter, may be used before the master.

LXXIV. The master shall be at liberty to examine any creditor or other person coming in to claim before him, either upon written interrogatories or *viva voce*, or in both modes, as the nature of the case may appear to him to require. The evidence upon such examination shall be taken down by the master, or by some other person by his order and in his presence, if either party requires it, in order that the same may be used by the court, if necessary.

LXXV. The courts may appoint standing masters in chancery in their respective jurisdictions,(*n*) and they may also appoint a master *pro hac vice*, in any particular case. The compensation to be allowed to every master in chancery for his services in any particular cause, shall be fixed by the court in its discretion, having regard to all the circumstances thereof; and the compensation shall be charged upon and borne by such of the parties in the cause as the court shall direct. The master shall not retain his report as security for his compensation; but when the compensation is allowed by the court, he shall be entitled to an attachment for the amount against the party who is ordered to pay the same, if, upon notice thereof, he does not pay it within the time prescribed by the court.

Exceptions to Report of Master.

LXXVI. No exception will be received to the report of any master, unless the party excepting has filed the same with the master by whom

---

(*n*) Under this rule the Supreme Court of Pennsylvania, by a commission dated 20th Dec. 1844, appointed JOHN W. WALLACE, Esq., standing master for their jurisdiction. The master's office is in the buildings at the S. E. corner of Sixth and Walnut streets.

the report has been made, whose duty it shall be, on such exception being filed, to re-examine the subject and amend his report, if in his opinion such exceptions are in whole or in part well founded. And in order to give all parties in interest an opportunity of entering such exception, no master shall file his report until ten days after he has notified to the parties his intention so to do on a day designated, and giving them an opportunity of having access to such report. On the hearing of the question of confirming or setting aside the master's report, the party excepting thereto shall be confined to the exception made by him before the master, according to the previous requisition of this rule; reserving to the court, however, the power of committing the report again, should justice require it. On the return of the master's final report, on the next succeeding rule day, either party may set down the cause for hearing on the next equity argument list.

[This rule is composed partially of the old rule of March 1844, and partially of a new one adopted January 1847. In the Court of Common Pleas, though not in the Supreme Court, the rule proceeds as follows:]

And it is further ordered, that all reports of auditors and masters in the Court of Common Pleas, shall be confirmed on the third Saturday next succeeding the day on which they shall have been respectively filed, unless in case of exceptions duly filed as provided by the foregoing rule.

Decrees.

LXXVII. Clerical mistakes in decrees, or decretal orders, or errors, arising from any accidental slip or omission, may be corrected by order of the court or a judge thereof, upon petition, without the form or expense of a rehearing.

LXXVIII. In drawing up decrees and orders, neither the bill, nor answer, nor other pleadings, nor any part thereof, nor the report of any master, nor any other prior proceeding, shall be recited or stated in the decree or order; but the decree and orders shall begin in substance as follows: "This cause came on to be heard (or to be further heard, as the case may be) at this term, and was argued by counsel; and, therefore, upon consideration thereof, it was ordered, adjudged, and decreed as follows, viz.:" (Here insert the decree or order.)

LXXIX. The decree shall be drawn by the solicitor of the party in whose favor it is, who shall serve a copy thereof on the solicitor of the adverse party, with notice of the time, which shall not be less than three days thereafter, when the same will be submitted to the court. If the opposite party shall not deem such draft of decree in conformity with the intentions of the court, he may file exceptions before the day of hearing designated in such notice, which shall be submitted with the draft of the decree on the day so prefixed, and thereupon the court approving of the draft or correcting the same in conformity with such exceptions or otherwise, the prothonotary shall enter it in his equity docket, and from thenceforth it shall become the act and decree of the court.

LXXX. If the decree be merely for the payment of money, the party in whose favor it is made shall be entitled to have a minute thereof (without waiting for the draft of a more formal decree) entered in the Equity Docket, and placed in the usual form of entering judgments, in the judgment index of the common law side of the court.

Guardians and Prochein Amis.

LXXXI. Guardians *ad litem* to defend a suit may be appointed by the court, or by any judge thereof, for infants or other persons, who are under guardianship, or otherwise incapable to sue for themselves; all infants and other persons so incapable, may sue by their guardians, if any, or by their *prochein ami*, subject, however, to such orders as the court may direct for the protection of infants and other persons.

LXXXII. Every petition for a rehearing, shall contain the special matter or cause on which such rehearing is applied for, shall be signed by the counsel, and the facts therein stated, if not apparent on the record, shall be verified by the oath of the party, or by some other person. A petition for rehearing may be granted at any time within the discretion of the court; but where the decree has been executed, parties who have acted on the faith of such decree shall not be injured by such decree being reversed or varied.

LXXXIII. The courts may make any other and further rules and regulations for the practice, proceedings, and process, mesne and final in their respective districts, not inconsistent with the rules hereby prescribed, in their discretion, and from time to time alter and amend the same.

LXXXIV. In all cases, when the rules prescribed by this court, or by the Court of Common Pleas, do not apply, the practice of the courts shall be regulated by the present practice of the High Court of Chancery in England, so far as the same may reasonably be applied consistently with the local circumstances and local convenience of the district where the court is held, not as positive rules, but as furnishing just analogies to regulate the practice.

LXXXV. Whenever under these rules an oath is or may be required to be taken, the party may, if conscientiously scrupulous of taking an oath, in lieu thereof make solemn affirmation to the truth of the facts stated by him.

FEE BILL.

SETTLED BY A COMMITTEE APPOINTED BY THE SUPREME COURT OF PENNSYLVANIA, AND THE COURT OF COMMON PLEAS FOR THE CITY AND COUNTY OF PHILADELPHIA.

Prothonotary's Fees.

Filing Bill, original or subsequent thereto	50
Docketing every cause	25
Subpœna, all names	1 50
Office copy of any paper for every line of ten words	$1\frac{1}{2}$
Certificate to office copy when made by a party	$37\frac{1}{2}$
Entering every motion, rule, and report, and filing exceptions	$12\frac{1}{2}$
Every order of reference to a master	25

Entering every order and decree on a cause and for
    every injunction and every line of ten words   . $1\frac{1}{2}$
Subpœna to testify, the same as at law.
Every other writ, same as at law.
Affixing the seal of the court, the same as at law.
Administering oath or affirmation .   .   .   . $12\frac{1}{2}$
Stationery in every cause in which decree is made .   75
Taxing bill of costs 1 50

Examiner's Fees.

Taking depositions per line of ten words   .   .   5
Exhibits, each   25
Administering oaths or affirmations   .   . $12\frac{1}{2}$
Subpœna, same as to Prothonotary.
Attesting and returning deposition   .   .   .   1 50
The Examiner is to be paid as for taking a deposition of one page of
thirty lines by a party who makes an appointment to take depositions,
and does not attend, or attends and does not examine a witness.

Fees of the Sheriff, Witnesses, Surveyors, and Commissioners in dower
    and partition, Sheriff's Fees for service of subpœna and to appear
    and answer and of injunction, the same as service of summons at law.

Witnesses' Fees, the same as at law.

Fees of Commissioners appointed to make partition, or to admeasure
    dower, and of Surveyors appointed to make surveys in such cases—
    for every day's actual and necessary service—Two dollars to each.—
    For necessary assistants to the same, one dollar per day.

Party's Costs.

For drawing bill, answer, or other pleading, demurrer, exceptions,
    interrogatories, and any decree, or order of the court, for every
    page of 30 lines, each of 10 words, ten cents for each line of the
    first page, and six cents per line for each subsequent page.
For every motion and notice thereof to the opposite party   .   .   20
For service of subpœna to testify, the same as at law.
Copy to keep, of any paper that shall be filed in the cause, one-half of
    the allowance for an office copy.

J. K. KANE,
EDWD. D. INGRAHAM,
BENJN. TILGHMAN,
WILLM. RAWLE,
H. B. WALLACE,
    Committee.

SECTION V.

OF THE POWERS TO GRANT RELIEF IN EQUITY, BY MEANS OF COMMON
LAW FORMS, DEPENDING UPON THE DECISIONS OF THE SUPREME
COURT.

IN no one of the preceding sections have we adverted to the powers
exercised from the beginning by the Supreme Court and Courts of
Common Pleas, of giving relief and administering equity through the
ordinary common law *remedies* and *forms;* that is, through the medium
of the usual *actions*, the *pleadings* appropriate to each; conditional *verdicts;* special *judgments*, and the *final* process adequate to enforce and
obtain the fruit of them.

A view of this branch of the subject of equity in Pennsylvania is,
however, of the utmost importance; because, in the recent changes in
our code, the legislature have not provided for the establishment of a
separate tribunal to exercise the new equity jurisdiction created, through
chancery forms; but have conferred it on the common law tribunals;
and in them are now vested, not only the new powers to grant relief in
equity, but those they before possessed, to be enforced according to the
old common law methods. The plan which the legislature seem to have
adopted was this: They found our legal system a mixed one; "com-
bining the use of certain chancery remedies, and the expansion of certain common law remedies, and their application to cases to which they
are not applied in England, and in other States of the Union possessing
a regular chancery organization:" And they thought, that it was safest
"to pursue the same course with respect to the *residuum* of equity
powers; that is, to give the necessary relief whenever it can be done by
the convenient application of some familiar common law remedy, or by
the revival of some one that has become obsolete; and whenever full
and complete relief cannot be obtained by such process, to resort without hesitation to the methods of the chancery courts, and employ them
either as they are to be found, or in a modified shape, as has been done
heretofore in useful and harmonious co-operation with those of the law."
Our civil tribunals are, therefore, to continue, as heretofore, to administer justice on the basis of the common law procedure, with common
law forms and materials, with the addition of the chancery forms and
materials, both in the cases in which they were specifically granted by
the legislature prior to the act of 1836, and also under the provisions
of that act. It is probable, therefore, that in every case in which the
direct chancery method is used to obtain the intervention of our courts
under their equity powers, it will be necessary that the usual allegation
in the bill, that the complainant is remediless at the common law, should
be true, or at all events, that he should have no convenient remedy at
common law.

It will be observed, too, that the District Court of this city and
county only partakes of the new equity powers, as far as the discovery
of evidence necessary to a just decision of the suits instituted in it is
involved, and, in every other respect, must proceed according to the old
methods in the exercise of its blended jurisdiction.

The common law *remedies*, that have been long made the vehicles of equitable rights in this State, are the actions of assumpsit; debt; covenant; replevin; ejectment; and partition. Perhaps, indeed, all the personal actions may be here called equitable remedies;(o) as, from the rights of a defendant to *plead* an equitable defence to any one of them, the *reply* to such a defence may take the same complexion, and thus at last the action may result in procuring for the plaintiff the fruits of a *merely* equitable right. This will be more fully seen hereafter.

I. *Of the Equity of a Plaintiff, as depending on the form of Action and Declaration.*

1. ASSUMPSIT, OR DEBT. In the case of Bixler *v.* Kunkle,(p) a majority of the court held that assumpsit was, in its *general* form, i. e. the declaration being in general *indebitatus assumpsit*, a good vehicle of a purely equitable claim. GIBSON, C. J. and HUSTON, J. dissented, and the former observed: "It would be but another step formally to entertain a bill for a specific execution. A power to decree a trust, or a contract, specifically, would, no doubt, be a most salutary one; for the very case before us is an instance of the impotence of attempts to give entire effect to the principles of equity while trammelled with common law forms. Yet, in the whole course of our juridical history, there is not an instance of an attempt to cast these forms off."(q) But in the subsequent case of Pidcock *v.* Bye,(r) all objections to this use of the action of assumpsit are removed by the unanimous decision of the court. It was held in that case, that an action of *assumpsit* may be maintained against the assignee of land to recover the principal of a widow's thirds, charged on such land by those entitled to it after her death, without an express promise to pay it on the part of the assignee; but the judgment must be entered so as to make the land only liable, and not the defendant personally. It is to be observed, however, that in this case the declaration was special.

The case of Irvine *v.* Bull,(s) was assumpsit on a parol agreement to convey land, in which the declaration was on the agreement, and under the equitable powers of the court, demanded conditional damages sufficiently large to compel the defendant to execute a conveyance; but, as the agreement was by parol and had not been partly executed, it was repugnant to the statute of frauds, and the plaintiff could not recover. The policy of requiring the title to relief to be specially set out was said to be strikingly evinced by that case; and it was held that it could produce neither injustice nor inconvenience to narrow the plaintiff's resource to a specific ground, as a count for equitable relief might be joined with a count for damages at law.

A and B, equitable tenants in common of land, the legal title to which was in A, sold the land to C. A afterwards died, having appointed C his executor. It was held, that an action of debt might be brought by B against C for his share of the purchase-money due by C, as a substitute for a bill in equity.(t)

(o) "I do not like the idea, that our equitable powers are more extensive in one form of action than another." Per HUSTON, J. 3 Rawle, 195.
(p) 17 S. & R. 298.
(q) Ibid. 311.
(r) 3 R. 183.
(s) 4 W. 287.
(t) Work *v.* Work, 2 H. 316.

A and B entered into an agreement with a corporation, that A should collect certain collaterals, and pay the avails over to the corporation in discharge of a debt due by him to it. A collected the money, but applied it to the payment of certain debts of B. It was held, that B thereby became the principal debtor, and that an action in the nature of a bill in equity could be maintained against his executors by the corporation, on the agreement;(u) and that the joinder in the action of A, who afterwards became bankrupt, was an irregularity which would be disregarded, the action being otherwise barred by the statute.(v)

It was said that where it is required by the justice of the case, the common law form of writ, count, or judgment may be disregarded.(w)

In the case of Butcher v. Metts,(x) the District Court of this city and county held a doctrine that does not seem in accordance with that laid down in Bixler v. Kunkle,(y) for they maintained that it was a general principle, that where the form of action is *ex contractu*, and the plaintiff founds his claim upon a *right merely equitable*, his declaration should be assimilated to a bill in equity, and should set forth distinctly the special circumstances upon which the equity he claims is supposed to arise.(z) In Irvine v. Bull,(a) the necessity for the existence of this doctrine is insisted on and illustrated by the chief justice.(b)

2. COVENANT.—Where by articles of agreement for the sale of land, a deed was to have been delivered at a certain time, and by a subsequent parol agreement, the vendee agreed to receive the deed at a later period, and accepted it accordingly, it was held that the vendor, who brought covenant for the non-payment of the purchase-money, might declare according to the circumstances of the case, by setting forth, in the first place, the covenants according to the articles of agreement, and then showing the alteration which had been made by consent of parties.(c)

3. REPLEVIN.—This action, from the liberal extension of it by the courts, has become a very effectual vehicle of an equitable right; it may be employed both to prevent and counteract fraud, and to compel the specific execution of a contract relating to personal property. It is applicable to every case in which goods and chattels, in the possession of one person, are claimed by another; and no distinction is made between those instances in which there has been a *tortious* deprivation of the *possession*, and others, in which the dispute is only as to the *title* or ownership.(d) By means of this action, not only may family pictures, for which an agreement has been made, be obtained, but also

(u) Loan Co. v. Elliot's Exrs. 3 H. 224.
(v) Ibid.
(w) Ibid.)
(x) 1 M. 153.
(y) 17 S. & R. 298.
(z) Jordon v. Cooper, 3 S. & R. 578, 579, 581; Witman v. Ely, 4 S. &. R. 266, 267; Reichart v. Beidleman, 17 S. & R. 43. See the method of framing an equitable declaration pointed out, Bixler v. Kunkle, 17 S. & R. 303. See the form of one, Pidcock v. Bye, 3 R. 183. But see this case reconsidered in Unangst v. Kroemer, 8 W. & S. 400.

(a) 4 W. 289.
(b) See *post*, vol. ii. Assumpsit.
(c) Jordan v. Cooper, 3 S. & R. 564, 578.
(d) Weaver v. Lawrence, 1 D. 157; Stoughton v. Rappale, 3 S. & R. 562; Shearick v. Huber, 6 Bin. 3; Snyder v. Vann, 2 R. 423. See vol. ii. Replevin.

merchandise, when the particular bales can be distinguished.(e) Nor is the plaintiff restricted to the continuance of the possession in the defendant; he may follow the property through successive transfers, and as the doctrine of market overt has been adjudged not to hold in Pennsylvania, he may replevy it, wherever found.(f)

In all of the preceding cases, a person who is clothed with the rights of the plaintiff by a previous transfer or assignment (who then obtains the name of his *assignee*), acquires through such a transfer, the privilege of enforcing it as well *equitably* as at law, by commencing his action in the name of the assignor " for his use."(g) This mode of instituting the action is not indispensable; but if omitted, may lead to inconvenience;(h) thus the assignor may release, or receive payment from the defendant, who is unapprised of the transfer.(i) When the action is brought in the name of the assignor, generally, the defendant may show the trust, and name in his plea the person to whose use the action is really brought, in order to avail himself of a set-off; so he may suggest his name on the record, to charge him with costs.(j)

4. EJECTMENT.—The *equitable* action of ejectment, as will hereafter be seen,(jj) forms, in this State, an important branch of the law. Through the liberality and ingenuity of the courts, it has become the most important and universal mode of enforcing the equity of a plaintiff relating to land. It is a remedy which has been substituted in this State for the bill in equity; though it is subject to all those considerations, by which a claim to have the land itself, may be defeated.(k) The rule is, that wherever equity will presume a trust to have arisen, and will compel its execution, or will enforce articles of agreement, our courts will, through the application of this remedy, administer the same relief.(l) Thus the vendee of lands by articles of agreement, who has complied with his part of the contract, as, by payment or tender of the purchase-money, may by ejectment obtain possession, if withheld by the vendor.(m) In exercising the right, the general form of this action in common use is adopted, and the articles are not required to be spread out upon the record.(n) The plaintiff is required to allege and prove *no more* than would induce a chancellor to decree a specific performance of the agreement;(o) though less would not avail him.(p)

5. PARTITION. An equitable estate is sufficient in Pennsylvania to support this action.(q) In the case of Stewart v. Browne,(r) the

(e) Shearick v. Huber, 6 Bin. 5.
(f) Hosack v. Weaver, 1 Y. 478; Hardy v. Metzgar, 2 Id. 347; Easton v. Worthington, 5 S. & R. 130.
(g) Morris v. Demars, 1 D. 140. Steele v. Phœnix Ins. Co. 3 Bin. 312. Rogers v. Old, 5 S. & R. 403.
(h) See Brindle v. McIlvain, 9 S. & R. 77; Bury v. Hartman, 4 Id. 184.
(i) See on this subject Christine v. Whitehill, 16 S. & R. 105.
(j) Canby v. Ridgway, 1 Bin. 496.
(jj) Vol. ii. Ejectment.
(k) Pennock v. Freeman, 1 W. 409. See Hawthorn v. Bronson, 16 S. & R.

278, 9, a description of this remedy by the late Mr. Justice Duncan.
(l) See Wh. Dig. tit. Equity and Ejectment, and *post*, vol. ii. Ejectment.
(m) Hawn v. Norris, 4. Bin. 78. Griffith v. Cochran, 5 Id. 105. Cope v. Smith's Ex's, 8 S. & R. 115.
(n) Hawn v. Norris, 4 Bin. 78.
(o) Irvine v. Bull, 4 W. 289.
(p) See *post*, vol. ii. Ejectment.
(q) See vol. ii. Partition. Willing v. Brown, 7 S. & R. 467; Miller et al. v. Schneider, 5 R. 140.
(r) 2 S. & R. 462.

defendant had bought lands under an agreement with the plaintiff, that the purchase when made should be for their equal, mutual interest; the latter had never been in possession; but the court held that the agreement of the defendant made him a trustee to the use of the plaintiff, as to one moiety, and that the action of partition was maintainable against him to obtain it.

Independently of the *forms* of actions, our courts will advance the equitable rights of plaintiffs, where, through some accident that occurred anterior to the institution of his suit, or that happens during its pendency, his common law remedy would be taken away or rendered nugatory. The first instance, is the case of a lost bond, which the owner could not maintain an action on, in a common law tribunal, because he could not say that he had the instrument to show the court—called, in technical language, making *profert* of it—and therefore would be obliged to recur to chancery, to obtain an injunction on the party, not to take advantage of its non-production. But in our courts, the plaintiff may state his claim on the bond, and explain the reason why he cannot produce it, *i. e.*, may declare without a *profert*.(s) Although in 1789, the Court of King's Bench in England, decided that this might be done in that court,(t) the Supreme Court of this State did not wholly proceed on the reason of that decision, but founded theirs on the necessity of the case occasioned by the want of a Court of Chancery. The benefit of the rule is, of course, open to defendants who may have to *plead* lost deeds. Another instance is the case of a plaintiff having a *joint* demand, *i. e.*, a demand against several jointly bound for it, one of the parties to which is dead, and the survivor insolvent. At common law, the plaintiff could only sue this survivor, and to get at the estate of the deceased party, he would have to recur to chancery. But our system allows suit to be brought against the executor or administrator of the latter, through whom a judgment may be obtained against the property of the decedent.(u) Should one of several codefendants jointly liable have died before judgment was obtained against all, his estate may be reached through an equitable *scire facias* against his executor or administrator.(v) Should he have died *after* judgment obtained against all, an equitable *scire facias* against his executor may issue.(w) Recently, however, by statute, the deceased party's estate is made primarily liable.(ww)

II. *Of the Equity of a Defendant as depending on the Form of a Plea.*

A defendant in Pennsylvania is permitted, as will hereafter be more fully seen,(x) to give evidence of equitable matters under the general issue : or if this mode be inconvenient or improper in his particular case, he may plead specially his equitable right, and thus obtain the advantages of a chancery answer so far as they relate to a complete statement of his

(s) Res. v. Ross, 1 Y. 2.
(t) 3 T. R. 151.
(u) Lang & Whitaker v. Keppele, 1 Bin. 123.
(v) Reed v. Garvin's Executors, 7 S. & R. 354, 355, 356, *et seq.*
(w) Id. 7 S. & R. 365. See the form, 1 Hall's Journ. of Jurisp. 248.
(ww) Vol. ii. "Partners."
(x) *Post*, "Plea," "Special matter."

case. In making, however, an equitable defence in a court of law, he is in effect a plaintiff in equity, and is bound to show such a state of things affirmatively as would authorize a chancellor to interfere by injunction.(y) Thus where to a *sci. fa.* on a mortgage to secure a joint and several bond by one of the obligors, the latter defended on the ground that the mort. gage and bond were only collateral security for notes given by the other obligors, which had been paid, it was *held*, that this was to be shown distinctly and affirmatively, and not by mere presumptions, so as to satisfy a jury of the fact.(z)   So in ejectment by one holding the legal title to land, it was *held*, that the defendant could not set up as a defence, that the land had been conveyed by himself to the plaintiff on a trust fraudulent as to creditors.(a)   The methods of asserting the equity of a defendant, therefore, resolve themselves into two kinds; 1st. That in which the defence is made by evidence of equity, given under a general plea; and 2d. That in which the equitable ground is specially pleaded.

I. Of general pleas to a personal demand.

PAYMENT.—The practice of giving in evidence under the plea of payment, matters relating to a defence, whose only foundation is equity, may be traced to the earliest stages of our jurisprudence, and is a branch of the common law that aroʒe out of the peculiar wants of the province of Pennsylvania.(b)   The general rule adopted by the courts is, that whatever would be sufficient in chancery to protect the party, will be admitted in evidence under the general plea of payment; and that shall be presumed to be *paid*, which in equity and good conscience, ought not to be *paid*.(c)   The cases in our reports serve very fully to illustrate and prove this general principle, as they include almost every species of defence usually made in a Court of Chancery.

The various defences permitted in equity may be classed under the heads of want of consideration, fraud, mistake, and accident; the equitable grounds specified in the rule of the Supreme Court, relating to the plea of payment, are the want of consideration, fraud, a suggestion of falsehood, and a suppression of truth.   The last two are but varieties of the second, and mistake and accident, although not included in the rule, are causes recognized by authorities, and make our equitable system agree with that of England.

1. *Want of Consideration.*—In Pennsylvania, the law relating to this subject has long been settled according to the principles of equity, in order to avoid the manifest injustice which would otherwise have ensued.   In Swift v. Hawkins,(d) the court said, that the want of consideration to a bond could be shown under the plea of payment, although in an English court of law such a defence would not be permitted; and the same principle has been asserted in succeeding cases.(e)

(y) Waln v. Smith, D. C. C. P. 9 Leg. Int. 87.   See Murphy v. Hubert, 4 H. 50.
(z) Ibid.
(a) Murphy v. Hubert, 4 H. 50.
(b) Sparks v. Garrigues, 1 Bin. 164; Swift v. Hawkins, 1 D. 17.
(c) Sparks v. Garrigues, 1 Bin. 164; Robinson v. Eldridge, 10 S. & R. 142; Cope v. Smith's Executors, 8 S. & R. 116; Gochenauer v. Cooper, 8 S. & R.

203; 2 Browne, 120; Hollingsworth v. Ogle, 1 D. 260; Griffith v. Chew's Executors, 8 S. & R. 25.
(d) 1 D. 17.
(e) Baring v. Shippen, 2 Bin. 166; Pipher v. Lodge, 4 S. & R. 309; Heck v. Shener, 4 S. & R. 256; Solomon v. Kimmel, 5 Bin. 234. *Post*, "PLEAS," "SPECIAL MATTER."

An act of assembly,(*f*) passed in 1715, rendered bonds and promissory notes assignable at law, and gave the assignee a right of suit in his own name, independently of his assignor. A question then arose, whether these two instruments were not to be placed upon a similar footing, as to the effects of a transfer: so that evidence of want of consideration to a bond, would be restricted to suits between the original parties, in the same manner as with promissory notes under the statute of 3 and 4 Ann. chap. 9. In Baynton *v.* Hughes,(*g*) the case in which this point was mooted, the court, observing the distinction between *assignability* and *negotiability*, decided that the assignee of a bond was here to be considered in the same light as in a Court of Chancery, and was liable to the equity of the obligor against the original obligee; the law has in consequence always been so held in Pennsylvania.(*h*)

2. *Fraud.*—That the fraud of a party who has obtained a bond either by a suggestion of falsehood, or a concealment of truth, may be given in evidence, under the general plea of payment, is a point so clearly settled by numerous authorities, that it will be only necessary to cite a few by way of examples.

In Baring *v.* Shippen,(*i*) a bond had been obtained from the defendant (a lady) by one Cutting, in order to raise money for her use; but being in embarrassed circumstances, he assigned it to the plaintiff as a security for his own private debts. The court held that under the plea of payment, the fraud might be given in evidence; and the defendant thus discharged herself from the obligation in the hands of the assignee.

In Carpenter *v.* Groff,(*j*) a case removed by writ of error into the Supreme Court, the plaintiff in error, in consequence of an oath taken by the defendant in a former judicial proceeding, had given a bond by way of compromise. The perjury of the plaintiff below having been ascertained, the obligor refused to discharge the bond; and on suit brought, he offered under the plea of payment, to give evidence of the fraud. The testimony was rejected by the Court of Common Pleas, but their decision was reversed in the Supreme Court.(*k*)

Fraud must be alleged specially in plea or notice of special matter.(*l*) It is not enough to state facts from which fraud may be inferred.(*m*)

3. *Mistake and Accident.*—The rule of the common law which directed the mode in which mistake in the execution of a bond should be pleaded, was extremely inequitable. A party who had executed an agreement contrary to his intention, was obliged to rely upon the plea of *layman and unlettered;*(*n*) so that on proof of his *ability to read*, a fraudulent plaintiff would be entitled to a recovery. The Court of Chancery proceeding upon broader principles of natural justice, would relieve a party wherever there was a plain mistake proved by irrefragable evidence.(*o*)

In Pennsylvania, the equitable principle has been adopted, and the

(*f*) 1 Smith's Laws, 90.
(*g*) 1 D. 23.
(*h*) Alexander *v.* Jameson, 5 Bin. 244; Bury *v.* Hartman, 4 S. & R. 177.
(*i*) 2 Bin. 154.
(*j*) 5 S. & R. 165.
(*k*) See also Heck *v.* Shener, 4 S. & R. 256; Robinson *v.* Eldridge, 10 S. & R.

142; Sparks *v.* Garrigues, 1 Bin. 164; Miller *v.* Henderson, 10 S. & R. 292.
(*l*) Clark *v.* Partridge, 2 Barr, 15.
(*m*) Clark *v.* Partridge, 2 Barr, 15.
(*n*) Thoroughgood's Case, 2 Rep. 96; Pigot's Case, 11 Rep. 27; Moore, 184; 2 Freem. 194.
(*o*) 1 Vez. 317; 2 Atk. 195.

plea of payment is made the medium of its enforcement. In Swift *v.* Hawkins,(*p*) Chief Justice Allen said, that within the scope of his re. collection, which extended as far back as the year 1727, this had always been the practice; and it has continued until the present day unimpaired, and without question or dispute.

The notice of an equitable defence is, in fact, a bill in chancery, and operates substantially as a bill for an injunction. To avoid injustice, it would seem necessary that the opposite party should have notice of the defence, for it is impossible to answer that of which he has been studiously kept ignorant.(*q*)

In a *scire facias* upon a recognizance of bail, the defendant cannot, under the plea of payment, take advantage of any want of form or substance in the recognizance given in evidence to support the writ which recited one in due and proper form.(*r*)

The plea of payment with leave is a general issue plea, within the purview of a rule of court requiring previous notice of a special defence under the general issue.(*s*)

Under the plea of payment, in an action of assumpsit on a promissory note, the defendant cannot, without notice of special matter, give evidence of facts which constitute a special equitable defence; yet he may show the consideration for the note, and that the debt has been discharged since the note was given.(*t*)

In Galbraith *v.* Ankrim,(*u*) the court said: "There can be no doubt of the principle, that in a suit on a bond in Pennsylvania, the defendant, under the plea of payment, may prove *mistake* and want of consideration: and that, in such case, the jury may and ought to presume everything to have been paid, which *ex æquo et bono,* in equity and good conscience ought not to be paid."(*v*)

As to the discharge of a party from an obligation, by an accident unforeseen at the time of its making, whenever such cases occur, the court will proceed upon the principles of equity, and will allow the facts to be given in evidence under the general plea of payment. In Solomon *v.* Kimmel,(*w*) Chief Justice Tilghman said that it had often been decided, that when a bond was given for the purchase-money of land, to which the title afterwards proved to be defective, the obligee could not recover. The decision in Pollard *v.* Shafer,(*x*) was grounded upon the principles of equity, relating to accidents; and though this was not done under the plea of payment, on account of the particular nature of the action (covenant), yet it shows that those rules have been adopted, and that facts which constitute such a defence, may therefore be given in evidence under this equitable general issue.

There was one difficulty for which it was necessary to make provision, in order to prevent the means of enforcing equity from becoming the instrument of fraud. If the general plea of payment were alone to be put in, without any other explanation of the defendant's intentions, it is obvious, from a view of the extensive varieties of defence which the

(*p*) 1 D. 17.
(*q*) Ellmaker *v.* Franklin Ins. Co. 5 Barr, 183; Covely *v.* Fox, 1 J. 174.
(*r*) Abbott *v.* Lyon, 4 W. & S. 38.
(*s*) Covely *v.* Fox, 1 J. 171.
(*t*) Hobson *v.* Croft, 9 Barr, 364.
(*u*) 2 Br. 120.
(*v*) Steele *v.* Phœnix Ins. Co. 3 Bin. 308; Baring *v.* Shippen, 2 Bin. 154.
(*w*) 5 Bin. 233.
(*x*) 1 D. 210.

courts in their liberality will permit to be made, that he would possess a highly inequitable advantage over the plaintiff who, at the day of trial, might be surprised by an answer against which he had had no previous cause to provide. A perception of this injustice has induced the several courts to make a rule requiring the defendant to give notice of the equitable matter which constitutes his true defence. Independently of this rule, too, this plea does not admit all the averments in the declaration. It admits nothing but what is admitted by the general issue in other actions. It is a special or general defence, as the notice given under it makes it one or the other.(y)

This notice, in substance, often amounts to a bill in equity, and if the defendant present and prove a case on which he would be entitled to relief in equity, he will be entitled to a verdict here. But if in his notice of special matter, he presents a case in which equity would afford no relief, the plaintiff, instead of putting the cause to the jury, may object to the evidence, and pray the opinion of the court on it. And if the court be of opinion that it is a case in which equity would not relieve, the evidence will be rejected in toto, as irrelevant; or if any part of it be such as would not be received in equity, that part will be rejected.(z)

The plea of payment with leave is only admissible where damages are claimed, and is therefore a nullity when pleaded to a sci. fa. to revive a judgment in ejectment or in dower, even after a replication of non solvit.(a)

The plea of payment with leave, &c., to an action of debt, against the acceptor of a bill, is an admission of the drawing and acceptance, and that the bill is in the hands of the plaintiff as indorsee and holder.(b)

Under the plea of payment with leave, the jury cannot find any sum due from the plaintiff to the defendant. They can only find a verdict for the defendant.(c)

When the equity of the case is opened by the plea of payment, the plaintiff in his turn, under the replication of non solvit, may give evidence of such special matters as would rebut the defendant's equity in a Court of Chancery ;(d) so that, although the forms of the common law are the only means employed, yet the decisions of our courts, and the determination of the cause, are in such cases entirely and completely guided by the principles of equity.

NON ASSUMPSIT.—As we have seen, any matter which would discharge the party in chancery from a personal claim, or would rebut his equity, may be given in evidence under the plea of payment, or the replication of non solvit, to the ordinary kinds of actions. In the case of Stansbury v. Marks,(e) there appeared to be a disposition in the judge, who delivered the opinion of the court, to extend the plea of non assumpsit, in the same manner, so as to render similar justice. He said: "The evidence (of infancy) is clearly admissible. Under the general issue, however, the jury may decide whether the evidence is sufficient to discharge him or not. The position is generally true, that an infant

(y) Roop v. Brubacker, 1 R. 304.
(z) Robinson v. Eldridge, 10 S. & R. 142.
(a) Shaw v. Boyd, 2 J. 215.
(b) Snyder v. Wilt, 3 H. 63.

(c) Glass v. Blair, 4 Barr, 196, citing 10 S. & R. 55.
(d) McCutchen v. Nigh, 10 S. & R. 344; Jordan v. Cooper, 3 S. & R. 589.
(e) 4 Dall. 130.

can only bind himself for necessaries; yet in the Court of Chancery cases occur, in which a payment would be decreed, contrary to the strict rule of the common law. In this form of action, equity is the principal consideration; and from necessity the courts of law in Penn. sylvania adopt the principles of the English courts of chancery.

Notwithstanding these favorable expressions, if a defendant intends to avail himself of a defence founded upon equity, it is most prudent to rely upon the plea of payment, which is the favorite equitable plea of the courts. The extension of *non assumpsit* to new cases, was severely reprobated by Chief Justice Tilghman, in Dunlap *v.* Miles,(*f*) and the decision there made may be considered as overruling that of Stansbury *v.* Marks. "Whether a Court of Equity, under such circumstances, would afford relief, there is no occasion *now* to determine; for the point is, was the evidence admissible or not, in a *court of law*, under the plea of *non assumpsit.*" A little farther he says: "If the circumstances of the case afforded ground for relief in equity, Dunlap ought to have given notice of the special matters, in consequence of which, under our practice, he might have brought forward all his *equity* under the *plea of payment*. I am not for extending the admissibility of evidence under the plea of *non assumpsit*. It has been carried far enough, and in my opinion too far already: so far as to involve plaintiffs in difficulties on trials, without any possibility of knowing the matter on which defendants rest their defence." Mr. Justice Yates said: "I have not the smallest difficulty in asserting, that on the general issue of *non assumpsit*, the equitable evidence offered upon the trial, could not be received at *common law*."

The general rule seems to result from these several dicta, that under the issue formed by *non assumpsit*, the courts will consider themselves as courts of common law; and that in those actions to which the plea of payment applies, it is only through the medium of that plea that the principles of equity may be called into action.

Under the plea, says Judge Bell, in a recent case, of *non assumpsit* to work and labor done, the defendant, without notice of special matter, may prove the work was done in an unworkmanlike manner.(*g*)

By this plea, the defendant puts his antagonist upon proving his whole case, and entitles himself to give in evidence anything which shows that, at the time the action was commenced, the plaintiff, *ex æquo et bono*, ought not to recover. This is especially true of everything going to the consideration, which is the gist of the action.(*h*)

Under the plea of *non assumpsit*, or of *payment*, the defendant, without notice of special matter, may show that the plaintiff has credited him in his account for goods sold to the plaintiff, thereby balancing the account. So he may give evidence of a former recovery.(*i*)

SET-OFFS.—Before proceeding to the consideration of this species of equitable plea (which will hereafter be treated in detail in reference to the practice in a common law suit),(*j*) as depending upon the resolutions of the Supreme Court made in the exercise of its inherent powers, it may be well to advert to the subject of set-off under our statute of

---

(*f*) 4 Y. 370.
(*g*) Gaw *v.* Wolcott, 10 Barr, 43. See Beals *v.* See, 10 Barr, 57.

(*h*) Id. 44. BELL, J.
(*i*) Carvill *v.* Garrigues, 5 Barr, 152.
(*j*) *Post*, chap. xviii.

defalcations, which is also an equitable defence, lest the two kinds of defence should be confounded. "Our act about defalcation is the first legislative provision giving chancery powers to the common law courts. It was intended to give the common law courts all the power which chancery had ever exercised over bond and other debts; to put an end to what had been said, that a demand was good at law, but would be relieved against in equity, and to do all at the trial of the cause, which a chancellor had been used to do afterwards; and it was intended to do and has done more; it has prevented cross actions, wherever one [action] will effect the ends of justice."(*k*) The substance of the act thus commented on is, that where there have been mutual dealings between the ǀparties, and the defendant cannot *gainsay* the claim of the plaintiff, he may plead payment of all or any part of the debt, and give any bond, bill, receipt, account, or *bargain* in evidence, and should there be an excess in his favor, a verdict and judgment may be rendered for it. In many of the cases in our reports, the courts say that they have adopted all the doctrine of chancery as to set-offs; if that doctrine be compared with the foregoing statute, it will be seen that the latter is even more liberal than it, and perhaps more liberal than the doctrine of *compensation* in the civil law.(*l*) But as to the cases about to be quoted, it will be difficult to bring the principles on which they rest within the statute, unless, indeed, the defences allowed as set-offs, can be brought within the term "*bargain*," contained in its text. If they cannot, then those cases must rest upon the inherent powers of the court to do equity,(*m*) and such set-offs may be denominated not statutable.

As to equitable set-offs, then, not *statutable*, our highest court, although having expressly decided that a demand arising out of the wrongful or *tortious* acts of the plaintiff cannot be set-off,(*n*) have, step after step, brought the law almost to the verge of such a doctrine.— Thus, the defendant may give evidence of acts of non-feasance or *misfeasance* by the plaintiff, where these acts are *immediately connected with his cause of action*, it not being admitted by way of defalcation, but for the purpose of *defeating*, in whole, or *in part*, the plaintiff's cause of action;(*o*) and so also, where the evidence, though held good under another *name*, was treated by one judge, who dissented, as matter of set-off and inadmissible.(*oo*) So, a bond conditioned for the delivery of goods "at any time when called on," may be set-off on proof that the goods had been refused.(*p*) So, in an action for the price of goods sold, the defendant may show, by way of set-off, a warranty of the articles and breach;(*q*) so, a warranty of a horse.(*r*) So, in an action to recover the price of cattle, the defendant may give in evidence, by way of set-off, *or equitable defence*, that he had sustained damage by reason of the plaintiff not having delivered to him certain sheep purchased by him at the same time of the plaintiff, in an entire contract.(*s*) So, unliquidated damages for deficiency of work in the

(*k*) HUSTON, J., Lee *v.* Dean, 3 R. 325.
(*l*) See 2 Story's Eq. 665, *et seq.*
(*m*) See this distinction adopted as to another form of equitable d f nc , in Sparks *v.* Haydock, 1 Bin. 152e   e
(*n*) Gogel *v.* Jacoby, 5 S. & R. 122.
(*o*) Ibid.

(*oo*) Heck *v.* Shener, 4 S. & R. 249.
(*p*) Leas *v.* Laird, 6 S. & R. 129.
(*q*) Steigleman *v.* Jeffries, 1 S. & R. 477.
(*r*) Sadler *v.* Slobaugh, 3 S. & R. 388.
(*s*) Shaw *v.* Badger, 12 S. & R. 275.

erection of a building, upon one contract, may be set-off against the plaintiff's claim for extra work, done under a subsequent contract.(*t*) It seems, too, that a set-off of the character of an *equitable defence in the nature of a counter demand*, arising out of the same transaction, may be pleaded in *replevin*;(*u*) and a set-off is admissible in replevin, on an issue made to determine whether any rent be due.(*v*) Perhaps most of the preceding defences may be thought to be admissible within the meaning of the term "bargain," in the statute, but those sustained in the cases referred to(*w*) certainly cannot be. But in Romig *v.* Romig,(*x*) there is a remarkable instance of a set-off allowed in an action founded wholly in *tort*. It was trover for bonds which the defendant had given the plaintiff's intestate in payment for land, and which he had surreptitiously got possession of, and he was allowed to plead by way of set-off, that he had paid for patenting the land, and also the funeral expenses of the intestate, and also a claim for work done for him in his lifetime. It is true, the court say that all this was not by way of set-off, but that it "went to destroy the consideration of the bonds;" yet this explanation does not change the fact inferable from the entire report.

For a full consideration of the practice in set-off, the reader is referred to a subsequent chapter (*post*, Chapter XVIII).

PERFORMANCE.—The plea of *performance*, or *covenants performed*— which, as a common law plea, will be hereafter more fully considered— though not unknown to the ancient common law, has long been obsolete in the English practice in consequence of its limited applicability.(*z*) Even at the time when this plea was in ordinary use, it was held to be a governing principle, that it could only be resorted to where the covenants were *affirmative ;* if one of the articles of the agreement had been *negative* or *disjunctive*, the answer of the defendant was informal, and liable to a demurrer.(*a*) Restricted as this plea was, by the action of these nice distinctions, to an insignificant and narrow operation, it is not surprising that it fell into gradual disuse ; and as the modern opinion appears to be that, by reason of its generality, it is now in all cases insufficient ;(*aa*) it is no longer enumerated in the books of pleading.(*b*)

As in actions of *debt* and of *assumpsit*, the courts of Pennsylvania, by a series of liberal decisions, have made a particular plea the vehicle of equity, so by rescuing the plea of performance from the neglect into which it had fallen, and giving it a more general application, they have avoided the intricacies of special pleading, and extended the benefit of an equitable defence to actions of covenant. It is a well-settled rule in our courts, that under this plea, aided by an informal notice, any matter may be given in evidence that would discharge the defendant in a Court of Chancery ; and that shall be presumed to have been performed, which in equity and good conscience ought not to be performed. There could be no stronger assurance of the liberal disposition of the judiciary

---

(*t*) Bayne *v.* Gaylord, 3 W. 301.
(*u*) Peterson *v.* Haight, 1 M. 250.
(*v*) Gray *v.* Wilson, 4 W. 39. See also Irwin *v.* Potter, 3 W. 271.
(*w*) *Ante*, notes (*n*), (*o*).
(*x*) 2 R. 241.
(*z*) See vol. ii. ch. i. ∤ 3.

(*a*) Bacon's Abridgment, tit. "Covenant." K.
(*aa*) 3 Woddes's Lectures, 93 ; Cowp. 575.
(*b*) Stephen on Pleading, 174, 176; 1 Chitty's Pleadings, 481.

towards the plea of performance, than the fact that its effects and operation have been compared to those of the plea of payment.(c)

By this method, which is peculiarly Pennsylvanian, we possess the certainty of special pleading, without its dangers, and the principles of equity without the dilatoriness of its forms.

II. Of the general plea where the claim is to the realty.

As an equitable title may be made the foundation of an action of ejectment, and is sufficient to ground a recovery, it follows as a natural consequence that it may protect the actual possession of a defendant. From the nature of the various species of defence before enumerated, they are necessarily confined to those cases in which the demand is *personal*; where the claim is *real*, recourse must be had to other methods, in order to render available the equity possessed by the party.

The action of ejectment, from the great improvements it has received, and its peculiar advantages, is almost the only method used in Pennsylvania to try a title to land.(d) Among other provisions made by acts of assembly,(e) to simplify its proceedings, it has been enacted that the general plea of "not guilty" shall be the only plea put in by the defendant; and, with certain exceptions to be hereafter considered, the special nature of the defence can therefore only be given in evidence.(ee)

If the equity of the defendant be merely founded on the non-performance of a particular act by the plaintiff, such as the payment of purchase-money, or making title to a part of land,(f) it is always made a prerequisite to the recovery of the possession of the land by the latter; and may be either relied on in the defence, or judgment will be arrested by the court until it is performed.(g) The pervading principle of chancery interference, that he who seeks equity should be compelled to do equity, was adopted by our courts when they extended their jurisdiction for the better administration of justice.

When the equity of a defendant goes to a total denial of the title of the plaintiff, it is supported by a recurrence to the principle which forms the groundwork of the equitable action of ejectment, that everything shall be presumed to be done, which in good conscience ought to have been done. If, therefore, the party ought to have received proper title deeds, he will be considered in the same situation as if they had been actually delivered to him; and the same course will be pursued with every other equity to which he may be entitled.(h) In the establishment of these liberal regulations, the courts appear to have been actuated by the same spirit with the legislature, which, so early as 1705, had enacted that a quiet possession of seven years under an *equitable* right, should give an unquestionable title to the land.(i)

III. Of special equitable pleas.

The last mode by which a defendant may avail himself of the assistance of equity, is when the facts of his case are specially pleaded.

(c) 4 D. 439; 2 Y. 108. See *post*, vol. i. chap. xviii., vol. ii. chap. i. sect. 3.

(d) Morris's Lessee v. Vanderen, 1 D. 67.

(e) Act of 13th April, 1807, 4 Sm. Laws, 476; Lewis v. Wallick, 3 S. & R. 409.

(ee) *Post*, vol. ii. "Ejectment."

(f) Mathers's Lessee v. Akewright, 2 Bin. 93.

(g) Ibid.

(h) Griffith v. Cochran, 5 Bin. 105; McCall v. Lenox, 9 S. & R. 315.

(i) 1 Smith's Laws, 48.

The act of assembly, which restricts the defendant in ejectment to the general plea of not guilty, deprives him of this mode of asserting his equity, and confines it in practice to those cases in which the demand is of a strictly personal nature. With this exception, wherever the pleas before enumerated would be inconvenient or improper, from the nature of the action, the defendant may state his equity specially, and the courts will support it as a sufficient defence. The general rule was es. tablished in Pollard v. Shafer,(j) and has been recognized as law by a number of succeeding decisions.(k) In the former case the defendant pleaded at length, that a house, which he had covenanted to keep in repair, had been destroyed by the British army under General Howe, in 1777 ; and the court, declaring that an enforcement would be inequitable, relieved him from his agreement.

The practice of pleading specially the equity of a defendant, possesses one of the most important advantages of the answer in chancery, in stating at length all the circumstances of the case, without regard to their intricacy or complication. But for this method, the operation of equity would be narrow and restricted : as the rule now is, it supplies all the chasms left by the general pleas, so that no case can possibly occur in which a defendant may not rely upon his equitable right, as fully and completely in a Pennsylvania court of law as in an English Court of Chancery.

Where the equitable defence may be, at the defendant's option, given in evidence under one of the preceding general pleas, with notice, or specially pleaded, he should be careful not to adopt the latter mode too hastily. The case of Bauer v. Roth,(l) will afford some hints as to the propriety or danger of either course. In that case, a special equitable plea to an action on a bond was held to be defective, "in not stating the transaction more fully, and giving to it some definite character," by showing particularly how the equity against the claim set up arose, whether by fraud or mistake, and whether this fraud or mistake were without the knowledge or assent of the defendant ; " for without all this, in case of a demurrer to his plea," he could not have judgment, unless the plea state " all the circumstances with such precision that the court may see whether it have arisen from fraud or mistake, and decide distinctly, upon which it is that he is entitled to relief." But though this plea was thus held to be defective, the court said that, from the difficulty they found in pronouncing it to be so, pleaders "ought to be very cautious in demurring to pleas which set forth special matters and circumstances from which fraud or mistake may be inferred to have been practised or to have taken place in the obtaining of the writings upon which the suits are brought."

EQUITABLE REPLICATIONS, REJOINDERS, &c.—As to replications, and other subsequent pleadings, if a plea be put in, founded in equity only, the plaintiff will be permitted to make a replication to it, stating any special matter sufficient to rebut or destroy that equity.(m) Thus, where a *scire facias* on a recognizance entered into under a decree of the Or-

(j) 1 D. 214.
(k) Murray v. Williamson, 3 Bin. 136 ; Hartzell v. Reiss, 1 Bin. 291 ; Jordan v. Cooper, 3 S. & R. 578.

(l) 4 R. 83, 95–6.
(m) McCutchen v. Nigh, 10 S. & R. 344.

phans' Court, conditioned for the payment of money to the plaintiff, the defendant pleads that he has paid off incumbrances on the land created by the plaintiff previously to his owning them, the plaintiff may reply, that though the defendant did pay them, he was not entitled to any allowance, because he had received rents and profits sufficient for their discharge, having been in possession of the land prior to the decree of the Orphans' Court.(n) To this replication, the defendants may make such a rejoinder as their case requires, and upon the point thus raised in issue, alone, the parties will go on to trial.(o) If, instead of the equitable special plea just described, the defendant pleads payment with leave, &c., and go into an equitable defence, the plaintiff may, under the replication of *non-solvit*, give evidence of other special matter to rebut the defendant's equity(p) without notice, for the defendant might have obviated the danger of surprise by pleading specially.

This replication of *non-solvit* to the equitable plea of payment, is a favorite vehicle of equity in this State in answer to the defendant's special case, as the plaintiff may under it enter as largely into the special matter of his answer (having, however, given precise notice of his grounds to the defendant)—as could be done under a plea of payment. And it does not seem necessary that any equitable pleadings should have been previously put in, to justify the use of *non-solvit* as an equitable replication, for it may happen that the plea of the defendant which is strictly at common law, may, for the first time, compel the plaintiff to rely upon equitable grounds for the establishment of his action.

CONDITIONAL VERDICTS.—Another method of obviating the want of a Court of Equity, when such a court would enjoin a party from proceeding at law, ·or when the specific execution of a contract, or the performance of a trust, is of right due to the plaintiff, is through the instrumentality of the jury, who may wield the damages so as to effect the desired end. It seems that in all actions, whether relating to personal or real property, the jury may, when the plaintiff sets out in his declaration the whole ground of his equitable right—for this has been held to be a prerequisite to secure a conditional verdict(q)—find large damages conditionally ; that is, to be released, on condition that the terms which the jury, and the jury alone, prescribe, are complied with.(r) Thus, in a case where chancery would enjoin an obligee in a bond from proceeding at law, while the obligor is a loser or in jeopardy as a surety of the former, the jury may produce the same result by a conditional verdict.(s) Thus, too, a specific performance of an agreement for the sale of land—provided the agreement be not within the statute of frauds, as being by parol or wholly unexecuted—may be enforced by a conditional verdict.(t) And there are many cases of ejectment, where such verdicts have been recommended by the court, in matters of trust and executory contracts.(u) The action itself, as we have seen, approaches

---

(n) Ibid, 345–6.
(o) Ibid.
(p) Ibid, 344.
(q) Irvine v. Bull, 4 W. 287 ; Butcher's Executor v. Metts, 1 M. 153.
(r) Decamp v. Feay, 5 S. & R. 323 ; Coolbaugh v. Pierce, 8 Id. 418. See

vol. ii. "Ejectment."
(s) Hart v. Withers, 1 Pa. Rep. 257. See also Gray v. Waln, 2 R. 227, a similar principle adopted in foreign attachment.
(t) Irvine v. Bull, 4 W. 287.
(u) Collins v. Rush, 7 S. & R. 155.

very near to a bill in equity; "and the verdict of a jury, imposing conditions on the party in whose favor it is rendered, performs the office, though imperfectly, of the decree.(v) In all these cases, the jury are to be governed by the rules and principles of equity, which they are to learn from the charge of the judge. This subject is thus summed up by the late Mr. Justice Duncan: "The court, in discharging this duty, are the judges whether the plaintiff is entitled to relief, and the extent, mode, and manner of this relief. Nothing is submitted to the jury, but that which is their proper province—the ascertainment of the facts, with instructions, that if they find the facts in a particular way, the plaintiff is entitled to relief or he is not; and if they find facts that would require the interposition of chancery powers, then it is the court's duty to instruct them, in what manner, to what extent, and on what terms, the relief is to be granted. Thus the verdict may be moulded, and equity substantially attained."(w) Juries may, however, under particular circumstances of hardship, inequality, and oppression, find a very small sum in damages, where chancery would not carry a contract so infected into specific execution.(x) Should the jury, however, in *equity cases*, draw inferences in matters of fact different from those a chancellor would probably have drawn, it does not follow that the court have for that reason a power to order a new trial; and it is said that the principles which must guide, in motions for new trials, are the same, whether the suit be an action strictly at the common law, or substantially a bill in equity.(y)

Although a verdict in the alternative would be erroneous, there are many instances in practice in which a cautionary verdict is allowed; as when a verdict is rendered for the plaintiff in ejectment, or for a penal sum in actions for damages, to be enforced unless the defendant pay a sum of money, or does certain specified things. The court can judge whether the defendants comply with the terms of the verdict, and mould the judgment accordingly. They are, for the most part, obliged to decide on affidavits and depositions; and as these constitute no part of the record they are, like the granting of a new trial, subjects not inquirable into on error.(z)

In debt or bond for purchase-money of land, a verdict may be given for plaintiff, conditioned that no execution shall issue for the amount until he removes an incumbrance on the land so sold.(a)

Conditional verdicts have been employed here to effect an equity not to be reached by the ordinary form of verdicts. But there is no instance of their adoption to relieve a plaintiff from a difficulty occasioned by his not being ready to establish those facts which are put in issue in the cause. Indulging this practice would gradually change our system of pleading, and proofs encourage remissness in suitors, and increase delays and litigation.(b)

When a conditional verdict is rendered to compel specific performance, it is not, of course, as in ordinary cases, to issue a *habere facias*. The

(v) Coolbaugh v. Pierce, 8 Id. 419.
(w) Peebles v. Reading, 8 S. & R. 489, 490. See Hawthorn v. Bronson, 16 Id. 278-9.
(x) Simpson v. Coon, 4 Id. 267.

(y) Kuhn v. Nixon, 15 S. & R. 125.
(z) Mager v. the Germantown R. R. Co., 3 W. & S. 91.
(a) Roland v. Miller, 3 W. & S. 390.
(b) McCormick v. Crall, 6 W. 213.

court will grant leave to issue it on being satisfied that the terms of the verdict have not been complied with.(c)

EQUITABLE JUDGMENTS AND EXECUTIONS.—Besides this use of conditional verdicts in actions at common law adopted here to enforce equitable rights, the courts must, in such cases, if necessary, mould their judgments and executions to suit the case ; and they will render them specially, to affect certain property only, and allow special executions to be levied on that property alone.(d)

EQUITABLE LIEN OF JUDGMENTS.—Equitable rights having thus by the liberality of the judiciary of Pennsylvania become vested and tangible interests at law, it was necessary to the complete attainment of justice, that the new advantage thus vested in the party should be attended with its corresponding burdens. Proceeding upon this just and natural principle, it has been decided in our courts, that every species of equitable right is subject to the lien of a judgment, and may be sold so fully and completely under an execution, that the sheriff's vendee will stand in precisely the same situation as the original defendant. This rule, resulting from a connected series of decisions, is thus stated by the late Chief Justice Tilghman :(e) "By the law of Pennsylvania all the real estate of the debtor, whether legal or equitable, is bound by a judgment against him, and may be taken in execution, and sold for the satisfaction of the debt. At common law, an equitable estate is not bound by a judgment, or subject to an execution. But the creditor may have relief in chancery. We have no Court of Chancery, and have therefore from necessity established it as a principle, that both judgments and execution have an immediate operation on equitable estates."(f)

As in the establishment of this rule, the courts were guided by the most liberal and enlightened views of relative justice, they have not suffered themselves to be deterred, by any technical niceties, from its steady application.

In Carkuff v. Anderson,(g) the right of pre-emption, vested by law in the settlers of Luzerne County, under the pretended Connecticut title, was held liable to the lien of judgment.

In Ely v. Beaumont,(h) the plaintiff in error had a leasehold estate with a condition that he might erect buildings upon the premises, and if, at the expiration of the term, they were not paid for by the lessor at a stipulated valuation, he might then hold them in fee simple. As buildings were erected accordingly, it was held that his interest ceased in equity to be a mere chattel real, and was subject to the lien of a judgment.

In Richter v. Selin,(i) the equitable right of a vendee by articles of agreement, was declared to be subject to a lien and to execution.

But in a later case, a majority of the Supreme Court held, that a judgment is not, under our peculiar usages, a lien on every possible interest

(c) Shaw v. Bayard, 4 Barr, 257.
(d) 3 R. 194.
(e) Aulwerter v. Mathist, 9 S. & R. 402.
(f) See also Stiles v. Bradford, 4 R. 402.

(g) 3 Bin. 8.
(h) 5 S. & R. 126.
(i) 8 S. & R. 440.

in land, whether immediate or remote, actual or contingent: that the interest of a mortgagee, judgment creditor, owner of a legacy charged on land, creditor of an intestate estate, mechanic or material man, or of a preferred creditor under an assignment to trustees (to each of whom the land is debtor), is not the subject of judgment and execution: that "*nothing is such*, but an immediate interest; as, for instance, the estate of a tenant by the courtesy initiate; or of a widow, whose interest is put by the intestate acts on the footing of a rent-charge: the only thing peculiar to a judgment with us, is, that it binds an equitable, or even an inchoate interest, but that interest must be an *estate* in´ the land."(*j*) Upon these principles, they decided, where a testator orders his real estate to be sold by his executors, as soon as convenient after his decease, the proceeds to be divided equally among his children, and empowers them to rent, if they cannot sell it, that no estate in the land vested in the children, and that a levy and sale of the share of one of the children under a judgment against him, did not pass his interest to the purchaser.(*k*) This subject, in its common law relations, will be considered more fully hereafter, when the doctrine of *scire facias* on judgments is considered.

MOTIONS FOR NEW TRIALS; TO OPEN JUDGMENTS, AND FOR OTHER PURPOSES, FOUNDED ON EQUITABLE CIRCUMSTANCES.

The chancery power to grant injunctions against an improper enforcement of a judgment, is, in some respect, supplied by the power vested in the courts to *open* them upon motion, and to ascertain the facts upon issues directed to be formed;(*m*) as also by their control over verdicts, either in setting them aside, and granting new trials, or putting the parties under terms in the use of them; setting off judgments against judgments, and generally by the extensive and all-pervading method by *motion*, and an issue to try disputed facts, to prevent injustice under the color of legal proceedings. In what way equity is enforced by these processes will be observed hereafter, when they come to be severally treated.

SECTION VI.

OF POWERS COMMON TO THE FOREGOING COURTS.

The subject of the authority and jurisdiction of the courts, whose organization we have treated of, will be aptly concluded by the introduction of the last eight sections of the act of 1836 (which has been already so often referred to), which confer upon all the courts certain powers, and ascertain and define others.

Each of the said courts shall have power to award process to levy and recover such fines, forfeitures, and amercements as shall be imposed, taxed, or adjudged by them, respectively. § 20.

(*j*) Morrow *v.* Brenizer, 2 R. 188.   (*m*) See Bower *v.* Blessing, 8 S. & R.
(*k*) Ibid. 185. HUSTON, J., dissent.   242.

Each of the said courts shall have full power and authority to establish such rules for regulating the practice thereof, respectively, and for expediting the determination of suits, causes, and proceedings therein, as in their discretion they shall judge necessary or proper: *Provided*, That such rules shall not be inconsistent with the constitution and laws of this commonwealth.(*n*) § 21.

Each of the said courts is empowered to issue writs of subpœna, under their official seal, into any county of this commonwealth, to summon and bring before the respective court, any person, to give testimony in any cause or matter depending before them, under the penalties hitherto appointed and allowed in any such case by the laws of this commonwealth. § 22.

The power of the several courts of this commonwealth to issue attachments, and to inflict summary punishments for contempts of court, shall be restricted to the following cases, to wit — ·:
I. To the official misconduct of the officers of such courts, respectively:
II. To disobedience or neglect by officers, parties, jurors, or witnesses of or to the lawful process of the court:
III. To the misbehavior of any person in the presence of the court, thereby obstructing the administration of justice. § 23.

The punishment of imprisonment for contempt, as aforesaid, shall extend only to such contempts as shall be committed in open court, and all other contempts shall be punished by fine only. § 24.

Provided, That the court may order the sheriff, or other proper officer, to take into custody, and commit to jail, any person fined for a contempt, until such fine shall be paid or discharged; but if such person shall be unable to pay such fine, he may be committed to prison by the court, for any time not exceeding three months. § 25.

No publication out of court, respecting the conduct of the judges, officers of the court, jurors, witnesses, parties, or any of them, of, in, or concerning any cause depending in such court, shall be construed into a contempt of the said court, so as to render the author, printer, publisher, or either of them, liable to attachment, and summary punishment for the same. § 26.

(*n*) The *rules* of the foregoing courts, constitute by no means an unimportant part of their system of procedure; for it is remarkable, that many regulations of practice, which were introduced into England by STATUTE, have been accomplished by RULES OF COURT in this country. See 3 Bin. 424. Independently of any statute, it has been settled in this State, that every court of record has an inherent power to make rules for the transaction of its business, provided such rules do not contravene the law of the land; 3 Bin. 277; and each is the most proper judge of the extent and application of its own rules, and is intrusted with a discretionary power of enforcing them. 8 S. & R. 336. If, however, a rule of court is contrary to an act of assembly, or illegal, a practice under it will be subjected to correction in the Supreme Court. 1 Pa. R. 232. See, generally, Wh. Dig. "Practice I."

If any such publication shall improperly tend to bias the minds of the public, or of the court, the officers, jurors, witnesses, or any of them, on a question depending before the court, it shall be lawful for any person who shall feel himself aggrieved thereby, to proceed against the author, printer, and publisher thereof, or either of them, by indictment, or he may bring an action at law against them, or either of them, and recover such damages as a jury may think fit to award. § 27.

Provided, That notwithstanding anything hereinbefore contained, the several courts aforesaid shall have power to make rules on sheriffs and coroners, for the return of all process in their hands, and for the payment of money, or delivery of any article of value in their possession, according to their respective duties, and also, to make rules upon attorneys for the payment of money, and the delivery of deeds, and other papers in their hands, belonging to their clients, and in every such case to enforce obedience to such rules, by attachment; and the courts shall have the same power against former sheriffs and coroners, if application be made for the purpose, within two years after the termination of their offices respectively. § 28.

Every court of record has an inherent power to make rules for the transaction of its business, provided such rules are not contradictory to the law of the land.(o)

A mistake by a court below, in the construction of one of its rules, must be very obvious, to induce the Supreme Court to reverse for that reason alone.(*p*)

(o) Barry *v.* Randolph, 3 Bin. 277;   (*p*) Dailey *v.* Green, 3 H. 128.
Snyder *v.* Bauchman, 8 S. & R. 336;
Mylin's Estate, 7 W. 64.

CHAPTER III.

OF THE OFFICERS OF THE COURTS.

SECTION I.

OF PROTHONOTARIES AND CLERKS, CRIERS, AND TIPSTAVES.

IN addition to the legislative provisions relating to prothonotaries, before quoted,(q) the following enactments also exist in the 76th and 77th sections of the act of 1834.(r)

The prothonotaries and clerks of the several courts of this commonwealth shall, before they enter upon the duties of their offices, respectively, make oath or affirmation to support the constitution of the United States and the constitution of this commonwealth, and to perform the duties of the respective office with fidelity; they shall, also, with one or more sureties, to be approved of by any two of the judges of the Court of Common Pleas of the respective county, and also by the governor, give a joint and several bond to the commonwealth, in such sum as the governor shall judge sufficient, with condition faithfully to execute the duties of their respective offices, and well and truly to account for and pay according to law all moneys which shall be received by them in their official capacity, and to deliver the books, seals, records, writings, and papers belonging to their respective offices whole, safe, and undefaced, to their successors therein. § 76.

The prothonotaries and clerks, aforesaid, shall have and exercise, respectively, in the courts to which they severally belong, and with full effect in term time and vacation, the powers and authorities following, to wit: They shall have power—

I. To assign and affix the seal of the respective court to all writs and process, and also to the exemplifications of all records and process therein:

II. To take bail in civil actions, depending in the respective court:

III. To enter judgments at the instance of plaintiffs, upon the confessions of defendants:

IV. To sign all judgments:

V. To take the acknowledgment of satisfaction of judgments or decrees entered on the record of the respective court:

(q) *Ante,* p. 4.　　　　　　　(r) Pamph. L. 355.

VI. To administer oaths and affirmations in conducting the business of their respective offices. § 77 :

They cannot practice in the courts of which they are prothonotaries. § 75.

The 7th section of the act organizing the District Court of this city and county provides, that there shall be a prothonotary appointed by the governor, for the said court, who shall perform all the duties of a prothonotary, and shall be entitled to receive like fees as other prothonotaries are entitled by law to receive for similar services, and be subject to the like account to the commonwealth, and give the like security as the prothonotary of the Court of Common Pleas of the City and County of Philadelphia is required by law to give for the due performance of the duties of his office; and it shall and may be lawful for the prothonotary, under the sanction of the court, to appoint one or more discreet persons as commissioners of bail, who are hereby empowered to take and receive recognizances of bail in any suit or action in the said court, and to administer oaths and affirmations, in case of the absence or sickness of the prothonotary, in the same manner as if the prothonotary was present.

The succeeding section of the act of 1834 provides for the appointment of criers, tipstaves, and constables.

The judges of the several courts of this commonwealth shall have power to appoint a crier for the respective court, and so many tipstaves or constables as may be necessary to attend upon the court, and the said officers shall be paid by the respective county, such sum for each day's attendance, as the said judges shall allow. § 78.

SECTION II.

OF SHERIFFS AND CORONERS.

These officers, of whom there is one for every county, are chosen by the electors of the respective counties once in every three years, and as often as vacancies occur. The sheriff is ineligible to the same office for the next three years after its termination.(s)

The following sections of the same act of 1834, prescribe the terms on which these officers shall hold and fulfil their offices.

Every sheriff, before he shall be commissioned or execute any of the duties of his office, shall enter into a recognizance, and become bound in a bond with at least two sufficient sureties, in the sums and manner hereinafter mentioned. § 62.

The recognizance and bond of the sheriff of this county shall be taken in the sum of $80,000. § 63.

The form of the recognizance to be taken from the sheriff of each county, and his sureties, shall be as follows, to wit : "You, (A B,

(s) Cons. art. VI. § 1.

C D, and E F,) do acknowledge that you owe unto the common-wealth of Pennsylvania, the sum of ———, to be levied and made of your several goods and chattels, lands and tenements, upon condition that if you (A B,) shall and do, without delay and according to law, well and truly serve and execute all writs and process of the common-wealth of Pennsylvania, to you directed, and shall and do, from time to time, upon request to you for that purpose made, well and truly pay or cause to be paid to the several suitors and parties interested in the execution of such writs and process, their lawful attorneys, factors, agents, or assigns, all and every sum and sums of money to them respectively belonging, which shall come to your hands, and shall and do, from time to time, and at all times during your continuance in the office of the sheriff of the county of ———, well and faithfully execute and perform all and singular the trusts and duties to the said office lawfully appertaining, then this recognizance to be void or else to be and remain in full force and virtue. Taken and acknowledged the ——— day of ———, A. D. ———, before me, ——— ———, recorder of deeds for the county of ———." § 64.

The form of the bond to be given by the sheriff and his sureties, shall be as follows, to wit: "Know all men by these presents, that we (A B, C D, and E F,) are held and firmly bound unto the common-wealth of Pennsylvania, in the sum of ——— dollars, to be paid to the said commonwealth, for the uses, intents, and purposes declared and appointed by law, to which payment well and truly to be made, we bind ourselves, our heirs, executors, and administrators, jointly and severally, firmly by these presents, sealed with our seals, dated the ——— day of ———, Anno Domini ———. The condition of the above obligation is such, that if the said A B shall and do, without delay, according to law, well and truly serve and execute all writs and process of the said commonwealth to him directed, and shall and do, from time to time, upon request to him for that purpose made, well and truly pay, or cause to be paid, to the several suitors and parties inte-rested in the execution of such writs or process, their lawful attorney, factors, agents, or assigns, all and every sum and sums of money to them respectively belonging, which shall come to his hands, and shall and do, from time to time, and at all times during his continuance in the said office, well and faithfully execute and perform all and every of the trusts and duties to the said office appertaining, then this obliga-tion to be void, or else to be and remain in full force and virtue." § 65.

The coroner of each county, before he shall be commissioned, or execute any of the duties of his office, shall enter into a recognizance and become bound in a bond, with at least two sufficient sureties, in one-fourth of the sum which shall be by law required from the sheriff of the same county. § 66.

The condition of the recognizance and bond to be given by the coro-ner, shall be, that such coroner will "well and truly perform all and singular the duties to the said office of coroner appertaining;" and such recognizance and bond shall be a security to the commonwealth, and to all persons whomsoever, for the faithful discharge and due performance of all the duties required by law from such coroner. § 67.

Every such recognizance entered into by a sheriff and coroner, shall be taken by the recorder of deeds of the proper county, and recorded in his office; and when so recorded, shall be by him transmitted to the secretary of the commonwealth, with a certificate, indorsed by such recorder, of its having been duly recorded. § 68.

Before any such bond or recognizance shall be taken by the recorder of deeds, the sufficiency of the sureties therein named shall be submitted to and approved of by the judges of the Court of Common Pleas of the proper county, or by any two of them, for that purpose convened, who shall certify their approbation of such sureties to the recorder; and no commission shall afterwards be granted until the governor shall have also approved of the sufficiency of such sureties. § 69.

Provided, That no judge, clerk, or prothonotary of any court, or attorney at law, shall be permitted to become a surety in such bond or recognizance, and that no person shall be received as surety for a sheriff and for a coroner at the same time. § 70.

Copies of the record of any such bond or recognizance, acknowledged and recorded as aforesaid, and duly certified by the recorder of deeds for the time being, shall be good evidence in any action brought against the obligors or cognizors, according to its form and effect, in the same manner as the original would be if produced and offered in evidence. § 71.

It shall be the duty of every sheriff and of every coroner, immediately after receiving his commission from the governor, to deliver the same to the recorder of deeds of the county, by whom the same shall be recorded at the expense of such sheriff or coroner. § 72.

No person elected or appointed to the office of sheriff or coroner, shall presume to execute any of the duties of such office, before a commission shall have been duly granted to him, and left for record as hereinbefore provided, under a penalty of imprisonment for a term not exceeding six months, at the discretion of the Court of Quarter Sessions of the county: *Provided*, That such person shall nevertheless be liable to any person injured by any acts done by him under color of such office. § 73.

All the real estate, within the same county, of a sheriff and coroner and their respective sureties, shall be bound by a recognizance, taken in manner aforesaid, as effectually as by a judgment to the same amount in any court of record of such county; and it shall be the duty of every recorder of deeds, so soon as a sheriff or coroner shall be commissioned, to certify the recognizance taken by him to the prothonotary of the Court of Common Pleas of the same county, who shall enter the names of the parties thereto upon his docket, in like manner as judgments are by law directed to be entered. § 74.

If any sheriff shall be legally removed from his office, or shall die before the expiration of the term for which he shall have been commissioned, the coroner of the same county shall execute the office of sheriff, and perform all things thereunto appertaining, until another sheriff shall be duly commissioned, and notice thereof given to such coroner. § 75.

Whenever a vacancy shall happen in the office of sheriff or coroner, which is to be filled by a new appointment, in the manner prescribed by the constitution of this commonwealth, the person so to be appointed shall enter into recognizance, and give bond with sureties, to be approved in manner aforesaid, in such sum as shall be determined on by the judges of the Court of Common Pleas of the same county, or by any two of them for that purpose convened. § 76.

In case of the sale of real estate by a sheriff or coroner, and an appropriation thereof by the court, under the act of the sixteenth of April, eighteen hundred and twenty-seven, entitled "An act relative to the distribution of money arising from sheriff and coroners' sales," it shall be the duty of the prothonotary to note on each judgment or lien, the amount paid thereon by such appropriation, with a reference to such appropriation. § 77.

It shall be the duty of every sheriff, and of every coroner acting as sheriff, to provide and keep in his office a proper book or books, in which he shall enter all writs that may come to his hands, and the proceedings thereon, and at the expiration of his term of office, such books shall be deposited in the office of the prothonotary of the Court of Common Pleas in the same county, for the inspection of all persons interested therein. § 78.

It shall be the duty of every sheriff, his deputy or agent, and of every coroner acting as sheriff, if a demand for that purpose shall be made immediately after receiving any of his fees, or any written security therefor, to deliver a bill of particulars specifying the several items contained therein and the amount thereof, and to give the party paying such fees a receipt in full therefor, or to indorse on such written security when taken, that the same was given for fees, and to sign the indorsement so to be made ; and if any sheriff, his deputy or agent, or coroner acting as aforesaid, shall refuse or neglect to give such bill of particulars or receipt, or to make such indorsement, he shall forfeit and pay any sum not exceeding fifty dollars to the commonwealth. § 79.

It shall be the duty of every sheriff to place and keep up in some conspicuous part of his office the seventy-ninth section of this act, for the inspection of all persons having business in such office, on pain of forfeiting for each day the same shall be missing through his neglect, the sum of ten dollars, one half of which penalty shall be for the use of the informer, and the other half for the use of the proper county. § 80.

The sheriff is, by the common law, the officer to whom all process ought to be directed, and he cannot be passed by without cause ; but if there be just cause of exception to him, the prothonotary may issue the process to the coroner.(t)   But the sheriff is the proper officer to exe. cute all writs, except in case of partiality, or where he himself is the defendant.   Thus if the action be against the bail of the sheriff, for his neglect of duty, it would be improper to trust him with the service of the process, whether original or final(u).   So too, it seems, that process against the sureties of the sheriff, in cases which are not founded on the sheriff's default or delinquency, should be directed to the coroner.(v) But whether the sheriff be or be not incompetent by reason of partiality, the coroner is bound to execute the process directed to him by a court having jurisdiction, at his peril, even though such direction be errone-ous.(w)   The process is not void ; but, when issued to the coroner when it ought not to be, is aided by the statutes of amendment.(x)   And the obligation of the sureties in the recognizance of the coroner compre-hends such process, where executed by the coroner(y).

The coroner is both a judicial and ministerial officer.   In his judicial capacity, he appears to be confined, in this State, to the holding of in-quests in cases where persons have been slain or have died suddenly, as to such death ; and in case of the vacancy of his office, the governor of the commonwealth is authorized by the constitution to appoint another in his place, to serve until the next general election.(z)

The ministerial office of the coroner is only as a substitute for the sheriff, and we have above seen in what cases this substitution may be needed or required.   For his neglect or unskilfulness in the perform-ance of any of these ministerial duties, or for his refusal to undertake them, he is, together with his sureties, liable as are the sheriff and his sureties; and the same rules of evidence apply in the actions that are instituted against him or them.(a)

For a view of the proceedings in actions against sheriffs and their sureties, we refer the inquirer to our second volume, where the subject is treated under the head of *scire facias* on official bonds.

(t) 8 Mod. Rep. 248.
(u) Beal's Executors v. The Common-wealth, 11 S. & R. 302.
(v) Ibid. 299.
(w) Ibid. 303.

(x) Ibid.
(y) Ibid.
(z) Const. Art. 6, § 1.
(a) Beal's Exe'rs v. Commonwealth. 11 S. & R. 299.

CHAPTER IV.

OF THE COURTS OF THE UNITED STATES.

CONSTITUTIONAL PROVISIONS.

THE jurisdiction of the courts of the United States is wholly derived under the constitution of the United States, which declares that "the judicial power shall extend to all cases in law and equity, arising under this constitution, the laws of the United States, and treaties made, or which shall be made under their authority; to all cases affecting ambassadors, other public ministers and consuls; to all cases of admiralty and maritime jurisdiction; to controversies to which the United States shall be a party; to controversies between two or more States, between a State and citizens of another State, between citizens of different States, between citizens of the same State claiming lands under grants of different States, and between a State or the citizens thereof, and foreign States, citizens or subjects.(a)

This provision has been qualified, in one of its particulars, by an amendatory article of the constitution, which declares that "the judicial power of the United States shall not be construed to extend to any suit in law or equity, commenced or prosecuted against one of the United States by citizens of another State, or by citizens or subjects of any foreign State."(b) This inhibition applies only to citizens or subjects, and does not extend to suits by a State, or by foreign States or powers against one of the United States.(c) The right of a State to assert as a plaintiff any interest it may have in a subject which forms matter of controversy, is in no way affected by this article of amendment.(d)

By the seventh article of amendments to the constitution it is further provided, that "In suits at common law, where the value in controversy shall exceed twenty dollars, the right of trial by jury shall be preserved; and no fact tried by a jury shall be otherwise re-examined in any court of the United States than according to the rules of the common law. The phrase common law, as used in this article, is construed to mean the same as cases in law in the third article of the constitution,(e) and to embrace all suits which are not of equity or admiralty jurisdiction;(f) and this right of trial by jury forbids a nonsuit except at consent of plaintiff.(g) And in furtherance of the provision of the

(a) Art. 3, § 2.
(b) Amendments, Art. 11. See 1 Kent's Com. 6 ed. p. 297.
(c) 5 Peters, 1; Ibid. 284.
(d) 5 Cranch, 115.

(e) Baldwin, 394, 405.
(f) 3 Peters, 433, 447.
(g) 1 Peters, 469; id. 476; 6 Peters, 598.

seventh article, by the 16th section of the act of 1789, the courts of the United States are forbidden to entertain suits in equity in any case where plain, adequate, and complete remedy may be had at law. But this section is held to be merely declaratory,(h) as where the case is cognizable at common law the defendant has a constitutional right to a trial by jury.(i)

Although all the courts of the United States thus owe their jurisdiction to the constitution, yet none of them, except the Supreme Court, were directly established by that instrument. The Supreme Court was established, and power given to Congress to establish inferior tribunals by the following provision of the constitution: "The judicial power of the United States shall be vested in one Supreme Court, and in such inferior courts as the Congress may from time to time ordain and establish."(j) It was thus left to Congress not only to decide what inferior tribunals should be established, but to allot to each such portions of the judicial power as it might deem expedient.

It may be remarked here that, although in the language of the constitution, the Circuit and District Courts of the United States are termed inferior courts, they are not to be deemed such in the technical sense of the term; they are courts of limited rather than inferior jurisdiction; their proceedings are not subject to the scrutiny of the narrow rules which the caution or jealousy of the courts at Westminster long applied to courts of that denomination; but are entitled to as liberal intendments or presumptions in favor of their regularity as those of any Supreme Court.(k) And although judgments, where the jurisdiction of the court is not shown, are erroneous, and may be reversed, yet they are not nullities, as in case of courts of inferior jurisdiction.(l)

Although the limits of the judicial powers of the federal courts are prescribed by the constitution, yet it requires that Congress should concur in conferring jurisdiction upon these courts, and it is not sufficient that a case falls within the scope of the judicial powers of the United States, as declared in the constitution, unless jurisdiction over it has been conferred by some act of Congress; and Congress is not bound to enlarge the jurisdiction of the federal courts in every form which the constitution might warrant.(m) And even to the Supreme Court, the constitution does not secure jurisdiction, in all those cases, to which it declares that the judicial power extends; but leaves it to Congress as to most of those cases, to limit its jurisdiction by making exceptions to them.(n) In conferring jurisdiction upon the Supreme Court, the constitution declares that "in all cases affecting ambassadors, other public ministers and consuls, and those in which a State shall be a party, the Supreme Court shall have original jurisdiction. In all the other cases before mentioned, the Supreme Court shall have appellate jurisdiction, both as to law and fact, with such exceptions, and under such regulations, as the Congress shall make."(o)

In order, therefore, to learn the appellate jurisdiction of the Supreme Court, and the organization, jurisdiction, and powers of the inferior

(h) 3 Peters, 210, 215; 1 Baldwin, 394.
(i) 1 Baldwin, 394, 405.
(j) Art. 3, § 1.
(k) 4 D. 8.
(l) 8 How. 611; 5 Cra. 185; 6 Cra. 267.

(m) 7 Cra. 506; 12 Peters, 616; 3 How. 245; 8 How. 441.
(n) See 3 D. 327; 6 Cranch, 313.
(o) Art. 3, § 2.

courts of the United States, it becomes necessary to refer to the acts of Congress by which they are regulated or established; and in doing this, each court will be considered separately. But before proceeding to the separate consideration of each court, it may not be amiss to take a more single and general view of them, as the united depositories of the entire judicial power.

The cases to which the judicial power relinquished by the State governments to the courts of the Union, as regulated by Congress, extends, are of four kinds: 1. Those which arise under the constitution, laws, and treaties of the nation, and which, therefore, seem to belong, naturally, to the jurisdiction of its courts; 2. Those which concern persons who, as representatives of foreign governments, are entitled to national protection; 3. Those which are of admiralty and maritime jurisdiction; the general regulation of commerce having been resigned to the nation; and 4. Certain particular cases in which there might be a bias in the State courts towards one of the parties, in consequence of such party's claiming title under the State, or being one of its citizens, or the State itself; or against him, on account of his being an alien.(p)

In establishing the inferior national courts, Congress has placed them, for the more convenient and ready administration of justice, in different portions of the Union, generally allotting two courts with different powers to each State; and in distributing the judicial power between the Supreme Court and such inferior courts, it has been done with particular reference to the locality and character of the tribunal. To the district or lower local court, which is organized for the greatest dispatch of business, has been assigned the jurisdiction of admiralty and maritime causes, and the collection and protection of the revenues of the nation. To the circuit or higher local court, has been given a supervisory power over the District Court; a concurrent jurisdiction with that court in matters of revenue; the adjudication upon private rights acquired under certain acts of Congress; and the jurisdiction of cases withdrawn from the State courts on account of apprehended partiality, except when a State is the party. To the Supreme Court has been confided the high and sometimes exclusive jurisdiction where a State is a party in certain cases; jurisdiction in suits where one of the parties is entitled to national protection; and a supervisory power over the Circuit Courts; and also over the State courts, so far as was necessary in order to prevent them, in administering justice, from misconstruing or disregarding the laws of the Union; securing by such supervisory power the uniform construction and paramount authority of those laws.

We shall proceed to consider the courts of the United States in the following order and under the following heads:—

I. District Court of the United States.
    (1.) Organization.
    (2.) Jurisdiction.
II. Circuit Court of the United States.
    (1.) Organization.
    (2.) Jurisdiction.

(p) See 2 D. 475.

(*a.*) Original Jurisdiction.
(*b.*) Jurisdiction by removal from the State courts.
(*c.*) Jurisdiction by removal from District Court.
(*d.*) Appellate Jurisdiction by writ of error to the District Court.
(3.) Process.
(4.) Practice.
(5.) Jails, and discharge from Imprisonment for debt.
III. Supreme Court of the United States.
   (1.) Organization.
   (2.) Jurisdiction.
      (*a.*) Original.
      (*b.*) Appellate Jurisdiction by writ of error to the Circuit Court.
      (*c.*) Appellate Jurisdiction by writ of error to the highest State Court.
      (*d.*) Appellate Jurisdiction by certificate of points of disagreement from the Circuit Court.
      (*e.*) Writs of prohibition, mandamus, habeas corpus, &c.

SECTION I.

DISTRICT COURTS OF THE UNITED STATES.

(1). *Organization.*

Under the authority contained in the first section of the third article of the Constitution, Congress has established Circuit and District Courts in different portions of the Union, upon which jurisdiction has been conferred according to the provisions of the Constitution.

The State of Pennsylvania originally composed but one judicial district,(*q*) and the District Court was directed to be held at Philadelphia.(*r*)

By the act of 20th April, 1818,(*s*) the State of Pennsylvania was divided into two districts—to be called the Eastern and Western Districts, and a District Court appointed for each—that for the Eastern District to be held at Philadelphia, and that for the Western at Pittsburg.

The Eastern District of Pennsylvania, as now constituted, is composed of the Counties of Adams, Berks, Bucks, Carbon, Chester, Cumberland, Dauphin, Delaware, Franklin, Lancaster, Lebanon, Lehigh, Monroe, Montgomery, Northampton, Perry, Philadelphia, Pike, Schuylkill, Wayne, York.

The sessions are held at Philadelphia on the third Mondays of February, May, August, and November.

The Western District is composed of the counties other than those enumerated as composing the Eastern District, and its sessions are held at Pittsburg on the first Monday of May and third Monday of October in every year; and at Williamsport on the third Monday in June and first Monday in October.

The District Court of each district consists of a single judge, called a District Judge, who resides in the district for which he is appointed ;(*t*)

(*q*) Act of Sept. 24, 1789, s. 2.
(*r*) Act of Aug. 11, 1790, s. 2, U. S. Stat. at large, v. i. p. 184.
(*s*) U. S. Stat. at large, v. iii. p. 462.
(*t*) Act of Sept. 24, 1789, s. 3. U. S. Stat. at large, v. i. p. 73.

and, like all other judges of the courts of the United States, he holds his office during good behavior.(u)   The judges of the District Courts are forbidden to practise law as attorneys or counsellors.(v)

The duration of the terms is not limited by law, and the district judges are authorized to hold special courts at their discretion, at such places within their respective districts as they may deem proper.(w)

In case of the inability of the judge to attend at the commencement of a session, or on the day appointed for the holding a special or an adjourned court, the court may, by virtue of a written order from the judge of the district, directed to the marshal, be adjourned by him, to such a day, antecedent to the next stated session of the court, as shall be appointed in the order;(x) or if it be a special or an adjourned court, to the next stated term, or to any day prior thereto, appointed in the order.(y)   In case of a vacancy by the death of a judge, all process, pleadings, and proceedings continue over until the next term after the office is again filled.(z)   And in case of contagious sickness, the district judge is authorized to issue his order to the marshal, directing him to adjourn the court to some convenient place within the district; which he is to do, by publishing the order in the newspapers until the commencement of the session.(a)

In case of the sickness or disability of the district judge to hold a term of a District Court, or of a Circuit Court, in the absence of the circuit judge, upon such fact being certified by the clerk to the circuit judge, such judge may appoint any other district judge of any other judicial district to hold such term—and in case of the non-residence or inability of the circuit judge to make the appointment—the Chief Justice of the United States is authorized to make the appointment.(b)

Clerk.—The clerk is appointed by the court, and gives security in the sum of two thousand dollars, in the same manner as the marshal.(c)

Whenever money is paid into court, or received by the officer of the court, it does not remain in the hands of the officers until the order of the court, whether it be in the Circuit or District Court; but an act of Congress requires that it should be immediately deposited in the branch bank within the district, if there be one, and if not, in some incorporated State bank within the district, in the name and to the credit of the court; and that no money, so deposited, shall be drawn from the bank, except by the order of the judge or judges of such court, respectively, in term or in vacation, to be signed by such judge or judges, and to be entered and certified of record by the clerk.   At each term of the court, it is the duty of the clerk to present to the court a particular account of all the moneys remaining in court or subject to its order.(d)

The clerks of the District and Circuit Courts are authorized, in the absence or in case of the disability of the judges, to take recognizances of special bail and depositions, *de bene esse,* in their courts.(e)   And in

(u) Const. Art. 3, s. 1.
(v) Act of Dec. 18, 1812. U. S. Stat. at large, v. ii. p. 788.
(w) Act of Sept. 24, 1789.
(x) Act of 1799, § 6.
(y) Act of March 26, 1804.
(z) Act of 1789, § 6.
(a) Act of Feb. 25, 1799, § 7. U. S. Stat. at large, v. i. p. 621.

(b) Act of July 29, 1850, § 1, 2, 4. U. S. Stat. at large, v. ix. p. 442.
(c) Act of 24th Sept. 1789, § 7.
(d) Act of March 3, 1817; U. S. Stat. at large, v. iii. p. 395.
(e) Act of May 8, 1792, § 10; U. S. Stat. at large, v. i. p. 278.

case of the disability of the judge to discharge his duties, they are authorized by leave or order of the circuit judge to take all examina- tions or depositions of witnesses and make all necessary rules or or- ders.(*f*) These provisions, though still in force, are in a great measure superseded by subsequent acts authorizing the appointment of commis- sioners.(*g*)

By act of May 15, 1820, § 8, it is made the duty of the clerks of the Circuit and District Courts, within thirty days after the adjournment of each term, to forward to the Solicitor of the Treasury a list of all judgments or decrees to which the United States are parties, showing he amount, and stating the term to which execution is made return- able.(*h*)

Marshal.—The marshal of the district is the ministerial officer of the court, and possesses the same powers generally as sheriffs. He is appointed by the President and Senate, for the term of four years, but is removable at pleasure.(*i*) He gives a bond for the performance of his duties, with two sureties, to be approved by the district judge, in the sum of twenty thousand dollars.(*j*) In actions in which the marshal, or his deputy, is a party, writs and precepts are to be directed to some disinterested person, to be appointed by the court or a judge.(*k*)

The official bond of the marshal is filed and recorded in the clerk's office, and a certified copy, under the seal of the court, is evidence in any court. In case of the breach of the condition of the bond, the party injured may put it in suit in his own name; the bond after- wards remains as security for future breaches, until the whole penalty shall have been recovered, and the proceedings are always to be the same as for the first breach. The time for bringing such suits is limited to six years after the right of action accrued, with a saving of the rights of infants, *femes covert*, and persons *non compos mentis*, until three years after disability removed.(*l*)

It is the duty of the marshal to execute all process which may be placed in his hands; but he performs this duty at his peril, and under the guidance of the law. He must, of course, exercise some judgment in the performance. Should he fail to obey the exigit of the writ with- out a legal excuse, or should he, in obeying its letter, violate the rights of others, he is liable to the action of the injured party.(*m*) The court will not dictate to the marshal what return shall be made to process— he must do it at his peril.(*n*) A marshal is not removed by the appoint- ment of a new one, until he receives notice of such appointment; all acts done by the old marshal, after the appointment of a new one, before notice, are good.(*o*)

The judiciary act of 1789 has the following provisions, in the event of the removal of the marshal by death or otherwise: "In case of the death of any marshal, his deputy or deputies shall continue in office, unless otherwise specially removed; and shall execute the same in the name of the deceased, until another marshal shall be appointed and

---

(*f*) Act of March 2, 1809, § 3.
(*g*) See *post*, Commissioners.
(*h*) U. S. Stat. at large, v. iii. p. 596.
(*i*) Act of Sept. 24, 1789, § 27; U. S. Stat. at large, v. i. p. 87.
(*j*) Ibid.

(*k*) Ibid. § 28.
(*l*) Act of April, 10, 1806, §§ 1, 2, 3, 4; U. S. Stat. at large, v. ii. p. 372.
(*m*) 9 Peters, 573.
(*n*) Peters, C. C. R. 241.
(*o*) Wallace, C. C. R. 119.

sworn; and the defaults or misfeasances in office of such deputy or deputies, in the mean time, as well as before, shall be adjudged a breach of the condition of the bond given, as before directed, by the marshal who appointed them; and the executor or administrator of the deceased marshal shall have like remedy for the defaults and misfeasances in office of such deputy or deputies, during such interval, as they would be entitled to if the marshal had continued in life, and in the exercise of his said office, until his successor was appointed and sworn or affirmed: And every marshal or his deputy, when removed from office, or when the term for which the marshal is appointed shall expire, shall have power, notwithstanding, to execute all such precepts, as may be in their hands, respectively, at the time of such removal or expiration of office; and the marshal shall be held answerable for the delivery to his successor of all prisoners which may be in his custody at the time of his removal, or when the term for which he is appointed shall expire, and for that purpose may retain such prisoners in his custody until his successor shall be appointed, and qualified as the law directs.(p)   § 28.

A marshal is bound, like a sheriff, after the expiration of his term of office, to complete an execution which has come to his hands during his term.(q)

By the act of May 7, 1800, where the marshal dies, or is removed from office, or where his commission expires, after the sale of land under judicial process, and before execution of a deed to the purchaser, the court may, on the application of the purchaser or plaintiff, direct the marshal for the time being to perfect the title and execute a deed; and the same proceedings may be had in case of the occurrence of the death, removal, or expiration of the commission of a marshal, after execution levied, and before sale.(r)   § 3.

Under the act of 18th September, 1850, commonly known as the Fugitive Slave Act, it is "the duty of all marshals and deputy marshals to obey and execute all warrants and precepts issued under the provisions of this act, when to them directed; and should any marshal or deputy marshal refuse to receive such warrant or other process, when tendered, or to use all proper means diligently to execute the same, he shall on conviction thereof be fined in the sum of one thousand dollars, to the use of such claimant, on the motion of such claimant, by the Circuit or District Court for the district of such marshal; and after arrest of such fugitive by such marshal or his deputy, or whilst at any time in his custody, under the provisions of this act, should such fugitive escape, whether with or without the assent of such marshal or his deputy, such marshal shall be liable on his official bond to be prosecuted for the benefit of such claimant, for the full value of the service or labor of said fugitive in the State, Territory, or District whence he escaped."(s)   § 4.

The deputy marshals are appointed by the marshal, but are removable by the judge of the District or the Circuit Court sitting in the district,

(p) U. S. Stat. at large, v. i. p. 87.   (r) U. S. Stat. at large, v. ii. p. 61.
(q) 3 How. 717.   (s) Stat. at large, v. ix. p. 462.

at the pleasure of either.(*t*)   They are officers of the court, and responsible as such.(*u*)

A marshal is liable on his bond for the failure of his deputy to serve original process to the extent of the injury sustained by the plaintiff;(*v*) but he is responsible for the acts of his deputy only when done in the line of his duty.(*w*)

Commissioners to take affidavits and special bail.—The Circuit Courts are authorized to appoint such and so many discreet persons in different parts of the district, as they shall deem necessary, to take acknowledgments of bail and affidavits;(*x*) and by another act, the commissioners so appointed are required to perform the same duties in the District Courts.   And such commissioners are authorized to exercise all of the powers that a justice or judge of any of the courts of the United States may exercise by virtue of the 30th section of the judicial act of 1789.(*y*) Under this act they exercise the power to take depositions to be read in evidence in civil causes.(*z*)

Attorneys, &c.—The attorney of the United States, for the district by whom the United States always appear, is appointed in the same manner as the marshal.   The other attorneys and counsellors of the court are admitted from the same grade in the Supreme Court of the State.

The following are the rules adopted in the District and Circuit Courts of the United States for the Eastern District of Pennsylvania, in relation to the attorneys of these courts.

Rule IV.—1. No person shall be admitted to practise as counsel or attorney of these courts, unless he shall have previously been admitted in the Supreme Court of a State.   Satisfactory evidence of moral character will be required.   He shall take the following oath, to wit: "I do swear that I will demean myself, as an attorney of this court, uprightly and according to law; and that I will support the constitution of the United States."

2. No attorney shall be accepted as security for costs, nor as bail of any kind, nor to testify in favor of his client, except as to matters which are provable by the affidavit of a party.

(2.) *Jurisdiction.*

The District Court of the United States derives its jurisdiction chiefly from the 9th section of the judicial act of September 24, 1789, by which it is constituted a court of criminal jurisdiction; of admiralty and maritime jurisdiction; and of common law jurisdiction.

The ninth section reads as follows:—

"The District Courts shall have, exclusively of the courts of the several States, cognizance of all crimes and offences that shall be cognizable under the authority of the United States, committed within their respective districts, or upon the high seas, where no other punishment than whipping, not exceeding thirty stripes, a fine not exceeding one hundred dollars, or a term of imprisonment not exceeding six months, is to be inflicted: and shall also have exclusive original cognizance of all civil

(*t*) Act 24th Sept. 1789, ¿ 27, U. S. Stat. at large, v. i. p. 87.
(*u*) 3 M'Lean, 465.
(*v*) 2 Prock, 317.
(*w*) 3 M'Lean, 465.

(*x*) Act of Feb. 20, 1812, ¿ 1; U. S. Stat. at large, v. ii. p. 679.
(*y*) Act March 1, 1817; U. S. Stat. at large, v. iii. 350.
(*z*) See *post*, Circuit Court, title Practice.

causes of admiralty and maritime jurisdiction, including all seizures under laws of impost, navigation or trade of the United States, where the seizures are made on waters which are navigable from the sea by vessels of ten or more tons burthen, within their respective districts, as well as upon the high seas; saving to suitors, in all cases, the right of a common law remedy, where the common law is competent to give it."

" And shall also have exclusive original cognizance of all seizures on land, or other waters than as aforesaid, made, and of all suits for penalties and forfeitures incurred, under the laws of the United States. And shall also have cognizance, concurrent with the courts of the several States, or the Circuit Courts, as the case may be, of all causes where an alien sues for a tort only in violation of the law of nations, or a treaty of the United States. And shall also have cognizance, concurrent, as last mentioned, of all suits at common law, where the United States sue, and the matter in dispute amounts, exclusive of costs, to the sum or value of one hundred dollars. And shall also have jurisdiction exclusively of the courts of the several States, of all suits against consuls or vice consuls, except for offences above the description aforesaid. And the trial of issues in fact, in the District Courts, in all causes, except civil causes of admiralty and maritime jurisdiction, shall be by jury."(a)

The grant of common law jurisdiction to the District Courts contained in the clause above cited, in cases where the United States are plaintiffs, has been extended by a subsequent act to suits in which the debt or claim may not amount to one hundred dollars, by the following provision : " The District Court of the United States shall have cognizance, concurrent with the courts and magistrates of the several States, and the Circuit Courts of the United States, of all suits at common law, where the United States, or any officer thereof, under the authority of any act of Congress, shall sue, although the debt, claim, or other matter in dispute shall not amount to one hundred dollars."(b)

The exclusive jurisdiction of the District Courts in suits for penalties and forfeitures incurred under the laws of the United States when they are passed for the collection of direct taxes and internal duties, has, by a subsequent act of Congress, been made concurrent with the State courts ; and the courts to which this concurrent jurisdiction is so extended, as well as those which are to exercise the concurrent jurisdiction before allowed to State courts, where the United States are plaintiffs, in suits arising under such collection laws, are particularly specified, and some of the proceedings in suits and prosecutions in such cases, prescribed by the following provisions.

" The respective State or county courts within or next adjoining a collection district, established by any act of Congress now in being or hereafter to be passed, for the collection of any direct tax or internal duties of the United States, shall be and are hereby authorized to take cognizance of all complaints, suits, and prosecutions for taxes, duties, fines, penalties, and forfeitures, arising and payable under any of the acts passed, or to be passed, as aforesaid, or where bonds are given under the said acts ; and the district attorneys of the United States are hereby authorized and directed to appoint by warrant, an attorney, as

(a) Act of Sept. 24, 1789, § 9.   (b) Act of March 3, 1815, § 4 ; U. S. Stat. at large, v. iii. p. 245.

their substitute or deputy, in all cases where necessary to sue or prosecute for the United States, in any of the said State or county courts,
within the sphere of whose jurisdiction the said district attorneys do not
themselves reside or practise ; and the said substitute or deputy shall be
sworn or affirmed to the faithful execution of his duty."(c)

" The jurisdiction conferred by the foregoing section shall be considered as attaching, in the cases therein specified, without regard to. the
amount or sum in controversy, and shall be concurrent with the jurisdiction of the District Courts of the United States ; but may nevertheless
be exercised in cases where the fine, penalty, or forfeiture may have been
incurred, or the cause of action or complaint have arisen, at a less as
well as a greater distance than fifty miles from the nearest place by law
established for the holding of a District Court of the United States.
But in all suits or prosecutions instituted by or on behalf of the United
States in any State or county court, the process, proceedings, judgment
and execution therein shall not be delayed, suspended, or in any way
barred or defeated by reason of any law of any State authorizing or
directing a stay or suspension of process, proceedings, judgment, or
execution : *Provided,* That final decrees and judgments in civil actions,
passed or rendered in any State court by virtue hereof, may be re-examined in the Circuit Court of the United States, in the same manner
and under the same limitations, as are prescribed by the twenty-second
section of the act to establish the judicial courts of the United States,
passed the twenty-fourth of September, seventeen hundred and eighty-
nine."(d)

In these cases in which the State courts are thus allowed to exercise
a concurrent jurisdiction with the District Courts, the former or the
presiding judges thereof are also invested with the same powers, for the
mitigation or remission of the fines, penalties, and forfeitures, imposed
by them, as are exercised by the district judges, in similar cases ; and
the proceedings for that purpose are to be the same, with this difference,
that the substitute of the district attorney in the State court is to have
notice of the application instead of the district attorney.(e)

The act regulating the post-office department also makes the jurisdiction of State tribunals concurrent with that of the District Courts in
suits for penalties and forfeitures under that act, by the following provisions : " All causes of action arising under this act may be sued, and
all offenders against this act may be prosecuted, before the justices of
the peace, magistrates, or other judicial courts of the several States, and
of the several territories of the United States, they having competent
jurisdiction, by the laws of such States or territories, to the trial of
claims and demands of as great value and of the prosecutions, where the
punishments are of as great extent ; and such justices, magistrates, or
judiciary shall take cognizance thereof, and proceed to judgment and
execution, as in other cases." (f)

The county courts of the State within or next adjoining certain
collection districts of the United States lying on the lakes, are authorized
to take cognizance of all complaints and prosecutions for fines, penalties,
and forfeitures arising under the revenue laws of the United States in

---

(c) Ibid. § 1.
(d) Ibid. § 2.
(e) Ibid. § 3.

(f) Act of March 3, 1825, § 37 ; U. S.
Stat. at large, v. iv. p. 113.

those districts, with the like powers as those of the District Courts in relation to the remission of penalties.(*g*)

The following section of the patent law provides for the cases in which patents may be repealed, and for some of the proceedings for that purpose :—

" Upon oath or affirmation being made, before the judge of the District Court, where the patentee, his executors, administrators, or assigns reside, that any patent which shall be issued in pursuance of this act, was obtained surreptitiously, or upon false suggestion, and motion made to the said court, within three years after issuing the said patent, but not afterwards, it shall and may be lawful for the judge of the said District Court, if the matter alleged shall appear to him to be sufficient, to grant a rule, that the patenteé, or his executor, administrator, or assign show cause why process should not issue against him, to repeal such patent. And if sufficient cause shall not be shown to the contrary, the rule shall be made absolute, and thereupon the said judge shall order-process to be issued against such patentee, or his executors, administrators, or assigns, with costs of suit. And in case no sufficient cause shall be shown to the contrary, or if it shall appear that the patentee was not the true inventor or discoverer, judgment shall be rendered by such court, for the repeal of such patent; and if the party at whose complaint the process issued shall have judgment given against him, he shall pay all such costs as the defendant shall be put to in defending the suit, to be taxed by the court, and recovered in due course of law."(*h*)

By the act of March 2, 1799, § 8, the District Court has jurisdiction concurrent with the Circuit Court, in actions brought by the possessor or assignee of assigned debentures against the person to whom such debentures were originally issued, or against any indorser thereof.(*i*)

Under these acts, the common law jurisdiction of the United States courts, in cases of a civil nature, is believed to be embraced under the following heads :—

First. Exclusive original cognizance of all seizures on land or waters not navigable from the ocean by boats of ten or more tons burthen, made under the law of the United States.

These cases are of common law jurisdiction ; the proceedings are instituted by proceedings *in rem*, and the trial of issues of fact is by jury.(*j*)

Second. Original jurisdiction of all suits for penalties and forfeitures incurred under the laws of the United States.

The original jurisdiction granted to the District Courts was exclusive, and still is, except in the cases mentioned in the acts before cited.(*k*)

Third. Original jurisdiction, concurrently with the courts of the several States and the Circuit Courts, of all causes wherein an alien

(*g*) Act March 8, 1806; Laws U. S. 988.

(*h*) Act of February 21, 1793, § 10; U. S. Stat. at large, v. i. p. 323.

(*i*) U. S. Stat. at large, v. i. p. 689.

(*j*) See Conkling, Prac. p. 156 ; 4 Cranch, 443 ; 8 Wheat. 391.

(*k*) *Ante*, p. 140.

sues for a tort only in violation of the laws of nations, or a treaty of the United States.

Fourth. Jurisdiction, concurrent, in like manner, of all suits at common law, brought by the United States, or an officer thereof, under the authority of an act of Congress.

Fifth. Jurisdiction, exclusively of the courts of the several States, of all suits against consuls or vice-consuls.

A State has no jurisdiction of a suit against a consul; and whenever this defect of jurisdiction is suggested, the court will quash the proceedings; it is not necessary that it should be by plea before general imparlance.(*l*) If a consul, being sued in a State court, omits to plead his privilege of exemption from the suit, and afterwards, on writ of error to a higher court, he claims the privilege, such an omission is not a waiver of the privilege;(*m*) but where a State court has jurisdiction of a suit at the time it was commenced, it is not divested of its jurisdiction by the defendant's afterwards voluntarily accepting the office of consul to a foreign power.(*n*)

Sixth. Jurisdiction concurrent with the Circuit Courts over suits brought by an assignee of assigned debentures.

Seventh. In proceedings for the repeal of letters patent for inventions. In which cases the process to be awarded is held to be in the nature of a *scire facias*.(*o*)

The District Courts of the United States have also power to issue injunctions in certain cases.

By the act of February 13, 1807, the judges of the District Courts of the United States are invested with as full power to grant writs of injunction, to operate within their respective districts, in all cases which may come before the Circuit Courts in their respective districts, as is now exercised by any of the judges of the Supreme Court of the United States under the same rules, &c. *Provided,* That the same shall not, unless so ordered by the Circuit Court, continue longer than to the Circuit Court next ensuing; nor shall an injunction be issued by a district judge in any case where a party has had a reasonable time to apply to the Circuit Court for the writ.(*p*)

This power is to be considered as conferred upon the district judge rather in his capacity as a member of the District Court than as the judge of the District Court, and it issues out of the Circuit Court.(*q*)

Under the act of May 15, 1820, § 6, authorizing and requiring the agent of the treasury to issue a warrant of distress against a delinquent public officer and his sureties—by the fourth section it is provided: "That if any person shall consider himself aggrieved by any warrant issued under this act—he may prefer a bill of complaint to any district judge of the United States, setting forth the nature and extent of the injury of which he complains; and thereupon the judge aforesaid may, if in his opinion the case requires it, grant an injunction to stay proceedings on such warrant altogether, or for so much thereof as the nature of the case requires," &c., and the fifth section provides, "that such

(*l*) 1 Bin. 138.
(*m*) 7 Peters, 276.
(*n*) 1 Barb. 19.

(*o*) 1 Mason, 153; 9 Wheat. 603.
(*p*) U. S. Stat. at large, v. il. p. 418.
(*q*) Conk. Prac. p. 162.

injunctions may be granted or dissolved by such judge—either in or out of court."(r)

Under the fugitive slave act,(s) the judges of the District Courts of the United States have concurrent jurisdiction with the judges of the Circuit Courts, and the commissioners named in that act to enforce its provisions.

The sixth section, providing for the manner of reclaiming fugitives from labor, is in the following words:—

That when a person held to service or labor in any State or Territory of the United States, has heretofore or shall hereafter escape into another State or Territory of the United States, the person or persons to whom such service or labor may be due, or his, her, or their agent or attorney, duly authorized, by power, of attorney, in writing, acknowledged and certified under the seal of some legal officer or court of the State or Territory in which the same may be executed, may pursue and reclaim such fugitive person, either by procuring a warrant from some one of the courts, judges, or commissioners aforesaid, of the proper circuit, district, or county for the apprehension of such fugitive from service or labor, or by seizing and arresting such fugitive, where the same can be done without process, and by taking, or causing such person to be taken, forthwith before such court, judge, or commissioner, whose duty it shall be to hear and determine the case of such claimant in a summary manner; and upon satisfactory proof being made, by deposition or affidavit, in writing, to be taken and certified by such court, judge, or commissioner, or by other satisfactory testimony, duly taken and certified by some court, magistrate, justice of the peace, or other legal officer authorized to administer an oath and take depositions under the laws of the State or Territory from which such person owing service or labor may have escaped, with a certificate of such magistracy or other authority, as aforesaid, with the seal of the proper court or officer thereto attached, which seal shall be sufficient to establish the competency of the proof, and with proof, also by affidavit, of the identity of the person whose service or labor is claimed to be due as aforesaid, that the person so arrested does in fact owe service or labor to the person or persons claiming him or her, in the State or Territory from which such fugitive may have escaped as aforesaid, and that said person escaped, to make out and deliver to such claimant his or her agent or attorney, a certificate setting forth the substantial facts as to the service or labor due from such fugitive to the claimant, and of his or her escape from the State or Territory in which such service or labor was due, to the State or Territory in which he or she was arrested, with authority to such claimant, or his or her agent or attorney, to use such reasonable force and restraint as may be necessary, under the circumstances of the case, to take and remove such fugitive person back to the State or Territory whence he or she may have escaped as aforesaid. In no trial or hearing under this act shall the testimony of such alleged fugitive be admitted in evidence; and the certificates in this and the first section mentioned shall be conclusive of the right of the person or persons in whose favor granted, to remove such fugitive to the State or Territory from which

(r) U. S. Stat. at large, v. iii. p. 595.   large, v. ix. p. 462.   See Wharton's Cr.
(s) Sept. 18, 1850. U. S. Stat. at   Law, 470, 777.

he escaped, and shall prevent all molestation of such person or persons by any process issued by any court, judge, magistrate, or other person whomsoever. § 6.

The District Court has also jurisdiction concurrent with the Circuit Court, of certain causes arising under the acts in relation to the slave-trade, in relation to the post-office, and under the steamboat and pas-senger acts, which will be referred to under the head of the Circuit Court.

It is not within the scope of the present work to treat of the criminal jurisdiction of this court, or of its jurisdiction as a Court of Admiralty; although the latter is that of the most frequent resort, in which case it has original jurisdiction without reference to the sum or value in con-troversy.(t)

Under the heads of Circuit and Supreme Courts of the United States, will be found several statutory provisions regulating the jurisdiction and process of the District Courts in certain respects, and empowering all the courts of the United States to issue writs of different kinds; and also such judicial decisions as have been made upon the various branches of the jurisdiction and practice of the courts of the United States.

Almost the whole civil business of the District Courts consists of suits in admiralty, which must be commenced in those courts, and of suits at common law in favor of the United States or their officers, or for penalties and seizures under their laws, and of proceedings for the repeal of patents, few occasions occurring which call for the exercise of their jurisdiction in relation to aliens and consuls.   And these courts have proved to be in practice, what they were, no doubt, designed to be, the Admiralty and Exchequer Courts of the nation.

Practice.—The statutes regulating practice in the United States courts affect the District and Circuit Courts alike where they are ap-plicable, and the reader is referred to the head of Practice in the suc-ceeding section in relation to the Circuit Court, where the subject will be treated.

The District and Circuit Courts for the Eastern District of Pennsyl-vania, by order of November 13, 1849, adopted the same rules at law for both courts.

SECTION II.

OF THE CIRCUIT COURT OF THE UNITED STATES.

(1.) *Organization.*

The Circuit Courts of the different districts consist of a justice of the Supreme Court and the district judge of such district; but no dis-trict judge of such district can give a vote in any case of appeal or writ of error from his own decision, but he is allowed to assign the reason of such his decision.   The Supreme Court may, however, direct two of its justices to hold a Circuit Court, in cases where special circumstances may require it.   Where only one of the judges attend, the court may

(t) 8 Pet. 4, 8.

be held by the judge so attending.(*u*)   And the district judge may alone hold a Circuit Court, though no justice of the Supreme Court be allotted to that circuit.(*v*)

The justice of the Supreme Court is not, however, required to attend more than one term of a circuit in any one year.   Such term is designated by him; and at such term appeals and writs of error from the District Court, questions of law arising upon statements of fact agreed by the parties, or specially reserved by the district judge, and cases at law and in equity of peculiar interest or difficulty, shall have precedence.(*w*)

Under the act of April 20, 1818, dividing the State of Pennsylvania into two districts, the Circuit Court for the eastern district was directed to be held at Philadelphia; and the District Court for the western district, which was directed to be held at Pittsburg, in addition to the ordinary powers of a District Court, had jurisdiction conferred upon it of all causes except appeals and writs of error, cognizable by the Circuit Courts; and the circuit powers of that court were re-enacted by the act of Feb. 19, 1831,

By a subsequent act, February 26, 1824, the judge of the District Court, for the western district, was directed to hold two terms, in every year, at Williamsport; but, by the act of March 3d, 1837, § 3,(*x*) the circuit powers of the District Court, for the western district of Pennsylvania, were taken away; and a Circuit Court was directed to be held at Pittsburg, on the third Mondays of May and November.   But it was provided by the third section that, nothing therein contained should prevent the judge of the western district from holding courts at Williamsport, at the same time and with the same power and jurisdiction as heretofore.   And by the act of March 3d, 1843,(*z*) the circuit powers of the District Court, for the western district, sitting at Williamsport, were repealed, and a Circuit Court directed to be held there by the associate justice of the Supreme Court, and the judge of the western district, either of whom might constitute a quorum, on the third Mondays of June and September.

The Circuit Courts hold their sessions at the times and places prescribed by law.

The Circuit Court for the eastern district is held at Philadelphia, on the first Monday in April and October; for the western district, at Pittsburg, on the second Monday in May and November; and at Williamsport on the third Monday in June and September.

Special sessions may also be appointed by the presiding judge, at which all the same powers may be exercised as at the stated sessions, except that of holding jury trials.(*a*)

Respecting adjournments, it is provided that the court may be adjourned from day to day, by any one of its judges, or if none are present, by the marshal of the district, until a quorum be convened.(*b*) Under this provision it has been held, that where a judge has once at-

(*u*) Acts 1793, ch. 22, § 1; 1789, ch. 20, § 4; 1802, ch. 31, § 4.
(*v*) 4 Cranch, 421.
(*w*) Act of June 17, 1844, § 2; U. S. Stat. at large, v. v. p. 676.

(*x*) U. S. Stat. at large, v. v. p. 177.
(*z*) Ibid. 618.
(*a*) Act July 4, 1840, § 2, U. S. Stat. at large, v. v. p. 393.
(*b*) Act of 1789, § 6.

tended and adjourned the court, the marshal cannot afterwards continue the court open by adjournment, and the term ceases.(c)

It is also provided that if the justice of the Supreme Court does not attend within four days after the commencement of the term, the court may be adjourned to the next stated term by the district judge, or, in case of his absence, by the marshal.(d)

Where neither of the judges of the Circuit Court attend at the commencement of a stated or adjourned session thereof, to open and adjourn the courts in person, either of such judge may, by a written order to the marshal, adjourn the court to any time antecedent to the next stated term.(e)

Whenever there is a contagious or a dangerous and general disease at the place where the Circuit Courts are usually holden, the judges may adjourn the same to some convenient place within the district, or may, by an order to the clerk, adjourn the same to some future day specified in the order.(f)

Officers.—The marshal of the district is the ministerial officer of the Circuit Court. The clerk of the Circuit Court is now appointed by that court. In case of disagreement, the appointment is made by the circuit judge.(g) The same rules in relation to the admission of attorneys, are adopted in the Circuit as the District Court for the Eastern District of Pennsylvania.(h)

(2.) *Jurisdiction.*

The Circuit Courts possess no powers except such as both the constitution and the acts of Congress concur in conferring upon them. A party, therefore, who has acquired rights under the laws of the United States, or is charged with any liability for acts performed under their sanction, although the cause of complaint for which redress is sought may come within the constitutional limits of the judicial powers of the United States, is not entitled to redress in these forums, unless by the express provision of some act of Congress.(i) Parties entitled to sue in the courts of the United States, are in general entitled to pursue in such courts all the remedies for the vindication of their rights which the local laws of the State authorize to be pursued in its own courts.(j)

The jurisdiction of the Circuit Court will be considered under the following heads:—

(a.) Original Jurisdiction.
(b.) Jurisdiction by removal from the State Courts.
(c.) Jurisdiction by removal from the District Courts.
(d.) Appellate Jurisdiction by writ of error to the District Courts.

(a.) *Original Jurisdiction.*

The following section of the judiciary act of 1789, conferred upon the Circuit Court its general original jurisdiction. This section also con-

(c) C. Ct. N. Y. May, 1829 ; 2 Paine.
(d) Act of May 19, 1794 ; Laws U. S. 339.
(e) Act July 4, 1840, sec. 1, U. S. Stat. at large, v. v. p. 392.
(f) Act 1799, ch. 12, § 7 ; Act 1839, ch. 3, § 9.

(g) Act Feb. 28, 1839, § 2, U. S. Stat. at large, v. v. p. 322.
(h) For an account of all these offices see District Court.
(i) 1 Mason, 520 ; 1 Paine, 45 ; 5 Cranch, 85 ; ibid. 303 ; 7 ibid. 504 ; 2 Wheat. 1 ; 9 ibid. 817.
(j) 2 Mason, 472 ; 3 M'Clean, 174.

tains some of the provisions regulating the jurisdiction of the District Courts, to which we have referred.

"The Circuit Courts shall have original cognizance, concurrent with the courts of the several States, of all suits of a civil nature, at common law, or in equity, where the matter in dispute exceeds, exclusive of costs, the sum or value of five hundred dollars, and the United States are plaintiffs, or petitioners; or an alien is a party, or the suit is between a citizen of the State where the suit is brought, and a citizen of another State. And shall have exclusive cognizance of all crimes and offences cognizable under the authority of the United States, except where this act otherwise provides, or the laws of the United States shall otherwise direct, and concurrent jurisdiction with the District Courts, of the crimes and offences cognizable therein. But no person shall be arrested in one district for trial in another, in any civil action, before a Circuit or District Court. And no civil suit shall be brought, before either of said courts, against an inhabitant of the United States, by any original process, in any other district than that whereof he is an inhabitant, or in which he shall be found at the time of serving the writ; nor shall any District or Circuit Court have cognizance of any suit to recover the contents of any promissory note, or other chose in action, in favor of an assignee, unless a suit might have been prosecuted in such court, to recover the said contents if no assignment had been made, except in cases of foreign bills of exchange. And the Circuit Courts shall also have appellate jurisdiction from the District Courts, under the regulations and restrictions hereinafter provided." § 11.

As has been already noticed, the limitation of five hundred dollars and upwards was abolished by the act of March 3d, 1815, in cases where the United States are plaintiffs.(k)

It is proposed to examine the jurisdiction of the Circuit Court, as conferred by the 11th section of the judiciary act of 1789, under the following heads:—

1. The amount required to give the court jurisdiction.

2. The jurisdiction where the United States are plaintiffs or petitioners.

3. Jurisdiction arising from the alienage of a party.

4. Jurisdiction arising from the citizenship of a party.

5. The right of the defendant to be sued only in the district where he lives, or is found when the process is served.

6. The restriction in the case of assignment of promissory notes, and other choses in action.

1. In order that the Circuit Court should have original jurisdiction of a cause, on account of the citizenship or alienage of parties, it is necessary that the matter in dispute should exceed five hundred dollars, and this is to be determined by the amount laid in the writ or declaration, and not by the amount finally recovered;(l) as well in original suits as those removed by petition from a State court.(m) The court may give costs

(k) U. S. Stat. at large, v. iii. p. 245.   64; 2 Wash. C. C. 463; 3 McLean, 463.
(l) 1 Wash. C. C. 1; 1 Peters, C. C.   (m) 16 Peters, 97, 104.

against the plaintiff where he recovers less than five hundred dollars, under the 20th section of the act of 1789; and this is the only penalty the law designed to impose in such cases.(n) In a writ of right, if the land demanded exceeds five hundred dollars, and the demandant recovers less, the court has jurisdiction.(o)

2. A question was made in the Supreme Court of the United States whether the Circuit Courts were to be considered as acquiring any jurisdiction under the act of 1815, in relation to suits brought by the United States, or any officer thereof, under the authority of any act of Congress, which they did not possess before; but it was held that the act gave the same jurisdiction to the Circuit as to the District Court, and that the postmaster-general, who was required by the post-office law(p) to sue his deputies in his own name, might sue in the Circuit Court.(q)

It does not appear, however, ever to have been decided whether this act embraces penalties and forfeitures, so as to give the Circuit Court jurisdiction of suits brought for their recovery by the United States, or their officers, under an act of Congress, over which, it will be observed, this act did not extend the jurisdiction of the District Court, as it was before unlimited as well as exclusive.(r)

It may be remarked here that, under this act, the United States are entitled to sue in the Circuit Court, unless the District Court has exclusive jurisdiction, in all cases where they can sue at all; and of course few questions of jurisdiction can arise. But a very important question was raised as to their right to sue, without an act of Congress for the purpose; but the Supreme Court declared that they entertained no doubt on the point; and that the United States could sue on all contracts made with them, including bills of exchange indorsed to the treasurer of the United States for their use,(s) unless a different mode were provided by law.(t) It is to be understood, however, that nothing in the article of the constitution extending the judicial power of the United States to controversies to which the United States is a party, or in this section of the judiciary act of 1789, confers upon any court cognizance of all controversies to which the United States shall be a party, so as to justify a suit to be brought against the United States.(u) But in an action brought by the United States to recover money in the hands of a party, the defendant may, by way of defence, set up any legal or equitable claim he has against the United States (v)

3. It has been held that the grant of jurisdiction to the Circuit Court, where an alien is a party, is to be construed, in subordination to the constitution, to mean that the opposite party must be a citizen of the United States.(w) An alien, therefore, cannot sue another alien in the Circuit Court.(x) Where the parties on one side are aliens and citizens

(n) 2 D. 358, 360.

(o) Sed quere—Where the action is for the recovery of land, whether the value alleged in the declaration is to govern ; 1 Peters, C. C. 64; 8 Cranch, 229.

(p) Act of April 30, 1810; see act of March 3, 1825.

(q) 12 Wheat. 144.

(r) And see 12 Wheat. 486, 498; 2 D. 366; 4 Ibid. 342; but see 1 Gall. 177, 4.

(s) 3 Wheat. 172, and see 1 Peters, C. C. R. 168; 1 Paine, 156.

(t) 12 Wheat. 143.

(u) 3 Story's Com. ? 1669 ; 6 Wheat. 411 ; 8 Peters, 444.

(v) 6 Wheat. 135, 143 ; 9 Wheat. 651; 7 Peters, 16 ; 2 How. 711.

(w) 4 D. 12 ; 4 Cranch, 46 ; 5 Cranch, 303 ; 2 Peters, 136.

(x) But see 2 Cranch, 240.

of one State, and those on the other are citizens of another State, the court has jurisdiction.(y)

And the courts of the United States have jurisdiction in a case between citizens of the same State if the plaintiffs are only nominal parties suing for the use of an alien.(z) But a trustee is not a nominal party, and therefore an alien executor is competent to sue upon the ground of his alienage.(a)

It is necessary to aver that one party is an alien and subject of a foreign government, and that the other is a citizen of a State with the same distinctness as that with which the citizenship of the parties in other cases must be averred.(b)

The residence of aliens within the State with the opposite party, constitutes no objection to the jurisdiction. Aliens need not reside abroad to be qualified to sue in the several courts.(c)

In cases of assignments of choses in action, the same rules apply where aliens are parties to the suit, or to the instrument, as where citizens are such parties.(d)

But the privilege secured to aliens of suing and being sued in these courts, does not supersede the disability of non-resident alien-enemies to sue, founded on general principles of law.(e)

4. Where the character of citizen is the ground of jurisdiction, it is necessary that one of the parties should be a citizen of the State where the suit is brought; the act of Congress not giving to the Circuit Court, in this respect, the whole judicial power provided for by the constitution."(f)

As the jurisdiction of the court depends on the character of the parties, it is necessary, if either party consists of a number of individuals, that each individual should possess the requisite character to give the court jurisdiction;(g) or in other words, that each of the plaintiffs should be capable of suing each of the defendants in the Circuit Court.(h) It was held in a case in Pennsylvania, where the plaintiff was a citizen of another State, and one of the defendants, a citizen of Pennsylvania, was taken, and the other defendant, a citizen of a third State, was returned *non est inventus*, that the former defendant could not plead the want of jurisdiction as to his codefendant; because by the statute of the State the former might in such case be proceeded against singly.(i)

In 5 Cranch, 61, it was held that a corporation composed of citizens of one State may sue in the Circuit Court, but the members must all be citizens of a different State from the other party, and the same point was decided in 14 Peters, 60—but this inconvenient and narrow doctrine was reviewed and overruled in the Louisville Railroad Company v. Letson, where it was held that a citizen of one State might sue a corporation which has been created by and transacts its business in another State, in the Circuit Courts of the United States (the suit being brought in the latter State), although some of the members of the corporation

(y) 1 Paine, 580.
(z) 5 Cranch, 303; 8 Wheat. 642; 2 How. 9.
(a) 4 Cranch, 306.
(b) 1 Paine, 580; 3 Day, 294.
(c) 7 Peters, 413.
(d) 4 Cranch, 46; 4 D. 11.

(e) 1 Gallison, 366.
(f) 1 Mason, 520; 1 Peters, C. C. R. 431, & n.
(g) 1 Paine, 410.
(h) 3 Cranch, 267.
(i) 1 Peters, C. C. R. 431, n.

are not citizens of the State in which the suit is brought, and although the State itself may be a member of the corporation.(*j*)

And where a suit is brought in such courts by or against a corporation, the State, in which the corporation is created and established, should be averred.(*k*)

It was held, however, previously to the ruling of the case in 2 Howard, that it was *prima facie* evidence of the citizenship of the members of a corporation, that it was incorporated by and transacted its business within the State.(*l*)

Executors or administrators, if they themselves possess the requisite character of citizenship, are entitled to sue and may be sued, in the Circuit Court, whatever may have been the character of those whom they represent;(*m*) such cases not being affected by the restrictive clause of the eleventh section of the act of 1789.(*n*)

In the following case, the court looked beyond the plaintiffs, considering them merely nominal, to the party in interest, in order to sustain its jurisdiction. The plaintiffs were citizens of Virginia, and the defendant, who was sued as an executor, upon his bond for the faithful execution of the will, was also a citizen of that State; but the object of the suit was to recover a debt due from the testator to a British subject; and the Supreme Court held, that the Circuit Court had jurisdiction;(*o*) but where the legal right to sue is in the plaintiff, the court will not inquire into the residence of those who may have an equitable interest in the claim.(*p*)

It is not necessary that a citizen, removing from a Territory of the United States, or a State, into another State, should acquire all the rights of a citizen of the State into which he removes, by the laws of such State: it is sufficient if he acquire a domicil there; a citizen of the United States being, in a manner, a citizen of each State; and although it is necessary to aver, in the language of the law, that the party is a citizen of the State, yet proof of residence only, is sufficient.(*q*) If a party removes into another State, with the avowed object of acquiring a right to sue in the Circuit Court, but with the intention of a permanent residence, and not to return, it is not a fraud upon the law;(*r*) and his right to sue is complete immediately upon such removal.(*s*) If a citizen of one State removes with his family into another State with a *bona fide* intention to reside there, he becomes instantly a citizen of that State, and may sue in the courts of the United States as such.(*t*)

Where the plaintiff was a citizen of the United States, and it was at-

---

(*j*) 2 How. 497.
(*k*) 3 Story, 76.
(*l*) 1 Paine, 611.
(*m*) 4 Cranch, 306, 307, 308. See 6 Cranch, 334, and *post*.
(*n*) 8 Wheat. 642.
(*o*) 5 Cranch, 303. There appears to be some imperfection in the report of this case. Unless there was some peculiarity in the case, taking it out of the general rule, it is clearly not law, and has been expressly overruled by the principles settled in Osborn *v.* The United States Bank, 9 Wheat. Rep. 856, where the doctrine is fully laid down, that in all

cases of this description the character of the parties on the record, and not of those whose interest is litigated, determines the jurisdiction. See 1 Wash. C. C. R. 149; where the court would not listen to the objection that the agent by whom the policy was effected was not entitled to sue.
(*p*) 2 Howard, 574.
(*q*) 1 Paine, 594; 4 Wash. 516; 4 Wash. C. C. 609.
(*r*) Ibid.
(*s*) Cooper's Lessee *v.* Galbraith, C. Ct. U. S. Penn. April, 1821. MS.
(*t*) 3 Wash. C. C. 568.

tempted to show that he was not a citizen of any particular State, the court held, that to deprive him of his right to sue in the Circuit Court, there ought to be very strong evidence of his being a mere wanderer, without a home.(*u*)

The jurisdiction of the Circuit Court, having once vested between citizens of different States, cannot be divested by a change of domicil of one of the parties, and his removal into the same State with the adverse party, *pendente lite.*(*v*)   So where the jurisdiction has once vested, the defendant will not be allowed to withdraw his name from the suit, and thereby deprive the court of jurisdiction, although he is no longer interested.   Thus, where the defendant, an alien, after the institution of an ejectment against him, and while it was pending, sold the property to a third person, a citizen of the same State as the plaintiff's lessor, and then desired to withdraw his name from the suit, by which the name of the vendee must necessarily be substituted, and the jurisdiction of the court would be taken away, the court ordered the name of the original defendant to be retained, the vendee being required to indemnify him against costs.(*w*)

A citizen of the District of Columbia,(*x*) or of a Territory of the United States, cannot sue in the Circuit Court in his character of citizen.(*y*)

The Circuit Courts have no jurisdiction of suits brought by a State against citizens of the same or any other State,(*z*) nor where a State is a party.(*a*)

In order to give the court jurisdiction on the ground that the parties are citizens of different States, their citizenship must be distinctly stated in the process and pleadings,(*b*) and it is not sufficient that it is averred that they reside in different States,(*c*) or are of different States;(*d*) but the allegation of citizenship in a declaration need not be proved unless denied specially.(*e*)   Nor where proceedings are commenced by petition is it sufficient that the petition states the petitioners to be citizens of one State, and that they are informed and believe that the adverse parties are citizens of another State.(*f*)   The averment of jurisdiction must be positive, and the declaration must state expressly the fact on which jurisdiction depends.   It is not sufficient that jurisdiction may be inferred, argumentatively, from its averments.(*g*)   The omission of such averment will be fatal at any stage of the cause.(*h*)

But where a declaration contained both special and money counts, although the jurisdiction of the court did not appear from the special counts, if the money counts sustained by evidence would have been sufficient, the Supreme Court will presume that such evidence was given, nothing to the contrary appearing on the record, and no objection to the jurisdiction having been made at the trial.(*i*)

(*u*) 1 Paine, 580; as to what constitutes citizenship, see also 4 D. 360, and 1 Paine, 594.
(*b*) 2 Wheat. 290; 2 Peters, 565; 9 Wheat. 537; 8 Peters, 331; 12 Peters, 165.
(*w*) Peters, C. C. R. 444.
(*x*) 2 Cranch, 445.
(*y*) 1 Wheat. 91; 2 Cranch, 445.
(*z*) 4 Wash. C. C. 199.

(*a*) Ibid. 344.
(*b*) 3 D. 382; 4 Ibid. 7; 6 Wheat. 151; 3 Cranch, 515; 8 Howard, 586.
(*c*) 1 Cranch, 343.
(*d*) 2 Cranch, 9.
(*e*) 1 M'Lean, 412.
(*f*) 2 Mason, 472.
(*g*) 8 Peters, 112.
(*h*) 1 Sumner, 578.
(*i*) 6 Howard, 31.

But where after a cause had gone up to the Supreme Court and been there decided upon its merits and remanded to the Circuit Court, it was discovered that the jurisdiction of the court did not appear upon the record; it was held that, as the mandate of the Supreme Court only required the execution of its decree, the Circuit Court were bound to carry it into execution, notwithstanding the defect of jurisdiction.(j)

When an amendment is made in the Supreme Court by consent of counsel, which amendment sets forth the facts giving jurisdiction, a mandate containing that amendment should prevent any subsequent objection to the jurisdiction in the Circuit Court.(k)

The courts of the United States being courts of limited jurisdiction, although not inferior courts, in the language of the common law,(l) their proceedings are erroneous unless their jurisdiction appears upon the record.(m) Their jurisdiction is so limited, that the presumption is that a cause is without their jurisdiction until the contrary appears; but their proceedings are not nullities, as in the case of inferior courts.(n)

But the question of citizenship to oust the jurisdiction of the court must be pleaded in abatement,(o) and under a plea in bar it cannot be raised at the trial on the merits.(p) Nor after final judgment for plaintiff is it competent for the court at a subsequent term to strike out the judgment on the ground of want of jurisdiction.(q)

5. It is not necessary to aver that the defendant is an inhabitant of the district where the action is brought, or that he was found therein. The exemption of the defendant from suit, except in the district where he is found or where he resides, is a privilege which he may waive by a voluntary appearance.(r) If the marshal, however, return that the defendant is not an inhabitant of the district, it is said that the law will abate the suit.(rr)

Neither the Circuit nor District Courts, either in suits at law or in equity, can send their process into another district, except where specially authorized by Congress.(s)

Nor can judgment be rendered against any defendant, not served with process issued against his person in the manner pointed out by the judiciary act, unless the defendant waive the necessity of such process.(t)

Under the clause in the 11th section of the judicial act which prohibits the bringing of a civil suit against an inhabitant of the United States by any original process in any other district than that whereof he is an inhabitant, or in which he shall be found at the time of serving the writ, it was held that a foreign attachment would not lie in the Circuit Court against the effects of an inhabitant of the United States.(u) And though in several cases in the Circuit Court for the Eastern District of Pennsylvania, where the defendant was an alien residing out of the

---

(j) 6 Cranch, 267.
(k) 8 Howard, 586.
(l) 4. D. 11.
(m) 5 Cranch, 185.
(n) Ibid.; 10 Wheat. 192; 2 D. 340; Ibid. 330.
(o) 1 Peters, 498; 11 Ibid. 80.
(p) 6 Howard, 1; 7 Howard, 198.
(q) 6 Howard, 41.

(r) 8 Wheat. 699; 3 Mason, 158; 4 Cranch, 421; 3 Ibid. 496; 5 Ibid. 288; 1 Peters, C. C. R. 489, 431; 5 Cranch, 288.
(rr) 7 Cranch, 201-2.
(s) 3, Wash. C. C. 456.
(t) 15 Peters, 167; 12 Ibid. 300.
(u) 2 D. 396.

United States,(v) writs of foreign attachment were adjudicated upon without any exception being taken to the jurisdiction of the court, yet the Supreme Court held, in Toland v. Sprague,(w) that the right to attach property to compel the appearance of persons can properly be used only in cases in which such persons are amenable to the process of the court in *personam*—that is, where they are inhabitants of, or found within, the United States ; and not where they are aliens or citizens resident abroad at the commencement of the suit, and have no habitancy here. It is proper to remark that the question of the jurisdiction of the courts in foreign attachments against non-resident aliens was not properly before the court, as the record stated the defendant to be a citizen of Massachusetts, the point before the court being the same as that in 5 Mason, 35, in which it was held that where a party defendant is a citizen of the United States, resident in a foreign country, and not having any inhabitancy in any State of the Union, the Circuit Courts of the United States have no power to maintain jurisdiction over him at the suit of an alien, although he has property in the district which may be attached.

An important change has been produced in the jurisdiction of this court, depending upon the residence of the parties, by the act of 1839,(x) which provides that where, in suits brought in the courts of the United States, at law or in equity, there shall be several defendants, any one or more of whom shall not be inhabitants of, or found within, the district where the suit is brought, or shall not voluntarily appear thereto, it shall be lawful for the court to entertain jurisdiction and proceed to trial and adjudication of such suit between the parties who may be properly before it ; but the judgment or decree rendered therein shall not conclude or prejudice other parties not regularly served with process or not voluntarily appearing to answer ; and the non-joinder of parties who are not so inhabitants or found within the district, shall constitute no matter of abatement or other objection to said suit. § 1.

Under this act it has been decided that the act of 1839 did not contemplate a change in the jurisdiction of the court as regards the character of the parties as prescribed by the judiciary act; that is, that each of the plaintiffs must be capable of suing, and each of the defendants of being sued.(y)

6. The provision of the eleventh section, that an assignee of a chose in action shall not sue in the Circuit Court, unless a suit might have been brought there, if no assignment had been made, was intended to prevent persons who have no right to sue in a Circuit Court, from acquiring such a right at their pleasure, by a colorable assignment. And this restriction has been decided not to be inconsistent with that part of the third article of the constitution which provides that the judicial power of the United States shall extend to controversies between citizens of different States.(z)

Under this clause it has been held that a note payable to a certain person or bearer was not a case within the provision. In such case there is no assignment, but the note passes by mere delivery, and the

(v) 2 Wash. C. C. 382; Ibid. 480 ; 3 Ibid. 560 ; 1 Peters, C. C. 245.
(w) 12 Peters, 300.

(x) Act of Feb. 28 ; U. S. Stat. at large, v. v. p. 521.
(y) 14 Peters, 60.
(z) 8 Howard, 441.

bearer is an original party to the contract.(a)   And a note made paya_ble to the maker's own order and by him indorsed, passes by delivery as if it were made payable to bearer, and the Circuit Courts have juris_diction of an action brought against the maker by the holder who is a citizen of another State, where the amount exceeds $500.(b)

Where the payees of a note given by citizens of the same State, removed from the State where it was given into another State, and became citizens thereof, before the note fell due, held, that they or their indorsees might sue in the Circuit Court.(c)

The indorsee of a promissory note may sue his immediate indorser in the Circuit Court, although he could not the maker; for he does not claim through an assignment, but the suit is brought on the new con-tract between the indorser and indorsee.(d)   But where the suit is against a remote indorser, it is necessary, in order to give the court jurisdiction, that the plaintiff should have been able to sue, in the Cir-cuit Court, every intermediate indorser through whom he traces his title in the declaration, as well as the indorser sued.(e)

And where an action is brought by the assignee, of a promissory note or bill, in the Circuit Court of the United States, the declaration must show that the assignee could have sued in that court.(f)

Where a mortgagor and mortgagee resided in the same State, and the mortgagee assigned the mortgage to a citizen of another State— held, that the assignee could not file a bill for foreclosure in the Circuit Court of the United States.(g)

The assignees of an insolvent debtor under the laws of a State can-not sue in the Circuit Court, unless a suit could have been brought there if no assignment had been made; for they are within the letter if not within the spirit of the law; and do not stand on the same prin-ciple as executors, who are not the assignees but the representatives of a party.(h)   Executors and administrators are not *assignees* within the meaning of this act.(i)   It was held in this case that open accounts and all other choses in action were equally within the act with promissory notes.   As the bank of the United States did not derive its right to sue from the eleventh section of the act of 1789, but from a different law, it might sue in this court on a chose in action assigned to it, not-withstanding a suit could not have been brought here if no assignment had been made.(j)

And even where the subject of the suit is not a chose in action, and, consequently, not within the letter of the law, but a party has, by an assignment, made for the purpose, endeavored to acquire the privilege of suing in the Circuit Court, the court has extended the spirit of the law to the case, and held that they had no jurisdiction.(k)   The assign-ments in these cases were conveyances of land, and merely colorable and collusive, and considered by the court as frauds upon the law.   In

---

(a) 1 Mason, 251; 9 Wheat. 908; 2 Peters, 318; 15 Ibid. 125; 3 Mason, 308; 3 Howard, 574.
  (b) 1 W. & M. 115.
  (c) 6 Peters, 20.
  (d) 6 Wheat. 151; 3 Day, 3.
  (e) 9 Wheat. 538.
  (f) 3 M'Lean, 106; 2 Ibid. 126.

(g) 8 Howard, 441; overruling 3 M'-Lean, 204.
  (h) 6 Cranch, 334.   But see 4 Cranch, 306.
  (i) 4 Wash. 349.
  (j) 9 Wheat. 908.
  (k) 2 D. 381; 4 Ibid. 330, S. C. 1 Wash. C. C. R. 70.

refusing to sustain the suits, the court did no more than was done in a case already noticed,(*l*) in order to support the jurisdiction of the court. They looked beyond the nominal parties, to the real parties to the controversy.

But to divest the court of its jurisdiction, it is necessary to bring home to the assignee a knowledge of this motive and purpose; till then he must be considered an innocent purchaser without notice.(*m*)

And where the conveyance, although made in order that a suit might be brought upon it in the Circuit Court, was not colorable, but from a trustee to his *cestui que* trust, and such a one as a Court of Equity would have decreed, it was held that the court had jurisdiction.(*n*)

As the different citizenship of the parties must be averred upon record, in order to give the court jurisdiction, so also it is equally necessary, where the suit is brought upon a chose in action, which has been assigned, that the citizenship of the assignors to, or through whom the plaintiff traces his title, should appear upon the record.(*o*)

In cases of violation of patent rights under either of the acts of 1793(*p*) or 1800,(*q*) original jurisdiction is given to the Circuit Court by the following section of the last-mentioned act: "Where any patent shall be, or shall have been, granted pursuant to this or the above-mentioned act, and any person, without the consent of the patentee, his or her executors, administrators, or assigns, first obtained, in writing, shall make, devise, use, or sell the thing whereof the exclusive right is secured to the said patentee by such patent, such person so offending shall forfeit and pay to the said patentee, his executors, administrators, or assigns, a sum equal to three times the actual damage sustained by such patentee, his executors, administrators, or assigns, from or by reason of such offence, which sum shall and may be recovered by action on the case, founded on this and the above-mentioned act, in the Circuit Court of the United States having jurisdiction thereof."(*r*) § 3.

The following section of the act of 1793 contains some provisions regulating the practice in actions under the above section: "The defendant in such action shall be permitted to plead the general issue, and give this act, and any special matter of which notice in writing may have been given, to the plaintiff or his attorney, thirty days before trial, in evidence, tending to prove that the specification filed by the plaintiff does not contain the whole truth relative to his discovery, or that it contains more than is necessary to produce the described effect, which concealment or addition shall fully appear to have been made for the purpose of deceiving the public, or that the thing thus secured by patent was not originally discovered by the patentee, but had been in use, or had been described in some public work, anterior to the supposed discovery of the patentee, or that he had surreptitiously obtained a patent for the discovery of another person; in either of which cases judgment shall be rendered for the defendant, with costs, and the patent shall be declared void."(*s*) § 6.

(*l*) 5 Cranch. 303.
(*m*) 7 Howard, 198.
(*n*) 1 Wash. C. C. R. 429; 4 D. 338, n.
(*o*) 4 D. 8; 4 Cranch, 47; 9 Wheat. 538.

(*p*) Act of Feb. 21.
(*q*) Act of April 17.
(*r*) U. S. Stat. at large, v. ll. p. 38.
(*s*) U. S. Stat. at large, v. i. p. 322.

Where a suit was brought in the Supreme Court of the State for the infringement of a patent right, and the defendant pleaded to the juris-diction of the court, the court sustained the plea, on the ground that the Circuit Court must have exclusive jurisdiction, for the reasons, that the judicial power of the United States extends to all cases arising under the laws of the United States, and the act declares that suits on patents shall be brought in the Circuit Court, and gives that court power to declare the patent void.(t) Nor will the fact that the defendant has agreed, upon a valuable consideration, to waive the objection of want of jurisdiction, make any difference, as consent cannot confer jurisdiction.(u) And it has been held that for the same reasons a patent right could not even be pleaded or set up as a defence or justification to an action in a State court, but that the party must be sent to the Circuit Court in order to test the validity of his patent, and seek the competent redress.(v) From the principles of these decisions, it would seem that a State court can never directly or indirectly inquire into the value or validity of a patent.

Under these acts it was held that the Circuit Courts had no juris-diction in equity upon a bill to restrain the infringement of rights secured by patent, because no such jurisdiction had been conferred by Congress.(w)

But a subsequent act,(x) gives the court original jurisdiction in all cases, as well in equity as at law, arising under the patent acts securing to authors or inventors the property in their writings, inventions, and discoveries, including, as will be seen by a reference to those acts, as well suits for forfeitures as for damages.(y)

The act is as follows: "The Circuit Courts of the United States shall have original cognizance, as well in equity as at law, of all actions, suits, controversies and cases, arising under any law of the United States, granting or confirming to authors or inventors the exclusive right to their respective writings, inventions and discoveries; and upon any bill in equity, filed by any party aggrieved in any such cases, shall have authority to grant injunctions, according to the course and principles of Courts of Equity, to prevent the violation of the rights of any authors or inventors, secured to them by any laws of the United States, on such terms and conditions as the said courts may deem fit and reasonable; *Provided*, however, that from all judgments and decrees of any Circuit Courts, rendered in the premises, a writ of error or appeal, as the case may require, shall lie to the Supreme Court of the United States, in the same manner, and under the same circumstances, as is now provided by law in other judgments and decrees of such Circuit Courts."

Under the general patent law of 1836(z) the same section is re-en-acted, being limited, however, in that act, to inventors.

The jurisdiction of the Circuit Courts of the United States under these acts is without regard to the character of the parties, or to the amount in controversy—or in other words, as well where the parties are

(t) 7 Johns. 144.
(u) 3 Coms. 9.
(v) 9 Johns. 567, 582.
(w) 1 Paine, 45.
(x) Act of Feb. 15, 1819; U. S. Stat. at large, v. iii. p. 481.

(y) Act of April 29, 1802; Act of May 31, 1790; Act of June 4, 1790; Act of April 29, 1802.
(z) July 4, U. S. Stat. at large, § 17, v. v. p. 124.

citizens of the same State as when they are citizens of different States, or one of them is an alien, and as where the sum claimed is less as when it is more than $500.(a)

The act of 1794,(b) prohibiting the slave-trade, gave the Circuit Court as well as District Courts cognizance of forfeitures incurred under its provisions, and the act of 1800 declares, that " the District and Circuit Courts of the United States shall have cognizance of all acts and offences against the prohibitions herein contained;" certain penalties being affixed to the prohibited acts.(c) And perhaps the Circuit Court has jurisdiction, as well as the District Court, of suits for forfeitures under the act of 1803, passed for the same object,(d) as it has under that of 1807,(e) but does not appear to have any under that of 1818.(f)

The act regulating passenger ships gives the Circuit as well as District Courts original jurisdiction in actions for penalties incurred by a ship's carrying more than the number of passengers allowed.(g)

The Circuit Court has jurisdiction conferred concurrent with the District Courts, under the act of 1838,(h) in causes under acts relating to steamboats, and by the act of 1845,(i) relating to the post-office. all causes of action arising under that act may be sued in any District or Circuit Court of the United States.

The following provision of the collection law of 1799,(j) gives the Circuit Court and District Courts original jurisdiction in actions by assignees of debentures, against the assignors or indorsers. "For the purpose of maintaining the credit of the said debentures, it is hereby declared, that the debentures, to be issued as aforesaid, shall be assignable by delivery and indorsement of the parties who may receive the same ; and in all cases where payment shall be refused by the collectors of the districts where the said debentures were granted, in consequence of the non-payment of the duties which accrued on the importation of the goods for which such debentures were issued, for a longer time than three days after the same shall have been due and payable, said refusal to be proved in the same manner as in the case of non-payment of bills of exchange, it shall be lawful for the possessor or assignee of any debenture, upon which payment has been refused as aforesaid, to institute and maintain, in the proper Circuit or District Court of the United States, a suit against the person to whom such debenture was originally granted, or against any indorser thereof, whereby to recover the amount of such debenture, with interest, at the rate of six *per centum per annum*, from the time when the same became due and payable. And in all suits for the recovery of money, upon debentures issued by the collectors of the customs as aforesaid, it shall be the duty of the court in

(a) Conkling, Practice, ed. 1831, p. 57. Curtis on Patents, § 406 ; and the better opinion is that this jurisdiction is exclusive, Ibid. 3 Kent's Com. 368.

(b) Act of March 22 ; U. S. Stat. at large, v. i. p. 347.

(c) Act of May 10, 1800, § 5; U. S. Stat. at large, v. ii. p. 71.

(d) Act of Feb. 28, § 1; U. S. Stat. at large, v. ii. p. 205.

(e) Act of March 2, § 2; U. S. Stat. at large, v. ii. p. 426.

(f) Act of April 20; U. S. Stat. at large, v. iii. p. 450.

(g) Act of March 2, 1819, § 1 ; Laws U. S. 1723.

(h) July 7, § 11; U. S. Stat. at large, v. v. p. 306.

(i) March 3, 1845 ; U. S. Stat. at large, v. v. p. 739.

(j) Act of March 2; U. S. Stat. at large, v. i. p. 689.

which such suits shall be pending, to grant judgment at the return term, unless the defendant or defendants shall, in open court, exhibit some plea, on oath or affirmation, by which the court shall be satisfied that a continuance, until the next succeeding term, is necessary to the attain. ment of justice; in which case, and not otherwise, a continuance until the next term may be granted."

By the act of 1833,(k) the jurisdiction of the Circuit Courts of the United States is declared to extend to all cases in law or in equity arising under the revenue laws of the United States for which other provisions are not made by law; and if any person shall receive any injury to his person or property, for or on account of any act done by him, under any law of the United States for the protection of the revenue or the collection of duties on imports, he shall be entitled to maintain suit for damage therefor in the Circuit Court of the United States in the district wherein the party doing the injury may reside or be found. § 2.

By the provisions of the act incorporating the Bank of the United States, the Circuit Court had original jurisdiction, concurrently with the State courts, of all actions in which the bank were plaintiffs or defendants.(l) Notwithstanding the plain terms in which this law allowed the bank to sue in the Circuit Court, its meaning was questioned; and its constitutionality was also most strongly contested in the Supreme Court of the United States, on the ground that suits to which the bank is a party, are not "cases arising under the laws of the United States." The court, however, decided in favor of its constitutionality.(m)

With regard to the mode of objecting to the want of jurisdiction of the Circuit Court, it has already been stated that if the jurisdiction of the court depends on the character of the parties, the objection must be taken by plea in abatement, as at any subsequent stage of the cause it will be considered as waived; and that this rule, however, does not dispense with the requisite averments in the declaration. If the jurisdiction of the court depend on the subject-matter, a plea in abatement is not necessary, but the objection may be taken at any time.(n)

After having observed so many cases in which different courts have concurrent jurisdiction, it may not be improper to refer here to the established principle, that in all such cases the court which first has possession of the subject, must decide it.(o)

The authorities of a State cannot annul the judgment of the courts of the United States, nor destroy the rights acquired under those judgments.(p)

(b) *Jurisdiction by removal from the State courts.*

The following section of the judiciary act of 1789, provides for the cases in which actions are allowed to be removed from the State courts into the Circuit Courts, and also prescribes the steps which a party must take in order to entitle himself to such removal.

"If a suit be commenced in any State court against an alien, or by

(k) March 2; U. S. Stat. at large, v. iv. p. 632.
(l) Act of April 10, 1816, § 7; U. S. Stat. at large, v. iii. p. 269.
(m) 9 Wheat. 738.

(n) 2 Gall. 345; 2 Peters, 250, 409; 2 D. 368.
(o) 9 Wheat. 535; 1 Paine, 620.
(p) 5 Cranch, 135.

a citizen of the State in which the suit is brought against a citizen of another State, and the matter in dispute exceeds the sum or value of five hundred dollars, exclusive of costs, to be made to appear to the satisfaction of the court, and the defendant shall, at the time of entering his appearance in such State court, file a petition for the removal of the cause for trial into the next Circuit Court, to be held in the district where the suit is pending, and offer good and sufficient surety for his entering, in such court, on the first day of its session, copies of said process against him, and also for his there appearing and entering special bail in the cause, if special bail was originally requisite therein, it shall then be the duty of the State court to accept the surety, and proceed no further in the cause; and any bail that may have been originally taken, shall be discharged; and the said copies being entered as aforesaid, in such court of the United States, the cause shall there proceed in the same manner as if it had been brought there by original process. And any attachment of the goods or estate of the defendant, by the original process, shall hold the goods or estate so attached, to answer the final judgment, in the same manner as by the laws of such State they would have been holden to answer final judgment, had it been rendered by the court in which the suit commenced."

"And if, in any action commenced in a State court, the title of land be concerned, and the parties are citizens of the same State, and the matter in dispute exceeds the sum or value of five hundred dollars, exclusive of costs, the sum or value being made to appear to the satisfaction of the court, either party, before the trial, shall state to the court and make affidavit, if they require it, that he claims, and shall rely upon a right or title to the land, under grant from a State, other than that in which the suit is pending, and produce the original grant, or an exemplification of it, except where the loss of public records shall put it out of his power, and shall move that the adverse party inform the court whether he claims a right or title to the land under a grant from the State in which the suit is pending; the said adverse party shall give such information, or otherwise not be allowed to plead such grant or give it in evidence upon the trial; and if he informs that he does claim under such grant, the party claiming under the grant first mentioned, may then, on motion, remove the cause for trial to the next Circuit Court to be holden in such district; but if he is the defendant, shall do it under the same regulations as in the before-mentioned case of the removal of a cause into such court by an alien; and neither party removing the cause, shall be allowed to plead or give evidence of any other title than that by him stated as aforesaid, as the ground of his claim. And the trial of issues in fact in the Circuit Court, shall, in all suits except those of equity, and of admiralty and maritime jurisdiction, be by jury." § 12.

It will be observed, that the jurisdiction which the court has, by removal of causes under this section, on account of the citizenship or alienage of parties, is not so extensive as that which is given by the eleventh section, on account of such character of parties; the jurisdiction under this section arising from such character, being confined to suits against aliens or by a citizen of this State against a citizen of another State. But the principles generally which have been settled under the eleventh section, as to whether the court is entitled to juris- diction on account of the character of the parties, apply equally to this section. And all questions under this section, as to the amount in controversy, necessary to give the court jurisdiction, are governed by the same rules as have been established under the eleventh section.

In drawing a petition for the removal of a cause, the same exactness should be observed in describing the character of the parties, as we have seen is required in process and pleadings under the eleventh section; and a motion for a removal was refused because the defendant described himself as a resident and not as a citizen of another State.(q)

If there be two defendants, the petition must be by both, or the cause cannot be removed.(r)

But where a *capias* in an action for a tort is served only upon one of the defendants, and the plaintiff declares against the defendant so served, such defendant may make application to have the cause re- moved to the Circuit Court, without joining the others named as defendants.(s)

Although the amount of damages laid in the declaration in *assumpsit* is *prima facie* to be considered the amount in dispute in determining whether a cause is removable into the Circuit Court of the United States, yet it seems that it is not conclusive, and that the plaintiff may show by affidavit that his claim amounts to less than $500, in order to prevent the removal.(t)

It is the course for the defendant in his petition and affidavit to swear that the matter in dispute exceeds the sum or value of $500 exclusive of costs.(u) The petition must be signed by the party himself, and not by attorney, and he must, at the time of entering his appearance, offer the security required by the act.(v)

It has been held, that the bond given on removing the cause should be a joint and several bond, in case of more than one person being bound; and that a merely joint bond is insufficient; and a joint bond of the defendant and one surety having been given at the time of filing the petition, the court refused to allow the cause to be removed; since such a bond was not unexceptionable at law, although in chancery it might probably have been enforced against the representatives of a de- ceased obligor in case of death.(w)

In a case in which the question arose, as to what is the appearance of a party under the statute, and when such appearance is to be considered as entered, the court were nearly divided; the minority holding that the appearance could only be entered in open court, as the court were to do other acts at the same time, which could not be done except during its session; but it was decided that the appearance spoken of in the act was the ordinary appearance of the defendant, according to the practice of the court; as by filing common or special bail, where the action was commenced by *capias;* that an appearance and filing the petition were to be simultaneous acts, and that Congress did not contemplate that the court should be thus in session, but intended to put the plaintiff to a

(q) 3 Johns. 145.
(r) 4 Wash. C. C. R. 286; 2 Sum. 338.
(s) 4 Denio, 243.
(t) Per Bronson, C. J. 2 Denio, 197.
(u) 12 Johns. 153; 2 Wash. C. C. 463.

(v) 2 M. 277.
(w) Carrington v. Roberts, in the Su- perior Court of the City of New York, Sept. 1829.

prompt election of his tribunal, and give the opposite party early notice of his intention.

Under this decision, the practice is for the defendant, at the time he puts in bail, to file his petition, affidavit, and bond, and give notice of motion for the earliest day in term thereafter, for leave to remove the cause. In a case before referred to,(x) the court observed, that it was necessary that they should approve the security before the removal was a matter of right, and this they could only do as a court, and that therefore merely filing the petition and bond was not sufficient of itself to stay the proceedings: to do this a judge's order was necessary, who should have some satisfaction given him as to the grounds of removal, and sufficiency of the surety, whereupon he might order the proceedings to be stayed, that the motion to the court might be made; and that unless this was followed up by a motion at the first opportunity afterwards, the petition might be dismissed, and the defendant thus lose his opportunity of having the cause removed.

Where five months, including two terms, had elapsed after the defendant's appearance was entered, and the State court then agreed to allow the petition to be filed, as of the time when the appearance was entered, the Circuit Court held, that they could not obtain jurisdiction of the cause by this consent of the State court to permit the petition to be filed *nunc pro tunc*, when they saw that, in point of fact, it was not filed until a subsequent term.(y)

It seems that it is the duty of the Circuit Court, where a cause is improperly removed, to remand it to the court from which it came; and that even after it had reached the Supreme Court by error, that court would direct it to be remanded.(z)

In ejectment, after a default and judgment against the casual ejector, the tenant, on moving at the next term to set aside the default, also petitioned to remove the cause, and was allowed to do so, as he had had no opportunity before to make the application, since the service of the notice of the declaration.(a) And where the landlord, under the same circumstances, made a motion for the same purposes, and also to be admitted to defend as landlord, the court held that he was entitled to be admitted to defend, and that such admission was his appearance, and that he was consequently in season to remove the cause, and was entitled to do so, notwithstanding the judgment against the casual ejector.(b)

In ejectment in the State court by A, a citizen of Pennsylvania, against B, also a citizen of that State, tenant in possession, judgment by default was obtained against B; after which C, a citizen of Massachusetts, was, in his petition to the court, admitted a defendant, and the default was set aside. It was held that C could not remove the cause into the Circuit Court of the United States, under the 12th section of the judiciary act.(c)

In an action by indorsee against the maker of a promissory note, the defendant presented a petition setting forth that the plaintiff was a citizen of Pennsylvania, and he, the defendant, a citizen of New Jersey, and

(x) Carrington v. Roberts, *supra.*
(y) 1 Peters, C. C. R. 44.
(z) 4 Cranch, 428, 429. See 2 Wheat. 221.

(a) 4 Johns. 492.
(b) Ibid.
(c) 4 Wash. C. C. R. 286.

praying a removal of the case to the Circuit Court of the United States. It was held, that as the petition did not aver that the indorser was also a citizen of Pennsylvania, the petitioner was not entitled to the removal.(d)

The Circuit Court will remand a suit removed from a State court, where the State is a party.(e)

The following points have been settled as to the practice in removing causes, under the first clause of this section, from the State courts, where there are several defendants, and their appearance in the State courts is entered at different times.

The defendants were both aliens, and one of them had appeared in the State court, but the appearance of the other had not been entered, when the petition of the one who had appeared, to remove the cause, was filed. The court held, that under these circumstances the cause could not be removed, and one defendant compelled to follow his co-defendant into the Circuit Court, possibly against his will. That the removal of the cause was intended by the judiciary act to be the voluntary act of the party, and that by party was to be understood all the individuals constituting such party. The court, however, limited the application of this rule, to cases where, from the subject-matter of the suit, the judgment must be joint.(f)

The court also held in this case, that although the application to remove the cause must be made at the time of entering the appearance in the State court, yet it was not necessary that the application should be made by all the defendants at the same time; and that there was no objection to their appearance being entered in the Circuit Court at different times. That this indeed was necessary, because where the defendants were brought into court, in the State court, at different times, that court could not allow the petition for a removal to be filed *nunc pro tunc*.(g)

It was also further ruled, that if all the defendants should not petition to have the cause removed into the Circuit Court, so as to enable it to proceed, the cause might be remanded to the State court, so as to give it possession of the whole case. And finally, that an original appearance of some of the defendants could not be entered in the Circuit Court; but that the mode prescribed by the act must be pursued, in order to divest the State court of its jurisdiction, and prevent both courts from proceeding in the cause at the same time.(h)

Where the plaintiff, after a cause had been removed from a State court, remitted on record a part of the damages laid in the declaration, the court declared that they could not be thus ousted of their jurisdiction;(i) but the plaintiff may amend his declaration in the State court after the defendant has presented his petition, by reducing the damages below five hundred dollars, after which the cause cannot be removed.(j)

It was held in the Supreme Court of Appeals of the State of Virginia, that if an inferior court refused to allow a defendant, on his complying with the terms of the act, to remove a cause which is within the act, to the Circuit Court, it might be compelled to allow the removal, by mandamus from the superior State court;(k) and if, in such a case, in

(d) 2 M. 459, & S. C. in C. C. U. S., n. p. 463.
(e) 4 Wash. C. C. 344.
(f) 1 Paine, 414, 415.
(g) Ibid. 1 Peters, C. C. R. 44.

(h) Ibid. and see 4 Cranch, 429.
(i) 1 Peters, C. C. R. 220.
(j) 2 Denio, 197.
(k) 4 Hen. & Mun. 173. *Sed quere—* Whether the Circuit Court, in such a

this State, the Supreme Court should refuse a mandamus, perhaps the course might be to bring a writ of error, upon their judgment, from the Court of Errors,(*l*) and carry it, if necessary, to the Supreme Court of the United States.(*m*)

The defendant being entitled to a right to have the cause removed, under the law of the United States, the judge of the State Court has no discretion to withhold the right; and the application having been made in the proper form, every step subsequently taken in the exercise of a jurisdiction in the case, is *coram non judice.*(*n*)

A case arose under the latter clause of this section, where one party claimed lands under a grant from the State of New Hampshire, and the other under a grant from the State of Vermont, Vermont having been, at the time of the first grant, a part of New Hampshire; and it was contended that the court, from this circumstance, had no jurisdiction; but on an appeal to the Supreme Court it was determined that they had.(*o*)

So also where both parties obtained inchoate titles from the same State before its separation into two States, and after such separation received conflicting grants from the two new States, these grants were held to be from different States, the constitution and laws looking to the grants as the test of jurisdiction, and to any equitable title previously acquired.(*p*)

The act of 1833(*q*) provides for the removal to the Circuit Court of the United States, of causes commenced in the State courts against any officer of the United States, or other person, for or on account of any act done under the revenue laws of the United States, or under color thereof, or for or on account of any right, authority, or title set up or claimed by such officer, or other person, under any such law of the United States.   § 3.

(c.) *Jurisdiction by removal from the District Court.*

Besides the jurisdiction which the Circuit Court exercises over suits commenced in the District Courts by writ of error, there is still another mode by which such suits may come before it, although rather in the exercise of a substituted original, than an appellate jurisdiction. This is when causes are removed from a District into the Circuit Court by reason of the disability of the district judge to hold the District Court, or on account of his supposed want of impartiality in a cause, arising from his being concerned in interest, or having been of counsel for a party, or related to him. The following acts contain the provisions for this purpose :—

" In case of the disability of the district judge of either of the districts of the United States, to hold a District Court, and to perform the duties of his office, and satisfactory evidence thereof being shown to the justice of the Supreme Court, allotted to that circuit in which such Dis_

---

case, might not grant a mandamus or certiorari, being necessary for the exercise of its jurisdiction? See 4 Hen. & Hun. 179; 1 Wheat. 302, and *ante;* 1 Cooke, 160.

(*l*) That it would lie, see 6 Johns. 337; 12 Johns. 31; 6 Wheat. 598; 7 Wheat. 534.

(*m*) But *quere*—If the cause were de_ pending in the Supreme Court of the State.

(*n*) 16 Peters, 97.
(*o*) 9 Cranch, 292.
(*p*) 2 Wheat. 377.
(*q*) March 2, 1833, U. S. Stat. at large, v. iv. p. 663.

trict Court ought by law to be holden ; and on application of the district attorney, or marshal of such district, in writing, to the said justice of the Supreme Court, said justice of the Supreme Court shall thereupon issue his order, in the nature of a *certiorari*, directed to the clerk of such District Court, requiring him forthwith to certify into the next Circuit Court to be holden in said district, all actions, suits, causes, pleas, or processes, civil or criminal, of what nature or kind soever, that may be depending in said District Court, and undetermined, with all the proceedings thereon, and all files and papers relating thereto ; which said orders shall be immediately published in one or more newspapers, printed in said district, and at least thirty days before the session of such Circuit Court, and shall be deemed a sufficient notification to all concerned. And the said Circuit Court shall thereupon have the same cognizance of all such actions, suits, causes, pleas, or processes, civil or criminal, of what nature or kind soever, and in the like manner as the District Court of said district by law, might have, or the Circuit Court, had the same been originally commenced therein ; and shall proceed to hear and determine the same accordingly ; and the said justice of the Supreme Court, during the continuance of such disability, shall, moreover, be invested with, and exercise all and singular the powers and authority vested by law in the judge of the District Court in said district. And all bonds and recognizances taken for, or returnable to, such District Court, shall be construed and taken to be to the Circuit Court, to be holden thereafter, in pursuance of this act, and shall have the same force and effect in such Circuit Court, as they could have had in the District Court to which they were taken. *Provided,* That nothing in this act contained shall be so construed as to require the judge of the Supreme Court, within whose circuit such district may lie, to hold any special court, or Court of Admiralty, at any other time than the legal time for holding the Circuit Court of the United States in and for such district."(*n*)

" The clerk of such District Court shall, during the continuance of the disability of the district judge, continue to certify as aforesaid, all suits or actions, of what nature or kind soever, which may thereafter be brought to such District Court, and the same transmit to the Circuit Court next thereafter to be holden in the same district ; and the said Circuit Court shall have cognizance of the same, in like manner as is hereinbefore provided in this act, and shall proceed to hear and determine the same : *Provided, nevertheless,* That when the disability of the district judge shall cease or be removed, all suits or actions then pending and undetermined in the Circuit Court, in which by law the District Courts have an exclusive original cognizance, shall be remanded, and the clerk of the said Circuit Court shall transmit the same, pursuant to the order of said court, with all matters and things relating thereto, to the District Court next thereafter to be holden in said district, and the same proceedings shall be had therein in said District Court, as would have been, had the same originated, or been continued, in the said District Court."(*o*)

" In all suits and actions in any District Court of the United States,

(*n*) Act of March 2, 1809, § 1; U. S.   (*o*) Ibid. § 2.
Stat. at large, v. ii. p. 534.

in which it shall appear that the judge of such court is anywise concerned in interest, or has been of counsel for either party, or is so related to, or connected with, either party, as to render it improper for him, in his opinion, to sit on the trial of such suit or action, it shall be the duty of such judge, on application of either party, to cause the fact to be entered on the records of the court; and also an order that an authenticated copy thereof, with all the proceedings in such suit or action, shall be forthwith certified to the next Circuit Court of the district; and if there be no Circuit Court in such district, to the next Circuit Court in the State; and if there be no Circuit Court in such State, to the most convenient Circuit Court in an adjacent State; which Circuit Court shall, upon such record being filed with the clerk thereof, take cognizance thereof, in the like manner as if such suit or action had been originally commenced in that court, and shall proceed to hear and determine the same accordingly; and the jurisdiction of such Circuit Court shall extend to all such cases so removed, as were cognizable in the District Court from which the same were removed."(p)

In a case which arose under the first of these acts, after the cause had been removed into the Circuit Court on account of the disability of the district judge, and before any determination of the cause in the Circuit Court, the district judge died: It was contended that, the disability having now become permanent, the court should go on and make a final disposition of the cause: But the court held, that on the contrary, the vacancy removed the disability, and that the cause must be remanded to the District Court for determination.(q)

(d.) *Appellate Jurisdiction by writ of error to the District Court.*

The appellate jurisdiction of the Circuit Courts, to take cognizance of causes brought before them for re-examination by writ of error to the District Courts, is conferred by the 22d section of the judiciary act of 1789,(r) which provides that final decrees and judgments in civil actions in a District Court, where the matter in dispute exceeds the sum or value of fifty dollars, exclusive of costs, may be re-examined and reversed or affirmed in a Circuit Court holden in the same district upon a writ of error, whereto shall be annexed and returned therewith, at the day and place therein mentioned, an authenticated transcript of the record, an assignment of errors, and prayer for reversal, with a citation to the adverse party, signed by the judge of such District Court, or a justice of the Supreme Court, the adverse party having at least twenty days' notice.

The same section also provides that writs of error shall be brought within five years after the rendering of the judgment, with an exception in the cases of infants, *femes covert*, persons *non compos mentis*, or imprisoned—in which cases the writ of error must be brought within five years, exclusive of the time of such disability.

The 23d section provides that a writ of error shall be a supersedeas and stay of execution only where the writ of error is served, in the manner therein provided, within ten days after rendering judgment, Sundays exclusive; until the expiration of which term of ten days, no execution shall issue in such cases where a writ of error operates as a supersedeas.

(p) Act of March 3, 1821; U. S. Stat. at large, v. iii. p. 643; see act of May 8, 1792, § 11; U. S. Stat. at large, v. i. p. 278.

(q) 1 Gall. 338.
(r) U. S. Stat. at large, v. i. p. 84.

The 22d section also requires the plaintiff in error to enter bail to prosecute his suit to effect, and answer all damages and costs if he fail to make his plea good.

The 24th section provides that when a judgment shall be reversed in a Circuit Court, such court shall proceed to render such judgment or pass such decree as the District Court should have rendered or passed. In cases of appeal or writ of error, the judgment is to be rendered in accordance with the opinion of the justice of the Supreme Court.(s)

Final judgments and decrees of the State courts authorized by the first section of act of March 3, 1815, to take cognizance of complaints, suits, and prosecutions, for taxes, duties, fines, penalties, and forfeitures, under the acts of Congress for the collection of taxes or internal duties of the United States, may be re-examined in the Circuit Court of the United States, under the same limitations as are prescribed by the twenty-second section of the judiciary act of 1789.(t)

The following rule has been adopted in the Circuit Court of the United States for the Eastern District of Pennsylvania: "Appeals and writs of error shall be heard, in the Circuit Court, at the return term, and shall not be continued, even by consent of counsel, unless for a legal reason assigned, or because the case is not reached. If, when the case is reached, a legal reason be not assigned for putting it off, judgment of *non pros* shall be entered, with double costs, in case the plaintiff be the appellant or plaintiff in error; and in case the defendant be the appellant or plaintiff in error, judgment shall be entered against him for the same sum, or in the same way for which the District Court had rendered it, with interest, double costs, and such damages for delay as the court may deem just."(u)

Proceedings in the District Court, under the tenth section of the patent act of 21st February, 1793,(v) are to be deemed civil actions, within the meaning of the judicial act, and a writ of error will lie on the judgment in such proceedings to the Circuit Court.

The twenty days' notice which the adverse party is to have upon the allowance of a writ of error, is understood to be twenty days before the return of the writ.(w)

By the act of 1803,(x) an appeal from all final judgments and decrees of the District Court, where the matter in dispute exceeds, exclusive of costs, the sum of fifty dollars, is allowed to the Circuit Court next to be holden in this district. A question arose under this section, whether it was not intended to confer upon suitors the privilege of electing the process of appeal, instead of the writ of error, in actions at common law; but it was held not to apply to them, but to have been designed for the purpose, only of diminishing the amount before required on appeals from decrees of the District Court in equity and admiralty causes, and of relieving such causes from the embarrassments attending their removal, by writ of error, into the Supreme Court, under the provisions of the act of 1789.(y)

(s) Act of April 29, 1802, § 5; U. S. Stat. at large, v. ii. p. 158.
(t) Act of March 3, 1815, § 2; U. S. Stat. at large, v. iii. p. 245.
(u) Rule 3, § 3.
(v) *Ante*, p. 142.
(w) 7 Peters, 220.
(x) Act of March 3, § 2; Laws U. S. 905.
(y) 1 Gall. 5; 2 Wheat. 132; see 7 Cranch, 108.

A fuller consideration of the subject of the appellate jurisdiction of this court, will be found by reference to the section of this chapter treating of the Supreme Court—the statutory provisions and practice in relation to writs of error being nearly the same in both courts.

Before closing the subject of the jurisdiction of the Circuit Courts, it is to be noticed, that these courts, as well as the other courts of the United States, are governed in the exercise of all branches of their jurisdiction by the laws of the State, where the constitution and laws of the United States are not applicable to the case. This is provided for by the following section of the act of 1789 : "The laws of the several States, except where the constitution, treaties, or statutes of the United States shall otherwise require or provide, shall be regarded as rules of decision in trials at common law, in the courts of the United States, in cases where they apply."(z)   It will presently be seen, however, that this provision is not construed to extend to the process and practice of the courts of the United States.

The acts of limitation of the several States, where no special provision has been made by Congress, form rules of decision in the courts of the United States, and the same effect is given to them as in the State courts.(a)   And the Supreme Court has uniformly adopted the decisions of the State tribunals, respectively, in all cases where the decisions of a State court have become a rule of property.(b)

Where the highest court of a State has given a decision that a corporation, chartered by the legislature of such State, has violated its charter in taking a certain mortgage, the courts of the United States, in a suit upon the same mortgage, will follow the decision of the State court.(c)

The acts of assembly limiting the lien of judgments to five years, unless revived by *scire facias*, has been considered a rule of property binding on the Circuit Court for the Eastern District of Pennsylvania, and therefore adopted by it, although passed subsequently to 1789 ;(d) and the Circuit Court of the United States, sitting in Pennsylvania, in a suit with regard to the assets of a decedent, are administering the laws of that State, and bound by the rules governing the local tribunals, as in requiring security from a devisee or legatee to refund on the discovery of debts against the estate.(e)

The courts of the United States are bound to take judicial cognizance of the laws of the several States;(f) and in cases depending on the construction of the laws of a particular State, will in general adopt the construction given to them by the courts of that State.(g)

The distinction between local and transitory actions is recognized in the courts of the United States, and actions in their nature local, according to the laws of the State where they arise, must be prosecuted only in the Circuit Court for the district where they originate.(h)   In a late case it was held, that a Pennsylvania plaintiff might sustain

(z) ∂ 34.
(a) 3 Peters, 270 ; 13 Peters, 245.
(b) 6 Peters, 291 ; 12 Wheat. 153 ; 9 Cranch, 89 ; 2 Wheat. 316.
(c) 7 How. 198.
(d) 1 Wallace, Jr. 196 ; 1 Baldwin, 259 ; see act of July 4, 1840, *post*, p. 173.

(e) 4 How. U. S. 498. CATRON, J.
(f) 2 Sumner, 402.
(g) 10 Wheat. 152 ; 7 How. 1.
(h) 4 Am. Law Jour. 78; 1 Brock, 203 ; 1 Wallace, Jr. 275.

an action in the Circuit Court of the United States for New Jersey, against a corporation chartered by the latter State, for consequential injuries done to the plaintiff's real property lying in Pennsylvania, the cause of the injury, the canal, being situated in New Jersey, on the ground that the action was not in its nature local.(*hh*)

With regard to the jurisdiction in equity of the Circuit Courts of the United States it is proper, also, here to remark, that their equity jurisdiction is independent of the local law of any State, and is the same in nature and extent as the equity jurisdiction of England, from whence it is derived; and the fact that there are no equity courts in the State of the district will not prevent the exercise of equity jurisdiction by the United States court,(*i*) and it is not sufficient to oust the equity jurisdiction of these courts, that the plaintiff has a remedy given at the common law by the local law of the State (*j*)

And in the Circuit Court of the United States for the Western District of Pennsylvania, in a late case, it was held, that the statute of April 13, 1807, making two verdicts and judgments thereon in ejectment conclusive, was intended to supply a want of equitable jurisdiction in the State courts, and that it did not affect the equity jurisdiction of that court, which would enjoin a plaintiff in ejectment on the law side of the court from proceeding further in his suit, a proper case being made out, though the identical title in question had not been settled in accordance with that act.(*k*)

As the constitution and laws of the United States are also the paramount law of the State courts, with a final appeal to the Supreme Court of the United States, in all cases where they come in question there can be but one rule of decision in all our courts, whether they be of federal or of State origin.

(3.) *Process.*

Before proceeding to consider the process and practice of the Circuit Court, it will be proper to present the reader with the following statutory provisions conferring on the courts of the United States the power to regulate those subjects :—

"It shall be lawful for the several courts of the United States, from time to time, as occasion may require, to make rules and orders for their respective courts, directing the returning of writs and processes, and filing of declarations and other pleadings, the taking of rules, the entering and making up judgments by default, and other matters in the vacation; and otherwise, in a manner not repugnant to the laws of the United States, to regulate the practice of the said courts, respectively, as shall be fit and necessary for the advancement of justice, and especially to that end to prevent delays in proceedings."(*l*)

"All the said courts of the United States shall have power to grant new trials, in cases where there has been a trial by jury, for reasons for which new trials have usually been granted in the courts of law, and

---

(*hh*) 1 Wallace Jr. 275.
(*i*) 15 Peters, 9; 2 M'Lean, 568, 571; 2 Story, 553.
(*j*) 4 Washington, C. C. 349; 2 Sumner, 401.

(*k*) Craft *v.* Lathrop, C. C. U. S. West. Dist. of Penna. 2 Wallace, Jr.
(*l*) Act of March 2, 1793, § 7; U. S. Stat. at large, v. i. p. 335.

shall have power to impose and administer all necessary oaths or affirmations, and to punish by fine or imprisonment, at the discretion of said courts, all contempts of authority in any cause or hearing before the same; and to make and establish all necessary rules for the orderly conducting business in the said courts, provided such rules are not repugnant to the laws of the United States."(*m*)

By the following provisions of an act of 1793,(*n*) the subpœnas of the courts of the United States are allowed to run into any other district: " Subpœnas for witnesses, who may be required to attend a court of the United States, in any district thereof, may run into any other district: *Provided*, That in civil causes, the witnesses living out of the district in which the court is holden, do not live at a greater distance than one hundred miles from the place of holding the same."

The judiciary act of 1789, § 14, provides: " That all the courts of the United States shall have power to issue writs of *scire facias, habeas corpus*, and all other writs not specially provided for by statute, which may be necessary for the exercise of their respective jurisdictions, and agreeable to the principles and usages of law. And that either of the justices of the Supreme Court, as well as judges of the District Courts, shall have power to grant writs of *habeas corpus*, for the purpose of an inquiry into the cause of commitment: *Provided*, That writs of *habeas corpus* shall, in no case, extend to prisoners in jail, unless where they are in custody, under, or by color of the authority of the United States, or are committed for trial before some court of the same, or are necessary to be brought into court to testify."

Under this section it has been held that the power of the Circuit Court to issue writs of mandamus is to be confined to those cases where it is necessary to the exercise of its jurisdiction; and the court has refused in cases over which it had undisputed jurisdiction from the character of the parties, to allow a mandamus on the ground that it was to be directed to an officer of the United States, or was to enforce some right arising under the laws of the United States.(*o*)

Where a District Court refuses to give judgment, a mandamus will lie from the Circuit Court to compel it; because the Circuit Court having jurisdiction over the final judgments of the District Court, a mandamus is in such a case necessary for the exercise of its jurisdiction; but as its jurisdiction is only to re-examine the judgments of the District Court on writ of error, it has no power to compel the court below by mandamus, to expunge amendments improperly made in the record returned with the writ of error.(*p*)

It has been decided that executions are comprehended within the words of this section,(*q*) as being equally necessary for the exercise of jurisdiction as process anterior to judgment: And that the words "agreeable to the principles and usages of law," embrace not only the principles and usages of the common law, but those of the State as they then existed.(*r*)

But the process of the Circuit Court and of the other courts of the

(*m*) Act of Sept. 24, 1789, § 17 ; U. S. Stat. at large. v. i. p. 83.
(*n*) Act of March 2, § 6.
(*o*) 7 Cranch, 504 ; 6 Wheat. 598.

(*p*) 1 Paine, 453.
(*q*) 10 Wheat. 23, 55.
(*r*) Ibid. 56.

United States, is principally regulated by the following provisions of the act of 1792: "All writs and processes issuing from the Supreme or a Circuit Court, shall bear teste of the Chief Justice of the Supreme Court, or (if that office shall be vacant), of the associate justice next in precedence; and all writs and processes issuing from a District Court, shall bear tests of the judge of such court, or (if that office shall be vacant), of the clerk thereof, which said writs and processes shall be under the seal of the court from whence they issue, and signed by the clerk thereof."(s)

"The forms of writs, executions, and other process except their style, and the forms and modes of proceeding in suits, in those of common law, shall be the same as are now used in the said courts, respectively, in pursuance of the act, entitled "An act to regulate processes in the courts of the United States;" in those of equity, and in those of admiralty and maritime jurisdiction, according to the principles, rules, and usages which belong to courts of equity and to courts of admiralty, respectively, as contradistinguished from courts of common law; except so far as may have been provided for by the act to establish the judiciary courts of the United States; subject, however, to such alterations and additions as the said courts, respectively, shall, in their discretion, deem expedient, or to such regulations as the Supreme Court of the United States shall think proper, from time to time, by rule, to prescribe to any Circuit or District Court concerning the same: *Provided*, That on judgments in any of the cases aforesaid, where different kinds of execution are issuable in succession, a *capias ad satisfaciendum* being one, the plaintiff shall have his election to take out a *capias ad satisfaciendum* in the first instance."(t)

The act referred to in the above act is the expired process act of 1789; the provisions of which, so far as they are material to a right understanding of the existing law, are as follows :—

"Until further provision shall be made, and except where, by this act or other statutes of the United States, is otherwise próvided, the forms of writs and executions, except their style and modes of process, and rates of fees, except fees to judges, in the Circuit and District Courts, in suits at common law, shall be the same in each State respectively as are now used, or allowed in the Supreme Courts of the same. And the forms and modes of proceedings in causes of equity, and of admiralty and maritime jurisdiction, shall be according to the course of the civil law. And the rates of fees the same as are or were last allowed by the States respectively, in the court exercising supreme jurisdiction in such cases. *Provided*, That on judgments in any of the cases aforesaid, where different kinds of executions are issuable in succession, a *capias ad satisfaciendum* being one, the plaintiff shall have his election, to take out a *capias ad satisfaciendum* in the first instance, and be at liberty to pursue the same, until a tender of the debt and costs in gold or silver shall be made."(u)

So far as the process act adopts the State laws, the adoption is expressly confined to those in force in 1789. It does not recognize the authority of any laws which might be afterwards passed by the States.

(s) Act of May 8, §1; U. S. Stat. at large, v. i. p. 275.
(t) Ibid. § 2.

(u) Act of Sept. 29, 1789, § 2; U. S. Stat. at large, v. i. p 93.

The system as it then stood is adopted; subject, however, to such alterations and additions as the said courts respectively in their discretion might deem expedient, or to such regulations as the Supreme Court shall think proper from time to time by rule to prescribe to any Circuit or District Court concerning the same,(v) and this provision enabled the several courts of the Union to make such improvements in the forms and modes of the proceedings as experience might suggest; and especially to adopt such State laws on the subject as might vary to advantage the forms and modes of proceeding which prevailed in September, 1789.(w)

The constitutional validity and extent of the power given to the courts of the United States to make alterations and additions in the process as well as in the modes of proceeding was fully considered in the cases of Wayman v. Southard,(x) and the Bank of the U. S. v. Halstead.(y) The delegation of power was regarded as constitutional, and that a power to alter and add embraced the whole progress of a suit from its commencement to its termination, and until the judgment should be satisfied. And it was held that the courts might so alter the form of process of execution used in the State courts as to subject to execution issuing out of the federal courts, lands and other property not thus subject by the State laws.(z)

But a material change in the final process of the United States courts was effected by the act of May 19th, 1828, the third section of which provides that "writs of execution and other final process issued in judgments and decrees rendered in any of the courts of the United States, and the proceedings thereupon shall be the same, except their style in each State, respectively as are now used in the courts of such State." * * * * "Provided, however, that it shall be in the power of the courts, if they see fit in their discretion, by rules of court, so far to alter final process in said courts as to conform the same to any change which may be adopted by the legislatures of the respective States for the State courts.(a)

The object of this act was to produce uniformity between final process issued out of the courts of the United States and that issued out of the State courts; and it is to be observed that the power of the courts to alter by rules, final process, was limited so as only to enable them to adopt subsequent alterations which might be made by the laws of the respective States.

Under this act of 1828, it was held that a discharge of the principal under the insolvent laws of the State of Ohio was a defence to an action brought against the bail in a suit against the principal in the Circuit Court of the United States,(b) and that this provision gives to debtors imprisoned under executions issued out of the courts of the United States, at the suit of the United States, the privilege of the jail limits in the several States, as they were fixed by laws of the several States at the date of that act.(c)

And it was held (d) that under the act of 1828, the forthcoming

(v) 10 Wheat. 51; 3 Wash. 328; 3 Wash. 503.

(w) 10 Wheat. 1; 10 Wheat. 51; 1 Peters. 604; 8 Peters, 123; 12 Peters, 300.

(x) 10 Wheat. 1.

(y) Ibid. 51.

(z) 10 Wheat. 51.

(a) U. S. Stat. at large, v. iv. p. 281.

(b) 9 Peters, 329; 13 Peters, 45.

(c) 14 Peters, 301.

(d) 16 Peters, 303.

bond taken for the restoration of personal levied upon by the marshal, according to a statute of Mississippi, is a part of final process within the meaning of the act.

It is held also that where the Circuit Court adopts the process pointed out by a State law, there must be no essential variance between them. Such a variance is a new rule unknown to any act of Congress or the State law professedly adopted; and no State law can be adopted under the act of 1828, which is in collision with any act of Congress.(e)

A late act(f) gives to the Supreme Court authority to prescribe and regulate, and alter the forms of writs, and other process to be used and issued in the District and Circuit Courts of the United States, in suits at common law, and in admiralty and equity, and generally to regulate the whole practice of the said courts.

The words of this act are sufficiently comprehensive to give that court a power to alter the forms of final process, beyond what is given to the Circuit Courts themselves by the act of 1828, which only admits of alterations in conformity with the State laws; and this delegation of power by Congress we have seen has been declared to be constitutional. In accordance with that act the Supreme Court has prescribed general rules for the regulation of practice and process in admiralty, but as yet no general rules have been prescribed to regulate the proceedings of these courts at common law.

By the act of February 28, 1839,(g) it is provided that no person shall be imprisoned for debt in any State, on process issuing out of a court of the United States, where, by the laws of such State, imprisonment for debt has been abolished; and where, by the laws of a State, imprisonment for debt shall be allowed under certain conditions and restrictions, the same conditions and restrictions shall be applicable to the process issuing out of the said courts of the United States; and the same proceedings shall be had therein as are adopted in the courts of such State.

And by the act of January 14, 1841,(h) the construction of this act is made to apply to all cases whatever, where, by the laws of the State in which the said court shall be held, imprisonment for debt has been or hereafter shall be abolished.

The lien of a judgment in the Circuit Court of the United States is coextensive with the district and not with the county in which it is held ;(i) and by the act of July 4, 1840,(j) it is provided that judgments and decrees entered in the District and Circuit Courts within any State shall cease to be liens in the same manner and at like periods as judgments and decrees of courts of such State.

By the act of August 23, 1842,(k) it is directed that the marshal shall levy interest on all judgments where, by the law of the State, interest may be levied under process of execution.

(e) 16 Peters, 89; ibid. 303; 2 How-ard, 608.

(f) August 23, 1842, § 6; U. S. Stat. at large, p. 518.

(g) U. S. Stat. at large, v. v. p. 321.

(h) U. S. Stat. at large, v. v. p. 410.

(i) 1 Wallace, 196; 2 M'Lean, 78; 5 Ohio, 400; 6 Paige, 466.

(j) § 4; U. S. Stat. at large, v. v. p. 393.

(k) § 8; U. S. Stat. at large, v. v. p. 321.

In general, writs of execution and other process from the District and Circuit Courts are operative only in the districts in which the judgment is rendered.

Exceptions to this rule have been made in the following cases :—

" All writs of execution, upon any judgment or decree, obtained in any of the District or Circuit Courts of the United States, in any one State, which shall have been, or may hereafter be, divided into two judicial districts, may run and be executed, in any part of such State; but shall be issued, and made returnable to the court where the judgment was obtained, any law to the contrary notwithstanding."(*l*)

Executions upon judgments obtained for the use of the United States, are allowed by the following statutory provisions to run into any other State, or into any of the territories of the United Sates: " All writs of execution upon any judgment obtained for the use of the United States, in any of the courts of the United States, in one State, may run and be executed in any other State, or in any of the territories of the United States, but shall be issued from, and made returnable to the court where the judgment was obtained, any law to the contrary notwithstanding."(*m*)

When judgment has been obtained upon verdict, a stay of execution is allowed for forty-two days, on the motion of either party, for the purpose of petitioning for a new trial, on the terms and conditions prescribed in the following section of the judiciary act: " When in a Circuit Court judgment upon a verdict in a civil action shall be entered, execution may, on motion of either party, at the discretion of the court, and on such conditions, for the security of the adverse party, as they may judge proper, be stayed forty-two days from the time of entering judgment, to give time to file in the clerk's office of said court, a petition for a new trial. And if such petition be there filed within said term of forty-two days, with a certificate thereon, from either of the judges of such court, that he allows the same to be filed, which certificate he may make or refuse at his discretion, execution shall, of course, be further stayed to the next session of said court. And if a new trial be granted, the former judgment shall be thereby rendered void."(*n*)

In any one of the United States where judgments are a lien upon the property of the defendants, and where, by the laws of such State, defendants are entitled in the courts thereof to an imparlance of one term or more, defendants in actions in the courts of the United States, holden in such State, shall be entitled to an imparlance of one term.(*o*)

The right to issue execution is also qualified by the 23d section of the judiciary act of 1789, which prohibits the issuing of an execution upon a judgment in the District or Circuit Courts, in any case in which a writ of error may be brought and may be a supersedeas until the expiration of ten days after judgment.

By a rule of the District and Circuit Courts for the Eastern District of Pennsylvania, the form of writs, service, and of the proceedings generally, in ejectment, may be as in the courts of the State, if the

(*l*) Act of May 20, 1826; U. S. Stat. at large, v. iv. p. 184.

(*m*) Act of March 3, 1797, § 6; U. S. Stat. at large, v. i. p. 515.

(*n*) § 18; U. S. Stat. at large, v. i. p. 83.

(*o*) Act May 19, 1828, § 2; U. S. Stat. at large, v. iv. p. 281.

plaintiff's counsel should prefer to proceed in that form. But no ejectment shall be brought on an equitable title.(*p*)

Garnishee Process.—A proceeding by this kind of process, not being
generally a part of the practice of the Circuit Court, can only be had
in one instance, viz., in suits by the United States against corporations.
This is allowed by the following statutory provisions :—

"In any suit or action which shall be hereafter instituted by the
United States against any corporate body, for the recovery of money
upon any bill, note or other security, it shall be lawful to summon as
garnishees, the debtors of such corporation ; and it shall be the duty of
any person so summoned, to appear in open court, and depose, in writing, to the amount which he or she was indebted to the said corporation, at the time of the service of the summons, and at the time of
making such deposition ; and it shall be lawful to enter up judgment in
favor of the United States, for the sum admitted by such garnishee to
be due to the said corporation, in the same manner as if it had been due
and owing to the United States : *Provided,* That no judgment shall be
entered against any garnishee, until after judgment shall have been
rendered against the corporation, defendant to the said action, nor until
the sum in which the said garnishee may stand indebted, be actually
due."(*q*)

"Where any person summoned as garnishee shall depose in open
court, that he or she is not indebted to such corporation, nor was not at
the time of the service of the summons, it shall be lawful for the United
States to tender an issue upon such demand, and if, upon the trial of
such issue, a verdict shall be rendered against such garnishee, judgment
shall be entered in favor of the United States, pursuant to such verdict,
with costs of suit."(*r*)

"If any person summoned as garnishee, under the provisions of this
act, shall fail to appear at the term of the court to which he has been
summoned, he shall be subject to attachment for contempt of the court."(*s*)

In the Circuit and District Courts of the United States for the Eastern
District of Pennsylvania, writs of process bear test the day they are
issued, and may be made returnable to any return day ; and the first
Monday of every month is made a return day.(*t*)

(4.) *Practice.*

The same acts of Congress, which we have before considered, regulating the process of the United States courts, regulate their practice also,
and in precisely the same manner; and the rules established by the cases
there cited on the subject of the process of the courts, apply equally to
their practice.

By the first act of 29th September, 1789, the then existing systems
of practice in the several States, were temporarily adopted as the practice of the Circuit and District Courts for those States respectively,
subject, however, to be modified by rules of court. By the act of 1792,
the system of practice thus introduced into the courts of the United

(*p*) Rule ix.
(*q*) Act of April 20, 1818, § 8; Laws
U. S. 1690.

(*r*) Ibid. § 9.
(*s*) Ibid. § 10.
(*t*) Rule xiv.

States, was sanctioned and permanently established, subject, however, to the like power of modification, as circumstances and convenience might require.

Subsequent changes in the modes of proceeding of the State courts, unless adopted by the United States courts themselves, are inapplicable to the United States courts, and will not authorize a departure from the former practice of the Circuit Court without first altering the general rule.(u)

Under the power, however, which we have seen that the Circuit Court possesses, of providing rules for its own practice, it has adopted rules which do not vary substantially, in most respects, from the rules of the Supreme Court of the State. The practice of both courts belongs to the same system ; that of the Circuit Court having sprung from the practice of the State court as it existed before 1792, with such variations as were made by the laws of the United States.

The practice of the Circuit Court may now be considered as resting upon the laws of the United States, the rules and decisions of the Supreme Court of the United States, its own rules and decisions, and so much of the practice of the Supreme Court of the State as it had adopted before the act of 1792, and not altered by subsequent rules.

It is to be observed here, that it is not necessary that any court, in establishing and changing its practice, should do so by written rules ; a practice may be established by an uniform mode of procedure for a number of years, and this forms the law of the court ;(v) and where a practice has existed for a series of years, it is to be presumed to have been established under an order of the court.(w)

Notwithstanding the differences which must exist between the practice of the Supreme Court of the State and that of the United States courts, it will not come within the compass of this work to notice any except what have been made by the enactments of Congress, and the decisions of the courts thereupon. For such as arise from the rules of the Circuit Court, we must generally refer the inquirer to those rules ; and for the rest, to the English books of practice, as the safest guides on this subject. In treating of the various branches of the jurisdiction of the Circuit Court, we have already considered the practice in certain particular cases, and have referred on those subjects to the laws of the United States, and the construction which they have received, and the practice in those cases will not be again noticed. It is proposed now to speak of such subjects merely as belong to the ordinary practice of the court, and in the order in which they arise in suits.

Appearance and Bail.—Having considered the subject of process, the next which occurs is that of appearance and bail.

Parties are expressly permitted by statute to appear and manage their causes, either in person or by attorney or counsel.(x)

The effect of appearance as a waiver of objections to the jurisdiction of this court, where the party is not an inhabitant of the district out of which the process issues, has already been considered under the head relating to the clause of the eleventh section of the judiciary act of 1789, providing that no civil suit shall be brought against an inhabi-

(u) Peters, C. C. 1.   (w) 1 Peters, 612.
(v) 7 Peters, 435 ; 1 Peters, 604.   (x) Act of 1789, § 35.

tant by any original process, in any other district than that whereof he is an inhabitant; and although much of the importance of the acts of Congress in relation to bail in civil actions, is taken away by the act to which we have already referred, abolishing imprisonment for debt in causes originating in the national courts, where by the laws of the respective States imprisonment for debt is abolished,(y) yet, as the same circumstances give a right to hold to bail in the United States courts as will entitle the defendant to be held to bail in the State courts, we shall proceed to give the enactments on the subject.

It is provided by statute, "That in all cases in which suits and prosecutions shall be commenced for the recovery of duties, or pecuniary penalties, prescribed by the laws of the United States, the person or persons against whom process may be issued, shall and may be held to special bail, subject to the rules and regulations which prevail in civil suits in which special bail is required."(z)

In order to provide for the relief of bail, where their principal has been arrested, after the commencement of the action, in another district, it is enacted that, "in all cases where a defendant who hath procured bail to respond to the judgment in a suit brought against him in any of the courts of the United States, shall afterwards be arrested in any district of the United States, other than that in which the first suit was brought, and shall be committed to a jail, the use of which shall have been ceded to the United States for the custody of prisoners, it shall be lawful for, and the duty of, any judge of the court, in which the suit is depending, wherein such defendant had so procured bail as aforesaid, at the request and for the indemnification of the bail, to order and direct that such defendant be held in the jail to which he shall have been committed a prisoner, in the custody of the marshal, within whose district such jail is, and upon the said order, duly authenticated, being delivered to the said marshal, it shall be his duty to receive such prisoner into his custody, and him safely to keep; and the marshal shall thereupon be chargeable, as in other cases, for an escape. And the said marshal thereupon shall make a certificate, under his hand and seal, of such commitment, and transmit the same to the court from which such order issued; and shall also, if required, make a duplicate thereof, and deliver the same to such bail, his or their agent or attorney, and upon the said certificate being returned to the court which made the said order, it shall be lawful for the said court, or any judge thereof, to direct that an *exoneretur* be entered upon the bail piece, where special bail shall have been found, or otherwise to discharge such bail, and such bail shall thereupon accordingly be discharged."(a)

"The marshal, or his deputy, serving such order as aforesaid, shall, therefor, receive the same fees and allowances, as for the service of an original process commitment thereon to the jail and the return thereof."(b)

"In every case of commitment as aforesaid, by virtue of such order as aforesaid, the person so committed shall, unless sooner discharged by law, be holden in jail until final judgment shall be rendered in the

(y) Act of Feb. 28, 1839; *ante*, p. 173.
(z) Act of March 2, 1799, § 65; U. S. Stat. at large, p. 630.

(a) Act of March 2, 1799, § 1; U. S. Stat. at large, v. i. p. 727.
(b) Ibid. § 2.

suit in which he procured bail as aforesaid, and sixty days thereafter, if such judgment shall be rendered against him, that he may be charged in execution, which may be directed to, and served by, the marshal in whose custody he is. *Provided always,* That nothing in this act contained shall affect any case wherein bail has been already given."(c)

In a case where the defendant had been arrested for a misdemeanor and let to bail, and was afterwards arrested and confined on State process in a civil suit; on a motion by the bail for a *habeas corpus* to the jailer who had him in custody, the court held that the fourteenth section of the judiciary act of 1789 did not extend to cases where the process was from a State court, or the object to surrender a party in discharge of bail; and they also refused to allow an *exoneretur* to be entered on the bail piece.(d)

Consolidation of Suits.—There is a statute expressly authorizing courts of the United States to consolidate suits conformably to the principles and usages of the courts, for avoiding unnecessary costs and delay.(e)

Evidence.—The rules of court provide for taking the testimony of non-resident witnesses, under a commission, very nearly according to the practice of the State courts; and in order to compel unwilling witnesses to testify, under a commission, where they reside within the United States or its territories, Congress have, by a recent act, provided that the clerk of any court of the United States of the district or territory into which the commission is issued, shall subpœna the witness to attend before the commissioners; and in case of his neglect to attend, the judge of such court is authorized to compel and punish the witness as he might do if the subpœna had issued in a cause depending in his own court; but a witness cannot be required to go out of his county, nor more than forty miles from the place of his residence, and is entitled to fees as if attending court;(f) and in order to bring him into contempt, it is necessary to tender him his fees as in ordinary cases. If the testimony of the witness is wanted as to books, papers, &c., the clerk is to issue a subpœna *duces tecum,* on the order of the judge obtained upon affidavit, and similar provisions are made in case of disobedience. On the production of the books, papers, &c., the commissioners, at the cost of the party, are to cause copies to be made of such parts as he may require.(g)

But the judiciary act of 1789, § 30, has provided a less formal mode of obtaining the depositions of witnesses, *de bene esse,* where they reside more than one hundred miles from the place of trial, or where the other causes contemplated by the act exist for taking their depositions. The provisions referred to are as follows:—

"When the testimony of any person shall be necessary in any civil cause depending in any district, in any court of the United States, who shall live at a greater distance from the place of trial than one hundred miles, or is bound on a voyage to sea, or is about to go out of the United States, or out of such district, and to a greater distance from the place of trial than as aforesaid, before the time of trial, or is ancient or very

(c) Ibid. § 3.
(d) 1 Gall. 1.
(e) Act of July 22, 1813, § 3; U. S. Stat. at large, v. iii. p. 21.

(f) Act of Jan. 24, 1827, § 1; U. S. Stat. at large, v. iv. p. 197.
(g) Ibid. § 2.

infirm, the deposition of such person may be taken, *de bene esse*, before any justice, or judge of any of the courts of the United States, or before any chancellor, justice, or judge of a Supreme or Superior Court, mayor, or chief magistrate of a city, or judge of a County Court, or Court of Common Pleas of any of the United States, not being of counsel or attorney to either of the parties, or interested in the event of the cause, provided that a notification from the magistrate before whom the deposition is to be taken to the adverse party, to be present at the taking of the same, and to put interrogatories, if he think fit, be first made out and served on the adverse party, or his attorney, as either may be nearest, if either is within one hundred miles of the place of such caption, allowing time for their attendance after notified, not less than at the rate of one day, Sundays exclusive, for every twenty miles travel."

" And every person deposing as aforesaid, shall be carefully examined and cautioned, and sworn or affirmed to testify the whole truth, and shall subscribe the testimony by him or her given, after the same shall be reduced to writing, which shall be done only by the magistrate taking the deposition, or by the deponent in his presence. And the depositions so taken, shall be retained by such magistrate, until he deliver the same, with his own hand, into the court for which they are taken, or shall, together with a certificate of the reasons as aforesaid, of their being taken, and of the notice, if any given, to the adverse party, be by him, the said magistrate, sealed up and directed to such court, and remain under his seal until opened in court. And any person may be compelled to appear and depose as aforesaid,(*h*) in the same manner as to appear and testify in court.

" And unless it shall be made to appear on the trial of any cause with respect to witnesses whose depositions may have been taken therein, that the witnesses are then dead, or gone out of the United States, or to a greater distance than as aforesaid, from the place where the court is sitting; or that by reason of age, sickness, bodily infirmity or imprisonment, they are unable to travel and appear at court, such depositions shall not be admitted or used in the cause. *Provided*, That nothing herein shall be construed to prevent any court of the United States from granting a *dedimus potestatem*, to take depositions according to common usage, when it may be necessary to prevent a failure or delay of justice; which power they shall severally possess; nor to extend to depositions taken in *perpetuam rei memoriam*, which, if they relate to matters that may be cognizable in any court of the United States, a Circuit Court, on application thereto made as a Court of Equity, may, according to the usages in chancery, direct to be taken."(*i*)

Upon these provisions for taking depositions, it was first held, that they were to be so construed as to confine their operation to depositions taken within the district, and where the witness lives more than one hundred miles from the place of trial; and that witnesses who live at a greater distance and out of the district, must be examined under a commission.(*j*) But the construction now is, that the provisions in question are not confined to depositions taken within the district where the court is held.(*k*)

(*h*) Ibid.
(*i*) Ibid.

(*j*) 3 Wash. C. C. R. 417, 531.
(*k*) 5 Peters, 604, 616, 617.

Where in the caption of a deposition, taken before the mayor of Norfolk, to be used in a cause pending and afterwards tried in the Circuit Court of the United States, held in Baltimore, the mayor stated the witness "to be a resident in Norfolk;" and in his certificate he stated that the reason for taking the deposition was, "that the witness lives at a greater distance than one hundred miles from the place of trial, to wit, in the borough of Norfolk:" Held, that it was sufficiently shown by this certificate, at least *prima facie*, that the witness lived at a greater distance than one hundred miles from the place of trial.(*l*)

Depositions taken *de bene esse*, under this act, cannot be read, except where the witness lives at a greater distance than one hundred miles from the place of trial;(*m*) unless it be shown that the witness has been served with a subpœna, and also that from some sufficient cause he cannot attend;(*n*) the disability being supposed temporary, and the only impediment to compulsory attendance.(*o*)

The testimony of witnesses residing within the reach of process may be taken under a commission by consent.(*p*)

The deposition of a witness living beyond one hundred miles from the place of trial, may not always be absolute; for the party against whom it is to be used may prove the witness has removed within the reach of a subpœna, after the deposition was taken; and if that fact were known to the party, he would be bound to procure his personal attendance. The burden of proving this would rest upon the party opposing the admission of the deposition in evidence. For a witness whose deposition is taken under such circumstances, it is not necessary to issue a subpœna.(*q*)

By the act of March 2, 1793,(*r*) subpœnas for witnesses may run into districts other than where the court is sitting, provided the witness do not live at a greater distance than one hundred miles from the place of holding the court.(*s*)

Although the act of Congress allows subpœnas to run from the Circuit Court into another circuit, yet where a witness who has been thus subpœnaed, shows no disposition to treat the process of the court with contempt, the issuing of an attachment is always a matter of discretion with the court; and where it would be oppressive or dangerous to the health of the witness; or where any strong reasons of business or family exists against his compulsory absence from home, the court will not compel his attendance, but will either postpone the cause or have his deposition taken.(*t*)

A subpœna will run from the C. C. U. S. for the Eastern District of Pennsylvania, into the City of New York.(*u*)

The liability of a witness to be ordered out of the reach of the court, is not one of the causes deemed sufficient by this act, for the taking of a deposition *de bene esse;* and it was accordingly held, that the reason assigned for the taking of the deposition, that the deponent was a seaman on board a gun-boat of the United States, and liable to be ordered

(*l*) 5 Peters, 604.
(*m*) 5 Peters, 604, 616.
(*n*) 1 Wheat. 16; 1 Peters, C. C. R. 294; 3 Wash. C. C. R. 244; 2 Ibid. 487.
(*o*) 5 Peters, 616, 617.
(*p*) 4 Wheat. 508.

(*q*) 5 Peters, 604, 617.
(*r*) 2 Laws U. S. 365.
(*s*) See 5 Peters, 604, 618.
(*t*) *Ex parte* Beebees, 2 Wall. Jr.
(*u*) Ibid.

to some other place, and not to be able to attend the court at the time of its sitting, was insufficient.(v) Where the United States are a party, notice of taking the depositions must be served on the district attorney, if he reside within one hundred miles of the place of the caption ; and the court intimated that where there was an attorney of record, they would require notice to be given to him, whatever might be his distance from such place.(w)

Objections to the competency of the witness should be made at the time of taking his deposition, if the party attend, and the objections are known to him, in order that they may be removed; otherwise he will be presumed to have intended to waive them ; but if the facts constituting the objection were not known to the party when the deposition was taken, the objection may be taken at the time of reading it.(x)

The authority given by this act is in derogation of the common law, and has always been construed strictly; and, therefore, it is necessary to establish, that all the requisites of the law have been complied with, before such testimony can be admitted.(y)

The officer taking the deposition, *prima facie*, is to be presumed *de facto* and *de jure*, to be such as he by his official act describes himself ; and if upon the face of his certificate it appears that he was an officer authorized by the act to take the deposition, it is all the proof that is required in the first instance of his authority.(z) It should plainly appear from the certificate, that all the requisites of the statute have been fully complied with ; and no presumption will be admitted to supply any defects in the taking of the deposition.(a) But a deposition cannot be read in evidence, unless the officer before whom it was taken, certify that it was reduced to writing by himself, or by the witness in his presence.(aa) If the deposition is opened out of court, it is a fatal objec-

---

(v) 1 Wheat. 9.

(w) 2 Gall. 314.

(x) 1 Paine, 400.

(y) 1 Peters, 351; 5 Peters, 604; 3 Wash. C. C. 408.

(z) 1 Paine, 362; 5 Peters, 604, 617, 618; 1 Id. 351.

(a) 1 Peters, 356. See 5 Peters, 617, 618.

(aa) Pettibone v. Derringer, C. C. Penn. Oct. 1818, MS. The following forms of caption and certificate were adopted on the return of a deposition reduced to writing by the witness himself:—

CAPTION.

Deposition of G. H. Esquire, a citizen of the State of Pennsylvania, residing in the City of Philadelphia, aged ——, reduced to writing by him, to serve as evidence in the case of I. K. v. L. M. in the Circuit Court of the United States for ——.

I, the said G. H. being duly sworn according to law, do depose and say as follows, &c.

CERTIFICATE.

I, I. S. mayor of the City of Philadel-

phia, do certify that the foregoing is the deposition of G. H. Esquire, of the said city, to me personally known, reduced to writing and subscribed by him in my presence, taken in the aforesaid case of I. K. v. L. M. pending in the said Circuit Court of the United States, under and by virtue of the provisions of the act of Congress of 1789, to serve as evidence in the said cause, he living at a greater distance than one hundred miles from the place for the trial thereof, to wit, at the City of Philadelphia aforesaid, and the said witness having been first duly sworn by me on the Holy Evangely of Almighty God, to tell the truth, the whole truth, and nothing but the truth. And the said deposition was duly sealed up by me and directed to the said court. I further certify that I am not of counsel, or the attorney of either of the aforesaid parties, nor am I interested in the event of the said cause.

In testimony whereof, I have hereunto set my hand and affixed the seal of the said city, this —— day of —— A. D. 1836.

tion.(*b*)　Where a deposition had been read in evidence, without opposition, and afterwards the plaintiff moved to have it rejected because not
taken according to the rules of the court, it was held that having been
once introduced with the acquiescence and consent of the plaintiff, he
could not afterwards avail himself of the objection.(*c*)

By a later act, it is provided that commissioners appointed to take
affidavits under the act of 1812,(*d*) may exercise all the powers that a
justice or judge of any of the courts of the United States may exercise
by virtue of the above thirtieth section of the judiciary act.(*e*)

It is provided by rule that depositions may be taken before an
examiner, or any one of the commissioners of these courts: and commissions may be executed in the same way or by any person qualified
to take testimony, according to the laws of the State or County to which
it issues.(*f*)

In relation to the depositions taken in *perpetuam rei memoriam*,
besides the provisions contained in the thirtieth section of the judiciary
act, the act of Feb. 20, 1812,(*g*) provides "that in any cause before a
court of the United States, it shall be lawful for such court, in its discretion, to admit in evidence any deposition taken in *perpetuam rei
memoriam*, which would be so admissible in a court of the State wherein
such cause is pending, according to the laws thereof."

Copies of records and papers in the office of the secretary of State,
authenticated under the seal of the department, are evidence equally as
the original records or papers.(*h*)

Copies of papers in the office of the Secretary of the Treasury, affecting land titles derived from the United States, authenticated under the
hand and seal of the Secretary of the Treasury, are evidence equally as
the original papers.(*i*)

Consular certificates of acts done before consuls, duly authenticated
under the consulate seal, are evidence equally as the originals would be.(*j*)

By the act of August 8th, 1846, extracts from the journals of the
Senate and House of Representatives, duly authenticated, and Little &
Brown's edition of the Laws of the United States, are made competent
evidence in the courts of the United States.(*k*)

The Circuit Court is not bound by an act of assembly of the State
regulating the mode of proof upon trial;(*l*) therefore the law of Pennsylvania of 1815, making the certificates of notaries public evidence in
certain cases, does not affect the common law mode of proof in force in
the Circuit Court.(*m*)

The Circuit and District Courts of the United States for the Eastern
District of Pennsylvania, have adopted the same rules as to admissions,
for the purpose of evidence, in actions brought upon instruments of writing and in suits against partners.(*n*)

(*b*) 8 Cranch, 70 ; 2 Wash. C. C. 356.
(*c*) 7 Wheat. 470.
(*d*) See *ante*, "District Courts," p. 139.
(*e*) Act of March 1, 1817 ; U. S. Stat.
at large, v. iii. p. 350.
(*f*) Rule 8.
(*g*) ? 3, *sup*.
(*h*) Act of September 15, 1789, ? 5 ;
U. S. Stat. at large, v. i. p. 69.

(*i*) Act of January 23, 1823; U. S. Stat.
at large, v. iii. p. 721.
(*j*) Act of April 14, 1792, ? 2 ; U. S.
Stat. at large, v. i. p. 255.
(*k*) U. S. Stat. at large, v. ix. p. 80.
(*l*) 3 Wash. C. C. 328.
(*m*) Ibid. 503.
(*n*) See Rule 1, D. C. and C. C. U. S.

Very important practical rules of evidence have been introduced by statute, in certain cases where the United States are parties.

The act of 1797, "to provide more effectually for the settlement of accounts between the United States and the receivers of public moneys," after directing the comptroller to institute suits against "any revenue officer or other person accountable for public money, when he neglects or refuses to pay into the treasury the sum or balance reported to be due to the United States, upon the adjustment of his account," proceeds to provide that, "in every case of delinquency, where suit has been, or shall be instituted, a transcript from the books and proceedings of the treasury, certified by the register, and authenticated under the seal of the department, shall be admitted as evidence, and the court trying the cause shall be thereupon authorized to grant judgment, and award execution accordingly. And all copies of bonds, contracts, or other papers, relating to, or connected with, the settlement of any account between the United States and an individual, when certified by the register to be true copies of the originals on file, and authenticated under the seal of the department, as aforesaid, may be annexed to such transcripts, and shall have equal validity, and be entitled to the same degree of credit, which would be due to the original papers it produced and authenticated in court : *Provided*, That where suit is brought upon a bond, or other sealed instrument, and the defendant shall plead " *non est factum*," or upon motion to the court, such plea or motion being verified by the oath or affirmation of the defendant, it shall be lawful for the court to take the same into consideration, and (if it shall appear to be necessary for the attainment of justice) to require the production of the original bond, contract, or other paper, specified in such affidavit.(o)

Another section of the same act provides for the exclusion in evidence of claims for credits against the United States, where they have not been first presented and disallowed at the treasury, as follows : " In suits between the United States and individuals, no claim for a credit shall be admitted upon trial, but such as shall appear to have been presented to the accounting officers of the treasury for their examination, and by them disallowed, in whole or in part, unless it should be proved, to the satisfaction of the court, that the defendant is, at the time of trial, in possession of vouchers not before in his power to procure, and that he was prevented from exhibiting a claim for such credit, at the treasury, by absence from the United States, or some unavoidable accident."(p)

It has been decided,(q) that it is not necessary in order to render the provisions of this act operative in a suit, that a notification should be given to the party from the treasury department, requiring him to render his accounts under the act of March 3, 1795.(r)

By the act of March 3, 1825, § 31, " certified statements under the seal of the general post-office, of the accounts of the several post-masters and contractors, after the same shall have been examined and adjusted at that office, shall be admitted as evidence in all suits brought by the Post-master-general for the recovery of balances or debts due from the post-

(o) Act of March 3, 1797, § 1, 2 ; U. S. Stat. at large, v. i. p. 512.
(p) Ibid. § 4.
(q) 9 Wheat. 652.
(r) U. S. Stat. at large, v. i. p. 441.

masters or contractors; and also certified copies of the quarterly accounts of post-masters; or if lodged in the treasury, copies certified by the register, under the seal of his office, shall be admitted as evidence.(s)

Production of Books, &c.—The judiciary act provides that, "all the said courts of the United States shall have power, in the trial of actions at law, on motion and due notice thereof being given, to require the parties to produce books or writings in their possession or power, which contain evidence pertinent to the issue, in cases and under circumstances where they might be compelled to produce the same by the ordinary rules of proceeding in chancery; and if a plaintiff shall fail to comply with such order to produce books or writings, it shall be lawful for the courts, respectively, on motion, to give the like judgment for the defendant as in cases of nonsuit; and if a defendant shall fail to comply with such order to produce books or writings, it shall be lawful for the courts, respectively, on motion, as aforesaid, to give judgment against him or her by default." § 15.

In a case under this section, the court stated that its provisions were intended to prevent the necessity of instituting suits in equity, merely to obtain from the adverse party the production of books and papers; and they declared that they would keep the cause under their control for the purposes of substantial justice, and not suffer either party to be entrapped; that if a client lived so far from the attorney that he could not get notice of the rule to produce books, it was a sufficient reason for postponing the trial; and that they would not indulge a party with a rule to produce deeds, where they were on record, merely as a cheap mode of procuring evidence.

This provision was intended as a substitute, so far as written documents are concerned, for a bill of discovery in equity in aid of a jurisdiction at law.(t)

It is sufficient for one party to suggest that the other is in possession of a paper, which he has given him notice to produce at the trial, without offering proof of the fact. If the possession is denied, the affirmative must be proved, to enable the party to derive any advantage from the non-production.(u)

Upon a notice of the defendant to the plaintiff to produce a title paper to the land in dispute, which is to defeat the plaintiff's title, the court will not compel such production unless the defendant first shows a title to the land in dispute. A right of possession is not sufficient.(v)

When either party wants papers in the possession of the other party, he must give notice to produce. If not produced he may give inferior evidence of their contents, or argue against the party not producing them. But in either case, he must show them in the possession or power of the other party, and give evidence of their contents. The oath of the party that he has them not, may be met by contrary proof of two witnesses.(w)

Whenever a judgment by default, or a nonsuit is intended to be claimed, the notice to produce papers must give the party information

---

(s) U. S. Stat. at large, v. iv. p. 112.
(t) 2 D. 332.
(u) 1 Wash. C. C. 298; Conk. Treatise, ed. 1842, 263.

(v) Ibid.
(w) 3 Wash. C. C. 381.

that it is intended to move for a nonsuit, or a judgment by default, as the case may be.(*x*)

To entitle the defendant to nonsuit, the plaintiff, for not producing papers which he was notified to produce, the defendant must first obtain an order of the court under a rule that they should be produced.— But this order need not be absolute, but may be *nisi*.(*y*)

A notice to produce at the trial all papers, letters, and books in one's possession relating to moneys received by him under a particular award, is sufficiently specific; the oath of a party that he had not such a letter in his possession, or had diligently searched for it and could not find it, is sufficient to prevent secondary evidence of its contents.(*z*)

Before the jury are sworn and the trial commenced, it is too soon for a party to call for a paper which the other party has been notified to produce.(*a*)

The affidavit of a party interested taken without cross-examination, is competent evidence on a motion for an order in the opposite party to produce books and writings under this act.(*aa*)

In the District Court, it has been held that a proceeding *in rem* is not within the provisions of the act of 1789, which authorizes an order to produce books and writings in an action at law.(*b*)

Pleadings.—The rules adopted by the Circuit and District Courts, under the heads of dilatory pleas, pleas of the general issue with leave to give the special matter in evidence, plea of payment to a bond or specialty, and the plea of set-off, are similar, except in the length of the notice required, to those adopted in the District Court for the City and County of Philadelphia.(*c*)

Rules to declare and plead, and for all other pleadings, may be entered from four weeks to four weeks, in the clerk's office, and on failure to declare, or plead, or enter other pleadings accordingly, judgments *nisi* may be entered, on motion, either in court or before a judge at chambers.(*d*)

After appearance, the defendant may call for a bill of particulars, and until it be furnished proceedings shall stay. Should the plaintiff not furnish it for two calendar months, a nonsuit may be entered by the clerk, on notice of two weeks.(*e*)

Where a feigned issue for the trial of a fact is directed by the Circuit Court of the United States, no pleadings of any sort are necessary. The case is put upon the trial list, and the jury sworn to try the issue in the words of the order of issue itself.(*f*)

Death of Parties.—In order to prevent the abatement of a suit on the death of parties, it is provided by the judiciary act of 1789, that " where any suit shall be depending in any court of the United States, and either of the parties shall die before final judgment, the executor or administrator of such deceased party, who was plaintiff, petitioner, or defendant, in case the cause of action doth by law survive, shall have full power to prosecute or defend any such suit, or action, until final judgment; and the defendant or defendants are hereby obliged to answer

---

(*x*) Ibid.
(*y*) 4 Wash. C. C. 126.
(*z*) Ibid. 519.
(*a*) 1 Wash. C. C. 298.
(*aa*) Gilpin, 306.

(*b*) Ibid. 306.
(*c*) See Rule xiii.
(*d*) Rule xv.
(*e*) Rule vi.
(*f*) 1 Wall. Jr. 345.

thereto accordingly; and the court before whom such cause may be depending, is hereby empowered and directed to hear and determine the same, and to render judgment for or against the executor or administrator, as the case may require. And if such executor or administrator, having been duly served with a *scire facias*, from the office of the clerk of the court where such suit is depending, twenty days beforehand, shall neglect or refuse to become a party to the suit, the court may render judgment against the estate of the deceased party, in the same manner as if the executor or administrator had voluntarily made himself a party to the suit: And the executor or administrator who shall become a party as aforesaid, shall, upon motion to the court where the suit is depending, be entitled to a continuance of the same until the next term of the said court. And if there be two or more plaintiffs or defendants,. and one or more of them shall die, if the cause of action shall survive to the surviving plaintiff or plaintiffs, or against the surviving defendant or defendants, the writ or action shall not be thereby abated; but such death being suggested upon the record, the action shall proceed at the suit of the surviving plaintiff or plaintiffs, against the surviving defendant or defendants." § 31.

In a case which arose under this section, it was held that where an executor wishes to avail himself of the privilege of becoming a party, a *scire facias* is unnecessary, and he may be made a party on motion *instanter*: That the *scire facias* was to be used only where the executor did not choose to become a party, in order to enable the court-to render judgment against the estate: That the opposite party is not to be indulged with any delay in consequence of an executor's becoming a party voluntarily; but that he may insist on the executor's proving his character and producing his letters testamentary, before he shall be permitted to prosecute.(*g*)

The statute embraces all cases of death before final judgment, and of course is more extensive than the English statutes on the same subject. The death may happen before or after the plea pleaded, or issue joined, or verdict, or interlocutory judgment; but in all these cases the proceedings are to be exactly as if the executor or administrator were a voluntary party to the suit.(*h*) The suit on the death of a party does not become the suit of his representatives, but remains his suit to be prosecuted by them.(*i*)

Where the administratrix of the plaintiff had revived the suit after issue joined, by *scire facias*, and afterwards intermarried, and upon the marriage being pleaded, the *scire facias* had been abated; it was held that the suit might still, notwithstanding the abatement, be revived by *scire facias* by the husband and wife, which was the proper course; for that the abatement of the *scire facias* did not affect the original suit, which always existed by force of the statute, and was still depending.(*j*)

It was said in this case, that as the act of Congress does not provide for the case of marriage, but only for that of death, the suit of a feme sole who marries abates as at common law; and it was admitted that had this been her suit, it would have abated; but that as it was the suit

(*g*) 3 Cranch, 206–7; 1 Paine, 484–5.   (*i*) 2 Wheat. 116.
(*h*) 1 Gall. 164.   (*j*) Ibid. 111, 116.

of the intestate, and not hers, her marriage did not affect it, except to render it necessary to join her husband with her in its prosecution by *scire facias*.(*k*)

If an administrator is made a party to a suit under this section, by *scire facias*, after verdict, as he can have no opportunity to plead a want of assets or any other matter of defence to the *scire facias*, an execution cannot be issued, until after a *scire facias* has been brought upon the judgment, in order to give the administrator an opportunity to plead any defence he may have ; and it was held that an execution in such case issued without a *scire facias* ought regularly to be quashed. From the principles of this decision, a *scire facias* upon the judgment would appear to be necessary in all cases where the executor becomes a party to the suit at such a stage of it, that he has no opportunity before judgment to plead his defence.(*l*)

This section is confined to personal actions, the power to prosecute or defend being given to the executor and administrator, and not to the heir or devisee. Where, therefore, the defendant in a writ of right died before appearance, it was held that his heirs could not be made parties to the suit, and that the action abated as at common law.(*m*)

Amendments.—The judiciary act provides that, " no summons, writ, declaration, return, process, judgment or other proceedings in civil causes, in any of the courts of the United States, shall be abated, arrested, quashed or reversed, for any defect or want of form, but the said courts, respectively, shall proceed and give judgment according as the right of the cause and matter in law shall appear unto them, without regarding any imperfections, defects, or want of form in such writ, declaration or other pleading, return, process, judgment, or course of proceeding whatsoever, except those only in cases of demurrer, which the party demurring shall specially set down and express, together with his demurrer as the cause thereof. And the said courts, respectively, shall and may, by virtue of this act, from time to time, amend all and every such imperfections, defects and wants of form other than those only which the party demurring shall express as aforesaid ; and may, at any time, permit either of the parties to amend any defect in the process or pleadings, upon such conditions as the said courts, respectively, shall, in their discretion, and by their rules, prescribe." § 32.

This section of the judiciary act of 1789, is not to be restricted to causes of original jurisdiction, nor is there anything in the nature of appellate jurisdiction which forbids the granting of amendments.(*n*)

The Circuit Court, on appeal from a District Court, has power under this section to allow any amendments of defects in form occurring in the court below, which could have been amended there, or to disregard them in giving judgment ; but this power does not extend to defects in substance.(*o*) Defects in substance may, however, be amended in the District Court on terms, but the amendments must be made before final judgment ; and the court remarked that amendments at common law were for trivial errors, and where there was something to amend by ;

(*k*) 2 Wheat. 111, 116.
(*l*) 1 Gall. 160.
(*m*) 7 Wheat. 530.

(*n*) 1 Gall. 22.
(*o*) 1 Paine, 486 ; but see 1 Gall. 257, 261 ; 2 D. 364.

that anciently, they could be made only during the term when the error occurred in the record; that afterwards they were allowed at any time pending the suit, but never after final judgment.(p)

The omission of the averment of citizenship, or of the value of the property in dispute, when necessary to give jurisdiction, are defects in substance, not cured by verdict, and cannot be amended after final judgment. And where a judgment had been entered in the court of the northern district of New York, sitting with Circuit Court powers, the record filed and execution issued, and eight months afterwards the cause was removed by writ of error into the Circuit Court, and the District Court subsequently allowed the record to be amended by inserting in the declaration the averment of citizenship, and of the matter in dispute, which were essential to jurisdiction; the court held that the amendments were irregular, and that it could not receive them after the original record had been sent up.(q) And an amendment will not be permitted which introduces a new subject of controversy.(r) But the Circuit Court may grant a motion to strike out the name of one of the defendants where its jurisdiction might otherwise be ousted; and the same practice also obtains in the Supreme Court, and is within the remedial action of the judiciary act of 1789.(s)

Where, in action against a bank, the writ was upon sixty-eight of their notes, but the declaration, although purporting to count upon the sixty-eight, had omitted one of them, and judgment was entered by default, for the whole sixty-eight: upon this being assigned in the Supreme Court for error, the court declared that they would adopt the English practice, and allow a *remittitur damma* to be entered in the court above, and not require the party to suggest diminution and resort to a *certiorari* to bring up the record after it had been amended in the Circuit Court.(t)

Where a cause came up on error to the Supreme Court, and was remanded to the Circuit Court, the court, on remanding the cause, refused to give any directions to the Circuit Court as to amendments, saying that they always considered that a subject for the court below, not being able to say whether the latter would be justified or not in granting leave to amend.(u)

If the amendment is made in the Circuit Court, the cause is heard and adjudicated in that court; if the amendment is allowed in the Supreme Court, the cause is remanded, with directions to allow the amendment to be made.(v)

The allowance or disallowance of amendments is not matter for which a writ of error will lie from a superior court,(w) as the permitting of them is a matter of discretion: But the court stated in this case, that they did not mean to say that a court might in all cases permit or refuse amendments without control; that a case might occur where it would be error in a court, after having allowed one party to amend, to refuse to suffer the other party to amend also before trial.(x)

(p) 1 Paine, 486.
(q) Ibid.
(r) 15 Peters, 40.
(s) 3 Story, 76.
(t) 2 Peters, 327.

(u) 6 Cranch, 267, n.
(v) 11 Wheat. 1.
(w) Ibid. 302.
(x) 5 Cranch, 15; 6 Ibid. 206; 9 Wheat. 576.

The Circuit Courts may amend judgments at a subsequent term in matters of form only.(y)

Judgment of first Term.—Where suits are brought for the United States against revenue officers or other persons accountable for public money, under the act before referred to, providing for the settlement of accounts between the United States and receivers of public moneys ;(z) or where suits are brought on bonds for duties due the United States,(a) and also in all actions arising under the post-office law ;(b) the court are required to give judgment the first term after the suit is commenced. The defendant may, however, by satisfying the court, in the manner provided for by each act, that a continuance is necessary, have a continuance until the next term, but no longer.

Assessment on Bonds, &c.—It is provided that : "In all causes brought before either of the courts of the United States, to recover the forfeiture annexed to any articles of agreement, covenant, bond or other specialty, where the forfeiture, breach or non-performance, shall appear by the default or confession of the defendant, or upon demurrer, the court before whom the action is shall render judgment therein for the plaintiff to recover so much as is due, according to equity. And when the sum for which judgment should be rendered is uncertain, the same shall, if either of the parties request it, be assessed by a jury."(c)

Costs.—There is no statute of the United States which expressly allows the plaintiff to recover costs in ordinary suits, nor the defendant, except in some particular cases. The existence of costs, however, in the federal courts, and the right to receive the same, are recognized generally, by the 9th, 11th, 20th, 21st, 22d, 23d, and 35th sections of the judiciary act of 1789, and in many other acts. And it has been the uniform practice that the prevailing party in civil actions should recover costs ;(d) and such has been recognized as the practice by the Supreme Court of the United States,(e) and that the rates of fees are the same as the State laws in the highest courts have been accustomed to allow under them.

The judiciary act of 1789 has the following provision on the subject of costs : "Where, in a Circuit Court, a plaintiff in an action originally brought there, other than the United States, recovers less than the sum or value of five hundred dollars, he shall not be allowed, but, at the discretion of the court, may be adjudged to pay costs." § 20.

Where a cause is removed from a State court into the Circuit Court, under the 12th section of the act of 1789, the plaintiff is entitled to costs, although he has a verdict for less than $500,(f) and where a plaintiff prevails the court will not tax costs against him, though he recovers less than $500, if he has good reason to suppose he was entitled to recover more than $500.(g)

Custom-house officers are, by the following provision, allowed to recover double costs, when sued for acts done under the collection law.

(y) 1 Story, 310; 3 Wheat. 591; 12 Wheat. 10; 3 Peters, 431.
(z) Act of March 3, 1797, § 3, *sup.*
(a) Act of March 2, 1799, *sup.* § 65.
(b) Act of March 3, 1825, § 38 ; U. S. Stat. at large, v. iv. p. 113.

(c) Act of 1789, § 26.
(d) 2 Wash. C. C. 71 ; 4 Wash. C. C. 546.
(e) 6 Cranch, 187.
(f) 3 Mason, 457.
(g) 3 Day. 289.

" If any officer, or other person, executing, or aiding, or assisting in the seizure of goods, shall be sued or molested, for anything done in virtue of the powers given by this act, or by virtue of a warrant-granted by any judge or justice, pursuant to law, such officer or other person may plead the general issue, and give this act and the special matter in evidence ; and if in such suit the plaintiff is nonsuited, or judgment pass against him, the defendant shall recover double costs."(h)

By the act of July 22, 1813, § 1,(i) it is provided that where several actions shall be brought against persons who might legally be joined in one suit—if judgment be given for the party pursuing the same, such party shall not recover more than the costs of one action, unless special cause for several actions shall be satisfactorily shown on motion in open court.   § 1.

And where any attorney, proctor, or other person, admitted to manage and conduct causes in the courts of the United States, shall appear to have multiplied proceedings in any cause before the court, so as to increase costs unreasonably, such person may be required, by order of court, to satisfy any excess of costs so incurred.   § 3.

A direct judgment for costs cannot be given against the United States ;(j) but where the government is a party to a suit, and fees of the marshal, or other officers, are chargeable to the United States, they are paid from the treasury, on a certificate of the amount made by the court, or one of the judges;(k) and where the United States owe a party who has a claim against the government of fees in relation to suits to which the United States are a party, the court will permit him to set up such claim by way of defence.(l)

Since the repeal of the process act of 1789, and the expiration of the act of 1793,(m) there has not been any law of the United States regulating the fees of attorneys ; in this State, the attorney's legal, or judgment fee, is eight dollars in common law cases ; and in admiralty causes, six dollars.   This practice is founded on the old order of adding one-third to the legal fee in the highest court of the State.   There are, however, several acts fixing the fees and compensation of the officers of the court, and of jurors and witnesses.(n)   And the marshal, or other officer,(o) or jurors and witnesses,(p) may have an attachment to compel the payment of their fees.

Where three attorneys appear for a defendant, to suits instituted against him, the attorney's fee is to be equally divided between them.(q)

The right to demand security for costs is governed by the following rule in the District and Circuit Courts for the Eastern District of Pennsylvania :—

In every action in which the plaintiff or complainant is not, at the time of suit brought, a citizen of the District of Pennsylvania ; or, being so, then afterwards removes from the district ; and in every other case

(h) Act of March 2, 1799, § 71 ; U. S. Stat. at large, v. i. p. 678.
(i) U. S. Stat. at large, v. iii. p. 19.
(j) 2 Wheat. 395 ; 3 Cranch, 73 ; 12 Wheat. 546 ; 8 Peters, 150.
(k) 12 Wheat. 546.
(l) 8 Peters, 150.
(m) Act of March 1, § 4.
(n) Act of Feb. 28, 1799 ; U. S. Stat.

at large, v. i. p. 629 ; Act of May 8, 1792; Ibid. p. 275 ; Act of April 18, 1814 ; Ibid. v. iii. p. 133 ; Act of March 8, 1824 ; Ibid. v. iv. p. 18.
(o) 6 Wheat. 194.
(p) Case of the Sailors' Snug Harbor, C. C. N. Y. Oct. 1827.
(q) 1 Wash. C. C. 348.

where a defendant, or other person for him, shall make affidavit that he believes the costs could not be recovered of the plaintiff by attachment or execution, a deposit or other security for costs shall be given, and proceedings shall be stayed until it is done.(*r*)

The defendant must demand security within a reasonable time, or it will not be a cause for a continuance, that such security is not given when the cause is called for trial.(*s*)

Costs are not allowed as of course in cases of reversal, but it is otherwise in case of affirmance.(*t*)   And it is said to be the common course not to allow costs to the prevailing party where the district judge differs from the circuit judge.(*u*)

With regard to interlocutory costs, it has been held that though costs are generally imposed upon a party who asks to amend the pleadings, yet in a case where the error which required amendment, arose from the irregularity of the practice in the courts of the State where the action was brought, the court did not allow costs on amendment.(*v*)

(5.) *Jails, and Discharge from Imprisonment.*

The United States have no jails of their own.   In 1789, Congress passed the following resolution,(*w*) for the purpose of obtaining the use of the State jails :—

"*Resolved, &c.*, That it be recommended to the legislatures of the several States to pass laws, making it expressly the duty of the keepers of their jails to receive, and safely keep therein, all prisoners committed under the authority of the United States, until they shall be discharged by due course of the laws thereof, under the like penalties as in the case of prisoners committed under the authority of such States, respectively."

The legislature of Pennsylvania, in compliance with this resolution, in 1789, passed an act giving the use of the State jails to the United States.(*x*)   The second and third sections of that act provide that "all sheriffs, jailers, prison-keepers, and their and each and every of their deputies, within this commonwealth, to whom any person or persons shall be sent or committed, by virtue of legal process issued by, or under the authority of the United States, shall be, and they are hereby enjoined and required, to receive such prisoners into custody, and to keep the same safely until they shall be discharged by due course of law; and all such sheriffs, jailers, prison-keepers, and their deputies, offending in the premises, shall be liable to the same pains and penalties, and the parties aggrieved shall be entitled to the same remedies against them, or any of them, as if such prisoners had been committed to their custody, by virtue of legal process issued under the authority of this State.

" A calendar of such prisoners shall, on the first day of January, in every year, be made out by the respective jailers and prison-keepers in each county, upon oath or affirmation, to be administered by the president of the Court of Common Pleas of the respective county, specifying particularly the names of such prisoners, the time of their commitment and discharge, and whether upon civil or criminal process, together with

(*r*) Rule vii.
(*s*) 4 Wash. C. C. 285.
(*t*) 4 Cranch, 46.
(*u*) 3 Story, 612.

(*v*) 4 Wash. C. C. 630.
(*w*) Sept. 23 ; U. S. Stat. at large, v. i. p. 96.
(*x*) Act of Dec. 5, Purd. Dig. 351.

the expense of subsisting such of the said prisoners as shall have been committed for offences ; which calendar shall be transmitted to the president and supreme executive council of this State, to the end that order may be taken for the payment of the allowances and expenses on the part of the United States, in and by the resolution (of Congress) assumed."

Under these laws, persons are imprisoned in the State jails, on process issued out of the United States courts.

The jail liberties are allowed to persons confined on United States process by the following provision: "Persons imprisoned on process issuing from any court of the United States, as well at the suit of the United States, as at the suit of any person or persons in civil actions, shall be entitled to like privileges of the yards or limits of the respective jails, as persons confined, in like cases, on process from the courts of the respective States, are entitled to, and under the like regulations and restrictions."(y)

In an action of escape, which arose under the State act of 1801, of a prisoner from the limits, on execution from the Circuit Court, it was held that that act and the resolution of Congress of 1789, and the above act of Congress, allowing the limits to prisoners confined on process of the United States court, were, being in *pari materia*, to be construed together ; that under these, the prisoner had a right to demand of the sheriff to be admitted to the privilege of the limits in the same manner as if he had been committed on process from a State court, and that the State law must be referred to to ascertain what that right was ; the act of Congress of 1800 having intended to adopt the State law in all respects, so as to place prisoners confined under process from the courts of the United States, on the same footing with those confined on process from the State courts ; and that false imprisonment would lie against a sheriff for refusing a prisoner the limits.

It was also held that the bond for the limits taken in this case had, in all respects, the same incidents and the like legal effect with a bond taken under the State laws ; that it was assignable, and that an assignment discharged the sheriff from liability for a subsequent escape ; that the United States were expressly named in the act of Congress, and bound by it, and that an assignment of the bond to them as plaintiffs was valid; and that the Secretary of the Treasury having accepted the assignment for them, he was to be presumed to have been authorized, and that the plaintiffs were bound by his acceptance.(z)

It is not perceived that the repeal of the former State law and adoption of the new one, or any difference in their provisions, affect the application of the principles of this decision to future cases.

The marshal is not liable for an escape after a prisoner has been committed to a State jail.(a)

In connection with the subject of jails, it may not be amiss to introduce such provisions as have been made by the laws of the United States for the relief of imprisoned debtors. The United States have no bankrupt or insolvent law, properly so called; but they have, by the follow-

(y) Act of Jan. 6, 1800, § 1; U. S.   (z) 1 Paine, 368.
Stat. at large, v. ii. p. 4.   (a) 8 Cranch, 84.

ing act, made provision for the discharge of debtors from imprisonment when reduced to a state of absolute indigence:—

"Any person imprisoned on process of execution issuing from any court of the United States, in civil actions, except at the suit of the United States, may have the oath or affirmation, hereinafter expressed, administered to him, by the judge of the District Court of the United States, within whose jurisdiction the debtor may be confined; and in case there shall be no district judge residing within twenty miles of the jail wherein such debtor may be confined, such oath or affirmation may be administered by any two persons who may be commissioned for that purpose by the district judge: The creditor, his agent, or attorney, if either live within one hundred miles of the place of imprisonment, or within the district in which the judgment was rendered, having had at least thirty days' previous notice, by a citation served on him, issued by the district judge, to appear at the time and place therein mentioned, if he see fit, to show cause why the said oath or affirmation should not be so administered; at which time and place, if no sufficient cause, in the opinion of the judge (or the commissioners appointed as aforesaid), be shown, or doth, from examination, appear to the contrary, he or they may, at the request of the debtor, proceed to administer to him the following oath or affirmation, as the case may be: viz. 'You ——— solemnly (swear or affirm) that you have no estate, real or personal, in possession, reversion, or remainder, to the amount or value of thirty dollars, other than necessary wearing apparel; and that you have not, directly or indirectly, given, sold, leased, or otherwise conveyed to, or intrusted, any person or persons, with all, or any part, of the estate, real or personal, whereof you have been the lawful owner or possessor, with any intent to secure the same, or to receive or expect, any profit or advantage therefrom, or to defraud your creditors, or have caused, or suffered to be done, anything else whatsoever whereby any of your creditors may be defrauded.' Which oath or affirmation being administered, the judge or commissioners shall certify the same, under his or their hands, to the prison-keeper, and the debtor shall be discharged from his imprisonment on such judgment, and shall not be liable to be imprisoned again for the said debt; but the judgment shall remain good and sufficient in law, and may be satisfied out of any estate which may then, or at any time afterwards, belong to the debtor. And the judge or commissioners, in addition to the certificate by them made and delivered to the prison-keeper, shall make return of their doings to the District Court, with the commission, in cases where a commission had been issued, to be kept upon the files and record of the same court.— And the said judge, or commissioners, may send for books and papers, and have the same authority as a court of record, to compel the appearance of witnesses, and administer to them, as well as to the debtor, the oaths or affirmations necessary for the inquiry into, and discovery of, the true state of the debtor's property, transactions, and affairs."

"When the examination and proceedings aforesaid, in the opinion of the said judge or commissioners, cannot be had with safety or convenience, in the prison wherein the debtor is confined, it shall be lawful for him or them, by warrant, under his or their hand and seals, to order the marshal or prison-keeper to remove the debtor to such other place, convenient and near to the prison, as he or they may see fit; and to remand the debtor to the same prison, if, upon examination or cause shown by the creditor, it shall appear that the debtor ought not to be admitted to take the above-recited oath or affirmation, or that he is holden for any other cause."

"If any person shall falsely take any oath or affirmation, authorized by this act, such person shall be deemed guilty of perjury, and, upon conviction thereof, shall suffer the pains and penalties in that case provided. And in case any false oath or affirmation be so taken by the debtor, the court, upon the motion of the creditor, shall recommit the debtor to the prison from whence he was liberated, there to be detained for the said debt, in the same manner as if such oath or affirmation had not been taken."

"Any person imprisoned upon process issuing from any court of the United States, except at the suit of the United States, in any civil action, against whom judgment has been, or shall be, recovered, shall be entitled to the privileges and relief provided by this act, after the expiration of thirty days from the time such judgment has been, or shall be recovered, though the creditor should not, within that time, sue out his execution, and charge the debtor therewith."(b)

By a subsequent act, it is provided that the oath prescribed by the above act of 1800, "may be, in all cases, administered to the person entitled to take the same, either by any judge of the Supreme Court of the United States, or by the district judge for the district within which such person may be, or by any person or persons commissioned by any judge of the Supreme Court, or the said district judge, for that purpose."(c)

And by a still later act, it is provided that the persons commissioned under the act of 1824, last cited, "may have full power and authority to issue a citation, directed to the creditor, his agent or attorney, if either lives within one hundred miles of the place of imprisonment, requiring him to appear at the time and place therein mentioned, if he see fit, to show cause why the said oath or affirmation should not be administered; and that if the creditor, his agent or attorney, lives within fifty miles of the place of imprisonment, only fifteen days' previous notice by citation shall be required."(d)

It will be observed that the above act of 1800, so far as it provides for the discharge of debtors from imprisonment, does not extend to debtors imprisoned at the suit of the United States. Such debtors, however, are not left without relief, but on the contrary, in their case, Congress have provided a sort of partial insolvent law, by which, on the debtor's making an assignment of his property to the Secretary of the Treasury for the use of the United States, the latter is authorized to discharge him from imprisonment. This relief is afforded by the act of 1798, which provides as follows:—

"Any person imprisoned upon execution issuing from any court of the United States, for a debt due to the United States, which he shall be unable to pay, may, at any time after commitment, make application, in writing, to the Secretary of the Treasury, stating the circumstances of

(b) Act of Jan. 6, 1800, §§ 2, 3, 4, 5;   (d) Act of April 22, 1824; U. S. Stat.
U. S. Stat. at large, v. ii. p. 4.   at large, v. iv. p. 19.
   (c) Act of Jan. 7, 1824; U. S. Stat. at
large, v. iv. p. 1.

his case, and his inability to discharge the debt; and it shall, thereupon, be lawful for the said Secretary to make, or require to be made, an examination and inquiry into the circumstances of the debtor, either by the oath or affirmation of the debtor (which the said Secretary, or any other person by him specially appointed, are hereby authorized to administer), or otherwise, as the said Secretary shall deem necessary and expedient, to ascertain the truth; and upon proof being made to his satisfaction, that such debtor is unable to pay the debt for which he is imprisoned, and that he hath not concealed, or made any conveyance of his estate in trust, for himself, or with an intent to defraud the United States, or deprive them of their legal priority, the said Secretary is hereby authorized to receive from such debtor, any deed, assignment, or conveyance, of the real or personal estate of such debtor, if any he hath, or any collateral security, to the use of the United States; and upon a compliance, by the debtor, with such terms and conditions as the said Secretary may judge reasonable and proper, under all the circumstances of the case, it shall be lawful for the said Secretary to issue his order, under his hand, to the keeper of the prison, directing him to discharge such debtor from his imprisonment under such execution, and he shall be accordingly discharged, and shall not be liable to be imprisoned again for the said debt; but the judgment shall remain good and sufficient in law, and may be satisfied out of any estate which may then, or at any time afterwards, belong to the debtor."

"If any person shall falsely take an oath or affirmation under this act, he shall be deemed guilty of perjury, and be subject to the pains and penalties provided in the third section of an act, entitled 'An act for the relief of persons imprisoned for debt.'"

"The benefit of this act shall not be extended to any person imprisoned for any fine, forfeiture, or penalty, incurred by a breach of any law of the United States, or for moneys had and received by any officer, agent, or other person, for their use."(e)

A later act makes provision for the discharge by the President of debtors, whose case does not warrant their discharge under the above act by the Secretary of the Treasury, as follows: "Any person, imprisoned upon execution for a debt due to the United States, which he shall be unable to pay, if his case shall be such as does not authorize his discharge by the Secretary of the Treasury, under the powers given him by the act, entitled 'An act providing for the relief of persons imprisoned for debts due to the United States,' may make application to the President of the United States, and upon proof being made to his satisfaction that such debtor is unable to pay the debt, and upon a compliance by the debtor with such terms and conditions as the President shall deem proper, he may order the discharge of such debtor from his imprisonment, and he shall be accordingly discharged, and shall not be liable to be imprisoned again for the same debt; but the judgment shall remain good and sufficient in law, and may be satisfied out of any estate which may then, or at any time afterwards, belong to the debtor."(f)

(e) Act of June 6, §§ 1, 2, 3; U. S. Stat. at large, v. i. p. 561.

(f) Act of March 3, 1817; U. S. Stat. at large, v. iii. p. 399.

SECTION III.

SUPREME COURT OF THE UNITED STATES.

(1). *Organization.*

The Supreme Court consists of a Chief Justice and eight Associate Justices,(*g*) any five of whom constitute a quorum. They are appointed by the President and Senate,(*h*) and hold their offices during good behavior.(*i*)   The Associate Justices take precedence according to the date of their commissions, or, where they bear date the same day, according to their ages.(*j*)

It holds, annually, one session, at the city of Washington, commencing on the first Monday of December.(*k*) If a quorum shall not attend on the appointed day, such justice or justices as may attend, may adjourn the court from day to day, for twenty days; and if a quorum does not convene by the expiration of that time, the business of the court shall be continued over to the next regular session. But any one or more of the justices so attending shall have power to make all necessary orders touching any suit, action, writ of error, process, pleadings, or proceedings returned to the said court, or depending therein, preparatory to the hearing, trial, or decision of such action, suit, appeal, writ of error, process, pleadings, or proceedings.(*l*) After a quorum has once been formed, any less number may adjourn the court from day to day until a quorum shall attend, and, when expedient and proper, may adjourn the same without day.(*m*)

The judiciary act of 1802,(*n*) provides "that it shall be the duty of the associate justice, resident in the fourth circuit formed by this act, to attend at the city of Washington, on the first Monday of August, each and every year, who shall have power to make all necessary orders touching any suit, action, appeal, writ of error, process, pleadings, or proceedings, returned to the said court, or depending therein, preparatory to the hearing, trial, or decision of such action, suit, appeal, writ of error, process, pleadings, or proceedings.

"And that all writs and process may be returnable to the said court on the said first Monday in August, in the same manner as to the session of the said court, hereinbefore directed to be holden on the first Monday in February,(*o*) and may also bear teste on the said first Monday in August, as though a session of the said court was holden on that day; and it shall be the duty of the clerk of the Supreme Court to attend the said justice on the said first Monday of August, in each and every year, who shall make the due entry of all such matters and things as shall or may be ordered as aforesaid by the said justice; and at each and every such August session, all actions, pleas, and other proceedings, relative to any cause, civil or criminal, shall be continued over to the ensuing February session."(*p*)

(*g*) Act of March 3, 1837.
(*h*) Const. Art. 2, § 2.
(*i*) Ibid. Art. 3, § 1.
(*j*) Act 1789, § 1.
(*k*) Act of June 17, 1844, § 1; U. S. Stat. at large, v. v. p. 676.

(*l*) Act of 1802, § 1; act of 1829, § 1.
(*m*) Act of 1829, § 2.
(*n*) April 29, § 2; U. S. Stat. at large, v. ii. p. 156.
(*o*) Altered 1st Monday of Dec., *supra.*
(*p*) Ibid. § 2.

The act of 1799,(p) provides for the adjournment of the court to some other place, in case of contagious sickness.

The court at an early period adopted the practice of the King's Bench as its guide, subject to such alterations as circumstances might render necessary.(q) And the reader is referred to the rules of the court for its practice generally.

Officers.—The clerk of the Supreme Court is appointed by the court, and gives a bond in the sum of two thousand dollars.(r) It is the duty of the marshal of the district where the court may sit, to attend its sessions; and the marshal of each district is the ministerial officer of the court in his district.(s)

(2). *Jurisdiction.*

The Supreme Court was established by the constitution.(t) Under that instrument its jurisdiction is original and appellate.

Original.—In all cases affecting ambassadors and other public ministers and consuls, and in all cases to which a State is a party.

Appellate.—In all cases within the jurisdiction of the courts of the United States, as prescribed by the constitution, both as to law and fact, with such exceptions and under such regulations as Congress shall make.(u)

We shall proceed to treat the jurisdiction of this court under these two separate heads.

(a). *Original Jurisdiction.*

We have already considered the limitation of the jurisdiction of the Federal courts, contained in the eleventh article of amendments to the constitution, by which it is provided that "the judicial power of the United States shall not be construed to extend to any suit, in law or equity, commenced or prosecuted against one of the United States, by citizens of another State, or by citizens or subjects of any foreign state;" and that this amendment does not affect their jurisdiction where a State as plaintiff asserts its claims, nor does it oust their jurisdiction where such claims are suggested, the State not being an actual party.(v) And it has been held that the eleventh amendment to the constitution is limited to those suits in which a State is a party on the record.(w)

Besides the provision contained in the second section of the third article of the constitution, the judiciary act of 1789, which was passed before the amendatory article had been adopted, has the following provisions relating to the original jurisdiction of the Supreme Court: "The Supreme Court shall have exclusive jurisdiction of all controversies of a civil nature, where a State is a party, except between a State and its citizens; and except also between a State and citizens of other States, or aliens, in which latter case it shall have original but not exclusive jurisdiction. And shall have, exclusively, all such jurisdiction of suits, or proceedings against ambassadors, or other public ministers, or their domestics, or domestic servants, as a court of law can have or exercise consistently with the law of nations; and original, but not exclusive

---

(p) Feb. 25, § 7; U. S. Stat. at large, v. i. p. 621.
(q) Rule of Aug. 1792.
(r) Act of Sept. 24, 1789, § 7.
(s) Ibid. § 27.
(t) Art. 3, § 1.

(u) Art. 3, § 2.
(v) 5 Cranch, 139; 2 D. 402; 3 Ibid. 411; 9 Wheat. 904, 855, 738; 1 Peters, 122; Ibid. 110; 2 Peters, 323.
(w) 9 Wheat. 904; 4 D. 3.

jurisdiction of all suits brought by ambassadors, or other public ministers, or in which a consul or vice-consul shall be a party. And the trial
of issues in fact in the Supreme Court, in all actions at law against citizens of the United States, shall be by jury."(x)

Congress has not passed any act for the special purpose of prescribing
the mode of proceeding in suits instituted against a State, or in any
suit in which the Supreme Court is to exercise this original jurisdiction.(y)
But at a very early period of our judicial history, suits being instituted
in this court against States, the questions concerning its jurisdiction
and mode of proceeding were necessarily considered.(z) And, this
court, having then settled that it could exercise its original jurisdiction
in suits against a State, under the authority conferred by the constitution and the existing acts of Congress, the rule respecting the process;
the persons on whom to be served; the time of service; and the course
of the court on the failure of the State to appear after a due service of
process, were prescribed and fixed.(a) And it is provided by rule, that
"Where process at common law or in equity shall issue against a State,
the same shall be served on the governor, or chief executive magistrate
and attorney-general of such State."(b) In respect to that class of cases
in which a State is sued by a foreign State, in only a single case has
the question been raised. But the point was not decided because the
plaintiffs in that case were held not to constitute a foreign State.(c)

It has been held, that a case which belongs to the jurisdiction of the
Supreme Court, on account of the interest which a State has in the controversy, must be one in which the State is, either nominally or substantially, the party.(d) And in this case the court declined to decide,
as the point was not before them, the important question, whether they
had jurisdiction of a suit between States, where the right of State jurisdiction only, abstractedly from the right of soil, was in question.
But if the claims of a State may be ultimately affected by the decision
of a cause, though the State may not necessarily be a defendant, the
court is bound to exercise jurisdiction.(e)

In 2 Dallas, 297, it was held that Congress might vest a concurrent
jurisdiction in the Circuit Courts in "cases affecting ambassadors and
other public ministers and consuls;" but in 11 Wheaton, 467, the question whether the grant of jurisdiction, under a true construction of the
second section of the third article of the constitution, was not exclusive
in the Supreme Court in such cases, was considered as still undecided.(f)

By another clause of the thirteenth section of the judiciary act, the
Supreme Court was empowered to issue writs of mandamus to persons
holding office under the authority of the United States; and under this
provision an application was made to the court for a mandamus to compel the Secretary of State of the United States to issue commissions to
certain officers of the United States: But the court held that the provision, so far as it attempted to confer such power, was unconstitutional;

(x) § 13, U. S. Stat. at large, v. i. p. 80.
(y) 5 Peters, 284.
(z) Ibid. 288.
(a) Ibid. And as to the jurisdiction
and modes of practice, where a State is
a party, see also 3 D. 1; 2 D. 419; 4 D.
3; 3 D. 320; 12 Peters, 657.

(b) Rules S. C. 10. Aug. 12, 1796.
(c) 5 Peters, 1.
(d) 3 D. 412; and see 4 Id. 1, 3; 2 Id.
407, 408.
(e) 5 Cranch, 115.
(f) See also 6 Wheat. 264.

as it could not be considered as an appellate power, being in its nature original; and as Congress could not assign original jurisdiction to the court in any other cases than those specified in the constitution: And the court observed that, "when an instrument, organizing fundamentally, a judicial system, divides it into one supreme, and so many inferior courts as the legislature may ordain and establish; then enumerates its powers, and proceeds so far to distribute them, as to define the jurisdiction of the Supreme Court, by declaring the cases in which it shall take original jurisdiction, and that in others, it shall take appellate jurisdiction; the plain import of the words seems to be, that in one class of cases its jurisdiction is original, and not appellate; in the other it is appellate, and not original."(*g*)

Under the head of "Circuit Court," will be found many powers conferred upon the courts of the United States, and also many provisions and decisions in relation to process and practice, which are applicable to the Supreme Court, when exercising either its original or appellate jurisdiction.

(*b*) *Appellate Jurisdiction.*

The court have determined that although its appellate powers are not given by the judiciary act, but by the constitution, yet that they are limited and regulated by that and other acts passed on the subject; and that although without the judiciary act, it would have possessed all the appellate powers conferred on it by the constitution, yet as that act has described affirmatively its jurisdiction, such description is to be understood to imply a negative on the exercise of such appellate power as is not comprehended within it.(*i*) And the appellate jurisdiction will only be exercised in cases where it is given by statute; the constitution and law must concur to vest it.(*j*)

Its original jurisdiction is founded on the character of the parties to a suit, its appellate jurisdiction on the character of the case.(*k*)

The judiciary act declares that, "the Supreme Court shall also have appellate jurisdiction from the Circuit Courts and courts of the several States, in the cases hereinafter specially provided for: and shall have power to issue writs of probation to the District Courts, when proceeding as courts of admiralty and maritime jurisdiction, and writs of mandamus, in cases warranted by the principles and usages of law, to any courts appointed, or persons holding office, under the authority of the United States." § 13.(*l*)

The cases in which appellate jurisdiction from the Circuit Courts and courts of the several States is afterwards specially provided for by the judiciary act, are those only in which a writ of error is allowed upon the final judgments of those courts.

The fourteenth section of the judiciary act, which empowers the courts of the United States to issue writs of *scire facias* and *habeas corpus* and other writs necessary for the exercise of their jurisdiction, has been construed to contain regulations of the appellate jurisdiction of the Supreme Court.

A novel kind of appellate jurisdiction was also given to the Supreme

(*g*) 1 Cranch, 137, 174, 175; 5 Peters, 190; 6 Wheat. 400, 401; 9 Wheat. 820.
(*i*) 6 Cranch, 312.
(*j*) 1 Cranch, 91; 3 Ibid. 159; 6 Ibid. 307; 3 D. 321.
(*k*) 6 Wheat. 269.
(*l*) U. S. Stat. at large, v. i. p. 81.

Court by the subsequent judiciary act of 1802, having its origin in the evil of a division of opinion which must so often occur between the two judges of the Circuit Court. This must be classed among the appellate powers of the court, although it may be, perhaps, termed rather a power of umpirage than of review.

Under this head of appellate jurisdiction, will be considered, 1. Writs of error to the Circuit Court; and at the same time will be considered, writs of error from the Circuit to the District Courts, which were, for convenience, omitted in their proper place: 2. Writs of error to the highest court of the State: 3. Certificates of points of disagreement from the Circuit Court: 4. Writs of mandamus, prohibition, *habeas corpus*, &c.

Error to the Circuit Court, &c.—The following sections of the judiciary act of 1789 provide for the cases in which writs of error may be brought upon the final judgments of the Circuit or District Courts, and also contain several directions as to the proceedings.

" Final decrees and judgments, in civil actions in a District Court, where the matter in dispute exceeds the sum or value of fifty dollars, exclusive of costs, may be re-examined, and reversed, or affirmed in a Circuit Court, holden in the same district, upon a writ of error, whereto shall be annexed and returned therewith, at the day and place therein mentioned, an authenticated transcript of the record, and assignment of errors, and prayer for reversal, with a citation to the adverse party, signed by the judge of such District Court, or a justice of the Supreme Court, the adverse party having at least twenty days' notice.

" And upon a like process may final judgments and decrees in civil actions and suits in equity, in a Circuit Court, brought there by original process, or removed there from courts of the several States, or removed there by appeal from a District Court, where the matter in dispute exceeds the sum or value of two thousand dollars, exclusive of costs, be re-examined and reversed, or affirmed, in the Supreme Court, the citation being in such case signed by a judge of such Circuit Court, or justice of the Supreme Court, and the adverse party having at least thirty days' notice.

" But there shall be no reversal in either court on such writ of error, for error in ruling any plea in abatement, other than a plea to the jurisdiction of the court, or such plea to a petition or bill in equity, as in the nature of a demurrer, or for any error in fact.   And writs of error shall not be brought but within five years after rendering or passing the judgment or decree complained of, or in case the person entitled to such writ of error be an infant, *feme covert, non compos mentis,* or imprisoned, then within five years as aforesaid, exclusive of the time of such disability. And every justice, or judge, signing a citation on any writ of error as aforesaid, shall take good and sufficient security, that the plaintiff in error shall prosecute his writ to effect, and answer all damages and costs, if he fail to make his plea good.   § 22.(*m*)

" A writ of error, as aforesaid, shall be a *supersedeas*, and stay execution, in cases only where the writ of error is served, by a copy thereof being lodged, for the adverse party, in the clerk's office, where the record remains, within ten days, Sundays exclusive, after rendering the judg-

(*m*) U. S. Stat. at large, v. i. p. 84.

ment or passing the decree complained of. Until the expiration of which term of ten days, executions shall not issue, in any case where a writ of error may be a *supersedeas ;* and where upon such writ of error the Supreme or a Circuit Court shall affirm a judgment or decree, they shall adjudge or decree to the respondent in error, just damages for his delay, and single or double costs, at their discretion. § 23.

"When a judgment or decree shall be reversed in a Circuit Court, such court shall proceed to render such judgment, or pass such decree, as the District Court should have rendered or passed; and the Supreme Court shall do the same on reversals therein, except where the reversal is in favor of the plaintiff or petitioner in the original suit, and the damages to be assessed, or matter to be decreed, are uncertain : in which case, they shall remand the cause for final decision. And the Supreme . Court shall not issue execution in causes that are removed before them by writs of error; but shall send a special mandate to the Circuit Court, to award execution thereupon."(*n*)

Doubts having arisen, under the twenty-second section, as to the extent of the security to be required on signing the citation on a writ of error, Congress passed an explanatory act, declaring that "the security to be required and taken, on the signing of a citation on any writ of error, which shall not be a *supersedeas,* and stay execution, shall be only to such an amount as, in the opinion of the justice or judge taking the same, shall be sufficient to answer all such costs as, upon an affirmance of the judgment or decree, may be adjudged or decreed to the respondent in error.(*o*)

The process act of 1792,(*p*) contains the following provision, allowing writs of error returnable in the Supreme Court, to issue from the Circuit Court :—

"It shall be the duty of the clerk of the Supreme Court of the United States, forthwith, to transmit to the clerks of the several Circuit Courts, the form of a writ of error, to be approved by any two of the judges of the Supreme Court; and it shall be lawful for the clerks of the said Circuit Courts, to issue writs of error agreeably to such forms, as nearly as the case may admit, under the seal of the said Circuit Courts, returnable to the Supreme Court, in the same manner as the clerk of the Supreme Court may issue such writs, in pursuance of the act, entitled ' An act to establish the judicial courts of the United States.' "

In cases of copyrights and patents, it is provided, that from all judgments and decrees of any Circuit Court, as well in equity as at law, rendered in all actions, suits, controversies, and cases arising under any law in the United States, granting or confirming to authors or inventors the exclusive right to their writings, inventions, and discoveries, a writ of error, or appeal, as the case may require, shall lie to the Supreme Court of the United States, in the same manner and under the same circumstances as is now provided by law in other judgments and decrees of such Circuit Courts.(*q*)

Final judgments in any Circuit Court in the United States, in any

---

(*n*) U. S. Stat. at large, v. i. p. 84, § 24.
(*o*) Act of Dec. 12, 1794; U. S. Stat. at large, v. i. p. 404.
(*p*) May 8; U. S. Stat. at large, v. i.

p. 278.
(*q*) Act 1819, Feb. 15; U. S. Stat. at large, v. iii. p. 481. (Re-enacted as to inventors, by the patent act of 1836, § 17.

civil action brought by the United States, for the enforcement of the revenue laws of the United States, or for the collection of the duties due, or alleged to be due, on merchandise imported therein, may be re-examined, and reversed, or affirmed, in the Supreme Court of the United States, upon writ of error, as in other cases, without regard to the sum or value in controversy in such action, at the instance of either party.(r)

In order to give the Supreme Court jurisdiction, the matter in dispute must exceed two thousand dollars, exclusive of costs. In an action instituted in a Circuit Court for the violation of a patent, the plaintiff claimed more than two thousand dollars in his declaration, but obtained a judgment for four hundred dollars. The Supreme Court ruled —expressly overruling the case of Wilson v. Daniel(s)—that its jurisdiction depends on the sum or value in dispute between the parties, as the case stands upon the writ of error in it; not on that which was in dispute in the Circuit Court.(ss)   If the writ of error be brought by the plaintiff below, then the sum which the declaration shows to be due may be still recovered, should the judgment for a smaller sum be reversed; and consequently, the whole sum claimed is in dispute.(t)   But if brought by the defendant below, this court can only affirm that of the Circuit Court.(u)   The party bringing the writ of error must prove that the value exceeds two thousand dollars.(v)

In a case where the penalty of the bond was twenty thousand dollars, but the breach assigned was the non-payment of only three hundred and twenty-eight dollars, the court held the latter to be the matter in dispute.(w)

In an action of dower, where the matter in dispute did not appear upon the record, the court ordered the same to be ascertained by affidavits to be taken on ten days' notice to the opposite party, the writ of error not to operate as a *supersedeas*.(x)

In an action of trover, where judgment had been rendered below for the defendants, it was contended that the court must be satisfied by evidence, other than the declaration, of the matter in dispute; but the court said that that rule applied only to cases where the property itself, and not damages, was the matter in dispute, such as actions of detinue, &c.; and observed further, that if the judgment below be for the plaintiff, that judgment ascertains the matter in dispute; but that where the judgment below was rendered for the defendant, the court had not, by any rule or practice, fixed the mode of ascertaining that value.(y)

In an action of replevin it was held that as in that action the damages were merely nominal, if the writ were issued as a means of trying the title to property it was in the nature of detinue, and the value of the article replevied was the matter in dispute; but that if the replevin was of goods distrained for rent, the amount for which avowry was made was the matter in dispute.(z)   And in another case in replevin, where the replevin bond was in the penal sum of twelve hundred

(r) Act 1844, May 31; U. S. Stat. at large, v. v. p. 658.
  (s) 3 Dall. 401.
  (ss) 3 Peters, 33.
  (t) Ibid.
  (u) Ibid. S. P. Ibid. 469.

(v) 10 Ibid. 160; 4 Cranch, 216.
  (w) 4 Cranch, 316.
  (x) 4 D. 20; and see rule of Aug. 15, 1800.
  (y) 5 Cranch, 14; 9 Wheat. 527.
  (z) 9 Wheat. 527.

dollars only, it was contended that this was conclusive evidence as to the matter in dispute, but the court allowed the plaintiff in error time to show by affidavits its real value.(a)

This court has not jurisdiction in a case in which separate decrees have been entered in the Circuit Court for the wages of seamen, the decree in no one of the cases amounting to $2000; although the amount of all exceeded that sum, and the seamen in each case claimed under the same contract with the owners.(b) So in the case of salvage apportioned amongst numerous claimants.(c)

In covenant for ground-rent, the plaintiff claimed in his declaration a sum over the jurisdiction of the Circuit Court, and laid his damages at a sum within their jurisdiction : a general verdict having been given against him, the matter in dispute is the sum which he claims in the *ad damnum*. The court will not judicially notice, that by computation, it may be inferred from the declaration, that the plaintiff's claim in reality must be without the jurisdiction of the court below, particularly where the plaintiff might be allowed interest enough to swell his claim beyond the jurisdiction.(d)

Where the prayer of a bill in equity shows that the demand of the complainant is susceptible of definite computation, and that there can be no recovery over the sum of $2000, the appeal will be dismissed on motion, for want of jurisdiction.

Where error was brought upon a peremptory mandamus to admit one to office, the court held that the salary was the value of the office and matter in dispute, and they allowed it to be shown by affidavits,(e) at the same time deciding that it was a case in which error would lie.(f)

A writ of error, by the provisions of the judiciary act, will only lie upon the final judgment of the court below ;(g) nor will it lie for any error in fact, and therefore where the judgment is upon the issue of *nul tiel* record, a writ of error will not lie, as such issue, although triable by the court, is an issue of fact.(h)

If a judgment is final, so that execution could issue upon it, and the defendant be thus injured by it, he is entitled to a writ of error, notwithstanding it may be defective.(i)

Under the act of 1789, it was held that where a cause had been removed from a District Court to the Circuit Court by writ of error, error would not lie to the Supreme Court upon the judgment of the Circuit Court; as the judiciary act of 1789, which alone regulates the subject, provides for such writs, in cases at common law, only in suits brought in the Circuit Court by original process, or removed there from the State courts.(j) But by the act of July 4th, 1840, § 3, this distinction was abolished, and writs of error now lie to the Supreme Court from all judgments of a Circuit Court, in cases brought there by writs of error from the District Courts in like manner as if the suit had been originally brought in the Circuit Court.(jj)

We have seen that the allowance or disallowance of amendments is

(a) 5 Cranch, 287, and as to amount see *ante*, " Circuit Court."
(b) 6 Peters, 143.
(c) 8 Ibid. 4.
(d) 6 Ibid. 349.
(e) 7 Wheat. 534.
(f) And see 6 Wheat. 598.

(g) 4 D. 22.
(h) 2 Mason, 28 ; and see 3 D. 54.
(i) 3 D. 404.
(j) 7 Cranch, 108, 287 ; 2 Wheat. 248, 395.
(jj) U. S. Stat. at large, v. v. p. 393.

not ground for error ;(*k*) nor will error lie for a refusal of the court below to grant a new trial.(*l*) Any defect appearing upon the record which would have been fatal on motion in arrest of judgment, is equally fatal upon a writ of error, and it is not too late to allege it in the court above.(*m*) But as these and the like principles are not peculiar to the courts of the United States, they will not be further considered in this place.

Where a writ of error was tested after the term had expired, the court allowed it to be amended ;(*n*) but where a writ was sued out of the day it was tested, and a term intervened between the teste and return, the court refused to allow it to be amended ;(*o*) but they allowed it to be done where it was not sued out until after the intervening term.(*p*) Where the writ was returnable of August term, but not returned, nor the record transmitted until the following February, the court said it was a nullity ;(*q*) but in a subsequent case the court held, that if the writ was served before the return day and while in full force, but not returned until afterwards, the return would be good, and that although it was not returned of the term when returnable, the appearance of the defendant waived all objection.(*r*) The court in this case said that the service of the writ was the lodging of a copy thereof for the adverse party in the office of the clerk of the court below ; and they held such service to be good, although made before the judgment below was signed.(*s*)

The security to be taken by the judge signing the citation, in order to operate as a *supersedeas*, must be sufficient to secure the whole judgment on which the writ is brought ; and where security had been taken to cover only such damages and costs as the court should adjudge for the delay, the court, on motion, ordered the cause to stand dismissed unless a proper bond were given in thirty days.(*t*) Where the defendant in error had intermarried after the judgment, service of the citation on her husband was held to be sufficient, the act not designating any person on whom it must be served.(*u*) Unless the citation be served thirty days before the first day of term, the court will not take up the cause without consent of parties.(*v*) If a citation do not accompany the writ of error it will be quashed or dismissed ;(*w*) but if the citation has been served, but the clerk has not returned it with the writ, a *certiorari* will be allowed to bring it up.(*x*)

It is not necessary that it should appear by the record that the judge signing the citation took the bond required by the act.(*y*) If the record be not filed within the first six days of term, as required by the rule, but is filed before a motion made to dismiss the writ, the rule does not apply.(*z*) The omission of the names of the jurors in the record was held to be immaterial.(*a*)

In a case which came up to have a judgment reversed which had been

(*k*) *Ante,* p. 188.
(*l*) 5 Cranch, 11, 280 ; 7 Ibid. 155.
(*m*) 6 Ibid. 221.
(*n*) 4 D. 25.
(*o*) 3 Ibid. 371.
(*p*) 7 Cranch, 277.
(*q*) 4 D. 21.
(*r*) 4 Cranch, 180.
(*s*) Ibid.

(*t*) 9 Wheat. 553.
(*u*) 5 Cranch, 21.
(*v*) 5 Ibid. 221 ; *sed. vide* 1 Ibid. 365.
(*w*) 1 Ibid. 365 ; 2 Ibid. 406.
(*x*) 3 Ibid. 514.
(*y*) 1 Wheat. 361.
(*z*) 7 Cranch, 99 ; and see Rules.
(*a*) 9 Ibid. 180.

rendered on a bond given to the marshal, conditioned that goods seized by him on execution should be forthcoming, on the ground that this court had already reversed the judgment upon which the execution was issued, a difficulty arose how the court were to be satisfied of the connection be- tween the judgments; there being no intrinsic error in the latter judg- ment, but a reversal being proper if it had the alleged dependence upon the first judgment. In order to avoid the difficulty, the court ordered a special writ to be framed, to suit also similar cases, directing the clerk of the court where the judgments were rendered to certify the execution, which, though no part of either record, would supply the link necessary to prove the connection between the judgments.(b)

It is incumbent on the plaintiff in error to show that the court has appellate jurisdiction,(c) and this must appear upon the record,(d) and the court refused to regard for this purpose the report of the judge who tried the cause, containing a statement of the facts, as it was no part of the record, but addressed merely to the discretion of the court.(e) The plaintiff below may assign for error the want of jurisdiction in the court to which he has chosen to resort,(f) as consent will not give jurisdiction; and the court above will not take cognizance of a case by consent of parties, but only when brought before them by the regular process of the law.(g) But where a cause had been removed by *certiorari* from the District to the Circuit Court in an entirely irregular and illegal manner, but the cause was within the jurisdiction of the latter court, and the parties appeared and litigated there, on error to the Supreme Court, it was held, that it was too late after verdict to object to the irregularity in the proceedings, and that the court would consider the suit as an original one in the Circuit Court, made so by consent of parties.(h)

A writ of error will lie from a judgment upon a general verdict taken subject to the opinion of the court, upon a case made, or case agreed ;(i) and as it would seem from these cases, without turning the case into a special verdict or bill of exceptions.

If the plaintiff in error does not appear, the defendant may have him called and dismiss the writ, or may open the record and pray for an affirmance ;(j) and where no appearance was entered on the docket for either party, and no counsel appeared, the court ordered the parties to be called, and dismissed the writ.(k)

Costs, in cases of reversal, do not go, of course ; but in all cases of affirmance they do ;(l) and where a judgment is reversed for want of jurisdiction, it is without costs.(m)

If the judgment of the court below is reversed upon a special verdict, or case agreed, the court above will proceed to give judgment; but where a judgment or verdict in favor of a plaintiff is reversed, on a bill of exceptions to instructions given to the jury, a new trial must be awarded by the court below ;(n) and the court applied the same rule to

(b) 7 Cranch, 288.
(c) 4 Ibid. 216.
(d) 2 Wheat. 368.
(e) Ibid. ; and see 7 Wheat. 426.
(f) 2 Cranch, 125.
(g) 3 D. 410.
(h) 2 Wheat. 221; see 1 Cranch, 428.

(i) 3 Cranch, 174; 5 Ibid. 358; 6 Id. 285 ; 6 Wheat. 268.
(j) 3 Cranch, 249.
(k) 5 Ibid. 289.
(l) 4 Ibid. 47.
(m) Ibid. ; but see 3 Id. 315 ; 2 Wheat. 368; 3 Id. 435.
(n) 6 Cranch, 285.

a case of a bill of exceptions to the opinion of the court, where there had been in reality no trial, but a case had been made and used as a bill of exceptions, in order to have the opinion of the court on certain questions of law.(o)   And where there was a special verdict, but it was too imperfect, on account of a material fact not being found to enable the court to render judgment upon it, the cause was remanded with directions that a *venire facias de novo* should be awarded.(p)   It has been held that this practice of remanding a cause from the Supreme Court for trial below, which is necessary in that court from the terms of the act,(q) need not be observed in cases of error from the District Court, but that the Circuit Court may, if justice require it, award a *venire de novo*, and try the cause at bar.(r)

If a judgment be reversed and a cause remanded, and the plaintiff in error obtain a judgment in the court below, the judgment is to be entered with the costs of that court; and in all cases of reversal, if the court direct the court below to enter judgment for the plaintiff in error, the latter enters the judgment of course, with the costs of the court below.(s)   After a cause has been remanded, the court below may receive additional pleas, or admit amendments to those already filed, and even after the court above has decided such pleas to be bad upon demurrer.(t)

In causes remanded to the Circuit Court, if the mandate be not correctly executed, a second writ of error lies thereupon to the Supreme Court.(u)

Most of these decisions on the subject of writs of error were made in the Supreme Court ; but their application to writs of error from the Circuit to District Courts, will be readily ascertained by a reference to the provisions of the judiciary act, where the differences made between writs from the Supreme and Circuit Courts will be found to be very small.

It has been held that error lies upon a judgment of the District Court for the repeal of a patent,(v) under the patent law, the value of the patent being admitted to be sufficient to give the court jurisdiction, and it appearing upon the record that each of the parties claimed the invention as his own ; but the court declined to decide whether error could have been had if the plaintiff had claimed no title to the invention ; suggesting the difficulty which would occur in such a case as to the matter in dispute.(w)

Error to the highest State Court.—The judiciary act of 1789 provides that " a final judgment or decree in any suit, in the highest court of law or equity of a State in which a decision in the suit could be had, where is drawn in question the validity of a treaty or statute of, or an authority exercised under, the United States, and the decision is against their validity ; or where is drawn in question the validity of a statute of, or an authority exercised under, any State, on the ground of their being repugnant to the constitution, treaties, or laws of the United States, and the decision is in favor of such their validity ; or where is drawn in

(o) 12 Wheat. 180.
(p) 11 Ibid. 415 ; and see 7 Cranch, 434.
(q) Act of 1789, § 24.
(r) 1 Gall. 86.
(s) 6 Cranch, 187.

(t) Ibid. 206.
(u) 1 Wheat. 352, 353.
(v) See act of Feb. 21, 1793, § 10; U. S. Stat. at large, v. i. p. 323.
(w) 1 Mason, 153, 167.

question the construction of any clause of the constitution, or of a treaty or statute of, or commission held under, the United States, and the decision is against the title, right, privilege, or exemption, specially set up or claimed by either party, under such clause of the said constitution, treaty, statute, or commission, may be re-examined, and reversed or affirmed in the Supreme Court of the United States, upon a writ of error, the citation being signed by the chief justice, or judge, or chancellor of the court rendering or passing the judgment or decree complained of, or by a justice of the Supreme Court of the United States, in the same manner and under the same regulations; and the writ shall have the same effect as if the judgment or decree complained of had been rendered or passed in a Circuit Court, and the proceeding upon the reversal shall also be the same, except that the Supreme Court, instead of remanding the cause for a final decision, as before provided, may, at their discretion, if the cause shall have been once remanded before, proceed to a final decision of the same, and award execution. But no other error shall be assigned or regarded as a ground of reversal, in any such case as aforesaid, than such as appears on the face of the record, and immediately respects the before-mentioned questions of validity or construction of the said constitution, treaties, statutes, commissions, or authorities in dispute." § 25.

This is the only statutory provision regulating the appellate jurisdiction of the Supreme Court over questions arising in the State courts, under the constitution, laws, and treaties of the United States.

The constitutionality of this provision having been called in question, it was held, after great consideration, that, as the appellate jurisdiction of the Supreme Court conferred by the constitution was unlimited, and declared to extend to certain cases, without any reference to the courts in which they might originate; and as the constitution had, moreover, expressly declared that the constitution, laws, and treaties of the United States should be binding upon the judges of the State courts,(x) and as State courts must continually be called upon, in cases coming within their ordinary jurisdiction, to pronounce upon the effect of the laws of the United States; and as there ought to be but one common interpretation of those laws, the constitution meant to extend the appellate jurisdiction of the Supreme Court to the State courts;(y) and it is no objection to the exercise of such jurisdiction that one party is a State and the other a citizen of that State.(z)

The judgment of the State court must be final; and therefore, where the highest State court had given judgment of reversal upon error from an inferior court, where judgment had been rendered for the plaintiff, and ordered a *venire de novo*, on remanding the cause; it was held that error would not lie to the Supreme Court, as the judgment might still be finally given for the plaintiff.(a) The judgment must be final, so as to determine the particular cause, but need not be such as finally to decide the right, so that it can never again be litigated between the parties.(b)

That provision of the act which requires that the court appealed from

(x) Art. 6.
(y) 1 Wheat. 337; 6 Wheat. 413.
(z) 6 Ibid. 264.

(a) 3 Ibid. 433; 12 Id. 135.
(b) 2 Peters, 449.

should be the highest court of the State in which a decision in the suit can be had, does not appear to have often called for the construction of the court; but in the case of Cohens v. Virginia,(c) the inferior court where the suit was depending, having refused to allow an appeal to a higher State court, on the ground that it was a case not subject to revision, it seems to have been taken for granted that a writ of error lay to the inferior court. In this case the jurisdiction of this court necessarily appeared upon the record; but there does not appear to be any case suggesting a mode of reviewing the decisions of inferior State courts, upon matters collateral in a suit, where the laws of the United States are in question, but which, not forming a part of the record, cannot be carried to the highest State court, where judgment may be finally given.

In order to bring a cause for a writ of error or appeal within the 25th section, it must appear on the face of the record, 1st, that one of the questions stated in that section did arise in the State court; 2d, that the question was decided in the State court, as required in that section.(d)

Where the record of a case in the Supreme Court of a State does not show that a constitutional question was raised, the Supreme Court of the United States will dismiss a writ of error issued thereon under the 25th section of the judiciary act, for want of jurisdiction.(e)

It is not indispensable that it should appear on the record in totidem verbis, or by direct or positive statement, that the question was made and the decision given by the court below on the very point; it is sufficient if it is clear, from the facts stated, by just and necessary inference, that the question was made, and that the court below must, in order to have arrived at the judgment pronounced by it, have come to the very decision of that question as indispensable to their judgment.(f)

In a case where both parties claimed title to land under the same act of Congress, but both were citizens of the same State, it was objected that the court, from this circumstance, had not jurisdiction; but it was held otherwise,(g) as the appellate jurisdiction arises wholly from the character of the case, and not of the parties.(h) And the court has also had occasion to decide that the value of the matter in dispute is immaterial;(i) that the writ need not purport to be issued upon the final judgment of the highest State court;(j) and that it may issue, like writs to the Circuit Court, out of the Circuit Court.(k) This court has no authority, on a writ of error from a State court, to declare a State law void on account of its collision with a State constitution; it not being a case embraced in the judiciary act, which gives the power of a writ of error to the highest judicial tribunal of the State.(l)

Where a municipal body had taxed United States stock, and an inferior State court, on the application of the stockholders, had granted a writ of prohibition to restrain the levying of the tax, and on a removal of the cause to the highest State court, the order for the prohibition had

---

(c) 6 Wheat. 290.
(d) 10 Peters, 368; 2 Wheat. 363; 4 Wheat. 311; 5 Howard, 317.
(e) 7 How. U. S. 279.
(f) 10 Peters, 368; 16 Ibid. 281; 2 Ibid. 245, 280.

(g) 4 Cranch, 382.
(h) 6 Wheat. 375, 264.
(i) 8 Wheat. 321.
(j) Ibid.
(k) Ibid.
(l) 3 Peters, 280.

been reversed; it was held, on error to the Supreme Court, that a writ of prohibition was a suit within the meaning of the act, and the judgment a final judgment, and within the appellate jurisdiction of the court.(m)

It has also been held, that a writ of error will lie upon the judgment of a court on a motion for a mandamus ;(n) and where a State court entertained, as within its jurisdiction, a motion for a mandamus to compel an officer of the United States to perform an alleged duty under the laws of the United States, but refused the mandamus on the merits of the case, and the relator brought a writ of error from their judgment to the Supreme Court, that court entertained the writ of error as within its jurisdiction, but holding that the State court had no jurisdiction in such a case, and affirming the judgment with costs.(o)

The jurisdiction of the Supreme Court of the United States, under the 25th section of the judiciary act, does not extend to a case where the alleged violation of the contract is, that a state has taken more land than was necessary for the easement which it wanted, and thus violated the contract under which the owner held his land by a patent.(p)

Where, upon the trial of a case in a State court, a party claimed the land in controversy under an authority which, he alleged, had been exercised by the Secretary of the Treasury in behalf of the United States, and the decision was against the validity of the authority, it was held that such party was entitled to have his case brought to the Supreme Court of the United States under the 25th section of the judiciary act.(q)

The proceedings on writs of error to the State court are, with a few exceptions, which will be readily seen by referring to the statute, the same as on writs of error to the Circuit Courts, which we have already considered, and to which the reader is referred.

If the cause has been once remanded before, and the State court declines or refuses to carry into effect the mandate of the Supreme Court thereon, this court will proceed to a final decision of the same, and award execution thereon.(r)

If the Court of Errors has given judgment and remanded the cause to an inferior court, where the record remains, so that the former court cannot return the record with the writ, a second writ may be issued to the court where the record is to be found, in order to bring it up.(s)

As to the costs of the writ, and the State court to which the mandate is to be directed, it was held, in a cause which came up on error from the judgment of the highest State court, reversing the judgment of an inferior court, which had been rendered in favor of the plaintiff in error, that on reversing the judgment of the highest court, and affirming that of the inferior court, the judgment of the former having become a nullity, the costs must follow the right as decided here, and that the costs of all the courts should be allowed to the plaintiff, and the mandate for execution be issued to the inferior court.(t)

Certificate of Points of Disagreement from the Circuit Court.—When

(m) 2 Peters, 463.
(n) 7 Wheat. 534.
(o) 6 Wheat. 598.
(p) M'LEAN, J., dissenting, 8 How.
U. S. 569.

(q) 7 How. U. S. 772.
(r) 1 Wheat. 304.
(s) 3 Wheat. 304, 305.
(t) 3 D. 342.

the judges of the Circuit Court differ in opinion upon any question, except in cases coming up on error, or by appeal from the District Courts, a summary and informal appeal for the determination of such question, is allowed to the Supreme Court of the United States, by the following statutory provision :—

"Whenever any question shall occur before a Circuit Court, upon which the opinions of the judges shall be opposed, the point upon which the disagreement shall happen, shall, during the same term, upon the request of either party, or their counsel, be stated under the direction of the judges, and certified under the seal of the court, to the Supreme Court, at their next session to be held thereafter; and shall, by the said court, be finally decided. And the decision of the Supreme Court, and their order in the premises, shall be remitted to the Circuit Court, and be there entered of record, and shall have effect according to the nature of the said judgment and order: *Provided*, That nothing herein contained shall prevent the cause from proceeding, if, in the opinion of the court, further proceedings can be had without prejudice to the merits."(v)

Upon this provision the following decisions have been made: When a question in a cause is certified to the Supreme Court, the law gives that court jurisdiction over the single point only on which the judges were divided, and not over the whole cause, or any other part of it. It is not necessary that any of the proceedings in the Circuit Court should be stated, upon which the questions certified do not arise, but only enough to show the principle on which the judges were divided.(w) But the court will entertain jurisdiction of several questions if they appear to have arisen at one time, at one stage of the cause, and substantially involve but one point.(x) But after a final judgment of the Circuit Court, the whole case may be brought before the Supreme Court by writ of error, in the same manner as if no question had been certified.(y)

But the whole cause cannot be certified on a division of the judges. The act intended to provide for a division of opinion on single points, which occur in the trial of a cause;(z) and a construction which would authorize a transfer of an entire cause before final judgment, would counteract the policy which forbids writs of error and appeals until a final judgment or decree.(a) And where it is evident from the record, that the whole case had been sent up to the Supreme Court, upon a certificate of division of opinion, the case must be dismissed for want of jurisdiction.(b)

As the district judge cannot vote in the Circuit Court, on a writ of error from the District Court, but judgment must be rendered according to the opinion of the presiding judge, the Supreme Court in such cases has no jurisdiction to entertain a certificate of a division of opinion of the judges, and consequently no division can be certified.(c) Nor has the Supreme Court any jurisdiction where the question certified arises upon some proceeding after the decision of the cause in the Circuit Court.(d) Nor where the question is, whether a new trial ought to be

(v) Act of April 29, 1802, § 6; U. S. Stat. at large, v. ii. p. 159.
(w) 10 Wheat. 1, 20, 21.
(x) 7 How. 185.
(y) 2 Cranch, 33.
(z) See 10 Peters, 286; 5 How. 208.

(a) 9 Peters, 267, 273 ; and see 10 Id. 286, 366.
(b) 6 How. 41; 7 How. 646.
(c) 5 Wheat. 434.
(d) 12 Wheat. 212; 6 Peters, 26.

granted, the motion for that purpose not being a part of the proceedings in the cause, but an application to the discretion of the court, and upon the decision of which a writ of error will not lie.(e)

The judges do not state in the certificate the reasons of their opinion, but merely the point of disagreement.(f) Where the questions are so imperfectly certified that the Supreme Court cannot pronounce upon them, the only step which they take in the case is, to certify to the court below, the fact of such imperfection.(g)

So, if the point on which the judges are divided in opinion be not certified, but the point of difference is only to be ascertained from the whole record, this court will remand the cause for that reason.(h)

Where a cause is brought before the Supreme Court of the United States on a division in opinion, between the judges of the Circuit Court, the points certified only are before the Supreme Court; the cause should remain on the docket of the Circuit Court, and at their discretion may be prosecuted.(i)

Writs of Prohibition, Mandamus, Habeas Corpus, &c.—We have seen that the thirteenth section of the judiciary act declares that the Supreme Court "shall have power to issue writs of prohibition to the District Courts when proceeding as courts of admiralty and maritime jurisdiction, and writs of mandamus, in cases warranted by the principles and usages of law, to any courts appointed, or persons holding office, under the authority of the United States."

The writ of mandamus, which the court is by this section allowed to issue, will be first considered. We have already had occasion to observe that the clause relating to the writ of mandamus, so far as it attempts to confer original jurisdiction upon the court, has been held to be unconstitutional. In the same case, however, in which this point was ruled,(j) it was held that the writ might be issued in cases where the jurisdiction was of an appellate nature.

On this subject the court observed: "It has been stated at the bar that the appellate jurisdiction may be exercised in a variety of forms, and that if it be the will of the legislature that a mandamus be used for that purpose, that will must be obeyed. This is true, yet the jurisdiction must be appellate, not original. It is the essential criterion of appellate jurisdiction, that it reviews and corrects the proceedings in a cause already instituted, and does not create that cause. Although, therefore, a mandamus may be directed to courts, yet to issue such a writ to an officer for the delivery of a paper, is in effect the same as to sustain an original action for that paper, and, therefore, seems not to belong to appellate, but to original jurisdiction."

This case, then, establishes the power of the court, under this provision of the judiciary act, to issue writs of mandamus to any courts of the United States; and that it is an independent branch of its appellate jurisdiction; while it denies generally that the court can have any power under it to issue such writs to persons holding office under the United States. The act, however, in this case, which it was sought by the mandamus to compel the officer to perform, was one of a merely minis-

(e) 6 Wheat. 547 ; 4 Wash. C. C. 332.
(f) Trial of Smith and Ogden, 47.
(g) 11 Wheat. 257.
(h) 3 Peters, 269 ;·S. P. 4 Id. 392.
(i) 8 How. 586.
(j) 1 Cranch, 137, 175 ; see *ante*, p. 198; 5 Peters, 190.

terial character,(*k*) and in no way connected with the judicial power: And it might, perhaps, be still considered open to inquiry whether a mandamus, under this section, will only lie to inferior courts to be ordained and established by Congress with permanent judges as the constitution requires, or may be also issued to persons holding office under the authority of the United States, where they are invested with and exercise any portion of the judicial power described by the constitution, and in cases where it allows this court appellate jurisdiction.

It will be observed that the mandamus of which we are now speaking, is in principle quite different from the ordinary writ of mandamus which the courts of the United States are allowed to issue.   This forms a distinct and independent branch of the appellate jurisdiction of the Supreme Court; the other it issues like the other courts, in cases where it is necessary for the exercise of a jurisdiction to which it is otherwise entitled, whether original or appellate ; and under a different section of the judiciary act.

The Supreme Court will not grant a mandamus to a district judge to grant an application resting in his discretion,(*l*) but it will to compel a judge to execute a sentence pronounced by him;(*m*) and it will lie to the Circuit Court requiring it to sign a bill of exceptions.(*n*)

Where an application was made for a mandamus to compel a Circuit Court to restore an attorney who had been suspended, the court observed that some doubts were felt respecting the extent of its authority as to the conduct of the Circuit and District Courts towards their officers, but denied the motion on other grounds.(*nn*)

On a mandamus, this court will not order an inferior tribunal to render judgment for or against either party; but it will, in a proper case, order such court to proceed to judgment.   To justify this mandate, however, a plain case of refusing to decide in the inferior court, ought to be made out.(*o*)

A writ of mandamus is not a proper process to correct an erroneous judgment or decree rendered in an inferior court.(*p*)

But one case has arisen under the above provision of the judiciary act, of a prohibition to a District Court proceeding as a court of admiralty and maritime jurisdiction, and no question was made in it as to the constitutionality or construction of the provision.(*q*)   The power conferred is of course of an appellate nature.

The fourteenth section of the judiciary act provides that "all the courts of the United States shall have power to issue writs of *scire facias*, *habeas corpus*, and all other writs not specially provided for by statute, which may be necessary for the exercise of their respective jurisdictions, and agreeable to the principles and usages of law.   And that either of the justices of the Supreme Court, as well as judges of the District Court, shall have power to grant writs of *habeas corpus*, for the purpose of an inquiry into the cause of commitment.   *Provided*, That writs of *habeas corpus* shall, in no case, extend to prisoners in jail, unless where they are in custody, under or by color of the authority of the

(*k*) See 8 Peters, 306.
(*l*) 6 Peters, 216, 661 ; 7 Peters, 637.
(*m*) 5 Cranch, 115.
(*n*) 5 Peters, 190.

(*nn*) 9 Wheat. 529.
(*o*) 9 Peters, 574, 602, 603.
(*p*) 13 Peters, 279.
(*q*) 3 D. 121.

United States, or are committed for trial before some court of the same, or are necessary to be brought into court to testify."

Under this act, the right of the Circuit and District Courts to issue the writ of mandamus is confined exclusively to those cases in which it may be necessary to the exercise of their jurisdiction.(r)   And that it would seem that the Circuit Court may issue a mandamus to a State court which refuses to transfer a cause under the act of Congress ;(s) and where a District Court refuses to give judgment, a mandamus lies to compel it.(t)   But a mandamus will not lie to a District Court to compel it to expunge amendments improperly made in the record returned to the Circuit Court on a writ of error.(u)

In 4 Cranch, 75, it was definitely settled that the Supreme Court possess power to issue the writ of *habeas corpus ad subjiciendum* to bring up a prisoner committed for trial, on a criminal charge under the authority of the United States.   But in 7 Wheaton, 38, it was held that it would not be granted where a prisoner has been committed for contempt by any court of competent jurisdiction, and, if granted, the court would not inquire into the sufficiency of the cause of the commitment— as the adjudication of the court below is a conviction, and the imprisonment an execution, and the Supreme Court has no appellate jurisdiction in criminal cases.

(r) 7 Cranch, 504; Paine, 453.   (t) 7 Cranch, 577.
(s) *Ante*, p. 163, n.   (u) Paine, 620.

CHAPTER V.

OF ATTORNEYS, AND OF THE PROSECUTION AND DEFENCE OF ACTIONS BY ATTORNEYS.

SECTION I.

OF ATTORNEYS.

AN attorney at law is a person put in the place, stead, or turn of another, to manage his matters of law.(a) By the act of assembly of 1806,(b) "in all civil suits or proceedings in any court within this commonwealth, every suitor and party concerned shall have a right to be heard, by himself and counsel, or either of them."

In the State of Pennsylvania, as is the almost general custom throughout the United States, the two capacities of counsel and attorney are combined.

It is not every person indiscriminately that is capable of exercising the functions of an attorney; but it is necessary for that purpose to possess certain qualifications, and to have conformed to certain regulations prescribed as well by statute, as by the rules of the court in which he is admitted to practise.

I. *Of the Admission of Attorneys, under the Act of Assembly and under the Rules of the Courts.*

The recent act of the 14th of April, 1834,(c) provides, on the subject of the admission, duties, and responsibilities of attorneys, as follows :—

The judges of the several courts of record of this commonwealth shall respectively have power to admit a competent number of persons of an honest disposition, and learned in the law, to practise as attorneys in their respective courts. § 68.

Before any attorney, admitted as aforesaid, shall make any plea at the bar except in his own case, he shall take an oath or affirmation, as follows, viz. :—

You do swear or affirm that you will support the constitution of the United States and the constitution of this commonwealth, and that you will behave yourself in the office of attorney within this court, according to the best of your learning and ability, and with all good fidelity, as

---

(a) 3 Bl. Com. 25.
(b) 4 Sm. Laws, 330.

(c) Pamph. L. p. 354, §§ 68 to 74.

well to the court as to the client; that you will use no falsehood, nor delay any person's cause for lucre or malice. § 69.

Every such attorney shall have power to commence, prosecute, and defend, all actions and suits in which he may be retained or concerned, from time to time, in the manner and with the effect hitherto allowed and practised. § 70.

The attorney for the plaintiff in every action, shall, if required, file his warrant of attorney in the office of the prothonotary or clerk of the court in which such action shall be depending, at the term of the court in which he declares; and the attorney for the defendant shall, if required, file in like manner his warrant of attorney, at the term of the court in which he appears. § 71.

If any attorney shall neglect or refuse to file his warrant of attorney in the manner required by law, he shall not be allowed a fee in the bill of costs, nor be suffered to speak in the cause until he shall have filed his warrant. § 72.

If any attorney at law shall misbehave himself in his office of attorney, he shall be liable to suspension, removal from office, or to such other penalties as have hitherto been allowed in such cases by the laws of this commonwealth. § 73.

If any such attorney shall retain money belonging to his client, after demand made by the client for the payment thereof, it shall be the duty of the court to cause the name of such attorney to be stricken from the record of attorneys, and to prevent him from prosecuting longer in the said court. § 74.

No judge of any court of this commonwealth shall practise as attorney or counsellor in any court of justice in this commonwealth or elsewhere, nor shall he hold or exercise the office of alderman or notary public. Nor shall any alderman or justice practise as aforesaid in any case which has been or may be removed from before him by appeal or writ of *certiorari*, nor act as agent in any such case. Nor shall any prothonotary or clerk of any court practise as aforesaid, in the court of which he shall be prothonotary or clerk. Nor shall the register of wills of any county practise as aforesaid, in the Orphans' Court of the same county. § 75.

By the act of the 14th of April, 1835, it is declared, that the above seventy-fifth section shall not be construed to extend to such person or persons as at the time of its passage held or exercised the office of alderman or notary public.

The periods of study requisite to obtain admission as an attorney into the several courts of this State are various.

The rules now in force in the District Court for the City and County of Philadelphia, in this respect, are as follows:—

VIII. It shall be the duty of every attorney of this court to register with the prothonotary, the name, age, and place of residence, of every person studying the law under his direction, and the time of clerkship shall be computed from the date of such registry.

IX. No person shall be permitted to practise as an attorney of this court, except upon the following conditions:—

1st. He shall be a citizen of the United States, and of full age.

2d. He shall have served a regular clerkship in the office and under the direction of a practising attorney of this, or some other court of this commonwealth, for three years, the last year of which clerkship shall have been passed in the office, and under the direction of a practising attorney, residing within the City or County of Philadelphia.—*Provided*, That if the applicant shall have been for a part of the said time in the office of a practising attorney of any other State, and the remaining par not being less than eighteen months in the office and under the direction of a practising attorney residing within the City or County of Philadelphia, the court may, in their discretion, allow him to be examined and admitted as if he had studied three years in the City or County of Philadelphia.

3d. His name shall have been registered with the prothonotary, as an applicant for admission, at least three, and not more than four calendar months before his admission; but no such registry shall be made except by permission of the court upon motion.

4th. He shall have undergone an examination before the board of examiners, appointed for such purpose, and shall produce and file with the prothonotary, at the time when his admission is moved for, a certificate signed by all the examiners who were present at his examination, that he is sufficiently qualified for admission to the bar, and that they have received satisfactory evidence, in writing, of his good moral character, which evidence of moral character shall also be at the same time produced, and filed as aforesaid.

X. Persons already admitted to practise in other courts of this commonwealth, may, at the discretion of this court, be admitted without an examination, on the production of a certificate, by the presiding judge of the Court of Common Pleas of the county wherein such person has been last admitted and practised, of the good moral character of the applicant for admission. No person shall be admitted without the examination and registries before mentioned, who has studied law in the City or County of Philadelphia, and has procured his admission elsewhere as a mere preliminary to his admission in this court.

XI. Attorneys from other States shall be admitted after a residence of two years within the State, the last year of which residence shall have been passed within the City or County of Philadelphia, upon producing satisfactory evidence of their admission into the Supreme or Superior Court of the State from which they came, and a certificate signed by the chief justice or presiding judge of such court, that they are of good standing at the bar, and of good moral character.(*d*)

XII. Persons in other respects qualified, who shall have studied the law in the office and under the direction of a practising attorney of the City and County of Philadelphia, two years after attaining the age of twenty-one years, shall be entitled to admission as attorneys on complying with the other rules of this court.

(*d*) See *post*, XII¾.

XII½. Attorneys at law from other States in which attorneys of this court are admitted to practise without any previous residence therein, upon producing satisfactory evidence of their admission into the Supreme or Superior Court of the State from which they came, and of their having practised in some one or more of the courts of record of that State during seven years or more, may be admitted to practise at the bar of this court, upon the recommendation of the board of examiners thereof.(e)

XII¾. No action shall be had by the board of examiners on any application for admission to the bar of this court, unless notice shall have been given of such application, by publication in the *Legal Intelligencer*, for four weeks immediately preceding the action of the board thereon.

XXVI. A board for the examination of applicants for admission to practise as attorneys of this court, to consist of nine members of the bar, of whom the eldest shall be chairman, and the youngest secretary, shall be appointed on the first Mondays of June and December in every year.

XXVII. No examination of a student of law for admission to practise shall take place except at a meeting of the said board, when six of the examiners shall be requisite to constitute a quorum.

XXVIII. All applications for examination, subject to the existing rules of court, shall be made to the chairman of the said board, whose duty it shall be to direct the secretary to summon the said board to meet at the earliest convenient time for the examination of the applicant, and to give written notice to him of the time and place of holding the said meeting.

XXIX. It shall be the duty of the said board to keep regular minutes of their proceedings, and to hand over the said minutes to their successors duly appointed as above provided, and no inspection, copy, or certificate of said minutes, or any part thereof, shall be allowed or given, except upon the order of the court, on motion to that effect.

The provisions of the fifth rule of the Common Pleas of Philadelphia County, are substantially similar to the foregoing rules of the District Court. The board of examiners consists of but seven members, of whom four constitute a quorum.

In the Supreme Court, the regulations for the admission of attorneys are as follows:—

No person shall be admitted to practise as an attorney or counsellor in this court, unless he hath served a regular clerkship, within this State, to some practising attorney, or gentleman of the law, of known abilities, for the term of four years, and afterwards practised as an attorney in some of the county Courts of Common Pleas for the term of one year; or served such clerkship for the term of three years and practised two years.

Provided always, that in the case of a person applying to be admitted, who shall appear to have studied the law with assiduity, under the direction of some practising attorney or gentleman of the law, of this State, for the term of two years after his arrival at the age of twenty-one years, and afterwards practised in some or one of the county Courts of Com-

(e) See *Ante*, XI.

mon Pleas, or District Courts for the term of two years, he may be admitted.

No person shall be admitted to practise as an attorney of this court, upon the ground that he has been admitted to practise in the courts of some other State, unless he be a citizen of the United States, and also unless it be shown that the attorneys of this court are entitled by the practice of the court where the applicant has been admitted, to admission under the like circumstances.

II. *Of the Punishment of Attorneys for Official Misconduct.*

The penalties inflicted for misconduct upon attorneys have been the same here as in England.(*f*)

The mode adopted there for the punishment of attorneys for misconduct (independently of the client's remedy by action, for misconduct or neglect, and where no other method is specifically pointed out by law) is by attachment, and in very gross cases by striking them off the roll; and if dismissed by one court, they shall not afterwards be admitted in any other.(*g*) Where an attorney is charged by affidavit, with any fraud or malpractice in his profession, contrary to the obvious rules of justice and common honesty, the court upon motion will order him to answer the matters of the affidavit. If he positively deny the matters alleged against him, the court will dismiss the complaint; otherwise they will award the attachment.(*h*) Yet where an attorney in his answer to interrogatories fully denied the matter of complaint, but in doing so, gave such an account of the transaction in question as was highly incredible, the court, notwithstanding the denial, granted the attachment.(*i*) The consequence of attachment may be fine and imprisonment, or either, at the court's discretion. It may be deemed an invariable rule, that the court will interfere in a summary way, where the misconduct complained of arises from want of integrity.(*j*)

By the third section of the act of 1808,(*k*) " the several courts of this commonwealth shall have power to enforce by attachment, the payment of moneys, had and received by any sheriff, coroner, or attorney, in his official capacity, and the delivery of all papers belonging to their clients." And by the seventy-fourth section of the act of 1834,(*l*) when any attorney has retained money belonging to his client, after demand made by the client for payment thereof, it shall be the duty of the court to prevent such attorney from prosecuting longer in the said court, and to have his name striken off the record of attorneys.

The District Courts and Courts of Common Pleas have exclusive jurisdiction and control over the conduct of their officers, and may strike an attorney who, in their discretion, misbehaves himself in his office, from the rolls, though such a discretion ought not to be exercised to redress a mere private grievance.(*m*) And in such case the Supreme

---

(*f*) See sections 73, 74, of the act previously quoted, *supra.* p. 215; see also Case of Austin *et al.* 5 R. 191.
(*g*) 1 Archb. Pr. 26.
(*h*) Tidd. Pr. 64.
(*i*) 6 T. R. 701.

(*j*) 1 Archb. Pr. 27; see 1 Dunl. Pr. 69.
(*k*) 4 Sm. Laws, 531.
(*l*) *Ante*, p. 215.
(*m*) Case of Austin *et al*, 5 R. 191.

Court has no authority to give relief in any form, whether it be certiorari, appeal, or writ of mandamus.(*n*)

An order of court ordering an attachment against an attorney to compel the payment over of money, part of which he claimed as fees, is no bar to a suit by such attorney for such fees.(*o*)

III. *Of the Duties, Privileges, and Liabilities of Attorneys.*

The principal duties of an attorney, are care, skill, and integrity. He will be protected, where he acts to the best of his skill and knowledge, and is not answerable for error or mistake, in cases where there is just room for doubt; he is only bound to use reasonable care and skill in managing the business of his client, and is not liable, unless he has been grossly negligent or ignorant.(*p*) But in ordinary cases, where there is no room for difficulty or doubt, if an attorney be deficient in skill or care, by which a loss arises to his client, he is liable to a special action on the case for damages.(*q*)

An attorney will, in some instances, be compelled to pay costs for his own neglect; as where a verdict, which had been taken by default, through the negligence of the defendant's attorney, was set aside, and a new trial granted on payment of costs, he was ordered to pay the costs.(*r*)

Attorneys were, at common law, entitled to a variety of privileges, most of which they yet possess in England. But in this State, the distinction between them and other classes of the community is not very strongly marked, and they must sue by the same process, and be sued in the same manner, as other persons. Counsellors, attorneys, and other officers of the court, are privileged from being summoned on juries ;(*s*) and an attorney at law is privileged from serving as an overseer of the poor, and it seems, as supervisor of the roads, constable, and in similar offices, but he is not privileged from arrest or militia duty.(*t*)

By rules of the several courts, no attorney of those or any other courts, or sheriff's officer, bailiff, or other person, concerned in the execution of process, shall be permitted or suffered to become special bail in any action or suit depending in either court, unless he shall obtain the leave of the court. The rule of the Supreme Court goes further, and prescribes that no attorney of that or any other court, sheriff's officer, bailiff, or other person concerned in the execution of process, shall become special bail, surety in a replevin bond, or for the stay of execution, or bail on an appeal or in error, except by special leave of the court previously obtained. In the Circuit Court of the United States of the

(*n*) McLaughlin *v.* The District Court, 5 W. & S. 272.

(*o*) Walton *v.* Dickerson, 7 Barr, 378.

(*p*) Burr. 2061; 3 Camph. 17, 19.

(*q*) 2 Wils. 325, as explained in Burr. 2060; 1 Dunl. Prac. 69; eee 1 Nev. & Man. 262. See an able essay, by KENNEDY, J., on the duties and obligations of an attorney to his client, and on his disability to purchase and set up any title, however doubtful, as to which he may have been consulted by, or obtained knowledge of, from the owner, no matter how long the interval, or complete the termination of his professional relation. Galbraith *v.* Elder, 8 W. 93. Such purchases must always, if claimed, enure to the client. Ibid. He cannot in any way take profits by knowledge thus obtained to the prejudice of his clients.

(*r*) 3 Taunt. 484.

(*s*) 3 Bac. Abr. 758.

(*t*) Res. *v.* Fisher, 1 Y. 350; 1 Wh. Dig. "Attorney."

third district, it is declared by rule, that attorneys shall not be received as bail in any form, and that they shall not be permitted to become security for costs.

An attorney, or counsellor at law, cannot be permitted to disclose confidential communications made to him by his client,(u) at any period of time—not in an action between third persons—nor after the proceeding, to which they referred, is at an end—nor after the dismissal of the attorney.(v) The privilege of not being examined to such points, as were communicated to the attorney while engaged in his professional capacity, is the privilege of the client, not of the attorney, and it never ceases. "It is not sufficient to say the cause is at an end ; the mouth of such a person is shut forever."(w)

The attorney of a party in the cause may be examined like any other witness, where he knew the fact before the retainer, that is, before he was addressed in his professional character, or where he has made himself a party to the transaction,(x) or where he is questioned as to collateral facts,(y) as, for instance, to the fact of the existence of the relation of client and attorney,(z) or to a fact which he might have known without being intrusted as attorney in the cause.(a) In such a case he may be examined, though his judgment fee depends upon his success,(b) or though he expects to receive a larger fee from his client, if the latter succeeds.(c) And an attorney who has a contract with a party for a certain sum as a fee in case of recovery, is a competent witness for him, if it do not appear that the contract is under seal or capable of being enforced.(d)

It cannot be denied, however, that there is a gross indelicacy in counsel thus interested, stepping from the bar to the witness-box, and after making their opening speech, swearing to the necessary facts in their clients' cases, and then summing up the evidence thus obtained. The general policy of frowning down the practice has been fully discussed elsewhere,(e) and it is needless to recapitulate the line of decisions by which the legal competency of counsel to testify is sustained by the Supreme Court. It is enough here to say, that when a verdict is obtained by such testimony, it is in the discretion of the court to grant a new trial.(f) It is clear that when the testimony of counsel thus given is material, the court should forbid his subsequently addressing the jury.(g)

"The law as to agents, is not generally applicable to attorneys: the relation of the latter to their clients and the court, renders their authority and responsibility peculiar in many respects. It is of an intimate and highly confidential character ; so much so, indeed, that the acts of the attorney in the suit will bind his client even to his prejudice, nor will the court look beyond the attorney to his authority. His fidelity, on the other hand, is secured by the obligation of an oath and the power of the court to inflict summary censure and punishment. The court

---

(u) Heister v. Davis, 3 Yeates, 4.
(v) 1 Phil. Evid. 108.
(w) Per Buller, J. 4 T. R. 759 ; see the cases cited in full in Wh. Dig. "Evidence," xix. s. ; 1 Phil. Evid. 108.
(x) 1 Phil. Evid. 110.
(y) Heister v. Davis, 3 Yeates, 4.
(z) 11 Wheat. 280.
(a) Bull. N. P. 284.

(b) Newman v. Bradley, 1 D. 241.
(c) Miles v. O'Hara, 1 S. & R. 32.
(d) Boulden v. Hebel, 17 S. & R. 312.
(e) 6 P. L. J. 405.
(f) See cases in Wh. Dig. Evidence, xix. (k.)
(g) Johns v. Bolton, 2 J. 339. See also post, "New Trials."

regard him in the light of an officer attached to their jurisdiction, no less than as the intimate representative of the party for whom he appears before them." These observations are extracted from the opinion of the Supreme Court delivered by SMITH, J. in the case of Boulden *v.* Hebel,(*h*) in which it was held, that, where a plaintiff's attorney having in his hands money recovered by a suit on a bond, and the plaintiff and a third person having, by a writing under seal, agreed to divide the money equally, the attorney, notwithstanding this agreement, was not bound to pay half the money to the third person, but was justifiable in paying it all to his client. And the learned judge said, that "it would be inconsistent with the duties of the attorney's situation, and the necessary economy of courts of justice, to subject him to the inconvenience of trying, in a suit against himself, the rights of different claimants to money which he had recovered for his client." But TOD, J. dissented, and held the following doctrine: "That an attorney is not bound to look beyond his own employer, is a rule which in equity and at law is liable to many exceptions. He who delivers to an attorney a bond for collection, whether payable to himself or another, whether with an assignment or not, may fairly be presumed the owner. But, if he afterwards, and before the money is paid over to him, is known not to be the real owner as to the whole, or as to part; or if he has sold it and got the amount from another person, or has in any way fairly disposed of it; or if it appear that he was only intrusted to convey the bond to the lawyer, or that he picked it up in the street, or defrauded some one out of it; or if in any other possible shape, it appears that he never had an interest, or that the interest which he had is vested in another person, then I do hold that the attorney, who, knowing these things, or knowing any one of them, shall go on, under an obligation of duty, or without it, to pay money voluntarily to a man who is not the owner, may, by the rules of law, be compelled to pay it over again to the man who is the owner. In Dottin's case,(*i*) the client had borrowed sundry deeds and delivered them to his attorney. The owner complained to the court; and nothing saved the attorney from an attachment but his having given the deeds back again to his client before he knew that they were not the client's property. In the common case of the attachment of a debt in suit, I do not know that it has ever been imagined that the attorney of the plaintiff, after notice, could with safety pay the money to his client."

Attorneys are entitled to certain specified fees, for the services which they perform, by particular acts of assembly; the second section of the act of February 22, 1821,(*j*) contains a table of their fees in common cases, as now regulated by law, to which we must content ourselves with referring the reader.

Formerly, an action could not be supported by an attorney or counsellor at law against his client, for advice and services in the trial of a cause, over and above the attorney's fees allowed by act of assembly,(*k*) and these fees they were allowed to retain out of the money recovered by them for their clients, or otherwise to maintain an action of *assump-*

(*h*) 17 S. & R. 312.
(*i*) 1 Stra. 547.

(*j*) 7 Re. Laws, 367.
(*k*) Mooney *v.* Lloyd, 5 S. & R. 412.

sit against their clients to recover them.(*l*)   But if a client gave a note or obligation, it was lawful for counsel to accept it, and in case of non-payment, an action might be supported on it.(*m*)   But now, by a later decision, he is entitled to recover on a *quantum meruit* for his services.(*n*) The subject is very fully investigated in this latter case, as also the applicability of the statute of limitations to such a claim.

A member of the bar may maintain an action on an implied *assump sit*, for professional services rendered by him, without regard to the character of the services.(*o*)

In *assumpsit*, by an attorney, to recover compensation for professional services, where it appeared that he had presented his demand to the defendant, who refused to pay on the ground that too much was charged, it was held that he was entitled to interest from the time of the demand.(*p*)

An attorney has no lien for his fees on money in the hands of the sheriff, belonging to his client or on his client's papers.(*q*)

In an action by the attorney for his legal fees or costs advanced, although the original retainer need not be proved, yet some recognition of the attorney in the progress of the suit ought to be shown to make the party liable.(*r*)   The negligence of the attorney in conducting the suit is, it seems, a defence in any action for fees or costs ;(*s*) but it cannot be given in evidence under the general issue, without notice.(*t*) Where an attorney receives money for his client, and neglects or refuses for a length of time to render an account of it, and his client is compelled to have recourse to a suit to recover his money, such attorney forfeits all right to claim any deduction as compensation for his services.(*u*)   He cannot receive compensation when he has performed no service.   It amounts to nothing more nor less than the substitution of one debtor for another.   The debt is not nearer collection than before; and it is apparent that if the plaintiff should be equally unfortunate in the selection of agents, the whole amount will be consumed under pretence of collection.   The retention of money by an attorney is a flagrant breach of trust, for which he renders himself liable to attachment, and, in some cases, to have his name stricken from the roll.   In the case of Leonard Ellmaker's estate,(*v*) the court ruled that an administrator was not entitled to commissions where he had been guilty of fraud.   The same principle was decided in Brackett *v.* Norton.(*w*)   It was there ruled that if an attorney, after having obtained final judgment and execution, prevent the collection of the execution by fraudulent conduct, this will be a violation of his duty as attorney, and will deprive him of all legal claim for his services in procuring such judgment and execution.   It is the duty of the attorney, in a reasonable time, to inform his client of the receipt of money, and either transmit it to him or

(*l*) 1 Dunl. Prac. 76.
(*m*) Mooney *v.* Lloyd, 5 S. & R. 416.
(*n*) Gray *v.* Brackenridge, 2 Pa. R. 75 ; Foster *v.* Jack, 4 W. 334.
(*o*) Foster *v.* Jack, 4 W. 334. See Kentucky Bank *v.* Combs, 7 Barr, 543.
(*p*) Gray *v.* Van Amringe, 2 W. &. S. 128.

(*q*) Irwin *v.* Workman, 3 W. 357; Walton *v.* Dickerson, 7 Barr, 376.
(*r*) See 9 Johns. 142.
(*s*) 11 Johns. 547 ; 1 Camp. 176 ; Starkie, 409 ; Contra, 2 New Rep. 136.
(*t*) 11 Johns. 547.
(*u*) Bredin *v.* Kingland, 4 W. 420.
(*v*) 4 W. 77.
(*w*) 4 Conn. Rep. 518.

hold it subject to his order. A neglect or refusal to do so, or to render an account, is such fraudulent conduct as to deprive him of all right to claim compensation for his services.(x) And even if the attorney does not offer to pay to his client in a reasonable time all the money which he was bound to pay, he is not entitled to compensation for his trouble.(y)

An attorney is not liable to suit for money collected for another, till demand, or direction to remit.(z)

An attorney is not liable to an action by his client for money collected until after demand made, unless there be special circumstances dispensing with the necessity therefor.(a)

A note was given to L, one of a legal firm, to collect, and a receipt in his individual name taken therefor. From negligence in bringing suit, the claim was lost. It was held that if the contract to collect the note was made with L, acting not individually, but on behalf of the firm, the action for a breach of it, occurring in his lifetime, should be brought against the surviving partner.(b)

In action brought by a creditor against his attorney for negligence in the collection of the debt, it is competent for the defendant to show that the plaintiff had given to the debtor time, and had received from him partial payments.(c)

If a loss has occurred through the negligence of an attorney, the negligence of one subsequently acting is no defence.(d)

In an action against an attorney for negligence in the collection of a claim, the measure of damages is the actual loss sustained by such negligence, and the subsequent negligence of another attorney, employed after his death to collect the same debt, is no excuse for his negligence.(e)

SECTION II.

OF THE PROSECUTION AND DEFENCE OF ACTIONS BY ATTORNEYS.

The authority of an attorney to prosecute or defend a suit, is derived from his warrant of attorney, or is rather supposed to be thus derived; for such a warrant is in fact never given, unless specially required. It is not the practice of Pennsylvania to file warrants of attorney;(f) but the act of assembly before quoted,(g) provides, that, *if required*, both the attorney for the plaintiff, in every action, shall file his warrant of attorney in the prothonotary's office the same court he declares; and the attorney for the defendant shall file his warrant of attorney the same court he appears; and if they neglect so to do, they shall have no fee allowed them in the bill of costs, nor be suffered to speak in the cause, until they file their warrants respectively.

Here, as in England, the practice of not filing and even of not taking warrants of attorney, is, for the most part, disused; a mere *parol*

(x) Bredin v. Kingland, 4 W. 420.
(y) Fisher v. Knox, 1 H. 622.
(z) Krause v. Dorrance, 10 Barr, 463. ROGERS, J.
(a) Krause v. Dorrance, 10 Barr, 462.
(b) Livingston v. Cox, 6 Barr, 360.

(c) Derrickson v. Cady, 7 Barr, 27.
(d) Ibid.; Livingston v. Cox, 7 Barr, 27.
(e) Livingston v. Cox, 7 Barr, 27.
(f) Coxe v. Nicholls, 2 Y. 547.
(g) Ante, p. 215, §§ 71 & 72.

retainer is deemed sufficient. Hence, courts are indulgent when rules to file them are taken. The defendant undoubtedly has the right to know the authority by which he is sued; but in ordinary cases, justice is obtained by merely staying the proceedings until it be filed. In no case can the writ be quashed upon this ground.(*h*)

A motion for a rule on the plaintiff to file his warrant of attorney, must be made before plea pleaded,(*i*) in the courts of this State. But in the Circuit Court of the United States, the defendant may, at any time, call upon the plaintiff's attorney for his warrant to sue; but if the court is satisfied, either by the production of the warrant of attorney, or even by parol evidence, that the attorney acts by authority, they will not in a summary way, arrest the proceedings.(*j*)

The mere appearance of the attorney is always deemed enough for the opposite party and the court, which will look no further, and will proceed as if he had sufficient authority, and leave the party injured to his action, unless there was fraud or collusion between a party and the opposite attorney.(*k*) Where there are two or more defendants, and an attorney enters his name on the docket, opposite the names of the defendants, this is a good appearance for all, though one of the defendants be not summoned.(*l*) Where a summons against two, was returned "*served*" as to one, and "*nihil habet*" as to the other, and afterwards an attorney entered his appearance generally, opposite the names of the defendants on the docket, and signed as their attorney an agreement to refer, it is a good appearance for both, to support a judgment against both.(*m*) Yet, though this general appearance by attorney, would amount by implication to an appearance for all, the parties may consider it otherwise, as an appearance only for those arrested or summoned.(*n*)

The filing of a declaration against one alone, would be a contradiction of the appearance of the other, and from that moment the proceedings must be against the one declared against alone, and a judgment against the other would be erroneous.(*o*) The case of Compher *v.* Anawalt,(*p*) exhibits so full and interesting a view of the incidents to and consequences of a general appearance by attorney for more than one defendant, that we shall here transcribe a large portion of the opinion of the court. "The case as it stands," proceeds SERGEANT, J. "in the court below, appears fraught with the most striking injustice to the defendant below. The sheriff comes to him in 1832, at his residence in Bedford County, with executions for a considerable sum of money, issued out of the Court of Common Pleas of Somerset County, and levies on his goods. He then learns for the first time that a suit had been brought against him and another person in that court in the year 1819; that in consequence of the entry without his direction or knowledge, by an attorney of the court, of his name on the margin of the docket, he was made a party to the suit, a rule of arbitration entered, and an award and judg-

(*h*) Meyer *v.* Littell, 2 Barr, 177.
(*i*) Mercier *v.* Mercier, 2 D. 142.
(*j*) C. Ct. 1810. MS. Wh. Dig. Attorney, vii.; and see ibid. for authorities generally.
(*k*) 6 Johns. 37, 302; 1 Dunl. Pr. 81.
(*l*) Scott *v.* Israel, 2 Binn. 145.

(*m*) M'Cullough *v.* Guetner, 1 Binn. 214.
(*n*) Hunt *v.* Breading, 6 S. & R. 38.
(*o*) Stewart *v.* Allison, 12 S. & R. 325, 326.
(*p*) 2 W. 492.

ment obtained against him; that this judgment, after having slept ten years, was revived by two writs of *scire facias* of which he had no notice, and he is now apprised that he must pay a large sum of money or submit to the seizure and sale of his goods; he at the same time being willing to make oath that he owes nothing to the plaintiff in the suit. Such is the case which appears on the affidavits of the defendant below, and also of Fleming the attorney; and if the facts stated in the affidavits are made out to the satisfaction of the court below, they imperiously demand the interference of that court. Of its power to grant relief in the case there can be no doubt. It is true that an attorney being an officer of the court, his acts are to be deemed the acts of the party for whom, in the course of legal proceedings, he assumes to appear. But the meaning of this rule merely is, that the acts of the attorney will be deemed regular though a want of authority be subsequently shown. The court will, notwithstanding, in every case interpose and grant relief, so far as it can be done without injury to the other party. In Coxe *v.* Nicholls,(*q*) in this court, an amicable action had been entered and judgment confessed by an attorney who afterwards absconded. On the defendant's affidavit, that he had never employed the attorney, and that the first notice he had of the proceedings was by a note from one of the plaintiffs some time after the date of the judgment; the court, though there was a counter affidavit by the plaintiff, allowed the judgment to stand as a security, and permitted the defendant to contest the demand in point of law. The same principle has been since adopted in New York, in the case of Denton *v.* Noyes,(*r*) where the subject is thoroughly examined by Chief Justice Kent, and all the cases reviewed. There an attorney appeared for a defendant against whom a writ had been issued and not served, and without the defendant's authority confessed a judgment. 'I am disposed,' said the chief justice, 'to prevent all possible injury to the defendant, and at the same time to save the plaintiffs from harm. This can be done only by preserving the lien, which the plaintiffs have acquired by their judgment, and in giving the defendant an opportunity to plead, if he has any plea to make, to the merits.' In the case of Brooke *v.*   decided at Philadelphia at the last term of this court, an attorney, by the direction of one defendant, in a suit against two, appeared and acted for both. It was discovered soon after that the direction was without authority; and the Court of Common Pleas, on the application of the attorney and proof, allowed the original appearance for both to be amended, by restricting it to a special appearance for one, and this court relieved the injured party from an award and execution against him. So strongly impressed is this court with the propriety and justice of granting such relief to the plaintiff in error in this case, that he is permitted to withdraw his writ of error, in order that he may make application to the court below for that purpose."

It is now held, that in an action against several partners, one may enter an appearance for the others, which may in its consequences lead to a judgment against all, and of course may substitute an attorney to do it for him.(*s*)   •

(*q*) Coxe *v.* Nicholls, 2 Y. 546.   (*s*) Taylor *v.* Coryell, 12 S. & R. 250.
(*r*) 6 Johns. 296.   See *post*, vol. ii. " Partnership."

To protect as well an innocent plaintiff as a defendant, from the consequences of a judgment suffered by default, or confessed by an attorney who has undertaken to appear without authority, the court, although the judgment must stand as security, will stay all proceedings, and permit the defendant to plead, if he has a defence.(t)   An attorney who enters an appearance in a suit, without authority, is answerable in damages, for the injury he may thereby have occasioned the parties;(u) and if he be not clearly able to answer in damages, they will be responsible.(v) Where attorneys enter judgments in different counties, under a warrant to confess judgment on the same bond, in such cases, having acted without authority, they are liable to the obligor for the consequences of the second judgment, which is only irregular and not void.(w)

It is a familiar principle that actual appearance is a waiver of defects in the process or service of it.(x)

Where an attorney accepts a warrant, or takes upon him to appear for any person, he cannot afterwards refuse to be his attorney, or withdraw himself from the cause; where he undertakes the recovery of the amount of a judgment, if it can be accomplished, he is bound to make good the collection so far as it is practicable by diligent skill and attention, although he does not reside or practise in the county where the judgment is entered;(y) but still, he is not bound to proceed and expend money for his client without being reimbursed or secured.(z)

The general authority or power of an attorney at law in this State does not allow him to ratify an unauthorized act of the prothonotary, such as the receiving payment of the debt, and interest on a judgment, and therefore the ratification by an attorney will not give validity to such payment without the assent, express or implied, of the principal.(a)

It is within the power and authority of an attorney at law to stay execution upon a judgment, in consideration of the promise of a third person to pay the debt; and such promise is binding, although not made to the creditor himself, nor expressly assented to by him at the time.(b)

An attorney at law in Pennsylvania has very extensive power in relation to conducting a suit, but after judgment this plenary power, in a great measure ceases, excepting as to his power of receiving the amount of the judgment, and giving a receipt for it.(c)   The limitations, as to his authority, imposed on him by the law, relate generally to compromises, such as substituting one thing for another, as land for money, or to acts after judgment.   These are without the range of that professional learning and skill which constitute, in fact, the groundwork of the relation of counsel and client.(d)

But the authority of an attorney is not limited here in the same manner that it is in England;(e) thus, his entire authority does not end with the judgment or with the issuing execution within a year and a

(t) Coxe v. Nicholls, 2 Y. 546; 6 Johns.' 296.
(u) 1 Peters, 155.
(v) Ibid. 158.
(w) Martin v. Rex, 6 S. & R. 296.
(x) Skidmore v. Bradford, 4 Barr, 300.
(y) Riddle v. Poorman, 3 Pa. Rep. 224; Com. Dig. Attorney, B. 9.
(z) 2 Johns. 296.

(a) Tompkins v. Woodford, 1 Barr, 156.
(b) Silvis v. Ely, 3 W. & S. 420; see Tompkins c. Woodford, 1 Barr, 158.
(c) Stackhouse v. O'Hara's Ex'rs, 2 II. 890. Coulter, J.
(d) Ibid.
(e) Reinholt v. Alberti, 1 Bin. 470.

day thereafter (as it does there);(*f*) and a payment to the plaintiff's attorney, long after judgment and without execution, has been held good upon argument.(*g*) It follows, therefore, that this authority extends to a *scire facias* against the bail, or to revive the judgment, contrary to the English rule.(*h*) But because this is a new action, and different record, it would seem that consonantly with that practice, execution, or a *scire facias*, or writ of error, may be sued out without any formal substitution, by a new attorney.(*i*) An attorney who receives a note from his client to collect, is warranted by his general retainer, to bring a second suit on the note, after being nonsuited in the first, for want of sufficient proof of the execution of the note.(*j*) His acts in general, bind his client;(*k*) but, his authority does not extend to discharge a defendant from execution,(*l*) without satisfaction of the debt, or to enter a *retraxit*, or to acknowledge satisfaction of record;(*m*) nor can he compromise the rights of his client,(*n*) although he may submit them to arbitration,(*o*) and may confess judgment, restore an action after *non pros*, without the consent of his client,(*p*) or enter a *remittitur damna*.(*q*) The plaintiff is bound by the act of his attorney, provided he acts within the sphere of his authority. If the attorney receive the debt, the plaintiff is bound, although the money never comes to his hands.(*r*) His general authority as attorney, does not warrant the purchase of land sold under an execution issued in the cause, in behalf of, and as trustee for, his client.(*s*)

He cannot, without express authority, convert his client's money into land, or *vice versa*,(*t*) and a judgment confessed by him by authority of a warrant from the wife of an absent debtor, is voidable when properly attacked.(*u*)

An attorney may submit a question of boundary to the decision of arbitrators chosen in an action of trespass between the parties; and where the decision is unappealed from it is competent as evidence to go to the jury, of submission by the client to the award.(*v*)

An agreement by an attorney at law to buy in the debtor's land at the sheriff's sale and to release the debt, is unauthorized, invalid, and without consideration, and where the debtor has suffered no damage it is no defence in an action brought to recover the debt.(*w*)

Where a claim is put in the hands of an attorney for enforcement, it is with the understanding that the suit shall be conducted in the usual way, and the attorney has no power to bind his client by a proceeding out of the ordinary course not recognized by custom.(*x*)

(*f*) 2 Bos. & P. 357, *n. b.*
(*g*) Reinholt *v.* Alberti, 1 Bin. 470.
(*h*) 1 Taunt. 46 ; 6 Johns. 106.
(*i*) See 2 B. & P. 357 ; 7 T. R. 333 ; 6 Johns. 106.
(*j*) 12 Johns. 317.
(*k*) Coxe *v.* Nicholls, 2 Y. 546.
(*l*) But when execution has issued, he often gives time to the defendant, and directs the sheriff to postpone a sale advertised, and so far as known, this has always been taken as a justification to the sheriff for not selling. Per Huston, J. Lynch *v.* Com., 16 S. & R. 369.
(*m*) 1 Dunl. Prac. 82.

(*n*) Ibid.
(*o*) McCullough *v.* Guetner, 7 Cranch, 436 ; 1 Bin. 214. See *post*, (*v*).
(*p*) Reinholt *v.* Alberti, 1 Bin. 469.
(*q*) Salk. 89, *pl.* 9.
(*r*) Pearson *v.* Morrison, 2 S. & R. 21.
(*s*) 11 Johns. 464.
(*t*) Miller *v.* Ralston, 1 S. & R. 307 : Gable *v.* Hain, 1 Pa. R. 264 ; Naglee *v.* Ingersoll, 7 Barr, 185.
(*u*) Campbell *v.* Kent, 3 Pa. R. 72; Hauer's Appeal, 5 W. & S. 473.
(*v*) Babb *v.* Stromberg, 2 H. 397.
(*w*) Stackhouse *v.* O'Hara, 2 H. 88.
(*x*) Willis *v.* Willis, 2 J. 162.

An auditor was appointed on a sale of the real estate of an intestate, who had previously been declared a lunatic, to ascertain what advancements had been made in his lifetime to his heirs. The attorney of one of the children, who had at the same time in his hands for collection, a single bill given by the decedent to his client, agreed that the auditor should determine the question of the sanity of the intestate and the validity of the client's note. The auditor reported against the sanity, and that the notes given by him to the children were consequently void. It was held, that the attorney had no power to bind his client by such a proceeding, and that she was not precluded by the report from contesting the lunacy in an action on the bill.(*y*)

The attorney at law of a debtor has no authority to bind him by a promise to pay a debt barred by the statute of limitations.(*z*)

He may purchase land at sheriff's sale, the condemnation of which he was employed to prevent.(*a*)

With regard to the agreements of attorneys, there is so much danger of mistake and difference in recollection, when they are to be enforced, that the courts have adopted a rule that " all agreements touching their business shall be in writing, otherwise they will be considered of no validity."(*b*) This rule is often enforced; but it does not apply to every case, as it has been decided that only *executory*, and not executed, agreements come within its meaning. Thus in a case in the federal Supreme Court, the verbal executory agreement of the plaintiff's attorney made with the party to another action on the same note, was enforced in equity.(*c*)

Where a cause, when it was reached on the trial-list, was referred, by consent of the attorneys of the parties in open court, to certain persons named as arbitrators, and such parol agreement was entered of record by the prothonotary; it was held, 1. That in such case the rule of court which requires all agreements of counsel to be in writing had no bearing. 2. That if a party make no application to the court to strike off such submission, the law will presume it to have been made with his approbation and consent, and the agreement in such case will not be set aside on a writ of error.(*d*)

We know of no practice which inhibits a party from countermanding the authority of an attorney who has undertaken to appear and appointing a new one, without the intervention of the court; though it would seem that notice of such a change ought to be given to the opposite party, as a measure of prudence. In the case of a change during the progress of the suit, it is unnecessary to file a new warrant.(*e*) The new attorney is bound to take notice of the previous rules and proceedings in the suit; and it would seem that until notice of the change has been given, the opposite party is justified in considering the former attorney as still continuing, and therefore payment to him will be good; though perhaps the doing of any act, recognizing the new attorney as attorney in the cause, would be a waiver of a defect of notice.(*f*) In the event of the death of an attorney, it appears to be

(*y*) Willis *v.* Willis, 2 J. 159.   Geary, 5 Peters, 99.
(*z*) Crist *v.* Garner, 2 P. R. 262.   (*d*) Millar *v.* Criswell, 3 Barr, 449.
(*a*) Devinney *v.* Norris, 8 W. 314.   (*e*) 1 Taunt. 44.
(*b*) D. C. Rule vii.   (*f*) See Doug. 217; 2 W. Bl. 1323; 6
(*c*) Union Bank of Georgetown *v.*   East. 549; 2 New R. 509.

sufficient, until the appointment of a new one with notice, to consider the client as in his place, and there is no necessity to warn him to appoint a successor, in the practice of this State.

In case of the death of an attorney prosecuting or defending a suit, another may enter his appearance upon the docket, without any formal motion to the court.

In the English and New York practice, in case of the change of an attorney, the person withdrawing from the suit must move the court for leave to withdraw his appearance, stating a sufficient reason, such as the assent or wish of his client, or that his client neglects or refuses to advance the fees and charges necessary for the prosecution or defence of the suit.   And where an attorney has been retained to defend a suit, and appears, the defendant is not allowed to countermand the appearance, or change his attorney without a rule of court ;(g) and the acts of the second attorney, unless a regular substitution be shown, will be disregarded by the court.(h)   But in our practice, any party may dismiss his attorney and appoint a new one at pleasure, without application to the court, and without, as we have stated above, any written substitution of another, but not so as to deprive the former of his lien for fees and disbursements.(i)   The proper course, however, when an attorney wishes to withdraw, is to take a rule on his client and the opposite party to show cause.   Such a rule made absolute relieves him from subsequent responsibility.   By a withdrawal of appearance the case stands as if no appearance had been entered.(k)

(g) 1 Arch. Prac. 29 ; 1 Paine & Duer, 196.

(h) Ibid.

(i) See Howe's Prac. 48.

(k) Michew v. McCoy, 3 W. & S. 501.

CHAPTER VI

OF THE MODES OF COMMENCING ACTIONS.

THE modes of commencing actions, of which we shall treat in this chapter, are by summons, by *capias ad respondendum*, and by the peculiar procedure established by the act of 1842, abolishing imprisonment for debt. These are the remedies of general use and application, although in particular cases and against particular persons, actions may be otherwise commenced, as, by attachment against absent or absconding debtors, and against convicts, under the act of 1836; by *scire facias*, on mortgages, and mechanics' liens; and by the agreement of parties without a writ. In the ensuing sections we shall consider the nature and incidents of the first-mentioned writs, and of the duties of the sheriff under them.

It will be proper to observe, first, that to commence any form of action in this State, the party, or his attorney, must address a *præcipe*,(a) to the prothonotary of the court for the writ applicable to the cause of action. It is the foundation of the proceedings; is considered part of the record, and the courts may order amendments by it.(b)

SECTION I.

OF THE SUMMONS FOR THE COMMENCEMENT OF PERSONAL ACTIONS.

The first section of the act of June 13, 1836, "relating to the commencement of actions,"(c) after declaring that personal actions, except in cases where other process shall be especially provided, shall be com-

---

(a) This is the term given in this State to the attorney's mandate to the clerk. In the English practice, the *præcipe* is filed with the clerk, before the writ is issued, from which he is supposed to make it out, though in fact it is made out by the attorney, and only given to the clerk to seal. The writ itself is a mere transcript of the *præcipe*, with the addition of the formal commencement and conclusion. In our practice, the *præcipe* is not only an order to the clerk of the court to issue the first or original process, whether it be a *capias* or a summons, whether it be for a writ in debt, or in case for a tort, but is likewise the name given to the order to the clerk to issue any other process, either mesne or final; as a *præcipe* for a *scire facias* against the garnishee in foreign attachment; for a *retorno habendo* in replevin; for a writ of error to remove a record; for a *fieri facias*, on a judgment; or for a *venditioni exponas*, after execution.— The *præcipe* is not usually returned as part of the record to the Supreme Court, unless when brought up on *certiorari*, or when referred to and read below for some purpose. Jones v. Hartly, 3 Wh. 189.

(b) Guhr v. Chambers, 2 Bin. 439; Fitzsimons v. Saloman, 8 S. & R. 157; *post*, vol. ii. "Amendments."

(c) Pamph. L. 572.

menced by a writ of summons, provides that it shall be in the following form, to wit:—

[L. S.] The commonwealth of Pennsylvania, ——— County, ss. to the sheriff of said county, greeting: We command you that you summon ———, so that he be and appear before our Court of ———, to be holden at ———, in and for said county, on the ——— day of ——— next, there to answer ——— of a plea, [setting forth briefly the cause of action or complaint,] and have you then there this writ: Witness ———, president [or as the case may be] judge of our said court, the ——— day of ———.

Prothonotary.

It appears to follow from the establishment of this form of writ, that the process in *debt* prescribed under the act of 1806, is abolished. The first decisions on this act did not hold this form to be exclusive;(*d*) but subsequent *dicta* would seem to question them.(*e*) The latter are, however, authorities in favor of the idea of abrogation by the preceding section.

Act of 4th April, 1837.(*f*) In all writs of summons issued by virtue of the act relating to the commencement of actions, passed the thirteenth June, eighteen hundred and thirty-six, the blank left for the cause of action, in the form prescribed in the first section of that act, shall be filled as directed for the corresponding part of writs of *capias ad respondendum*, in the third section of said act,(*ff*) and that all writs of summons issued since the passage of the said act, in the form previously thereto used, shall not be held or deemed defective for want of form according to said writ. § 3.

As will be hereafter seen, when we come to the subject of the *capias ad respondendum*, the writ of summons is to be the process against all persons who are *inhabitants* of the State, and that a *capias* can only be issued against strangers, or such citizens as have no known place of residence in the commonwealth, or are about to quit it without leaving sufficient estate to answer for their debts or liabilities; and further, that when an action has already been instituted by summons, against an inhabitant, if by any change in his affairs, he can be shown, by affidavit, to be within the scope or terms of the law, a *special capias ad respondendum* or warrant of arrest, may be taken against him.(*g*)

I. *Date and Return Days of the Summons.*

The 30th, 31st, and 32d sections of this act provide on these subjects as follows:—

Every writ used for the commencement of an action shall bear date on the day of the issuing thereof, and shall be made returnable on the first day of the term next succeeding the time at which it shall be issued. § 30.

Provided, That in the case of a writ of summons, if there shall not

---

(*d*) See Miles *v.* O'Hara, 1 S. & R. 32; Ib. 35; Bonn *v.* Heister, 6 Ibid. 20, 289.
(*e*) See Wike *v.* Lightner, 1 R. 290; Roop *v.* Brubacker, Ibid. 309.

(*f*) Pamph. L. 377.
(*ff*) *Post*, p. 245.
(*g*) See *post*, chap. v. § 24, of the act of 1836; and *post*, act of 1842.

be ten days between the issuing thereof and the first day of the term as aforesaid, the writ may be made returnable on the next day preceding the last day of such term, or upon the first day of the second term next after the issuing of the writ.   § 31.

In the courts for the City and County of Philadelphia, and County of Alleghany, all writs used for the commencement of actions may be made returnable on the first day of the next term as aforesaid, or on the first Monday of any intermediate month, at the election of the party suing out the writ.   § 32.

II. *Mode of Service of the Summons by the Sheriff.*

The 2d section of the foregoing act declares that a writ of summons shall be executed by reading the same in the hearing of the defendant, or by giving him notice of its contents, and by giving him a true and attested copy thereof; or if the defendant cannot conveniently be found, by leaving such copy at his dwelling-house, in the presence of one or more of the adult members of his family; or if the defendant resides in the family of another, with one of the adult members of the family in which he resides.   § 2.

Where the sheriff returned to a summons issued under this law, " summoned by leaving a copy at place of residence," the District Court of Philadelphia, upon a rule to show cause, set aside the service of the writ, upon the ground that the sheriff had not, in his return, sufficiently stated *the manner* in which the service of the writ had been made.(h) PETTIT, President, delivering the opinion of the court, said:—

" The second section authorizes either of two modes of personal service : the one ' by reading the writ in the hearing of the defendant,' and the other ' by giving the defendant notice of the contents of the writ, and by giving him a true and attested copy thereof.'   It also authorizes, if the defendant cannot conveniently be found, either of two modes of executing the writ by leaving a copy : the one ' by leaving a true and attested copy at the defendant's dwelling-house in the presence of one of the adult members of his family,' and the other, if the defendant resides in the family of another, ' by leaving a true and attested copy at the house in which the defendant resides with one of the adult members of the family in which he resides.

" The question now submitted appears to be, whether the return of the sheriff is sufficiently made, when he states a *personal service*, without particularly specifying *which* of the *two* modes of personal service; or when he designates an execution of the writ by *leaving a copy*, without detailing by *which* of the *two* modes of service by leaving a copy.

" The legislature have thought it proper to point out with precision four modes of executing a writ of summons.   They have presumed it to be practicable for the officer to pursue one of these four modes thus carefully described, and they have expressly required him in all cases to state in his return not only the *time* but the *manner* of service.   The injunction is so clear, that without any inquiry or speculation in regard to the motives which induced the passage of the law, it

(h) Weaver *v.* Springer, D. C. Dec. 17, 1836, 2 M. 42.

would seem to be the obvious duty of the officer to yield, and of the court to exact, obedience.

"But there are sound reasons why the mode of executing a writ of summons should be distinctly stated. In default of an appearance, the court may be called upon by the plaintiff to allow a judgment against the defendant: and before thus visiting a party with the penalty of a default, common and equal justice may demand that it should be unequivocally exhibited to the court by the record, that the writ was served on a proper day and in a legal manner—while strict attention to the form of the return, will do much to prevent remissness or negligence on the part of the officer charged with the important duty of executing the writ.

"The suggestion that it may not be easy for the officer to ascertain, as to service by leaving a copy, whether the place is the dwelling-house of the defendant or the residence of another in whose family the defendant lives, and, in either case, to find an adult member of the family, is answered by the fact that the legislature have assumed the feasibility of the sheriff's performing such a duty, and have devolved the responsibility of it upon him. It may be added, too, that with ordinary intelligence and reasonable diligence in the officer, and with the aid of such direction as can be procured from the plaintiff, it is not probable that any real difficulty will occur in practice in carrying into effect the purpose of the law.'

The service of a summons against a defendant who is out of the State (under circumstances which prevented a foreign or domestic attachment from issuing against his property), by leaving a copy with his partner, with whom he lived before he went abroad on a trading concern, whence he was daily expected to return, and with whom his wife and children were then living, was held good under the act of 1724.(i)

The service of a summons on a defendant, by leaving a copy at his boarding-house, in the presence of one of the adult members of the family, and by leaving a copy at the store of the defendant in the presence of his clerk, and by leaving a copy at the dwelling-house of the defendant's father in the presence of adult members of the family, was held by the District Court to be sufficient, although it appeared that the defendant, a few days before the service of the summons, had left the County of Philadelphia, and gone on a temporary visit to Europe.(ii)

If the summons be issued against several defendants, and one of them cannot be found, and the sheriff so returns, the plaintiff may proceed against the others; but if the process have been served on all of the defendants, he cannot omit or drop one, and proceed against the others.(j)

A sheriff will be permitted to amend his return, when the application is made in reasonable time, and when the return was made by a mistake as to matter out of his personal notice.(k)

(i) Bujac v. Morgan, 3 Y. 258.
(ii) Farnum v. Walton, Dist. Ct. C. C. P. Jan. 1847.
(j) Marshall v. Lowry, 6 S. & R. 281.
(k) Anspach v. Carr, D. C. Dec. 9, 1848. Why the sheriff should not have leave to amend his return of "served," by altering it to "nihil habet." Per curiam.

It appears clearly in this case, by depositions, that the sheriff by mistake served the summons upon the wrong person. It may be that he did not exercise due diligence to ascertain and serve it upon the right one. If so, the plaintiff has his remedy against him, if he has suffered.

A sheriff's return will not be set aside unless it appear on its face to be defective, though a judgment will be opened and a defendant let into a defence on the merits, when he shows as an excuse for non-appearing that the return was false.(*kk*)

fered damage. It is not right that this judgment should be enforced against either the person who really was not intended to be sued, or the real defendant who was served with no process, and turn them round to an action against the sheriff. The case of Ibbotson *v.* Tindal (1 Bing. 156), cited and relied on by the plaintiff's counsel, and which comes nearest to the point before us, does not sustain his position. In that case, a *capias* was placed in the sheriff's hand against a defendant who was already in custody under other process, but who subsequently escaped. The sheriff had returned *cepi corpus*, but afterwards asked to be permitted to amend his return by setting out the facts specially. The court refused to do this, deeming the first return substantially correct. On the other hand, in Scott *v.* Sailer (5 W. 542), in which it was recognized as the practice that sheriffs, upon application made to the court within a reasonable time, have been permitted frequently to amend their return to writs, where it has been shown clearly that they were made through mistake in regard to some matter of fact, which, from its nature, might not be within their own notice, Judge Kennedy puts the very case of the arrest and return of the wrong person, as defendant, as within the rule.

(*kk*) Kennard *v.* The Railroad Co., Monday, March 4, 1850.—Why service should not be set aside and writ quashed. *Per curiam.* This is an action against the New Jersey Railroad and Transportation Company, commenced by summons, the return to which is as follows : " Served by leaving a true and attested copy of the within writ with an agent of the defendant's, Dec. 22, 1849, and by leaving a certified copy in the office attached to the depot Jan. 7, 1850."

It is important in practice to settle in what cases the court will set aside the service of a writ by the sheriff.

Nothing seems better settled than that the sheriff's return is conclusive in the suit in which it is made. It is settled in numerous cases in Pennsylvania: Zion Church *v.* St. Peter's Church (5 W. & S. 215) ; Freeman *v.* Caldwell (10 W. 11) ; Frick *v.* Troxsell (7 W. & S. 65). The application of this plain principle would seem to require that in no case might the court go beyond the face of the return, or in the same case, either di-

rectly or collaterally to admit extraneous evidence to impeach.

Bujac *v.* Morgon (3 Y. 258) ; Weaver *v.* Springer (2 M. 42) ; Brobst *v.* Bank of Pennsylvania (5 W. & S. 379) ; Combs *v.* The Bank of Kentucky (3 L. J. 58) ; Nash *v.* The Rector, &c. (1 M. 78) ; Winrow *v.* Raymond (4 Barr, 501), are all cases in which the defect appeared on the face of the return. In Kleckner *v.* The County of Lehigh (6 Wh. 66), in which the return was of service upon two persons as commissioners of the county, evidence was taken in the court below to show that these persons were not commissioners ; and upon this ground the service was set aside. But the Supreme Court reversed the judgment because " as the return must be considered absolute and conclusive between the parties to the action, the court erred in setting aside the service of the writ by the introduction of extraneous proofs."

Dawson *v.* Campbell (2 M. 170) may be hard to reconcile with this decision, but must give way before it. In Combs *v.* The Bank of Kentucky (3 L. J. 58), at *nisi prius* before Judge Kennedy, and Nash *v.* The Rector, &c. (1 M. 78) the fact that the defendant was a foreign corporation seems either to have been admitted or proved, and was certainly in both these cases an extraneous fact, necessary to make the return bad on its face.

In the case before us, however, that extraneous fact does not impeach but support the return. We think, therefore, that the rule is a well established and sound one that the sheriff's return will not be set aside unless it appears upon its face to be defective. The facts stated in it must be taken to be true, and if they are false the remedy of the party is by action against the sheriff.

This decision does not interfere at all with a practice which has been long used to open a judgment by default, and let a defendant into a defence upon the merits where he shows as an excuse for not appearing that the return of the sheriff is false and that he never had notice of the proceeding.

We must take it then as true in point of fact that the summons in this case was served upon an agent of defendant, and that a certified copy was left at the office of the depot of defendant ;

An error in the service of a summons will be cured by appearance ;(*l*) but the obtaining of a stay of execution after judgment by default will not aid an error in the service of the summons ;(*m*) though an appearance *de bene esse* reserves exceptions.(*mm*)   After a writ of inquiry executed, judgment on that, and *a long acquiescence*, it will not be presumed that the summons was irregularly served.(*n*)

The defendant or his attorney sometimes agrees to accept service of the writ, and this dispenses with the agency of the sheriff, though accepting service of the writ will not be considered as an appearance.(*o*)

A summons issued on the return day cannot be made returnable on the same day;(*p*) though a service of a summons at any time on the return day is good.(*q*)   But it is otherwise with a summons made returnable on the Saturday next preceding the first Monday of the term of the District Court.(*r*)

Though, strictly speaking, an *alias* writ should recite the mandate and return of its predecessor; yet in practice, an *alias* which is a mere transcript of the original, though docketed as an *alias*, will be sustained.(*s*)

If the sheriff reads a writ of summons in the hearing of the defendant, it is sufficient without leaving a copy of the writ with him.(*t*)

The service of a summons will be set aside, if it appear that the copy served was not attested by the officer.(*u*)

The 37th and 38th sections provide further as to the service of writs of summons, as follows :—

1. In cases of trespass or nuisance affecting real estate.

In cases where a trespass or nuisance has been or may be committed on real estate, by non-residents of the county wherein such real estate is situated, it shall be lawful for the sheriff to go beyond his bailiwick into an adjoining county, for the purpose of serving any process which may be issued out of the court of the proper county, in suits instituted for the recovery of damages, or abatement of the nuisance, and such service shall be as good and valid as if the same had been made by the sheriff within his bailiwick.   § 37.

2. In regard to the form of return.

The sheriff or other officer serving any writ of summons, shall in all cases state in his return, the time and manner in which the service thereof was made.   § 38.

Act of April 14th, 1851.(*v*)—The remedy provided by the 37th section of the act passed the 13th day of June, 1836, entitled " An act relating to the commencement of actions," be, and the same is hereby extended to actions by mortgagees for injuries in the nature of waste that have been or may hereafter be committed to the mortgaged premises ; and

---

that the person served was a person competent to receive service, and the place was the *depot* of the defendant. See vol. ii. "Corporations."

(*l*) Gibbs *v.* Albert, 4 Y. 374 ; Stroup *v.* McClure, ibid. 523 ; Zion Church *v.* St. Peter's Church, 5 W. & S. 215.

(*m*) Ranck *v.* Becker, 12 S. & R. 417, *sed. vide* ibid. 424.

(*mm*) Blair *v.* Weaver, 11 S. & R. 84. See Bright R. 67.

(*n*) Morrison *v.* Wetherill, 8 S. & R. 502.
(*o*) 2 Nott & M'Cord's Rep. 548.
(*p*) Dyott *v.* Pennock, 2 M. 213.
(*q*) Heberton *v.* Stockton, 2 M. 164 ; Cashee *v.* Wisner, 2 Br. 245 ; Boyd *v.* Serrill, 4 P. L. J. 114.
(*r*) Thompson *v.* Patterson, 2 M. 146.
(*s*) Davidson *v.* Thornton, 7 Barr, 128.
(*t*) Klechner *v.* Lehigh Co., 6 Wh. 66.
(*u*) Bank *v.* Perdriaux, Bright. R. 67.
(*v*) Pamph. L. 612.

the sheriff of the proper county, or his deputy, shall be authorized to serve the process in any other, although such other shall not be adjoining to the county wherein such real estate is situated. § 1.

Act of May 4th, 1852.—That the fifteenth section of an act entitled "An act relative to the commencement of actions, and for other purposes," approved the fourteenth day of April, A. D. one thousand eight hundred and fifty-one, is hereby construed to extend to and apply only to writs of right and other writs pertaining to manorial lands in the City and County of Philadelphia. § 7.

Act of May 4th, 1852.—Where any person or persons being residents of the commonwealth, shall engage in business in any other county than the one in which he, she, or they shall reside, and not being in the county at the time of issuing the writ or process, it shall be lawful for the officer charged with the service thereof, to serve any writ of summons, or any other mesne process, upon the agent or clerk of such defendant, at the usual place of business or residence of such agent or clerk, and to have the same effect as if served upon the principal personally. § 1.

Act of April 10th, 1848.(r)—In all cases of suits against the sheriff, or his sureties, of any county of this commonwealth, when there is no coroner in commission to serve process, it shall be lawful for any constable, in the county where such process has issued, to serve the same, and perform the duties which coroners are authorized to do under the laws of this State. § 2.

The manner of serving process on a corporation will be hereafter fully considered.(s)

III. *Judgment on Default of Appearance after Service of the Summons.*

This subject, with reference to writs of summons in personal actions, is regulated by the 33d and 34th sections of the act of 1836, in regard to the usual personal actions, as follows :—

If the defendant in any writ of summons as aforesaid, shall not appear at the return day thereof, and the officer to whom such writ was directed, shall make return that it was served upon the defendant ten days before the return day aforesaid, it shall be lawful for the plaintiff, having filed his declaration, to take judgment thereon for default of appearance, according to the rules established by the court to regulate the practice in this respect. § 33.

In case such writ shall not be served ten days before the return day thereof, if the defendant therein shall not appear in ten days after the day of service, it shall be lawful for the plaintiff, having filed his declaration, to take judgment thereon at any subsequent day in term time, for default of appearance, according to the rules established by the court to regulate the practice in this respect. § 34.

As nothing appears in any of the revised acts repealing that part of

(r) Pamph. L. 441.   (s) *Post*, vol. ii. "Corporations."

the act of 1806, which allows a statement to be filed instead of a declaration, it is probable that the spirit of these sections would be complied with if a statement were filed instead of a declaration. It was held in a case decided nineteen years after the passing of that act (and the decision went on the principle that it was the duty of the court to support the law, a principle that has recently been very emphatically promulgated),(t) that where the writ is issued under this act in debt, the plaintiff has his choice of filing either a declaration or a statement. And where the writ is debt on a simple contract, the declaration or statement may be in assumpsit; at least it will not be error.(u) It would, however, be most prudent for a plaintiff who designs to take such a judgment, to file a formal declaration.

The court will not order a judgment for want of an appearance, where an affidavit of defence has been filed by the defendant in person, but will direct the defendant's appearance in *propriâ personâ*, to be entered on the docket.(v)

The mere acting by an attorney in the cause for a defendant, without entering his appearance, as, the making of a motion to set aside a judgment by default, is not an appearance for such defendant.(w)

The 39th section, with reference to writs of *scire facias*, is as follows:—

In every case in which a writ of *scire facias* may by law be issued, it shall be served and returned in the same manner as is herein provided in the case of a summons in a personal action, and judgment for default of appearance may be taken at the same time, and in the same manner, as in the case of a summons as aforesaid, unless it be otherwise especially provided.   § 39.

The following decisions, regulating the practice as to this species of judgment, will apply, it is conceived, to the present law:—

If two are jointly sued and summoned, and only one appears, the course is (the declaration having been previously filed against both) to take judgment by default against the one not appearing, and go on to trial of the issue tendered by the other.(x)

The preceding case supposes a service of the summons upon all the defendants, in a case where there are several. But where a service has only been effected upon some of them, the practice is different, and should be attended to. Where a summons is issued against several, six, for example, and is only served on three, the declaration ought to be against the three who have been summoned, with an averment, that the process was issued against the three others who were not to be found, &c.(y) The judgment may then be entered against the three declared against.(z)

If the plaintiff declare against the six defendants, and take judgment against the three summoned, it will be erroneous.(a) It will be equally erroneous if it be entered against them all.(b)

(t) See White v. Leightner, 1 R. 290, 309.

(u) Pedan v. Hopkins, 13 S. & R. 46.
(v) Morton v. Hoodless, 1 M. 46.
(w) Chalroon v. Hollenback, 16 S. & R. 425.
(x) Marshall v. Gougler, 10 S. & R.

164; see Wh. Dig. Judgment, ii. iii. *Post*, vol. ii. "Partners."
(y) Latshaw v. Steinman, 11 S. & R. 357.
(z) Boaz v. Heister, 6 S. & R. 19.
(a) Latshaw v. Steinman, 11 S. & R. 357.
(b) Boaz v. Heister, 6 S. & R. 19.

The court may, in their discretion, amend a judgment by default, and whether that discretion were judiciously exercised cannot be inquired into by a Court of Error.(c)

The proper practice is to enter the judgment in the office of the prothonotary.(d)

To entitle a party to judgment by default, under the act of 13th June, 1836, a declaration must be filed at the prescribed time. The defendant is not bound to appear without.(e)

Where a summons was issued, January 31st, returnable first Monday, February 4th, and on February 13th a narr. was filed, and on February 14th a judgment taken, it was held that the judgment was regular. In cases where the writ is not served ten days before the return day, it is necessary that the declaration should be filed within four days after the ten days from service.(f)   Where the writ is served ten days before the return day, the narr. must be filed within four days.(g)

---

* (c) Latshaw v. Steinman, 11 S. & R. 357. But see Crosby v. Massey, 1 Pa. R. 230. *Post*, " Amendment."

(d) Sheerer v. Adams, D. C. Phil. March, 1848.

(e) Foreman v. Schrieon, 8 W. & S. 43; Dennison v. Leech, 9 Barr, 164.

(f) May v. Sharp, Dist. Ct. C. C. P. September, 1848.

(g) Ibid. The following cases are of interest on this point:—

Buckley v. Eastman, D. C. Sep. 8, 1849. Rule to set aside judgment. *Per curiam.* The summons was served on the 2d July, and the judgment signed in the office on the 14th day, according to our practice, adopted in conformity to the practice where the summons was required to have been ten days before the return, and the English rule which *ex gratia curiâ* allowed the party until the fourth day after the return day *quarto die post.* This, in England, is the first day of the term in which the court sits for business, except in Trinity term, when the court, by act of Parliament, does not sit till the fifth day. 1 Tidd's Pr. 122. With us the practice of taking judgment on the fifth day, or Saturday, has resulted from the fact of its being the first general motion day; but a judgment entered on Friday, is, nevertheless, regular. Applying the same rule to the case before us, judgment on the 14th day, exclusive of the day of service, was not premature. See Fisher v. Potter, 2 Miles, 148.

May v. Sharp, Saturday, Sept. 23, D. C. Why the judgment should not be opened and defendant let into a defence. *Per curiam.* One ground of this rule, or rather that the judgment should be set aside as irregular, is, that it was taken by default for want of appearance, though the narr. was not filed in time.

The summons issued January 31, 1846, returnable to 1st Mond. February, which was February 4. The narr. was filed February 13, 1846, and judgment taken February 14. It is evident that, allowing the summons to have been served on the day it issued, judgment could not have been taken, according to the established practice of the court, until fourteen days thereafter, and the narr., therefore, was filed at the time appointed for giving judgment, so that this judgment is regular even under the case of Foreman v. Schrieon (8 W. & S. 43). It is very desirable, however, that the point decided in that case should be reconsidered by the Supreme Court. The case of Foreman v. Schricon, seems entirely based upon the idea that the act of June 13, 1836, reiterates the provisions of the act of March 20, 1724–5—a statute which, as the court say, was " effectively repealed by the indolence of the profession." "But nearly the same provision," say they, " has been repeated in the existing statute, and the legislature certainly intended it should be executed." But this is a mistake, as an examination of the acts will clearly show. The act of 1724–5, after providing for the summons and return, proceeds to enact, " Upon which return, if the defendant (making default), has been so served ten days, and the plaintiff had filed his declaration in the office of the prothonotary, *within the space of five days, before the court to which such writ is returnable,* it shall be lawful to, and for the plaintiff in such action, to file a common appearance for the defendant so making default, and proceed to judgment and execution by *nihil dicit.*" (Smith, 164; Purd. 56, ed. of 1830.) On the other hand, the 33d and 34th sections of the act of June

IV. *Opening Judgments for want of an Appearance.*

The old practice, as stated in our first edition, was as follows :—

If judgment be taken for default of appearance and execution sued out and even served, still the defendant may open the judgment and execution on terms to be prescribed by the court under the circumstances ; the most usual of which are, paying costs, and pleading the general issue, so as to have the cause set down for trial at the next opportunity. This, however, is to be effected by motion in court, accompanied with an affidavit that the defendant has a good defence. This motion, even under these circumstances, is not granted of course. The great and leading question upon it, is, whether the plaintiff have lost a trial, that is, whether the trial would have been over if the defendant had made no default, but had appeared and pleaded. If the plaintiff have not lost a term, no hardship can accrue to him from setting aside the judgment. The motion must of course be made at the third term at furthest (though in general that delay would be fatal), when by the course of the courts the cause is entitled to a trial. But as this is a privilege not due *ex debito justitiæ*, but granted *ex speciali gratia* to the defendant, the court will always insist upon the strict performance of those conditions. Care should be taken to have the sheriff apprised of the execution having been set aside, in order to prevent his further proceeding upon it. In the place of opening and setting aside the judgment in the manner before mentioned, it was customary for the attorneys

31, 1836 (Purd. 48)—one section applying to cases where the summons has been served ten days before the return—and the other to the case when it has not—both provide that, upon the sheriff's return, " it shall be lawful for the plaintiff, *having filed his declaration,* to take judgment thereon for default of appearance, *according to the rules established by the court, to regulate the practice in this respect."* The 34th section, which relates to a summons not served ten days before the return day, adds, to prevent a judgment being taken before the expiration of ten days after service, "at any subsequent day in term time." How can this be said to be nearly the same provision as that in the act of 1724–5, when that act expressly requires that the narr. shall have been filed within the space of five days before the court, and the existing statute only requires that the narr. shall have been filed to authorize a judgment by default? The commissioners of the revised code report their sections without remark ; and it is as plain as words can make it, that they meant to affirm simply the practical repeal which had taken place of the act of 1724–5, and which has been sanctioned by the Supreme Court. Considering, however, as we have always done, that the last clauses of the 33d and 34th sections of the act of June 13, 1836, " according to the rules established by this court, to regulate the practice in this respect, extended the time for appearance to the *quarto die post*—and the narr., in this case, was filed on that day—we think this judgment strictly regular, even according to the case of Foreman *v.* Schricon.

We do not think, upon the depositions, there is any case made out for opening the judgment. It is true that in ordinary cases of judgment by default for want of appearance, the court will open the judgment upon a sufficient affidavit of defence, and excusing the default without going into the question of merits. But that is where the application is made within a reasonable time, when, if the appearance had been entered, the plaintiff, in the ordinary course of the court, would not have had a trial. Here, however, more than two years have elapsed since the judgment was rendered. The allegation of the defendant's affidavit that he was incapable, from intemperate habits, of attending to business at the time the settlement was made, and notice given upon which the suit was brought, is not sustained by the deposition. Rule dismissed.

to agree that the judgment should stand as a security, in order to prevent private sales made by the defendant to defraud the plaintiff, and merely to set aside the execution.

Since the law was so stated, however, a great change has taken place in practice, which will be fully considered hereafter, when judgments are considered generally.(i)

Where the defendant, being informed of a judgment by default, neglected or refused for two terms, and until after inquiry executed, to apply for relief, although the judgment *was irregularly entered*, such judgment would not be reversed on error.(j)

The common law abhors an *ex parte* proceeding, whose end is not to compel a contumacious surety to come in; and it consequently knows no such thing as a judgment for want of an appearance. It does not permit a judgment *in personum* to be rendered against an absent party in any case; and every judgment, for want of an appearance, which is not supported by a statute, is consequently irregular. Hence, where a defendant appears and pleads to issue by attorney, who subsequently withdraws his appearance and pleas at the trial, by leave of court without opposition, and the court thereupon give judgment for the plaintiff, such judgment is irregular because unauthorized by the common law or by any statutory provision. When the exigence of the writ has been answered by an appearance recorded but subsequently vacated by the attorney's death, removal, or retirement from the court, the course is not to sign judgment for what the client could not prevent, but to rule him into court by a fresh appearance in person, or by counsel. Such a rule is a monition for his benefit, which he may disregard without incurring any other penalty than suffering the other party to have an appearance entered for him; and the practice is the same whether the defendant's or the plaintiff's appearance has been vacated. Instances of such rules are not unknown, though seldom resorted to. The withdrawal of an appearance and plea do not amount to a confession of judgment which presupposes an appearance. In such case, therefore, nothing remains but to rule the defendant into court to try the cause in the usual way.(k)

The court will set aside a judgment in an action of ejectment as well as in common actions, though a distinction has been offered between them, as, that in the former the right was not bound, but a new ejectment might be brought; but it was held, that that distinction obtained formerly in many instances where it is now exploded, a new trial could not then be had as it now may; and great inconveniences may arise from changing the possession, as timber may be felled, &c.;(l) moreover, the possession ought not to be changed by a judgment in ejectment, where there has been no trial or opportunity of trying.(m)

The court will never open a regular judgment to give the defendant advantage of a nicety in pleading,(n) or to let him have an opportunity of pleading the statute of limitations;(o) but if the defendant, although judgment by default has been regularly entered against him, will state the nature of his defence, and swear that the money was actually paid,

(i) See *post*, chapter xxvii.
(j) Crosby *v.* Massey, 1 Pa. R. 229.
(k) Michew *v.* McCoy, 3 W. & S. 502.
(l) 2 Stra. 975.

(m) 4 Burr. 1997.
(n) 2 Stra. 1242.
(o) Brown *v.* Sutter, 1 D. 239; Willet *v.* Atterton, 1 Bl. Rep. 35.

or in any way settled and accounted for, as will be hereafter seen, the court will not restrain him from pleading the statute, but they will not open the judgment on a general affidavit of defence only, to give the defendant an opportunity of pleading it.(*p*)   No dilatory plea would be allowed after the opening of a judgment by default for want of an appearance, from analogy to the English decisions, which forbid it on the setting aside a judgment incurred for want of a plea.(*q*)

SECTION II.

OF THE MODE OF COMMENCING PERSONAL ACTIONS AGAINST SEVERAL DEFENDANTS WHERE ONE IS A CITIZEN OF ANOTHER COUNTRY.

This subject is provided for by the act of 1836, §§ 70—76; but as those sections refer to others preceding them, which establish the mode of proceeding by what is called, in the act, "foreign attachment against non-residents," it will be necessary for the inquirer or reader to bear the circumstance in mind, otherwise the phraseology of the succeeding extracts from the law will appear confused or unintelligible.

In all cases where two or more persons shall be jointly, but not severally liable to the suit of another, if one or more of such persons shall be liable to process of attachment as aforesaid, and another or others of them shall not be liable to such process, it shall be lawful for the persons to whom such liability is due to sue out and prosecute thereon a writ of attachment and summons, in the following form, to wit:—

[L. S.]   ———— County, ss.
    The Commonwealth of Pennsylvania,
                            To the sheriff of said county, greeting:
We command you that you summon ————, so that they and every of them, be and appear before our Court of ————, to be holden at ————, in and for said county, on the ———— day of ———— next, there to answer ———— of a ———— [setting forth briefly the cause of action or complaint as in the præcipe], and that you attach ————, late of your county, by all and singular, his goods and chattels, in whose hands or possession soever the same may be found, and also, that you summon the person and persons, and every of them, in whose hands the goods or effects, or any of them, of the said ———— may be found, so that they be and appear before the said court, at the day and place aforesaid, to answer what shall be objected to them, and abide the judgment of the court in the premises, and have you then there this writ; witness, &c.   § 70.

Instead of a clause of summons against defendants not liable to attachment as aforesaid, it shall be lawful for the plaintiff to have against them a *capias ad respondendum*, in all cases where they would

(*p*) 2 Br. 311.   2 Call. 49; and see fully *post*, chapter
(*q*) See 3 Tuck. Bl. App. x. n.; *contra,*   xxvii. and Wh. Dig.—Judgment, iv.

otherwise be liable to arrest, and thereupon, the like proceedings shall be had as in other cases of such writ, and the garnishees shall be liable to arrest upon a *capias*, in the manner hereinbefore provided, where all the defendants in the writ are liable to such attachment.   § 71.

The plaintiff in such writ shall be entitled to proceed thereon against the defendants named in the clause of summons or *capias*, in like manner, and with like effect, as if one writ of summons or *capias* had been issued against all the defendants, instead of a writ in the form aforesaid; and he shall also be entitled to proceed against the defend- ants named in the clause of attachment, and their estate or effects, seized or bound thereby, in the manner hereinbefore provided where all the defendants in such writ are attached.   § 72.

If a judgment be rendered against the defendants who shall have appeared as aforesaid, execution thereof may be had, in like manner as in the case of a judgment rendered upon the confession of the defend- ant; and if such defendants have nothing, or not sufficient whereof to levy such judgment, it shall be lawful for the plaintiff to levy his judg- ment, or the residue thereof, of the goods and effects which may remain, subject to the attachment, proceeding therein in all respects in the manner hereinbefore provided, where none of the defendants enter bail as aforesaid.   § 73.

Provided, nevertheless, that the court may, if they see cause, award execution of the whole or any part of such judgment, against the goods or effects of the defendants attached in the first instance, saving never- theless, to all the defendants, their respective rights and claims against each other in that behalf.   § 74.

If any of such defendants against whom a summons or *capias* shall issue as aforesaid, shall plead any plea in bar of the whole action, in the manner and form in which it is brought, and a verdict and judg- ment absolute thereon be rendered for such defendant, the attachment against the other defendant shall, upon the motion of any person in- terested, be dissolved, and the goods and effects thereby bound shall be discharged, unless the plaintiff shall, within a year and a day thereafter, sue out and prosecute a writ of error to reverse such judgment, and in the mean time, and until such judgment be reversed, no further pro- ceedings shall be had upon any judgment which may have been rendered against any defendant attached.   § 75.

A writ of attachment, in the form aforesaid, may be issued against any foreign corporation, aggregate or sole, and the proceedings afore- said may be had thereon, so far as the case will permit; and such at- tachment and proceedings may be dissolved as aforesaid, upon an appearance by an attorney, and a deposit made as aforesaid, or security given for the debt or demand in lieu thereof, in such sum and form as the court from which such writ issues shall direct.   § 76.

The mode of commencing personal actions against convicts, is by writ of attachment, in the form prescribed by the act of 1836; but as it is a subject which belongs to the head of actions, by and against particular persons, we will postpone the consideration of it until we come to that part of this work.

SECTION III.

OF THE SUMMONS FOR THE COMMENCEMENT OF REAL ACTIONS, AND OF THE SERVICE OF IT.

This subject is regulated by the latter sections of the act of 1836, commencing with the seventy-ninth. The various provisions contained in them are so precise and explicit, that nothing is left for us to do but to introduce them in their order.

Actions of dower, partition, waste, ejectment, nuisance, and all other pleas of land, may be commenced in any court of the county, wherein the lands or tenements in question are situate, having original jurisdiction thereof, either by agreement of the parties, in the manner and with the effect provided in the case of personal actions, or by writ. § 79.

In cases where the subject of controversy shall be a tract of land, or any other single tenement, situate in different counties, it shall be lawful to commence an action as aforesaid, in either of the counties; and in such case, the sheriff of the county in which such writ shall issue, shall have power to execute the same, and all other process, whether original or final, which may be issued in such action, in like manner, and with like effect as if the said counties were within his proper bailiwick. § 80.

Whenever any action shall in such case be commenced in any such county, no other action between the same parties, for the same cause, shall be instituted, during the pendency thereof, in any other county. § 81.

The writ which shall be used for the commencement of any such action, shall be in all cases, unless otherwise especially provided, a writ of summons, which shall be directed to the sheriff of the county in which the action is commenced, and shall be made returnable in the manner, and according to the rules provided in the case of personal actions. § 82.

If any defendant in any real action as aforesaid, shall be a minor, service of the writ shall be as follows:—
I. If any such defendant have a guardian of his estate, service thereof shall be made upon such guardian, in the manner directed by law.
II. If any such defendant be above the age of fourteen years, service thereof shall also be made upon him, in the same manner as is directed by law in the case of adults.
III. If any such defendant be under the age of fourteen years, and have no guardian as aforesaid, service thereof shall be made upon the next of kin of such defendant, residing in the county wherein such defendant shall reside, in the manner aforesaid.
But in every case in which any such defendant shall not have a guardian as aforesaid, it shall be the duty of the plaintiff, upon or after the day on which he might take judgment by default, against such minor,

if he were of full age, and before any plea pleaded, or rule taken in the action, to make application to the court in which such action shall be brought, for the appointment of a guardian of such minor in that cause, if such minor shall not have appeared by his guardian as aforesaid, and such appointment being made, he shall give notice thereof to the person appointed. § 83.

The court which shall appoint a guardian *ad litem* of a minor, defendant in any cause, shall have power to require security of such guardians for the faithful execution of the trust, and in all cases, whether such security shall be given or not, such guardians shall be responsible to their wards, in like manner as guardians appointed by the Orphans' Court, and they shall also be entitled to a reasonable compensation for their services. § 84.

If damages shall be recoverable, and shall be demanded, in any such action, it shall be lawful for the plaintiff by a rule, to require the defendant, if he would be liable to arrest in a personal action, to enter bail, or give security, in such sum as shall be sufficient, in the judgment of the court, to satisfy the damages and costs to which such plaintiff may be entitled, and the proceedings for that purpose shall be conducted in such manner as the court in which such action may be depending by their rules shall direct. § 85.

The officer serving any such writ, shall in all cases state in his return the time and manner in which the service thereof was made, and in case the publication of the writ, or of the substance thereof, shall be required by law, or by any order of the court, compliance therewith shall be shown by affidavit, or otherwise, to the satisfaction of the court. § 86.

After the service of any such writ, or notice thereof, given as aforesaid, if the defendant shall not appear, it shall be lawful for the plaintiff, without other process, to file his declaration or statement, as by law shall be required or allowed, and at such time and manner as may be allowed by law, have judgment thereon for such default of appearance, and no essoin or saver-default in any such case be received or allowed. § 87.

Whenever it shall be lawful to cause service of any writ as aforesaid, to be made upon any defendant out of the county in which the action may be commenced, the sheriff of the county in which such defendant may reside or be found, shall, by virtue of his office, have within his county the power of a deputy to the sheriff of the county in which such writ shall have issued, for the purpose of executing such writ, without any special deputation for the purpose. § 88.

That all laws hereby altered or supplied, so far as are inconsistent with this act, are hereby repealed. § 89.

The mode of service of writs of right and other writs pertaining to manorial lands in Philadelphia, is specified in the act of May 4, 1852.(r)

(r) *Ante*, p. 236.

CHAPTER VII.

OF THE CAPIAS AD RESPONDENDUM FOR THE COMMENCEMENT OF PERSONAL ACTIONS.

The act of June 13, 1836, by which the practice in regard to this kind of process was settled, is as follows:—

SECTION I.

OF THE FORM OF THE WRIT, ITS DATE, AND RETURN.

The 3d section declares, that it shall be the duty of the prothonotary of any court having jurisdiction of the action, on the application of the plaintiff in any personal action, his agent or attorney, instead of the writ of summons as aforesaid, to issue a writ of *capias ad respondendum*, in the following form, to wit:—

The Commonwealth of Pennsylvania, ———— [L. S.] County of ————, to the sheriff of ———— County, greeting:

We command you that you take ————, if he shall be found in your bailiwick, and him safely keep until he shall have given bail, or made deposit according to law, so that he be and appear in our court of ———— on the ———— day of ———— next, then and there, to answer ———— in an action of debt [or as the case may be] in our court of ————, at the suit of ————, or until the said ———— shall by other lawful means be discharged from your custody, and have you then there this writ; witness ———— president of said court [or as the case may be], the ———— day of ————, A. D.

Prothonotary.

As we have seen, the 30th section of this act directs that these writs shall bear date on the day of the issuing of them, and shall be returnable on the first day of the term next succeeding the time at which they are issued.

By the 24th and 25th sections of the act, it is provided that, in any personal action, commenced by summons as aforesaid, if the plaintiff, his agent or attorney, shall, during the pendency of such action, make affidavit, to be filed of record, of his cause of action as aforesaid, and that the defendant is about to quit the commonwealth, as the deponent verily believes, without leaving sufficient real or personal estate therein to satisfy the demand, he may have a special *capias ad respondendum* against the defendant, in the following form:—

—— County, ss.

The Commonwealth of Pennsylvania,

To the sheriff of —— County, greeting:

Whereas, An action of debt (or as the case may be) has been commenced in our court of ——, and is depending between A B and C D, and the said A B (*or as the case may be*) has made affidavit that the said C D is justly and truly indebted to him (or as the case may be, reciting the cause of action), and that the said C D is about to quit the commonwealth, as he verily believes, without leaving sufficient real or personal estate therein, to satisfy the demand, therefore, we command you that you take the said C D, and him safely keep until he shall have given bail, or made deposit according to law, in the said action, or until the said —— shall, by other lawful means, be discharged from your custody; and you are to make return of this within ten days after the execution thereof, together with the manner in which you shall have executed the same, and the day of the execution thereof:

Witness ——, President of the said court (or as the case may be), the —— day of —— A. D.

Prothonotary.   § 24.

The proceedings upon such special *capias ad respondendum*, shall be the same as are hereinbefore provided in the case where the action is commenced by a *capias*.   § 25.

The 24th section has reference only to personal actions commenced by summons issued after the date on which the law went into operation, viz., the 1st of September, 1836: therefore, where in an action of account render to the term of December, 1835, commenced by writ of summons, the plaintiff, in October, 1836, made and filed of record an affidavit within the terms of this section, and issued a special *capias* against the defendant under which he was arrested, the court, upon a rule to show cause, quashed the latter writ.(*a*)

The 28th section makes it the duty of every prothonotary issuing a *capias ad respondendum*, whether original or special, to indorse upon it the amount of bail required by the plaintiff.   And the succeeding section empowers the courts to inquire into the cause of action, to quash the writ, *with or without costs*, and to mitigate the bail or refuse it altogether, as they were before wont to do.

By the 36th section it is provided that, whenever any writ of *capias* as aforesaid, shall be issued against any person who may be confined in the jail of the county, a copy thereof shall be delivered to the defendant, by the officer holding the same, and another copy thereof shall be left by such officer with the jailer, and thereupon, such writ shall operate to detain such person, after the other cause or causes of his confinement shall have ceased, in like manner as if he had been arrested and imprisoned by virtue of such writ.

The return days of the courts of this county have been stated in the chapter devoted to the consideration of their jurisdiction.

(*a*) Robinett *v.* Pollard, D. C. Phila. Nov. 19, 1836, 2 M. 99.

The *capias* may be sued out on the very return day,(*b*) and of course made returnable the same day; and it is immaterial whether the defendant be arrested before or after the rising of the court, there being no fractions of a day.(*c*)

SECTION II.

OF THE MODE OF EXECUTING ITS MANDATE AGAINST ONE OR MORE DEFENDANTS.

As will be seen hereafter, in the section upon the subject of privilege from arrest, this writ may be issued, under certain circumstances, against defendants whose names are unknown, when it becomes the duty of the officer, on the arrest, to inquire their names and insert them in the writ.(*d*)

If the sheriff, after receiving the writ, cannot find the defendant, he returns it with *non est inventus*, or N. E. I. indorsed upon it, in which case the plaintiff may sue out an *alias capias*, commanding him as *before* he had been commanded to take the defendant, or a *pluries capias*, commanding him as *oftentimes* he had been commanded, into the same county, and the *pluries* may be repeated from time to time until the defendant be arrested.(*e*)

It is the rule in the practice of some States, that a second writ cannot be considered as an *alias*, if it be issued more than a year and a day after the first writ.(*f*)

If the sheriff can find the defendant he is bound to arrest him; if he cannot, and it is ascertained that the defendant is not in the county, the proceedings must be dropped, for a *testatum capias* cannot be issued into another county, as in England, suggesting that it has been *testified* the defendant lurks and wanders in that county; but the plaintiff must go himself, or send his warrant of attorney therein, for the purpose of issuing the writ from the Common Pleas of such county.

If the writ be issued against several defendants, and one only is arrested, or all cannot be found, the practice in regard to them differs in this State from that pursued in England.

In England, when a *capias ad respondendum* has issued against several, and *non est inventus* has been returned as to one, the process does not stop there against him, but the plaintiff proceeds to outlaw him.(*g*) But it is now even there a mere form to compel an appearance, and when it has been completed, any plausible excuse will be sufficient to reverse it. But in Pennsylvania, their being no process of outlawry in civil actions, the return of *non est inventus* for all purposes of pleading has the same effect. When the plaintiff has done *all he can* to bring into court all the defendants, he may proceed against the one who has been arrested, stating in his declaration the writ and the return.(*h*) If he declare against two defendants jointly, one of whom

(*b*) Salk. 422, *n. a.* 4 T. R. 610.
(*c*) 2 Br. 245.
(*d*) See §§ 7 and 8, *post*, § 3.
(*e*) 1 Dunl. Pr. 119.
(*f*) 1 Nott & M'Cord, 171.

(*g*) The mode of doing it is described in the third volume of Blackstone's Commentaries, pp. 283–284.
(*h*) Dilman *v.* Schultz, 5 S. & R. 36 ; Taylor *v.* Henderson, 17 Id. 456.

only has been arrested, without the usual clause as to the return of *non est inventus* as to the other, and enter judgment by default against both, the judgment will be erroneous,(*i*) unless there had been a general appearance by attorney, which would be considered as an appearance for both; and the judgment against both would, according to our practice, be regular.(*j*) And where the appearance by attorney is special for some of the defendants only, and the others do not appear, either by attorney or entering bail to the action, the plaintiff may, even though he have declared against all, have a verdict and judgment against those only who are in court.(*k*)

Where a *capias* had issued in the Circuit Court of the United States for the Pennsylvania district, returnable to April term, 1792, against three defendants, and only one was arrested, who gave bail, and a declaration was filed against him, on which issue was joined, and the cause was continued till August, 1796, it was held that an *alias capias* could not then be issued against another of the three defendants, returnable to October, 1796, bearing teste of April, 1792. And it was even doubted whether such an *alias* would be good in that court, if regularly taken out (that is, tested of the term to which the original was returned), returnable at the next ensuing term and continued from term to term.(*l*) In this case, it was said by MR. JUSTICE IREDELL, that "the practice of Pennsylvania went no further than to give to the plaintiff an option, either to suspend his proceedings until the non-appearing defendant can be arrested, or to waive, on filing a declaration, all chance against him, and enforce the suit only against the defendant who is taken on the *capias*." If the plaintiff adopt the latter course of the alternative, he cannot arrest the other defendant without discontinuing the first action;(*m*) for, were a different rule to prevail, it might operate to the injustice and oppression of the defendant first arrested, in a variety of ways.(*n*) By a recent act of assembly, this waiver of the liability of one joint defendant in the proceeding against another, is remedied, and the plaintiff may pursue his claim in subsequent actions against such of the defendants as could not be served with process in the first action, notwithstanding a judgment may have already been obtained on the joint claim against one.

The plaintiff is not bound to drop a defendant who has not been served or taken, but may bring him in by an *alias* engrafted on the original writ.(*o*) The *alias* is a continuance of the original process, and the entries in the action may be under the original or any subsequent writ. The practice has been to continue them under that on which the defendant has been brought in; but this, though convenient, is not to have the effect of changing a supplementary writ into an original. If, therefore, special bail be entered in time in the original suit, in which the writ was returned *non est inventus*, it will be a compliance with the condition of the bail-bond given upon an *alias capias*.(*p*)

(*i*) Boax *v.* Heister, 6 S. & R. 18.
(*j*) Id. 20.
(*k*) Taylor *v.* Henderson, 17 Id. 453.
(*l*) United States *v.* Parker, 2 D. 373.
(*m*) Ibid. 378–9.

(*n*) See further, the remarks of IRE-DELL, J., ibid. 379.
(*o*) Taylor *v.* Henderson, 17 S. & R. 456.
(*p*) Lynn *v.* McMillen, 3 Pa. R. 170.

The following rules of the District Court, as they still govern all proceedings sounding in *tort* commenced with *capias*, will be found important here :—

XX. No bail shall be required in actions of trespass *vi et armis*, in actions for libel, slanderous words, malicious prosecution, conspiracy, or false imprisonment, unless an affidavit of the cause of action be made and filed before the issuing of the writ.

XXI. No attorney of this or any court, or sheriff's officer, bailiff, or other person, concerned in the execution of process, shall be permitted or suffered to become special bail in any action or suit depending in this court, unless by leave of the court.

XXII. Exceptions to bail, under the act of assembly of the 13th of June, 1836, relating to the commencement of actions, must be made in writing and filed with the prothonotary; and notice thereof in writing shall be given by the plaintiff to the defendant or his attorney, and to the sheriff, within forty-eight hours from the filing of such exceptions.

XXIII. Notice of the justification, addition, or substitution of bail must be given in writing to the plaintiff or his attorney at least forty-eight hours before the time designated in the notice of such justification, addition, or substitution; and when bail is to be added or substituted, the notice must state the name, occupation, or profession, and place of residence of such proposed bail.(*q*)

XXIV.(*r*) Hereafter the prothonotary shall issue no *capias ad respondendum* indorsed with bail in more than five hundred dollars, without a special *allocatur* from one of the judges.

SECTION III.

OF PRIVILEGE FROM ARREST, UNDER THE ACT OF 1836.

The 4th, 5th, and 6th sections provide as follows :—

That no writ of *capias ad respondendum* shall issue in any case, unless the plaintiff, his agent or attorney, shall previously thereto make affidavit, setting forth :—

First : The cause of action, and the amount in which the defendant is indebted to the plaintiff, or the value of the property taken or detained, or the damages sustained, as the case may be, to the best of the deponent's knowledge and belief; and,

Second : That to the best of the deponent's knowledge or belief, the defendant is not an inhabitant of this commonwealth, or if such inhabitant, that he has no place of residence therein to the knowledge of the deponent, or that he is about to quit the commonwealth, without leaving sufficient real or personal estate therein to satisfy the demand; which affidavit shall be filed of record in the suit. § 4.

Provided, That it shall be lawful for a plaintiff in any action founded upon actual force, or which shall be brought by reason of actual fraud

(*q*) The District Court has given notice that a judge will be in attendance on Saturday morning, at 9½ o'clock, for the purpose of justifying bail, and that surety must be offered at that hour.
(*r*) Adopted March 7, 1849.

or deceit, upon affidavit of the facts, to have a *capias* as aforesaid, against any person not otherwise liable to arrest. § 5.

By the act of April 14, 1838,(s) these two sections were repealed, and the acts formerly existing revived. As, however, these are again superseded by the act abolishing imprisonment for debt, to be considered presently, it will be unnecessary here to give more than a brief recapitulation.

The following sections, of the act of 1836, continue in force except so far as they conflict with the act abolishing imprisonment for debt:—

Nothing herein contained shall be taken to authorize the issuing of a *capias ad respondendum* against any female for any debt contracted since the 8th of February, 1819; nor against any executor, or other person sued in a representative character, unless such person shall have become personally liable for the debt or demand alleged; nor against any person whomsoever, for any sum of money. § 6.

The 7th and 8th sections provide, that whenever the cause of action shall be founded upon an injury done to the persons or property of the plaintiff by a person whose name is unknown to him, or upon a fraud practised by such person, to the prejudice of the plaintiff, it shall be lawful for the plaintiff, whether such person would otherwise be liable to arrest or not, on affidavit of that fact, to have a writ of *capias*, in the form aforesaid, against such person, without naming him, but such writ shall be executed by the sheriff or other officer, only under the direction of the plaintiff, and at his risk. § 7.

Upon the arrest of any person against whom a writ of *capias* shall be issued as aforesaid, it shall be the duty of the officer to inquire of him his name, and if given, he shall insert the same in such writ, and thereupon, the same proceedings shall be had as if such writ had issued in the usual form. § 8.

By the act of 1838, the act of 1725, exempting freeholders in certain cases from arrest, is revived.(ss)

As will be presently fully considered,(t) the plaintiff should be particular, in framing his affidavit, to pursue the words of the act, and to bring himself as nearly as possible within its spirit and meaning.

An affidavit made under this section, in which the plaintiff merely averred that "to the best of his belief the defendant was about to quit the commonwealth," without more, was held to be insufficient.(u)

(s) Purdon, 52.
(ss) Lynd v. Biggs, 1 P. L. J. 47.
(t) Post, chap. x.
(u) Diehl v. Perie, Dist. Court, Philad. Dec. T. 1836, 2 M. 47; see also 2 Wh. 499. Jones, J., delivering the opinion of the court, said: "The phrase, 'to the best of the deponent's knowledge and belief,' is of judicial origin. We have also from the same source the formal expression, 'so far as the deponent knows and as he verily believes.' The intent and import of both are the same. Both imply that the deponent has information or evidence of the fact asserted, which, although it may not amount to certain knowledge, is in his judgment sufficient to justify a conclusion of the fact he swears to; and both forms are intended to express a positive belief. Affidavits in this form, are allowed for the purpose of avoiding an inconvenient detail of evidence; and usually, when there is no opportunity of submitting the evidence of the requisite fact to judicial examination and inference; or when it would be inconvenient to do so. The effect of allowing

SECTION IV.

OF PRIVILEGE FROM SUIT, INDEPENDENTLY OF ACT OF 1842.

Besides the exemption from arrest of inhabitants under the act of 1836, there is a privilege from this process extended to other persons, which will constitute the immediate subject of this section. And as this immunity, whether it be perpetual, temporary or local, generally amounts, during its continuance, to a total privilege from suit,(v) the

affidavits in this form, is to substitute the probity and intelligence of the deponent for the judgment of the court or of a judge, inasmuch as the law, without inquiry, assumes that to be true which he says he knows or has reason to know and verily believes.

"A person, therefore, who should, in this form, swear to a fact upon information or evidence which does not induce his own belief of it; or upon a belief of the fact which is not founded upon what he deems sufficient evidence of it (if we can suppose the mind can believe under such circumstances), would be guilty of a degree of rashness which would be evidence of a criminal purpose: Nor could he, in such circumstances, legally or conscientiously swear to the fact, either to the best of his knowledge, or upon his belief: For if his knowledge be not such as actually produces in his own mind a belief of the fact, the qualification of the affirmation, as it would refer to that which has no existence, or which exists without any rational foundation, would be nugatory in conscience and illusory as it respects the public justice: It would in reality be without meaning, and therefore would give us nothing to subtract from the unqualified affirmation.

"If then we take this phrase in the disjunctive or alternative form, as it occurs in the clause under consideration, and construct an affidavit upon either branch of it, still, the deponent must be deemed to affirm both his belief of the fact, and that he has such knowledge concerning it as he conscientiously deems sufficient to justify his belief. For these reasons we must construe the word " or," in this place to signify " and." Indeed, we cannot suppose the legislature intentionally adopted this unusual form of expression. The spirit of the act certainly confirms the use of the *capias* to cases in which the plaintiff has reason to know and verily believes the defendant is about to quit the commonwealth: And it may not be improper to suggest that affidavits under this section should hereafter be drawn so as to make the expression conform to this view of the sense, otherwise a door may be opened to questions of casuistry depending on distinctions too refined for practical purposes.

"But it is not necessary to rule the point raised in this case, upon these reasons. The legislature certainly did not intend that anything less than the deponent's full belief of the fact sworn to, should be sufficient to justify the arrest: For although the act does not require him to swear to the absolute certainty of his knowledge, or that his conclusions from facts certainly known are infallibly true, yet he must aver that his knowledge is such, that *se judice, et in foro conscientiæ suæ,* it proves the fact and induces his own positive belief of it. There is nothing unreasonable in this; for every man certainly knows whether he believes that which he asserts or not. He can discriminate between his belief, suspicion, unbelief, and disbelief. But a qualified or partial belief or such a state of the mind as the words ' to the best of his belief,' would seem to describe, is impossible. The expression is a solecism. We cannot determine from it what precisely was the state of the deponent's mind, nor how far it was short of positive belief: But when those qualifying words are applied, as in the act they are, to the knowledge or the evidence which the deponent possesses of the fact which he affirms, we are allowed to suppose that it does not fall very far short of certain proof, if it produces a conscientious belief in a reasonable mind. On the ground, then, that the plaintiff has not sworn positively that he believed the defendant was about to quit the commonwealth, this rule is made absolute."

(v) 1 Dunl. Pr. 92.

consideration of privilege from summons will also with propriety enter
into the subject of the present section.

By the law of nations the ambassador of a foreign state is privileged
from arrest for any cause whatever, and the same privilege is extended
to his domestics or servants.(w)   These privileges are recognized, regulated, and enforced by the act of Congress of April 30, 1790, §§ 25 and
26.(x)

A defendant claiming the benefit of the act of Congress as domestic
servant to a public minister must be really and *bona fide* his servant at
the time of arrest.(y)   A secretary of legation is entitled to all the
immunities of a minister.(z)

Consuls are not considered as public ministers, nor consequently
privileged from arrest;(a) if they were, it would be attended with much
inconvenience, for such persons are generally engaged in trade, and are
frequently subjects of the countries in which their office is exercised.(b)

By the sixth section of the first article of the constitution of the
United States, the senators and representatives in Congress "shall in
all cases, except treason, felony, and breach of the peace, be privileged
from arrest during their attendance at the session of their respective
houses, and in going to or returning from the same."   There is no
statute fixing the time during which a member of Congress is to be
privileged before or after the session of Congress; and it has been held
that this privilege is to be taken strictly, and is to be allowed only while
the party is attending Congress, or is actually on his journey, going or
returning from the seat of government.(c)

In regard to the privilege of members of the senate and house of representatives of this State, it has been decided that they are privileged
from arrest, summons, citation, or other civil process during their attendance on the public business confided to them; and it seems their suits
cannot be forced to trial during the session of the legislature.(d)   So a
member of a State convention is privileged from a summons or arrest,
during the sitting of the convention, and for a reasonable period before
and after the session.(e)

The members of a corporation aggregate cannot be arrested, or sued
individually, for any matter relating to their corporate concerns.(f)

In an action against husband and wife, the husband alone is liable to
be arrested; and shall not be discharged until he have put in bail for
himself and his wife.(g)   Women, by the sixth section of the act of
June 13th, 1836,(h) are not liable to be arrested or imprisoned for any
debt contracted after the 8th of February 1819; but it leaves them still
liable to arrest in actions founded upon *tort*, or claims arising otherwise
than *ex contractu*, when sole, or living as feme sole traders.

The parties to a suit, their attorneys, counsel and witnesses, are, for
the sake of public justice, privileged from arrest in coming to, attending

---

(w) Com. Dig. Ambassador, B.
(x) 2 Laws U. S. 97.
(y) 1 Dunl. Pr. 95, 96.
(z) Wh. Dig. "Privilege;" Res. v.
Keating, 1 Dal. 117.
(a) United States v. Revara, 2 Dal.
297–299, n.; 1 Bac. Abr. 144.
(b) 1 Dunl. Pr. 96.

(c) 2 Johns. Cas. 222; 1 Dunl. Pr. 96.
(d) Bolton v. Martin, 4 Dal. 107.
(e) Ibid. 1 Dal. 296.
(f) Tidd. Pr. 200.
(g) 6 Mod. 17, 87; Str. 1272; 1 Lev.
216.   See further 3 Bl. Com. 414; 7
Taunt. 55; 1 Dunl. Pr. 99.
(h) *Ante*, p. 250, 251.

upon, and returning from the court ; or as it is usually termed, *eundo, morando, et redeundo.*(*i*) In the Supreme Court, a party attending court as a suitor is privileged from the service of a summons, as well as from a *capias.*(*j*) But in the Circuit Court of the United States, it has been held that the privilege of a suitor or witness extends only to exemption from arrest, though the service of process, whether a *capias* or summons, in the actual or constructive presence of the court (as on the steps of the court-house) would be a contempt.(*k*) A suitor lawfully in custody, on the surrender of his special bail in another action, and who, of course, could not attend his cause even if the trial were going on, is not privileged from either process in a third action.(*l*) If a party coming to attend the trial of his cause, be arrested, he may move the court, out of which the process issued, to discharge him on common bail. But on application to the court for the discharge of the defendant notice must be given to the opposite party ; otherwise only a rule to show cause why he should not be discharged, with stay of proceedings in the mean time, will be granted.(*m*) Or, the court or judge at *nisi prius* will grant a *habeas corpus* to discharge him, and will likewise put off the trial.(*n*) Where the Common Pleas had decided that one of its suitors was not entitled to privilege from arrest, the Supreme Court refused to interfere on a *habeas corpus.*(*o*)

The common law term, "privilege from arrest," is with us substantially equivalent to the expression "privilege from suit."(*p*)

A counsellor-at-law, coming from another county to attend to the cause of his clients before the Supreme Court, is exempt from the service of a summons in a civil action, in going, remaining, and returning.(*q*)

(*i*) Com. Dig. Privilege, A. Miles *v.* McCullough, 4 Dal. 487 ; 1 Dunl. Pr. 100. Dunton *v.* Halstead, 4 P. L. S. 237.

(*j*) Miles *v.* McCullough, 1 Bin. 77 ; Hayes *v.* Shields, 2 Y. 222.

(*k*) 1 Peters, Rep. 41.

(*l*) 3 Y. 387.

(*m*) 1 Dunl. Pr. 102; 1 Caine's Rep. 116.

(*n*) 1 Campb. 229.

(*o*) Com. *v.* Hambright, 4 S. & R. 149.

(*p*) Wicks *v.* Brown (D. C. All., LOWRIE, J.)

(*q*) Ibid. Austin *v.* Brown, Dec. 9, 1848. D. C. C. C. P. Why writ of summons should not be quashed. *Per curiam.* The defendant, an attorney at law, resides at Easton, and in the course of his professional duties was in this city in attendance upon the trial of a cause in the Circuit Court of the United States, in which he was concerned. While so in attendance he was served with the writ of summons. It is too well settled to be now questioned with us that a witness, party, or attorney, attending the trial of a cause at a distance from his home, and at another jurisdiction, is privileged as well from the service of a summons as of a *capias.* (Hayes *v.* Shields, 2 Y. 222. Miles *v.* McCullough, 1 Bin.

77. Wetherill *v.* Lutzinger, 1 M. 240.)

The question has been made (unimportant, indeed, in this case), what in practice is the proper order to quash the writ or set aside the service. In Wetherill *v.* Lutzinger (1 M. 240), the rule was as in this case to show cause why writ should not be quashed. This point was not raised, and the rule was made absolute. In Miles *v.* McCullough (1 Bin. 77), the eminent counsel for the defendant, the late Judge Hopkinson, moved to set aside the service upon the ground of privilege ; and the order of the court was made accordingly. In Hayes *v.* Shields (2 Y. 222), a case which was at *Nisi Prius*, in Greensburg, held by two of the justices of the Supreme Court, and in which the defendant, a suitor, was served with a summons issuing out of the Common Pleas of Westmoreland County, the motion by Mr. Ross was that the defendant should be discharged from the action, and the order was made in the terms of the motion. In Bolton *v.* Martin (1 D. 296), which is the only other and earliest case reported, the rule was to show cause why the process should not be quashed, but the order of

Judge Duncan, in the Supreme Court,(r) points out the practice to be pursued when a privileged person has been arrested, in the following words: "The power to discharge suitors and witnesses is necessarily inherent in every court, and though the court from which the process issues may discharge, for the abuse of their process on the privileges of suitors and parties in other courts, yet the court on which the contempt has been committed is the most suitable forum, and the practice generally is to apply there for redress. A chancellor exercises this authority whenever the proceeding under which the privilege is claimed issues from that court. Indeed, some doubts have been of late entertained whether the application must not be made to that court, of which the arrest is a contempt, and there can be no doubt of the power of that court to discharge, though the court from which the process issues have declined or refused to discharge; and as this power is necessary for their own protection, it cannot depend upon another tribunal to grant or withhold it. It is the privilege of the court, yet it is the protection of the suitor or witness to whom the common law gave a writ of privilege in that case, in lieu of which summary relief on motion is now substituted, and this cannot be denied on proper grounds shown, for there is no such thing in the law as writs of grace and favor issuing from the judges; they are all writs of right, but not writs of course. The giving a bail-bond is so far from waiving this privilege, that the court when they discharge will order it to be delivered up to be cancelled. The defendant is not obliged to apply in person, his bail or his attorney may. Nor must he continue in custody, or give up his own lawful pursuits and remain stationary until the sitting of the court." The law is the same, though the arrest were made by the United States. "Protection to a witness ought to be at least as extensive as to a party; and when the privilege is not a mere cover to a skulking debtor, it ought to be considered liberally. Origi-

the court was that he should be discharged from the action.

It appears to us upon reflection, that the most proper practice is that pursued in Miles v. McCullough, which is the last decision of the Supreme Court. The writ itself was not irregular. If, after having completed his business as attorney, the defendant had unnecessarily remained for his pleasure or private affairs, he surely could have been served, with the process, or if he had gone and returned before the return day. It is not the issuing of the writ, but the service which is the breach of privilege. Thus it would be competent, as well for the court issuing the process as the court in contempt of whom it was served, to set aside and to enforce their order in the case of the latter court by an attachment against the officer, but to quash the writ could only be done by the court issuing it. This makes one think that both Hayes v. Shields and Bolton v. Martin are authorities in favor of the practice of simply setting aside the service. In the latter case, though the rule was to

quash the writ, the order was that the defendant be discharged from the action. And in the former case the order was made by a different court from that which issued the writ; and of course, had no power to quash it. In cases of arrests of privileged persons, the uniform practice in England, as well as this country, appears to be not to quash the writ, but to discharge the defendant from the custody of the sheriff, or order the bail-bond to be delivered up to be cancelled. (See 6 Taunt. 356; 11 East, 439; 2 Blackst. Rep. 1113; Ex parte Edme, 9 S. & R. 147.) It is true that in Kinsman v. Reinen (2 M. 200), the rule was to show cause why the capias should not be quashed, but then the court discharged the rule, referring the defendant for redress to the court upon whom the contempt had been committed; whose power surely could not extend to quashing the process of another court.

Service set aside and R. D.

(r) United States v. Edme, 9 S. & R. 147.

nally, indeed, it embraced only attendants on courts, but it has extended itself in process of time to every case where the attendance was a duty in conducting any proceedings of a judicial nature, as commissions of bankrupt, or before a judge at his chambers; and whatever doubts might have been entertained as to a witness attending on arbitrations under a rule of court, he is now just as much protected as a witness attending a judge at *nisi prius.*"

A witness attending without subpœna is equally privileged;(s) so, in general, all persons who have relation to a cause which calls for their attendance in court, and who attend in the course of that cause, though not compelled by process so to do, are privileged from arrest, provided their attendance be not for any unfair purpose.(t) Nor have the courts been nice in scanning this privilege, whether relating to the coming, attendance, or returning of any one concerned in the trial, but have given it a large and liberal construction.(u) Wherever it exists *eundo*, it extends *redeundo*.(v)

The law now, both in the federal and State courts, is that the privilege of the suitor when in court exempts him equally from a summons and a *capias*.(w) But a party under arrest in another suit is not protected.(ww)

Though it is said that a party attending a criminal court, is not privileged from service of process,(x) yet, where it appears that a criminal pro-

---

(s) United States *v.* Edme, 9 S. & R. 147; 8 T. R. 536; 1 H. Blac. 636.

(t) 1 Dunl. Pr. 101; 1 Campb. 230, n.; Barnes, 27; 1 H. Blac. 636.

(u) Stra. 986, 1094; 11 East, 439; 4 D. 387; Hayes *v.* Shields, 2 Y. 222; Com. Dig. Privilege, A.; 1 W. Blac. 1113; 5 Bac. Abr. 617; 6 Taunt. 358; 4 D. 329.

(v) Dunton *v.* Halstead, 4 P. L. J. 237.

(w) Miles *v.* McCullough, 1 Bin. 77; Parker *v.* Hotchkiss, 1 Wall. Jun. 268. See Wh. Dig. "PRIVILEGE."

(ww) Stryker *v.* Patterson, Baum *v.* Patterson, D. C. Feb. 10, 1849. Why the service of the *alias* summons should not be set aside. *Per curiam.* It appears that the writ in these cases was served on the defendant after he had been arrested, and was in custody on warrant of arrest under the act of 12th July, 1842, issued in these same cases. It is not pretended that the defendant, when arrested and in custody under a warrant of arrest, cannot be served with the summons in the same case—but it is contended that being under arrest in the one suit, he is privileged from the service of a summons in another suit. This is a misunderstanding of the doctrine of privilege, which entitles a person to be free from molestation when in actual attendance upon court, either as party or witness, but does not extend to exempt him, when he is merely attending to his law business, for the reason of it would then extend to his going and returning from the office of his counsel. It is plain

that when a party is arrested under process, he may be properly served with any other process in the hands of the sheriff. Several writs of *capias* may be placed together in the sheriff's hands, and the sheriff may arrest the defendant upon all of them, and cannot safely let him go until he has given bail on all of them. *A fortiori* he cannot claim exemption from the service of a summons. Rules discharged.

(x) Addicks *v.* Bush, D.C. Dec. 22, 1849. Motion to set aside the service of certain writs of summons. *Per curiam.* It appears that the defendant was indicted for conspiracy with one Chadwick to obtain goods on false pretences. The plaintiffs were the prosecutors, or active in carrying on the proceeding. The defendant was a resident of Tioga County, in this State, and was brought here to be tried on the indictment. He was acquitted. On the day of the acquittal, he was served with these writs. It seems settled that a person in custody, on a criminal charge, is not privileged from the service of process. Were it necessary, however, we should hesitate long before carrying this exception to the general rule to the extent of saying, that a man at large on bail was not privileged *eundo redeundo et morando.* A man may be in custody in default of bail a long time before his trial—to extend the privilege to that case would lengthen it from a few days to as many months. But there seems no good reason why a man attending a trial in-

ceeding is made use of only for the purpose of bringing the defendant within reach of process, the court will set aside the service of a writ of summons.(y)

A person privileged from arrest, on the ground that he was attending the Court of Quarter Sessions, as prosecutor and witness in an indictment, cannot be discharged from imprisonment on *ca. resp.* on a *habeas corpus,* before a judge of the Common Pleas in vacation; but must be put to his application to the court from which the *capias* issued.(z)

Soldiers in the service of the United States are privileged from arrest for debts under twenty dollars;(a) and to some extent bail may avail themselves of the privilege of their principal, a soldier.(b) United States seamen and marines are privileged from arrest for any debt or contract without limitation.(c)

By the seventieth section of the act of 1822,(d) " No civil process shall be served upon any officer, non-commissioned officer, or private, when going to, whilst attending at, or when returning from any parade, for disciplining any part of the volunteers or militia. "

The sheriff is not bound to take notice that the party is protected from arrest; but if he chooses to notice it, or neglects to take a person privileged from arrest, and can show that he is so privileged, it is a good defence in an action against him for an escape.(e)　A defendant will not be discharged out of custody, on common bail, on the ground of infancy, or that he was insane at the time of the arrest, or afterwards became so.(f)

In case of a mere contempt, the court will not set aside a service when the defendant omits to move until after he leaves the jurisdiction.(g)

---

volving life, liberty, or character, should not as well be unembarrassed during the necessary period of time occupied in the trial, and in going to and returning from the same, as in civil suits. It is unnecessary to decide that question here; because it is agreed that if the prosecution was instituted for the purpose of getting the defendant away from his home, and then serving him with the process—the court will set aside the service. We think there is sufficient evidence that such was the case here. Service set aside.—Though see Com. v. Daniel, 6 P. L. J. 330.

(y) Ibid.

(z) Com. v. Adams, 10 P. L. J. 134.

(a) As to this privilege, see 3 Laws U. S. 456 ; 4 Id. 163 and 826.

(b) See 4 Taunt. 557.

(c) 3 Laws U. S. 97.

(d) 7 Re. Laws, 646.

(e) 11 Johns. 433 ; *sed vide,* 4 Taunt. 631.

(f) 1 Bos. & P. 480 ; 4 T. R. 121 ; 2 Bos. & P. 362 ; 2 T. R. 390.

(g) Souder v. Burling, D. C. Saturday, April 24, 1852. Rule to set aside service of summons. *Per curiam.* The defendant, a non-resident, was attending before an alderman to have his deposition taken, when the summons was served. It may be considered, perhaps, as having been served *constructively* in the presence of the court, otherwise, as the defendant does not appear to have come into this State for the purpose of giving his testimony, it would have been no breach of privilege within the principles settled by our decisions. However, the defendant did not apply until he had left the State, though he had the opportunity. This would have made no difference if he had had his privilege during his reasonable stay, as if he had come expressly to be examined ; but here it was all-important to the plaintiff to be at once informed that he meant to insist on his privilege: for he might have had the process legally served afterwards and before he left. Rule dismissed.

SECTION V.

WHEN THE DEFENDANT MAY BE HELD TO BAIL.

By the act of 1842, abolishing imprisonment for debt, as will be pre-sently seen, no *capias* can issue except in an action sounding in *tort*. So far as concerns actions arising on contract, therefore, the following section is no longer authoritative. As, however, it is in many points applicable to *torts*, and as it supplies illustrations for the construction of the act of 1842, it is here retained.

In many cases the defendant, upon being arrested, may be detained in custody until he has given bail or security for his appearance; in others, he ought to be discharged on his own written engagement or that of his attorney, to appear. It is a general rule in the practice of the English courts, that whenever the defendant may be arrested he may be held to bail;(*h*) but this rule does not apply in our practice: and it is a general principle, that whenever a *capias* lies, the defendant may be arrested, but whether he shall be held to bail or not depends on other considerations.(*i*)

The actions wherein bail is of course, or wherein discretionary, have been in this State generally regulated by the English practice.

The general rule adopted in England, in the construction of the stat-utes regulating bail, is, that when the cause of action arises from a debt or money demand; or where it sounds in damages, but the damages may be ascertained with certainty; the defendant may be held to bail, as of course. But where the cause of action sounds merely in damages, and those damages are unliquidated, or cannot possibly be reduced to any degree of certainty without the intervention of a jury; the defendant shall not be held to bail, unless a judge's order be first obtained for that purpose.(*j*) It must here be observed, that this practice as to a judge's order does not prevail in this State, in cases where bail is not of course, but the right to bail is discussed after the arrest, upon a citation, or rule to show cause of action, and why the defendant should not be discharged on common bail;(*k*) as will be more particularly seen in a subsequent chapter.

In *assumpsit*, where the action sounds in debt, as where it is brought for goods sold, money lent, or on a bill of exchange or promissory note, or the like, the defendant could formerly be held to bail as of course: but where it sounded merely in damages, and those damages were un-liquidated, as for breach of an agreement to receive or deliver goods, or the like, bail could not be required, unless on a judge's order.(*l*)

In actions of *debt*, the defendant could be held to bail as of course ; and if the debt be secured by bond, the defendant would be held to bail merely for the principal and interest due on it, and not for the penalty.(*m*) But in all cases where the penalty is in the nature of liquidated dam-ages, as where a bond is conditioned for the performance of a promise

(*h*) Tidd. 245.
(*i*) 1 Dunl. Pr. 94, n.
(*j*) 1 Arch. Pr. 48.
(*k*) Jack *v*. Shoemaker, 3 Bin. 280.

(*l*) 1 Arch. Pr. 49 ; 5 Taunt. 201; and see further, 1 H. Bl. 301; 4 Burr. 1996; 5 Taunt. 259.
(*m*) 1 Arch. Pr. 49.

to marry,(n) or the like, the defendant could be held to bail for the penalty, it being in such a case the debt in law.(o)

The defendant could not be held to bail in an action upon a penal statute,(p) for it is a maxim that every man shall be presumed innocent of an offence till he be found guilty ; nor on a recognizance of bail, because on taking the bail, they are admitted to be sufficient;(q) but in an action of debt on a recognizance to prosecute a writ of error, bail had to be put in.(r)   The defendant could not be held to bail in *debt* on a bail or replevin bond,(s) whether the action be brought in the name of the sheriff or his assignee. Though after judgment has been obtained against the bail in such action, the defendant might be held to bail in an action on the judgment.(t)   In debt on a judgment, special bail could not in general be required, if the defendant had been held to bail in the original action.(u)   But if the defendant were not held to bail in that action, he might in general be held to bail in an action on the judgment,(v) even though a writ of error were pending on it ;(w) provided the original cause of action were such that the defendant might have been held to bail on it.(x)   A defendant who pleaded non-joinder in abatement of an action in which he was arrested, might be again arrested in a new action against all the contractors.(y)

In an action brought in the courts of this State against the subject of a foreign country, on a contract or cause of action arising in that country, the plaintiff was entitled to bail, although by the laws of such country the defendant was not liable to imprisonment for debt except in certain cases,(z) for though the *lex loci contractus* applies to the interpretation of contracts, it does not govern as to the mode of enforcing them.(a)— But in an action between foreigners, the laws of whose country suspend the action to a period not yet arrived, special bail could not be required.(b)

The defendant might also be held to bail in an action of trover or detinue,(c) for although these are in form actions of *tort*, yet as they relate to property, they are not merely actions for the recovery of uncertain damages ; and this continues still to be the law, such cases being excepted out of the act of 1842.   In detinue of charters, the defendant was discharged on common bail, because it did not appear that he had tortiously possessed himself thereof.(d)

In slander, the court will hold to bail if the plaintiff swear positively to special damage, although the amount of damage is not specified.(e) But the court will uniformly discharge a defendant in slander, on common bail, unless special damage be proved, or the words charge the plaintiff with a crime of a gross nature,(f) or the defendant is about to leave the State.   When common bail has been ordered by a judge at his

(n) 1 Doug. 449.
(o) 1 Arch. Pr. 50.
(p) Gilb. C. P. 37.
(q) 1 Tidd. Pr. 33.
(r) 2 Y. 280.
(s) 2 Saund. 61, b ; 6 T. R. 336 ; Salk. 99, pl. 8.
(t) 2 Saund. 61, b.
(u) 2 Wm. Bl. 768; and see 2 T. R. 756.
(v) 1 New Rep. 133.

(w) 2 Wm. Bl. 768.
(x) 1 Arch. Pr. 50.
(y) 1 Chit. Rep. 207, n.
(z) Milne v. Moreton, 6 Bin. 360.
(a) Ibid.
(b) 4 D. 419 ; 1 Wh. Dig. Tit. Bail.
(c) 1 Tidd. Pr. 173.
(d) Burnbridge v. Turner, 2 Y. 429.
(e) 1 Br. 297.
(f) McCawley v. Smith, 4 Y. 193.

chambers, on a citation to show cause of bail in slander, the plaintiff cannot recur to the court in term, although, under the authority of a *dictum* of Lord HOLT,(g) he has declared to the defendant his intention of so doing.(h)

In actions of trespass, the general rule is, that bail is not demandable, because there is no standard by which the damages can be measured.— But there are exceptions to this rule. One is, where the defendant is about to depart out of the jurisdiction of the court. Another is, where there has been a violent battery, in which the plaintiff may sometimes swear to damages to a certain amount, and it may be evident, from a view of the wounds, that considerable damage must have been sustained. There are other cases where it is presumable that large damages will be given, because the subject may have been discussed in an action against others for a similar trespass.(i)

Persons sued in *auter droit*, as heirs, executors, and administrators, when sued for the debt of their ancestor, testator, or intestate, cannot be held to bail; for the demand is not on their persons, but on the assets of the deceased; and it would be unreasonable to subject their persons to an execution for the debt of another.(j)

The defendant shall not be held twice to bail for the same cause of action, unless under very special circumstances.(k) Therefore a defendant who was under bail in the State of Delaware, for the same cause of action, was discharged from bail in a suit in Pennsylvania.(l) Where a former suit had been brought against the defendant for the same cause of action, in which no bail was required, special bail was exacted.(m)

But where, in consequence of a mere inadvertence or mistake on the part of the plaintiff, the defendant was discharged, and there appeared no actual oppression or design to harass, the court refused to discharge a defendant arrested a second time for the same cause.(n)

So where a special *capias* had issued under the act of 1836, and was quashed on the ground that the action was brought before the act of 1836 went into operation, and the plaintiff then discontinued the action and commenced a new one by *capias*, the court refused to discharge the defendant on common bail.(o)

An arrest of the defendant in a new action, during the pendency of another action in a foreign country, is justifiable by the common law.(p)

By the 48th section of the act of 1836,(q) "every person who shall be confined in any jail of this commonwealth, in execution or otherwise, for any debt, sum of money, fine, or forfeiture, not exceeding the sum of fifteen dollars exclusive of costs, and who shall have remained so confined for thirty days, shall be discharged from such confinement, if there be no other cause of confinement, and shall not be liable to *imprisonment again for the same reason*, and the sheriff or jailer shall discharge such person from confinement, if confined for such debt, sum of money, fine, or forfeiture, and for no other cause."

(g) 12 Mod. 526.
(h) Ruled by CHEW, C. J. in 1774, on a case stated for his opinion, MS. Rep.
(i) Duffield v. Smith, 6 Bin. 304.
(j) Gilb. C. P. 37; see § 6 of the act of 1836, *ante*, sect. iii.
(k) Clark v. Weldo, 4 Y. 206, *vide infra*, p. 293.

(l) Ibid. see Parasset v. Gantier, 2 D. 330.
(m) Field v. Colerick, 3 Y. 56.
(n) Butterworth v. White, 2 M. 141.
(o) Robinett v. Pollard, 2 M. 99.
(p) Stouffer v. Latshaw, 2 W. 167, GIBSON, C. J.
(q) Pamph. L. 741.

By the nineteenth section of the act of 1814,(r) it is made "the duty of the several Courts of Common Pleas to fix and order a daily allowance, not exceeding twenty cents, for all such *poor* and insolvent debtors as shall or may be confined in the prison of their respective counties, and have not property sufficient to support themselves, and it shall be the duty of the plaintiff, at whose suit any such debtor may be imprisoned, his agent or attorney, upon notice given by the keeper of the prison, to pay the said daily allowance at the prison on every Monday morning, while the debtor continue in prison, on failure whereof for the space of three days, the debtor may apply to the Court of Common Pleas, if it be in session, or if not, then to a judge of the same, who, upon inquiry, and finding the said debtor to be destitute of property, for his support in prison, and failure of payment to have been made as aforesaid, shall forthwith discharge the said debtor from imprisonment, and such debtor shall not be *again imprisoned for the same debt or debts.*"

It has been seen that a defendant shall not be twice held to bail, unless under special circumstances: as, where the plaintiff is non-prossed for want of declaring, or regularly discontinues his suit on payment of costs, he may hold the defendant to bail *de novo.*(s)   So, if the plaintiff be nonsuited in an action of debt on bond, for not sufficiently proving the execution of it, on *non est factum*, the defendant may be held to bail again, in an action upon the same bond.(t)   And if the defendant were discharged from the first arrest for some act for which the plaintiff is not answerable, as an irregularity on the part of the officer, he may be held to bail in a second.(u)

This rule is also affected in Pennsylvania by arrests without the jurisdiction of the State, as was before shown ;(v) so if the defendant had been discharged from imprisonment by the insolvent laws of his own State, of which the plaintiff was also a citizen : for it would be highly mischievous as well as incongruous, that, when a debtor has been so discharged, a fellow-citizen should follow him to other parts of the Union, and there arrest him again by new process.(w)   When persons, discharged by insolvent laws in other States of the Union, were arrested in Pennsylvania, by virtue of process issued out of its courts, the rule seems to be to discharge them on common bail, unless the States in which they resided and were discharged, refused to extend the same courtesy to the citizens of Pennsylvania, which would be presumed, until some reason be shown to the contrary.(x)

(r) 6 Sm. Laws, 201.
(s) 2 T. R. 756.
(t) 14 Johns. 347.
(u) 6 T. R. 218.
(v) *Ante*, p. 259.
(w) Jeffries v. Thompson, 2 Y. 482.
(x) Smith v. Brown, 3 Bin. 201 ; Millar v. Hall, 1 D. 229 ; Hilliard v. Greenleaf, 2 Y. 533 ; Boggs v. Teackle, 5 Bin. 336 ; Ing. on Insolv. 171, *et seq.*
But this doctrine of reciprocity, as it is called, has been questioned and much shaken by a recent decision of the District Court of this city and county, in the case of Mount v. Bradford, special bail

of Larned, of September Term, 1836. The judgment of the court was pronounced by PETTIT, President, in the course of which, after stating the facts of the case to be, in substance, that the contract on which the original action was founded was made in the District of Columbia, to be executed there, and that the parties resided there at the date of the contract, and at the time of the defendant's discharge under the insolvent law of the district; that the original defendant (Larned) was arrested in this city, and judgment obtained against him *before* his discharge in the District of

When a person, discharged by the insolvent law of this State, is arrested on any cause of action from which he may have been dis-

Columbia, and that the question was whether his bail were entitled to have an *exoneretur* entered on the bail-piece, he thus proceeded:—

"The rule of reciprocity by which the same regard is paid to the insolvent laws of our sister States, which their courts pay to ours, was stated for the first time in Smith *v.* Brown, 3 Bin. 203; and though Millar *v.* Hall, 1 D. 228, was there cited as furnishing the date of the doctrine, yet it is difficult to find in the report of that case any foundation for the reference. In Boggs *v.* Treacle, 5 Bin. 339, the rule was repeated upon the authority of Smith *v.* Brown. In Walsh *v.* Nourse, 5 Bin. 385, Chief Justice TILGHMAN intimated his regret that it was so authoritatively established as to be then beyond judicial control. In this court the judges have occasionally felt themselves embarrassed by it, and though the rule, if still in force, would be restricted in its operation, to but a few of the States, yet cases sometimes occur, presenting facts, which would cause no small degree of reluctance in the enforcement of it. Indeed, now that we have the benefit of the views of the Supreme Court of the United States in Ogden *v.* Saunders, as confirmed by Boyle *v.* Zacharie (as will be more particularly noticed directly), it may be questioned whether the rule should be any longer recognized at all. This point, however, will be open for further consideration should a proper case be presented.

"In Walsh *v.* Nourse, the Supreme Court of Pennsylvania refused to give effect to a discharge obtained in the District of Columbia, the debt having been contracted, and the plaintiffs residing out of that District. Though it was shown that 'the practice of the District Court of Columbia gave the same validity and effect to the insolvent law of any State as it would have in the courts of that State,' yet it was inferred, from what had actually taken place in the Supreme Court of the United States, that that court, to which there was an appeal from the District Court of Columbia, would, whenever the point should be distinctly brought up, make a decision unfavorable to the debtor.

"The two cases in this court in 1826, cited by Mr. Ingraham in his valuable work on the Insolvent Laws, page 201, were determined under the impression that as fifteen years had elapsed without producing any action on the subject by

the Supreme Court of the United States, the unaltered practice of the District Court of Columbia should be recognized notwithstanding the case of Walsh *v.* Nourse. All difficulty on this point may however be considered as removed by the case of Ogden *v.* Saunders, determined in 1827, and reported in 12 Wheat. 213. It was there decided, that though a State insolvent law was valid if limited to the *controversies of citizens of the State*, yet as between parties of different States, it had no application, and this too without regard to the place in which the contract originated. In Boyle *v.* Zacharie, 6 Peters's Rep. 643, Mr. Justice STORY, in pronouncing the judgment of the court, where the effect of the discharge under a State insolvent law was distinctly presented, says: 'The ultimate opinion delivered by Mr. Justice JOHNSON, in the case of Ogden *v.* Saunders, 12 Wheat. 213, 358, was concurred in and adopted by the three judges, who were in the minority upon the general question of the constitutionality of State insolvent laws, so largely discussed in that case. It is proper to make this remark, in order to remove an erroneous impression of the bar, that it was his single opinion, and not of the three other judges who concurred in the judgment. So far, then, as decisions upon the subject of State insolvent laws have been made by this court, they are to be deemed final and conclusive.' The language of Judge JOHNSON, thus adopted and confirmed, is as follows: 'All this mockery of justice, and the jealousies, recriminations, and perhaps retaliations which might grow out of it, are avoided, if the power of the States over contracts, after they become the subject exclusively of judicial cognizance, is *limited to the controversies of their own citizens*. And it does appear to me almost incontrovertible, that the States cannot proceed one step farther, without exercising a power incompatible with the acknowledged powers of other States, or of the United States, and with the rights of the citizens of other States. *Every bankrupt or insolvent system in the world, must partake of the character of a judicial investigation: Parties whose rights are to be affected are entitled to a hearing.* Hence every system, in common with the particular system now before us, professes to summon the creditors before some tribunal, to show cause against granting a discharge to the bankrupt. *But on what principle can a citizen of another State be forced into the courts of a State for this investigation?* The judgment to be passed is to prostrate his rights; and on the subject of these rights, the constitution exempts him from the jurisdiction of the State tribunals, *without regard to the place* where the *contract may originate.* In the only tribunal to which he owes allegiance, the State insolvent or bankrupt laws cannot be carried into effect.' He subsequently adds, ' when in the exercise of that power' (passing insolvent laws), 'the States pass beyond their own limits, and the rights of their own citizens, and act upon the rights of citizens of other States, there arises a conflict of sovereign power, and a collision with the judicial powers granted to the United States, which renders the exercise of such a power incompatible with the rights of other States, and of the constitution of the United States.'

"Whether the decisions of the Supreme Court of the United States, prior to 1826, were in that year carefully examined by the judges of this court, does not distinctly appear; but in 1831, the Circuit Court of the United States for Pennsylvania, in the case of Woodhull *v.* Wagner, 1 Baldwin's Rep. 296, very elaborately reviewed the whole series of cases in the Supreme Court, and the two learned judges, Baldwin and Hopkinson, concurred upon what they called the *settled principles* of the Supreme Court of the United States, in refusing to recognize a discharge under the insolvent law of Pennsylvania, where the defendant, a resident of Pennsylvania, contracted a debt payable in New York, to citizens of New York. The city of New York being the place where the debt was payable, and the plaintiffs being citizens of the State of New York, it was held that ' the discharge of the defendant by the insolvent laws of Pennsylvania, could have no operation on the contract, or the remedies to enforce performance.' It was upon the same ground, and with reference to this train of decisions, that, in the courts of the United States, that, in the case of M'Strakin *v.* Hamilton, in May, 1835, this court, composed of the present judges, adhered to the authority of Walsh *v.* Nourse, and refused to give effect to a discharge obtained in the District of Columbia, the debt having been contracted in Philadelphia, and the plaintiff being a citizen of Pennsylvania.

"The same reasons, however, which induced the Circuit Court of the United States for Pennsylvania, to inquire as to the place where the contract was to be executed, and where the parties resided, are sufficient to prove that where both parties reside, and the debt was contracted in the State in which the discharge was obtained, the discharge would be held valid to precisely the same extent as within that State. This, too, is in accordance with what Chief Justice TILGHMAN, in Walsh *v.* Nourse, states to be the true principle, to wit, ' that every State has power over the persons residing within its territory; and, therefore, where a debt is discharged by the law of a State in which both plaintiff and defendant reside, another State ought to pay regard to it;' a position which is independent of the doctrine of mere reciprocity or comity. See also Walsh *v.* Farrand, 13 Mass. Rep. 19, to the same effect.

"It may be remarked that Woodhull *v.* Wagner, 1 Baldwin, was determined before Boyle *v.* Zacharie, 6 Peters. If the declaration made by Judge Story, in 6 Peters, 643, that the final opinion of Judge Johnson in Ogden *v.* Saunders, was concurred in and adopted by the three other judges, and that the decision was to be deemed final and conclusive, had been uttered before the adjudication of Woodhull *v.* Wagner, it might have been a question, whether the Circuit Court of the United States for Pennsylvania, would not have been authorized to narrow the ground of their opinion in the last-mentioned case, and to have confined it to the mere fact of the place of residence of each party. It is clear, however, that as the *facts* gave them the broader ground, they did not assume the restricted one.

"In the case before us, then, as the contract was made in the District of Columbia, to be executed there, and the parties resided there at the date of the contract and the time of the discharge, the discharge is to be regarded; unless the fact that judgment was obtained in Pennsylvania before the date of the discharge, prevents this conclusion.

"Upon principle, no good reason can be suggested why this circumstance should make a difference. Were this allowed, indeed, the effect on the contrary might be to confer upon a citizen of another State suing here a citizen of his own State during a temporary visit, and obtaining a judgment against him, an advantage which our own citizens would not possess in regard to each other. The case before us furnishes a full illustration. In the District of Columbia, where the contract was made, and where both parties reside, the judgment in Pennsylvania would not be allowed to defeat the discharge. As be-

charged, he may be released from custody, under the 16th section of the act of 1836, on giving a warrant of attorney to appear to the action on which he is arrested, and to plead thereto.(y)

With respect to the effect of a new promise made by an insolvent, after his discharge, to pay a debt which he owed previously to it, the case of Earnest v. Parke(z) settles the law in this State. It decides, that an absolute and unconditional promise by one who has been discharged by the insolvent law of this commonwealth, to pay a debt which existed before his discharge, creates a new contract upon which suit may be brought. The court below had ruled that this promise was without consideration and void, and in the Supreme Court, the learned judge who delivered its opinion, said: "This is the first time the question has arisen in this shape. It has been presented heretofore on applications to discharge debtors from arrest on mesne process, upon common bail; sometimes, though rarely, on final process, or in cases where suit had been brought on the old debt, and not on the new promise. All these may be distinguishable from the present." The learned judge then observes that the principle decided in the Common

tween two of our own citizens, a judgment here would not control a discharge obtained here. Here is, then, no sound reason why the force now claimed for this judgment should be accorded to it. In acknowledging the validity of the discharge at all, as to contracts made within the territories of the State granting the discharge, and between parties resident there, the true principle is, to yield to it the precise extent and effect which is allowed to it by that State itself. If this principle be departed from, it would be better to adopt at once the rule of the New York cases, 2 Johns. 198; 18 Johns. 194; 3 Cowen, 626, and utterly reject in every instance the discharge obtained in another State, no matter where the contract originated, nor of what State or States the parties were citizens: a rule, however, which is equally opposed to the true principles of general jurisprudence, and to the current of decisions in the United States courts.

"The fact of obtaining a judgment ought, then, to be entirely disregarded. Accordingly we find, notwithstanding anything which may have been said in Green v. Sarmiento, 3 Wash. C. C. Rep. 17, that, in the whole train of cases in the Supreme Court of the United States, no effect whatever is referred to such a circumstance, nor is any allusion made to a distinction founded upon it. So far as relates to this question, therefore, Green v. Sarmiento cannot be held to be law. In the case of Woodhull v. Wagner, in the Circuit Court, before cited, judgment had been obtained eleven months before the discharge under the

insolvent law of Pennsylvania: and yet this was not deemed to be an extinguishment of the original contract, but the court felt themselves called upon to investigate a complicated state of facts, and ascertain where the debt was originally payable and where the parties resided. In an earlier case, Thibault v. Bassavillaso, 1 Baldwin, 9, in which Judge Hopkinson, holding the Circuit Court of the United States, allowed an exoneretur to be entered on the bail-piece, the defendant having been discharged under the insolvent law of Pennsylvania, that eminent judge had also disregarded the circumstance of the entry of a judgment, and had inquired fully into the character and place of the original contract. However true it may be, then, that for some purposes a judgment extinguishes the original contract, yet it is not now to be considered that, as regards the effect of a discharge under the insolvent law of a State or of the District of Columbia, such force is to be given to it.

"According to the case of Boggs v. Bancker, 5 Bin. 507, the bail should pay the costs of the scire facias. Upon this being done, the rule will be made absolute."

(y) For an exposition of the meaning of this section as regards the causes of action comprehended by its terms, and the persons discharged by insolvent or bankrupt laws other than those of Pennsylvania, we refer to pp. 156–171, 2d ed. of Mr. Ingraham's Treatise on Insolvency.

(z) 4 R. 452. See Wh. Dig. "Contract," I (a).

Pleas, that the new promise was without consideration, "may be a distinct question from the legal effect which may result from a new promise or contract, as regards the right of arrest, either on mesne or final process:" and that this, though a parol promise, had in this State the same legal effect as if made in writing in the most solemn form.   After reviewing the various adjudged cases applicable to the subject, at length, the learned judge proceeds to notice, collaterally, its connection with the question of bail, and says: "These questions have generally arisen on a parol promise to pay the debt, and as the fact of the promise may admit of dispute, the court will not, in this stage of the proceeding, inquire whether the parties have entered into a contract, and particularly when the suit is brought upon the old debt.   And although the plaintiff makes a positive affidavit of the debt, yet this being in its nature *ex parte*, has not been considered such evidence of the fact of indebtedness as to justify holding the defendant to special bail.   The courts have felt it their duty to discharge on common bail, and leave the fact of a new promise to be ascertained by a jury.   This is a decision in favor of liberty, and, as far as it goes, I have nothing to urge against its correctness.   The cases bearing on this question in England, before and since 1776, have been cited by Mr. Ingraham in his Treatise on Insolvency, p. 202, and are very much at variance with each other; so much so, that it is difficult to know what the law now is in that country. Since 1776, they are not authority in this State, nor have they much to recommend them from the intrinsic merits of the decisions themselves."—
"In Shippey v. Henderson,(a) it is said that when a debt has been barred by the defendant's discharge under the insolvent act, it is proper for the plaintiff to declare upon the original cause of action without noticing the subsequent promise.   And when this is done, the court will of course discharge the defendant from arrest, on common bail, and this is perhaps the reason that we have such contrariety of decisions on this point. It has been viewed merely as the revival of the old debt, as in the case of the act of limitations.   Had it been considered in the light of a new contract, as it has uniformly been in Pennsylvania, difficulties would have been avoided.   The defendant has the same power to make this as any other contract, and the contract being made, it would have created a valid debt, recoverable at law, *by all the remedies common to other actions.*"   From the preceding quotations, it is easy to perceive that there was a doubt in the mind of the court whether they should say, that a debtor, on such a new promise, could be *held to bail*, although it seems that the learned judge who delivered its opinion inclined to think that he would only be subject to arrest on final process.   The inclination of his mind may be discovered in parts of his reasoning on other cases, particularly on that called Field's case.(b)   "It was there held, that a debt discharged by a certificate of bankruptcy, does not revive the original debt as a debt by specialty, but that the original debt is a consideration which renders the new promise available.   The court were of the opinion, that the creditor had a right to come upon the fund on the new contract, as a simple contract creditor, but not on the footing of a debt due by specialty; and that, by the promise to pay, a new debt was contracted.   Lord Mansfield says, in one of the cases cited, "that

(a) 14 Johns. 178.   (b) 2 R. 351.

where a remedy is taken away and not the debt, the debt is a debt in conscience, and may be the ground of a future promise or security." The counsel for the defendant in error seem to feel the force of this position, the truth of which they admit in relation to a case in which all remedies are taken away, as in the case of infancy, a debt barred by the statute of limitations, or by the bankruptcy and certificate of the defendant, but they deny it as regards a case when only *one* remedy is gone. No reason has been given for the distinction at the bar, and it is not easy to understand why a promise should revive *several* remedies, and yet should not have the legal effect of reviving *one* remedy. I can perceive no good reason for any anxiety to exempt insolvents from liability on account of their contracts. If, as in Field's case, it is a new contract, the defendant, by the new engagement into which he has voluntarily entered, has rendered himself liable to suit, and to all the remedies pursued in the collection of debts, among which, in the eye of the law, the right to arrest the person on final process, and its consequences, are not the least important. This remedy may sometimes enable a creditor, by appealing to the oath of his debtor, to recover a just debt. It gives a right to the legal assignee to collect the assets of the insolvent, whether it be property in possession, or choses in action."

CHAPTER VIII.

PRIVILEGE FROM ARREST UNDER ACT ABOLISHING IMPRISONMENT FOR DEBT.

THE act of 12th July, 1842,(a) declares that from and after the passage of this act no person shall be arrested or imprisoned on any civil process issuing out of any court of this commonwealth, in any suit or proceeding instituted for the recovery of any money due upon any judgment or decree founded upon contract, or due upon any contract, express or implied, or for the recovery of any damages for the non-performance of any contract, excepting in proceeding, as for contempt, to enforce civil remedies, action for fines or penalties, or on promises to marry, on moneys collected by any public officer, or for any misconduct or neglect in office, or in any professional employment, in which cases the remedies shall remain as heretofore : [*Provided*, That this section shall not extend to any person who shall not have resided in this State for twenty days previous to the commencement of a suit against him.] § 1.(b)

In all cases where, by the preceding provisions of this act, a party to a suit cannot be arrested or imprisoned, it shall be lawful for the party who shall have commenced a suit, or obtained a judgment in any court of record, to apply to any judge of the court in which the suit shall have been brought for a warrant to arrest a party against whom the suit shall have been commenced, or the judgment shall have been obtained; whereupon the said judge shall require of the said party satisfactory evidence, either by the affidavit of the party making such application or some other person or persons, that there is a debt or demand due to the party making such application from the other party in the suit or judgment, in which affidavit the nature and amount of the indebtedness shall be set forth as near as may be.   § 2.

If the demand set forth in the affidavit be such that the party could not, according to the provisions of this act, be arrested, and if the affidavit shall establish, to the satisfaction of the judge, one or more of the following particulars, to wit :—

That the party is about to remove any of his property out of the jurisdiction of the court in which such suit is brought, with intent to defraud his creditors;

Or, that he has property which he fraudulently conceals;

Or, that he has rights in action, or some interest in any public or cor.

(a) Pamph. L. 339.   (b) Repealed, *post*.

porate stock, money, or evidence of debt, which he unjustly refuses to apply to the payment of any such judgment or judgments, which shall have been rendered against him, belonging to the complainant;

Or, that he has assigned, removed, or disposed of, or is about to dispose of, any of his property with the intent to defraud his creditors:

Or, that he fraudulently contracted the debt or incurred the obligation respecting which suit is brought.

It shall be the duty of the said judge to issue a warrant of arrest in the form following, to wit:— § 3.

County, ss.

The commonwealth of Pennsylvania, to the sheriff or any constable of county, Greeting:

Whereas, complaint has this day been made before me, on the oath (or affirmation, as the case may be) of (here insert the name of the party making the affidavit), setting forth (here briefly set forth the complaint).

These are, therefore, to command you to arrest the said and bring him (or them, as the case may be) before me, at my office in (here insert the residence of the judge), without delay, to be dealt with according to law. And have you there also this precept.

Witness my hand at this day of

, Judge.

Which warrant shall be accompanied by a copy of all affidavits presented to the judge, upon which the warrant is issued, which shall be certified by such judge, and shall be delivered to the party at the time of serving the warrant by the officer serving the same. § 4.

The officer to whom such warrant shall be delivered, shall execute the same by arresting the person or persons therein named, and bringing him or them before the judge issuing the warrant, and shall keep him in custody until he shall be duly discharged or committed as hereinafter provided. § 5.

On the appearance of the person so arrested, before the judge, he may controvert any of the facts and circumstances, on which such warrant issued, and may, at his option, verify his allegations by his affidavit, and in case of his so verifying the same, the complainant may examine him on oath, touching any fact or circumstance material to the inquiry, and the answers on such examination shall be reduced to writing, and subscribed by him; and the officer conducting such inquiry shall also receive such other proof as the parties may offer, either at the time of such first appearance, or at such other times as such hearing shall be adjourned to; and in case of an adjournment, the judge may take a bond, with or without surety, for the appearance of the party arrested at the adjourned hearing. § 6.

The judge conducting such inquiry, shall have the same powers to issue subpœna to enforce the attendance of witnesses, and to punish witnesses refusing to testify, as is vested in the court of which he is a judge. § 7.

If such judge is satisfied that the allegations of the complainant are substantiated, and that the party arrested has done, or is about to do any one of the acts specified in the third section of this act, he shall issue a commitment under his hand, reciting the facts of the case, and directing that such party be committed to the jail of the county in which such hearing is had, to be there detained until he shall be discharged by law, and such party shall be committed and detained accordingly. § 8.

Such commitment shall not be granted if the defendant shall pay the debt or demand claimed with cost of suit, and of the proceedings against him, or give security to the satisfaction of the judge before whom the hearing shall be had, that the debt, or demand, with the costs of the suit and proceedings against him, shall be paid, with interest, within sixty days, if the demand be in judgment, and the length of time for stay of execution given by law on debts of like amount has expired, and if the said length of time has not elapsed then, that the same shall be paid at the expiration of that time, if that shall be sixty days distant from the time of giving said surety; and if not then, that the same shall be paid within sixty days from the time of giving the same. If the demand be not in judgment at the time of giving said surety, the day of payment shall be regulated by the same rule; but in no case shall the party be required to give surety for the payment of the debt before the recovering of judgment. § 9.

Such commitment shall not be granted if the party arrested shall give bond to the complainant in a penalty of not less than twice the amount of the debt, or demand claimed, with such sureties as shall be approved by such judge, conditioned that he will not remove any property which he then has, out of the jurisdiction of the court in which suit is brought, with the intent to defraud any of his creditors; and that he will not assign, sell, convey, or dispose of any of his property with such intent, or with a view to give a preference to any creditor for any debt antecedent to such assignment, sale, conveyance, or disposition, until the demand of the complainant, with costs, shall be satisfied, or until thirty days after final judgment shall be rendered in the suit brought for the recovery of such demand: *Provided, however,* That this section shall apply only to cases where the only fraudulent design established against the party arrested is, that he is about to remove any of his property out of the jurisdiction of the court in which suit is brought with intent to defraud his creditors. § 10.

Such commitment shall not be granted if the person arrested shall enter into a bond to the complainant in the penalty and with the securities prescribed in the preceding section, conditioned that he will, within thirty days, apply by petition, to the Court of Common Pleas of the county, or to a judge thereof, if the court shall not within that time be in session, for the benefit of the insolvent laws of this commonwealth; and that he will comply with all the requisitions of the said law, and abide all orders of the said court in that behalf, or in default thereof; and if he fail in obtaining his discharge as an insolvent debtor, that he shall, on the day of his so failing, surrender himself to the jail of said county. § 11.

Any defendant committed agreeably to the eighth section of this act, shall remain in custody until a final judgment shall have been rendered in his favor in the suit prosecuted by the creditor, at whose instance he shall have been committed, or until he shall have assigned his property and obtained his discharge, as provided in the subsequent sections of this act; but such person may, at any time, be discharged by any judge of the county, on his paying the debt or demand claimed, and costs, or by giving the security for the payment thereof, as provided in the ninth section of this act, or on his executing either of the bonds mentioned in the tenth and eleventh sections of this act. § 12.

Any person committed as above provided, or who shall have given the bond specified in the eleventh section of this act, or against whom any suit shall have been commenced in a court of record, in which such person, by the provisions of this act, cannot be arrested or imprisoned, may present a petition to the Court of Common Pleas of the county in which he shall be imprisoned, or in which the said suit is pending, or to the judge thereof, praying that he may assign his property and have the benefit of the provisions of this act. § 13.

The petition aforesaid shall set forth all the matters required to be set forth by the ninth section of the act of the sixteenth day of June, one thousand eight hundred and thirty-six, entitled "An act relating to insolvent debtors," and shall be verified in like manner. Upon the presentation of the said petition, the court or judge shall fix a time for the hearing of the same, which shall be during the next session of the Court of Common Pleas: *Provided*, Thirty days shall intervene between the presentation of the petition and the time for hearing the same; and the petitioner and his creditors shall be heard before the judges of the Court of Common Pleas, unless the said court shall make an order that a single judge shall hear the case and decide it, in which case the judge shall have all the powers herein conferred upon the court. § 14.

The court or judge shall proceed agreeably to the provisions of the aforesaid act of the sixteenth day of June, one thousand eight hundred and thirty-six, in causing the notice to be given to the creditors of the petitioner, in deciding upon his case, in making orders, in permitting an assignment to be made by said petitioner in the oath to be administered to him, and in all the proceedings thereafter touching his property, and shall have the same power over the trustees to whom an assignment shall be made as is therein specified. § 15.

The trustee of any debtor, to whom an assignment shall be made under this act, shall have the same powers, shall be liable to the same duties, and shall proceed in the same manner in all respects, to discharge the same as is given, imposed upon, and required of the trustees under the aforesaid act; and the rights of creditors and their remedies, shall be the same as under the said act; and the effect of a discharge of the petitioner by the said court, shall be the same as under the said act, so far as regards both his person and property; and all rights and remedies given by the said act, and all proceedings, both civil and criminal, thereby authorized, may be had the same as if they were herein fully enacted at length, so far as the same can be applied to the case of a debtor upon a contract only. § 16.

Any person who shall be imprisoned on civil process at the time of this act taking effect as a law, in a case where, by the preceding provisions of this act, such person could not be arrested or imprisoned, may give ten days' notice in writing to the plaintiff, his agent or attorney, of his intention to apply to a judge of the Court of Common Pleas of the county in which he is imprisoned for a discharge from confinement.— Upon proof of such notice having been given, it shall be the duty of any judge of said court to issue a writ of *habeas corpus* to the officer having such person in custody to bring him before the said judge at a time and place to be named, not less than two or more than six days thereafter. If the plaintiff, or his agent or attorney, shall not have filed with said judge an affidavit setting forth such facts as are required by section third of this act, in order to obtain a warrant of arrest, and the case be such an one that the party, by the preceding provisions of this act, could not be imprisoned, it shall be the duty of the said judge to make an order discharging the party from imprisonment; but if such affidavit shall have been filed, and the judge on hearing the case shall be satisfied that the imprisoned party, if at liberty, would be liable to an arrest under the provisions of this act, then and in that case the judge shall proceed in the same manner as if the party had been brought before him upon such warrant of arrest as hereinbefore provided. § 17.

When a complaint shall be made and a warrant of arrest issued, or upon a hearing under the seventeenth section of this act, and the complaint shall be dismissed, the party making the same shall be liable for all fees to officers and for all costs which the party arrested shall have incurred, and the fees of the officers shall be the same as for similar services in other cases. Witnesses shall receive the same fees as are allowed before justices of the peace, but if the complaint shall be sustained, the party making the same shall recover the costs of the party arrested, upon the same being taxed or allowed by the proper officer, and shall be recovered with the other costs in the suit. § 18.

Whenever any bond given under the preceding sections of this act shall become forfeited by the non-performance of the condition thereof, the obligee shall be entitled to recover thereon the amount due to him on the judgment with costs obtained in the original suit. § 19.

Any person who shall remove any of his property out of any county with the intent to prevent the same from being levied upon by any execution, or who shall secrete, assign, convey, or otherwise dispose of any of his property with intent to defraud any creditor, or to prevent such property being made liable for the payment of his debts, and any person who shall receive such property with such intent, or who shall, with like intent, collude with any debtor for the concealment of any part of his estate or effects, or for giving a false color thereto, or shall conceal any grant, sale, lease, bond, or other instrument or proceeding, either in writing or by parol, or shall become a grantee, purchaser, lessee, obligee, or other like party in any such instrument or proceeding, with the like fraudulent intent, or shall act as broker, scrivener, agent, or witness in regard to such instrument or proceeding, with the like intent, such person or persons, on conviction thereof in the court of Quarter Sessions of the proper county, shall be deemed guilty of misdemeanor, and shall forfeit and pay a sum not exceeding the value of the property or effects, so secreted, assigned, conveyed, or otherwise disposed of, or concealed, or in respect to which such collusion shall have taken place, and shall suffer imprisonment not exceeding one year. § 20.

No person shall be excused from answering any bill seeking a discovery in relation to any fraud prohibited by this act, or from answering as a witness in relation to any such fraud, but no such answer shall be used in evidence in any other suit or prosecution. § 22.

No execution issued on any judgment rendered by any alderman or justice of the peace, upon any demand arising upon contract, express or implied, shall contain a clause authorizing an arrest or imprisonment of the person against whom the same shall issue, unless it shall be proved by the affidavit of the person in whose favor such execution shall issue, or that of some other person, to the satisfaction of the alderman or justice of the peace, either that such judgment was for the recovery of money collected by any public officer, or for official misconduct. § 23.

No *capias* or warrant of arrest shall issue against any defendant in any case in which, by the provisions of the preceding section, an execution on the judgment recovered could not be issued against the body; and whenever a *capias* or warrant of arrest in such case shall issue, the like affidavit shall be required as for the issuing of an execution by the provisions of said section. § 24.

Whenever a plaintiff shall reside out of this commonwealth, he may, upon giving bond, with sufficient surety, for the payment of all costs which he may become liable to pay, in the event of his failing to recover judgment against the defendant, have a *capias* or warrant of arrest, if he shall be entitled to such writ, on making the affidavit required in the twenty-third section of this act, or a summons, which may be made returnable not less than two nor more than four days from the date thereof, which shall be served at least two days before the time of appearance mentioned therein, and if the same shall be returned, personally served, the justice or alderman issuing the same may proceed to hear and determine the case in the manner heretofore allowed by law. § 25.

Whenever, by the provisions of the twenty-fourth section of this act, no *capias* can issue, and the defendant shall reside out of the county, he shall be proceeded against by summons or attachment returnable not less than two nor more than four days from the date thereof, which shall be served at least two days before the time of appearance mentioned therein. § 26.

It shall be the duty of any alderman or justice of the peace, to issue an attachment against any defendant, on the application of the plaintiff in any case whereby the provisions of this act, no *capias* can issue upon proof, by the affidavit of the plaintiff or some other person or persons to the satisfaction of the alderman or justice, that the defendant is about to remove from the county any of his property with intent to defraud his creditors, or has assigned, disposed of, or secreted, or is about to assign, dispose of, or secrete, any of his property, with the like fraudulent intent, which affidavit shall also specify the amount of the plaintiff's claim, or the balance thereof, over and above all discounts, which the defendant may have against him: *Provided,* That before such attachment shall issue, the plaintiff, or some one in his behalf, shall execute a bond in the penalty of at least double the amount of the claim, with good and sufficient securities conditioned that in case the plaintiff shall fail to recover a judgment of at least one-half the amount of his claim, he shall pay to the defendant his damages for the wrongful taking of any property over and above an amount sufficient to satisfy the judgment and costs, and that, if the plaintiff shall fail in his action, he shall pay to the defendant his legal costs and all damages which he may sustain by reason of said attachment.   § 27.

Every such attachment shall be made returnable not less than two nor more than four days from the date thereof, and shall be served by the constable to whom the same shall be directed ; by attaching so much of the defendant's property, not exempt by law from sale upon execution, as will be sufficient to pay the debt demanded, and by delivering to him a copy of the said attachment, and an inventory of the property attached, if he can be found in the county, and if not so to be found, then by leaving a copy of the same at his place of residence with some adult member of his family, or the family where he shall reside ; or if he be a non-resident of the county, and cannot be found, then by leaving a copy of said attachment and inventory with the person in whose possession the said property may be.   § 28.

The constable shall state specifically in his turn the manner in which he shall have served such attachment, and it shall be his duty to take the property attached into his possession, unless the defendant, or some other person for him, shall enter into a bond with sufficient surety in the penalty of double the amount of the claim, conditioned that, in the event of the plaintiff recovering judgment against him, he will pay the debt and costs at the expiration of the stay of execution given by law to freeholders, or that he will surrender up the property attached to any officer having an execution against him on any judgment recorded in such attachment.   § 29.

If such attachment shall be returned personally served upon the defendant, at least two days before the return day thereof, the alderman or justice shall, on the return day proceed to hear and determine the same, in the same manner as upon a summons returned personally served. But if the same shall not have been so served, the alderman or justice shall issue a summons against the defendant, returnable as summonses issued by justices of the peace are now by law returnable, and if the said summons shall be returned personally served, or by leaving a copy at the residence of the defendant, or that the defendant, after diligent inquiry, cannot be found in the county, then, in either case, the alderman or justice of the peace shall proceed to hear and determine the cause, in the same manner as upon a summons personally served. § 30.

Any defendant against whom a judgment shall have been rendered in any case where the attachment or summons shall not have been per_sonally served, may, within thirty days after the rendition of the same, apply to the alderman or justice rendering the same, for a hearing of the matter, and if he, or some other person, knowing the facts, shall, for him, make an affidavit setting forth that he has a just defence to the whole or part of the plaintiff's demand, it shall be the duty of the alderman or justice to open the judgment, and give notice to the plain_tiff of the time when he will hear the parties, which time shall be not less than four nor more than eight days distant. On the said hearing the justice shall proceed in the manner directed in the thirtieth section of this act. § 31.

A judgment obtained before any alderman or justice, in any suit commenced by attachment, when the defendant shall not be personally served with the attachment or summons, and shall not appear, shall be only presumptive evidence of indebtedness in any *scire facias* that may be brought thereon, and may be disproved by the defendant, and no exe_cution issued upon such judgment shall be levied upon any other pro_perty than such as was seized under the attachment, nor shall any de_fendant in such case be barred of any set-off which he may have against the plaintiff. § 32.

A defendant against whose body, by the provisions of this act, an execution cannot be issued by an alderman or justice of the peace, shall be required, in order to obtain an appeal, stay of execution, or adjourn_ment, to give a bond of recognizance in the nature of special bail; con_ditioned that no part of the property of the defendant which is liable to be taken in execution, shall be removed, secreted, assigned, or in any way disposed of, except for the necessary support of himself and family, until the plaintiff's demand shall be satisfied, or until the expiration of ten days after such plaintiff shall be entitled to have an execution issued on the judgment obtained in such cause, if he shall obtain such judg_ment; and if the condition of such bond or recognizance be broken, and an execution on such judgment be returned unsatisfied in whole or in part, the plaintiff in an action on such bond or recognizance shall be entitled to recover the value of the property so removed, secreted, or assigned. § 33.

This act shall not be construed to extend the jurisdiction of justices of the peace and aldermen to demands above one hundred dollars; and the same right which is given to the parties respectively, to appeal from the decision of an alderman or justice of the peace, by the act of the twentieth day of March, one thousand eight hundred and ten, relat_ing to the proceedings of justices of the peace, is hereby given to the parties respectively, in proceedings upon sums or attachments issued by aldermen or justices of the peace under this act. And all and singular the provisions of the said act, and its several supplements not hereby expressly repealed, and not inconsistent with the provisions of this act,

I.—18

are hereby declared to be in full force, and to apply to the provisions of this act so far as the same relates to proceedings before aldermen or justices of the peace, and to the powers of the courts of record over the proceedings of justices of the peace. § 34.

After the defendant in any case shall have executed the bond required by the eleventh section of this act, he shall not sell, assign, or dispose of any part of his property which is not exempt by law from execution, except so far as may be necessary for the support of himself and family, until he shall be discharged.   And if proof shall be made on the hearing before the judge, or the court, that the applicant has so sold, assigned, or disposed of his property, it shall be the duty of said judge or of the court to refuse to make the order directed by the aforesaid act of the 16th day of June, one thousand eight hundred and thirty-six. § 35.

So much of any act as is hereby altered or supplied is hereby repealed. § 37.

The act of 16th July, 1842,(b) provides that in all cases of imprisonment for debt, the plaintiff or plaintiffs shall be liable for the boarding and jailer's fees, from the time of the commitment, if the defendant shall make affidavit that he is unable to support himself, and the sheriff or jailer may recover the same as debts of similar amount are by law recoverable.   § 11.

The cases which have heretofore arisen under this act may be arranged as follows:—

   1. *Where the plaintiff might have sued on contract, but where he elects the tort.*
   In an action on the case, one of the defendants was held to bail on an affidavit charging him with having fraudulently and with intent to cheat, induced the plaintiff to agree to a compromise of a debt due him by the former, and to release a portion thereof and give up the evidences of indebtedness held by him, on certain terms, one of which was the acceptance, as cash, of a draft on the other defendant, which he falsely and fraudulently represented would be paid at maturity, knowing that it would not be so paid, which draft was consequently protested at maturity: and the affidavit further alleged that the defendant was merely a sojourner in the State, and was about to withdraw himself from the jurisdiction of its courts.   Judge Rogers, at Nisi Prius, notwithstanding the act of 1842 to abolish imprisonment for debt, refused to discharge the defendant on common bail, and also declined hearing counter affidavits or entering on the merits of the case.(c)   He went so far as to doubt whether under this act, even in cases of contract, the court has not a discretion to hold to bail on proper cause being shown, as that a *capias* is necessary to enable the plaintiff to reap the fruits of any judgment he may afterwards obtain; and he intimated the opinion that

(b) Pamph L. 391.   (c) Sedgbeer v. Moore, Sup. Ct. N. P.
                         7 Leg. Int. 194; Bright. R. 197.

where the defendant in an action on contract is about to abandon the country without leaving property to meet the debt, he may be arrested and held to bail.(*d*)

In the District Court for Philadelphia, it is held, that though a plaintiff cannot now have a *capias* where there is a contract, even though the contract be fraudulent, yet this will not be applied to cases where the proceeding was throughout a tort.(*e*)

Where an affidavit to hold to bail, set forth that the defendant had fraudulently obtained from the plaintiff a negotiable note, under the pretence of getting it discounted, but with the actual intention of appropriating its proceeds, the District Court for the City and County of Philadelphia, refused to quash the *capias*, holding that though the plaintiff might have waived the *tort* and brought *assumpsit*, yet he had his election, and the court would not compel him to sue on the contract merely.(*f*)

On an application for the discharge of a defendant from custody on a bail-piece in an action of deceit, it was held by the same court that as the action was *ex delicto*, the defendant was not entitled to his discharge under the act of 1842, abolishing imprisonment for debt.(*g*)

So it was further said by Judge Sharswood, that where a debt has been contracted fraudulently, the plaintiff may bring either an action in form *ex delicto*, or an action on the contract; but he cannot by his election deprive the defendant of any substantial privilege or defence; and, therefore, since the act of 12th July, 1842, an action in form *ex delicto* cannot be commenced by a writ of *capias* for a debt contracted fraudulently.(*h*)

2. *Practice of warrant of arrest.*

In an application to a judge for a warrant of arrest, "under the third section of the act of 1842, abolishing imprisonment for debt," &c., the

---

(*d*) Id.

(*e*) Barger *v.* Radley, Saturday, March 23, 1850. D. C. C. P. Rule to show cause of action. *Per curiam.* The affidavit discloses a case of deceit in the sale of chattels. The question is again presented, which was formerly decided after careful deliberation in Bowen *et al. v.* Burdick, 5 L. Journ. 113. It is true there have been cases since in which, perhaps, the principle of that decision has been departed from, but we now re-affirm it. Whenever the foundation of the action is a contract between the parties, in which it is alleged the defendant cheated the plaintiff, the case is within the provisions of the act of July 12, 1842, without reference to the form of action adopted. The proper recourse of the injured party is the warrant of arrest, provided by the third section of the act. The case before us, however, is one of some nicety as to the question, whether it falls within the principle of this decision. The contract was made according

to the affidavit with one Kooher, who had been introduced to the plaintiff by the defendant under the fictitious name of Andrews. The receipt was signed by him in that name—and although the affidavit does aver that Kooher had acted with and for the defendant in the transaction, and had received $100, and his expenses from Radley, for his services—so that, perhaps, the plaintiff would pursue defendant in an action for money had and received—yet that could only be on the footing of a recision of the contract and a waiver of the tort. It is, therefore, a case not within the provisions of the act of July 12, 1842. R. A.

(*f*) Hopper *v.* Williams, D. C. C. P. 2 P. L. J. 382.

(*g*) Tyron *v.* Hassinger, D. C. C. P. 2 P. L. J. 43. See remarks of GIBSON, C. J., Lopeman *v.* Henderson, 4 Barr, 231.

(*h*) SHARSWOOD, J., Bowen *v.* Burdick, 5 P. L. J. 113. As to form of affidavit, see *post*, chapter x.

plaintiff must set out in his affidavit, the facts from which the judge is to infer whether such a case is made out as justifies a warrant.(i)

Pending a levy on real estate, by virtue of a *fi. fa.*, a warrant of arrest under the second section of act of 12th July, 1842, cannot issue against the defendant.(j)

Where a warrant of arrest had been issued under the act of 12th July, 1842, against a debtor upon the ground that he had property which he had fraudulently concealed, and that he had disposed of property with intent to defraud his creditors; and it appeared that the defendant had previously filed his petition for the benefit of the bankrupt law; the court on motion quashed the warrant of arrest.(k)   And so of an intermediate discharge under the insolvent law.(l)

The fraud contemplated by the act as sufficient to justify an arrest, must be actual, not constructive; and therefore one cannot be arrested for fraud committed by his copartner, without his actual participation.(m)

3. *Attachment before justices.*

The 25th section of the act of 1842 does not authorize attachment before a justice against non-residents.(n)

There is nothing in the act which prohibits a justice of the peace from issuing a warrant of arrest after suit brought or judgment rendered, even though a transcript had been filed in the Common Pleas.(o)

Upon a transcript filed in the Court of Common Pleas from the judgment of a magistrate, a judge of that court has no authority to issue a warrant under the 3d section of the act.(p)

Though the affidavit made and bonds executed by the plaintiff, under the provisions of the 27th section of the act, to found an attachment, be defective, the defendant waives the irregularity by appearing and confessing a judgment.(q)

Act of 22d March, 1850,(r) no attachment hereafter issued by any alderman or justice of the peace of this commonwealth, in pursuance of the 17th section of the act, entitled "An act to abolish imprisonment for debt and to punish fraudulent debtors," approved the 12th day of July, Anno Domini 1842, shall remain and continue a lien on the property attached for a longer period than sixty days, from and after the time when the plaintiff might legally have had execution issued on said judgment; but the said property shall, after the expiration of the said time, be discharged from such attachment: *Provided*, That the said property shall remain liable to be seized and taken in execution as in other cases: *And provided further*, That whenever an appeal shall be entered and taken from the judgment of the justice, the lien on the property attached as aforesaid, shall remain for the period of sixty days after final judgment.   § 1.(rr)

(i) Dougherty v. Dougherty, D. C. C. P. 6 P. L. J. 153.

(j) Neall v. Perry, 4 P. L. J. 410.

(k) Bishop v. Loewen, 2 P. L. J. 364. BANKS, P. J.

(l) Bassett v. Davis, D. C. C. P. 2 P. L. J. 287.

(m) Bassett v. Davis, D. C. C. P. 2 P.

L. J. 287.

(n) Vansyckel's Appeal, 1 H. 128.

(o) Wraith v. Van Dewater, 2 Par. 251.

(p) Ibid.

(q) Quay v. Kuckner, C. C. P. of Chester, 3 P. L. J. 307.

(r) Pamph. L. 233.

(rr) For Bail, see *post*, chapter xi.

CHAPTER IX.

OF THE COMMENCEMENT OF ACTIONS BY THE AGREEMENT OF PARTIES WITHOUT A WRIT.

There is in Pennsylvania a mode of instituting an action, without the intervention of the sheriff, which seems peculiar to its practice, by amicable agreement signed by the parties or their attorneys, and filed in the prothonotary's office, to be by him entered on record.

The 40th section of the act of 1836, provides on this subject as follows:—

It shall be lawful for any persons, willing to become parties to an amicable action, to enter into an agreement, in writing, for that purpose, either in their proper persons, or by their respective agents, or attorneys, and on the production of such agreement to the prothonotary of any court having jurisdiction of the subject matter, he shall enter the same on his docket, and from the time of such entry, the action shall be deemed to be depending, in like manner as if the defendant had appeared to a summons issued against him by the plaintiff.

By the 8th section of the act of March, 1806,(a) "it shall be the duty of the prothonotaries, respectively, on the application of any persons willing to become parties in an amicable suit, to enter the same without the agency of an attorney, and when thereunto required, and on confession in writing, executed in presence of two or more witnesses, expressing the amount due to the plaintiff (which confession shall be filed in his office), he shall enter judgment against the defendant, for the amount expressed as aforesaid, with stay of execution as may be agreed upon by the parties, and the prothonotary shall receive fifty (by a late act now twenty-five) cents for every such entry, to be paid by the defendant in the suit, and when any suit is ended, the clerk of the court before which it was pending, shall, on the request of the plaintiff expressed in writing, enter satisfaction thereon." When judgment is confessed in this manner, care should always be taken to express the cause of action in the agreement,(b) and to have it attested by two witnesses, as an omission of this would be a good exception to its validity.(c) This act is affirmative, and does not prohibit the entry of judgments according to the pre-existing practice; accordingly, judgment may be entered up by the prothonotary upon a written order sent to him by the defendant, confessing judgment in an action of debt, and directing him to enter judgment against him.(d)

(a) 4 Sm. Laws, 328.
(b) See Cooke v. Gilbert, 8 S. & R. 567.
(c) McCalmont v. Peters, 13 S. & R. 197–8.
(d) Ibid.

An amicable action of ejectment is good, although the twelfth section of the act declares that all writs of ejectment shall be in the form prescribed therein, and not otherwise;(e) because this is to be understood as applicable only to cases in which the suit is commenced by writ, and by no means as impairing the force of those sections by which all persons are permitted to enter suits without writs.(f) By such entry of an amicable action, the defendant waives the necessity of issuing a writ, and of course everything contained in it.(g) But it does not also follow that he has waived the filing of a declaration or statement, by the mere agreement to enter an amicable action. That the necessity of doing this in certain cases is not taken away by such an agreement, will be seen at the conclusion of the present chapter.

An amicable action may be entered whenever a husband and wife can sue or be sued by adversary process, and she and her rights are as much bound as if the proceeding had been adverse.(h)

It is sometimes the practice of attorneys to enter amicable actions in one term, as of the preceding term; which is adopted in order to gain precedence; as, when a confession of judgment accompanies such an agreement, the judgment, as against the defendant, is dated from the time to which the action is entered.

The fifth section of the act of 1836, which (in the third and fourth sections) provides for a stay of execution upon judgments obtained in suits instituted by *capias* or summons, puts amicable actions upon a similar footing, and extends the like stay of execution on judgments obtained in them, unless when it is differently provided by the parties in the terms of their agreement, counting from its date.

All that remains to be said on the subject of amicable actions is, that it is a mode to which frequent recurrence is had in beginning suits in this State, because it not only comports with the milder feelings of parties, but it is a saving of the expense of an original writ, and the sheriff's fees for serving it. It is also said to be a very ancient practice in Pennsylvania. Though the issuing of the writ is dispensed with, it is considered as having been issued, and may be filed at any time.(i) Upon this principle it was determined, that where an amicable action of *scire facias* upon a mortgage was entered by the agreement of the parties, which agreement contained a description of the mortgage, it was not error, that the cause had been tried without writ, declaration, or statement.(j) For the writ being *supposed* to be filed, and it being the constant practice to plead to the *scire facias* without a declaration, in which writ the cause of action is always sufficiently described, it cannot be said that there is no writ upon which issue cannot be well joined. The inference from this case is, that amicable agreements in actions wherein the writ does not contain the substance of the declaration, are no waiver of the necessity of a declaration. When this is omitted to be put in, therefore, either party, who has not relinquished the exception by some subsequent act, such as, for example, putting the cause at issue, or calling for a plea or replication, may make the omission ground of error. It is, however, perfectly competent for the parties to stipulate in the amicable

(e) **Massey** v. Thomas, 6 Bin. 333.
(f) Ibid. 336.
(g) Ibid. 338.

(h) Gratz v. Phillips *et al*. 1 Pa. R. 333.
(i) Morris v. Buckley, 11 S. & R. 173.
(j) Id.; Ibid. 168.

agreement for such an omission; and it might, in the majority of cases, be found most convenient to state the cause of action in the amicable writing, with a view to such a convention.

Upon the entry of this form of action, a case may be stated for the opinion of the court, when the cause will be placed on the argument list.

By the 49th rule of the District Court: "No judgment by confession shall be entered in any amicable suit unless there be filed, at the time of filing the agreement, a specific statement of the cause of action signed by the parties or their attorneys; and where said statement is signed by the attorney of the defendant, there shall also be filed with the same his warrant of attorney; it being understood, that this rule does not apply to judgments on warrants by attorney, or to revivals of judgments by agreement."

An agreement to an amicable action, is in effect an appearance by the defendant.(k)

(k) Crossby v. Massy, 1 P. R. 229.

CHAPTER X.

OF THE ARREST; OF THE BAIL TO BE TAKEN BY THE SHERIFF; AND OF DEPOSITS OF MONEY IN LIEU OF BAIL.

SECTION I.

OF THE ARREST.

An arrest, upon process directed to the sheriff, is to be made by him, or one of his deputies (as all his officers are),(a) and it can only be made in the county to the sheriff of which it is directed.(b)

No civil process can be served upon Sunday, it being prohibited by the "act to restrain people from labor on the first day of the week," § 1 ;(c) and the person serving or executing it shall be liable for damages, at the suit of the party grieved.

If a person be detained against his will on Sunday, to be served with a process on Monday, the arrest will be void.(d) After a voluntary escape of a defendant in custody, he cannot be retaken, on a Sunday, but after a negligent escape he may ; for this is not an original taking, but the party is still in custody on the old commitment.(e)

No man can be arrested in his own house, provided the outer door be shut ; but if the outer door be open, the officer having gained admittance, may break open an inner door, to arrest the defendant ;(f) and if a man let out part of his house, reserving for himself, and occupying an inner room, an officer entering through the outer door of the house, being open, may break open the inner door to arrest him.(g) Yet he cannot break open the inner doors of the house of a third person, on suspicion that the defendant is there, in order to arrest him.(h) But bail may break open the outer door of their principal, in order to arrest, as may a sheriff, to take a prisoner who has escaped from arrest.(i)

In making the arrest, the sheriff, or his officer, it has been said, must actually seize or touch the defendant's body ;(j) but this does not seem to be absolutely necessary ; for, if the defendant submit himself to the arrest, or be completely in the power of the officer, it is sufficient ; as

---

(a) As to the relative responsibility and duties of the sheriff and his deputies, see Wheeler v. Hambright, S. & R. 393, 394-7, in which the subject, as regards this State, is thoroughly discussed and determined. And see Pemberton v. Hicks, 1 Bin. 24.

(b) 7 Taunt. 233 ; Doug. 384; 1 T. R. 187; 2 New Rep. 167.

(c) 1 Sm. Laws, 25.
(d) 1 Anstr. 85.
(e) 7 Johns. 155 ; Ld. Ray. 1028 ; 5 T. R. 25.
(f) Cowp. 1 ; 16 John. 287.
(g) Cowp. 1.
(h) 6 Taunt. 246.
(i) 7 Johns. 156.
(j) Salk. 79, pl. 2.

if an officer come into a room, and tell the defendant that he arrests him, and lock the door, that is held to be an arrest.(*k*)

When the defendant is arrested, by virtue of any writ, process, or warrant, it is declared unlawful for the officer, by the act of 1729–30, § 14,(*l*) to take or convey him to any tavern, or other public victualling or drinking house, or to the private house of the officer, without the prisoner's voluntary consent; or with his consent to keep him above twenty days at either of those places; or to demand or receive, directly or indirectly, any greater sum of money than is allowed by law, for the arrest, or waiting till the prisoner shall have given in an appearance or bail, as the case shall require, or agreed with the person, at whose suit or prosecution he shall be arrested, or until he shall be sent to the proper jail; or to take any reward, gratuity, or money, for keeping the prisoner out of jail; or to receive any greater sum of money, for each night's lodging, or for a day's diet, or other expenses, than what shall be allowed as reasonable, in such cases, by some order to be made by the justices of the respective Courts of Common Pleas, at some court to be held for such place where the arrest may be.

Where a defendant, arrested upon *mesne* process, is rescued as he is going to prison, the sheriff may return the rescue, and it is a good defence to an action for an escape.(*m*) The plaintiff has several remedies against the rescuers; either by an action on the case, an indictment, or by attachment on the sheriff's return of a rescue, which not being traversable, is of itself a conviction.(*n*) But an attachment will not be granted, without the sheriff's return, on affidavits of the fact;(*o*) and as the return is not traversable, the rescuers are not to be examined upon interrogatories, as in ordinary cases.(*p*)

The officer, having received special directions from the plaintiff, or his attorney, either in writing or by parol, is bound to arrest the defendant, if to be found within his precinct. For a return, that the defendant *cannot* be arrested, or, that the precept *cannot* be served, for *resistance*, can never be justified, inasmuch as the officer, in the execution of such process, may command the *posse comitatus*.(*q*)

For the same reason an officer, when he has once arrested, must, at his peril, retain the defendant. It is presumed, however, that in both cases, were the officer overcome by the actual force of the defendant, he would be liable to nominal damages only.(*r*)

If the defendant be known, or can be easily ascertained, the officer must arrest him, upon the mere direction of the plaintiff. If otherwise, and there be a question as to the identity of the defendant, the plaintiff is bound, as in the attachment of property, upon demand, to point him out, and to indemnify the officer against the consequences of a mistake.(*s*)

Should there be several persons, of precisely the same name and

(*k*) 1 Dunl. Pr. 153; 2 New Rep. 211, 212; Rep. T. Har. 301; 6 Mod. 178; 2 Hawk. P. C. ch. 19, § 1.
(*l*) 1 Sm. Laws, 186.
(*m*) Cro. Eliz. 868; Cro. Jac. 419; 3 Lev. 46; Str. 435; Gilb. C. P. 23.
(*n*) Com. Dig. Rescous. D. i. 6; Cro. Jac. 419; 1 Dunl. Pr. 154.

(*o*) Salk. 586, pl. 3; 6 Mod. 141; Str. 531.
(*p*) Burr. 2129; *Sed vide* 5 T. R. 362.
(*q*) 2 Inst. 193, 453; Bac. Abr. Shff. N. 2.
(*r*) Howe's Prac. 151.
(*s*) Marsh *v.* Gold et al. 2 Pick. Rep. 285.

occupation, in his precinct, and the officer be unable, by any means, to ascertain which is the defendant named in the writ, the safest return for him to make would be, that he did not know upon whom to serve, for a return of "*non est*" would be false.(*t*)

An officer, generally known as such, is not bound to show his writ before he serves it; but after service, or when the defendant has submitted to the arrest, if the defendant demand it, and not otherwise, he is bound to make known the cause of the arrest.(*u*) A *special* deputy, however, and perhaps a newly appointed officer, also, ought to show the writ before executing it.(*v*)

The refusal of the officer to show his writ, when bound so to do, will not make him a trespasser *ab initio*. But the service, in such a case, may be set aside for irregularity.(*w*)

If the defendant he rightly named in the writ, but the sheriff execute his process upon the wrong person, though of the same name with the right one, he will be a trespasser. And it would be the same though the person arrested declared that he was the individual named in the writ.(*x*)

If the writ describe the defendant by a wrong name, unless he be known as well by that given him as by his true one, the officer cannot arrest him. If he do, the defendant may not only plead in abatement, but may also maintain an action of trespass against the officer for false imprisonment.(*y*) In one such case the court discharged the defendant upon motion.(*z*)

The difference between the names, however, must be a material one; for when there is only an inaccuracy in the spelling, so that the name is still *idem sonans*, the rule does not apply.(*a*)

But an appearance by the defendant in the suit, either by his wrong name or his right, without pleading in abatement, will render him liable to be taken on the execution by the wrong name.(*b*)

SECTION II.

OF THE BAIL TO BE TAKEN BY THE SHERIFF.

The practice on this subject has undergone a very material change by the operation of the act of 1834. In some respects, the bail to be given to the sheriff is also the bail to the action, and the old practice of taking an assignment of the bail-bond from the sheriff is done away with. Before quoting the provisions of the act upon this branch of the law of arrests, it will be better to state the old practice.

(*t*) Dalt. Shff. 112, 113.
(*u*) Blatch *v.* Archer, 1 Cowp. Rep. 63; Crowther *v.* Ramsbottom, et als. 7 Term Rep. 654; Bac. Abr. Shff. N. 1; 9 Co. 66; Commonwealth *v.* Field, 13 Mass. Rep. 321; Countess of Rutland's case, 6 Co. 53.
(*v*) Bac. Abr. Shff. N. 1.
(*w*) Thomas *v.* Pearce, 2 Barn. & Cress. 761.

(*x*) 1 Burr. Rep. 210; Moore, 457.
(*y*) Cole *v.* Hindson, 6 Term Rep. 234; Shadgett *v.* Clipson, 8 East's Rep. 328; Coffall *v.* Hentley, 1 Marsh. Rep. 75.
(*z*) Wilks *v.* Lorck, 2 Taunt. Rep. 400.
(*a*) Ahitbol *v.* Beniditto, 2 Taunt. Rep. 401.
(*b*) Crawford *v.* Satchwell, 2 Strange, 1218.

The defendant, having been arrested, had either to go to jail or give security to the sheriff for his appearance at the return of the writ. This was called bail to the sheriff, or bail below, in order to distinguish it from bail to the action, bail above, or special bail, which was afterwards required to be put in to abide the event of the suit. Bail to the sheriff was given by executing to him a bond with one or more sureties, conditioned for the party's appearance at the return of the writ, and for no other purpose.(c) The sheriff had to take reasonable bail if tendered, otherwise a special action on the case lay against him by the defendant.(d) But, in order to maintain such an action, it was requisite to show that the parties who were offered as bail had sufficient in the county where the arrest was made.(e)

If the sheriff took insufficient sureties, or persons who did not inhabit within the county, he was not liable to an action for an escape ;(f) but the plaintiff had to proceed by attachment, after having ruled him to bring in the body of the defendant.(g) To relieve himself, it was the sheriff's practice, when thus ruled, to put in special bail to the action, which the court permitted at any time, and without notice to the plaintiff, for the purpose merely of a surrender. The sheriff then arrested and imprisoned the defendant upon a bail-piece, from which he could not be relieved without putting in and justifying fresh bail on notice to the plaintiff. The bond was to be taken by the sheriff before the return of the writ, otherwise it was void,(h) and might be avoided on the plea of *non est factum*.(i)

The defendant having given a bail-bond, might surrender himself to the sheriff before the return of the writ, and the bond might be cancelled, after which the plaintiff could neither proceed against the sheriff nor maintain an action against him for not assigning it.(j) It was optional in the sheriff whether he would accept the surrender of the party, in discharge of the bail-bond ;(k) and when a surrender was made, the defendant had to give notice of it to the plaintiff.(l) After the return of the writ, bail above could only surrender the principal, and a surrender by the bail below would not discharge them ;(m) therefore, if the defendant would not put in special bail, the bail below had to do it, which they might do against the consent of the defendant, and then the special bail might discharge themselves by surrendering the principal.(n)

The sheriff or his officer might, if he wished, discharge the defendant, without taking a bail-bond, or any other security for his appearance, provided he had him at the return of the writ. But if he had him not

(c) 6 Bac. Abr. 181 ; 1 T. R. 422.

(d) At common law, the sheriff was not obliged to bail a defendant arrested upon mesne process, unless he sued out a writ of mainprize, though he might have taken bail of his own accord ; 2 Saund. 60, c. ; this defect in the law was remedied by the statute 23 Hen. VI. c. 9. This statute is omitted in the report of the judges to the legislature of the State ; but the twentieth section of the statute 4 Anne, c. 16, which directs the sheriff to assign such bail-bond, is reported to be in force. See Rob. Dig. 83. The statute of Henry was once deemed a private law ; Bull. N. P. 224 ; but it is now determined to be a public act, of which the courts will judicially take notice. 2 Saund. 155, b. ; 15 East, 320 ; 1 Cromp. Pr. 51 ; 2 Saund. 59, 61, c. d.

(e) 15 East, 320.

(f) 2 Saund. 60, c, 61, d.

(g) 1 Dunl. Pr. 157.

(h) 2 Saund. 60, a.

(i) 4 M. & S. 338 ; 2 T. R. 569.

(j) 2 Saund. 61, c.

(k) 1 East, 383.

(l) 1 B. & P. 325.

(m) 1 Dunl. Pr. 161.

(n) Str. 876.

then, that is, if he had him not in custody, and neither put in special bail, nor rendered the defendant in due time, he would then be answerable in an action for an escape;(o) and having been guilty of a breach of duty, could not recover over against the defendant,(p) unless he subsequently promised to indemnify the sheriff;(q) for which promise the previous moral obligation to indemnify was a sufficient consideration.(r)

If the sheriff permitted the defendant to go at large without bail, he might protect himself by putting in and perfecting bail, as of the term in which the writ was returnable ; but after an action for an escape had been commenced, he could not defeat it by putting in bail in a subsequent term;(s) even admitting that he would be allowed to put in bail as of the proper term.(t)

If the sheriff had, in fact, taken a bail-bond, his denial that he had taken one did not subject him to an action for an escape.(u) But in an action for an escape upon mesne process, the sheriff's return of *cepi corpus*, and proof that the party did not put in bail above, and was not in the sheriff's custody at the return of the writ, was sufficient evidence on the part of the plaintiff.(v)

We will now introduce the several sections of the act of 1836, regulating the present practice.

It shall be the duty of the officer charged with the execution of any writ of *capias ad respondendum*, to let to bail any person arrested or detained by him by force thereof, on his giving bond, with reasonable sureties, having sufficient estate within the county, in the manner hereinafter provided, under the penalty of treble damages to the party aggrieved. § 9.

The bond to be taken by the officer as aforesaid, shall be in the name of the commonwealth, and in the amount of the bail demanded ; and the condition thereof shall be, that if the defendant therein named shall be condemned in the action, at the suit of the plaintiff, he shall satisfy the condemnation money and costs, or surrender himself into the custody of the sheriff of the county ; or in default thereof, that the bail will do so for him; and such bond shall be for the use of the plaintiff in the action, or of the sheriff, or other officer, as the case may be. § 10.

Upon the execution of a bond, in the form aforesaid, it shall be lawful for the bail therein, to have, from the officer by whom it was taken, a bail-piece, to be made according to the following form : —— County, ss. in the Court of ——, C D, of the county aforesaid, delivered to bail upon a bond taken by me, J S, sheriff [or other officer, as the case may be], of said county, the —— day of ——, to E F, of the township of ——, in said county [yeoman], and G H, of the township of ——, in said county [merchant], at the suit of A B, in a plea of [describing the action as described in the bond]. § 11.

(o) 2 Saund. 61, c; 1 Arch. Pr. 77.
(p) Peake's N. P. C. 144, n; 8 East, 161.
(q) 14 Johns, 378.
(r) 1 Dunl. Pr. 162.

(s) 4 M. & S. 397 ; 6 Taunt. 554.
(t) 1 Esp. Rep. 87; 2 B. & P. 38; *sed vide* 7 T. R. 105.
(u) 5 Taunt. 325.
(v) 3 Camp. 397.

It shall be the duty of the officer taking such bond, to make return of the same, at or before the return day of the writ, together with the *capias ad respondendum*, to the office of the prothonotary issuing the capias, who shall file the same, and enter upon his docket the names of the bail. § 12.

It shall be the duty of every sheriff, taking bond as aforesaid, to give notice, in writing, of the names and places of residence of the bail, to the plaintiff in the action, his agent, or attorney. § 13.

The bail taken by the sheriff as aforesaid, may be excepted to by the plaintiff, his agent, or attorney, at any time within twenty days after the return day of the writ; and notice given to him by the sheriff as aforesaid, and the bail so entered may justify, or new bail be added or substituted, and justify, within ten days after notice of the exception as aforesaid, according to the practice hitherto allowed with respect to special bail. § 14.

Provided, nevertheless, That it shall be lawful for any court to make such rules respecting the time and manner of giving notice of bail, excepting to bail, and justifying bail as aforesaid, taken upon process out of such court, as the convenient administration of justice in such court may require. § 15.

The sheriff taking any bond as aforesaid, shall be responsible to the plaintiff for the sufficiency of the bail therein, but such responsibility shall cease and determine :—

First, If the plaintiff shall not except to the bail within the time allowed for that purpose ; or

Second, If, upon exception made, the bail shall justify, to the satisfaction of the court, or of the commissioner authorized for the purpose ; or

Third, If, upon such exception, other bail shall be added or substituted, and justify as aforesaid. § 16.

If a defendant, arrested or detained on a *capias ad respondendum* as aforesaid, shall not give bail as aforesaid, it shall be the duty of the sheriff to state the fact in his return, according to the practice now prevailing and allowed. § 17.

If the officer charged with the execution of such writ, shall make return that he has taken the body of the defendant in such writ, or that such defendant hath surrendered himself to his custody, he shall be chargeable to have the body of such defendant at the day of the return of such writ, in the manner heretofore practised. § 18.

It shall be lawful for any defendant committed to prison by virtue of any *capias ad respondendum*, or surrendered by his bail as aforesaid, to enter special bail to the action, in the manner now practised and allowed, at any time before final judgment obtained against him. § 19.

In a subsequent chapter we shall consider the subject of the sheriff's liability, generally, and under the provisions of the foregoing law.(w)

It will be observed, that, when the defendant is unable to find bail, and must necessarily go to prison, unless the sheriff choose to keep him in his own private custody, the 18th and 19th sections of the above act allow the defendant to proceed according to the old practice, and to obtain his release from imprisonment by putting in bail to the action, that is, by procuring some sufficient person to enter into a recognizance of special bail before the prothonotary. This subject will also be considered in the same chapter.(x)

The ensuing section will treat of the method by which the defendant may obtain his liberty after the arrest, by depositing money with the sheriff as security for his appearance.

SECTION III.

OF DEPOSITS OF MONEY WITH THE SHERIFF IN LIEU OF BAIL.

This subject is regulated by the 20th, 21st, 22d, 23d, 29th, and 35th sections of the same act of 1836. Those sections are as follows :—

It shall be lawful for the defendant in any writ of *capias ad respondendum*, either before or after arrest, or after bail given, and before the return of the writ, to deposit in the hands of the sheriff, in lieu of all bail, the sum in which bail is demanded, to abide the event of the suit, for which he shall be entitled to demand of such officer a receipt ; and upon making such deposit, he shall be forthwith discharged from arrest in the action in which such deposit shall be made, and the liability of the bail, if any have been given, shall cease and determine. § 20.

It shall be the duty of the officer receiving such deposit, to make return of the fact, and to pay the sum deposited with him thereon, into court; and if the plaintiff in such writ shall fail in his action, the money so deposited shall be forthwith returned to the defendant, upon application made to the court for that purpose. § 21.

If judgment be rendered against the defendant in such action, the money deposited as aforesaid, or so much thereof as may be necessary, shall be applied by order of the court towards the satisfaction of such judgments, in like manner as money paid into court by a defendant in other cases. § 22.

It shall also be lawful for any defendant, after the return of the writ, by the leave of the court, to deposit and pay into court the sum in which bail may be demanded as aforesaid, to bide the event of the suit, and to be disposed of in manner aforesaid; and thereupon, it shall be lawful for the said court to make an order for the discharge of the defendant from imprisonment, or of his bail, as the case may be, from liability. § 23.

(w) Vide *post*, ch. xii.   (x) Ibid.

The court from which any original or special writ of *capias ad respondendum* shall issue, shall have the like power and authority to
inquire into the cause of action, to quash the writ, with or without costs,
to reduce the amount of bail required, or to discharge without bail, as
are now possessed and exercised by the several courts of this commonwealth; and if any deposit shall have been made as aforesaid, and the
court shall decide that the plaintiff was not entitled to bail, or shall
reduce the amount for which bail was demanded, the defendant shall be
entitled to the repayment of the money deposited, or so much thereof
as shall remain beyond the amount of bail authorized by the court.
§ 29.

If the defendant shall have deposited in the hands of the officer a
sum of money in lieu of bail as aforesaid, he shall be deemed to have
appeared in court at the return day, in like manner as if he had entered
special bail to the action.   § 35.(*y*)

(*y*) See, for recent cases on bail generally, Wh. Dig. tit. "Bail."

CHAPTER XI.

OF THE RULE TO SHOW CAUSE OF ACTION, AND WHY THE DEFENDANT SHOULD NOT BE DISCHARGED ON COMMON BAIL.

As the law and practice of this State stood before the act of 1836, no affidavit or other proof of the debt, or of its amount, was required to be made by the plaintiff before issuing process in *bailable* actions, it often happened that a defendant would be arrested, and compelled to give bail to the sheriff, or go to prison, where there was not even *prima facie* a cause of action, or where the sum claimed in the writ was exaggerated beyond the amount justly due, and the power of the defendant to obtain security.(*a*) Again, although in actions *sounding in damages*, it was necessary to file an affidavit of the cause of action previously to issuing the writ, when the defendant might be held to bail, it might be that the affidavit showed no ground of action, or that it was too generally or informally worded, or the damages alleged might be exaggerated, or might not be stated in any particular sum.

To obviate the injustice which might be done to the defendant when thus held to bail, his attorney, or he himself, could serve the plaintiff or his attorney with a citation or rule to show his cause of action, and why the defendant should not be discharged on common bail ;(*b*) under which rule the bail might be either discharged or mitigated.(*c*)

And now, although the right to arrest and hold to bail in civil actions has been so much restricted by the act of 1836 and 1842, above alluded to, and it can in no case be exercised without the previous making and filing of an affidavit, yet, when a *capias ad respondendum*, general or special, has been properly issued and served under this act, the same

---

(*a*) 1 Dun. Pr. 166.

(*b*) 3 Bin. 280.

(*c*) Mr. Roberts, in his "Digest of British Statutes appearing to be in force in Pennsylvania," p. 89, after stating that, according to the English practice, no writ can be marked for bail, in actions for uncertain damages, or where, from the nature of the case, proof cannot be exhibited of the amount of the plaintiff's demand, without the court's or a judge's order previously made ; but that in Pennsylvania, in the cases of this kind, the *capias* is at once issued, marked for bail in a certain sum, and the defendant may, upon a rule to show cause of action, be relieved from bail, has these remarks : ' Whether the English practice or our own, in this particular, is to be preferred, may perhaps be questionable. According to the former, the order is made on an *ex parte* hearing ; whereas by the latter the parties are confronted. Where a previous order is requisite, opportunities may be afforded to elude justice, yet, on the other hand, some temporary inconveniences may arise from allowing bail to be required without such an order. But perhaps wanton abuses are seldom to be apprehended, where redress may so speedily be obtained, and where the consequence of such abuses may be serious to the author."

practice must be pursued as to citing the plaintiff to show his cause of action, in order to effect a discharge of the defendant without giving bail, or a diminution of its amount.   And this privilege so to cite the plaintiff, may be asserted in the case of attachments of the property of an absent debtor, and the court will inquire into the cause of action in the same manner as is done in cases of *capias*, as the abuse of process may be as great, and the necessity of providing against a wanton and ground. less seizure of the defendant's effects, as obvious.   In the case of *specific articles* attached, a stranger's ship, or other effects may be taken out of his hands, and detained for such a length of time as to ruin his voyage and embarrass his affairs beyond redress.   So, in the case of *debts* attached, his property may be locked up, his remittances prevented, and the injury nearly as great as in the other case.   The bail marked by an attorney, or a malicious plaintiff, may be out of all bounds disproportioned to the debt; and if there were no way of examining into the justice or extent of the demand, a defendant might be at the mercy of the plaintiff, to be ruined at his pleasure.(*b*)

The rules of the District Court in this respect are as follows:—
XXX. The manner of giving notice to the plaintiff to show cause before a single judge shall be by application to the judge himself, who will issue his citation for that purpose, appointing such time and place for the hearing as he shall find convenient to himself and the parties concerned.
XXXI. A rule to show cause of action, and why the defendant shall not be discharged on common bail, must be moved for before the end of the first week of the term to which the process is returnable.(*c*)

When common bail has been ordered by a judge at his chambers, upon a citation, the plaintiff cannot, though he there give notice of his intention, recur to the court in term to obtain special bail.(*d*)   The court, notwithstanding the above rules, received a motion for a rule to show cause of action after the expiration of the first week, in a case where the defendant had been confined in jail, and had no counsel until after the first week of the term.(*e*)
On the hearing, the court or judge will make the proper order, according to the nature of the action, or the cause for holding to bail, which the plaintiff may show.   Cause of action may be shown by the plaintiff, or by some other person for him, qualified by knowledge and situation, making affidavit of the subsisting debt.   The only legal mode of showing cause is by affidavit, which, if drawn with a sufficient degree of precision, is conclusive.   It must, in general, state the facts so much at large, that the judge may be enabled to decide on the *quantum* of bail required by the plaintiff, and that he may be indicted for perjury, if the facts are not truly stated by him.(*f*)   It must be *positive*. Swearing to the best of the plaintiff's belief is not sufficient.(*g*)   In trespass, assault and battery, &c., the plaintiff need not swear that he

(*b*) 1 D. 154–5.
(*c*) See Boyer *v.* Searle, 2 D. 110.
(*d*) Chryster *v.* Jackson, Sup. C. Dec. 1774, MS. Reps. *Contra*, 12 Mod. Rep. 526.

(*e*) 2 Br. 261.
(*f*) 1 Br. 33.
(*g*) Ibid. Diehl *v.* Perie, 2 M. 47, *ante*, p. 250.

has sustained damage to any *precise* amount. He swears to the particular facts, and the court or judge fix the amount of bail. In covenant, and special actions for the non-performance of contracts, the plaintiff must not only state in his affidavit the material circumstances of the case, but he must state the *amount* of his damage in positive terms.(*h*) After the plaintiff has sworn to facts sufficient to hold to bail, the court will not inquire how he became acquainted with those facts.(*i*)

To entitle a plaintiff to hold a defendant to bail under the 4th section of the act of 13th June, 1836, it was held that the cause of action must be positively sworn to; though the amount in which the defendant was indebted, or the value of the property taken or detained, or the damages sustained, might be set forth to the best of the defendant's knowledge and belief.(*j*)

An executor may hold a defendant to bail without swearing positively to a subsisting debt; an affidavit of his belief of the existence of the debt is sufficient; for the nature of his situation will not admit of his being more positive.(*k*)

"In all cases where a positive affidavit of a real subsisting debt shall be made by the plaintiff in the cause, or by a third person, whose knowledge and situation shall enable him to make such positive affidavit, it shall be so far conclusive that no counter affidavit shall be admitted; but the judge will, at his discretion, ask such further questions of the person making such affidavit, as shall be necessary to satisfy his conscience, as well to the cause of action as to the *quantum* of bail." But the court will not interrogate the witness who makes the affidavit, unless, *on the face of the affidavit itself*, further satisfaction be deemed necessary.(*l*)

"When the affidavit is not positive, yet sufficient to convince the judge that a good cause of action actually exists, particularly where it is founded on a bond, note, letters, or other papers signed by the defendant, he may, at his discretion, hold the defendant to bail; and where satisfaction cannot, in such cases, be otherwise obtained, counter affidavits may be admitted; so, nevertheless, that the merits of the cause be not any further inquired into, than shall be absolutely necessary to decide the question of bail." In inquiries relative to bail, the evidence of a party, or person interested in the event of the suit, has always been received.(*m*)

Affidavits to hold to bail made by the plaintiff (residing in New York), and his clerk in Philadelphia, which set forth that the defendant was indebted to the plaintiff in a certain sum, "part of which" was for money lent and advanced by the plaintiff to the defendant, and "the rest of the principal sum" was due "for the balance which the defendant owes the plaintiff, on settlement, in transactions in which the plaintiff, by the defendant's request, and as his agent, made purchases and sales for the defendant, but in the plaintiff's name, by which he stands

(*h*) 1 Br. 35, 206.
(*i*) 1 Br. 341.
(*j*) Nevins *v.* Merric, 2 Wh. 499.
(*k*) Com. Dig. Pleader, 2 D. 1; 3 Leon. 212.
(*l*) C. C. 1810, MS. Wh. Dig. p. 69; 1 Br. 286. We have been informed that in the time of Mr. J. Shippen, who drafted these rules when he was president of the Court of Common Pleas for the City and County of Philadelphia, the right of the defendant to ask questions of the plaintiff was almost unlimited, and the court and judge, on questions of bail, went very far by means of these questions, into the merits of the cause; but a different practice has since prevailed.
(*m*) 3 Y. 560; 1 Bin. 224.

indebted to third persons, and the defendant is indebted to him in the said sum; the precise amount and extent of which balance cannot be stated now, because the defendant suddenly left New York, without coming to any settlement, &c.," and that the defendant, on being required to pay, did not deny the debt or the amount: held to be sufficient.(n)

In consequence of a determination in the Court of Common Pleas, of this county, in 1785, a rule was adopted in the courts, that "when the plaintiff himself is not present, and the evidence of the debt is brought from a foreign country, founded on any bonds, notes, bills of exchange, or other papers, executed, signed, or acknowledged by the defendant himself, if it shall appear that due proof has been made of the execution, signature, or acknowledgment before a lawful magistrate or other public officer, according to the forms of the country whence they came, and certified under some known and public seal of that country, the judge being satisfied that a good cause of action appears, may, at his discretion, hold the defendant to bail; but no affidavit of the plaintiff himself, or any other person, taken in such foreign country, to prove any demands or accounts not accompanied with such writings, executed, signed, or acknowledged by the defendant, and proved as aforesaid, shall be sufficient to hold the defendant to bail, although such affidavit be certified under any public seal, unless it shall likewise appear in evidence to the judge that the defendant has acknowledged such demands or accounts to be just."(o)   But now, by a very late decision in the Supreme Court, a positive affidavit of a debt, made before a justice of the peace in a foreign country, who is certified to be duly commissioned, is sufficient to hold a party to special bail, without any acknowledgment of the debt by the defendant.(p) And in consequence of this decision, the District Court of this county, held the foregoing rule to be null, and on other grounds to be obsolete.(q)   The act of the 16th of January, 1827,(r) applies, it is apprehended, under the words, *instruments of writing*, to such affidavits. That act is as follows:—

Whereas, difficulties have been experienced by reason of the want of a convenient mode of proving and acknowledging deeds, made and executed abroad: Therefore, all deeds and conveyances, whether of *femes covert*, or otherwise, made, granted, and executed out of the United States, brought into this commonwealth to be recorded, in the county where the lands lie, and all letters of attorney and instruments of writing, made and executed out of the United States, and intended to have effect in this commonwealth, the execution of such deeds, conveyances, letters of attorney, or instruments of writing, being first proved, or the acknowledgment thereof being first duly taken and made, in the manner directed and provided by the laws of this commonwealth, before any consul or vice-consul of the United States, duly appointed for, and exercising consular functions in, the State, kingdom, country, or place where such deeds or conveyances, letters of attorney, or instruments of writing, may, or shall be made and executed, and certified under the

---

(n) Cammann v. Hind, 1 Wh. 320.
(o) 1 D. 159, 160.
(p) Walker v. Bamber, 8 S. & R. 61; and see the liberal and correct view there taken of the whole subject by the Chief Justice, delivering the opinion of the court.
(q) Baker et al. v. Croft, Dem. Press. March 19, 1825.
(r) Pamph. L. p. 9; Troub. & H. Dig. 36.

public official seal of such consul or vice-consul of the United States, shall be as valid and effectual in law as if the same had been made and duly proved or acknowledged before a justice of the peace, or other officer within this commonwealth, having authority to take such proof or acknowledgments, according to the existing laws of this commonwealth.

When the plaintiff resides in some other State of the Union, and is not present at the time of showing cause of action, a positive affidavit, of a subsisting debt, being made before any judge, mayor, or chief magistrate of the city, town or place, where the plaintiff resides, and certified under the common or public seal of such city, town or place, shall be admitted to show cause of action, and shall have the same force and effect as if made in this State before a judge of the court.(s)

The Supreme Court and Common Pleas, at their discretion, will hear supplemental affidavits; but the practice was not formerly allowed in the Supreme Court, on the ground that the rejection of supplemental affidavits was better adapted to produce certainty, and to take away the temptation to commit perjury.(t)   If the plaintiff, when cited, could not at once make out a sufficient cause of action, could he then make another affidavit, it would be giving him, if an unprincipled man, an opportunity of learning how far he must go, in order to swear up to the mark.(u)

To entitle the defendant to a discharge on common bail, after a rule to show cause of action, in cases where the reason alleged for discharging the bail is *dehors* the plaintiff's affidavit, or depends on particular merits, the defendant's evidence must not be of a doubtful nature.(v) And where sufficient reasonable ground has been shown to bring a cause before a jury, the court will not so discharge him.(w)

Upon a question of bail, the court will not inquire into an objection of fraud in the original contract ;(x) nor into the fact of the defendant's infancy, where there is no suggestion of fraud ;(y) neither when the *defendant* shows a discharge under the insolvent laws of the State, which is always conclusive evidence on a question of bail, will the court at that stage inquire whether due notice of the petition had been given to the plaintiff ;(z) nor hear evidence that the defendant had acted unfairly and fraudulently in obtaining his discharge.(a)

The court, indeed, appears bound so to act by the sixteenth section of the act of assembly of June 16, 1836,(b) which directs, in express terms, that "the order of the court as aforesaid, shall be a sufficient warrant for the discharge of the petitioner from imprisonment, if he shall be in confinement at the time of such order, or shall be at any time afterwards arrested, by virtue of process, in any action or proceeding for the recovery of any debt or demand, as aforesaid, on his giving a warrant of attorney, if arrested on mesne process, to appear to the action, and plead thereto."

(s) Walker *v.* Bamber, 8 S. & R. 63. The rules above quoted as to bail, have been abolished in the District Court.
(t) Parke *v.* Graham, 4 S. & R. 548
(u) *Vide* Ibid.
(v) 1 Peters's Rep. 352.
(w) Waters *v.* Collot, 2 D. 247, S. C.; Waters *v.* Collot, 2 Y. 26 ; Parasset *v.* Gautier, 2 D. 330 ; in note.
(x) Parasset *v.* Gautier, 2 D. 330 ; in note.
(y) Clemson *v.* Bush, 3 Bin. 413.
(z) D. C. Phila. 1821 ; MS.
(a) 1 Peters's Rep. 484.
(b) Pamph. L. 734.

The seventeenth section, however, contains this proviso: " That if the petitioner shall be in custody or confinement at the time of such order, by virtue of process issued upon any judgment obtained against him in an action founded upon actual force, or upon actual fraud or deceit, or in an action for a libel or slander, malicious prosecution or conspiracy, or in an action for seduction, or criminal conversation, where the damages found by the jury shall exceed the sum of one hundred dollars ; or if such petitioner shall be afterwards arrested by virtue of process issued upon any such judgment obtained against him previously to such order, he shall not be entitled to be discharged from such imprisonment or arrest, until he shall have been in actual confinement, during a term of at least sixty days."

On a question of bail, the court, it seems, will go into an inquiry whether another suit be depending for the same cause of action.(c)

The Circuit Court will not discharge a defendant on common bail, on the ground of want of jurisdiction, if the question be attended with doubts of law or fact, but will put the defendant to a plea in abatement.(d)

In the case of an arrest, where no cause of action is shown, the cause is still continued in court by the ordering of a common appearance ; but in attachments, the defendant being absent, cannot enter a common appearance, or give a warrant of attorney for that purpose : therefore, all that can be done, where no cause of action is shown, is to dissolve the attachment, which it is only in the power of the court, whence the writ issues, to do.(e)

Where a party undertakes, in an affidavit to hold to bail, to set forth the circumstances, he must do so with reasonable precision, though there might otherwise have been no necessity for him to do so.(f)

An affidavit to hold to bail, which does not name the defendant in its body, is bad: to describe him as the "said defendant" is not sufficient.(g)

In the Supreme Court at Nisi Prius, it is said that the court will not discharge on common bail for a mere interlineation in the affidavit,(h) though in the District Court, when the alteration is material, the practice is otherwise.(i)

(c) Clark v. Weldo, 4 Y. 206 ; vide ante, p. 259 ; Contra, Post et al. v. Sarmiento, 2 W. C. C. R. 198 ; Wh. Dig. "Bail."

(d) Wallace, 10.

(e) Vienne v. McCarty, 1 D. 155, n.

(f) Donahue v. Keller, D. C. C. P. 7 Leg. Int. 183.

(g) Smith v. Bible, D. C. C. P. Saturday, Sept. 21, 1850. Rule to show cause of action. Per curiam. The defendant is not named in the body of the affidavit. The style of the action is placed at the head, and the affidavit uses the words, "the said defendant" throughout. Now when the affidavit was sworn to and filed, there was no defendant. Perjury could not be assigned on such an affidavit. In England, if an affidavit to hold to bail is even entitled in a cause, it is bad, and the defendant discharged on common bail. Our practice is not so strict. But certainly the affidavit must name the defendant, and not refer merely to the title, which, at best, is surplusage. R. A.

(h) Sedgbeer v. Moore, S. C. N. P. 7 Leg. Int. 194 ; Bright. R. 197.

(i) Ohio Life Ins. Co. v. Folwell, Mss. act, 1849. Berry v. Carman, March 17, 1849. Rule to show cause of action. Per curiam. We adhere, after the fullest reflection, to the rule of practice which we have adopted and followed in some time past, that a material interlineation or erasure in an affidavit to hold to bail, not noted in the Jurat, is a sufficient reason to make the rule absolute. If one result of the practice should be to oblige the attorney to take

An affidavit sworn to more than a year before, is insufficient to hold to bail unless process had been taken out in time and continued.(*j*)

An affidavit averring that the defendant "did make use of the following false and scandalous words," and then proceeding not to set out the words, but to narrate the substance of them, has been held to be insufficient.(*k*)

An affidavit in trover that the defendant "hath possessed himself of divers goods and chattels of the plaintiff, of the value of $300, which he hath refused to deliver to the plaintiff, and hath converted to his own use," was held to be sufficient.(*l*)

An affidavit to hold to bail in an action for malicious prosecution before an alderman, which sets forth that the defendant, after the arrest, neglected to prosecute his suit, and that it was ended and determined, is insufficient; it must state what was the action of the alderman, and leave it to the court to say whether the suit was ended and determined.(*m*)

It is not necessary in an affidavit in trover to set forth that the cause of action accrued within six years.(*n*)

Where sufficient reasonable ground has been shown to bring a case before a jury, the court will not discharge a defendant on common bail.(*o*)

---

a little more time before issuing the *capias*, we do not know that that forms any objection to the rule. R. A.

(*j*) Carin *v.* Millington, 2 M. 267.

(*k*) Vanderslice *v.* Spear, 2 M. 392.

(*l*) Carey *v.* Henry, 2 M. 295.

(*m*) Walker *v.* Curran, D. C. C. P. 7 Leg. Int. 187.

(*n*) Young *v.* Wall, D. C. C. P. 7 Leg. Int. 98.

(*o*) Waters *v.* Collot *et al.*, 2 D. 247, S. C. 2 Y. 26; Parasset *v.* Gautier, C. C. 2 D. 330, in note.

The following cases in the District Court will be found of interest on this point:—

Gruninger *v.* Culbertson, *et al.*, Dec. 16, 1848. Rule to show cause of action. *Per curiam.* The affidavit sets forth a conspiracy to defame and destroy the reputation of plaintiff's wife, by accusing her of a want of chastity. If there was a conspiracy to accomplish this object by the means set forth in the affidavit, it certainly presents an aggravated case. That such an action lies, we have no doubt. The case of Mott *v.* Danforth (6 W. 304), establishes the general principle that an action on the case lies wherever the plaintiff is aggrieved or damnified by unlawful acts done by the defendants in pursuance of a combination or conspiracy for that purpose. It comprehends any confederacy to prejudice a third person. It is objected that the affidavit does not use the word *false* as applied to the con-

spiracy. Undoubtedly, the declaration in this action must aver the fact to be false and malicious. But it is sufficient if it appear upon the whole declaration taken together to be so. Thus, when the declaration was that the defendant *maliciously intending to defame the plaintiff, caused him to be indicted, and falsely deposed,* &c. (1 Leon. 108; 1 Com. Dig. 343. Action on the case for conspiracy. C. 3.) Applying this rule to the affidavit before us, it begins by the usual averment of chastity and innocence of the plaintiff's wife of the alleged crime, and avers that the defendants conspired and combined, *of their mere malice,* &c., and then that in pursuance of the said conspiracy, one of the defendants did *falsely,* maliciously, and without any reasonable or probable cause, accuse her, &c. We hold the affidavit therefore to be sufficient. Rule discharged.

Parke *v.* Bolivar, Jan. 20, 1849. Rule to show cause of action. *Per curiam.* This is an action for a breach of promise of marriage. The affidavit is defective in not stating any request by the plaintiff and refusal by the defendant to marry her. It is perfectly clear, that to support an action for a breach of promise of marriage, if the defendant has not married another, there must be evidence of an offer to marry on the part of the plaintiff, and a refusal by the defendant. Gough *v.* Farr, 2 Carr & P. 631. The affidavit before us avers that

As has been already observed, it is necessary that the affidavit should be positive. "To the best of deponent's knowledge and belief," &c., is not enough.(*p*)

"the defendant wishing to deceive this plaintiff, does now maliciously and falsely, and without any cause, refuse to marry this plaintiff, and declares that he never will marry her." We are not informed how, when, to whom, or under what circumstances, this declaration was, or rather is made (for the plaintiff, making use of a figure very allowable in fine writing, but not at all proper in an affidavit, has employed the present tense). Without a knowledge of the circumstances, it is impossible to say whether it is such as to dispense with the necessity of an offer. R. A.

Newall *v.* Stiles, Saturday, Feb. 2, 1850. Rule to show cause of action. *Per curiam.* This is an action of trover to recover damages for the conversion of a paper, belonging to defendants, purporting to be a certificate of the interest of plaintiff in the proceeds of certain lands, and which is alleged to be of the value of $5000. The affidavit states a demand and refusal, without adding the deponent's oath as to the fact of conversion. It is said in one part, that defendant has admitted the right of plaintiff, but upon demand refused to deliver it up, "and again, through his agent, deponent on the 23d day of November, 1849, demanded of said Stiles to deliver up to him possession of said certificate, but said Stiles refused to do so, pretending that he had sent it to some person in New York." Now, putting aside the question, whether it is sufficient to swear to a simple demand and refusal—that being mere evidence of conversion—and whether the *affiant* must not take upon himself to swear to the conversion, it is clear that there is here no unqualified refusal stated. The defendant gives as a reason for his refusal, that he was not in possession. It is true, the deponent goes on to allege *his belief* that this was untrue. But this is not sufficient in an affidavit to hold to bail, which, as to all material facts, must be direct and positive. Therefore, in Thynne *v.* Protheros (2 M. & S. 563), it was decided that an affidavit to hold to bail in trover, by the assignees of a bankrupt, stating that "the defendant possessed himself of the goods, which he refused to deliver, and has converted them to his own use, as appears by the bankrupt's books of account, and by the letters of S (the agent), and letters of the plaintiff, *as deponent believes*," was not sufficiently certain to show a conversion; and therefore the court discharged the defendant on common bail. R. A.

George *v.* Graham, Saturday, June 8, 1850. Rule to show cause of action. *Per curiam.* The affidavit is in trover. It alleges property in the plaintiff—that the defendant unlawfully and fraudulently possessed himself of the goods and converted them to his own use, and it states the value. This is all that is requisite to sustain the action. It is objected, that as the time is not stated, it does not appear that the cause of action accrued within six years. But this is a matter of defence, which must be specially set up, and may be replied to. Such a general affidavit as the one in question was the common practice in England, until the courts interfered by a general rule, 48 George III., which requires that the affidavit should fully set forth the circumstances under which the defendant has possessed himself of the goods, the particulars of which they consist, and the value, and in what manner the defendant has converted them to his own use. It will be a matter for the court to consider upon the propriety of framing and adopting such a rule, but without it we of course cannot inquire whether the affidavit is not itself consistent with a state of circumstances which if they appeared would, under the practice of the court now settled, deprive the plaintiff of the power to hold the defendant to bail. R. D.

(*p*) *Ante,* pp. 250, 289.

CHAPTER XII.

OF SPECIAL BAIL, AND BAIL UNDER THE ACT OF 1842.

ALTHOUGH this branch of practice has ceased, under the operation of the act of 1836, to be of the same prominent importance that it was before, yet, in some cases, even under that act, the whole of the old doctrine may become applicable, after an arrest. After stating the old practice, we shall proceed to consider when such cases may occur.

Bail to the action is either common or special. Common bail, in the strict English practice, are fictitious persons, as John Doe and Richard Roe, to whose keeping it is supposed that the defendant has been delivered, and are requisite in cases where special bail is not or cannot be demanded; and may be sometimes entered by the plaintiff himself, in order to effect the defendant's appearance in court, without which the plaintiff is not entitled to any judgment.(a) With us, in all cases where common bail is ordered by a judge, it is sufficient that the defendant subscribe a note to the prothonotary in these, or the like words: "I hereby empower the prothonotary to enter my appearance to this action," which must be attested by the sheriff or his officer. In other cases, the defendant, if not already in custody, may be compelled to put in bail to the action, unless the plaintiff elect to file common bail for him (in other words, to waive real bail altogether), to warrant further proceedings in the suit. Special bail are real and responsible persons, who undertake in a recognizance entered on the records of the court, that if the defendant be convicted, he shall satisfy the plaintiff, or render himself to the custody of the sheriff.(b) Where the defendant has been unsuccessful in an attempt to be discharged on common bail, upon a rule to show cause of action, in the manner described in the last chapter, or where the action requires bail of course, he must put in special bail within the time required by the practice of the court; and if it be not put in, or the defendant has not surrendered himself, and been accepted, in discharge of the bail-bond, or was not taken into custody on the arrest, the plaintiff may either file common bail for him, which is done in this State by simply accepting the defendant's appearance by an entry on record, and proceed to judgment against him, or may avail himself of the forfeiture of the condition of the bail-bond, and commence an action against the parties to it.

(a) Com. Dig. Pleader, B. 1; 6 Johns.   (b) Tidd's Pr. 244.
328; 12 Johns. 154.

SECTION I.

OF PUTTING IN AND JUSTIFYING SPECIAL BAIL.

We will now consider the cases in which the common law practice as to putting in and justifying special bail to the action may become applicable here, under some of the provisions of the act of 1836.(c) These provisions are contained in the 17th, 18th, and 19th sections.

If a defendant, arrested or detained on a *capias ad respondendum*, as aforesaid, shall not give bail as aforesaid, it shall be the duty of the sheriff to state the fact in his return, according to the practice now prevailing and allowed. § 17.

If the officer charged with the execution of such writ, shall make return that he has taken the body of the defendant in such writ, or that such defendant hath surrendered himself to his custody, he shall be chargeable to have the body of such defendant at the day of the return of such writ, in the manner heretofore practised. § 18.

It shall be lawful for any defendant committed to prison by virtue of any *capias ad respondendum*, or surrendered by his bail as aforesaid, to enter special bail to the action, in the manner now practised and allowed, at any time before final judgment obtained against him. § 19.

When the defendant has been arrested, and his case comes within the purview of the three preceding sections, that is, when he is in the sheriff's custody for want of bail, he may obtain his liberty, if he has not been discharged on a common appearance by order of a judge, or of the court, or exonerated by the insolvent act,(d) by putting in and perfecting special bail to the action, or bail above, so called in contradistinction to the sheriff's bail, or bail below. He is, however, considered in court while in prison.

Special bail, in this State, is only required to be one real and sub-

---

(c) The practice as to freehold is illustrated by the following case in the District Court of Philadelphia: Bidichimer *v.* Sterne, Saturday, June, 19, 1852. Why *capias* should not be quashed. *Per curiam.* The defendant's freehold has been clearly made out by the deeds and depositions. We have never required a defendant in these cases to deduce and prove title as in ejectment. Possession. under color of title, is, in general, all that has been required. As to the party on whom the onus of showing incumbrances devolves, it is settled by Hill *v.* Ramsey, 2 M. 342, that if the estate of freehold is within the jurisdiction of the court, the defendant need only show its existence and value; it then rests on the plaintiff, if he objects, to show an incumbrance ; but if the estate of freehold is in another county, the defendant must not only show its existence and value, but must produce evidence, by the usual certificates of search, of its being clear from incumbrances. R. A. with costs.

(d) King *v.* Bank, 2 R. 197. If the defendant, after being arrested and giving a bail-bond, is discharged by the insolvent act, then he need not enter special bail; the proper course is to enter a common appearance. In such case, the plaintiff cannot be subjected to delay, because he may enter judgment if there is no appearance, or demand a plea if there is. In this case, the court said that it was unnecessary to determine, " whether the name of an attorney in the margin of the docket, without an explicit minute among the docket entries, be such an appearance."

stantial person; his general qualification is, that he should be a house-keeper, or freeholder, and worth the amount in which the defendant is held to bail, after payment of all his debts. It is a rule of the courts, that no attorney of those, or any other court, shall be special bail in any action depending in them, without obtaining the leave of the court.(e) A person privileged from arrest (other than an *inhabitant* of this county) is objectionable as bail, on account of the difficulty of proceeding against him.(f) Foreigners are not admitted to be bail, merely in respect to property abroad, which is not liable to the process of the court ;(g) though it has been said, that this is not a sufficient objection without other auxiliary circumstances.(h) This is the practice as settled in England, but here it seems to be very different; for the prothonotary sometimes scruples to take bail domiciled in another county, and his rejection of such bail has been sanctioned by the District Court.

Special bail may be acknowledged before a judge of the court, or prothonotary of each court respectively, as is usually the case, or, in the Supreme Court, before such other commissioners of bail as that court may appoint.(i) We have already seen,(j) that the prothonotaries of the several courts within this commonwealth, have power to take bail in all actions in their respective courts.

If the plaintiff be not satisfied with the bail, he may except to him, and thereby compel a justification. When exception is taken to bail, such exception must be entered with the prothonotary, and also notice in writing given thereof to the defendant or his attorney. The filing of a declaration, though it be not marked *de bene esse, i. e.* conditionally, provided good bail be put in, or the bail already put in do justify,(k) is no waiver of bail by the practice of Pennsylvania.(l) The defendant cannot, by entering a rule for arbitration, deprive the plaintiff of special bail.(m) If the plaintiff take out a rule for arbitration, before special bail is entered, it is a waiver of bail; but the defendant has no right to enter a rule before he has put in bail. If he does, and obtains an award in his favor, the court will set it aside, unless the plaintiff consents to the proceedings of the arbitrators.(n) The former rule, that the defendant might arbitrate before special bail entered, though it was not to dispense with bail, is of course changed; inasmuch as he cannot now enter any rule at all.

The filing of a declaration is a waiver of exceptions to bail, but does not operate as a discharge of the bail.(nn)

When the bail already put in does not mean to justify, other should be added within the time allowed for justification; upon notice in writ-

---

(e) If a person, who is not permitted by these rules, which have been copied from the English rule, and which also exclude sheriff's officers, or other persons concerned in the execution of process, be put into the bail-piece, and not excepted to, can the plaintiff take an assignment of the bail-bond, and proceed upon it, as if no bail had been put in? In B. R. he cannot. Doug. Rep. 466, n. 1, 2 East, 181. In C. B. the bail are regarded as an absolute nullity, and no exception is necessary. 1 Bos. & P. 356; 2 Bos. & P. 49, 5641; Taunt. 162, 164.

(f) 4 Taunt. 249.
(g) 4 Burr. 2526; 4 M. & S. 371.
(h) 1 W. Blac. 444; 4 M. & S. 173.
(i) 2 Sm. Laws, 393.
(j) *Ante*, pp. 126, 127.
(k) Tidd's Pr. 261.
(l) Caton *v.* McCarty, 2 D. 141, S. C.; Caton *v.* McCarty, 1 Y. 103; see Blair *v.* Weaver, 11 S. & R. 85.
(m) Maas *v.* Sitesinger, 2 S. & R. 421.
(n) Nones *v.* Gelband, 11 S. & R. 9.
(nn) Commonwealth *v.* Heilman, 4 Barr, 455.

ing to the plaintiff, setting forth the residence and addition of the bail, proposed to be added or substituted, and if there be not time enough, the defendant's attorney may obtain an order for further time. If he intend to justify, it must be also upon written notice to the plaintiff, stating the time and place. The justification of bail is usually before the prothonotary. For the purpose of justifying, the bail, whether justifying before the prothonotary or in court, must appear personally, and may be examined *viva voce*, as to his sufficiency, by the opposite party. Where the sum is considerable, three or more bail may justify, and in different sums.(*o*) The court refused to permit affidavits to be read, containing sweeping attacks upon the characters of the bail, without stating any particulars to justify the imputations.(*p*)

SECTION II.

OF PROCEEDINGS AGAINST THE SHERIFF.

The responsibility of this officer, after taking bail on an arrest upon original process, ceases, as we have already seen,(*q*) provided he has complied with the injunction contained in the thirteenth section of the act of 1836, which declares, that it shall be the duty of every sheriff, taking bond as aforesaid, to give notice in writing of the names and places of residence of the bail to the plaintiff in the action, his agent or attorney, if the plaintiff shall not except to the bail within the time allowed for that purpose; or if upon exception made, other bail shall justify, to the satisfaction of the court, or of the commissioner authorized for the purpose; or if upon such exception other bail shall be added or substituted, and justify as aforesaid.

It will be recollected that by the fourteenth section of this act, the bail taken by the sheriff as aforesaid, may be excepted to by the plaintiff, his agent or attorney, at any time within twenty days after the return day of the writ, and notice given to him by the sheriff as aforesaid; and the bail so entered may justify, or new bail be added or substituted, and justify, within ten days after notice of the exception as aforesaid, according to the practice hitherto allowed with respect to special bail. It follows, that if the plaintiff have complied with the requisition of this section, and the second and third conditions of the sixteenth section are not performed, that the sheriff becomes responsible to him. How and when this responsibility is to be enforced, is not designated by the statute; neither is it stated whether the sheriff may retake, or surrender the defendant to prison, or whether the rejected bail may do it. It is, however, very certain that, unless sufficient bail be put in, or the defendant be in prison, there is no appearance to the action, and the plaintiff is prevented from going on to judgment. It would seem then, that the old practice, as far as analogous, must be resorted to; we will therefore endeavor to present a view of that practice, modified by the act of assembly in question.

When process against the body of the defendant has been issued and delivered to the sheriff, he is bound to cause the arrest to be made; and

(*o*) 1 Chit. Rep. 601.　　　　　　　(*q*) *Ante*, p. 285.
(*p*) Ibid. 676.

the day on which the writ is returnable is the latest period allowed for making the arrest.(r) If by any corrupt practice he omits to serve the writ, he is liable to an attachment, which will be awarded by the court, in which the writ is returnable, upon a bare suggestion, or its own knowledge. This, however, is altogether an unusual course in our practice. If the sheriff were known to have corruptly omitted to serve the writ, the remedy here would be by action.

If the sheriff make no return to the writ, he may be proceeded against by attachment, after being ruled to return the writ,(s) the object of this rule being to bring him into contempt. It is, however, the duty of the sheriff to return the writ without being ruled to do it; and in case of his neglect, the party is not confined to his remedy by attachment, but may, at his election, bring an action on the case for not returning it; to which the sheriff cannot plead that he had never been ruled to return it.(t) If the sheriff make a false return, that is, if he return *non est inventus*, to the writ, where he might have taken, but has neglected to take the defendant, he is liable to an action for a false return, at the suit of the plaintiff in the writ.(u) Should he refuse to arrest a defendant who claims privilege by reason of dignity, station, or other circumstance, the plaintiff may maintain an action against him, or rule him to return the writ: and in either case the question of the defendant's title to the privilege he claims, will be brought fully before the court.(v)

Where there has been no omission or neglect to arrest or to return the writ, but the sheriff has discharged the defendant without taking a bail-bond, or the latter has escaped from the sheriff's custody, without giving bail, it is a breach of his duty; for which he is answerable in an action for an escape.(w) In this action, if the escape were *involuntary*, evidence of the original defendant's circumstances or insolvency at the time of the escape, would be competent in order to show the extent of the plaintiff's actual loss,(x) and nominal damages may be given.(y) This doctrine applies only to escapes or false returns on mesne process and not on final.(z)

If there be no bail-bond, or if there be one, the bail, being excepted to, do not justify, the plaintiff proceeds to compel the sheriff to bring in the defendant's body. This course, however, can only be pursued, after the writ has been returned, and therefore, if the sheriff has not returned it, he must be ruled to do so.(a)

When a rule is taken against the sheriff to return the writ, a copy of the rule, which is obtained on motion of counsel, must be served on the sheriff or one of his deputies or officers. The sheriff must return the writ on or before the day on which the rule expires, otherwise the plaintiff may move for an attachment the day following.(b) The sheriff's return to a writ of *capias ad respondendum* is, either that the defendant

---

(r) 9 Johns. 117; 2 Burr. 812; 1 T. R. 191.

　(s) See 2 Saund. 61, e.
　(t) 15 Johns. 456.
　(u) 1 Esp. Rep. 475.
　(v) 1 Arch. Pr. 140.
　(w) 2 Saund. 61, c.
　(x) Huron et al. v. Proctor, Sup. C.

1787; MS. See also Kauffelt v. Treichtler, 7 S. & R. 278; 2 Bay's S. C. Rep. 395; 10 Mass. 470; 7 Johns. 189.

　(y) 10 Mass. 470; and see 2 Mass. 526; 7 Johns. 189.
　(z) *Sed vide* 11 Mass. 207.
　(a) 3 Bl. Com. 291.
　(b) 1 Arch. Pr. 95.

is not found in his bailiwick, or if he has taken him, and let him to bail, *cepi corpus;* or if in custody, *cepi corpus in custodia;* or, *committitur:* or he may return that the defendant was sick, *languidus;* or dead, *mortuus;* or that he had been rescued.(*c*) When the time limited by the rule has expired, it is expedient to examine in the prothonotary's office whether it has been returned. If the sheriff have returned that he has taken the body and holds it ready, and no bail be yet put in, the sheriff may be ruled to bring in the body.(*d*)

But if on examination at the office, it appears that the sheriff has not returned the writ, the court may be moved for an attachment against him. If the rule to return the writ expire in term, it has been just seen that the motion for the attachment may be made on the day following; if on the last day of the term, then, on that day, at the rising of the court.(*e*) This attachment is moved for, upon an affidavit stating a personal service of a copy of the rule, and that the writ has not been filed.(*f*)

The informal return "served and delivered to court," is in substance the formal return in the English practice where the prisoner is not too sick to be removed. It would seem that it is better than the one established by our practice, although loosely worded, and is sufficient in case of an escape to fix the sheriff's sureties.(*g*)

The sheriff, having arrested the party, and let him go at large on bail, must return *cepi corpus,* and if bail above be not put in, and perfected, the next step for the plaintiff to take is to rule the sheriff to bring in the body.(*h*) The object of this rule is to compel the sheriff, when the defendant is at large, to put in and perfect bail above.(*i*) It may be taken out on the day the sheriff returns the writ, provided the time for putting in bail have then expired;(*j*) but not before the time for putting in bail has expired.(*k*)

The sheriff being thus called upon to bring in the body, must either bring it into court (that is, show that it is in his custody), or put in bail above, within the time allowed him by the rule. This bail may immediately take the defendant and render him in their discharge,(*l*) without justifying.(*m*) If the rule expire, the sheriff is considered as in contempt, and the court will, on an affidavit of the service of the rule, and that no bail has been put in, grant an attachment against him. But he has the whole of the day, on which the rule to bring in the body expires, to bring it in, therefore the contempt is not incurred till that day be past, and of course an attachment cannot be moved for until the next day.(*n*)

If the sheriff be called upon in due time (that is, whilst in office, or within two years after the termination of his office),(*o*) to bring in the body, and neglect to do so, he is liable to an attachment; or to a *distringas;* the proceeding in which is regulated by the eighth section of the act of 1803,(*p*) which declares, that "whereas the process by *dis-*

(*c*) 6 Bac. Abr. 180.
(*d*) 1 Arch. Pr. 95.
(*e*) 11 East, 591.
(*f*) 1 Arch. Pr. 95.
(*g*) Beale *v.* Com., 7 W. 187.
(*h*) 2 Saund. 61, e.
(*i*) Ibid.

(*j*) 4 M. & S. 427; *contra*, 5 T. R. 479; 2 East, 241.
(*k*) 8 East, 525; 2 H. Bl. 276.
(*l*) Peake, 169.
(*m*) 7 T. R. 527.
(*n*) 2 Saund. 61, e.
(*o*) Act of 1822, 7 Sm. Laws, 55.
(*p*) 4 Sm. Laws, 45.

tringas is dilatory and expensive, and it is necessary to provide some adequate remedy therein, to prevent the delays of sheriffs and others in the duties of their respective offices," it is enacted: "That the court out of which any writ of *distringas vice-comitem*, or *distringas nuper vice-comitem*, or other writ of *distringas*, proceeds, may, by a rule for that purpose made, order and direct that the issues levied from time to time shall be sold, and the money arising thereby be applied in the first instance to pay such costs to the plaintiff, as the said court shall think just, under all the circumstances, to order, and have the remainder thereof in court to be retained until the defendant shall have appeared, or other purpose of the writ answered, or to be rendered to the plaintiff for his debt, damages, and costs where the same shall be ascertained. *Provided*, That where the purpose of writ is answered, the said issues shall be returned, or if sold, what shall remain of the money arising by such sale shall be returned to the party distrained upon."

The attachment, either for not returning the writ, or not bringing in the body, is a criminal process, directed to the coroner, when it issues against the present sheriff; or when against the late one, to his successor,(*q*) commanding him to attach the sheriff. The proceeding by attachment against the sheriff is more usual than by *distringas*.

The sheriff cannot be discharged from the attachment for not bringing in the body, but upon the payment of the whole debt and costs;(*r*) neither can he be relieved on the ground of the defendant's death, after the contempt was incurred, and before the attachment issued.(*s*) But he is not liable beyond the penalty of the bail-bond.(*t*) It is incumbent on the plaintiff to pursue his remedy against the sheriff within a reasonable time after the defendant's neglect to enter bail, otherwise it may be lost by delay.(*u*) So, if an attachment be granted, the writ must be sued out within a reasonable time, or the sheriff is discharged.(*v*)

The proceedings against the sheriff may be stayed upon terms, in order to let in a trial of the merits; these terms vary with the circumstances.(*w*) If the plaintiff has not lost a trial, the practice of the English courts is, to set aside the proceedings upon putting in and perfecting bail above, and payment of costs.(*x*) But if a trial have been lost, they further require that the attachment shall remain in the office, and stand as a security for the sum recovered, in case the plaintiff should obtain judgment.(*y*) If the application be made on the behalf of the defendant, it is necessary that there should be an affidavit of merits; or if made by the sheriff or the bail, though it cannot be expected that they should swear to merits, they require an affidavit that the application originated from them, and was not made in collusion with, or on indemnity from the defendant in the cause.(*z*) But upon setting aside a regular attachment, upon payment of costs, the question, whether or not the attachment shall stand as security, depending upon the fact, whether a trial has been lost; it is for the plaintiff who seeks to qualify the rule, to

(*q*) 1 Sellon, 201.
(*r*) 2 Saund. 61, f.
(*s*) 3 T. R. 133.
(*t*) 3 East, 604.
(*u*) 1 Taunt. 111; 9 East, 468; 1 Dunl. Pr. 197.

(*v*) 3 B. & P. 151; 9 East, 468.
(*w*) 1 Dunl. Pr. 198.
(*x*) 4 T. R. 352; 2 H. Bl. 235.
(*y*) 4 T. R. 352.
(*z*) 2 Saund. 61, f; 1 New Rep. 123.

show by his affidavit the necessary facts which may entitle him so to do; such as the date of the delivery of the declaration.(*a*)

Where the sheriff has been guilty of a breach of duty, in discharging the defendant from custody, without the plaintiff's assent, upon his own undertaking to appear and put in bail, instead of taking a bail-bond, the court will not assist him, by staying the proceedings in an action for an escape, or by setting aside the attachment.(*b*)   The sheriff, after being obliged to pay the debt and costs, may put the bail-bond in suit against the bail; though in general he is reimbursed by his officer, and the latter then brings the action in the sheriff's name.(*c*)

SECTION III.

OF THE LIABILITY OF SPECIAL BAIL AND BAIL UNDER THE ACT OF 1842 UPON THEIR BOND, AND HOW EXONERATED.

Under the act of 1836, the bond to be taken by the sheriff on an arrest seems, in its nature, to be similar to a recognizance of special bail, though it combines some of the qualities of a bail-bond, as far as relates to the sheriff.   For the sake of perspicuity we will here again introduce the particular section alluded to:—

The bond to be taken by the officer as aforesaid shall be in the name of the commonwealth, and in the amount of the bail demanded; and the condition thereof shall be, that if the defendant therein named shall be condemned in the action, at the suit of the plaintiff, he shall satisfy the condemnation money and costs, or surrender himself into the custody of the sheriff of the county, or, in default thereof, that the bail will do so for him, and such bond shall be for the use of the plaintiff in the action, or of the sheriff or other officer as the case may be.   § 10.

Yet, though such *appears* to be the double nature and quality of the form of bail-bond prescribed by the statute, it is nowhere declared in it, whether, how, or when, the bail is relievable, in default of the defendant's voluntarily surrendering himself or in case of his absence or concealment.   Consequently, if the bail be entitled to the same privileges, rights, or relief, that bail to the action formerly were, such a doctrine must exist solely by implication.   If, however, there could be any doubts on the subject, they would be removed by a consideration of the case of Kelly *v.* Stepney,(*d*) in which it was held, that, from the nature and terms of an insolvent bond, a surrender of the principal before the day of appearance would not exonerate the bail from his obligation. The language of the chief justice, who delivered the opinion of the court, was as follows: "It is supposed that there is something *inherent* in the relation which entitles bail to an *exoneretur*, having surrendered the principal at any time before they are fixed.   The recognizance of special bail has, indeed, that peculiarity.   Being moulded by practice into a contract of indemnity, the bail, who have become keepers of the prin-

(*a*) 5 Taunt. 606.   (*c*) 2 Saund. 61, f.
(*b*) 7 T. R. 236.   (*d*) 4 W. 69.

cipal by the delivery of his person to them, as the name imports, are relievable from their undertaking by restoring the plaintiff to the advantages he would have had if the defendant had remained in prison. But there is no discretionary power, anywhere, to relieve against the contract of one whose responsibility has been incurred, not by an engagement to the court attended with peculiar incidents, but by an obligation on conditions prescribed by a statute; in which the party who undertakes for performance by the principal is but a surety, and not bail in the proper sense of the word. The condition of a bail-bond to the sheriff would require performance as strictly as does the condition of any other obligation, did not the 4 Anne, c. 16, § 20, authorize the court to give such relief by a rule 'in the nature and effect of a defeasance,' as justice and reason may require—a provision engrafted on our act of 1772, in order to enable the courts to grant the like relief against the forfeiture of a replevin bond. Now, that bail to the sheriff, as they are improperly called, are not keepers of the defendant's person, is proved by the means to which they resort to put off their responsibility; they become special bail to perform the condition of their bond, and they surrendered him on the new authority of a bail-piece to perform the condition of their recognizance, a circuity which would be superfluous if they might surrender him directly in performance of the bond. But were the surety even the keeper of his insolvent principal, it would seldom be in his power to restore the parties to their original footing, as at least a part of the object of a commitment in execution would be frustrated. The purpose of it being satisfaction, and not security for the debtor's appearance at a day certain, he would gain an advantage by the temporary liberation of his person, which is certainly not the end designed to be accomplished by the proceeding, and for which the debtor would be without compensation."

Supposing, then, that the old practice as to the fixing and exoneration of bail for appearance to the action is still applicable, we will proceed to a review of it, with this preliminary remark, that a notice of the law as to writs of *scire facias* on recognizances of special bail is incidentally indispensable.

The bail is liable for the sum recovered by the plaintiff, with the costs of suit; and if the plaintiff, after judgment, fail in obtaining satisfaction from the principal, he may resort to the bail, by instituting an action of debt on his bond; but still, the latter may have recourse to the alternative of his undertaking, and exonerate himself by the surrender of his principal within the period established by the practice of the courts.

The defendant may render himself, or be rendered in the bail's discharge, before or after judgment,(e) until the latter has become fixed in law, and within a certain time thereafter, allowed him, *ex gratia*, that is, by the favor of the court.

A surrender is made *of right*, before the return of a *capias ad satisfaciendum* against the principal, but on a surrender after its return, the bail is only relievable on motion.(f) When the ca. sa. is returned *non est inventus*, the condition of the recognizance is broken, and the bail is fixed in law, though further time, as just mentioned, is allowed

(e) 1 Str. 198.

(f) 1 L. Ray. 156; Salk. 101, pl. 13; 1 Dunl. Pr. 201.

him, *ex gratia*, by the practice of the courts. But he is so far fixed that he remains liable, unless the body of the principal is surrendered within that time. If the principal die there is no relief.(*g*) But if he become entitled, by the benefit of the insolvent law, to a discharge on the *ca. sa.*, an *exoneretur* will be entered without an actual surrender by the bail, on application at any time before the return of the *scire facias* against him.(*h*) The plaintiff cannot proceed against the bail without previ. ously issuing an execution against the defendant in the original suit,(*i*) and delivering it to the sheriff, so as to lie in his office at least for four days prior to the return day.(*j*) In the courts of Common Pleas of this State, on an appeal from a justice, the bail has until the first day of the next term after judgment to surrender the principal; in default of which a *scire facias* is in practice issued, without an execution previously had against the principal (*k*)

Bail may surrender their principal to the District Court at any time within fourteen days after the service of the writ upon them.(*l*)

The service of a bail-piece may be deputed, or one of two bail may depute the other to serve it.(*m*) Whilst in arrest under it, he cannot be taken out of custody by civil process here while on his way for surrender in another State.(*n*) Of course, if in custody here *previously*, he cannot be delivered to such bail, but must abide his previous arrest.(*o*)

Where the bail to the sheriff entered special bail, it was held that he was entitled to surrender the principal before the return of the writ in the suit against him, on the bail-bond, although he had failed to justify as special bail.(*p*)

Special bail are bound to surrender all the defendants.(*q*)

Where a court, after fixing bail at a particular grade, by a subsequent order reduces it, the latter order is the only one which can be recognized as obligatory.(*r*)

The bail is discharged by the discharge of the principal under bail-piece, though erroneously,(*s*) and when such discharge is in bankruptcy the bail is consequently entitled to an *exoneretur*.(*t*)

(*g*) 12 Wheat. 604.

(*h*) Boggs *v.* Teackle, 5 Bin. 332, 338.

(*i*) In the State of New York, by a statutory provision, it is made the duty of the sheriff to endeavor to serve such writ upon the defendant, notwithstanding any directions of the plaintiff to the contrary; 1 Dunl. Pr. 202; and this is said to have reference to the English practice, by which the sheriff is accustomed to return *non est inventus* to the *ca. sa.* merely by the direction of the plaintiff, without attempting to serve the writ; though, if the defendant were actually in the custody of the sheriff, he would not be justified in returning *non est*, and the return, and all the proceedings against the bail, would be set aside. 1 New Rep. 151; 2 M. & S. 238. In Pennsylvania, the English practice as to this does not seem to obtain, though there is no express law against it. But the sheriff is bound with sureties, "without delay and according to law, *well and truly* to serve and execute all writs and process to him directed."

(*j*) 13 East. 592; 16 Johns. 117.

(*k*) See act of 1810, § 5; 5 Sm. L. 161.

(*l*) Still *v.* Howard, 2 M. 274.

(*m*) Holsey *v.* Trevillo, 6 W. 402.

(*n*) Holsey *v.* Trevillo, 6 W. 402.

(*o*) Ibid.

(*p*) Stockton *v.* Throgmorton, 1 Bald. 148.

(*q*) Bombaugh *v.* Robinson, 1 W. & S. 159.

(*r*) Potts *v.* Fitch, 2 Barr, 173.

(*s*) Lopeman *v.* Henderson, 4 Barr, 232.

(*t*) Com. *v.* Huber, 5 P. L. J. 331.

If the principal is discharged before the bail is fixed, an *exoneretur* will be entered at any time.(*u*)

If by the terms of a recognizance the plaintiff has a right to demand the surrender of all the defendants, the bail is answerable for the non-production of any of them, as the sheriff would be when one escapes though the other remains in prison, because each body is a separate pledge for the debt. For the same reason, when one escapes from his bail, they are liable for the whole.(*v*)

The bail may, by the English practice, be proceeded against on his recognizance by action of debt, as well as by *scire facias*, and the time allowed him, *ex gratia*, for surrendering his principal, varies as the one or the other course is adopted.

If the plaintiff proceed against the bail, by action of debt, it is the settled practice in the king's bench in England, that he shall have eight entire days in full term after the return of the process against him, in which to surrender his principal;(*w*) and this he may do without any previous application to the court.(*x*) If there be not eight days in the term in which the writ is returnable, the deficiency is to be supplied from the next term,(*y*) so that the bail, in such case, will have all the intermediate vacation.(*z*)

When the surrender is made, and an *exoneretur* entered, the suit against the bail is not thereby put an end to, but he must apply to the court for a stay of proceedings, which will be only granted on payment of the costs of the action against him. If the bail, without surrendering his principal, apply for a stay of proceedings, it will only be granted on payment of the debt and costs in the original action, and of the costs in the action on the recognizance.(*a*) When he has paid the debt, with his own funds, without action, and the judgment against the principal has been assigned to third persons, at the request of the bail, the court will not, against his wish, at the instance of the principal, order an *exoneretur* on the bail-piece before the principal has been taken.(*b*)

When the proceeding against the bail is by *scire facias* on the recognizance (which, in this State, before the act of 1836, was almost the only process used against special bail), the writ is issued commanding him to show cause why the plaintiff should not have execution against him for his debt and damages, and on such writ, if he show no sufficient cause, or the defendant does not surrender himself on the day of the return, or of showing cause, the plaintiff may have judgment against the bail, and take out a *ca. sa.* or other process of execution against him.(*c*) In practice, the bail may surrender *ex gratia*, at any time before the rising of the court, on the appearance day, or *quarto die post* of the return of the second *sci. fa.*,(*d*) or of the first, where *scire feci* is returned, and not after.(*dd*) If the principal be in court within the four days ready to be surrendered, and the court, on a rule to show cause why he should

(*u*) Kelly *v*. Com. 9 W. 43.
(*v*) Bombaugh *v*. Robinson, 1 W. & S. 159.
(*w*) Ld. Ray. 721; 6 Mod. 132; 8 Mod. 340.
(*x*) 1 Dunl. Pr. 204.
(*y*) Ld. Ray. 721.
(*z*) 1 Dunl. Pr. 204. For the cases, when the time for surrendering the Principal, will, on application, be enlarged, see 1 Dunl. Pr. 205, 206.
(*a*) 5 T. R. 363.
(*b*) Kesland *v*. Medford, 1 Bin. 497.
(*c*) 3 Bl. Com. 417.
(*d*) 1 Arch. Pr. 284.
(*dd*) McClurg *v*. Bowers, 9 S. & R. 24.

not be surrendered, hold the matter under advisement, without committing the principal, he may be surrendered when the court make the rule absolute, although the four days have expired.(e)

The defendant, if at large, may come and surrender himself, or he may be surrendered by his bail, and if he will not voluntarily submit to be surrendered, the bail may arrest and take him *at any time, and in any place,* for the purpose of rendering him. Thus, bail in a suit entered in another State, may seize and take the principal in this State, by virtue of a bail-piece,(f) and he may depute his power to another, to take and surrender the principal;(g) and in case of the death of the bail, his executor or administrator may make the surrender.(h) Bail may take up his principal when attending court as a suitor, or at any other time.(i) Where the defendant is in custody on a charge of felony, a writ of *habeas corpus* will be allowed returnable immediately, and the defendant having been brought up, and surrendered, the court will order an *exoneretur* to be entered on the bail-piece, and then remand him.(j) But in general, when the defendant is in prison, it does not appear to be necessary to bring him up on a *habeas corpus,* and the sheriff's acknowledgment of his being in custody is sufficient.(k) If the defendant obtain his discharge under an insolvent law, before the bail is completely fixed, the court will order an *exoneretur* to be entered on payment of costs (of the *sci. fa.* and not of the original suit),(l) without the formality of a surrender, to avoid the unnecessary circuity of surrendering a person who would be immediately entitled to his liberation.(m) The discharge of an insolvent debtor, by the proper court, is *prima facie* evidence of the service of notices on his creditors, in a *scire facias* against the bail, but the evidence may be repelled by other proof.(n)

Where on a citation to show cause of action, &c., the defendant had been ordered to be discharged on common bail, but before the citation, and without the knowledge of the defendant, the bail to the sheriff had entered special bail, the court, at the instance of the defendant, ordered an *exoneretur* to be entered.(o)

The bail having taken out a bail-piece, and arrested his principal, may commit him at once to prison—from the keeper of which he will obtain a certificate of surrender, which will authorize the entry of an *exoneretur* on the bail-piece. Until an *exoneretur* be entered, the surrender is incomplete, and the bail is not discharged.(p)

One of the conditions of the recognizance being, that the defendant shall surrender himself to prison, if he be arrested on a *ca. sa.* the condition is strictly complied with, and the bail is discharged from responsibility; and where he is discharged by the taking of the defendant in the execution, it is not usual nor necessary to enter an *exoneretur* on the bail-piece.(q) If the principal die before the return of the *ca. sa.,*

(e) Ibid.
(f) Res. v. The Jailer of the City and County of Philadelphia, 2 Y. 263; 7 Johns. 145.
(g) 1 Johns. Cas. 413; 3 Taunt. 425. In the third section of the Fee-bill, 7 Rev. Laws, 369, seventy-five cents are allowed the sheriff for executing a bail-piece.
(h) 7 Johns. 153; 7 Mass. 169.

(i) Broome v. Hurst, 4 Y. 123.
(j) 3 Burr. 1875; 2 Johns. 482.
(k) 1 Dunl. Pr. 209.
(l) Boggs v. Banker, 5 Bin. 507.
(m) 1 Dunl. Pr. 209; Boggs v. Teackle, 5 Bin. 332, 338.
(n) 4 Y. 352.
(o) Myers v. Young, 2 D. 79.
(p) Salk. 98, pl. 3; 8 Mod. Rep. 281.
(q) 1 Dunl. Pr. 214.

the bail is also discharged; but afterwards he takes the risk of his death.(r) He is not discharged on the ground of the insanity of his principal, and that he is confined in a hospital;(s) though he may have a *habeas corpus* to bring up the principal, notwithstanding his lunacy, in order to surrender him in the bail's discharge.(t)

A discharge of a party by the court, from arrest, on a bail-piece, is conclusive in an action against the bail, however erroneous may be the reasons for the order. It may be pleaded to the *sci. fa.* against the bail, or an *exoneretur* may be entered on the bail-piece.(u)

Bail sued on the bail-bond, cannot defend upon the ground that the *ca. sa.* was not issued and delivered to the sheriff four days before the return of the writ. To avail themselves of the circumstance they must move to quash the writ against them.(v)

In debt upon recognizance of bail, there was a plea of *nul tiel* record; but no declaration or replication, and the docket entry was merely "Judgment for plaintiff, sum due liquidated at," &c. The judgment was affirmed.(w)

On a *scire facias* against bail, to enable the defendant to take advantage of the fact that no *ca. sa.* had issued against the principal, he must plead the fact; but if evidence be given without such plea, and without objection, and the court err in their opinion upon the effect of that evidence, the judgment will be reversed.(x)

The plea of *nul tiel* record to a *sci. fa. sur* recognizance of bail, puts in issue only the recognizance. If there be a variance between the recital of the original action and the record, it ought to be specially pleaded, and the same rule applies to the defence.(z) It is on the same principle that it is held that it must be specially pleaded that the *scire facias* issued before the stay of execution was out.(a)

Where a *scire facias* on a recognizance stated that the recognizance was acknowledged on the second of March, and the recognizance stated that it was dated and acknowledged in February, and the prothonotary's docket stated that it was acknowledged on the 2d of March, it was held that the variance was not material.(b)

Parol evidence may be received in an action on a recognizance under the act of July 12, 1842, section 33, to the effect that the defendant had goods at the time the recognizance was entered into.(c)

In an action on a bond given in accordance with the provisions of the act of 1842, abolishing imprisonment for debt, an omission in the bond which is in ease of the obligor, does not make it void; nor is such bond void because the penalty exceeds double the amount of the plaintiff's claim.(d)

Where bond has been given with surety, in accordance to the 27th section of the act of 1842, it is not necessary to pursue the principal, and fix his liability before action brought against the surety.(e)

A nonsuit granted by a justice of the peace in an attachment under

(r) Boggs v. Teackle, 5 Bin. 322.
(s) 6 T. R. 133 ; 2 W. C. C. R. 464.
(t) 3 B. & P. 550.
(u) Lopeman v. Henderson, 4 Barr, 231.
(v) Rodney v. Hoskins, 2 M. 465.
(w) Glenn v. Copeland, 2 W. & S. 261.

(x) Brotherline v. Mallory, 8 W. 132.
(z) Cooper v. Gray, 10 W. 440.
(a) Ibid.
(b) Ibid.
(c) Hallowell v. Williams, 4 Barr, 339.
(d) Hibbs v. Blair, 2 H. 413.
(e) Ibid.

the act of 1842, unappealed from, is conclusive, so as to create a forfeiture of the bond given therein.(*f*)

A stranger's levying on and selling property covered by a recognizance under the 33d section of the act, does not relieve the recognizor.(*g*)

Bail for stay of execution under this act, is bound to account for the goods of the defendant, after the expiration of the stay, as against all the world.(*h*)

In a suit against the surety in a bond, given in an attachment before a justice, under the act of 1842, by the defendant in the attachment, on a breach of the conditions, evidence that the latter obtained credit from the plaintiff in the attachment, on false representations, and had confessed judgments to other creditors than the attachment creditor, and had requested them to issue execution, is irrelevant.(*i*)

Under the act of 1842, the bond to appear on a warrant of arrest, is well taken in the name of the judge.(*j*)

The act of 1842 requires the defendant, in a warrant of arrest, to give bond to appear; but not to appear, answer, and abide the decision. If he appears on the day fixed, it is enough: in case of a second adjournment, there should be a second bond.(*k*)

The entry of security to obtain a stay of execution under the act of assembly, operates as a discharge of a recognizance of special bail.(*l*) So, if the plaintiff take a confession of judgment for payment by instalments, if any instalment is postponed to a later day than the time in which, with diligence, he could have obtained a judgment and execution, he discharges the special bail.(*m*) So, if the defendant be ordered out of the country; or be banished, or transported for crimes. Or if he become a member of the [legislature], or be sent abroad by the government in their service, and there detained, so that he could not be rendered, this would be held sufficient to discharge the bail; " because the bail only engaged for the principal in the then situation of the parties."(*n*)

No one shall suffer by a mistake of the officer of the court : therefore bail was relieved on payment of costs of the *scire facias,* where the principal offered to surrender himself in due time, but was prevented by the *scire facias* being entered as of a prior term.(*o*)

If a *fi. fa.* be issued by the plaintiff, on the judgment against the principal, he is not precluded from afterwards resorting to the bail, even though part of the debt be levied.(*p*) It is from the date of the judgment against the bail, on his recognizance that his lands are bound, and not from the caption of the recognizance.(*q*) But a recognizance of bail, where the bail was *fixed* for the debt in his lifetime, was entitled to a preference in the order of payment over bond and simple contract debts, under the act of 1794.(*r*) This preference, however, was abrogated by a recent act of assembly. If the bail have no property, the plaintiff may elect to proceed against his body ; but if that be taken in

(*f*) Ibid.
(*g*) Lerch *v.* Stichter, 1 H. 86.
(*h*) Id. 89.
(*i*) Hibbs *v.* Blair, 2 H. 413.
(*j*) McClelland *v.* Smith, 2 J. 303.
(*k*) Ibid.
(*l*) Roup *v.* Waldhouer, 12 S. & R. 24.

(*m*) Ibid. 26.
(*n*) Ibid. 27–28; citing 1 Sel. Pr. 173.
(*o*) Hamilton *v.* Taylor, 3 Y. 389.
(*p*) 4 Johns, 407 ; 1 Dunl. Pr. 214.
(*q*) Campbell *v.* Richardson, 1 D. 131 ; Patterson *v.* Sample, 4 Y. 308.
(*r*) Dorsey *v.* Tunis, 4 Y. 93.

execution, the plaintiff can never afterwards proceed against the principal.(s)

The act of July 12, 1842, which abolished imprisonment for debt in all but a few excepted cases, abolished special bail in all but those cases, and consequently every recognizance with condition to surrender the body.(t) It did not, however, work the discharge of a bond previously executed to take the benefit of the insolvent laws.(u)

(s) 6 Johns, 97; 2 M. & S. 341.
(t) Beers v. West Branch Bank, 7 W. & S. 365. See Gillespie v. Hewlings, 2 Barr, 492; Kelley v. Henderson, 1 Barr, 495.
(u) Lilley v. Torbet, 8 W. & S. 89; M'Fadden v. Dilley, 2 Barr, 61.

CHAPTER XIII.

OF THE DECLARATION, AND OF THE STATEMENT UNDER THE ACT OF 1806.

THE defendant being in court, by entering his appearance, or by the filing of the bail-bond given to the sheriff, under the 12th section of the act of 1836, or as a prisoner, the next step is for the plaintiff to file his declaration, or, under the act of 21st March, 1806, § 5, a statement of his cause of action.

The declaration is a specification, in a methodical and legal form, of the circumstances which constitute the plaintiff's cause of action.(a) A description of its general requisites, or qualities, and of its nature and form, belongs properly to treatises on the science of pleading, and cannot be attempted in a work on practice, without swelling it to an inconvenient bulk; and after touching briefly upon one or two points of practice connected with the narr. generally, we shall proceed to the consideration of the statement.

A declaration, though filed after the rendition of judgment, is part of the record, and is admissible in evidence as such. An irregular practice exists in portions of the State of entering judgment by default without narr., and curing the defect by filing one subsequently. The Supreme Court, whilst censuring the practice, have said that such judgments are good, until reversed on error, and that the courts below are most competent to decide on the circumstances of each case, as to the allowance of amendments of their records.(b)

If the narr. contain several counts, and there is evidence to support any one of them, the Supreme Court will not reverse if the count on which judgment is rendered be good.(c)

If it contain the essentials of a good cause of action, it will be sufficient after verdict, although bad if objected to seasonably.(d)

In general, the declaration ought to state the agreement, where it is special; but where it has been so far performed that nothing remains but a mere duty to pay money, which it is for the plaintiff to show, a general count is all that is required.(e)

Where there is a doubt as to the character of an averment, immaterial in itself, in a declaration, whether it is so far connected with the cause of action as to make it necessary to be proved as laid, or whether it is

(a) 1 Chit. Plead. 278; 6 S. & R. 28.
(b) Corn v. Schaeffer, 9 W. 251.
(c) McCredy v. James, 6 Wh. 547.
(d) Irvine v. Bull, 7 W. 323.
(e) Bomeisler v. Dobson, 5 Wh. 405.

surplusage; it is best to class it with those subject to rejection as surplusage.(*f*) Immaterial matter, which must be proved, is that which enters into the foundation of the action, though the plaintiff might have succeeded without stating it. But if the matter introduced have no necessary connection with the action, and would be stricken out on motion, it is deemed impertinent, and need not be proved.(*g*)

Where the inference from the record is plain that both parties were heard, and judgment was given after argument, it will not be reversed because there was no declaration or replication to the plea. This rule is as applicable to an issue in law as to one of fact. The only remedy in such cases is an application to the court below to set the judgment aside.(*h*)

If the plaintiff files two narrs., the court may order him to elect which he will go to trial on, and if he refuses, they may continue the cause, or, on special demurrer, turn him out of court.(*i*)

A judgment for a greater sum than is declared for is erroneous.(*j*)

Where the defect in the narr. is title, and not a title defectively stated, the error is not cured by verdict, as in an action for taking illegal fees, where the narr. charges that he took other and greater fees than were allowed by the act, without averring the particular services for which he so overcharged.(*k*)

The general rule as to the use of the *videlicet*, appears to be, that it will save an immaterial description from becoming material.(*l*)

Where judgment was arrested below because no title to sue appeared in the narr. filed as a supposed copy of the original mislaid, but which was subsequently found, containing proper averments, the Supreme Court on error, treated the substituted narr. as a second count, and the verdict as a general one on both counts, and entered judgment on the original and sound count, being satisfied that the plaintiff's title had been proved upon the trial.(*m*)

In several districts of the State the bar have agreed on a rule recognized by the courts, that all appeals from justices shall be tried on a declaration for money had and received, which, however awkward where the first is in trespass, the Superior Court has sustained.

In other districts they are tried on the transcripts without any declaration, which the Superior Court have said is not quite so bad as the other rule. In neither case will exceptions lie to the pleading when taken there on error, and they can only decide them on the supposition that a suitable narr. and pleadings were filed.(*n*)

It is a general principle that a plaintiff cannot join in the same declaration a demand as executor or administrator with another which accrued in his own right; but if the money recovered in each of the counts will be assets, the counts may be joined.(*o*)

The action of a surviving partner being his own, a count for what

(*f*) Grubb *v*. The Mahoning Navigation Co., 2 H. 302.
(*g*) Id. 305. BELL, J.
(*h*) Glenn *v*. Copeland, 2 W. & S. 261.
(*i*) Gould *v*. Crawford, 2 Barr, 89.
(*j*) Dennison *v*. Leech, 9 Barr, 164.
(*k*) Valchternacht *v*. Watmough, 8 W. & S. 162.

(*l*) Moritz *v*. Melhorn, 1 H. 335. COULTER, J.
(*m*) Catherwood *v*. Kohn, 7 Barr, 393.
(*n*) Rundel *v*. Keeler, 7 W. 237. See, however, remarks of GIBSON, C. J., in Huffsmith *v*. Levering, 3 Wh. 110.
(*o*) Peries *v*. Aycinena, 3 W. & S. 64.

was at first a copartnership demand may be joined with another for the surviving partner's separate cause of action.(*p*)

The court will not give leave to file an additional count which would be bad on general demurrer.(*q*)

The plaintiff cannot be forced to elect as to which of the additional counts filed by him he will proceed on.(*r*)

The act of assembly authorizing a statement, it has been said, was intended by the legislature to enable suitors, if they should think proper, to conduct their causes, in plain cases, without the intervention of counsel. They have, therefore, so far from intending that a plaintiff should disclose his cause of action in a statement with the same nicety and precision of averment that is necessary in a declaration, only required the plaintiff to specify "the date of the promise, book account, penal, or single bill, and the whole amount that he may believe is justly due."(*s*) When a statement is filed in an action on a contract, if it follow the directions of the act, it is good, although the plaintiff does not state performance on his part,(*t*) or does not aver performance of precedent conditions; for that is implied by the very act of bringing suit for money that could not otherwise be demandable.(*u*)

If a statement within the meaning of this act be filed, and it set forth no cause of action, the plaintiff cannot recover,(*v*) though if it be merely too general,(*w*) or not sufficiently explicit to enable a defendant to meet a demand, the courts would, both before and since this act, direct a special statement of the items, or a bill of particulars to be filed; and this in matters of account was always done, if the party required it;(*x*) but when a *statement* alone does not contain a sufficiently accurate specification of the plaintiff's demand, the court would only compel him to file a more accurate and particular statement;(*y*) and would stay the proceedings until a proper statement was furnished,(*z*) for an imperfect statement is not to be scanned as minutely or examined as critically, as a declaration.(*a*) Yet, if it appear on the face of it, that the plaintiff has no cause of action at all, he cannot recover.(*b*)

In one case, it would seem that the statement ought to be full and certain, in order to insure the plaintiff a benefit under the act, to which he would not otherwise be so certainly entitled.(*c*) In a suit on a

---

(*p*) Davis *v.* Church, 1 W. & S. 242.

(*q*) Kensington Bank *v.* Patton.—District Court, Saturday, Sept. 16, 1848.—Why plaintiff should not have leave to file additional counts. *Per curiam.* The court are not compelled to allow a count to be filed which would clearly be bad on general demurrer. We think this is the case in the present instance. A promise to call and make some arrangements to pay a debt is not an absolute nor a conditional promise to pay, nor can it prevent the bar of the statute, as this court has already decided. How, then, can it be the ground of an action itself. It means merely that the defendant will take time to consider how much, when, and in what manner, he will pay the claim, which leaves everything—time, amount, and means of payment uncertain. Rule dismissed.

See generally, v. ii. "AMENDMENT."

(*r*) Frederick *v.* Gilbert, 8 Barr. 454.

(*s*) Boyd *v.* Gordon, 6 S. & R. 53; see Cook *v.* Gilbert, 8 S. & R. 567.

(*t*) Riddle *v.* Stevens, 2 S. & R. 537.

(*u*) Dixon *v.* Sturgeon, 6 S. & R. 28; Boyd *v.* Gordon, Ib. 54.

(*v*) Buck *v.* Nicholas, 8 S. & R. 316.

(*w*) 2 Br. 46.

(*x*) Brack. Law Mis. 461.

(*y*) 2 Br. 46.

(*z*) Girard *v.* Rhodes *et al.* D. C. Phila. Feb. 18, 1823, MS.

(*a*) Reed *v.* Pedan, 8 S. & R. 263.

(*b*) Buck *v.* Nicholas, 8 S. & R. 317.

(*c*) The following was decided to be a good form of statement, viz.:

A B *v.* C D & E F.

bond conditioned for the payment of money by instalments, judgment may be rendered for the penalty, notwithstanding the act directs judgment to be entered for the sum that is due. The reason is, that as the act comprehends a suit on such an obligation, and as there can be but one action brought upon it, the court, in entering judgment, must protect the party, and this could not be done without entering a judgment for the penalty: for if it be entered only for the instalment due, all further right of action would be gone, and the residue would be lost. The court would take care of the defendant, by requiring that their leave should be first asked to take out execution, and by letting him into a trial, if he alleged payment of subsequent instalments. But in addition to this, it would seem that the statement filed by the plaintiff should be in every respect certain and consistent with the obligation, spreading on the record the real nature of the obligation, and thus putting it out of his power to misuse the judgment for the penalty.(d)

The statement must, however, accord with the evidence, for a variance between them would be as fatal as a variance between a declaration and the evidence.(e) But the rule is not stricter in the former case than in the latter. Thus, if the plaintiff state an agreement, he must prove it. But whether he prove an agreement *express* or *implied*, is immaterial. For a declaration, in an action on an implied assumption, avers a positive assumption.(f) So also, the evidence, though agreeing with the statement, should not vary from the writ. But where the writ stated the plaintiff to be executor of A, who was a surviving obligee with B, it is no variance, though the statement describe the bond as given to A and B, executors of C, and the bond is in that form.(g) If the plaintiff set forth in his statement matters which are not necessary, he is not bound to prove them.(h)

A proceeding by declaration and statement in the same case is incongruous, but if a statement be filed with a declaration, the former can neither vitiate the latter, nor cure a defective title in it. But after verdict the statement might be rejected as surplusage.(i)

As the act directs a statement to be filed in suits "for the recovery of any debt founded on a verbal promise, book account, note, bond, penal or single bill," the demand must be included in one or other of the above expressions, and must be likewise of a *debt.*(j) It was said by TILGHMAN, C. J., in this case, that "these statements are less *certain*

The plaintiff's demand is founded on the assumption of the defendants, C D & E F, to pay the said plaintiff the sum of one thousand dollars, with interest from the 4th November, 1806. The said defendants then being indebted to the said plaintiff, for the like sum of one thousand dollars, before that time paid, laid out and expended, to the use of the defendants, by the said plaintiff, at the special instance and request of the said defendants, as well as for the like sum had and received by the defendants to the use of the plaintiff, one thousand dollars. Interest from the 4th of November, 1806. 3 S. & R. 402. In this case, the process was issued against both the defendants, but one was not summoned and did not appear.—See also 3 Pa. R. 391, another form held good.

(d) See Underwood v. Lilly, 10 S. & R. 100-1.

(e) Church v. Feterow, 2 Penns. Rep. 301.

(f) Slaymaker v. Gundacker's Executors, 10 S. & R. 83.

(g) Crotzer v. Russel, 9 S. & R. 78; see Graff v. Graybill, 1 Watts, 430.

(h) Sidwell v. Evans, 1 Pa. R. 383.

(i) Riddle v. The County of Bedford, 7 S. & R. 395; Ely v. Beaumont, 5 R. 124.

(j) Allen v. Irvin, 1 S. & R. 555.

than a declaration, and therefore not to be encouraged by an equitable construction of the act of assembly. As far as the legislature has thought proper to authorize them, the court is bound to support them. But it would be wrong to extend the law to cases not within its plain intent." If, however, the defendant accept a statement in such a case (which is good in point of form and matter), and proceed to issue upon it, the judgment will not be reversed for want of a declaration.(k) But the same judge afterwards took another view of the act, and decided that a statement may be admitted in the case of an *implied* promise, as well as an *express* one,(l) and therefore supported a statement that the plaintiff paid a sum of money as bail of the defendant, whence arose an implied assumption of the defendant to pay it.(m) A legacy is not among the cases enumerated in the act, nor is it founded on any kind of contract, and is therefore not within the meaning of the act.(n)

So, the cause of action on a due bill in these words: " On the 1st October next, due A. B. R. two bureaus at Carnahan's shop in Butler," is not the subject of a statement, because no certain *sum* can be alleged as the foundation of the judgment.(o) In this case, "the rule was laid down, that, to authorize the filing of a statement, the demand must be one not only of the description mentioned in the act, but must also be of such a nature, that a fixed and determinate sum may appear to be due with sufficient certainty; so that, if the defendant neglects to appear, the court may ascertain the amount without the intervention of a jury, and give judgment for such sum."(p) A note given for the payment of a certain amount of money in furniture or other specific articles, within a certain time, is the subject of a statement, when the day of delivery is past, and there has been no tender of the article.(q)

It seems that a statement is proper in an action of debt on a recognizance of bail in error.(r)

The act of 1806 is limited to suits for debt on verbal promise, book account, note, bond, penal or single bill, or all, or any of them ; and although construed liberally, yet a demand for rent, due on a lease, by a sealed instrument, is not comprised within the words of the act. The act embraces a class of debts simple in character, and plain in the evidence to prove them, and involving usually no more than the right to money, not nice complicated questions, to which the ancient mode of pleading is more appropriate.(s)

Nothing is indispensable to it which is not made so by the statute which substituted it for the declaration, and that requires no more to be specified than the date of the contract, and the amount supposed to be due by it. The terms must be set out intelligibly, so as to show an available cause of action; but performance of conditions precedent, and anything beyond defendant's engagement to pay, may be omitted.(t)

A statement may be filed in an action brought into court by appeal

(k) Id. Ibid.
(l) Thompson *v.* Gifford, 12 S. & R. 75.
(m) Ibid.
(n) Meals *v.* Wiley, 12 S. & R. 96.
(o) Roberts *v.* Beatty, 2 Pa. R. 63.
(p) Church *v.* Feterow, Id. 304.

(q) Ibid. See also Gray *v.* Cunningham, 17 S. & R. 425.
(r) Ibid. See Donohue *v.* Dougherty, 5 R. 124, as to a statement in an action on a penal statute.
(s) Lomis *v.* Ruetter, 9 W. 516.
(t) Snevily *v.* Jones, 9 W. 436.

from the judgment of a magistrate.(*u*)   And in one case, the transcript of a justice, which set forth that the plaintiffs demanded of the defendant $98, due on book account, was held to be a sufficient statement of the plaintiff's claim.(*v*)

When a statement is filed by the plaintiff, it appears not to be obligatory on the defendant to put in a counter-statement, within the meaning of the act of assembly; and it seems that he can plead, technically, to it, as he could to a declaration; it has also been said, in a recent case in error, that a plea of payment to a statement, with notice of the special matter, which special matter was proved at the trial without objection, would be considered as a counter-statement.(*w*)

The rules of pleading seem to apply to statements as well as to declarations.   Averments in the former may be admitted unless met by the form of the counter-statement; and on the other hand, the latter will not admit any facts not mentioned in the statement, by implication.(*x*)

Defects in statements may also be cured by a verdict.   Thus, a statement, in an action of *assumpsit*, which is defective for want of the date of the assumption, or of an averment of the consideration for it, is cured by a verdict.(*y*)   See also another case.(*z*)   It is agreed in this case that a statement may be demurred to, but it is at the same time intimated that, from the same scope for amendment under the act of 1806, a demurrer would be of little use.   This, of course, cannot apply to cases wherein the statement on its face shows no cause of action.

The statement under the act of 1806, may be filed as well by the attorney who institutes the action, as by the party who brings suit without his intervention.(*a*)

It has been seen that under the act of 1836, a declaration must be filed, if the defendant do not appear at the return day of the summons, before the plaintiff can take judgment by default; and to enable him to enter a rule to arbitrate, after the return of the writ, he must file a declaration previously to the rule.   Anterior to the act of 1820, § 3,(*b*) the plaintiff might have taken out a rule of reference after the entry of the suit on the prothonotary's docket, though before the service of the summons or capias;(*c*) and though it was not necessary, prior to that act, to file a declaration or statement before the rule to arbitrate, the plaintiff was at liberty to do so.(*d*)

The preceding observations may serve to show that there is nothing in this State to prevent the plaintiff from declaring before the return day of the writ, as in England, where he can in no case declare against the defendant until. then.(*e*)

The declaration must be filed in the office of the prothonotary of the court, and at the same time (an appearance having been effected), a rule may be entered that the defendant plead thereto, within the time specified by the rules of the respective courts, which are quoted in this chap-

(*u*) Thompson *v.* Gifford, 12 S. & R. 74.

(*v*) Holden *v.* Wiggins, 3 Pa. R. 469.

(*w*) Schlatter *v.* Etter, 13 S. & R. 36; see Graff *v.* Graybill, 1 W. 430.

(*x*) *Vide* Ibid.

(*y*) Ibid.

(*z*) Gray *v.* Cunningham, 17 S. & R. 424.

(*a*) 2 Browne, 40.

(*b*) 7 Sm. Laws, 323.

(*c*) Sadler *v.* Slobaugh, 3 S. & R. 387; Flanegan *v.* Negley, Id. 498.

(*d*) Buck *v.* Nicholas, 8 S. & R. 316.

(*e*) 1 Tidd, 421.

ter, after the service of notice of the rule; for, without such rule, the defendant cannot be compelled to answer.(*f*)

The following rules of the District Court are important in this connection:—

LXIII. In every case where the defendant's appearance is recorded, rules to declare and plead, and for other pleadings, may be entered in the prothonotary's office, at any time after the return day of the process, and on eight days' notice thereof in writing to the adverse party, or his, her, or their attorney on record; and on failure to declare, plead, or enter other pleadings accordingly, a judgment in the nature of a judgment by default, or *non pros.* may be entered, which judgment may be opened or set aside, at the discretion of the court, when deemed necessary for the purposes of justice.

Provided, the above rule is not to preclude the plaintiff or defendant, in special cases, from applying either to the court or a single judge, for enlarging the time to declare or plead, having first given reasonable notice in writing to the opposite party or attorney of the intended application.

LXXIV. The time of filing the declaration, pleas, replications, and all other pleadings and papers, shall be distinctly marked in the prothonotary's docket.

LXXIV½. Ordered, that in all suits hereafter to be instituted, a copy of the narr., and every subsequent pleading, shall be served by the party or his attorney filing the same, on the opposite party or his attorney, - of record; otherwise, such narr. or other pleading may be treated as a nullity: *Provided*, however, that it shall not be necessary to serve a copy of the narr. upon a defendant or defendants who have not appeared to the action.

If the papers in a cause are mislaid or lost, and cannot be found when the case is called for trial, they may be supplied by such copies, or other duly authenticated copies of the pleadings.(*g*)

Ordered, That notwithstanding no appearance may have been entered at the time of filing the declaration, no judgment for want of a plea shall be entered, unless a copy of the declaration has been served on the defendant or his attorney, with the rule to plead.(*h*)

If, on the appearance of the defendant, the plaintiff, being previously ruled to file a declaration, omit to declare against him, he is liable to be non-prossed, or have judgment signed against him for not prosecuting his suit. It is called a judgment of *non-pros.* from the words *non prosequitur*, &c., formerly used in entering it up. And this is said, by a writer on the English practice, to be the proper appellation of the judgment in actions by bill; but in actions by original, it is more commonly called a judgment of nonsuit, the language of the judgment being *non prosequitur breve vel sectam.*(*i*) In order to obtain this judgment, the defendant must, in the first place, as has been seen, rule the plaintiff to declare.

The court refused to take off a *non pros.* where a declaration was filed on the same day, but at a later hour than that on which the *non pros.* was signed.(*j*)

(*f*) Com. Dig. Pleader, E. 42.
(*g*) Adopted Dec. 29, 1849.
(*h*) Adopted Monday, March 4, 1850.
(*i*) Tidd, 470.
(*j*) 1 Br. 83.

The defendant might formerly have pleaded to the action, before any declaration had been filed, and then lay a rule for trial or *non-pros.*; and the court would enforce the *non pros.*, unless the plaintiff filed a declaration, joined issue, and put the cause on the trial-list, before the rule had expired, because all these things were necessary to bring the cause on to trial.(*k*)　But this practice is no longer adopted.

When a cause has been submitted to arbitration by one of the parties, under the act of 1810, all the rules that have been entered are suspended during the time the cause is actually before the arbitrators; but the moment it is brought into court again, by appeal, they are revived in the same manner and with the same efficacy and effect as if the case had never been arbitrated.(*l*)

A rule formerly prevailed in the courts, " that unless a declaration be filed in twelve months from the first day of the term, to which an action is brought, a *non pros.* shall be entered by the prothonotary as a matter of course, unless the parties otherwise agree by writing filed." In England, it is a general rule of law that a plaintiff must declare within twelve months after the return of the writ, or he will be out of court;(*m*) though it is otherwise as to the practice in this State.

If the plaintiff, after being ruled, neglect to declare in due time, and his default in not declaring be not set aside, the defendant may have his judgment of *non pros.* entered; upon which he may issue execution or maintain an action of debt to recover his costs.(*n*)　The cases in which judgments by default may be entered and will be opened, will be considered presently.

(*k*) Fitzgerald *v.* Caldwell, 2 D. 215; Galloway *v.* Saunders, 2 S. & R. 405.

(*l*) 1 Br. 141, 115; see McCall *v.* Crousillat, 2 S. & R. 167.

(*m*) 1 Sellon, 221; 2 T. R. 112; 3 T. R. 123; 5 T. R. 35; but see Davis *v.* Jones, 12 S. & R. 60.

(*n*) 1 Dunl. Pr. 303.

CHAPTER XIV.

OF JUDGMENT BY DEFAULT.

In the present chapter, we shall consider the subject of judgment by default, after appearance, which, in this State, is either for want of an affidavit of defence, by *non sum informatus*, where the defendant's attorney having appeared, says that he is not informed of any answer to be given to the action—or by *nil dicit*, where the defendant himself appears, but says nothing in bar or preclusion thereof.(*a*)

SECTION I.(*aa*)

JUDGMENT BY DEFAULT FOR WANT OF AN AFFIDAVIT OF DEFENCE.

No part of our system is more effective to the speedy administration than the one now to be considered. Its origin was an agreement of all the members of the bar in 1795, with the exception of two, that judgments should be confessed unless the defendant in the action made an affidavit, " that, to the best of his knowledge and belief, there was a just cause of defence to the action."(*b*)

After some time, the rules of the Supreme Court and Common Pleas embodied this agreement, thus rendering the practice compulsory. The power of the court to make the rule was contested, but sustained.(*c*)

After the establishment of the District Court, a similar rule was adopted there.

While a very large number of suits were thus terminated, it is obvious that two classes of cases, and they very extensive, were withdrawn from its operation. Those in which a supposed defence existed, and those in which a defendant, who might hesitate to misstate particular facts, saw but little risk under the vagueness and generality required by the rule.

To compel the defendant, against whom a *prima facie* obligation was shown, to exhibit, under oath, the facts on which he rested his defence, and allow the court to draw the legal conclusions, was very desirable, and was at length accorded by the legislature in 1835, to the District Court for the City and County of Philadelphia.

The system is so useful and so free from all objections, that it has

---

(*a*) Tidd. 587.
(*aa*) For this section, the publishers are indebted to R. C. McMurtrie, Esq.

(*b*) Vannatta *v.* Anderson, 3 Bin. 422.
(*c*) Id.

gradually been extended to embrace new subjects, to other counties and courts of the State.

The act of 1835, § 2, the first of the acts of assembly on the subject, provides that: " In all actions instituted in the said court on bills, notes, bonds, or other instruments of writing for the payment of money, and for the recovery of book debts, and in all actions of *scire facias* on judgments, and on liens of mechanics and material men, under the act of 17th of March, 1806, and the various supplements thereto, it shall be lawful for the plaintiff, on or at any time after the third Saturday succeeding the several return days hereinbefore designated, on motion, to enter a judgment by default, notwithstanding an appearance by attorney, unless the defendant shall previously have filed an affidavit of defence, stating therein the nature and character of the same: *Provided*, That in all such cases, no judgment shall be entered by virtue of this section, unless the said plaintiff shall, within two weeks after the return of original process, file in the office of the prothonotary of the court hereby erected a copy of the instrument of writing, book entries, record, or claim on which the action has been brought."

By the 14th section of the act of March 11th, 1836, it is declared: " That the provisions of the foregoing section shall be extended to all actions brought on contracts for the loan or advance of money, whether the same be reduced to writing or not: *Provided*, That in all such cases, no judgment shall be entered by virtue of this section unless the plaintiff shall, within two weeks after the return of the original process, file in the office of the prothonotary of said court an affidavit setting forth the terms of the said loan or advance, with the date thereof."

And the 1st section of the latter act provides, that "in all actions which have been or shall be brought in the said court upon any record remaining therein, it shall not be deemed or held to have been, or to be necessary for the plaintiff to file, in the office of the prothonotary of the said court, a copy of such record to enable him to enter judgment under the second section of the act to which this is a supplement, provided he shall have complied with the other requisitions of the said act."

By this act any one of the judges of the court is authorized to enter the judgment by default.

By the supplementary act of 1842, § 1, it was provided that the § 2 of the act of 1835, "shall be construed to embrace actions of *scire facias* on liens of mechanics and material men, under the act of June 16, 1836; and under any other act extending the provisions of the said last-mentioned act, and all former proceedings in said court, so far as they are founded on such construction, are hereby confirmed."

And by § 2, it is " declared to embrace all actions brought in said court, on bonds, or recognizances of bail in error, or bonds of sureties for stay of execution, and is hereby extended to all actions brought in the said court, on bonds or recognizances of special bail, or bonds given by debtors, and their sureties, with the condition prescribed in the sixth section of the act of the sixteenth of June, 1836, entitled, 'An act relating to insolvent debtors.' "

In any action of *scire facias* upon mortgage, it shall not be deemed necessary for the plaintiff to file in the office of the prothonotary of said court, a copy of the mortgage, to entitle him to enter judgment under the second section of the act to which this act is a supplement: *Pro_vided*, That the writ of *scire facias* shall contain a statement of the date of the recording of said mortgage: *And provided, also*, That the plaintiff shall have complied with the other requisitions of the said act. § 3.

Where the plaintiff in any action brought in said court, sues as assignee in fact or in law, of an instrument of writing for the payment of money, it shall not be deemed necessary for him to file in the office of the prothonotary of said court, a copy of any assignment of said instrument, in order to entitle him to enter judgment under the second section of the act to which this act is a supplement: *Provided*, That the plaintiff shall, within two weeks after the return day of the original process, have filed in the office of the prothonotary a sufficient declaration setting forth the grounds of the plaintiff's claim, and of the defendant's liability: *And provided, also*, That the plaintiff shall have complied with the other requisitions of the said act. § 4.

The provisions of these several acts are, by the act of 1846,(*d*) "extended to all actions brought, and appeals filed in the Court of Common Pleas, for the County of Philadelphia, wherever the cause of action would, in a like case, have authorized the entry of such judgment in said District Court: *Provided*, That the writing or affidavit to be filed by the plaintiff, to entitle him to such judgment, shall be filed within two weeks after the return day of the suit, or the first day of the term to which an appeal may be entered; and the affidavit of defence shall be made before the third Saturday succeeding such return day, or term day, as the case may require; and all writs of execution issued out of said Court of Common Pleas, shall be returnable to the first Monday of the next month, or the first day of the term, at the option of the party issuing the same."

By the 7th section of the act of 1842, establishing the present Nisi Prius Court, they are also extended to that court.

The act of 1851,(*e*) extended the system generally throughout the commonwealth.

But by the act of March 8, 1852, this is repealed.

By the 9th section of the act of 1851, the District Court is continued indefinitely, and the several acts of assembly relating thereto are continued until abolished.

The rules of court which preceded these statutes have now been repealed.

By the rules adopted since the acts of assembly, the court, on the hearing of a motion for judgment for want of a sufficient affidavit of defence, require to be furnished with copies of the instruments or affidavits on which judgment is asked, and also of the affidavit of defence. And by another rule, where the copy has not been filed within one week from the return day, but has been filed on the second week, forty-eight hours' written notice thereof is required to be given to the defendant, or his attorney, before the motion for judgment is made.

(*d*) P. L. p. 328.

(*e*) P. L. p. 307.

It is now proposed to consider: 1. What instruments or evidences of obligations are within the meaning of the various acts of assembly. 2. The parties who are subject to the acts or entitled to the benefits thereof. 3. The various conditions precedent, and the acts required from the defendant to avoid the judgment. 4. The general rules of construction applied to the affidavits, and the usage with respect to supplemental affidavits. 5. The time for filing copies, and in what cases they are dispensed with. 6. The effect of an affidavit of defence if it is sufficient to prevent a judgment by default.

The instruments or grounds of action on which the courts are authorized to grant this summary judgment are:—

1. *Bills* and *notes*, which include checks.(*f*) And it is settled that all the parties to such instruments are within the act, as well drawers of bills and checks and indorsers of notes as the acceptors and makers; and this, though they are but contingently liable, and the fact of dishonor and notice is not averred in the copy filed.(*g*) And the right to costs of protest follows where the form of the instrument renders it usual and proper, as where there is an indorser to be charged.(*h*) Bank bills and bank post notes are also included.(*i*) But there must appear a legal liability on the face of the instrument. Hence an indorsement on an instrument, not negotiable, is not within the act.(*j*)

2. *Bonds.*—By these are meant bonds for the payment of money absolutely, and not those coupled with a defeasance for the performing of any collateral act; hence a bail-bond is not included.(*k*) But this has been altered by statute; and now, by the act of 1842, section 2d, actions on bail-bonds, bonds for stay of execution, bonds by parties arrested to apply for the benefit of the insolvent law, are within the act. But by the present rule of construction, hereafter noticed, the act applies equally to bonds with a collateral condition.

3. *Other instruments in writing for the payment of money.*—Under this are included leases,(*l*) ground-rent deeds,(*m*) submission and award,(*n*) entries in a bank book,(*o*) recognizance of bail in error and *remittitur,*(*p*) records of judgment in another State, founded on an instrument which itself is within the act, a copy of which was there filed.(*q*) But a judgment by default in another State is not within the act.(*r*) Nor a judgment confessed by one partner in an action against those without their assent.(*s*)

By the practice of the District Court, the principle of McCleary v. Faber is confined to cases under exactly similar circumstances. It is not every judgment of another State that is within the meaning of the law. There must be an instrument within the meaning of the act upon the record, a copy of which is filed, to entitle the plaintiff to a judgment

(*f*) Walker v. Geisse, 4 Wh. 252; Hill v. Gaw, 4 Barr, 493.

(*g*) Sleeper v. Dougherty, 2 Wh. 177; Hall v. Bk. of the U. S. 6 Wh. 585; Bk. of the U. S. v. Thayer, 2 W. & S. 443.

(*h*) Ibid.

(*i*) Ibid.

(*j*) Patterson v. Poindexter, 6 W. & S. 227.

(*k*) Elkinton v. Bomeister, D. C. C. C. P. April 8, 1837.

(*l*) Dewey v. Depuy, 2 W. & S. 553.

(*m*) Watkins v. Phillips, 2 Wh. 210.

(*n*) Bayard v. Gillespie, 1 M. 256.

(*o*) Harley v. Caldwell, 2 M. 334.

(*p*) Baker v. Olwine, 2 M. 404.

(*q*) McCleary v. Faber, 6 Barr, 476.

(*r*) Anon. Appx. to form. ed. 2 vol.

(*s*) Wood v. Nevius, 2 M. 113.

for want of an affidavit of defence. Thus in Lynch *v.* Rogers,(*t*) which was the record of a judgment in Mississippi against a plaintiff for costs, which had been taxed, a copy of the record was filed and judgment taken. The court, September 8, 1849, opened it on this ground. And in Walker *v.* Del. Mutual Ins. Co., cited Wh. Dig. Supplement. Prac. v. 18, the record contained a submission, signed by the defendant's attorney, an award, and judgment thereon, but the District Court refused a judgment, saying the act of assembly did not apply in such cases. In a recent case in the Supreme Court, however, the record of a judgment in an action of assumpsit was considered of itself an instrument within the act.(*u*) Nor will the court take notice of a private act of assembly avoiding the defence set up,(*v*) when the defence set up was usury; and an act of assembly, in effect repealing the usury laws as to the bonds of that company, was relied upon by the plaintiff.

The construction originally put upon the act of assembly as to the character or form of the contract required to come within its operation, has been very materially changed. With the exception of actions against parties liable only secondarily upon negotiable instruments, it was at first considered that no contract was within the purview of the act if the plaintiff would be required to aver and prove any fact not apparent on the face of the writing. The exception of bills and notes was grounded on the express language of the statute, and the reasonable inference that it looked to all actions thereon without regard to the character of the parties.

In conformity with this rule, it was said the act did not include recognizances of special bail;(*w*) for an averment that the defendant had not been surrendered was necessary to a recovery. Nor a contract to pay at a future day for goods to be delivered at that day,(*x*) for proof of delivery was essential to a recovery. Nor where the covenants were dependent.(*y*) Nor a guarantee of a note,(*z*) under the peculiar effect given to that contract in Pennsylvania. In Mechanics Bk. *v.* Pringle, D. C., Dec. 6, 1847, the copy filed was of a mortgage on its face not then due; accompanying this was a copy of an agreement that the mortgage should become due at an earlier period, on certain conditions, coupled with an averment that the conditions had been performed. But judgment was refused, the court saying this would be to permit the plaintiff to confess and avoid, as in a declaration, and require the defendant to deny matters *dehors* the instrument.

In the case of the Bank of the United States *v.* Thayer,(*a*) an observation fell from Mr. Justice ROGERS, which, with a *dictum* of Mr. Justice SERGEANT, has led to an important change in the rule of construction by the District Court.

The action was upon bank notes and post notes. On the former, no action lies under the act of 1817, without previous demand at the banking house of the drawer defendant. By a clause in the charter, the holder was authorized to recover interest at twelve per cent. per annum

(*t*) D. C. J. 49, 309.
(*u*) Winner *v.* Carter, Apl. 1852; Wh. Dig. Sup. Practice, § 20. *Post*, p. 335.
(*v*) Handy *v.* Reading R. R. Co., Leg. Intel. Feb. 15, 1850.
(*w*) Stokes *v.* Sayre, 1 M. 25.

(*x*) Montgomery *v.* Johnston, 1 M. 324.
(*y*) Dugan *v.* Lloyd, 2 M. 259.
(*z*) Ogden *v.* Root, D. C. March 10, 1849.
(*a*) 2 W. & S. 447.

from such demand until payment. Together with the copies, the plaintiff filed a statement of a demand made previous to the bringing of the suit. The District Court considered the defendants were not required to deny this averment, but that, under the construction put upon the act in suits against indorsers of notes, &c., the suit was such evidence of a demand as of that day as required a denial. Upon error brought by the Bank, the judgment, which was for twelve per cent. interest from the commencement of the suit, was affirmed, ROGERS, J. saying: "If it be necessary to make averments *dehors* the instrument, on which suit is brought, whether it be a bill, note, or other instrument for the payment of money, the fact so set forth may be denied in the affidavit; if not denied, it is admitted; and the court can say with certainty whether, taking the statement with the affidavit, the defendant has any defence to the action."

Dewey *v.* Depui,(*b*) was an action on a lease. The objection taken was that a narr. or statement of the claim should have been filed. It is probable the argument was that a statement was necessary to indicate the precise sum claimed, as it is apparent that a part of the rent had been paid. The objection was overruled. SERGEANT, J., after remarking that the act did not require any such thing, nor would a declaration necessarily give the required information, saying: "Where a copy of the instrument is filed, it is in the power of the defendant to deny all indebtedness upon it, or to explain the nature of his defence against all and any claims *that might arise* upon the face of the instrument. It would seem as if the legislature intended that the propriety of entering a judgment was to be tested, not so much by the plaintiff's claim as by the defendant's affidavit, which is on that account required to state specially the nature and character of the defence." The District Court, following these suggestions, have very much enlarged the operation of the act. And it is believed, that where upon the face of the instrument there is an obligation to pay expressed, whether dependent on the performance of a condition precedent by the plaintiff, or the non-performance by the defendant of any condition, the defendant will be required to deny that the contingencies have occurred upon which the obligation becomes absolute, otherwise they will be presumed against him.

In such cases it is usual to file with the copy a brief statement of the facts, proof of which would be required on the trial.

In Frazier *v.* Fitler,(*c*) the copy filed was of a receipt of a sum of money, "which I hold to pay over to N. F. as certain liens for which said money is retained are removed from the record." The court declined hearing argument, that this was such an instrument as was within the act, saying: "The Supreme Court have settled, whatever may have been the practice of this court, that the promise being conditional the non-performance must be denied." In Rile *v.* Wort,(*d*) the agreement was that the plaintiff would give the defendant such necessary instructions "as will enable him to meet the requirements of the Jefferson Medical College in 1850:" and the court held that the defendant must swear that he did not enjoy the benefits he was entitled to under the contract.

(*b*) 2 W. & S. 553.   (*d*) Dig. Intel. March 16, 1850.
(*c*) D. C. Jan. 26, 1850, MSS.

In Curtis *v.* Jacobs, the agreement recited that certain indorsements and loans to U. had been for the benefit of the firm of J. C. & U. and contained a promise to pay the plaintiff after the estate of U. should have been settled, the balance remaining due after deducting the dividends received from U.'s estate. And it was considered to be within the act. In this case there was a statement that U.'s estate had been settled, and of the dividends received therefrom. In Girard Ins. Co. *v.* Finley, a guarantee of rent was held within the act.(*e*)

The amount due must also be ascertainable from the face of the instrument, or from another referred to therein, of which a copy is filed.(*f*) Privity of contract between the parties must appear on the face of the instruments. Thus a written agreement to accept all drafts drawn by A, not addressed to any one, was held insufficient to entitle the holder to have judgment.(*g*)

An unsigned indorsement on a written instrument, which determines the amount due thereon, may be averred to be in the handwriting of the defendant.(*h*)

4. *Book Debts.*—Under which are included only such debts as are proveable by the parties' book of original entries. Hence a copy of entries in the ledger is not a compliance with the act,(*i*) and does not entitle the plaintiff to judgment.

5. *Actions of scire facias on judgments and on the liens of mechanics and material men* (extended to such actions under the act of 1836, by act 1842, § 1).

6. *Contracts for the loan or advance of money, whether the same be reduced to writing or not.*—Here the act requires an affidavit by plaintiff of the terms of the said loan or advance, with the date thereof. The act of 1835 has been extended to this class of contracts by the act of 1836, § 14. It was said, in Sylva *v.* Bond,(*j*) that this act only includes express contracts for the loan of money. In that case the loan was to a captain, and the affidavit alleged a promise to pay by the manager of the ship. But in Farmers *v.* Sellers,(*k*) it was so held, and an overdraft of a bank account, not by virtue of any express agreement, was held not within the act; and in George *v.* Lewis,(*l*) there was an admission of the receipt of the loan, but a denial that there were any terms settled for the repayment, and it was held a sufficient defence, the act being confined to express contracts. But if verbal contracts of loan are put on the same footing as written ones, as they seem to be by the act, it is difficult to see why the legal obligation to pay inferable in the one case should not be held of equal efficacy in the other. Entries in a bank book, for instance, are an instrument in writing for the payment of money, because the law infers the obligation and promise. Precisely the same obligation and promise are inferred from the admission of a loan without any stipulation respecting the time or mode of payment.

7. *Recognizances and bonds of bail in error; bonds of sureties for stay of execution; bonds or recognizances of special bail; bonds by*

(*e*) Wh. Dig. Suppl. Practice, i. 16.
(*f*) Kearney *v.* Collins, 2 M. 13 ; Bayard *v.* Gillespie, 1 M. 256.
(*g*) Miners *v.* Blackiston, 2 M. 358.
(*h*) Hallowell *v.* Whiteman, D. C. Nov. 2, 1848.

(*i*) Hamilton *v.* O'Donnell, 2 M. 101.
(*j*) 2 M. 422.
(*k*) 2 M. 329.
(*l*) D. C. March 10, 1849 ; *post*, p. 334.

debtors and their sureties conditioned to apply for the benefit of the insolvent laws, are now included in provisions of the act of 1835 by the act of 1842, § 2. As has been stated, all of these instruments which were conditioned absolutely for the payment of money, and not dependent on the non-performance of a collateral act, were held to be included in the term "instruments for the payment of money."

8. Claims filed by the Board of Health, are also included within the provisions of this act ;(*m*) and by most, if not all, of the charters of the incorporated districts of Philadelphia County, they are authorized to file claims for expenses of curbing, paving, &c., and proceed under this act.

9. In Pennsylvania Savings Institution *v.* Smith,(*n*) an instrument was filed on which no judgment would have been taken had the facts been brought to the notice of the court. No affidavit or suggestion having been filed judgment was granted by the court, which was sustained in error, under an intimation there that the party had waived his defence, or had not complied with the statutory provision.

It is difficult to perceive how a defendant who is required to put in a defence under oath to one class of cases only is in default where the case is not one of that class. The statute gives a summary remedy on certain conditions ; the defendant knowing that it was impossible to comply with the conditions, waited till he was called upon to answer in due course of law. The plaintiff filed a copy of an instrument on which the law distinctly says, that from grounds of public policy there shall be no right of action in such a case. Yet the defendant was held to be in default for not setting up that as a defence.

An additional objection is, that in a Court of Error, where the plaintiff had by his own showing no case, and where there had been no trial on the merits, a judgment by default was sustained. The profession were doubtless misled on this point by the strong expression of Mr. Justice KENNEDY, in Thomas *v.* Shoemaker.(*o*) In reply to the argument that an objection was waived by not having been taken in the affidavit, he says : " It would be preposterous to hold that the defendant was bound or could be required, under the act of assembly, or act of the court, to file an affidavit of defence, when it appeared from the plaintiff's own showing that he had no cause of action at the time of commencing his suit."

The practice of the District Court prevents the evil which would otherwise ensue from this construction. If a judgment is obtained on any instrument, not within the act of assembly, it will be invariably opened, on the plain principle that the court had no jurisdiction to give it, and this without affidavit or suggestion of defence.(*p*) It is, however, the usual practice where anything styled "a copy" is filed, and the instrument is not within the meaning of the act, to file a suggestion to that effect. The effect of this is simply to require the copy to be looked at by the court, and a decision given as to its validity in form.

II. *Parties.*—The words of the act are general. But exceptions have been made by construction. Thus it is held that executors, adminis-

(*m*) Act of 1845, § 1.
(*n*) 10 Barr, 13.
(*o*) 2 W. & S. 183. *G. W. & S. 179.*

(*p*) McFate *v.* Shallcross, Wh. Dig. Prac. vol. 33.

trators, defendants, are not within the act where the action is upon a contract made by their testator or intestate.(q) But where the action is on a contract made by an executor, though in his representative capacity, as a submission and award, then being presumed to be acquainted with the defence, he is within the act.(r) So where a contractor is dead, and his administrator is served with a *scire facias* on a mechanic's claim ;(s) and the same rule is applied in an action against a lunatic or his committee.(t) Where, too, the defendant is not in default for not appearing until after the time allowed for filing an affidavit, as a defendant in foreign attachment he is not within the act.(u) As to the case of assignees see *post*, IV. 3.

III. The plaintiff shall be entitled to judgment by default unless the defendant shall previously have filed an affidavit of defence, stating therein the nature and character of the same.

1. *Judgment by default.*—This judgment when entered is final, and the subsequent assessment of damages relates to the date of the entry.(v) This is done by the prothonotary, where it is a mere matter of calculation.(w) It has always been the practice of the District Court, where the defendant admitted part of the amount claimed to be due, to permit the plaintiff to take judgment for so much, and this was considered a termination of the suit. This practice was overruled in McKinney v. Mitchell,(x) where it was held that payment of such judgment was no waiver of the right to proceed for the residue. But the difficulties attending this practice would seem to require it to be restrained to exactly similar cases. If, as there said, the judgment is interlocutory, of course no execution could issue, and if execution may issue it would seem that the plaintiff thereby elected to consider the judgment as final. But at whose risk is the subsequent prosecution of the suit ? If the plaintiff fails, he still has a judgment and must recover full costs ; and if he is nonsuited, will he be permitted to fall back on his original judgment ? If a matter of defence subsequent should occur or be discovered, is the defendant concluded by the judgment, or may he disprove the correctness of his own admissions? The practice of the District Court is certainly much recommended for simplicity, and it cannot certainly be said that a plaintiff may *issue execution* for the amount confessed and retain his right of action for the residue.

In accordance with this practice was the course taken in Potts v. Smith,(y) where the court, reversing the judgment of the District Court on the ground that a partial defence had been sworn to, *with the plaintiff's consent,* gave judgment for the amount admitted to be due ; whereas, either his consent was not required, or there should have been a *procedendo* awarded as to the residue of the claim.

If one of several joint defendants admits his separate liability for the debt sued upon, and judgment is taken against him for that amount, the plaintiff will not be permitted, at a subsequent day, to take judgment against the others, for want of a sufficient affidavit of defence. Whether

(q) Leibert v. Hoelser, 1 M. 263.
(r) Bayard v. Gillespie, 1 M. 256.
(s) Richards v. Reed, D. C. Sept. 19, 1851, Leg. Intel.
(t) Alexander v. Ticknor, Whart. Dig. Supplement. Prac. sec. 27.

(u) Roberts v. Hugg, 2 M. 283.
(v) McCleirg v. Sansom. 2 M. 177.
(w) Watkins v. Phillips, 2 Wh. 210.
(x) 4 W. & S. 25.
(y) 2 Wh. 183–4.

he is concluded, or may proceed against the other parties, was not decided.(z)

2. *Unless the defendant shall have previously filed, &c.*—The act requires the defendant to file but not to make the affidavit. Hence the affidavit by a third person, is sufficient.(a) But where a stranger makes the affidavit, it should appear that he had some reason for doing so—as that he was the agent of the defendant, &c.(b)

Previously filed.—The construction put upon this clause in the District Court was, that after the motion for the judgment, no affidavit could be received unless filed by leave of the court.(c) But this was overruled ;(d) and it was said that great injustice would be done if defendants were precluded from setting out their defences by supplemental affidavits, and obtaining a trial by jury. It is, therefore, the rule of this court, that all affidavits filed before the judgment is given, must be noticed.

In the Common Pleas.—The act of 1846, extending these acts to this court, requires an affidavit to be made *before* certain days, &c. The construction put upon this clause in this court was, that the affidavit is insufficient if filed on or after the days on which the plaintiff is entitled to judgment.(e)

This construction, though it must be conceded to accord with the words of the act, is unfortunate. It violates the analogy which ought to exist in the practice of the two courts. But what is much more important, it deprives the court, and the parties, of the advantage of supplemental affidavits—the use of which, as settled in the District Court, is one of the most common methods of testing the fairness of the original affidavit ; and thus enabling the court to see whether that was defective, through inadvertence or design.

Since this was written, however, the ruling of the Common Pleas has been reversed, and the practice now accords with that of the District Court.(f) And the court will stay the proceedings, and thus enlarge the time for making an affidavit of defence, until inspection of the original instrument, or of the book of original entries, a copy of which is filed.(g)

3. *An affidavit of defence, stating the nature and character of the same.*—The obvious intention of this extension of the old rule of court, was to compel the defendant to submit his defence in his own language to the court ; and if, on his own showing, he had no available defence, to allow the court to enter judgment. Such has been the construction, and to it the beneficial character of the act is owing.(h)

But there are some cases in which no affidavit is necessary. 1. Where on the face of the record the plaintiff is not entitled to judgment, as where the suit was prematurely brought ;(i) where the instrument is one from which no legal liability by defendant to plaintiff is inferable ;(j) where

(z) Welsh v. Hirst, Leg. Intel. March 23, 1850 ; Wh. Dig. Suppl. Practice, § 36.
(a) Sleeper v. Dougherty, 2 Wh. 177.
(b) Marshall v. Witte, Leg. Int. March 23, 1850 ; Wh. Dig. Suppl. Practice, § 28.
(c) Simmons v. West, 1 M. 165.
(d) West v. Simmons, 2 Wh. 261.
(e) Sharpless v. Schneebly, 6 L. J. 284.

(f) Gillespie v. Smith, 1 Harris, 65.
(g) Taylor v. Montgomery, D. C. S. 51, 1919.
(h) West v. Simmons, 2 Wh. 261.
(i) Thompson v. Shoemaker, 6 W. & S. 179.
(j) Patterson v. Poindexter, 6 W. & S. 227.

the plaintiff has appealed from the judgment of a justice for defendant ;(*k*) by proceeding under the arbitration law, which had not been
repealed as to this court.(*l*)   2. Where the plaintiff has waived his
right, as by declaring, calling for, and accepting a plea.(*m*)

IV. In the examination of these affidavits, some general rules of construction have been adopted ; so far as we are able to collect them from
the cases within our reach, we propose to state them.

Where they are requisite, they must contain legal grounds of defence
—that is, such a state of facts which, if proved, would constitute a legal
defence.(*n*)

An obvious rule would be to consider the affidavit as containing a
plea in substance, divested of all the formal or technical parts. This
rule, though not directly stated, has been so far alluded to as to make
it not improperly considered as a general principle. Thus, in West *v.*
Simmons,(*o*) it is said the defendant has the same advantages as if the
forms of a demurrer were used ; and in Hugg *v.* Scott,(*p*) it is said certainty to a common interest is all that is required. This is all that is
required in pleas in bar.(*q*)   The analogy of the rules will be perceived
on examining the several decisions on this class of cases.

1. *Facts must be stated*, from which legal inferences can be drawn ;
and the inferences or conclusions of law, though sworn to, will not constitute a defence. This was laid down in Stitt *v.* Garett,(*r*) where, after
a defence to a bill as between the original parties was stated, it was
averred that the holder took the bill, not in the usual course of business,
but under circumstances of suspicion, such as ought to have put him on
inquiry ; and it was said to be insufficient, because the circumstances
should have been stated, to enable the court to say whether they were
sufficient ; and that all taking, out of the usual course of business, did
not affect the party with notice ; and in Brown *v.* Street,(*s*) the defendant swore that he believed the payee, as to whom he had a defence, was
the real plaintiff—that the plaintiff was the particular friend of drawee ;
and it was held to be insufficient, because no facts were stated going to
show the plaintiff's want of right to sue.

In Moore *v.* Somerset,(*t*) to an action on a note, dated at Philadelphia, defence was taken that there had been delay in giving notice to
the drawer. The delay stated would have discharged the indorsers, had
the drawer resided at Philadelphia. But the court said the affidavit
should contain facts, not inferences, and the defendant was bound to
show the residence of the drawer to have been within such a distance as
made out a case of legal delay in giving the notice.

2. *Time and place, where essential, must be averred.*—Thus, where
the consideration of a note was shown to be illegal, under the lottery
act, it was required that defendant should state the illegal act was done
within the State ;(*u*) and in Reising *v.* Patterson,(*v*) the defendant set
out an accord and tender "in full, upon the terms specified." The terms

(*k*) Gifford *v.* Bockius, C. P. October
23, 1847.
   (*l*) Lusk *v.* Garrett, 6 W. & S. 89.
   (*m*) Hauer *v.* Humphreys, 2 M. 28.
   (*n*) Hill *v.* Bromall, 1 M. 352 ; West *v.*
Simmons, 2 Wh. 261.
   (*o*) 2 Wh. 261.

(*p*) 6 Ibid. 274.
(*q*) 1 Chitty Pl. 237.
(*r*) 3 Wh. 281.
(*s*) 6 W. & S. 222.
(*t*) Ibid. 262.
(*u*) Dows *v.* White, 2 M. 140.
(*v*) 5 Wh. 316.

were payment of a certain sum, part of which had been paid; and it was held insufficient, because not averred to have been at the time and place agreed upon. This accords with the rule of pleading.(w) It is proper to observe that a more obvious objection occurred in this case— it was an accord without averment of a receipt in satisfaction.

3. *The averments are construed most favorably for the plaintiff;* it being reasonable, as has been said, to suppose that the defendant would state his case most favorably for himself; and the possibility of evasion or duplicity must be excluded.(x) Thus, in Walker v. Geisse,(y) it was said that the averment that payee *had said* he had passed the checks to the holder before the day of their date, was no averment that the fact was so. And in the same case, the averment that they were passed to the holder for an antecedent debt (there being a defence as to the payee), was held bad for uncertainty, whether as collateral security or in payment; for in the latter event no defence existed. In Comly v. Bryan,(z) where the general principle was stated, the original affidavit set forth that the bill in suit had been forwarded to A'after it fell due, the supplemental affidavit setting up a defence as to A, who was said to have been the holder after maturity, was held defective, in not stating in what capacity he was holder, viz., as owner or agent for collection. And in Dewey v. Depuy,(a) where in the lease sued on there was a covenant that the lessees should have the use of a road, and the affidavit averred that they had not the use of it; it was held bad, for not showing how they were deprived of it; for it might have been by acts for which the lessor was irresponsible. And in Ogden v. Offerman,(b) the lessee averred that the lessor had occupied the premises and not the lessee, and it was held insufficient, there being nothing alleged amounting to an ouster, surrender, &c. And in Harris v. Mason,(c) an action on a sealed indorsement, the defendant said he was not conscious of ever having indorsed the note with a seal, and did not believe he ever did, and it was held to be equivocal. In Hugg v. Brown,(d) however, there was a defence, by way of set-off, set up, and in the affidavit it was also stated that defendant had brought an action against the plaintiff, in which there had been an award and appeal; and it was held sufficient, though there was no averment that the set-off and the action were for different matters, which, it was admitted, was essential to the validity of the defence. Under this rule, an averment of an agreement existing is held to imply that it is by parol, and not in writing, unless so stated. Thus, in an action on a post-dated 'check, an agreement made at the time of giving the check, that at maturity the drawer might have further time to pay it, was held immaterial, as tending to alter the terms of a written agreement.(e)

4. *As to the particularity* required in the statement of the facts, it has been held that where a set-off is sworn to, it is not essential that the items and amount should be set forth ;(f) provided, that it is said

(w) Halsey v. Carpenter, Crp. Jac. 359, Steph. 382-3.
(x) Ogden v. Offerman, 2 M. 40.
(y) 4 Wh. 257.
(z) 5 Wh. 261.
(a) 2 W. & S. 553.

(b) 2 M. 40.
(c) Ibid. 270.
(d) 6 Wh. 472.
(e) Hill v. Gaw, 4 Barr, 493.
(f) Runyan v. Crawford, D. C. April 1, 1848.

to exceed the plaintiff's claim.(*g*) But where there are circumstances connected with the formation of the instrument sued on, or arising out of it, which form a defence, they must be set forth. Thus, in Riley *v.* Bullock,(*h*) the defendant, a drawer of a note, stated he had received no value, and owed the plaintiff nothing; he was required to set forth his defence with greater particularity, doubtless to explain how he came to give the note, &c. In Fisher *v.* Stokes,(*i*) defendant stated he had paid the plaintiff to the amount of $500, and he was required to specify the time, place, and manner. And in Thompson *v.* Daniels,(*j*) to an action on a physician's bill, an affidavit that the charges were too high, was held insufficient, as defendant should have added they were higher than usual.

5. *The defendant's belief* of the facts stated, is all that is required when these facts form part of the plaintiff's case.(*k*) But where the facts forming part of the defendant's case are averred upon information and belief, the defendant must add that he expects to prove them.(*l*) And in M'Laughlin *v.* Diamond,(*m*) it was said, that where facts founded on mere belief are spoken of, he must add "expects to be able to prove;" and where he said, "will endeavor to prove," it was clearly insufficient. In Berrill *v.* Zeigefaus,(*n*) the defendant averred that the note was held by the payee at maturity, "as defendant believes;" and it was held not sufficiently positive. This rule was adopted in Brown *v.* Street,(*o*) where defendant having stated a defence to the payee, added, that he believed the payee was the real plaintiff; and the court said this was immaterial, for his belief would not avail without proof, and there were no facts stated from which such an inference could be drawn. Moore *v.* Somersett,(*p*) is to the same effect.

6. *The affidavit is to receive a reasonable construction in favor of the defendant.*(*q*)—Where, in an action on a bill drawn by an agent on his principal, in payment of certain goods, it was averred that the goods were sold to the principal, and on his credit, his name being disclosed, the defendant acting but as agent, and the bill was in payment of that debt; and it was held a sufficient averment that the goods were sold on the credit of the principal alone.

7. *A primâ facie case for the defendant* is sufficient. What would require a replication to a plea, or rebutting evidence by plaintiff to avoid the defence, need not be negatived. Thus, in an action on a lease, the defendant averred that the rent for quarters subsequent to those sued for had been recovered in an action in the lessor's name, to the use of the sheriff's vendee, of the lessor's title, and that that judgment had been paid. It was held to be *primâ facie* evidence of payment of the previous arrears, though it was open to explanation, by showing that the lessor's name had been used by the purchaser merely to recover the rent accruing since the equitable plaintiff had acquired title.(*r*) And in an action on a recognizance of bail, it was averred that the plaintiff had issued a *fi. fa.* in the original action, and enough

(*g*) Fletcher *v.* Bancroft, Ib. Oct. 14.
(*h*) Ib. Sept. 23.
(*i*) Ib. Oct. 21.
(*j*) Ib. Dec. 9.
(*k*) Anon. D. C. Dec. 9, 1848.
(*l*) McClure *v.* Bingham, *post,* 334, 336.
(*m*) Ib. Dec. 23.
(*n*) C. C. P. Nov. 1847.
(*o*) 6 W. & S. 222.
(*p*) 6 W. & S. 263.
(*q*) Roberts *v.* Austin, 5 Wh. 313.
(*r*) Hemphill *v.* Eckfeldt, 5 Wh. 274.

money was collected to pay the debt, interest, and costs; and it was held not necessary to deny that the landlord had received the same, or was entitled to receive it. It was urged, that in point of fact the landlord's priority of claim had exhausted the fund, but the court said this was matter for replication, and that the defence was *primâ facie* made out by showing a levy of sufficient to answer the debt.(s) So, in an action on a note, the affidavit alleged facts which, if proved on the trial, would have required the plaintiff to prove that he was a *bonâ fide* holder for value before maturity; and it was held sufficient.(t)

8. It is sufficient if at the expiration of the period for filing an affidavit, a defence existed which is set up. Subsequent amendments of the record cannot have a retroactive effect. This was decided in a case of *misnomer*, which was amended under the act of assembly.(u) So, where a variance between the copy and the instrument is alleged, if it is such that the court must take notice of it, it operates as a bar to the judgment.(v) It was there stated, that the practice is for the defendant to rule the plaintiff to produce the original.(vv) Averment of another action for the same cause in a sister State, is a bar,(w) but there is nothing in the case warranting the latter part of the syllabus—"until discontinuance." The remark of the judge refers to the validity of a plea in abatement, which might be filed, and hence the affidavit showed a good defence at the time.

9. Judgment was also refused in an action for purchase-money, where the defence set up was a defect in title, and the question on which the title depended was about to be argued in the Supreme Court.(x)

The affidavit is received as absolute, and cannot be contradicted or explained by counter affidavits. Thus, where the defendant averred that plaintiff had not the note sued on, but it had been delivered to the defendant's agent to transmit to defendant, the court refused to hear affidavits that their agent was also the agent of the plaintiff.(y)

10. *Supplemental affidavits* are very generally used in the District Court, and it may be stated as the general rule to require them, or rather to allow the defendant to file them, when, from the affidavit filed, it is probable that a defence exists, but it has been stated defectively. It is also used where the defence is set up in terms so general that the court cannot determine from the facts whether a defence exists. It has already been shown that the court must notice all supplemental affidavits filed before judgment is given. And in Hill v. Gaw,(z) it was intimated that no inference was to be made against a defendant who refused to give a supplemental affidavit, but that he had a right to rest himself upon his original affidavit.

V. *Provided that judgment shall not be entered unless the plaintiff shall within two weeks from the return day of the original process file a copy, &c.* By the rule of the District Court and Common Pleas, this

(s) Christy v. Bohlen, 5 Barr, 38.

(t) Purves v. Corfield, Wh. Dig. Suppl. Prac. See also Forchheimer v. Feistman, Bright. R. 87.

(u) Brown v. Hackney, D. C. March 25, 1848; Durar v. Carrigan, Ib. March 10.

(v) Reiger v. Briedenhart, D. C. Dec. 16, 1848.

(vv) See *post*, p. 336.

(w) Hopkins v. Ludlow, 11 P. L. J. 344.

(x) Moss v. Hauson, ib. June 21, 1848.

(y) Brown v. Merriweather, ib. June 17, 1848.

(z) 4 Barr, 495.

is qualified, and it is ordered that where the copy is not filed within one week from the return day, the plaintiff, to entitle himself to judgment, must give to the defendant or his attorney a written notice, forty-eight hours before applying to the court for judgment, and in default of such notice he will not be entitled to judgment.

Where the action is upon a record of the same court, it is not requisite to file a copy thereof,(a) and though mechanics' claims, Board of Health claims, district claims, &c., are not records, in the proper sense of the word,(b) it has never been the practice to do more than issue a *scire facias* reciting the claim filed, and treat that as a copy filed within the meaning of this act.

§ 2. *In suits on mortgages* it is no longer necessary to file a copy of the instrument if it has been recorded. For by the act of 1842, §. 3, a statement of the date of the recording contained in the *scire facias* is equivalent. And though not required by the statute, the place of recording seems equally necessary, otherwise the record would be very defective in pointing out matters essential; as the instrument might not have been recorded in the county, and bidders at the sale would not have reasonable information as to the nature and extent of the lien and title passing by the sale.

3. By the same act, an assignee filing a copy need not file a copy of the assignment, if, within the two weeks, he files a declaration containing the necessary averments.

Perhaps the only instances in which this provision is practically applicable are a *scire facias* on a mortgage by an assignee thereof, covenant by an assignee of a ground-rent, and debt by an assignee of a bond assigned under the act of 1715.

It has never been pretended that this act was intended to alter the rules of the common law respecting parties to actions. Any other construction would extend the range of negotiable contracts which has never been done, but under statutes having that object distinctly in view, and cautiously defining the particular form of contract intended to be thus affected, as in the instances above mentioned of mortgages and bonds. Covenant by an assignee of a rent reserved on a grant in fee is sustained under Streaper v. Fisher.(c) An assignee of the land was always liable in covenant in virtue of his estate, and though he may not have acquired his estate by any written instrument, the latter part of this section seems to have been intended for such a case. There being no necessity for a declaration setting forth the grounds of a defendant's liability if he were a party, on the face of an instrument for the payment of money.

The object and effect of the affidavit of defence is complete when the plaintiff is thus compelled to go to trial. Thus the averments there will not obviate the necessity of notice of special matter of defence intended to be given in evidence under the general issue ;(d) nor does it stand in lieu of a plea, and therefore admissions there made may be used against the defendant on the trial.(e)

Neither is it proper to take defence by affidavit on grounds which are strictly preliminary to a defence—as that the plaintiff on the record has

(a) Act 1835, § 1.
(b) Davis v. Church, 1 W. & S. 240.
(c) 1 R. 155.

(d) Sullivan v. Johns, 5 Wh. 369.
(e) Bowen v. De Lattre, 6 Wh. 430.

not authorized the action—that should be done by ruling the attorney to file his warrant.(*f*)

(*f*) Zeibert *v.* Grew, 6 Wh. 404.

The following decisions of the District Court for Philadelphia, will be found important in this branch of practice:—

Carter *v.* Winner, April 5, 1851. Why judgment should not be set aside. *Per curiam.* We have not acted, in our practice, either upon McCleary *v.* Faber, 6 Barr, 476, or Philadelphia Savings Insti. *v.* Smith, 10 Barr, 13. On the contrary, we have held that debt upon judgment is not within the affidavit section, and that when the copy filed is not of the kind mentioned, we will not give judgment, though affidavit be not made. But this motion is an appeal to our discretion. We cannot, under these decisions in the Supreme Court, consider this judgment as irregular—and set it aside on that ground. We ought not to interfere, therefore, except upon an affidavit of merits. R. D.

Shaw *v.* Baildon, D. C., Saturday, Sept. 16, 1848. Rule for judgment. *Per curiam.* When a defendant wishes to take advantage of an alleged difference between the paper filed and the instrument or book of which it purports to be a copy, his proper course is to take a rule on him to produce the original in court on the return day of the rule for judgment. The court must otherwise act upon the assumption that the copy filed is a true copy. Here the defect suggested in the copy is the want of the year in the year, and it is said the date at the top is the date of the bill, or account, and is no part of the entries, because the month and day there given are subsequent to the other entries, on the supposition that the year is the same. We must take it, however, that the whole is a copy, and if so, the year sufficiently appears. It is to be regretted that counsel are in the habit of filing accounts and copies furnished by their clients, without themselves examining to see if they are correct. The filing a copy ought to be what it purports to be on its face—a professional affirmation that it is a copy, where the original is in the attorney's possession or within his reach. Rule absolute. (See p. 336.)

McClure *v.* Bringham, D. C., March 25, 1848. Rule for judgment. *Per curiam.* Where the defendant cannot speak from his own knowledge, the formulæ used in this case, "that he believes and expects to be able to prove," has heretofore received the sanction of this court. A defendant is not required, in his affidavit, to make a development of the evidence by which he expects to prove his defence. He may have a belief, founded on circumstances within his own knowledge, which it would be laying down an inconvenient rule to say he shall in all cases fully set forth. If we require him to say that he has derived his belief from information of others, it would aid the case of a prosecution very little, unless, in addition, we could compel him to state the names of the persons from whom his information was derived. Assuming, then, Reed & Brothers to be the real plaintiffs, and judging upon this case, as we are bound to do, from the matter contained within the four corners of the affidavit, we think that it discloses a full defence. If it were, indeed, a set-off of damages arising on defendant's guarantee, it might be doubtful whether the insolvency of the parties to the draft in question is alleged in such a manner as to relieve defendant from the necessity of proceeding against them before resorting to Reed & Brother. But we look upon this defence as a failure of the consideration of the note. This affidavit distinctly denies that the note was given in payment, or absolutely in exchange for a draft. Requiring Reed & Brothers, subsequently, to give a guarantee, is by no means conclusive against this view. Why did Reed & Brothers give the guarantee, if the transaction were one simply of payment or exchange? On the other hand, there was every reason why the defendants should require a written guarantee, as their note had passed from Reed & Brothers, and they might be called upon and obliged to pay it to a *bona fide* holder, without notice, against whom the failure of consideration would be unavailable. Rule dismissed.

George *v.* Levis, March 10, 1849. Rule for judgment. *Per curiam.* The plaintiff has filed an affidavit of loan. Although he avers that he lent and advanced to the defendant, at his express request, the money in question, yet the defendant denies, positively, that there was any express contract by him to repay the money, and that, though he received the money, it was not as a loan or advance. It may be that, upon the case as presented by these two affidavits, the plaintiff, on the trial, would be entitled to have the instruction of the court, that the evidence is sufficient to authorize a verdict in his favor, upon a count, for money lent and advanced. But that is a different question from the one now presented, whether the court can enter judgment, for want of an affidavit of defence, under the 14th section of the act of March 11, 1836, Purd. 268. That section provides that the affidavit shall set forth the terms of the loan or advance, evidently looking to the case of an express contract, and not one to be merely implied from the receipt of the money at defendant's request. Such have been the decisions of this court heretofore, in Farmers' & Mechanics' Bank v. Seller, 2 M. 329, and Sylva v. Bond, 2 M. 421. The defendant has distinctly denied that he received this money as a loan or advance, or with any agreement to repay it. R. D.

Durar v. Charagan, March 10, 1849. Rule for judgment. *Per curiam.* Defendant was sued by a wrong name, and filed his affidavit making this his ground of defence. Plaintiff then had the record amended under the act of April 16, 1843, and now asks for judgment for want of a sufficient affidavit of defence. At the time the affidavit was filed, however, the defence was a good one, and we have heretofore held in Owen v. Hackney, 1 M. S. Cases, 194, that an amendment, subsequently made in such a case, will not entitle the plaintiff to a judgment. R. D.

Peters v. Vanderwerken, Jan. 25, 1851. Rule for judgment. *Per curiam.* In this case an amendment was allowed in the name of defendant after the time for filing the copy had expired. Had the defendant filed an affidavit of the misnomer when the copy was filed, it would have been a good defence, and, as we have heretofore decided, the subsequent amendment will not help the plaintiff. We think this case falls within the reason of that decision. The amendment here expressly admits that defendant had (not) a defence when the copy was filed. R. D.

Walker v. Delaware Ins. Co. Saturday, Oct. 5, 1850. Rule for judgment. *Per curiam.* We have always held that judgment for want of an affidavit of defence could not be entered in an action of debt on foreign judgments or judgments of sister States. The words of the act are expressly *scire facias* in judgments and *expressio unius est exclusio alterius.* An examination of the opinion in McCleary v. Faber, 6 Barr, 476, shows that the court in that case went upon the ground, that the cause of action in the original action, as set forth in the record filed, was within the act. Here, however, that

cannot be pretended. It is said, however, that there was a reference and award upon which the original judgment was obtained, and that such reference and award are instruments of writing for the payment of money within previous decisions of this court. Upon referring to the record we find there was, by agreement of the court, a simple reference to an arbitrator "to hear and try the same and report thereon to the court." Upon the report the judgment was entered. It was evidently, therefore, a proceeding in that cause, no award, but merely a report to the court. We are of opinion, therefore, that the plaintiff is not entitled to judgment. R. D.

Reed v. Keech, Saturday, Jan. 4, 1851. Rule for judgment. *Per curiam.* It has been held uniformly by us, that in an action of debt on a judgment, upon filing a copy of a record, the plaintiff is not entitled to a judgment for want of an affidavit of defence. We have recognized also an exception to this upon the authority of McCleary v. Faber, 6 Barr, 470, that when the record filed also shows a copy of such an instrument of writing as the foundation of that judgment, as would have entitled the plaintiff to what is now sought had it been filed alone, then judgment will be given. And this seems perfectly reasonable. A plaintiff may add to a count upon a judgment, one upon the original cause of action. The only question in this case then is, whether the agreement to confess the judgment in Chester County is an instrument of writing within the act. It seems to us that it could not be used as evidence of indebtedness against defendant. It is a confession of judgment in Chester County, confined to that county on its face, and to use it for any other purpose is aside altogether from the obvious intention of the parties to it. R. D.

Kaulter v. U. S. Bank, June 14, 1851. M. L. 119. Rule for judgment. *Per curiam.* Though an attempt has been made to distinguish it, we are of opinion that this case does not materially differ from the former case decided by this court between the same parties. It seems clear from the affidavit, and from the statement of the balance by the plaintiff, that some of the collaterals deposited by defendants have been realized, and defendant is certainly entitled to have an account of them. Indeed, it would seem by far the best practice for a plaintiff to state on the face of his copy filed, the securities which he still holds, in order to enable the court to exercise that proper control over the money raised by

In what way judgment for default of appearance may be taken, has already been considered ;(*g*) and how such, as well as other judgments, may be opened, will be hereafter fully examined.(*h*)

the execution which it has been held that they have. Without it the grossest injustice might be perpetrated through the instrumentality of legal proceedings, and without it a defendant, ignorant of what a plaintiff has received on collaterals, and what he still holds, is necessarily embarrassed in his defence. We think, therefore, this case ought to go to a jury.

Lynch *v.* Rogers, Sept. 8, 1849. Why judgment should not be set aside. *Per curiam.* Although the case of McCleary *v.* Faber, 6 Barr, 476, which was decided under a special act of assembly, copied *verbatim* from the 2d section of the act of 28th March, 1835, appears to go the length of deciding that judgment for want of an affidavit of defence under that section may be entered in an action of debt on judgment, we think it was not intended to be so broad, and that it must be confined to cases where the judgment sued upon is founded, and so appears on its face, "on a contract and cause of action covered by the terms of the act" of assembly. It then becomes in effect an action upon such contract, and the fact that it has already passed *in rem judicatam,* so that he can no longer resort to an original action, ought not to deprive the plaintiff of the privileges of this section. But the same reason does not exist where this does not appear. The words of the act are very express in confining the authority of the court to enter judgment to the case of *scire facias* on judgment. This writ issues only on a record of the same court, and there appears to have been most reason for making the distinction. To give a summary judgment in debt on the judgment of another State, or in debt or assumpsit on a foreign judgment, without affording the defendant opportunity to inquire into the case, would be very unjust. His property might be levied on and sold before he could obtain or convey to the court the information that a writ of error had issued and suspended execution on the judgment, or before he could ascertain the fairness of the proceeding. No doubt in just such a case as McCleary *v.* Faber, the court, upon a sufficient affidavit of defence to the original cause of action, would give the party further time to ascertain if there existed any ground to avoid the effect of the conclusiveness of the judgment. R. D.

Reigel *v.* Breidenhart, Dec. 16, 1848.

Rule for judgment. *Per curiam.* The proper practice where there is a variance between the copy filed and the original, is to call for the production of the original. Here the affidavit sets up the variance, and although it presents the case of a necessary admission of the fact that defendent knew what the instrument was upon which she was sued, and was not taken by surprise, yet we are not disposed to say that defendant is thereby estopped from taking advantage of it. It would undoubtedly be a variance if the note was described in the narr. as indorsed E. A. Breidenhart, and it appeared on the trial as indorsed E. Breidenhart, Chitty on Bills, 560. We consider it of the highest importance to lay down and maintain a strict rule in requiring that the copy filed should be a true copy of the instrument sued upon. If we should begin to relax it, who can say where we would be landed? Rule discharged. (See p. 334.)

McLaughlin *v.* Dimond, Dec. 23, 1848. Rule for judgment. *Per curiam.* Where a party defendant says he is informed of and verily believes a certain state of facts constituting a defence, he is bound either to add that he expects to be able to prove the defence or show the court specially the grounds of his belief, when, if those grounds are such as are reasonably calculated to raise such belief, the court will give him the delay the law allows, even though he may not be able to say at present that he expects to be able to make out his evidence. Time may help him to the evidence, and he is entitled in an honest case to the benefit of it. In this case the defendant, after setting out his defence, evidently aware of the rule, says he will endeavor to prove it; but he may not have been aware that if he could not say he expected to prove it, it was lawful for him to adopt the other, and inform the court why he entertained the belief to which he has sworn.

Suppl. aff. allowed to be filed within ten days after service of a copy of this order on defendant or his attorney, in which defendant shall state either that he expects to be able to prove the defence set up, or shall set forth specially the sources of his information, and the facts upon which he grounds the belief expressed in his affidavit.

(*g*) See *ante*, p. 236.
(*h*) *Post*, chap. xxvii.

SECTION II.

JUDGMENT ON NON SUM INFORMATUS, NIL DICIT, ETC.

When judgment by default or *non sum informatus* is taken (for it is said to be now seldom or never used),(*i*) it is only in cases where judgment is entered in pursuance of a previous agreement between the parties ;(*j*) or when the plaintiff's attorney *accepts* a judgment of this kind after a plea put in by the defendant, which he allows the latter to retract.(*k*) This form of judgment is unknown in practice here.

Judgment by *nil dicit* is either for want of any plea at all, or for want of a plea adapted to the nature of the action or circumstances of the case, or for not pleading in a proper manner, or within the times limited by the rules of court.(*l*)

When judgment by default for want of a plea may be taken after a rule to plead has been given, may be seen from the rules of court introduced and considered when we were treating of filing the declaration.(*m*) When the defendant pleads before he has appeared, or where his plea is not adapted to the nature of the action, as *nil debet* in *assumpsit* or *non assumpsit* in debt, the plaintiff may treat the plea as a nullity, and have judgment by default.(*n*) So, if the defendant, after craving *oyer* of a deed, do not set forth the whole deed, the plaintiff is entitled to judgment as for want of a plea.(*o*)

Where no rule to plead is entered on the docket, the proceeding is nugatory, though the defendant have notice of it.(*p*)

Where the rules of court require two consecutive rules to plead to be taken before judgment by default can be taken, one rule will not entitle the party to his judgment.(*q*)

A notice of a rule to plead is sufficient, if the party served cannot mistake its object or the suit in which the plea is demanded ; hence, a notice requiring defendant to plead is sufficient under the rule.(*r*)

According to the English practice, if the plea do not answer the whole of the declaration, judgment by *nil dicit* may in general be signed for the part not answered, and the action may be proceeded in for the residue. The rule upon this subject is thus : if a plea begin as an answer to part only, and is in truth an answer only to that part,(*s*) or if it begin as an answer to part, but afterwards answer more,(*t*) the plaintiff should sign judgment for that part of the cause of action, which the plea in its commencement does not profess to answer ; otherwise, if, instead of doing so, he demur or plead over, the whole action will be discontinued.(*u*) If, on the contrary, the plea begin as an answer to the whole, but in truth be only an answer to part, the plain-

(*i*) Tidd, 587.
(*j*) 2 Arch. Pr. 8.
(*k*) Vasse *v.* Spicer, 2 D. 111.
(*l*) Tidd, 588 ; 2 Arch. Pr. 8.
(*m*) *Ante*, 317.
(*n*) 4 T. R. 578 ; Barnes, 257 ; 4 Taunt. 164.
(*o*) 4 T. R. 370.

(*p*) Bisbing *v.* Albertson, 6 W. & S. 450.
(*q*) Green *v.* Hallowell, 9 Barr, 53.
(*r*) Stroop *v.* Gross, 1 W. & S. 139.
(*s*) 1 Saund. 28, n. 1, 2, 3.
(*t*) 1 Saund. 28, n. 3, *sed vide* 2 B. & P. 427.
(*u*) 2 Arch. Pr. 8, 9.

tiff cannot sign judgment for the part not answered, but should demur, because the whole plea is bad.(v) If a plea be bad or frivolous, the plaintiff may either demur to it, or treat it as a nullity, and enter judgment by default ;(w) but if it be not palpably bad and void on the face of it, he must resort to his demurrer.(x)

If the defendant plead a plea in abatement(y) without a verification by affidavit, or if he plead a tender without paying the money into court,(z) as will be seen when pleas come to be particularly considered, the plaintiff may enter judgment by default. In like manner, he may enter the defendant's default for not rejoining ;(a) or for not pleading to a new assignment, or joining in demurrer when necessary.(b)

If the defendant make default at the trial, this is not such a default as will entitle the plaintiff to sign judgment ; but he must proceed regularly to verdict and judgment, in the same manner as if the action were defended.(c)

A judgment by default is interlocutory, in assumpsit, covenant, trespass, case, and replevin, where the sole object of the action is damages ; but in debt and ejectment, damages not being the principal object of the action, the plaintiff usually signs final judgment in the first instance,(d) except in actions of debt within the statute of 8 & 9 W. III. c. 11, § 8, which is in force in this State.(e)

After appearance and plea, if the court, without objection by the plaintiff, permit the defendant's attorney to withdraw his appearance and plea, no judgment can be given until a new appearance is entered by or for him ; and for that purpose a rule may be obtained by the plaintiff. No judgment is authorized by the common law or statute in such a state of the case. As the court would not allow an appearance to be retracted against the plaintiff's consent, nothing remains for him in such case but to rule the defendant into court to try the cause in the usual way.(f)

A judgment in an action on the case, for want of an appearance without declaration or anything to indicate the amount, is interlocutory in the first instance, and is not final until the amount is stated and entered : and if between these acts other judgments intervene, they obtain priority as liens.(g)

If any of the proceedings on the part of the plaintiff be irregular, and the irregularity be not waived by any act of the defendant, or if judgment be signed when in fact the defendant has not been guilty of any default, the court upon motion will set aside the judgment.(h) But if the defendant, being informed of a judgment irregularly entered for want of an appearance, neglects for two terms and until after inquiry executed to make such motion, it will not be reversed on error.(i) The plaintiff, also, may waive or relinquish judgment by default, whether

(v) 1 Saund. 28, n. 1, 2, 3 ; 296, n. 1.
(w) 1 B. & P. 646 ; 3 B. & P. 398 ; Barnes, 338.
(x) 5 T. R. 152 ; Wh. Dig. Prac. § 398.
(y) 2 Saund. 210 (e).
(z) Stra. 638, Com. Dig. Pleader, E. 42.
(a) 5 T. K. 152.
(b) Tidd, Pr. 588.

(c) 2 Arch. Pr. 9.
(d) 2 Arch. Pr. 9, and see Tidd, 508.
(e) Report of the Judges, 3 Bin. 625 ; Rob. Dig. 142 ; see 2 Arch. Pr. 11.
(f) Michew v. McCoy, 3 W. & S. 502 ; see ante, p. 229.
(g) Phillips v. Hellings, 5 W. & S. 44.
(h) 2 Arch. Pr. 11.
(i) Crosby v. Massey, 1 Pa. R. 229.

irregularly(j) or regularly entered,(k) by getting the clerk to strike it out.

On a judgment obtained in one State against a person residing in another, who was never served with process, or notified of the existence of the suit, his remedy was by motion, accompanied with sufficient proof to the court, in which the judgment was entered, who would stay the execution if issued, and set aside the judgment,(l) though, as will hereafter be noticed, by a recent statute, the non-service, by special plea, may be taken advantage of here. The attorney and the plaintiff are answerable in damages to the defendant; so also is the officer to whom the process was delivered, if the judgment were entered by default, for non-appearance upon a false return.(m)

As will hereafter be considered at greater length,(n) the court will also, in some cases, on the defendant's application, set aside a regular judgment, upon an affidavit of merits, if the plaintiff have not lost a trial.(o) This is, however, wholly discretionary in the court to do or not. And where it appeared that the defendant had refused to accede to equitable terms of compromise, the Court of Common Pleas in England would not set aside a regular judgment by default.(q) When the court set aside a regular judgment, it is usually upon the terms of the defendant's paying costs,(r) pleading issuably *instanter*,(s) that is, giving a plea in chief to the merits upon which the plaintiff may take issue and go to trial, or by demurring for some defect in substance,(t) and giving judgment of the term(u) when necessary; and in some cases also they will order the defendant to bring the money into court.(v)

(j) 2 Arch. Pr. 11.
(k) 1 Dunl. Pr. 378.
(l) 1 Peters, Rep. 155.
(m) Ibid.
(n) *Post*, chap. xxvii.
(o) 2 Salk. 518; 1 Salk. 402.

(q) 4 Taunt. 885.
(r) 1 Salk. 402; see Barnes, 256.
(s) 1 Burr. 586.
(t) 1 Chit. Plead. 505.
(u) 2 Stra. 823.
(v) Barnes, 243.

CHAPTER XV.

OF JUDGMENT BY CONFESSION.

JUDGMENT by confession is either by *cognovit actionem*, or by warrant of attorney; the former applying where an action has been commenced, and the latter being generally given as a security for a debt where no suit is pending, though sometimes given on compromising a suit. In the present chapter, we will treat first of the *cognovit*, and secondly of the warrant of attorney.

SECTION I.

OF A COGNOVIT.

Where the defendant has no available defence to make to the action, it is usual for him, instead of proceeding to trial, or of allowing judgment to pass against him by default, to give the plaintiff a *cognovit* or written confession of the action, usually upon condition that he shall be allowed a certain time for the payment of the debt or damages, the amount of such debt and damages being first ascertained and agreed upon.(a) If no time be stipulated in the *cognovit* for payment, the defendant, if a freeholder, was then entitled under the seventh section of the act of March, 1806,(b) to the usual stay of execution according to the amount of the judgment confessed; if he were not a freeholder, then by complying with the requisitions of the act. But the third section of the act of 1836,(c) which supersedes the former law, only gives a stay of execution " on judgments recovered in actions instituted by writ," and does not speak of judgments by confession, as did the act of 1806. The *cognovit* also generally contains an agreement upon the part of the defendant that no writ of error shall be brought.(d)

A *cognovit*, in the English practice, is given either where there has been no plea, or after plea pleaded. If given before plea, it merely states the confession, the amount of the debt or damages, the terms upon which the confession is given, and the defendant's agreement not to bring a writ of error;(e) but if given after plea pleaded, it also contains an agreement to withdraw the plea; in which case it is termed a *cognovit actionem relicta verificatione* from the form of the entry of it upon

(a) 2 Arch. Pr. 5.
(b) 4 Sm. L. 326.
(c) Pamph. L. 762.
(d) 2 Arch. Pr. 5.

(e) 2 Arch. Pr. 5, where Tidd, Forms, 156, §§ 1, 2, and Sellon, 372, are referred to for a form.

the roll.(f) The confession of the action may, it is said, be given before the plaintiff has declared,(g) particularly where the cause of action is expressed in the process (which original writs in Pennsylvania always do), but in England it is more regular, if the parties compromise before declaration, to take a warrant of attorney to confess judgment, as security for the debt and costs.(h) When the defendant has appeared by attorney and judgment is entered against him, it will be taken to be by confession.(i) If the amount of damages be not ascertained by the *cognovit*, the plaintiff must enter interlocutory judgment, and proceed to assess his damages as on a default.(j) "If the plaintiff's demand is in nature of a debt, which may be ascertained by calculation, whether it arise on a note or other writing, or on an account, it is sufficient to enter *judgment generally*. The judgment is supposed to be for the amount of damages laid in the declaration, and the execution issues accordingly. But the plaintiff indorses on the execution the amount of the *actual debt*, and if the defendant complains that injustice has been done, the court are always ready to give immediate and liberal relief on *motion*. Relief may likewise be given by a judge at his chambers before the return of the execution, a proper case being laid before him verified by oath."(k) This doctrine was adverted to with approbation by the Supreme Court, in a later case,(l) in which it was held that a confession of judgment, "sum to be liquidated by attorneys," operates as a lien upon the defendant's real estate, although not afterwards liquidated. The action in this case was stated to be in debt at the common law, for a specific sum, and that, even if a declaration were not filed, the judgment would be rendered certain by relation to the writ. The case of the Philadelphia Bank *v.* Craft,(m) was said to want the feature of certainty in the judgment in the first instance, it not having been rendered even for a nominal sum. In this case, it was held, that a judgment by confession "for a sum to be ascertained by the prothonotary," bound the real estate of the defendant only from the time of the liquidation of the sum by the prothonotary. At the first blush, these cases would appear to be exactly alike, but the court have pointed out the distinction.(n)

A judgment confessed by the defendant with an agreement that he be at liberty to have a trial, *whether anything, and how much may be due,*

(f) 2 Arch. Pr. 5.
(g) Ib. *cites* 7 Taunt. 701.
(h) Tidd, 585. The practice in reference to the form and nature of a *cognovit*, as above stated, is that which prevails in England, and would be regular in Pennsylvania, but it is seldom that the same practice is observed here, either as to the form of a confession of judgment, or as to the entering of it on record. Frequently, immediately after the institution of an action, both before and after the return of the writ, the defendant's attorney confesses judgment generally in words to the following effect: " I appear for the defendant, and confess judgment to the plaintiff for the sum of——, to take effect as if given on an award of arbitrators for the same sum, filed this day. A B, attorney for defendant—July

—th, 1825. It is not always that the latter clause has a determinate meaning; though, when a rule to arbitrate has been entered, it may be presumed to be a reservation by the defendant of his right to appeal within twenty days; or, it may be intended to give the defendant an opportunity, during twenty days, of entering security for a stay of execution, under the third and fourth sections of the act of 1836.

(i) Barde *v.* Wilson, 3 Y. 149.
(j) 1 Dunl. Pr. 357; 2 Arch. Pr. 7.
(k) Per TILGHMAN, C. J., Lewis *v.* Smith, 2 S. & R. 155.
(l) Com. *v.* Baldwin, 1 W. 54.
(m) 16 S. & R. 347.
(n) See Arrison *v.* Com., 1 W. 374, 378.

admits nothing, but the plaintiff is, nevertheless, bound to prove his case as laid in the declaration.(*o*) It has been usual at the bar thus to enter judgments, in order to bind lands or for the purpose of proceeding to charge the special bail, and under these judgments to try or refer the suits. In many instances, after such judgments confessed to plaintiff, verdicts, reports of referees, and judgments for the defendants have succeeded. Such appears to have been the old practice, though the cases just referred to have much affected it. Thus, in the Philadelphia Bank *v.* Craft,(*p*) it was held, that a judgment by confession for a sum to be ascertained by the prothonotary, binds the real estate of the defendant only from the time of the liquidation of the sum by the prothonotary. And the court said, that "secret incumbrances on real estate are not permitted by our law;" that a confession of judgment for debt or damages uncertain in amount, without any statement of the cause of action, and without any declaration or document on the record, by which the amount can possibly be known, is not from the time of such confession a lien upon land valid for whatever sum may be afterwards fixed.(*q*) Where an attorney appears specially for one defendant in a suit against two, and afterwards, as attorney "for the defendant," acknowledges judgment in favor of the plaintiff, it is a good judgment only as to the defendant for whom such attorney appeared, and a joint execution is erroneous. Although the acknowledgment is made in behalf of the "defendant," in the singular number, which in strictness is applicable only to one, yet if the attorney who confessed the judgment had appeared for both there might perhaps be a difference.(*r*)

A judgment entered in the District Court, by agreement, without the specific statement of the cause of action signed by the parties or their attorneys under the rule of court, which has heretofore been given, is a nullity, and may be set aside on the motion of any one who has an interest.(*s*)

A judgment which on the face of it is confessed by one partner, is a nullity as to the other, and the court will set it aside, together with a *fi. fa.* issued on it against the firm.(*t*)

When the legal or the stipulated stay of execution on a confession of judgment has expired, the plaintiff sues out execution, to recover the amount confessed, and if the *cognovit* be only of part of the cause of

(*o*) Gorgerat *v.* McCarty, 1 Y. 253.

(*p*) 16 S. & R. 347.

(*q*) See The Com. *v.* Baldwin, 1 W. 54, *supra*, 341. If the plaintiff take a *cognovit* for payment by instalments, if any instalment is postponed to a later day, than the time in which with diligence he could have obtained a judgment and execution, this discharges the special bail." Roup *v.* Waldhoner, 12 S. & R. 26.

(*r*) Kimmel *v.* Kimmel, 5 S. & R. 294.

(*s*) Baidee *v.* Murray, D. C. Phil. 9 Leg. Int. 239. See as to rule, *ante*, p. 279.

(*t*) Walker *v.* Bradley, D. C., Saturday, Sept. 16, 1848. Why judgment should not be opened and *fi. fa.* Set aside.— *Per curiam.* The judgment was con-

fessed, as appears by the record, by one member of the firm, and of course the judgment against the other is a nullity, and must be set aside. The *fi. fa.* of course recites judgment against the firm which never existed, and is, therefore, irregular. It is said, however, to have been levied only on Bradley's interest, and we are asked to amend. This we think we ought not to do. The writ is in the sheriff's hands, and, without consent, it is questionable whether we can amend. However that may be, we think we ought not to amend, and thereby encourage such irregularities. Judgment set aside as to Williams, and *fi. fa.* quashed. See *post*, chap. xxvii.

action (as it may), and not of the entire, he must levy for that part, and proceed in the original action for the residue.(*u*)

In cases under the act of 21st March, 1806, where a defendant is willing to confess judgment for a certain amount, "if the plaintiff, on trial being had, do not recover more than the amount for which the defendant was willing to confess judgment, he shall not recover any costs that accrued on the cause subsequent to the offer of confessing judgment, excepting the costs of issuing and serving a writ of execution when the same may be necessary."(*v*)

While a judgment may be confessed in writing in the presence of two witnesses upon the entry of an amicable action, conformably to the act of March, 1806,(*w*) an entry or confession of judgment by the prothonotary, in pursuance of an agreement, that an amicable action shall be entered, and that he shall enter judgment against the defendants in a certain sum, is independent of that act, and is valid; for the agreement is a sufficient authority to the prothonotary to enter an appearance of the defendants *in proper persons*, and a confession of judgment by them for the sum mentioned in the agreement.(*x*) So, too, is a judgment entered up by the prothonotary upon a written order sent to him by the defendant confessing judgment as in an action of debt, and directing the officer to enter judgment against him.(*y*) The assent of the plaintiff to such judgment may be presumed. The act just referred to is affirmative, and does not prohibit the entry of judgments according to a practice existing prior to its date.(*z*) The power of the prothonotary to sign judgment rests on a statutory grant of it when that officer was *ex officio* a judge of the Common Pleas, which has not been revoked.(*a*) And a defendant may appear before him and confess judgment in person; for he may do in person whatever he can by deed authorize another to do for him; and judgments in vacation by confession, on warrant of attorney, have been recognized as valid since the foundation of the province. But judgments by confession, on the appearance of the party in the office, have, from time immemorial, also been frequent, and their validity has never been contested.(*b*) The rule of the District Court on this point has been given.(*bb*)

Besides the case of judgment by default, where the defendant's default is deemed tantamount to a confession (and which was considered in the preceding chapter), there is also a confession of action in some cases implied in the defendant's pleading; as when an executor or administrator pleads *plene administravit* or *plene administravit præter*, without pleading in bar, this is impliedly a confession of the action; and upon the plea of *plene administravit*, the plaintiff may take judgment of assets *in futuro;* or upon *plene administravit præter* take judgment presently of the assets acknowledged to be in the hands of the defendant, and of assets *in futuro* for the residue.(*c*)

It is no objection to the validity of a judgment, entered under the 28th section of the act of 24th February, 1806, that no declaration was

(*u*) 1 Sellon, 373; Tidd, 495.
(*v*) § 5, 4 Sm. L. 329.
(*w*) *Vide ante,* p. 277.
(*x*) Cook *v.* Gilbert, 8 S. & R. 567.
(*y*) McCalmont *v.* Peters, 13 S. & R. 196.

(*z*) Ibid.
(*a*) Reed *v.* Hamet, 4 W. 441-2.
(*b*) Ibid.
(*bb*) *Ante,* p. 279.
(*c*) 2 Arch. Pr. 7, 131-132.

filed; although the warrant of attorney required that one shall be filed.(*g*)

A warrant of attorney is a written authority to the attorney or attorneys to whom it is directed, to appear for the party executing it, receive a declaration for him in an action, at the suit of a person therein mentioned, and thereupon to confess the action, or suffer judgment to pass by default ; and to sign a release of all errors and defects touching such proceedings.(*h*) Where a party gives a warrant of attorney as security for a debt on which no suit is pending, it is usual at the same time to execute a bond, conditioned for the payment of the debt, with interest, either immediately, or within a stipulated time after the date, to which bond the warrant refers, and authorizes a confession of judgment for the penalty.(*i*) The person to whom the warrant of attorney is given has all the benefit of a judgment and execution against the debtor's person and property, without being delayed by any intermediate process, as in the case of a regular suit.(*j*) It is as much an act of the court as if it were formally pronounced on *nil dicit* or a *cognovit* ; and, till it is reversed or set aside, it has all the qualities and effect of a judgment on verdict ;(*k*) and if it be given to confess a judgment unconditionally, or without delay of execution, judgment may be signed, and execution may be taken out upon the same day it is given; and thus a debtor may give one creditor a preference to another, who has obtained a judgment after long litigation(*.l*)

A warrant to confess judgment, should contain not only a grant of the authority, expressed clearly and intelligibly, but a designation by name, or description of the person who is to execute it.   The act of assembly merely substitutes the prothonotary, though not named or described in the warrant, for an attorney of the court ; but it supplies no deficiency which may exist in the power.   A writing expressing a *desire* that the judgment be *recorded*, is an insufficient authority for the prothonotary—nothing can cure the want of it.(*m*)

A warrant of attorney, accompanying a bond, authorizes the entry of but one judgment.(*n*)   The delivery of the warrant of attorney is not necessary to the validity of the judgment as to strangers.(*o*)

The warrant of attorney must be subscribed by the defendant, and it is generally by deed, with an attesting witness ; but it has been held that an attesting witness was not necessary, and that it was not even requisite that it should be by deed.(*p*)

(*g*) Montelius *v.* Montelius, Bright. R. 79.

(*h*) 2 Arch. Pr. 12; Bing. on Judgments, 38.

(*i*) 1 Dunl. Pr. 359 ; see Shoemaker *v.* Shutliffe, 1 D. 133.

(*j*) 1 Cromp. Pr. 316.

(*k*) Braddee *v.* Brownfield, 4 W. 474.

(*l*) 5 T. R. 235.

(*m*) Rabe *v.* Heislip, 4 Barr, 139.

(*n*) Ulrich *v.* Voneida, 1 P. R. 250; Hauer's Appeal, 5 W. & S. 474.

(*o*) Parmentier *v.* Gillespie, 9 Barr, 87.

(*p*) 5 Taunt. 264.   As to when a judgment confessed under a warrant of attorney is void or voidable, as to whom void, and as to the effect of a warrant given by the agent or one of the family of the

The manner of entering up judgment on a warrant of attorney by the English practice, is as follows : A declaration in debt is made out by the plaintiff's attorney, at the end of which judgment is confessed for the defendant, and signed by the attorney to whom the warrant is directed (which is usually the attorney for the plaintiff). If the warrant of attorney justify immediate execution, a *præcipe* for this may be written on the back of the declaration. The declaration thus prepared, with the warrant of attorney, must be filed with the prothonotary ; all this may be performed at once ; and judgment may be entered in vacation, as well as in term ; but if in vacation, the judgment must be entered as of the preceding term.(*q*) If a bond have been given with a warrant of attorney, the declaration is made out in debt on bond; if not, it is usually made out on a *mutuatus*, that is, as on an instrument not under seal ; but in all cases the warrant of attorney must be strictly pursued in entering up the judgment.(*r*) Therefore, if, on a warrant to enter up judgment in debt on bond, judgment be entered up in debt on a *mutuatus*, the court will set it aside as irregular.(*s*)

In our practice, the prothonotary will enter up the judgment on simply taking to him the bond and warrant ; and retaining the latter, he will return the bond with the date of the entry of the judgment indorsed on it. This practice seems to owe its origin to the act of assembly next referred to.

By the act of February 24, 1806, § 28,(*t*) "it shall be the duty of the prothonotary of any court of record within this commonwealth, on the application of any person, being the original holder (or assignee of such holder) of a note, bond, or other instrument of writing, in which judgment is confessed, or containing a warrant for an attorney at law, or other person to confess judgment, to enter judgment against the person or persons, who executed the same for the amount, which, from the face of the instrument, may appear to be due, without the agency of an attorney, or declaration filed, with such stay of execution as may be therein mentioned, for the fee of one dollar, to be paid by the defendant ; particularly entering on his docket the date and tenor of the instrument of writing, on which the judgment may be founded, which shall have the same force and effect as if a declaration had been filed, and judgment confessed by an attorney, or judgment obtained in open court, and in term time ; and the defendant shall not be compelled to pay any costs, or fee to the plaintiff's attorney, when judgment is entered on any instrument of writing as aforesaid." When a judgment, entered pursuant to this act, is opened, and the defendant let into a defence, neither declaration nor statement is necessary.(*u*) The evident and sole end of this act, was, it is said, to exempt the obligor from the payment of costs to an attorney.(*v*) And no set form of words is prescribed, in which the prothonotary shall enter judgment, as it is to be desired there should have been, both for the sake of uniformity and pre-

---

obligor, to an attorney at law, see, without reference to the syllabus, the case of Campbell *v.* Kent, 3 Pa. R. 72, in which the whole subject is thoroughly discussed in the opinion of the majority of the court, and also in that of the two dissenting judges.

(*q*) 2 Ld. Raym. 766, 850.
(*r*) 2 Arch. Pr. 17.
(*s*) 8 T. R. 153.
(*t*) 4 Sm. Laws, 278.
(*u*) Reed *v.* Pedan, 8 S. & R. 263.
(*v*) Helvete *v.* Rapp, 7 S. & R. 307.

cision. There being no literal form directed, and no precedent to guide the prothonotaries in the exercise of this duty, each has adopted his own mode.(w)

The party giving a warrant of attorney, cannot revoke it by his own act ;(x) but the death of either party is, generally speaking, a counter-mand of the warrant of attorney ;(y) and on a warrant to confess judgment given *by* two, the death of one is a revocation of the authority, and judgment cannot be entered against the other ;(z) but if it be given *to* two or more, and one of them die, judgment may be entered up by the survivor ;(a) and if the warrant authorize a judgment to be entered at the suit of A, his executors and administrators, it is not revoked by the death of A, and his executors may enter judgment.(b) The general rule does not apply where the judgment can be made good by relation : therefore, if the defendant die during vacation, judgment may be entered against him in that vacation, as of the preceding term, and it will be valid by the common law ;(c) but it will not affect lands or tenements as regards purchasers, or mortgagees, or have any preference against heirs, executors or administrators, except from the time of filing or docketing.(d) Neither can judgment be entered up against two defendants, on a warrant purporting to be an authority to confess judgment against three persons, one of whom has refused to execute.(e)

A warrant of attorney to enter judgment as of the last, next, or any subsequent term, authorizes the entry of a judgment in the present term.(f)

Judgment was entered on a bond and warrant of attorney, which stipulated that execution should not issue before default in the payment of several promissory notes, unless the partnership existing between defendant and A B should be dissolved. It was held, that an execution issued before the maturity of the notes, without a *scire facias* having been first sued out, to ascertain whether the partnership had been dissolved, was irregular, and it was accordingly set aside.(g)

As between the plaintiff and defendant, it was said by SERGEANT, J., it is no objection to the validity of a judgment, that the prothonotary has not fully complied with the act which requires him to enter on his docket the date and tenor of the instrument of writing on which the judgment is founded.(h)

It is held in the State of New Jersey, that, where a bond has been legally assigned, judgment must be entered in the name of the assignee, though the warrant be not in its terms assignable.(i)

A prothonotary who has entered judgment on a bond by virtue of the warrant of attorney accompanying it, under the provisions of the act of 1806, is not the agent either of the party or of the law, and if the defendant pay the money to him, it is a mispayment which cannot be set up as a discharge of the debt.(j)

(w) Ibid.
(x) Ld. Raym. 850 ; Salk. 87, pl. 6.
(y) Co. Littl. 52, b.; Bing. on Judg. 43.
(z) 15 East, 592 ; 7 Taunt. 453.
(a) 2 M. & R. 76 ; 2 W. Bl. 1301.
(b) 8 T. R. 257.
(c) Salk. 87 pl.; 6 Willes, 427 ; Barnes, 267, 268, 270 ; 8 T. R. 257.

(d) Ld. Raym. 850 ; Stra. 882 ; 3 P. Wms. 399.
(e) 1 Chit. Rep. 322.
(f) Montelius v. Montelius, Bright. R. 79.
(g) Ibid.
(h) Ibid.
(i) 1 South. 351.
(j) Bear v. Kistler, 4 R. 364.

A warrant of attorney, whether given by a feme sole,(h) or to her,(i) is not revoked or countermanded by her marriage, and judgment may be entered up in the names of husband and wife.(j) Where a bond and warrant of attorney were given to a feme *dum sola*, who afterwards married, the court, upon affidavit of the fact, allowed judgment to be entered in favor of the baron and feme.(k) A judgment entered up under such circumstances, without leave, would be irregular.(l)

The judgment cannot be entered before the warrants reach the office.(m)

A judgment confessed by attorney of court is valid although done without authority.(n)

A warrant of attorney to confess judgment must be express.(o)

A prothonotary complies substantially with the directions of the act of 1806, requiring him to enter judgment on a bond with warrant of attorney, upon the application of the party, when he enters on his docket the names of the obligor and obligee in the form of an action as parties; the date of the bond and warrant of attorney, the penal sum, the real debt, and the time of entering the judgment, and the date of the entry of the judgment on the margin of the record, according to the act of 21st March, 1772.(p)

Within a year and a day next after the date of the warrant, judgment may be entered of course, by the English practice, without applying to the court or a judge; but not after that time, without moving the court in term time, unless the warrant be but ten or under ten years old, and then application may be made to a judge in vacation;(q) but here, by our rules of court, if a warrant of attorney to enter judgment be above ten years old, and under twenty, the court in term time, or a judge in the vacation, must be moved for leave to enter judgment, which motion must be grounded on an affidavit of the due execution of the warrant, that the money is unpaid and the party living; but if the warrant be above twenty years old, there must be a rule to show cause, and served on the party, if to be found within the State.(r)

In the absence of Pennsylvania cases on the subject, we will state some of the English decisions, relative to entering up judgment on an old warrant of attorney. The party must be sworn to have been alive on a day within the term.(s) And an affidavit, stating that the party was alive on the 5th November, and that deponent verily believed him to be now alive, was held insufficient.(t) So where it stated that the party was alive the 22d January, the first day of the term being the 23d January, on a Sunday. So an affidavit, that the party was alive, "about ten days ago," which, by computation, would be within the term.(u) But an affidavit stating that deponent had received a letter from the party dated on a day within the term, and that he believed it to be his handwriting, was held sufficient.(v) Where the party lives

(h) 1 Show, 89; 3 Burr. 1470; 4 East, 522; Bingh. on Judg. 42, 43.
(i) Salk. 117, pl. 9.
(j) 3 Burr. 1471; Eneu v. Clark, 2 Barr, 421.
(k) 1 Br. 253.
(l) 3 Burr. 1471.
(m) Chambers v. Denie, 2 Barr, 421.
(n) King v. Carter, 1 Barr, 153.

(o) Rabe v. Heslip 4 Barr, 140.
(p) Com. v. Conrad, 1 R. 249.
(q) Tidd, 578.
(r) Dist. Ct. Rule c ii.
(s) 3 Moore, C. P. 606.
(t) 1 Chit. K. B. 617.
(u) Ibid. *notis.*
(v) Ibid.

abroad, and no affidavit can be made of his being alive within the term in which the application is made, the court will give judgment as of the term to which the affidavit can apply.(w) On a motion to enter up judgment on a warrant of attorney, an affidavit, verifying the hand-writing of the defendant, is not sufficient to dispense with that of the attesting witness, or an affidavit verifying his handwriting, if he alone cannot be found.(x) So, if the attesting witness be out of the juris-diction of the court.(y) If the warrant be above twenty years old, the rule is only *nisi* in the first instance; and a warrant to secure payment after the death of the defendant's father, is within the rule.(z) The affidavit should state some facts showing that the legal presumption of payment has not attached.(a)

Where a judgment has been irregularly or improperly entered upon a warrant of attorney, the remedy of the defendant, as will be hereafter fully seen,(b) is by motion to set aside the judgment.(c) The court pos-sesses an equitable jurisdiction over judgments entered on bond and warrant of attorney; and therefore, if the requisites necessary to ren-der them valid be wanting, they will be set aside.(d) The rules in re-lation to contracts apply to a warrant of attorney. It must not only be founded on a valid consideration, but the parties by, and to whom it is executed must possess legal capacity.(e) And not only the immediate parties to it, but those whose estate is affected by the judgment, may impeach the judgment; therefore it is competent for a terre tenant, who is brought in on a *scire facias* issued to revive a judgment, to show on the trial (after an unsuccessful application to the court to strike the entry of the judgment from the record) that it was entered without authority, that it was fraudulent, or otherwise wholly irregular, as, that it had been previously entered in another county.(f) When the bond, upon which judgment is confessed by virtue of a warrant of attorney, is invalid or illegal, the party should apply to the court *in which it is entered* to open the judgment; for if it be regularly confessed and entered, the Supreme Court on a writ of error, will not inquire further.(g)

It is when the facts, on which the defendant seeks relief, are not de-nied, or rendered doubtful by the counter affidavits on the part of the plaintiff, that the court will set aside the warrant of attorney, and the proceedings which have been taken upon it.(h) But where the affidavits are contradictory, the court will not weigh the credit of those who made them, but *will award a feigned issue* to ascertain the truth; and this was done, in one case, in order to try the fact whether the bond and warrant of attorney, on which judgment was entered, were forgeries.(i) So, on an application by a creditor to set aside a judgment alleged to have been fraudulently confessed by the defendant to the plaintiff, on a warrant of attorney, the court directed an issue to try the charge of fraud, and permitted the creditor to *subpœna* witnesses to attend the

(w) Ibid. *notis*.
(x) Ib. 743.
(y) Ib. 744.
(z) Ib. 617, *notis*.
(a) 2 Barn. & Cress. 556; 9 S. & Low. 177.
(b) *Post*, chap. xxvii.
(c) Cowp. 729.
(d) 9 Johns. 80, 253; See 1 Dunl. Pr. 367.

(e) See on this subject 1 Dunl. Pr. 359, 367; Young v. Reuben, 1 D. 119–122; 2 Arch. Pr. 14.
(f) Ulrich v. Voneida, 1 Pa. R. 245; See Davis v. Barr, 9 S. & R. 137, 141.
(g) Carlisle v. Woods, 7 S. & R. 207.
(h) 3 Johns. 250; 1 Taunt. 415.
(i) 3 Johns. 142.

trial, in the name of the defendant.(*j*)   The court have sometimes given special directions as to the manner in which the issue shall be made up, and the county in which it is to be tried.(*k*)   On awarding the issue, the court will stay execution until their further order.(*l*)   With us, a feigned issue is to every legal intent an action ; the motion for a new trial be. ing entertained by the court in which the question has been tried, and the practice being to render a judgment on the verdict for the purpose of enabling the unsuccessful party to have the proceedings reversed on a writ of error.   And when sent by the Orphans' Court to the Common Pleas, the former court is to be governed exclusively by the opinion of the court to which the issue is sent, nor does it exercise any power of selection.(*m*)

The contradiction or doubt, which will induce the court to direct a feigned issue, must not be such as arises only from the assertion of one party, and the denial of the other ; for, if the plaintiff's affidavit positively contradict the allegations in the defendant's affidavit, and no other testimony be produced, the court will not interfere in any way ; but it is where the subject is rendered doubtful or obscure by the evidence of third persons, that the court will send it to a jury to be tried. Where the warrant of attorney, and the proceedings thereon, have been set aside, the party is, notwithstanding, at liberty to proceed by action on the bond.(*n*)

A feigned issue being a proceeding, directed by the court, to ascertain the truth of facts for its own information,(*o*) either party may notice it for trial, and there can be no judgment, as in case of nonsuit, for not proceeding to trial.(*p*)   Neither can the plaintiff discontinue it.(*q*)   The court, on the award of a feigned issue, part with their power over the facts of the case ; but they are not bound by the verdict, and may, therefore, direct a new trial.(*r*)

For a more general discussion of the nature of feigned issues, and the manner of conducting them, the reader is referred to a subsequent chapter.(*s*)

Great frauds are often committed under color of these bonds and warrants of attorney, and in some of the States they are absolutely prohibited, on experience of the abuse made of them.   They could be nowhere tolerated without the exercise of a liberal discretion by the court in inquiring into them.   Feigned issues should be encouraged, because, without them, the court must draw the trial of all facts to itself. If the court decides the whole on motion, there is no redress in case of error.   But should there be a mistake in the admission or rejection of evidence, or in charging the jury, on a feigned issue, a writ of error lies.(*t*)   But the mode in which a feigned issue is made up is not the subject of a writ of error, and the court below may mould it as their discretion dictates.(*u*)

After judgment has been entered on a bond in one county, by virtue

(*j*) 9 Johns. 80.
(*k*) 3 Johns. 140.
(*l*) 2 Johns. Cas. 260.
(*m*) Woods *v.* Woods, 17 S. & R. 13.
(*n*) 6 Johns. 331; 1 B. & P. 270 ; 1 Dunl. Pr. 369.
(*o*) See Davis *v.* Barr, 5 S. & R. 516.
(*p*) 17 Johns. 267.

(*q*) Semb. 1 Bin. 448.
(*r*) Graham *v.* Graham, 1 S. & R. 331, 332.
(*s*) See Index, " Feigned Issues."
(*t*) See Kellogg *v.* Krauser, 14 S. & R. 143, 144 ; Neff *v.* Barr, Id. 166.
(*u*) Ibid.

of a warrant of attorney to confess a judgment, a judgment entered on the same bond, under the same warrant, in another county, is irregular ;(v) as soon as the judgment is entered in one county, the power contained in the warrant is fully complied with; the debt is then merged into a debt of a higher nature, and the judgment must be pursued, either by bringing an action of debt upon it in another county, or proceeding in the usual way, by *testatum fi. fa.* or *ca. sá.*(w) A judgment, however, entered under such a warrant, in another county, is not void, for, if a sale have been made under it, the purchaser from the sheriff has a good title. The attorney, who entered such judgment, or the obligee, if entered by him, is answerable for the consequences.(x) Where two judgments have been entered under the same power, in different counties, and an issue is directed by the court in which one of the judgments is entered, to determine whether it be valid, the party who alleges that it is not valid, may give in evidence an entry on the docket, stating the hour and minute when the judgment was entered, if it appear from other evidence that such entry was made by the opposite party or his agent. But, it seems, that the burden of showing which of the judgments was first entered, properly lies on him by whom they were entered.(y)

The entry of a second judgment, in another county, under the same warrant, is not the subject of a writ of error. The court in which it is entered must, and will, under ordinary circumstances, vacate it.(z) But it is a question how far the court will exercise their discretionary power to let in the subsequent judgment of a third person.(a)

When an agreement, in restraint or enlargement of the right of execution, takes place between the parties, it should be made part of the condition of the bond, or of the warrant,(b) or the subject of a separate instrument under seal, for, parol evidence, to contradict or to construe the bond differently from the plain import of the condition or indorsement, cannot be admitted. Thus, on a motion to set aside an execution, which had issued on a judgment entered up on a bond, by warrant of attorney, on the ground that the first instalment was paid, evidence to prove that it had been verbally agreed by the parties that execution might issue for protecting the whole sum, was rejected by the court.(c) So, in an action for a malicious abuse of legal process, where the plaintiff was allowed, *in support of his declaration,* to give evidence of a parol agreement not to issue execution on a bond with a warrant of attorney, until after notice, the court said that whether *such* an agreement is *a good cause of action* was another matter, of which the defendant may avail himself by demurrer, or motion in arrest of judgment.(d) Any agreement between the original parties, inconsistent with the purport or legal effect of the warrant, will not affect the assignee of the bond. The assignee is not bound to call on the obligor for information

(v) Martin v. Rex, 6 S. & R. 296, S. P.; 2 Br. 321; Addis. 267; Neff v. Barr, 14 S. & R. 166; Ulrich v. Voneida, 1 Pa. R. 245; 3 W. C. C. R. 558; Campbell v. Kent, 3 Pa. R. 76.

(w) 2 Br. 321.
(x) Martin v. Rex, 6 S. & R. 296.
(y) Neff v. Barr, 14 S. & R. 166.
(z) Id. ibid.

(a) Ibid.
(b) See Shoemaker v. Shutliffe, 1 D. 133.
(c) Plankinhorn v. Cave, 2 Y. 370.
(d) Sommer v. Wilt, 4 S. & R. 19. See as to an agreement in restraint of the right to enter up judgment, Davis v. Barr, 9 S. & R. 137. See also Anderson v. Neff, 11 S. & R. 220–1, particularly.

about matters, the existence of which he has no reason to suspect, such as collateral agreements; the necessity of inquiry being limited by the act authorizing the assignment of bonds to want of consideration and set-off.(e)

If the amount payable on the bond be unliquidated, execution must not be issued until it be first ascertained; if it is, the process will be set aside on error.(f)

In the next chapter will be considered the practice in assessing damages on bonds generally.

(e) Davis v. Barr, 9 S. & R. 137, 141.   (f) Holden v. Bull, 1 Pa. R. 460.

CHAPTER XVI.

OF THE WRIT OF INQUIRY AND ASSESSMENT OF DAMAGES, AND HEREIN OF THE PRACTICE IN ASSESSING DAMAGES ON BONDS.

AFTER an interlocutory judgment, a writ of inquiry of damages is in general awarded; which is a judicial writ, directed to the sheriff of the county where the action is laid, setting forth the proceedings which have been had in the cause, "and that the plaintiff ought to recover his damages, by occasion of the premises; but because it is unknown what damages he hath sustained by occasion" thereof, the sheriff is commanded, that by the oath of twelve honest and lawful men he diligently inquire the same, and return the inquisition into court at the next term. This writ is sued out by præcipe to the prothonotary.(a)

It is customary to have all those writs awarded the same term executed together, in order to save charges. In such case, the time fixed upon is usually some few days before the next term. It is said to have been the uniform practice to give a defendant eight days' notice of the execution of a writ of inquiry of damages, which must be served personally,(b) or left at his place of abode; but in a foreign attachment the notices are put up in the prothonotary's office.(c) If notice of the time, and likewise of the place, of executing the writ be not given, the court will, on motion and affidavit of the fact, set aside the writ and *all the subsequent proceedings*.(d) But the present rule of the Supreme Court only requires four days' notice of the execution of a writ of inquiry.

The writ must be executed against all the defendants, jointly, who have suffered judgment to go by default.(e)

To prevent the excessive charges which arose upon executing writs of inquiry, it was provided by an act passed the 22d of May, 1772 :(f) "That the justices who give any interlocutory judgment shall, at the motion of the plaintiff, or his attorney in the action where such judgment is given, make an order, in the nature of a writ of inquiry, to charge the jury attending at the same or next court, after such judgment is given, to inquire of the damages and costs sustained by the plaintiff in such action, which inquiry shall be made and evidence given in open court; and after the inquest consider thereof, they shall forth-

(a) See for forms 2 Grayd. Forms, 232; and see Wh. Dig. "Practice," xii.

(b) Moore v. Heiss, 4 Y. 261; Duncan v. Lloyd, 1 M. 350. In 2 Graydon's Forms, p. 237, it is said that the defendant must have eight days' notice of the execution of the writ, if he live within forty miles; if further, fourteen days.

(c) Ibid.; *et vide* Penrose v. Hart, 1 D. 378. See *post*, p. 361.

(d) Sheetz v. Hopkins, C. P., June, 1784, MS. Reports.

(e) Cridland v. Floyd, 6 S. & R. 414.

(f) 1 Sm. Laws, 144.

with return their inquisition, under their hands and seals, whereupon the court may proceed to judgment, as upon inquisitions of that kind returned by the sheriff." This course, however, as has been said,(*g*) is never pursued in our practice; for what signifies it to the plaintiff, it is asked, that charges are made heavy, since it is the defendant who is to pay them? But this is not a good reason under all circumstances, for the costs being first to be deducted, if an execution be not very productive, there is danger of losing the debt; it is good policy, therefore, in the plaintiff, always to have the costs low. The true reason why suitors do not avail themselves of this act in practice, is from the fact of only one jury being summoned for all the cases of each term, by which all inquests are held, and also from the increase of business which has occasioned reductions in the fee bill; so that now this course is as cheap as the other, perhaps cheaper. By a recent decision, this act has been declared to be still in full force, notwithstanding non-user, and that its provisions may be adopted according to the pleasure of courts or suitors.(*h*) We have seen, however, two attempts made in the District Court to obtain the benefit of the provision of this act, which were both abandoned in consequence of the evident disinclination evinced by the court to sanction the course. In one of those cases the reasons offered by the counsel who asked for the taking of the inquisition by the court, were, that several important questions of law would arise, both as to the evidence to be given, and the amount of damages to be assessed, which he thought the sheriff incompetent to decide; and further, there was always so much hurry before a sheriff's jury of inquiry, that in a disputed case there was no chance of having a full and adequate investigation. In the case of Wright *v.* Crane, above referred to, the objection was, that after the judgment by default a writ of inquiry should have been issued in the usual form, instead of the proceeding under this act of assembly, which had been exactly complied with, but which was alleged to be obsolete. But the eminent judge who delivered the opinion of the court observed: "The provisions of this act are not unsuited to modern times. It imposes no hardship on the defendant, who is secured a fair trial. And, indeed, it has this advantage, that the proceedings are conducted under the eye of the court. There is no pretence, therefore, for saying that it is obsolete."(*i*)

When judgment is obtained in actions instituted and conducted under the act of March, 1806, in consequence of the defendant's default in not appearing at the second term, and making defence against the plaintiff's demand, it is made the duty of the court by the fifth section, on a precise day in the term, to give judgment by default against the defendant for the sum which shall appear to be due.(*j*) But it being very questionable whether the act of 1836, providing new forms of original process, have not impliedly abrogated the form of writ given by the act of 1806, this practice seems obsolete.

After appeal by defendant from award of arbitrators and judgment for want of a plea, no writ of inquiry is necessary.(*jj*)

Judgment by default is always interlocutory in assumpsit, covenant, trespass, case, and replevin, the sole object of these actions being da-

(*g*) MS. on Prac.
(*h*) Wright *v.* Crane, 13 S. & R. 447.
(*i*) Per TILGHMAN, C. J., ibid. 452.

(*j*) 6 Id. 21.
(*jj*) Green *v.* Hallowell, 9 Barr, 54.

mages.(*k*) Such judgment merely establishes the plaintiff's title to damages; but their amount still remains to be ascertained. This is usually done by writ of inquiry.(*l*) As the inquest, however, is only for the purpose of informing the conscience of the court, the court themselves may, in all cases, if they please, assess the damages, and thereupon give final judgment;(*m*) and it is accordingly the practice, in actions upon bills of exchange and promissory notes, to refer it to the prothonotary to compute the amount of principal and interest due on the bill or note, without a writ of inquiry;(*n*) and the same in an action of covenant for non-payment of a liquidated sum,(*o*) as for non-payment of money lent upon mortgage,(*p*) or for non-payment of rent,(*q*) or the like. In suits on bonds for performance of written agreements, within the provisions of the act of 14th June, 1836, no power is given to grant summary or equitable relief; and hence in judgments by default for the penalty, the damages sustained by breach of the condition to appear ought to be assessed by writ of inquiry.(*r*)

According to the English practice, in order to a reference to the prothonotary, it is proper to make an affidavit of the cause of action, and that interlocutory judgment has been signed, and then to move the court to have the matter referred to that officer, who will grant a rule to show cause, or absolute at their discretion. If the former, the copy must be served on the opposite attorney.(*s*) When a reference is granted, it is also proper for the plaintiff to give notice to the defendant of the time appointed by the prothonotary for computing the principal and interest, &c., in analogy to the practice upon writs of inquiry.(*t*) The principal and interest being computed, and the costs being taxed, final judgment is entered for the sum thus found, and execution may issue.(*u*) But the foregoing is not the practice here.

In Pennsylvania, however, the practice used to be pretty general to issue writs of inquiry even in cases where the damages are capable of arithmetical computation.(*v*) An express rule of the Supreme Court, and the unbroken practice of the courts of original jurisdiction, now authorize the prothonotary to ascertain the damages in all cases of judgment by default, where the suit is on a promissory note, bill of exchange, or book account, and, also, in all other cases founded on contract, and sounding in damages, when the defendant does not object. But if the defendant object in the two last-mentioned cases, or if the action be founded on a tort, the damages shall be ascertained by a jury of inquiry.

In the District Court, in all cases of judgment taken under the second section of the act which organizes it, for want of a special affidavit of defence, the prothonotary assesses the damages, upon which execution may immediately be issued. Where damages had been assessed on one only out of several notes, the court, on motion, vacated the assessment, and permitted the damages to be reassessed.(*w*)

(*k*) 2 Arch. Pr. 20.
(*l*) Ibid.
(*m*) 3 Wils. 61, 62; 2 Id. 372, 374; 1 Doug. 316, *n.*; 4 Taunt. 148.
(*n*) 4 T. R. 275; 2 Saund. 107, *a.*; and see 12 East, 420; 4 Taunt. 148.
(*o*) 1 Doug. 316.
(*p*) 8 T. R. 326.
(*q*) 8 T. R. 410; 6 Taunt. 336.

(*r*) O'Neal *v.* O'Neal, 4 W. & S. 130; Thornton *v.* Bonham, 2 Barr, 102.
(*s*) See 2 Arch. Pr. 31.
(*t*) 4 Taunt. 487.
(*u*) 2 Arch. Pr. 31.
(*v*) See Serg. on Attach. 20, *n.*
(*w*) Kensington *v.* Vandusen, D. Ct. C. C. P. Sept. 1848.

The case of Lewis *v.* Smith,*(x)* before quoted,*(y)* confirms another mode of practice highly convenient, which, although founded on a judgment *confessed*, may be extended, it is apprehended, to all judgments by default, which are themselves *implied* confessions of judgments. And where judgment is confessed for the penalty of a bond, execution may issue for the condition, with interest, and costs, without a writ of inquiry.*(z)*

But when the computation of damages is not a mere matter of calculation, the court will not thus refer it, but will put the plaintiff to sue out his writ of inquiry: thus, in an action on a bill of exchange for foreign money,*(a)* in an action on a foreign judgment,*(b)* in an action on a bond to save harmless,*(c)* or on a covenant to indemnify,*(d)* in an action on a bottomry bond,*(e)* or in assumpsit for a sum certain due upon an agreement,*(f)* the court have refused to refer it to the clerk. But in covenant for non-payment of ground-rent, the prothonotary may assess the damages.*(g)*

If there be judgment by default as to part, and issue joined as to the residue, a special *venire* is awarded *tam ad triandum quam ad inquirendum*, as well to try the issue as to inquire of the damages; and the jury who try the issue, in that case assess the damages.*(h)* So, where there are several defendants; if some let judgment go by default, either of appearance or plea, and some plead to issue, the present uniform practice is for the, jury who try the issue to assess the damages against all the defendants.*(i)* Thus, in an action on a penal bond against two, where one suffers judgment by default, and the other pleads to issue, the judgment against the former is interlocutory, and damages for breaches are assessed against both on the trial of the issue.*(j)* In such cases, says GIBSON, C. J., where the judgment by default has been given erroneously for the penalty, but special damages are assessed on the trial of the issue, it seems that the court may strike off the sum added to the first judgment, take the damages assessed on the trial to be the amount for which each is liable, and give final judgment against them jointly.*(k)* But in actions where the plea of one defendant enures to the benefit of all, as in actions upon contracts, if the plaintiff fail of obtaining a verdict against those who have pleaded, he cannot have damages assessed against the others who let judgment go by default; for the contract being entire, the plaintiffs must succeed against all the defendants or none.*(l)* In actions *ex delicto*, on the contrary, if the plaintiff do not succeed against the defendants who plead, he may still have his damages assessed against those who allowed judgment to go by default,*(m)* unless the plea of those who pleaded prove that the plaintiff could have no cause of action against any of them;*(n)* for the tort is several as well

(x) 2 S. & R. 142.
(y) Supra, p. 341.
(z) Grubb *v.* Willis, 11 S. & R. 107. See Douredoure *v.* Krambaar, 1 M. 264.
(a) 5 T. R. 87.
(b) 4 T. R. 493.
(c) 2 Wils. 5.
(d) 14 East, 622.
(e) Tidd, 504.
(f) Ibid.
(g) Watkins *v.* Phillips, 2 Wh. 209;

ante, p. 354.
(h) 2 Arch. Pr. 9.
(i) Cridland *v.* Floyd; 6 S. & R. 414, 416, 417, 418; Ridgely *v.* Dobson, 3 W. & S. 118.
(j) O'Neal *v.* O'Neal, 4 W. & S. 130.
(k) Ibid.
(l) 2 Arch. Pr. 9.
(m) 2 Stra. 1108, 1222; Cridland *v.* Floyd; 6 S. & R. 416.
(n) 2 Ld. Ray. 1372.

as joint. So, also, where one of the defendants demurs, a *venire* is awarded as well to try the issue as to assess contingent damages;(*o*) and if issue be joined on one of the pleas, and judgment be entered by default on two others, the plaintiff cannot execute a writ of inquiry on those pleas on which he has judgment, but must award jury process, *tam ad triandum quam inquirendum*.(*p*) If joint defendants suffer judgment by default, and the plaintiff execute several writs of inquiry, and several damages are given, judgment for such damages would be erroneous; but before final judgment, the court will suffer a plaintiff to cure the defect by setting aside his own proceedings and issuing a new writ of inquiry.(*q*)

Writs of inquiry, to use the language of Judge Burnside in a recent case, are not usual in Pennsylvania after judgment by default in action by debt, but the practice is when the demand can be ascertained by calculation, to issue executions for the amount laid in the declaration, and for the plaintiff's attorney to indorse on the execution the real debt.(*r*) But if there be several years' interest to calculate on the amount of the debt, it should be referred to the prothonotary to ascertain what is due to the plaintiff.(*s*)

By the stat. 8 & 9, W. III. c. 11, § 8 :(*t*) "In all actions in any court of record upon any bond, or on any penal sum, for non-performance of any covenants or agreements contained in any indenture, deed, or writing," (whether the covenant, &c., be contained in the same, or in any other deed or writing ;(*u*) and the statute extends to bonds, &c., for the payment of money by instalments,(*v*) for the payment of an annuity),(*w*) "for the performance of an award,(*x*) or for the performance of any other specific act, excepting for the payment of a sum of money in gross, and excepting the case of a bail-bond,(*y*) and replevin-bond,(*z*) the plaintiff may assign as many breaches as he shall think fit, and the jury shall assess not only such damages and costs as have heretofore been usually done, but also damages for such of the breaches of covenants, &c., as the plaintiff upon the trial of the issues shall prove to have been broken; and the like judgment shall be entered on such verdict, as heretofore has been usually done. And if judgment shall be given for the plaintiff on demurrer, or by confession or *nil dicit*, he may suggest upon the roll as many breaches as he shall think fit; upon which a writ shall issue to the sheriff of the county where the action is brought, to summon a jury before the justices of assize of that county, to inquire of the truth of those breaches and to assess the damages; in which writ the said justices of assize shall be commanded to make return thereof to the court whence the same shall issue, at the time mentioned in such writ. And in case the defendant, after such judgment, and before exe-

(*o*) See 2 Arch. Pr. 20, 21.
(*p*) Cridland *v.* Floyd ; 6 S. & R. 414.
(*q*) Ibid.
(*r*) Gray *v.* Coulter, 4 Barr, 188. BURN-SIDE, J. See 2 B. & P. 446 ; 6 S. & R. 18.
(*s*) See 2 Arch. Pr. 21 ; 14 East, 442. See the practice in the C. C. U. S., Armstrong *v.* Carson's Executors, 2 D. 302. Wherever the action is for a *sum certain*, or that can be made certain by computation, judgment for *damages* may be

entered without a writ of inquiry. 1 Wheat. 215 ; Brown *v.* Vanbraam, 3 D. 348, 355. 1 Chit. Rep. 627.
(*t*) Rob. Dig. 142.
(*u*) 2 Burr. 824, 826.
(*v*) 6 East, 550.
(*w*) 8 T. R. 126.
(*x*) 6 East, 613 ; 14 East, 401.
(*y*) 2 B. & P. 446.
(*z*) 2 Saund. 187.

cution, shall pay into court to the use of the plaintiff the damages assessed and costs, a stay of execution shall be entered on the record; or if by reason of an execution the plaintiff shall be fully paid all the damages and costs, and the charges of the execution, the defendant's body, land, or goods shall be thereupon forthwith discharged from the execution, which shall likewise be entered upon the record; but in each case the judgment shall notwithstanding remain as a further security to answer to the plaintiff such damages as he may sustain by any further breach of a covenant contained in the same indenture, deed, or writing; upon which the plaintiff may have a *scire facias* upon the said judgment against the defendant, his heirs, terre-tenants, or executors or administrators, suggesting other breaches of the said covenants or agreements, and to summon him or them respectively to show cause why execution should not be awarded upon the said judgment, in which there shall be the same proceeding as there was in the action of debt upon the said bond, for assessing of damages upon the trial of issues joined upon such breaches, or inquiring thereof upon a writ to be awarded in manner aforesaid and upon payment or satisfaction as aforesaid of such further damages, costs, and charges as aforesaid, all further proceedings on the judgment aforesaid are again to be stayed, and so *toties quoties*, and the defendant's body, land, or goods shall be discharged out of execution as aforesaid." The defendant, however, is accountable only to the extent of the penalty; and as soon as that is recovered, or if the defendant choose to pay it into court, the plaintiff can proceed no further, but on the contrary may be compelled to enter satisfaction on the record.(*a*) It has also been ruled that the statute is obligatory; and although it enacts that the plaintiff "may" assign, "may" suggest, &c., yet the word "may" is compulsory, and the plaintiff *must* assign or suggest the breaches, otherwise the proceedings will be erroneous.(*b*) Before this statute, the plaintiff, in an action on a penalty for the performance of covenants, not only had judgment to recover the penalty, but was entitled to take out execution for the whole; but the statute introduced a new practice, the assignment of breaches, and damages to be assessed thereon.(*c*) The great object of the statute was, to take away the necessity of applying for relief to a Court of Equity; and on this principle, replevin-bonds and bail-bonds are held not to be within this act, because the court can then relieve the defendant without his being compelled to file a bill in equity; and on the same ground, money bonds are not within it, against the penalty of which the courts give relief by the statute of 4 Ann. ch. 16, § 13, which empowers the court pending an action on a money bond, if the defendant bring into court the principal and interest due on such bond, and all costs incurred, to discharge him from such bond altogether. Where a bond was conditioned for the payment of money pursuant to the stipulations of an indenture bearing even date with it, which bond was put in suit after both interest and principal became due, it was held not to be within the statute, and that breaches need not be assigned.(*d*)

(*a*) 1 Saund. 58, a.
(*b*) 5 T. R. 636, 538; 2 Wils. 377; Cowp. 359; see the proceedings after judgment by default, under this statute, fully stated, 2 Arch. Pr. 28, 29.

(*c*) Dunn *v.* The Commonwealth, 14 S. & R. 429.
(*d*) 10 Bing. 133; S. C. 25 Com. Law Rep. 56. See Arrison *v.* Com. 1 W. 378, 379, as to the judgment.

If the plaintiff, instead of the usual mode of declaring as on a common money-bond, have set forth the condition of the bond in the declaration, and assigned the breaches (which is advisable for the sake of expedition), there is no necessity for a suggestion of breaches on the roll as directed by the statute.(e)

Actions on official bonds ought to be brought under, and conducted according to the provisions of this statute, and in truth are, but not in the regular manner. An action is brought in the name of the commonwealth, and if no defence be made to this action, the course of proceeding under the statute would be to suggest breaches and issue a writ of inquiry; but instead of this, a *scire facias* is in our practice issued on the judgment thus obtained by default, in order to ascertain the damages sustained, for which execution is taken out, and the judgment stands as security for further breaches.(f)

If after the first inquisition or trial, the defendant be guilty of any further breaches, as the statute says that in such a case the judgment already signed, shall remain as a security to the plaintiff, the plaintiff in order to obtain damages may sue out a *scire facias* on the judgment, and thereupon suggest the further breaches ;(g) or, as it appears from the case of Sparks *v.* Garrigues,(h) the plaintiff may move for leave to take out execution for the principal and interest accruing since the action, when the defendant may make any defence (on an issue framed, if necessary), other than that which has been tried. However, this, the old practice in this State, was afterwards reconsidered and condemned by a decision of the Supreme Court. This decision(i) (ROGERS, J., strongly objecting to it) was as follows: "In an action on a bond conditioned for the payment of several sums at different times, in which breaches had not been assigned, judgment was signed for want of an affidavit of defence, upon which the plaintiff took out execution, as well for the instalments due at the time suit was brought, as for those not then due, but which had become due afterwards: This execution was set aside, and the plaintiff's motion for execution for the sums which became due after suit brought was refused, and he was put to a *scire facias.*"(j)

It may now be considered as settled that judgments entered by virtue of warrants of attorney are not within the statute 8 & 9 Will.(k)

But it is otherwise upon a judgment bond and warrant of attorney without writ for the payment of money by instalments; for then, though the better course is to move the court for leave to issue execution for a particular sum in the first instance, yet this is not the only course, and an inquiry as to whether too much is demanded is equally open to the defendant after execution as before.(l)

In a late case in the Supreme Court, an action was brought against A, a surety on an assignee's bond, and a verdict and judgment had for certain damages. A thereupon brought suit and obtained a verdict

---

(e) 2 Arch. Prac. ibid. 29.

(f) As to the practice in suits on administration-bonds, and on sheriff's-bonds, in which judgment is not entered up for the penalty, but the verdict and judgment pass for whatever damages are proved to have been suffered. See *post,* vol. ii. under those titles in this index. Also, the title of *Scire Facias.*

(g) 2 Arch. Pr. 30; *post,* p. 359.
(h) 1 Bin. 152.
(i) Longstreth v. Gray, 1 W. 60.
(j) See Arrison v. Com. 1 W. 378, 379, as to the nature and form of judgment under this statute.
(k) Longstreth v. Gray, 1 W. 60; Harger v. Commissioners, 2 J. 253.
(l) Skidmore v. Bradford, 4 Barr, 296.

against one who had promised to indemnify him against loss as surety. Entry of judgment on this verdict was opposed because the judgment against A was irregular, for want of the cautionary judgment prescribed by the act of 1836; but it was held, that the court would have entered the proper judgment for the penalty, and also judgment for damages, had A sued out a writ of error in the original action, and what would have been done would be considered as done to effect the justice of the case.(m)

After a judgment was entered on a bond and warrant of attorney, which stipulated that execution should not issue before default in the payment of several promissory notes, unless the partnership existing between defendant and A B should be dissolved: it was held, that an execution issued before the maturity of the notes, without a *scire facias* having been first sued out, to ascertain whether the partnership had been dissolved, was irregular, and it was accordingly set aside.(n)

Upon a bond of indemnity there can be but one judgment against the same party; and that must be for the amount of penalty with an assessment of damages upon the breaches assigned. If subsequent breaches occur, the remedy is by *scire facias* upon that judgment, the assignment of additional breaches, and the assessment of damages upon them.(o)

Where a bond was given to the guardians of the poor in a certain penalty for which judgment might be entered and execution issued and the judgment afterwards to remain as security, with condition for the payment of a weekly sum for the support of the obligor's wife; and judgment was entered upon the bond and the obligor had made divers weekly payments, after which his real estate was sold under execution upon a subsequent mortgage, it was held, that the mortgagee was not entitled to receive out of the proceeds the amount of the payments so made; but that the judgment was in the nature of a continuous security and to stand as a security for the performance of the condition after payments made.(p)

In another case it appeared that L., a retiring partner received from the other members of the firm, a bond with warrant of attorney, &c., conditioned to pay the debts of the firm, and to indemnify and keep the said L. harmless. The bond also contained an agreement that on failure of the obligors to indemnify the said L., he should be at liberty as often as he should pay or become liable to pay any of the debts, to file a statement with the record of the judgment, and to issue execution and collect the amount. Judgment was entered on the bond in May, 1846, and in August following, a statement of debts which L. was liable to pay as one of the firm, was filed, and execution issued: It was held by the Supreme Court, that as judgment was entered on a warrant of attorney, without writ, no *scire facias*, or application to the court for leave to issue execution for the instalment was necessary.(q)

On the death of either of the parties between interlocutory and final judgment, a *scire facias* against his personal representatives must first issue to show cause why damages should not be assessed, under the 6th

(m) Carman v. Noble, 9 Barr, 366.
(n) Montelius v. Montelius, 5 P. L. J. 88. SERGEANT, J. Bright. R. 79.
(o) Duffy v. Lytle, 5 W. 120; Adams
v. Bush, 5 W. 289; 5 P. L. J. 93; *ante*, p. 358.
(p) Vogel v. Hughes, 2 M. 399.
(q) Reynolds v. Lowry, 6 Barr, 465.

section of this statute of William, before a writ of inquiry can be awarded.(r)

After giving notice of inquiry, the next step to be taken is for each party to subpœna his witnesses. At the time appointed, the inquest will be taken by the sheriff and jury,(s) in nearly the same manner as at a trial in court, excepting that the jurors cannot be challenged.(t) They must hear the evidence on both sides, and if the sheriff should refuse to admit such evidence, the court will direct a new writ of inquiry ;(u) excepting in *foreign attachment*, when the defendant is not entitled to produce evidence before the jury on the execution of a writ of inquiry,(v) because the purpose of the proceedings is merely to compel an appearance.

All the plaintiff has to prove, or the defendant is permitted to controvert, is the amount of the damages ;(w) for the cause of action itself, as stated in the declaration, is impliedly admitted by the defendant, by his suffering judgment to pass against him by default.(x) Thus in an action on a bill of exchange against the defendant as acceptor, it admits that he accepted it ; and that the bill is as stated in the declaration ; and he cannot afterwards show on the execution of a writ of inquiry, that he has not accepted it : the bill must, indeed, be produced, for the purpose of seeing whether there is any indorsement of money having been paid upon it.(y) So, in an action for goods sold and delivered, or for money had and received, the defendant, by suffering judgment to go by default, admits that something is due ; and he cannot afterwards dispute the contract of sale, or show fraud on the part of the plaintiff in making the contract.(z) So, in case for words, the plaintiff need not, at the execution of the writ of inquiry, offer any evidence ; neither is the jury bound to assess nominal damages only, but may measure them by the enormity of the charge declared on and admitted by the judgment by default.(a)

So, the defendant will not be allowed to give in evidence, in mitigation of damages, any matter which might have been made the subject of a set-off.(b)

It is said, that in this State, facts may be determined by a majority of the jury of inquiry, though their verdict should be signed by them all.(c) But this is questionable. The proper method seems to be this : the return and verdict must be the act of at least twelve ; therefore the sheriff must at least summon twelve jurors, but he may summon as many more as he chooses, provided the whole number do not exceed twenty-three, so that twelve will always be a majority.

The verdicts of juries of inquiry when rendered, are much respected by the courts ; for it has been decided that they will not set them aside on frivolous grounds, and that they will not examine into the effect of any particular piece of evidence upon the jury's mind ; for unless it

(r) As to this practice, see 2 Arch. Pr. 79, and *post*, vol. ii. *Tit. Scire Facias.*

(s) See Doug. 198.

(t) 3 Salk. 81; but see 15 Johns. 177.

(u) McClenachan v. McCarty, 1 D. 377.

(v) Ibid. Serg. on Attach. 21.

(w) 1 Bos. & P. 368.

(x) 1 Stra. 612; and see 2 Saund. 107, n. 2.

(y) 3 T. R. 301 ; Doug. 316, n.

(z) 1 Str. 612 ; 1 Phil. Ev. 148.

(a) 3 Barn. & Cress. 427 ; 10 Serg. & Low. 139.

(b) 2 Arch. Pr. 25 ; 14 East, 548.

(c) MS. on Prac.

appears that there was *no* proper evidence before them, the court will presume that they had sufficient grounds for their inquest.(*d*)

In the case of Leib *v.* Bolton,(*e*) two of the jurors were admitted to depose what kind of evidence had been submitted on the inquest.

Under the old act of 1724–5, which is now repealed, if the summons had not been served on the defendant ten days before the return, a judgment by default against him would have been irregular ; but after a writ of inquiry executed, and judgment on that, and a long acquiescence, it was held that it was not to be presumed that the summons was irregularly served.(*f*)

The practice, as has been seen,(*g*) now is for a defendant to have eight days' notice at least, of the execution of the writ ; and the notice must be served on the defendant in person if practicable, or if not, by reason of absence or concealment, by leaving it with his family, or at his usual place of abode. If he is not in the bailiwick, and has no family or residence therein, the practice is to post the notice in the prothonotary's office, as in the case of writs of inquiry on judgments in foreign attachment.(*h*)

The thirty days given for entering for security stay of execution, run from the judgment for want of affidavit, and not from the assessment of damages.(*i*)

A judgment entered for want of an appearance where a declaration and copy of a promissory note had been filed, is final and a lien.(*j*)

Upon the return of the writ and inquisition, the prothonotary will enter judgment *nisi causa* within four days. The defendant is allowed these four days to move to set aside the inquisition, or in arrest of judgment. If this time expire, and the defendant has not moved to set aside the inquisition, or in arrest of judgment ; or if he have moved, and the inquisition be not set aside, nor the judgment arrested, the plaintiff may have the costs taxed, and proceed to sue out execution.(*k*)

If the inquisition be defective, it is amendable ; and upon a rule to show cause, the court will allow it to go back to the sheriff, to be amended according to the truth of the case ;(*l*) even after exception taken to the inquisition.(*m*)

Where more damages are found by the jury than are laid in the declaration, the plaintiff may release the excess.(*n*)

Upon motion to set aside a writ of inquiry, for excessive damages in an action for a trifling assault, the court of K. B. imposed the terms of bringing part into court, where a long interval must occur before cause could be shown against the rule.(*o*) Such terms are extremely equitable, and might be insisted on with advantage in many cases in our practice.

(*d*) Leib *v.* Bolton, 1 D. 82 ; see 1 Dunl. Pr. 395, 396, 397.

(*e*) 1 D. 82.

(*f*) Morrison *v.* Wetherill, 8 S. R. 502. S e also Crosby *v.* Massey, 1 Pa. R. 229, a case similar in principle, where the irregular judgment had existed for two terms, the defendant knowing of its irregularity. This case was commenced by amicable action.

(*g*) See *ante*, p. 352.

(*h*) Duncan *v.* Lloyd, 1 M. 350.

(*i*) M'Clung *v.* Murphey, 2 M. 177.

(*j*) Hays *v.* Tryon, 2 M. 208.

(*k*) 2 Arch. Pr. 26.

(*l*) Moore *v.* Heiss, 4 Y. 378.

(*m*) 1 Har. & M'Hen. 175.

(*n*) Ibid. 159.

(*o*) 1 Chit. Rep. 729.

CHAPTER XVII.

OF PROCEEDINGS BETWEEN THE DECLARATION AND PLEA.

WHERE the defendant intends to contest the plaintiff's action, he may find it necessary or convenient, before pleading, to take certain intermediate steps, in order the better to prepare himself for his defence. These vary according to circumstances: thus, where the plaintiff declares upon a deed, it may be requisite for him to obtain a copy of the deed, which he does by craving *oyer*. Or if the declaration be not sufficiently explicit to apprise him of the precise items of the plaintiff's claim, he may call upon him for the particulars of his demand, which are furnished in a *bill of particulars*. In England, another step may at this stage be taken, which is to move the court to *change the venue,* into a county in which it is more proper that it should be tried than where the plaintiff has laid his action; but there never was a power in Pennsylvania, under its judiciary system, as at first adopted, nor since, to change the *venue;* and this owing to the organization of the courts, and the laws providing for the return of jurors.(a) But a third step, which the defendant may take before pleading is, to move to *consolidate actions* unnecessarily divided; and a fourth, to require the interpleader of the plaintiff with a third party, in respect to funds of which he may allege he is a mere stakeholder. And, if he do not deny the plaintiff's right to recover to a certain amount, he may, by *paying that amount into court,* discharge himself of all further costs, unless the plaintiff can show a right to more than the defendant has admitted to be due. These several subjects will be briefly treated in this chapter.

SECTION I.

OF OYER.

Wherever the plaintiff, in his declaration, necessarily makes a *profert in curiam* (which is an allegation by a party who states a deed in pleading, that he *brings it into court*),(b) of any deed, writing, letters of administration, or the like, the defendant may crave *oyer;* that is, may pray or request that he may *hear* the deed read to him (which is done by directing the prothonotary, in writing, so to enter the request on his docket, and giving notice of it), and it is accordingly supposed to be

---

(a) Brac. L. Mis. 191. For a very full and satisfactory history and explanation of the doctrine of venue, see Steph. on Plead. 280–291, 3d edit.; also Oliphant *v.* Smith, 3 Pa. R. 160.

(b) Lawes on Pl. 77.

read in court;(c) but in practice oyer is usually given by delivering a copy of the deed. But *profert* ought only to be made of a deed or grant of administration, and oyer cannot be demanded of a private statute even where *profert* is made of it.(d) The entry on the docket of the demand of oyer is, it is apprehended, only to enable the party to plead a short plea. For instance, in an action on a bond, if it be wished to plead performance of the condition, an entry may be made on the docket in these words : "*Defendant craves oyer of bond and condition,*" the instantaneous effect of which entry is *fictione legis*, to spread the bond and its condition upon the record. The defendant has, therefore, merely to plead in short, "*performance,*" when the record is complete thus far. But, by thus craving oyer, the defendant precludes himself from excepting to any variance on the trial between the bond and declaration,(e) although he does not choose to avail himself of the oyer. If the supposition be correct, that this practice is the result of, and subsidiary to short pleading,(f) it will follow that it may be dropped where the privilege of short pleading is not used. The course then would be, for the defendant to make a demand of oyer in writing of the plaintiff's attorney, who will give him a copy of the instrument, which he may use or not, as he thinks proper ; if used, he states in his plea the oyer and the words of the deed ; if not used, he takes no notice of the deed or oyer in his plea, and may take advantage of any variance between the deed and declaration on the trial where it is necessary to produce the deed to show that there were no indorsements of payment.(g)

By the present English practice, the attorney for the party by whom it is demanded, before he answers the pleading in which the *profert* is made, sends a note to the attorney on the other side, containing a demand of oyer; on which the latter is bound to carry to him the deed, and deliver to him a copy of it, if required, at the expense of the party demanding; and this is considered as oyer, or an actual reading of the deed in the court.(h) And the party demanding is entitled to a copy of the attestation and names of the witnesses.(i)

Oyer is demandable in all actions, real, personal, and mixed. Oyer is said to have been formerly demandable not only of *deeds*, but of *records* alleged in pleading; but, by the present practice, it is not now granted of a record; and can be had only in the cases of *deeds*, *probates*, and *letters of administration*, &c., of which profert is made on the other side. Of *private writings not under seal*, oyer has never been demandable.(j) But where an action is founded on a written instrument not under seal, though the defendant cannot pray oyer, yet the court will, in some cases, make an order for delivery of a copy of it to the defendant or his attorney, and that all proceedings in the mean time be stayed.(k) It seems that oyer is not demandable of an act of parliament ;(l) nor of letters patent ;(m) nor of recognizance.(n) But it is

(c) 3 Salk. 119, pl. 2, 5.
(d) Zion Church *v.* St. Peter's Church, 5 W. & S. 215.
(e) Douglass *v.* Beam, 2 Bin. 76.
(f) On the subject of *short pleading*, *vide post*, c. xvii. § 2.
(g) 2 Stra. 1241.
(h) Steph. on Plead. 68, 3d edit. ; 2 T. R. 40 ; 1 Tidd, 635, 8th edit. ; 1 Sel. 264.

(i) 1 Saund. 9, b. n.
(j) Steph. on Plead. 69, 3d edit.
(k) 1 Tidd, 639, 8th edit. ; 1 Saund. 9, d. n. See Zion Church *v.* St. Peter's Church, 5 W. & S. 215.
(l) 1 Tidd, 634.
(m) 1 Arch. 164.
(n) Ibid.

demandable of a deed enrolled, or of the exemplification of the enrolment, according to the terms of the profert.(o)

Advantage of variances between a recognizance and the declaration and writ can only be availed of by oyer of the writ and pleading the variance in abatement.(p)

Oyer can be demanded only where a profert is made. In all cases where profert is necessary, and where it is also in fact made, the opposite party has a right, if he pleases, to demand oyer; but if it be unnecessarily made, this does not entitle to oyer; and so, if profert be omitted where it ought to have been made, the adversary cannot have oyer, but must demur.(q)

A party having a right to demand oyer, is yet not obliged, in all cases, to exercise that right; nor is he obliged, in all cases, after demanding it, to notice it in the pleading that he afterwards files or delivers.—Sometimes, however, he is obliged to do both, viz. where he has occasion to found his answer upon any matter contained in the deed of which profert is made, and not set forth by his adversary. In these cases, the only admissible method of making such matter appear to the court, is to demand oyer, and from the copy given set forth the whole deed *verbatim* in his pleading.(r)

It is in some cases absolutely necessary that the defendant should crave oyer, and set forth the deed upon the record; as for instance, where he pleads performance of a condition or covenant,(s) or demurs to a declaration for a variance from the instrument on which it is founded.(t) If the defendant, not being furnished with oyer in an action of covenant on articles of agreement, puts in a plea of "*covenants performed*," he dispenses with oyer, because his plea, if formally drawn up at length, must have set out the material parts of the argument.(u)

After a demand of oyer, where the defendant is entitled to have it, he cannot be compelled to plead without it, even though the deed be lost.(v)

In like manner, as the plaintiff must give oyer to the defendant, so, if the defendant, in his plea, make a necessary *profert in curiam* of any deed, &c., the plaintiff may pray oyer, and is entitled to a copy.(w)

The demand of oyer is a kind of plea,(x) and should regularly be made in writing before the time for pleading is expired;(y) and if made afterwards, the demand is a nullity, and the other party may sign judgment.(z) If the plaintiff will not give oyer when demanded, he may counterplead or demur to the defendant's prayer, and the court will give judgment thereupon. If the court deny oyer when it ought to be granted, it is error, and a writ of error lies upon their judgment; but it is no error to grant oyer where it ought not to be.(a)

There is no settled time prescribed for the plaintiff to give oyer; but the defendant has the same time to plead, after the delivery of oyer, as he had when he demanded it;(b) therefore it is generally the plain-

(o) Ibid.
(p) Slocum *v.* Slocum, 8 W. & S. 369.
(q) Steph. on Plead. 69, 3d edit.
(r) Steph. on Plead. 70, 3d edit.
(s) Com. Dig. Plead. P. 2; 2 Saund. 408, n. 2; 5 Cranch, 253.
(t) 1 Dunl. Pr. 399.
(u) Litle *v.* Henderson, 2 Y. 295.

(v) 1 Saund, 9 a; and see 1 Dunl. Pr. 399, 400; Dunbar *v.* Jumper, 2 Y. 74.
(w) 6 Mod. 122.
(x) 3 Salk. 119 pl. 4.
(y) Barnes, 263; Tidd. 521, 522.
(z) Barnes, 326.
(a) 1 Saund. 9, b; 2 ibid. 46, n. 7.
(b) 8 T. R. 356; Com. Dig. Plead. E. 41; 14 Johns. 329.

tiff's interest to grant it without delay.(c)   The time allowed the defendant to give oyer to the plaintiff is, according to the practice of the English courts, two days, which are both reckoned exclusive ;(d) and if it be not given it that time, the plaintiff may sign judgment, as for want of a plea.(e)

SECTION II.

OF BILLS OF PARTICULARS.

The defendant has a right to call on the plaintiff for the particulars of his demand, where they are not disclosed in his declaration ;(g) and this is peculiarly proper in actions of *assumpsit,* or debt for goods sold and delivered, for work and labor, &c. (though not requisite in special *assumpsit,* nor, in general, in actions for torts, the particulars of the demand in the former, and the specific injury in the latter, being set forth in the declaration),(h) since, from the very general manner in which the plaintiff is allowed to declare, the defendant cannot be apprised of the items which constitute his demand ;(i) or if, proceeding under the act of 1806, he were to deliver a statement which in itself did not contain a sufficiently accurate specification of his demand, the court would `com-pel him to file a more accurate and particular statement.(j)   For this purpose, the defendant may, on motion, obtain from the court a direction to the plaintiff to file a bill of particulars in the one case, or a more particular statement in the other.(k)   This may be done in an early stage of the cause, so as to afford the defendant an opportunity to plead.(l)   By the English practice, a bill of particulars is obtained by the order of a judge to the plaintiff to deliver one at a certain day, or show cause why it should not be delivered, and that all proceedings should in the mean time be stayed.   If neither a bill of particulars be then delivered, nor any cause to the contrary shown, the judge will, on proof of the service of the former order, grant an absolute order for a bill of particulars, with an indefinite stay of proceedings until it be delivered.   If an insufficient bill be delivered, the party may in like manner proceed to obtain further particulars.(m)   After serving the bill of particulars, or of further particulars, where the first is insufficient, the plaintiff is at liberty to proceed in the action, the judge's order being thereby complied with ; and the defendant must plead within the time which he had for pleading when the order was granted.(n)   If the plaintiff neglect to deliver to the defendant the particulars of his demand, pursuant to an order for that purpose, the defendant may move the court for judgment, as in case of *non pros.,* and a rule will be granted that the plaintiff furnish to the defendant the particulars of his demand within some given time, or that a judgment of *non pros.*

(c) 2 Arch. Pr. 195.
(d) 2 T. R. 40.
(e) Com. Dig. Plead. P. 1.   And see generally, Frey v. Wells, 4 Y. 505, 506.
(g) 2 Br. 46, 47 ; 3 Johns. 248 ; 1 Campb. 294, n.
(h) Tidd. 621, 622.

(i) 1 Dunl. Pr. 402.
(j) 2 Br. 46.
(k) Ibid. 47.
(l) Ibid. 3 Burr. 1389.
(m) 1 Dunl. Pr. 403 ; 2 Arch. Pr. 198; *post,* p. 368.
(n) 13 East, 508.

be entered.(o) The Supreme Court has an express rule on this subject, in these words : At any time after the entry of an appearance to a summons, or of special bail, justified or not excepted to, the defendant may call for a bill of particulars, and, until it be furnished, proceedings shall stay. Should the plaintiff not comply for three months, a nonsuit may be entered by the prothonotary on due notice of ten days.

At the trial, the particulars of the plaintiff's demand, if delivered, are considered as incorporated with the declaration,(p) and then he is not allowed to give any evidence out of the bill ;(q) but, though he cannot himself give evidence out of it, yet if the defendant's evidence show that there were other items which he might have included in his demand, he is entitled to recover all that appears due him.(r)

The bill should be as precise as a special declaration, and is insufficient if it fail to disclose the gist of the plaintiff's action.(s)

A bill of particulars, in an action by a justice to recover fees earned, was held to be sufficient, which set out the number and names of the cases, with the prices of services short, as follows : " J. & J. 25 ; E. 12½; C. 6 ; H. & D. 50 ; O. 6."(t)

When the plaintiff is conscious that his bill of particulars filed does not detail his entire cause of action, his course is to move to amend, so as to let in the omitted items. Leave will be granted by the court, unless it appear that the original cause of action is changed.(u)

(o) 14 Johns. 329; 15 Johns. 222.

(p) Ibid.

(q) 1 Camp. 69 ; Peake's N. P. C. 172; 2 Bos. & P. 243.

(r) 1 Camp. 69.

(s) Gilpin v. Howell, 5 Barr, 41, post, n. (u)

(t) Harris v. Christian, 10 Barr, 233.

(u) Hartell v. Seybert, D. C., Saturday, March 11, 1848. Why plaintiff should not be allowed to amend his bill of particulars. Per curiam. In this case, a bill of particulars was originally furnished to the defendant, upon which he pleaded to the narr. In such case, the proper practice is that which has been adopted here, of applying to the court for leave to amend the bill.

A second bill of particulars, not delivered under a judge's order, has been held, in England, not to cure a defect in a previous bill. Brown v. Watts, 1 Taunt. 353 ; 1 Tidd's Pr. 644.

We have been furnished with a copy of the proposed amendment, and we think that it is insufficient. A bill of particulars ought to be as certain, and convey as much information, as a special declaration. Gilpin v. Howell, 5 Barr, 53. It ought not to be a mere echo of the common counts ; and in one case, already cited, the Court of Common Pleas are stated to have severely animadverted on the too frequent practice of delivering particulars which were so general as to convey no further information to the parties than they could gain from the declaration itself. Brown v. Watts, 1 Taunt. 353.

We think the amendment proposed falls under this objection ; and as to the difficulty suggested, that a particular specification of details would discover the ingredients or materials of a secret art possessed by plaintiff, the only answer to be made to it is, that there are no secrets in courts of justice. The plaintiff will certainly be obliged, before the jury, to show the nature and quantity of the articles and materials furnished, if he ever expects to recover for them, and the disclosure might just as well be made now as then. Rule dismissed.

Hartell v. Seybert, D. C., March 25, 1848. Why plaintiff should not amend his bill of particulars. Per curiam. We see no reason, under the circumstances, why the plaintiff should not be allowed to amend as he desires. This, indeed, has not been objected to by the defendant. The discussion before us related to the point whether the form in which the amendment was asked and allowed might not bear upon the question whether the defendant, on the trial, should be allowed to give in evidence the plaintiff's former bill of particulars to show that he had varied from time to time the nature of his claim.

The authorities are by no means clear upon this question. A bill of particulars is a mere creature of the court, and is no part of the record. Blunt *v.* Cooke, 4 Man. and Gran. 458. The object of it is to give the defendant more specific and precise information as to the nature and extent of the demand made upon him by the plaintiff, than is announced by the declaration, in a mode unincumbered by the technical formalities of pleading. 3 Starkie on Ev. 1055. It ought to be as certain, and convey as much information as a special declaration. Gilpin *v.* Howell, 5 Barr, 53. Thus it has been held, that if a bill of particulars state the plaintiff's demand to be for goods sold and delivered to the defendant, no evidence can be received of goods sold by the defendant as plaintiff's agent. Holland *v.* Hopkins, 2 Bos. & Pal. 243. Hence Mr. Chitty recommends the practitioner to describe the claim in the particulars in every possible shape that could be admissible under the counts in the declaration. 3 Chitty, Gen. Pr. 616. Yet this and other elementary writers seem- to consider that, like every other matter *in pais*, the bill of particulars may be used against the party who has furnished it; and there are reported cases which sustain this view. Ibid. 617; 3 Starkie on Ev. 1058; Colson *v.* Selby, 1 Esp. N. P. C. 452; Rymer *v.* Cook, Moody & Malkin, 86. In the case of Harrington *v.* MacMorris, 5 Taunt. 228, however, it was decided that the plaintiff cannot use one plea of a defendant as evidence of the fact which the defendant denies in another plea. Nor can he use a notice of set-off for evidence of the debt on the issue of *non-assumpsit*, because the statute gives the notice of set-off in the nature and place of a plea; nor can he use a particular of set-off for that purpose, because it is incorporated with the notice of set-off. See, also, Miller *v.* Johnson, 2 Esp. N. P. C. 602; Short *v.* Edward, 1 Esp. N. P. C. 374. So it has been held in other cases that one count of a declaration cannot be called in as proof by the defendant to contradict or affect the evidence in respect to another. Cowen & Hill's Notes to Phillips on Evid. 331, and the cases there cited. Upon these grounds, and considering the bill of particulars as a part of the pleadings, a very respectable court in New York has denied any effect to them as evidence. Brittingham *v.* Stevens, 1 Hall, 379; Cowen & Hill's notes to Phillips on Ev.

361, and cases there referred to. We think this is the sounder and practically the more just and convenient doctrine. In providing that defendant shall be furnished with a previous knowledge of the nature of the claim which he must prepare to meet on the trial, we must take care that the plaintiff be not trammelled by the mere forms of the proceedings, so that substantial justice may in all cases, so far as possible, be attained.

We make this rule absolute, therefore, without any qualification or condition in regard to the use, by defendant in evidence, of the plaintiff's former bill of particulars. Rule absolute.

Spencer *v.* Tams. D. C. Saturday, June 24, 1848. Why plaintiff should not amend his bill of particulars. *Per curiam.* We must be careful, in motions of this kind, to see that no new cause of action is introduced, while we should be liberal in allowing amendments which only vary the form in which the claim is stated. We think the amended bill, as prayed for, exceptionable in this respect; but we have stricken out the objectionable parts, and, as amended, it is allowed, and ordered to be filed. Rule absolute.

Howell *v.* Gilpin, D. C. Saturday, May 20, 1848. Why plaintiff should not be allowed to amend his bill of particulars. *Per curiam.* We have settled (Hartell *v.* Seybert, *ante*) that a bill of particulars may be amended, with the leave of the court, and the opinion delivered in the Supreme Court, in this very case, recognizes the practice (Gilpin *v.* Howell, 5 Barr, 41). Undoubtedly we will not allow a new and entirely different controversy to be incorporated or substituted; but we see nothing of that kind attempted. In the proposed bill, it is stated that the note, or notes, the proceeds of which are sued for, was either without consideration, or the consideration thereof had failed, and it is objected that this alternative statement vitiates the bill. It appears to be the practice in England to vary the grounds of the claim in different items, in the same manner as the different counts of a narr. The whole effect of our giving ear to this objection would be that the plaintiff would furnish two copies of his bill, in one of which he would state the fact in one way, in the other differently. We are not hampered by rules of pleading, as in the case of a narr.; the bill of particulars is a mere creature of the court. We think it would be highly inconvenient in practice to apply the rules of pleading to these bills, which are re-

When the bill of particulars is too vague, the opposite party may by rule obtain more exact specification.(v)

SECTION III.

OF CONSOLIDATING ACTIONS.

The consolidation of actions is intended to save expense, and may be ordered by the court on motion.(w) When separate actions are brought by the same plaintiff against the same defendant, for causes which might all have been joined in the same suit, it has been the practice of the court to consolidate them all in one suit.(x) Thus the Court of Common Pleas ordered three actions between the same parties, on three separate promissory notes, of a similar date, to be consolidated.(y) It is a matter of discretion, however, with the court to order such actions to be consolidated; and they will always do so, if it appears that the actions were brought separately, without any necessity for the purpose of vexation or oppression.(z) In the exercise of this discretion, the court will either consolidate many actions in one, or more: thus the

quired to give a party notice of the adversary's case, that he may come prepared to encounter it. Rule absolute.

(v) McClain v. Henry, Saturday, September 21, 1850. Rule for more specific bill of particulars. *Per curiam.* Although the rule of practice be, in general, that a bill of particulars must be demanded before the plea pleaded, yet the court have undoubtedly the power to interfere at any stage of the cause where they see that justice demands it. The first item of the bill stands upon peculiar ground, and as its correctness was admitted judicially on the former trial, we will not interfere with that. The next four items seem sufficiently explicit. The last five items, however, we think, ought to be stated with day and date, and the items given. Rule absolute as to the last five items of the bill.

Sargeant v. Gilbert, Saturday, March 30, 1850. Rule for sufficient bill of particulars. *Per curiam.* We have heretofore held in Hartell v. Seybert (*ante*, p. 366) in accordance with the English practice, that a bill of particulars must not be a mere echo to the common counts. Where the claim is susceptible of it, it must give particulars. It is not difficult to do this in a case for goods sold. If in fact the plaintiff has sold and delivered a number of articles in the lump, he can remember and specify the nature more particularly. Now the bill of particulars before us is simply the " good-will and fixtures of a certain store." The only common count under which this can be supposed to avail defendant is

that for goods sold and delivered; and as to that, it is very well settled that the price of fixtures to a house cannot be received under a declaration for goods sold and delivered. Lee v. Risden (7 Taunt, 188). It is evident, if the defendant had not stirred in the matter, the plaintiff could have given this as evidence under the bill of particulars. As it is, he had better rely on his special count alone, or furnish a more detailed statement of goods and chattels, *not fixtures*, under the common count.—R. A.

Brown v. Bradford, Saturday, December 29, 1849. Why plaintiff should not furnish a further bill of particulars. *Per curiam.* In this case, the plaintiff having asked leave to amend by giving a date and amount to each item, we think the bill will then be sufficient, whether, supposing the dates or amounts to be merely fictitious, the bill will be of any service at all to the plaintiff it is not for us now to say. That will appear on the trial. Where a plaintiff sues for work done under a special contract, and yet desires to retain the right to recover on the common counts, it is the best course, undoubtedly, to have the work valued in as specific and detailed a manner as is possible, and furnish a bill of particulars accordingly. Amendment allowed, and therefore R. D.

(w) Morris v. Tarrin. 1 D. 147.
(x) Towanda Bank v. Ballard, 7 W. & S. 434. See *post*, Costs.
(y) 1 Br. Appx. lxvii.
(z) 2 Arch. Pr. 108.

Supreme Court, where seven suits had been brought on protested bills, drawn by the defendant, and taken up for the honor of one of the in-dorsors, considering the length of the declarations, consolidated them in three.(a) So, where five suits were brought returnable to the same term, upon bonds, between the same parties, this court consolidated them in three, although the defendant's counsel applied for a rule to show cause why they should not be consolidated in two.(b)

The court will never order a consolidation without the consent of the defendant,(c) who may have good reasons for withholding it.

In actions upon a policy of insurance against several underwriters, the court, upon application of the defendants and with the consent of the plaintiff, will grant a rule, which is called the consolidation rule, to stay the proceedings in all the actions but one, the defendants under-taking to be bound by the verdict in such action, and to pay the amount of their several subscriptions and costs, if the plaintiff should recover; together with such other terms as the court may think proper to impose upon them.(d) Or, if the plaintiff refuse his consent, the court will then grant imparlances in all the actions but one, until that one have been determined;(e) and if determined in favor of the plaintiff, the other defendants may (if necessary) obtain a stay of proceedings in their several actions, upon payment of the amount of their subscriptions and costs.(f)

SECTION IV.

INTERPLEADER.

By the act of March 11, 1836, relating to the District Court, for the City and County of Philadelphia, it is provided :—

The defendant, in any action which shall be brought in the said court for the recovery of money, or of any goods, chattels, or the value thereof in damages, which shall have come lawfully to his hands or possession, may, at any time after the declaration filed, and before plea pleaded, by a suggestion to be filed of record, disclaim all interest in the subject matter of such action, and offer to bring the same into court, or to pay or dispose thereof, as the court shall order ; and if he shall also allege under oath or affirmation, that the right thereto is claimed by, or sup-posed to belong to some person not party to the action (naming him or them) who has sued, or is expected to sue for the same, or shall show some probable matter to the court to believe that such suggestion is true, the said court may, thereupon, order the plaintiff to interplead with such third person, and make such rules and orders in the cause, and issue such process for the purpose of making such third person party to the action, and for carrying such proceeding to interplead into full and complete effect, and may render such judgment or judgments thereon, as shall be agreeable to the rules and practices of the law in like cases.(g) § 4.

(a) Morgan v. Biddle, 1 Y. 5.
(b) Donaldson v Maginnes, 4 Y. 128.
(c) Groff v. Musser, 3 S. & R. 262, 265.
(d) Park, Ins. Intrud. p. xliv.
(e) Ibid.
(f) 2 Arch. Pr. 180.
(g) See 3 M. & Scott, 180. 2 M. & G. 876.

I.—24

If the process issued upon an order to interplead, as aforesaid, shall not be actually served, or personal notice thereof shall not be given to such third person, the said court shall have power, upon giving judgment for the plaintiff, to require him to enter into a recognizance, and if they shall think it necessary, with sufficient surety, to interplead with such third person, if afterwards, and before the expiration of the time which would be allowed to him to prosecute his claim against the defendant, such third person should appear in the said court, and claim such money, or such goods or chattels, or the value thereof.   § 5.

The same provisions are, by the act of March 27, 1848, extended to Berks and Schuylkill counties.

But it would seem that the doctrine of interpleader, independently of these acts, exists in Pennsylvania at common law.   Thus, as far back as 1833, Judge Huston(h) said: " There was certainly a time in England when the practice in the courts of law was very different from what it always was and is here.   That practice gave constant employment to the courts of chancery ; and even the courts of chancery have extended their powers, and applied them to subjects not formerly known.   When bills of interpleader were first used, I shall not inquire.   Lord Hardwicke speaks of them in 1 Vezey, 249, as a new invention, and not to be encouraged ; they have, however, been applied much more extensively than in his time, and now parties are compelled to interplead by the courts of law, without the trouble, delay, and expense of a bill of chancery.

"We are told(i) a bill of interpleader lies where a person claiming no right in the subject, not knowing to whom to render a debt or duty, apprehends injury from claims made by two or more claiming, in different rights, the same debt or duty.   A mere claim is now the subject of such bill, and that the one claims in a legal and the other an equitable right. It is granted, on an affidavit, that the bill is not exhibited by fraud or collusion, but for his own security; but it need not state it is done at his own expense, nor that it is filed without the knowledge of either party. The bill must show that there are two persons in existence, each of whom claims the property; if one of them does not appear, or will not support his claim, the debt is given to the one who does appear, and a perpetual injunction is granted as to the other.   I shall not go into the inquiry as to all the cases to which it applies ; it is the appropriate remedy for a mere stakeholder.   Sometimes a trial at law is directed; and after the plaintiff in the bill has no more concern in the matter, his death does not stay the proceedings, and the cause will be decided between the claimants without a bill of revivor.(j)

"We have no Court of Chancery; but as it often happens that more than one person claims an interest in, or right to the same goods or money, and as it would be a disgrace to the administration of justice that the law should levy a sum of money from a defendant for one person, and the same law should, without any fault of the defendant, compel him to pay the same debt to another ; the practice of permitting a party to interplead has long been well known, and in some cases, the courts compelled a person to interplead, or more properly, to appear and take

(h) Coates v. Roberts, 4 R. 109.   (j) 1 Vernon, 351.
(i) See Maddock's Ch. 173.

defence in a suit, or to be forever barred. And by an act of assembly,(k) for distributing money raised by sales on execution, the court are required to give notice to all who may claim; and if any person neglects to appear and take defence against any claimant, such person is forever barred; and by the decision of this court, it is not necessary nor proper that each claimant should bring an action; if one sues, and an issue is directed, every claimant must interplead, or be forever barred.(l) This act of assembly is only a recognition of what was always the law and the practice, with the addition of prescribing what shall be notice to all concerned, of giving an appeal to the Supreme Court. So, under the 14th section of the act of March 20, 1810, giving jurisdiction to justices of the peace, it is provided that a judgment may be entered before a justice by confession, &c., for a sum exceeding one hundred dollars; if, however, any creditor of the defendant shall make oath before the justice, that there is just cause to believe such judgment was confessed with a view to defraud creditors, it is made the duty of the justice to transmit a transcript of his judgment to the prothonotary of the Common Pleas, whose adjudication thereon shall be final. Under this act, the practice has been in some counties to order a feigned issue; in others, the courts, on proper affidavits, open the judgment, and permit the creditor or creditors to plead, and the plea is entered as being made by some creditors; the verdict and judgment in either form, in the words of the act, are final.

"The case of Heller and Jones,(m) is the earliest recognition I have found in our books of interpleading, and the effects of it. The proceeding began by a judgment confessed in 1787. On a *scire facias* to revive his judgment, Miller, who claimed under a younger judgment, on which he had sold the land, was permitted to enter a plea, and he gave notice of special matter. This was before Rush, then president of that district, and who had been a justice of the Supreme Court, under the former constitution. The cause was removed to the Supreme Court, and tried at Nisi Prius in 1795. No objection was made to his right to interplead, though eminent counsel were concerned; but for some cause, he did not appear at the trial; no witnesses were examined, and a verdict and judgment were rendered for the plaintiff, who levied on and sold the land, and brought ejectment against Heller, who had bought from Miller. Heller offered to prove the same matter which Miller had alleged in his plea, and it was held he could not: that Miller, under whom he claimed, having been admitted to interplead, and put in a plea, &c., was barred, although he afterwards neglected the defence; and Heller, claiming under him, was also barred. In the argument, the right of Miller to appear and interplead was denied, and also the effect of it if he had been heard, and Judge Breckenridge was with them; but the chief justice and Judge Yeates, whose practice began in 1762, and had been, perhaps, more extensive than that of any other man, then or since, in this State, had no doubt as to this point; and I have never heard the right of a party interested to interplead, denied since. The acts of assembly above referred to, are predicated on the existence of such practice; they did not introduce it."

(k) April 16, 1827.
(l) Boal's Appeal, 2 R. 37.
(m) 4 Bin. 61.

"The only difference between the practice here and in England is, that there, when one claimant sues, and interpleading is ordered, the name of the other claimant is substituted as defendant, and the name of the bail or stakeholder, is struck out; here, so far as I have known the practice, one claimant sues him who has the money or property, and the other claimant is permitted or compelled to defend the suit, and show his right. If, after appearing and pleading, the defence is neglected or abandoned, the party is forever barred. Much more will this be the case if a party defends the cause and loses it."

The same doctrine was held by Judge LOWRIE, when sitting in the District Court of Alleghany County;(n) and very recently, by Judge SHARSWOOD, in Philadelphia. "I conceive," said he, "that by the common law of Pennsylvania, of which equity is a part, a stakeholder could protect himself by a notice *in pais* to the adverse claimant in every case in which a chancellor would decree an interpleader. The advantages of the interpleader act are first, that he is relieved by its provisions from primary liability for costs, and secondly from the contingency and risks of his defence in a subsequent action by the adverse claimant."(nn)

Under the act of 1831, the court will not grant a rule to interplead, unless it be stated in the petition that the third party who makes claim to the same fund as the plaintiff, has sued or is expected to sue.(o)

An attachment execution cannot be considered a suit, under the provisions of the act.(p)

To grant an interpleader, it is necessary that there should be a declaration or statement filed; a copy of book entries, filed as such, will not be enough.(q)

(n) McMunn v. Carothers, 9 P. L. J. 134.

(nn) Bird v. Neff, *post*, p. 374.

(o) Stewart v. Smith, D. C. C. P. Saturday March 9, 1850. Rule to interplead. *Per curiam.* In this case the petition of the defendant, praying an award of interpleader, is defective in not alleging that the third person who claims the fund "has sued, or is expected to sue for the same." It is very important to adhere strictly to the act in this respect, as no provision is made that the defendant shall deny collusion, as is the practice in equity. Rule discharged.

(p) Snyder v. Wetherby, D. C. C. P. 9 Leg. Int. 46.

(q) Howell v. The Farmers' & Mechanics' Bank, D.C. March 6, 1848. Why suggestion and prayer of interpleader should not be allowed. *Per curiam.* The words of the 4th section of the act of 11th March, 1836, under which this court possesses the power of awarding an interpleader, are express that the suggestion and proceedings thereon are to be "after the declaration filed, and before plea pleaded." No declaration has been filed in this case; but a copy of entries in a bank book have been filed under the 2d section of the act of March 28,

1815, and it is contended that such a copy takes the place of a declaration, is a sufficient statement of the plaintiff's demand under the 5th section of the act of 21st March, 1806, puts the defendant and court in as complete possession of the nature of the plaintiff's claim, as a declaration would do; that the reason of the provision of the law is thereby satisfied, and that otherwise the defendant upon whom a *bona fide* adverse claim is made, would be subjected to a judgment for want of an affidavit of defence, and thus be left without remedy. These arguments have not convinced us that we ought to depart in our practice from the express words of the law. No doubt, a statement under the act of 1806 would be a declaration within the interpleader act, and as little doubt that the copy filed in this case, had it been filed as a statement, would have been sufficient under the decisions, particularly Bailey v. Bailey (14 S. &. R. 199). But the plaintiff has not filed it as a statement, nor has he taken any step, such as a rule to plead, which shows that he regards it in any other light, than as a copy under the 2d section of the act of 28th March, 1835. Nor is there any difficulty in practice arising from the right of the

Where an agent deposits money as such in a bank, the latter, in a suit by the former, may compel an interpleader with his principal.(r)

To entitle a defendant in trover to the benefit of the interpleader act, it is necessary, 1. That the goods or chattels in controversy came lawfully into his hands; 2. That he shall offer to bring them into court, or dispose of them as the court may direct.(s)

When the suit is determined, the order to pay the money to the winning party is made in the original suit.(t)

plaintiff to demand a judgment for want of an affidavit of defence. We have held in many cases, that we will not give a judgment against one who shows by his own affidavit, or that of others cognizant of the facts that there is an adverse claim made to the subject matter of the suit, and it does not appear on its face to be wanton and collusive. It is competent for the court in such cases to suspend their decision of the rule for judgment until a declaration is filed in order that the defendant may have the opportunity of suggesting his interpleader, and paying the money into court. Prior to the interpleader act, it may have been necessary for the defendant in his affidavit of defence to show the court that the adverse claim was valid, or some probable ground for so believing. The check to collusive claims set up for the purpose of delaying judgment in the provision for the payment of money into court was not then in existence. The plaintiff may prevent any delay by filing his narr. with his copy. There is now no difficulty whatever, in doing entire justice to both parties, and no reason why in this or any other case, the words of the act should not be the rule of our practice. Rule dismissed.

(r) Ware v. The Western Bank, D. C. May 5, 1849. Rule to interplead. Per curiam. The plaintiff sues for the use of the trustees of a certain corporation. The defendant shows that the debt sued for was a deposit specially made by the plaintiff as secretary of that corporation. The corporation might have sued in its own name. The defendant avers that other persons claim to be the trustees of that corporation. It is said that this is a mere matter of use, and that the plaintiff having made the deposit in his own name, is entitled to recover at all events, whichever party may be the true corporation. We consider, however, the act of the plaintiff as that of a mere agent; his agency known and avowed at the time, and that the corporation, his constituent, could at any time revoke his authority and sue for the money themselves. The money being theirs, and, without ques-

tion, traced and identified as theirs, unmixed with any of the agent's, they have a right to receive and recover it from the depositary, without the intervention of the agent or the use of his name. It is then, we conceive, a case for a interpleader. R. A.

(s) Tiernan v. Stille, D. C. Saturday, April 22, 1848. Motion for a rule to interplead. Per curiam. This is an action of trover, and the defendants have filed a petition disclaiming all title or interest in the goods, and setting forth that they are claimed by one Jones, to whom, it seems, they had been delivered upon a writ of replevin before this action of trover was commenced. The petition then proceeds to pray that an order may be made on the plaintiff and Jones, to interplead conformably with the 4th and 5th sections of the act of 11th March, 1836, relating to this court, commonly called the Interpleader act. There is no doubt the provisions of that act extend to the action of trover; but to entitle a party to the benefit of them, two things are absolutely essential:—

1. That the goods or chattels for which the action is brought came lawfully to the hands or possession of the defendant.

2. That he shall offer to bring them into court or dispose thereof as the court shall order.

Neither of these are set forth in the petition and affidavit; and, indeed, if the goods have been delivered on the replevin to the plaintiff in that suit, it is plainly no longer in the power of the defendant to bring them into court or dispose of them as the court shall direct.— Motion refused.

(t) Stewart v. Smith, D. C. March 22, 1851. Why plaintiff should not take money out of court. Per curiam. This was a proceeding under the 4th section of the act of 11th March, 1836, giving this court power in certain cases to compel parties to interplead. The issue directed between the plaintiff and third person, claimants, has been tried and found in favor of the plaintiff, and he now asks an order to take money out of court,

The act does not apply to cases where the entire claim of the plaintiff is not admitted; nor, it seems, to a suit by a principal against an agent.*(tt)*

Proceedings under the sheriff's interpleader act will be hereafter considered.*(u)*

SECTION V.

PAYMENT OF MONEY INTO COURT.

A defendant may answer the merits of an action by confessing or denying it; but a confession of the *whole* complaint is not very usual, for then the defendant would probably end the matter sooner; or not plead at all, but suffer judgment by default. Yet sometimes, after tender and refusal of a debt, if the creditor harasses his debtor with an action, it then becomes necessary for the defendant to acknowledge the debt, and plead the tender,*(uu)* adding that he has always been and still is ready to pay it; which is called a plea of tender and *toujours et uncore prist*, from those words having been used in the plea when the proceedings were in the French language;*(v)* for a tender by the debtor and refusal by the creditor will, in all cases, discharge the costs, but not the debt itself.

"The prudence of paying money into court, is one of the most anxious points on which counsel can be asked to advise; between the care lest the party should admit the terms of a special contract, on the one hand; or, on the other, lest he should proceed with a consciousness that something must ultimately be recovered. But whatever course be adopted, it must be followed by all its legal consequences."*(w)*

which was paid in by defendant when the original order of interpleader was made. The only point of practice worthy of note in regard to it, and which has been settled in England under the analogous statute provision there, is, that the order for the payment of the money be made in the original suit, and not in the issue framed under the order of interpleader.   R. A.

(tt) Bird *v.* Neff, D. C. Saturday, Sept. 25, 1852. Rule for interpleader. *Per curiam.* The plaintiff's claim is $448 06. The defendant admits but $337 85. A certain amount of this difference is commissions; the residue, however, is said to be a distinct claim. It appears to us that there would be a great difficulty in holding the interpleader act applicable except where the defendant admits the entire amount of plaintiff's claim. The act does not contemplate that the action should branch off into several issues with different parties. Even the payment of the whole sum into court, unaccompanied by a disclaimer of interest in the whole of it, would not meet the difficulty. Indeed, it is questionable whether an agent or commission merchant can turn his acknowledged constituent over to a contract with a third person having or making a claim. Such a power might be used very unjustly and disastrously; especially if we allow the question of commissions to be reserved and decided separately. I conceive that by the common law of Pennsylvania, of which equity is a part, a stakeholder could protect himself by a notice *in pais* to the adverse claimant in every case in which a chancellor would decree an interpleader. The advantages of the interpleader act are first, that he is relieved by its provisions from primary liability for costs, and secondly from the contingency and risks of his defence in a subsequent action by the adverse claimant. But the reason does not hold in the case of an agent sued by his principal, especially where it may possibly be that the adverse claim is founded on the agent's own acts or admissions.

(u) Post, "Execution."
(uu) 3 Bl. Com. 303.
(v) Lawes on Plead. 124.
(w) Per GARROW, Baron, 4 Price, 64; 2 Condens. Exch. Rep. 39. *Vide post,* 378.

By § 2 of the act of 1705,(x) it is provided, "that in all cases where a tender shall be made, and full payment offered by discount or other. wise, in such specie as the party by contract ought to do, and the party to whom such tender shall be made, refuses the same, and yet afterwards will sue for the debt, or goods so tendered, the plaintiff shall not recover any costs in such suit." A mere offer to pay money is not, in legal strictness, a tender, and of a legal tender the defendant is not entitled to take advantage, unless he pleads it, and brings money into court.(y) No tender is a substantial one but a legal tender, and the only effect of a tender and refusal, where the plaintiff has a direct cause of action, is to expose him to the loss of the costs, if the defendant pleads the tender, and brings the money into court.(z) Gold and silver coin is the only *legal* tender; but where current bank notes are tendered, and the defendant makes no objection to the tender on that account, but refuses it on another, the proffered notes will be considered as an *equitable* tender in the courts of Pennsylvania.(a) It is necessary that the difference between a tender *before* and *after* suit brought should be always adverted to; for in the latter case the costs must be paid up to the time of paying the money into court; in the former, if the plaintiff do not recover beyond the tender, he loses all claim to costs. But frequently the defendant confesses one *part* of the complaint, by *payment of money into court;* and pleads to the residue of it, which is for the most part necessary upon pleading a tender, and is of itself a kind of tender to the plaintiff; by paying into the hands of the proper officer of the court as much as the defendant acknowledges to be due, together with the costs hitherto incurred, in order to prevent the expense of any further proceedings. This may be done upon motion.(b) The practice of bringing money into court is said to have been introduced to avoid the hazard and difficulty of pleading a tender.(c) This "difficulty and hazard" would seem to attend rather the *proving* of a tender and a *legal* tender too, than the "*pleading*" of one. For as there is no complexity or intricacy in the construction of such a plea, it is not easy to see how the mere *pleading* of it can be difficult or hazardous. But the tender must be proved as any other *fact*, while the paying of money into court, which is tantamount to a tender, is a fact that proves itself. And when a tender is proved as a fact, a question may arise as to its being a *legal* tender; as, whether the *kind* of money tendered were proper and sufficient; whether when bank notes are offered, the party waived his objection to the tender's not being in gold or silver coin; whether the defendant did not impose terms on his antagonist (such as the giving of a receipt in full) which destroyed the validity of the tender; whether the tender were made on behalf of the defendant; and finally, whether the plaintiff refused the tender which his antagonist has set up.(d)

The practice of bringing money into court is allowed as a general rule, in cases where an action is brought upon contract for the recovery of a debt, which is either certain or capable of being ascertained by mere computation, without leaving any other sort of discretion to be exercised

(x) 1 Sm. Laws, 49.
(y) Sheredine v. Gaul, 2 D. 190; Seibert v. Kline, 1 Barr, 38.
(z) Cornell v. Green, 10 S. & R. 14.

(a) Decamp v. Feay, 5 S. & R. 322. See Wh. Dig. "Tender."
(b) 3 Bl. Com. 304.
(c) 1 Tidd, 669, 8th edit.
(d) 2 Carr. & Payne, 50, 51, 77.

by the jury.(e) In these cases when the dispute is not, whether any-thing, but how much is due to the plaintiff, the defendant may have leave to bring into court any sum of money he thinks fit ;(f) and where there are several counts or breaches in the declaration, and the defend-ant may bring money into court as to some of them, but not as to others, he may obtain a rule for bringing it in *specially*, upon some of the counts or breaches only.(g)

Where, however, the action is on a *tort* it cannot be allowed.(h)

The Supreme Court has the following rules upon the subject of pay-ing money into court :—

A defendant may, upon motion and before he pleads, pay into court the amount which he admits to be due, together with costs up to that time. The plaintiff may receive the amount so paid, and either enter a discontinuance or proceed to trial at his option. But in the latter case he shall pay all costs subsequently accruing, unless he recover judgment for a sum independently of that so admitted to be due and paid into court.

Upon the payment of any money into court to abide the order of the court, the same shall be deposited in such incorporated bank as the court may designate, to the credit of the court in the particular cause, and shall be drawn out only upon an order of the court, attested by the pro-thonotary : *Provided*, That nothing herein shall be construed to pre-vent a disposition of the money by agreement of the parties. A copy of the rule shall be inserted in the bank book in which the deposits are inscribed.

The prothonotary shall receive, for all sums of money paid into court from the party paying in the same, at the rate of one per cent. on an amount not exceeding three hundred dollars, of one-half per cent. on an amount not exceeding one thousand dollars, and of one-quarter of one per cent. on sums exceeding that amount.(i)

On the second Monday of each term of this court, and on the return day in July in each year, the prothonotary shall exhibit to the court an account of all moneys paid into the court, and also his bank book con-taining his account with the bank in which such moneys are deposited, settled up to the time when it is exhibited.

Bringing money into court is an acknowledgment of the right of ac-tion, to the amount of the sum brought in,(j) which the plaintiff is en-titled to receive at all events, whether he proceed in the action or not, and even though he be nonsuited, or have a verdict against him ; and being an acknowledgment of record, the party can never recover it back

---

(e) 2 Burr. 1120.

(f) 1 Tidd, 655.

(g) Ibid. ; and see 2 Arch. Pr. 182.

(h) McArther *v.* McRean, D. C. C. P. Feb. 21, 1852. Why defendant should not have leave to pay money into court. *Per curiam*. In assumpsit or covenant for the payment of money, the defendant may bring money into court. But on any action for general damages upon a contract, or for a tort, as a tender cannot be pleaded, so the defendant is not al-lowed to bring money into court. 1 Tidd,

669, 670. This general principle is well settled. It was stated in the argument that this was an action for general un-liquidated damages. We were not fur-nished, however, with a copy of the narr.; and all that we can do, therefore, is to dismiss the rule.

(i) Quere, as to the right of the court to allow the prothonotary fees not author-ized by the fee bill. See Irwin *v.* The Commissioners of Northumberland coun-ty, 1 S. & R. 506, 507.

(j) 2 Arch. Pr. 183.

again, though it afterwards appear that he paid it wrongfully. But beyond the amount of the sum brought in, bringing money into court is no acknowledgment of the right of action; and therefore if the plaintiff proceed further it is at his peril. If he proceed to trial otherwise than for the non-payment of costs, and do not prove more to be due to him than the sum brought in, he shall be nonsuited or have a verdict against him, and pay costs to the defendant. But if more appear to be due to him, he shall have a verdict for the overplus and costs.(k)

The payment of money into court on several general counts, one of which only is applicable to the plaintiff's demand, admits a right of action on that count only.(l) It must be observed, too, that where the declaration is on a special contract, payment of money into court generally admits the contract, and is conclusive on the defendant. Such payment is an acknowledgment of the specialties of the declaration, and an admission of the plaintiff's right to recover such amount at least upon the contract he has set forth.(m)

It used to be thought that the plaintiff cannot become voluntarily nonsuited after a plea of tender sufficient to cover the debt proved on the trial; otherwise, he might take the money out of court, and renew the action with a view to adduce additional testimony.(n) But such is not now the law, it being held that under such circumstances the plaintiff may become nonsuited.(o)

Though after the payment of money into court, the defendant can never afterwards take it out, even though it were paid by mistake,(p) yet the court, it should seem, if the plaintiff failed in his action, and the money had not been already taken out of court by him, would impound it to answer the defendant's costs.

In a very recent case in the Supreme Court, it appeared that under a mistake as to the amount of the debts against an estate, money was lent on bond and mortgage by a third person to one of the heirs, who had taken the real estate at the valuation, and entered into a recognizance for the payment of the distributive shares of his co-heirs, the mortgage being given on such real estate, and a part of the mortgage money was paid into court to the use of one of the heirs, a married woman. The whole of the estate was subsequently sold to pay after-accruing debts of the decedent, and the mortgagor became insolvent. It was held, that the party to whose use the money was paid into court, not being entitled by law to take it out, it should be decreed to the mortgagor, unless he had made fraudulent representations as to the solvency of the estate to the mortgagee, ignorant of the facts, in which case the latter would be entitled to follow the money as though surreptitiously obtained.(q)

As has been already observed, a defendant cannot take advantage of a tender, unless he pleads it and pays the money into court, with the costs to that time.(r)

(k) Tidd, 656.
(l) 2 Bing. 377; 9 S. & Low. 437.
(m) 4 Price, 58; 2 Condens. Exch. Rep. 35.
(n) Lewis v. Cublertson, 11 S. & R. 60; see also, 3 Cowen, 336.

(o) Jenkins v. Cutchins, 2 Miles, 65; McCredy v. Fly, 7 W. 499.
(p) 2 Bos. & P. 392; 2 T. R. 645.
(q) Goepp's Appeal, 3 H. 421.
(r) Sheredine v. Gaul, 2 D. 190; Harvey v. Hackley, 6 W. 265; see Seibert v. Kline, 1 Barr, 38.

Payment into court, under a plea of tender, by one of several joint defendants, is a payment for all, and the money may be impounded, in such case, for the costs of all.(t)

In an action of ejectment by a vendor, to compel specific performance of a contract for the sale of land, where there has been a tender of the purchase-money, the defendant may bring the money into court, and entitle himself to costs, even, perhaps, without pleading the tender.(u)

Where ejectment is brought to enforce specific performance, or to execute a trust, the money to be paid by the plaintiff must be brought into court on the trial.(v)

In order to entitle him to costs, the defendant must not only have tendered the amount, but also have obtained a rule to pay it into court, otherwise such a payment is irregular, and not to be recognized; and hence, where on a plea of tender, and other pleas, there was a verdict for the defendant, "the plaintiff to receive $26, tendered before suit brought, and now in court," but no rule of court appeared for the purpose, and the plaintiff took the money out of court, judgment was entered for the defendant without costs.(w)

A payment into court, or tender in the notes of a bank, as between the bank itself and its debtors, is equivalent to payment in specie.(x)

A voluntary payment into court by the garnishee in attachment-execution, which is applied by the prothonotary to the payment of other debts of the defendant, will not discharge the garnishee.(y)

It seems, that a voluntary payment into court, where a debt in suit is attached, is a payment to the plaintiff as against the attaching creditor.(z)

An order for the payment of money out of court, after the trial of an issue of interpleader between the plaintiff in the original action and third parties claimants, must be entitled of the original action, and not of the issue founded on the interpleader.(a)

A payment into court, where it is not authorized by statute, is, *it seems*, not payment to the party entitled.(b)

(t) Ibid.
(u) Cornell v. Green, 10 S. & R. 17. GIBSON, J.
(v) Peebles v. Reading, 8 S. & R. 484; see Lessee of Diermond v. Robinson, 2 Y. 329; and Small v. Jones, 1 W. & S. 138.
(w) Harvey v. Hackley, 6 W. 264.
(x) Northampton Bank v. Balliet, 8 W. & S. 311.
(y) Baldy v. Brady, 3 H. 103; and see Stoner v. Com. 4 H. 387.
(z) Daly v. Derringer, D. C. Phil. 9 Leg. Int. 46.
(a) Stewart v. Smith, D. C. C. P., *ante*, p. 373.
(b) Goepp's Appeal, 3 H. 427. See Hawes, v. Hackley, 6 W. 265.

The case of Jenkins v. Cutchens, and two other defendants in the District Court of this city and county (2 M. 65), which was a rule to show cause why money in court should not be impounded to answer the defendant's costs, has been already noticed, and illustrates several important points on the subject of this section.

It was an action of debt on a joint and several bond of the defendants, conditioned for the payment of one hundred and twenty-five dollars. The defendant, Cutchens, pleaded payment and a set-off; the other defendants pleaded payment and a release.

When the cause was reached in April, 1835, and before the jury were sworn, the defendant, Cutchens, paid into court the sum of one hundred and ten dollars and seventy-one cents; and pleaded, that on the 19th of September, 1833, he had made a tender of that sum, and that the money was now paid into court.

The parties went on to a trial, and the jury not agreeing were discharged by the court. The plaintiff died, and his administrator was substituted. A new *venire* was issued; when the cause was again reached in September term, 1836, the plaintiff was called and did not appear; and, on motion of the defendant's counsel, a nonsuit was entered.

The defendant's counsel then obtained a rule to show cause why the money in court should not be impounded to answer the defendant's costs. After argument,

The opinion of the court was delivered by PETTIT, President: "After payment of money into court, the defendant can never take it out; yet the court, if the plaintiff failed in his action, and the money has not been already taken out of court by him, will impound it to answer the defendant's costs. 2 Arch. Pr. 184. Whatever difficulty there may be in regard to a nonsuit after a plea of tender, where there is no payment into court, yet it is settled that the plaintiff may be nonsuited after payment of money into court. 1 Arch. Pr. 188; 1 Camp. Rep. 327, and cases cited in note; 7 T. R. 368. Upon general principles, then, it would seem to be proper for the court to make this rule absolute. But the plaintiff alleges, 1st, that the cause was not at issue; 2d, that, as administrator, the plaintiff is not responsible for costs; and 3d, that the plea of tender, and the payment into court were by one only of the defendants. First. The only difficulty here is, that the plaintiff never entered in form a replication to either of the pleas, in regard to the difference between the amount claimed and the sum paid into court. The plaintiff went to trial under the first venire, as if the prothonotary had, under the rule of court, entered the proper replications. The defendant had a right to consider that act of the prothonotary as done; and it is too late for the plaintiff to avail himself of this suggestion now. Second. The case of Muntorf *v.* Muntorf, 2 R. 180, decides, that though in England executors and administrators are by judicial construction excepted out of the statute of 23 Hen. 8, ch. 15, giving the defendant judgment and execution for costs against the plaintiff, in case of nonsuit or of verdict for the defendant, yet that a different interpretation has been uniformly given to the statute since its extension to Pennsylvania. Executors and administrators here are bound for costs. There is nothing then in this point. Third. The *third* objection rests upon the assumption that the money never was, in legal contemplation, paid into court. No sound reason can be assigned why one of several defendants, where each is liable for the whole debt, and where payment by one is payment for all, should not be allowed to pay money into court. It is in entire unison with the spirit of the original understanding of the parties. Though in the case of Kay *v.* Panchiman, *et al.* 2 Wm. Blacks. 1029, one of three defendants was not permitted to bring money into court; yet it appears, from the unsatisfactory report of the facts, that of the other two defendants one had suffered judgment to go by default, and the other had been outlawed; and further, that it was thought that confusion would be introduced into the record, and the plaintiff be unjustly put in jeopardy of costs by such a proceeding. The reasoning of the decision in that case has no application to the one before us."

CHAPTER XVIII.

OF PLEAS.

THE plaintiff having declared, and every precautionary measure in proceedings between the declaration and plea being first taken, it is for the defendant to determine the manner of his defence. For this purpose, he considers whether, on the face of the declaration, and supposing the facts to be true, the plaintiff appears to be entitled, in point of *law*, to the redress he seeks, and in the form of action which he has chosen. If he appears to be not so entitled in point of law, and this by defect either in the substance or the form of the declaration, that is, as disclosing a case insufficient on the merits, or as framed in violation of any of the rules of pleading, the defendant is entitled to except to the declaration on such ground. In so doing, he is said to *demur;* and this kind of objection is called a demurrer.(*a*)

If the defendant do not demur, his only alternative method of defence is, to oppose or answer the declaration by matter of *fact*. In doing so, he is said to *plead* (by way of distinction from *demurring*), and the answer of fact, so made, is called the plea.(*b*)

Pleas are divided into pleas *dilatory* and *peremptory;* and this is the most general division to which they are subject.(*c*)

Subordinate to this is another division. Pleas are either *to the jurisdiction of the court; in suspension of the action; in abatement of the writ; or, in bar of the action:* the first three of which belong to the dilatory class; the last is of the peremptory kind.(*d*) In the succeeding sections we shall consider briefly as much of the nature of these pleas as is connected with their adoption in practice.

SECTION I.

OF DILATORY PLEAS.

By the 68th rule of the District Court, no dilatory plea shall be received, unless the party offering such plea does by affidavit prove the truth thereof, or show some probable matter to the court to induce them to believe that the fact of such dilatory plea is true.

(*a*) Steph. on Plead. 61, 1st edit.
(*b*) Ibid. Of the considerations which determine the defendant in his election to demur or to plead, and of the aider of faults in pleading, by pleading over by verdict, and by the statutes of jeofails and amendments, see Steph. on Plead. 164, 170, 1st edit.
(*c*) Ibid. 63.
(*d*) Ibid.

Rules to the same effect exist in the Supreme Court, and in the several Courts of Common Pleas.

A plea to the jurisdiction is one by which the defendant excepts to the jurisdiction of the court to entertain the action. In a local action it is a good plea to the jurisdiction, that the land out of which the debt or duty accrued, lies in a foreign country.(e) So it is good plea that the cognizance of the cause belongs to the Circuit or District Court of the United States.(f) In pleading a ground for refusing to answer, in a court of general jurisdiction, it is a rule that exclusive jurisdiction in some peculiar court must be set forth.(g) This, however, is an objection which it is, in this State, unnecessary to *plead*, for if a want of jurisdiction appear in any stage of the cause, the plaintiff must fail.(gg) But in England, it is too late to except to the jurisdiction of the court after a plea in bar; for by pleading, it is said the defendant has submitted himself to the court's jurisdiction;(h) but the operation of this rule is there confined almost exclusively to those cases in which a defendant, by reason of some local or personal exemption, is privileged from being sued except in a particular place or court.(i) In this State there are no exempt jurisdictions, like the courts of the counties palatine, cinque ports, or universities in England;(j) neither is any personal exemption of a judge, attorney, or officer of a court of record, from being sued elsewhere than in his own court, in existence here. If, then, there be a defect of jurisdiction as to the subject matter of the suit, the court cannot entertain the action; and such courts as are of limited jurisdiction must not only act within the scope of their authority, but it must appear on the face of their proceedings that they did so; if this does not appear, all they do is *coram non judice ;*(k) and no consent or acquiescence of the parties can give the court a jurisdiction which it did not originally possess.(l) Thus, where the cause of action is strictly local, as ejectment or trespass in relation to lands situate without the State,(m) or the foundation of an action in the court of a State is exclusively of prize or admiralty jurisdiction, or is exclusively within the cognizance of the courts of the United States,(n) or where a common law right is made the direct subject of a suit in a prize or admiralty court ;(o) or where an action is brought in the courts of the United States upon a cause of action not arising under the laws of the United States, the parties being neither aliens nor citizens of different States ;(p) in these and similar cases, the want of jurisdiction is an inherent and incurable defect, of which the defendant may avail himself at any stage of the proceedings ;(q) so that if the defect of jurisdiction should appear after the declaration is filed, it would be sufficient with a plea in bar to file a suggestion that the court ought not to take cognizance of the case for want of jurisdiction ;(r) or, if the de-

(e) Oliphant v. Smith, 3 Pa. R. 180; Salk. 80, pl. 1; Steph. on Plead. 290, 291, 3d edit.
(f) 7 Johns. 144; 17 ibid. 4.
(g) Palmer v. The Com. 6 S. & R. 246.
(gg) Ante, p. 23.
(h) 1 Mad. Chan. 13.
(i) 1 Dunl. Pr. 429.
(j) 3 Bl. Com. c. 6.
(k) 1 Peters's Rep. 36.

(l) 3 Caine's Rep. 129 ; 12 Johns. 466; 13 ibid. 218 ; 18 ibid. 22, 27.
(m) 1 Dunl. Pr. 429.
(n) 7 Johns. 144.
(o) Com. Dig. Adm. F. 9.
(p) Bingham v. Cabot, 3 D. 382; 4 ibid. 8; 5 Cranch, 303.
(q) Mannhardt v. Soderstrom, 1 Bin. 142. See ante, p. 23.
(r) Vide ibid. 133.

fect of jurisdiction appear at the trial, the defendant may then avail himself of it ;(s) or, if it appear upon the record, may demur, or move in arrest of judgment, or bring a writ of error.(t)   So the want of jurisdiction of a justice may be taken advantage of in every stage of the cause, after plea, trial on the merits and judgment, or on appeal entered, and the cause in court.(u)

Where a want of jurisdiction is not apparent on the record, it cannot be shown on the trial of a *scire facias quare executio non*, which is a collateral proceeding.

Want of jurisdiction in the District Court of Philadelphia can only be taken advantage of by a special plea to the jurisdiction, which, however, can be filed at any time during trial.(v)

A plea in suspension of the action is one which shows some ground for not proceeding in the suit at the present period, and prays that the pleading may be stayed, until that ground has been removed.   The number of these pleas is small.   Among them is that which is founded on the nonage or infancy of one of the parties ; and is termed *parol demurrer.*(w)   It may be founded on the nonage of *either* party in some *real* actions.(x)   In *personal* actions, it extends to the case of the *defendant* only,(y) as when an action of debt is brought against him, as heir to any deceased ancestor.(z)   But the necessity of such pleas can seldom arise in this State, and they are consequently not known in its practice.

The pendency of a bill for discovery of a debtor's effects, in another State, and an injunction to prevent his selling them, is not the subject of a plea in abatement of a subsequent suit here for the same cause.(a)

A plea in abatement of the writ is one which shows some ground for *abating* or *quashing* the original writ ; and makes prayer to that effect.(b)

The grounds for so abating the writ are any matters of fact tending to impeach the correctness of that instrument ; *i. e.* to show that it is improperly framed or sued out, without, at the same time, tending to deny the right of action itself.   Thus, if there be a variance between the declaration and the writ, this shows that the writ was not properly adapted to the action, and is, therefore, a ground for abating it.   So, if the writ appear to have been sued out pending another action already brought for the same cause, if it name only one person as defendant, when it should have named several, or if it appear to have been defaced in a material part, it is for any of these reasons abateable.(c)

Pleas in abatement relate either : To the person of the plaintiff, to the person of the defendant, to the count or declaration, or to the writ.(d)

(s) Maxfield *v.* Levy, 4 D. 338 ; Cheriot *v.* Foussat, 3 Bin. 239, n.

(t) 1 Dunl. Pr. 430.

(u) 5 Sm. Laws, 177, n. ; Moore *v.* Wait, 1 Bin. 220.

(v) *Ante*, p. 23.

(w) *Vide* Steph. on Plead. 64.

(x) See Rob. Dig. 319, 320.

(y) Steph. on Plead. Appx. xxvi.

(z) 3 Bl. Com. 300.

(a) Ralph *v.* Brown, 3 W. & S. 395.

(b) See Steph. on Plead. 65, 66, 1st edit.

(c) Steph. on Plead. 65.

(d) Ibid.

To the person of the plaintiff they are, either that he is not in exist.
ence (being only a fictitious person, or dead), or else that, being in ex.
istence, he is an alien enemy,(e) attainted of treason or felony,(f) or an
infant. The disability of the plaintiff as an alien enemy, may be pleaded
either in abatement or in bar; but, whichever way pleaded, the judg.
ment thereon is not a bar to a new suit on the return of peace.(g)   The
plea must allege that the plaintiff is himself an enemy, or adhering to
the enemy, but it is not necessary to aver that he is resident in the
enemy's country.(h)   It is not always necessary to plead the plaintiff's
alienage, but in some cases it may be given in evidence under the general
issue.(i)   The objection that the plaintiff is an infant, not suing by prochein amy or guardian, can only be pleaded in abatement, and is not a
proper ground of nonsuit at the trial; for by pleading in chief, the defendant admits the due appearance of the plaintiff, and after verdict the
error is cured by the statute of jeofails.(j)

A defendant may plead minority to an action of debt on a judgment
confessed before a justice, and it is an available defence of necessity,
because in such case no writ of error lies, and a certiorari would correct
only errors on the face of the record—and the fact of infancy is triable
per pais instead of by inspection.(k)

Pleading to the action after the defendant has attained twenty-one,
waives any defect in the service of the writ during his minority.(l)

Pleas in abatement to the person of the defendant are, when he alleges
that he is privileged, or that he is an infant.   The coverture of a feme,
plaintiff or defendant, suing without her husband, or coverture occurring
after suit brought, may be pleaded in abatement, and this is the only
way in which the objection can be taken advantage of, where she would,
if joined with her husband, be a proper party to the suit.(m)

A plea of coverture in abatement may be struck off if filed after a
plea in bar, although the latter was withdrawn and the other plea substituted by leave of court.(n)

Under the head of pleas in abatement to the person may be included
a plea, that the plaintiffs or defendants, suing or being sued as husband
and wife, are not married;(o) and any other plea for want of proper
parties, whether plaintiffs or defendants.(oo)

When the plaintiff's disability not only suspends the right of action,
but destroys it altogether, it seems that it may be pleaded in bar as well
as in abatement.(p)

The act of 24th February, 1834, renders the tender of a refunding
bond unnecessary before suit for a legacy; and, therefore, its absence
is no ground for plea in abatement.(q)

(e) See Wilcox v. Henry, 1 D. 69; 1
Peters, 107; Russel v. Skipwith, 6 Bin.
241; 10 Johns. 69.
(f) Com. Dig. Abatement, E. 3, 4, 16,
17.
(g) 10 Johns. 183; 6 Taunt. 237; 11
Johns. 418; see Russel v. Skipwith, 1 S.
& R. 310.
(h) Id.; 6 Bin. 241; contra, 10 Johns.
70; 1 Bac. Abr. 6; 2 Galison, 105.
(i) 11 Johns. 418; 6 T. R. 35.
(j) 7 Johns. 373. See post, "Infants."

(k) Etter v. Curtis, 7 W. & S. 170.
(l) Hilligas v. Hilligas, 5 Barr, 97.
(m) 3 T. R. 631; 4 T. R. 627; 1 Bac.
Abr. 503; Wilson v. Hamilton, 4 S. &
R. 238; Perry v. Boileau, 10 S. & R.
208; 11 Wheat. 303.
(n) Beitler v. Study, 10 Barr, 418. See
post, p. 386.
(o) Com. Dig. Abatement, E. 6.
(oo) Wh. Dig. "Pleading," vi. (c)
(p) Sandback v. Quigley, 8 W. 460.
(q) Bixter v. Blankenbiller, 8 W. 64.

A plea in abatement to the *count* or declaration is such as is founded on some objection applying immediately to the declaration, and only by consequence affecting the writ. The only frequent case in which this kind of plea has occurred, is where the objection is that of a variance in the declaration from the writ; which was always a fatal fault. Even in this case, however, the plea is now out of use, in consequence of a change of practice relative to the original writ, that will be presently noticed.

A plea in abatement of the writ, is such as is founded on some objection that applies to the writ itself; for example, that in an action on a joint contract, it does not name as defendants all the joint contractors, but omits one or more of them.(*r*) It is a general rule, that an omission of this kind can only be taken advantage of by such a plea;(*s*) but this rule is confined to those species of actions in which the plaintiff gives notice to the defendant of the nature of his demand, as in actions on bonds or special actions on the case, and does not extend to actions of general *indebitatus assumpsit*, unless in such suits the plaintiff before plea furnishes the defendant with a copy of the account, which he means to offer at the trial.(*t*) Pleas of this latter kind have been very anciently divided into such as relate to the *form of the writ*, and such as relate to the *action of the writ;* and those relating to its *form*, have been again subdivided into such as are founded on objections *apparent on the writ itself*, and such as are founded *on matter extraneous.*(*u*) By § 6 of the act of 1806, " in all cases where any suit has been brought in any court of record within this commonwealth, the same shall not be set aside for informality, if it appear that the process has issued in the name of the commonwealth, against the defendant for moneys owing or due, or for damages by trespass, or otherwise, as the case may be, that said process was served on the defendant, by the proper officer, and in due time."(*v*)

In all actions, not of contract, but proceeding *ex delicto*, where one who ought to be named, is omitted, it can only be taken advantage of by plea in abatement; otherwise, the damages will be apportioned on the trial.(*w*)

The actual power of using these pleas in abatement has been much abridged, and the whole law of original writs consequently rendered of less prominent importance than formerly, by a rule of practice laid down in modern times. With respect to such pleas in abatement, as were *founded on facts that could only be ascertained by examination of the writ itself*, as for example, variance between the writ and declaration, or erasure of the writ, it was always held a necessary matter of form, preparatory to pleading them, *to demand oyer* of the writ, that is, to *hear it read;* which, in the days of oral pleading, was complied with, by reading it aloud in open court, and after the establishment of written pleadings by delivering a copy of the instrument. The Court of Common Pleas, however, in the 11 & 12 Geo. II., and the King's Bench, in

<hr>

(*r*) Steph. on Plead. 65, 66.
(*s*) 3 W. C. C. R. 110.
(*t*) Ibid.
(*u*) See Steph. on Plead. 67, n. 1st edit., where it is said that these divisions of pleas in abatement to the *writ* are

more subtle than useful, and do not, in the modern English practice, often come under consideration.
(*v*) 4 Sm. Laws, 329.
(*w*) Railroad *v.* Boyer, 1 H. 501. COULTER, J.

the 19th Geo. III.;(x) thought fit to establish it as a rule, that thenceforth oyer should not be granted of the original writ; and the indirect effect of this has consequently been, in England, to abolish in practice all pleas in abatement, founded on objections of the kind here stated.(y) In this State, though not yet fully settled, it seems that a variance between the writ and declaration, where the cause of action appears to be the same, cannot be taken advantage of in any stage of the suit.(z) But there are pleas in abatement, which *do not require any examination of the writ itself*. For example, if in the declaration one only of two joint contractors is named defendant, this is sufficient to show that the same non-joinder exists in the writ; for as a variance between the writ and declaration is a fault, the defendant is entitled to assume that they agree with each other; and he may consequently, without the production of the writ, *plead* this non-joinder as certainly existing in the latter instrument. So the plea that the writ was sued out pending another action,(a) or pleas to the person of the plaintiff or defendant, require no examination of the writ itself, and there are many others to which the same remark applies. In all such cases no oyer is necessary; and, therefore, pleas of this latter description may be, and are, in fact, still pleaded, notwithstanding the rule of practice which denies oyer of the writ.(b) But no advantage can be taken of a variance between the writ and declaration, after the defendant has *pleaded in bar*.(c)

A plea in abatement must give the plaintiff a better writ; that is, in pleading a mistake of form, in abatement of the writ, the plea must, at the same time, *correct* the mistake, so as to enable the plaintiff to avoid the same objection in framing his new writ.(d) It must also, as all dilatory pleas must, be pleaded at a preliminary stage of the suit,(e) and must be put in within four days after the declaration has been delivered.(f) A plea in abatement cannot be put in after a *general imparlance*,(g) and accordingly, if the defendant wish to preserve his right to do this, he must vary his form of prayer, by making it with a reservation of his right, and asking a *special* imparlance,(h) which must be entered on the record.(i) Nor can it be pleaded after oyer,(j) or a *view ;*(k) nor after a plea in bar, unless under special circumstances, of which the court must judge ;(l) and if a plea in abatement be put in after a plea in bar, the plaintiff is not bound to reply to it,(m) even though the first plea was bad. (n)

(x) 1 Saund. 318, n. 3.

(y) Steph. on Plead. 69; see Gratz v. Phillips, 1 Bin. 588.

(z) Dillman v. Schultz, 5 S. & R. 35; Latimer v. Hodgson, Id. 514; Gratz v. Phillips, 1 Bin. 588.

(a) See 2 Br. 175.

(b) Steph. on Plead. 70.

(c) Dillman v. Schultz, 5 S. & R. 35; Newlin v. Palmer, 11 Id. 100; Overseers of Poor of Roxborough v. Bunn, 12 Id. 295.

(d) Steph. on Plead. 435; Witmer v. Schlatter, 15 S. & R. 150.

(e) Ibid.

(f) Stoever v. Gloninger, 6 S. & R. 69; Williams v. Etzell, 6 P. L. J. 294.

(g) Witmer v. Schlatter, 15 S. & R. 150; Coates v. McCamm, 2 Br. 173; Chamberlain v. Hite, 5 W. 373; Fritz v. Thomas, 5 P. L. J. 423; Thomas v. Hitner, 9 Barr, 441. See 3 Bl. Com. 301; 2 Saund. 2, n. 2; 2 Br. 173, 176; 2 D. 263, 184.

(h) Steph. on Plead. 91.

(i) Coates v. McCamm, 2 Browne, 176; Chamberlain v. Hite, 5 W. 373.

(j) Com. Dig. Abatement. I. 22.

(k) Ibid. I. 25.

(l) Riddle v. Stevens, 2 S. & R. 537.

(m) Wilson v. Hamilton, 4 S. & R. 238.

(n) Chamberlain v. Hite, *supra*.

When a plea in abatement, and a plea in bar are filed together, the plea in abatement will be stricken off by the court.(o)

After permission to withdraw a plea in bar, and file a new plea, the defendant pleaded coverture in abatement. It was held that the plea came too late, and that the court were right in striking it off.(p) But although the practice is to strike off a plea in abatement put in after a plea in bar, or unsupported by an affidavit of its truth, yet this will not be done when the plea is in form pleaded in bar, and it is a question whether the matter is or is not pleaded in abatement.(q) It seems that in this sense the defence that the suit has been prematurely brought, or that the action has been misconceived, can be taken advantage of upon the general issue.(r)

A plea to further maintenance, &c., may be entered after the general issue. (rr)

(o) Maitland v. McGonigle, D. C., Saturday, Sept. 30, 1848. Why defendant's plea should not be stricken off. Per curiam. When the court opened the judgment in this case, they decided that the defence of presumption of payment from the lapse of time, was like the statute of limitations—a defence upon the merits. Had their attention been called to it, they certainly would have placed this defendant upon the terms of not pleading the death of one of the defendants in abatement. The court have the power, no doubt, of still so modifying their former order; but it is not necessary to exercise it in this case. The defendant has pleaded the death of his codefendant in abatement, together with non-assumpsit and payment—pleas in bar. It is perfectly clear that a plea in abatement cannot be pleaded at the same time with a plea in bar. (1 Bac. Abr. Tit. Abatement, a.) If issue is taken upon a plea in abatement, and it is found for plaintiff, the jury proceed at once to assess the damages without an inquiry into the merits. It is the first penalty which the law annexes to a false dilatory plea. On the other hand, a verdict for defendant ends the case. It is evident, then, that a plea in bar is incongruous and inconsistent with a plea in abatement, and the plaintiff may elect which he will have struck off. The Supreme Court of the State of New York have refused to permit the general issue to be withdrawn to let in a plea of coverture in abatement, though the defendant swore that the general issue was pleaded without his knowledge, by a person whom he never meant to retain as attorney. (Anon, 3 Caine's Rep. 102.) Nor is the power of our courts affected, in this respect, by the 6th section of the Act of March 21, 1806 (Purd. 67), which was only intended to compel the allowance of amendments of informalities affecting the merits

of the cause in controversy. Rule absolute.

(p) Beitler v. Study, 10 Barr, 418; Lacroix v. Macquarts, 1 M. 42.

(q) Machette v. Musgrave, D. C. C. P. 8 Leg. Int. 74.

(r) Ibid. Machette v. Musgrave, April 26, 1851. Motion to strike off plea. Per curiam. Although undoubtedly the practice is to strike off a plea in abatement put in after a plea in bar, or unsupported by an affidavit of its truth, yet this will not be done when the plea is in form pleaded in bar, and it is a question whether the matter is or is not pleadable in abatement. It amounts to this—that the suit has been prematurely brought; such matter may be properly pleaded in abatement—and, perhaps, if specially pleaded at all, it should be so pleaded. In that respect it is like the defence, that the action has been misconceived. Yet the books are unanimous in holding that these are matters which may be taken advantage of upon the general issue; and the reason, perhaps, why it is not to be found pleaded except in abatement is, that it amounts to the general issue. The principle, however, is well settled, that matters only pleadable in abatement, if not so pleaded, are waived—a principle taken in connection with the authorities, that such a defence as this is available on the general issue, is decisive upon the question as far as regards this motion. R. D.

(rr) Folwell v. Norvell, Dec. 30, 1848. Why the plea should not be stricken off. Per curiam. In this case, after the action was commenced, and before the declaration was filed, a foreign attachment was commenced against the plaintiff, and the defendant was served as garnishee. Defendant has pleaded it not in abatement, which it is not, because there was no disability to sue when the suit was brought, nor in bar, generally, because

A plea of misnomer was struck off where the record has been pre- viously amended so as to correct the mistake. (s)

A plea in abatement must be verified by affidavit, which must be filed at the time of pleading ;(ss) and as has been seen, " no dilatory plea shall be received, unless the party offering such plea does, by affidavit, prove ¬the truth thereof, or show some probable matter to the court, to induce them to believe that the fact of such dilatory plea is true." The facts set forth in a dilatory plea, must be stated in positive terms, and the plea must be positively sworn to ; swearing that the facts set forth in the plea are true, " to the best of the defendant's knowledge and belief," is not sufficient.(t)

If the above-enumerated requisites be not attended to or wanting, that is, if the plea be not filed in time or verified by oath, or if the affidavit be defective, it may be treated as a nullity,(u) or the plaintiff may move to set it aside.(v)

But though a plea in abatement may thus be set aside or treated as a nullity if pleaded out of time, or if it be otherwise irregular, this cannot be done for insufficiency ; a demurrer is then the proper course.(w)

After a plea in abatement, if it be sufficient in form, and the plaintiff cannot contest the facts which it alleges, he may discontinue on pay- ment of costs ; otherwise, he must reply or demur. If he reply, and take issue upon the plea, and it be found in his favor, the judgment is final for the plaintiff, *that he recover*,(x) and the jury ought to assess the damages.(y) If he demur to the defendant's plea,(z) or the defend- ant demur to the plaintiff's replication,(a) and the issue in law be in either case decided in favor of the plaintiff, judgment *quod respondeat ouster*, that he (the defendant) *answer over*, only is awarded. After judgment of *respondeat ouster* on a demurrer to a plea in abatement, the defendant may be ruled *de novo* within the time indicated by the rule of court, or within such shorter time as the court (who are not bound by their rule) may prescribe on application.

A second plea in abatement may be pleaded after a former ; as, if a plea to the person of the plaintiff be overruled, the defendant may next plead to the form of the writ ; and it appears that he may plead as

the mere pendency of a foreign attach- ment cannot be pleaded in bar ; but he has pleaded it in bar to the further main- tenance of the suit. It appears to us that, according to the case of Le Bret v. Papillon (4 East, 502), that is the proper mode of pleading in such cases. R. D.

(s) Owen v. Hackney, D. C., Saturday, May 20, 1848. Why the pleas in abate- ment should not be stricken off. *Per curiam.* In this case the defendant was sued by the name of J. N. Hackney. He filed a⅓ affidavit of defence that his name was Joseph N. Hackney. Under the act of April 16, 1846, the court allowed the record to be amended. No actual altera- tion was made in the narr., however, and the plaintiff pleaded the matter of his affidavit in abatement. No actual altera- tion of the record was necessary ; nor is

it proper that there should be any erasure or alteration of the record of the court. The entry of the allowance of the amend- ment is all that is necessary, and the amendment is considered as actually made accordingly. Rule absolute.

(ss) Rapp v. Elliot, 1 Y. 185, S. C. Id. 2 D. 184. See Vicary v. Moore, 2 W. 458.

(t) 1 Br. 77.

(u) 1 Dunl. Pr. 377, 443.

(v) Rapp v. Elliot, 1 Y. 185, S. C. Ibid. 2 D. 184.

(w) Ralph v. Brown, 3 W. & S. 395 ; Cooper v. Comfort, 8 Leg. Int. 187, *post*, p. 409.

(x) 2 Saund. 210, n. 3.

(y) Mehaffy v. Share, 2 Pa. R. 361 ; Wallace's Rep. 57, 58.

(z) 2 Saund. 210, n. 3.

(a) 1 East, 542.

many different pleas in abatement, in succession, as he pleases, under these restrictions: 1st. That he do not invert the established order of pleading; 2dly. That the latter plea be not repugnant to the former; and, 3dly. That the latter be not such as is waived by the former.(*b*) Hence, where judgment of *respondeas ouster* is given on a plea in abatement of the writ, the defendant can only plead next in bar of the action.

Pleas of this description being considered as dilatory, are not much favored by the courts; and in one case, where a defendant pleaded in abatement, that others were jointly liable with himself, and the plaintiff applied to the defendant's attorney to give the places of abode and additions of those persons, which he refused to do unless the action were discontinued, the Court of King's Bench held, that if the defendant persevered in such refusal, the plea might be set aside.(*c*)

Where the defendants have, in one action, abated the suit by pleading that other persons are joint contractors, not named in the writ, and a new suit is brought, a similar plea, in abatement, will not be allowed in such second suit, though put in by the defendants who were not parties to the first suit.(*d*)

The subject of non-joinder of parties will be considered under a future head. (*dd*)

SECTION II.

OF PEREMPTORY PLEAS, OR PLEAS IN BAR.

1. Peremptory pleas generally.
2. *Non-assumpsit.*
3. *Non est factum*, *nil debet*, and covenants performed.
4. Payment, &c.
5. Not guilty, *non detinet, non cepit, &c.*
6. Special matter and set-off.
7. Double pleas.
8. Former action, attachment.
9. Short pleadings.
10. Striking off, adding, and altering pleas.

1. *Peremptory pleas generally.*

A peremptory plea, or *plea in bar of the action*, may be defined as one which shows *some ground* for barring or defeating the action; and makes prayer to that effect. A plea in bar is, therefore, distinguished from all pleas of the dilatory class, as impugning the right of action altogether, instead of merely tending to divert the proceedings to another jurisdiction, or abate the particular writ. It is, in short, a substantial and conclusive answer to the action. It follows from this property, that in general it must either deny all, or some essential part of the averments of facts in the declaration, or, admitting them to be true, allege new facts, which obviate or repel their legal effect. In the

(*b*) Com. Dig. Abatement, 1, 4.
(*c*) 4 B. & Ald. 93; Gow on Partn. 222, Am. ed.
(*d*) Whelen *v.* Watmough, 15 S. & R.

159. For pleas *puis darrien continuance*, see *post*. chapter xxiv. sec. 2.
(*dd*) *Post*, vol. ii. "Partners."

first case, the defendant is said, in the language of pleading, to *traverse*, that is, *deny*, the matter of the declaration; in the latter, to *confess and avoid* it. Pleas in bar are, consequently, divided into pleas *by way of traverse*, and pleas *by way of confession and avoidance.*(e)

The defendant, as may be gathered from the rules of court previously quoted,(f) may be ruled to plead by the plaintiff (when the latter has complied with the exigencies of those rules), in eight days, or five or four weeks (this depending on what court the action has been brought in), under the penalty of judgment by *nil dicit*, for want of a plea.(g) In proceedings under the fifth section of the act of 1806, which, we have already seen,(h) authorizes a filing of a statement of the cause of action in lieu of a declaration, the defendant, by not appearing, and by neglecting to make his defence, at the second term, consonantly with the same section, is presumed not to gainsay the plaintiff's demand, but to confess it; he is supposed to confess a judgment, which may therefore be entered, without a rule to plead.(i)

The time and manner of appearing, pleading, and signing judgment for want of a plea, &c., are matters of practice regulated by the rules of the various courts, and irregularities therein must be sought to be remedied by applications to the court, whose rules or practice have been violated, as soon as the complainant has notice of the injury.(j)

If the defendant plead in bar to the declaration, by way of *traverse*, a question is at once raised between the parties, and it is a question of *fact*, viz., whether the facts in the declaration, which the traverse denies, be true. A question being thus raised, or, in other words, the parties having arrived at a specific point or matter, affirmed on the one side and denied on the other, the defendant is, in general, obliged to offer to refer this question to some *mode of trial*, and does this by annexing to the traverse an appropriate formula, proposing either a trial by the *country* (i. e. by a jury), or such other method of decision as by law belongs to the particular point. If this be accepted by his adversary, the parties are then said to be *at issue*, and the question itself is called the *issue*. Consequently, the party who thus traverses, annexing such formula, is said to *tender issue*, and the issue so tendered, is called an issue in fact.(k) This practice, it will be observed, is that which is

(e) Steph. on Plead. 70, 71, first ed.

(f) *Supra*, p. 317.

(g) See Shaffer v. Brobst, 9 S. & R. 85.

(h) *Ante*, p. 312.

(i) Boaz v. Heister, 6 S. & R. 18.

(j) Crosby v. Massey, 1 Pa. R. 231.

(k) Steph. on Plead. 72, 73. The following rules of the District Court of Philadelphia are important here:—

PLEADING IN PARTICULAR ACTIONS.

Ordered: That the following rules relative to pleading be adopted, to take effect on the 1st April, 1842.

I. *Assumpsit.*

LXXV. In all actions of *assumpsit*, except on bills of exchange and promissory notes, the plea of *non-assumpsit* shall operate only as a denial in fact of the *express* contract or promise alleged, or of the matters of fact from which the contract or promise alleged may be *implied* by law.

Ex. gr. 1. In an action on a warranty, the plea will operate as a denial of the fact of the warranty having been given upon the alleged consideration, but not of the breach, and in an action on a policy of insurance, of the subscription to the alleged policy by the defendant, but not of the interest, of the commencement of the risk of the loss, or of the alleged compliance with warranties.

2. In actions against carriers and other bailees for not delivering, or not keeping goods safe, or not returning them on request, and in actions against agents for not accounting, the plea will operate as a denial of any express con-

pursued in England, and would be *regular* here; though it is by no means actually adopted. For, as will be subsequently shown, the defendant, on pleading a general plea, may merely plead the plea by name, thus: "*defendant pleads non-assumpsit*," or, "*non-culpabilis*," without tendering issue, and the prothonotary is then authorized by rule of court to put the cause at issue; or the defendant may simply add to the above plea "and issue," without, as in England, traversing at length and annexing a formula proposing a trial by jury.(*l*) But though it is not usual to conclude pleas to the country or to the court, the court will direct them to be put in a legal form, if the plaintiff require it.(*m*)

tract to the effect alleged in the declaration of such bailment or employment, as would raise a promise in law to the effect alleged, but not of the breach.

3. In an action of *indebitatus assumpsit* for goods sold and delivered, the plea of *non-assumpsit* will operate as a denial of the sale and delivery in point of fact; in the like action for money had and received, it will operate as a denial both of the receipt of the money and the existence of those facts which make such receipt by the defendant a receipt to the use of plaintiff.

LXXVI. In all actions upon bills of exchange and promissory notes, the plea of *non-assumpsit* shall be inadmissible. In such actions, therefore, a plea in denial must traverse some matter of fact, *e. g.*, the drawing, or making, or indorsing, or accepting, or presenting, or notice of dishonor of the bill or note.

LXXVII. In every species of *assumpsit*, all matters in confession and avoidance, including not only those by way of discharge, but those which show the transaction to be either void or voidable in point of law, on the ground of fraud or otherwise, shall be specially pleaded —*Ex. gr.* Infancy, coverture, release, payment, performance, illegality of *consideration*, either by statute or common law; drawing, indorsing, accepting, &c., bills or notes by way of accommodation, set-off, mutual credit, unseaworthiness, misrepresentation, concealment, deviation, and various other defences must be pleaded.

LXXVIII. In actions of policies of insurance, the interest of the assured may be avoided thus: "That A, B, C, and D (or some one of them), were or was interested," &c.; and it may also be averred, "that the insurance was made for the use and benefit, and on the account, of the person and persons so interested."

II. *In Covenant and Debt.*

LXXIX. In debt on specialty, or covenant, the plea of *non est factum* shall operate as a denial of the execution of the deed in point of fact only, and all other defences shall be specially pleaded, including matters which make the deed absolutely void, as well as those which make it voidable.

LXXX. The plea of "*nil debet*" shall not be allowed in any action.

LXXXI. In actions of debt on simple contract, other than on bills of exchange and promissory notes, the defendant may plead that "he never was indebted in manner and form as in the declaration alleged;" and such a plea shall have the same operation as the plea of *non-assumpsit* in *indebitatus assumpsit*, and all matters in confession and avoidance shall be pleaded specially as above directed in actions of *assumpsit*.

LXXXII. In other actions of debt, in which the plea of *nil debet* has been hitherto allowed, including those on bills of exchange and promissory notes, the defendant shall deny specifically some particular matter of fact alleged in the declaration, or plead specially in confession and avoidance.

November 12, 1845.

LXXXIII. 1. The rules relative to pleading in *assumpsit*, covenant, and debt, adopted on the first day of April, 1842, are repealed so far as they are compulsory on defendants, and pleas in the said actions may be pleaded in such forms as were used and approved before the adoption of the said rules, and with like effect.

2. The said rules are continued in force as rules to be observed at the election of defendants.

3. The plea of *non-assumpsit* and the plea of *non est factum*, when pleaded under the said rules, must appear to be so pleaded either on the face of the plea or by indorsement thereon signed by the party or his attorney.

(*l*) See Shaffer *v.* Brobst, 9 S. & R. 87.
(*m*) Share *v.* Becker, 8 S. & R. 241.

If, instead of traversing, the defendant *demur*, a question of law is raised, whether the declaration be sufficient in point of law to maintain the action, which is referred to *the judgment of the court;* and as the plaintiff cannot object to this *question*, he is obliged to accept or join in the *issue in law*, which is tendered by a set form of words, called a *joinder in demurrer*.

But the tender of the *issue in fact* is *not* necessarily accepted by the plaintiff; for, first, he may consider the *traverse itself* as insufficient in law. It must be understood that, by the traverse, the defendant may deny either the *whole* or a *part* of the declaration; and in the latter case, the traverse may, in the opinion of the plaintiff, be so framed as to involve a *part immaterial* or *insufficient* to *decide the action*. Again, he may consider the traverse as defective in point of form, and object to its sufficiency in law on that ground. So, in his opinion, the *mode of trial proposed* may, in point of law, be inapplicable to the particular kind of issue. On such grounds, therefore, he has an option to *demur* to the traverse, as insufficient in law. The effect of this demurrer, however, would only be to postpone the acceptance of issue by a single stage; for, by the demurrer, he tenders an issue in law, and his adversary would be obliged to join in demurrer, that is, to accept the issue in law in the next pleading. On the other hand, supposing a demurrer not to be adopted, the alternative course will be to accept the tendered issue of fact, and also the mode of trial which the traverse proposes; and this is done (in case of trial by jury), by a set form of words, called a *joinder in issue* or a *similiter;* that is, the defendant having put himself upon the country, the plaintiff *doth the like*.(n) The issue in law or fact being thus tendered, and accepted on the other side, the parties are at issue, and the pleading is at an end.(o)

The making up of issue and the settling of the record is in our practice simple, when compared with that prevailing in England, being unincumbered and unattended with stamps, with issue or demurrer-books, or with plea rolls and *nisi prius* rolls.(p) Thus, to exhibit a common example, when the declaration is drawn (suppose it to be in debt on a bond), the plaintiff's attorney may file it and lay a rule to plead; or, before filing it, may take it to the attorney for the defendant, and request him to plead to it. If the latter will give a plea, he may indorse the plea on the declaration; thus, if the plea be payment, "*the defendant pleads payment*," and then signs it for the defendant. The former then indorses his replication under this plea; thus: "*The plaintiff replies non solvit.—And issue*," which he likewise signs as attorney for the plaintiff. These pleadings are then filed by him in the prothonotary's office, the cause goes on to trial in due time, at which this record is alone produced.(pp)

It may sometimes happen that even this short form of pleading is not observed, and a plea may have been put in after the declaration has been filed, which has not been replied to, and of course no joinder in issue entered: but this will not retard the proceedings.

Unless where a special plea is drawn by counsel and filed, the plea

---

(n) Steph. on Plead. 75, 76.
(o) Ibid. 76.
(p) See Eunom. Dial. II. ₴ 29; Steph. on Plead. 99–101.

(pp) See Beale v. Buchanan, 9 Barr, 123.

is entered on the docket, which is for many purposes the record in this State.(q)

A party cannot be compelled to try until the cause is put into legal form by an issue properly framed between all the parties on the record. And if it be not at issue as to any one defendant, whose plea has been overruled by the court irregularly, it is error to proceed to trial against him. He does not thereby necessarily adopt the pleas of the other defendants.(r)

In the District Court and Common Pleas of Philadelphia rules formerly existed on this point, which still obtain in other counties. Thus, in the latter court, it was ordered, "that in all cases in which the defendant pleads 'payment,' the prothonotary shall enter the replication '*non solvit*,' unless otherwise directed by the plaintiff's attorney; and issue shall be thereupon entered and considered as joined." In the former court, "upon a *plea* or *pleas being* entered, the prothonotary shall of course put the cause to issue, and enter the proper replications and other pleadings for that purpose; but the act of the prothonotary herein' shall not prejudice either of the parties. Each party shall have it in his power to enter other pleadings, or demur, as they may deem most eligible; provided, to prevent surprise and secure a fair trial, they give reasonable notice thereof in writing to the adverse party. The time of filing the declaration, pleas, replications, and all other pleadings and papers, shall be distinctly marked in the prothonotary's docket." Such rules, of course, do not apply where there is a plea of confession and avoidance filed, with no replication; in which case it is error to non-suit the plaintiff for not proceeding to trial.(rr)

The non-joinder of issue, discovered after trial, would not, in this State, be sufficient to reverse a judgment, if the parties had gone on to trial upon the presumption that it was joined, where the prothonotary is directed by rule of court to join issue without prejudice to the parties, after a plea is put in, as they may, if they please, join issue in a different manner.(s) Again, if in covenant the defendant pleads covenants performed, and an entry is made on the docket "and issue," it is to be considered as a direction to the prothonotary to make a *formal* entry of the issue, and the omission to do so is no more than a clerical error, which may be amended.(t) It was formerly held in this State, that where issue was not joined, and the entry was not made on the docket, the judgment would be reversed.(u) It was with reluctance, however (it was said), that the court hearkened to the objection of no issue being joined, though they were obliged to adhere to some principle, lest in an attempt to do justice in a particular case they might do a public injury, by taking away all certainty. But in a late case,(v) the Supreme Court determined, that, after going to trial on the merits, they would not reverse the judgment because there had been no plea nor issue, and blanks had been left for dates in the declaration. The court

---

(q) See Black *v.* Dobson, 3 Wh. 189; See *post,* 408.

(r) Britton *v.* Mitchell, 5 W. 69; Roberts *v.* Williams, 5 Wh. 186.

(rr) Maxwell *v.* Beltzhoover, 9 Barr, 139. See p. 421-2, and as to present rules, p. 450.

(s) Jordan *v.* Cooper, 3 S. & R. 577.

(t) Hanna *v.* Burkholder, 7 Id. 228; see also Carl *v.* Com. 9 Id. 67; Shaw *v.* Redmond, 11 Id. 27.

(u) 2 Bin. 33.

(v) Sauerman *v.* Weckerly, 17 S. & R. 116.

observed that the necessity of reconsidering their decisions on this subject had been intimated in late cases, particularly in Carl v. The Commonwealth,(w) where it was said: "To reverse for a mere formal defect of this sort after a trial on the merits is a grievance; and to avoid it, we say once for all, we will lay hold on the most trifling circumstance. Whether we may not even go further, when we are driven to it by the absence of all pretext, it is unnecessary to say." That the alternative thus spoken of presented itself in the case before them, and that, on mature reflection, they were resolved to disregard such exceptions altogether. Notwithstanding this case, however, it has never been supposed that a party can be *compelled* to try until the cause is put into legal form by an issue, properly formed between the parties on the record. Where an objection is made, there is no room for presumption of any kind, and it would be against right and justice to infer an agreement to waive form, in opposition to the protestation of the party against the trial;(x) or in his absence.(xx) There is no occasion, under the act of 1806, for a formal joinder of issue when the cause goes to trial on the statement and counter-statement of the parties.(y)

When the writ is served on one defendant, who appears by attorney specially, and then a general appearance by another attorney is marked, and the party served pleads to issue, upon which a trial on the merits is had, and a verdict and judgment are rendered against both, a substituted attorney being present at the trial, an objection that issue was joined by one defendant only will be disregarded upon error.(z)

The issue or trial lists in the practice of the courts of the Western District, are recognized as monuments of the record and process of trial and judgment in the cases thereon, from which the records in the cases may be made up at any distance of time; and the Supreme Court will consider as amended what might have been amended below by such issue lists.(a)

Issues, which may be divided into general and special, result from *traverses*, and these are of various kinds. The most ordinary kind is that which may be called a common traverse. It consists of a *tender of issue*; that is, of a denial, accompanied by a formal offer of the point denied for decision; and the denial that it makes is by way of *express contradiction in terms of the allegation traversed.*

Besides this, the common kind, there is a class of traverses both frequent and important in practice, which is that of the *general issues*. In most of the usual actions there is an appropriate plea, fixed by ancient usage, as the proper method of traversing the declaration, in cases where the defendant means to deny the whole or the principal part of its allegations. This form of plea, or traverse, is called the *general issue* in that action; and it appears to be so called, because the issue that it tenders, involving the whole declaration, or the principal part of it, is of a more general and comprehensive kind than that usually tendered on a common traverse, and also differs from it somewhat in point of form; for though, like the common traverse, it *tenders issue*, yet in several

(w) 9 S. & R. 67. S. P. Beale v. Buchanan, 9 Barr, 123.

(x) Per ROGERS, J., Bratton v. Mitchell, 5 W. 70; and see Maxwell v. Beltzhoover, 9 Barr, 139.

(xx) Ensley v. Wright, 3 Barr, 501.

(y) Riddle v. Stevens, 2 S. & R. 544; Reed v. Pedan, 8 Id. 266.

(z) Hall v. Law, 2 W. & S. 121.

(a) Wilkins v. Anderson, 1 J. 406.

instances it does not contradict *in terms of the allegation traversed*, but in a more general form of expression.(b) As, in personal actions, where the defendant pleads *nil debet*, that he owes the plaintiff nothing, or *non culpabilis*, that he is not guilty of the facts alleged in the declaration.

- Other pleas are ordinarily distinguished from general issues by the appellation of *special pleas;* and when resort is had to the latter kind the party is said to plead *specially*, in opposition to pleading the *general issue*. So the issues produced upon special pleas, as being usually more specific and particular than those of *not guilty*, *nil debet*, &c., are sometimes described as *special issues*, by way of distinction from the others, which were called *general issues*, the latter term having been afterwards applied, not only to the issues themselves, but to the pleas which tendered and produced them.(c)

Formerly, the general issue was seldom pleaded, except where the defendant meant wholly to deny the charge alleged against him ; for when he meant to avoid or justify the charge, it was usual for him to set forth the particular ground of his defence in a *special plea*, which appears to have been necessary to apprise the court and the plaintiff of the particular nature and circumstances of the defendant's case, and was originally intended to keep the law and the fact distinct. And even now, as it is an invariable rule, that every defence which cannot be specially pleaded, may be given in evidence at the trial upon the general issue ; so the defendant is, in many cases, *e. g.* fraud, in altering an instrument,(cc) obliged to plead the particular circumstances of his defence specially, and cannot give them in evidence on that general plea. But the science of special pleading having been frequently perverted to the purposes of chicane and delay, the court have, in some instances, and the legislature in others, permitted the general issue to be pleaded, and special matter to be given in evidence under it at the trial ; which at once includes the facts, the equity, and the law of the case.(d)

It is a rule in pleading, that a special plea, which amounts to the general issue, is bad.(e) But it would seem from the case of Bauer *v.* Roth,(f) that, in Pennsylvania, it is no cause of demurrer to a special plea that the facts which it alleges may be given in evidence under the general issue. In that State, "the defendant is at liberty to plead as many pleas in the same action as he pleases, just as the plaintiff may insert counts in his declaration ; and I am not aware that the circumstance of two counts in the same declaration, or that of two pleas in the same action, being substantially the same, will render either bad on demurrer."(g) But the case of M'Bride *v.* Duncan(h) seems to have established a different doctrine. In that case, it was said by SERGEANT, J., delivering the opinion of the court : "Though the general rule is that a defendant is not permitted to put in special pleas which amount to the general issue, and the court will strike them off, yet there are exceptions. For in some cases by the English rules, the defendant may take his choice and frame his plea so as to escape being liable to the objec-

---

(b) Steph. on Plead. 172, 173.
(c) Ibid. 185, 186.
(cc) Clark *v.* Partridge, 2 Barr, 13 ; Renshaw *v.* Gans, 7 Barr, 114. As to fraud in other cases, see *ante*, p. 112.

(d) 3 Bl. Com. 306.
(e) Strawn *v.* Park, D. C. 8 Leg. Int. 63.
(f) 4 R. 83.
(g) *Per* KENNEDY, J., ibid. 94.
(h) 1 Wh. 269.

tion. This is effected by the device of giving color, as in these pleas is done, by alleging that the plaintiff was in possession of the goods by a bailment from Linn for safe keeping, and by fraudulent conveyances from him. And where such course preserves to the defendant any serious advantage he might otherwise lose, he would, strictly speaking, be entitled to take his choice, and resort to the circuity of special pleading instead of this plain path of not guilty.

"No important advantage can attend the defendant's special pleading in the case before us, while it leads to delay, and burthens the records with volumes which serve little or no purpose but the exercise of ingenuity and learning. It is said,(i) that it is a good reason for pressing the general issue, instead of special pleading, that 'it makes long records where there is no cause.' In Pennsylvania, this remark applies with peculiar force. The genius of our jurisprudence is not favorable to the practice of special pleading, and the cases are rare in which the time and attention of the court has been occupied by disputes upon it. There is no class of the profession employed peculiarly in its study, nor would our trivial attorney's fee compensate for the labor of it. Our system has been to try causes on the general issue, with notice of the special matter; to that system our laws and practice conform; and justice, it is believed, is as well administered as where another system prevails. It is remarkable that in some of the actions which the courts have invented and fostered as best calculated for the trial of right, such as ejectment and trover, there is no special pleading; and in *assumpsit* it is not required. It is not meant, by these remarks, to intimate that there are not cases on which special pleas are necessary and proper, and in which the law of the case cannot be administered without them; or that an intimate knowledge of that branch of the law is not indispensable to the advocate. But where justice may be fully attained without it; where special pleading involves the cause in prolixity and delay, without conferring any real benefit on him who resorts to it, the court ought, in the exercise of their legal discretion, and for the prevention of the evils that would result, to enforce the rule, that the defendant shall not plead specially what amounts to the general issue."

The rules now in force in reference to notice of special matter, will be hereafter given at large.(ii)

2. *Non-assumpsit.*

In *assumpsit*, the general issue is *non-assumpsit*, under which the defendant may give in evidence everything, even a general release, which shows that the plaintiff has no right to recover, notwithstanding that no notice has been given under this rule of the court.(j) Under the plea of *non-assumpsit* to work and labor done, the defendant, without notice of special matter, may prove the work was done in an unworkmanlike manner.(k) By this plea, says Judge BELL, the defendant puts his antagonist upon proving his whole case, and entitles himself to give in evidence anything which shows that, at the time the action

(i) Hob. 127.

(ii) *Post*, 398, 401.

(j) Henry v. Norwood, 4 Y. 349. See further as to this plea, and what may be given in evidence under it, Wh. Dig. Pleading vi,(f) and Assumpsit v.; Steph.

on Plead. 179, 182; Kennedy v. Ferris, 5 S. & R. 394; and particularly *ante*, p. 115; and *post*, p. 404, and vol. ii. "Assumpsit."

(k) Gaw v. Wolcott, 10 Barr, 43. See Beals v. See, 10 Barr, 57.

was commenced, the plaintiff, *ex æquo et bono*, ought not to recover. This is especially true of everything going to the consideration, which is the gist of the action.(*l*)   In *indebitatus assumpsit*, the defendant may demand of the plaintiff to specify the nature of the evidence he means to offer; and until this is done, the court will not suffer the plaintiff to bring on the trial.(*m*)

3. *Non est factum, nil debet, and covenants performed.*

In *debt* on *specialty*, and in *covenant*, the general issue is *non est factum*, which denies that the deed mentioned in the declaration is the deed of the defendant.   Under this, the defendant at the trial may contend, either that he never executed such deed as alleged, or that its execution was absolutely void in law; as, for example, on the ground that the alleged obligor or covenantor was a married woman, or a lunatic; but if the defendant's case consist of anything but the denial of the execution of the deed, or some fact impeaching the validity of its execution, the plea will be improper.(*n*)   Under a rule of court requiring the plea of *non est factum* to be verified under oath, a plea without such affidavit is a nullity.(*o*)   Where interlineations or erasures appear in a bond, and the defendant would oblige the plaintiff to show, before reading it in evidence, that they were made before execution, he ought to plead *non est factum*.   *Nil debet* admits the execution of the bond.(*p*.) In our practice, the most efficacious and frequent plea to a declaration in debt on a specialty, is that of payment, under which the same advantages, together with many more, may be had as under the general issue of *non est factum;* as under the plea of payment with notice (besides the numerous defences which may be set up, hereafter mentioned),(*q*) it has been decided that fraud in its *execution* may be given in evidence.(*r*)

In debt on matter of record, as a judgment, the general issue is *nul tiel record*, that there is *no such record*.   This plea merely puts in issue the existence of the record, and therefore is only proper where there is either no record at all, or one different from that which the plaintiff has declared on; and any matter in discharge of the action, as payment, or a release, must be specially pleaded.(*s*)   The general rule of law is, that a plea which contradicts a record is bad; therefore *nil debet* cannot be pleaded to a judgment; and as a judgment rendered in another State, if a record there, must, under the constitution of the United States,(*t*) and the act of Congress of 1790,(*u*) have the same force and effect in the courts of this State,(*v*) it follows, that the only plea by which the existence of the record can be put in issue, is not *nil debet*, but *nul tiel record.*(*w*)   Lately, however, an act of assembly has been adopted on this point, which will be considered in the second volume.(*ww*)

(*l*) Id. 44. BELL, J.

(*m*) Kelly *v.* Foster, 2 Bin. 7.

(*n*) Steph. on Plead. 176–7; Bradley *v.* Grosh, 8 Barr, 45; see vol. ii. "Debt."

(*o*) McAdam *v.* Stilwell, 1 H. 90.

(*p*) Barrington *v.* Bank, 14 S. & R. 473; Smith *v.* Weld, 2 Barr, 55; Zeigler *v.* Sprinkle, 7 W. & S. 179; see vol. ii. "Debt."

(*q*) And see also *ante*, p. 110, *post*, vol. ii. "Debt."

(*r*) Baring *v.* Shippen, 2 Bin. 154. See further as to this plea, Sharp *v.* United States, 4 W. 21.

(*s*) 1 Chit. Plead. 481. See Eichelberger *v.* Smyser, 8 W. 181; Hersch *v.* Groff, 2 W. & S. 449.

(*t*) Art. 4, § 1.

(*u*) Ing. Dig. 26.

(*v*) Brudenell *v.* Vaux, 2 D. 302; 7 Cranch, 481; 3 Wheat. 234; 1 Peters, 155.

(*w*) Ibid.

(*ww*) *Post*, vol. ii. "Debt."

Though *non est factum* is, in most cases, the general issue in debt on a specialty; and *nul tiel record*, in debt on a record: yet when the deed or the record is only *inducement* to the action, that is, introductory to some matter of fact on which the action is mainly founded, the general issue is *nil debet*. As in debt for rent by indenture, the indenture is but inducement, and the arrears of rent are the foundation of the action.(*x*)

Where there are issues to the country, and a verdict for the plaintiff thereon, and a plea of *nul tiel record*, a record being the foundation of the action, on which the replication of *habetur tale recordum* is sustained, the course is to enter the judgment for the plaintiff generally; but if the plea be sustained, judgment is entered for the defendant *non obstante veredicto.*(*y*)

There is, in this State, a plea in *covenant*, which is peculiarly of the nature of a plea of the general issue; it is that of *covenants performed with leave, &c.*, that is, with leave to give in evidence everything that amounts to a legal defence. This plea is peculiar to Pennsylvania, and has been sanctioned by very long usage. Under this plea, upon notice to the plaintiff, without form, the defendant may give anything in evidence which he might have pleaded.(*z*) . The plea of covenants performed, admits the execution of the instrument, and supersedes the necessity of other proof, but it does not admit that the adverse party had performed his agreement.(*a*) In covenant on articles of agreement, where the covenants are independent, evidence on the part of the defendant of breaches by the plaintiff, are inadmissible, either by way of bar, offset, or in mitigation of damages.(*b*) In a case of this description,(*c*) it was determined by the Supreme Court, that a release of the cause of action cannot be given in evidence, without having been pleaded.

The plea of covenants performed is not altogether equivalent to the plea of payment, but it admits the foundation of the suit. The usual mode of putting a plaintiff on proof of performance, is by the addition of *absque hoc*, &c., to the plea of covenants performed.(*d*)

Covenants performed, though not strictly the general issue, is yet in the nature of the general issue.(*e*) Under it, without notice of special matter, it is not competent (under a rule of court requiring notice of the special matter) to show a breach of contract between the covenantor and a stranger, which, if performed, would have enured to the benefit of the covenantor.(*f*)

Under the plea of "covenants performed," with notice, &c., to an action of covenant on a ground-rent, evidence of the breach of a collateral agreement at the time of the execution of the deed, but not appearing on its face, that the grantor, within a certain time afterwards, should do certain acts to improve the value of the property, is inadmissible,(*g*) and it seems generally that, under this plea, with notice, &c., the defendant may give evidence of a failure of consideration, which would entitle him to relief in equity.(*h*)

(*x*) 1 Chit. Plead. 477.
(*y*) Rhoads *v.* Com. 3 H. 276. GIBSON, C. J.
(*z*) 4 D. 439. *Ante*, p. 117; *post*, vol. ii. " Covenant."
(*a*) 2 Y. 107.
(*b*) 2 W. C. C. R. 456.

(*c*) Johnson *v.* Kerr, 1 S. & R. 25.
(*d*) Martin *v.* Hammon, 8 Barr, 272.
(*e*) Ellmaker *v.* Franklin Ins. Co. 5 Barr, 189.
(*f*) Ibid.
(*g*) Kates *v.* Dougherty, D. C. C. P. 8 Leg. Int. 238.
(*h*) Ibid.

But a breach of a collateral agreement, which may in fact have formed the real consideration of a deed, can only be taken advantage of by set-off or cross action.(*i*)

In *debt on simple contract* the general issue is *nil debet*, which alleges that the defendant *does not owe, &c.;* this plea is adapted to any kind of defence that tends to deny *an existing debt;*—and, therefore, not only to a defence consisting in a denial of the consideration of the debt, but to the defences of *release, satisfaction,* the *statute of limitations,* and a multitude of others, to which a general issue of a narrower kind, for example, that of *non est factum,* would, in its appropriate actions, be inapplicable. In short, there is hardly any matter of defence to an action of debt, to which the plea of *nil debet* may not be applied; because almost all defences resolve themselves into a denial *of the debt.*(*j*)

4. *Payment, &c.*

On a plea of payment in an action of debt, justice is promoted by the universal rule in the courts of this State, that under this plea, evidence may be given which shows that *ex æquo et bono* the plaintiff ought not to recover; and accordingly a rule of court, to be noticed more fully presently, (*jj*) after reciting an adjudication in that court, "that on a plea of 'payment' to a specialty, the defendant may on the trial, in avoidance of the deed, give in evidence that it was given without any, or a good consideration, or obtained by fraud, or by suggestion of a falsehood, or suppression of the truth, orders that in all such cases the defendant shall give the plaintiff at least notice in writing, before the the trial, of the matter intended to be objected in avoidance of the same, or else to be precluded from using it." The reason of this rule is, that, from the want of a Court of Chancery in this State, the special matter may be regarded as the substance of a bill in equity, and the notice gives ample opportunity to the plaintiff to meet the allegations contained in the special matter ;(*k*) the more, as it has been decided that the spirit of the rule obliges the defendant to specify the *particulars* of the defence as to want of consideration, fraud, falsehood, or a suppression of the truth, if required by the plaintiff ;(*l*) and it has been ruled that there is no distinction, as to notice of the special matter intended to be objected in avoidance of a bond, between a *total* and *partial* want of consideration.(*m*) Where the special matter is the ground of the controversy, or reason or cause of the issue, notice of it cannot be exacted.(*n*)

The general character of the plea of payment with leave, &c., as the means of introducing an equitable defence, has already been fully examined,(*o*) and it remains now to consider but a few practical points.

The plea of payment with leave is a general issue plea within the purview of a rule of court requiring previous notice of a special defence under the general issue.(*p*)

(*i*) Ibid.
(*j*) Steph. on Plead. 177–8. *Post,* vol. ii. "Debt." *Ante,* p. 110.
(*jj*) *Post,* 401–402.
(*k*) See *ante,* p. 111, Griffith *v.* Chew's Executors, 8 S. & R. 25, 26.
(*l*) Greenwalt *v.* Ensminger, 3 Y. 6; Swift *v.* Hawkins, 1 D. 17.

(*m*) Brown *v.* Herron, 4 Y. 561; Hessner *v.* Helm, 8 S. & R. 179.
(*n*) 1 Br. 272; see further of the plea of payment, with leave, &c., and what may be given in evidence under it, *ante,* pp. 56–59; and particularly 4 W. 21.
(*o*) *Ante,* p. 111.
(*p*) Covely *v.* Fox, 1 J. 171; see cases in full, in Wh. Dig. Pleading, vi. (e)

It should be observed, however, that the plea of payment with leave is only admissible where damages are claimed, and is therefore a nullity when pleaded to a *sci. fa.* to revive a judgment in ejectment or in dower, even after a replication of *non solvit.*(q)

The plea of payment with leave, &c., to an action of debt, against the acceptor of a bill, is an admission of the drawing and acceptance, and that the bill is in the hands of the plaintiff as indorsee and holder.(r)

The replication *non solvit* to the plea of payment is merely formal, and the cause is at issue within a rule of court, which dispenses with a formal joinder when a substantial issue has been raised.(s)

Under this plea, the jury cannot find any sum due from the plaintiff to the defendant.(t) To authorize this finding, notice of defalcation must have been given; for an equitable defence under the plea of payment is very different from defalcation under that plea. Under the former plea and notice, therefore, the defendant can only give such matters in evidence as show that the plaintiff has no right to recover. He may defeat the plaintiff's action, but there must stop. But when he pleads payment, with leave to give defalcation in evidence, he may give evidence of matter which entitles him to a recovery against the plaintiff.(u)

5. *Not guilty, non detinet, non cepit, &c.*

In an action on the case, the general issue is *not guilty*, under which the plaintiff is bound to prove the whole charge in his declaration.(v) In this action, the plaintiff's claim is founded on the justice and equity of his case: and therefore, whatever will, in justice and conscience, according to the circumstances of the case, mitigate or bar the claim, may be received in evidence, on the part of the defendant, under the general issue.(w) And it is not only competent for the defendant to show any matter in excuse or justification, but he may also give in evidence any matter in discharge of the action, as payment, a release, or accord and satisfaction.(x) In an action for verbal or written slander, the truth of the words cannot be given in evidence under the general issue, either as a justification or in mitigation of damages, but it must be pleaded specially, or notice must be given.(y) In *trover*, almost every defence may be given in evidence under *not guilty.*(z)

The general issue in *detinue*, is *non detinet*, under which the defendant may give in evidence a gift from the plaintiff; but he cannot give in evidence that the goods were pawned to him for money which is not paid; but he must plead it.(a)

In *trespass*, the general issue is *not guilty*, and amounts to a denial of the trespass alleged; but wherever the act is *prima facie* a trespass, matter of justification or of excuse must be specially pleaded;(b) or sub-

(q) Shaw v. Boyd, 2 J. 215.
(r) Snyder v. Wilt, 3 H. 63.
(s) Beale v. Buchanan, 9 Barr, 123. *Ante*, p. 391.
(t) 10 S. & R. 55. See *post*, 401.
(u) King v. Deal, 9 S. & R. 409, 422; and see ibid. Henderson v. Lewis, 382.
(v) 4 Mod. 424. *Post*, vol. ii. "Trespass on the case."

(w) 14 Johns. 389; 1 Dunl. Pr. 455.
(x) 1 Stark. R. 97; 3 Burr. 1353.
(y) 13 Johns. 475; 1 Johns. 47, 49.
(z) 1 Chit. Pl. 490; and see vol. ii. "Trover."
(a) Co. Litt. 283, a.
(b) 1 Chit. on Plead. 491, 492. *Post*, vol. ii. "Trespass."

stantial notice of the special matter given with the plea of the general issue.(c)

In replevin, the general issue is called the plea of *non cepit;* and applies to the case where the defendant has not, in fact, taken the property, or, where he did not take it, or have it, in the *place* mentioned in the declaration. For, the declaration alleges that the property was taken "in a certain place called," &c.; and the general issue states that it was not taken "in manner and form as alleged;" which involves a denial both of the taking and of the place in which the taking was alleged to have been—the *place* being a material point in the action.(d) *Non cepit,* and *property* (which is also a plea in bar), may be pleaded together.(e) And under the plea of property, the defendant is at liberty to show either a general or special property in himself, either by bill of sale, delivery from the plaintiff, or otherwise, and the rule of court respecting notice does not apply to this plea.(f)

6. *Special matter and set-off.*

Besides the instances already mentioned, in which the defendant, under the rules of court,(g) is allowed to give the special matter of his defence in evidence under the general issue, on giving to the opposite party notice of the particulars of his defence, he is allowed, under a similar notice, to avail himself of debts and demands which he may have against the plaintiff, by way of set-off (which is in the nature of an action), or defalcation,(h) unless he prefer to plead it specially, when notice is not necessary.(i)

It is enacted by the first section of the act of 1705,(j) that "if two or more persons dealing together be indebted to each other upon bonds, bills, bargains, promises, accounts, or the like, and one of them commence an action in any court of this province, if the defendant cannot gainsay the deed, bargain, or assumption upon which he is sued, it shall be lawful for such defendant to plead payment of all or part of the debt or sum demanded, and give any bond, bill, receipt, account, or bargain in evidence; and if it shall appear that the defendant hath fully paid or satisfied the debt or sum demanded, the jury shall find for the defendant, and judgment shall be entered, that the plaintiff shall take nothing by his writ, and shall pay the costs. And if it shall appear that any part of the sum demanded be paid, then so much as is found to be paid shall be defalked, and the plaintiff shall have judgment for the residue only, with costs of suit. But if it appear to the jury that the plaintiff is overpaid, then they shall give in their verdict for the defendant, and withal certify to the court how much they find the plaintiff to be indebted or in arrears to the defendant more than will answer the debt or sum demanded; and the sum or sums so certified shall be recorded with the verdict, and shall be deemed as a debt of record; and if the plaintiff refuse to pay the same, the defendant, for recovery thereof, shall have a *scire facias* against the plaintiff in the

---

(c) See Kerlin v. Heacock, 3 Bin. 215; 1 Br. 197; and see vol. ii. "Trespass."

(d) Steph. on Plead. 183, 184. *Post,* vol. ii. "Replevin."

(e) 11 Johns. 196.

(f) Murray v. Paisley, 1 Y. 197; see vol. ii. "Replevin."

(g) *Supra,* 395, 398; *post,* 401-2.

(h) Gazer v. Lowrie, 8 S. & R. 499.

(i) Commissioners of Berks County v. Ross, 3 Bin. 539; Jacks v. More, 1 Y. 391; see, also, Boyd v. Thompson, 2 Y. 217. See *ante,* p. 115.

(j) 1 Sm. Laws, 49.

said action, and have execution for the same, with the costs of that action."(*k*)

Under the 23d section of the act of 1836,(*l*) relating to insolvent debtors, it is provided that the trustees of such insolvent shall have power to compound with his debtors, in case of controversy, and to settle the same by arbitration or otherwise, and the same right to set-off shall exist where there shall be mutual debts between the insolvent and such debtors, as in other cases. § 23.

Two acts of assembly formerly obtained in this State on this subject. The first was the old act for defalcation, of 1765; the second was the 10th section of the act for the relief of insolvent debtors, passed in 1730; but the first thirteen sections of this latter act having been repealed by the 20th section of the insolvent law of 1814, the defalcation law now principally regulates this subject. It will be observed that the terms defalcation and set-off are used. as convertible in the present discussion, as in all the cases on the subject they are generally used without discrimination, and therefore it may be taken as a general rule that the defendant has the same right and remedy under a plea of set-off as under a plea of defalcation, except where the set-off is what the books denominate an equitable one, when he may defeat the plaintiff's claim, but can *recover* nothing from him.(*m*)

The difference between the British and Pennsylvania defalcation statutes is, that under the former the defendant cannot have a verdict for the balance due him, as he may under the latter; if, therefore, the plaintiff fail to make out his claim, the defendant may still go on and establish his set-off, and take a verdict.(*n*)

The rules of the several courts in reference to the notice of set-off, and of special defences, under the general issue, are as follows:—

SUPREME COURT AND COMMON PLEAS.

XXII (S. C.), XXIX (C. P.). *Sec.* 3. When a defendant has pleaded the general issue with leave to give the special matter in evidence or to justify, he shall, at least ten days before trial, give notice of the special facts or matter on which he intends to rely, otherwise he shall be confined strictly to evidence admissible on a general issue plea.

Sec. 4. When there have been mutual dealings between a plaintiff and defendant, in order to enable the latter on the general issue to defalk his own account against the plaintiff's demand, or any part of it, he shall give notice at least ten days before the trial, and at the same time furnish a copy of the account, to be given in evidence. When a set-off is *pleaded*, it shall be fully and specially set forth in the plea or in a notice, to be given ten days before the trial.

Sec. 5. A defendant shall not be allowed, under the plea of payment to an action of debt, to give evidence that the bond or specialty was obtained by fraud, or a suggestion of falsehood or suppression of the truth, or without sufficient consideration; unless at least twenty (C. P. "ten")

(*k*) See an important statutory provision in relation to set-offs before justices of the peace, 5 Sm. Laws, 165; act of 1810, 7.

(*l*) Pamph. L. 735.

(*m*) *Vide supra,* 398, *post,* 406; Morgan *v.* Bank of North America, 8 S. & R. 73.

(*n*) See Lewis *v.* Culbertson, 11 S. & R. 59.

days before the trial he give notice of the matter upon which he intends to rely.

DISTRICT COURT.

LXIX. It having been the common practice to plead the general issue, with leave to give the special matter in evidence at the trial of the cause or to justify, in order, for the future, that neither party may be taken by surprise, and that a fair opportunity may be offered to encounter the evidence intended to be offered under such pleas, *it is ordered,* that the party who proposes to take the benefit of it shall, at least ten days before the trial, give notice in writing to the other, what are the special facts or matters on which he will rely, and which he intends to urge in support of his action, or by way of defence or qualification; otherwise, he shall give no other evidence than what is by law admissible on a general issue plea, or what has been received on such plea.

LXXI. On a plea of payment to a bond or specialty, the defendant, at least thirty days before the trial, shall give the plaintiff notice in writing of the matter intended to be objected in evidence of the same, or else he shall be precluded therefrom.

LXXII. When the defendant pleads a set-off, unless the matter be fully and specially set forth in the plea, or where he intends, on the plea of payment, to defalk his own account against the plaintiff's demand, or any part of it, he shall give a full and particular notice in writing of such intended set-off at least ten days before the first day of the period for which the cause is set down for trial, or he shall not be allowed to give in evidence, under such plea, any set-off, nor under such notice, any matter of set-off not therein particularly set forth.

The tendency of the Supreme Court is to encourage this method of pleading, GIBSON, C. J., in one case going so far as to say that policy requires that special pleading be abolished, and the general issue, with notice of special matter, substituted as less cumbrous and better suited to the habits of the bar.(o)

A defendant who has neglected to give notice under the rule of court, of a set-off, or of special matter which he intends to prove, cannot, at the trial, introduce a plea of set-off, and produce evidence to sustain it.(p)

In the Supreme Court, when the defendant pleads a set-off or defalcation *generally,* the plaintiff may *insist* on a particular statement of the items meant to be defalked,(q) or on a specification of the defendant's demand,(r) and if he refuse to render this, evidence of matters of set-off cannot be given;(s) but if the plaintiff take issue on the plea of set-off or defalcation entered in short, it is not necessary for the defendant to give notice of the matter intended to be set off.(t)

The notice of set-off must describe the demand intended to be set off with reasonable certainty, and on the trial the defendant cannot give evidence in contradiction of it.(u)

(o) Sherk v. Endress, 3 W. & S. 257.
(p) Thom v. Hough, 9 Leg. Int. 46; Wilson v. Irwin, 14 S. & R. 176; McCay v. Burr, 6 Barr, 153.
(q) Commissioners v. Ross, 3 Bin. 539.
(r) Rogers v. Old, 5 S. & R. 404.
(s) Ibid.
(t) Commissioners v Ross, 3 Bin. 539.
(u) Gogel v. Jacoby, 5 S. & R. 117; see 1 Y. 391; Lewis v. Culbertson, 11 S. & R. 48.

To make the admission of evidence error, on the ground that no prior special notice of it was given, it must appear that the objection was specifically taken on trial.(x)

Where a plaintiff used on trial a notice of withdrawal and change of pleas, to show such fact alone, it was held, he was not thereby estopped from setting-off a want of the proper preliminary notice to special matter, which was also contained in said first-mentioned notice.(y)

A notice of special matter, under a plea of payment, &c., to assumpsit in a feigned issue, to try the right to the proceeds of land sold under a mortgage, was given as follows: "That the mortgage was in due form of law assigned to the defendant, for a full and fair consideration by P. K. (the mortgagee)." Under this, the evidence offered, was that a witness "had lent to P. K., on the 1st of February, 1846, as the agent of L., the sum of $2600, for which he took a note signed by P. K., and by his brother, A. K. (the defendant), as security, at K. (in the State of New York), and that the note had been paid to him by A. K." It was held that the evidence was inadmissible.(z)

Notice of special matter must be given notwithstanding an agreement by an attorney employed by the plaintiff for the purpose of attending at the taking of a deposition which contains the special matter, that it may be read in evidence;(b) notwithstanding an affidavit of defence has been filed, setting forth in substance the matter offered in evidence;(c) and notwithstanding that the evidence offered to establish such matter has been given on a former trial of the cause before arbitrators.(d) Neither a deposit of a formal notice of special matter in the office of the prothonotary, nor an informal suggestion in the pleadings by reference to the affidavit of defence filed, is a compliance with the rule of court.(e)

When special matter is offered by the defendant by way of set-off, or in diminution of the plaintiff's demand, it should set forth with reasonable certainty the grounds of the plaintiff's liability. It has been held that the notice of set-off need not be so certain, and by no means so formal as a declaration, but it must describe the demand with reasonable certainty, so as not to take the plaintiff by surprise.(f) It would be dangerous to allow a deviation from this rule, and to permit a defendant, upon the statement of remote and conjectural possibilities, to enter into the pursuit of a defence, rather than the proof of one.(g)

If the set-off is to be proved by the acknowledgments of the plaintiff, it must be so expressed in the notice;(h) and on calling upon the plaintiff to produce books and papers, at the trial, the defendant cannot go into evidence of their contents to prove a set-off, without special notice beforehand of the set-off.(i)

In pleading payment under the defalcation law, it is important to the defendant, if he expects to recover a balance, to note the difference be-

(x) Rearich v. Swinehart, 1 J. 233.
(y) Coverly v. Fox, 1 J. 171.
(z) Moatz v. Knox, 1 J. 268. See this case again on other points, 3 H. 79.
(b) McClurg v. Willard, 5 W. 275.
(c) Sullivan v. Johns, 5 Wh. 366; S. P. Simmons v. West, 2 M. 196; Reintzheimer v. Bush, 2 Barr, 88.
(d) Beyer v. Fenstermacher, 2 Wh. 95; Reintzheimer v. Bush, 2 Barr, 88.
(e) Erwin v. Leibert, 5 W. & S. 103.

(f) Gogel v. Jacoby, 5 S. & R. 120; Lewis v. Culbertson, 11 S. & R. 50. See McDowell v. Meredith, 4 Wh. 311; Hale v. Fenn, 3 W. & S. 364; Gilpin v. Howell, 5 Barr, 54; Appleton v. Donaldson, 3 Barr, 381; Moatz v. Knox, 1 J. 278.
(g) Irwin v. Potter, 3 W. 271.
(h) 4 Y. 102.
(i) Latimer v. Hodgdon, 5 S. & R. 514.

fore stated,(j) between this plea with notice of defalcation, and that of payment with leave to give an equitable defence in evidence, and that under the latter form of allegation he cannot *recover* anything against the plaintiff.

In respect to set-off, the decisions may be classified as follows :—(k)
(1.) *As to Claim.*
The assignee of a bond, or the indorsee of a bill or note, may, doubtless, set it off against a demand by the obligor or drawer, without having had any transaction with him ; for such assignee or indorsee stands in the place of the assignor or indorser, as the transferee of a right growing out of a personal responsibility.(l)

But the liability of the assignee of land subject to ground-rent, depends on privity of estate alone ; and therefore in an action by the assignee of a bond, the defendant cannot set off arrears of ground-rent due by the plaintiff, as assignee of a ground tenant.(m)

A judgment having been recovered by A against B, B took a writ of error to the Supreme Court, where the judgment was affirmed, when A assigned the judgment to T ; but pending the writ of error, B purchased a judgment against A from a third person ; it was held that the latter judgment could not be set off against the former, in the hands of T, who was an innocent purchaser, without notice.(n)

In an action of covenant upon a lease, the breach of a subsequent agreement with the tenant to continue the lease may be set off.(o)

Where it is agreed in a contract for the performance of work, that a note, previously given by one party to the other, shall go in part payment therefor, the defendant in an action on the note may set off the substantial completion of the work.(p)

A claim acquired after suit, cannot be set off therein.(q)

In replevin for rent, set-off is not allowable, except under the act of assembly, which applies only to cases under one hundred dollars.(r)

Set-off is, in substance, a cross action ; and a cross demand, also, must have been complete when the action was instituted.(s)

There can be no set-off when plaintiff has no cause of action.(t)

The plaintiff cannot set off a fresh claim, against a set-off introduced by the defendant, set-off against set-off being inadmissible.(u)

In a very recent case, where the action was of debt on one of two promissory notes given for the price of a canal-boat, evidence was held admissible under the general issue with notice, as an equitable defence, on the part of defendant, to show that the plaintiff, who sold the boat, at the time of the sale fraudulently represented the boat to be a good boat and worth the money ; and, to prove that the boat was leaky, was rotten in its timbers and frame ; that no diligence on the part of the

(j) *Supra*, p. 398, *post*, p. 407.
(k) See more fully, Wh. Dig. "Set-off."
(l) Irish *v.* Johnston, 1 J. 487. Gibson, C. J.
(m) Id. 483.
(n) Mervine *v.* Greble, 2 Par. 271.
(o) Kelly *v.* Bogue, D. C. C. P. 7 Leg. Int. 166.
(p) Truesdale *v.* Watts, 2 J. 73.

(q) Stewart *v.* U. S. Ins. Co. 9 W. 126. See Huling *v.* Hugg, 1 W. & S. 418.
(r) Ashton *v.* Clapier, Bright. R. 481.
(s) Pennell *v.* Grubb, 1 H. 554.
(t) Claridge *v.* Klett, 3 H. 255. But see Shoup *v.* Shoup. Id. 351.
(u) Gable *v.* Parry, 1 H. 181 ; see Ulrich *v.* Berger, 4 W. & S. 19.

defendants could have enabled them to discover the condition of the boat, and that it was known to the plaintiff.(*uu*) "The court below," said BELL, J., " rejected the proffered proof in this case because it did not show *a warranty*. But we have seen this is unnecessary. If it tended to establish an injurious fraud perpetrated by the plaintiff on his vendee, in a point where the latter was not in a position to judge for himself, it is enough for the purposes of a defence, which may wholly or partially defeat the action, as the boat sold may turn out to be wholly worthless, or only of less value than the price induced by the misrepresentation."(*v*)

(2.) *As to Parties.*

On a *sci. fa.* sur mechanic's lien against owner and contractor, the defendants may offer as set-off, a debt due by the plaintiff to the contractor.(*vv*)

In an action brought to recover tolls which had accrued after the appointment of a sequestrator, to a turnpike company, the defendant cannot defalk a debt due to him by the company, arising out of a transaction anterior to the appointment of a sequestrator, as the subsequently accruing tolls are dedicated by law to the payment of all debts *pro rata*.(*w*)

In an action for the income of a fund which has been set apart by the executor, under the provisions of a will, the executor may set off rent due to himself and another, on a lease made by them, as executors of another estate, to the plaintiff, the coexecutor assenting to such set-off.(*x*)

There can be no set-off by the defendant in a suit by the United States in the Circuit Court, which, under the Pennsylvania practice, can, in its effect, oblige the United States, or any of its officers, to pay over money to him.(*y*)

A cross demand against the defendant in an attachment may be set off by the garnishee, as it may by a defendant in any other suit, but subject to the same rules and restrictions.(*z*)

Thus, a garnishee may not set off a cross demand, without proving that it was acquired before the attachment was laid.(*a*)

A debt due by an intestate cannot be set off to an action on a note given by the defendant to the administrator for goods bought at the sale of the decedent's effects.(*b*)

Several defendants may set off a debt due by the plaintiff to a company or partnership of which they were members, the other members consenting thereto.(*c*)

On an action of replevin brought by one partner against another, the defendant was held not entitled to set off a debt paid by him on the partnership account, there being no allegation of a settlement between the partners, &c., or a balance due the defendant.(*d*)

Where the plaintiff claimed to recover $800, being the amount advanced by him on a note of the defendants, for $1864, which the defendant had deposited with O, a note-broker, " for sale or an advance."

(*uu*) Price *v.* Lewis, 5 H. 51; *ante*, pp. 115, 395.
(*v*) Price *v.* Lewis, 5 H. 54.
(*vv*) Gable *v.* Parry, 1 H. 181.
(*w*) Beeler *v.* The Turnpike Co. 2 H. 162.
(*x*) Solliday *v.* Bissey, 2 J. 347.

(*y*) Reeside *v.* Walker, 11 How. U. S. 272.
(*z*) Pennell *v.* Grubb, 1 H. 554.
(*a*) Ibid.
(*b*) Steel *v.* Steel, 2 J. 64.
(*c*) Tustin *v.* Cameron, 5 Wh. 379.
(*d*) Roberts *v.* Fitler, 1 H. 265.

It was ruled that the defendant could not set off a debt claimed to be due by the plaintiff to O.(e)

Defalcations between opposite claimants are permissive, not compulsory. The right to defalk is a privilege given by our act of 1705, and afterwards by the English statutes of set-off, not an obligation. The only exception is where, by legislative enactment, defendant is required to set off his claim, as in sections seven and twenty of the act of March 20, 1810, relative to justices of the peace.(f)

(3.) *Practice.*

An omission of the notice to give evidence of a set-off, is, under our practice, a retraction of the notice ; but where it is followed up with evidence at the trial, a verdict upon it concludes the defendant.(g)

When the short pleas of payment and set-off with leave, are pleaded, and defendant has gone to trial without demanding a replication to his plea of set-off, the defence to the set-off is left at large, and the plaintiff may avail himself of the statute of limitations, or any other defence.(h)

Under the Pennsylvania statute a defendant may plead payment, and give in evidence as a set-off, any bond, note, bill, or book account, in evidence. The special plea of set-off is not warranted here by anything but long practice.(i)

A set-off is in the nature of a cross action, and may be withdrawn in analogy to suffering a nonsuit when the evidence is found too weak to support it ; but, like a nonsuit, the withdrawal ought to be explicit.(j)

A defendant must be able to show that the debt claimed to be set off by him was his at the time suit was begun.(k)

The defendant is required, by the act of 1810, to set off his claim before a justice, or lose it, only when it does not exceed $100. Nor need he split up his claim and set off a portion of it. He may sue for his claim after a judgment against him by the justice, although he may have offered it to him as a set-off and it has been rejected.(l)

In an action of debt, on a bond, it was held that an assignment by the plaintiff to a third party, between suit brought and trial, did not prevent the defendant from obtaining judgment for a set-off in his favor, the pleas being payment and set-off.(m)

A defendant who has omitted to give notice under a short plea of set-off, cannot amend on the trial, by filing a special plea of set-off, setting forth the matter with particularity.(n)

By the act of April 11, 1848, § 12 : "In all cases where, by the verdict of a jury, any debt or damages shall have been found or certified in favor of the defendant, he shall be entitled to judgment and execution in like manner as if the verdict were in favor of the plaintiff; and the defendant need not resort to *scire facias,* as required by the act of 1705, for defalcation."

By the 18th section of the act of April 9, 1849, the above section is declared not to extend to suits pending at its passage.

(e) Carman v. Garrison, 1 H. 158.
(f) Himes v. Barnitz, 8 W. 43.
(g) Good v. Good, 9 W. 567.
(h) Coulter v. Repplier, 3 H. 208.
(i) Id. 211, GIBSON, C. J.
(j) Muirhead v. Fitzpatrick, 3 W. & S. 508.

(k) Huling v. Hugg, 1 W. & S. 418.
See Stewart v. U. S. Ins. Co. 9 W. 126.
(l) Simpson v. Lapsley, 3 Barr, 459.
See Wh. Dig. " Justice,"iv. (e)
(m) Kline v. Gundrum, 1 J. 243.
(n) Thom v. Hough, D. C. Phil. 9 Leg. Int. 46. See *ante,* 402, n. (p)

7. *Double pleas.*

At common law, the defendant could only have pleaded one plea to the whole declaration ; though where the declaration consisted of distinct parts, he might have pleaded a distinct answer to each of those parts ;(*p*) but by the Stat. 4 Ann. c. 16, §§ 4, 5,(*q*) " It shall be lawful for any defendant or tenant, in any action or suit, or for any plaintiff in replevin, in any court of record, with leave of the court, to plead as many several matters as he shall think necessary for his defence ; *Provided*, nevertheless, if any such matter shall, upon a demurrer joined, be judged insufficient, costs shall be given at the discretion of the court; or if a verdict shall be found upon any issue in the said cause for the plaintiff or demandant, costs shall also be given in the like manner, unless the judge, who tried the said issue, shall certify that the said defendant, or tenant, or plaintiff in replevin, had a probable cause to plead such matter which upon the said issue shall be found against him." Since this act, the defendant may plead whatever pleas he thinks proper, and in practice, without applying to the court for leave ; subject, however, if his pleas be inconsistent, and such as ought not to be joined, to be compelled, on motion of the plaintiff, to elect the plea by which he will abide.(*r*)

This statute giving the courts a *discretionary* power to permit several matters to be pleaded, they have determined, that in a *qui tam* action the defendant cannot plead double.(*s*) So, in an action on a penal statute,(*t*) and in an information in nature of a *quo warranto.*(*u*) So, at one time, the defendant was often refused leave to plead several pleas, where the proposed subject of plea appeared to be *inconsistent ;* but in modern practice, such pleas, notwithstanding the apparent repugnancy between them, are permitted. Therefore, with *non assumpsit*, he may plead the statute of limitations, or a discharge by bankruptcy, or infancy, or with *non est factum*, payment, or a discharge by bankruptcy ;(*v*) and in trespass, " not guilty, with leave to justify."(*w*) So other defences may be combined, and the only pleas, perhaps, which are now disallowed, on the mere ground of inconsistency, are those of the general issue, and a *tender ;*(*x*) otherwise, if a verdict were found for the defendant on the general issue, this incongruity would appear upon the record : that nothing was due, when the defendant himself admitted that there was something due from him.(*y*)

Pleas going to the whole count or declaration, but which answer only a part of it, are bad on general demurrer, as nullities, and this whether the cause of action be set out in one or more counts.(*z*)

A special plea setting out a defence only to part of the declaration is bad on demurrer.(*a*)

Multifarious matters, if they go to make up only one point, will not make a plea double.(*b*)

(*p*) Steph. on Plead. 289.
(*q*) 3 Bin. 625.
(*r*) 1 Dunl. Pr. 470.
(*s*) 2 Wils. 21. See Wh. Dig. "Pleading."
(*t*) Barnes, 15, 365.
(*u*) Sayer's Rep. 96.
(*v*) Com. Dig. Plead. E. 2 ; 5 Taunt. 340.

(*w*) Kerlin *v.* Heacock, 3 Bin. 215.
(*x*) Steph. on Plead. 293.
(*y*) 4 T. R. 194.
(*z*) Naglee *v.* Ingersoll, 7 Burr. 205.
(*a*) Garrison *v.* Moore, D. C. C. P. 9 Leg. Int. 2.
(*b*) Brown *v.* Young, D. C. C. P. 7 Leg. Int. 114.

A party cannot plead and demur to the same count; if he does so, and the issues in fact are tried, the demurrers will be dismissed.(c)

It is also to be observed, that the power of pleading several matters extends to pleas in *bar* only, and not to those of the *dilatory* class; with respect to which the leave of the court will not be granted.(d)

8. *Former action and attachment.*

To sustain a plea of the pendency of a prior action, it is necessary not only that the cause of action, but the parties also be the same. Thus, when an administrator is compelled to bring a new action in consequence of having paid a wrong party, he will be allowed to proceed on the second suit without paying the costs of the former.(e)

It is not to be disputed that an attachment laid in the hands of a defendant must be pleaded specially, either in abatement or in bar, according to the nature of the attachment or the progress made in the proceedings under it at the time of plea pleaded. The attachment execution given by our statute should, it seems, be pleaded by a garnishee in bar, for the foundation of it is a judgment which concludes those who are parties to it.(f)

9. *Short pleadings.*

It may be proper here to notice a very common but informal practice prevailing in this State, which consists *in the entry of short pleadings*, as they are called, or " memoranda of the substance of the defence,"(g) and which is allowed for the sake of brevity and dispatch. Thus, we plead *Non assumpsit—Nil debet—Non cul.*—Usury—The Statute of Limitations, &c.—No Award—Set-off—and other pleas of a similar form; and sometimes several pleas are thus pleaded together in short entries. And when a special defence is intended to be set up under a plea of the general issue, after notice according to the rules of court, the plea is accompanied with a declaration of such intention in in the following manner: " Defendant pleads *non assumpsit,* with leave to give the special matter in evidence," or, " Defendant pleads *non cul.,* with leave to justify," and so in other cases. It is a course of pleading in Pennsylvania too long established now to be overturned, to plead in short. As this mode does not conduce always to certainty, but often causes confusion, and sometimes injustice,(h) short pleas ought not to be received but by consent. If either party request his adversary to draw up his plea at large, and it is refused, it will be good cause of demurrer, assigning the same specially for cause,(i) or, on " motion the court would enter a rule to draw up the pleadings at large."(j) But, in order to support the judgments of the inferior courts, which have been given after a trial of the merits, the Supreme Court will consider the short entries of pleadings in the same light as if they were formally drawn up, provided there is *enough* to show the

---

(c) M'Fate *v.* Shallcross, D. C. C.P.7. Leg. Int. 114.

(d) Steph. on Plead. 295.

(e) Cornelias *v.* Vanarsdallon, 3 Barr, 435. See Wh. Dig. " Pleading," vi. (g) " Actions," v.

(f) Maynard *v.* Neckervis, 9 Barr, 82.

(g) See Sauerman *v.* Weckerley, 17 S.

& R. 117; Sherk *v.* Endress, 3 W. & S. 257, and *ante*, p. 391.

(h) Weidell *v.* Roseberry, 13 S. & R. 180.

(i) 6 Bin. 15.

(j) Per DUNCAN, Jordan *v.* Cooper, 3 S. & R. 583; Weidell *v.* Roseberry, 13 S. & R. 180.

meaning of the parties.(*k*) In pleading such pleas, therefore, the defendant should guard against a brevity, which may obscure their meaning or render them insensible; thus, a plea of "The Lottery Act," without *more*, is an insensible plea, and need not be replied to.(*l*)

10. *Striking off, adding, or altering pleas.*

To induce the court to strike off a plea, it must be clearly frivolous —*e. g.*—when unsuited to the form of action,(*m*) or must be irregular in time or place.(*mm*)

When one of several pleas is thus insensible and void, or when sufficient and proper, the defendant is persuaded that he cannot support it, he may, either with leave of the court or consent of the adverse party, alter or strike it out. But without this leave or this consent, he cannot withdraw any of his pleas, where it may be supposed that he gains any advantage thereby:(*n*) therefore, where issue was joined on the pleas of *non assumpsit* and payment, and the jury was about to be impannelled, the court refused the defendant leave to strike out the former plea, the plaintiff having been put to expense in obtaining proof

---

(*k*) Ibid. See Sauermann *v.* Weckerly, 17 S. & R. 116.

(*l*) Reed *v.* Pedan, 8 S. & R. 263.

(*m*) Marseilles *v.* Kenton.—D. C. Saturday, Sept. 16, 1848.—Rule to show cause why defendant's pleas of the statute of limitation, filed June 24, 1848, should be stricken off. *Per curiam.* There may be cases in our practice in which the court would strike off pleas as impertinent and frivolous. It would have to be, however, in a very clear case, such as a plea not adapted to the form of action, as *non assumpsit* to an action of trespass, and where the plaintiff might regard it as a nullity, and sign judgment for want of a plea. Perhaps, moreover, there might be other cases: we do not mean to lay down any general rule. Here, to a count alleging that the plaintiff was a merchant, and the defendant his factor, and a promise to account, the defendant has pleaded the statute, *non assumpsit infra sex annos* and *actio non accrevit infra*, and these pleas the defendant asks leave to strike off. The exception in the statute of "such accounts as concern the trade of merchandise between merchant and merchant, their factors and servants," has rarely been presented to the consideration of the courts either of this country or England. The cases of what are termed *mutual accounts*, in which some of the items, being within six years, are held to save the bar of the statute, seem referable to the head of implied acknowledgment rather than to the saving clause of *merchants' accounts.* In many of the cases these two claims are evidently confounded,

and it would require much consideration and examination to determine whether these pleas to this count are insufficient pleas. It is, therefore, clearly a case in which the court ought not summarily to interfere on motion. Rule dismissed. See also *ante*, 387.

Commonwealth *v.* Smiley. — D. C. Saturday, Oct. 21, 1848.—Why judgment should not be entered for want of a proper plea. *Per curiam.* This is an action of debt upon the official bond of a constable, in which the narr. sets out the breaches. Upon a rule to plead, the defendant has pleaded *nil debit.*

When the defendant pleads a plea not adapted to the action, as *nil debit* in *assumpsit* or *non assumpsit* in debt, the plaintiff may either move the court to strike it off or treat it as a nullity. If he elects the latter course, if the defendant is under a rule, he may enter judgment for want of a plea; if not, he must put him under a rule. The more usual practice with us has been to move the court to strike off the plea.

Where, however, the plea is adapted to the nature of the action, though it may be bad on demurrer, or informal and irregular, it is not such a nullity as will warrant the plaintiff in signing judgment. Thus, it has been held in the K. B., in England, that *nil debet* to an action of debt on a judgment, though a bad plea, is not to be treated as a nullity. Anon. 2 Chitty's Rep. 239. Rule dismissed.

(*mm*) Ralph *v.* Brown, 3 W. & S. 398.

(*n*) Jackson *v.* Winchester, 2 Y. 529; S. C. 4 D. 205.

of the assumption.(o) If this were not the practice, such pleas "would be put in by defendants as stratagems to take the chance of the plaintiff's not being able to procure witnesses to prove the issue, and, after putting them to the expense and trouble of bringing their witnesses, would all at once assume the appearance of candour in relinquishing a defence which could not in reality be supported."(p) It has also been ruled that the defendant cannot withdraw a plea at the time of trial, to give him the benefit of conclusion to the jury.(q) But where the plaintiff had not been put to any inconvenience in procuring testimony to prove the *assumpsit*, the District Court allowed the plea to be struck out after the jury was sworn.(r) So, likewise, where the defendant tenders full compensation to the plaintiff for the trouble and expense which he has incurred by reason of any plea upon which issue has been taken, the court will permit him to retract the plea.(s) When the witnesses for the defendant, on the closing of the evidence, have been dismissed, it is too late for the defendant to add a plea requiring new evidence on the part of the plaintiff to repel it.(ss)

"If a defendant, in the progress of the cause, finds that one of his pleas will not serve him, and that, in all probability, he will be subjected to an increase of costs by insisting on it, he may apply to the court at a previous term to strike out the plea, and the plaintiff, on such leave being granted, is saved the trouble and expense of adducing proof in support of that issue."(t) He may also, on a rule to show cause, obtain leave to *add* a plea ;(u) and on such a rule, a plea of the act of limitations was allowed to be added in trespass for mesne profits.(v)

In many of the cases upon the subject of withdrawing and adding pleas, it appears that the 6th section of the act of 1806 has been relied on by practitioners, as countenancing a system of amendment it never intended. This section provides, that when any informality in entering a plea will, in the opinion of the court, affect the merits of the cause, the defendant may alter his plea or defence on or before the trial of the cause ; and if, by such alteration, the plaintiff is taken by surprise, the trial shall be postponed to the next court ; and the construction of it is, that when the plea is not sufficient to cover the *merits of the case*, an amendment may be made before or even *during* the trial;(w) but the court are to judge whether the amendment be necessary,(x) and it is not in every instance that it will or must be granted, and many cases may occur not within the scope and intent of the act. Thus, "where a plea *in abatement* is kept back until after the swearing of the jury, it was not the intention of the act that the defendant should be permitted to alter his plea, and thus defeat the plaintiff's action. So, where a plea is kept back, which ought to have been put in *since the last continuance*."(y) So, where the defendant offers a plea of set-

---

(o) Ibid. *sed vide* 4 D. 205, 206, n.

(p) Waggoner v. Line, 3 Bin. 590.

(q) Wikoff v. Perot, 1 Y. 38.

(r) 2 Br. 13.

(s) Jackson v. Winchester, 2 Y. 529.

(ss) Ridgely v. Dobson, 3 W. & S. 118. See Fox v. Foster, 4 Barr, 122.

(t) Per YEATES, J., Waggoner v. Line, 3 Bin. 591.

(u) 4 D. 205, 206, n. See Vol. ii. on "Amendments."

(v) Peaceable v. Whitehill, 2 Y. 279.

(w) This law also embraces declarations. See 4 Sm. Laws, 329. 'The object of it was to prevent nonsuits of plaintiffs, where the declarations were informal, and to attain the justice of every case on a full trial." *Per* YEATES, J., Waggoner v. Line, 3 Bin. 591.

(x) Waggoner v. Line, 3 Bin. 590.

(y) Clymer v. Thomas, 7 S. & R. 181.

off, after the plaintiff has closed his evidence,(z) the defendant having a remedy by an action on his claim of set-off. And where the defendant offers to plead *specially* a matter of law necessary to his defence, after having already pleaded, it is *not* error to refuse it, when it is put in at such a time as shows that the object is delay.(a) So likewise this act does not extend to actions upon penal statutes, but only to actions for money owing, or due, or for damages by trespass or otherwise.(b)

By the 6th section of the act of 1836, relative to the powers and organization of the District Court,(c) it is provided, that the said court sitting in bank, shall have power from time to time, by general rules and orders, to make such alterations and regulations in respect to the time and manner of pleading, and the form and effect of pleadings, and the verification and amendment thereof, and to variances occurring between the cause or causes of action alleged, and the evidence offered in support thereof, in suits brought in the said court; and such rules for carrying the same into effect, either by way of staying proceeding in the action, or by the payment of costs or otherwise, as shall be conducive to fairness, economy, and dispatch in the trial of such actions: *Provided*, That nothing herein contained shall be so construed as in any way to impair the 5th section of the act of 1806, to regulate proceedings in courts of justice. The important object of this section appears to have been, to empower the court to remedy the injustice often produced by an application of the common law doctrine of *variance*.

When defendant has pleaded in bar, it is in the discretion of the court to refuse leave to withdraw his plea and demur, and this is consequently not a subject of inquiry on a writ of error.(d)

The defendant is entitled to add a plea after issue joined, though he might prove the same fact under a general plea on the record; as where, to a *sci. fa.* on a mechanic's lien, the defendant pleaded payment, and the terre-tenant no lien, it was held to be error to refuse, after issue joined thereon, to permit the terre-tenant to plead, that since the issuing of the writ the land had been sold under judicial process.(e)

Where a plaintiff in his replication had admitted rent to be due, but when the case was called for trial, asked to put in a plea of *no rent in arrear*, it was *held*, that the judge was right in refusing permission so to do, as the amendment would have changed the whole nature of the proceeding, and forced the defendant to a continuance.(f)

On an appeal from an award of arbitrators, the defendants may be permitted to withdraw their general plea of not guilty, and may sever in their pleas, and take separate defences for the portions of the premises they respectively claim.(g)

If the parties to an action enter into an agreement that the cause shall be tried upon a certain plea, it is not in the power of the court afterwards to admit any other plea, without the consent of both parties.(h)

(z) Glazer v. Lowrie. 8 S. & R. 499.

(a) Young v. The Commonwealth, 6 Bin. 88.

(b) Buckwalter v. United States, 11 S. & R. 197. *Per* Duncan, J.

(c) Pamph. L. 76.

(d) Payran v. McWilliams, 9 W. & S. 155.

(e) Johns v. Bolton, 2 J. 339. See generally on this head, Vol. ii., "Amendment."

(f) Crowell v. Vandyke, D. Ct. C. C. P. Dec. 1848.

(g) Keeler v. Vantuyle, 6 Barr, 250.

(h) Fursht v. Overdeer, 3 W. & S. 470.

CHAPTER XIX.

OF DISCONTINUANCE AND NOLLE PROSEQUI.

WHERE the defendant pleads the general issue, or any other plea which properly concludes to the country, there are no further pleadings between the parties, and there is an issue joined in the cause, on which they may proceed to trial. But if the plea present some new fact, it is incumbent on the plaintiff to reply; or, if he cannot support his action, he may discontinue, or enter a *nolle prosequi*, and in the two ensuing sections, these subjects are considered at large. Or in an action against an executor or administrator, where the original cause of action is not denied by the plea, he may take judgment of assets *in futuro*. So, in an action against an insolvent debtor, whose future effects remain liable to the payment of his debts, the plaintiff may take judgment for his demand, to be levied of those effects.(a)

SECTION I.

OF DISCONTINUANCE.

When the plaintiff finds that he has misconceived his action, sued a wrong party, or that for some defect in the pleadings, or other reason, he will not be able to maintain it, he may obtain a rule for leave to discontinue, which, however, is effectual only on payment of costs,(b) which should be paid forthwith; for until paid the action is not discontinued.(c) The plaintiff, however, is not liable to an attachment for the non-payment of them.(d) An executor or administrator may discontinue without paying the *costs* of the opposite party; though not without paying the *fees* of the officers of the court for services rendered.(e) If a cause be discontinued, and afterwards the defendant appears and takes defence, he cannot, at the trial, take advantage of the discontinuance.(f)

Regularly, there can be no discontinuance without leave of the court, and this rule holds with peculiar force in replevins; there both parties are *actors*, and yet the avowant cannot discontinue;(g) and where the goods are delivered to the plaintiff in replevin, he will not be permitted to discontinue.(h) So, where the defendant claims property, and the

(a) Burns's K. B. 339.
(b) See Stat. 8 El. ch. 2, § 2, Rob. Dig. 126; Comb. 299.
(c) 3 M. & S. 153.
(d) 7 T. R. 6; 10 Johns. 367.

(e) Musser v. Good, 11 S. & R. 247.
(f) 2 W. C. C. R. 180.
(g) Broom v. Fox, 2 Y. 531; 1 Str. 112.
(h) Ibid.

goods remain in his hands, there may be cases in which the court would refuse such leave.(*i*) So, neither, on the same principle, can the plaintiff discontinue, after a set-off has been pleaded; for, under the defalcation act of this State, the defendant, where his demand overreaches that of the plaintiff, becomes an actor, and is entitled to a verdict for the balance;(*j*) besides, if the action were on a specialty, and the set-off by simple contract, the six years might expire while the matter was *sub lite;* if then the plaintiff could discontinue, he might renew his action, and to the plea of set-off reply the statute of limitations.(*k*) A plaintiff cannot discontinue his cause after a *bona fide* assignment of the debt, for a valuable consideration, to another person. In such case, it ought to be mentioned on the docket, for whose use the suit is brought.(*l*) After a general verdict, or a writ of inquiry executed and returned,(*m*) the plaintiff will not be allowed to discontinue (unless with the defendant's consent), for if he were permitted this privilege, it would be granting him as many new trials as he pleased.(*n*) The court may probably give this leave, as matter of especial favor, after a special verdict, because it is not complete and final,(*o*) but they will not do so in a hard action,(*p*) or to give the plaintiff an opportunity to adduce fresh proof in contradiction to the verdict.(*q*) The court have allowed the plaintiff to discontinue, on payment of costs, after a demurrer argued and allowed, where there was a mistake in the plaintiff's pleading; but they now usually give the party leave to amend, upon payment of costs.(*r*)

A discontinuance must be founded on the express or implied leave of the court. In England, leave is obtained on motion; here it is taken without the formality of an application, but it is subject to be set aside by the court on cause shown. When the propriety of the discontinuance is contested, it must have the court's sanction.(*s*)

A discontinuance will not be permitted where it will give the plaintiff an advantage, or tend to oppress the defendant.(*t*) As the law of discontinuance is well considered in this case, we will introduce the judgment of the court which was delivered by SMITH, J. "The right of a party to discontinue his suit, under proper restrictions, is not denied; indeed, generally speaking, it is the right of the party, but is not always a matter of course, for the plaintiff will not be permitted to discontinue where he will gain an advantage by it; nor will he be indulged in doing so, if prejudicial to his opponent, or when leading to vexation or oppression.

"In England, in the King's Bench and Common Pleas, it is generally done by obtaining a side bar rule 'for leave to discontinue the action upon the payment of costs.' But from the case of Belchier *v.* Gansell,(*u*) not cited at the bar, it is clear that the rule to discontinue will not be granted, if it be intended to oppress the defendant by another suit. To me it appears, the case of Belchier *v.* Gansell, if not exactly the same as the one before us, is very analogous to it. In that case, a

(*i*) Ibid.
(*j*) Lewis *v.* Culbertson, 11 S. & R. 60.
Ante, p. 406.
(*k*) Ibid.
(*l*) McCullum *v.* Coxe, 1 D. 139.
(*m*) 2 Saund. 73, n. 1.
(*n*) Salk. 178, pl. 4.
(*o*) Ibid.

(*p*) Hardw. 200, 201.
(*q*) 2 W. Bl. 815.
(*r*) 2 Arch. Pr. 208; 2 Saund. 73, n. 1.
(*s*) Schuyl. Bank *v.* Macalester, 6 W. & S. 149; Ibid. *v.* Wager, 6 W. & S. 147.
(*t*) Mechanics Bank *v.* Fisher, 1 R.. 341.
(*u*) 4 Burr. 2502.

discontinuance had been entered on a side bar rule, and then the plaintiff arrested the defendant again on the very same bonds, only laying the new suit in Middlesex instead of London ; but on motion, the discontinuance was set aside, on the ground that it was a *trick*, and an unwarrantable conduct in the attorney, and that it ought not to have the intended effect.

" In this country, in our own courts, the law is established in the same way. In Pollock *v.* Hall,(*v*) Chief Justice SHIPPEN says, discontinuances are the acts of the court, and subject to their discretion. And in Broom *v.* Fox,(*w*) the court says, ' regularly, there can be no discontinuance without leave of the court.' In addition to these cases, there are others, which, by a parity of reason, bear on the present case. In Wikoff *v.* Perott,(*x*) and Jackson *v.* Winchester,(*y*) it is decided that the defendant cannot withdraw his plea, at the time of trial, to give him the benefit of the conclusion to the jury without the leave of the court; or, wherever trouble or expense has been incurred by any plea of the defendant's, the court will not give leave to retract the plea. So, in M'Cullough *v.* M'Cullough,(*z*) after an inquest has returned that the rents and profits will pay in seven years, the plaintiff cannot discontinue his *fieri facias*, and take out a new one, without leave of the court. I take the result of this doctrine to be, that courts will protect their suitors from vexation, oppression, or an undue advantage, and will not suffer either party to do any act which may have this tendency. In this case, the advantage the plaintiffs proposed to themselves, must be obvious to all, for by discontinuing the suit in Dauphin County, where the defendant was at home, and by suing him immediately for the same cause of action in Philadelphia, where the plaintiffs resided, they would, of course, get rid of some inconvenience, expense, and trouble ; to all which, the defendant would necessarily be exposed, if compelled to attend at Philadelphia. I would then ask, was not this a contrivance, or an attempt on the part of the plaintiffs, not only to gain an advantage over their opponent, but was it not also calculated to vex, and oppress, and expose him to unnecessary expense and inconvenience ? Whenever, therefore, it appears a party discontinues one suit for the purpose merely of instituting another for the same cause of action elsewhere, the court, on motion, will set aside the discontinuance, and reinstate the former suit, and subject the party to the consequences of his own acts. Here the plaintiffs had chosen the place and the tribunal where, and before which, to sue their debtor ; having done so, the defendant, on his part, as he had a right, moved in the suit, and filed his determination of record to have the suit decided by arbitrators, of which he noticed the plaintiffs ; but before he had returned home from this service, the plaintiffs gave directions to discontinue their suit : it was discontinued by one not authorized, and without the permission of the court. Under these circumstances, I am not disposed to favor the discontinuance of a suit. The rule to arbitrate was not stricken from the record, but remained on the same, when the discontinuance was entered. In the case of Landis *v.* Bigler (I believe not reported), in which a rule to arbitrate had been

(*v*) 3 Y. 42.   (*y*) 2 Y. 529.
(*w*) 2 Y. 531.   (*z*) 1 Bin. 214.
(*x*) 1 Y. 38.

taken out, but never acted on, but still remained on record, and the case afterwards tried, and a verdict and judgment rendered for the plaintiff, this court, on error, reversed the judgment, declaring the law to be, that whilst the rule to arbitrate remained, the cause was out of court. If this be so, and the discontinuance of a suit be the act of the court, then there could be no discontinuance in the suit before us. The arbitrators were afterwards appointed and met (the bank having been previously duly notified of the time and place of their meeting), made an award, and filed the same of record, according to law. The act of assembly, under which these proceedings were had, directs that the report of the arbitrators shall be entered on the docket of the prothonotary, and from the time of such entry shall have the effect of a judgment against the party against whom it is made, and be a lien on the party's real estate, until such judgment be reversed on an appeal; and the appeal is to be made within twenty days after the entry of the award. In the case before us the plaintiffs did not appeal; but on the 8th day of April, 1829, moved the Circuit Court to strike off the rule of reference, and the subsequent proceedings, which motion the court granted. Upon the whole, then, this court is of opinion, that where it appears a discontinuance is entered with a view to vex and oppress a defendant, by suing him elsewhere for the same cause of action, and the party, under such circumstances, applies to the court to sanction the discontinuance of the suit, and set aside all subsequent proceedings in the cause, the application should not succeed, unless founded in justice and equity; and not, as in the present case, where an advantage is the obvious and necessary consequence to the plaintiffs, and great expense, besides inconvenience to the defendant."

The court will not allow a discontinuance to be entered by one of several plaintiffs in ejectment, in such manner as to defeat the action as to the other plaintiffs.(a)

In ordinary cases, however, the plaintiff may, upon payment of the costs, enter a discontinuance without leave of the court, though after an interlocutory judgment.(b)

(a) Cooper v. Cooper (D.C. Alleghany, Lowrie, J.).

(b) Lacroix v. Marquait, 1 M. 156, Stroud, J. "At the time of the discontinuance, interlocutory judgment had been obtained, but no steps had been taken to ascertain the damages. A writ of inquiry had not been sued out. Was it competent to the plaintiff's attorney, in this stage of the proceedings, to repair to the prothonotary's office, get a taxation of the costs there, and without application to the court, on payment of these, to discontinue the scire facias?— We are of opinion it was. It is every day's practice to do so in any stage of the cause, previous to the signing of judgment. And it is plain from the books of practice in the English courts, that an action may be discontinued by the plaintiff after interlocutory judgment, but before a writ of inquiry has been executed. 2 Arch. Prac. 208; 2 Sellon's Prac. 335. A rule for discontinuance, however, is necessary there in all cases; but this may be a "side-bar rule, which is of course before verdict, or argument on demurrer, or execution of inquiry."— Ibid. And the only purpose of this requisition is the taxation of costs, a matter of great moment there, as is well known to every one at all conversant with their practice, but of none with us, since the only fees allowed by our laws are specially fixed by act of assembly, and can be ascertained by the prothonotary at once by inspection of his docket. In England, it is deemed of so much advantage to the defendant's attorney to be present at the taxation, preliminary to a discontinuance, that, by the rule in the Common Pleas, the plaintiff is under the necessity of repeating the service of notice on the defendant's attorney of the

Before argument on demurrer, verdict, or execution of a writ of inquiry, a rule to discontinue is a matter of course. In other cases it is obtained upon application to the court.(c)

After the costs have been taxed and paid, the plaintiff may commence a new action for the same cause, and may again hold the defendant to bail;(d) provided the discontinuance of the first action did not arise from any gross laches on the part of the plaintiff, and the second arrest do not appear to be vexatious.(e)

A plaintiff *before declaration filed* addressed the following authorization and requirement in writing, signed by her, to the prothonotary of the court in which her action was brought: "E. M'M. *v.* J. F. L. In the Court of Common Pleas of H. County: Sir, you are hereby authorized and required to *discontinue forever,* and *withdraw* the above-stated suit forever, on the presentation of this paper." This paper was filed on record by the prothonotary. It was held that it was not a *retraxit,* but simply a discontinuance or nonsuit, and consequently neither a bar nor estoppel to a subsequent suit for the same cause of action.(f)

If the plaintiff agree to discontinue, in consideration of a promise by the defendant not to file a bill against him, and the defendant performs his part, the court will stay proceedings in the suit at common law, and order an *exoneretur* to be entered on the bail-piece.(g)

---

time appointed for taxation no less than *three* times, according to Sellon, before the prothonotary will consider him in neglect, so as to proceed to the taxation without his attendance. Ibid. With us, a similar rule would be preposterous.— No notice to the defendant's attorney is required; but the prothonotary makes out the bill of costs silently, by a recollection of the fee bill, and examination of his docket entries in the particular action. The Mechanics' Bank *v.* Fisher, 1 R. 343, has been relied upon as an authority contravening the position that a *discontinuance* may be effected on payment of costs, without application to the court; and without doubt an opinion of considerable length is reported there in which it is attempted to be shown that it is not consonant with our law to permit a *discontinuance* without leave of the court. This, however, was not a point in the cause, and, according to the declared doctrine of that court, is to be regarded merely as the *dictum* of the individual who expressed it. Hickman *v.* Caldwell, 4 R. 380. Two cases are referred to in the Mechanics' Bank *v.* Fisher, in support of the extra-judicial

discussion there on the subject of discontinuance. The first is Brown *v.* Fox, 2 Y. 530, in which the court say: "*regularly,* there can be no discontinuance without leave of the court." The other case is Pollock *v.* Hall, 3 Y. 42, in which the same doctrine is again enumerated. It is plain, however, from an examination of the whole scope of these opinions, that it was not intended to impugn the practice of entering discontinuances in the prothonotary's office without application to the court, *but merely to assert the right of the court to set aside a discontinuance so entered,* if the circumstances under which it was entered were such as rendered it manifestly unjust and injurious to the defendant. With this qualification we have no disposition to question the soundness of the principle. In the present case, there is no allegation of *injury* to the defendants by the discontinuance."

(c) 2 Arch. Pr. 208.
(d) 2 Str. 1209.
(e) 5 M. & S. 93 ; Doane's Administrators *v.* Penhallow, 1 D. 220.
(f) Lowrey *v.* M'Millan, 8 Barr, 157.
(g) Wilkins *v.* Burr, 6 Bin. 389.

SECTION II.

NOLLE PROSEQUI.

A *nolle prosequi* is an acknowledgment or agreement by the plaintiff entered upon the record, that he will not further prosecute his suit as to the whole or a part of the cause of action; or as to some one of the counts in his declaration, or as to some or one of the issues joined; or, where there are several defendants, against some or one of them.(*h*).

A *nolle prosequi* is not regarded as a confession of the plaintiff that he has no cause of action, nor is it considered in the nature of a *retraxit* or release, for it may be entered as to one of several defendants, and the plaintiff may still proceed against the others, in which respect it differs from a judgment of *non pros.*, whereby the plaintiff is put out of court as regards all the defendants.(*i*) But it rather resembles a discontinuance :(*j*) for, when the plaintiff has misconceived his action, or made a mistake as to the party sued (as where he sues a feme covert, and she pleads coverture; or where he discovers that the defendant is an infant, and the action is not for necessaries, or the like), he may enter a *nolle prosequi* as to the whole cause of action.(*k*) But in cases where both the parties are actors (as in replevin or in a feigned issue),(*l*) the plaintiff cannot defeat the suit by entering a *nolle prosequi*.(*m*)

Where the defendant pleads one plea to the whole declaration, and that plea happens to be a complete bar to one or more of the counts, but not to others, the plaintiff may enter a *nolle prosequi* as to the counts to which the plea is a bar. Thus, where assumpsit is brought for goods sold, &c., and upon an account stated, and infancy is pleaded to the whole of the declaration, the plaintiff may enter a *nolle prosequi* as to the count upon an account stated (no action upon an account stated lying against an infant), and rely on the other counts.(*n*) But where there is a demurrer to a whole declaration, the plaintiff will not be allowed to rectify his error, by entering a *nolle prosequi* as to some of the counts :(*o*) Thus, where there was a demurrer to a declaration against two defendants, because one of them was not named in one of the counts, the court held that the plaintiff could not enter a *nolle prosequi* as to that count, and proceed on the others.(*p*) So, where there was a demurrer to a declaration for a misjoinder of counts, the court held that the plaintiff could not rectify his mistake by entering a *nolle prosequi* as to some of the counts.(*q*) But if the defendant demur or plead separately to several counts, the plaintiff may enter a *nolle prosequi* as to some of the counts, and proceed to trial or argument on the others.(*r*)

When the plaintiff wishes to withdraw part of the cause of action contained in a single count, he may enter a *nolle prosequi* for that part,

(*h*) 2 Ro. Abr. 100, pl. 5; Bing. on Judg. 49; 7 Cranch, 176.
(*i*) 1 Saund. 207, n. 2.
(*j*) 3 T. R. 511.
(*k*) Ibid.; 2 Arch. Pr. 218; *post*, 418.
(*l*) Lessee of Penn *v.* Divellin, 2 Y. 310.

(*m*) Vansant *v.* Boileau, 1 Bin. 448.
(*n*) 1 Saund. 207, b. c.
(*o*) Ibid.
(*p*) 4 T. R. 360.
(*q*) 1 H. Bl. 108.
(*r*) 1 Saund. 207; a. 203, 339.

which will show on the record, exactly what was submitted to the jury, and will be no bar to a subsequent suit.(*s*)   Thus, in trespass, where the plaintiff declares that the defendant took and carried away the plaintiff's hay, grass, and corn, he may enter a *nolle prosequi* as to the hay and grass, and proceed for the taking of the corn.(*t*)

In actions upon *contracts* against several defendants, if the defendants *join* in their pleas, the plaintiff cannot enter a *nolle prosequi* as to any one of them, without releasing the others;(*u*) but if they *sever* in their pleas, and one of them plead bankruptcy, *ne unques executor*, infancy, or any other matter not denying the cause of action, but merely in his personal discharge, the plaintiff may enter a *nolle prosequi* as to him, and proceed against the others.(*v*) So, also, if a feme covert be one of the defendants, a *nolle prosequi* may be entered as to her.(*w*) And again, where one of two obligors was a bankrupt, plaintiff was allowed on the trial to enter a *nolle prosequi* as to him, and proceed to trial against the other.(*x*)   *Nolle prosequi* may be entered after verdict in an action of ejectment, there being no contribution.(*y*)

In a late case in the District Court, E. K. was sued as the wife of H. K., on a paper signed by her alone. The court allowed a *non pros.* to be entered as to her, but without expressing an opinion as to its effect in remedying any mistake that had been made.(*z*)

In actions founded upon *torts* against several defendants, the plaintiff may enter a *nolle prosequi* as to some of them, and proceed against the others, *at any time before final judgment*, even although they all join in the same plea, and be found jointly guilty; and *à fortiori*, he may do so, where they plead severally.(*a*) The reason of this seems to be, because such actions being in their nature joint and several, as the plaintiff might therefore have originally commenced his action against *one only*, and proceed to judgment and execution against him alone; so he may after verdict against several, elect to take his damages against either of them.(*b*)   And upon this ground it is, that where a jury give a wrong verdict in point of law, the plaintiff may, in some cases, cure the defect in the verdict, by entering a *nolle prosequi* before judgment.(*c*) As where several persons are jointly charged in an action of assault, battery, and false imprisonment, who either pleaded jointly or sever in their pleas, or one suffers judgment to go by default (for it is immaterial which is the case), if the jury assess *several* damages, the ver-

---

(*s*) Hess *v.* Heevle, 6 S. & R. 61.
(*t*) 1 Saund. 207, n. 2.
(*u*) Ibid.
(*v*) Ibid. 2 M. & S. 444; 5 Johns. 160; 1 Peters's S. C. Rep. 46.
(*w*) Beidman *v.* Vanderslice, 2 R. 334. See also Lacroix *v.* Macquart, 1 M. 45; Lefevre *v.* Lefevre, 4 S. & R. 240; Engle *v.* Nelson, 1 Pa. R. 442; Montgomery *v.* Patterson, 15 S. & R. 150.
(*x*) Com *v.* Nesbit, 2 Barr, 16.
(*y*) Freedly *v.* Mitchell, 2 Barr, 101.
(*z*) Grace *v.* Kurtz, D. C. C. P. 7 Leg. Int. 183.   *Per curiam.*   Elizabeth Kurtz is sued as the wife of Henry Kurtz, the other defendant. The note is signed by

her alone.   A suggestion is filed by Henry Kurtz of the coverture as a defence to the note. It is settled that in assumpsit if one of the defendants is a feme covert, a *nolle prosequi* may be entered as to her. We allow this *nolle prosequi* to be entered without expressing any opinion as to its effect in remedying the mistake, if one has been committed in bringing the action against husband and wife, where the husband ought to have been sued alone.   R. A.

(*a*) Ibid. 2 Arch. Pr. 220.
(*b*) Carth. 20; Cridland *v.* Floyd, 6 S. & R. 413.
(*c*) 1 Saund. 207, n. 2.

dict is wrong, and the judgment will be erroneous.(*d*)   But the plaintiff may cure the verdict by entering a *nolle prosequi* against all the defendants but one, and taking judgment against him only.(*e*)   And in these cases, it should seem, that the *nolle prosequi* so entered against some of the defendants, must, from the nature of the actions, be an absolute bar to any further action for the same cause.(*f*)

Where a *nolle prosequi* is entered as to the whole declaration, the defendant is entitled to costs, and in the same manner as upon a discontinuance.   And where entered as to some of several counts, the plaintiff is not entitled to costs as to these counts, although he have a verdict on the others.(*g*)

A technical *retraxit* is it seems nearly unknown in this State.   It is where a plaintiff, *after declaration filed*, comes *personally* into the court where the action is, and declares he will not proceed further in it; and this is a bar to any subsequent suit for the same cause of action.   A written authority given before declaration filed, " to discontinue forever, and withdraw the suit forever," is not a *retraxit*—but a mere discontinuance or nonsuit, and therefore no bar to a subsequent action.(*h*)

(*d*) 5 Burr. 2792; Cridland *v.* Floyd,   (*f*) 1 Saund. 207, n. 2.
6 S. & R. 413.   (*g*) 2 Arch. Pr. 220.
  (*e*) Cro. Car. 239, 243.   (*h*) Lowry *v.* McMillan, 8 Barr, 157.

CHAPTER XX.

OF THE REPLICATION, AND THE SUBSEQUENT PLEADINGS.

WHEN the defendant has pleaded, either in abatement or in bar, by way of confession and avoidance, as a release, the plaintiff has the option of demurring to the plea—as being, in substance or form, an insufficient answer in point of *law* to the declaration—or of *pleading* to it, by way of *traverse,* or by way of confession and avoidance of its allegations. Such pleading on the part of the plaintiff is called *the replication.(a)*

If the replication be by way of traverse (that is, in *denial* of the whole or part of the defendant's plea), it is in general necessary (as in the case of the plea) that it should tender issue. So, if the plaintiff demur, an issue in law is necessarily tendered; and, in either case, the result is a joinder in issue; upon the same principles as heretofore stated(*aa*) with respect to the plea. But if the replication be also in confession and avoidance (as, that the release alleged in the plea was made by duress and force of imprisonment), the defendant may then, in his turn, either demur, or, by a *pleading,* either traverse, or confess and avoid, its allegations. If such pleading take place it is called the *rejoinder.(b)*

In the same manner, and subject to the same law of proceeding, viz. that of *demurring,* or *pleading* either in denial of the truth of the adverse allegation, or confessing and avoiding it, is conducted all the subsequent altercation to which the nature of the case may lead; and the order and denominations of the alternate *allegations of facts* or *pleadings* throughout the whole series are as follows: *declaration, plea, replication, rejoinder, surrejoinder, rebutter,* and *surrebutter.(c)* After the surrebutter, the allegations of the respective parties, in the English system of pleading, have no distinctive names, for beyond that stage, as it is said, they never occur in practice.(*d*) And, indeed, in those cases where the parties in pleading do actually arrive at the two last-known stages of the system, that is, of rebutter and surrebutter, it is said to be very seldom that either of these is a special allegation, or, in other words, contains anything more than a tender of, or joinder in issue.(*e*) In our practice, it is rare that a defendant finds it necessary to rejoin specially, and much more so a plaintiff to surrejoin specially; but issue is most frequently attained either on a general plea to the declaration, or on a replication to the plea.

(*a*) Steph. on Plead. 77, 1st edit.
(*aa*) *Ante,* chap. xviii.
(*b*) Ibid.

(*c*) Ibid.
(*d*) 1 Arch. Plead.
(*e*) Lawes on Plead. 161.

With regard to the form and qualities of the replication and the subsequent pleadings, and therein of a *new assignment* (which is in the nature of a replication),(*f*) and of *departure* in pleading, which can never occur till the replication,(*g*) we shall content ourselves with referring the reader to any of the recent treatises on pleading, and merely mention the rule in reference to these pleadings, which forbids the joinder of several replications to the same plea, or of several rejoinders to the same replication; and so to the end of the series. The reason of this is, that the statute of Anne extends to the cases of pleas *only*, and not to replications or subsequent pleadings.(*h*) So that, when several pleas are pleaded, the plaintiff can only make one replication to each plea; therefore, a replication to a plea of the statute of limitations, stating that six years had not run since a nonsuit in a previous action; that the debt arose on an account between merchant and merchant; and that the plaintiff was beyond sea when the cause of action arose, is bad for duplicity.(*i*)

There is no time fixed upon by law for replying: when the defendant, therefore, has put in his plea he may rule the plaintiff to reply, in the same time and manner as directed by the rules of court previously quoted,(*j*) with regard to rules to declare and plead; or he may pray the court to grant a rule on the plaintiff to reply in a less time than is prescribed in their standing rules. If the plaintiff be not ready to reply within the time limited by the rule, he may apply to the court and obtain an order for further time. But if he neglect to reply within the time required by the rule, or order, for further time, the defendant may sign a judgment of *non pros*. On the other hand, the plaintiff, on filing a replication without joining issue, that is, concluding with a verification, may enter a rule requiring the defendant to rejoin; or, if there be a new assignment, to plead thereto, in like manner as to the original declaration, and, in case of his neglect to comply with the rule, may have judgment in the same manner as on a default for want of a plea. And so rules may be entered by each party respectively, until an issue is attained, or one of them incurs a judgment by default.

When several pleas are pleaded, to one of which there has been no replication, and the cause has been tried without a joinder in issue upon that plea, the following distinction made by the Supreme Court, will indicate whether this has produced any error in the record: Where the defendant has pleaded the general issue, and with it, has pleaded specially a matter which might have been given in evidence under such general issue, the want of a replication to the special plea, would not, it seems, be error.(*k*) In other words, if the latter plea could be struck out of the record, without injury to the defendant, it would, if not conclusive with the court, operate with them as a strong auxiliary argument, where there are other grounds to overrule the objection.(*l*)

The entry on the docket by the clerk, of the words "and issue," or "issues," at the close of the short minute of the pleadings, is considered to be a sufficient joinder of issue; it is "always held to be a memorandum

(*f*) Steph. on Plead. 244.
(*g*) *Vide* id. 405.
(*h*) *Vide* Steph. on Plead. 293, 294.
(*i*) 1 Peters's Rep. 443.

(*j*) *Ante*, p. 317.
(*k*) Reed *v.* Pedan, 8 S. & R. 263.
(*l*) Ibid. 266.

for the clerk to join the issue formally, the want of which, under such circumstances, is a clerical slip, and amendable."(*m*)

The replication *de injuria* to a plea of *son assault demesne* in assault and battery, confines the defendant to proving an excuse for the battery: he cannot give evidence in mitigation of damages, or contradict the averments of aggravated injuries laid in the narr.(*n*)

Where there is a plea in confession and avoidance, the plaintiff cannot be forced to trial or nonsuit without a replication, although a rule of court dispenses with one, where a substantial issue is raised by the pleadings.(*o*)

If the defendant does not object to go to trial without a formal joinder of issue, and has had the chance of a verdict, he cannot afterwards object.(*p*)

Although after trial on the merits the court will not listen to an objection of want of replication or issue, yet the court will not intend that a plea of law was disposed of, where the verdict is only on the issue of fact, and judgment is on the verdict. Hence, an execution on such judgment cannot be sustained.(*q*)

By replying to a dilatory plea which is defective for want of an affidavit, the plaintiff waives the defect, and cannot ask judgment for want of an affidavit.(*r*)

The replication *de injuria* is proper when the plea consists merely of matter of *excuse* or *justification*, and it cannot be applied so as to include in the denial any matter alleged on the other side in the nature of *title*, *interest*, *commandment*, *authority*, or *matter of record*.(*s*)

Where a plea avers that the note declared on had been attached as the property of the original payee, a replication setting forth that such payee's interest was divested at the time of the attachment, without stating that it was vested in the plaintiff, is bad.(*t*)

(*m*) Carl *v.* The Commonwealth, 9 S. & R. 67; see particularly, 127; Sauerman *v.* Weckerly, 17 S. & R. 116; see also *ante*, p. 392.

(*n*) Frederick *v.* Gilbert, 8 Barr, 450.

(*o*) Maxwell *v.* Beltzhover, 9 Barr, 139.

(*p*) Clement *v.* Hayden, 4 Barr, 138.

(*q*) Beale *v.* Buckman, 9 Barr, 123. See *ante*, p. 392.

(*r*) Casporus *v.* Jones, 7 Barr, 120.

(*s*) Lincoln *v.* Souder, 4 P. L. J. 107.

(*t*) Doty *v.* Sturdevant, 1 Barr, 399.

CHAPTER XXI.

OF DEMURRERS.(a)

IF the declaration, plea, or other pleading, of either of the parties, be defective, the other party, instead of answering it, or joining issue where no answer is requisite, may demur, admitting the facts alleged in the pleading, and referring it to the judgment of the court to determine whether those facts are either in substance, or in the form in which they are stated, sufficient to maintain the plaintiff's action, or support the defendant's defence.(b)

When there are several counts in a declaration, some of which are good in point of law, and the rest defective, the defendant should only demur to the latter, and plead to the former; for if he demur to the whole declaration, the plaintiff shall have judgment on the good counts.(c) So, if the defendant plead several pleas, all of which are demurred to, if one be good, judgment must be given for the defendant.(d) A party cannot plead and demur to the same count.(e)

A demurrer is either general or special. A general demurrer excepts to the sufficiency in general terms, without showing specifically the nature of the objection: a special demurrer adds to this a specification of the particular ground of exception. A general demurrer is sufficient where the objection is on matter of *substance*. A special demurrer is necessary where it turns on matter of *form* only; that is, where, notwithstanding such objection, enough appears to entitle the opposite party to judgment, as far as relates to the merits of the cause.(f) For, by two statutes,(g) passed with a view to the discouragement of merely formal objections, it is provided, in nearly the same terms, that the judges " shall give judgment according as the very right of the cause and matter in law shall appear unto them, without regarding any imperfections, omission, defect or want of form, except those only which the party demurring shall specially and particularly set down and express,

(a) This subject has already been partially explained, *supra*, pp. 389, 390.
(b) Co. Litt. 71, b.; 1 Chit. Pl. 638.
(c) 1 Saund. 286, n. 9; 18 Johns, 457.
(d) 2 Mass. Rep. 541.
(e) McFate *v.* Shallcross, D. C., Saturday, June 29, 1850. Demurrer. *Per curiam.* To a narr. upon a replevin bond by the plaintiff, as assignee of the sheriff, the defendant put in several pleas upon which issues of fact were taken, tried, and decided, and at the same time demurred specially. It is one of the oldest and best-settled rules that it is not allowable both to plead and to demur to the same matter. A man may plead to one count and demur to another. Here the declaration consisted of a single count. The statute of Anne, which authorizes the pleading of *several pleas*, gives no authority for *demurring and pleading* to the same matter. (Stephens on Pl. 327 and 328.) Demurrer dismissed.

(f) Steph. on Plead. 159.
(g) 27 Eliz. c. 5, Rob. Dig. 367, and 4 Anne, c. 16; ibid. 43.

together with his demurrer, as causes of the same,"—the latter statute adding this proviso, " so as sufficient matter appear in the said pleadings, upon which the court may give judgment, according to the very right of the cause." Since these statutes, therefore, no mere matter of form can be objected on a general demurrer; but the demurrer must be in the special form, and the objection specifically stated.(h) But, on the other hand, it is to be observed, that, under a special demurrer, the party may, on the argument, not only take advantage of the particular faults which his demurrer specifies, but also of all such objections in substance, or regarding " the very right of the cause," (as the statute expresses it,) as do not require, under those statutes, to be particularly set down. It follows, therefore, that, unless the objection be clearly of this substantial kind, it is the safer course, in all cases, to demur specially.(i) Indeed, it is advised by Lord Hale(j) and Lord Coke,(k) to demur specially in all cases, and never generally. Yet, it is said, where a general demurrer is plainly sufficient, it is more usually adopted in practice; because the effect of the special form being to apprise the opposite party more distinctly of the nature of the objection, it is attended with the inconvenience of enabling him to prepare to maintain his pleading in argument, or of leading him to apply-the earlier to amend.(l) When objections, which are well founded, *though merely formal*, are stated specifically as causes of demurrer, and it is shown *in what respect* the pleading is defective or informal,(m) the party taking them is entitled to the benefit of the exceptions; and the cause may be decided on them alone.(n)

With respect to the *effect* of a demurrer, it is a rule that a demurrer admits all such matters of fact as are sufficiently pleaded,(o) or which, if informally pleaded, are not specially excepted to on that account,(p) though a special demurrer is no admission of a fact not pleaded in a formal and sufficient manner, and a party may, on the argument, not only take advantage of the faults specified in his demurrer, but also of such objections in substance as do not require to be particularly set down.(q)

It is also a rule that, on demurrer, *the court will consider the whole record*, and give judgment for the party who, on the whole, appears to be entitled to it.(r) Thus, on demurrer to the replication, if the court think the replication bad, but perceive a substantial fault in the *plea*, they will give judgment, not for the defendant, but the plaintiff,(s) provided the *declaration* be good; but if the declaration also be bad in substance (and not in form merely),(t) then, upon the same principle, judgment would be given for the defendant.(u) This rule, however, has reference to pleas in bar only; for if the plaintiff demur to a *plea in abatement*, and the court decide against the plea, they will give judg-

(h)Steph. on Plead. 160.
(i) Ibid.
(j) 1 Vent. 240.
(k) 2 Bulst. 267.
(l) Steph on Plead. 160–1.
(m) 1 Saund. 161, n. 1–327, b. n. 3.
(n) 1 Peters's Rep. 475 ; *post*, 425–6.
(o) Sid. 10, ca. 5.
(p) 1 Saund. 337, b. n. 3 ; Com. v.

Primrose, 2 W. & S. 407; Ellmaker v. Ins. Co. 6 W. & S. 445.
(q) Fisher v. Lewis, D. Ct. C. C. P. 3 P. L. J. 73.
(r) Saund. 285, n. 5 ; Murphy v. Richards, 5 W. & S. 280.
(s) 2 Wils. 150 ; Hall v. Hurford, 4 P. L. J. 44.
(t) 2 Vent. 198, 222.
(u) 5 Rep. 29, a.

ment of *respondeat ouster*, without regard to any defect in the declaration.(v)

A demurrer must be filed in the same manner as any of the pleadings. As, if a rule be entered to plead or rejoin, the party must file his demurrer within the time granted by the rule.(w) When the prothonotary has, under the rules of court,(x) put the cause to issue, upon a plea or pleas being filed, and entered the proper pleadings for that purpose, the other party has still a right to put in a demurrer, provided, to prevent surprise, he gives notice of it to his adversary. Either party, on demurring, may at once add the joinder, or it may be done by the prothonotary.

It seems that an objection to a declaration good in substance but defective in form, cannot be taken by praying instructions to the jury to that effect, but there should be a special demurrer.(y)

Two narrs. are demurrable.(z)

The demurrer and joinder constitute an issue in law, which is referred to the decision of the court, and for this purpose placed on the argument list (according to the seniority of the cause on the docket),(a) to be discussed before them. The counsel for the party who is entitled to begin and conclude the argument, must make up and deliver to each of the judges a paper-book, containing a full and distinct statement of all facts conducive to a ready comprehension of the matter to be argued.(b) Upon some day in that portion of the term which remains after trials by special jury, the demurrer will be called on for argument, in the order in which it stands on the list. If there be no argument, the counsel moves for judgment, as of course. But if argued, the counsel for the party demurring is first heard in support of the demurrer. Next, the counsel for the other party is heard in answer; and lastly, the former counsel is heard in reply.(c)

Where there are several issues, both in law and in fact, the plaintiff may, without waiting for a decision on the issues in law, go to trial on the issues in fact, and at the same time have contingent damages assessed on the counts in his declaration, to which the demurrer replies; or he may wait the result of the issue in law, and then proceed to trial if necessary.(d) It is, however, advisable to determine the demurrer first; for if it go to the whole cause of action, and is determined against the plaintiff, it is conclusive; and there is no occasion afterwards to try the issue in fact; whereas, if the issue in fact be first tried and found for the plaintiff, he must still proceed to the determination of the demurrer, and if that be determined against him, he will not be allowed his costs of the trial of the issue in fact, but final judgment will be entered upon the demurrer against him, notwithstanding a judgment on the issue of fact in his favor.(dd) If the issue be tried before the demurrer is argued, the damages are said to be *contingent*, depending upon the event of the demurrer, and it is necessary for the jury to assess contingent damages; and the award of the *venire* is *tam quam*, that is, as well to try the issue as to inquire of the contingent damages.(e) But notwith-

---

(v) Lutw. 1592, 1667.
(w) 1 Dunl. Pr. 518.
(x) *Ante*, 393, 422.
(y) Halderman *v.* Martin, 10 Barr, 369.
(z) Gould *v.* Crawford, 2 Barr, 89.

(a) 1 Br. 214; R. Sup. C.
(b) R. D. C. Philad.; see *post*, 427.
(c) 2 Arch. Pr. 35.
(d) 2 Saund. 300, n. 3.
(dd) Willard *v.* Morris, 1 P. R. 480.
(e) 2 Saund. 300, n. 3.

standing the general right of the plaintiff to pursue whichever course he may think proper, yet in many cases, where there have been issues in law and in fact upon the same record, the demurrer has been ordered to be first argued, in order that the parties might not go to the trial of the issue under the necessity of assessing the contingent damages; but that the judge who may have to direct the jury may do so without hesitation as to the final measure of damages.(f)

The settled rule in Pennsylvania now is, where there are two issues, one of fact and the other of law, it is discretionary with the court which they will try first. The same has been repeatedly held with regard to demurrers.(g) In Philadelphia, the practice in the District Court is to take the argument of the law issue last; in the Common Pleas, the contrary.(h) The practice of the former has very recently received the approval of the Supreme Court.(i)

The court refused a preference to the argument of a demurrer to a plea in *quo warranto*, though the office was an annual one.(ii)

Judgment upon demurrer is interlocutory or final in the same manner and in the same cases as judgment by default.(j) After judgment on demurrer, the defendant cannot move to arrest the judgment for an exception that might have been taken on arguing the demurrer, but he may for a fault arising on the writ of inquiry or verdict.(k)

If a defendant plead several pleas to the same or several counts of a declaration, and the plaintiff demur to some of the pleas, and take issue upon others, if the defendant succeed upon any of the pleas demurred to, and that plea be an answer to the whole action, the plaintiff shall not have judgment upon the issue in fact should they be found for him; but the only judgment that shall be entered is *nil capiat per breve.*(l)

Where judgment is given in favor of the plaintiff on a demurrer to a plea in bar, it should be a judgment *quod recuperet,* and not *quod respondeat ouster;* but if the latter judgment be entered, it is an error of which the defendant cannot complain, for it is in his favor.(m) Where the action sounds in damages, as in covenant, trover, trespass, &c., judgment for the plaintiff on demurrer is interlocutory, and it is necessary before final judgment that damages should be assessed by a jury. And until final judgment a writ of error cannot be taken.(n)

After demurrer, general or special, it is said to be usual to give the other party leave to amend; and it has been given even after demurrer argued, but before judgment, where the justice of the case required it,(o) upon payment of costs. It has been refused, however, to a plain-

---

(f) 13 East, 41, 47; *vide etiam* id. 27; Eckart v. Wilson, 10 S. & R. 52.

(g) Beale v. Buchanan, 9 Barr, 123.

(h) Wh. Dig. "Practice," xix.

(i) "The court," said LEWIS, J., "in our opinion, properly exercised its discretion in postponing the determination of the issues in *law* until the issues in *fact* were found by the jury.— Such a course tends to promote accuracy in pleading, and prevents frivolous demurrers. It is, also, the means of saving time, because the finding of any one of the issues in fact for the defendant, as already remarked, disposes of the whole case. The action of the court, however, affected but the *order* of *proceeding,* not the *rights* of the *parties,* and was an exercise of discretion which is not the subject of revision here." Marseilles v. Kenton, 5 Harris, 248.

(ii) Com. v. Sparks, 6 Wh. 416.

(j) *Vide ante,* 337, *et seq.*

(k) 1 Str. 425.

(l) 1 Saund. 80, n. 1; 2 Burr. 753.

(m) Bauer v. Roth, 4 R. 83.

(n) Logan v. Jennings, Id. 355.

(o) 2 Arch. Pr. 231; 1 Peters, 443.

tiff in a *qui tam* action; (*p*) in an action against bail ;(*q*) and in hard actions ;(*r*) and to a defendant after the plaintiff had lost a trial.(*rr*)— Under particular circumstances, also, the party has been allowed to withdraw his demurrer, on payment of costs, and plead *de novo*, even after argument ;(*s*) but not in a case where the court are of opinion that the party demurring could not plead successfully.(*t*) So if there be issues in law and in fact, and the latter be tried first, and contingent damages assessed as to the demurrer, the court, it seems, will not in that case allow either of an amendment, or of the demurrer being withdrawn.(*u*) The proper course is for the court, except under peculiar circumstances, to proceed after argument to enter judgment in the demurrer.(*v*)

Where a demurrer is well founded, it is important for the opposite party at once to ask leave to amend, as he cannot patch up the error in his joinder in demurrer;(*vv*) and, as has just been seen, leave to amend after judgment will rarely be given.

After a party has once amended on a demurrer, the court will not permit him to amend again on a second demurrer.(*w*)

If either party have judgment upon demurrer, he is entitled to costs, and may have execution for the same by stat. 8 and 9 W. III. c. 11, § 2.(*x*) This statute, however, does not extend to demurrers to pleas in abatement, its intention being only to give costs, where the merits of the cause are determined upon the demurrer; (*y*) neither does it extend to actions where the plaintiff would not be entitled to damages if he had a verdict,(*z*) as in actions of partition.

By the practice of the District Court of Philadelphia, when the demurrant fails to furnish the court with paper-books, the other party, if he asks for a decision, must be prepared to do so, and where no books are furnished, the court will refuse to act.(*a*)

(*p*) 4 T. R. 459.
(*q*) Say. Rep. 117.
(*r*) 1 H. Bl. 37.
(*rr*) Hardw. 171.
(*s*) 4 T. R. 690 ; Say. 316,317 ; Barnes, 155 ; 2 Burr. 820, 756 ; 2 Wils. 173 ; 1 Doug. 385, 452.
(*t*) 2 Hals. N. J. Rep. 278.
(*u*) 1 Burr. 316.
(*v*) Stephens *v.* Myers, 2 J. 302 ; Young *v.* Parkam, D. C. Jan. 11, 1852. Why judgment on the demurrer should be opened. *Per curiam.* It has the appearance of trifling with the court ; for a party, after a solemn admission by demurrer of facts set up in a plea, and after a decision by the court that these facts amounted to a bar, to ask to be permitted to withdraw that admission. We do not suspect the very respectable gentleman concerned in this case of such an intention. There are circumstances connected with this case of a peculiar character, which have induced us, by the consent of the opposite party, to agree that this rule be made absolute. The case is not to be drawn into a precedent. The bar will perceive that there can be no assignable limit to the privilege of

raising and discussing abstract questions upon general demurrers, if, after the judgment has been pronounced, the parties may go in and try the case afterwards on the general issue. If the facts are unquestionable, and the only thing which remains is to determine the law, there is no imaginable benefit. If the facts are questionable, then the only true professional course is to try and determine the question of fact first. The question of law will then be out of the way, or, it may be, much more satisfactorily disposed of afterwards.
(*vv*) Gibson *v.* Todd, 1 R. 452.
(*w*) 2 H. Bl. 561 ; 2 Arch. Pr. 231.
(*x*) Rob. Dig. 140.
(*y*) Say. Costs, 86–7 ; 2 Ld. Raym. 992.
(*z*) Hullock, 145–6.
(*a*) Etting *v.* Potter, July 1, 1848.
For a carefully drawn form of a judgment at length in the Supreme Court for plaintiff in error who succeeded in reversing a judgment against him on demurrer to his replications, and where other pleas remain to be tried, see Watmough *v.* Fruners, 7 Barr, 220; and for rules, see *ante*, p. 425.

CHAPTER XXII.

OF TRIAL BY THE RECORD.

WHEREVER a record is alleged on one side as the foundation, or in bar or abatement of the action, and the opposite party denies its existence by pleading or replying that *there is no such record* upon which issue is taken (*habetur tale recordum*), it is called an issue of *nul tiel record*, the trial of which must be by the court, and not by the country;(*a*) for a record is a monument of so high a nature, and imports in itself such absolute verity, that if it be pleaded there is no such record, it shall not receive a trial by witnesses, jury, or arbitrators, but only by itself; and as the evidence of its existence depends, from its nature, on ocular demonstration, the law refers it to the judgment of the court alone.(*b*) But where the plea consists both of matter of fact, and matter of record, the issue must then be to the country;(*c*) as, for instance, where two persons having committed a joint *tort* or trespass, and judgment having been recovered against the one, and satisfaction obtained from him, the other pleads the recovery and satisfaction in bar of a separate action against himself.(*d*) So, when the judgment of a court in another State, or of a Circuit or District Court of the United States, for either of the districts into which this State is divided, is put in issue by the plea of *nul tiel record*, the issue must be to the country, and the verity of the record is triable only by a jury.(*e*)

A plea of *nul tiel record* to a judgment of an alderman, is triable by the record and not by a jury.(*f*)

In a *scire facias* on a recognizance of bail on appeal from a justice, the transcript filed is conclusive evidence of the record, on an issue upon that point, and cannot be contradicted by the justice's docket, which is no record of the Common Pleas.(*g*)

Where the declaration is founded on a matter of record, which is traversed in the plea, the plea should allege that there is no such record, and conclude to the court, and the plaintiff must reply, reasserting the existence of the record, and concluding with a prayer that it may be viewed and inspected by the court, and a day is given to the parties;(*h*) or if it be the record of another court, the replication re-

(*a*) Share *v.* Becker, 8 S. & R. 241; 1 Chit. Pl. 480, 571; 3 Bl. Com. 330, 331.
(*b*) Roop *v.* Meek, 6 S. & R. 545.
(*c*) Share *v.* Becker, 8 S. & R. 242.
(*d*) 6 Johns. 26. See Bul. N. P. 230.
(*e*) 17 Johns. 272. *Contra*, the opinion of Mr. Justice BRACKENRIDGE, Frey *v.* Wells, 4 Y. 503.
(*f*) Oliver *v.* Foster, 5 P. L. J. 335.
(*g*) Bell *v.* Murphy, 6 W. & S. 50.
(*h*) Share *v.* Becker, 8 S. & R. 241; 4 W. C. C. R. 388; see 7 Taunt. 30.

asserts it, and a day is given to the plaintiff to bring it in.(*i*) If matter of record, as a judgment recovered for the same demand, be pleaded,
the plaintiff, instead of replying *nul tiel record*, may demand of the defendant a note in writing of the term and number of the roll whereon
such judgment is entered, or in default thereof the plea is not to be received, and the plaintiff may sign judgment. But this cannot be done,
when the defendant pleads a record of another court.(*j*)

As a void record is no record, the plea of *nul tiel record* to it is sus-
tainable.(*k*)

In debt on judgment, a variance as to amount is fatal on *nul tiel
record.*(*l*)

Where the plaintiff replies *nul tiel record*, he may obtain a rule on
the defendant to produce the record ;(*m*) and when he replies to a plea
of *nul tiel record*, a rule will be granted upon him to bring in the record, and a day to bring it in ;(*n*) but the English practice requires
notice in writing to be given to the defendant's attorney, that he (the
plaintiff) will produce the record on a day certain therein mentioned.(*o*)

The party on whom it is incumbent to produce the record, may obtain
it from the prothonotary, who will have it brought into court; and upon
the day appointed by the rule or notice above mentioned, the crier makes
proclamation in court for the party to bring forth the record by him in
pleading alleged, or else he shall be condemned.(*p*)

The plea of *nul tiel record* is dispensed with, and the cause is put on
the trial of its merits by an agreement to try on the plea of payment
with leave, &c., or notice of special matter. After such an agreement,
the court ought not to allow the plea of *nul tiel record* to be added
without consent of both parties, and it is then too late to object that
the writ recites a judgment for $500, when it was in fact for $1500.
At best, this is but a clerical error, which the court would allow the
plaintiff to amend.(*q*)

Scire facias on mortgage is not a proceeding on a record, but on a
deed, hence the plea of *nul tiel record* is a nullity in this action. If a
variance exists between the writ and the mortgage, the proper mode of
taking advantage of it is by objecting to the admission of the mortgage
in evidence, on the trial, under the plea of *non est factum.*(*r*)

On the trial of the issue of *nul tiel record*, the record itself must be
produced, if it be a record of the same court, or the tenor of it, *sub
pede sigilli*, if it be the record of another court within the jurisdiction
of this State.(*s*) The seals of all public courts established here, are received in evidence, without extrinsic proof of their genuineness.(*t*)

If the record of a court of another State be put in issue, it must be
exemplified in the manner pointed out by the act of Congress of May
26, 1790,(*u*) which provides, that "the records and judicial proceedings of the courts of any State shall be proved or admitted in any other
court in the United States, by the attestation of the clerk, and the seal

(*i*) 1 Saund. 92, n. 3 ; 4 W. C. C. R.
338.

(*j*) 2 Arch. Pr. 38. See 1 Saund. 92,
n. 3.

(*k*) Donley v. Brownlee, 7 Barr, 109.

(*l*) Eichelberger v. Smyser, 8 W. 181.

(*m*) 2 Arch. Pr. 39.

(*n*) Smith v. Ramsey, 6 S. & R. 576.

(*o*) Tidd, 680.

(*p*) Smith v. Ramsey, 6 S. & R. 576.

(*q*) Fursht v. Overdeer, 3 W. & S. 471.

(*r*) Frear v. Drinker, 8 Barr, 520.
Roberts v. Halstead, 9 Barr, 34.

(*s*) Bull. N. P. 230 ; 3 Salk. 296, pl. 5.

(*t*) Foster v. Shaw, 7 S. & R. 163.

(*u*) 2 L. U. S. 102;

of the court annexed, if there be a seal, together with a certificate of the judge, chief justice, or presiding magistrate, as the case may be, that the said attestation is in due form." But a copy of a record from another State, not certified according to this act, may still be received as *prima facie* evidence.(v)

If the record be not produced, or if there be a *material* variance between the record produced to the court, and that pleaded, as in the names or numbers of the parties, the amount of damages, &c., it is a failure of the record, and judgment will be rendered in favor of the party pleading *nul tiel record.*(w)

Upon a *scire facias* to revive a judgment and *nul tiel record* pleaded, the original judgment which was for want of an appearance, and without any declaration, will not be treated as a nullity; although erroneous, yet the only point to be examined under the issue is whether there is a substantial variance between the judgment and the *scire facias*. In the absence of a declaration, the original judgment goes for the sum stated in the writ, and stands as if rendered on a declaration. It is no variance that a different sum was indorsed on the execution on the original judgment, which is immaterial, forming as it does no part of the record.(x)

On a replication of *nul tiel record* to a plea in abatement, the judgment for the plaintiff is not final, but only *respondeat ouster*, for failure of record in this case is not peremptory.(y) In other cases, the judgment is interlocutory or final, according to the nature of the action. If the former, a writ of inquiry must be executed, or damages assessed by the clerk in the same manner as on a judgment by default.(z) Judgment for the defendant is of course final.(zz) Where, after an issue on a plea of payment, a plea of *nul tiel record* was added the day before the trial, to which was replied, *quod habetur tale recordum*, and issue, and a verdict was found for the plaintiffs, the mere entry of judgment by the court, generally (where the record is of the same court), without its appearing that a day was given to produce the record, or that the court decided the issue on inspection, is regular, under our practice, though informal.(a) ·

A bill of exceptions to the judgment of the court, on a plea of *nul tiel record*, may be taken, it is said, where an exemplification of a record of another State has been offered in evidence, unless the exception has been set forth in the pleadings; and by this means the paper offered had been tacked to the record.(b)

Where a defendant pleads former recovery, setting out a record of a judgment which he avers to have been for the same cause of action, and the plaintiff replies *nul tiel record*, he admits by so doing the averment in the plea of the identity of the cause of action, and only puts in issue the existence of the record. His proper course, if he wishes to deny such identity, is to traverse the averment.(c)

(v) Backer *et al. v.* Field, 2 Y. 532. See Wh. Dig. "Evidence," ii. iii. "Judgment," xi.

(w) Com. Dig. Record, C. 7, T. R. 443. n. d.   2 Root, Con. Rep. 90, 437.

(x) Hirsch *v.* Groff, 2 W. & S. 449; see Eichelberger *v.* Smyser, 8 W. 182.

(y) Ld. Ray. 550.

(z) 2 Arch. Pr. 39.

(zz) Eichelberger *v.* Smyser, 8 W. 182.

(a) Share *v.* Hunt, 9 S. & R. 404.

(b) Per BRACKENRIDGE, J., Frey *v.* Wells, 4 Y. 505.

(c) U. S. *v.* Ashmead, U. S. Dist. Ct. 1848. KANE, J.

If there be pleas concluding to the country, and also a plea of *nul tiel record*, and it appears that the parties went to trial generally, the Supreme Court will presume that the issues were respectively decided by the proper tribunal.(*d*)

Error lies to the judgment of the court below on an issue of *nul tiel record*. It is too late to doubt the power of the court to review, in such cases, the decisions of inferior tribunals.(*e*)

When removed, it has been the practice for the record to be certified by the court below without a bill of exceptions; evidence short of record evidence suffices to identify the papers, without requiring the record brought in for inspection to be made a formal part of the proceedings. ·This practice has, however, been objected to as inconvenient, and the record on which issue is joined ought, in such cases, to be attached by means of a bill of exceptions or certificate, or otherwise, so as to form part of the record returned.(*f*)

(*d*) Baxter *v.* Graham, 5 W. 418.
(*e*) Crutcher *v.* Com. 6 Wh. 350.

(*f*) Crutcher *v.* Com. 6 Wh. 350.

CHAPTER XXIII.

OF THE PROCEEDINGS FROM ISSUE TO TRIAL.

THE cause being at issue, it is incumbent on the plaintiff to proceed to trial at the first opportunity, or in case of his neglect, the defendant may move for judgment, as in case of nonsuit, unless the proceedings are suspended by some legal cause, as by a commission to examine witnesses residing out of the State. By the constitution of Pennsylvania,(a) the Supreme Court, together with the several Courts of Common Pleas, have the power of a Court of Chancery, which relates to the obtaining of evidence from places not within the State. The mode in which this power is exercised, we shall briefly consider in the present chapter, after having, as a preliminary subject, first treated of the rule to take the depositions of witnesses residing within the State.

SECTION I.

OF THE RULE TO TAKE DEPOSITIONS ;—THE NOTICE OF TAKING THEM ;— BEFORE WHOM, AND THE MANNER IN WHICH THEY ARE TO BE TAKEN, —AND WHEN THEY MAY BE READ IN EVIDENCE.

I. *Of the Rule to take Depositions.*

In England, when a party in a cause is fearful of losing the testimony of a material witness, who is perhaps so old or so infirm that he may not live until the trial takes place (which may be, and is frequently deferred by the other party for his own convenience), or perhaps his necessary business, as a trading voyage or employment abroad, obliges him to leave the country immediately, *a motion is made in term time, or an application to a judge in vacation, to examine such witness de bene esse (that is, conditionally);* the consequence of which is to admit the depositions so taken as evidence, if the person cannot afterwards be produced and examined in chief at the trial.(b) But in this State, "rules to take the depositions of ancient, infirm, and going witnesses, to be read in evidence, on the usual terms, *are of course,* and may be entered by either party, stipulating a reasonable notice to the adversary." The *just* construction of this rule is, that it should stipulate itself, that is, fix and ascertain the number of days' notice; but the construction

---

(a) Art. v. § 6.   (b) Euno. Dial. II. § 30.

must now, so far as respects this, depend on the usage and practice of the courts.(c)

The rule of the Supreme Court is, that there must be forty-eight hours' notice within this city or county, and four days' notice out of the city and county, and within forty miles of the city. And in the same court, rules to take the depositions of witnesses within the State, at a greater distance than forty miles, may be entered of course, and the depositions may be taken before any person legally authorized to administer oaths or affirmations, on fifteen days' notice. § 1.

No rule to take depositions (except in the case of ancient, infirm, or going witnesses, or for a commission) shall be entered by the plaintiff until a declaration be filed, and a bill of particulars furnished (in cases where it is necessary); or by the defendant until he has entered special bail in suits commenced by *capias*, or an appearance in suits commenced by summons. § 4.

The rules of the District Court are as follows:—

XXXV. Notwithstanding a rule of court has been obtained for taking depositions of witnesses, and that they shall be read in evidence at the trial of the cause, in case of the death, absence out of the State, or other legal inability of such witness to attend; yet, in case the witness is resident within this State, and within forty miles of the place of trial, it is ordered, that the deposition shall not be read in evidence, unless the party offering it shall satisfy the court that a subpœna has been actually taken out (except in case the witness is out of the State), and that the witness has been duly subpœnaed, or could not be found, after reasonable pains taken for that purpose.

XXXVI. A rule to take the depositions of ancient, infirm, and going witnesses, to be read in evidence on the usual terms, is of course, and may be entered by either party, stipulating a reasonable notice to the adversary: so of a rule for a commission to any of the United States, or to foreign parts. But the interrogatories must be filed in the prothonotary's office at the time, and written notice of this last rule, and of the names of the commissioners, must be served on the adverse party at least fifteen days before the commission issues, in order that he may file cross-interrogatories, or nominate commissioners on his part.

The 36th rule is hereby extended to all witnesses, without regard to the circumstance of their being ancient, infirm, or going witnesses, stipulating, however, eight days' notice to the adverse party; subject, nevertheless, in all other respects, to the existing rules and regulations.

Saturday, December 12, 1846. The court made the following order, to wit: *Order of Court explanatory of 35th Rule of Court.*—Whereas, by a rule of July 3d, 1837, the former practice of taking depositions of witnesses to be read in evidence on the usual terms under a rule for that purpose, entered of course, by either party, was extended to all witnesses without regard to the circumstance of their being ancient, infirm, or going witnesses, stipulating, however, eight days' notice to the adverse party, and subject in all other respects to existing rules and regulations, but the said rule not having been transcribed in the revisal of the rules of court, recognized by the court's order of 24th March, 1842, doubts having been suggested whether the said rule may not have been impliedly

(c) M'Connell v. M'Coy, 7 S. & R. 223; S. P., Cunningham v. Irwin, ibid. 247.

I.—28

repealed by the said order, it is hereby declared, that the said rule is still in force.

XXXVII. All depositions of witnesses under a rule of this court, to be used in evidence on the trial, shall be taken before a judge, justice of the peace, alderman, or an examiner appointed by the court, upon due notice to the opposite party or his attorney.

XXXVIII. On all motions or rules to show cause, on the hearing of which facts are to be investigated, the testimony of the witnesses shall be taken by depositions in writing before a judge, justice of the peace, alderman, or an examiner appointed by the court, upon reasonable notice in writing to the opposite party or his attorney; and no witnesses shall be examined at the bar, but by a special and previous order of the court.

XXXIX. On the return and opening of any commission, or filing of any deposition, either party may give notice thereof to the opposite party, who shall within ten days after service of such notice, file with the prothonotary a specification of his exceptions, if he have any, to the form or execution of the commission or taking of the deposition, or to the mode of swearing the witnesses, or to any of the acts or omissions of the commissioners, examiners, or officers, or of any other person or persons, in or about the same. No exception to the admissibility of the evidence so returned or filed, not included in such specification, shall be taken on the trial of the cause, unless it be an exception that might be taken to the evidence, if the witness were offered for examination orally in court: *Provided*, That nothing herein be construed to permit or sanction the reading on trial, in any case, of the answers or deposition of a witness resident within the State, and within forty miles of the City of Philadelphia. In all cases of exception filed as above, by either party, the other party may, before the trial of the cause, on motion, obtain a decision of the court upon the sufficiency or insufficiency of the exceptions; and such decisions shall not be reconsidered upon the trial, but a bill of exceptions thereto shall be signed, if required, at the trial in the same manner as if the decision had taken place during the trial. *Provided*, That the motion for such a decision be made within ten days after the exceptions are filed; and that, if the same be not made within that time, the decision thereon can only be had upon the trial.(*cc*)

XL. Subpœnas for witnesses residing within the City or County of Philadelphia shall be taken at least five days previously to the day assigned for the trial of the action in which their attendance shall be required, or such action shall not be continued on account of the absence of any such witness, if he were or might be found at his residence within that period. But this rule will not dispense with the obligation to take the deposition of any such witness, where the party requiring his attendance knows, previously to that period, that such witness intends to be absent from the county at the time of the trial.

A deposition taken *under a rule of court*, and executed by a *justice of the peace*, may be read in the Circuit Court, the 30th section of the judicial act of 1789 relating merely to depositions taken without such rule.(*d*)

(*cc*) See *post*, 448.   (*d*) Banert *v.* Day, 3 W. C. C. R. 243.

On appeals to the Supreme Court, a party may, at any time, without a special order, have a rule to take depositions on ten days' notice; but if a shorter notice be requisite, the rule for it must be obtained on motion.(*dd*)

A rule to take the depositions of such persons *de bene esse*, may be granted before the return of the writ.(*e*) It may also be entered in the court below, while the cause is pending in the Supreme Court, on a writ of error.(*f*) The act of 26th of March, 1827, provides expressly for entering a rule in such a case. The action remains stated on the docket; and it is proper that a party should have power to perpetuate his testimony while his cause is pending anywhere.(*g*)

There is no process by which a witness can be compelled to attend for the purpose of being examined *de bene esse*;(*h*) but the court must be applied to for an order in the nature of a subpœna. A witness attending before a magistrate, whether voluntarily or by compulsory process, to give his deposition under a rule of court, in a suit depending, will be discharged by the court, of which the arrest is a contempt, if arrested on his return from the magistrate's office, under a writ from the District Court of the United States.(*i*) And such application may be made in the absence of the witness defendant, and after bail given.(*j*)

II. *Of the Notice of taking Depositions.*

As the rules just quoted require notice to be given to the adverse party, notice to his attorney is not sufficient.(*k*) However, in practice, "service of notice on the attorney is held insufficient in the case of depositions, only where the attorney has objected at the time of service. To be exempt from the trouble and responsibility of transmitting the notice to his client, is a personal privilege, which, if he please, he may waive; and he does tacitly waive it, by not objecting; otherwise, the adverse party might be taken by surprise. The silence of the attorney, therefore, is equivalent to an agreement; which will bind his client."(*l*) When the rule is entered before the return of the writ, notice should be given to the defendant.(*m*)

Service of notice on the special bail of the defendant is not good, although he attends and cross-examines the witness, if another person has usually acted as agent in the absence of the defendant.(*n*) So, service on the plaintiff's wife, though a party to the process, the husband being out of the State, is not good, if she have not acted in the business.(*o*) So, service on the defendant's daughter, more than ten days before the appointed time, was held insufficient, both parties living near each other in the same town, and the defendant being absent at the time of service.(*p*) But a service, by leaving notice at the dwelling-

(*dd*) Armstrong's Est. 6 W. 234.
(*e*) Gilpin *v.* Semple, 1 D. 251; Stotesbury *v.* Covenhoven, ibid. 164; see, also, Anonymous, 1 Y. 404; —— *v.* Galbraith, 2 D. 78.
(*f*) Huidekoper *v.* Cotton, 3 W. 56.
(*g*) Ibid.
(*h*) 1 Dunl. Pr. 552.
(*i*) United States *v.* Edme, 9 S. & R. 147.

(*j*) Ibid. See *ante*, p. 255.
(*k*) Nash *v.* Gilkeson, 5 S. & R. 352.
(*l*) Newlin *v.* Newlin, 8 S. & R. 41; Snyder *v.* Wilt, 3 H. 65.
(*m*) Gilpin *v.* Semple, 1 D. 251.
(*n*) Weaver *v.* Cochran, 3 Y. 168.
(*o*) Bauman *v.* Zinn, Id. 157; though see Cunningham *v.* Jordan, 1 Barr, 443.
(*p*) Lemon *v.* Bishop, 1 Pa. R. 485.

house of the party with his son, is sufficient.(*q*)   Where the defendant is merely a stakeholder, and the suit is instituted by agreement,. to try the right of the plaintiff or a third person to money in the defendant's hands, notice of taking a deposition on behalf of the plaintiff should be given to such third person; a notice to the defendant is not sufficient.(*r*) But notice to an agent has always been considered good; and where a suit has been marked to the use of another, notice to the plaintiff on the record, of the time and place of taking a deposition, is sufficient, where he has always appeared in the suit either as party or agent.(*s*)

A notice, not signed by any one, though regularly served, is insufficient to enable a deposition to be read in evidence.(*t*)

Where a rule of court empowers depositions to be taken on notice as of course, providing, that either party may send written interrogatories to the commissioner; and notice was given that depositions would be taken before A, at, &c., or some other person competent to administer an oath, and the depositions were taken before B, a person competent to administer an oath, at the time and place appointed, which was the office of A; it was held, that the depositions were regular.(*tt*)

Where the sheriff returns to a notice of the time and place of taking a deposition, that he served it on the opposite party by leaving a copy with his wife, it is sufficient, the presumption being that he served it at the dwelling-house.(*u*)

It is no objection to the admissibility of a deposition, that notice of the taking of it was served on the attorney on the other side, it appearing that he acquiesced in it, and that the deposition had been admitted in a former trial of the same case without objection.(*v*)   Where the rule of court requires service of notice of a rule on the party, service on the attorney, it is true, has been held insufficient, though he do not expressly object to the service at the time; and it was said that the general rule to the contrary, stated in Newlin *v.* Newlin,(*w*) was so laid down for cases in which no such express rule of court intervenes.(*x*) But the sound rule seems to be, that whether a notice to take depositions be rightly served upon the party or his attorney, depends upon the rule of the court in which the cause is depending, and that in the absence of proof of any rule on the subject, it will be presumed that the court below decided rightly in respect to it.(*y*)   And the inclination now is to return to the old rule that the objection to the service by the attorney must be immediate and unequivocal.

Notice to take depositions on consecutive days is not necessarily bad in every instance; but merely where one witness is to be examined and the notice wants precision.   But where there are many witnesses, notice to take their depositions, under a common rule, on three consecutive days, is good, where it indicates that the business is to be commenced on a day certain, and continued throughout the period.(*z*)

(*q*) Campbell *v.* Shrum, 3 W. 60.
(*r*) Nicholson *v.* Eichelberger, 6 S. & R. 546.
(*s*) Dennis *v.* Barber, 8 Id. 425.
(*t*) McDonald *v.* Adams,7 W. & S. 371.
(*tt*) Alexander *v.* Alexander, 5 Barr, 277.
(*u*) Snyder *v.* Wilt, 3 H. 65.

(*v*) Ibid.
(*w*) 8 S. &. R. 41.
(*x*) Cunningham *v.* Jordan, 1 Barr, 443.
(*y*) Ives *v.* Niles, 5 W. 323 ; Snyder *v.* Wilt, *supra.*
(*z*) Phillipi *v.* Bowen, 2 Barr, 21.

A rule of court requiring fifteen days' notice of a commission for the opposite parties to file interrogatories, it was held that the latter had the whole of the fifteen days for the purpose, and that a commission taken out at the close of the fifteenth day, though after the prothonotary's office had closed, was irregular.(zz)

And where a rule requires, "if the notice be in pursuance of any rule of court, a copy of it shall be prefixed to the notice and proved in like manner," and no copy of the rule to take depositions was served with the notice to take the depositions, it was held, that depositions, without such copy prefixed, could not be read.(a)

Where the rule of court does not require the names of witnesses to be inserted in notices of taking depositions, depositions taken without such insertion in the notice, will be received.(aa)

A deposition taken under a rule of court, but without notice to the opposite party, is not admissible, although a person, said to have had an interest in the land, attended at the taking of the deposition, and cross-examined the witness.(b)

It is unusual, and productive of uncertainty, to assign two days for the attendance of the opposite party, though they be consecutive. It is better to give notice only of the time of commencement, leaving the other side to take notice of the adjournments.

The examiner's name should appear in the notice, to enable the party to send cross-interrogatories to him in a sealed envelop.

When taken by the magistrate, the testimony must be orally delivered before him in a regular course of judicial examination, and reduced to writing by him, or some one by his authority.(bb)

A notice of the taking of depositions of witnesses under a rule of court, should contain *convenient certainty* as to the time and place of taking them; and, therefore, a notice that they would be taken "at the house of Thomas Fanneghan, in Bedford county, on the 20th of February," is not sufficiently certain.(c) Where the rule was for taking depositions on reasonable notice, a notice on the 11th, for taking depositions at ten in the morning of the 13th, was held to be too short, in the country.(cc) As to the time requisite in a notice in the country, there appears to be no fixed rule or uniform practice throughout the State regulating it; ten days' notice appears to be the usual time given, and therefore it might be prudent, *ex majore cautelâ*, always to afford this time, if possible; though a less time, as nine, and even six days' notice, where the parties lived near each other, has been held to be sufficient.(d)

It seems to be, and certainly ought to be a rule, that if the party notified has had reasonable time for preparation to attend at the taking of depositions under a rule of court, they will be received in evidence at the trial. In case, then, a rule be entered in vacation for taking depositions, and the notice to the other party stipulate a time which he may

(zz) Van Arminge v. Ellmaker, 4 Barr, 281.

(a) Alexander v. Alexander, 5 Barr, 277.

(aa) Cadbury v. Volen, 5 Barr, 320.
(b) Vincent v. Lessee of Huff, 4 S. & R. 298.

(bb) Carmalt v. Post, 8 W. 409.
(c) Sheeler v. Speer, 3 Bin. 130.
(cc) Hamilton v. M'Guire, 2 S. & R. 478.

(d) Carpenter v. Groof, 5 S. & R. 162.

think too short, or unreasonable, he ought to apply, at the *next* term, to the court to suppress them.(*dd*)

Where a notice to take depositions in pursuance of a rule of court specifies a particular place for the purpose, the depositions cannot be read in evidence, unless it appear from the certificate of the justice that they were taken at the place appointed.(*e*)

A party who has notified a justice of the peace before whom depositions were taken on behalf of the opposite party, and who requested the justice in his absence to ask certain questions, will not be permitted to allege want of notice.(*ee*)

Filing cross-interrogatories waives notice of rule.(*f*)

A misdirection of the notice to the plaintiff instead of the defendant, though served on the right party, is, although a clerical error, calculated to mislead, and a deposition taken under it will be rejected.(*ff*)

As to notices in general, any defect in them is cured, if the adverse party attend at the taking of the depositions.(*g*)

III. *Before whom, and the manner in which Depositions are to be taken.*

It is expressly ordered by the District Court, " that all depositions of witnesses, under a rule of that court, to be used in evidence on the trial, shall be taken before a judge, justice of the peace, alderman, or an examiner appointed by the court, upon due notice to the opposite party or his attorney." It has been decided that a rule to take depositions, implies, without its being so expressed in it, that they are to be taken before some judge or justice, having authority to administer an oath.(*h*) A deposition taken under a rule of court, before a justice of the peace, is evidence, although it does not appear on the face of the deposition that the person before whom it was taken was a justice, if the fact can be sufficiently shown by other proof.(*i*) The taking of depositions before examiners, specially appointed by the court, is not frequent in practice, in consequence of the expense attending it ; neither is it in general expedient, unless the testimony be perplexed and voluminous, or belong to a cause of an important character.

The court, on a preliminary rule taken, will strike off depositions in which there are material interlineations not noted in the *jurat.*(*j*)

Though the rule to take depositions implies that the examiner be a

---

(*dd*) Ibid.
(*e*) M'Cleary *v.* Sankey, 4 W. & S. 113.
(*ee*) Barnet *v.* School Directors, 6 W. & S. 46.
(*f*) Insurance Co. *v.* Francia, 9 Barr, 395.
(*ff*) Adams *v.* Easton, 6 W. 463.
(*g*) Selin *v.* Snyder, 7 S. & R. 172; Lessee of Porter *v.* Johnson, 2 Y. 92. See Wh. Dig. " Practice," xiii.(*b*)
(*h*) Keller *v.* Nutz, 5 S. & R. 246.
(*i*) Berks County Commissioners *v.* Ross, 3 Bin. 539.
(*j*) Williams *v.* Pool, Saturday, Sept. 23, 1848. D. C. Exceptions to deposition. *Per curiam.* There appear to be

alterations of which no note or memorandum was made by the alderman as having been made at the time. They are, also, in very material parts of the testimony. We do not say that, upon parol evidence of the magistrate, at the trial, these alterations were made at the time, and that the deposition was duly taken at the hour named in the notice (in regard to which, also, there is an erasure), that the deposition would be inadmissible. But the plaintiff has put these exceptions down for argument, and unexplained they are certainly fatal. The fifth and ninth exceptions sustained, and the other exceptions dismissed.

judge or justice, though it be not so set down; and though the prothonotary has no power to administer oaths in matters that do not belong to his office; still, such a power may be delegated to him by rule as fully as by commission, or by appointment, or by a verbal direction to a bystander in the presence of the court. If the rule contain such a delegation, it is sufficient; and the want of this may be supplied by consent, which makes testimony competent under an extra-judicial oath, or without any oath. Liability to prosecution for perjury is not always the test of competency. Appearance and cross-examination, therefore, will waive all objection to the examiners' authority.(*k*)

A rule to take depositions before any judge or justice, on ten ·days' notice, does not authorize the taking of depositions in another county,(*l*) although the notice to take them mention that county. It appears that it should be expressed in the rule.

The certificate of a justice that the witness was duly qualified and examined at the time and place stated in the caption, the caption being in the ordinary form, shows sufficiently that the witness was sworn before he was examined.(*m*)

It is not necessary in depositions before a justice, that there should be a certificate at the end of each deposition, that the witness was sworn, and had subscribed it. The general caption and certificate are sufficient.(*n*)

A deposition taken *ex parte* under a rule of court, *after* the hour named in the rule, cannot be read in evidence.(*o*) But it seems that it may, if the opposite party had notice, and did not attend *at* the hour named.(*p*) So, a deposition taken *before* the hour indicated by the rule and notice, was admitted in evidence, there being no proof that the adverse party had attended at *any* hour of the appointed day.(*q*)

A deposition ought to be reduced to writing from the mouth of the witness, in the presence of the justice or magistrate, and in general ought, though it need not in all cases, be drawn by him. In case of difference of opinion in taking down the words of the witness, the magistrate should decide. Depositions are sometimes drawn by the counsel of the party by consent, or where both parties attend. But without such consent, a deposition in the handwriting of the counsel is inadmissible in evidence.(*r*) In still later decisions, the court lay down the rule to be, that the whole deposition should be in the handwriting of the magistrate, unless by agreement on the face of it otherwise.(*s*) And it is immaterial whether the counsel who pens the deposition was concerned in the conduct of the cause, or was merely employed to take the deposition, or specially authorized to write it. The magistrate cannot make him his clerk for that purpose, unless by the express consent or acquiescence of the other party.(*t*) So, if it has been drawn by an agent, party, or relation of a party having or feeling an interest in the

(*k*) Phillipi *v.* Bowen, 2 Barr, 20.
(*l*) 1 Br. 255.
(*m*) Sample *v.* Robb, 4 H. 305.
(*n*) Morss *v.* Palmer, 3 H. 51.
(*o*) Bachman's case, 2 Bin. 72.
(*p*) Ibid.
(*q*) Lessee of Sweitzer *v.* Meese, 6 Bin. 500.

(*r*) Summers *v.* McKim, 12 S. & R. 405.
(*s*) Patterson *v.* Patterson, 2 Pa. R. 200.
(*t*) Addleman *v.* Masterson, 1 Pa. R. 457.

cause; and the fact that such a deposition had been filed a number of years, and read on a former trial before arbitrators, and in court, without objection, does not alter the case.(*u*)

Though the justice may employ the witness to write down his own testimony, it must appear that he actually did so, his testimony being orally delivered in the justice's hearing and presence. A deposition previously written by the witness, the caption being prefixed to it by the justice, is inadmissible.(*v*) And the rule now is, that it is not fatal to the admissibility of depositions that they are in the handwriting of one of the counsel concerned, if it appear that they were so written with the assent of the counsel of the opposing interest.(*w*)

It is not necessary that a copy of the rule to take depositions should be produced to the magistrate, unless he require it, nor that it should be served on the opposite attorney.(*x*)

The person before whom a deposition is to be taken, has no power to adjourn, from time to time, without consent and without notice, although the defendant have neglected to appear at the time first appointed by the notice; because *then* the depositions might have been taken *ex parte*; and the defendant is not bound to take notice of the adjournments.(*y*)

Where a deposition is taken before a justice, on interrogatories, it is the duty of the justice to put the interrogatories severally to the witnesses, and obtain distinct answers to each; and if the witness refuse to answer, he must certify the matter at the foot of the deposition.(*z*)

The parties or their counsel, when before the magistrate, may respectively examine and cross-examine the witness, but the questions or interrogatories put to him need not be stated in the deposition.(*a*)

It is a fatal exception that witness was not sworn until after deposition taken, where he refused to answer on cross-examination.(*b*)

It is no objection to the admissibility of a deposition, that the witness testifies to its containing the substance of a memorandum, then before him, made to aid his recollection, but which memorandum does not accompany the deposition;(*c*) nor will an admission by the witness that he had made a previous deposition in the case, from a memorandum in the handwriting of one of the parties to the suit, but which was a copy of one of his own, and the substance of which is contained in the deposition in question, invalidate the latter.(*d*)

Depositions are not admissible, being *ex parte*, if it appear that the witness was not sworn until after his testimony had been reduced to writing. The error is waived by the opposite party's not objecting to it before the justice or examiner.(*e*)

The exhibits spoken of by the deponent should be referred to in the

(*u*) Swearingen *v.* Pendleton, 3 Pa. R. 41; Grayson's Bannon, 8 W. 524.
(*v*) McEntire *v.* Henderson,1 Barr,402.
(*w*) Farm. and Mech. Bk. *v.* Woods, 1 J. 99.
(*x*) 1 Br. 273.
(*y*) Hamilton *v.* Menor, 2 S. & R. 73.
(*z*) Vincent *v.* Lessee of Huff, 4 S. & R. 298.
(*a*) 1 Dunl. Pr. 551.

(*b*) McDonald *v.* Adams, 7 W. & S. 371; Stonebreaker *v.* Short, 8 Barr, 155.
(*c*) Craig *v.* Sibbett, 3 H. 241.
(*d*) Ibid. [The two preceding points were decided in this case, but the facts on which the decision was based not appearing in the report, are taken from the paper-book.]
(*e*) Armstrong *v.* Burrows, 6 W. 266.

body of the deposition, and either annexed to the deposition or so marked as to be identified.(f)

But where such exhibits have been annexed to a previous deposition, and are properly referred to in the subsequent one, and marked by the justice, the identification may be by parol testimony; and this need not be that of the justice himself.(g)

A deposition taken for the purpose of proving the execution of a paper, is not admissible, unless the paper be described with such precision as to identify it with ease and certainty. Thus, where a deposition, taken for the purpose of proving the execution of a due-bill, stated, "that the due-bill dated 28th December, 1839, signed P. M. & Co., is in the handwriting of M.," it was held that the deposition did not describe the due-bill with sufficient certainty, and therefore could not be read in evidence.(gg)

The court, as a general rule, will not compel a party to produce books and papers before a magistrate taking depositions under a pending rule,(h) though where a nominal plaintiff offers himself to testify, he will be compelled to produce his papers.(hh)

It is usual in practice for the party obtaining the rule (and also where no rule has been entered, but it has been agreed by the opposite attorneys to take the deposition without a rule), to examine and draw up the deposition of the witness by consent at office, in the first instance, and to produce it, together with the witness, before the magistrate; and if the witness swear or affirm to the truth of the deposition thus prepared, it will be regarded as if it were the result of an examination in the presence of the former. But this can only be by consent of attorneys.

Although an alderman or commissioner before whom depositions are taken under rule of court, may commit a witness who refuses to testify, yet the proper course is for the alderman to report the question to the

---

(f) Petriken v. Collier, 7 W. & S. 392; Dailey v. Green, 3 H. 127. BELL, J.

(g) Dailey v. Green, 3 H. 118.

(gg) Petriken v. Collier, 7 W. & S. 392.

(h) Thomas v. Smith, D. C. Oct. 27, 1849. Why plaintiff should not produce books and papers before the magistrate who takes the deposition. *Per curiam.* The act of Feb. 27, 1798, is a highly penal statute, and although it does not in terms confine the rule to produce books and papers to the trial of the cause, yet the uniform practice under the act has so confined it. To extend it farther would be accompanied with great danger and inconvenience. The right to inspect books and papers before the trial has, therefore, been confined to the cases where the parties have a common interest in the instrument of evidence called for. Where books and papers are produced before the court and jury in a public court, there is an evident restraint upon making a bad use of them. Were we to establish the precedent asked for, every defendant who was unwilling to pay the plaintiff's demand would resort to this mode for the purpose of fishing up a defence or attack upon the plaintiff from his books and papers. There are few merchants who would be willing, with such a power hanging over them, to have all their letter-books and account-books taken to the office of a justice of the peace, and then overhauled, studied, and copied by their adversary or his lawyer. I can only conceive of one case in which the court might safely make a rule to produce a paper in which the parties had not a common interest, before a magistrate or commissioner, and that would be in the case of a deed or other paper, to which the person proposed to be examined was a subscribing witness, and necessary to prove it.

R. D.

(hh) Borton v. Streeper, 2 M. 4.

court for their action. Where the attempt in such case is to interrogate a party, the court will refuse an attachment.(*i*)

The contents of a former deposition may, with the consent of the parties, be read to a witness for the purpose of refreshing his memory. But the answers to questions put on the taking of a second deposition, must be taken according to the present recollection of a witness ; and, therefore, if a witness does not recollect *all* the matters contained in a former deposition, and such former deposition be, nevertheless, copied into the second deposition, the latter will not be evidence.(*j*) A leading interrogatory (that is, one expressed in such a manner as to indicate to the witness the answer which it is wished he should make)(*k*) must be

(*i*) Pfiel *v.* Elmes, D. C., Friday, March 24, 1848. Motion for attachment against *Charles E. Elmes. Per curiam.* In this case a *fi. fa.* having been placed in the hands of the sheriff against Abner Elmes, and a levy made upon certain personal property, a claim thereto has been made by Charles E. Elmes. The sheriff has a rule pending to show cause why the time for making return of the *fi. fa.* should not be enlarged until he is indemnified by the plaintiff against the claim thus made. Under that rule, the plaintiff is taking depositions before Alderman Thomas D. Smith, and having subpœnaed the claimant, Charles E. Elmes, he appeared before the alderman, but refused to give evidence, by the advice of his counsel, upon the ground that, being a party to the proceeding, he could not be compelled to testify against himself. The alderman was thereupon asked to commit Mr. Elmes, but he refused, and has certified the proceeding for our determination.

In this case, the alderman has acted with entire propriety. However, in cases in which the witness should be compelled to appear and to testify, it is the province of the alderman or commissioner to issue an attachment or commit the witness. (Act of 26th Feb., 1831, Purd. 428.) Where this is refused by him, the party laying the proper ground by affidavit, may obtain, by special motion, a subpœna, directed to the witness, to appear and testify at the bar of the court, upon which an attachment may issue or the witness be committed, according as the circumstances require. So that the motion in this case should have been for a subpœna, and not for an attachment. However, we would refuse the subpœna, as we do not think the witness, in this case, ought to be compelled to give testimony against himself. The general rule is, that neither the party on record nor the party in interest can be compelled to testify. Thus, where a suit was instituted on a check,

in the name of the plaintiff, who had no interest, for the benefit of another, the defendant was not allowed to examine, nor either to prove usury. (Mauran *v.* Lame, 7 Cowan, 74; 1 Greenl. Ev. 330.) So in the common case of a hearing before an auditor, a claimant on the fund cannot be compelled to testify against his own claim, as it appears to us, though there is really, in strictness, no suit pending to which he is either party on the record or in interest. Still, he is substantially a party in a proceeding by the result of which he is to be directly affected; for a feigned issue may be awarded in the very case to try the validity of his claim, to which, of course, he would be made a party; and his evidence, forced from him on the hearing before the auditor, would be employed against him on the trial of the issue, just as effectually as if he had been compelled then to testify. This case is entirely analogous. If the sheriff had empannelled a jury *de proprietate probanda,* the issue would have been between the claimant and the plaintiff in the execution, asserting the property to be in the defendant. If the sheriff is indemnified, or otherwise proceeds with his levy, the claimant's only remedy will be an action of trespass against the sheriff, or trover against his vendee, in which actions the evidence now extracted from him may be used against him. A bill of discovery against a party is quite a different affair. He has time for deliberation and counsel in framing his answer. He is not brought up and answers elicited upon a *viva voce* examination to sudden, unexpected questions, and taken down in his unpremeditated language. An honest mistake, the result of embarrassment, may often in this way be fatal to him. It will be safest, then, to hold this case to be within the general rule. Motion denied.

(*j*) Bovard *v.* Wallace, 4 S. & R. 500.
(*k*) Selin *v.* Snyder, 7 S. & R. 166; and see Wogan *v.* Small, 11 S. & R. 143.

objected to at the time it is put to the witness. If no exception be then taken, the answer of the witness to the leading interrogatory cannot be opposed on that ground, when his deposition is read on the trial.(*l*)

Where testimony is taken on depositions as to the genuineness of an instrument, the original must be exhibited to the witness.(*m*)

The proper course is, on taking the deposition of a witness residing more than forty miles distant, or of a going witness, to insert in the deposition itself the preliminary proof of the witness's disability.(*n*)

Where a particular house is specified in the notice of the rule, at which depositions are to be taken, the justice's certificate must state it. It must appear to have been taken at the very spot—its omission is fatal.(*nn*)

Where a witness has been examined on interrogatories they must be attached to the return, so that the court may see whether the answers are pertinent.(*o*)

When the examination is concluded, the witness signs the deposition, and the judge or magistrate adds his *jurat*, and delivers the deposition to the party at whose instance it was taken, by whom it must be filed.(*oo*) As will presently be seen, an omission in this respect is attended with great risks.

IV. *When a Deposition regularly taken may be read.*

A deposition not taken or filed according to the rules established by the court, is not evidence ;(*p*) and it is important in this connection to keep in mind the very salutary rules now in force in most of the courts by which a party, by promptly filing the return, may exact from the other side an immediate disclosure of any technical exception. As has already been noticed, the court will then, if the exceptions be well founded, permit the commission or depositions to be sent back for amendment.(*pp*)

It is incumbent on the party who offers a deposition in evidence, at the taking of which the adverse party did not attend, to prove that it was taken according to notice. This may be done by parol evidence, or by certificate from the magistrate who swore the witnesses.(*q*)

Our rules of court severally order, that "notwithstanding a rule of the court has been obtained for taking the depositions of witnesses, and that they shall be read in evidence at the trial of the cause in case of the death, absence out of the State, or other legal inability of such witnesses to attend, yet it is required that the party offering such deposition in evidence shall satisfy the court that the witness, if resident within this State, and within forty miles of the place of trial, was duly subpœnaed, or could not be found after reasonable pains taken for that purpose ; otherwise the same may not be admitted."(*qq*)   A party to the

(*l*) Sheeler *v.* Speer, 3 Bin. 130, S. P.; Snyder *v.* Snyder, 6 Bin. 483; Strickler *v.* Todd, 10 S. & R. 63.

(*m*) Weidner *v.* Conner, 9 Barr, 78.

(*n*) Poole *v.* Williams, D. Ct. C. C. P. Dec. 1848.

(*nn*) McCleary *v.* Saubry, 4 W. & S. 113.

(*o*) Weidner *v.* Conner, 9 Barr, 78.

(*oo*) See, generally, Wh. Dig. " Practice," xiii. (c)

(*p*) Rambler *v.* Tryon, 7 S. & R. 90.

(*pp*) See pp. 434, 443, 452, 453.

(*q*) Selin *v.* Snyder, ibid. 172.

(*qq*) See *ante*, 443-4.

suit is competent to prove that a material witness was unable to attend, by reason of advanced age and indisposition, in order to entitle him to read his deposition.(r)

"When the deposition is taken it ought to be filed. It is not the property of the party on whose behalf it was taken, nor has he any right to withhold it. But it often happens that the party, at whose instance it was taken, finds himself mistaken, and the testimony proves unfavorable to him. In such case the adverse party has a right to make use of it, subject, nevertheless, to the rule of the court, which forbids the reading of it, if the witness lives beyond a certain distance, unless the court be satisfied that due diligence has been used to procure his attendance. This is a good rule, because the truth cannot be so completely elicited by a deposition as by a *viva voce* examination."(s)

If, then, he wish to secure testimony which he may think favorable to himself, it is his business to do it, by taking out a subpœna for the witness, and endeavoring to procure his personal attendance; for the party who took the rule to obtain the deposition of the witnesses may not like it, and if he do not, he is under no obligation to summon him.(t)

Whether the witness, whose deposition is offered in evidence, be able to attend the trial or not, is a matter which the court who try the cause are to inquire into and decide; and if they be satisfied of his inability, their admission of the deposition will not be a ground of error.(u)

The deposition of a witness far advanced in pregnancy may be read, where it was shown she resided eight miles from the court-house, and it was said it would not be proper for her to attend, though it was shown she was not at the time in ill health.(v)

When the witness has no stated home or family, his deposition taken in another State, at the place where he was at work at the time, may be read, and it will be presumed that he is out of the reach of a subpœna at the time of trial.(w) Under these circumstances depositions are always received in evidence.(x)

The deposition of a person lying in prison awaiting the decision of a criminal court upon a motion for a new trial, after conviction of a misdemeanor, may be taken under the rule of court in relation to ancient, infirm, and going witnesses.(xx)

It is the practice to take the depositions of non-residents temporarily here, under rules for that purpose, as going witnesses; and such depositions may be read, though subsequently retaken under commissions.(y)

(r) Lessee of Douglass v. Sanderson, 2 D. 117; 1 Y. 16.

(s) *Per* TILGHMAN, C. J., Gordon v. Little, 8 S. & R. 549; but see the opinion of GIBSON, J., ib. p. 655. As to the right of compelling the party to file a deposition in the office of the prothonotary, by a rule obtained on motion, see the opinions of the judges in this case, particularly that of GIBSON, J., against it. In a very recent case it was said by TILGHMAN, C. J., "We are told that counsel are in the habit of keeping possession of depositions taken under rule of court as if they were the property of the party who obtained the rule. This is all wrong. The depositions belong to neither party, but are for the use of both, and should be delivered to the prothonotary with all convenient speed as soon as they have been taken," Nussear v. Arnold, 13 S. & R. 327.

(t) Gordon v. Little, 8 S. & R. 549.
(u) Vinc n v. Lessee of Huff, 8 S. & R. 381.   e t
(v) Beitler v. Study, 10 Barr, 418.
(w) Gould v. Crawford, 2 Barr, 91.
(x) Ibid.
(xx) Crosby v. Williams, 4 P. L. J. 235.
(y) Schoneman v. Fegeley, 7 Barr, 437.

Whether a deposition may be read in consequence of the witnesses' inability to appear, is in the discretion of the court, subject, however, to review on error.(z) The court, however, intimated that it must be a strong case in which they would reverse for error.(a)

The rule requiring a subpœna to be thus taken out, and if possible served, is not meant, it will be at once observed, to direct an useless thing; such as issuing a subpœna for a witness actually residing in London, or any other distant country; though even this was once required in strict practice.(b) For the rule only exacts it when the witness is "resident within this State, and within forty-miles of the place of trial." In accordance with the spirit of this rule, therefore, the deposition of a witness residing out of the jurisdiction of the court is allowed to be read in the District Court, without the prior issuing of a subpœna.(c)

A deposition which was agreed to be read, but "*subject to all legal exceptions*," is not evidence in the Common Pleas, if the witness be within the jurisdiction of the court at the trial, although he has been subpœnaed, and neglected to attend.(d)

Although a deposition is stated to be taken by consent, yet it remains open to all legal exceptions, unless the contrary is expressly declared.(e)

A deposition taken by consent while a cause is depending before arbitrators, from whose award an appeal has been entered, cannot be read in evidence on the trial of the appeal, unless the witness be dead, or not within the State.(f) The ground of this decision is, that on an appeal the proceedings in court are *de novo ;* such a deposition, therefore, is to be considered as if taken in *another* suit, between the same parties, for the same cause of action ; and in that case the rule is, that the deposition would be evidence if the witness were dead, or if he were not within the State.(g)

A party cannot allege ignorance of the time and place of taking the deposition who has authorized the justice, in his absence, to cross-examine.(h)

If cross-interrogatories be not sent under the rule of court, the party cannot object that the notice did not give the name of the alternative magistrate before whom, in the absence of the commissioner named, the deposition is finally taken.(i)

When the rule of court directs that a copy of the rule to take the depositions be prefixed thereto, the depositions cannot be read without it.(j)

A cross-examination of a witness under a rule of court is not on the same footing with an examination upon the *voir dire,* and does not preclude the party from taking any legal exception at the trial, to the competency of the witness.(k)

(z) Dennison v. Fairchild, 7 W. 309.
(a) Pipher v. Lodge, 16 S. & R. 214; Dietrich v. Dietrich, 1 P. R. 318, and Vincent v. Huff, 8 S. & R. 387.
(b) Mifflin v. Bingham, 1 D. 276.
(c) 2 Br. 13.
(d) 1 Br. 252.
(e) Burke v. Lessee of Young, 2 S. & R. 383.
(f) Forney v. Hallagher, 11 S. & R.203.
(g) Id. ibid.
(h) Barnet v. School Directors, 6 W. & S. 49.
(i) Alexander v. Alexander, 5 Barr, 277.
(j) Ibid.
(k) Mifflin v. Bingham, 1 D. 275.

The deposition of a witness who afterwards becomes interested, and is in full life at the time of the trial, is admissible ;(*l*) but interest at the time incapacitates the deposition, though the witness afterwards becomes competent.(*ll*)

A deposition read by one party on the argument of a rule to show cause why a feigned issue should not be directed to try his right to money in court, cannot be read in evidence by the opposite party on the trial of the issue, when the witness is himself in court, and capable of being examined.(*m*) Perhaps, the reading of the deposition might be deemed an admission of the competency of the witness, so far as respected existing objections on the side of the party reading it, but it cannot be deemed such an admission of the contents of the deposition as to supersede the usual and salutary rule, that the best evidence in the power of the party must be given.(*n*)

It is to be presumed that a rule for depositions has been faithfully executed ; and at all events the party himself is competent to prove the time when they were taken.(*o*)

A notice having been given that a deposition would be taken at the office of Joseph *Stormer*, Esq., in a certain township, a deposition taken at the time and place appointed, and otherwise unobjectionable, at the office of Joseph *Stermer*, Esq., is admissible, it not being shown that there were two justices of these names in that township.(*p*)

Where a plaintiff took depositions to prove the handwriting of the maker of a note on which he had brought suit, and from facts contained in the depositions, an inference might have been drawn of the infancy of the defendant at the time the notes were made, whereupon the defendant added the plea of infancy, and afterwards, *without the leave of the court*, the plaintiff took other depositions of the same witness to explain and qualify the facts in the former depositions, and to prove the age of the defendant : It was held, that both depositions might be given in evidence by the plaintiff.(*pp*)

A deposition taken before amendment of name of party is not admissible.(*q*)

Where a deposition refers to books of account, copies of the entries referred to, duly authenticated, should be produced, at least, to entitle the deposition to be read.(*qq*)

It is no objection to a deposition, that it was not entitled, or expressed to have been taken under a rule of court, if it be annexed to a certified copy of the rule of court under which it was taken.(*r*) Nor is it a valid objection to reading a second deposition, that a former one has been taken.(*s*)

A party has a right to take a second deposition of the same witness without leave of the court or cause shown.(*t*) Should abuses of the rule to take depositions occur, the court will correct them ; but the

(*l*) Wolfinger *v.* Fortman, 6 Barr, 294; *contra*, Irwin *v.* Reed, 4 Y. 512.

(*ll*) Sch. Nav. *v.* Harris, 5 W. & S. 29.

(*m*) Stiles *v.* Bradford, 4 R. 394.

(*n*) Id. ibid.

(*o*) Black *v.* Moor, 1 Barr, 344.

(*p*) Sample *v.* Robb, 4 H. 305.

(*pp*) Watson *v.* Brewster, 1 Barr, 381.

(*q*) Horback *v.* Knox, Boggs, & Co. 6 Barr, 377.

(*qq*) Christie *v.* Woods, 2 Y. 213.

(*r*) Vincent *v.* Lessee of Huff, 8 S. & R. 381.

(*s*) 2 W. C. C. R. 7.

(*t*) Martin *v.* Caffroth, 16 S. & R. 120 ; Schoneman *v.* Fegeley, 7 Barr, 437.

practice to re-examine as often as occasion may require, is general, if not universal.(*u*)

A deposition is but secondary evidence, and admissible on proof of its having been taken under a competent authority, on due notice, and in a proper manner; and also, on proof that the contingency, for which it was intended to provide, has *actually* happened; and if it be admitted without this, it is error. Therefore, where a deposition was admitted on the ground of inability to attend, and the proof was that the witness had broken her leg eight years before, and had again been hurt the preceding autumn, but was a stout, active woman of her age, and had come a few days before to within ten miles of the court-house; that she was not able to walk to court, nor would it have been prudent to bring her to court on a wet day, such as that on which the cause was tried, unless in a covered carriage, in which she might have been safely brought: it was held that the deposition ought to have been rejected.(*v*)

A copy of a deposition, no account being given of the loss of the original, nothing proved but that due search had been made for it, the introductory evidence particularly defective in not showing that the paper was truly copied from the original, and the usual ground not laid to make way for the original itself, had it been produced, cannot be admitted in evidence.(*w*)

In cases of secondary evidence (such as a deposition is, as we have just seen), the question whether a sufficient introductory ground was laid, has always been the subject of a writ of error. In Lamberton *v.* Sanderson,(*x*) the Supreme Court reversed the judgment, because the court below had rejected evidence of an obligor's handwriting, although evidence had been given that the subscribing witness was out of the jurisdiction; and that, after *diligent inquiry*, no person could be found to prove his signature. So, a question of what was *reasonable notice*, where no particular time was specified in the rule, was entertained in Hamilton *v.* M'Guire, (*y*) and the same principle was involved in Sweitzer *v.* Meese,(*z*) and also in Carpenter *v.* Groff,(*a*) where the decision of the court below was reversed. There is an endless list of other cases where a court of error will inquire into the sufficiency of introductory evidence, as, for instance, of the existence, loss of, and search for deeds or other writings; of the notice to produce them; of evidence of interest, or an objection to a witness; or evidence of the execution of deeds or writings offered in evidence collaterally.(*b*)

When one party takes the deposition of a witness, and reads so much of it as supports his case, and stops, the other party may, generally speaking, read the rest of the deposition which is in his favor.(*c*) But where one party reads only part of a deposition without objection, the other will not be permitted in his turn to read the omitted parts for the sole purpose of contradicting them by other evidence.(*d*)

By the act of 28th March, 1814,(*e*) any deposition taken in any

(*u*) Ibid.
(*v*) Pipher *v.* Lodge, 16 S. & R. 214.
(*w*) Id. ibid.
(*x*) 4 Bin. 192.
(*y*) 2 S. & R. 478.
(*z*) 6 Bin. 500.

(*a*) 5 S. & R. 162.
(*b*) Pipher *v.* Lodge, 16 S. & R. 220.
(*c*) Breyfogler *v.* Breckley, 16 S. & R. 264.
(*d*) Logan *v.* McGinnis, 2 J. 2.
(*e*) 6 Sm. Laws, 208.

cause, which by the rules of law may be read in evidence on the trial of the cause in which it was taken, may be read in evidence in any subsequent cause between the same parties, their heirs, executors, administrators, or assigns.

In an ejectment against A for the use of the heirs of B, a deposition taken in a former ejectment by B against the same defendant for the same land, but in which the plaintiff claimed under a different title, cannot be read (*f*)

That depositions taken in a former ejectment may be read in a subsequent one, the latter cause must be between the same parties, or those claiming under the same parties, and the matter in issue must be the same, or at least part of the same property.(*g*) And the plaintiff cannot, by joining in one ejectment two defendants who hold by separate titles, read in evidence depositions taken in a former suit, in which one only of these defendants was party; especially if the land in controversy in the different suits be not the same.(*h*)

Under the rule of court by which objections to depositions on trial, other than to relevancy or competency, are excluded, unless notice of the objections in writing is given to the opposite counsel within ten days after notice of filing the deposition, or a motion is made on the first opportunity to suppress it, it was held, upon a deposition which was filed on Friday, notice of the filing having been given on Saturday, the term commencing on Monday, and on Tuesday exceptions being filed, and afterwards, on the same day, a jury being sworn in the case, the exceptions were in time.(*hh*)

A party objecting to a deposition, should state the ground of his objection, so that if it be but to a part, his opponent may withdraw the exceptionable matter, or that the court may overrule it; therefore, where objection is made to a deposition *in toto*, or there is a refusal to specify the particular exceptions to it, it will not be error to read it, if any part of it be legal evidence, though other parts of it may be inadmissible. This rule, however, may have exceptions.(*i*) Thus, it is said that the matter excepted to may be so very palpable, so directly opposed to every principle of justice, as to strike every man on the slightest investigation.(*j*)

SECTION II.

OF COMMISSIONS TO EXAMINE WITNESSES, AND OF LETTERS ROGATORY.

I. *Of Commissions.*

When the necessary witnesses in a cause reside altogether abroad, whether in another State, or in a foreign country, it is necessary to ob-

---

(*f*) Cluggage *v.* Duncan, 1 S. & R. 111. But see the observations of YEATES, J., Ib. 121, and see Wharton's Dig. "Evidence," iv. (*b*)

(*g*) Walker *v.* Walker, 16 S. & R. 380.

(*h*) Ibid.

(*hh*) Cunningham *v.* Jordan, 1 Barr, 442.

(*i*) Anderson *v.* Neff, 11 S. & R. 208. 219.

(*j*) Ibid. See Wharton's Dig. "Error," iv. (*b*) (*c*)

tain a commission from the court, directed to certain persons appointed and approved by the parties, *to examine such witnesses on interrogatories*. We shall consider the subject of commissions in this section with reference first to the manner of obtaining and preparing it; secondly, to the manner of executing it, and the costs of execution; and thirdly, to the subject of letters rogatory.

First—Of the manner of obtaining the rule for a commission and preparing the same:—

In England, a party has no means of obtaining the benefit of the testimony of a witness residing out of the jurisdiction of the court, if he cannot procure his personal attendance on the trial, unless his adversary will consent to the issuing of a commission; and the court cannot compel him (if the plaintiff) to give his consent, otherwise than by putting off the trial from time to time, until the defendant by a bill in equity, or the recovery of his witnesses, can have the benefit of their evidence; or (if it be the defendant who refuses), by denying him judgment as in case of a nonsuit.(*k*) But our practice is different; for our courts, as has been seen, have, under the constitution of the State, the power of a court of equity, which relates to the obtaining of evidence from places not within the State: and by their standing orders, "a rule for a commission to any of the United States, or to foreign parts, shall be of course, and may be entered by either party in the clerk's office; but the interrogatories must be filed in the clerk's office at the time, and a copy thereof, and written notice of the rule, and of the names of the commissioners must be served on the adverse party, at least fifteen days before the commission issues, in order that he may file cross-interrogatories, or nominate commissioners on his own part, if he shall deem it eligible."(*l*) In strict practice, a commission ought not to be taken out before the facts in dispute between the parties are put in issue;(*m*) but our practice justifies the rule before issue has been joined.(*n*)

The respective parties have a right to propose supplemental, direct, or cross-interrogatories, where new or further subjects of inquiry arise out of the preceding interrogatories of the other party. The interrogatories, together with the cross-interrogatories, if any, are then annexed to the commission, which is a writ sued out by the party who has entered the rule, and to whom it belongs to transmit it to the commissioners, and to do whatever else is requisite to obtain a speedy and regular examination, and return of the commission.(*o*)

Where a commission to take testimony has been returned with the last general interrogatory unanswered, the party issuing it, upon notice to the opposite side, may take a rule for its return in order that the interrogatory should be answered.(*oo*)

After the plaintiff has had a commission executed, the defendant may send a new commission, to examine the same witnesses on matters not inquired of by the plaintiff's interrogatories.(*p*) If the defendant cannot put cross-interrogatories as to a matter upon which the plaintiff

---

(*k*) See 1 Arch. Pr. 153.
(*l*) Lessee of Coxe *v.* Ewing, 4 Y. 429.
See *ante*, p. 433.
  (*m*) See 1 Har. Chan. Pr. 430.
  I.—29

(*n*) See 1 Caines's Rep. 73; 2 Id. 259.
(*o*) 1 Dunl. Pr. 547.
(*oo*) Hinckley *v.* Ins. Co. 4 Barr, 470.
(*p*) Hook *v.* Hackney, 16 S. & R. 385.

does not interrogate his witness in chief, the defendant may issue a commission to examine the witness *de novo.*(*q*)   But, it seems, that even if the objection lay to a commission, that it is only a commission to cross-examine, the objections to it should be made before the trial, in order to give the defendant an opportunity to issue a new one.(*r*)

If the commission be *ex parte*, that is, where one party will not join in it, no notice of the time and place of execution need be given to him.(*s*)

Although no rule for a commission appears on the docket, yet if the parties have joined in a commission, and filed their interrogatories, the deposition taken under it is evidence.(*t*)

A deposition, taken under a commission, in an action against two defendants, one of whom had not been summoned, and did not appear, was entitled against *both* defendants, but the actual defendant filed cross-interrogatories, it was held that this was merely a clerical error, and that the Supreme Court would consider it as if it had been amended by the court below.(*u*)

Without an order of court, it is not necessary to name the witnesses to be examined under a foreign commission, either in the rule, the interrogatories, or the commission itself.(*v*)

But where a case has been twice on the trial-list, and the defendant took out commissions to Nantucket and Boston on filing interrogatories, and gave notice to the plaintiff that the commissions would issue in fifteen days, if cross-interrogatories were not filed within that time, and an application being made to the defendant for the names of the witnesses, he declined giving them, the court on motion granted a rule upon the defendant to file the names of his witnesses, and enlarge the time of filing cross-interrogatories until fifteen days after the names should be given.(*vv*)

When any of the interrogatories filed appear irrelevant, the opposite party is at liberty to move the court to strike off such interrogatories. Except, however, in a clear case, the court will refuse thus to exclude evidence on any contingent issue.(*w*)

A commission regularly issued, is a stay of all proceedings, so that the plaintiff cannot proceed to trial, or the defendant move for judgment as in case of nonsuit, until the court, on application, vacate the rule, though(*x*) if the party who sues out a commission, does not use due diligence to get it returned in proper time, the court will permit the

---

(*q*) Ibid.

(*r*) Id. ibid.

(*s*) Nussear *v.* Arnold, 13 S. & R. 326; 4 Cranch, 224.

(*t*) Dawson *v.* Tibbs, 4 Y. 349.

(*u*) 3 S. & R. 402.

(*v*) Heaton *v.* Findlay, 2 J. 310; see Packer *v.* Nixon, 1 Bald. 291; Leggett *v.* Austin, 2 P. L. J. 247.

(*vv*) Leggett *v.* Austin, Dist. Ct. C. C. P., 2 P. L. J. 247.

(*w*) Pingree *v.* Griffin, D. C., Saturday, May 27, 1848.   Why the interrogatories filed should not be stricken off. *Per curiam.* Where the pleas are so general as *non assumpsit* and payment, it is impossible to say beforehand what may, or may not be relevant to the question to be finally determined. The matter which at this stage may seem to us the most remote, may turn out in reality to lie at the very heart of the controversy. Every party takes his depositions under a commission under the penalty of bearing not only his own costs, but those of his adversary, if the evidence should turn out to be impertinent. We must, however, wait to see the result before we can determine that. Rule dismissed, and rule for the commission extended fifteen days from this date.

(*x*) 1 Caines's Rep. 73.

trial to proceed, notwithstanding the commission.(*y*) What shall be a reasonable time for the execution and return of a commission, depends upon the circumstances of the case, such as the remoteness or proximity of the place where the commissioners and witnesses reside, the frequency and facility of intercourse, &c. The period of eight months from the time of obtaining the rule, seems to be sufficient for the return of a commission to be executed in Great Britain, or other maritime country in Europe; and it has been held that three months was a sufficient time for executing and returning a commission arrived in London.(*z*)

By the act of March 30, 1829,(*a*) entitled, " A further supplement to the act entitled, ' An act to amend and consolidate, with its several supplements, the act entitled, An act for the recovery of debts and demands not exceeding one hundred dollars, before a justice of the peace, and for the election of constables, and for other purposes,' " it is provided that, " in all cases when a suit shall be pending before a justice of the peace, it shall be lawful for either party to obtain testimony out of the State, in the same manner as is directed by the eighth section of the act to which this is a supplement."

" In all such cases, where it shall not be convenient to take the testimony of witnesses before a justice of the peace, it shall be lawful for the party or parties to name a commissioner, who, on receiving a certificate of his appointment, with a copy of the rule and interrogatories, certified by the alderman or justice of the peace, shall have authority to administer oaths and affirmations, and take the answers of witnesses therein named; and depositions so taken shall be as good, to all intents and purposes, as if the same were taken before a justice of the peace." And by the act of February 26, 1831,(*b*) the commissioners may issue subpœnas to witnesses in the same manner as in a court of record, and the witness is liable for the penalty named in the subpœna, and to an attachment when refusing to testify. This latter act consists of four sections, which, with the preceding one, makes the system for obtaining evidence in suits before justices and aldermen very complete.

Secondly—Of the manner of executing a commission :—

Many commissions are excluded from being read on account of their not being executed regularly. It is therefore usual to accompany a commission with minute instructions to the commissioners, both as to the manner in which they are to proceed to take the examination of the witnesses, and as to the cautions to be observed in returning the commission after the depositions have been taken. Commissioners can seldom commit an error if they read their authority with care, which it is their duty strictly to pursue, and recollect that though nominated by a party, they are not his agents, but are appointed by the court.(*c*)

A commission issued before the expiration of the last of the days

---

(*y*) 2 Johns. Cas. 70. But see *post*, 486.
(*z*) 1 Caines's Rep. 517; 1 Dunl. Pr. 548.
(*a*) Pamph. L. 115.
(*b*) Ibid. 92; P. & J. Dig. 195.
(*c*) Hastings *v.* Eckby, 8 Barr, 194;
Hall's Adm. 57, n.; 1 Dunl. Pr. 547; Boudereau *v.* Montgomery, 4 W. C. C. R. 186; 1 Peters's Rep. 88. See Withers *v.* Gillespy, 7 S. & R. 16; 1 Har. Ch. Pr. 462, 477.

allowed by rule of court for filing interrogatories, is inadmissible, although taken out after the office was closed.(*d*)

Although the time for filing cross-interrogatories has elapsed, yet if filed in time to annex them to the commission they ought to be sent, and it would be error to admit the evidence taken without the cross-interrogatories, especially if the counsel's permission to annex them has been required. And although exceptions on that ground had not been filed under the rule of court until the trial, yet the Supreme Court inclined in such a case to think that the commission, executed *ex parte*, ought not to have been admitted, and that it was taking an advantage of the party, which ought not to be tolerated by a court of justice.(*e*)

The witnesses are not to be sworn in chief, but to answer the interrogatories which accompany the commission ; and it is the business of the commissioners distinctly to put to them all the questions proposed by the parties, and separately to note the answer to each.(*f*) In their return to the commission, the commissioners ought to certify when and *where* the depositions were taken ;(*g*) that they examined the witnesses on oath, upon the interrogatories annexed to the commission, and that they caused the examination to be reduced to writing, signed the same, and affixed their seals on the envelop.(*h*) Where commissioners to take depositions had not made the return under seal, and the envelop was indorsed by one only, there being one commissioner on each side, the court sustained exceptions to the execution of the commission, but ordered that it be returned to the commissioners to be properly executed, &c.(*hh*)

Although exhibits come in the same envelop with the commission, yet it seems that if they are not annexed to the depositions, or identified by marks or references, they ought not to be received.(*i*)

If the county in which the depositions are taken be noted in the margin, it will be a sufficient designation of the place of taking.(*ii*) It is not necessary that they should be signed by the witnesses.(*j*)

If the execution of the commission appear by the return to be defective, or irregular, the exception to the depositions may be taken *at the trial,*(*k*) though in Philadelphia by rule of court it is otherwise.(*kk*)

Commissions for the examination of witnesses now run *jointly* and *severally.* Notice is given to all the commissioners, and if any neglect or refuse to attend, or cannot be found, the others are at liberty to proceed without him.(*l*) But a deposition taken under a commission, directed to five persons, or any *one* of them, is not admissible, if another person, not named in the commission, assisted the commissioner in taking the examination.(*m*)

Where a commission is directed to several commissioners residing in different counties, or either of them, one may take depositions in one of

(*d*) Vanamringe *v.* Ellmaker, 4 Barr, 283.

(*e*) Case *v.* Cushman, 1 Barr, 241.

(*f*) Withers *v.* Gillespy, 7 S. & R. 10.

(*g*) Scott *v.* Horn, 9 Barr, 407 ; see Boudereau *v.* Montgomery, 4 W. C. C. R. 186.

(*h*) Nussear *v.* Arnold, 13 S. & R. 323 ; see Scott *v.* Horn, 9 Barr, 469.

(*hh*) Waln *v.* Freedlan, 2 M. 161.

(*i*) Dodge *v.* Israel, 4 W. C. C. R. 323.

(*ii*) Id. ibid. ; 1 Dunl. Pr. 547.

(*j*) Moulson *v.* Hargrave, 1 S. & R. 201.

(*k*) Withers *v.* Gillespy, 7 S. & R. 13.

(*kk*) *Ante*, 434, 448.

(*l*) See Pigot *v.* Holloway, 1 Bin. 436 ; Hall's Adm. 56–57, n. See *post.*(*ww*)

(*m*) 1 Peters's Rep. 309.

the counties named, though he do not reside therein.(*n*) If joint and several, it may be read, although the commissioner named by the defendant did not attend at the execution.(*o*)

Where a commission is returned with an interrogatory unanswered, the court will, on notice to the other side, permit the party issuing it to return it to have the answer taken.(*p*)

It seems that where a commission is directed to three persons as commissioners, or either of them, and it is executed by one only, it need not appear that notice was given to the other two.(*q*)

Depositions taken by others than those named in the commission, cannot be read even to prove pedigree.(*s*) But where they were taken by a judge of one of the courts of the country where the witnesses lived, in the presence of the commissioners, and it appeared that the government of the country did not permit the execution by individuals, the commission was ruled to be sufficiently executed.(*t*) If there be a mistake in the name of the commissioner, it may sometimes be fatal to it. Where a commission was directed to *George Dunlair*, it was held not admissible because taken by *George Dunbar*, though there was reason to believe it was executed by the person intended.(*u*)

Where the rule and notice of the commission were to R. C. H. and T. R., and the commission was to R. H. C. and T. R., and gave power to them, "or either" of them, it was held not to be a valid objection that the commission was executed by R. H. C. alone.(*uu*)

It is not a valid objection to the return of a commission that the commissioners or clerk were not sworn.(*v*) It is not necessary that commissioners should administer the oath to witnesses themselves. If a return to a commission states that a witness was duly sworn by a justice of the peace, it may be presumed to have been done in their presence.(*w*)

It is not a good objection to a deposition on a commission that it was not marked filed in the office upon its return, if it was filed in fact, and brought into court by the officer upon the trial.(*x*)

Testimony cannot be read if the agent or attorney of one party was present when it was taken, though he took no part in the examination, and was not employed to attend,(*y*) though in a case in the District Court the court dismissed exceptions to a commission, on the ground that an agent of the other party was present at the taking of the depositions, it not appearing that he took any part in putting the interrogatories, &c.(*yy*)

Where the return to a commission was, by mistake, directed to the defendant's attorney, the court made a rule on the attorney to file the return with the same effect as if originally directed to the prothonotary.(*z*)

If the witnesses do not answer interrogatories substantially, it is fatal to the whole commission, though the answers to the general interroga-

(*n*) Nussear *v.* Arnold, 13 S. & R. 323; see Waln *v.* Friedland, 1 M. 61.
(*o*) Pennock *v.* Freeman, 1 W. 401.
(*p*) Hinckley *v.* Ins. Co. 4 Barr, 470.
(*q*) Louden *v.* Blythe, 4 H. 352.
(*s*) Banert *v.* Day, 3 W. C. C. R. 243.
(*t*) 2 Id. 7.
(*u*) Breyfogle *v.* Beckley, 16 S. & R. 264.

(*uu*) Berghaus *v.* Alter, 9 W. 385.
(*v*) 1 Peters's Rep. 85, 88.
(*w*) Vaughan *v.* Blanchard, 2 D. 192, S. C.; Ibid. 1 Y. 175.
(*x*) Summers *v.* Wallace, 9 W. 161.
(*y*) Hollister *v.* Hollister, 6 Barr, 449.
(*yy*) Otis *v.* Clark, 2 M. 272.
(*z*) N. Y. State Bank *v.* Western Bank, 2 M. 16.

tory are, that they know nothing further material to either party.(*zz*) But if all the interrogatories which accompany a commission are substantially, though not formally answered, it is sufficient.(*a*) And interrogatories which are directed to be put to the witnesses on behalf of one party, need not be put to the witnesses of the other.(*b*) And where the commissioners on both sides attended, and one of the plaintiffs was also present, the depositions were allowed to be read, though all the interrogatories had not been·answered, the objection to reading them having been taken by the plaintiff, who was present at the execution of the commission, and who did not then object.(*c*) It has been said that if a witness do not answer the general interrogatory, his deposition cannot be read,(*d*) though this has been doubted.(*dd*) It is a fatal objection to a deposition that the cross-interrogatories were not put to a witness,(*e*) although it was the fault of the commissioners nominated by the opposing party.(*f*) But it is not a valid objection that the cross-interrogatories were not put to each witness immediately after he had answered the direct interrogatories, but after the direct interrogatories had been answered by all the witnesses.(*g*) It is no objection to a deposition that it is in English, though the commissioners were Dutch, and it does not appear that they had a sworn interpreter.(*h*)

The expenses of a commission are usually paid by the party at whose instance it is issued, or in such other manner as has been agreed upon previously to the issuing of it.(*i*) In a case in the Common Pleas in the time of President Shippen, the plaintiff claimed a variety of expenses which had been incurred in the execution of a commission that had been issued for him *ex parte*. The court allowed the charges for swearing the witnesses, and for their attendance; but rejected those for agency and for travelling to collect the testimony.(*j*) In the District Court, it is the practice to allow the party successful in the suit, all the expenses which he has necessarily incurred, in obtaining the execution of a commission. In the absence, indeed, of any express rule on the subject, the English chancery practice as to the costs of a commission, seems to govern and regulate that of the courts of this judicial district.(*k*)

In the Supreme Court, it is ordered, "that the actual expenses of executing a commission, including postage and of taking depositions before an examiner, or commissioner appointed by this court, shall be allowed in the costs, provided they do not exceed $100 in any case."

The rules of the District Court have been already given.

II. *Of Commissions sub mutuæ vicissitudinis, or Letters Rogatory.*

Where the government of a foreign country (as, for example, that of the Island of Cuba), will not permit a commission to be executed, the

(*zz*) Ketland *v.* Bisset, 1 W. C. C. R. 144; Winthrop *v.* Ins. Co. 2 Id. 7; Miller *v.* Dowdle, 1 Y. 404.

(*a*) 1 Peters's Rep. 235, 237.

(*b*) Pigott *v.* Holloway, 1 Bin. 436.

(*c*) Stewart *v.* Ross, 1 Y. 148, S. C.; Ibid. 2 D. 157.

(*d*) Richardson *v.* Golder, 3 W. C. C. R. 109.

(*dd*) Louden *v.* Blythe, 4 H. 532.

(*e*) Withers *v.* Gillespy, 7 S. & R. 10.

(*f*) Gilpin *v.* Conesqua, 1 Peters's Rep. 85, 88.

(*g*) Ibid.

(*h*) Ibid.

(*i*) Hall's Adm. 57, n.

(*j*) Lynch *v.* Woods, 1 D. 310; see 2 Johns. 107.

(*k*) See 1 Har. Ch. Pr. 442, 477–479, Tappan *v.* Columbia Bank, 4 P. L. J. 224. As to examiner's costs, see *ante*, p. 105.

court will issue letters rogatory after the form and practice of the civil law,(*l*) on the application of either party, to take depositions, in any cause depending therein.(*m*)

"By the law of nations, the courts of justice of different countries are bound to be mutually aiding and assisting to each other for the furtherance of justice. Hence, when the testimony of witnesses who reside abroad is necessary in a cause, the court where the action is pending, may send to the court or tribunal within whose jurisdiction the witnesses reside, a writ patent or close, as they may think proper, denominated by civilians a commission *sub mutuæ vicissitudinis*, from a clause which it generally contains. By that instrument, the court abroad is informed that a certain claim is pending in which the testimony of certain witnesses who reside within its jurisdiction is required, and it is requested to take their depositions or cause them to be taken, in due course and form of law, for the furtherance of justice and *sub mutuæ vicissitudinis obtentu*: that is, *with an offer*, on the part of the court making the request, *to do the like for the other in a similar case*. If these letters rogatory be received by an inferior judge, he proceeds to call the witnesses before him, by the process commonly employed within his jurisdiction, examines them on interrogatories or takes their depositions, as the case may be, and the proceedings being filed in the registry of his court, authentic copies thereof, duly certified, are transmitted to the court *à quo*, and are legal evidence in the cause. If the letters are directed to a court of superior jurisdiction, they appoint an examiner or commissioners for the purpose of executing them, and the proceedings are filed and returned in the same manner."(*n*)

"It is to be regretted," it is said, "that the principle of the civil law with respect to letters rogatory, has not been introduced into our practice. Commissions of *dedimus protestatem* are liable to great objections. It is sometimes difficult to procure the names of commissioners, and when they are obtained, it is often impossible to prevail upon them to act. They have no power to compel the attendance of witnesses, and as they rarely receive a compensation for their services, they do not care much about attending themselves. Thus the return of the commission is protracted, the attorney is unable to account for the delay, his opponent is ordered to press for a trial, and an honest creditor is frequently deprived of a just claim. We may add that the witnesses cannot be prosecuted for perjury before the tribunal of their own country, nor, while they remain there, can they be prosecuted in that in which the cause was tried. It often happens, too, that the constituted authorities of the place consider these commissions as an encroachment upon their jurisdiction, and refuse to permit them to be executed. Instances of this kind have sometimes happened in cases of commissions which have been issued by the courts of the United States, the commissioners having been threatened with punishment if they proceeded to act under them."(*o*)

Where letters rogatory are regularly issued from another State, the court here will compel the witnesses summoned to testify, holding it to

(*l*) 1 Peters's Rep. 236, n.
(*m*) See the form, ibid. Rules, Sup. Ct. 1828.

(*n*) Hall's Adm. Pr. 37–38, n.
(*o*) Ibid. 41–42.

be no objection to a witness being compelled to testify that his testimony is alleged to be irrelevant.(*p*)

If it be objected that the letters rogatory are not issued according to law and the practice of the court from whence they purport to come, the court executing the commission will not decide the point, but will give an opportunity to the party objecting to apply to that tribunal, to have them vacated, holding them to be regular unless so vacated.(*q*)

SECTION III.

OF THE RULE FOR TRIAL OR NON PROS. ; AND OF NONSUIT UNDER THE ACT OF 1812.

I. *Of the Rule for Trial or Non Pros.*

When assizes were held in the several counties of this State by the judges of the Supreme Court, the defendant had no mode, at common law, of compelling the plaintiff to bring on his cause for trial : although he was permitted, in case of the plaintiff's neglect, to proceed himself to trial by *proviso*. The trial by *proviso* took its name from a clause in the jury process, which provided that if two writs came to the sheriff, he should only execute and return one of them : that is, if two writs came to him in the same cause (the one being supposed to be delivered on the part of the plaintiff, and the other on the part of the defendant), he should summon but one jury for the trial of the issue ; but the trial should, in all cases, be by the plaintiff's record, if he entered it in time, after giving due notice of trial.(*r*) But the defendant could not carry the cause down by *proviso*, until there was laches in the plaintiff ;(*s*) except in a cause where the defendant is regarded as an actor, as in feigned issues or actions of replevin.(*t*)

The trial by proviso being then the only way which the defendant had to get rid of the action, where the plaintiff neglected to proceed to trial, and the expense and delay attending such trial being a great inconvenience and vexation,(*u*) an act of assembly was passed in the year 1767 to remedy such mischiefs in future, the title of which is a copy of that of the statute of 14 Geo. II. c 17, viz. : "*An act to prevent inconveniences arising from delays of causes, after issue joined;*" and, indeed, the whole tenor of the act assimilates it to the English statute. In consequence of this statute, the trial by proviso has in England fallen into desuetude ;(*v*) and in this State it has ceased to exist since the abolition of the Courts of *Nisi Prius* for the entire State.

By this act,(*w*) it is declared, "That where any issue shall be joined, in any action, in any court, and the plaintiff shall neglect to bring such issue on, to be tried according to the course and practice of the said courts respectively, the judges of the said courts, respectively, at any time after such neglect, upon motion made in open court, due notice

(*p*) McKenzie's Case, 2 Par. 227.
(*q*) Ibid.
(*r*) 3 Bl. Com. 356, 357; 2 Saund. 336, n. 4.
(*s*) Penn *v.* Keigler, 2 Y. 241.

(*t*) Leather *v.* Leather, ibid. 310.
(*u*) 2 Saund. 336, b.
(*v*) 3 Bl. Com. 357.
(*w*) 1 Sm. Laws, 271.

having been given thereof, in open court, the preceding term, to give the like judgment for the defendant, in every such action, as in cases of nonsuit, unless the said judges shall, upon just cause, and reasonable terms, allow any further time for the trial of such issue; and if the plaintiff shall neglect to try such issue, within the time so allowed, then the judges shall proceed to give such judgment as aforesaid; which shall be of like force and effect as judgments upon nonsuit, and of no other force or effect; and costs shall be awarded to the defendant in any action or suit where he would, upon nonsuit, be entitled to the same, and in no action or suit whatsoever."

"The only material difference between the English statute and ours seems to be in respect to the notice to be given to a plaintiff. The statute provides that *due notice* of such intended motion shall be given to the plaintiff; whereas the act of assembly requires that due notice should have been given in open court the *preceding term;* hence a difference of practice has necessarily arisen in this particular."(x)

The practice under the statute is to move the court for a rule to show cause why judgment should not be given for the defendant as *in case of a nonsuit* (which motion is held to be *notice* within the act),(y) on affidavit of the state of the proceedings, and of plaintiff's default in proceeding to trial; the rule *nisi* for judgment is then made out for the next day, which will be made absolute on motion, if sufficient cause be not shown against it, or the plaintiff do not undertake to try his action within the time the court shall think proper to allow him.(z) "But with us, a term's notice being required, the course is to obtain, *on motion,* a rule for trial at the next term, or *non pros.*, which will be made absolute, unless sufficient cause to the contrary be then shown."(a)

"In other respects, the construction which the statute has received is not dissimilar to that which has been applied to our act of assembly: neither does there appear to be much difference in the practice which has obtained under the one and the other.(b)

In general, a slight cause is deemed sufficient to induce the court to enlarge the rule, even in a *qui tam* action, if the plaintiff will undertake peremptorily to try at the next sittings or assizes.(c) It is usual to put off the trial only to the next term: but where there is no probability of the defendant's being ready to try till a more distant time, he may apply to put off the trial until then.(d)

There must be a previous neglect on the part of the plaintiff to entitle the defendant to a rule for trial or *non pros.*;(e) thus, where the plaintiff had been guilty of *laches* in obtaining an exemplification of a record from another State, to serve him as evidence here, the rule was granted.(f) After the rule is obtained, it seems that the court will oblige a plaintiff who asks a postponement of the trial, to agree to the taking of depositions, to be read in evidence at all events.(g)

It has been ruled in the Circuit Court of the United States that if the cause be not at issue, a rule to try or *non pros.* cannot be enforced against the plaintiff.(h) But a different practice has been sanctioned

(x) Rob. Dig. 130.
(y) Lofft's Rep. 265.
(z) 1 Cromp. Pr. 256.
(a) Rob. Dig. 131.
(b) Ibid.
(c) 7 T. R. 174; 1 East, 554.

(d) 2 Tidd's Pr. 706.
(e) Penn v. Keigler, 2 Y. 240.
(f) Todd v. Thompson, 2 D. 105.
(g) Lessee Welsh v. Baker, 1 Y. 171.
(h) 2 W. C. C. R. 204.

by the Supreme Court of this State in two cases. The reason of the practice in the former court may be deduced from a clause in the English statute, and likewise our act, referring to the "*course and practice*" of the court; this is that which before regulated the trial by *proviso ;* and as the defendant could not have had such trial until the plaintiff had been guilty of *laches,* nor *until after the issue was entered on record,* so neither till then is he entitled to judgment as in case of a nonsuit.(*i*) But the Supreme Court have determined that a *non pros.* may be entered in ejectment, after a plea of not guilty, and a rule for trial or *non pros.,* although the plaintiff has not filed a description of the land according to the act of 1806, and *issue has not been joined.(j)* The court relied on the authority of Wenn v. Adams,(*k*) which was an action of *assumpsit.* "There," says Chief Justice TILGHMAN, "the defendant pleaded, and laid a rule for trial or *non pros.* before a declaration was filed; and the court enforced the *non pros.* because the plaintiff, by receiving the plea, and submitting to the rule, had waived the objection arising from the want of a declaration; and it was his business, after the rule was laid, to fill a declaration and prepare the cause for trial. So in the present case, the rule being laid, the plaintiff was bound to file a description of the land, to join the issue, and put the cause on the trial-list; because all these things were necessary in order to bring the cause to trial."

If the court, on the application of the plaintiff, put off the trial, but grant a rule for trial of *non pros.* at the next term, it will non-preclude the plaintiff from showing reasonable cause of delay at the next term.(*l*)

A rule to try or *non pros.* is in force from the time it is taken, until the cause is concluded, notwithstanding that the cause may have been once tried during the existence of the rule, or continued at the instance of the defendant.(*m*) The continuance of a cause by consent, or by order of the court, while it is under a rule for trial or *non pros.,* does not discharge the rule; but the rule continues until it is expressly discharged.(*n*) In a case where the State is plaintiff and affects delay, the court will assign a day for trial; and a subsequent amendment of the declaration by the plaintiff shall not deprive the defendant of the benefit of the rule.(*o*) But where there is a rule for trial or *non pros.,* if a plea be subsequently added, and particular facts be referred, the previous rule for trial is vacated.(*p*) Where a continuance was entered by mistake of the defendant, who immediately after discovered that he had a rule on the plaintiff, to try or *non pros.,* the court held that the entry was not conclusive, and that the rule was still in force.(*q*)

Where a rule for trial or *non pros.* has been pending several years, the defendant is bound to give reasonable notice of his intention to proceed under the rule.(*r*)

Upon the expiration of the rule, judgment as of *non pros.* cannot be signed in the prothonotary's office, but must be moved for in open

(*i*) 2 Tidd's Pr. 703, 704; 2 Saund. 336, c.

(*j*) Galloway v. Saunders, 2 S. & R. 405.

(*k*) 2 D. 156, S. C.; Haldane v. Fisher, 1 Y. 156.

(*l*) Schlosser v. Lesher, 1 D. 251.

(*m*) Thurston v. Murray, 3 Bin. 413.

(*n*) 1 Peters's Rep. 217, 219; Smith v. Davids, 1 D. 410.

(*o*) Respublica v. Coates, 1 Y. 35.

(*p*) Halhead v. Ross, 1 D. 405.

(*q*) Leshit v. Pope, 2 D. 143.

(*r*) Wallace v. Boyd, Sup. C. Lancaster, 1 Sm. Laws, 156.

court ;(s) and the motion will then be granted, unless the plaintiff can show some precise legal ground for the postponement of the trial, or some circumstances of hardship not arising from his own inattention, or that of his attorney or agent.(t) A *non pros.* entered on a mistaken supposition that a rule for trial or *non pros.* had been obtained, was taken off, on an agreement that the rule should be entered as of the preceding term.(u)

Judgment of *non pros.* is a final judgment for costs only, signed by the defendant. The act only gives costs to the defendant, where he would have been entitled to them upon a nonsuit; and, therefore, the tenant is not entitled to costs, in a writ of right.(v)

II. *Of Nonsuit under the Act of* 1812.

By an act of the 30th March, 1812,(w) passed "*for the facilitating the due administration of justice,*' it is provided : " That when a cause at issue shall be regularly set down for trial in any court of record within this commonwealth, either by the plaintiff or the defendant, and the plaintiff is not ready for trial, when the cause is called up in its order, the court, on motion of the defendant, may order a nonsuit to be entered, without previously granting a rule to try, or *non pros.*, unless the plaintiff shall adduce such reasons for postponing the said cause as would have been a sufficient ground for postponement, if the application therefor had been made on the behalf of the defendant."

" The ordering a nonsuit is, by this act, authorized only in causes 'at issue regularly set down for trial.' To ascertain the regularity, the rules of court seem to be the only criteria contemplated by the legislature."(x)

" The chief advantage given by this act, seems to be that of preventing a plaintiff, who had regularly set down his cause for trial, from continuing it without sufficient cause shown, although he had been guilty of no previous laches, which would have authorized a rule for trial or *non pros.*"(y)

The compulsory nonsuit, under the acts of 1836 and 1846, will be considered hereafter.(z)

SECTION IV.

OF THE JURY PROCESS; OF JURIES COMMON AND SPECIAL; AND OF VIEWS.

I. *Of the Venire.*

The cause being ready for trial by jury, the prothonotary is required by a general law, passed on the 14th day of April, 1834, to prepare and deliver to the sheriff, as soon as conveniently may be after the list

(s) McKegg v. Crawford, 1 D. 347.
(t) Wallace's Rep. 1.
(u) German v. Wainwright, 2 D. 266.
(v) 2 Tidd, 708 ; 2 W. Bl. 1093.

(w) 5 Sm. Laws, 361.
(x) Rob. Dig. 133.
(y) Ibid.
(z) *Post*, chapter 24, § 7.

of causes at issue shall have been settled,(*b*) a writ, called a *venire*, commanding him and the county commissioners to summon a jury, or a jury of special jurors, as the case may be, for the trial of all such issues. Every writ of *venire* must be awarded of the body of the county where the issue is triable, according to a form prescribed by the 97th section.(*c*)

"We command you, and every of you, that in your proper persons you draw from the wheel (or from the proper wheel if there be several), containing the names of the persons selected according to law to be jurors (or special jurors, as the case may be), in the courts of the said county, the names of ——— persons to be jurors in our ——— court ——— to be holden at ——— in and for said county, the ——— day of ——— at ——— o'clock, in the ———noon of that day; *And, further*, That you, the said sheriff, do summon the persons whose names shall be so drawn, and every one of them, to come before our said court at the same time and place, to make up the juries requisite for the trial of all issues in the pleas depending and for trial by a jury in our said court; and that you, the said sheriff, have then there this writ; and the names of the persons so summoned, with their additions respectively in a panel hereto annexed, and otherwise make return, at the day and place aforesaid, how you shall have executed this writ. Witness (J. B.) &c., at, &c.

In contemplation of law, a *venire* is issued and returned with a panel annexed, in every cause set down for trial; but in actual practice only one writ is made out, and one panel of jurors summoned upon it, annexed, which serves for the trial of every cause so set down.

By § 100, the Supreme Court are directed to award such process in all issues in fact depending thereon returnable during its sitting, at *nisi prius*, at such times as they shall see fit.

By § 101, it is made returnable to the District Court and Common Pleas of the City and County of Philadelphia, at such particular day of the term as the court shall direct. The District Court may direct that one or more panels of general or common jurors, and also one or more panels of special jurors, be selected and returned for any one term thereof. And by § 2, of the act of 1836(*d*), it is enabled to award writs of *venire* at any time not less than thirty days before the day appointed for the return thereof, notwithstanding the term shall have commenced.

When the Common Pleas of that county shall appoint a court to be holden by one of the judges, a separate *venire* shall be awarded return-able before him at the day to be appointed by the court. § 106.

(*b*) No cause shall be placed on the trial-list until after issue joined, nor without the written order of the parties or his counsel, nor shall any cause be placed on the trial-list for any period, unless the same shall be at issue before the issuing of the *venire* for such period. Rule 101, D. C. Philad.

A cause cannot be put on the argu-ment-list and on the issue-list at the same term, except by consent or special order of the court on notice to all the parties. A contrary practice would lead to surprise and injustice. Therefore, while a motion to quash an appeal is pending, neither party can be compelled to prepare for trial of the issue. Keller *v.* Cuningham, 6 Barr, 376. See, as to "issue," *ante*, 392; *post*, 481, 482, 485.

(*c*) Pamph. L. p. 359.
(*d*) Pamph. L. p. 76.

The District Court for Lancaster county may direct the *venires* to issue for each week during the time it may be necessary to continue the terms thereof, returnable on the Monday in each week of said terms respectively. § 103.

And in any county wherein the term of the Common Pleas is to continue two weeks, it is directed to be returnable on the first day of the second week of the term, unless the court specially order otherwise. § 104.

If they shall be of opinion at any term that the criminal business to be before them during the next succeeding court will interfere with the civil issues, they may order that no *venire* shall be awarded for such succeeding term of the Common Pleas. § 105.

For an adjourned or special court of Common Pleas in any county, a majority of the judges thereof may direct a *venire* to issue, thirty days before the time of holding thereof, returnable thereto, notwithstanding a regular term or return day may intervene between the issuing and return of such writ. § 107.

Wherever the number of jurors to be returned to any court shall not be fixed by law, it is made the duty of the respective courts, by a standing order, to direct the number of jurors which shall be returned at each successive term; subject to be enlarged by order of the judges or any two of them, in vacation, if emergencies require it. § 116.

The number of persons to be summoned and returned as special jurors in the District Court and Court of Common Pleas of Philadelphia County, or in the Supreme Court, is fixed at forty-eight: that of the general or common jurors at not less than forty-eight, nor more than sixty; and in the Courts of Common Pleas and District Courts of any other county at not less than thirty-six nor more than sixty. § 99.

Whenever the array of jurors is successfully challenged, the court is empowered to award, at the instance of either party to a cause, a *venire*, returnable forthwith for the trial thereof. § 146. Such *venire* shall be directed to the sheriff or coroner of the respective county, or if the case require it to two elisors; it shall require him or them to summon and return forthwith twenty-four good and lawful men to be jurors in such cause, and on the return thereof with a panel of jurors annexed, the trial shall proceed in like manner and with like effect, as if the jurors had been selected and summoned as is prescribed in the previous parts of the act. § 147.

II. *Of the Selecting, Summoning, and Returning of Juries.*

The juries for the trial of all issues in fact, shall be selected by the sheriff and commissioners, and summoned and returned to the respective court in the manner following, and not otherwise, to wit:—

The commissioners of the several counties, except the County of Philadelphia, shall, as occasion requires, provide, and at all times keep, one wheel for the purpose of containing the names of jurors for the courts of the respective county. §§ 80, 81. The next section directs wheels to be kept for the grand and petit jurors of certain criminal courts, and also one other wheel for the names of special jurors of the County of Philadelphia, which wheel shall be marked No. 3. § 82.

Each wheel shall be provided with a sufficient lock and key; the whole shall remain in the custody of the county commissioners, and the keys in that of the sheriff of the respective county. § 83. The 84th section prescribes a fine for the sheriffs' or commissioners' neglect in this behalf.

The sheriff, and at least two of the commissioners of every county, shall, at least thirty days previously to the first term in every year of the Court of Common Pleas of the respective county, meet, and thereupon proceed with due diligence, to select, at the seat of justice thereof, from the taxable citizens of the county, a sufficient number of sober, intelligent, and judicious persons, to serve as jurors in the several courts of such county, in which juries shall be required to be holden therein during that year. § 85.

But before the sheriff and commissioners shall make any such selection of jurors, they shall severally take an oath or affirmation, before some person having authority to administer oaths, to use their utmost endeavors and diligence in making an impartial selection of competent persons for jurors during the ensuing year, and not to suffer partiality, favor, affection, hatred, malice, or ill-will, in any case or respect whatever, to influence them in the selecting, drawing, or returning of jurors; but, in all respects, honestly to conform to the true intent and meaning of the acts of assembly, in such case made and provided. § 87.

The sheriff and commissioners shall provide a sufficient number of small slips, or pieces of paper, upon each of which they shall write, or cause to be written, the name, surname, and addition, or occupation, and place of abode, of one of the persons selected; they shall roll up, or fold the said slips, so that the name shall not appear, without unfolding thereof, and thereupon they shall deposit the names of the persons so selected, in the appropriate wheel, as aforesaid. § 88.

Provided, That the sheriffs and commissioners of the several counties shall, in every year, select such a number of persons, and deposit their names in the proper wheel, as aforesaid, that at the end of the year there shall remain in each wheel, as near as may be, the number of names requisite to compose the panels of jurors for one court at the least, and not any greater number. § 89.

As soon as the selection of jurors and the depositing of their names in the wheel, as aforesaid, shall be completed, the sheriff shall cause the same to be locked and secured by sealing-wax, and thereon the said sheriff and commissioners shall impress distinctly their respective seals. § 90.

The sheriff, in the absence of the commissioners of the respective county, or of at least two of them, and the commissioners, in the absence of the sheriff of the county, shall not at any time open any of the wheels, nor shall the sheriff and commissioners open any such wheel, except for the purpose of depositing therein the names of persons to be jurors, in pursuance of law, or an order of court, or of drawing a panel or panels of jurors therefrom, in compliance with a precept directed to them for that purpose.   And if any sheriff or commissioner shall offend herein, he shall forfeit, for the use of the respective county, a sum not exceeding five hundred dollars, at the discretion of the court having jurisdiction of the offence.   § 91.

If at any time the names in any of the wheels aforesaid, shall be exhausted before the end of the current year, it shall be the duty of the sheriff and commissioners, upon the order of the Court of Common Pleas, or two of the judges thereof, to make a new selection of persons, and deposit their names in the proper wheel, for the remainder of such year : *Provided*, That in the counties wherein more than one wheel is provided, the judges of the court in which such jurors shall be required shall make the order aforesaid.   § 92.

When the array of jurors returned at any court shall be quashed by reason of any fault or irregularity in the selection of persons, or depositing their names in the wheel, as aforesaid, the sheriff and commissioners of the respective county shall, upon the order of such court, forthwith take out of the wheel, from which such jurors were drawn, all the names therein deposited, and make a new selection of persons, and deposit their names in the wheel for the remainder of the current year, in the manner aforesaid.   § 93.

If at any time any such wheel shall be broken open or destroyed, so that no jury can be drawn from it, a new selection of persons shall be made, and their names deposited in such wheel, or in a new wheel to be prepared for that purpose, for the remainder of the current year, thirty days before the court at which such jurors shall be summoned to serve, if so many days shall intervene.   § 94.

If by any accident, mistake, or neglect of the sheriff or commissioners of any county, or either of them, any of the wheels shall be opened, unlocked, or unsealed, except in the presence of such sheriff or commissioners, it shall be the duty of the court, upon sustaining a challenge to the array for any such cause, to direct the sheriff and commissioners, forthwith, to take out of the wheel the names therein deposited, and to make a new selection of persons, and deposit their names in such wheel for the remainder of the current year, in the manner aforesaid.   § 95.

Whenever any writ of venire shall be delivered to any sheriff, he shall give immediate notice thereof to the commissioners of the respective county ; and the sheriff and at least two of the commissioners shall, without delay, draw from the proper wheel, after having turned the same sufficiently to intermix the papers deposited therein, the names of so many persons to be jurors as shall be required by such writ.   § 118.

The moment jurors are thus drawn, they become, in contemplation of law, the legal jury, as much so as if returned to the court. The sheriff and commissioners have no right, therefore, to make any selection, or to exclude a single name on the score of its being an unsuitable or incompetent character, or on any pretext whatever.(e) The act, however, authorizes them, in case any of the persons whose names shall be drawn, shall have removed from the county, or shall be dead, or absent, to destroy the slips containing the names of persons so removed or dead, and proceed to draw other names, until the several panels shall be completed; and thereupon they shall lock and seal up, in the manner aforesaid, the said wheel. § 119.

Whenever writs of venire for a grand jury and petit jury in the Court of Quarter Sessions, and also, a writ of venire from the Court of Common Pleas in any county, except the County of Philadelphia, shall be in the hands of the sheriff and commissioners at the same time for execution, the required number of names first drawn shall be annexed in a panel to the venire for a grand jury, and the required number of names next drawn shall be annexed in a panel to the venire for a petit jury in the Court of Quarter Sessions; and thereupon the said sheriff and commissioners shall proceed to draw and annex the panel required, to be returned into the Court of Common Pleas. § 120.

In every county wherein the terms of the Courts of Common Pleas and Quarter Sessions of the peace are limited, by law, to one and the same week; the sheriff and commissioners of such county shall annex and return one and the same panel of names to the venires issuing as aforesaid, for the summoning and returning of petit and general jurors in the said courts. § 121.

If thirty days shall not intervene between the time of depositing the names of jurors in the wheel or wheels as aforesaid, and the next court in any county, the jurors shall be drawn, as aforesaid, for such court from the names deposited in the wheel for the preceding year. § 122.

The commissioners of the several counties, respectively, shall make out, in alphabetical order, two lists of the names of the persons so drawn, to serve as grand, petit, or special jurors; and one of the said lists they shall deliver to the sheriff of the respective county, and the other to the prothonotary or clerk of the proper court, to be set up by them in their respective offices for the inspection of all persons concerned. § 123.

It shall be the duty of the sheriff to summon, at least ten days before the return day of the venire, the persons whose attendance shall be thereby required, by delivering to each of the said persons a separate ticket, in the customary form, specifying the duty enjoined, or by leaving such ticket at their usual places of abode, respectively. § 125.

It shall not be lawful for the sheriff and commissioners, of any county, to return or put into the wheels aforesaid, or any of them, the name of

(e) 1 Br. 121.

any person privileged or exempted from serving upon juries, as aforesaid. § 126.

The sheriff of each county shall enter, in alphabetical order, in a book to be kept by him for that purpose, the surnames of all persons, together with their christian names, and additions, who shall be summoned by him or by any officer or other person legally authorized for the purpose, and who shall duly attend and serve upon any jury in any of the said courts, and also the times of their services respectively; and said book shall be delivered by him to his successor in office. § 127.

The several duties hereby enjoined upon the sheriffs of the several counties, relative to the selecting, summoning, and returning of jurors as aforesaid, shall, in case of the death, resignation, removal from office, inability, or incompetency of any sheriff to act, be performed by the coroner of the respective county; and the coroner performing such duties shall be subject to all and singular the provisions herein enacted in relation to the sheriffs; and in case of the death, resignation, removal from office, inability, or incompetency of the sheriff and coroner to act, by a disinterested person, to be appointed for that purpose by the court, or by two of the judges of the Court of Common Pleas of the respective county. § 131.

By the one hundred and thirty-third section, any two of the judges of the Common Pleas are empowered to appoint persons to act in place of the commissioners or sheriff, in case of the death, sickness, resignation, or removal from office of two of the commissioners, or of the sheriff or coroner, for the purpose of discharging these duties.

By the act of 21st February, 1814,(*f*) all errors relative to the venire, drawing, summoning, and returning of jurors, are cured by a trial, or an agreement to try on the merits, or by a plea of the general issue.

III. *Of Special Juries.*

The jurors contained in the panel and summoned by the sheriff are either common or special. A common jury is that returned by the sheriff in one and the same panel for the trial of all causes at issue not marked for trial by special jury. A special jury in England is so called, because chosen specially for the trial of a particular cause; and from the manner in which it is selected, it is also called a struck jury. The object of such a jury was originally to have one composed of gentlemen of superior understanding for the trial of a cause of intricacy or importance; or to prevent the sheriff, when suspected of partiality to a party, from summoning jurors open to corrupt influence or biased.(*g*) In this State there are, strictly speaking, no special juries, although the act of assembly above cited mentions them, and it is nominally the privilege of either party to enter a rule for trial by special jury.(*h*) But in

(*f*) 6 Re. Laws, 111. (*h*) Neff *v.* Neff, 1 Bin. 350.
(*g*) Euno. Dial. II. ₰ 31; 3 Bl. Com. 357.

I.—30

practice, the only selection allowed, is that of striking twelve names each from the panel of general or common jurors—instead, therefore, of entering a rule for trial by special jury, the party enters a rule for striking a special jury. In such case, the 157th section of the act already cited, directs the parties to "strike the same in the office of the prothonotary, or clerk, from the list of jurors which shall have been drawn from the proper wheel as aforesaid for the ensuing court." This is done by the parties respectively striking any number not exceeding twelve names each from the general panel. The prothonotary draws twelve names from the residue, and they constitute the jury, unless challenged, as will be hereafter stated.

The rules of the District Court in this respect are as follows :—

L. 1. The prothonotary shall cause a list of jurors, in each cause set down for trial by jury, to be delivered to the attorney on each side, at least eight days before the time appointed for striking, and he shall subjoin thereto a notice of the time and place of striking the same.

The notice of the prothonotary shall be considered as entitling the plaintiff or defendant to strike the same *ex parte*, at the time appointed without further notice: *Provided*, That the striking of a jury is not to be considered as entitling either party to trial if not otherwise entitled.

LI. 2. Neither party shall be required to strike from the list of jurors twelve names, but may omit to strike out any, or may strike out any less number than twelve, provided the list must be struck, if at all, at the time and place appointed by the prothonotary, according to the existing rules of this court, and no jury shall be struck at the bar; but if the list be not struck according to the rules of the court, the jury shall be taken from the panel as returned.

LII. 3. Every challenge to the array of jurors returned for the trial of any issue in fact shall be made on the first day of the period at which the said issue shall be set down for trial.

4. The prothonotary shall indorse upon every writ of *venire facias* which shall be specially awarded in any cause, the day assigned in the trial-list for the trial of the said cause.

5. The sheriff or other officer to whom any writ of *venire facias* specially awarded in any cause shall be directed, shall summon the jury to appear in court at ten o'clock in the forenoon of the day so indorsed on the said writ.

If, after a rule for a struck jury, a party goes on to a trial before a general jury, it is a waiver of the rule for a struck jury; and if he wish a subsequent trial of his cause to be before such a jury, he must obtain a new rule.(*i*)

IV. *Of Views.*

The nature of the cause will sometimes require the jury or some of them to see the very spot where the matter in dispute arises; in which case, after issue joined, either party may move the court for a view. By the act of 1834, §§ 158, 159,(*j*) "where a view shall be allowed in any cause, six of the first twelve of the jurors named in the panel, or more of them, shall be taken by the sheriff, or other officer, to the place

(*i*) White *v.* Kyle, 6. S. & R. 107.   (*j*) Pamph. L. 368.

in question, and they shall have view thereof. And at the calling of the jury to try any cause in which a view shall have been had, those of the viewers who shall appear shall first be sworn or affirmed, and so many jurors only shall be drawn as aforesaid, and added to the said viewers, as shall, after default and challenges allowed, make up the number twelve, to be sworn or affirmed for the trial of such cause.(k) The courts have established a regulation with respect to viewers, "that no trial shall be put off on account of a view not being had by six of the first twelve of the jury as they stand in the panel, provided any of them have viewed, and some of them do appear to try the cause, and such of them who have viewed and appear, shall be first sworn on the trial, and the form of venire shall be altered accordingly."(l)

A motion for a view must be founded on an affidavit of the particular circumstances which render it necessary, unless the propriety of granting it appears on the face of the pleadings;(m) and if applied for in ejectment, it must be stated, that boundaries were in question.(n) The expense of a view is not chargeable to the county, but is to be paid by the parties; and like other costs, it must fall ultimately on the losing party.(o) A jury drawn and struck at a previous court, when they held a view, and, to save the expense of another view, were continued over by consent to the next court, at which they tried the cause, are not entitled to be paid by the county, but by the losing party.(p) No evidence can be given on either side, at the time of taking the view, and the places, to which, on the trial, the evidence is to be adapted, can only be shown to the viewers.(q)

The act of 4th April, 1809, does not authorize a party to challenge peremptorily any of the viewers provided under the act of 29th March, 1805.(qq)

The viewers must be of the first twelve.(r) The view ought regularly to be allowed, but attendance waives irregularity.(rr)

V. Of the Exemption, Liability, and Pay of Jurors.

Certain persons are exempted in Pennsylvania from serving as jurors, among whom are the guardians of the poor of the City of Philadelphia, District of Southwark, and Township of the Northern Liberties; as also the wardens of the port of Philadelphia, while in office;(s) and by act of Congress 2d March, 1799, postmasters and persons occupied in the transportation of the mail. And by St. 5 Hen. viii. c. 6,(ss) surgeons are likewise exempted. There are others who are privileged, on account of their professions or offices, as those whose attendance is required in the courts of justice, such as counsellors, attorneys, and other officers of the courts.(t) So, persons will be excused from serving as

---

(k) See Lessee of Nesbit v. Kerr, 3 Y. 194; Stat. 4 Anne, c. 16, § 8; Rob. Dig. 45.

(l) Schwenk v. Umstead, 6 S. & R. 354; et vide ibid.

(m) Tidd, 844; see Barnes, 467.

(n) 1 Dunl. Pr. 603; Lessee of Nesbit v. Kerr, 3 Y. 194.

(o) Sherer v. Hodgson, 1 Bin. 535.

(p) Ibid.

(q) Tidd, 844; Barnes, 458.

(qq) Schwenk v. Umsted, 6 S. & R. 351; see act of 1834, and Schuylkill. Nav. Co. v. Farr, 4 W. & S. 371.

(r) Brown v. O'Brien, 4 L. J. 501.

(rr) Ibid.

(s) Purd. Dig. 446, n.

(ss) Rob. Dig. 337.

(t) 3 Bac. Ab. 758.

jurors, who hold offices of a public nature, and who have no power to act by deputy; but not if the trust be of a private nature, or the person has power to act by deputy.(u)

By the one hundred and thirty-sixth section of the act of 1834, above cited, it is declared unlawful to return to the wheel or to any of them (if there be several), the name of any person who may have served as a juror during the year in which such service shall be rendered; nor shall it be lawful to put the name of the same person during the same year into two or more different wheels containing the names of jurors for the courts of the respective county; and every sheriff and commissioner who shall intentionally offend herein, or shall consent thereto, shall forfeit and pay to the respective county, for the use of the fund aforesaid, a sum not less than ten dollars nor more than thirty dollars, at the discretion of the Court of Quarter Sessions of the peace for the respective county. On the other hand, the name of every person selected, drawn, summoned, and making default as aforesaid, also the name of every person who shall be excused from serving, shall be returned by the sheriff and commissioners to the wheel from which it was taken, at the time of the next drawing from the said wheel for any of the courts of such county : *Provided,* Such person is resident within the respective county, and competent and liable to perform the duties of a juror.   § 135.

Every person selected and summoned, who shall, after being called three times in open court, fail to appear at the time and place appointed, shall, upon due proof of lawful summons, forfeit and pay for every such default to the respective county, to be appropriated towards a fund for defraying the expenses of jurors, a sum not exceeding thirty dollars, at the discretion of the court at which his attendance shall be required : *Provided,* That the said court shall remit any fine which may be so imposed by them, at the same or the next succeeding term thereof, if reasonable cause for the absence of such person shall be shown.   § 134.

The prothonotaries and clerks of the several courts aforesaid, shall respectively certify to the sheriff and commissioners of the respective county, at the end of each term or session of the respective courts, the names of the jurors who shall have appeared and served at such court, also the names of those who shall have made default or were excused from serving as jurors at that term, and also the names of those who were privileged or exempted from serving on juries.   § 128.

Every person who shall be summoned, or who shall serve upon a jury as aforesaid, shall be entitled to demand and receive from the sheriff, without fee or reward, a certificate, testifying his attendance and service, and the time thereof, as aforesaid.   § 129.

The prothonotaries and clerks of the several courts of the commonwealth shall, without fee or reward, certify to the commissioners of the respective county, the number of days each person shall have served or attended as aforesaid, either as grand, petit, or general jurors at the respective court.   § 130.

(u) 2 Br. 59.

Every person who shall serve or attend as a juror in any court, shall be entitled to receive from the treasurer of the county, upon a warrant drawn by the commissioners thereof, one dollar for each day's service or attendance as aforesaid. § 137.

Every person who shall be summoned, and who shall serve as a juror in any court of this commonwealth, shall be entitled to six and a quarter cents for each mile he shall travel, going to and returning from the same, to be paid out of the county treasury in the usual manner. § 138.

SECTION V.

OF EVIDENCE AND WITNESSES, AND OF COMPELLING THE PRODUCTION OF BOOKS AND WRITINGS UNDER THE ACT OF 1798.

I. *Of Evidence and Witnesses.*

Another step introductory to a trial by jury, is the procuring testimony by the respective parties, in support or denial of the allegations put in issue by the pleadings; the general rule being, that the proof must conform to the issue, and that everything which is put in issue must be proved and no more.(v) The evidence, also, must be the best of which the nature of the case is susceptible. Secondary evidence cannot be given, as long as proof of a better kind can be had. Thus, a copy of an instrument, or parol evidence of its contents, cannot be admitted if the original be in existence, and capable of being produced by the party who relies upon it.(w) On the general issue, the plaintiff must prove the whole of his case; but on a special issue, it is only necessary to prove the particular point referred to the jury; for whatever is not expressly denied, is admitted by the pleadings.

Evidence is either written or parol. Written evidence consists either of public writings, whether of record, such as statutes or judgments, or not of record; and of private writings, such as bonds, bills, notes, and other instruments, sealed or unsealed; and these may be in the custody and possession of the party intending to use them as evidence, or of a third person, or of the adverse party in the suit. Parol evidence consists in the testimony of competent and disinterested witnesses, which is either delivered openly in court, in the presence of the judge, jury, and parties, or is taken out of court, previous to the trial, upon a commission, or upon a rule for the examination of witnesses *de bene esse;* in which last case, as we have seen,(x) the party offering the deposition must show, that the personal attendance of the witness at the trial could not be procured.

Witnesses must be persons possessed of reason and understanding, and acquainted with the nature and obligation of an oath: children of a very early age, idiots, and lunatics, therefore, cannot be witnesses.(y) A

(v) 1 Phil. Ev. 126, 150.   (x) *Ante,* p. 443.
(w) Id. 167; see Clark *v.* Sanderson,   (y) 1 Phil. Ev. 14; 10 Johns. 362.
3 Bin. 192.

person laboring under a temporary privation of understanding from intoxication is regarded as a voluntary madman, whom the court will not permit to testify; but as there are various degrees of intoxication, all of which do not disqualify a man to remember and relate the truth, it belongs to the judge to determine whether the situation of the witness is such as to require that he should be excluded from giving testimony.(z) A slave cannot be a witness in Pennsylvania.(a) And a person who has been stigmatized by a conviction for felony, perjury, or other infamous crime, is not permitted to testify.(b) The objection to the competency of a witness, which most frequently occurs in practice, is on account of interest in the event of the suit.(c) An interest in the question involved in the suit is no reason for excluding him, however much it may affect his credit.(d) To render a witness incompetent, on the ground of interest, there must be a *direct* interest, that is, he must be immediately benefited or injured by the event of the suit; or the verdict to be obtained by his evidence, or given against it, must be evidence for or against him in another action, in which he may afterwards be a party.(e) But where a person renders himself interested by a voluntary act, for the purpose of depriving a party of the benefit of his testimony, he may be compelled to be a witness.(f)

The mode of procuring the attendance of witnesses is by writ of *subpœna ad testificandum*, which is a judicial writ, requiring the persons named in it to appear on a certain day in court, in order to testify, under a certain penalty in case of disobedience. Any number of names may be inserted in one subpœna (unless separate subpœnas should be required by the party,(g) and they need not be restricted to four only, as in the practice of the English courts.(h) If the witness, whose attendance is required, be in another county, resort may, notwithstanding, be had to a subpœna, for it has been ruled that the Courts of Common Pleas have the power of issuing subpœnas to any part of the State;(i) and this power has also been expressly given by a recent act of assembly.(j) But if the testimony of the witness be essential to success in the cause, it would be expedient, lest the process of subpœna should be disregarded, to obtain a rule to take his deposition in that county before a magistrate, with notice to the opposite party of the time and place of taking it; after which the party may repair there with a copy of the rule under the seal of the court, or may transmit it with instructions to his agent, to take the deposition; or the parties, by agreement, may annex interrogatories to it, and send it to commissioners nominated by them for execution.(k)

By rule of the District Court, " subpœnas for witnesses residing within the City or County of Philadelphia, shall be taken at least five days previously to the day assigned for the trial of the action in which their

(z) 16 Johns. 143.
(a) 4 D. 145, n.
(b) 10 Johns. 132; 2 Bin. 165.
(c) 1 Phil. Ev. 22.
(d) Cas. T. Hardw. 358; 3 T. R. 27; Wakely v. Hart, 6 Bin. 319; Cornogg v. Abraham, 1 Y. 84.
(e) Hayes v. Grier, 4 Bin. 83; and see Conrad v. Keyser, 5 S. & R. 371.
(f) Long v. Bailie, 4 S. & R. 222; see

further, Wh. Dig. "Evidence," xix., and as to the evidence of counsel, *ante*, p. 220.
(g) Act of 1821, § 6; 7 Re. Laws, 371.
(h) See Tidd, 846.
(i) Bell v. Lessee of Wetherill, 2 S. & R. 350.
(j) *Ante*, p. 124.
(k) See 4 Wheat. 508; *ante*, 432, 448.

attendance shall be required, or such action shall not be continued on account of the absence of any such witness, if he were or might be found at his residence within that period. But this rule will not dispense with the obligation to take the deposition of any such witness, where the party requiring his attendance knows previously to that period that such witness intends to be absent from the county at the time of the trial."(*kk*)

If a witness have in his possession any deeds or writings which are thought necessary at the trial, a special clause must be inserted in the subpœna, commanding him to bring them with him.(*l*) The writ of *subpœna duces tecum* (as it is denominated) is of compulsory obligation on a witness to have the papers thereby demanded, which he has in his possession, ready to be produced : he is bound to bring them into court with him, according to the command of the writ; but then, if there be any sufficient reason or excuse for their not being read in evidence (the validity of which is to be determined by the court exclusively, and not by the witnesses), the judge will permit them to be withheld.(*m*) In general, a witness is not excused from producing a paper because it belongs to a third person,(*n*) though if the reading of it will operate to the prejudice of a third person, the court will, it is said, direct it not to be read.(*o*) A witness, who, without sufficient excuse, disobeys a writ of *subpœna duces tecum*, is liable to a special action on the case,(*p*) or to an attachment on an affidavit of service of the subpœna.(*q*) A *subpœna duces tecum* cannot issue to a public officer to bring original papers into court, when certified copies would be evidence.(*r*)

By the 3d section of the act of April 22, 1846,(*s*) " in all cases wherein any person has been or may be subpœnaed with a *subpœna duces tecum*, requiring the production of any title papers, or other documents whatsoever, on the trial of any suit, and said person has, or shall refuse to produce any such papers or documents, and for such refusal has been or may be attached and imprisoned by the court, and subsequently discharged, persisting in such refusal, parol evidence shall be received in relation to the existence and contents of such papers and documents."

To prevent surprise, notice to produce papers must be given, though they be in court at the trial in the hands of the opposite party; otherwise he cannot give secondary evidence of its contents. The object of the notice is not only to produce the paper, but to give the party an opportunity to support or impeach it by testimony.(*t*)

The subpœna must be served personally on the witness,(*u*) either by delivering the writ itself, or by delivering him a copy or a ticket which is in the nature of a notice addressed to the witness, and informing him of the substance of the writ.(*v*) When service is made by delivering a copy or ticket, it is of no avail unless the writ is at the same time shown to the witness.(*w*) The subpœna ought to be served a reasonable time before the trial, that the witness may have an opportunity to put his own affairs in such order that his attendance may be of as little preju-

(*kk*) See *post*, 486.
(*l*) 1 Phil. Ev. 11.
(*m*) 9 East, 473, S. C. ; 1 Campb. 14 ;
sed vide 1 Esp. Rep. 405.
(*n*) Holt's N. P. R. 239.
(*o*) 1 Stark. Rep. 95.
(*p*) 9 East, 473, S. C. ; 1 Campb. 14.

(*q*) See Shippen *v*. Wells, 2 Y. 260.
(*r*) Delaney *v*. Regulators, 1 Y. 403.
(*s*) Pamph. L. p. 483.
(*t*) Millikin *v*. Burr, 7 Barr, 23.
(*u*) 2 Str. 1054 ; 1 Phil. Ev. 4.
(*v*) See the form, 2 Grayd. Forms, 188.
(*w*) 2 Caines's Rep. 335.

dice to himself as possible.(x) No witness is bound to appear in civil cases, unless his expenses for going to, attending at, and returning from the trial, at the rate fixed by law, be tendered him at the time of serving the subpœna; nor if he appear, is he bound to give evidence till such charges are actually paid or tendered.(y) A subpœna is not necessary, if the witness will attend without one.(z)

The fees to be received by witnesses are regulated by the act of 22d February, 1821, § 13,(a) as follows: "For each day's attendance at court, when the witness does not reside in nor within one mile of the county seat, sixty-two and a half cents; but when the witness resides in or within one mile of the county town, fifty cents per day; and mileage, each mile circular in travelling to and from, three cents. For these fees, the witness may maintain an action against the party sub-pœnaing him;(b) but the witness can demand no fees of the party sub-pœnaing him, for his expenses and attendance, beyond the sum above specified,(c) which will be allowed, in taxation of costs, to the party obtaining judgment, on showing the attendance and travel of the wit-nesses.(d) Where witnesses are brought from another State, the time of their attendance can only be computed from the place of trial, coming and returning to the boundary line of the State.(e) A witness attending voluntarily, is entitled to his fees equally as if he attended on sub-pœna.(f) And witnesses subpœnaed though not examined, and examined though not subpœnaed, are entitled to payment;(g) for a party has a right to call as many witnesses as he thinks necessary to make out his case; and the court will not interfere unless there is proof of oppression.(h) To entitle a party to the costs of his witnesses, and of the service of subpœnas upon them, it is not necessary that their names should have been inserted in the subpœnas by the prothonotary, before delivering them to the party.(i)

If the witness, not having a sufficient excuse, neglect to attend upon the subpœna, he is liable to be proceeded against, first by attachment, for a contempt of the process of the court, whether the cause were called on or not;(j) or, secondly, by a special action on the case for damages, at common law.(k) The more usual way is, to proceed by

(x) 1 Str. 510.
(y) 2 Str. 1150, S. C.; 13 East, 16, n. a.; 1 H. Bl. 49; 1 Phil. Ev. 3.
(z) 1 Bin. 46.
(a) 7 Sm. Laws, 367.
(b) See 15 Johns. 260.
(c) See 14 Johns. 357.
(d) 6 Johns. 330; 7 Taunt. 337; 1 B. Moore, 76. See post, "Costs."
(e) 4 Johns. 311. But see 4 Taunt. 55, 699; 6 Taunt. 88; 1 Marshall, 563, S. C.; 1 Phil. Ev. 5.
(f) 1 Bin. 46; Bac. Ab. Evidence, D.
(g) Ibid.; 1 Bin. 46, S. C.; Debene-ville v. Debeneville, 3 Y. 558.
(h) Ibid.
(i) McWilliams v. Hopkins, Esq., 1 Wh. 276.
(j) 1 Arch. Pr. 152; see Lessee of Knight v. Pechen, 1 Y. 18; and post, 481.
(k) Doug. 561. An additional remedy

is given in England by the Stat. 5 Eliz. c. 9, § 12, but this section of the statute has been declared to be inapplicable to this commonwealth. Report of the Judges, 3 Bin. 621.

See, particularly, McGlinsey v. Mc-Glinsey, D. C., March 25, 1848. Why the entry of "Settled defendant for costs" should not be stricken off, and the case restored to the trial-list. Per curiam. With every disposition to assist a party standing, as the plaintiff does, in a representative character, we think we have not the power to do so. When the case was called, the plaintiff found herself without witnesses; nor was her agent, who had served the sub-pœna, present, to lay the necessary ground for an attachment. She might have submitted to a nonsuit, but in the trouble and embarrassment of the mo-

attachment: and in order to ground this summary mode of proceeding, it is necessary to prove that the witness was personally served with the subpœna ;(*l*) and that his reasonable expenses were paid or tendered him.(*m*) But a witness may, by his own act, dispense with the legal form of serving a subpœna, and may, under such service, be subjected to an attachment.(*n*) The party must, as in ordinary cases, apply in the first instance for a rule on the witness to show cause why an attachment should not issue ; though where the witness has positively refused to attend, the attachment will be granted without a previous rule to show cause.(*o*) Though the Common Pleas may issue subpœnas to any part of the State,(*p*) it is questionable whether they have power to issue writs of attachment into another county ;(*q*) this, therefore, is a reason for the practice above stated,(*r*) where the testimony is important, and it is wished to avoid delay and trouble incident to a proceeding against a witness in another county, for disobeying the subpœna.

An attachment has been refused, where the witness was very old, weak, and infirm, and it was sworn that he could not attend without danger of his life.(*s*) And where it appeared that witnesses, against whom an attachment had issued for disobedience to a subpœna, had been so much indisposed as to be incapable of attending, they were discharged, and the costs of the attachment directed to abide the event of the suit.(*t*) The general rule appears to be, that the party applying for an attachment, must make out a clear case of contempt :. and it seems that, by delay, he loses his right of proceeding summarily against the witness.(*u*)

Where the witness is detained in prison, a *habeas corpus ad testificandum* is necessary to bring him up : for which an application is made to a judge, or the court, upon an affidavit stating the materiality of the witness ; and thereupon the judge or court has a discretion to allow the writ or not, as may appear most proper. If it be allowed, it must, after having been sealed, be served on the sheriff or other officer, in whose custody the witness is.(*v*) It is said that the danger of the prisoner's escape will be at the risk of the party who brings him up ; the charge of which, and also of his being carried back again, must be borne by such party.(*w*)

---

ment, she made a compromise, which she now regrets. We think we cannot relieve her. An action will lie for damages against a material witness who absents himself without any excuse. (Pearson *v.* Iles, Dougl. 561 ; Amey *v.* Long, 9 East, 473 ; Hasbrouch *v.* Baker, 10 Johns. 248.) The application of this salutary rule of law in some proper case would have a very good practical effect in reminding the community that witnesses are responsible for the consequences if they do not obey a subpœna. Much delay and trouble in the trial of causes arise from the neglect and carelessness of witnesses. Rule dismissed.

(*l*) 2 Str. 1054; *sed vide* Barnes, 35.

(*m*) 13 East, 16, n. a.; 1 H. Bl. 49; 1 W. Bl. 36.

(*n*) Feree *v.* Strome, 1 Y. 303.

(*o*) 1 Dunl. Pr. 611.

(*p*) Bell *v.* Lessee of Wetherill, 2 S. & R. 350.

(*q*) Bowen *v.* Douglas, 2 D. 45.

(*r*) *Supra*, 470, 471.

(*s*) Barnes, 497.

(*t*) Butcher *v.* Coats, 1 D. 340.

(*u*) 6 Taunt. 9 ; Barnes, 33, 35, 497 ; 1 H. Bl. 49 ; 5 Taunt. 262.

(*v*) 1 Dunl. Pr. 612.

(*w*) 2 Grad. Forms, 194 ; cites Rich. Pr. K. B. 179; see 5 Johns. 357; 18 Id. 48.

II. *Of compelling the Production of Books and Papers.*

Where writings are in possession of a party to the suit, the other party may either proceed to compel their production under the act of 1798, or, after giving notice to produce them, on non-production may proceed to prove their contents by secondary evidence. By the act just alluded to,(x) the Supreme Court, and the several Courts of Common Pleas in this State, are empowered " in any action depending before them, on motion, and sufficient cause shown by affidavit, and due notice thereof being given, to require the parties, or either of them, to produce books or writings in their possession or power, which contain evidence pertinent to the issue ; and if either party shall fail to comply with·such order, and to produce such books or writings, or to satisfy the courts why the same is not in the party's power so to do, it shall be lawful for them, if the party so failing shall be a plaintiff, to give judgment for the defendant as in cases of nonsuit, and if a defendant, to give judgment against him or her by default, as far as relates to such parts of the plaintiff's demand, or the defendant's defence, to which the documents of the party are alleged to apply."(y) It has very recently been decided by the Supreme Court, that this act does not extend to actions of slander, or other actions founded on *tort ;*(yy) and it seems a proceeding *in rem* is not within the act.(z) The rule may be obtained against executors.(zz)

The correct practice under this law would seem to be this : the party seeking its benefit should obtain from the court in bank previous to the trial, a rule to show cause why such an order should not be made, notice of which should be given to the other party. If the rule be made absolute, and the papers ordered are not produced at the trial, the judge may withdraw a juror'; and the whole proceedings appearing on the *postea*, the court in bank may enter judgment according to the act of assembly.(a) Or if it be the defendant who is in default, the court may discharge the jury, award judgment against him, and make an order in the nature of a writ of inquiry, under the act of 1722,(b) to assess the plaintiff's damages.(c)

" Every order to produce papers under this act must be founded on a previous affidavit ; which, as the law is highly penal, should set forth, with precision, every fact necessary to authorize the court to proceed.(d) The party is to have due notice of the motion,(e) and as he is to come prepared to contest the truth of the facts, he ought to have the same length of time previous to the hearing as would be sufficient for preparation for the trial of an issue before a jury. The notice should describe the book or paper required with sufficient certainty,

---

(x) 3 Sm. Laws, 303.
(y) See 3 Bl. Com. 382.
(yy) Morgan *v.* Watson, 2 Wh. 10.
(z) Epler *v.* Funk, 8 Barr, 470.
(zz) Kuhn *v.* Elmaker, D. Ct. C. C. P. 2 P. L. J. 299.
(a) See McDermot *v.* United States Ins. Co. 1 S. & R. 357.
(b) *Vide ante*, p. 352.
(c) Wright *v.* Crane, 13 S. & R. 447. See the form of judgment and order, ibid.
(d) See a form, ibid.

(e) In a case under the 15th section of the judiciary act of the United States, 2 Laws. U. S. 60, which is very similar in its terms to our act of assembly, it was decided that notice of the rule was well served on the opposite party's attorney, but that, if his client lived at a great distance, the court would pos on the trial until full opportunity had been afforded to the attorney to communicate with his client. Geyger's Lessee *v.* Geyger, 2 D. 332.

and the question on the motion, being only incidental, should be decided previously to the trial of the issue."(*f*) The affidavit should describe with reasonable certainty the books or papers alleged to be withheld, and contain a positive averment, that they are material to the issue, and exclusively in the power of the party against whom relief is sought.(*g*) This rule, as to a positive averment in the affidavit, has, by a very recent decision, been mitigated, and it will now be sufficient if there be an averment that the deponent verily believes that the documents required are material to the issue, and exclusively in the adverse party's power.(*h*) It is also said to be a proceeding in the nature of a bill of discovery, and as such should be viewed with a favorable eye.(*i*) The order of the court ought to be made on the plaintiff on record; and is bad, if directed to a third person, though he is the plaintiff's agent.(*j*) If deeds are on record, the court will not grant a rule on the party in whose possession the originals are to produce them, unless a special reason be assigned.(*k*) The order of the court on making the rule absolute is not peremptory, but in the alternative to produce the papers, or satisfy them *why* it is not in the party's power. Therefore, an affidavit of a party, that it was not in his power to produce the documents called for, would not be sufficient without showing the reason why not, if the court were not otherwise satisfied.(*l*)

The affidavit of one party is sufficient to put the other on determining whether he will deny on oath that the books and papers referred to are in his custody or power : if the latter do so deny, the former must produce proof by *other evidence* before he can have the rule or order made ; but if the denial be not so made, the party's own affidavit, if sufficiently full, is conclusive.(*m*)

An order under the act of 1748, to produce papers is conclusive only of the pertinency of the documents. At the trial, the party may show his inability to produce them by himself, or *per testes.*(*n*) Circumstances have been held to be a sufficient answer to such an order. And it would seem that reading a copy of the paper required waives objections to non-compliance with it.(*o*)

Proceedings under this act are in the sound discretion of the courts ; and when it is exercised, it will require a strong case to induce the Supreme Court to reverse their judgments.(*p*)

It is no answer to a rule taken upon an administrator to produce that such administrator is merely a nominal party, auxiliary to a foreign administrator, and having no custody of the papers.(*q*)

(*f*) Rose *v.* King, 5 S. & R. 244.
(*g*) Ibid.
(*h*) Wright *v.* Crane, 13 S. & R. 450–1.
(*i*) Cowles *v.* Cowles, 2 Pa. R. 139.
(*j*) Houk *v.* Foley, ibid. 245.
(*k*) Geyger's Lessee *v.* Geyger, 2 D. 332.
(*l*) Wright *v.* Crane, 13 S. & R. 451.
(*m*) Skinner *v.* Perit *et al.* C. P. Phila. Jan. 24, 1824, Rep. Dem. Press; U. S. *v.* 28 Packages, G. 306.
(*n*) Gilpin *v.* Howell, 5 Barr, 42.
(*o*) Ibid.
(*p*) Cowles *v.* Cowles, 2 Pa. R. 139.
(*q*) Elliott *v.* Ruddach. D. C. Saturday, Feb. 19, 1848. Why plaintiff should not produce papers on trial. *Per curiam.* The plaintiff is an administrator. His intestate died in Virginia, where the principal administration of course was granted. The administration here, though independent in some respects, is ultimately but ancillary to the administration of the domicil. The plaintiff says that the books and papers called for are not in his possession, but that of the principal administrator. We think this is no answer to the rule, and if the principal administrator refuses to give the plaintiff here the means of complying with the order of the court upon this

A judgment under this act, against a defendant in an action on the case, is interlocutory,˙and the damages may be ascertained by a writ of inquiry.(*r*)

The rule of court and the act of assembly are to govern, and not the reason for which the court may have thought it proper to make the rule. Hence, the court will not go beyond the rule itself and inquire into the items specified in the affidavit of the applicant for the rule, to find some equivalent for the actual production of the books required, such as his adversary's admission that the books contain no entry against him. The rule is peremptory without qualification or condition, and when once made, the directions of the act must govern. Affidavits to account for non-production of the books, such as their destruction, &c., must be produced at the time of trial. Reasons for not making the rule absolute for their production should be offered on the hearing of the rule to show cause, or before the trial the court may be applied to to rescind the rule on adequate grounds.(*s*)

This act of assembly does not affect the common law principle as to the admission of parol evidence of books and papers, which the party has refused to produce on notice. And the remedies by the act, and by the common law, must be considered as concurrent.(*t*)   In cases, therefore, "where the common law principle would be efficacious,˙ but the act of assembly would give no adequate relief," or where the party does not deem it eligible to proceed under the act, he may give notice to his opponent to produce writings in his possession, or that parol evidence would be given of their contents ; and on the trial, before secondary proof can be admitted, it ought to be clearly shown that the writing required is in the possession or power of the other party, and that a notice to produce it has been regularly served :(*u*) but the non-production of books or papers affords no legal ground for any inference respecting their contents, and merely entitles the opposite party to prove their contents by parol evidence.(*v*)   If, in compliance with a notice, the party produce the writings in his possession, he is entitled to have the whole read, if any part of them be given in evidence :(*w*) and if a writing produced refer to others with such particularity as to

rule, the estate must abide the consequences.   As far as this *forum* is concerned, we must consider the plaintiff as fully representing the deceased, and bound, therefore, to produce his books, which he does not aver to be wrongfully withheld.

What the effect of a wrongfully withholding of papers from the party ordered to produce them, must be decided by the judge on the trial.   The order made upon this rule under the act of 27th February, 1798, is an alternative one necessarily, " to produce the books or writings, or to satisfy the court why the same is not in the party's power, so to do :" but it would have to be a case without the least shadow of a suspicion of collusion to make such an excuse available.

The Supreme Court have said (Rose

v. King, 5 S. & R. 246), however, that the order under this act of assembly must be made on such service of notice as would be sufficient for preparation to try an issue of fact.   In conformity with this decision, this court has adopted the practice of requiring thirty days' service of notice before making the rule when the party lives here.   Here the rule was taken, and notice served on the 5th of February.   We enlarge the rule until Saturday, March 11th.

(*r*) Cowles *v.* Cowles, *supra.*
(*s*) McNair *v.* Wilkins, 3.Wh. 551.
' (*t*) Steinmetz *v.* the United States Ins. Co. 2 S. & R. 496.
(*u*) 1 Phil. Ev. 338. See Wh. Dig. " Evidence," xviii.
(*v*) 3 Camp. 363.
(*w*) 1 Phil. Ev. 338 ; 11 Johns. 260.

make it necessary to inspect them, that the sense may be complete, he may insist on having these also read in evidence.(*x*) So, when books are produced on notice, and entries are read in evidence by the party calling for them, the party producing them may read other entries necessarily connected with the former entries, if made prior to the commencement of the suit.(*y*) But the production of papers at the trial, on notice, does not make them evidence for the party producing them, if the opposite party choose to waive the reading of them, which he has a right to do ;(*z*) or if, as it seems, he merely inspect them,(*a*) without using them in evidence.

Where books and papers are produced pursuant to notice, and used, proof of their authenticity is dispensed with, and they are in evidence for both parties.(*b*) But the non-production of books is not proof of facts alleged by the opposite party to be contained in them.(*c*)

When from the form of the action, or the pleadings, the defendant must know that the contents of a written instrument in his possession will come into question, or where the instrument is itself the immediate subject of the action (as in trover, replevin, or detinue), it is not necessary to give any notice for its production, preparatory to its proof by parol evidence.(*e*) But it is not enough that the instrument *is referred to* in the declaration.(*f*)

It is not necessary that the notice should be given to the party himself; it is sufficient to serve it upon his attorney.(*g*) No rule has ever been laid down as to the time previous to the trial that notice must be given; it ought, however, to be a notice reasonable under the circumstances of the case, and will principally depend on the distance of the party, or his papers, from the place of trial.(*h*) The opposite attorney may be called as a witness to prove the contents of a notice which he had received, to produce a paper in the hands of his client.(*i*) And the proof of notice, as in other cases of testimony preparatory to the introduction of secondary evidence, being addressed solely to the judge, and not to the jury, the rule excluding the admission of an interested witness does not apply; and the practice is universal in Pennsylvania for a party to testify as to the service and contents of his own notice.(*j*)

In replevin, upon a distress for rent, where the lease is in the hands of the plaintiff, it will be ordered to be produced and placed in the hands of a proper person, and in default thereof, defendant will be entitled to judgment in his favor for the rent due.(*k*)

Compelling the production of papers under the act of 1798, is a feature of chancery practice as to discovery, and is governed by the same principles.(*l*)

When two papers, mutually dependent, are produced on call, both

(*x*) 4 Esp. Rep. 21.
(*y*) Withers *v.* Gillespy, 7 S. & R. 10.
(*z*) 1 Peters's Rep. 15, 22.
(*a*) Withers *v.* Gillespy, 7 S. & R. 10. See generally Wh. Dig. "Evidence," xviii.
(*b*) Withers *v.* Gillespy, 7 S. & R. 11 ; See also 12 Johns. 223 ; 17 Id. 158.
(*c*) Epler *v.* Funk, 8 Barr, 470.
(*e*) Alexander *v.* Coulter, 2 S. & R. 496 ; 14 East, 274 ; 4 Taunt. 865 ; 2 Merivale, 464 ; 17 Johns. 293 ; 1 Phil. Ev. 339.

(*f*) Alexander *v.* Coulter, 2 S. & R. 497.
(*g*) 3 T. R. 306.
(*h*) 1 Dunl. Pr. 614 ; 1 Caines's Rep. 153 ; See 6 Johns. 19.
(*i*) 7 East, 357.
(*j*) Jordan *v.* Cooper, 3 S. & R. 575.
(*k*) Hurd *v.* Ryan (D. C. All., Lowrie, J.
(*l*) Ibid.

must be read, or neither, if insisted on by the party who produces them.(*m*)

When the court in bank have, under the act of 1798, made an order to produce certain writings on the trial, the judge at *nisi prius* cannot inquire whether they are pertinent to the issue, or whether, if produced, they would or would not be evidence; the order is peremptory and conclusive; though a case might perhaps arise where it would be rescinded by the court in bank. Whilst it lasts, it is presumed that when made, the court were satisfied that the evidence was pertinent, and ought to be produced; whether on its production it is competent evidence, is another question, which cannot arise where the party refuses to produce it on the trial.(*n*)

When books and papers are of a public nature, or are on record, certified entries in the former, and copies of the latter, will in general be evidence; but as our limits will not permit the introduction of the various acts of assembly on this subject, we refer the inquirer for a connected view of the whole to the several acts of assembly, and to the decisions of the courts of this State, which have been elsewhere abundantly collated.(*nn*)

On a rule to produce books and papers, the party on whom it is taken cannot allege that he has transferred them to another; if they be in reality beyond his control he can show it on the trial.(*o*)

The rule to produce books and papers, when absolute, is only a rule nisi.(*p*)

Books produced at a trial, in obedience to an order of the court, are in its custody; and it may allow such access to them, or make such other disposition of them as, in the exercise of a sound discretion, it may deem necessary to fairness and justice. Its orders in respect to them, are, consequently, not subject to a writ of error.(*q*) In general, a party will be allowed the inspection of a document wherever he has a common interest in it, without regard to the right of custody, and at a convenient period before the trial. Thus, in an action to recover certain money alleged to have been received by the defendant to the use of the plaintiff, being the proceeds of sale in a foreign port, of

---

(*m*) Smith's Appeal, 2 Barr, 331. See Wh. Dig. "Practice," xvii.

(*n*) Tuttle *v.* Mechanics' Loan Co. 6 Wh. 218.‛ George *v.* George. D. C. Rule to produce papers. *Per curiam.* The answer admits the possession of the papers asked to be produced, but denies the materiality or relevancy of it to the issue. According to Tuttle *v.* The Mechanics' & Tradesman's Loan Co. (6 Wh. 216), the rule is conclusive upon the judge on the trial on the question of pertinency; but that "whether, on being produced, it would be competent evidence is another question, which cannot arise when the party withholds the evidence at the trial, and refuses to produce it under the rule." It is plain, then, that on the trial, the materiality or relevancy of the papers as well as its proof, if the

custody from which it comes is not enough to prove it, must be decided, because these are all involved in the question of its competence. What is decided there by the rule or order, is, that the paper ought to be produced or its absence accounted for, and this decision cannot be reviewed on the trial by arguments addressed to the pertinency of the paper, without the production of it, though these arguments urged against its competence may exclude it from the jury. R. A.

(*nn*) Purd. Dig. "Evidence;" Wh. Dig. "Evidence," iii. vii.

(*o*) Coleman *v.* Spencer, D. C. Phil. 8 Leg. Int. 239.

(*p*) Ibid.

(*q*) Beales *v.* See, 10 Barr, 58. GIBSON, C. J.

the goods on board of a certain vessel, part of which goods were owned by the plaintiff, and part by the defendant; the court made an order that the plaintiff permit the defendant, on reasonable notice, to inspect a certain paper, being the account-sales of the goods on board the vessel, which had been obtained by the plaintiff from a third person; and to have a copy of it made at his (the defendant's) charge, by a person designated by the plaintiff.(*qq*)

The court will not order that the paper produced be read on the trial without further identification.(*r*)

(*qq*) Arrott *v.* Pratt, 2 Wh. 566.

(*r*) Straun *v.* Park, D. C. Saturday, Oct. 12, 1850. Rule to produce papers, and why they should not be read on the trial without further identification. *Per curiam.* As to the latter part of the rule, it is a novelty in our practice, and we are not prepared to sanction it. It often happens that the production of a paper from the possession of one who is part party to it, dispenses with any proof of its execution; and if that should be the case here, to make the order asked, would be unnecessary; where, according to the rules of evidence, this would not be the case, the party would seem entitled to have it proved, when by his pleading he has denied it. In the English courts, there is a very good practice by which a party is called upon by a rule before a judge at chambers, either to admit or deny the execution of a paper upon the penalty of costs. In the case of Arrott *v.* Pratt, 2 Wh. 566, referred to in the argument, the case was of a paper, the common property of both parties, and when an inspection previous to the trial was ordered. That is not this case. Rule to produce absolute, and residue discharged.

CHAPTER XXIV.

OF TRIAL, AND ITS INCIDENTS.

THE proceedings, introductory or preparatory to the trial of the cause, which have been stated in the preceding chapter, having been had, it is to be tried in the order in which it stands upon the list,(*a*) unless the court continue the cause until the next term, on the application of either party, or leave it open until a day subsequent to that on which it ought, according to the regular course, to be brought on. The trial may also be prevented when the plaintiff, being unprepared, at the time the cause is called on by the judge, suffers a *non pros.* or nonsuit to be entered against him.(*b*) And if a matter of defence has arisen subsequent to the commencement of the suit, and after plea pleaded, so that it could not have been set up as a bar to the further maintenance of the suit,(*c*) and the defendant has had no opportunity to plead it *puis darrein continuance*, he may plead when the cause is called on, and thus prevent the trial. In the present chapter, will be considered as incidents to the trial by jury, in the first place, the subject of continuing and leaving open the cause, and in the next, pleas *puis darrein continuance;* the drawing, challenging, and swearing of the jury; talesmen; proceedings before the jury; bills of exceptions, and filing of opinions; demurrers to evidence; nonsuit, verdict, and damages; special cases and cases stated, and points reserved by the court.

SECTION I.

OF THE CONTINUING OR LEAVING OPEN A CAUSE ON THE LIST.

The rules of the District Court now in force in this connection, are as follows:—

Trial by Jury.

XCVI. No cause, when reached in order on the trial-list, shall be hereafter left open or continued in consequence of a pending engagement of counsel in any other than a court of this commonwealth, of civil jurisdiction, except in the case of any member of the bar, practising in

---

(*a*) But see Wh. Dig. "Practice," xxii. (*o*) as to priority of trial in favor of some causes at Nisi Prius.

(*b*) *Vide ante,* 456.
(*c*) 1 Chit. Plead. 532, 634; Holt's N. P. R. 6.

this court, who shall elect, and so signify in writing to be filed with the prothonotary, and entered on the minute-book, to substitute for the courts of civil jurisdiction before mentioned, either the Court of General Sessions in this city, or the Circuit Court of the United States for the Eastern District of this State.

XCVII. Where more than one counsel are concerned on the same side, the cause shall not be left open on account of the sickness or absence of one of them, nor on account of any engagement out of this court; but in such case the cause may, by consent, be placed at the foot of the list. And if any counsel shall be actually engaged before one of the judges of this court at the time of the calling of a cause for trial before another judge of this court, in which he is also retained as counsel, such cause shall be left open with the privilege of being called on by either party, immediately after the engagement before such other judge shall be terminated, in preference to any other cause not then under trial, or previously left open under this rule.(*d*)

XCVIII. Whenever an action which has been marked for trial shall be reached in order on the trial-list, and either or both parties shall be absent, or, being present, shall assign no legal reason for a continuance, the judge, at his discretion, may order such action to be stricken off the list and marked, "Not to be brought forward," or direct a nonsuit, whether the nonsuit be applied for by the defendant or not: *Provided*, That where a case is stricken off the list, the plaintiff may, during the sitting of the court on that day, upon motion, come under a peremptory rule to try at the next term, or whenever the cause shall be again reached on the trial-list, or be *non pros'd*, as a matter of course.

XCIX. No cause when reached in its order, upon either the trial or argument list, shall be continued, left open, or put at the foot of the list, unless no one of the counsel concerned on the same side shall be able to conduct the trial or argument by reason of sickness, or occasional absence on public business, or an engagement in another court, or before another judge of this court: *Provided*, That where more than one counsel are concerned on the same side of a cause on trial before another court, no one shall be considered as *engaged* within the meaning of this rule, who having a colleague in the cause at liberty to remain till the end of the trial, shall have concluded his address to the jury. And where more than one counsel are concerned on the same side of a cause on trial before another judge of this court, after the evidence is closed in such cause, no one shall be considered as engaged within the meaning of this rule, except the counsel on whom the duty of addressing the jury shall devolve: *Provided, also*, That nothing in this rule contained shall prevent the continuance of a cause, where the usual legal grounds therefor shall be laid before the court.

I.(*e*) No case, when reached on the trial-list, shall be passed on account of an attachment for witnesses, unless it shall have been applied for and issued within one hour after the opening of the court on the day on which the case is marked for trial, except it be shown that the witness or witnesses were in attendance at that time and departed.

LXXIII. No cause shall be placed on the trial-list until after issue joined, nor without the written order of one of the parties or his coun-

(*d*) July 6, 1835.   (*e*) Made January, 1852.

sel; nor shall any cause be placed on the trial-list, for any period, unless the same shall be at issue before the issuing of the *venire* for such period.(*ee*)

Undefended Causes.

CV. Whenever any cause on the trial-list shall not be reached on the day to which it may be assigned, the plaintiff's counsel may, upon filing his own certificate, that he has reason to believe and does verily believe that there is no defence in the said cause, give direction in writing to the prothonotary, that such cause shall be put down upon a list to be called *the list of undefended causes;* and it shall be the duty of the plaintiff's counsel, within twenty-four hours after giving such direction, to give notice thereof to the defendant or his attorney.

The last week of the third period of each term of the list No. 2, is hereby appropriated to undefended causes, and each cause thereon shall be liable to be called up on any day of said week, at the discretion of the judge.

If after the calling of any cause upon the list of undefended causes, it shall appear to the judge that there is a defence, or if the defendant's counsel shall certify in writing to be filed of record, that he has reason to believe, and does verily believe, that there is a defence in the said cause, the same shall not then be tried, but shall be restored to its proper place on the trial-list.

The decisions of the courts on the subject of continuing or forcing on the trial of causes, are these:—

The rules for bringing on causes must be influenced by a legal discretion, applicable to the peculiar circumstances of every case,(*f*) by exercising which, care will be taken by the courts that injustice is not done either by precipitate trials or wanton delays.(*g*) Our courts, sitting to do substantial justice, are fully disposed to bring on causes as early as it may be done, yet this must necessarily be in those cases where the parties are prepared, or have not been guilty of manifest negligence. Therefore, the discovery of a material witness in another State, will, when there is no affectation of delay, be a ground to put off the trial.(*h*)

"It is the duty of a party, if he knows that a witness is about to leave the country, to take his deposition. If he has failed to do so, and knows to what place the witness has gone, he ought to obtain a commission without loss of time, and endeavor to get it executed; and if the witness has departed without the knowledge of the party, of his intention to do so, or of the place to which he has gone, the party is entitled to a reasonable indulgence."(*i*) An affidavit by a defendant, that A (the affirmant's brother) was *a material witness, that he had sailed for a foreign port, "upon a sudden determination, known to the affirmant only three or four days before his departure, and that the affirmant did not advert at the time to the circumstance of his testimony being material,"* is not a sufficient ground for postponing the trial.(*j*) In order to put off the trial, the court must be satisfied that in-

---

(*ee*) See *ante*, 392, 460.
(*f*) Lesher's Lessee *v.* Levan, 2 D. 96.
(*g*) United States *v.* Worral, ibid. 384.
(*h*) Lessee of Campbell *v.* Sproat, 1 Y. 20; see 15 Johns. 293.

(*i*) 1 Peters's Rep. 217, 218.
(*j*) Davidson *v.* Brown, 4 Bin. 243; see 2 Caines's Rep. 384; Symes's Lessee *v.* Irvine, 2 D. 383.

justice would be done, if the application were refused, and it will not be granted if the defendant has conducted himself unfairly;(k) or if the testimony of the witness be intended to support an odious defence.(l) And a postponement was denied where the witness went out of town, after notice of trial given, when he might have been subpœnaed.(m)— But where an attorney of the court is a material witness, and promised to attend, a subpœna is not necessary to entitle a party to a postponement of the trial.(n) A motion for a postponement was granted, the defendant, as soon as he had notice of trial, having taken out a subpœna for a witness at a great distance, neither the witness nor the person employed to serve the subpœna having attended.(o) A cause which had been continued (on account of the absence of material witnesses residing in another county, to whom a subpœna had issued), from a term to which the subpœna was returnable, and again continued at the next term, because an attachment had been issued returnable to that term, which could not be served, was, notwithstanding a rule to try or *non pros.*, continued a third time, subject to the same rule, the defendant having refused to have the depositions taken.(p) The trial of a cause shall not be postponed for the non-attendance of a witness whose deposition has been taken, where the adverse party agrees it may be read in evidence.(q)

The affidavit in support of the motion, generally states that the person absent is a material witness, as the party is advised and verily believes, without whose testimony he cannot safely proceed to trial; that he had endeavored to find the witness, and have him subpœnaed, but without effect, and that he expects to be able to procure his attendance hereafter.(r)

(k) 1 B. & P. 33.
(l) 1 B. & P. 455.
(m) Barnes, 442.
(n) White v. Lynch, 2 D. 183.
(o) Bowen v. Douglas, 2 D. 94.
(p) Pennington v. Scott, 2 D. 44; see Wallace's Rep. 29.
(q) Bond's Lessee v. Hunter, 1 Y. 284; 1 Br. 272.
(r) 1 Sell. Pr. 421; see Wallace's Rep. 46.

The case of Clark v. Cochran, 1 Miles, 282, so fully and ably discusses the subject of granting continuances upon the usual affidavit, that we will here introduce a large portion of the opinion of the court, which was delivered by STROUD, J. The particular point decided in the case will be found stated in precise terms in the course of the ensuing extracts.

"The materiality of the testimony of the absent witness is sworn to in the usual manner, as also the belief of the defendant that his testimony (not his presence) might be had at the next session of the court for jury trials. These are the commonplaces of every application of the kind, and though essential to its success, are of themselves of no avail unless the party can acquit himself of *laches* in not procuring the witness, or his testimony by deposition, on the trial. What then are the facts which bear upon this point? 1. It is sworn that 'the witness has been absent from Pennsylvania more than nine months.' The action was brought on the 16th of April, 1835, by summons returnable on the first Monday of May ensuing. The declaration was filed within four days afterwards. The defendant, therefore, was fully apprised from that time of the cause of action, and it was competent for him to take the deposition of the witness whilst he resided here, which appears to have been about four months after the issuing of the writ, as a *going* witness, upon the knowledge of his intention to remove to New York. In Stotesbury v. Covenhoven, 1 D. 164, this was allowed to a defendant *before* the return of the writ, and a similar privilege has been from early times accorded even to the plaintiff. —— v. Galbraith, 2 D. 78; Anon. 1 Y. 404; Harlan v. Stewart, 2 R. 333. As the defendant has not ventured to swear that he was ignorant of the nature of the testimony of the wit-

Although it has been held,(s) that the affidavit can only be made by the defendant himself, yet this is not absolutely necessary, for if the defendant be abroad, or the facts on which the motion is founded lie exclusively in the knowledge of a third person, the affidavit of a third person will be sufficient.(t) When an affidavit is made of the absence

ness whilst he resided here, nor that he effected his change of residence without his knowledge, he is, upon the principle that he must *discharge* himself of all *laches*, presumed to have been cognizant of both these facts in proper season, and therefore the application is brought fully within the decision of Davidson *v.* Browne, 4 Bin. 243, where the Supreme Court held the party chargeable with *laches*, and that the cause had been rightly ordered on to trial. See also King of Spain *v.* Oliver, Peters's C. C. R. 218. This point was not adverted to when the application for a postponement of the cause was made, and it was not therefore the ground on which the *laches* of the defendant was then affirmed. It was stated orally by counsel at that time, as indeed is to be inferred from the *affidavit*, that the witness had removed from this city and settled in New York in August, 1835, and that he continued in the latter place till sometime in November following—about three months. It was not pretended that any effort had been made during the whole of that period to obtain his testimony by commission or otherwise. On the contrary, the ground distinctly assumed in the trial, and reiterated on the argument of the rule, was, that no obligation rested on the defendant to procure his testimony at New York; that a party circumstanced like the defendant was justified in relying upon the expectation of inducing the personal attendance of a witness on the trial, if in *his* opinion this expectation was well founded; and of consequence, a disappointment in this particular constituted a *legal* cause for a continuance. The *affidavit*, in accordance with this assumption, states, ' whether in Philadelphia or in New York, defendant is certain that at his request said Wilson would attend at the trial of this cause.' We have then this case. A material witness for the defendant, domiciled in a neighboring State, and *actually* resident there for three months subsequent to declaration filed, without any effort having been made to procure his testimony, afterwards leaves that State and is at the time of trial in a remote State, but expected, according to the belief of the party desiring his testimony, to return to his domicil

so that his personal attendance may be *voluntarily* had at the next court for jury trials; and we are called upon to say that this exhibits a legal ground for the continuance of the cause against the will of the plaintiff."

" As to the circumstance of the witness being domiciled at New York, between which and this city the intercourse is so easy and frequent, it is plain that no practical reliance could be placed upon it. A witness there is as much out of the jurisdiction of the court as if he were in Europe. Where the only subscribing witness to a bond was traced to Baltimore, and from the evidence it might fairly be inferred that he was there at the time of the trial of a suit on the bond in the Court of Common Pleas of Cumberland County, he was regarded as dead, because inaccessible to the process of the court, and secondary evidence of the execution of the bond admitted. This was sustained on error to the Supreme Court, although the very question of the proximity of Baltimore was relied on by counsel then, as it has been before us in the present case. ' A general rule,' says YEATES, J., 'must be laid down as to witnesses residing in our sister States, however near or remote from the place of trial.' And the foundation of the rule then established, and followed ever since, was separately and distinctly stated by each of the judges to be the residence of the witness without the jurisdiction of the court. This is a plain and rational test, eminently recommended by its practical convenience. Clark *v.* Sanderson, 3 Bin. 192. Upon the same principle, that a witness out of the jurisdiction of the court is to be regarded as dead, the evidence of a witness on a former trial between the same parties, who, at the time of the second trial, was a resident of another State, was permitted to be proved without any effort having been made to procure his testimony by commission. Magill *v.* Kauffman, 4 S. & R. 317."

(s) Barnes, 437.
(t) Barnes, 448 ; Peake's N. P. C. 97; Jackson *v.* Mason, Jackson *v.* Keely, 1 D. 135 ; Hunter's Lessee *v.* Kenneday, 81.

of a material witness, in order to the postponement of a trial, the court will not inquire into the testimony of the witness, to determine whether he be *really* material.(*u*) But a contrary practice prevails in England.(*v*)

There are other cases in which the trial will be put off if justice require it, as where the costs of a former suit between the same parties, in which the plaintiff was nonsuited, or a verdict passed against him, remain unpaid. So when an amendment of the pleadings is made. But in no case can a continuance be demanded by reason of an amendment, unless where the opposite party is thereby taken by surprise, and of that matter, generally, the court must judge.(*w*) So a trial will not be ordered on where the party has not prepared, making affidavit that he expected a compromise, from the declarations of his adversary; and the costs of the term will, in such case, be ordered to continue on the *remanet*;(*x*) that is, the costs are to *abide* the event of the cause, which *remains untried* at the end of the term, without the fault of either party. It seems, also, that a case in which a member of assembly is a party, cannot be forced to a trial while the session of the legislature continues.(*y*) So, where a party was absent in the service of the State, the trial was postponed.(*z*) But it is not a sufficient ground to continue a cause, that the party, who asks a continuance, has been summoned and sworn as a grand-juror, in the mayor's court;(*a*) or that he is dangerously ill, unless there is an affidavit stating that there were material witnesses, who had not been summoned in consequence of this sickness, or unless the party himself were a witness to prove books or the like.(*aa*)

By the second section of the act of April 14, 1846:(*b*) "From and after the first Monday in December next, it shall and may be lawful for the several courts in the City and County of Philadelphia, whenever a cause is reached in its order, on the trial-list, and the plaintiff or his counsel does not appear, or if he appear, does not proceed to the trial of the cause, and does not assign and prove a sufficient legal cause for the continuance thereof, to enter a nonsuit without motion; and no nonsuit shall be taken off by agreement, nor any cause continued by agreement, without the payment of four dollars to the prothonotary of the said court, for the use of the County of Philadelphia; said payment not to be taxed as part of the costs of the cause, unless so agreed by writing filed; *Provided, nevertheless*, That the parties may, by agreement, at any time before the issuing of the *venire*, for any period, withdraw any case from the trial-list, but the same shall not be entitled to be put down for trial at any subsequent period of the same term, without a special order of the court."

Where a case is not at issue, it is error for a court, in the absence, and without the consent of counsel, to go to trial on it.(*bb*)

Accidental absence of the plaintiff's counsel, when a case is called,

(*u*) Wharton *v.* Morris, 1 D. 125.
(*v*) 3 Burr. 1514; 8 East, 31.
(*w*) Folker *v.* Satterlee, 2 R. 213; 4 D. 353; 1 Br. 38.
(*x*) Cornogg *v.* Abraham, 1 Y. 18.
(*y*) 4 D. 107.
(*z*) Respublica *v.* Matlack, 2 D. 180.

(*a*) 1 Br. 272.
(*aa*) Jones *v.* Little, 2 D. 182; see Phillips *v.* Gratz, 2 Pa. R. 412.
(*b*) Pamph. L. 328.
(*bb*) Ensley *v.* Wright, 3 Barr, 501; see *ante*, 392, 460.

is no ground for taking off nonsuit, as the interest of parties and witnesses demand that a case should be tried when called.(c)

The defendant is not bound to prepare for trial while a motion to quash appeal is pending.(cc)

On granting a continuance, the court will sometimes require that the party shall pay the costs of the term, which will not be refunded to him in case he should ultimately prevail.(d) The costs of the term are principally the prothonotary's and witnesses' fees. When a cause is thus continued, the party may either wait the event of the suit or may demand them immediately, and if not paid, he may proceed to trial; or he may waive this privilege, and resort to an attachment; but if he do so, he must first have the costs regularly taxed on notice.(e)

By the act of April 25, 1850,(f) continuance fees can only be charged on cases actually on the trial-list.

An executor or administrator, who has been substituted under the act of 1791, for a party deceased before final judgment, is entitled to a continuance of the cause until the next term.(g)

It is too late to move for a continuance after one of the jury has been sworn.(h)

The rule that requires a subpœna in the District Court to be taken out and served five days before the trial, applies only to applications for a continuance on account of the absence of witnesses who might have been found within reach of the process within the five days.(i)

The professional business that forms a legal ground for the continuance of a cause, is confined to an engagement in another court, and does not comprehend a professional engagement in another city.(j)

In order to entitle a suit to be continued on account of an outstanding commission, it must appear that no unnecessary delay was suffered to intervene after the commencement of the suit; therefore, where an action was brought in March, 1849, and a commission to examine a witness was not issued till January, 1850, and the case was called for trial on April 9, 1850, and the witness in the mean time had left the city, it was held that a continuance was rightly refused.(k)

The question what is a good ground for continuance will be more

---

(c) Shelley v. Kelly, D. Ct. C. C. P. June, 1848. See post, "New Trial," where the question how far such excuses should prevail is elaborately considered.

(cc) Keller v. Cunningham, 6 Barr, 376.

(d) 1 Hayw. N. C. Rep. 26, 179, 222.

(e) 2 Johns. Cas. 114.

(f) Pamph. L. 627.

(g) 3 Sm. Laws, 30, § 8; see Christine v. Whitehill, 16 S. & R. 98.

(h) 1 Br. 240.

(i) Scriber v. Reeves, D. C. C. P. 9 Leg. Int. 2. See ante, 470.

(j) Olden v. Litzenburg, D. C. C. P. 8 Leg. Int. 106.

(k) Cooper v. Mitchell, Saturday, June 22, 1850. Motion for a rule for a new trial. Per curiam. The court refused to continue the cause on the ground of

an outstanding commission, although it was shown that reasonable diligence had been used in endeavoring to get it executed. The action was brought to March, 1849. The commission to Boston was not issued till Jan. 26, 1850, and the cause was not tried until April 9, 1850. It is said that the commission was still outstanding, owing to temporary absence of the witness from Boston, after his exact residence was ascertained. In other words, the defendant left the business of hunting up the witness to the very last moment, and then found he was temporarily away; and asks that the plaintiff may be delayed a term on that account. It is a plain case of negligence on his part. Rule refused. But see ante, 450.

fully examined in a subsequent chapter, where motions for new trials are considered.

SECTION II.

OF PLEAS PUIS DARREIN CONTINUANCE.

When the cause is called on, the defendant may plead any matter of defence arising *puis darrein continuance,* that is, *after the last continuance,* and such a plea may be pleaded after the jury are gone from the bar, but not after they have given their verdict.(*m*) Neither can it be pleaded after a *relictâ* and *cognovit,*(*n*) given by the defendant.(*o*) This plea admits the original merits to be with the plaintiff, and rests the defence on something that has occurred, or some act that has been done by the defendant since the last continuance of the cause.(*p*) The general rule with regard to a plea of this description is, that it must be pleaded without delay,(*q*) and, therefore, the defendant must not suffer a term to intervene between the happening and pleading of this new matter ; and this is the rule as to all matters arising after issue joined, whether going to the merits or disclosing a personal disability to maintain the suit.(*r*) But for extrinsic reasons, the court may exercise a discretion in receiving such a plea even after a continuance, when, to preserve consistency, they would permit the defendant to enter it *nunc pro tunc,* an affidavit of the truth of the plea and the extrinsic matter first being made.(*s*) The court may, at any time, to prevent injustice, or for special reasons, permit a plea to be put in *nunc pro tunc,* and a plea *puis darrein continuance,* although a continuance has intervened.(*t*) And full satisfaction received by the plaintiff of the claim for which his action was instituted, *before the trial,* need not be pleaded, but may be given in evidence under the general issue.(*u*) If a plea *puis darrein continuance* be well pleaded, issue must be taken on it, or there will be a mis-trial ; if it be bad on its face, the plaintiff must demur ; but if good, in point of form, though pleaded out of due time, the proper course is to move to have it set aside.(*v*) Should a matter, which ought properly to have been pleaded *puis darrein continuance,* be given in evidence without objection, it is not error that it was not pleaded.(*w*) In pleading this plea, extreme certainty is required ; it must contain a precise specification of the day of continuance. To plead that the matter arose since the issue was joined, is a defect for which the plea may be rejected on motion.(*x*)

This plea is either in abatement or in bar. If anything happen pending the suit to abate it, this may be pleaded *puis darrein continu-*

(*m*) Bull. N. P. 310; 1 Chit. Plead. 637.
(*n*) *Vide ante,* p. 340.
(*o*) 1 Cowen, 42.
(*p*) Wilson *v.* Hamilton, 4 S. & R. 239.
(*q*) 7 Johns. 195.
(*r*) Wilson *v.* Hamilton, 4 S.˙ & R. 239.
(*s*) Ibid. 239, 240; 10 Johns. 161; Lyon *v.* Marclay, 1 W. 276 ; Hostetter *v.* Kaufman, 11 S. & R. 146; and see particularly, Bauer *v.* Roth, 4 R. 83.
(*t*) Lyon *v.* Marclay, 1 W. 271.
(*u*) Id.
(*v*) Wilson *v.* Hamilton, 4 S. & R. 239.
(*w*) Hostetter *v.* Kaufman, 11 S. & R. 146.
(*x*) Bleary *v.* Moore, 2 W. 451.

ance, though there is a plea in bar; for this can only waive all pleas in abatement that were in being at the time of the bar pleaded, but not subsequent matter: and judgment thereon, if against the defendant, is peremptory, as well on demurrer as on trial, because after a bar pleaded, he has answered in chief, and therefore can never have judgment to answer over.(*y*)   At common law, the death of a 'plaintiff or demandant, or of a defendant or tenant, might be pleaded after the last continuance.(*z*)   But by the act of April 13, 1791,(*a*) the executor or administrator of a deceased party may be substituted in a suit, in case the cause of action survives by law.(*b*)   So, by section third of the act of April 13, 1807,(*c*) in ejectment, the person next in interest may be substituted for a deceased plaintiff or defendant.   In actions in which there are two or more plaintiffs or defendants, a remedy is provided in case of the death of one or more of them, by the statute 8 & 9 W. III. c. 11, § 7.(*d*)   By the act of March 24, 1818, § 7,(*e*) no suit is to abate by reason of the death or removal of administrators, executors, trustees, or assignees, *pendente lite*, but may be proceeded in by their legal representative or successor.(*f*)   By section four of the act of April 7, 1807,(*g*) no plea in abatement shall be admitted in any suit for partition, nor shall the same be abated by reason of the death of any defendant.(*h*)

If a personal action, which does not survive, is brought after the death of the party, the court may abate it on motion; or if there be doubt about the fact, should put the party to his plea, and that without regard to the previous state of the pleadings, whether the defendant had pleaded in bar or not.(*i*)

In an action by husband and wife, if the husband die pending the suit, but the cause of action survives to the wife, it will not abate, and the wife may proceed to judgment and execution, the death of the husband being suggested upon the record.(*j*)   But in an action against husband and wife, for a contract of the wife *dum sola*, the cause of action does not survive against the husband, and consequently the death of the wife *pendente lite* abates the suit.(*k*)

By the first section of the act of April 12, 1845,(*l*) "no suit, or

---

(*y*) Gilb. C. P. 105; 1 Wheat. 215; Wilson *v.* Hamilton, 4 S. & R. 239.

(*z*) Com. Dig. Abatement, H. 32, 33, 34, 35.

(*a*) ¿ 8, 3 Sm. Laws, 30.

(*b*) Therefore, where in an action for assault and battery, the plaintiff died after an appeal by the defendant from an award of arbitrators in favor of the plaintiff, it was decided that his representatives could not be substituted, and that the award was annihilated: 10 S. & R. 31, Miller *v.* Umbehower. If it be the plaintiff who has died, his representative may make himself party by substitution, without any citation to the opposite party. But if he neglect to do so, the defendant, on suggesting the death of the plaintiff, can, by *scire facias*, compel him to appear, and to prosecute or dispose of the deceased plaintiff's suit:

Reist *v.* Heilbrenner, 11 S. & R. 132. If there be no such representative, the defendant may raise one in the same manner that a creditor or plaintiff might raise one. Ibid. This would be by suggesting the death of the plaintiff, and bringing his representatives in upon process. Ibid. See Clow *v.* Brown, 1 Y. 324; Serg. Cons. Law, 165, 167.

(*c*) 4 Sm. Laws, 476.

(*d*) Rob. Dig. 142; see 2 Saund. 72, *i. k.*

(*e*) 7 Re. Laws, 131.

(*f*) See Wilson *v.* Wallace, 8 S. & R. 56.

(*g*) 4 Sm. Laws, 398.

(*h*) See McKee *v.* Straub, 2 Bin. 1.

(*i*) Sandbach *v.* Quigley, 8 W. 460.

(*j*) 1 Chit. Plead. 22.

(*k*) Id. 43, 44.

(*l*) Pamph. L. 386.

other legal proceeding, in any court of this commonwealth, brought by a feme sole, now or hereafter pending, shall abate by the marriage of the plaintiff or petitioner, contracted after the commencement of the same; but the husband of such plaintiff or petitioner shall have the power to become a party thereto, and prosecute the same to final judgment or decree."

When a plaintiff's representative has been substituted, the defendant is obliged to defend without further ado. A *scire facias*, or citation, when necessary to be issued, must be served sixty days before the meeting of the court wherein the suit is depending.(*m*)

The marriage of a feme plaintiff, during the pendency of the suit, before the act of 1845, could be pleaded *puis darrein continuance.(n)* But the marriage of a feme defendant does not abate the suit, and the plaintiff may proceed to execution without noticing the suit.(*o*) So, it may be pleaded to an action by husband and wife, that they are divorced pending the writ.(*p*) The insolvency of a plaintiff does not abate the suit, but it may be continued by the trustees or assignees.(*q*)

There appears to be no exception to the rule that, in actions real, personal, or mixed, a defence arising after the last continuance may be pleaded in bar to the plaintiff's right.(*r*)

Since the act of 1806, a plea in bar of matter subsequent to the issuing of the writ, need not be pleaded *puis darrein continuance;* nor does it waive any former pleas.(*s*)

The defendant may plead in bar, *puis darrein continuance,* payment,(*t*) or that the plaintiff has given him a release, or that he has obtained a discharge under an insolvent act;(*u*) or a judgment recovered against him as executor.(*v*) So, in debt by an administrator, it may be pleaded that the plaintiff's letters of administration are revoked *puis darrein continuance;(w)* and a recovery and satisfaction in another suit for the same cause may be pleaded in like manner.(*x*) A plea *puis darrein continuance,* waives all former pleas; the defendant must stand or fall by it; and if put in issue it forms the only subject of inquiry before the jury.(*y*) This plea must be drawn with great certainty, and must be verified by affidavit.(*z*)

If the defendant succeeds on this plea, he is entitled to the costs incurred after its interposition, but not to the costs of the whole cause; for the plea shows that the action was rightfully commenced.(*a*)

(*m*) Act of 1791, § 8.
(*n*) Wilson *v.* Hamilton, 4 S. & R. 238; 2 Wheat. 111.
(*o*) 1 Bac. Abr. 16; Str. 811; 4 East, 521.
(*p*) Com. Dig. Abatement, H. 42.
(*q*) Act of March, 1814, § 4; 6 Re. Laws, 195.
(*r*) Brownfield *v.* Braddee, 9 W. 149.
(*s*) Johns *v.* Bolton, 2 J. 339.
(*t*) Salk. 519, *pl.* 16.

(*u*) 2 Dunl. Pr. 626.
(*v*) 5 Taunt. 333, 665.
(*w*) Bull. N. P. 309.
(*x*) 9 Johns. 221.
(*y*) Wilson *v.* Hamilton, 4 S. & R. 239. [*Quere,* whether, in Pennsylvania, such a plea is a waiver of a previous plea in bar? See 4 R. 83.]
(*z*) Ibid; 1 Chit. Pl. 636; 1 Br. 77.
(*a*) 4 Barn. & Cress. 117; 10 S. & Low. 285.

SECTION III.

OF BALLOTING FOR, CHALLENGING, AND SWEARING THE JURY; AND OF TALESMEN.

If neither party take any step by which the trial of the cause is prevented, the jurors are to be balloted for and called, and when twelve of the panel appear, are to be sworn. But before the jury are called either party may challenge the array, that is, except to the whole panel in which the jury are arrayed, or set in order, by the sheriff, in his return; or, as each juror is called he may be challenged, which is termed a challenge to the polls.(*b*) In addition to this right of making challenges to the array or to the polls, for cause, it is provided by the act of April 4, 1809, § 2,(*c*) re-enacted by § 150, act of 14th April, 1834,(*d*) "that in all civil suits, each party shall be allowed to challenge two jurors *peremptorily*." "The spirit of this privilege is, that a party shall possess the power of challenging at least two persons who may be obnoxious to him, but against whom there is no legal exception as jurors."(*e*) But it does not permit the challenge of viewers.(*f*) This act does not direct the mode in which the challenge shall be made when both parties wish to challenge, but it has been the general practice for the plaintiff to challenge one juror from the whole panel first, after which the defendant may challenge one; the right of making a second challenge then comes to the plaintiff; and then to the defendant. If the plaintiff waive the second challenge, when it comes to his turn to make it, he cannot resume it again.(*g*) So, too, if he waive his right to challenge altogether, and the defendant challenge two jurors, whose places are supplied by two others, the plaintiff cannot resume his right and challenge the latter.(*h*) Either party may waive his first or second challenge.(*i*)

Though a jury has been struck on both sides, each party is, *it seems*, nevertheless, entitled to two more peremptory challenges under the act of assembly.(*j*)

The right is a valuable one, and should not be fancifully restricted; hence the waiver of the first challenge of a juror by each party, is not a waiver of the second also. There is no reason why a party should be precluded by a waiver of the entire right on both sides, provided the panel has not been closed by swearing the jurors in the mean time.(*k*)

It is not cause of principal challenge to a juror, that his sister is the wife of the nephew of a party; but if made to the favor of the juror it would be sufficient, with evidence of great intimacy between the juror and party, to induce triers to exclude him from the jury.(*l*) Nor is it cause of challenge that the juror is brother to the counsel of one of the

(*b*) See Co. Litt. 156, *a.*; 3 Bl. Com. 359; 1 Arch. Pr. 169.
(*c*) 5 Sm. Laws, 59.
(*d*) Pamph. L. 368.
(*e*) Schwenk *v.* Umsted, 6 S. & R. 354.
(*f*) Ibid. 351.
(*g*) Patton *v.* Ash, 7 S. & R. 116.
(*h*) Wenrick *v.* Hall, 11 S. & R. 153.

(*i*) Ibid.
(*j*) Schwenck *v.* Umsted, 6 S. & R. 351. [But see the remarks of GRIER, J., on this case, in Blanchard *v.* Brown, 1 Wall. Jr. 309.]
(*k*) Kennedy *v.* Dole, 4 W. & S. 176.
(*l*) Rank *v.* Shewey, 4 W. 218.

parties.(*m*) Nor, in ejectment for land sold for taxes, that the juror purchased other land sold at a subsequent period for taxes.(*n*)

But it is good cause of principal challenge, in an action for mesne profits, that he had acted as an arbitrator on the trial of an ejectment for the same land, brought by the same defendant, and had awarded in his favor.(*o*) So, if he has been subpœnaed as a witness by the plaintiff, and had given evidence on a former trial.(*p*) So, a tenant who holds from year to year as a cropper is disqualified, in an action to which his landlord is party.(*q*)

It is not error to allow a challenge of a juror for cause, upon its appearing that he is interested in the result, although it should, on further progression in the trial, appear that he had no interest.(*r*)

It is cause of challenge, that the juror is tenant to one of the parties.(*s*)

By § 151 of the act last cited, no person shall be deemed incompetent to serve as a juror in any suit on any official bond or forfeited recognizance, or on any penal act of assembly, by reason of his being subject to any tax which would be diminished by a recovery in the case.

By § 149, no alien shall be entitled in any case to a jury *de medietate linguæ*, or party of strangers.

By § 139, on the return of the *venire*, the prothonotary shall cause the names of the jurors summoned to be written separately, on distinct slips or pieces of paper, as nearly alike in size and appearance as may be; he shall, by direction and under notice of the judge presiding, roll or fold up the said slips separately, and as nearly in the same manner as may be, and put them in a box to be provided by him for that purpose.

And by § 140, where the cause shall be ready for trial, some disinterested person shall, by direction of the court, in open court, draw from the said box, after having well mixed the papers deposited therein as aforesaid, twelve of the said papers, one after another; and if any of the jurors whose names shall be so drawn shall not appear, or shall be challenged or set aside, such person shall proceed to draw as aforesaid a further number of the said papers, until twelve jurors shall appear and be approved; and the said jurors, having been sworn or affirmed, as the law directs, shall be the jury to try such cause.

The oath or affirmation to be administered to jurors impanelled in any cause as aforesaid, shall be in the following form, to wit:—

You, and each of you, do [swear or affirm], that you will well and truly try the issue joined between C D, plaintiff, and E F, defendant, and a true verdict give according to the evidence, unless dismissed by the court, or the cause be withdrawn by the parties. So, &c. § 141.

If the jury be sworn irregularly, through the oversight of both parties, and the verdict be rendered without objection against two, one of whom

(*m*) Zeiter *v.* Zeiter, 16 S. & R. 214.
(*n*) McCall *v.* Larimer, ibid. 351.
(*o*) 2 R. 492; 14 S. & R. 292.
(*p*) 1 Pa. R. 32.

(*q*) 16 S. & R. 214.
(*r*) Silvis *v.* Ely, 3 W. & S. 420.
(*s*) H. Bank *v.* Forster, 8 W. 304.

had not appeared, the Supreme Court will correct the error without ordering a new trial, where the merits are not thereby affected.(t)

The names of the jurors drawn and sworn, or affirmed, in any cause as aforesaid, shall be written on a panel, and the slips or papers which bear those names shall be kept apart by themselves in some other box, to be provided as aforesaid and kept for that purpose, until such jury shall give in their verdict and the same be recorded, or until the said jury shall, by consent of the parties, or by the order of the court, be discharged from the cause, and thereupon the names of the said jurors shall be again rolled up as aforesaid, and returned to the box first above mentioned, and mingled with the names of the jurors remaining at that time undrawn; and the like proceedings in all respects shall be had so often as any cause shall be called on for trial during the holding of the court.

If a second or any subsequent cause shall be called for trial, before the jury charged as aforesaid with the first or any former cause shall have given in their verdict, or shall be otherwise discharged, it shall be lawful for the court to proceed as aforesaid to impanel a jury in such second or subsequent cause of the jurors remaining for the trial thereof; and so in like manner as long as any of the jurors aforesaid shall remain. § 143.

After a juror is sworn a challenge cannot be permitted for cause pre-existing. The proper course is, in such case, to direct a juror to be withdrawn, and to call a fresh jury.(u)

The presumption is, that a jury is properly sworn; and where, in an action of trespass against three defendants, only one of whom had pleaded, the entry on loose memoranda kept by the clerk, and transferred to the docket, that the jury were sworn to try the issue between plaintiff and the defendant, who had pleaded "et al.," will not overcome that presumption.(v)

Jurors are sworn to try not a particular issue, but all the issues, when more than one; and can be relieved of this duty only by one of the parties, with leave of court to withdraw a count or plea.(w)

When a person is called as a juror, whose name is not in the venire, and a party suffers him to remain on the jury without objection, and takes his chance of a verdict, it is a waiver of the objection.(x)

At common law, if a sufficient number of jurymen did not appear at the trial, or so many of them were challenged and set aside, as that the remainder could not make up a full jury, there issued a writ to the sheriff, of undecim, decem, or octo tales, according to the number that was deficient, in order to complete the jury.(y) But now, by the act just cited, § 144, " If a sufficient number of the persons summoned and returned, shall not appear as required, or if by reason of challenges or otherwise, there shall not be a sufficient number of jurors present, competent for the trial of any cause which shall be called for trial, the sheriff or coroner, or if the case require it, two citizens to be appointed by the court for that purpose, shall, upon the order of the court, immediately summon and return from the bystanders, or from the county at

(t) Haas v. Evans, 5 W. & S. 253.
(u) Gearheart v. Jordan, 1 J. 326.
(v) Breidenthal v. McKenna, 2 H. 160.

(w) Good v. Good, 9 W. 567.
(x) Burton v. Ehrlich, 3 H. 236.
(y) Gilb. C. P. 73; 2 Saund. 349, n. 1.

large, so many qualified and competent persons as shall be necessary to fill up the jury for the trial of such cause;" and in case of their neglect to attend shall be liable to the same fine as the court would inflict on jurors regularly summoned who make default; the fine to be collected in like manner. § 145.

On a *tales de circumstantibus,* bystanders only, or those actually present in court, can be selected or returned as jurors.(z)

SECTION IV.

OF PROCEEDINGS BEFORE THE JURY.

I. *Opening the Case and Examination of Witnesses.*

Before the enactment of the act of March 21, 1806,(a) every man had a right, by the constitution, to be heard by himself and counsel, in *criminal* prosecutions; but it is said there existed no law which gave him the same right in civil cases;(b) the 9th section of this act, therefore, gives him the same right in all *civil* suits and proceedings in courts, to be heard by himself and counsel or either of them. When the jury have been called and sworn, if the affirmative of the issue be on the part of the plaintiff,(c) as it usually is where the general issue is pleaded, the plaintiff or his counsel states his case to the jury, and then calls and examines his witnesses, who may be cross-examined by the counsel for the defendant. After the plaintiff has gone through with his evidence, and rested his cause, the defendant or his counsel opens the defence, and produces and examines his witnesses, who may be cross-examined on the part of the plaintiff.

A party cannot, before he has opened his case, introduce it to the jury, by cross-examining the witnesses of the adverse party.(d) And "a witness cannot be cross-examined to facts which are wholly foreign to the points (and I would add, to what he has already testified), for the purpose of contradicting him by other evidence. And here," said GIB-SON, C. J., in a leading case, "I take occasion, in broad terms, to dissent from the doctrine broached in Mr. Phillips's Law of Evidence, p. 211, that a witness actually sworn, though not examined by the party who has called him, is subject to cross-examination by the adverse party; and that the right to cross-examine is continued through all the subsequent stages of the cause, so that the adverse party may call the same witness to prove his case, and for that purpose ask him leading questions."(e)

The rules of the District Court in this respect are as follows:—

C. The party calling a witness shall in all cases state briefly the point or points which he proposes to establish by his testimony.

CI. The detention for the purpose of noting his testimony, of a wit-

---

(z) Philips v. Gratz, 2 Pa. R. 412.
(a) 4 Sm. Laws, 330.
(b) 2 Br. Appx. 25; *sed vide* Steph. on Plead. 28, 1st edit.
(c) See Leech v. Armitage, 2 D. 125; Delaney v. Regulators, 1 Y. 403.

(d) Ellmaker v. Buckley, 16 S. & R. 72.
(e) *Per* GIBSON, C. J., delivering the opinion of the court. Id. 77. See Wh. Dig. "Evidence," xxii. xx.; "Practice," xxii.(f)

ness under examination, shall be regulated by the discretion of the judge, in the particular cause on trial.

CII. The entire examination of a witness shall be conducted by one only of the counsel of each party. The re-examination by the party calling him shall be confined to the matter of the cross-examination.

After a witness has been examined and cross-examined, the court may, at their discretion, permit either party to examine him again, even as to new matter, at any time during the trial.(*f*)

When a witness is called, the opposite party may, first, examine him on his *voire dire*, before he is sworn in chief, as to his interest in the event of the cause; still, if, without his being examined on the *voire dire*, it appears in any part of the trial that he is interested, the court will reject his testimony.(*g*) The ancient rule, that an objection to a witness is waived by permitting him to be sworn, does not now hold.(*h*) If a witness has been sworn on his *voire dire*, no other evidence to prove him incompetent can be given.(*i*) But if it should appear, in any subsequent stage of his examination, that he was incompetent, the court will set him aside.(*j*) Or, secondly, the opposite party may show the witness's interest by other evidence. And if one party has proved by evidence *aliunde*, that a witness is interested, the other cannot offer the witness's own oath to show that he has no interest.(*k*) In most cases a witness may be divested of interest by a release or payment, or any other means, when he is ready to be sworn, there is no objection to his competency.(*l*) A release to a person otherwise interested will restore his competency, though made at the bar during the trial;(*m*) unless, by the policy of the law, he be incompetent.(*n*)

"If a person, not a party on the record, be called as a witness and objected to by the adverse party on the score of interest, the party making the objection must show the interest, and if it should *clearly* appear to be so from the testimony adduced for the purpose of proving it, the *court* will decide upon it and reject the witness: but if it be in the *least degree doubtful*, the court will not decide the question of interest in the witness, but will receive his testimony and leave it to the *jury* to determine whether he has an interest or not in the event of it, and if they should be of opinion that he has such an interest, then instruct them to pay no regard whatever to his testimony, and to leave it altogether out of view."(*o*) So, where a person who is a party plaintiff on the record, after having at the trial assigned all his interest in the

(*f*) Curren *v.* Connery, 5 Bin. 488.

(*g*) Phil. Ev. 96, 204; Bank of North America *v.* Wikoff, 2 Y. 39, S. C.; 4 D. 151.

(*h*) Ibid.

(*i*) 1 Peters's Rep. 338; Mifflin *v.* Bingham, 1 D. 275; see Shannon *v.* Com. 8 S. & R. 444. A party to a cause, sworn on his *voire dire* to his book of original entries, cannot be examined *generally*, by the opposite party, without his own consent or that of his counsel; but can only be examined to show it was not his book of original entries, or that the entries were not made at the time. Shaw *v.* Levy, 17 S. & R. 99.

(*j*) 1 Peters's Rep. 338.

(*k*) Vincent *v.* The Lessee of Huff, 4 S. & R. 298.

(*l*) Phil. Ev. 97; 1 Peters's Rep. 307.

(*m*) Lilly *v.* Kitzmiller, 1 Y. 28; see further as to the release of a witness, Wh. Dig. "Evidence," xix.(*p*); 14 Johns. 387; 16 Johns. 270; 18 Johns. 60; Richter *v.* Selin, 8 S. & R. 425; Patton's Administrators *v.* Ash, 7 S. & R. 116; Hart *v.* Heilner, 3 R. 407.

(*n*) See fully, Wh. Dig. "Evidence," xix.(*p*)

(*o*) Hart *v.* Heilner, 3 R. 410.

suit to a coplaintiff, and paid into court all the costs of suit, is called as a witness, if the assignment "be made to appear *clearly* to the *court* to be collusive, *they* would interpose and reject the witness; and where there occurred *any difficulty as to the fact*, they would instruct the *jury* to pay no regard to the testimony of the witness, if they were satisfied that the assignment was merely colorable."(*p*)

"A party offering evidence, when called on, should state the purpose for which it is offered, for, on the main question, it might be wholly irrelevant, yet an incident might have occurred, during the trial, which would render it material; as, where the credit of a witness is impeached, that might be evidence to corroborate him, which would not be received on the issue."(*q*) Where the party, offering evidence, is called upon to state for what purpose it is offered, he will be confined to the point which he states it is proposed to prove by such evidence; but if it be objected to *generally*, all that is incumbent upon the party offering it is to show that it is proper for some purpose.(*r*)

It has grown into practice, within these few years, for counsel to propose a chain of evidence, the first links of which depend on those that follow, and would not be supportable without them. When, therefore, evidence, in itself irrelevant, has been given to the jury, with a promise that it should be followed by other evidence, connected with which, it would be relevant, but such evidence is not given, the former cannot be argued upon by counsel, or if written, be taken out by the jury, and the court should instruct the jury to pay no regard to it in making up their verdict.(*s*)

The time and manner of examining witnesses is a matter very much in the discretion of the court before whom the trial is had.(*t*) It is not regular to introduce evidence after the counsel have begun their address to the jury, although, where circumstances render it proper, the court may permit it.(*u*) Thus, it seems, if a new witness arrived, who had been subpœnaed and failed to appear before the evidence was closed, his evidence would be admitted.(*v*) And where the evidence was not discovered before the time it was offered, it ought to be admitted.(*w*) The law, however, leaves this case wholly to the discretion of the court by whom the cause is tried; and whether that discretion be exercised one way or the other, it is not the subject of a writ of error. Therefore, where an attachment of contempt had issued against a witness who had been subpœnaed on the part of the defendant, and being brought in, after the evidence was closed and one counsel on each side had spoken, the court rejected his testimony, on error alleged, the Supreme Court refused to interfere.(*x*) If, after the plaintiff has closed his evidence, without having made out such a case as will entitle him to recover, evidence is given on the part of the defendant, the plaintiff may give

(*p*) Ibid.
(*q*) Anderson *v.* Neff, 11 S. & R. 219.
(*r*) 11 S. & R. 352.
(*s*) Stewart *v.* The Huntington Bank, 11 S. & R. 267.
(*t*) Duncan *v.* McCullough, 4 S. & R. 480; Devall *v.* Burbridge, 4 W. & S. 529.
(*u*) Ibid.

(*v*) Ibid.
(*w*) 7 Johns. 306; Richardson *v.* Lessee of Stewart, 4 Bin. 198. See, further, as to the time and order in which evidence is to be offered, Wh. Dig. "Evidence," xx.; Richardson *v.* Lessee of Stewart, 4 S. & R. 480; Starkie, 117.
(*x*) Frederick *v.* Gray, 10 S. & R. 182.

evidence to rebut that of the defendant, although, by so doing, he cures the defects of the case on which he originally rested.(y)

If the court be divided in opinion on the admissibility of evidence, it must be admitted.(z)

The following important rules exist in the District Court:—

I. In all actions brought in this court upon any deed, bond, bill, note, or other instrument of writing, a copy of which shall have been filed within two weeks from the return day to which the action is brought, it shall not be necessary for the plaintiff, on the trial, to prove the execution thereof, but the same shall be taken to be admitted, unless the defendant, by affidavit, filed at or before the time of filing his plea, shall have denied that such deed, bond, bill, note, or other instrument of writing was executed by him.

II. In all actions by or against partners, it shall not be necessary for the plaintiff, on the trial, to prove the partnership; but the same shall be taken to be admitted as alleged on the record, unless one or more of the defendants shall, at or before the time of filing their plea, make and file an affidavit denying the existence of the partnership as alleged, and stating, to the best of his or their knowledge and belief, whether there is any partnership in relation to the subject matter of the action, and who are parties to it.

II. *Withdrawing a Juror.*

During the trial, either after the jury are sworn, and have heard the evidence, or before it has been submitted to them, parties sometimes agree to *withdraw a juror;* the effect of which is, that the cause goes off, without impairing the rights of either party,(a) until the next term. This is usually done at the recommendation of the judge, in cases where it is doubtful whether the action will lie, or where the judge intimates an opinion, that, under the peculiar circumstances of the case, the action should proceed no further.(b) It seems to have been once doubted whether, in civil cases, the court had power to direct a juror to be withdrawn, without consent of the parties. But it is now settled that this may be done, in the exercise of a sound discretion, instead of nonsuiting the plaintiff; thus saving him from the consequences of a fatal defect in his testimony. And it is proper to do so, in case of a surprise or mistake on his part, in the preparation of his cause for trial, even where he has not been wilfully misled by the defendant.(c) Where the interest of a party is in danger of being sacrificed, the court can prevent injustice by withdrawing a juror—a power which, in the opinion of able judges, should be liberally but judiciously exercised.(d) Where a cause had been tried before arbitrators, and a deed admitted without objection, and on appeal, the same deed being offered, was rejected by the court on the ground that the seal of a foreign corporation, attesting its acknowledgment, and not proved; this is not sufficient reason for withdrawing a juror on the ground of surprise.(e) In our practice, where a juror is withdrawn, the costs abide the ultimate event of the

(y) Cutbush v. Gilbert, 4 S. & R. 551.
(z) 1 Peters, 434, n.
(a) 1 Arch. Prac. 196.
(b) Ibid.
(c) 8 Cowen's Rep. 127; and see 5 Id. 30.
(d) Rentzheimer v. Bush, 2 Barr, 89.
(e) Chew v. Keck, 4 R. 163.

suit. In England, it seems that each party pays his own costs.(f) This case was one of a payment of money into court, which the plaintiff refused to take till after the jury were sworn, and the whole cause was thus disposed of.

Where a juror, after being sworn, fails to appear, the cause cannot be proceeded with without consent. No substitution can be made; his attendance must be compelled, or the jury dismissed and another impanelled.(g)

III. *Summing up of Counsel.*

The defendant having closed, sums up his cause to the jury,(h) and the plaintiff's counsel may then reply. If the affirmative of the issue be on the defendant, as where, without pleading the general issue, he pleads some other matter which confesses and avoids the cause of action, he is entitled to open and reply.(i) Thus, if to a declaration in waste, the defendant plead *liberum tenementum,* he is entitled to the opening.(j) So, in covenant on the plea of *covenants performed,* the defendant's counsel have a right to begin the evidence and to conclude.(k) So, where the defendant pleads payment, without the general issue, he has the conclusion to the jury; but the court will not permit him to withdraw a plea of the general issue, at bar, for the purpose of obtaining that right. The general rule is, that whoever maintains the affirmative of the issue begins and concludes.(l) But where there are two pleas, one affirmative and the other negative, the plaintiff shall always open the cause.(m) And, although in most cases where the defendant pleads merely an affirmative plea, he is, by the course of practice, entitled to the conclusion; yet the plea of *property* does not, as it seems, produce this effect in the action of *replevin.* The plaintiff ought, notwithstanding, first to prove that he has a right to maintain his writ of *replevin,* by showing that he has either an absolute or special property in himself.(n) Under the practice of Pennsylvania, the defendant in ejectment is not entitled to the general reply, where the plaintiff, claiming by descent, proves his pedigree and stops, and the defendant sets up a new case in his defence, which is answered by evidence on the part of the plaintiff.(o)

By the rules of the District Court:—

CIII. After the evidence in a cause on trial is closed, neither party

---

(f) 3 T. R. 659.

(g) Pennell *v.* Percival, 1 H. 200.

(h) In the English courts the defendant's counsel, upon the trial of an issue of fact, is never allowed to address the jury but once, and that in opening the defence. In doing this, he must make all the comments he has to offer to the jury, both upon his adversary's evidence and his own. He then examines his witnesses, and the counsel for the plaintiff replies upon the whole case. If the defendant examines no witnesses, there is no reply, and the cause goes immediately to the jury, upon the charge of the judge. From this rule there is no deviation, except, perhaps, in trials for treason, and some other state prosecutions. U. S. Law Journ. No. V. Jan. 1826, p. 135.

(i) 2 Dunl. Pr. 637; Delaney *v.* Regulators of Philadelphia, 1 Y. 403.

(j) Leech *v.* Armitage, 2 D. 125.

(k) Norris *v.* Ins. Co. of North America, 3 Y. 84.

(l) *Per curiam,* Delaney *v.* Regulators of Philadelphia, 1 Y. 404.

(m) Inglis *v.* Inglis, 2 D. 47.

(n) Marsh *v.* Pier, 4 R. 283; *per* KENNEDY, J.

(o) Lessee of William M'Causland *v.* M'Causland, 1 Y. 304; *contra,* 4 T. R. 497.

shall be entitled to address the jury by more than one counsel. If evidence has been received on behalf of each party, the counsel having the right on the pleadings to begin, shall sum up, stating explicitly the grounds upon which he intends to rely, and citing such authorities as he may deem pertinent. One of the counsel of the opposite party may then address the jury as fully as the nature of the defence may require. Afterwards, the counsel who commenced the summing up may conclude, restricting himself to enforcing the grounds previously taken by him, and combating the views of the opposite counsel. When the party *not* entitled to begin shall produce no testimony, the counsel of the other party shall be confined to his address in summing up, and shall not be heard in reply.

The rule which prohibits the parties from addressing the jury by more than one counsel after the evidence in the cause on trial is closed, is repealed in cases when all the issues in fact to be tried by a jury are upon special pleas, and in cases when the plea of non assumpsit, or the plea of *non est factum* is pleaded under the said rules, either with or without other special pleas.

It is not the subject of error to refuse to allow counsel to address the jury unless excepted to.(*p*)

The court cannot prevent an attorney in the case from being a witness; but, after testifying for his client, it may, in a sound discretion, forbid his addressing the jury.(*q*)

A refusal to let the opinion of the Supreme Court be read to the jury as the law of the case, is not error.(*r*)

After the evidence on both sides has been closed, and the counsel have summed up, the judge usually charges or instructs the jury. The court has a right to instruct the jury as to all questions of law growing out of the facts of the cause; a party, also, has a right to ask the opinion of the court on any point of law relevant to the issue.(*s*) And it is the duty of the court to answer fully the points upon which they are requested by counsel to charge the jury.(*t*) But it is not necessary that they should answer the propositions submitted, in the very words of the proposition. It is enough if the answers be sufficiently full to be understood. Nor is it necessary, when the same proposition is repeated, though in different words, to answer every repetition of it, one full answer is enough.(*u*)

The court is not bound to answer points proposed, which according to the rules of court are out of time.(*v*)

The court ought not to answer questions propounded by counsel, unnecessary to the decision of the cause.(*w*)

If the judge answers the points by a general direction, a special response to each is unnecessary. His recognition of a number of disjointed propositions would give the jury but little instruction. It is

---

(*p*) Wilkins *v.* Anderson, J. 399.
(*q*) Johns *v.* Bolton, 2 J. 339. See *ante*, p. 220.
(*r*) Good *v.* Mylin, 1 H. 538 ; affirming Noble *v.* McClintock, 6 W. & S. 58.
(*s*) Shaeffer *v.* Landis, 1 S. & R. 449, 176 ; Hamilton *v.* Menor, 2 S. & R. 70; Vincent *v.* Lessee of Huff, 4 S. & R. 298 ;

Bellas *v.* Hays, 5 S. & R. 427 ; see also *post*, " Error."
(*t*) See Wh. Dig. "Error," iv. (b)
(*u*) See Wh. Dig. "Error," iv. (b)
(*v*) Kinley *v.* Slite, 4 W. & S. 426.
(*w*) Fox *v.* The Union Academy, 4 W. & S. 353.

therefore not error to extract the law contained in them, and apply it in a connected form to the evidence.(*x*)

By the rules of the District Court :—

XXXII. Points upon which the opinion of the court is desired on the trial of the cause, shall be plainly written and so framed that the answer of the court will be full, direct, and explicit, by a simple affirmation or negation. A copy of the points shall also be presented to the court at the close of the evidence and before the commencement of the summing up, or the court will at their discretion refuse to charge the jury upon the points proposed.(*y*)

XXXIII. Either party excepting to the charge of the court to the jury shall, before the rendition of the verdict, state distinctly the several matters of law in such charge to which he excepts; and no general exception to the whole of the charge shall be allowed by the court, but the exceptions to the matters of law so distinctly stated, and those only, shall be allowed in the bill of exceptions.(*z*)

By the rules of the Common Pleas (C. C. P.):—

XIII. Sec. 1. If on the trial of a cause the counsel on either side wish the charge of the court on any point or points of law arising in the case, and which were made in the argument, the point or points on which the charge is required shall be distinctly stated in writing, and delivered to the court as soon as the evidence in the case is closed, and before the summing up is commenced; but the court will not hold themselves bound to charge upon any point which shall not have been previously made in the course of the trial.

Sec. 2. Exception must be taken to the charge before the jury retire from court, or proceed to consider their verdict.

The court are not bound to give an opinion on facts ;(*a*) they may give an opinion to the jury on the weight of evidence, or they may decline to do so, if they think proper; if it be doubtful, it is in general most proper to leave it to the jury.(*b*) But nothing should appear in the charge from which the jury might reasonably infer they were precluded from considering the facts.(*c*) When the whole case is mixed up of law and fact, the judge may leave the whole to the jury, unless the counsel select some particular point for his opinion.(*d*)

SECTION V.

OF BILLS OF EXCEPTIONS; AND OF FILING OPINIONS UNDER THE ACT OF 1806.

I. *Bills of Exceptions.*

If on the trial of a cause, the judge deliver an erroneous opinion in some matters of law properly within the decision of the court, and

---

(*x*) Lynch *v.* Welsh, 3 Barr, 297.

(*y*) Note by J. Miles, Esq.—See 1 S. & R. 519–20; and S. & R. 228, 232; 8 S. & R. 150; 7 S. & R. 273, 277; 14 Peters, 321; 15 Peters, 378 and 405.

(*z*) See *Ex parte* Crane, 5 Peters, 180; 12 S. & R. 196.

(*a*) Galbraith *v.* Black, 4 S. & R. 210.

(*b*) 1 Peters's R. 229. See *post*, "Error."

(*c*) Sampson *v.* Sampson, 4 S. & R. 329; see further 1st and 2d Wh. Dig. tit. "Error."

(*d*) Poorman *v.* Smith's Executor, 2 S. & R. 464; see further as to the charge,

which would not otherwise appear upon the record, the party aggrieved, although he may in general avail himself of the error by moving for a new trial, has notwithstanding an option to tender a bill of exceptions, which may become parcel of the record, and on which a writ of error will lie. A bill of exceptions ought to be on some point of law, either in admitting improper,(e) or rejecting proper evidence,(f) or on a challenge to the jury, or in refusing to allow an amendment at the trial, under the act of 1806,(g) or on some matter of law arising upon a fact not denied, in which either party is overruled by the court,(h) or where the court, in charging the jury, expresses an incorrect opinion upon a question of law ;(i) in these and other cases,(j) it is enacted by Stat. 13, Ed. I. c. 31,(k) " if one impleaded before any of the justices allege an exception, praying that the justices will allow it, that if they will not, and if he write the exception and require the justices to put their seals to it, the justices shall do so, and if one will not, another shall."(l) If the record then be brought into a Court of Error, " and the same exceptions be not found in the roll, and the plaintiff show the exception written, with the seal of a justice put to it, the justice shall be commanded that he appear at a certain day, either to confess or deny his seal. If he cannot deny it, they shall proceed to judgment according to the same exception, as it ought to be allowed or disallowed."(m)

The statute of Westm. 2, which gives a bill of exceptions to "any one impleaded before the judges," does not extend to an inquiry of damages executed at the bar. The absence of any precedent proves that the statute has been restrained in practice to the letter, which embraces no more than a proceeding in which the party is "impleaded :" that is, the trial of an issue of fact. Although the execution of a writ of inquiry at bar resembles such a trial, yet it is only an inquest in which, by legal intendment, the sheriff sits as judge ; and there is nothing in the 27th section of the act of 1722 giving a bill of exceptions in such a proceeding.(n)

A bill of exceptions does not lie to the opinion of the court in receiving or rejecting testimony on a motion for summary relief.(o) Neither is the granting or refusal of the court to order a new trial,(p) the refusal to direct a nonsuit,(q) the subject of a bill of exceptions. At common law, if it be wished to have the opinion of the Common

---

Fisher v. Larick, 7 S. & R. 99 ; Irish v. Smith, 8 S. & R. 573, 150. See a full statement of the authorities in Wh. Dig. "Error," iv. (b) Courts I. ; and *post*, "Error."

(e) Salk. 284, pl. 16.

(f) See Zeigler v. Houtz, 1 W. & S. 533, for a merited rebuke, by Mr. Justice HUSTON, to the practice of taking bills of exception to all evidence offered, which he characterizes, justly, as absurd in every aspect, and indicative at once of want of respect to the court, and of confidence in the counsel's ability to discriminate between what is and what is not legal testimony. Of twenty bills in that case one or two only deserved even notice.

(g) Clymer v. Thomas, 7 S. & R. 178 ;

Man's Lessee v. Montgomery, 10 S. & R. 192.

(h) 2 Dunl. Pr. 641 ; Bull. N. P. 316.

(i) 4 Cranch, 62.

(j) See 1st and 2d Wh. Dig. "Error."

(k) Rob. Dig. 93.

(l) See Wolverton v. Com. 7 S. & R. 277, 278.

(m) See Downing v. Baldwin, 1 S. & R. 302 ; and see the authorities collected, Wh. Dig. "Error," iv. and *post*, chap. xxviii.

(n) Bell v. Bell, 9 W. 47.

(o) Shortz v. Quigley, 1 Bin. 222 ; see, also, Miller v. Sprecher, 2 Y. 162.

(p) Burke v. Lessee of Young, 2 S. & R. 383 ; Wright v. Lessee of Small, 2 Bin. 93.

(q) Girard v. Gettig, 2 Bin. 234.

Pleas examined on a writ of error, it will be necessary, instead of asking for a nonsuit, to state some specific point, and pray their opinion on it to be given in charge to the jury.(r) If the judge, in his charge, express an opinion on facts not warranted by the evidence, the only remedy is by a motion for a new trial.(s) No advantage can be taken by bill of exceptions of an erroneous opinion, on a point of law immaterial to the issue ; but the plaintiff in error may assign error in an opinion on any point material to the issue appearing on the bill of exceptions, although it was not particularized in stating the exceptions below.(t)

" The statute does not expressly mention at what time the exception is to be tendered, but the reason of the thing, the practice of most courts, and the precedents and authorities on the subject, prove that it must be *at the time of the trial.*"(u) Exceptions to *evidence* must be taken, as soon as the court has decided to admit or reject the evidence. It is sufficient, however, if a note be made of the exception, and submitted to the court at the time it is taken. It may afterwards be reduced to form.(v) If the evidence be withdrawn after the court has decided to admit it, that should be stated in the bill of exceptions : for, if the bill state that the court permitted evidence to be given, and then exception was taken on error brought, it cannot be alleged that no such evidence was afterwards given.(w) If an exception be taken to the opinion of the court rejecting evidence, and the evidence is afterwards admitted, the exception cannot avail the party.(x) A bill of exceptions to the *charge* of the court, may be tendered at any time before the jury have delivered their verdict in open court, even after they have agreed upon it and sealed it up.(y) In that case, also, it will be sufficient if the substance of the exception be reduced to writing and tendered to the court at the time, which may afterwards be reduced to form.(z) " But in all such cases the bill of exceptions is signed *nunc pro tunc;* and it purports on its face to be the same as if actually reduced to form and signed, pending the trial. And it would be a fatal error, if it were to appear otherwise ; for the original authority under which bills of exceptions are allowed, has always been considered to be restricted to matters of exception taken pending the trial, and ascertained before the verdict."(a) But the court is not bound to suspend the trial of a cause, until a bill is drawn in form and sealed. A note in writing, made at the time the exception is taken, containing the substance of the exception, to be reduced to form afterwards, is sufficient.(b)

A bill of exceptions to the charge, if taken after verdict, is in time, if sealed by the court and sent up with the record.(c)

(r) Widdifield v. Widdifield. ibid. 249.

(s) Burd v. Dansdale, 2 Bin. 80 ; Long v. Ramsay, 1 S. & R. 72; Brown v. Campbell, ibid. 176 ; Graham v. Graham, ibid. 330; Hamilton v. Menor, 2 S. & R. 70; Renn. v. Penna. Hospital, ibid. 413; Poorman v. Smith's Executors, ibid. 464; Henwood v. Cheeseman, 3 S. & R. 500.

(t) Phœnix Ins. Co. v. Pratt, 2 Bin. 308.

(u) Morris v. Buckley, 8 S. & R. 216.

(v) Ibid.

(w) Brindle v. McIlvaine, 9 S. & R. 74.

(x) Crouse v. Miller, 10 S. & R. 155.

(y) Jones v. North America Ins. Co. 4 D. 249; S. C. Jones v. North America Ins. Co. 1 Bin. 38. See *ante*, p. 500.

(z) Morris v. Buckley, 8 S. & R. 216.

(a) 9 Wheat. 651.

(b) Stewart v. Huntingdon Bank, 11 S. & R. 267.

(c) Dock v. Hart, 7 W. & S. 172.

A bill of exceptions(*d*) does not draw the whole matter again into examination, but only the specific points, to which the attention of the court is directed, by their having been the subject of exception at the trial.(*e*)　And when several exceptions are taken by the same party at the trial, all are not included in the same bill of exceptions, but are separately stated.(*f*)　All discussions must be confined to, and no notice can be taken of, matter not appearing on the face of the bill of exceptions.(*g*)　In examining the admissibility of evidence in the court above, the party excepting is to be confined to the specific objection taken at the trial.(*h*)

On tendering the bill, if the exceptions therein are truly stated, the judges ought to set their seals in testimony that such exceptions were taken at the trial; but if the bill contain matter false or untruly stated, or matters wherein the party was not overruled, the judges are not obliged to affix their seals; for that would be to command them to attest a falsity.(*i*)　If the judges of a Court of Common Pleas refuse to seal a bill of exceptions, the only effectual mode to compel them is by writ of mandamus, under the 10th section of the act of 1836.(*j*)

But the law is now settled that the Supreme Court have no power to issue a mandamus to the District Court, to compel them to sign a bill of exceptions.(*k*)

After the bill is sealed, and judgment has been rendered in the cause,(*l*) a writ of error is brought to remove the proceedings into the Supreme Court, upon which the points excepted to may be argued and decided in that court.　In England, upon the return of the writ of error, the judge is called upon by writ, to come in and confess or deny his seal.(*m*)　But, in our practice, the bill of exceptions is part of the

---

(*d*) As to the form of a bill of exceptions, and the statements which it should contain, see Bull. N. P. 317, 319, 320; 6 Cranch, 226; Tidd, 902; Newlin *v.* Newlin, 1 S. & R. 275; Richardson *v.* Lessee of Stewart, 4 Bin. 198.　"The reference in the bill of exceptions to the notes of the counsel concerned for the parties, and the notes of the evidence of the judges before whom the cause was tried, does not answer the design of a bill of exceptions, which is to desire the opinion of the court on certain points of law propounded to them on some given state of evidence.　To refer them to the notes of several gentlemen, however accurate and correct they may be in noting the evidence, cannot be said to afford a precise statement of facts.　The notes will not always agree, nor is it to be expected that they should.　If they disagree, what is the reviewing court to do?　They cannot decide upon their relative accuracy and exactness.　Besides, it is imposing on the courts a task which their duty does not require of them, of wading through volumes of notes, where only a small portion of them relates to the particular point, in which the opin-

ion of the court is required.　This, besides consuming time unnecessarily, creates confusion and incertitude as to the facts, for the bill does not draw the whole matter into examination; but only the point on which it is taken; it is a practice which ought not to be countenanced.　It saves a little labor at the moment, but finally wastes much time."　Per DUNCAN, J., delivering the opinion of the court, Thomas *v.* Wright, 9 S. & R. 91-92.

(*e*) 8 Johns. 495; Bull. N. P. 316.

(*f*) 2 Dunl. Pr. 644.

(*g*) 8 East, 280; Bingham *v.* Cabbot, 3 D. 38; ibid. 422, n.; Baring *v.* Shippen, 2 Bin. 168; see Withers *v.* Gillespy, 7 S. & R. 15.

(*h*) 11 Wheat. 119, 209.　See fully Wh. Dig. "Error," and *post,* chap. xxviii.

(*i*) Bull. N. P. 316; 3 Bl. Com. 372.

(*j*) *Vide ante,* p. 10; Morris *v.* Buckley, 8 S. & R. 211; Com. *v.* Court of C. C. of Cumberland County, 1 S. & R. 195, 199.

(*k*) Duxel *v.* Man, 6 W. & S. 386.

(*l*) See Eichelberger *v.* Nicholson, 1 S. & R. 430; Bull. N. P. 317.

(*m*) See 3 Burr. 1693.

record, and always comes up with it; and for that reason the judge is never called on to acknowledge his seal, which is necessary only where the bill of exceptions has not been tacked to the record.(n)

If the commission of the judge have expired, or his death have occurred before the return of the bill of exceptions, the mode of procuring a return is by moving the Supreme Court for a *certiorari* directed to him in the first case, and his executors or administrators in the second to return the bill.(o) So, where either event takes place, after an exception taken and immediately noted by the judge, though not reduced to form.(p)

In England, the proceeding by bill of exceptions, it is said, has become almost obsolete, being commonly declined partly from an apprehension of disrespect, and partly from considerations of the expense attendant on making up the record; and the course of moving for a new trial, or to set aside the verdict, is usually substituted.(q) In this State, neither the one nor the other reason operates to discontinue the practice; the idea of disrespect if ever entertained, being always disavowed, and the additional expense being in our system very inconsiderable; so that with us bills of exceptions are universal media through which to try, in the supreme tribunal of the State, the correctness of opinions delivered in the several Courts of Common Pleas.

By the act of March, 1812, § 2, (r) "When more than one exception is taken, or point made in any Court of Common Pleas, or other court of inferior jurisdiction, and the same has been duly removed to the Supreme Court for their decision, the judges of the Supreme Court are enjoined and required to give their opinion on every point and exception, taken and signed in the inferior court, which opinion so delivered, if required by either plaintiff or defendant, or any third person, interested in the event of the cause, shall be filed in writing by the said judges, with the prothonotary of the proper district."(s)

The rules of the District Court, in this respect, are as follows:—

XXV. In every case where a bill of exceptions is tendered, the same shall be prepared in form, and presented to the judge, within ten days after the verdict.

XXVI½. In every case of a bill of exceptions, it shall be the duty of the party presenting the bill, within thirty days thereafter, to have the same settled by the judge before whom the case was tried, on forty-eight hours' notice, with a copy of the bill served on the opposite party; otherwise, the judge shall not be required to seal the same: *Provided,* That the rule now in force, requiring the bill to be presented within ten days, be not affected by the adoption of this rule.(t)

II. *Filing Opinions.*

The act of 24th February, 1806, § 25,(u) has made some alteration in the practice of this State, with regard to bills of exceptions. By

(n) Withers v. Gillespy, 7 S. & R. 15; Clark v. Russell, 3 D. 419, n; Bull. N. P. 317.
(o) Galbraith v. Greene, 13 S. & R. 85.
(p) Ibid. 87; see fully Wh. Dig. "Error," and *post,* chap. xxviii.

(q) 2 Ev. Poth. on Oblig. 328.
(r) 5 Sm. Laws, 308.
(s) See as to this law, Brac. L. Mis. 198; Ibid. 93.
(t) Adopted Jan. 1852.
(u) 4 Sm. Laws, 276.

this act, "in all cases in which the judge holding the Court of *Nisi Prius*, or presidents of the Courts of Common Pleas, shall deliver the opinion of the court, if either party by himself or counsel require it, it shall be the duty of the said judges respectively, to reduce the opinion so given, with their reasons therefor, to writing, and file the same of record in the cause."(v) The opinion of the court being thus placed upon the record, supersedes the necessity of a bill of exceptions,(vv) and any error in the opinion may be taken advantage of, when brought before the Supreme Court on a writ of error.(w) The opinion, however, should always be accompanied by a statement of such facts as are necessary to understand it, and it is the business of the party who objects to it to see that the necessary facts are placed on the record.(x) There is nothing in the act which prevents the counsel proceeding by a bill of exceptions, although the opinion of the judge is filed. So that the evidence may always be introduced, whether contained in the judge's opinion or not.(y) But it seems it would be the duty of the court, if required, to permit the necessary evidence to be placed on the record, without a tender of a bill of exceptions. Such request, however, should be made immediately on the delivery of the opinion, and the statement of the evidence should be prepared by the counsel, and submitted to the court, in the same manner as in a bill of exceptions.(z) But the judge is not obliged to return the evidence on which his opinion is founded.(a) In many instances the judge's notes have been sent up, with consent of both parties. This practice was introduced to save trouble, and in that respect is said to have its use; but the Supreme Court have frequently expressed their disapprobation of it; because it presents a mass of useless matter, which must be separated from that which is relevant, and thus increases the labor and expense of the proceedings. When it is intended to have the opinion of a Court of Common Pleas reviewed in the Supreme Court, it should be the object of the counsel to have the necessary evidence stated as clearly and concisely as possible, and no more need ever be stated than is necessary for the elucidation of the opinion to which exception is taken.(b)

As to the filing of the entire charge of the court, the following are the sentiments of the Supreme Court: "There is great truth in the ob-

(v) See the observations of Mr. Justice Duncan, upon this law. Collins v. Rush, 7 S. & R. 151; and particularly Brown v. Caldwell, 10 S. & R. 114; see, also, Brac. L. Mis. 531, 92; also, Reigart v. Ellmaker, 14 S. & R. 124.

(vv) In May, 1807, it was determined by the president of the first judicial district (Rush), that the act did not extend to cases where there existed previously to it a legal remedy to obtain the opinion of a judge in *writing*, as on bills of exceptions, where evidence is admitted or rejected, or points of law stated in a charge to the jury; but that it should be confined to questions arising on special verdicts, demurrers, cases stated, points reserved, and such other cases as the court, in its discretion, and for its own character, may deem of sufficient magni-

tude to merit an accurate statement, in order to settle and adjust an important principle. 1 Br. 43, 47; but see *supra*, 503.

It is held by the District Court of this city and county, that the act, being passed before that court's existence, does not comprehend it, and if the law operate so inconveniently in practice, as is represented by Mr. J. Duncan, the construction put upon the act by the District Court cannot be complained of.

(w) Downing v. Baldwin, 1 S. & R. 298.

(x) Ibid.

(y) Bassler v. Niesly, ibid. 431.

(z) Ibid.

(a) Ibid.

(b) Ibid. 432; and see Wenrick v. Hall, 11 S. & R. 154.

servation of Mr. Justice STORY, in Evans v. Eaton,(c) that spreading a charge *in extenso*, on the record, is an inconvenient practice, and may give rise to minute criticisms and observations upon points incidentally introduced for purposes of argument and illustration, by no means essential to the merits of the cause. And the principle laid down by the Supreme Court of the United States, in that case, is perfectly just, and ought to be applied to opinions filed under the act of assembly, that, in causes of this nature, the substance only of the charge is to be examined; and if it appears on the whole, that the law was justly expounded to the jury, general expressions, which may need and would receive qualification, if they were the direct point in judgment, are to be understood in such restricted sense."(d)

If the opinion, when requested to be filed, be not accompanied with the reasons therefor, it will not be held as error, in the Supreme Court, but as the act is positive in that particular, every judge in executing it acts on his own responsibility.(e)

It was formerly thought and ruled, that if the opinion of the president of the court below is filed of record, with the reasons, the court above in error are bound to notice it, though it do not appear to have been filed at the request of either party, as they cannot presume that this was his own voluntary officious act, and done without such request.(f) "It matters not which party requested it. It is of record, and consequently the subject of revision. It differs, in this respect, from a bill of exceptions, which the party taking the exception may use or not as he pleases. The statute of Westminster 2d, giving the bill of exceptions, is different in its provisions from the act of assembly. The bill of exceptions does not form a part of the record. It is tacked to it. Its authenticity depends on the acknowledgment by the judge of his seal. It is called, emphatically, his bill of exceptions; that is, the bill of exceptions of him who takes it. Being for the benefit of the party who tenders it, remaining in his possession, it is in his breast to employ it or not. If the bill be tacked to the record, and certified by the judges below, it is then a part of the record, and comes up with it. But if it be not, then it seems necessary for the judge to come into court, and acknowledge his seal affixed to the bill. But an opinion filed, instantly becomes a part of the record, and subject to revision."(g) But in a more recent decision it was ruled, that the Supreme Court will not consider any paper annexed to the record, as furnishing the opinion of the court below, under this act, unless it also appears by the record, that the paper was filed at the request of one of the parties or of his counsel.(h) This request may appear by a certificate of the judge, filed with his opinion, or a memorandum at the foot of it; for, as a Court of Error can inspect nothing but the record, it cannot receive information of the fact elsewhere. It is the business of counsel, therefore, to see that the proper evidence be sent up; for where the fault cannot be repaired by

(c) 7 Wheat. 426.

(d) *Per* DUNCAN, J., delivering the opinion of the court, Gibbs v. Cannon, 9 S. & R. 202. See Wh. Dig. "Error."

(e) Moreberger v. Hackenberg, 13 S. & R. 26, 28.

(f) Brown v. Caldwell, 10 S. & R. 114.

(g) Ibid. 115, *Per* DUNCAN, J., delivering the opinion of the court.

(h) Lancaster v. De Normandie, 1 Wh. 49.

a supplementary certificate, he will else lose the benefit of his exception.(i) It does not alter the case that the charge has been since filed at the request of counsel, when this appears to have been done at a subsequent term; in this respect it is like a bill of exceptions, which must be tendered at the trial, for if the party then acquiesce he waives it. The statute of Westminster 2 is very general, and appoints no time for taking the bill; but it has been required, from the nature and reason of the thing, that the exception should be reduced to writing, when taken and disallowed, like a special verdict, or demurrer to evidence. It need not, it is true, be drawn up in form, but the substance must be reduced to writing while the thing is transacting, because it is to become a record. When, therefore, a party wishes to except to the charge of the court, his exception must be noted at the trial, and must be accompanied with a request to file the charge; otherwise, the party will be deemed to have waived it.(j)

Unless exception be taken at the trial, the charge, filed pursuant to request made on the following day, is not the subject of error.(k)

The opinions of a judge filed under the act of 1806, says Judge BELL, become thereby incorporated with, and are of the body of the record, and not merely tacked to it, like a bill of exceptions; and the Supreme Court, in a very recent case, distinctly reaffirmed the rule that, to bring the opinion of the court properly on the record, it must appear to have been filed by the judge, at the express request of a party to the action, preferred at the time of the trial. A subsequent prayer comes too late, though only a day intervenes.(l)

Though it is not necessary that there should be an exception recorded to a filed charge; yet the party making the request may be called on to specify what portions of the charge he asks to be reduced to writing.(m)

The judge is not, when called on to comply with this act, bound to reduce to writing his whole charge to the jury, and file it.(n) Nor is he bound to annex to the record a copy of the evidence taken by him, and transcribed by the party making the request. But it is his duty, if requested, to permit so much of the evidence as may be necessary to understand his opinion to be placed on the record;(o) reciting and confirming the doctrine above quoted.(p) This act does not apply to the rejecting or admitting of evidence, so as to oblige a judge to file his *reasons* in writing for such rejection or admission.(q)

This act makes no alteration as to those matters which are the object of revision in the Supreme Court, by writ of error. Therefore, the decision of an inferior court, on a motion for a new trial, is not the subject of a writ of error, although the reasons of the judges may be filed of record, conformably to the act.(r)

(i) Ibid. 51; Bratton v. Mitchell, 5 W. 71.

(j) Ibid. See Wh. Dig. "Error."
(k) Holden v. Cole, 1 Barr, 303.
(l) Meese v. Levis, 1 H. 385.
(m) Id. 386.
(n) Reigart v. Ellmaker, 14 S. & R. 121; id. 125.
(o) Id.

(p) Downing v. Baldwin, 1 S. & R. 298; and see in p. 124 of the same book, some comments of the Chief Justice on the nature and use of this act.

(q) Morrison v. Moreland, 15 S. & R. 61. See Wh. Dig. "Error."

(r) Burd v. Dansdale, 2 Bin. 80; ibid. 93; see Wh. Dig. "Error."

The judgment on the writ of error is, that the former judgment either be affirmed or reversed: if it be reversed, a *venire de novo* issues, if the error corrected took place in the course of the trial.(s)

SECTION VI.

OF DEMURRERS TO EVIDENCE.

A demurrer to evidence is a proceeding by which the judges, whose province it is to answer to all questions of law, are called upon to declare what the law is, upon the facts shown in evidence, analogous to the demurrer, upon facts alleged in pleading.(t) For, if the party wishes to withdraw from the jury, the application of the law to the fact, and all consideration of what the law is upon the fact, he then demurs in law upon the evidence; the effect of which is, to take from the jury, and to refer to the judge, the application of the law to the fact.(u)

Where the court is asked to direct the jury to disregard the testimony of a particular witness, it is the duty of the court to compel a demurrer by the party so applying, or else to permit the opposite party to address the jury.(uu)

The demurrer to evidence originally grew out of necessity; and fell into disuse only when the increasing liberality of the English judges, in granting new trials, afforded a more convenient method of obtaining the judgments of the Superior Courts at Westminster. With us, there is perhaps some reason why it should be retained and even encouraged, inasmuch as the opinion of the court in the last resort cannot be had on a motion for a new trial in the Common Pleas.(v)

As it is the peculiar province of the jury to ascertain the truth of facts, and the credibility of witnesses, the party ought not to be allowed, by a demurrer to evidence, or any other means, to take that province from them, and draw such questions *ad aliud examen.*(w) The rule, therefore, is, that the demurrer must admit the truth of all facts, which the jury might find in favor of the other party upon the evidence laid before them, whatever the nature of that evidence may be, whether of record, or in writing, or by parol.(x) Where the evidence is *written,* and where, though *parol,* it is certain, the party who offers it must join

---

(s) Ebersoll *v.* Krug, 5 Bin. 53; Miller *v.* Ralston, 1 S. & R. 309; Nash *v.* Gilkeson, 5 Ib. 351; see Wh. Dig. "Error," and *post,* chap. xxviii.

(t) 2 H. Bl. 205.

(u) Bank *v.* Donaldson, 6 Barr, 179; 3 Bl. Com. 372.

(uu) Lee *v.* Lee, 9 Barr, 169.

(v) Crawford *v.* Jackson, 1 R. 431; Per GIBSON, C. J. See 11 Wheat. 72, 179, 184, and the reporter's note, p. 183, where it is said, that the demurrer to evidence is an unusual and antiquated practice, which the courts have recently endeavored to discourage, as inconvenient, and calculated to suppress the truth and justice of the cause; also,

that it is allowed or denied by the court where the cause is tried, in the exercise of sound discretion, under all the circumstances of the case; and that, as it seems, the exercise of this discretion cannot be made the foundation of a writ of error. See also the case of Fowle *v.* The Common Council of Alexandria, ibid. 320; and in criminal cases, Com. *v.* Parr, 5 W. & S. 345.

(w) Doug. 134.

(x) 5 Rep. 104; Alleyn, 18; Hurst v. Dippo, 1 D. 20; Peaceable *v.* Eason, 4 Y. 54; Snowden *v.* Phœnix Ins. Co., 3 Bin. 457; Dickey *v.* Schreider, 3 S. & R. 413.

in the demurrer, or waive the testimony. If the plaintiff refuse to join in demurrer, except on terms which the court disapproves, the plaintiff's evidence must be considered as withdrawn, and the jury must find a verdict for the defendant.(y) But where the evidence is uncertain or circumstantial, the party by whom it is offered may specify the facts which he wishes to be expressly admitted, before he joins in the demurrer. The judge must decide upon that matter, and every fact should be admitted which the evidence conduces to prove, though but in a slight degree.(z) So, if the evidence conflict, the party demurring must admit that of his adversary to be true, so far as it conflicts with his own.(a) So, if the plaintiff call several witnesses to prove the same transaction, some of whom testify unfavorably to him, and others in his favor, the defendant, by demurring to the evidence, admits that the latter have told the truth, and so the court must take it, though the jury would have believed the former.(b) So, if one fact tends to the induction of another, the last fact should also be admitted. Under these restrictions, it is the right of the party demurring to insist on the demurrer being joined.(c) Where there is parol evidence of a fact, which is not evidence of any other fact, but itself a substantive ingredient in the case, a party may be required to join in demurrer.(d) It is the duty of the judge to be liberal in directing the admission of facts, and if he err in judgment, it will be good cause for the court in bank to order a *venire facias de novo*.(e) The court will, also, on the argument of the demurrer, make every inference of fact in favor of the party offering the evidence, which the evidence warrants, and which the jury might with the least degree of propriety inferred ;(f) but they ought not to make forced inferences ;(g) or, if upon consideration of the record, the court should be of opinion that there are not facts sufficient to warrant a judgment, they may order a *venire de novo*.(h)

On a demurrer to evidence, the damages may be assessed conditionally by the principal jury before they are discharged; or they may be assessed by another jury upon a writ of inquiry, after the demurrer is determined.(i) The judgment of the court in bank on such demurrer, is, that the evidence is or is not sufficient to maintain the issue joined.(j)

The judgment of the court, on a demurrer to evidence, stands in the place of the verdict of the jury, and the defendant may take advantage of any defects in the declaration, by motion in arrest of judgment, or by writ of error.(k) Though on a demurrer to evidence, judgment will

---

(y) Crawford v. Jackson, 1 R. 427 (the inquirer is referred to the judgment of the court in this case, as it particularly considers the character of demurrers to evidence in Pennsylvania jurisprudence); 2 H. Bl. 206; 2 Arch. Pr. 185.

(z) Duerhagen v. U. S. Ins. Co. 2 S. & R. 185; Davis v. Steiner, 2 H. 275; see 4 Cranch, 219.

(a) Morrison v. Berkey, 7 S. & R. 245.

(b) Feay v. Decamp, 15 S. & R. 228.
(c) Duerhagen v. U. S. Ins. Co. 2 S. & R. 185; see 11 Wheat. 320.

(d) Crawford v. Jackson, 1 R. 427.
(e) Ibid.
(f) Ibid; Peaceable v. Eason, 4 Y. 54; McKinley v. McGregor, 3 Wh. 370.
(g) Morrison v. Berkey, 7 S. & R. 245; see 1 Stark. Ev. 439.
(h) Duerhagen v. U. S. Ins. Co. 2 S. & R. 185; 2 H. Bl. 187; 11 Wheat. 320, 324; see Wh. Dig. "Practice," xxiv.
(i) Bull. N. P. 314; Doug. 222; Bingh. on Judgm. 8.
(j) Bull. N. P. 313. See the form of a demurrer to evidence and joinder therein, Bull. N. P. 314.
(k) 11 Wheat. 171; *contra*, Doug. 208.

not be given if the declaration set forth an illegal cause of action, or no cause of action at all, yet it waives all objections merely formal; and what would be cured by verdict, is cured by a demurrer to evidence.(*l*)

On a demurrer to evidence, variance between the declaration and proof will not be considered very critically.(*m*)

SECTION VII.

CONDUCT OF JURY, NONSUIT, DAMAGES, AND VERDICT.

1. *Conduct of Jury, and herein of what papers they may take out.*

The jury having been charged, may, if they think proper, withdraw from the bar to deliberate on their verdict.(*n*)

By section 160, of the act of 1834, it is declared that every juror, impanelled in any cause, who shall know anything relative to the matter in controversy in such cause, shall disclose the same in open court, before the jury shall retire to consider of their verdict.

And by § 161, if any juror, drawn or summoned, shall, in any cause, directly or indirectly, take anything to give a verdict, or shall take or receive, as aforesaid, any gift or gratuity, whatever, from either party to such cause, such juror shall forfeit and pay ten times the value of the thing so taken, one half to the commonwealth and the other half to the person that will sue for the same, and shall also be liable to prosecution by indictment, as for a misdemeanor: *Provided*, That nothing in this section shall debar the party aggrieved, of his action to recover the damages he shall sustain, in all cases where the penalty aforesaid shall be recovered at the suit of any other person.

Every person who shall procure any such juror to take, gain, or profit in the manner or for the purpose aforesaid, shall be deemed guilty of embracery, and shall be subject to the same pains and penalties, to be adjudged or recovered by indictment or action as aforesaid.

The practice of permitting a party to file papers, even during the trial, stipulating to avoid errors, and affecting the merits of matters in issue, ought to be discountenanced; and it is error if exception be taken when the papers are offered or sanctioned by the charge of the court; after judgment, defects or errors in the trial affecting the merits, cannot be amended in this way, and hence the practice is still more objectionable in the Supreme Court.(*o*)

A written disclaimer by a defendant in slander, although given in evidence by consent, ought not to be sent out with the jury. The rule is said to be that all papers given in evidence, except depositions, are to be sent out, but such a paper as a disclaimer is more like a deposition than a document. The refusal to send out papers may in the discretion of the court be good ground for a new trial; but it is no cause for reversal on error.(*p*)

The jury are allowed, by the practice of this State, to take out with

---

(*l*) Caldwell *v.* Stileman, 1 R. 212.
(*m*) Emerick *v.* Kroh, 2 H. 315.
(*n*) See 1 Arch. Pr. 175.
(*o*) Solms *v.* McCulloch, 5 Barr, 473.

(*p*) Hamilton *v.* Plum, 1 Barr, 341, citing 4 W. 169. See Mullen *v.* Morris, 2 Barr, 86.

them any written papers that have been given in evidence, although not under seal, except the depositions of witnesses ;(q) these have been withheld, because it would be unequal, that while the jury were not permitted to call the witnesses before them who had been examined in court, they should take with them the depositions of other witnesses not examined in court.(r) Therefore, where a record has been given in evidence without objection, to the jury, even though not legally, it is error to refuse to allow it to go out with the jury.(s)

In a recent case, it was held that the refusal to permit depositions, taken before the register to prove a will, to be sent out with the jury, trying its validity, is not the subject of error. And per GIBSON, C. J.: "Ordinarily, depositions are not sent out with the jury, because the testimony of witnesses examined at the bar cannot be sent; and to put the testimony of those examined previously on any other footing, would give it an unfair advantage. Such are the reasons given for it in Alexander v. Jamieson.(t) But according to Sholly v. Diller,(u) depositions taken before the register, standing not upon the ordinary footing, as said in Ottinger v. Ottinger,(v) *may* be sent out as a part of the proceedings ; but the refusal of leave to do so, has been held, in several instances, to be no reason for a new trial; and why should it be the subject of error? 'If the jury,' says Lord Coke, 'carry away any writing unsealed which was given in evidence in open court, this shall not avoid their verdict, albeit they should not have carried it with them.'(w) In Alexander v. Jamieson, the question was not considered in this aspect, the judges affirming the judgment of the Common Pleas because the permission to take out the papers was right, without determining whether it would have been ground of reversal had it been wrong; but they may have done so to settle the principle, which contained an interesting point of practice. On the other hand, it might seem that Lord Coke had in view the case of papers handed to the jury without the knowledge of the court. But it is the fact that the evidence was in the jury-room, and not the means by which it came there, that can affect the event or be material to the question; and if the judge who tried the cause ought not to disturb the verdict for it when happening by inadvertence, neither ought a Court of Error to disturb it when happening with his assent. It would seem to be one of those matters that are dependent on the discretion of the trial-court, and therefore not a subject for a writ of error." The parties are also allowed to send out with the jury, calculations made by them, showing the items on which they rely, or by which they arrived at the result they claim, in all cases where calculation is requisite, in making up the verdict.(x) But no item should be inserted, unless there has been evidence given of it, to which the court ought to see, and also that the paper is in fact, what it purports to be, a mere statement of particulars, subservient only to purposes of calculation.(y)

(q) Alexander v. Jamieson, 5 Bin. 238.
(r) Ibid.
(s) Hendel v. Turnpike Road, 16 S. & R. 92.
(t) 5 Bin. 238, and see McCully v. Barr, 17 S. & R. 445.
(u) 2 R. 177.

(v) 17 S. & R. 142; Spence v. Spence, 4 W. 165.
(w) 1 Inst. 227, b.
(x) Conn v. Lebo, 13 S. & R. 175.
(y) Frazier v. Funk, 15 S. & R. 26; Id. 61.

While statements of their respective claims may be sent out to the jury,(z) it is the duty of counsel to examine such statements, and if there is anything wrong in any item or number of items, to call the attention of the court on the trial thereto, and request them to be stricken out; unless such request be made, the Supreme Court will not reverse for error in this respect.(a)

But it is error in the court to permit the jury to take out a statement made by either party, containing items as to which no evidence was offered.(b)

It is no objection in any action where the question is as to the ownership of goods, to admit a printed catalogue of goods, to go to the jury, that certain of them have been marked by the plaintiff as his property.(c)

The jury may come back into court, and hear evidence of any matter of which they have doubts;(d) or to ask the information of the court as to a point of law.(e)

2. *Nonsuit.*

When the jury have agreed, they return to the bar, and by their foreman, publicly give their verdict, which is recorded by the clerk in his minutes, who then reads the entry to the jury, that if he has made a mistake in taking down the verdict, it may immediately be corrected. There is no verdict of any force but a public verdict given openly in court;(f) but the jurors are allowed, in civil cases, when the court has irsen before they are agreed, to give a privy verdict before any of the judges of the court; but if the court be adjourned to the judge's chamber, it is not privy but public. At the subsequent meeting of the court, in the afternoon or the next morning, the jury may either affirm or alter their privy verdict, and that which is thus given in open court shall stand; so that, as Sir Wm. Blackstone remarks, the privy verdict is a mere nullity, and it is a dangerous practice, allowing time for the parties to tamper with the jury, and therefore very seldom indulged.(g) "With us a practice has obtained, of permitting the jury to reduce their finding to writing, and after sealing it up to separate till the meeting of the court, when the paper being handed to the judge, their verdict is received from the lips of the foreman, and recorded in the usual way. But this difference is unimportant, for neither in the one cause nor the other, is a privy verdict, thus delivered, recorded. As the jury may depart from it, their finding in court is what decides the rights of the parties, and what is admitted of record. The paper delivered to the judge, having performed its office, is never filed or preserved; and if it even should be, it would form no part of the record."(h) After the verdict is received the jury may be polled, that is, by each juror being

(z) Kline v. Gundrum, 1 J. 253.
(a) Ibid.
(b) Hall v. Rupley, 10 Barr, 231. See Frazier v. Funk, 15 S. & R. 26; Morrison v. Moreland, id. 61.
(c) Striker v. McMichael, D. C. C. P. 7 Leg. Int. 154.

(d) Bull. N. P. 308.
(e) 7 Bac. Abr. 12; Barnes, 441.
(f) 3 Bl. Com. 377.
(g) Id. ibid.
(h) Dornick v. Reichenback, 10 S. & R. 84, 90.

separately examined and interrogated as to his concurrence in the verdict delivered by the foreman, and then either of the jurors may disagree to the verdict.(*i*). The court may, also, of its own accord, send the jury back to reconsider their verdict, if it appear to be a mistaken one, and before it is received and recorded.(*j*) So, where on the jury's being polled, some of them dissent from the verdict, or where they come into court, and declare that they cannot agree, the judge may again send them out to deliberate further.(*k*) A verdict may be received on Sunday.(*l*) But after the jury have rendered their verdict, which is received and recorded, and they are dismissed, they cannot alter their verdict on a certificate of mistake in making it.(*m*) Nor can the court do it upon such certificate. Should they so do, it would be the ground for a motion in arrest of judgment, or for a writ of error to the Supreme Court.(*n*) In England, "before the jury deliver their verdict, the plaintiff is bound to appear in court, by himself, attorney, or counsel, in order to answer the amercement from the crown, to which, by the old law, he was liable, in case he failed in his suit, as a punishment for his false claim. The amercement is disused, but the form still continues; and if the plaintiff do not appear, no verdict can be given, but the plaintiff is said to be *nonsuit, not to follow up his claim.* Therefore, it is usual for a plaintiff, when he, or rather his counsel, perceives that he has not given evidence sufficient to maintain his issue, to be voluntarily nonsuited, or withdraw himself; whereupon, the crier is ordered to *call the plaintiff;* and if neither he, nor anybody for him appears, he is nonsuited, the jurors are discharged, the action is at an end, and the defendant shall recover his costs.

The reason of this practice is, that a nonsuit is more eligible for the plaintiff, than a verdict against him; for after a nonsuit, which is only a default, he may commence the same suit again for the same cause of action; but after a verdict had and judgment consequent thereon, he is forever barred from attacking the defendant upon the same ground of complaint.(*nn*) But in this State, by the act of March 28, 1814, § 2,(*o*) it is declared that, "whenever, on the trial of any cause, the jury shall be ready to give in their verdict, the plaintiff shall not be called, nor shall he then be permitted to suffer a nonsuit." At any previous part of the trial, however, and at any time before the jury have signified to the court their readiness to give their verdict,(*p*) the plaintiff may suffer a nonsuit for defect of evidence; and if, when he has gone through with his evidence, he has not shown, in point of law, a right to recover, the judge may direct him to be nonsuited, without requiring the defendant to enter upon his defence. Yet, at common law, the court cannot order a nonsuit against the consent of a plaintiff who has given evidence in support of his claim, for he may answer on being called and insist upon taking a verdict.(*q*)

(*i*) 7 Johns. 32; 6 Id. 68.
(*j*) 7 Johns. 32.
(*k*) 3 Johns. 255.
(*l*) 15 Johns. 119, 179.
(*m*) Walters *v.* Junkins, 16 S. & R. 414.
(*n*) Id. ibid.

(*nn*) 3 Bl. Com. 376.
(*o*) 6 Re. Laws, 208.
(*p*) Miclaghan *v.* Bovard, 4 W. 308.
(*q*) Irving *v.* Taggart, 1 S. & R. 360; Girard *v.* Gettig, 2 Bin. 234; Widdefield *v.* Widdefield, ib. 248; Hayes *v.* Greer, 4 Bin. 84; Lyon *v.* Davis, 2 H. 197.

In our own practice the plaintiff may suffer a nonsuit at any time during the trial, and just as the jury are about to deliver their verdict, although the defendant has pleaded set-off, and given evidence of it.(r) And the privilege was held rightly allowed where the jury had repaired to the box, and when none of them had been called.(s)

The plaintiff cannot suffer a nonsuit if there be anything on the record to prevent him from abandoning his suit, such as a judgment on an award, finding money due to the defendant,(t) or a set-off; or plea of tender sufficient to cover the debt proved on the trial; otherwise, he might take the money out of court and commence a fresh action to procure additional proof.(u)

Great hardships to both parties, it was said recently, have been experienced under the 25th section of the act of 16th June, 1836, which provides that the court may, after appeal from arbitrators, allow the plaintiff to suffer a nonsuit with like effect as if the cause had not been referred, if the special circumstances seem to require it. Thus, where an award was for the defendant for a certain sum, and plaintiff appealed, and afterwards, by leave of court, improvidently granted, and not resisted by the defendant, the plaintiff was allowed to suffer a nonsuit, the award for defendant was necessarily held to be wholly defeated and irrecoverable by a *scire facias* against the plaintiff. In such a state of things, the court, instead of allowing the nonsuit, ought, under their plenary powers, have afforded redress to either party, by permitting the withdrawal of a juror, or continuing the cause.(v)

By the seventh section of the act of March 11, 1836,(w) it is provided that, whenever the defendant upon the trial of a cause in the District Court of this city and county, shall offer no evidence, the judge presiding at the trial may order a judgment of nonsuit to be entered, if, in his opinion, the plaintiff shall have given no such evidence as in law is sufficient to maintain the action, with leave, nevertheless, to move the court in bank to set aside such judgment of nonsuit; and in case the said court in bank shall refuse to set aside the nonsuit, the plaintiff may remove the record by a writ of error into the Supreme Court for revision and reversal, in like manner and with like effect as he might remove a judgment rendered against him upon a demurrer to evidence.

On the subject of compulsory nonsuit, the following points may be considered settled:—(x)

In the District Court of this city and county, whenever a nonsuit is ordered, with leave to move to take it off, a motion to take the nonsuit off must be made within the time prescribed for motions for new trials, which is four days after verdict; and to enable a writ of error to be taken, the motion to take off the nonsuit must be made and refused by the court below.

The prayer for a nonsuit is effectively a demurrer to evidence, except

---

(r) McCardy v. Fey, 7 W. 496.
(s) Easton Bank v. Coryell, 9 W. & S. 153.
(t) Lewis v. Culbertson, 11 S. & R. 60, sed vide ib. 146.
(u) Id 60

(v) McKinnan v. Henderson, 5 W. & S. 371.
(w) Pamph. L. 76.
(x) See, more fully, Wh. Dig. " Practice," xxii. (g.)

that the judge cannot give judgment for the defendant, though he should think the nonsuit not grantable.(y)

The discretion of the court in taking off nonsuits is strictly a legal discretion guided by fixed rules.(a)

The act is a useful one, as it facilitates dispatch, concentrates the opinions of all the judges upon the legal points which the judge, sitting at the trial, may deem worth consideration, and often prevents a case from being carried further. The Supreme Court will give the act liberal scope, so as not to cut off from either party an important right under it.(b)

A compulsory nonsuit is no bar to another proceeding for the same cause.(c)

Where the plaintiff had filed a copy of notes, but neither declaration nor statement, and the defendant put in a plea and set the case down for trial without a replication, and when the case was called the plaintiff was nonsuited, the court in motion took off the nonsuit.(d)

Where a plaintiff gave evidence from which a contract charging the defendant might be inferred, which evidence referred to an instrument in the defendant's possession, in which the terms of such contract were settled by the parties themselves, and afterwards, on the defendant offering such instrument and tendering it to the plaintiff to be given in evidence, the latter declined so to do, it was held that a nonsuit was rightly ordered.(e)

By § 2, act of 14th April, 1846:(f) "From and after the first Monday in December next, it shall and may be lawful for the several courts in the City and County of Philadelphia, whenever a cause is reached in its order, on the trial-list, and the plaintiff or his counsel does not appear, or, if he appear, does not proceed to the trial of the cause, and does not assign and prove a sufficient legal cause for the continuance thereof, to enter a nonsuit without motion; and no nonsuit shall be taken off by agreement, nor any cause continued by agreement without the payment of four dollars to the prothonotary of the said . court, for the use of the County of Philadelphia; said payment not to be taxed as part of the costs of the cause, unless so agreed by writing filed: *Provided, nevertheless,* That the parties may by agreement, at any time before the issuing of the venire, for any period withdraw any case from the trial-list, but the same shall not be entitled to be put down for trial, at any subsequent period of the same term, without a special order of the court."

Under the Nisi Prius act of 26th July, 1842, where the judge directs a nonsuit on the trial of a cause, it comes up to the Supreme Court by certificate, in the same manner as it does by writ of error, from the District Court, under the 7th section of the act of 11th March, 1836. And it is, therefore, to be considered as a demurrer to evidence, except that the judge is not at liberty to give judgment for the plaintiff, should he think the case made out, but should refuse the nonsuit.

(y) Fleming v. Ins. Co. 6 Pa. L. J. 373.

(a) Walton v. Heald, D. C. C. P. 8 Leg. Int. 3. The rules by which that discretion will be governed will be found hereafter under New Trials, *post*, p. 527.

(b) Wharton v. Williamson, 1 H. 275.

(c) Bournonville v. Goodall, 10 Barr, 133.

(d) Taylor v. Pearl, 2 M. 291.

(e) Cunningham v. Shaw, 7 Barr, 401.

(f) Pamph. L. 328.

If, therefore, there be some evidence, though slight, from which a jury may draw an inference favorable to the plaintiff, the case should be left to the jury.(*g*)

3. *General Verdict.*

The verdict being rendered, is either general or special; a general verdict is a finding by the jury, in the terms of the issue or issues referred to them; and it is either wholly or in part, for the plaintiff or for the defendant.(*h*) A verdict must be certain;(*i*) though certainty to a common intent is sufficient,(*j*) it must conform to the issue joined between the parties,(*k*) or at least must find the substance of it.(*l*) It must not contradict facts admitted by the parties on record;(*m*) and it must determine all the matters put in issue by the pleadings.(*n*) But if, in addition to their verdict, the jury find matter merely superfluous, such finding does not affect the verdict.(*o*) At the request of the parties, the jury may express an opinion distinct from their verdict.(*p*)

When the court adjourns, no one is bound to appear until the time of meeting fixed by the court; consequently, it cannot, without consent, receive and enter a verdict of a jury in the interval. The losing party has a right to be there and tender a bill of exceptions at the last moment, before verdict is taken, or to poll the jury before it is recorded.(*q*)

Where a jury, through mistake, bring in such a verdict as, if entered, will be set aside, the court will send them out again, notwithstanding they had separated, and sent a sealed verdict into court.(*r*)

It is an insurmountable objection to the verdict that there is no means of compelling its performance.(*s*)

When, in an action of debt on a recognizance for the appearance of the recognizor in the Quarter Sessions, the defendant pleaded that there was no such record, and also other pleas to the country, when the jury finding a general verdict for the amount of the recognizance, the court rendered judgment for the plaintiff on the plea of *nul tiel* record, it was held not erroneous.(*t*)

At common law, a verdict cannot find a sum of money to be recovered by the defendant of the plaintiff. But by the "*act for defalcation*," passed in the year 1705, "if it appear to the jury that the plaintiff is overpaid, they shall give their verdict for the defendant, and withal, certify to the court, how much they find the plaintiff to be indebted or in arrear to the defendant, more than will answer the debt or sum demanded, and the sum so certified shall be recorded with the verdict, and deemed a debt of record, and if the plaintiff refuse to pay the

---

(*g*) Bevan *v.* Ins. Co. 9 W. & S. 187.

(*h*) See Thompson *v.* Musser, 1 D. 458, 462. As to conditional verdicts, *vide ante*, 120.

(*i*) See Diehl *v.* Evans, 1 S. & R. 367; Smith *v.* Jenks, 10 Id. 153; see also 2 Y. 133.

(*j*) Lessee of Hubley *v.* White, 2 Wheat. 306; 1 Mason, 153.

(*k*) 2 Wheat. 221.

(*l*) Co. Litt. 114, b; Duane *v.* Simmons, 4 Y. 441.

(*m*) 3 Cranch, 270.

(*n*) Lessee of Sherman *v.* Dill, 4 Y. 295; 2 Wheat. 221; 5 Cranch, 19.

(*o*) Cavene *v.* McMichael, 8 S. & R. 441; see 16 Johns. 307.

(*p*) 1 Peters's Rep. 72; Friedley *v.* Sheetz, 9 S. & R. 165.

(*q*) Shomakin Co. *v.* Mitman, 3 Barr, 379.

(*r*) Hemphill *v.* Mon. Nav. Co., D. C. Allegheny. LOWRIE, J.

(*s*) Glass *v.* Blair, 4 Barr, 196.

(*t*) Rhoads *v.* Com. 3 H. 272.

same, the defendant for recovery thereof shall have a *scire facias* against the plaintiff and have execution for the same, with the costs of that action." This, however, supposes the defalcation to have been pleaded, or notice given of it under the plea of payment. The jury, however, could not, under any plea or notice, find a sum due from the plaintiff to the defendant, to be deducted from another debt due from the defendant to the plaintiff.(*u*)

But by the act of April 11, 1848, section 12 : "In all cases where, by the verdict of a jury, any debt or damages shall have been found or certified in favor of the defendant, he shall be entitled to judgment and execution, in like manner as if the verdict were in favor of the plaintiff; and the defendant need not resort to *scire facias*, as required by the act of 1705, for defalcation."

The jury have no right to throw the facts, and the law, on the court, though they may find the facts and submit the law. But in such case, the facts appearing of record, either party may have a writ of error. It would, therefore, be an imperfect verdict, where the jury find for a party, "*subject to the opinion of the court*," without any mention of facts ; or, where they find, "*subject to the opinion of the court on the facts proved*," without stating those facts ; for, if such a verdict were to stand, the party against whom judgment was given would lose the benefit of a writ of error.(*v*)

It is the practice of the English and American courts, where evidence has not been given on bad counts, to enter the verdict on those which are good, and supported by the proof. It is a matter of legal discretion, of which, where the whole evidence is not embodied in the bill of exceptions, a court of error cannot judge.(*w*)

Where in an action on the case the general issue is pleaded, and afterwards other counts are filed, which are demurred to, and the case is tried before a judgment on the demurrers; it will be considered that the verdict is rendered on the first count only, though in fact given generally.(*x*)

If the verdict be for the plaintiff, or in replevin, for the defendant, the jury should regularly assess the damages.

4. *Damages.*

The subject of damages will more particularly be considered in the second volume, under the heads of the several forms of actions in which damages are sought. At present, the attention of the student is called to a few general observations.(*y*)

Damages are a pecuniary compensation for an injury, and may be

---

(*u*) Anderson's Executors *v.* Long, 10 S. & R. 55; see *ante*, 406.

(*v*) Roberts *v.* Hopkins, 11 S. & R. 202.

(*w*) Haldeman *v.* Martin, 10 Barr, 372. GIBSON, C. J.

(*x*) Goodman *v.* Gay, 3 H. 188. See, for special verdict, *post*, 521.

(*y*) In aid of the general inquiry, the following references may be of use :—

Measure of damages, when performance of contract is prevented, see Alex-

ander *v.* Hoffman, 5 W. & S. 384. When vendee covenants to pay off incumbrances, see Young *v.* Stone, 4 W. & S. 51. For injury to mill property from navigation; company dam; see Schuylkill Navigation Co. *v.* Farr, 4 W. & S. 376. On a re-sale by sheriff, difference is the measure against the first purchaser, see Gaskell *v.* Morris, 7 W. & S. 40. Upon covenant of joint owner to pay his share of incumbrances, see Bre-

recovered in all personal actions, with the exception of actions upon statutes by common informers for penalties.(z) In most cases, damages are the sole object of the action; in some, however, they are merely nominal.

In *assumpsit, covenant, case, trover* and *trespass*, damages are the sole object of the action.(a)

In *debt*, the damages are in general merely nominal, the recovery of the debt itself being the principal object of the action. In this case, the jury first find the matter of the issue; as, upon *nil debet*, that the defendant owes to the plaintiff the amount of the debt proved; and then they assess nominal·damages (six cents) for the detention of the debt.(b) So, in debt on a bond for the payment of money, it is usual to give the plaintiff six cents damages; and, though in general he cannot recover beyond the penalty of the bond, yet, where the debt and *interest* exceed the penalty, damages beyond its amount may be given.(c) So, where the penalty is not in nature of stated and ascertained damages for non-performance, the injured party may· recover damages beyond the penalty.(d) And the jury may give damages beyond the penalty of a bond conditioned for the conveyance of land.(e)

din *v.* Agnew, 3 W. & S. 303. Against carrier for refusing to convey, see O'Conner *v.* Forster, 10 W. 421. In trespass for mesne profits, see Drexel *v.* Man, 2 Barr, 276. In trover, see Farmers' Bank *v.* McKee, 2 Barr, 322. In breach of warranty of horse, see Cothers *v.* Keever, 4 Barr, 168. Against railroad company taking earth and gravel to make embankment, see Railroad Co. *v.* Gibson, 8 W. 243. Against company for taking land to make road, see Railroad Co. *v.* Gibson, 8 W. 244. Upon contract of sale, where value at the time of delivery is the measure of damages, see Smethurst *v.* Woolston, 5 W. & S. 109. In case against sheriff for escape, see Shuler *v.* Garrison, 5 W. & S. 456. For not conveying when vendee has done his part is the value of the land, see Rohr *v.* Kindt, 3 W. & S. 565. In trespass for seizing goods, see Rogers *v.* Fales, 5 Barr, 154; overruled, Good *v.* Mylin, 8 Barr, 55. Damages after action brought, see Hoover *v.* Heim, 7 W. 62. Liquidated damages, see Curry *v.* Larex, 7 Barr, 470. In action on a parole contract for sale of land, Hastings' Adm'r *v.* Eckleys' Adm'r, 8 Barr, 197. For services to be paid in land, see Jack *v.* McKee, 9 Barr, 235; Bash *v.* Bash, 9 Barr, 260.

In an action for services, the value of services need not be proved, on *quantum meruit*, plaintiff entitled to nominal damages, Bash *v.* Bash, 9 Barr, 260. When case is one for compensation, the jury cannot give vindictive damages, Amer *v.* Longstreth, 10 Barr, 145.

Measure of damages in action by ven-dee against vendor for non-conveying, see Bitner *v.* Brough, 1 J. 136. In action for breach of promise of marriage, see Baldy *v.* Stratton, 1 J. 321. Exemplary damages in replevin, see M'Donald *v.* Scaife, 1 J. 381. In action by heir against administrator for fraudulently procuring land to be sold by sheriff, see Weiting and Wife *v.* Nissley, 1 H. 654. When vendor of chattel, who has been paid in part, brings trespass, see Rose *et al. v.* Story, 1 Barr, 196. Damages when vindictive, see Wilt *v.* Vickers, 8 W. 233; Taylor *v.* Parkhurst, 1 Barr, 197. Resale not only, nor conclusive mode of settling difference between the contract price and the true value, see Andrews *v.* Hoover, 8 W. 239; M'Combs *v.* M'Kennan, 2 W. & S. 219. Price paid measure of damages in covenant of title, see Good *v.* Good, 9 W. 572. Damages in action by father for injury to his child, see Wilt *v.* Vickers, 8 W. 232. When expenses of suit may be included, see Wilt *v.* Vickers, 8 W. 235; overruled, Good *v.* Mylin, 8 Barr, 55; Alexander *v.* Herr, 1 J. 538.

(z) 4 Burr. 2018, 2489.
(a) 1 Arch. Pr. 193. See these heads in vol. ii.
(b) Ibid.
(c) 2 T. R. 388; see 8 S. & R. 263.
(d) Graham *v.* Bickham, 4 D. 149; S. C. 2 Y. 32.
(e) 2 D. 252; but see 1 Wh. Dig. "Bond," E. 31. This subject is well discussed by Mr. Evans in his valuable appendix to Pothier on Obligations, pp. 101, 109, vol. ii.

In *detinue*, the damages are merely nominal; but the jury find the value of the articles detained, and the judgment is, that the plaintiff recover the articles or their value, together with the damages and costs, found by the verdict, and the costs of increase.(*f*)

In *replevin*, a verdict for the plaintiff gives damages precisely as in trespass.(*g*) If the verdict be for the defendant, damages are given as in a verdict for a plaintiff in trespass.(*h*)

Where the defendants in trespass join in pleading, the jury, if they find them jointly guilty, cannot sever the damages.(*i*) But they may find one of them guilty of the trespass, at one time, and the other at another ;(*j*) or one of them guilty of part of the trespass or trover, and the other of another ;(*k*) or, some guilty of the whole trespass, and the others guilty of part only ;(*l*) in all which cases, the jury may assess several damages. Also, where the defendants plead severally, if they be found guilty of the same act of trespass, the jury cannot sever the damages ;(*m*) but the jury who try the first issue, shall assess damages against all ; and there shall be a *cesset executio* until the other issues are tried, when the other defendants, if found guilty, shall be contributory to those damages.(*n*) If the jury sever, and judgment be entered for the several damages, it will be erroneous ;(*o*) yet, before judgment, the plaintiff may cure the defect by taking judgment *de melioribus damnis* against one, and entering a *nolle prosequi* as to the other ;(*p*) or, by entering a *remittitur* as to the lesser damages, he may have judgment for the greater damages against both.(*q*) As the damages in the joint action cannot be severed so as to give more damages against A than B, the damages ought to be given against both to the amount the jury think the most culpable ought to pay.(*r*)

When the declaration contains several counts, the jury may assess either entire damages upon all, or any of the counts, or several damages upon each.(*s*) But it is a settled rule, that if a verdict be entered generally on all the counts, and entire damages given, and one count be bad, it is fatal, and judgment shall be arrested ;(*t*) and it shall be arrested *in toto*, and no *venire de novo* awarded.(*u*) However, where a general verdict has been taken, and evidence been given only on the good counts, the court has permitted the verdict to be amended by the judge's notes. So, where it appears by the judge's notes that the jury calculated the damages on evidence applicable to the good counts only, the court will amend the verdict by entering it on those counts, though evidence was given applicable to the bad count also.(*v*) The court will not allow a verdict to be entered on a particular count, where the

(*f*) 1 Arch. Pr. 194. See vol. ii. "Detinue."

(*g*) 1 Arch. Pr. 194.

(*h*) Ib.; see 2 Arch. Pr. 73; Stat. 7 H. viii. c. 4; Rob. Dig. 117; 14 Johns. 386. See vol. ii. "Replevin."

(*i*) 5 Burr. 2790.

(*j*) 11 Co. 5, 6.

(*k*) Cro. Car. 54.

(*l*) Cro. El. 860.

(*m*) 11 Co. 6 a, 7 a; Cridland *v.* Floyd, 6 S. & R. 413.

(*n*) 11 Co. 6 a, 7 a.

(*o*) Cridland *v.* Floyd, 6 S. & R. 413.

(*p*) Carth. 19; ibid. 413; 6 T. R. 199. 200.

(*q*) Cro. Car. 192; 1 Wils. 30; 1 Arch. Pr. 195.

(*r*) Cridland *v.* Floyd, 6 S. & R. 413.

(*s*) 1 Ro. Abr. 570, F. pl. 1.

(*t*) Doug. 730; 3 M. & S. 110.

(*u*) 2 Saund. 171, b.

(*v*) Ibid. ; see, also, Paul *v.* Harden, 9 S. & R. 23.

jury have given their verdict on the whole matter and no one of the other counts is bad or inconsistent.(*w*)

Where there are several issues upon several pleas, as, for example, on the pleas of *non assumpsit, plene administravit*, and debts of a higher nature, it is a general rule that the jury must dispose of all of them; and there seems to be no difference, in this respect, between issues that are affirmative as regards the party who obtains the verdict, and those that are negative. It is necessary to show that every allegation material to the cause has been considered and determined, and this, whether it were made on the one part or the other. The English practice requires a particular finding of each issue, although the rule is not of universal application; and where the truth will warrant it, an issue taken on the plea of *plene administravit* is to be disposed of by finding a particular amount of assets unadministered in the hands of the executor. But as the plaintiff is not interested in proving assets beyond the amount of his demand, it is not usual to find the whole of what is unadministered, but only a sum sufficient to cover what is found due. By our practice, which is more loose than the English or that of almost any other State, it is unusual to pass on all the issues in the cause separately (although on the issues of fully administered, and debts of a higher nature, it is usual to find the amount of the assets specially), but a general finding for the plaintiff is considered as equivalent to an express negative to each particular plea.(*x*) Therefore, where there was a general verdict for the plaintiff on these issues and *non assumpsit*, it was held to be substantially a finding of assets to the amount of the demand, and good.(*y*)

In an action for words, if the words be set forth in one count, and some of them be actionable, and others not, entire damages may be given; for it shall be intended that the damages were given for the words which were actionable, and that the others were inserted only for aggravation.(*z*) But in an action of trespass, or on a contract, where the plaintiff introduces into his declaration matter for which, on his own showing, there was no cause of action, and which he had no occasion to introduce, the court cannot intend that the damages, if assessed generally, were given only for that matter in the count which was actionable.(*a*)

A verdict is not vitiated by the finding of superfluous matter by the jury: It is often proper and necessary that their verdict should state the grounds on which it is founded.(*b*)

As to the measure of the damages, it must be observed that where there is a penalty expressed for the non-performance of a contract, and it appears evident that such penalty is the precise sum fixed and agreed upon between the parties as liquidated damages for the non-performance of the contract, the jury are confined to that sum.(*c*) But where it does not appear clear that the parties intended the sum stated in the agree-

(*w*) Descamps *v.* Dutihl, 4 Y. 442.
(*x*) Stroheeker *v.* Drinkle, 16 S. & R. 39, 40.
(*y*) Id. 38.
(*z*) 1 Arch. Pr. 196; Gordon *v.* Kennedy, 2 Bin. 292, 293; see 2 Saund. 171, d.

(*a*) Gordon *v.* Kennedy, 2 Bin. 292, 293.
(*b*) Fisher *v.* Kean, 1 W. 259.
(*c*) See 4 Burr. 22, 25; 1 Holt, N. P. C. 43.

ment, as liquidated damages, it must then be deemed a mere penalty, in which case, although the jury cannot exceed that sum, yet they may find a less sum as a measure of the damages the plaintiff has sustained.(*d*) In all other cases, the jury are at liberty to give what damages they may think proper, proportioned to the degree of injury they may judge the plaintiff to have sustained from the *tort*, or breach of contract complained of.(*e*) And in an action for seduction, in ascertaining the damages, they are not obliged to confine themselves to such a sum as would be a sufficient compensation for the mere loss of service complained of, but they may also allow damages for the injury sustained by the daughter, and inflicted on the feelings of her parent.(*f*) On the other hand, it is a general rule, that the jury cannot take into consideration, in mitigation of damages, any fact or circumstance not pleaded, which could and should have been pleaded, as a defence to the action.(*g*) It is also a general rule, that the jury can in no case exceed the damages laid in the declaration;(*h*) but if a verdict be found for more, the plaintiff may release the overplus, and take judgment for the amount declared for. If judgment be entered for a greater amount, it is error.(*i*) And the court will not, on the removal of the record by writ of error, suffer a *remittitur* of the surplus damages to be entered; but will, without reversing the judgment, send back the record to the court below, to be amended, if they think proper, and if it be returned to the court above, amended by a release of the excess of damages, they will affirm the judgment.(*j*)

When damages or costs, or both, ought to be assessed, if the jury omit to assess either, the plaintiff may still make the verdict good, by releasing his right to either or both.(*k*) And where the jury omit to give costs only, being *ex officio* bound to give them, the court will supply the deficiency.(*l*)

At common law, single damages only are recoverable, but in certain instances, double, and even treble damages have been given by statute. Thus, in actions for malicious prosecution, double damages may be recovered, under the act of 1705.(*m*) So, under the act of 1772,(*n*) double damages are recoverable for distraining when no rent is in arrear.(*o*) And under the same act, treble damages upon any poundbreach, or rescous of goods or chattels distrained for rent, may be recovered in a special action on the case. The proper course in such case is, for the jury to find the single damages, and the court will then double or treble them.(*p*) It seems, however, that a verdict for double or treble damages will be good, if expressly so found by the jury.(*q*) It would seem to be, under the act of 1705, rather the province of the jury than the court to find the double damages. When the plaintiff counts on the statute with a demand for double damages, the presump-

---

(*d*) See 2 B. & P. 346; 1 Campb. 78.
(*e*) 1 Arch. Pr. 197.
(*f*) 2 T. R. 4; Hornkesh *v.* Barr, 8 S. & R. 39.
(*g*) 1 Arch. Pr. 197.
(*h*) Gratz *v.* Phillips, 5 Bin. 564; 2 W. Bl. 1300.
(*i*) Gratz *v.* Phillips, 5 Bin. 564.
(*j*) Spackman *v.* Byers, 6 S. & R. 385; Ordroneaux *v.* Prady, Id. 511.

(*k*) Allen *v.* Flock, 2 Pa. R. 159.
(*l*) Zell *v.* Arnold, Id. 292.
(*m*) 1 Sm. Laws, 56.
(*n*) Ibid. 370.
(*o*) Murray *v.* Bruner, 6 S. & R. 276.
(*p*) 1 Galison, 26, 479; Cas. Tem. Hardw. 138, n.; 4 Barn. & Cress. 154; 10 S. & Low. 298.
(*q*) 1 Galison, 26.

tion is that the jury have doubled them; and this presumption can only be negatived by a special finding of the jury themselves. The court have the power to double the damages only where they are not doubled by the jury; but the jury must find the facts by which it is to be determined whether the defendant be liable to double damages.(r)

5. *Special Verdict.*

A special verdict, which is grounded on the statute Westminster 2, 13 Edw. I. c. 30, § 2,(s) is a finding by the jury of all the facts of the case as disclosed upon the evidence before them; and after so setting them forth, concludes, when formally drawn up, to the following effect: "That they are ignorant, in point of law, on which side they ought, upon these facts, to find the issue; that if, upon the whole matter, the court shall be of opinion that the issue is proved for the plaintiff, they find for the plaintiff accordingly, and assess the damages at such a sum, &c.; but if the court are of an opposite opinion, then *vice versa.*"(t) On a special verdict the court are confined to the facts found therein, and will render judgment on it, if it be substantially good, though inartificially worded.(u) But they cannot supply the want of facts, by any argument or implication from what is expressly found. As if a question be submitted to the jury, in an action on a policy, whether the conduct of the master of the ship increased the risk of the insurer, and the jury find certain acts of misconduct, the court cannot infer that the risk of the insurer was increased, though their private judgments may be fully satisfied on the point.(v) If the jury, in a special verdict, find the issue, all that they find afterwards is surplusage. But if, meaning to find a special verdict, they introduce words which would amount to a general verdict contrary to their intention, the court will grant a new trial.(w) " However, as on a general verdict, the jury do not themselves actually frame the *postea,* so they have, for the most part, nothing to do with the formal preparation of the special verdict. When it is agreed that a verdict of that kind is to be given, the jury merely declare their opinion as to any fact remaining in doubt; and then the verdict is adjusted without their further interference. It is settled, under the correction of the judge, by the counsel on either side, according to the state of facts as found by the jury, with respect to all particulars on which they have delivered an opinion, and with respect to other particulars, according to the state of facts which, it is agreed, that they *ought* to find upon the evidence before them. The special verdict, when its form is thus settled, is, together with the whole proceedings on the trial, then entered on record; and the question of law arising on the facts found, is argued before the court in bank, and decided by that court as in case of demurrer. If the party be dissatisfied with their decision, they may afterwards resort to a Court of Error."(x) And by the act of March 11, 1800, § 6,(y) when the record is brought before the Supreme Court, if they deem the facts in the special verdict to be insufficiently or uncertainly found, they may remand the record, and direct another trial to ascertain the facts.

(r) Campbell v. Finney, 3 W. 84.
(s) Rob. Dig. 326.
(t) Steph. on Plead. 112.
(u) Fenn v. Blanchard, 2 Y. 543.
(v) Croussillat v. Ball, 3 ibid. 375.

(w) U. S. v. Bright et al. C. C. Oct. 1809, Pamph. L. p. 199.
(x) Steph. on Plead. 113.
(y) 5 Sm. Laws, 17.

A special verdict, says Judge COULTER, is where the jury find the facts of the case, leaving the ultimate decision of the cause upon those facts to the court, concluding conditionally, that if, upon the whole matter thus found, the court should be of opinion that the plaintiff had a good cause of action, they then find for the plaintiff, and assess his damages; if otherwise, then for the defendant.(z)

If the jury have omitted undisputed facts by mistake, the court may, upon motion and full evidence, amend the special verdict.(a)

A special verdict ought to include both undisputed and disputed facts. Therefore, where certain facts were stated by the court to be undisputed, and the jury were directed to find a special verdict on the disputed facts alone, it is error in the court to enter a judgment on the undisputed facts and facts as found by the jury.(b)

Where, in a special verdict, the essential facts were not distinctly found by the jury, although there was sufficient evidence to establish them, the Supreme Court of the United States would not render a judgment upon such verdict, but remanded the cause to the court below for another trial.(c)

Where a special verdict is defective, the practice is to move to amend from notes of counsel or on affidavit; and in order to sustain the merits, the court will so amend.(d) If it be so defective that the court cannot give judgment, they will grant a new trial, in order to have it restated.(e)

In a case, in 1836, in the District Court, upon a plea of discharge under the insolvent laws, the jury found, specially, the fact of the defendant's discharge, that the notice to the plaintiff of his application was given by leaving it at plaintiff's counting-house; and that the plaintiff's attorney marked, and subsequently withdrew his opposition before the hearing. When the case was reached on the argument-list, the court refused to hear the question discussed of the validity of such a discharge, as to the plaintiff saying that there was no special verdict; and that the regular mode of raising the point was by issuing a *ca. sa.*, and moving the court to set it aside; the plaintiff, of course, proceeding at his peril.(f)

SECTION VIII.

OF SPECIAL CASES, AND CASES STATED.

According to the English practice, which is adopted here in this respect, a special case is used instead of a special verdict, of which it is a species, and leave is sometimes granted to turn it into one. But in both the facts ought to be stated, and not merely the evidence of facts. Counsel cannot go out of it, and the court must judge upon it as stated.(g)

Where there is a suit actually pending in court, whether commenced by amicable agreement, or by the suing out of original process, the parties or their counsel may, without proceeding to trial, state a case,

(z) Wallingford v. Dunlap, 2 H. 31.
(a) Id. 33.
(b) Wallingford v. Dunlap, 2 H. 31.
(c) 11 Wheat. 415.
(d) Morse v. Chase, 4 W. 458.

(e) Whitesides v. Russell, 8 W. & S. 114, 1 Tidd's Pr. 930.
(f) Linn v. Fulmer, D. C. Philad. Dec. Term, 1836, MS.
(g) Diehl v. Ihrie, 3 Wh. 149.

by consent, for the opinion and decision of the court. This may consist either of one written statement of all the facts of the case, or of several statements of the facts, each involving a different question of law,(h) drawn up for the opinion of the court in bank, and signed by the parties or their counsel. A case stated is a substitute for a verdict, resorted to for convenience, and to save the expense of a trial; its purpose being not to make evidence for a jury, but to supersede the action of a jury altogether, by imparting to facts ascertained by consent, the judicial certainty requisite to enable the court to pass upon the law, and give judgment on the whole; and its existence is consequently inconsistent with an issue to draw the facts again into contest. Upon the statement of a case in a Circuit Court, there was the unusual agreement, " that the question of the admissibility, competency, and sufficiency of the evidence to maintain the action, should be submitted to the court; and that, in considering the evidence, the court should draw from it, so far as it was admissible and competent, every inference of fact and law which it would have been competent for a jury to draw from it." On error from the Supreme Court of the United States, it was declared by the latter court, that they did not admit the right of the parties, by such an agreement, to impose upon the court such duties as came properly or solely within the cognizance of a jury.(i) A case stated may be agreed on and submitted before an issue is attained, and indeed, before any of the pleadings have been filed; though a declaration is, in general, filed previously.

In the case of Bixler *et ux. v.* Kunkle,(j) it was held by Tod, J., delivering the opinion of the court, that, after a case stated, the declaration is waived and superseded. And he said: "The parties have agreed to put, and actually have put before us, the facts of the case. True, the counsel did reserve their exceptions. But it is a reservation incompatible with the agreement. They cannot, at the very time they are placing all the facts specifically on the record, object because all the parts are not specifically upon the record [in the declaration]. It is an attempt to mix a special demurrer with a case stated."

An agreement to a case stated may be rescinded either by tacit or express consent: the abandonment of it is satisfactorily evinced by the parties subsequently pleading to issue; and when thus abandoned, it is not evidence which may be given to the jury upon the trial of the cause.(k)

A case stated having been read to a jury as evidence of the facts contained in it, it is competent to prove by the attorney, who signed it, that the client's assent was not had;(l) and the better opinion is that the paper is not evidence at all.(ll)

The statement of a case being agreed on and signed, it is filed in the office of the prothonotary; after which it is placed, as an issue in law, upon the list, and comes on for argument as soon as reached, when the questions of law arising on the facts found, are discussed by the re-

(h) See examples, Dacosta *v.* Guieu, 7 S. & R. 462.
(i) 5 Peters's Rep. 390.
(j) Bixler *v.* Kunkle, 17 S. & R. 310.
(k) McLughan *v.* Bovard, 4 W. 308.
(l) Ibid.
(ll) Hart's Appeal, 8 Barr, 32.

spective counsel, and decided by the court.(m) "If the parties submit their case to the opinion of a Court of Common Pleas, they must be bound by its decision, unless it be agreed that it shall be subject to a writ of error. This has been settled with respect to cases stated, and submitted to a Court of Common Pleas; of which the Supreme Court will not take cognizance, unless it be the agreement of the parties that the case shall be considered as of the nature of a special verdict, and subject to a writ of error."(n)

Rules on the subject of cases stated exist in the Supreme Court, and in the District Court of this county only.(o) In the District Court, it is ordered that in all law arguments on cases stated for the opinion of the court, the party who is entitled to begin and conclude the argument, shall furnish to each of the judges a paper-book containing a full and distinct statement of all facts conducive to a ready comprehension of the matter to be argued. It has been held, that if a case stated consist of a cumbrous narration of evidence, the court will refuse to hear it; it being requisite to present, in brief terms, a statement of the facts themselves—not the evidence from which they can be drawn.(p)

An agreed case in the nature of a special verdict, is to be considered as a special verdict found by a jury, and if defective in substance, e. g., where there is no sum fixed for damages in case of the plaintiff's succeeding, the judgment on it will be reversed, and a *venire de novo* awarded.(q)

SECTION IX.

OF POINTS RESERVED.

By § 5 of the act of March, 1835, reconstituting the District Court, any one of the judges of that court, when he thinks expedient, may reserve questions of law which may arise on the trial of a cause, for the consideration and judgment of all the judges of the court, sitting together, provided that either party shall have a right to a bill of exceptions to the opinion of the court, as if the point had been ruled and decided on the trial of the cause.(r)

(m) Ibid. 312.
(n) Fuller *v.* Trevor, 8 S. & R. 529; see Brac. L. Mis. 193–4.
(o) For those of the former court, which it is here unnecessary to insert, we refer to 6 S. R. 600, and to the printed rules of that court.

(p) Long *v.* Thornley, D. C. MSS. 1850. Diehl *v.* Ihrie, 3 Wh. 13.
(q) Whitesides *v.* Russell, 8 W. & S. 44.
(r) Pamph. L. 88.

CHAPTER XXV.

OF MOTIONS FOR NEW TRIALS, AND TO TAKE OFF NONSUITS, AND ARREST OF JUDGMENT.

THE party who has obtained a verdict is immediately entitled to judgment, but before he can avail himself of it, a period of four days must, by the practice of the courts, elapse. And, during this period, certain proceedings may be taken by the unsuccessful party to avoid the effect of the verdict, the principal of which is, in our practice, a motion for a new trial, or, in arrest of judgment.

SECTION I.

OF MOTIONS FOR NEW TRIALS, AND TO TAKE OFF NONSUIT.(a)

"It may happen that one of the parties may be dissatisfied with the opinion of the judge expressed on the trial, whether relating to the effect of the admissibility of evidence; or may think the evidence against him insufficient in law, where no adverse opinion has been expressed by the judge, and yet may not have obtained a special verdict, or demurred to the evidence, or tendered a bill of exceptions.(b) He is at liberty, therefore, after the trial, and during the period above mentioned, to move the court in bank to grant a new trial, on the ground of the judge's having misdirected the jury, or having admitted or refused evidence contrary to law; or, where there was no adverse direction of the judge, on the ground that the jury gave their verdict contrary to the evidence, or on evidence insufficient in law.(c) And resort may be had to the same remedy, in other cases, where justice appears not to have been done at the first trial; as, where the verdict, though not wholly contrary to evidence, or on insufficient evidence in point of law, is manifestly wrong in point of discretion, as contrary to the weight of the evidence, and on that ground disapproved by the judge at the trial.(d) So a new trial may be moved for where a new and material fact has come to light since the trial, which the party did

(a) For an interesting view of the origin and reason of new trials, see 3 Bl. Com. 386, 393; Brac. Law Mis. 549, 560.

(b) A motion for a new trial, however, may be made after a bill of exceptions taken, and is not a waiver of the bill, though founded upon the same matter for which the bill is taken. Shaeffer v. Landis, 1 S. & R. 449.

(c) See Rose v. Turnpike Co. 3 W. 48.

(d) Bartholomew v. Judykunst, 3 Pa. R. 493.

not know, and had not the means of proving before the jury; or where the damages given by the verdict are excessive, or where the jury have misconducted themselves, as by casting lots to determine their verdict, &c.   In these, and the like instances, the court will, on motion, and in the exercise of their discretion, under all the circumstances of the case, grant a new trial, that opportunity may be given for a more satisfactory decision of the issue.   A new jury process consequently issues, and the cause comes on to be tried *de novo*.   But, except on such grounds as these, tending manifestly to show that the discretion of the jury has not been legally or properly exercised, a new trial can never be obtained; for it is a great principle of law, that the decision of a jury, upon an issue in fact, is in general irreversible and conclusive."(e)

In considering the general question, there are two classes of cases to be considered, in which there is an inflection of the rules by which, as will presently be seen, the discretion of the court is governed.

The first class comprises those cases where a nonsuit is entered, and where the only injury to the plaintiff from continuing it will be the loss of costs, in which case the court will adhere with the greater rigor to its rules, unless it should appear that intermediately the statute of limitations drops.(f)

The other class is thus described by Judge SHARSWOOD:(g) "It is evident that if a new trial were granted in every case in which a party should think that he might have presented his case more advantageously, we might as well say that we would grant a new trial in every case in which either plaintiff or defendant is dissatisfied.   There are cases, however, in which a party has been surprised by evidence which he had no reason to expect; in which a new trial will be granted.   There is an evident distinction to be drawn, however, between the case of a plaintiff against whose claim the statute of limitations has not run, and a defendant.   The former has the game in his own hands.   If surprised by evidence from the defendant which he is not prepared to meet and rebut, he can and therefore ought to suffer a nonsuit.   A defendant has no privilege of that character; and his application to the court for a new trial, under such circumstances, stands upon a different footing.   The party plaintiff here elected to take his chance with the jury upon the evidence as it stood, and hence is bound by that election.

"Cases upon the subject of new trials," said the same learned judge, "are not, in the nature of things, of much authority, except as to the mere laying down of the general principles.   The general principle upon which this decision rests has been recognized, and it by no means weakens it to show that in some cases a new trial has been awarded to a plaintiff on the ground of surprise.—Wherever a plaintiff is so situated that he cannot bring a new action, as when the defendant is beyond the jurisdiction of the court, or his claim is barred by the statute or any other cause, he may show that by suffering a nonsuit he would have irreparably lost the case, it may be in a case in which the costs have been unusually heavy, when especially if they were incurred by the fault, or delays of the opposite party, the rule ought not to be applied.   In

(e) Steph. on Plead. 115, 117.   (g) Martin *v.* Marvine, D. C. P. Dec.
(f) See Vandergrift *v.* Malcomson, 20, 1851.
post, 539.

short, to make a case in regard to the rules of granting new trials, of binding authority, we should have to know a variety of circumstances in regard to it, which cannot always be gathered from the printed report."

A motion for a new trial is not a waiver of a bill of exceptions, though founded upon the same matter for which the bill is taken.(i)

The practice with regard to new trials will be considered under the following heads :—(j)

1. Misdirection of court.
2. Error in admission or rejection of evidence.
3. Verdict against law.
4. Verdict against evidence.
5. Irregularity of jurors.
6. Misconduct by prevailing party.
7. After discovered evidence.
8. Absence.
9. Want of notice.
10. Mistake.
11. Surprise.
12. Irregularity in impanelling jury.
13. Unsuitable damages.
14. Time and form of notice.
15. Terms and costs.

1. *Misdirection of court.*

Any misdirection by the court trying the case, in point of law, on matters material to the issue, is a good ground for a new trial;(k) and such misdirection, even upon one point, is sufficient, although the jury may have properly found their verdict upon another point, as to which there was no misdirection ;(l) though, it is said, that if, on the trial of a civil issue, the court see that justice has been done between the parties, they will not set aside the verdict, nor enter into a discussion of the question of law.(m) Error committed by the court in the allowance or refusal of challenges,(n) or the allowance or refusal of a motion, either

---

(i) Shaeffer v. Landis, 1 S. & R. 449.

(j) The analysis, and a considerable part of the references, of this section are taken from Wh. Am. Crim. Law, 1st ed. p. 636.

(k) Doe d. Bath v. Clarke, 3 Hodg. 49; Doe d. Read v. Harris, 1 Will. Wol. & D. 106; Haine v. Davey, 4 Ad. & El. 892; 6 Nev. & Man. 356; 2 Har. & Wol. 30; Lyons v. Tomkies, 1 Mee. & W. 603; Anon. 6 Mod. 242; How. v. Stride, 2 Wils. 269; 10 Johns. R. 447; 5 Day, 479; 5 Mass. 487; Wilson v. Rastall, 4 T. R. 753; 4 Connec. 356; 3 Cranch, 298; Calcraft v. Gibbs, 5 T. R. 19; Crofts v. Waterhouse, 3 Bingham, 319; Young v. Spencer, 10 Barn. & C. 145; Holiday v. Atkinson, 5 Barn. & C. 501; Boyden v. Moore, 5 Mass. 365; Wardell v. Hughes, 3 Wendell, 418; Baylies v. Davis, 1 Pick. 206; Lane v. Crombie, 12 Pick. 177;

Doe v. Paine, 4 Hawks, 64; West v. Anderson, 9 Conn. 107; M'Faden v. Parker, 3 Y. 496.

(l) Doe d. Read v. Harris, Will. Wol. & D. 106; People v. Bodine, 1 Denio, 280.

(m) Edmonson v. Machell, 2 T. R. 4; How. v. Strode, 2 Wils. 269; Smith v. Page, 2 Salk. 644; Denly v. Masarine, 2 Salk. 646; Cox v. Kitchen, 1 Bos. & Pul. 338; Brazier v. Clap, 5 Mass. 1; Remington v. Congdon, 2 Pick. 310; State v. Tudor, 5 Day, 329; Rogers v. Page, Brayt. 169; Breckenridge v. Anderson, 3 J. J. Marshall, 710; Ingraham v. Ins. Co. Const. R. 717; Johnson v. Blackman, 11 Conn. 32; Coit v. Tracy, 9 Conn. 1; Peters v. Bamhill, 1 Hill's S. C. 234.

(n) Com. v. Lesher, 17 S. & R. 155; People v. Mather, 4 Wendell, 229; People v. Bodine, 1 Denio, 281; Heath's

for continuance,(o) or if any other peremptory motion,(p) will be ground for a new trial.

The due degree of weight to be given by a judge directing the jury, to particular evidence, which has been properly admitted, must be left to his own discretion ; and his discretion, in that respect, will not be revised,(q) though, if the court instruct a jury that they may indulge a presumption not warranted by the evidence, a new trial will be awarded.(r)

A new trial will not be granted on a point of law, not made at the trial, unless perhaps the party would be without remedy otherwise.(s)

Where a judge falls into an error of fact, on supposing evidence to be given which, although treated by counsel as offered, was not really so, a new trial will be granted.(t)

It is never a reason for a new trial that the judge refused to nonsuit the plaintiff. If, upon the trial, the plaintiff fails to make out his case, the judge should be requested so to charge the jury.(u)

A new trial will not be granted merely because a case is a proper one for the jury to view the premises, which they have not done.(v)

The omission, by the judge, in summing up, specifically to leave to the jury a point made in the course of the trial (his attention not being expressly called to it), is no ground for a motion for a new trial, if the whole of the case was substantially left to them.(w)

Where, however, from the absence of proper instructions, the jury fall into error, a new trial will be granted.(x)   But the judge cannot be required to give an opinion on a mixed question of law and fact, and a refusal to do so is no error. In an action for maliciously and without reasonable or probable cause, charging the plaintiff with felony before a magistrate, it appeared that the plaintiff had lived in the service of the defendant, and, on being discharged, took away with her a trunk and bag, the property of the defendant; that on the following day, the defendant wrote to desire the plaintiff to return those articles, stating, that unless she did so, he would, on the following Monday, cause her to be apprehended; that the letter being, in consequence of the plaintiff's absence, unanswered, the defendant obtained a warrant for the apprehension of the plaintiff, and carried her before a magistrate, who dismissed her, the defendant declining to press the charge; the judge, be-

case, 1 Robinson, 735 ; People v. Rathbun, 21 Wend. 509 ; Armistead v. Com. 11 Leigh, 657 ; though see Henry v. State, 4 Humphrey, 549.

(o) State v. Fyles, 3 Brevard, 304; Vance v. Com. 2 Va. Cases, 162 ; Com. v. Gwatkin, 10 Leigh, 687 ; Bledsoe v. Com. 6 Rand. 674 ; People v. Vermilyea, 7 Cowen, 369.

(p) Com. v. Church, 1 Barr, 105.

(q) Post, ch. xxviii. Attorney-General v. Good, M'Clel. & Y. 286; 4 Ch. Gen. Practice, 42 ; People v. Genung, 11 Wendell, 18.

(r) Post, ch. xxviii.; Harris v. Wilson, 1 Wendell, 511 ; Haine v. Davey, 4 Ad. & El. 899 ; 4 Wendell, 639 ; 10 Wend. 461 ; Levingsworth v. Fox, 1 Bay. 520 ; Handly v. Harrison, 3 Bibb, 481.

(s) Peters v. Phœnix Ins. Co. 3 S. & R. 25.

(t) Bodine v. R. R. Co., D. C. C. P. 7 Leg. Int. 19.

(u) Shields v. Windsor, D. C. C. P. 7 Leg. Int. 110.

(v) Phillips v. Kreitzer, D. C. C. P. 7 Leg. Int. 7.

(w) See Wh. Dig. "Error;" Robinson v. Gleadow, 2 Scott, 250; Den. v. Sinnickson, 4 Halst. 149.

(x) Wh. Dig. "Error;" Morrison v. Muspratt, 12 Moore, 231; Calbreath v. Gracey, 1 Wash. C. C. R. 198; Page v. Pattee, 6 Mass. 459; Dunlap v. Patterson, 5 Cowen, 243 ; see Scott v. Lunt, 7 Peters, 596.

fore whom the cause was tried, left it to the jury to say whether or not the defendant had reasonable or probable cause for apprehending the plaintiff, and whether he was actuated by malice or not, and it was decided that this direction was proper, and that the judge was not bound to take upon himself to decide as to whether or not there was reasonable or probable cause, it being a mixed question of law and fact.(y) In this country, however, it has been more than once held, that it is the duty of the court exclusively to determine whether the circumstances proved by the defendant amount to probable cause, leaving it to the jury to decide whether such circumstances are in proof or not.(z)

2. *Error in admission or rejection of evidence.*

Though there is exceptionable testimony, yet if there be sufficient legal evidence to support the verdict, and justice appear to have been done, the verdict will not be set aside;(a) and the same rule applies where legal evidence has been excluded, but where, had it been admitted, it would have produced no variation in the result;(b) though, in Pennsylvania, it may be questioned whether this liberality has been extended beyond testimony which was only irrelevant.(c) In such cases, however, the court must see that the evidence did not weigh with the jury in forming their opinion, or that an opposite verdict, given upon the remainder of the evidence, must have been set aside as against evidence.(d) And DENMAN, C. J., went so far once as to say to the counsel who had put in such inadmissible evidence: "It is not enough for you to say that the reception of this evidence could have made no difference; you should have taken care not to put in bad evidence. The alleged unimportance of a piece of evidence improperly rejected or admitted, is no ground for refusing to send a case down for a new trial.(e)

Where three actions against the same defendant were tried by the same jury, and the plaintiff in one of the actions gave evidence applicable to a case in which he was not a party, but which tended to swell the damages in his own case, the court granted a new trial in all the cases.(f)

3. *Verdict against law.*

Wherever the finding of the jury, in point of law, is against the charge of the court, the verdict will be set aside.(g)

(y) Macdonald v. Booke, 2 Scott, 359 ; Shaw v. Wallace, 2 Stew. & Porter, 193 ; see 1 Greenl. R. 135 ; 4 Ch. Gen. Practice, 40.

(z) Wh. Digest, "Error," iv. (b) "Courts," i.; Whitney v. Peckham, 15 Mass. 243 ; Munns v. Dupont, 3 Wash. C. C. R. 32.

(a) Tullidge v. Wade, 3 Wils. 18; Herford v. Wilson, 1 Taunt. 12; Doe v. Tyler, 6 Bingham, 561; Nathan v. Buckley, 2 Moore, 153 ; Smith v. Harmanson, 1 Wash. R. 6 ; Prince v. Shepherd, 9 Pick. 176; Stiles v. Tilford, 10 Wend. 388.

(b) Com. v. Irwin, 2 P. L. J. 329, BELL, J.; Edwards v. Evans, 3 East, 451; Fitch v. Chapman, 10 Conn. 8; Landon v. Humphrey, 9 Conn. 209.

(c) Boyd v. Boyd, 1 W. 366, ROGERS, J.

(d) De Butzen v. Farr, 5 N. & M. 617.

I.—34

(e) Ibid. 618.

(f) Consequa v. Willing, 1 P. C. C. 225, 231.

(g) Pierce v. Woodward, 6 Pick. 172 ; Payne v. Trevesant, 2 Bay. 23 ; Hine v. Robbins, 2 Conn. 342; Dillingham v. Snow, 5 Mass. 547 ; Cunningham v. Magoun, 18 Pick. 13 ; Hall v. Downs, Brayt. 168; U. S. v. Duval, Gilpin, 356 ; Ross v. Eason, 1 Y. 14; Bank v. Marchand, Charlton, 247 ; Moore v. Cherry, 1 Bay. 269 ; Thomas v. Brown, 1 McCord, 557 ; Mears v. Moor, 3 McCord, 282, ibid. 131 ;. Hyckman v. Shotbolt, Dyer, 279 ; Watkins v. Oliver, Cro. Jac. 558 ; Bright v. Eynon, 1 Burr. 390 ; Edie v. East India Company, 2 Burr. 1216 ; Hodgson v. Richardson, 1 Term. R. 167 ; Tindal v. Brown, 1 W. Black. 463 ; Farrant v. Olmius, 3 Barn. & Adol. 693 ; Turner v.

Where the court has instructed the jury to disregard evidence which afterwards appears to have been improperly admitted, and the jury does not follow the instruction;(h) where the jury finds for the plaintiff, against the charge of the court, that the act of limitations barred the action;(i) and generally, where the verdict is for the defendant against law, and the directions of the court;(j) new trials will be granted.

Although a judge may be wrong in his charge to the jury, even in stating to them that there was no evidence upon a particular point, when in fact there was some evidence, yet if the jury find against the charge, a new trial will be granted.(k)

Where a jury, in a very hard action, disregard an instruction that plaintiff is entitled to nominal damages, and find for defendant, it is not sufficient ground for a new trial.(l)

4. *Verdict against evidence.*

Where the verdict in the opinion of the court is against the weight of evidence, it will be set aside, if injustice be thereby done; and this is particularly the case where one of the material allegations of the succeeding party's case remains unproved.(m)

If, however, there be conflicting evidence on both sides, and the question be one of doubt, it seems the verdict will generally be permitted to stand.(n)

It has been said, that though the judge who tried the cause, inclined that the weight of evidence was with the plaintiff, yet it is no ground

Meymott, 1 Bingham, 158; Gibbons v. Phillips, 8 Barn. & Cress. 437. In Pennsylvania and Virginia, upon the trial of a defendant charged with a criminal offence, he may demur to the evidence, but the commonwealth will not be compelled to join in the demurrer. (Commonwealth v. Parr, 5 W. & S. 345; Doss v. Com. 1 Grattan, 557.)

(h) Unangst v. Kramer, 8 W. & S. 391.

(i) Cresman v. Caster, 2 Br. 123.

(j) Ross v. Eason et al. 1 Y. 14. Emmet v. Robinson, 2 Y. 514.

(k) Flemming v. Marine Ins. Co. 4 Wh. 59. See 2 Bin. 467; 3 Bin. 26; Id. 520.

(l) Mishler v. Baumgardner (C. P. Lancaster, per LEWIS, P. J.), 8 P. L. J. 304. Todd v. Jones, D. C. C. P. 7 Leg. Int. 42.

(m) Emmet v. Robinson, 2 Y. 514. Kohne v. Ins. Co. 1 W. C. C. R. 123. Dayrolles v. Howard, 3 Burr. 1385; R. v. Malden, 4 Burr. 2135; Farriant v. Olmius, 3 Barn. & Ald. 692; Corbett v. Brown, 8 Bingham, 33; U. S. v. Duval, Gilpin, 356; State v. Sims, 2 Bailey, 29; State v. Hooper, 2 Bailey 37; State v. Fisher, 2 N. & M. 261; Respublica v. Lacare, 2 D. 118; Wait v. McNeil, 7 Mass. 261; Curtis v. Jackson, 13 Mass. 507; Bartholomew v. Clark, 1 Conn. 472; Cockfield v. Daniel, 1 Rep. Con. Ct. 193; Ring v. Huntington, 1 Rep. Con. Ct. 162; Starke v. Cockerd, 2 Rep. Con. Ct. 337;

Kinnie v. Kinnie, 4 Conn. 102; Talcott v. Wilcox, 9 Conn. 134; Bacon v. Parker, 12 Conn. 212; Zaleer v. Geiger, 2 Y. 522; Snearingen v. Birch, 4 Y. 322; Thomas v. Brown, 1 McCord, 557; Newson v. Lycar, 3 J. J. Marsh. 440.

(n) Douglass v. Tousey, 2 Wend. 352; Jeffreys v. State, 3 Murphey, 480; Motley v. Montgomery, 2 Bailey, 11; Laval v. Cromwell, Const. Rep. 593; Darby v. Calhoun, 1 Rep. Con. Ct. 398; Miller v. McBurney, 1 Rep. Con. Ct. 237; Cohen v. Simmons, 1 Rep. Con. Ct. 446; Caldwell v. Barkley, 2 Rep. Con. Ct. 452; Palmer v. Hyde, 4 Conn. 426; Lafflin v. Pomeroy, 11 Conn. 440; Trowbridge v. Baker, 1 Cow. 251; Winchell v. Latham, 6 Cowen, 682; McKnight v. Wells, 1 Miss. 13; Clasky v. January, Hardin, 539; Nelson v. Chalfant, 3 Litt. 165; Lee v. Banks, 4 Ibid. 11; Johnson v. Davenport, 3 J. J. Marsh. 390; Reid v. Langford, 3 J. J. Marshall, 420; Creel v. Bell, 2 J. J. Marshall, 309; Talbot v. Talbot, 2 J. J. Marshall, 3; Fitzgerald v. Barker, 4 J. J. Marshall, 398; Swain v. Hall, 3 Wilson, 45; Gregory v. Tufts, 1 Crom. M. & R. 310; 1 Camp. 450; Melin v. Taylor, 2 Hodg. 125; 3 Bing. N. C. 109; Empson v. Fariford, 1 Wilm. Woll. & Dav. 10; Stanley v. Wharton, 8 Price, 301; Lofft. 147; Hankey v. Trotman, 1 W. Bla. 1; Wilton v. Stephenson, 2 Price, 282; Farewell v. Chaffey, 1 Burr. 54.

for awarding a new trial that the jury have differed from him in opinion ;(o) but the cases were frequent, as has just been seen, where new trials are granted upon the mere certificate of the judge trying the cause, that he is dissatisfied with the result.(p)

Although the court have a right to grant a second new trial, yet it must be a very extraordinary case to induce a judge to grant a new trial after two concurring verdicts on matters of *fact* ;(q) though it is otherwise where matter of law has been disregarded by the jury.(r)

Where a plaintiff is entitled only to nominal damages, the court will not grant a new trial when the verdict is for defendant.(s)

On a motion for a new trial, the court must judge not only of the competency, but of the effect of evidence ; and the question is not, whether on the new facts before them, the jury *might* not be *induced* to give a contrary verdict, but whether the legitimate effect of the whole evidence would require them to do so.(t)

5. *Irregularity of jurors.*

New trials were granted where the jury received new evidence after leaving the bar ;(u) where parol evidence had been allowed to be given of the contents of a deed and of a will, without previous notice to the

---

(o) Campbell v. Sproat, 1 Y. 327. McIntire v. Cunningham, id. 363.

(p) Swearingen v. Birch, 4 Y. 322. Pringle v. Gaw, 6 S. & R. 298.

(q) Burkart v. Bucher, 2 Bin. 467. Keble v. Arthurs, 3 Bin. 26.

(r) Ibid. Commissioners of Berks v. Ross, id. 520.

(s) Todd v. Jones, D. C. C. P. 7 Leg. Int. 42.

(t) Martin v. Marvine, 9 Leg. Int. 2. The practice of the District Court of Philadelphia, in this respect, is thus stated by Judge Sharswood : Hansell v. Lutz, Saturday, March 13, 1852. Motion for a new trial. There is no question so embarassing to a judicial tribunal, as to determine when it is or is not their duty to interfere with the verdict of a jury, upon a mere question of the weight of evidence. The single opinion of one man upon a mere question of fact, ought not, except in a clear case, to weigh down that of twelve. Evidence presents itself to different minds in different lights, and in no case is the remark more applicable than upon a question of fraud. Now there certainly were many circumstances, besides the incongruous and unexplained declarations of the plaintiff, which were calculated to confirm the impression these declarations were likely to produce. The fact that the mortgage was of the same date as the deed of the mortgagor, for a sum much larger than the property was worth, or the mortgagor had given for it, and the hot haste with which the mortgage was sued out the moment the sale took place,

before the time for which the interest was paid in advance had expired—linked with the fact that the mortgagor, immediately upon the sheriff's sale, had given notice to the tenant to pay no rent to the purchaser, as he intended to get the property *back*—were certainly circumstances calculated to fasten collusion and fraud. When all this is taken into consideration, with the fact that no evidence whatever was given of actual consideration and *bona fides*, but the plaintiff was compelled to rely upon the paper alone, it cannot in any view, be a case in which the verdict of the jury, contrary to the *prima facie* case presented by the mortgage, ought to be set aside. It may be unfortunate that the plaintiff could only prove the consideration and *bona fides* of the papers by a witness clearly incompetent to testify. It is not the first just cause—if it be a just cause, which has been lost by the arbitrary rule which excludes a witness pecuniarily interested in the result, and permits the admission of the testimony of a father in favor of a son, whose temptation to color and distort is as great, if not greater, than one whose interest is mere money. As to the allegation of surprise, the game was in the plaintiff's own hands. He might have suffered a nonsuit ; but as he has elected to take his chance with the jury upon the evidence as presented, we must, in consistency with established principles, hold him bound by that election. Rule refused.

(u) Brunson v. Graham, 2 Y. 166.

defendant to produce it, and where it appeared that two of the jury had testified to their brethren on the question in issue, after the jury had withdrawn ;(v) and where it appeared by the affidavit of one of the jurors, that after the jury had received the charge of the court, and retired to consider of their verdict, the foreman of the jury declared that the prevailing party had satisfied him with regard to a difficulty in the plaintiff's account, in a conversation he had with him out of court, and after the jury had been sworn.(w)

But it is not sufficient ground to grant a new trial, that one of the jurors, after they had agreed upon a verdict for the plaintiff, sealed it up and separated, heard a third person express his opinion that the plaintiff ought to recover ;(x) nor that the jury, in an action of *tort*, determined the amount of damages by each setting down the particular sum he thought just, and then dividing the aggregate by the number of jurymen, unless some fraudulent abuse of the mode adopted appears ; (y) nor that one of the jurors was an alien ;(z) nor that a special juror was struck off, and then sworn as a talesman, if done with the knowledge of the party who struck him off ;(a) nor that a brother-in-law of the plaintiff was sworn on the jury, and the plaintiff's attorney agreed to waive the juror, and swear another in his room, which the defendant refused, no injustice having been done by the verdict.(b)

There must be clear and full proof of the juror's having eaten and drunk at the expense of the party, and undue management, or a criminal intention must appear, or the court will not grant a new trial.(c)

A new trial will not be granted where it appears that a juror had betted on both sides of a cause, unless an evident bias was produced, nor where some of them have expressed an opinion on the opening of a cause.(d)

The English rule now is, that a juror is inadmissible to impeach the verdict of his fellows, and the courts of this country incline to the same result,(e) though the affidavits of jurors will be entertained for the purpose of explaining, correcting, or enforcing their verdict.(f)   Thus

(v) Bradley v. Bradley, 4 D. 112. [But in Cluggage v. Swan, 4 Bin. 157, it is said by YEATES, J., "This case is reported erroneously. The *plaintiff* obtained judgment on his verdict, the court being divided in opinion, and it is thus entered on the record. Nothing dropped from either of the members of the court respecting the conduct of the jury."]

(w) Ritchie v. Holbrook, 7 S. & R. 458.

(x) Willing v. Swasey, 1 Br. 123.

(y) Cowperthwaite v. Jones, 2 D. 55. In assumpsit, the rule seems otherwise : Zuber v. Geiger, 2 Y. 522.

(z) Hollingsworth v. Duane, C. C. 4 D. 353.

(a) Jordan v. Meredith, 3 Y. 318 ; S. C. 1 Bin. 27.

(b) Spong v. Lesher, 1 Y. 326.

(c) Goodright v. M'Cousland, 1 Y. 373.

(d) Ibid.

(e) Cluggage v. Swan ; 4 Bin. 150 ;

Willing v. Swasey, 1 Br. 123 ; Dana v. Tucker, 4 Johns. 487 ; Sergeant v. Deniston, 5 Cowen, 106 ; *ex parte* Caykendall, 6 Cowan, 53 ; People v. Columbia, &c. 1 Wendell, 297 ; State v. Freeman, 5 Connect. 348 ; Cochran v. Steel, 1 Wash. 79 ; Price v. Tugna, 1 Hen. & Mun. 385 ; Robbins v. Wendover, 2 Tyler, 11 ; Bladen v. Cockey, 1 Har. & M'Henry, 230 ; State v. Doom, Charlton, 1 ; Taylor v. Giger, Hardin. 586 ; Steele v. Logan, 3 A. K. Marshall, 394 ; Heath v. Conway, 1 Bibb, 398 ; Den v. M'Allister, 2 Halst, 46 ; Johnson v. Davenport, 3 J. J. Marshall, 390 ; Briggs v. Eggleston, 14 Mass. 245 ; Com. v. Drew, 4 Mass. 439 ; Forester v. Guard, Breese, 49 ; though see Sawyer v. Stephenson, Breese, 6 ; Grinnill v. Phillips, 1 Mass. 530 ; Hudson v. State, 9 Yerger, 408 ; Crawford v. State, 2 Yerger, 60.

(f) Cogan v. Ebden, 1 Burr. 383 ; R. v. Woodfall, 5 Burr. 2667 ; Dana v.

where a doubt existed, in consequence of confusion in the court-room, as to what the exact verdict was, the affidavits of jurors and bystanders were received for the purpose of showing the facts of the case, though all reference was excluded as to the motives or intentions with which such verdict was agreed to, or the circumstances attending the deliberations which led to it.(g) And so it is held that the affidavit of a juror is admissible to prove misconduct of one of the *parties.(h)*

6. *Misconduct by prevailing party.*

Any misconduct by the prevailing party, intended to affect the jury, and tending so to do, will be cause for a new trial.(i)

Evidence that a party, by exhibiting papers at places where the jury boarded, had been attempting to bias and influence them, has been held sufficient to sustain the motion(j)

Where papers, not in evidence, are surreptitiously handed to the jury, the verdict will be avoided;(k) and the same result will take place where it appears that a witness on one side has been spirited away by the opposite party.(l) Such efforts, however, must be traced to the party or his agents.(m) In fine, any unfair trick, if successful, will be ground for the motion.(n)

A new trial was granted where the plaintiff delivered a paper to the jury relating to his demand, without consent or leave of the court.(o)

The declaration by counsel on trial on his own knowledge, of a fact not proven in the case, is a sufficient cause for a new trial, if the verdict goes in favor of the party through whom such declarations are made.(p) Where, however, this irregularity is induced by a prior irregularity of the opposite party, the rule is otherwise.(q)

Tucker, 4 Johns. 487; Jackson v. Dickenson, 15 Johnson, 309; Cochran v. Street, 1 Wash. R. 79.

(g) R. v. Woodfall, 5 Burr. 2667; R. v. Simons, Sayre, 35.

(h) Ritchie v. Holbrook, 7 S. & R. 458.

(i) 2 Hale, P. C. 303; State v. Hascall, 6 N. Hamp. 352; Knight v. Inhabitants, &c. 13 Mass. 218; Lee's Rep. Tem. Hardwicke, 116; Bennett v. Howard, 3 Day, 223; Perkins v. Knight, 2 N. Hamp. 474; Jeffries v. Randall, 14 Mass. 205; Amherst v. Hadley, 1 Pick. 38, 42; Ritchie v. Holbrooke, 7 S. & R. 458; Metcalf v. Dean, Cro. Eliz. 189; Thompson v. Mallet, 1 Bay. 94; Knight v. Inhabitants, 13 Mass. 218; Blaize v. Chambers, 1 S. & R. 169; Cottle v. Cottle, 6 Greenleaf, 146.

(j) State v. Hascall, 6 N. Hamp. 352; Coster v. Merest, 3 Brod. & Bing. 272; 7 Moore, 87; Spenceley v. De Willot, 7 East, 108.

(k) Co. Lit. 272; Graves v. Short, Cro. Eliz. 616; Palmer, 325.

(l) Bull. N. P. 328.

(m) Grovenor v. Fernwick, 7 Mod. 156.

(n) Anderson v. George, 1 Barr, 352; Graham on New Trials, 56; Bodington v. Harris, 1 Bing. 187; Jackson v. Waterford, 7 Wend. 62; Hylliard v. Nickols, 2 Root, 176; Niles c. Brackett, 15 Mass. 378.

(o) Sheaffe v. Gray, 2 Y. 273.

(p) Fulmer v. Scott, D. Ct. C. P. Dec. 1848. See also *ante*, 220.

(q) Hart v. Dickerson, D. C., Saturday, July 8, 1848. Rule for a new trial. *Per curiam.* We have had considerable difficulty in this case, arising not so much from the verdict itself as from the irregular introduction of a fact in the course of the trial, which was calculated to have undue weight with the jury, but which really had nothing to do with the merits. Where the plaintiff is guilty of such an irregularity, as, for example, by stating a former verdict or award in his favor, the proper remedy of a defendant is to ask that the jury may be discharged and the cause continued. It is evident, however, that this cannot be applied to the case of a defendant who, by that means, may forever postpone the trial. However, in such a case, it ought to appear that the immaterial fact had been before the jury only in consequence of the irregularity committed by the party. Here the irregular statement was made by the defendant in his opening, and as a mere statement, without any evidence

7. *After-discovered evidence.*

Before discussing the several requisites of this ground for new trial, one or two preliminary points of practice may be noticed.

As a general rule, the party should mention, in his affidavit, the witnesses by name, and what he expects to prove by them; and either the witnesses themselves should state, on oath, the evidence they can give, or the party should add his own belief to the statement made by the witnesses.(r)

A new trial will not be granted unless depositions be taken to sustain the motion;(s) and the evidence is to be taken before a commissioner, in the presence of counsel, with the liberty to cross-examine.(t)

The rule, in general, will not be granted, if supported only by the affidavit of the party, or one interested. The motion must be accompanied by the affidavit of the newly-discovered witnesses.(u)

The adverse party may show, by affidavits, or cross-depositions, that the witnesses, whose testimony is stated to be material, are wholly unworthy of credit.(v)

A motion for a new trial will not be heard after a judgment has been regularly perfected, although it be on the ground of evidence newly discovered since the judgment.(w)

---

to support it, we are bound to suppose would have had but little if any weight. Still, if it stood upon that alone, we would feel disposed to listen to the objection. When Birkey, however, was on the stand as a witness for the defendant, he was asked, in cross-examination, whether he had not paid the note which he had given, being a part of the same transaction for which the note in suit was in question. This undoubtedly gave the defendant a right to ask why he had paid the note. And his answer, that he had paid it under the terror of a prosecution for perjury, to calm the natural anxieties of an aged parent, thus brought the fact clearly before the jury. Uninfluenced, then, by any considerations arising out of this irregularity, we see no sufficient cause to disturb the verdict. It was put to the jury mainly upon a question of fact, whether Nichuals had possession of the articles sold as agent for the defendant. Both parties agreed in going to the jury upon that question; and in regard to it, the evidence was contradictory. It appeared that, when the bill of sale was handed to defendant, he demanded possession, and the answer made by plaintiff's agent, according to his own testimony, was, that he had all the possession he could give him. The possession which Nichuals had was under a prior contract with Badger, in which he did not act as defendant's agent, but as vendee himself. It may be doubted whether, with such possession continued in Nichuals, the bill of sale would have

protected it from execution for his debts. The bill of sale was not a mere conveyance of the right of the vendor to the chattels, but of the chattels themselves; and in such a case, the vendee has a right to object unless possession can be immediately delivered. He is not bound to accept a lawsuit, even though the right of the vendor be unquestionable. It was then the true question, whether Nichuals, to whom alone possession had been given, was the agent of defendant? This it was incumbent on the plaintiff to make out. We cannot say consistently with the principles upon which the court have hitherto acted, that the weight of the evidence so preponderates that the verdict should be set aside on that account. Rule dismissed.

(r) Kenderdine *v.* Phelin, GIBSON, C. J., 9 Leg. Int. 54; Hollingsworth *v.* Napier, 3 Cai. 182; Denn *v.* Morrell *et al.* 1 Ham. 382; Brown *v.* Swan, 1 Mass. 202; Adams *v.* Ashley, 2 Bibb, 287; Andre *v.* Beinvenu, 1 Mart. Lo. 148; Locard *v.* Bullitt, 3 Mast. N. S. 170.

(s) Greenwood *v.* Iddings, D. C. C. P. 7 Leg. Int. 19.

(t) Kenderdine *v.* Phelin, S. C. N. P. 9 Leg. Int. 54. GIBSON, J.

(u) Webber *v.* Tres, 1 Tyler, 441; Noyce *v.* Huntington, Kirby, 282; though see Chambers *v.* Brown, Cooke, 292; Scott *v.* Willon, Cooke, 315.

(v) Williams *v.* Baldwin, 18 Johns. 489; Pomroy *v.* Colum. Ins. Co. 2 Caines, 260; Parker *v.* Hardy, 24 Pick. 246.

(w) Jackson *v.* Chase, 15 Johns. 355;

(1.) *The evidence must have been discovered since the former trial.*(x)

Where on an action in assumpsit on a policy of insurance, the jury rendered a verdict for a total loss, and a new trial was moved for partly on the ground of newly-discovered evidence, but from the affidavit it did not appear that this testimony had been discovered since the last trial, but only that it had arrived in New York since that time ; it was held that, as from the nature of the evidence, it must have been discovered as soon as the cause of the loss was known, and as there must have been a want of due diligence in procuring it, the verdict could not be disturbed.(y)

But in another case,(z) where the new evidence consisted of documents, from the custom-house at New York, tending to invalidate some of the testimony given at the trial, and to show the sale was not *bona fide*, but a mere cover, and the goods not neutral property, it was held that this was sufficient ground for granting the motion for a new trial, notwithstanding that the defendant's counsel, upon seeing the New York commission, which had come to hand a few days before the trial, suspected, from some parts of it, that some useful information might be collected.

If new evidence be discovered before the verdict is rendered, it should be submitted to the jury; and if neglected, a new trial will not be granted.(a) The judge, at the trial, has discretion as to the admission of evidence out of the regular and usual course. Thus, after the defendant's counsel had summed up, and while the counsel for the plain-

---

Evans v. Rogers, 2 N. & M. 563 ; Eckfert v. Des Coudes, 1 Rep. Con. Ct. 69.

Thus, where judgment had been perfected, a motion for new trial was made, on ground of newly-discovered evidence. From the affidavits that were read, it appeared that the suit was commenced in 1807, and after a trial and verdict for plaintiff, judgment was entered for plaintiff, in Oct. 1816, there being no order to stay proceedings, but no execution was issued until some time in July, 1818 ; and that the new evidence was not known or discovered by defendant until April, 1818. The motion was denied. Jackson v. Chace, 15 Johns. 355. But see Case v. Sheppard, 1 Johns. Cases, 245 ; Birh v. Barlow, 1 Doug. 170.

(x) Moore v. Phila. Bank, 5 S. & R. 41 ; Knox v. Work, C. P. 2 Bin. 582 ; Auber v. Ealer, ibid. ; Marshall v. Union Ins. Co. 2 W. C. C. R. 411 ; 15 Johns. 293 ; Vandevoort v. Smith, 2 Cai. 155 ; Hollingsworth v. Napier, 3 Cai. 182 ; Thurtell v. Beaumont, 8 Moore, 612 ; Palmer v. Mulligan, ibid. 307 ; Vernon v. Hankey, 2 T. R. 113 ; Ingram v. Croft, 7 Lo. R. 84 ; State v. Harding, 2 Bay, 267 ; Dixon v. Graham, 5 Dow, 267 ; Doe v. Roe, 1 Johns. Ca. 402 ; Williams v. Baldwin, 15 Johns. 489 ; Brayt, 170 ; 1 Greenleaf, 32 ; Standen v. Edwards, 1 Ves. Jun. 133.

Edwards v. Nicholas, D. C., June 14, 1851. M. for new trial. *Per curiam.* We are asked to grant a new trial in this case, mainly on the ground of after-discovered evidence. But it could not, and has not been pretended that the alleged evidence could not have been produced at the trial, for though the defendant might not have known what the witness, Glenn, would testify, or, indeed, that he would be called to give evidence at all, he undoubtedly did know that the note sued upon had passed through his hands, and that he alleged that he bought it and sold it to plaintiff. He knew, then, or ought to have known, that his *bona fides*, as the holder, might just as well arise in the case as the *bona fides* of the plaintiff. The rule being perfectly well settled that an indorsee, who has taken a note with full notice of the equities between the original parties, can shield himself under the *bona fides* of any previous holder, R. refused.

(y) Vandevoort v. Smith, 2 Caines, 155 ; Rogers v. Simons, 1 Rep. Con. Ct. 143.

(z) Marshall v. Union Ins. Co. 2 Wash. C. C. R. 411.

(a) Higden v. Higden, 2 A. K. Marsh. 42 ; U. S. v. Gilbert, 2 Sumner, 19 ; People v. Vermilyea, 7 Cow. 369.

tiff were speaking, the counsel for defendant informed the judge that he had just discovered, from a paper in the possession of one of the plaintiff's witnesses, that the money, &c., was not, in fact, received, &c., and asked leave to introduce the new evidence ; upon the judge's refusal, the court granted a new trial, with costs to abide the event of the suit.(b)

(2.) *It must be such as could not have been secured at the former trial by reasonable diligence on the part of the losing party.*(c)

It is not such newly-discovered evidence, that the party applying for a new trial could not procure in time the witness whom he seeks to introduce, as will entitle him to a new trial. He should have applied to the court for a postponement; and if he has gone to the trial without the testimony, a new trial will not be granted for the purpose of letting in such evidence.(d) Nor is the absence of a witness who had not been subpœnaed, a good cause for granting a new trial ;(e) but it seems that the sudden illness of a witness is.(f) Nor will a new trial be granted to admit newly-discovered evidence to points of which the party was before apprised, and had not shaped his pleas to admit it ;(g) nor on account of the want of recollection of a fact, which, by due attention, might have been remembered ; want of recollection being easy to be pretended, and hard to be disproved.(h)

Where the plaintiff had refused to produce a letter at the time, thinking the defendant had put in a sham plea, the court refused to grant a new trial, because it appeared that the evidence might have been produced had it not been for his own default.(i) Nor will the court grant a new trial on the ground of a claim which the party might have brought forward on the trial, but did not.(j)

(b) Mercer v. Sayre, 7 Johns. 306.

(c) Moore v. Phila. Bank, 5 S. & R. 41 ; Knox v. Work, C. P. 2 Bin. 582 ; S. C. 1 Br. 101 ; Auber v. Ealer, C. P. 2 Bin. 582, in note; S. C. 1 Br. 105, in note ; Turnbull v. O'Hara, 4 Y. 446 ; Waln v. Wilkins, 4 Y. 461 ; State v. Harding, 5 Bay, 267 ; Com. v. Drew, 4 Mass. 399 ; Lesher v. State, 11 Connect. 415 ; Com. v. Williams, 2 Ashmead, 69 ; Price v. Brown, H. 12 G. ; Cook v. Berry, 1 Wils. 98 ; Stanford v. Cullihan, 3 Mart. N. S. 124 ; Findley v. Nancy, 3 Monr. R. 403 ; Findley v. Com. 2 Bibb, 18 ; People v. Vermilyea, 7 Cowen, 369 ; Gordon v. Harvey, 4 Call. 450 ; Palmer v. Mulligan, 3 Cai. 307 ; Wilbor v. M'Gullicuddy, 3 Lo. R. 383 ; Rawle v. Skipurtt, 8 Mast. N. S. 593 ; Dixon v. Graham, 5 Dow, 267 ; Coe v. Givan, 1 Blackf. 367 ; William v. Baldwin, 18 Johns. 489; Sheppard v. Sheppard, 5 Halst. 250 ; Deacon v. Allen, 1 South. 338 ; Litcomb v. Potter, 2 Fairf. 218 ; Vandervoort v. Smith, 2 Cai. R. 155 ; Den v. Geiger, 4 Halst. 225 ; Lesher v. State, 11 Conn. 15 ; Drayton v. Thompson, 1 Bay, 263 ; State v. Gordon, ibid. 491 ; Hollingsworth v. Napier, 3 Cai. 182 ; Trumbull v. O'Hara, 4 Halst. 446 ; Waln v. Wilkins, ibid. 461 ;

Howe v. Work, 2 Bin. 582 ; S. C. 1 Br. 101 ; Aubell v. Ealer, 2 ibid. 582, note; Hawley v. Blanton, 1 Miss. 49 ; Hope v. Atkins, 1 Price, 143 ; Anonymous, 6 Mod. 222 ; Watson v. Sutton, 12 Mod. 583 ; 1 Salk. 273.

(d) Jackson v. Malin, 15 Johns. 293 ; Gordon v. Harvey, 4 Call, 450.

(e) Kelly v. Holdchip, 1 Br. 36 ; Lister v. Goode, 2 Murph. 37.

(f) Fiss v. Smith, 1 Br. App. 61 ; Gorgerat v. McCarty, 1 Y. 253. See *post*, 541.

(g) Eccles v. Shackleford, 1 Litt. 35.

(h) Bond v. Cutler, 7 Mass. 205 ; Durgnan v. Wyatt, 3 Blackf. 385.

(i) Cooke v. Berry, 1 Wils. 98. In another case, in an action upon a policy, the verdict was given for plaintiff, and the defendants moved for a new trial, assigning, as the reason why the evidence had not been offered at the trial, a presumption that the jury, of their own knowledge, must have taken notice of the fact. This was held an insufficient reason, and a new trial was refused.— (Gist v. Mason, *et al.* 1 T. R. 84.)

(j) McDermott v. U. S. Ins. Co. 3 S. & R. 604.

(3.) *It must be material in its object, and not merely cumulative and corroborative, or collateral.(k)*

Cumulative evidence is such as goes to support the facts principally controverted on the former trial, and respecting which, the party asking for a new trial, as well as the adverse party, produced testimony.

Where the object is to discredit a witness on the opposite side, the general rule is that a new trial will not be granted.(l) Thus, where the defendant was convicted of forgery, chiefly on the evidence of B. R., and on a motion for a new trial, evidence was produced to show the bias of B. R., it was held, by the Supreme Court of Massachusetts, that such evidence was no ground for the motion.(m)

Where a witness, whose testimony was not unexpected, was discredited by the party against whom he was produced, a new trial will not be granted, on the ground that the party has since discovered further evidence of his want of credit ;(n) nor will a new trial be granted for newly-discovered evidence which goes only to discredit a witness sworn on the trial, and might have been proved by other witnesses who were sworn.(o)

It has, however, been decided, that where a witness on whose testimony a verdict was found, denied, on the *voir dire*, having an interest in the case, newly-discovered evidence that he was interested, was admissible on an application for a new trial; and it being proved, by similar evidence of declarations of the witness and of the prevailing party, that the witness's evidence was untrue, that a new trial should be granted.(p)

(4.) *It must be such as ought to produce, on another trial, an opposite result on the merits.(q)*

"After the verdict," said ROGERS, J., on a motion for a new trial, "when the motion for a new trial is considered, the court must judge not only of the competency, but of the effect of evidence. If, with the newly-discovered evidence before them, the jury ought not to come to the same conclusion, then a new trial may be granted; otherwise, they are bound to refuse the application. And in Lewellen v. Parker,(r) it is ruled that, in considering the motion, the court will not inquire whether, taking the newly-discovered testimony in connection with that

(k) Moore v. Phila. Bank, 5 S. & R. 41 ; Com. v. Flannagan, 8 W. & S. 415 ; Gardner v. Mitchell, 6 Pick. 114 ; Yarmouth v. Dennis, ibid. 116, note ; Sawyer v. Merrill, 10 Pick. 16 ; Chambers v. Chambers, 2 A. K. Marsh, 348 ; Ames v. Howard, 1 Sumner, 482 ; Alsop v. Ins. Co. ibid. 451 ; Bullock v. Beach, 3 Verm. 72 ; Den v. Geiger, 4 Halst. 228 ; Pike v. Evans, 15 Johns. 210 ; Steinback v. Ins. Co. 2 Caines, 129 ; Smith v. Brush, 8 Johns. 84 ; Whiteback v. Whiteback, 9 Cow. 266 ; Reed v. Grew, 5 Ham. 375 ; Wheelwright v. Beers, 2 Hall, 391 ; Guyot v. Butts, 4 Wend. 579 ; People v. Superior Court of New York, 10 Wend. 285 ; Com. v. Williams, 2 Ashm. 69 ; Moore v. Phila. Bank, 5 S. & R. 41.

(l) People v. Sup. Court of N. Y. 10 Wend. 292 ; Shummey v. Fowler, 4 John. R. 425 ; Duryee v. Dennison, 5 John. R.

248 ; Rowley v. Kinney, 14 John. R. 186 ; Turner v. Pearle, 1 T. R. 717 ; Hammond v. Wadhams, 5 Mass. 353 ; Com. v. Green, 17 Mass. 515.

(m) Com. v. Waite, 5 Mass. 261.

(n) Hammond v. Wadhams, 5 Mass. 353.

(o) Dodge v. Kendall, 4 Verm. 31.

(p) Chatfield v. Lathrop, 6 Pick. 417.

(q) Moore v. Phila. Bank, 5 S. & R. 41 ; Ewing v. McConnell, 1 A. K. Marsh, 188 ; Ludlow v. Parke, 4 Ham. 5 ; Sheppard v. Sheppard, 5 Halst. 250 ; Kendrick v. Delafield, 2 Cai. 67 ; Halley v. Watson, 1 Caines, 24 ; Com. v. Manson, et al. 2 Ashm. 31 ; State v. Greenwood, 1 Hay. 141 ; Earl v. Sharldee, 6 Ham. 409 ; Jessup v. Cook, 1 Halst. 434.

(r) 4 Harr. O. R. 5 ; Ludlow v. Parke, 4 Ham. 5.

exhibited on the trial, a jury might be induced to give a different verdict, but whether the legitimate effect of such evidence would require a different verdict. The question, therefore, is (supposing all the testimony, new and old, before another jury), not whether they might, but whether they ought to give another verdict. It is manifest, therefore, if these principles be correct, granting a new trial would be almost, if not quite, equivalent to a verdict of acquittal."(s)

8. *Absence.*

The sudden illness of counsel, as well as the sudden illness of a witness, would be a good reason for a new trial.(t)

A new trial was refused, where a verdict had passed for the plaintiff, on the evidence of one witness; and the defendant being absent from home at the time of the trial, was unprepared to meet it.(u)

It is a general rule, that neither the mistake nor the absence of counsel, if voluntary or accidental, is a ground for a new trial.(v)

Where the defendant's attorney had conversed with the partner of the plaintiff's attorney, whom he supposed to be also attorney for the plaintiff, and was misled by him as to the time when the case would be called in, a new trial was ordered, on payment of all the costs by the defendant.(w)

Where the defendant was out of the commonwealth, his witnesses absent, and his attorney prevented, by sudden indisposition, from being present, it was held, that a new trial should be granted.(x)

It is no ground, however, for a new trial, that the defendant did not know on what day of the term his case would be tried; nor that the defendant's attorney was absent when the case went to the jury, and the plaintiff's counsel agreed before the recording of the verdict to open the case.(xx)

No mere engagement of a business character will be received as an excuse for the non-appearance of counsel. Thus, where the counsel for the defendant made oath, that in his capacity as counsel for the Humane Society of New York, he was obliged to visit the jail on the very day that the trial took place, and offered to pay all costs, a new trial was refused.(y)

Absence of counsel, to be a good ground, must be on an engagement in another court. A new trial was consequently refused where counsel was telegraphed for to Harrisburg from Philadelphia, "on professional business," and had communicated the fact (though not the cause) to the judge.(z)

Motions were refused in the District Court of Philadelphia, where

---

(s) Com. v. Flannagan, 7 W. & S. 423.

(t) Fiss v. Smith's Ex'rs, *ut supra*.

(u) Leedom v. Pancake, 4 Y. 183.

(v) Fiss v. Smith's Ex'rs, 1 Br. Appx. lxxi; Gorgeret v. M'Carty, 1 Y. 253.

(w) Sayer v. Finck, 2 Caines, 336.

(x) Honone v. Murray, 3 Dana, 31; see 2 ibid. 334; 4 Litt. 1.

(xx) Allen v. Donelly, 1 McCord, 113; Greatwood v. Sims, 2 Chitty, 269.

(y) Post v. Wright, 1 Caines, 111.

(z) Olden v. Litzenburg, June 14, 1851. M. to take off nonsuit. *Per curiam.* There was no trial in this case. The plaintiff's counsel says he was called to Harrisburg, by a telegraphic dispatch, on professional business. He communicated the fact of his absence to the judge, but did not state then that it was upon professional business; nor does he now state what the nature of the professional business was. It seems to be forgotten, that the professional business which forms a legal ground for continuance, is an engagement in another court. We see no reason, therefore, for disturbing the nonsuit. M. dismissed.

the attorney of one party was, by an accidental interchange of cases, misled as to the position of his cause and was thus absent ;(a) where the plaintiff took a verdict in the absence of the defendant and his attorney, who were out of court, endeavoring to obtain the Christian name of a material witness in the case, when the case was called ;(b) where the defendant's counsel was absent at the time of the trial of a case, relying on the promise of his adversary to notify him ;(c) where the defendant, his attorney and witnesses, were absent at the time of the verdict, in consequence of an erroneous impression that the case was continued ;(d) and where the verdict was taken when the defendant and his witnesses went, by mistake, into the wrong court-room, while his counsel was absent in another court, under the promise of plaintiff's counsel to send for him when the case was called.(e)

(a) Vandegrift v. Malcomson. Motion to take off nonsuit. *Per curiam.* With every disposition to assist counsel, where a mistake has occurred, by which a nonsuit has been entered, we cannot do so in this case. It might present a different case, were it shown to us that the claim is now barred by the statute of limitations. That, however, is not the case, and the only matter is one merely of costs. We think it best to adhere strictly to rule. The counsel left the court while the first case was on trial. He left no one in charge of the case ; no memorandum of where he was going. It was said, he went to his office. When he returned, No. 10 was on trial; when concluded, he was told that No. 11 had been nonsuited. All this was true. No. 10 had been reached and passed, on account of the engagement of counsel, or some other cause; No. 11 was called, no one answered for plaintiff; plaintiff's counsel was sent for in the other courts, without success ; and a nonsuit was entered. And then the counsel in No. 10 having come in, or other reason for its having been passed removed, the judge returned to No. 10. It is a lesson which, perhaps, it may require some time and experience thoroughly to teach, that counsel cannot safely leave the court, for any space of time, or for any purpose, without taking the precaution to leave their cases in care of somebody. Motion dismissed.

(b) Field v. Sergeant, D. C. C. P. 7 Leg. Int. 110.

(c) Tams v. Graef, D. C. C. P. 7 Leg. Int. 98.

(d) Duffy v. McGelligan, D. C., Saturday, June 15, 1850. Motion for a rule for a new trial. *Per curiam.* The reason assigned for a new trial is, that the case was called up and tried by plaintiff's attorney, in the absence of the defendant's attorney, defendant, and

his witnesses, after the plaintiff's attorney had requested defendant's attorney to have the cause continued, on account of the inability of plaintiff's attorney to try, and the case had been accordingly so continued. The fact appears by the record to be, that when the case was called, it was left open on account of the engagement of plaintiff's attorney, and never was continued. Such is the well-established practice of the court, nor would a case be continued on account of the engagement of counsel, without the payment of the continuance fee, unless it appeared highly probable that the engagement would continue for the whole period assigned for the trial of the case. It is clear, therefore, that defendant's attorney acted under a mistake in dismissing his client and witnesses. It would be dangerous to give effect to such a ground for a new trial. In cases of this character, the counsel must necessarily be thrown upon courtesy of his opponent. Rule refused.

Rambo v. Chambers, Saturday, March 20, 1852. Motion to take off nonsuit. *Per curiam.* This is a case in which, however disposed to relieve parties who have lost a trial, we do not feel at liberty to interfere when the defendant objects. No depositions have been taken, and we have been compelled to rely on the statements of counsel at the bar. A gentleman who leaves the court-room on an errand of business, ought to take the precaution to mention where he is going. Here, indeed, the plaintiff's attorney took that precaution, but the nonsuit occurred from the ignorance or mistake of his client. The defendant and his counsel were in no default, and their statement does not, in all respects, accord with that of the plaintiff. Motion dismissed.

(e) Woodward v. Hindley, D. C., Saturday, June 15, 1850. Motion for a rule

It is not a good reason that the verdict was taken during the temporary absence of counsel, waiting for a cause in another court.(*f*)

9. *Want of notice.*

Where the party or his counsel have had no notice of the trial, or such notice has been imperfect, or had a tendency to mislead, or been insufficient for their information, a new trial should be granted;(*g*) but where the party has gone astray from his own negligence, or appeared and taken defence without notice, the practice is otherwise.(*h*)

Where, in a feigned issue on a sheriff's levy, the case was put down on the trial-list under the name of the original execution and not of the issue, with the word ex. and the name of counsel subjoined, and the verdict was entered on the trial for defendant, the plaintiff not appearing, it was held no ground for a new trial;(*i*) and so, where the defendant's name was misspelled on the trial-list;(*j*) and where the defendant, having made an assignment, his assignee received the notice of trial, but did not forward it to the defendant.(*k*) But where the cause was put on the trial-list without an order, without the plaintiff's knowledge, the court took off a nonsuit.(*l*)

10. *Mistake.*

Where the cause has been prejudiced, from some misconception of the judge, or mistake of the party or his counsel, which could not have been avoided by ordinary prudence and care, a new trial will be allowed. Thus, where the counsel were misled by a positive intimation from the court, and refrained from offering evidence;(*m*) and where the judge

---

for a new trial. *Per curiam.* The allegation is, that the defendant went, by mistake, to the wrong court-room, with his witnesses, and that his counsel, being engaged in the Criminal Court, depended upon the promise of plaintiff's counsel to send for him in the event of the case being called. Neither reason is of any avail, and both together make the case no stronger. If we aim at regularity, certainty, and dispatch in the trial of causes, we must have rigid rules, and rigidly adhere to them. Rule refused.

(*f*) Dickson *v.* Elson, Dec. 23, 1848. Motion for a rule for a new trial. *Per curiam.* We should be glad to help the plaintiff in this case, but it would be a precedent too dangerous to establish, that a counsel waiting for a cause in another court, should be deemed a sufficient apology for not answering for the cause here. The proper mode of avoiding all difficulty, is to let his client, or some one else, answer to the case, and then send for him. Motion dismissed.

(*g*) Bingley *v.* Mollison, 3 Doug. 402; Watson *v.* Gowen, 8 D. & Ryl. 456; Atty. Gen. *v.* Stevens *et al.* 3 Price, 72; Yate *v.* Swaine, Barnes, 233; Lisher *v.* Parmellee *et al.* 1 Wend. 22.

(*h*) Wolfe *v.* Horton, 3 Caines, 86;

Bander *v.* Covill, 4 Cowen, 60; Doe *v.* Kighley, 7 Term 1359.

(*i*) Lincoln *v.* Parmentier, D. C. C. P. 7 Leg. Int. 15.

(*j*) Ivins *v.* Huber, March 15, 1851. Motion for new trial. *Per curiam.* The defendant's name was misspelled on the trial-list. The plaintiff's name and both the counsel were printed correctly. Were we to listen to such reasons as grounds for a new trial, there is no case in which a new trial might not be had—when the party had neglected to attend to his case. Rule refused.

(*k*) Mussi *v.* Lorain, 2 Br. 99.

(*l*) Myers *v.* Riot, D. C., Saturday, March 18, 1848. Motion to take off nonsuit. *Per curiam.* The plaintiff, it appears by the affidavit, was led astray by the refusal of the clerk to put the cause on the trial-list for the third period of September term. The clerk was right, for the order was not given until after the venire had issued. It went down for the succeeding term without an order, and of this the plaintiff was ignorant. Nonsuit taken off.

(*m*) Le Flemming *v.* Simpson, 1 M. & Ryl. 269; Durham *v.* Baxter, 4 Mass. Rep. 79; though see Beekman *v.* Reemins, 7 Cow n, 29; Jackson *v.* Cody, 9 Cowen, 140. e

misapprehended a material fact, and misdirected the jury;(n) a new trial has been granted.(o)

A verdict, in a penal action, however, will not be set aside where given for the defendant, unless it has been procured by mistake of the judge.(p)

A new trial will be granted where it appears that there was such a mistake in the bill of particulars as to mislead the defendant.(q)

A new trial was granted for a mistake by the jury, in the value of foreign money.(r)

The court will not grant a new trial on the ground of a claim, which the party might have brought forward at the trial, but did not.(s)

Although relief will be granted when an innocent mistake of counsel is made, this will not be the case when it appears that the same result would have taken place from a want of evidence on the merits.(t)

11. *Surprise.*

Where a party, or his counsel, has been taken by surprise, in the course of a cause, by some accidental circumstance, which could not have been foreseen, and in which no laches could be ascribed to either of them, a new trial will be awarded,(u) particularly if the court think the verdict against the weight of evidence.(v) Thus, a new trial has been granted where the plaintiff is surprised by the testimony of two witnesses who appeared to have been tampered with;(w) where a witness has been so much disconcerted as to be unable to testify at the trial;(x) where the jury gave a verdict against the plaintiff's claim, on a bill indorsed without the words, "or order," apprehending that, by the usage of merchants, it was not assignable, which usage the plaintiff did not expect to have to prove;(y) and where a material witness, regularly subpœnaed and in attendance, absented himself shortly before the case was called.(z) In a case of seduction, where the principal witness laid the seduction on a day which the defendant had no reason to anticipate,

---

(n) Jackson v. Harth, 1 Bailey, 482; Jones v. McNeill, id. 235; Murden v. Ins. Co. 1 Rep. Con. Ct. 200.

(o) Handley v. Harrison, 3 Bibb, 481.

(p) Clay v. Sweet, 4 Bibb, 255.

(q) Pfeffer v. Martin, D. Ct. C. C. P. July, 1848.

(r) Betts v. Death, Add. 267.

(s) M'Dermot v. United States Ins. Co. 3 S. & R. 604.

(t) Gault v. Mitchell, D. C. Saturday, June 10, 1848. Motion to take off nonsuit. *Per curiam.* We are disposed to be liberal in taking off a nonsuit where it has been a mere mistake of counsel. Here the nonsuit would be taken off on the surmise of the plaintiff's counsel, that he did not hear or understand the direction of the judge to call another witness, after he had declined stating what he proposed to prove by the witness then on the stand, if there were any evidence that there was any material witness actually in court whom he could have called. But the truth is he had called over several names on his subpœna, and it was only upon being urged to proceed that he called John J. Taylor to the stand—and as to him, after having been asked once by defendant's counsel and twice by the judge—what he proposed to prove—either declined to answer or stated that he was endeavoring to ascertain. It is plain that the case failed from no fault of the counsel, but because it was not ready for trial. Motion refused.

(u) Guthrie v, Bogart, 1 A. K. Marsh. 334; Blythe v. Sutherland, 3 McCord, 288; Libenintz v. Greenland, 2 ib. 315; Comply v. Brown, Const. Rep. 100.

(v) Hughes v. McGee, 1 A. K. Marsh. 28.

(w) Peterson v. Barry, 4 Bin. 481.

(x) Ainsworth v. Sessions, 1 Root, 175.

(y) Edie v. East India Company, 1 Wm. Black. 295.

(z) Ruggles v. Hall, 14 Johns. 112.

being at a time when he was absent from the place, and could easily prove an alibi, a new trial was granted.(a)

The mere fact of a party being surprised by the introduction of unexpected evidence, however, is no ground for a new trial;(b) nor can surprise be alleged as a sufficient reason, if the declaration and exhibits give notice.(c) Where a material witness for the government had declared that he would hang the prisoner by his testimony, if he could, which declaration the prisoner did not hear until after the trial, the court refused a new trial.(d) In general, as has been seen, the production of unexpected evidence, impeaching the character of a witness, is no reason to set aside the verdict.(e)

There are but few cases in which the verdict will be set aside, where neglect is ascribable to the party or his attorney, or if a good reason for a new trial on the merits is not shown.(f) There is an exception, however, which is sometimes made, where the case is strong on the merits, and has been lost, owing to the culpable negligence of the counsel employed. In such case a new trial will be granted, accompanied by the condition that the counsel be compelled to pay the costs.(g)

Surprise cannot be set up as a cause for a new trial, where the cause was tried at a day of the term subsequent to that at which the party expected it to come on;(h) and if a party knowing a witness to be absent, hazards a trial, no new trial can be granted on account of alleged surprise arising from the absence of such witness;(i) nor is it good ground for a new trial, that the party failed to summon material witnesses at the trial, under advice of counsel that their attendance was unnecessary.(j)

Where the pleadings do not distinctly state the extent and character of the plaintiff's claim (as in a *scire facias* on a mechanic's claim); and upon the trial, the plaintiff opens his case upon a certain basis, which is successfully met by the defendant; and the plaintiff, in conclusion, relies upon a different case, arising out of the testimony, so as to produce a material surprise upon the defendant, and the jury find for the plaintiff, the court will grant a new trial.(k)

But the court will not grant a new trial, if the amount in controversy,

---

(a) Sargent v. ——, 5 Cowen, 106. See *ante*, 537, as to what cases the defendant can be relieved in, on the ground of after-discovered evidence of the incompetency or bias of witnesses.

(b) Willard v. Wetherbee, 4 N. Hamp. 118; Bell v. Howard, 4 Litt. 117.

(c) Harrison v. Wilson, 2 A. K. Marsh. 547; Dodge v. Kendall, 4 Verm. 31; Bitting v. Mowry, 1 Miles, 216; Smith v. Morrison, 3 A. K. Marsh. 81; see *ante*, 538-9.

(d) Com. v. Drew, 4 Mass. 391.

(e) Ball v. Howard, 4 Litt. 117; Den v. Geiger, 4 Halst. 225; Shummay v. Fowler, 4 Johns. 425; Com. v. Green. 17 Mass. 515; see *ante*, 537.

(f) Com. v. Benesh, Thacher's C. C. 684; Patterson v. Matthews, 3 Bibb, 80; Barry v. Willbourne, 2 Bailey, 91; Lee-

den v. Pancake, 4 Y. 183; Hawley v. Blanton, 1 Miss. 49; McLane v. Harris, ib. 700; McLane v. Com. 2 Bibb, 17; Smith v. Morrison, 3 A. K. Marsh. 81; Blackhurst v. Bremer, 1 Dowl. & Ry. 553. Blake v. How, 1 Aik. 306; Smith v. Morrison, 3 A. K. Marsh, 81; Jackson v. Roe, 9 Johns. 77; Cockerill v. Calhoun, 1 Nott & McCord, 285; Steinbech v. Col. Ins. Co. 2 Caines, 129; Jackson v. Van Antwerp, 8 Cowen, 273.

(g) Martyn v. Podger, 5 Burr. 2631; *sed contra*, De Roufigny v. Peale, 3 Taunt. 484.

(h) Cotton v. Brashiers, 2 A. K. Marsh. 153.

(i) Gill v. Warren, 1 J. J. Marsh. 590.

(j) Pleasants v. Clements, 2 Leigh, 174.

(k) Bitting v. Mowry, 1 M. 216.

arising out of such matter of surprise, is so small as not to exceed the costs to the parties of another trial.(*l*)

It is not a sufficient reason for a new trial, that the plaintiff's principal witness stated as a fact that which appeared afterwards to have been mere hearsay;(*m*) nor that an unsubpœnaed witness was absent from trial.(*n*)

Where the plaintiff, on the trial, was led to believe that to the plea of *non est factum*, an affidavit denying execution had been added, and being surprised, was unable to give proof of execution, and it turned out that no denial had been made of execution, the court granted a new trial.(*o*)

A new trial was granted where the plaintiff was surprised at the trial by an allegation of a payment, sworn to by two witnesses whom there was reason to suspect of perjury.(*p*)

Where the plaintiff, on trial, having produced on trial an agreement by the defendant to settle and pay costs, of which the defendant's counsel denied all knowledge, and required proof, which the plaintiff was unable to produce, and was, consequently, nonsuited, the court refused to take off the nonsuit.(*q*)

A new trial, on the ground of surprise, will not, in general, be granted to a plaintiff, unless his claim is barred by the statute, or the defendant is beyond the jurisdiction of the court, or is able, for some reason, to show that, if he had suffered a nonsuit, he would have irreparably lost the case, especially where the costs are unusually heavy.(*r*)

    12. *Irregularity in impanelling the jury.*

Generally speaking, the mistake or informality of the officers charged with summoning, returning, and impanelling the jury, will be no ground for a new trial, unless there has been fraud or collusion, or material injury to the defendant.(*s*)

(*l*) Ibid.

(*m*) M'Gee *v.* M'Kinney, 9 Leg. Int. 46.

(*n*) Kelly *v.* Holdship, 1 Br. 36. Robinett *et al. v.* Lair, D. C. Dec. 23, 1848. Motion for a rule for a new trial. *Per curiam.* This motion is made because of the temporary absence of a witness, who was attending voluntarily without a subpœna. It is clear that a party under our system is never safe unless he has all witnesses under subpœna. Here no attachment would have been sent, and to have continued the cause on such ground would be to open the doors to an evasion of all the rules which have been made for the purpose of enforcing the trial of a cause, and of obviating, to some extent at least, the vexatious delays in the administration of justice, of which so much just complaint has been made. R. refused.

(*o*) Com. *v.* Farrell, D. Ct. C. C. P. Ap. 1847.

(*p*) Peterson *v.* Barry, 4 Bin. 481.

(*q*) Milke *v.* Kurlbaum, D. C. Saturday, March 18, 1848. Motion to take off nonsuit. *Per curiam.* We would be glad to help the plaintiff in this case, but we cannot do so. On the trial, he produced an agreement by the defendant to settle and pay the costs. He had no proof of the agreement; defendant's counsel denied all knowledge of his client's signature; the plaintiff had no evidence to prove his case, and of course was nonsuited. He ought to have been ready at all events to have proved the settlement. It is absolutely necessary to enforce upon parties and their counsel active vigilance in preparation for and attention to their cases on the list. The rights of other suitors as well as their own are involved. Motion refused.

(*r*) Martin *v.* Marvine, D. C. Phil. 9 Leg. Int. 2. See *ante*, 526.

(*s*) R. *v.* Hunt, 4 Barn. & Ald. 430; Com. *v.* Chauncey, 2 Ashm. 90; Amherst *v.* Hadley, 1 Pick. 38 ; Cole *v.* Perry, 6 Cowen, 584 ; People *v.* Ransom, 7 Wend. 417 ; Dewar *v.* Spencer, 2 Wh. 211 ; Com. *v.* Gallagher, 4 Pa. L. Jour. 58.

By the act of 21st February, 1814, no verdict can be set aside, nor shall any judgment be arrested for any defect or error in the jury process, "but a trial, or an agreement to try on the merits, or pleading guilty, or the general issue, shall be a waiver of all errors and defects in, or relative and appertaining to the said precept, venire, drawing, and summoning of jurors."

13. *Unsuitable damages.*

Except in an overwhelming case of excessive damages, a court is not at liberty to give the losing party, in an action for personal injury, a second chance.(t)

Though a jury give liberal damages in assumpsit, yet if they are not outrageous, the court will not order a new trial.(u)

The court will not grant a new trial, because the jury have exceeded legal interest in the measure of damages, for delaying payment of money, unless it be excessive.(v)

While the courts possess the power to grant new trials for excessive damages in cases of *torts*, there is no precedent of a new trial for this reason in *crim. con.*(w) And the case must be a rank one to induce the court to set aside a verdict, in an action for a *tort*, on account of the excessiveness of the damages.(x)

It is not correct to say, that a new trial will never be granted where the jury find only nominal damages.(y)

Where, in trespass for taking the plaintiff's goods, of the value of only forty dollars, 5000 dollars damages were given, and no affront had been offered, by battery or menaces, to the plaintiff's person, a new trial was granted;(z) and so, where, in an action against the sheriff, for levying an execution (which it was contended was satisfied) on the plaintiff's property, the jury gave 950 dollars damages, and there was no evidence of a design to oppress, but the conduct of the officer was mild and moderate, and a new trial was granted, on the terms of the verdict standing as a security, and the action not to abate.(a)

Where a plaintiff is entitled only to nominal damages, the court will not grant a new trial when the verdict is for defendant.(b)

Where a jury, in a very hard action, disregard an instruction that plaintiff is entitled to nominal damages only, it is not sufficient ground for a new trial.(c)

In contracts, which can be enforced specifically, or where damages are to be given for their non-performance, there is always a measure of damages. In actions affecting the reputation, the person, or the liberty of a man, they must depend, in some measure, on the discretion of the jury. If the jury go beyond the standard, the value ascertained by the evidence of the thing contracted for, or under its value, the court will set aside the verdict; but in the vindictive class of actions, the da-

(t) Kenderdine v. Phelin, S. C. N. P. 9 Leg. Int. 54.

(u) Roberts v. Swift, 1 Y. 209.

(v) Respublica v. Lacaze, 2 D. 118; S. C. 1 Y. 15.

(w) Shoemaker v. Livezly, 2 Br. 286.

(x) Summer v. Wilt, 4 S. & R. 27; Kuhn v. North, 10 S. & R. 409.

(y) Shenk v. Munday, 2 Br. 106.

(z) Shoemaker v. Livezly, 2 Br. 286; ibid.

(a) Kuhn v. North, 10 S. & R. 399.

(b) Todd v. Jones, D. C. C. P. 7 Leg. Int. 42.

(c) Mishler v. Baumgardner (C. P. Lancaster, per Lewis, P. J.), 8 P. L. J. 304.

mages must be outrageous to justify the interference of the court; seldom, if ever, for smallness of damages. There is a great difference between damages which can be ascertained, as in assumpsit, trover, &c., where there is a measure and personal *torts*, as false imprisonment, slander, malicious prosecution, where damages are matter of opinion.(*d*)

The court has power to compel a release of a portion of the damages, or to grant a new trial.

14. *Time and form of motion.*

By a former rule of the Supreme Court, "all motions in arrest of judgment, or for a new trial, in causes tried at *nisi prius*, shall be made within the first four days of the next succeeding term; but no such motion shall even then be received or admitted, unless notice in writing of such intended motion has been first given to the adverse party, or his attorney, ten days, at least, before the term commences;"(*e*) though, when a point is reserved at the trial, this notice was dispensed with.(*f*) "The counsel who makes a motion for a new trial, or in arrest of judgment, is required, before the commencement of the argument, to file in the prothonotary's office, and also to deliver to each of the judges, a written specification of the points on which he means to rely in support of his motion."(*g*)

As will hereafter be more fully seen, in motions and rules for new trials, the party who obtains the same must furnish to each of the judges a copy of the reasons filed. Every motion for a rule for a new trial must be heard upon the motion-list, and one counsel only is heard in support of the motion. If the rule shall be granted, the party who is to show cause against the rule is first heard by one counsel only in reply. But the court will order a further argument by other counsel, in cases which, in their opinion, require it.

The motion is, for a rule to show cause why a new trial should not be granted. The established practice is to place the motion for a new trial on what is denominated the motion-list, upon which are entered motions, for example, to discharge on common bail; why judgments should not be opened; why appeals from awards should not be struck off; for rules to take money out of court; together with such others as the course of practice may give rise to. This list is usually taken up towards the end of each period of the term; or, as in the District Court, every Saturday during the periods of jury trials. The causes rank by the date of the motions; not by their terms and numbers. Until the list has been gone through, the argument-list is not made out completely, as the clerk must be governed by the manner in which the motions are decided, in placing the causes upon it. If the court decline granting the rule (after hearing the applicant only), the motion is marked dismissed, or refused. If granted, it is immediately transferred to the argument-list, according to its term and number, and argued during that portion of the term allotted by the court for the discussion and decision of questions of law. The time set apart for arguments is always indicated in the printed regulations for the conduct of the business of each

(*d*) Per Duncan, J. 17 S. & R. 50.
(*e*) Foxcraft *v.* Nagle, 2 D. 150, S. C.; Galloway *v.* Negle, 1 Y. 103, S. P.; Furry *v.* Stone, 1 Y. 186; Henry *v.* Kennedy, 1 Bin. 458; Briton *v.* Stanley, 1 Wh.. 267.
(*f*) Reinoldt *v.* Aublai, 4 Bin. 378.
(*g*) Rules of court, 6 S. & R. 600.

I.—35

succeeding term. By the act of 1835, § 8, reorganizing the District Court, "motions for new trials and in arrest of judgment, and questions on reserved points, which may be made and sustained before any one of the judges of the said court, shall be reserved by the said judges, and heard and decided by the three judges of the said court, or any two of them sitting together for that purpose."(h)

In the Supreme Court, the day upon which a verdict is given is to be computed as one of the four days within which a motion for a new trial must be made.(i) It has been held otherwise in the District Court, and that if Sunday intervene it is *dies non juridicus*, and not included in the four days.(j) And so in the Common Pleas, by an express rule. In the latter court, the rules in relation to new trials, are as follows: "Motions for new trials shall be made within four days after the verdict; and unless such motion shall be made, and a rule to show cause granted by the court within that time, judgment shall be entered absolute. The day on which the verdict is given, and Sunday, are to be excluded in calculating the four days. On a motion for a new trial, the court will determine on the showing of the party by whom it is made, whether to grant a rule to show cause or not, without hearing the opposite party. If a rule be granted, the cause will be set down for argument; if not, judgment will be entered on the verdict, unless stayed by motion in arrest of judgment. When, in the course of a trial, a bill of exceptions shall have been taken to the opinion of the court, either in their charge, or the admission or rejection of testimony, the court, in their discretion, may permit a motion for a new trial to be made and argued upon the same grounds as those on which the bill of exceptions shall have been taken. This, however, is entirely discretionary, and, in general, will not be allowed, unless the court desire a further argument, or wish further time to deliberate on the subject.

It is a general rule that a motion for a new trial shall not be made after a motion in arrest of judgment.(k)

The decision of an inferior court, on a motion for a new trial, is not the subject of a writ of errror.(l)

In the District Court, by rule LXIX. All motions for new trials, and reasons in arrest of judgment, in causes tried in this court, shall be made and offered within four days after the verdict, and the motion must be made as aforesaid, notwithstanding the points have been reserved; and whenever a nonsuit is ordered with leave to move to take it off, a motion to take the nonsuit off must be made within the times aforesaid.

No motion shall be made for a new trial after a motion in arrest of judgment.

LX. Every motion for a rule for a new trial shall be heard upon the motion-list, and one counsel only shall be heard in support of the motion. If the rule shall be granted, the party who is to show cause against the rule shall be first heard by one counsel only in reply. But the court will order a further argument by other counsel, in cases which, in their opinion, require it.

(h) Pamph. L. 88.
(i) Lane v. Shreiner, 1 Bin. 292.
(j) Golder v. Blackstone, Dec. 1820, MS. Wh. Dig. "New Trials."

(k) Rules S. Ct. R. 32, D. Ct.; 2 Salk. 647; 1 Burr. 334; Bull. N. P. 326.
(l) Burd v. Lessee of Dansdale, 2 Bin. 90, Wh. Dig. "Error."

Unless good ground of surprise, or the like, is laid, the court will refuse to allow a motion for a new trial to be entered *nunc pro tunc,* when the four days have been let pass without entering the motion.(*m*)

The reasons filed must specially set forth the grounds on which the application rests.(*n*)

15. *Terms and costs.*

The court may impose a condition on the defendant on granting a new trial, to try the cause on its merits, without objecting to the form of the action, or to the declaration ;(*o*) or may order the verdict to remain as security for the damages which may be found on another trial ; and the action (if in tort) not to abate by the death of any party, or as to any party.(*p*) So they may grant a new trial upon the terms that the defendant shall pay all the costs which have accrued up to the time of trial, and may enforce that rule by entering judgment upon the verdict against the non-complying party.(*q*) But if the other party acquiesce in their non-payment, or proceed to enforce payment by citation and attachment, he cannot afterwards have judgment by default of payment of such costs.(*r*)

Where, in an action for money had and received, brought by one partner against another, before a balance had been struck, a trial had been had on the merits, and a motion for a new trial was made, on the

---

(*m*) Wetherill *v.* Woodruff, D. C. Dec. 23, 1848. Why a motion for a rule for a new trial shall not be entered *nunc pro tunc. Per curiam.* We must adhere to the old and well-established rules of the court, unless the circumstances of the particular case address themselves to our legal discretion. Though the depositions might show some ground for the absence of both the counsel when the cause was tried, yet no reason, whatever, is assigned for not having made the motion for a new trial within the four days. The fact of the trial having taken place, was known to one of the counsel on the same day, and to the other on the day after. Rule discharged.

Smith *v.* Fauner. Why a rule for a new trial should not be entered *nunc pro tunc. Per curiam.* The rule, that a new trial must be moved for within four days, is an invaluable one; but to say that it may be dispensed with in every case of forgetfulness or inattention, would be, practically, to repeal it. No doubt the court can order a new trial after four days, where they see that injustice has been done. Here, however, no reasons for a new trial have been shown which we think require the unusual interposition of the court. R. D.

(*n*) Sweeney *v.* Hamblin, D. C. March 16, 1850. Motion for a new trial. *Per curiam.* This case, not being answered to on the third calling of the list, was marked submitted. Of course, in such case, we have no guide but the report of

the judge, before whom the cause was tried, and the reasons. It is especially important, therefore, under the present practice, that the reasons filed should be special, and explain the grounds meant to be presented. In the case before us, the judge reports that it was an action of *assumpsit,* and involved a matter of account between the plaintiff and defendant, which was submitted to the jury without any charge ; and he sees no reason to be dissatisfied with the result. The reasons filed are : 1. The verdict of the jury was contrary to the weight of the evidence ; 2. The jury erred in their calculation of the accounts between the plaintiff and defendant ; 3. That the accounts in the books admitted to the jury were miscalculated, and, therefore, the jury were misled. These reasons afford no clue to enable us to understand the defendant's objections. We take this occasion, once again, to give a caution to gentlemen of the bar, as we have done before, on this subject. It may happen to the most careful and attentive practitioner, to be absent on the third calling, and have his case marked submitted. If his reasons are specially set forth, his chance of success, in such case, on having his rule at least granted, is considerably increased. Rule refused.

(*o*) 3 Bin. 337 ; Walker *v.* Long, 2 Br. 135.

(*p*) 10 S. & R. 411.

(*q*) Devinney *v.* Reeder, 1 Pa. R. 399.

(*r*) Ibid.

ground that the plaintiff could not recover in *indebitatus assumpsit*, the court granted a new trial, on condition that the defendant consented that the form of action should be changed to *account render*, and that the costs of the former action should abide the event of the cause ;(s) and so, where an error occurred on the trial, as to the value of foreign money, and also in the amount of interest, the court decided that the plaintiff might correct the errors ; but if he refused to do so, they awarded a new trial, on condition that the defendant should confine himself to those points in which the mistake occurred.(t)　As has just been seen, where a new trial is granted upon the terms of the payment of costs, the court, after a rule granted for the purpose, may render judgment of the verdict, if the party applying for the new trial fail to pay the costs; but such rule and judgment must be the act of the court, and cannot be entered in vacation ;(u) and if a plaintiff, after a new trial granted upon such terms, enters a rule for a commission to take the testimony of witnesses, he will be considered as waiving the right of making the payment of costs a condition precedent to a new trial.(v)

As to costs on granting a new trial, the act of the 21st March, 1806, § 3,(w) has made some variation from what the law was in this State before.　It provides that, " in all cases where a verdict of a jury shall be set aside, a new trial shall be had on the same conditions, as to costs and daily pay, as are prescribed by that act in cases of a new trial, on the report of referees being set aside ;" that is, if the plaintiff obtain a new trial, and do not recover a sum equal, or greater, than was first given, he shall not have judgment for costs, and shall pay the defendant seventy-five cents per day, while attending on the same ; but, if the defendant obtain the new trial, and the plaintiff then recover a sum equal to or greater than the original verdict, the latter shall have judgment for all the costs accrued on such suit, together with seventy-five cents per day whilst attending the same.

This section, it is thought, does not refer to actions where *land* is to be recovered, speaking, as it does, of the recovery of " a *sum* equal or greater," &c., and that, consequently, the law remains the same as it was before, as to costs, on setting aside a verdict in ejectment.(x)

SECTION II.

OF ARREST OF JUDGMENT.

Act of 2d August, 1842.(y)　From and after the first day of September next, in all cases where judgment shall be arrested on account of the insufficiency of the declaration, a new suit shall not be commenced for the same cause of action, until the costs shall be paid in the first suit, as in cases of a verdict and judgment for defendant.　§ 12.

The rules of court regulating the practice in obtaining new trials, in the Supreme and District Courts, govern, for the most part, that

---

(s) Walker v. Long, 2 Br. 135.
(t) Lee v. Wilcocks, 5 S. & R. 48.
(u) Devinney v. Reeder, 1 Pa. R. 399.
(v) Ibid.

(w) 4 Sm. Laws, 326.
(x) Brac. L. Mis. 465, 466 ; see 2 Arch.
Pr. 228, as to costs on new trial; see
post, " Costs."
(y) Pamph. L. 458.

pertaining to motions in arrest of judgment, and have already been noticed.(z) In the Common Pleas, "no judgment shall be stayed beyond the time when it should regularly be entered, by a motion in arrest of judgment, unless the court shall previously have granted a rule to show cause why the judgment should not be arrested; in proceeding upon such motion, the same course will be observed as in cases of motion for new trials—and on every such motion, reasons, in writing, must be exhibited to the court, and filed if the rule be granted."

"A motion in arrest of judgment is an application to the court on the part of the defendant to withhold judgment for the plaintiff on the ground that there is *error appearing on the face of the record*, which vitiates the proceedings. In consequence of such error, on whatever part of the record it may arise, from the commencement of the suit to this period, the court are bound to arrest the judgment. It is, however, only with respect to objections apparent on the *record*, that such motions can be made, nor can it be made, generally speaking, in respect to *formal* objections. This was formerly otherwise, and judgments were constantly arrested for errors of mere form;(a) but this abuse has been long remedied by certain statutes, passed at different periods, to correct inconveniences of this kind, and commonly called the *statutes* of *amendment* and *jeofails*, by the effect of which, judgment at the present day cannot, in general, be arrested for any objection of form."(b)

The reasons or causes appearing on the record which will suffice to arrest a judgment, are, first, where the declaration varies totally from the original writ, as where the writ is in debt, and the plaintiff declares in an action on the case for an *assumpsit*.(c) The defendant cannot move in arrest of judgment for anything which might have been pleaded in abatement;(d) and if there be a misjoinder of counts, and a verdict for the plaintiff on the counts well joined, and for the defendant on the other, the misjoinder is not a cause for arresting the judgment.(e)

Also, secondly, where the verdict materially differs from the pleadings and issue thereon.(f)

And thirdly, if it appear by the declaration, that the plaintiff had not a cause of action, as, if he declare as indorsee on a promissory note, which he stated to have been made payable to one V. and not to order.(g) This defect of title (which will always be apparent from the record) would likewise cause the judgment to be arrested in a Court of Error; therefore it is a general rule that any exception which may be taken advantage of on a writ of error, may also be taken advantage of on a motion in arrest of judgment.(h) It is also a general and invariable rule with regard to arrests of judgment, upon matter of law, that whatever is alleged in arrest of judgment must be such matter as would upon *demurrer* have been sufficient to overturn the action or plea. Therefore in slander, judgment cannot be arrested, because the words were proved on the trial to have been spoken after the writ issued.(i)

(z) *Vide supra*, 545, 6.
(a) See 2 Reeves, H. E. L. 448; 3 Bl. Com. 407.
(b) Steph. on Plead. 117, 1st edit.
(c) 3 Bl. Com. 393.
(d) Bingh. on Judg. 80.

(e) 2 M. & S. 533; Wenberg *v.* Horner, 6 Bin. 307.
(f) 3 Bl. Com. 393.
(g) Hartshorne's Lessees *v.* Patton, 2 D. 252.
(h) Ibid.
(i) Skinner *v.* Robison, 4 Y. 375.

But the rule will not hold *e converso*, "that everything that may be alleged as cause of demurrer will be good in arrest of judgment," for if a declaration or plea omit to state some particular circumstance, without proving of which, at the trial, it is impossible to support the action of defence, this omission shall be aided by a verdict.(*j*) For a verdict ascertains those facts, which before, from the inaccuracy of the pleadings, might be dubious ; since the law will not suppose that a jury under the direction of a judge would find a verdict for the plaintiff or defendant, unless he had proved those circumstances, without which his general allegation is defective.(*k*) Exceptions, therefore, that are moved in arrest of judgment, must be much more material and glaring than such as will maintain a demurrer; or, in other words, many inaccuracies and omissions, which would be fatal, if early observed, are cured by a subsequent verdict ; and not suffered, in the last stage of a cause, to unravel the whole proceedings.(*l*) But if the thing omitted be essential to the action or defence, as if the plaintiff does not merely state his title in a defective manner, but sets forth a title that is totally defective in itself, or if to an action of debt the defendant pleads *not guilty* instead of *nil debet*, these cannot be cured by a verdict for the plaintiff in the first case, or for the defendant in the second.(*m*) But the plea of *not guilty* in *assumpsit*, is cured by a verdict *for the plaintiff ;*(*n*) for the defendant cannot take advantage of his own mispleading to arrest the judgment.(*o*)

After judgment on a demurrer, the judgment cannot be arrested, whether the demurrer were argued or not ;(*p*) but it is otherwise in case of judgment by default.(*q*)

Where the declaration consists of two counts, and there is a general verdict for the plaintiff, and the action can be maintained only on one, the court will allow the plaintiff, after motion in arrest of judgment, to enter the verdict on the proper count.(*r*)

If the judgment be arrested erroneously, the Supreme Court will, on error, enter judgment upon the verdict.(*s*)

Judgment may be arrested for an objection on the face of the record, though it was not assigned at the time of filing the motion.(*t*) The day on which the verdict is entered is one of the four days, within which a motion in arrest of judgment must be made.(*u*) Before the act of 1842, above given, if judgment was arrested, each party paid his own costs.(*v*)

A writ of error will lie on a judgment arrested ; because the order to arrest the judgment is in nature of a judgment.(*w*)

As has already been observed, judgment will be arrested when, after verdict, it appears that the court has no jurisdiction.(*x*)

(*j*) 3 Bl. Com. 394.
(*k*) Ibid.
(*l*) Ibid.
(*m*) Ibid. 395.
(*n*) Cavene *v.* McMichael, 8 S. & R. 441.
(*o*) 12 Johns. 353.
(*p*) 1 Str. 425; 6 Taunt. 650.
(*q*) 1 Str. 425 ; 1 Caines's Rep. 104.
(*r*) Burrall *v.* Dublois, 2 D. 229.
(*s*) Wilson *v.* Gray, 8 W. 25.
(*t*) Grasser *v.* Eckhart, 1 Bin. 575.

(*u*) Burrall *v.* Dublois, 2 D. 229.
(*v*) Cowp. 407 ; 11 Johns. 141.
(*w*) Benjamin *v.* Armstrong, 2 S. & R. 392.
(*x*) Baugh *v.* Bartram, D. C. Saturday, July 1, 1848. Motion in arrest of judgment. *Per curiam.* It appears by the record, that on the trial the judge refused to permit the defendant to plead specially to the jurisdiction of the court, that the amount in controversy was under $100. He did this upon the ground that a

plea to the jurisdiction is in abatement, and cannot be put in after a plea in bar. In this we think there was error. Objections to the jurisdiction of a court of limited jurisdiction as to the nature of the actions instituted in it, and not where it is a mere matter of personal privilege in a defendant to be sued in a particular court, may be pleaded in bar or abatement (1 Chitty's Pl. 426, p. 6). As this is an error appearing upon the face of the record for which the judgment would be reversible, we think the proper course is to arrest the judgment, set aside the verdict, and award a *venire de novo*. Accordingly, defendant has leave to file the special plea; leave to do which was refused on the trial. Judgment arrested, verdict set aside, *venire de novo* awarded, and leave granted defendant to file special plea to the jurisdiction. See *ante*, 23.

CHAPTER XXVI.

OF JUDGMENT.

UPON the verdict of a jury, four days are allowed by our practice generally throughout the State, for the entry of a motion for a new trial, or in arrest of judgment. A specific rule of each particular court regulates the whole subject. It is a doctrine of the common law, that a reasonable delay after verdict should be permitted before judgment is signed, and would exist in the absence of a rule of court.(a) The same time is allowed the defendant in the case of an award of referees under the third section of the act of 1705;(aa) and upon an award of arbitrators under the compulsory act, he has twenty days after judgment *nisi*, within which to enter an appeal, in default of which the judgment becomes final. On the subject of the computation of time it is settled, that whenever, by a rule of court or an act of assembly, a given number of days are allowed to do an act, or where it is said that an act may be done within a given number of days, the day in which the rule is taken or the decision made, is excluded; and if one or more Sundays occur within the time they are counted, unless the last day falls on Sunday, in which case the act may be done on the next day;(b) therefore, in computing the twenty days, the rule is, that the day on which the report is filed, or the day on which the appeal is entered, should be excluded.(bb)

"According to our practice, judgment is signed by writing that word in the docket, to serve as a memorandum for making up the record in form, which, however, is seldom if ever done."(c) In general, the pleadings, issue, and verdict, show plainly enough what the judgment ought to be, in cases where any question arises as to what the word in the docket extends, whether it affects lands and persons, or lands alone.(d) So, the word refers to another part of the record, where a right is confessed subject to which the judgment is entered.(e)

The manner of taking judgment by default and for want of an affidavit of defence having been already considered, the practical questions connected with this branch of inquiry will be noticed under the following heads :—

(a) Burrall v. Dublois, 2 D. 229; Lane v. Schreiner, 1 Bin. 292; Maguire v. Burton, 1 M. 17.

(aa) 1 Sm. Laws, 50.

(b) Simms v. Hampton, 1 S. & R. 411; Gosweiler's Estate, 3 Pa. R. 201.

(bb) Frantz v. Kaser, 3 S. & R. 395.

(c) Hussey v. White, 10 S. & R. 347.

(d) Coyle v. Reynold's Executors, 7 S. & R. 329, 330.

(e) Reidenauer v. Killinger, 11 S. & R. 119, 121.

1. *Entering judgment.*

In order to secure a judgment upon a verdict, the successful party is required by the act 29th March, 1805,(*f*) to pay the sheriff the sum of four dollars, the jury fee. This form is rendered essential in some, and would seem to be generally observed in all courts. In the District Court of Philadelphia County, the rule further directs that the judgment be dated on the day of its entry, which cannot be made without a special order until payment of the fee.(*g*) It does not follow, however, that judgment may be entered during the four days by paying the fee. That court has recently decided that it cannot be done without their special order, and if the prothonotary enter judgment *nisi* it has no legal effect. The rule allows four days for a motion for a new trial or in arrest of judgment, and by construction this excludes the day in which the verdict is rendered, and if a Sunday intervene it is also excluded. It was formerly supposed that the entry of judgment *nisi* had a peculiar meaning, and though made within the four days, operated as a lien—but it never was judicially recognized, and was wholly at variance with principle. The practice of the King's Bench is however not in force, which requires a rule for judgment to be entered. No rule is necessary, nor need the court be applied to for leave to enter judgment, but after the four days, should no motion be pending, the prevailing party on paying the fee is entitled to have judgment signed by the prothonotary, not *nisi*, but *absolutely.*(*h*) And in connection with the former Court of Nisi Prius, it was decided that, under the 4th section of the 18th rule of that court, judgment could not be entered on a verdict rendered at Nisi Prius within the first four days of the term, nor during the pendency of a motion for a new trial, unless the court should have ordered judgment to be entered to stand as a security.(*i*) Under this rule, therefore, the plaintiff might at the first day of the court move for judgment, and if by the report of the judge who tried the cause it was deemed proper he should have it as a security, it was immediately ordered. In no case, however, could it be entered until the jury fee was paid, nor until the sitting of the court in bank.(*j*)

To give an award of referees under the act of 1705, the same effect as the verdict of a jury, it is necessary that it should be submitted to the court for their approbation, unless it is agreed that judgment be entered on the award: the first Saturday succeeding their filing is fixed for

(*f*) 4 Sm. Laws, 237.
(*g*) Rule 52, D. C. Phil. See Ash *v.* Patton, 3 S. & R. 303.

(*h*) Maguire *v.* Burton, 1 M. 14; 2 Tidd's Pr. 644.
(*i*) Britton *v.* Stanley, 1 Wh. 267.
(*j*) Ibid.

reading the reports of referees in open court.(*k*) And the rule is that, unless exceptions to the report be filed within four days afterwards, the judgment *nisi* becomes absolute.(*l*) Particular circumstances will, however, induce the court to hear motions to set aside reports of referees, though exceptions have not been filed within that time.(*m*) Under the rule of court, it is not necessary that notice should be given of reading the report in court; it is sufficient if notice is given that the report is *filed*, and the four days run from the time of such notice.(*n*) As to reports not read on that day, whether brought into court or not, filed in the office in term time or vacation, no executions are to issue thereon until notice in writing is given to the opposite party, after which notice, such party has four days to file his reasons.(*o*)

By the act for the prevention of frauds and perjuries,(*p*) it is enacted that any judge, or officer of any of the courts of record, shall at the signing of any judgments, without fee, set down the day of the month and year of his so doing upon the paper, book, docket, or record, which he shall sign, which date shall be entered upon the margin of the record where the said judgment shall be entered. In addition to the entries made by the prothonotaries of the several courts in their respective appearance, continuance, or judgment dockets, an entry of the parties names, term and number, date and amount of the judgment is made in a docket, called the judgment-index, in alphabetical order, commencing with the name of the debtor; and referring to the judgment itself. It was originally invented by courts for their own ease, as well as the security of purchasers, to avoid the inconvenience of turning over the rolls at large ;(*q*) and the practice of docketing judgments, appears to have first obtained in the Court of Common Pleas, where the dockets were entered on a separate roll, called the docket roll.(*r*) In entering judgments on bonds and warrants of attorney, the prothonotary complies substantially with the act of 24th February, 1806, by entering the names of the obligors and obligees in the form of an action as parties, the date of the bond and warrant, the penal sum, the real debt, the time of entering judgment, and the date of the judgment, on the margin of the record.(*s*) A judgment entered by him under this act, on the application of the *obligor*, without authority from or notice to the obligee or assignee, was lately decided to be irregular and was therefore struck off.(*t*) The prothonotary is not the agent of either party or of the law, and if the defendant in the judgment pays him the amount, it is no discharge of the debt.(*u*) The judgment-index may be referred to at reasonable times by the attorneys of the courts, and presents to creditors, purchasers, and others a ready access to information, important to their respective interests. As the officers are liable for the consequences of neglect in the entering or searching for judgments, particular accuracy is requisite in the discharge of this branch of their duties.

By our practice, final judgment on an inquisition or liquidation by

---

(*k*) Rule 84, D. C. Phil.
(*l*) Shewell *v.* Wycoff, 1 D. 312.
(*m*) Boyer *v.* Rees, 4 Y. 202 ; and see Davis *v.* Canal Navigation Co. 4 Bin. 296.
(*n*) 1 Br. 14.
(*o*) See Barre *v.* Affleck, 2 Y. 274.

(*p*) 1 Sm. Laws, 390.
(*q*) Gilb. C. P. 164.
(*r*) Cro. Car. 74; Sid. 70.
(*s*) Com. *v.* Conard, 1 R. 249.
(*t*) Ingersoll *v.* Dyott, 1 M. 245.
(*u*) Baer *v.* Kistler, 4 R. 364.

the prothonotary, is seldom formally entered, though it may be done at any time, if required, on application to the court. These interlocutory judgments are afterwards liquidated, and whether by inquest, or by the prothonotary, under the court's guidance, is immaterial.(v)

An entry by a prothonotary on his docket, as follows: "A v. B, plaintiff files of record a judgment bond, under the hand and seal of the defendant, for the sum of $5,450, conditioned for the payment of $2,725, on or before November 5th next; entered the 17th May, 1815," is a good entry of judgment, under the act of 24th February, 1806.(w)

The amount for which the judgment is entered in the "lien or judgment" docket, kept by the prothonotary in accordance with the act of 1827,(ww) and not that stated in the appearance or continuance docket, determines the party's claim.(x)

So far as concerns the sheriff, and as will presently be seen, subsequent judgment creditors, this doctrine is by no means shaken, either in principle or application, by the act of 1843.(xx) In 1845, the Supreme Court expressly ruled that the sheriff, in order to ascertain the judgments that were liens upon the land, was not bound to look further than the judgment-docket, and was relieved from any responsibility as to a misapplication of the proceeds by the prothonotary's certificate. So far from there being any breach of duty in paying the fund in court to a creditor whose judgment, though subsequent, was indexed antecedently, it was declared that in so doing he had faithfully and properly performed it ;(y) though in the same year it was ruled that where the entry in the index was greater than the amount actually due, the creditor can take only the actual debt.(z) And again, as late as 1850, it was determined that if the Christian names of defendants in a judgment are not entered on the judgment-docket, the judgment, though valid as between the parties, cannot affect subsequent purchasers or judgment-creditors. It is the duty of the judgment-creditor to see that his judgment is rightly entered in the judgment-docket.(a)

The court will enter judgment specially, so as to show that it binds only property held in trust by the defendant, and which was the sole purpose of the suit.(b)

It is discretionary to enter the verdict on particular counts, and unless the whole testimony is brought up on error this cannot be examined above.(c)

Where, in an action pending, the president judge marked on the margin of the trial-list, "Judgment for plaintiff; sum to be liquidated by the prothonotary," it will be presumed that the judgment was entered with the assent and acquiescence of the defendant.(d)

Where the record stated that "a jury was called and sworn, and the same day the jury was discharged, and judgment given for plaintiff,"

(v) Bennet v. Rind, 10 W. 396.
(w) Helvete v. Rapp, 7 S. & R. 306.
(ww) Purd. 994. [This was a defect in the execution of the power, not in the want of it: Rabe v. Heslip, 4 Barr, 140.]
(x) Bear v. Patterson, 3 W. & S. 233; though see acts of 1843, 9, post, 558–9.
(xx) Post, 558.

(y) Mann's Appeal, 1 Barr, 25.
(z) Hance's Appeal, 1 Barr, 408.
(a) Ridgway's Appeal, 3 H. 177. See post, 558–9.
(b) Aysinena v. Perics, 2 Barr, 286.
(c) Hildeman v. Martin, 10 Barr, 369.
(d) Hays v. The Comm. 2 H. 39; Seybert v. Bank, 5 W. 305.

it was held in error that the court below had given judgment on an agreement or with the acquiescence of parties.(e)

Judgment entered two days before verdict is not void.(f)

By the various acts of assembly, the docket is recognized as the proper and only place for the entry of the judgment, and its entries cannot be controlled by memoranda on loose scraps of paper filed as parts of the proceedings.(g)

When a case, when called for trial, is stated by counsel to be settled, the proper practice is for the judge to enter a formal judgment for the costs, if there be an agreement to that effect. If there be not, the plaintiff will be nonsuited, under the 2d section of the act of April 14, 1846, unless a legal ground for continuance be shown.(h)

Where a feme gives bond and warrant, and marries, the practice is, to move the court for leave to enter it against her and her husband, on filing a declaration and an affidavit of the facts. Though he had given no express authority, yet it is implied from the fact of marriage, his own voluntary act. If the agreement be entered without leave of court, it will be set aside. And where it can be done without risk, it is better to give previous notice to the husband, although the ruled cases seem not to require this.(i)

There can be but one final judgment in any personal action, whether founded in contract or tort, because the simplicity of the common law allows no incongruity in its forms, and requires that all the various

---

(e) Seybert v. Bank, 5 W. 307; Hays v. Comm. 2 H. 39.

(f) Myers v. Clark, 3 W. & S. 536.

(g) See Rogers, J., Crotcher v. Com. 6 Wh. 347.

(h) Thomas v. Kast, D. C. Feb. 26, 1848. Why fi. fa. should not be set aside and judgment opened. Per curiam. When this case was called for trial, during the present term, it was stated to the court, by the plaintiff's counsel, that it had been settled—that entry was accordingly made on the judge's trial-list. One of the judges of the Supreme Court, in delivering the opinion of that court (Moore v. Kline, 1 P. R. 133), has condemned this as "certainly a loose mode of doing business," though he adds, that he is not prepared to say it is a nullity when on the record. "It would, perhaps, amount to an entry of satisfaction, or a discontinuance." It is on this account that the judge before whom this cause was called, when such a suggestion is made, requires to be informed by the counsel if any agreement has been made as to the costs, and enters a formal judgment for the costs accordingly. Otherwise, he nonsuits the plaintiff, under the second section of the act of 14th April, 1846, unless a legal cause for continuance is shown. In this way all doubts as to the character of the entry is avoided, and the suit is finally and conclusively determined and ended.

In accordance with this practice, in the case before us, the counsel for plaintiff informed the judge that the defendant was to pay the costs, and taking it for granted that such was the arrangement, judgment was entered accordingly. It now appears that this was a misapprehension on the part of the plaintiff's counsel, and that the case had been settled by the parties, out of court, without their counsel, and a receipt in full given by the plaintiff, without any mention of the subject of costs. It is clear that, in such a case, each party bears his own costs: Watson v. Depeyster, 1 Caines, 66; Johnston v. Brannan, 5 Johns. 268; Herkimer Co. v. Small, 2 Hill, 127. Such a settlement is in effect an agreement to discontinue, and judgment might be entered that the plaintiff pay the costs of the office, that is, those which have not been already advanced as the suit proceeded, but not the costs of the defendant or his attorney. The entry in this case, then, is clearly wrong. The court, therefore, make absolute this rule, so far as regards setting aside the execution issued by the plaintiff for costs, and instead of opening the judgment as asked for, they direct it "to be set aside as having been improvidently rendered." Execution and judgment against defendant for costs set aside.

(i) Enau v. Clark, 2 Barr, 236.

entries on the record should exhibit a consistent whole. The symmetry of legal proceedings, however marred by legislative inconsistencies and professional looseness, has not yielded so far as to admit of distinct judgments of the same kind in the same action.(*j*)

The 8th section of the act of 1806, authorizing the prothonotary to enter judgment on a confession in writing by the defendant, attested by two witnesses, is affirmative, and does not prohibit the entry of judgment according to a practice existing prior to its date, and(*k*)

Therefore, an agreement of the parties, not under seal, nor attested by witnesses, for an amicable action, and that the prothonotary should enter judgment for a certain sum, was *held* sufficient.(*l*)

Act of 2d August, 1842.(*m*) In all original actions and proceedings to revive judgment, which have been or hereafter may be instituted against two or more defendants, in which judgment has been entered on record, at different periods, against one or more of said defendants, by confession or otherwise, or hereafter may be so entered, the entries so made or to be made shall be considered good and valid judgments against all the defendants, as of the date of the respective entries thereof, and the day of the date of the last entry shall be recited in any subsequent proceeding, by *scire facias* or otherwise, as to the date of judgment against all of them, and judgment rendered accordingly: *Provided*, That the provisions of this section shall not affect the liens of any such judgment. § 6.

From and after the passage of this act, where an entry of judgment has or shall be made on the records of any court against two or more defendants, at different periods, such entries shall operate as good and valid judgment against all the defendants, and the plaintiff may proceed to the collection of the money due thereon, with costs, as if the entries had all been made at the date of the latest entry. § 7.

The entry of judgment *nunc pro tunc* is not of right but of favor. It rests in discretion, influenced in its exercise by peculiarity of circumstances, and its propriety is not, therefore, to be inquired into by writ of error. It might be otherwise by appeal, were that form of removal provided. A party seeking to avoid the consequences of delay, must not appear to have consented, much less contributed, to its production; thus, if the judgment were suspended by exceptions on both sides, of which the procrastination, attempted to be charged exclusively on one party, was an inevitable consequence, the rule does not apply.(*n*)

The strict form in verdict formerly required, is now unnecessary. It needs only to be understood what the intention of the jury is, agreeably to which the clerk may mould it into form: and if the verdict is good, the judgment must likewise be so; for being entered generally, when drawn at large it may be put into form.(*o*) In our practice, judgments are all entered in short memoranda, the prothonotary merely writing the word "judgment" on the record. In general, the pleadings, issue,

---

(*j*) O'Neal *v.* O'Neal, Jr. W. & S. 131.
(*k*) Cook *v.* Gilbert, 8 S. & R. 567.
M'Calmont *v.* Peters, 13 S. & R. 196.
See *ante*, 276, 343.

(*l*) Cook *v.* Gilbert, *ut supra*.

(*m*) Pamph. L. 458.
(*n*) Bley *v.* Union Canal Co. 5 W. 104.
(*o*) Per M'KEAN, C. J., Thompson *v.* Musser, 1 D. 462: see Easton *v.* Worthington, 5 S. & R. 133.

and verdict, show plainly enough what the judgment ought to be ; but any uncertainty or obscurity in the judgment, as, for example, on a *scire facias* against heirs and terre-tenants, the courts, when called upon, must explain. Should plaintiffs attempt to injure the defendants under such a judgment, by taking execution against their persons, or other lands than those bound by it, the court will interfere and do justice in a summary way.(*p*)

The act of 1806 directed some peculiarities in the mode of entering judgment, as well as in the other proceedings in a suit ; but as it is left to the party to pursue its provisions or not, at his pleasure, a further notice of it is not deemed necessary.(*q*)

Act of 3d April, 1843.(*r*)　The omission or failure heretofore of the prothonotaries, clerks, or other proper officers of the courts of the several counties of this commonwealth, to transcribe into or enter upon the judgment or lien dockets of their respective courts, any judgment or judgments or other liens, according to the third section of the act of one thousand eight hundred and twenty-seven aforesaid, which have been properly entered upon the appearance or continuance dockets, shall in nowise invalidate or impair such judgments or liens. And all such judgments and liens which shall have been so entered upon the appearance or continuance dockets shall be deemed good and valid to all intents and purposes, as though they had been duly entered upon the judgment or lien dockets according to the requirements of the act aforesaid : *Provided*, That nothing contained in this act shall hereafter release prothonotaries or other proper officers of the courts of this commonwealth from keeping a judgment or lien dockets according to the requirements and provisions of the act of twenty-ninth of March, one thousand eight hundred and twenty-seven aforesaid : *And provided further*, That purchasers *bona fide*, without notice of the omission to make the entry upon such judgment-docket, shall not in any way be affected by the provisions of this act.(*s*)　§ 1.

Act of 16th April, 1849.(*t*)　The act approved 3d day of April, Anno Domini 1843, entitled, " An act to preserve and perfect the validity of judgments entered upon the continuance or appearance dockets of the courts," shall not be so construed as to impair the right of a plaintiff or plaintiffs, whose judgment had been properly entered on the judgment-docket in any of the courts of this commonwealth.

In all cases, when a judgment has been or shall be regularly revived between the original parties, the period of five years, during which the lien of the judgment continues, shall only commence to run in favor of the terre-tenant from the time that he or she has placed their deed on record : *Provided*, That this act shall not apply to any cases which have been finally adjudicated, or when the terre-tenant is in actual possession of the land bound by such judgment by himself or tenant. § 8.

(*p*) Coyle *v.* Reynolds's Executors, 7 S. & R. 329, 330 ; and see Lewis *v.* Smith, 2 S. & R. 155 ; Bower *v.* Blessing, 8 ibid. 243 ; Reidenauer *v.* Killinger, 11 ibid. 119.

(*q*) Miles *v.* O'Hara, 1 S. & R. 32 ; Hawk *v.* Senseman, 6 ibid. 21.
(*r*) Pamph. L. 127. See, for act of 1827, Purd. 994, and see *ante*, 555.
(*s*) 7 W. & S. 200.
(*t*) Pamph. L. 664.

Act of 16th April, 1845.(v) The omission or failure of the prothonotaries of the Courts of Common Pleas of Cambria and Union counties, subsequent to the passage of an act of assembly of this commonwealth, entitled, "An act to preserve and perfect the validity of judgments entered upon the continuance or appearance dockets of the courts," and approved the third day of April, one thousand eight hundred and forty-three, to transcribe into or enter upon the judgment or other lien dockets of said counties, any judgment or judgments, or other liens, according to the third section of the act of one thousand eight hundred and twenty-seven, which have been properly entered upon the appearance or continuance dockets of said counties, or which appear upon the minutes of the president judges of the courts of said counties, shall in nowise invalidate or impair such judgments or liens; and all such judgments and liens which shall have been so entered upon the appearance or continuance dockets of said counties, or which appear on the minutes of the president judge of the courts of said counties, shall be deemed good and valid to all intents and purposes, as though they had been duly entered upon the judgment or other lien dockets: *Provided*, That all transcripts of judgments, confessions of judgments, and judgment bonds which are now on file in the prothonotaries' offices of the counties aforesaid, shall have the same validity, and shall be deemed good to all intents and purposes, as though they had been duly entered upon the continuance and judgment dockets of said county : *And provided*, That purchasers *bona fide*, without notice of the omission to make the proper entries of judgments upon the judgment-docket, shall not be affected by the provisions of this act : *And provided further*, That no judgment entered in any of the said books shall be deemed irregular or invalid, unless it shall be made to appear that the same was entered by a person who then had a knowledge of entering the same contrary to law : *And provided further*, That nothing contained in this act shall be construed to release the prothonotaries of the said counties of Cambria and Union from keeping a judgment or lien docket, according to the provisions of the existing laws. § 1.

2. *When lien of judgment begins to run.*

A judgment regularly entered, has a preference over subsequent judgments against the same defendant as a lien upon his lands.(w) In Pennsylvania, the lien of judgments has been extended beyond the limits of the common law, embracing every kind of equitable and even an inchoate interest in land, and every right vested in the debtor at the time of the judgment;(x) but that interest must be an *estate* in the land.(y) But it does not attach to lands acquired by the defendant after judgment and aliened *bona fide* before execution.(z) This latter doctrine, it is believed, could not be supported upon the principles of the common law, but rests solely on a supposed general understanding, and a silent practice prevailing in this State; and though the question is at

(v) Pamph. L. 542.
(w) 2 Wheat. 396.
(x) Carkhuff v. Anderson, 3 Bin. 4; Richster v. Selen, 8 S. & R. 440.
(y) Per GIBSON, C. J., Morrow v. Bre-

nizer, 2 R. 188 ; see Share v. Lythe, 16 S. & R. 8 ; Chahoon v. Hollenback, ibid. 425 ; Andrews v. Lee, 2 Pa. R. 101.
(z) Rundle v. Ettwein, 2 Y. 23 ; Calhoun v. Snider, 6 Bin. 135 ; Br. 304.

rest, the rule, being considered an innovation on the law rather than an improvement, is confined most strictly to the point decided, and to the circumstances under which it was established.(a)   It has been therefore held, that a judgment binds land, for the sale of which articles of agreement have been entered into *before*, but which have not been conveyed until after judgment.(b)   And the revival of a judgment by *scire facias post annum et diem* creates a lien on real property of the defendant acquired after the entry of the original judgment.(c)

Under this head, it is not intended to consider what interest a judgment binds, or the extent and duration of the lien.   The authorities on these points will be found fully collected elsewhere.(d) `The present object is to touch merely on those decisions which concern the practical duties of counsel in perfecting judgment.

By the third section of the act of 1772, it is enacted that such judgments, as against purchasers *bona fide* for valuable consideration of lands, tenements, or hereditaments, to be charged thereby, shall, in consideration of law, be judgments only from such time as they shall be so signed, and shall not relate to the first day of the term whereof they are entered, or the day of return of the original or filing of the bail, any law, usage, or course of any court to the contrary notwithstanding.(e)

It would appear that this provision originally copied from the fifteenth section of the statute of Charles, is merely intended for the protection of *bona fide* purchasers, and not to prevent the technical relation of the judgment to the first day of the term in a contest between the judgment-creditor and the plaintiff in a domestic attachment. And it has been decided that, in such a case, the judgment does relate back to the first day of the term, so as to exclude a domestic attachment.(f) As between conflicting creditors, the priority of their judgments is governed by the times of their entry, and not by relation to the preceding term; the uniform, uninterrupted practice in Pennsylvania has been, to consider the binding effect of judgments upon lands, to take place only from the *actual entry* of the judgments, and thus entered, they have never been supposed liable to be affected by fictions or relations.(g) Between judgments entered on the same day, there is no priority, and, therefore, the proceeds of sale under them are divided *pro rata*.(h)   In regard to the entry of judgment and their priority of lien, a day is not susceptible of judicial division; therefore, it gives one no priority that his judgment appears to have been entered at an hour earlier than the others; consequently, they must be paid *pro rata*, if the fund is insufficient.(i)

And it makes no difference that the prothonotary has made an entry of the hour of entering judgment in each case.(j)

But, where two judgments have been entered on the same day, in different counties, by virtue of the same warrant of attorney, evidence is admissible of the exact time at which the first was entered; and, for

---

(a) Richter *v.* Selin, 8 S. & R. 440.
(b) Ibid.
(c) Clippinger *v.* Miller, 1 Pa. R. 64.
(d) Wh. Dig. "Judgment," iv. v.
(e) 1 Sm. Laws, 390.
(f) Hooton *v.* Will, 1 D. 450.

(g) Welsh *v.* Murray, 4 Y. 201.
(h) 1 Br. 20 ; Dupont *v.* Pichon, 4 D. 321, in note.
(i) Metzler *v.* Kilgore, 3 Pa. R. 245.
(j) Ibid.

this purpose, an entry on the docket, made in pursuance of instructions from the plaintiff, is competent evidence.(k)

Though, as between two judgments entered on the same day, *parol* evidence is inadmissible to show that one was taken before the other; yet the principle is different when a conveyance and a judgment conflict, in which case evidence *in pais* is receivable, to show that, though both bear date on the same day, one was in point of time prior to the other.(l)

When the vendee receives a deed, and at the same time gives a mortgage for the purchase-money, a judgment entered against him binds his entire interest; and, if the mortgage be not placed in the proper office, to be recorded within the time prescribed by the statute, the judgment will take precedence of it.(m)

Where a court opens a judgment, and lets the party into a defence, the lien of the judgment-from the date of the original entry, is not thereby impaired.(n)

Judgments against an equitable estate in land rank, like others, according to dates.(o)

A judgment for arrears of ground-rent, like a judgment against an administrator, creates no new lien. The lien of a ground-rent is not limited by any positive enactment.(p)

In order to give a judgment for purchase-money any peculiar merit, it must be entered at the same time the deed is delivered, or so near it as to constitute it one transaction. Otherwise, it will have no precedence of liens on the equitable estate held by the defendant under articles, or on the subsequently acquired legal estate.(q)

When transcripts of judgments obtained before a magistrate are filed in the prothonotary's office of the Court of Common Pleas, they become liens on lands, and are on a footing with judgments in courts of record, by virtue of the act of March, 1810, § 10.(r) They are in effect judgments of the Court of Common Pleas, and may be so called in a writ of *scire facias* to revive them.(s) The five years within which a *scire facias* should issue to preserve this lien must be computed from the first day of the term to which it is entered, and not from the actual date of the entry.(t) The court has no authority to strike off such judgments from the docket, or to take any cognizance of the judgments thus entered for the purpose of reserving them, unless brought before it by appeal or certiorari.(u) As regards real estate, it is virtually a judgment of that court,(v) consequently it may be set aside on motion with or without an issue, where it has been obtained surreptitiously, or it may be only opened to let the party into a defence, when he has missed his time by accident or mistake; a practice extremely beneficial, and founded on the chancery powers which our courts are in the daily habit of exercising. The matters, however, which constitute the defendant's title to relief, must have existed previous to or at the time

(k) Neff *v.* Barr, 14 S. & R. 166.

(l) Mechanic's Bank *v.* Gorman, 8 W. & S. 304.

(m) Foster's Appeal, 3 Barr, 79.

(n) Steinbridge's Appeal, 1 Pa. R. 481.

(o) Wilson *v.* Stupe, 10 W. 434.

(p) Wills *v.* Gibson, 7 Barr, 156.

(q) Lyon *v.* McGuffy, 4 Barr, 126.

(r) 5 Sm. L. 161.

(s) Walker *v.* Lyon, 3 Pa. R. 98.

(t) Betz's Appeal, 1 Pa. R. 271.

(u) Dailey *v.* Gifford, 12 S. & R. 72; see O'Donnel *v.* Seybert, 13 S. & R. 57; *sed vide* Walker *v.* Lyon, 3 Pa. R. 98.

(v) Brannan *v.* Kelley, 8 S. & R. 479.

of rendering judgment. If they be subsequent, the court will not interfere in a summary way further than to stay the execution, because they may be pleaded to a *scire facias*, which, if it be necessary, the plaintiff will be ordered to bring.(*w*) In this action the validity of the judgment ought, it seems, to be questioned upon the plea of *nul tiel record*, where the amount of the judgment exceeds the magistrate's jurisdiction. But when such a transcript is filed, the proper remedy is, a motion to strike it off, or, perhaps, a writ of error. It cannot be treated as a nullity;(*x*) a transcript, however, creates no lien on defendant's real estate, if an appeal has been duly entered before the alderman.(*y*)

No judgment rendered in the Supreme Court, or in the Circuit Courts shall be a lien on real estates, excepting in the county in which such judgment shall be rendered.(*z*)

3. *Judgment against deceased person.*

By statute 17 C. II. c. 8 (made perpetual by 1 J. II. c. 17, § 5, and reported to be in force in Pennsylvania),(*a*) where either party dies between the verdict and judgment, "in any action personal, real, or mixed," his death shall not be alleged for error, so that the judgment be entered within two terms after verdict. Under this statute it has been held in England, that the death of either party *before* the assizes is not remedied; but if he die *after* their commencement, although *before the trial*, that is within the remedy of the statute; for it is a remedial act, and shall be construed favorably; the assizes being considered as but one day.(*b*) And even at common law, if either party die after special verdict and pending the argument, motion for a new trial or other proceeding, whereby entry of judgment is suspended, judgment may be entered *nunc pro tunc* as of the term when the party would have been entitled to it on the return of the *postea*,(*c*) that the act, arising from the delay of the court, may not turn to the prejudice of the party. In the case of Griffith v. Ogle *et al.*,(*d*) the plaintiff having died after verdict, judgment was entered as of a term when he was living, and on an appeal this proceeding was sustained. And said TILGHMAN, C. J., "direct authorities have been cited by the plaintiff's counsel in support of this practice. It tends much to the attainment of justice, and we have no doubt but it is perfectly regular." Independently of the statute, the court has power to enter judgment at their discretion, as of a past time, when it ought to have been entered in order to do justice, without injury to third persons. Where, therefore, upon *nul tiel record* pleaded, the court decided that there was such a record, but the prothonotary omitted to enter judgment, and after this decision the defendant died, it was held that the court, in order to do justice, might enter judgment after his death, as of the time when it ought to have been entered, although nearly eight years had elapsed between the determination of the issue and the actual entry of the judgment. The rights of third persons will, however, be protected against any consequences which might result from the entry of the judgment as of *a past*

'(*w*) King v. King, 1 Pa. R. 20.
(*x*) Walker v. Lyon, 3 Pa. R. 98.
(*y*) Hastings v. Lolaugh, 7 W. 540.
(*z*) Act of March, 1779, 3 Sm. Laws, 358.

(*a*) Rob. Dig. 369.
(*b*) 2 Tidd. 847.
(*c*) 1 Johns. Cas. 410; Bingh. on Judgm. 95.
(*d*) Griffith v. Ogle, 1 Binn. 172.

time.(*e*) So it was held that an agreement to enter judgment as of a particular term, is complied with by an entry of judgment as of a subsequent term, provided, no third person is injured thereby. At all events, a judgment erroneously entered cannot be said to be void, upon a collateral examination. It is valid until reversed.(*f*) If the plaintiff die after the verdict for the defendant, and the latter do not enter up judgment within two terms after the verdict, the court has no authority to permit it to be entered afterwards *nunc pro tunc*.(*g*)

Although, at common law, the judgment being personal survives, when one of the several defendants dies, as to the personalty, yet it does not survive as to the real estate bound by it. It does not lie wholly on the survivor, but the lands of all are equally chargeable, and execution must be equally made ; and if one dies, the creditor must bring a *sci. fa.* against his heirs and terre tenants, and also against the survivors. But it is otherwise where the lands are not bound ; as if two enter into a bond, and one dies before judgment, the survivor shall be charged alone.(*h*)

By the practice of this State, the creditor of a decedent may enter judgment and issue execution after the death of his debtor ; and as between the plaintiff and the representatives of the decedent, the execution is considered as relating back to the first day of the term.(*i*)

But the plaintiff, in such execution, gains no priority thereby over other creditors, and is entitled to no more than is given to him by the intestate act.(*j*)

4. *Joint judgment.*

A judgment against one partner in a suit against two, without any service or return of *nihil habet*, &c., against the other, is erroneous ; but a *bona fide* payment of such judgment by the sheriff, out of proceeds of land sold by him, on which it was a lien, is a protection to the sheriff in an action brought against him by the judgment debtor, or his subsequent judgment creditors, after a reversal of the judgment.(*k*)

In *assumpsit* against several, if some are served and appear and plead to issue, and some make default, plaintiff takes judgment against the latter ; and under the 27th section of the act of 1722, the jury which tries the issue against the former may assess damages against all, and execution issues against all.(*l*)

In an action on contract the plaintiff should be careful not to sever the joint action by proceeding against them separately. He has his election, either to wait till all the defendants come in, and then proceed to joint judgment, or, if he believes either of them sufficient, to seek the recovery of his demand by a proceeding against that one. But if he adopt the latter course, taking a judgment from one for a sum certain, and the other defendant pleads, goes on to trial, and a verdict passes against him, the plaintiff cannot obtain judgment on such verdict; his only

---

(*e*) Murray *v.* Cooper, 6 S. & R. 126.
(*f*) Lewis *v.* Smith, 2 S. & R. 142.
(*g*) 4 Taunt. 702.
(*h*) See Stiles *v.* Brock, 1 Barr, 216.
(*i*) Leiper *v.* Levis, 15 S. & R. 108.
(*j*) Ibid. M'Millan *v.* Rod, 4 W. & S. 237 ; Bosler *v.* Exchange Bank, 4 Barr, 34. See 33d sect. act of Feb. 24, 1834.

See for the manner of collecting claims against a decedent's estate, vol. ii. "Executors," and Wh. Dig. "Decedent," iii.
(*k*) Com. *v.* Rogers, S. Ct., Penn. 1 Am. L. J. 208 ; Bright. R. 109.
(*l*) Ridgely *v.* Dobson, 3 W. & S. 118. See, as to opening joint judgment, *post*, 575.

recourse is to the judgment confessed, which remains good ;(m) but in such a case the *defendant* is not entitled to judgment.(n) So where, two defendants in an action of trespass against six, pleaded to issue, and judgment was signed against the others for want of a plea, and on the trial, damages were assessed against the two who pleaded, and judgment was entered on the verdict, it was considered as a separation of the defendants, and the verdict as equivalent to a formal entry of *nolle prosequi* as to the others, and the judgment against all, but the two who joined issue, was held erroneous.(o) In such cases the course is, after taking judgment by default against those defendants who do not plead, to issue a *venire*, as well to try the issue with those who have pleaded, as to assess the damages against *all* the defendants: and in order to fix the defaulters, the *venire* must so issue, and the jury must so be sworn.(p)

There are instances in which there may be distinct judgments on the same record. If the court see two separate causes of action in the same record, on one of which the plaintiff succeeds, and the other is found for the defendant, they are bound to give distinct judgments ;(q) So, in an action for an assault and battery against two defendants, if one suffer judgment by default, and the other justify and obtain a verdict, there must be two separate judgments on the record.(r) But where an action is brought on a joint contract against two, and one has suffered a default, and the other obtains a verdict, it is held that judgment must be entered up for both defendants.(s)

There would appear to be no case in which a court would render judgment on a verdict for damages payable by instalments. Even on *debt* for a penalty, the judgment is for the whole penalty as a *personal* debt, although the court having a control over the execution, permits the instalments to be recovered separately as they fall due.(t)

Where, in a default, suffered by one of two defendants in an action on a penal bond, the interlocutory form of judgment is made to assume, erroneously, a definite one, by adding the amount of the penalty, instead of assessing damages, the court will strike off this inadvertent addition, or the Supreme Court, on error, will treat it as a nullity, as they did an administrator's confession of judgment *de bonis*, where no confession of assets was intended.(u) The court distinguished this case from that of Williams *v.* McFall,(v) where the first judgment was not, as here, inadvertently made final, but was a regular confession of judgment by one, and an attempt, after execution, to obtain another judgment against a codefendant in the same action, which the court would not allow.

Where one of two defendants is in default, judgment must be signed against him, in order to proceed against the other. This is so where the default is after return of two nihils to a *sci. fa.* as to one, and appearances on both writs for the other defendant.(w)

(m) Williams *v.* McFall, 2 S. & R. 280.

(n) See *ante*, 388 ; and see vol. ii. "Partners," and Wh. Dig. "Debtor," i. iii., where the cases concerning the merger of a simple contract debt into a judgment, are considered.

(o) Cridland *v.* Floyd, 6 S. & R. 412.

(p) *Per cur.* ibid. 416 ; *vide ante*, 355.

(q) 3 T. R. 656 ; 2 Caines's Rep. 218.

(r) 3 T. R. 656.

(s) 3 Day's Rep. 307.

(t) *Per* GIBSON, J., Shoemaker *v.* Meyer, 4 S. & R. 452 ; see § 8, Stat. 8 & 9 W. III. Rob. Dig. 142 ; *ante*, 358, 9.

(u) O'Neal *v.* O'Neal, 4 W. & S. 132.

(v) 2 S. & R. 280.

(w) Bennet *v.* Reed, 10 W. 376.

To assess damages is the exclusive business of the jury, who, if they assess them conditionally, should also render them conditionally. It is not competent to the court to instruct the jury to find damages sufficient to insure a specific execution of a contract, and that the court will control the plaintiff in the use of the verdict ; they may be instructed to find the damages conditionally, they prescribing the terms on which they shall be released, and with us this mode of effecting an equitable object is, from necessity, frequently resorted to.(x)

If in an action of debt the sum found by the verdict does not exceed the sum *in numero* demanded in the writ, the verdict must be taken all in debt; but where the debt and interest exceed that sum, the verdict should be in debt for the whole sum demanded, and in damages for the sum *ultra.*(y) An action for a legacy charged upon real estate should be brought against the executor and terre-tenants, and the judgment in such case should be entered so as to charge the *land* and *not* the *persons* of the defendants.(z)

5. *Amendment of judgment.*(a)

The judgment is amendable at common law, in substance or in form, at any time during the term of which it is signed, and after that time, even after error brought, and *in nullo est erratum* pleaded.(b) It is amendable for misprision of the clerk, by 8 H. VI. c. 12 & 15, declared to be principally in force in Pennsylvania.(c) Where a judgment *de bonis propriis* was entered against an executor, instead of judgment *de bonis testatoris*, the court ordered it to be amended,(d) even after error brought.(e)

Although after the term is ended at which judgment is entered on a case stated, or verdict, the court cannot alter it so as to correct what, on reconsideration, may be deemed an error ; yet they may, before error brought, correct a mere mistake on entering it, such as an entry of judgment for one party, where the other party was in fact intended. Whenever there is anything to correct by, such as the judge's notes, no danger need be apprehended, and it is justified by the general rule on the subject, as well as by the reason of the thing.(f)

The act of 16th June, 1836, gives the Supreme Court power to *modify* as well as to reverse and affirm judgments. Under it, the court feel authorized to disregard slips in practice where it is not inconsistent with law and the rights of parties; such, for example, as a general judgment against two, where one had not been served, and had not appeared to the writ, and in which the court reversed the judgment as to him, and affirmed it as to the others.(g)

The doctrine of amendments appears to be without limitation in Pennsylvania, and has, in modern practice, been applied upon very liberal principles : thus an amendment was permitted in the verdict, in an ejectment, although nothing appeared to amend it by.(h) So, where the

---

(x) Decamp *v.* Feay, 5 S. & R. 328.
(y) Reed *v.* Pedan ; 8 S. & R. 267.
(z) Brown *v.* Furer; 4 S. & R. 213.
(a) See *post*, vol. ii. title, ' Amendment," for general principles, &c., concerning amendment; and see 7 W. & S. 140.
(b) 4 M. & S. 94; Barnes, 7.

(c) *Vide* Rob. Dig., 29, 33–4, 49.
(d) 5 Burr. 2730.
(e) 1 T. R. 783 ; and see 2 Arch. Pr. 243.
(f) Stephens *v.* Cowan, 6 Watts, 513.
(g) Jamieson *v.* Pomeroy, 9 Burr. 231.
(h) Scott *v.* Galbraith, cited Burrows *v.* Huysham, 1 D. 134.

verdict exceeded the amount of damages laid in the declaration, a *remittitur* for the excess was permitted, although after error brought, and judgment was entered for the residue.(*j*) If, however, the record be removed by writ of error, the Supreme Court will not suffer a *remittitur* of the surplus damages to be entered, but will send back the record to the court below for amendment, if they think proper to amend. This objection being removed, and the amended record returned, the judgment will be affirmed.(*k*) And where a plaintiff obtained a verdict, and the judges being equally divided on a motion for a new trial, the clerk entered judgment on the order of one of the judges, but objected to by the other: the judgment was held good, the court presuming that the dissenting judge merely wished his opinion against the verdict to be entered of record, and not to arrest the course of law.(*l*) Where one defendant died after suit brought, and judgment was entered against both, an amendment was permitted by entering a suggestion of his death, with the same effect as if entered before judgment, though after error *coram vobis* upon which his death before judgment had been assigned; and per TILGHMAN, C. J.: " The cases cited in support of the motion are sufficient to show the power of the court, and it is a power which, generally speaking, tends very much to the promotion of justice; the court feel themselves bound to adopt amendments of this nature, as far as is consistent with their lawful authority, nor will they be disposed to fetter them with conditions except in extraordinary cases."(*m*) The court will not presume anything against judgments, and do not incline to set them aside unless for manifest error ;(*n*) and whilst they remain in full force and unreversed, the court cannot *collaterally* in a new action brought against a different defendant, declare them to be illegal and of no effect.(*o*)

When an executor or administrator has rendered himself liable by pleading a matter which would be a perpetual bar, which lies within his own knowledge, and is false, the judgment is entered *de bonis testatoris si*, &c., *et si non, de bonis propriis;* as if he pleads *ne unques executor*, or that he *renounced*, and *nulla bona devenerunt ad manus;* and upon a judgment thus obtained, where an executor so charges himself, though the first execution must be *de bonis testatoris*, yet the sheriff cannot return *nulla bona testatoris*, simply, but must also return a *devastavit*.(*p*) If the defendant pleads *administravit*, plaintiff may pray judgment *quando acciderint;* but if he takes issue on the plea, and it be found against him, there shall be judgment *quod querens nil capiat*, &c. If the verdict be against the defendant on this plea, it is necessary that the jury should find the amount of the assets, for which alone the plaintiff shall obtain judgment. It is necessary too that the plaintiff should have proved the amount of this claim, for though the plea admits the debt it does not admit the amount of it.(*q*) Upon the plea of *plene administravit*, and verdict for the plaintiff, the judgment for all but the

(*j*) Rapp *v.* Elliot, 2 D. 184; and see Furry *v.* Stone, 1 Y. 186; Addis. 114.

(*k*) Lausatt *v.* Lippincott, 6 S. & R. 386.

(*l*) Cahill *v.* Benn, 6 Bin. 99.

(*m*) Lessee of Hill *v.* West, 1 Bin. 486.

(*n*) *Per cur.* Bradley *v.* Flowers, 4 Y. 436.

(*o*) Per YEATES, J., Bond *v.* Gardiner, 4 Bin. 281.

(*p*) Cro. Eliz. 102.

(*q*) Ibid.

costs is to be *of the goods of the testator.*(*r*)   On such an issue, the jury are not authorized to find that the defendant had wasted the goods, and the court cannot on such verdict order judgment for the whole amount of damages and costs to be entered *de bonis testatoris si,* &c., *et si non de bonis propriis* of the defendant, unless an issue have been joined on such wasting.(*s*)   When the defendant establishes his plea of no assets, the settled practice is to find for the defendant on the plea, and then for the plaintiff to pray judgment *de terris,* &c., and of assets *quando acciderint.*(*t*)   Where the administrator does not plead want of assets, and judgment goes against him, and an execution is levied on the personal estate, the plaintiff is entitled to payment of his whole debt; nor will the court enter into any consideration of the nature of the debt.(*u*)   When the creditor, having entered judgment *de terris,* &c., takes out execution and sells the land, upon payment of the money into court, in order to prevent a failure of justice, the court must assume the power of carrying the act of assembly, prescribing the order of paying debts, into effect, and make all orders necessary for the purpose, as the Orphans' Court would do.(*v*)

If judgment has been regularly entered against an administrator on a plea of *plene administravit præter,* it will not be set aside to give him an opportunity to come in and plead a judgment recovered.(*w*)

6. *Interest on judgments.*(*x*)

By the second section of the act of 1700,(*y*) lawful interest is allowed to the creditor on the amount of his judgment, from the time it is obtained until satisfaction.   Interest may, in general, be considered as legally incident to every judgment in this State ;(*z*) but where a plaintiff obtained a verdict, and a new trial was granted upon condition that a judgment should be entered as a security, for whatever might be ultimately recovered, the court upon the second trial, instructed the jury, that where a judgment was given merely as a security, the interest ought not to be calculated on the amount of the judgment (which included principal and interest), but only on the sum originally due.(*a*)   Under our act of assembly, the practice is stated to have been, both before and since the Revolution, to ascertain the real debt at the time of the judgment entered, and to calculate interest thereon as a new principal ;(*b*) and when credit for partial payments is allowed, the principle of calculation is thus decided.   Interest is always calculated on a judgment to the time of the first payment, which is applied in the first instance to discharge the interest, and afterwards, if there be a surplus, to sink the principal, and so *toties quoties,* care being taken that the principal, at any time thus reduced, be not suffered to accumulate by the accruing interest.   This rule is sustained not only by usage, but by decision.(*c*)

(*r*) Swearingen *v.* Pendleton, 4 S. & R. 336.

(*s*) Ibid.

(*t*) 1 Peters's Rep. 442 ; Penna. Agricultural and Manufacturing Bank *v.* Stanbaugh's Administrators, 13 S. & R. 299.

(*u*) Ibid.

(*v*) Ibid.

(*w*) 2 Caines's Rep. 101 ; see further on this subject, 2 Arch. Pr. 131, 132.

(*x*) See, for the cases under this head, Wh. Dig. "Interest."

(*y*) 1 Sm. Laws, 7.

(*z*) Fitzgerald *v.* Caldwell's Executors, 4 D. 252.

(*a*) Roberts *v.* Wheelen, 3 D. 506.

(*b*) Berryhill *v.* Wells, 5 Bin. 61.

(*c*) Per GIBSON, J., Com. *v.* Miller's Administrators, 8 S. & R. 458; see also Shaller *v.* Brand, 6 Bin. 435 ; Phillips *v.* Schaffer, 5 S. & R. 220.

On the affirmance of a judgment in the Supreme Court after a writ of error, interest is to be charged on the judgment below till affirmance, and then the aggregate is to bear interest.(*d*) The plaintiff should not, however, charge interest on the costs, unless he has paid them, and then only from the time of payment.(*e*)

7. *Judgment on balance found due defendant.*

Under the defalcation act of 1705,(*f*) if it appears to the jury, in an action wherein the parties have mutual accounts against each other, that the plaintiff is overpaid, they are directed to find their verdict for the defendant, and to certify to the court how much they find the plaintiff to be indebted, which sum so certified is recorded with the verdict, and deemed as a debt of record. If the plaintiff refuse to pay it, the defendant shall have a *scire facias* and execution for the same, with the costs of that action. By the third section of the same act, the report of referees chosen by the parties in open court, is put on a footing with the verdict under the former section. If, therefore, on such report, or on a verdict, a sum is found due by the plaintiff to the defendant, the latter, until lately, could not enter judgment and issue execution, but was obliged to take a *scire facias*, on which he had judgment and execution for the sum found due.(*g*) But now, by the act of April 11, 1848,(*h*) he is entitled to judgment and execution upon the balance found due him.(*hh*)

No judgment can be entered, in an action on a note, on a verdict "for the defendant," with a certificate in his favor for a sum certain, there having been no evidence of set-off, "and that plaintiff receive back the machine," which was the consideration of the note, the verdict being defective.(*i*)

The assignment of plaintiff's claim before trial does not deprive the defendant of his right to judgment on a verdict for a balance in his favor when the pleas were payment and set-off.(*j*)

8. *Opening judgments.*

(1.) By whom the motion may be made, and for whose use.
(2.) What character of defence must be shown.
(3.) What excuse given for the default.
(4.) Within what time the motion must be made.
(5.) Practice generally.

(1.) *By whom the motion may be made, and for whose use.*

Although an irregular judgment, which has been put upon the records of the court without authority, may be reversed on a writ of error, or set aside, on motion in the court where it has been entered; yet this can only be done at the instance of the defendant himself; a third party only is entitled to interfere where the judgment was collusive;(*k*) though, except in case of collusion, it is not competent for the court, upon application of a third person, to vacate and annul a

(*d*) McCausland's Administrators *v.* Bell, 9 S. & R. 388.
(*e*) Id. 389.
(*f*) 1 Sm. Laws, 49.
(*g*) Ramsey's Appeal, 2 W. 228.
(*h*) *Vide* Blackburn *v.* Markle, 6 Bin. 174; Kunckle *v.* Kunckle, 1 D. 364;

Kyd on Awards, 326, a.; 326, h.; Am. Editor's note.
(*hh*) See *ante*, 406.
(*i*) Glass *v.* Blair, 4 Barr, 196.
(*j*) Kline *v.* Gundrum, 11 St. R. 253.
(*k*) Drexel's Appeal, 6 Barr, 272; Hauer's Appeal, 5 W. & S. 473.

judgment between other parties, who ask no action, and attempt by the process of the court no injury to his rights, and which judgment, though fraudulent and inoperative as to him, is perfectly good as to all the world beside.(*l*)

It may be considered as settled, that a judgment can be impeached collaterally, in another court than that in which it was rendered, by third persons, for covin or collusion between the parties to it in fraud of their rights ;(*m*) and such a question may be determined in Pennsylvania by the Orphans' Court, upon the settlement of the account of an executor, or the distribution of the funds in his hands. And that court may direct an issue to the Common Pleas for the trial of the facts contested, although the judgment in dispute be entered in the District Court.(*n*)

But while a creditor, or a terre-tenant, may avoid, collaterally, a fraudulent judgment for a pretended debt, he cannot abate an erroneous one for a real debt, to gain priority by so doing, or to discharge his land ; for he was entitled to no priority at the date of the judgment, and its erroneousness was no wrong to him.(*o*) The law, in this respect, is thus comprehensively stated by GIBSON, C. J. : "A creditor may, indeed, be injured by a *collusive* judgment for a *fictitious* debt, which would sweep away his source of payment, and may, consequently, avoid it collaterally for the fraud ; and a terre-tenant, also, may avoid such a judgment in the same way, where it would be a fraud upon his title, as was shown by authority, in Campbell *v.* Kent. The question, in a contest with strangers, is not whether the judgment is erroneous ; but, whether it is fraudulent ; and Lord HOLT, doubtless, meant no more in Proctor *v.* Johnson,(*p*) when he said, in reference to a defence by terre-tenants to a *scire facias* on a judgment in ejectment, ' that strangers may *falsify*, but those that claim under the judgment, are estopped and bound by the judgment'—a *dictum* which seems to have been misapplied in Ulrich *v.* Voneida. A creditor, as I have said, may abate a fraudulent judgment for a pretended debt ; but he cannot abate an erroneous one for a *bona fide* debt, to gain priority by it, for he was entitled to no priority at the date of the judgment, and its erroneousness was no wrong to him. Priority is in the gift of the debtor, and where it is obtained from him, by means of an erroneous security, with which both parties are content, no one has room to complain of it. Where there is no interest of a third person to be defrauded at the entry of a judgment, want of authority to confess it, concerning as it

(*l*) Rowland's Estate, D. Ct. C. C. P. 7 P. L. J. 312.

(*m*) Dickerson's Appeal, 7 Barr, 257 ; Walson *v.* Willard, 9 Barr, 94 ; Postens *v.* Postens, 3 W. & S. 135.

(*n*) Ibid. ; see Johnson's Appeal, 9 Barr, 415 ; and as to Feigned Issues, Maynard *v.* Esher, 5 H. 222 ; and Brown *v.* Simpson, 2 W. 239, where it was said by KENNEDY, J.: "The practice of opening judgments upon the application of the creditors of the defendants, alleging that they were entered or obtained by collusion between the plaintiff and defendants, for the purpose of defrauding the creditors, is objectionable in principle. The proper course is to direct a feigned issue to be joined to try the question of fraud, leaving the judgment to stand as against the defendant."

Where a terre-tenant applied to the court to open a judgment in ejectment, and let him into a defence, so far as respected the alleged lien of the judgment on his land, and he was accordingly admitted ; this did not in effect make him a party to the *scire facias* as from the beginning. 5 W. 239.

(*o*) Hauer's Appeal, 5 W. & S. 473.

(*p*) 2 Salk. 600.

does only the parties to it, may be supplied by subsequent ratification, which is equivalent to a precedent authority, or by acquiescence, which is equivalent to ratification; but want of an actual debt, as a foundation for it, is an incurable vice. And, where an interest is subsequently acquired by a third person, with his eyes open, he is not defrauded by what has been done before his time. The conclusion of the whole matter is, that as a creditor has not a vested right to come in, even *pari passu*, without his debtor's consent, he cannot object to the means by which a preference is given to another; and that a terre-tenant, being a purchaser from the debtor, subsequently to the judgment, must not be allowed to disturb it where it does not wrongfully affect his title. The principle is an elementary one, which has never been disputed. Even in the contested cases to which I have referred, the ground assumed by the majority was, not that the judgment was erroneous, but that, for want of authority, it was absolutely void; an assumption, which the preceding considerations are equally proper to repel. But the principle rests not on argument alone; for it was broadly asserted in Lewis *v.* Smith,(*q*) as well as in Martin *v.* Rea,(*r*) and thus the decision in our own court, in regard to it, stands poised. But decisions are to be tried, not *numero*, but *pondere;* and the point was ruled in Ulrich *v.* Voneida, as well as in Campbell *v.* Kent, by a casting vote. But nothing is better fortified by authority, both British and American, than that an actual judgment of a court, of a competent jurisdiction, is never to be treated as a nullity in the first instance. There is an almost endless train of decisions for it, a few of which, but enough to set the •point at rest, were adduced in the contested cases; and there are many *dicta*, to the same effect, in our own books. Even Mr. Justice HUSTON, who delivered the opinion of the majority in Campbell *v.* Kent, has since recognized it in Humphreys *v.* Rawn ; and his opinion is now to be numbered with the authorities on the other side."(*s*)

In the District Court of Philadelphia, a judgment irregularly confessed by a mortgagor, after an assignment, will be opened on application of the terre-tenant.(*t*) The practice now is to permit a judgment to be attacked collaterally, before an auditor, "for fraud or collusion, and if an issue is demanded, he is bound to report such issue; but if no issue is demanded, he may decide that it is fraudulent as to the party impeaching, and exclude it from the distribution, or postpone it. It is not competent, however, for any third person to attack a judgment on the ground of error or irregularity, which can only be taken advantage of by a party or privy to a writ of error. When, however, a creditor has a lien prior to the date of the judgment, and it is claimed that the

---

(*q*) 2 S. & R. 142.
(*r*) 6 S. & R. 296.
(*s*) 5 W. & S. 474.
(*t*) Elkinton *v.* Fithion, D. C., Saturday, Oct. 14, 1848. Why sheriff's sale should not be set aside, judgment opened, and terre-tenant let into defence. *Per curiam.* The mortgage falls due Feb. 2, 1848, and the *sci. fa.* upon it could not regularly be issued until after the expiration of twelve months from that day. On the 20th April, 1848, the

defendant made a deed to John H. Benton, and then agreed to confess a judgment on the mortgage, waiving the privilege given by the law. He could not divest his alienee of his rights under the law, without his consent. No evidence has been offered to impeach the deed to Benton ; and the rule itself gave sufficient notice to put the other party upon inquiry as to his right to interfere. Rule absolute.

judgment takes priority of him, because rendered upon a debt which was a lien prior to the judgment, there it is competent to the creditor, holding a lien prior to the date of the judgment, to dispute the validity of the prior lien."(u)

The court, however, will not open a judgment to suffer a terre-tenant to try an issue whether the judgment be a lien.(v).

In the same court, a judgment, irregularly confessed, without a statement of the cause of action, will be set aside on motion of any one in interest.(w)

(2.) *What character of defence must be shown.*

Judgment will be opened when, from examination of the depositions, the court thinks there is a question of fact for a jury.(x)

When a judgment entered on a bond and warrant of attorney is opened, it is only to let in matters of defence which existed at the time of the rendition; never to let in matters subsequent to it, which are determinable in a trial on a *scire facias quare executio non*, or in a summary way, when the facts are not disputed, or the parties do not demand a trial by jury. A converse principle is, that on the trial of a *sci. fa.* the defendant shall not be permitted to go behind the judgment, and set up any matters prior to its entering.(y)

If a judgment be opened upon an affidavit of defence, and the defendant let into a defence upon the merits, he will not, upon the trial, be permitted to take advantage of a technical exception to the form of action, viz.: that the action had been brought in the name of the assignee of a *chose* in action, instead of an assignor.(z)

A judgment will be opened to let in a plea of bankruptcy.(a)

It seems that a judgment may be opened to let in a plea of the statute of limitations;(aa) and in the District Court of Philadelphia, a judgment

(u) SHARSWOOD, J.; see Cadwalader v. Montgomery, *post*, Execution, v. 9 (3), where this subject is fully discussed.

(v) Darrach v. Darrach, D. C., Saturday, Feb. 17, 1849. *Per curiam.* The question presented in this case is one of some practical interest. It is whether, upon a motion to set aside an execution, we will suffer a terre-tenant to try by an issue whether the judgment, upon which the execution has issued, is a lien. After the fullest consideration, we are of opinion that we ought not to do so. It comes back, practically, to the question, whether we will direct an issue to try the title of the defendant. There are inconveniences and risks, undoubtedly, in letting the sale go on, and putting the parties to their ejectment. The probability is the property will be sacrificed, and some one be a loser. But how can we, in any case, prevent a plaintiff from selling, by execution, the right, title, and interest of the defendant in any property? and were we to order an issue, it might not be conclusive in an ejectment subsequently brought

by the sheriff's vendee, and thus all the expense, time, and trouble of the proceedings, would absolutely go for nothing. R. D.

(w) Kaider v. Murray, Dec. 13, 1851. Why judgment should not be stricken off. *Per curiam.* This rule has been obtained on the ground that the judgment, entered by agreement, is without the specific statement of the cause of action, signed by the parties or their attorneys, required by the rule of the court. It is supposed that this is an irregularity which can only be taken advantage of by the defendant; as, however, the rule is an explicit direction to the prothonotary to enter no such judgment, we cannot but regard the entry of it as an absolute nullity, and must set it aside on the motion of any one who has an interest. R. A. See *ante*, 279, 342.

(x) Massey v. Buck, D. C. C. P. 8 Leg. Int. 124.

(y) Curtis v. Slosson, 6 Barr, 265.

(z) Ekel v. Snevily, 3 W. & S. 272.

(a) Comm. v. Huber & Co. 5 L. J. 331.

(aa) Ekel v. Snevily, 3 W. & S. 272.

of revival, entered on two *nihils*, was lately opened, on the ground of the presumption of payment arising from the lapse of twenty years.(*b*)

But a judgment will not be opened to let in a plea of infancy, when the defendant was of full age when the judgment was taken.(*bb*)

(*b*) Maitland *v.* McGonigle, D. C., Saturday, June 17, 1848. Why the judgment and execution should not be set aside. *Per curiam.* This was a judgment obtained upon two returns of *nihil* to a *sci. fa.* to revive a judgment. The judgment was originally entered upon a bond and warrant of attorney, upon the 30th December, 1816, against John and Bernard McGonigle. This was revived by a *sci. fa.* returned, "made known," and a judgment by default for want of appearance, July 26, 1822. It was again revived by *sci. fa.* and a judgment taken upon two *nihils*, upon the 20th May, 1825. The *sci. fa.* upon the judgment which we are now asked to open, was issued upon the 29th December, 1847. In the mean time, John, one of the defendants, died, say in June, 1827. The courts will always open a judgment upon two returns of *nihil*, where timely application, after knowledge, is made by defendant, and a probable *prima facie* defence is made out. Here, even from the last movement in the cause, the motion to set aside the *alias fi. fa.* levied upon the goods of John McGonigle, the deceased defendant, which motion was made June 13, 1827, more than twenty years elapsed. This is a legal presumption of payment. If we refuse to open this judgment, the defendant will be debarred from a perfectly legal defence, and from aught that it appears, and we can possibly know, from loss of vouchers and death of witnesses, a perfectly just defence; and that, too, without any fault or negligence on his part. He has resided during all this period in another county. It is true that there is a short note of a case decided in the Common Pleas of this county, in 1788 (Brown *v.* Sutter, 1 D. 239), in which President SHIPPEN is reported to have said that the court would never open a regular judgment to let in a plea of the statute of limitations. It was held, however, in this court, in 1813, during the presidency of Judge HEMPHILL, in Distich *v.* Miller (2 Br. 311), that the court would exercise a discretion on this subject, and would not restrict a defendant from pleading the statute in such cases, provided he would declare, on oath, the nature of his defence, and showed that he had just ground for putting in the plea.

They affirmed the case of Brown *v.* Sutter, however, so far as to say, the court ought not to interfere to give defendant the advantage of the plea, upon a general affidavit of defence. However, the present Chief Justice, in the recent case of Ekel *v.* Snively (3 W. & S. 272), uses the following language on this subject: "It was said, in Brown *v.* Sutter (1 D. 239), that a judgment will not be opened to let in the statute of limitations, but as the plea of that statute has since been considered, in Shock *v.* McChesney (4 Y. 507), and the Bank *v.* Israel (6 S. & R. 294), to be no longer an unconscionable one, the rule of practice would scarcely be held so now. So that Brown *v.* Sutter is to be considered as considerably shaken, if not overruled. The case before us is much stronger—the lapse of time being so much greater—and the defence arising from presumption of payment equally a legal defence as the statute of limitation, though the one has been introduced, and makes a part of the common law, by the decisions of the courts, and the other by the enactment of the legislature." Judgment opened, and defendant let into defence.

—Upon the judgment being opened, the defendant pleaded simultaneously a plea in abatement, to the effect that a code-fendant was dead, and non assumpsit and payment. The court struck off the plea in abatement, saying they would have put the defendant on terms had their attention been called to it, and that they had no doubt of their power to modify their order afterwards. See *ante*, 386.

(*bb*) Poulson *v.* Addis, D. C., Saturday, Nov. 4, 1848. Why judgment should not be set aside. *Per curiam.* The defendant appeared by attorney and suffered judgment to be entered against him for want of affidavit of defence, Jan. 24, 1848. He was then of full age. A *fi. fa.* issued; the property was condemned; a *vend. exp.* and a sale; and now defendant asks to be let in to take the defence that he was a minor when the deed was executed upon which the suit was brought. We think he is too late. The judgment is regular; for although the entry on the appearance-docket is simply "Copy of ground-rent deed filed," yet the copy filed was indorsed, "Copy of ground-

(3.) *What excuse given for the default.*

Unless some good reason be given, the court will not move, for a party cannot be permitted to set the process of law at contempt. Pending negotiations are no excuse for the delay.(c)

Any mistake or accident, however, will be enough, where it is promptly made, and when there is no contempt.(d)

Where the defendant was absent from home at the proper time for appearing, and, though served before he left, was detained away unexpectedly, so that judgment was taken against him, the court opened the judgment, on a defence being shown.(e)

rent and other deeds," and the other deeds were the assignments of the ground-rent. Rule dismissed.

(c) McQuillan v. Hunter, D. C., Saturday, March 23, 1850. Why judgment should not be opened. *Per curiam.* The allegation is, that the consideration of the bond and warrant upon which this judgment was confessed, is the balance of the contract price for building a house, which has turned out to have been so badly built as to be worthless to defendant. That there are defects in the house, seems evident enough upon the depositions, though there may be some doubt as to whether the fault is to be imputed to the plaintiff. However that may be, a party must show due diligence in making an appeal to the discretion of the court for relief in this way. He cannot wait until there has been a levy and condemnation, a *venditioni*, and all the expenses of advertisement incurred. Some good reason should be shown for such delay—some act of plaintiff to lull him into security. None has been shown in this case. It is said that hopes were entertained of a settlement; but the proper practice is, the moment that notice of the *fi. fa.* or levy is received by the defendant, to apply for the rule, and to carry on the negotiations for a compromise or settlement pending the rule. R. D.

(d) Blackwood v. Finley, D. C., Saturday, Oct. 7, 1848. Why judgment and *fi. fa.* should not be set aside. *Per curiam.* This judgment was taken September 23, 1848, for want of an affidavit of defence. In such cases, where the application for relief is prompt, the court is liberal. It is true, the affidavit in excuse of the default shows some negligence or stupidity, but it is evident that the defendants were embarrassed by the fact of two suits being brought in different courts, and thinking they had done all that was necessary by retaining counsel, supposed the summons to relate to the first suit, in which there had been no service. The affidavit shows a set-off, and in cases of prompt application for relief, especially, we make no distinction between this and any other kind of defence. The law of Pennsylvania pre-eminently favors defalcation. The plaintiff is in no worse position than if defendants had appeared and taken this defence. Indeed, he is in a better situation, for he has the lien of a judgment as a security; for in these cases, where the proceeding is regular on its face, we do not *set aside*, but only *open* the judgment, and let the defendant into a defence. *Fi. fa.* set aside, judgment opened, and defendant let into a defence.

(e) Sheerer v. Adams, D. C., Monday March 6, 1848. Why judgment should not be opened; execution set aside. *Per curiam.* This was a judgment taken for want of an appearance which was entered by plaintiff's attorney in the office. It has been objected that it is irregular on that account. We are, however, of a different opinion. It is the most convenient and proper practice to take such a judgment as well as a judgment for want of a plea in the office. The prothonotary is entirely competent to see that such a judgment is not entered, when in point of fact there is an appearance or a plea. However, it has been the uniform practice of this court to open even regular judgments by default, where the defendant comes in promptly, excuses his default, and shows that he has a defence. Here the defendant says he was absent from home at the proper time for appearing; and though he was served before he went away, that he was detained unexpectedly. He has also sworn to a defence. The plaintiff here has lost nothing; he could not have had a trial; the judgment will stand as security for what may ultimately be recovered; and the defendant must pay the costs of the execution.

Rule absolute on payment of the costs of the execution by defendant.

*   (4.) *Within what time the motion must be made.*

In the United States Circuit Court it was held that a judgment obtained at a former court cannot be set aside, however erroneous, unless it was entered by misprision of the clerk, by fraud, or the like.(*f*)

The power of the Court of Common Pleas in relation to the opening of judgments is most ample; and policy requires that it should be liberally used. It is a matter depending on the sound discretion of the court, who are not prevented by lapse of time, or the fact of a judgment having been renewed by successive *scire faciases*, from affording relief,(*g*) though it is said that, after the end of the term in which the court has rendered judgment upon a case stated on a special or general verdict, from which an appeal may be taken by writ of error or otherwise, it cannot alter or change it, with a view to correct what the court upon further reflection may consider an error therein.(*h*)

"On general principles," says Judge SERGEANT, "a judgment is binding and conclusive until reversed or set aside by a legal proceeding; and it is very questionable whether the court in which a judgment has been entered, can open the judgment where it was obtained several years before in an adverse proceeding, and afterwards duly revived."(*i*)

"I will not say," says Chief Justice GIBSON, "that a judgment by default, or on confession may not be opened at a succeeding term, on the ground of a defence arising *subsequently*, provided it do not interfere with rights acquired under the judgment, and by third persons; but the security of titles founded on judicial proceedings might be invaded by the exercise of an arbitrary and unconstitutional discretion of the courts over their own records."(*j*)

The practice of the District Court in Philadelphia is, where a defendant comes forward in a reasonable time, and makes a proper excuse for his non-appearance, to open judgment by default, and let him into a defence;(*k*) though, as has already been noticed, the court will not, under ordinary circumstances, open a judgment and set aside an execution, unless the party asking relief applies immediately on receiving notice of the levy.(*l*)

(*f*) Medford *v.* Dorsey, 2 W. C. C. R. 433.

(*g*) Kalbach *v.* Fisher, 1 R. 323.

(*h*) Stephens *v.* Cowan, 6 W. 513.

(*i*) Stiles *v.* Bradford, 4 R. 401.

(*j*) 2 W. 380.

(*k*) Emerson *v.* Knight, D. C. C. P. 7 Leg. Int. 199; *ante*, 573.

(*l*) McQuillan *v.* Hunter, D. C. C. P. 7 Leg. Int. 50.

Seibert *v.* Jones, Saturday, Feb. 19, 1848. Why judgment should not be stricken off; execution to stay. *Per curiam.* Where a party has cause to open a judgment or set aside an execution, he must not, by his supineness, allow plaintiff to go on incurring costs, and at the very last moment interpose the objection. Here the defendant alleges that the judgment, which was entered upon a bond and warrant, was given with the express understanding that it was not to be entered up until the costs of a former suit between the same parties was paid, which never has been done. He says, also, that it is for more than was justly due, and he was overreached in the settlement upon which it was given. Yet the judgment was entered May 27, 1844, and a *fi. fa.* was issued to Sept. 1847, upon which a levy was made, and the defendant made an affidavit that the goods levied on were not his, but belonged to an adverse claimant. An *alias fi. fa.* was issued and levied on defendant's real estate, notice given to him, inquisition and condemnation, and then a *vend. exp.*

(5.) *Practice in opening judgment.*

Where money has been brought into court, and a judgment opened to let the defendant into a defence, if the parties do not proceed within a reasonable time, the court ought to permit the next judgment creditor to appear as defendant, and rule the plaintiff to trial.(*m*)

A rule, to show cause why a judgment should not be opened, does not stay proceedings without an order to that effect.(*n*)

When a judgment on which a sheriff's sale is founded is set aside, the setting aside of the sale follows as of course on the ground of *restitution.*(*o*)

The principle, that a pretermitted defence can only be heard on a motion to open the judgment addressed to the court that entered it, is not affected by the fact that the judgment is entered by the prothonotary on a warrant of attorney.(*p*)

The practice in this State is to *open* a judgment confessed where there is an allegation of a pretermitted defence, and to try the question by issue in the cause; the judgment continuing to be a lien.(*q*)

A judgment will be set aside only for matter appearing on the face of the record.(*r*)

If there is any case in which a court can strike off a judgment, it must be a very special case, as of fraud, or perjury, or of a judgment entered on a cancelled bond, or the like; and then only where the facts are admitted or established on a trial. The court may open a judgment or direct an issue to ascertain whether anything is due, or direct an issue to decide who is entitled to the money, where that is disputed.(*s*)

Where a joint judgment against two defendants has been opened as to one, it is error in the court to permit execution to issue as to the other, before the trial of the issue to determine whether the defendant, as to

---

He now applies to have this judgment stricken off on the grounds stated. We think it is too late. See *ante*, 573.

(*m*) Fricker's Appeal, 1 W. 393.

(*n*) Spang *v.* Com. 2 J. 358.

(*o*) Stephens *v.* Stephens. (D. C. All.), 7 Leg. Int. 183.

(*p*) M'Veagh *v.* Little, 7 Barr, 279.

(*q*) Gallup *v.* Reynolds, 8 W. 424. GIBSON, C. J.

(*r*) Devereux *v.* Roper, January 25, 1851. R. to set aside judgment. *Per curiam.* It is the established practice of the court only to set aside a judgment for matter appearing upon the face of the record. It has not been adopted arbitrarily, but has sound reason in its support. An order of a court setting aside a judgment is subject to a writ of error, and if it be done upon matter *dehors* the record, how can the grounds of it appear to the court above. It is true, we proceed by depositions, but that is not essential. We might hear testimony at bar, and there is no bill of exceptions

nor any mode by which, as a matter of right, the party aggrieved could have the evidence spread upon the record. If the depositions were filed, it is doubtful whether the court of errors could or would re-examine the decision as far as matters of facts. There are two things which, in all our rules of practice, it is the especial duty of the court to take care of: 1. To maintain in its purity the constitutional right of trial by jury; and, 2. To preserve carefully to every suitor his right to have the law in regard to his case determined in the court of the last resort. Any practice which tends to impair either of these must necessarily be bad. The party seeking to have this judgment set aside has his legal remedies, in the pursuit of which his opponent will have his right of trial by jury, and his writ of error to the Supreme Court, with the benefit of a bill of exceptions. R. D.

(*s*) Humphreys *v.* Rann, 8 W. 80. HUSTON, J.

whom the judgment has been opened, has been discharged from his joint liability.(t)

Although since the decision of the case of Talmadge v. Burlinghame and Ivons,(u) and the practice which has so generally obtained, it is too late to question the order of a court in opening a joint judgment as to one defendant, and permitting it to remain as to the other, yet this course is not to be recommended. It would be much better in joint judgments, at least, to pursue the English practice of ordering a collateral issue with the proper parties to try the matters alleged by way of defence, staying the proceedings, if necessary, or permitting execution to issue to bring the money into court, according to the circumstances and equity of the case.(v)

Where a joint judgment is set aside as to one defendant after levy and sale of joint property, it will not affect the title of the purchaser.(w)

A feigned issue will not be granted to try the validity of a judgment, unless to inform the conscience of the court in the decision of some question before them.(x)

Wherever the writ of *audita querela* would lie, the court will grant relief on *motion;* but it is too late to apply for relief after judgment, when the party might have applied before, and neglected it. In such case, relief can be obtained only by the writ of error, *coram nobis.*(y)

It is clear that the Court of Common Pleas have a discretionary power to impose terms as a condition of their interference in opening judgments, and they ought to prescribe the issue, so as to draw into contest no more than the matters alleged as a defence in the affidavit, and to exclude pleas of the statute of limitations not relied upon therein.(z)

The court have unlimited power to impose terms on opening a judgment, and may direct an affidavit of defence to stand as a plea, and that the parties shall go to trial on the facts stated in it; where this, however, is omitted by the court, the defendant cannot be presumed to have waived the benefit of a formal plea and issue, and it would be error to try the case in his absence on such affidavit.(a)

This practice is peculiar to us, and, from its looseness, its nature is not very distinctly perceived. There is no trace of it in the English books; for where sufficient cause is shown, their practice is to order the warrant of attorney to be given up, and the judgment set aside if entered; and this, whether the judgment be irregular or by default on affidavit of merits. No instance exists of an English court opening a judgment, in our sense of the term; their practice is to award a collateral issue, and only when facts are alleged to be in contest, instead of an issue in the cause. Our practice gives the defendant all proper benefit of his defence, without depriving the plaintiff of the lien of his judgment. We overturn the judgment for irregularity or collusion in its rendition; but for pretermitted matter of defence it is opened, it being impossible to say what may be found due. Collusion is tried by a collateral issue; matter

(t) Struthers v. Lloyd, 2 H. 216.
(u) 9 Barr, 21.
(v) Id. 217. ROGERS, J.
(w) Kelly's Appeal, 4 H. 62.
(x) Rowland's Estate, 7 L. J. 312.

(y) Durand v. Halbach, 1 M. 46.
(z) Gilkyson v. Larue, 6 W. & S. 217;
Ekel v. Snevily, 3 W. & S. 272.
(a) Ensly v. Wright, 3 Barr, 502.

of defence by an issue in the cause. To open, is not to set aside; for when closed again by finding a sum due, execution issues upon it, as if it had not been disturbed. It may be opened upon terms; and it is usual to direct it to stand as a security, though this is unnecessary, as opening it deprives it of no quality but its maturity for execution.(b)

Where a judgment has been opened for the purpose of giving the defendant an opportunity of showing that he is entitled to a deduction for matter arising subsequently to the judgment, a verdict finding a balance in favor of the *defendant* is erroneous, and a judgment in favor of the defendant for such balance, will be reversed.(c)

Where a judgment is opened for the purpose of trying whether the bond on which the judgment was entered was not given by collusion between the plaintiff and the defendant to defraud creditors, it is not necessary that the creditors should be made parties to the suit.(d)

Where proceedings are stayed, on a rule to open a judgment after a levy on a *fi. fa.*, it is incumbent on the sheriff to preserve the property, to meet the exigencies of the contest; or, if of a perishable nature, permission may be obtained to dispose of it, paying the avails into court.(e)

Under the act of April 16, 1849 (since repealed), on the subject of fraudulent judgments, the practice was to let the execution go on, order the proceeds into court, and then award an issue to determine the question of fraud.(f)

(b) See Gallup v. Reynolds, 8 W. 424.

(c) Harper v. Kean, 11 S. & R. 280.

(d) Whiting v. Johnson, 11 S. & R. 328. See 1 Barr, 254.

(e) Spang v. Com. 2 J. 358. See generally as to practice as to opening judgments, Curtis v. Slosson, 6 Barr, 266; Drexel's Appeal, 275; Harrison v. Soles, 395; Rowland's Estate, 7 L. J. 312.

(f) Brown v. Herring, D. C., June 14, 1851. Why judgment should not be opened. *Per curiam.* The ground of this motion is the provision of the 4th section of the act of 16th April, 1849, which has recently received a construction by the Supreme Court, to the effect that, however awkwardly drawn, the plain meaning of it is to make void all preferences by insolvents, whether through the instrumentality of assignments for the benefit of creditors, or otherwise. It is evident, however, that the instrument is good between the parties. The lien of it only is avoided as to creditors. It seems too—at all events it is a question—that an assignee for the benefit is entitled to take advantage of the law, especially as it is a proviso to an act to prevent preferences in assignments. It would not be proper, therefore, to open the judgment, which is only done to let parties and privies into a defence. The true practice is to let the execution go on, order the proceeds into court, and then award an

issue to determine the question. We think there is sufficient ground laid by the depositions for that course in this case. At present, however, rule dismissed.

Prowattain v. Gillingham, Dec. 13, 1851. Why execution should not be set aside. *Per curiam.* This application is on behalf of an assignee for the benefit of creditors to set aside two judgments alleged by him to have been given by the assignees when they were in insolvent circumstances—with knowledge of the fact, and with intent to evade the act against preferences in assignments.

In regard to the judgment entered D. S. B. No. 80, and the act of 16th of Aug. 1851, we are of opinion that it appears by the evidence, and on the argument was conceded by the counsel for the rule —that the judgment note in question was given to secure an advance of money made contemporaneously with it. It is clear that such a judgment is not within the act—which touches only securities given for precedent debts. There was, indeed, a prior note held by plaintiff to same amount—which note had been paid at maturity by money borrowed by defendant of third persons. Subsequently, to enable the defendants to repay the borrowed money, this new advance was made. It was certainly a new debt. Plaintiff had been paid—he had a right to say, I will not advance the money you wish unless you give me this security—

A tenant who applies to the court to open a judgment, and to be let into a defence as to its lien on his land, does not thereby become a party *qua* party to the writ of *scire facias*, upon which the judgment was entered.(*h*) In delivering the opinion of the court in this case, KENNEDY, J., animadverted with great severity upon the practice generally prevailing, of making the opening of a·judgment absolute and unconditional.

"Why open a judgment," he said, "that is perfectly good and available as against the defendant, notwithstanding all that is alleged against it be true? If what be alleged of it be true, then the payment of it only ought to be postponed until all the just debts of the defendant shall be satisfied; and if after that, he shall have property still remaining, sufficient to satisfy the judgment entered with a view to defraud his creditors, the plaintiff therein may levy the amount of the judgment out of it. It seems to me that opening a judgment for any purpose whatever, must necessarily stay all further proceedings upon it until it shall be closed again in some way; but I take it that the plaintiff in such fraudulent judgment, is entitled in law to have execution at any time against the body of the defendant, unless the defendant can show property sufficient to satisfy that judgment, together with all just claims against him; and if so, what right has the court to tie up the hands of the plaintiff by making an order to open the judgment? None whatever, that I can perceive, and I should be much pleased to see all anomalous practices reformed."

It has been decided that a judgment cannot be opened by a court after their power over it is at end. Thus, a judgment on a mortgage was rendered at November term, 1826, and the premises bound by it were sold on a *levari facias* to the succeeding term. At November term, 1829, settlers on the land obtained a rule to show cause why the judgment should not be opened and they let into a defence, which was made absolute at the next term, the purchaser having in the interval recovered in ejectment against them on his legal title, which it was their object to destroy. It was held by the Supreme Court, that, although the opening of a judgment is not the subject of a writ of error, when the discretion of the court below is exercised in time, the *excess* of power in such a case, may be annulled on error brought.(*i*) And the court observed: " This seems to have been recognized in Bailey *v.* Musgrave,(*j*) where an amendment after verdict was held not ·to be cognizable on writ of error, only because the court had not exceeded its power;

and such appears to have been the transaction in this instance.

The case, however, of the note of Sept. 10, entered D. S. B. s. 51, No. 81, is different. That appears to have been given to secure a note which was a mere direct renewal of a former note of the same amount, between the same parties.

Since these decisions, however, by the act of May 4, 1852, section 5. That the proviso to the fourth section of the act of the sixteenth of April, one thousand eight hundred and forty-nine, entitled " An act relating to habitual drunkards,"

et cetera, which enacts " That no *bona fide* judgment or lien acquired against the property of any debtor, or any sale, or transfer of the property of such debtor, unless the same shall have been obtained, acquired or made with intent to evade the provisions of the said act, shall be avoided or defeated by the subsequent discovery that such debtor was insolvent at the time such judgment was obtained, lien acquired, or transfer made," be, and the same is hereby repealed.

(*h*) Brown *v.* Simpson, 2 W. 253.(h)
(*i*) Catlin *v.* Robinson, 2 W. 379.
(*j*) 2 S. & R. 220.

and the principle was still more distinctly announced in Huston v. Mitchell,(k) where the court below had opened a judgment at the term succeeding the verdict. "I shall give no opinion," said the Chief Justice, "on the power of the Common Pleas to set aside a verdict and judgment, and order a new trial on a motion not made till the second term after the entry of the judgment. But granting, for the sake of the argument, that they have the power, is the order made in this case lawful?" It was held to be unlawful, because it did not amount to a judgment for the defendant, and yet left the plaintiff without the means of proceeding in his suit. Here, then, was an order in the nature of a final judgment, reversed for an excess of power in the exercise of a discretionary function. In respect to the power to set aside a judgment on verdict, and award a new trial at a subsequent term, when the record had ceased to be in the breast of the court, not to speak of my own recollection of the sentiments of the judges when the cause came up at consultation, it is not difficult to say what ground would have been taken had the cause required it; and I mention this to show that the guarded terms in which the Chief Justice delivered the opinion of the court were not dictated by any doubt of the principle. I will not say that a judgment by default, or on confession, may not be opened at a succeeding term on the ground of a defence arising subsequently, provided it do not interfere with rights acquired under the judgment by third persons; but it must be obvious that it would be attended with extreme danger, if the security of titles founded on judicial proceedings, might be invaded by the exercise of an arbitrary and uncontrollable discretion of the courts over their own records. The act imposing a limitation on writs of error would be of little account, if an inferior court might do at discretion what the court of the last resort dare not do by an exercise of its legitimate prerogative. Nor would the act to prevent purchasers at sheriffs' sales from being dispossessed on reversal of the judgment, afford that perfect protection it was intended to do, if the foundation of the title might be expunged from the record by an act of power."

In the case of Compher v. Anawalt,(l) a writ of error was taken on the refusal of the Common Pleas to open a judgment; this was declared not to be assignable for error, but the court, after examining the merits of the case, expressed their sentiments in favor of the plaintiff in error, and permitted him to withdraw his writ of error, in order that he might apply to the court below for relief. In the case of Kalbach v. Fisher,(m) it was ruled that no writ of error lies to the opening of a judgment of the court below. It is a matter depending on the sound discretion of that court, who are not prevented from affording relief by lapse of time. "The power of the Court of Common Pleas," said ROGERS, J., "in relation to opening judgments, is most ample, and policy requires that it should be liberally used, otherwise great and manifest injustice would be the consequence, from the great variety of shapes which fraud may assume in the complicated transactions of men. It depends upon the sound discretion of the court, which must be regulated more by the particular circumstances of every case than by any *precise* and *known* rule of law. From the constitution of this court, it is impossible that

(k) 14 S. & R. 310.
(l) 2 W. 490.

(m) 1 R. 323.

we can be made fully acquainted with all the circumstances, and there would be more danger of injury from revising matters of this kind than would result now and then from an improper or arbitrary exercise of this discretion. If the court had refused to open the judgment, the defendant would have been without remedy, and yet there is less danger in opening than in refusing to open a judgment. The practice of opening judgments without stint or limit, except the sound discretion of the court, has obtained since the first settlement of the province, without injustice to suitors. On the contrary, it has frequently been the means of unravelling the most secret and unjust schemes of fraud, which could not have been reached without a liberal exercise of this extraordinary power of the court."(n)

As will hereafter be more fully seen, when treating of feigned issues,(nn) a writ of error now lies to the proceedings of the court in which the issue is tried.

9. *Assignment of judgments.*

A sale of a judgment is good though made by parol.(o)

Where a judgment was assigned in general terms, and at the foot of the assignment a certain amount was set down in figures, it was held that the statement of the amount was only matter of description, and did not amount to a warranty that so much was due.(p)

On the trial of a feigned issue to determine whether a judgment assigned to the plaintiff was a lien, it was held not to be error to charge the jury, that "if the assignor agreed not to enter judgment, and declared to the defendant that no judgment had been entered, the effect would be to render the judgment null and void, and it would be a fraud to proceed on the judgment under such circumstances.(q)

One who pays the amount of a judgment to the holder of it, is entitled to control it, and issue execution upon it, without an actual assignment of it.(r)

The assignment of a judgment does not imply a covenant or warranty that it will be paid.(s)

The assignor of a judgment is not liable for the failure of the debtor to pay, unless there have been fraud, or an express warranty.(t)

In 1816, A confessed a judgment in favor of B, his sister, who was tenant in common with him of certain real estate. In 1818, A and B conveyed their real estate to assignees, for the benefit of creditors. Afterwards, the same estate was sold under a prior mortgage. It was held that the judgment in favor of B must be postponed to the debts provided by the assignment, though the judgment was subsequently transferred to one who had paid full value for it.(u)

The assignee of a judgment takes it subject to all equities subsisting between the assignor and other persons at the time of the assignment.(v)

It seems that the assignment of a judgment in Pennsylvania, or the

---

(n) See *post*, 598.
(nn) Execution, II., 9 (3). V. 9 (3).
(o) Levering v. Phillips, 7 Barr, 387.
(p) Oyster v. Waugh, 4 W. 158.
(q) Kellogg v. Kranser, 14 S. & R. 137.
(r) Gratz v. Farmers' Bank, 5 W. 99; Fleming v. Beaver, cited ibid.

(s) Mohler's "Appeal," 5 Barr, 418.
(t) Jackson v. Crawford, 12 S. & R. 165; S. C. and S. P. 14 S. & R. 290.
(u) Mifflin v. Rasey, 3 R. 483.
(v) Himes v. Barnitz, 8 W. 39; Porter v. Boone, 1 W. & S. 252.

marking of a judgment to the use of another, does not imply any covenant or warranty that the said judgment will be paid.(*w*)

An entry, such as this, on the record, "These judgments stand for the use of M. F.," amounts to an assignment of the judgments with all their incidents; and such an entry, made by the attorney, is as binding as if by the principal; and such an assignment embraces the judgments against *terre-tenants*, as well as those against the obligors, though separately rendered.(*x*)   "The entry," said ROGERS, J., "amounts to a common assignment of the judgment, with all its incidents; and although made by the attorney, yet it is entitled to the same consideration as if made by the principal."

If the assignee of a moiety of a judgment entered on a bond, does not have his interest therein marked on the docket, and the bond being subsequently in the possession of the obligee, the latter assigns all his interest in the judgment bond, without notice being had by the second assignee of the former assignment, and notice of assignment to the second assignee is marked on the record, the first assignee will be postponed in favor of the second.(*z*)

10. *Transfer of judgments to other counties.*

A creditor, or heir of a deceased judgment creditor, may transfer the judgment, by transcript, to another county, so as to secure the assets, under the act of April 16, 1840; the suggestion of death and substitution of personal representative, may be before or after the transfer in either county, for the purpose of proceeding to execution.(*a*)

The 1st section of the act of April 16, 1840, enabling a judgment to be transferred from one county to another within this State, requires the whole record to be certified by the prothonotary. The certificate must purport to authenticate an exemplification of the record. A mere copy of the docket entry, certified to be as full and complete as the same remains of record in the court, is not such a transcript as the act requires, and a judgment and execution upon it are invalid.(*b*)

The transcript of a judgment in the Common Pleas, entered in another county, in pursuance of the act of April 16, 1840, is not an actual judgment of the court of the county in which it is entered, but a *quasi* judgment for limited purposes; it is evidence of a judgment in the court in which it was originally obtained.(*c*)

Where the original judgment was set aside at the instance of the defendant, for irregularity, and the execution in the second county stayed, it was held, that the judgment on the transcript fell with it; and that the plaintiff having obtained a new judgment, but no transcript of it having been entered, this last judgment had no lien in the county in which the transcript had been first entered.(*d*)

(*w*) Mohler's "Appeal," 5 Barr, 418. See, as to an assignment of part of judgment, Porter *v.* Boone, 1 W. & S. 251.

(*x*) Ibid. 420.

(*z*) Fisher *v.* Knox, 1 H. 622.

(*a*) Watt *v.* Swinehart, 8 Barr, 97.

(*b*) Updergraff *v.* Perry, 4 Barr, 291; see Bank of Chester *v.* Olwine, 6 P. L. J. 154.   Brandt's Appeal, *infra.*

(*c*) Brandt's "Appeal, 4 H. 343.

(*d*) Ibid.

SECTION II.

OF THE STAY OF EXECUTION UPON THE JUDGMENT.

When the judgment is entered, the defendant has it in his power to delay its execution, by a compliance with the conditions of the act of June 16, 1836,(f) the first section of which declares, that, "in all actions instituted by writ for the recovery of money due by contract, or of damages arising from a breach of a contract, except actions of debt and *scire facias* upon judgments, and actions of *scire facias* upon mortgages, if the defendant shall be possessed of an estate in fee simple, within the respective county, worth, in the opinion of the court, the amount of the judgment recovered therein, or the sum for which the plaintiff may be entitled to have execution by virtue thereof, clear of all incumbrances, he shall be entitled to a stay of execution upon such judgment, to be computed from the first day of the term to which the action was commenced, as follows, to wit :—

   I. If the amount, or sum aforesaid, shall not exceed two hundred dollars, six months.

   II. If such amount, or sum, shall exceed two hundred dollars, and be less than five hundred dollars, nine months.

   III. If such amount, or sum, shall exceed five hundred dollars, twelve months.

Every defendant, in any judgment obtained as aforesaid, may, upon entering security, in the nature of special bail, have a stay of execution thereon, during thirty days from the rendition of such judgment; and if, during that period, he shall give security, to be approved of by the court, or by a judge thereof, for the sum recovered, together with interest and cost, he shall be entitled to the stay of execution hereinbefore provided, in the case of a person owning real estate. § 4.

In amicable actions, the defendant shall be entitled to like stay of execution, if he possess an estate in fee simple, or give security as aforesaid ; in such cases, the stay shall be computed from the date of their agreement, unless it be otherwise provided therein by the party. § 5.

Under the act of 1806, for which the above is a substitute, it was ruled that the benefit of this stay is also extended to cases where judgment has been rendered for a sum awarded by arbitrators under the act of 1810.(g)

By the 1st section of the act of March 20, 1845, " the bail in all cases where bail is now required for the stay of execution, shall be bail absolute, with one or more sufficient sureties, in double the amount of the debt or damages, interest and costs recovered, conditioned for the payment thereof in the event that the defendant fail to pay the same at the expiration of the stay of execution."

(f) Pamph. L. 762.   (g) See ¿ 11, act of March 20, 1810.

By the 33d section of the act of April 25, 1850, "from and after the passage of this act, no defendant shall be entitled to stay of execution upon a judgment obtained against him as bail for stay of execution on any former judgment."

By the 92d rule of the District Court, " the defendant in every judgment in which there may be a stay of execution under the act relating to executions, passed the 16th day of June, 1836, may, at any time within seven days from the rendition thereof, but not afterwards, enter security in the nature of special bail for a stay of execution during thirty days; or he may enter security for the sum of money recovered, with the interest and costs, at any time within thirty days from the rendition of the judgment. And in case any execution shall have been issued, the same may be set aside upon the payment of the costs thereof. But this rule does not extend to cases in which the money has been made upon the execution, nor to cases of execution issued into another county after seven days from the rendition of the judgment."(h)

The bail required by the act for the stay of execution for thirty days, need not be entered, if special bail has been entered at the commencement of the action in a sum sufficient to secure the amount found due. It would be no advantage to the plaintiff to have bail *de novo* entered, but would increase the costs and oppress the defendant for no useful purpose.(i) The entry of security for the money, operates as a discharge of the recognizance of special bail, if the suit were instituted by *capias*.(j)

It has been determined that the entering of this security is no waiver of the right to a writ of error.(k) It is, therefore, now a question, whether, if in such a case the judgment be reversed, and a *venire de novo* awarded, the plaintiff loses the benefit of such special bail to the action (as we have seen above), or of bail on an appeal from an award, or the security for the *cesset;* or any, or all of them.(l) It may be well to remark, that in civil cases within a magistrate's jurisdiction, the stay of execution commences from the date of the judgment, differing from the cases mentioned in the act, by which it appears that the stay is counted from the first day of the term to which the action was commenced. A *fi. fa.* issued within the period of the stay, after security entered under this act, is a nullity, and trespass lies against the plaintiff or prothonotary for issuing it.(m) But if, after a recognizance entered into for a stay of execution, the plaintiff issue a *fi. fa.* against the defendants in the original suit, within the time of stay allowed by law, and obtain part of the debt from one of the original defendants, under a menace of levying the execution, this does not annul the recognizance.(n)

In a suit against the surety in a recognizance for a *cesset*, one of the defendants against whom judgment was obtained in the original suit, is not a competent witness for the defendant.(o)

If the recognizance for payment of the judgment be entered into

---

(h) See, for authorities generally under this head, Wh. Dig. " Execution," i.

(i) Perlasca v. Spargella, 3 Bin. 429.

(j) Roup v. Waldbouer, 12 S. & R. 24.

(k) Bank v. Becker, 12 S. & R. 412. DUNCAN, J., dissent.

(l) *Vide* ibid. 426.

(m) Milliken v. Brown, 10 S. & R. 188.

(n) Id. ibid.

(o) Id. ibid.

after the expiration of the time limited for a stay of execution, and the plaintiff proceed upon it, he cannot afterwards treat it as a nullity.(*p*)

The act above quoted, like that of 1806, does not designate the *kind* or *form* of the security; "nor whether it shall be by bond or recognizance; whether on the docket, or *in pais*; whether it shall be filed in the prothonotary's office or kept by the plaintiff. The practice has been general to enter it on the docket, and for the surety to sign it. It is in some counties drawn more at large [than in others], and stated to be for the purpose of obtaining for the defendant the stay of execution allowed by law. In some counties it is taken in double the amount of debt; in some in the amount; and in some, it is, '*becomes* security for debt, interest, and costs.' Where the stipulation is entered on the docket annexed to the suit, and the money not paid at the expiration of the stay of execution, *scire facias* or debt have been brought promiscuously."(*q*) Therefore, a recognizance, entered on the docket below the entry of the judgment, in this form: "S. F. of, &c., bound in the sum $3008 98, conditioned for the payment of the debt, interest and costs," signed by him, and attested by the prothonotary's clerk, is a valid recognizance under this act.(*r*)

It seems that the 77th section of the act of 14th April, 1834, enabling prothonotaries to take bail in civil actions *depending* in the respective courts, does not authorize them to take recognizance for stay of execution. It was the practice throughout the State to do so under the act of 1806, though not expressly made their duty. The act of 16th June, 1836, § 4, in addition, requires the security to be approved by the court, or a judge thereof, but also omits to direct by whom the recognizance shall be taken. It may, however, be taken by the prothonotary, and be afterwards perfected. The approval is for the benefit of the creditor, and he may waive it expressly or impliedly; but neither the debtor nor the bail can take advantage of the want of it.(*s*)

A recognizance taken in the mere amount of a judgment, together with the interest that may accrue, and costs, is substantially good. No form is prescribed by the act, whether by bond or recognizance, whether on the docket or *in pais*, whether to be filed or kept by the plaintiff. The practice, in general, has been to enter it on the docket, and for the surety to sign it. In some counties it is taken in double the amount; in some, in the mere amount; in others, he becomes surety for debt, interest and costs.(*t*)

An entry on the docket, under the proper action, "Defendants offer D. as bail for stay of execution for six months," signed by D., bears no resemblance to a recognizance of bail; it is a mere offer to assume bail.(*u*)

Before a magistrate, under the act of 20th March, 1845, is bound to account for the defendant's goods at the expiring of the stay or against all the world, a levy and sale under subsequent process are no excuse.(*v*)

The stay in appeals from magistrates, runs from the first day of the

(*p*) Reed *v.* Morrison, 12 S. & R. 24.
(*q*) Per HUSTON, J., Gratz *v.* Lancaster Bank, 17 S. & R. 283–4.
(*r*) Id. 282.
(*s*) Stroop *v.* Gross, 1 W. & S. 139.

(*t*) Bank of Penn. *v.* Reed, 1 W. & S. 104.
(*u*) Bieber *v.* Buh, 6 Barr, 198.
(*v*) Leich *v.* Stichter, 1 H. 87.

term to which they are entered, because the case begins *de novo* from the first day of the term to which it is entered.(*w*)

By the act of 20th March, 1810, § 11,(*x*) twenty days are allowed for the entry of an appeal from an award of arbitrators, and under it the prothonotary has no power to issue executions until the expiration of that period, whether the defendant be a freeholder or not. If he omit to appeal or give the prescribed security within that time, judgment is final, and execution may then be issued, unless special bail has been already entered, when, as we have seen, the defendant has a stay for thirty days. But in the cases mentioned in the acts of 1806 and 1836,(*y*) executions may issue *immediately* after judgment,(*z*) unless they fall within the provisions of the *cesset*. To prevent this, it is the practice, when confessing judgments, to stipulate that they shall be considered as being entered upon awards of arbitrators. By this means the defendants are entitled to a stay for twenty days without any security.

In order that every party may have sufficient opportunity of taking out a writ of error, it is directed by the act of March, 1809, § 6,(*a*) that no execution shall issue upon any judgment, on any special verdict, demurrer, or case stated, unless by leave of the court, in special cases for security of the demand, within three weeks from the day on which such judgment shall be pronounced.

The rule of the District Court in this respect is as follows:—

LXXXVIII. The defendant in every judgment in which there may be a stay of execution under the act relating to executions, passed the 16th day of June, 1836, may at any time within seven days from the rendition thereof, but not afterwards, enter security in the nature of special bail for a stay of execution during thirty days, or he may enter security for the sum of money recovered with interest and costs, at any time within thirty days from the rendition of the judgment. And in case any execution shall have been issued, the same may be set aside upon the payment of the costs thereof. But this rule does not extend to cases in which the money has been made upon the execution, nor to cases of execution issued into another county after seven days from the rendition of the judgment.

In the Common Pleas:—

IX. 3. Exceptions may be taken to the sufficiency of security for stay of execution, within four days after the expiration of thirty days from the entry of the judgment; and the defendant, within eight days after notice of exception, shall justify the security before the prothonotary, giving twenty-four hours' notice of justification, subject to appeal to a judge.

It is not sufficient that the defendant is a freeholder in another county. The freehold mentioned in the act must be situate in the county where the judgment is entered, to enable him to plead it successfully.(*c*) The freehold must moreover be entirely unincumbered; and it is not enough that it be considered equal to the judgment after paying all incumbrances, since any incumbrance on the estate has been held sufficient to deprive the defendant of this privilege.(*d*) The provi-

(*w*) Woods *v.* Conner, 6 Barr, 433.
(*x*) 5 Sm. Laws.
(*y*) *Supra,* 582–3.
(*z*) *Vide* Perlasca *v.* Spargella, 3 Bin. 429.

(*a*) 5 Sm. Laws, 17.
(*c*) Com. *v.* Meredith, 5 Bin. 432.
(*d*) Girard *v.* Heyl, 6 Bin. 253.

sions of the acts regulating stay of execution do not embrace the case of a defendant in a *scire facias* on a mortgage.(*e*) But a plaintiff in replevin is entitled to the stay, and, therefore, a *retorno habendo* cannot issue until it be expired.(*f*)

The plea of freehold will be stricken off, where the estate is not worth, in the opinion of the court, the amount of the judgment.(*g*)

The time of stay is to be dated from the return day of the first original process which is effective in bringing the defendant into court.(*h*)

(*e*) Anon. D. C. Philad. 1821, MS. Wh. Dig.

(*f*) Rose *v.* M'Crea, C. P. Philad. Jan. 1820, MS. ib. 521.

(*g*) Harrison *v.* Hyneman, D. C. C. P. 8 Leg. Int. 106. Hansell *v.* Garwood, D. C., Monday, March 6, 1848. Why plea of freehold should not be stricken off. *Per curiam.* It was settled in the Supreme Court, in Girard *v.* Heyl, 6 B. 253, that under the 7th section of the act of 21st March, 1806, to entitle a defendant to stay of execution, he must show a freehold not merely worth the amount of the judgment above, or more than the incumbrances upon it, but clear of all incumbrances. The words of this section are identically the same with those of the 3d section of the act of 16th June, 1836, the act now in force, though there is a slight transposition, so far at least as regards the point involved in this application. The legislature, by changing the law from requiring in the defendant "a freehold estate" to "an estate in fee simple," leaving words which had received a judicial construction to remain precisely the same, have shown no disposition to extend this privilege of the defendant Rule absolute.

(*h*) Morris *v.* Cameron, Dec. 15, 1849. Why security for stay should not be entered from the return day of the original process. *Per curiam.* In this case a summons was issued returnable to the 1st Monday of October, to which the sheriff made return of *"nihil habet."* An alias summons was issued returnable to the 1st Monday of November, to which the sheriff returned " served." Afterwards a judgment was entered, for want of an affidavit of defence, and the defendant having tendered security for stay of execution, which has been approved, the question has now been presented, from what period the stay of execution shall date—the return day of the first, or the second summons? The third section of the act of 16th June, 1836, relating to executions (Purd. p. 442), enacts that the stay of execution shall be computed " from the first day of the term to which the action was commenced;" and by the

proviso of the first section of the act of 28th March, 1835 : "An act. to establish the District Court for the city and county of Philadelphia," (Purd. 265,) it is declared that the stay of execution allowed by the seventh section of the act entitled "An act to regulate arbitrations and proceedings in courts of justice, passed 21st March, 1806, shall count from the return day to which the original process issued was returnable." Though the seventh section of the act of 1806 had been superseded and supplied by the third section of the act of 1836, it is plain that this provision, though it refers to an act repealed by having been supplied, does not thereby fall to the ground, but stands good still, and is to be applied to cases under the new act. By the strict letter of both these acts, the stay of execution would have to be computed from the return day of the first summons; but when we look at the reason and spirit which is to be liberally construed in favor of the indulgence therein accorded to the defendant, the conclusion must be that it was the intention of the legislature to accord to the defendant a certain delay, proportional to the sum received, to be computed from the time when he was first called on to answer, and had an opportunity, by at once confessing its justice, to avoid further trouble and expense. We think, therefore, that it is from the return day of the original process which is effective in bringing the defendant into court, that the stay ought to be computed. The reason of this determination will be more readily recognized if it be considered that an alias summons, according to our practice, may be issued at any indefinite period of time, grounded upon an original summons, the continuance being mere matter of form, which may be filled up afterwards. In this way the bar of the statute of limitations may be avoided. But in such case, if the law relating to executors were differently construed, the property of the defendant would be liable to be seized and swept from him at a sacrifice, without allowing him that time to look around and make provision to save

type

Agreements, stipulating for stay of execution, independently of that allowed by law, are frequently made, and courts will see that the proceedings are conducted according to good faith and the understanding of the parties ;(i) and, if an agreement for a stay of execution be made, it seems to be now settled that the court will receive evidence of it, although not entered on the record.(j) So, if a plaintiff is bound in equity to make a title to defendant for a portion of the premises, execution will be stayed upon the judgment in ejectment until such title is secured.(k) If, after judgment, an agreement is made between parties that execution shall not be taken out till the next term, and it is sued out before, the court will set aside the proceedings.(l) So, where judgment was entered upon a bond payable at a time certain, execution cannot issue until that time is expired, though no provision for a stay of execution, until that time, has been inserted in the warrant.(m) On the other hand, the court will not interpose, unless it appears that the execution issued contrary to good faith; upon this principle they refused to set aside an execution, issued before the expiration of the stay, agreed to by plaintiff, on condition that there were then no other judgments, but one, against defendant, when, in fact, there were others, as appeared in evidence upon the hearing.(n) So, where judgment was entered, with an agreement that it should be released on the defendant's performing a certain act, without expressly providing for any stay of execution, a _fi. fa._, issued after allowing a reasonable time, is regular, the defendant having neglected to fulfil the agreement, and no injury could arise from supporting such a proceeding, because the court would always interfere in a summary way to prevent injustice, and enforce the terms on which the judgment was entered. If, however, it had issued immediately after judgment, no doubt the court would have set it aside.(o) An omission by the prothonotary to enter on the record a stay of execution, provided for in the warrant of attorney, is not such neglect as to work a forfeiture of his official bond, or make him liable for the amount.(p)

The surety for _cesset_, who pays the judgment, is not thereby entitled to be substituted as plaintiff, and have priority to subsequent judgment, because he has intervened to hinder execution, and is, therefore, without equity against those injured by the stay. It would, however, be otherwise as between the bail and principal debtor, but the doctrine of subrogation has never been applied to a mere volunteer.(q)

Until the act of 1850, the bail for _cesset executio_ when sued, was entitled, like any other defendant, to the usual stay of execution. The recognizance is a _contract_ within the act regulating the stay.(r)

The principal and surety being both liable for the same debt, although by different responsibilities, it is clear that the plaintiff may pursue either, or both, at the same time, after the expiration of the _cesset_. And

himself, which it was evidently the great aim of the act to give him. R. D.

(i) 2 T. R. 163.
(j) Lessee of Dunlop v. Speer, 3 Bin. 172.
(k) Lessee of Mathers v. Akewright, 2 Bin. 93.
(l) 1 Mod. 20.
(m) Shoemaker v. Shirtliff, 1 D. 133.
(n) 1 Br. 130.
(o) Miller v. Milford, 2 S. & R. 36.
(p) 1 R. 249.
(q) Armstrong's Appeal, 5 W. & S. 356.
(r) Wolfe v. Nesbit, 4 W. & S. 313.

even after a levy on the real estate of the principal, he may proceed by *scire facias* against the bill, though he can recover but one satisfaction. The remedies being concurrent, the doctrine of election is not applicable.(*s*) So identified with, and undistinguishable from, his principal, does the bail become, that after judgment obtained against them, a surety of the principal, on the original obligation, who has paid a part of the debt, is entitled to an assignment of the judgment against the principal and his bail, to indemnify himself for the amount so paid.(*t*) But one, after placing himself on record as principal, and after the lapse of several years, and many judgment creditors have acquired rights, will not be permitted to be substituted as surety and have his situation and character changed so as to affect them.(*u*) And an order of court, marking the judgment against him and his codefendant to his use, would not be binding on other creditors not parties to it.(*v*)

SECTION III.

ENTRY OF SATISFACTION OF JUDGMENT.

When the judgment is satisfied by payment, voluntarily made, or enforced by execution, the defendant is entitled to have satisfaction acknowledged and entered of record. The attorney of the plaintiff, under his general authority, may enter satisfaction, and his authority is not limited here, as it is in England, to a year and a day after judgment ;(*w*) but it is usually done by the plaintiff himself, in the office of the prothonotary of the court where the judgment is entered, upon the docket containing the full entries ; from which the clerk makes an entry of satisfaction upon the margin of the judgment-index.

To enforce the entry of satisfaction, the act of April, 1791, § 14,(*x*) directs the plaintiff to acknowledge it upon the record within eighty days after request made, payment of the costs of suit and tender of his reasonable charges of office, under the penalty of a sum not exceeding one half the debt recovered. After the original debt has been fully satisfied, the judgment cannot be left open to cover new and distinct engagements between the parties.(*y*)

If the plaintiff enter on the docket, "Ended, and debt and costs paid," it is equivalent to an entry of satisfaction, and may be pleaded in bar of a new suit for the same cause of action.(*z*) If the entry have been procured by improper means, such as giving the plaintiff a worthless mortgage, he should apply to the court for leave to expunge the entry, which upon good cause shown might be done.(*a*) The entry " settled," on the record, would perhaps amount to an entry of satisfaction or discontinuance ; but such an entry on the trial-list of a judge never transferred to the docket, and afterwards ordered to be stricken out, verdict and judgment being rendered for the plaintiff, has no such

---

(*s*) Patterson *v.* Swan, 9 S. & R. 16.
(*t*) Burns *v.* Huntingdon Bank, 1 Pa. R. 398 ; 2 Vern. 608.
(*u*) Goswiler's Estate, 3 Pa. R. 202, 203.
(*v*) Ibid.

(*w*) Gibson *v.* Philad. Ins. Co. 1 Bin. 470 ; *ante*, 219.
(*x*) 3 Sm. Laws, 32.
(*y*) 4 Johns. Ch. R. 247.
(*z*) Phillips *v.* Israel, 10 S. & R. 391.
(*a*) Ibid. 392.

effect, and the lien of such a judgment would not be postponed to a judgment obtained, after such entries had been made and before they were stricken out.(b)　The trial-list certified under an act for holding a special court forms no part of the record.(c)

A defendant cannot be discharged by the court for any sum less than what is contained in a judgment entered, on a plain and fair agreement of the parties.(d)　But where judgment was entered on an award that the defendant pay so much to the plaintiff on receiving indemnity against certain claims, and the plaintiff afterwards refused giving this indemnity, the court ordered satisfaction to be entered on the judgment, upon payment by the defendant of those claims against which he was to be indemnified.(e)

A judgment in a *scire facias* upon a mortgage, for the amount of the money due upon the mortgage, is a judgment for "debt or damages," within the 14th section of the act of 13th April, 1791; which provides for entering satisfaction of such judgment, and gives a penalty to the party aggrieved by the refusal to enter satisfaction.(f)

It is not necessary that the party suing for such penalty should prove that he has sustained *actual* damage by the refusal to enter satisfaction; the jury may take into consideration all the circumstances by which the party has suffered vexation and inconvenience.(g)

In contemplation of law, a judgment entered by warrant of attorney is as much an act of the court, as if it were formally pronounced on *nil dicit* or *cognovit;* and until it is reversed or set aside, it has all the qualities and effect of a judgment on verdict,(h) and, therefore, such judgment is within the act of 13th April, 1791, providing a penalty for refusing to enter satisfaction thereof.(i)

A plaintiff in such action is not entitled to recover on proving that the *debt* was paid before the judgment was entered.　He is estopped by the judgment from showing that the debt did not exist at the time it was entered.(j)

Where satisfaction has been entered fraudulently, the court will order it to be vacated.　So where the plaintiff, after he had assigned a judgment to a third person, and given notice to the defendant of such assignment, entered up satisfaction, it was ordered to be vacated.(k)　But if, after the satisfaction is entered and before it is vacated, the defendant confesses judgment to a *bona fide* creditor, the second judgment is entitled to priority.(l)

The act of April 11, 1851,(m) is important in this connection:—

Whereas, it often happens that judgments and decrees for the payment of money are obtained, in the City and County of Philadelphia, against persons who subsequently pay the same in full, or settle the same by the payment of less sums, which are received in full satisfaction, or by the transfer of property, rights or credits received as full

---

(b) Moore v. Kline; 1 Pa. R. 129.
(c) Ibid., see also Wood v. Vanarsdale, 3 R. 401.
(d) Addis. 119.
(e) 2 W. C. C. R. 433, 467.
(f) Henry v. Sims, 1 Wh. 187.
(g) Ibid.

(h) Braddee v. Brownfield, 4 W. 474.
(i) Ibid.
(j) Ibid.
(k) 1 Johns. Ca. 121, 258.
(l) 1 Johns. 529.
(m) Pamph L. 612.

payment, settlement, or satisfaction, by the plaintiffs, but satisfaction has not been entered on the records thereof, and great inconvenience, trouble, and injustice has been occasioned thereby to children, heirs, and purchasers; therefore,

When it shall be made known by petition to any court in the said city and county in which any judgment or decree for the payment of money has been obtained, that more than ten years have elapsed since the rendition of said judgment or making of said decree, and that the same has been paid by the defendant or defendants, person or persons, against whom the same has been rendered or made, or by some other person, or has been settled or compromised by the payment of a less sum than the amount of such judgment or decree, or by the transfer of property, rights or credits, received in full thereof, or in settlement and satisfaction thereof, it shall be the duty of said court to examine into the facts set forth in such petition; and upon being satisfied of the truth thereof, to direct the prothonotary of said court, upon the payment of the costs, if any due to him upon such judgment or decree, to enter satisfaction upon the record thereof, which entry of satisfaction shall have the same effect as if made by the plaintiff or plaintiffs in such judgment, or the person or persons entitled to the benefit of the same, or by the complainant or complainants, or person or persons, entitled to the benefit of such decree.   § 2.

It shall be the duty of the court to which any such petition shall be so, as aforesaid, presented, to direct notice of the presenting of the same to be given to the attorney-at-law by whom the action, suit, bill, or proceeding in which said judgment or decree has been obtained was brought or instituted; and if he be dead, then to the plaintiff or plaintiffs, complainant or complainants, or to his or their executors or administrators, if any there be; or if he, she, or they cannot be found in the county where said judgment or decree has been obtained, and the fact shall be so returned by the sheriff of said county, notice to all parties interested in said judgment or decree shall be directed by said court to be published in one or more newspapers published in said county, or in any other place or places in addition thereto, so often as shall be deemed proper.   § 3.

CHAPTER XXVII.

PROCEEDINGS IN ERROR.

Rules announced, September 6, 1852, by the Supreme Court for the Western District of Pennsylvania.

I. In a case where the writ of error is to a judgment on a verdict, the paper-book of the plaintiff in error should contain the following matters in the following order:—

1. The names of all the parties as they stood on the record of the court below, at the time of the trial, and the form of the action.

2. An abstract of the proceedings, showing the issue, and how it was made.

3. The verdict of the jury and the judgment thereon.

4. A history of the case.

5. The points, if any, which were submitted in writing to the court below.

6. The charge of the court.

7. The specification of error.

8. A brief of the argument for the plaintiff in error.

9. An appendix, containing the evidence, and, if necessary, the pleading, in full.

II. Where the judgment below, is on a case stated in the nature of a special verdict, the facts as agreed on by the parties, the opinion of the board, and the argument of counsel, will be sufficient.

III. In appeals, the arrangement of the appellant paper-book shall be as follows:—

1. The names of the parties and the nature of the proceeding.

2. A short abstract of the bill or petition, and answer.

3. A history of the case.

4. The report of the auditor, or master, if there was one.

5. The exceptions taken to the report in the court below.

6. The opinion of the court on the exceptions, and decree made.

7. Assignments of error.

8. Argument on part of appellant.

9. Appendix, containing such documentary or other evidence as may be necessary.

IV. In a certiorari to the Court of Quarter Sessions, the paper-book shall contain:—

1. An abstract list or brief of all the petitions, motions, orders, reports, exceptions, &c., which may be necessary to give the court here

a full view of the record at once; and this in the precise order of their respective dates, and with the date of each prefixed.

2. The exceptions which were overruled or sustained by the final order or judgment of the court.

3. The opinion of the court, if it was filed in writing.

4. The assignment of errors.

5. The argument.

6. An appendix, containing the record in full.

V. The history of the case must contain a closely condensed statement of all the facts of which a knowledge may be necessary in order to determine the points in controversy here; and the want of such a statement cannot be supplied by reference to another part of the paper-book.

VI. Each error relied on must be specified particularly, and by itself. If any specification embrace more than one point, or refer to more than one bill of exceptions, or raise more than one distinct question, it shall · be considered a waiver of all the errors so alleged.

VII. When the error assigned is to be the charge of the court, the part of the charge referred to must be quoted *totidem verbis* in the specification.

VIII. When the error assigned is to the admission or rejection of evidence, the specification must quote the full substance of the bill of exceptions, or copy the bill in immediate connection with the specification. Any assignment of error not according to this and the last rule will be held the same as none.

IX. The brief of the argument shall contain a clear statement of the points on which the party relies, with such reasons and arguments as he may see proper to add; together with all the authorities which he thinks pertinent.

X. When an authority is cited, the principle intended to be proved by it must be stated. A naked reference to the book will not be sufficient.

XI. The paper-book of the defendant in error or appellee may, if he chooses, contain no more than his argument, to which rules IX. and X. will be held to apply.

XII. But he may make it embrace a counter statement, giving such version of the facts as he asserts to be the true one.

XIII. Where the paper-book of the appellee or defendant in error does not contain a counter statement, he will be taken as consenting to and concurring in the history of the case given by the other party.

XIV. The plaintiff in error, or appellant, shall serve a copy of his paper-book on the opposite party, or his attorney, at least ten days before the argument; and when the cause is called, shall furnish one copy to each of the judges, and file two with the prothonotary for the reporter.

XV. The defendant in error, or appellee, shall serve a copy of his paper-book on the opposite party, or his attorney, at least three days before the argument, furnish a copy to each judge, and file two with the prothonotary.

XVI. When the plaintiff in error, or appellant, is in default according to these rules, he may be nonsuited on motion; and when the defendant in error, or appellee, is in default, he will not be heard by the court, except on the request of his adversary, and not then if his negligence has been gross.

XVII. When paper-books are furnished which differ in any material respect from those here prescribed, the parties furnishing them shall be considered in the same default as if none had been furnished, and on proper occasion the court will of its own motion nonsuit or silence the defaulting party.

XVIII. Paper-books shall be furnished in the shape and size of a common octavo pamphlet, on ordinary printing paper.

XIX. Rule VI. does not apply to cases of judgment on facts which agree in the nature of a special verdict. In such cases, it is enough to say that the judgment is erroneous, without more. But that rule has no other exception.

XX. The prothonotary of each district shall keep a separate list for short causes.

XXI. To this list all causes shall be transferred in which the attorney of either party shall certify that it is a short cause.

XXII. The causes on this list shall have precedence over all others, on the Wednesday of every week in which the same causes might be heard if they had remained on the general list and had been reached in their order.

XXIII. Where a cause has been certified to be a short cause by the attorney of one party, and the attorney of the other party will certify that it is not so, and that injustice may be done to his client by placing it on the list of short causes, it shall be put back again on the regular list.

XXIV. On the hearing of short causes, the speeches of the counsel shall be limited to fifteen minutes on each side.

XXV. The hearing of short causes shall not be the exclusive business of Wednesdays. When they are disposed of, the general list shall be called as on other days; but the short list shall be finished before any other business. It shall be the duty of the prothonotary to put in the court-room a copy of the short list, and this shall be notice of the transfer of the causes which are on it. No party shall be permitted to certify any cause back to the regular list after three days from the time it has been placed on the short list.

XXVI. These rules shall not abrogate any former rules, except those with which they are inconsistent.

XXVII. They apply to all the districts in the State.

XXVIII. They shall go into operation from and after the 14th day of September inst.; but, until the first day of January next, no party shall be considered in default for non-compliance with them, if his attorney will certify that the cause was prepared and the paper-book made out before he had actual notice of them.

XXIX. The prothonotary of the western district is directed to send a copy of them to each of the other prothonotaries; and all prothonotaries are charged with the duty of printing and publishing them.

Independently of these rules, which in some respects vary the preexisting practice, the decisions may be classified as follows:—

I.—38

1. Within what time writ must issue.
2. Preliminary affidavit.
3. Form of writ.
4. To what proceedings error lies.
5. Parties to the writ.
6. Error to the federal Supreme Court.
7. Issuing of writ and bail in error.
8. *Supersedeas.*
9. Return of writ to Supreme Court.
10. Quashing writ by Supreme Court.
11. Abatement of writ.
12. Diminution of record.
13. Assignment of error, and what may be assigned.
14. Pleas in error.
15. Judgment in error, and herein of *venire facias de novo.*
16. *Remittitur* of record.
17. Costs in error.
18. Restitution.
19. Limitation as to new suit.
20. Error *coram vobis.*
21. Proceedings on *certiorari* to aldermen, &c.

1. *Within what time writ must issue.*

After final judgment has been entered, the unsuccessful party may bring a writ of error; and this suspends the execution until the former is determined. If execution has been issued and executed, the writ of error supersedes it on payment of costs, and restitution will be decreed, provided that the writ of error is issued, served, and bail entered within three weeks from the day of entering the judgment.(a)

It had been previously provided by the act of March, 1809, § 6,(b) in order that every party may have sufficient opportunity to take out a writ of error, that "no execution shall issue upon any judgment, on any special verdict, demurrer, or case stated, unless by leave of the court, in special cases for security of the demand, within three weeks from the day on which such judgment shall be pronounced.(c) Upon judgments on general verdicts, four days must elapse before execution can be sued out, which is the time, as has been seen,(d) within which a motion for a new trial, or in arrest of judgment, must be made, and during this time a writ of error ought to be taken, and bail given, else an execution may be issued and levied, and the defendant thus subjected to costs. It is not, however, to be implied from this that a writ of error, issued before execution actually taken out, although after the three weeks above mentioned, if bail be entered on it, is not a stay of the latter process, as in such case it undoubtedly would be. There the law, as it stood prior to the enactment above mentioned, would control the final process; that is to say, that so long as the execution was executable but not executed, the allowance of a writ of error would be a *supersedeas*, but not after-

(a) § 7, act of 16th June, 1836. Pamph. L. 762.
(b) 5 Sm. Laws, 17.
(c) The 6th section of the act of 16th June, 1836, Pamph. L. 762, was intended as a substitute; but by a clerical error in drafting, the bill has been rendered unintelligible.
(d) *Ante*, 525, 545.

wards.(e) Therefore, if in such case a levy be made under a *fieri facias*, a writ of error issued before the sale of the property is not a *supersedeas*.(f) Yet even here, if the case required it, the money levied by the execution would be retained in court till the event of the writ of error were known.(g) In the case of proceedings between landlord and tenant, in the Court of Common Pleas, a writ of error never operates as a *supersedeas*.(h)

But no judgment can be reversed unless the writ of error be obtained within seven years after the signing of the judgment, where the latter is only erroneous or irregular. But where it is a void judgment, error may be brought even afterwards,(i) and if infancy, coverture, imprisonment, insanity, or being beyond the limits of the United States, have prevented it, then within five years after the disability has ceased to exist.(j)

The time for taking out a writ of error, runs only from the time of the defendant having notice of the judgment.(k)

The proper course when a writ of error is too late is, not to quash the writ, but disregard the assignment of error.(l)

2. *Preliminary affidavit.*

The party purchasing the writ, who is called the plaintiff in error, must make oath or affirmation, to be filed with the record, that the same is not intended for delay.(m) By an act passed 11th of June, 1832,(n) this affidavit may be made by the party's agent or attorney; as the prothonotary of the court to whose judgment the writ is to be taken (thereafter called the court *below*) has nothing to do with expediting the writs of the Supreme Court, further than returning the record according to its mandate, the affidavit must necessarily be made before the prothonotary of the Supreme Court, or some officer having a general power to administer oaths.(o) In order to promote the convenience of parties residing at a distance from the office it is allowed to be made previously to the trial.(p) But if not filed until after the writ issues, and the record is returned, it is too late, and the writ may be quashed.(q) There is no distinction between administrators and others as regards the affidavit, for there is no reason why they should not swear that the writ of error was not prosecuted for delay.(r)

By the 4th section of the act of 22d March, 1817,(s) regulating suits against corporations, it is enacted "that in case of appeal, *certiorari*, or writ of error by any corporation, the oath or affirmation required by law, shall be made by the president or other chief officer of the corporation, or in his absence by the cashier, treasurer, or secretary."

Corporations are within the 3d section of the act of 11th June, 1832, allowing the affidavit required in the case of a writ of error to be made by an agent, and it does not require that the agent should be especially deputed.(t)

(e) Salk. 321, pl. 8. Willes, 271. S. C.; Barnes, 205.
(f) 9 Johns. 66, 17 ; Id. 34.
(g) Kirk v. Eaton; 10 S. & R. 108 ; Saund. 101. b.
(h) Grubb v. Fox, 6 Bin. 460.
(i) Brown v. Kelso's Executors, 2 Pa. R. 429.
(j) 3 Sm. Laws, 34.
(k) Camp v. Willis, 1 J. 206.

(l) Ibid.
(m) 5 Sm. Laws, 17.
(n) Pamph. L. 611.
(o) Pumroy v. Lewis, 1 Pa. R. 14.
(p) Creigh v. Wilson, 1 S. & R. 38.
(q) Beale v. Patterson, 6 S. & R. 89.
(r) Ibid.
(s) 6 Re. Laws, 438.
(t) Academy of Fine Arts v. Power, 2 H. 442.

The 3d section of the act of 11th June, 1832, allowing the affidavit in case of a writ of error, to be made by the party, his agent or attorney, enlarges, but does not repeal the 4th section of the act of 22d March, 1817, requiring the affidavit to be made by the president, or other chief officer, &c., of a corporation.(u)

3. *Form of writ.*

A writ of error, like an original writ, is sued either out of the court in which the judgment was given, or out of a superior court, by præcipe to the prothonotary, and is directed to the judges of the court in which the judgment was given,(v) commanding them, in the first case, themselves to examine the record; in the second, to send it to the court of appellate jurisdiction, to be examined, in order that some alleged error in the proceedings may be corrected. The first form of writ, called a writ of error *coram vobis*, is, where the alleged error consists of matter of *fact;* the second, called a writ of error, generally, where it consists of matter of *law.*(w) The object of this latter writ, therefore, being to correct errors in law, it cannot bring again into examination a mere matter of fact which has been passed upon by a jury in the court below;(x) except indirectly, in those cases in which the appellate court may award a *venire facias de novo:* and a writ of error, and not an appeal (as the word is applied to the practice of courts proceeding according to the course of the civil law), is the only mode of reviewing the decision of a court of record, proceeding according to the course of the common law.(y) By the act of May 22, 1772, § 9,(z) it is declared, that, "if any person or persons shall find him or themselves aggrieved with the judgment of any of the courts of general Quarter Sessions of the peace and jail delivery, or any other courts of record within this province, it shall be lawful to and for the party or parties aggrieved to have his or their writ or writs of error, which shall be granted them of course, in manner as other writs of error are to be granted, and made returnable to the Supreme Court." In a civil action, a writ of error is as much a writ of right and of course, as a summons in debt. It does not depend on any special *allocatur* as one to remove a judgment or an indictment; therefore, after appearance to a writ of error and argument commenced, the want of an *allocatur* is no objection.(a) The question whether a writ of error were properly sued out, or whether it lie in the particular case, belongs alone to the court in which it is returnable, on a motion made to quash it; or if it be too late for a motion, the court may quash it on their own motion, if they think injustice likely to be done.(aa)

4. *To what proceedings error lies.*(b)

For an error in law, a writ of error lies on every judgment of the District Court or Common Pleas (except on some particular judgments of the latter court, which will be noticed hereafter), from the Supreme Court, which is now the highest tribunal in the State. In the year

(u) Academy of Fine Arts v. Power, 2 H. 242.

(v) Fitzsimmons v. Salomon,2 Bin. 439.
(w) Steph. on Plead. 139.
(x) 1 Gallison, 14, 15, 18, 20, 21; 7 Cranch, 111.
(y) 1 Gallison, 5.

(z) 1 Sm. Laws, 138.
(a) Eckart v. Wilson, 10 S. & R. 44; Anderson's Executors v. Long, Id. 59.
(aa) Downing v. Baldwin, 1 S. & R. 298.
(b) See *post,* § 13, "Assignments of Error."

1791, a Court of Errors and Appeals was constituted, consisting of the presidents of the several Courts of Common Pleas, and justices of the Supreme Court, from which writs of error were directed to the latter court; but being found greatly to increase the expense and delay of litigation, without any equivalent benefit, it was suspended in 1806, as to sustaining any new cause, and after holding two terms for unfinished business, it was abolished, and its powers and duties were vested in the Supreme Court. So that no writ of error now lies from the final decision of the Supreme Court, except (in cases within its jurisdiction) to the Supreme Court of the United States. For an error in law, likewise, a *certiorari* lies from the Common Pleas on a judgment rendered by an alderman or justice of the peace, and as it only lies *after* his judgment, it is consequently in the nature of a writ of error, and will be briefly treated in the course of the present chapter.

Wherever a new jurisdiction is created by statute, and the court or judge that exercises this jurisdiction acts as a court or judge of record, according to the course of the common law, a writ of error lies on their judgment; but where they act in a summary way, or in a new course different from the common law, there a writ of error lies not, but a *certiorari*.(c) Thus, a *certiorari*, and not a writ of error, lies from the Supreme Court, to the judgment of the Court of Quarter Sessions, upon an appeal by supervisors of roads from a summary conviction by a justice of the peace, the proceedings in such cases not being according to the course of the common law.(d) A *certiorari* also lies from the former court to remove the proceedings before two aldermen or justices of the peace, under the act of the 6th April, 1802, to enable purchasers at sheriffs' and coroners' sales, to obtain possession.(e) In these cases, the Supreme Court has a concurrent jurisdiction with the Common Pleas; and a party has therefore his choice of jurisdictions: he may either remove by *certiorari* into the former court *per saltum*, or he may elect the inferior court.(f) If he remove the proceedings to the Common Pleas, a writ of error upon their judgment will lie from the Supreme Court;(g) and that is the proper remedy for the correction of errors in the Common Pleas. If, however, a *certiorari* has issued instead of a writ of error, and the record is actually certified, the writ will not be quashed after a delay of two terms.(h)

No writ of error can be brought but on a judgment, or on an award in nature of a judgment.(i) Thus, a judgment of *quod computet*, in an action of account render, being merely interlocutory, error will not lie on it.(j) And a writ of error was quashed where the judgment in the court below was entered *pro forma*, and without prejudice to either party, the court considering it no judgment, and not entitled to notice.(k) But an order of the Common Pleas, dismissing an appeal from a justice, is a judgment on which a writ of error lies;(l) because the

(c) 2 Bac. Abr. 456; 3 Bl. Com. 406; Ruhlman v. Com. 5 Bin. 24; Com. v. Beaumont, 4 R. 366; Baker v. Williamson, 2 Barr, 116.

(d) Ruhlman v. Com. 5 Bin. 24.

(e) Lenox v. McCall, 3 S. & R. 95.

(f) Snyder v. Bauchman, 8 S. & R. 340.

(g) Schuylkill Nav. Co. v. Thoburn, 7 S. & R. 418; Steeley v. Irvine, 6 Bin. 128.

(h) Cook v. Reinhart, 1 R. 321·

(i) Co. Litt. 288, b.; 6 East, 336; Com. v. Common Pleas of Philadelphia County, 3 Bin. 273; Davis v. Barr, 5 S. & R. 516.

(j) Beitler v. Zeigler, 1 Pa. R. 135.

(k) Kerr v. City of Pittsburg, 11 S. & R. 359.

(l) Com. v. Common Pleas of Philadelphia County, 3 Bin. 273.

dismissal of the appeal is in nature of a judgment, which, while it remains in force, prevents all further proceedings in the suit.(m) It is otherwise, however, when the order overrules a motion to strike off the appeal, because the case is still pending, and there is no final judgment.(n) But an order of court making an assignment of a judgment against a principal and bail, to the sureties of such principal, is the subject of a writ of error.(o) So a writ of error lies on an order of the court, lessening the amount of a judgment; for, though such order be no judgment, it has all the effects of one.(p) So, as we have seen,(q) a writ of error will lie in a case where judgment has been arrested. And error lies to an award of arbitrators under the act of 1810, upon which the judgment has become absolute by a failure to appeal within twenty days.(r)

There are many proceedings of an inferior court on which error is not maintainable.(rr) Thus it is not maintainable on a refusal by the court below to strike off an appeal from an award of arbitrators, no final judgment being entered;(s) nor upon a decision of the court below upon an issue of *nul tiel record*;(t) nor on a decision setting aside an award of referees, on exceptions founded both on law and fact, though the award was set aside exclusively upon the points of law;(u) nor to a judgment on an award under the compulsory arbitration act;(uu) nor to a refusal of the court to set aside a levy.(v)

Neither will error lie to the refusal of the court to open judgment.(vv) There are many cases in which writs of error do not lie from the decisions of the Common Pleas—such as granting or refusing a new trial, opening or refusing to open a judgment and motions of various kinds.(w) Neither is error maintainable upon the court's receiving or rejecting testimony on motions for summary relief,(x) such as motions to discharge on common bail, &c.; nor upon a judge or court's discharging a defendant on common bail, or a privileged person held to bail on a *capias*, nor upon moderating bail, and receiving the justification of bail, &c.,(y) nor upon staying proceedings in a bail-bond suit;(z) nor, as it would seem, upon ordering an *exoneretur* on the bail-piece.(a) And, in addition to these cases, it may be here stated, that "nothing, which is matter of pure discretion, is the subject of error: and when it is peculiarly the province of the court below to decide on a matter by exercising a sound discretion under all the circumstances of the case, a writ of error does not lie."(b) There are cases, too, in which the right to review a judgment on a writ of error is taken away by legis-

(m) Beale v. Dougherty, ibid. 436.
(n) Gardner v. Lefevre, 1 Pa. R. 73.
(o) Burns v. Huntingdon Bank, 1 Pa. R. 395.
(p) Court of Errors, Addis. 119, 121.
(q) *Ante*, "Arrest of Judgment."
(r) Frantz v. Kaser, 3 S. & R. 395.
(rr) See, generally, *post*, 618.
(s) Galbraith v. Fenton, 3 S. & R. 357.
(t) Taggart v. Cooper, 1 S. & R. 502.
(u) Gratz v. Phillips, 14 S. & R. 144; Kniseley v. Shenberger, 7 W. 194; Berg v. Moore, 7 Barr, 94.
(uu) LeBarron v. Harriott, 2 P. R. 154; Sullivan v. Weaver, 9 Barr, 223.

(v) Lewis v. Amor, 3 Barr, 460.
(vv) Kalbach v. Fisher, 1 R. 323; Allen v. Myers, 5 R. 335; Gratz v. Phillips, *ante*, 518.
(w) Ibid. Wakheiser v. Wakheiser, 6 W. & S. 184.
(x) Shrotz v. Quigley, 1 Bin. 222.
(y) Miller v. Spreeher, 2 Y. 162.
(z) Roop v. Meek, 6 S. & R. 542.
(a) McClurg v. Bowers, see 9 S. & R. 24.
(b) Renninger v. Thompson, 6 S. & R. 1 : see also Clymer v. Thomas, 7 S. & R. 180; Wh. Dig. "Error," ii. (c), *post*, 617, 8.

lative enactment; thus, error does not lie to the judgment of the Common Pleas, upon a *certiorari* to a justice of the peace, the act of March 20, 1810, having made their judgment final.(c) Neither does it lie in cases of divorce, the jurisdiction in such cases being vested in the Quarter Sessions or Common Pleas, and the mode of redress prescribed by that act being by appeal.(d) So, in actions of debt on forfeited recognizances, brought in the Common Pleas, where the judges have a power to moderate and remit according to equity and legal discretion, by the act of 1783,(e) no writ of error is given, an appeal only lying from their decision.(f) So a writ of error was held not to lie to remove a judgment in the Circuit Court to the Supreme Court, in any case in which the party might have had a remedy by appeal.(g) But an appeal might be taken in every case of demurrer, special verdict, case stated, point reserved, motion in arrest of judgment, or for a new trial, or to set aside a judgment, discontinuance, or *non pros.*, and it was, therefore, more extensively remedial than even the writ of error.(h) Error will not lie to a judgment upon a *habeas corpus.*(i) But, with the exception of these cases, a writ of error is a universal mean, in this State, to avoid the effect of a judgment.(j) It is to be observed, however, that the judgment must be a final judgment, that is, such a one as, if undisturbed, would preclude any further proceedings in the cause; and the reason of this rule is, that "there would be no end to suits, if they might be removed to the Superior Court on suggestion of error, in every stage of the proceedings."(k) This being the rule and its reason, it is obvious that a judgment *nisi* is final, though before the expiration of the four days, for the purposes of a writ of error. But in the case of error to an award of arbitrators upon which the judgment, as above intimated, does not become final until after the expiration of twenty days from the entry of the award, by failure to appeal; a writ of error cannot be delivered, and bail in error entered, until that time; and in computing the twenty days, either the day on which the report is filed, or the day on which the writ of error is filed in the court below, must be excluded.(l)

An agreement not to prosecute a writ of error, is binding upon the parties, and if any such agreement, either express or fairly to be implied, can be shown, it will be enforced by the court and the writ quashed.(m) The entry of security to obtain a stay of execution, is not, however, such a proceeding as will amount to a waiver of the party's right to a writ of error.(n)

(c) Cozens *v.* Dewees, 2 S. & R. 112; Johnson *v.* Hibbard, 3 Wh. 12; *sed vide* Clark *v.* Yeat, 4 Bin. 185.

(d) Miller *v.* Miller, 3 Bin. 30; *vide ante*, 24.

(e) 2 Sm. Laws, 82.

(f) Kellinger *v.* Reidenbauer, 6 S. & R. 545; *vide ante*, 24.

(g) Elliot *v.* Sanderson, 1 Pa. R. 74; Wike *v.* Lightner, 1 R. 290.

(h) Wike *v.* Lightner, 1 R. 290. We have seen, however, that Circuit Courts are now abolished.

(i) Elliot *v.* Sanderson, 1 Pa. R. 74.

(j) In a recent case in the Supreme

Court, it was contended that a writ of error did not lie upon a judgment on a *scire facias post annum et diem*, because it was only a derivatory suit; but the court, without noticing the point, reversed the judgment. Kirk *v.* Eaton, 10 S. & R. 105, 109.

(k) Lewis *v.* Wallick, 3 S. & R. 411; see also 1 Arch. Pr. 208.

(l) Frantz *v.* Kaser, 3 S. & R. 395.

(m) Com. *v.* Thum, 10 S. & R. 418; Cuncle *v.* Dripps, 3 Pa. R. 291. See *post*, 600.

(n) Ibid.

Where an act of assembly authorizes the Orphans' Court, *if they deem it expedient*, to appoint a trustee to make sale at once of certain real estate, held under a devise to sell on the happening of a contingency, the matter is discretionary with the court below, and not, it *would seem*, the subject of an appeal to the Supreme Court.(*o*)

Error lies on a summary conviction, which has been removed to the Court of Common Pleas, and decided by that tribunal.(*p*)

Error does not lie on an order to quash a foreign attachment, the affidavits, &c., on which the order was made, not being part of the record, though in fact sent up with it.(*q*)

The refusal of a court to direct an issue at the request of a party interested, on the distribution of the proceeds of an execution, is error.(*r*) But if there were no facts to submit on the issue, or their determination would not alter the result, the Supreme Court will not reverse.(*s*)

Error lies on an award of execution, that the question whether it was improvidently issued, may be determined.(*t*)

It is not the subject of a writ of error to refuse a stay of proceedings until payment of costs of a former suit; nor is the refusal to open a judgment or grant an issue because the former points had been decided in a former suit to which an appeal was taken.(*u*)

An appeal does not lie from an order of court appointing or refusing to appoint a sequestrator.(*v*)

The refusal to set aside a levy and all subsequent proceedings is not the subject of error.(*w*)

The Supreme Court cannot correct errors in an award of referees under the act of 1806, resting on facts extrinsic to the record; such as an adjournment to another place without consent, or negligence in not sealing up the award before giving it to the prothonotary, though the depositions and other evidence in the court below be sent up therewith.(*x*)

The refusal of the court below to make an order of subrogation, is not the subject of a writ of error. The application should be by bill or petition, and, if reviewed, it must be on an appeal.(*y*)

The Supreme Court will not disturb the liquidation by the prothonotary of the amount of a judgment obtained by default, under the 73d rule of the District Court of Alleghany County.(*z*)

A stipulation saving the rights of the defendant below, notwithstanding the entry of the judgment by consent, would enable him to maintain a writ of error;(*a*) but where the defendant below took a writ of error to a judgment entered on a judgment bond with the usual stipulation for the release of errors, the court, on motion of the plaintiff below, quashed the writ before the return day, it being manifest there was no error.(*b*)

(*o*) Anon. cited in Ervine's Appeal, 4 H. 267.

(*p*) Com. *v.* Cane, 2 Par. 265.

(*q*) Brown *v.* Ridgway, 10 Barr, 42.

(*r*) Reigart's Appeal, 7 W. & S. 267; Trimble's Appeal, 6 W. 138; Overholt's Appeal, 2 J. 224.

(*s*) Dougherty's Estate, 9 W. & S. 192; Dickerson's Appeal, 7 Barr, 250; Overholt's Appeal, 2 J. 224.

(*t*) Harger *v.* Commissioners, &c. 2 J. 251.

(*u*) Withers *v.* Haines, 2 Barr, 435.

(*v*) Lefever *v.* Witmer, 10 Barr, 505; Lancaster Bank *v.* Stouffer, ib. 398.

(*w*) Lewis *v.* Amar, 3 Barr, 461.

(*x*) Rogers *v.* Playford, 2 J. 181.

(*y*) Carpenter *v.* Koons, Sup. Ct. May, 1852.

(*z*) Hampton *v.* Matthews, 2 H. 105.

(*a*) Weidner *v.* Matthews, 1 J. 339. BELL, J. See *ante*, 599.

(*b*) Davis *v.* Hood, 1 H. 171.

Permission to file papers affecting the matter in issue, is error, if excepted to when offered, or when sanctioned by the charge of the court.(c)

A motion to set aside an original judgment, after *sci. fa.* issued, is not a ground of error. If the facts, on which the motion is made, are doubtful, it would be discretionary with the court to award an issue; but it would be rash to destroy the foundation of the *sci. fa.* by a summary inteference on the trial of an issue raised by the pleadings under it.(d)

5. *Parties to a writ of error.*

The writ of error is usually brought by the party or parties against whom the judgment was given; or it may be brought by a plaintiff to reverse his own judgment, if erroneous, in order to enable him to bring another action.(e) But the defendant is not allowed to bring it, contrary to his own agreement, or that of his attorney;(f) hence the utility of the agreement in most warrants of attorney to confess judgments, not to bring a writ of error.(g)

It is a general rule, that no person can bring a writ of error to reverse a judgment, who was not party or privy to the record, or prejudiced by the judgment, and therefore to receive advantage by the reversal of it. Third persons are not bound by the judgment.(h) An executor or administrator, however, may have a writ of error on a judgment against the testator or intestate;(i) and if an erroneous judgment be given against the ancestor, by which he loses the land, the heir may bring a writ of error.(j)

A writ of error can be sued only by one intrusted in the judgment sought to be recovered.(k)

In an ejectment removed into the Supreme Court by writ of error, a motion was made to quash the writ, because it was not sued out by the plaintiff in error. The facts were, that the writ of error was sued out by one of the landlords of the tenant; but the tenant, alone, was the defendant on record. He had taken no active part in the business, but had suffered his landlord to carry on the suit. This was proved by the attorney for the plaintiff in error. The landlord who sued out the writ of error, made the oath required by the act of assembly, and gave security on taking out the writ of error. Upon this evidence, TILGHMAN, C. J., was of opinion, that the writ of error was well taken out, as the landlord might be considered as the agent of the tenant. But YEATES, J., was of a contrary opinion. The court being divided, the counsel for the defendant in error took nothing by his motion.(l)

" The rule that there can be no severance of parties in personal actions applies to plaintiffs and not to defendants; and the same distinction prevails in writs of error in personal actions. Where the plaintiffs bring the writ of error, they must all join, and there can be no severance, because, as they have a joint right to the debt or damages, which they

(c) Hamilton *v.* Glenn, 1 Barr, 340; see 2 W. 401; *ante,* 509.

(d) McKinney *v.* Mehaffy, 7 W. & S. 277.

(e) 3 Burr. 1772.

(f) 2 T. R. 183; and see 1 T. R. 388; Smith *v.* Com. 14 S. & R. 69.

(g) *Ante,* 599, 600.

(h) 2 Saund. 45, n. 6, 101, e.; 1 W. C. C. R. 343.

(i) Com. Dig. Plead. 3 B. 9.

(j) 2 Bac. Abr. 457.

(k) Steel *v.* Bridenbach, 7 W. & S. 150.

(l) Vanhorn *v.* Fricke, 3 S. & R. 278.

are proceeding to recover, the release of one would bar them all, and, on the same principle, the dissent of one to the writ of error, shall bar the others from prosecuting it. But when the defendants bring the writ of error, the object is to discharge themselves from the judgment, and not to recover anything. There is, therefore, no joint right. If one defendant could prevent the other from bringing a writ of error, it would not only be a great hardship, but might be of most mischievous consequence; for the plaintiff, having a right to make any persons defendants whom he thinks proper, might by collusion introduce a defendant for the purpose of avoiding a writ of error."(*m*) But the writ of error must be brought in the names of all the defendants, provided they are all living, and aggrieved by the judgment; for, otherwise, this inconvenience would ensue, that every defendant might bring a writ of error by himself, and by that means delay the plaintiff from his execution for a long time, and from having any benefit of his judgment, though it might be affirmed once or oftener :(*n*) and if the writ of error be brought by one or more of the defendants only, it may be quashed;(*o*) or the court will give the plaintiff leave to take out execution.(*p*) But where judgment is given against several parties, and one or more of them dies, the writ of error may be brought by the survivors.(*q*) And in trespass against three, if there be judgment by default against two of them, and the third plead to issue, and it be found for him, the two only may bring a writ of error, for the party in whose favor the judgment was given cannot say that it was to his prejudice.(*r*) So, where there are five defendants, of whom three are acquitted, and verdict and judgment against the other two, it is evident that only those against whom judgment passes can have error.(*s*) For the same reason, where the plaintiff enters a *nolle prosequi* against one, and takes judgment against the others, he, against whom there was a *nolle prosequi*, shall not join in a writ of error.(*t*) Should any of the defendants refuse to join in the prosecution, they must be summoned to the Court of Error, and severed; after which, they never again can maintain a writ of error, but he who sued out the writ, may go on alone. It does not appear that the process of summons and severance has ever been used in the Supreme Court. It is probable that that court would proceed in a less formal and less expensive way, by laying a rule on those persons named as plaintiffs in the writ of error and not appearing, either to appear and join in the prosecution, or submit to be severed.(*u*)

By the act of 22d March, 1850,(*v*) § 2, "No act of the legislature of this commonwealth heretofore passed shall be so construed as to prevent either party in a cause from obtaining his, her, or their writ of error, and a decision by the Supreme Court thereon, as well after a decision by the said court on a writ of error previously obtained by the adverse party in such cause, as if both parties had obtained their respective writs returnable to the same term of the Supreme Court; and

(*m*) *Per* TILGHMAN, C. J., Gallagher *v.* Jackson, 1 S. & R. 493.

(*n*) 6 Rep. 25, S. C. Cro. Eliz. 648; 9 Carth. 8; 3 Burr. 1789; Fotterall *v.* Floyd, 6 S. & R. 320; 11 Wheat. 414.

(*o*) Ibid.

(*p*) Barnes, 262.

(*q*) Palm. 151; 1 Str. 234.

(*r*) 1 Str. 683.

(*s*) Fotterall *v.* Floyd, 6 S. & R. 320-1.

(*t*) Ibid.

(*u*) Ibid.

(*v*) Pamph. L. 230.

any writ of error heretofore taken under such circumstances and not yet acted on, shall entitle the plaintiff in error to a hearing and action of the Supreme Court thereon, as fully as if no former decision had been made on a previous writ of error obtained by the adverse party."(*vv*)

6. *Error to the federal Supreme Court.*

From an erroneous judgment of the Supreme Court of this State, a writ of error in certain cases lies to the Supreme Court of the United States. The third article of the constitution of the United States, § 1, declares that, "the judicial power of the United States shall be vested in one Supreme Court, and in such inferior courts as the Congress may from time to time ordain and establish." And by the same article, § 2, it is declared that, "the judicial power shall extend to all cases in law and equity arising under this consitution, the laws of the United States, and treaties made, or which shall be made under their authority." By the same article, original jurisdiction is given to the Supreme Court in all cases affecting ambassadors, other public ministers, and consuls, and those in which a State shall be a party; but in other cases, in which the Supreme Court has jurisdiction, it has appellate jurisdiction only, both as to law and fact, with such exceptions, and under such regulations as the Congress shall make.

By the judiciary act of September 24, 1789, § 25,(*w*) it is enacted, "that a final judgment or decree in any suit, in the highest court of law or equity of a State in which a decision in the suit could be had, where is drawn in question the validity of a treaty or statute of, or an authority exercised under, the United States, and the decision is against their validity; or where is drawn in question the validity of a statute of, or an authority exercised under, any State, on the ground of their being repugnant to the constitution, treaties, or laws of the United States, and the decision is in favor of such their validity; or where is drawn in question the construction of any clause of the constitution, or of a treaty, or statute of, or commission held under, the United States, and the decision is against the title, right, privilege or exemption, specially set up or claimed by either party, under such clause of the said constitution, treaty, statute, or commission, may be re-examined, and reversed or affirmed in the Supreme Court of the United States upon a writ of error." And further, "no error shall be assigned or regarded as a ground of reversal in any such case as aforesaid, than such as appears on the face of the record, and immediately respects the before-mentioned questions of validity or construction of the said constitution, treaties, statutes, commissions or authorities, in dispute."(*x*)

If the judgment of a State court be in favor of the privilege claimed under an act of Congress, the Supreme Court of the United States has no appellate jurisdiction;(*y*) and no writ of error lies to a State court, unless there is something apparent on the record bringing the case within the appellate jurisdiction of the Supreme Court.(*z*) But it is not required that the record should, in terms, state a misconstruction of an act of Congress, or that it was drawn into question; it is sufficient to give the Supreme Court of the United States jurisdiction of the cause, that the record should show that an act of Congress was applicable to

---

(*vv*) See for this head, discussed at large, *ante*, 206, 7.
(*w*) 2 Laws U. S. 65.

(*x*) See vol. i. 138, 139.
(*y*) 3 Cranch, 268.
(*z*) 2 Wheat. 363.

the case.(a) If the record does not continue in the highest court of the State, but has been removed to an inferior court, the Supreme Court of the United States is not deprived of its jurisdiction, and it may issue a writ of error directed to any State court in which the record may be found; thus, where a judgment of the Supreme Court of New York was affirmed in the Court of Errors, and the transcript of the record remitted to the Supreme Court, and the Court of Errors had returned to a writ of error from the Supreme Court of the United States, directed to them, that the transcript had been remitted, it was held that the Supreme Court of the United States might issue a writ of error to the Supreme Court of the State of New York to bring up the record.(b) It is only on the final judgment of the State court that a writ of error lies; and a judgment reversing that of an inferior court and awarding a *venire facias de novo*, is not a final judgment.(c)

     7. *Issuing of the writ and bail.*

The writ of error is made out, signed, and sealed by the prothonotary of the Supreme Court on filing a *præcipe* with him, which, after stating the names of the parties respectively as plaintiff and defendant in error, directs him to issue a writ of error to remove the record and proceedings in the particular court in which the judgment is obtained. The writ is directed to the judges of the court in which the judgment has been rendered, commanding them that, if judgment be rendered, then the record and process and all things touching the same, under their seal distinctly and openly they have before the justices of the Supreme Court on the next return day, together with the writ itself; that the record and process being inspected, they may further cause to be done what of right and according to the laws and customs ought. The allowance of one of the justices of the Supreme Court is also marked upon the writ, which is tested and made returnable like other writs issuing from the Supreme Court.

A special *allocatur* is still necessary in cases of *certiorari* to remove proceedings in the Quarter Sessions relating to opening roads in Philadelphia County, notwithstanding the act of 13th June, 1836, relating to Highways, Bridges, and Roads from Thomas's Creek.(d)

At common law no bail in error was required, so that the defendant by bringing a writ of error, might have delayed the plaintiff without giving any security for the prosecution of the writ, or payment of the debt or costs in case of an affirmance of the judgment.(e) To avoid unnecessary delays of execution, it was enacted by the statute, 3 Jac. I. c. 8 (made perpetual by 3 Car. I. c. 4, § 4, and reported to be in force in Pennsylvania),(f) that in all actions of debt upon " any single bond for debt, or upon any other obligation with condition for the payment of money only, or upon any action or bill of debt for rent, or upon any contract," the execution shall not be stayed by any writ of error, unless the party bringing the writ of error, together with two such sufficient sureties as the court shall approve of, shall first be bound by recognizance in double the sum recovered by the judgment, to prosecute the said writ of error with effect, and also to satisfy and pay the debt, damages, and costs, awarded by the former judgment, and also the

(a) 4 Wheat. 311.   (d) 3 Wh. 11.
(b) 3 Wheat. 303.   (e) 2 Tidd. 1074.
(c) Ibid. 433. See 206–7.   (f) Rob. Dig. 245.

costs and damages to be awarded for delaying of execution, if the said former judgment should be affirmed. It is material to observe that this statute extends to all judgments, as well by default on demurrer or on *nul tiel record*, as after verdict; all the other statutes on this subject relate to judgments after verdict only.(*g*)

By statute 13 Car. II. st. 2, c. 2, § 9,(*h*) bail in error is in like manner required, after verdict in actions on the case upon a promise for payment of money, in trover, covenant, detinue, and trespass, but it is provided by section eleven, that the act shall not extend to actions popular, actions upon penal statutes, or to indictments; and by statute 16 and 17 Car. II. c. 8, § 3 (made perpetual by 22 and 23 C. II. c. 4),(*i*) bail in error is now required after verdict in all personal actions whatsoever; provided, by the 5th section, that this act shall not extend to any writ of error brought by an executor or administrator, nor to any action popular, or upon a penal statute, nor to indictments. A *scire facias* against bail is a personal action within the meaning of this act.(*j*) Also, when a judgment is given against an executor *de bonis propriis*, it is not protected by the saving in the statute, but the executor must put in bail in error;(*k*) and where the judgment is *de bonis testatoris* and protected by the statute, yet, if the executor do put in bail, the court may take it, and the bail will be bound by it.(*l*) These statutes, it must be observed, extend only to cases where a writ of error is brought after verdict, and not after judgment by default, or judgment upon demurrer or *nul tiel record*.

In our practice, the plaintiff in error is now regulated by the 7th and 8th sections of the act of 16th June, 1836,(*m*) which provides that execution shall not be stayed upon any judgment in any civil action or proceeding, by reason of any writ of error from the Supreme Court to any other court of this commonwealth, unless the plaintiff in such writ, or some one in his behalf, with sufficient sureties, shall become bound by recognizance, to the party in whose favor such judgment shall be given, with condition to prosecute such writ of error with effect, and if the judgment be affirmed, or the writ of error be discontinued, or *non-prossed*, to pay the debt, damages, and costs (as the case may be) adjudged accruing upon such judgment and all other damages and costs that may be awarded upon such writ of error : § 7. *Provided*, that the preceding section shall not extend to any writ of error brought by any executor or administrator or by any guardian in behalf of his ward, or by any other person suing or defending in a representative character. § 8.

And when any corporation (municipal excepted) shall take a writ of error, the bail requisite in that case shall be taken absolute for the payment of debt, interest and costs on affirmance of the judgment.(*n*)

Corporations are like natural persons under the act of 1817 requiring bail in error; and any one may sue out the writ without bail if he chooses to let execution issue against him pending the writ.(*o*)

Bail in error may take an assignment of the judgment for costs in an

(*g*) See 1 Arch. Pr. 221, and the cases there cited.
   (*h*) Rob. Dig. 137.
   (*i*) Ibid. 41.
   (*j*) 2 W. Bl. 1227.

(*k*) 1 Sid. 368 ; 1 Lev. 245.
(*l*) 2 Str. 745 ; 2 L. Raym. 1459.
(*m*) Pamph. L. 762.
(*n*) Act of March 15, 1847.
(*o*) Savings *v.* Smith, 7 Barr, 241.

action of ejectment, and recover the same by an execution to indemnify themselves for the costs paid by them.(p)

A loose practice formerly prevailed to some extent as to the number of sureties on writs of error, which has been checked in Philadelphia County by a decision of the District Court, declaring a recognizance with less than *two* sureties, to be insufficient as a *supersedeas* ;(q) and it has been recently decided that if bail in error be not given, the judgment below may be revived by *scire facias*, notwithstanding the pendency of the writ of error.(r)

The second proviso of the foregoing section 8, directs that if the writ of error be issued, served, and bail be entered as aforesaid within three weeks from the day on which judgment shall be entered, the execution shall be stayed and superseded upon the payment of costs, although the service or execution thereof shall have begun, and if it shall have been fully executed, the defendant may have from the court which issued it a writ of restitution of the proceeds thereof, as the case may require. The recognizance is directed to be taken by the commissioners of bail when applied to within their respective counties. The prothonotary of the Supreme Court, and such other discreet person as the justices thereof shall nominate from time to time, are constituted commissioners of bail within the counties where they respectively reside, and are empowered to receive recognizances in the same manner as the judges of the Supreme Court, and for the same fees as formerly allowed by law.(s) Bail in error may also be entered into before any of the judges of the court from, or upon, whose judgment or decree the writ of error shall be taken, and shall be duly certified and transmitted with the record.(t) The authority of the Supreme Court to take bail on a writ of error is unquestionable. "The construction of this act has been that their power is concurrent with that of the Common Pleas. So that the recognizances are taken in the Supreme Court, or by the commissioners of bail, or by one of the judges of the Common Pleas of the proper county, as suits the convenience of the party."(u)

By section fifteen of rule sixth of the Supreme Court, the plaintiff's attorney may, within twenty days after notice of the taking of the bail in error, except to the sufficiency thereof, when the defendant must either put in new bail or the old bail must justify within ten days after exception taken, in default whereof, the prothonotary shall *non pros.* such writ. The prothonotary is, by act of assembly, commissioner of bail, and a justification before him within ten days is esteemed sufficient; otherwise, the party would be unable to justify in case the court did not sit during the ten days mentioned in the rule. If the court should be sitting, it would, however, be more prudent to justify in court. If the writ is taken without offering bail, or if the recognizance is irregular, the writ will not operate as·a *supersedeas*, and the plaintiff suffers no delay of execution.(v) The cause.is, nevertheless, well removed. But if the plaintiff has been delayed by the entering of insufficient bail, such conduct deserves some punishment, and that is the reason why the rule of court above stated directs a *non pros.* to be entered in such cases.(w)

(p) Bank v. Harper, 8 Barr, 249.
(q) 1 M. 386.
(r) Boyer v. Rees, 4 W. 205.
(s) ¿ 8, Act of 1786; 2 Sm. Laws, 393.
(t) ¿ 7, Act March, 1809; 5 Sm. L. 17.

(u) Per Duncan, J., Smith v. Ramsay, 6 S. & R. 574.
(v) Boyer v. Rees, 4 W. 205.
(w) Taggart v. Cooper, 3 Bin. 34.

It is the duty of the appellee, dissatisfied with the recognizance, to rule the appellant to perfect his bail, within a prescribed period, or in default thereof, to suffer a dismissal of his appeal.(x)

If bail in error be not perfected within ten days after exception, the writ of error may be *non-prossed*.(y)

The provisions for an oath and recognizance of bail being intended for the benefit of the suitor whose cause is delayed by a writ of error, may be waived by him, both expressly and impliedly, as in the latter case, by coming in and acting in the court of error; or, by delaying, to take the objection for an unreasonable length of time. Such objections ought to be taken at a preliminary stage, in the same manner as pleas in abatement, before the defendant in error has done any act admitting the writ to be in court.(z)

Amendments in the recognizance will sometimes be permitted, such as by adding the name of cognizor and altering that of the cognizee.(a)

Bail in error cannot discharge themselves by surrendering the plaintiff in error, and consequently are not entitled to relief, if their principal should become insolvent, pending the writ of error.(b)

8. *Supersedeas.*

After final judgment, and before execution executed, a writ of error by the English practice is, generally speaking, a *supersedeas* of execution from the time of its allowance; provided bail be put in and perfected in due time,(c) although no notice of the allowance be given to the opposite party.(d) With us the writ takes effect, not from the time of its issuing, which is immaterial, but from its delivery to the prothonotary of the court below. Therefore, where an award of arbitrators was filed on the 2d of April, the writ of error issued on the 11th, the recognizance of bail was taken on the 22d, and the writ of error filed in the prothonotary's office of the court below on the 5th May ensuing, the writ was supported, upon a motion made to quash it on the ground that no writ could be issued within twenty days after the award, and that the bail was also too soon.(e)

It is an established principle, that a second writ of error is not a *supersedeas* of execution, although bail has been given, if the first writ abated by the act of the party as by *non pros.*, otherwise a party might baffle his antagonist interminably.(f) It is otherwise where it abates by the act of God.(g)

A writ of error is a *supersedeas* at common law, but its operation *per se* is restrained by the 3 Jac. 1, c. 8; 13 Car. 2, St. 2, c. 2, and 16 & 17 Car. 2, c. 8, which require bail to be superadded, to prevent execution, in most cases, without application to the court. These statutes are enforced here, and, indeed, all our law is identical with the English, as it stood at the Declaration of Independence, except the act of 1834, which makes a writ of error with bail and service in three weeks from the date of the judgment a *supersedeas* even of an execution executed.(h)

(x) Weidner v. Matthews, 1 J. 339. BELL, J.

(y) Campbell v. Gregg, Bright. R. 440.

(z) Heckert's Appeal, 13 S. & R. 104, 105, 106.

(a) Welsh v. Vanbebber, 4 Y. 559.

(b) 1 T. R. 624.

(c) Tidd, 1172–3; Bing. on Ex'ns, 265.

(d) 5 Taunt. 204.

(e) 3 S. & R. 395.

(f) Sheerer v. Grier, 3 Wh. 14.

(g) Id.

(h) Id.

The writ is a *supersedeas* if served at any time before execution is levied.(*i*)

When there has been a *fi. fa.* and condemnation, and a *vend. ex.* but no sale, a writ of error is not a *supersedeas*.(*j*)

(*i*) Patterson *v.* Juvenal, D. C., Dec. 9, 1848. Why the *fi. fa.* should not be set aside. *Per curiam.* A writ of error was issued in this case on the 6th Oct., and bail in error given. On the 9th Oct. it was filed in the office. On the same day a *fi. fa.* was issued. Whether it was placed in the sheriff's hands before or after the writ of error was lodged in the office, does not appear, nor do we consider it material. On the 24th Nov. notice was given to defendant that the sheriff had levied on his real estate, when the present rule was taken.

This court has decided, in Bryan *v.* Comly (2 M. 271), and Adams *v.* Hindman (4 M. 464), that a writ of error, on which bail has been duly entered and served at any time before execution issued, or if issued before it is *executed* (which, it is said in the case of a *fi. fa.*, is so considered if *levied*), is a *supersedeas*. It is argued, however, in this case, that, as the judgment was a lien, the delivery to the sheriff is to be considered as *ipso facto* as a levy on real estate. And the case of Wood *v.* Calvin (5 Hill, 228), is cited to that effect. However it may be in the State of New York, it is clear that it cannot be so considered in Pennsylvania; for, by the 43d section of the act of 13th June, 1836 (Purd, 447), it is provided that, "If sufficient personal estate cannot be found by such officer, he shall proceed to levy upon the defendant's real estate, or such part thereof as he may deem sufficient to pay the sum to be levied." It is evident that no levy had been made at the time the writ of error in this case was lodged in the office; for on the 4th Nov. a rule was applied "to grant the sheriff four weeks to levy on real estate," which, though inartificially worded, was evidently intended and allowed as an enlargement of the time of making his return to enable him to make a levy on real estate.   R. A.

(*j*) Bozarth *v.* Marshall, D. C. C. P., Saturday, March 22, 1851. *Per curiam.* The question presented on this matter is, whether, where there has been a *fieri facias* and condemnation, and a *venditioni expon.*, but no sale, a writ of error is a *supersedeas*. The case of Roberts *v.* Springer, formerly decided by this court, is not at all to the point. There the writ of error was brought into the office before the pluries *fi. fa.* upon

which the condemnation was, had issued, there having been a *fi. fa.* previously upon which there had been a levy on personal property, a claim by a third person, levy withdrawn, and the writ returned *nulla bona*.

All that the court decided was, that a *fi. fa.* returned *nulla bona*, and an alias *fi. fa.* returned *stayed*, did not hinder the *supersedeas* of a writ of error. The general rule of law upon this subject, as laid down in the text-books, is, that an execution being an entire thing, cannot be superseded after it is once begun. The difficulty seems to be, whether the *vend. expo.* is to be considered as a separate and distinct execution from the *fi. fa.* The *fi. fa.*, in this case, has certainly been executed, but nothing has been done under the *vend. expo.*

The English cases settle the matter so far as relates to a levy on personal property, and there is no reason for making a distinction as to a levy and condemnation of real estate. In Cro. Eliz. 597, Charter *v.* Porter, a *fi. fa.* was awarded, by virtue of which the sheriff took the defendant's goods, and before sale the record was removed into the Exchequer Chamber by writ of error, and a *supersedeas* awarded; the sheriff returned a seizure of the goods, and that they remained in his hands *pro defectu empronum;* a restitution was prayed, but denied; and it was holden, *per totam curiam,* that as the plaintiff had begun the execution, he must complete it as far as he had gone, and a *venditioni expo.* was awarded to perfect it. In Yelv. 6, French *v.* Henryman, a writ of error, and *supersedeas* to the sheriff after a *fi. fa.*, he shall proceed to the sale of the goods which he has before the *supersedeas*, but shall levy no more, *per totam curiam.* In Vent. 255, Baker *v.* Balstrode, it was held that, if before the writ of error, the sheriff returns, *fieri feci et non inveni emptores,* the execution is not to be undone. These cases, and others, are cited and relied on in Mereton *v.* Stevens, Willis, 271. It is true, there is a reason given for this by Lord Mansfield, in Copper *v.* Chitty (1 Sir W. Bl. Rep. 69), that goods being of a perishable nature, cannot wait the determination of the suit, which may be thought inapplicable to the case of a levy on real estate. But that reason is not given in any other case—but they are all put upon the foot-

9. *Return of writ to Supreme Court.*

When the writ of error is allowed and filed with the prothonotary of the court by which the judgment was rendered, he returns it to the prothonotary of the Supreme Court, together with the whole record, including the original *præcipe*, which constitutes a portion of it. With us, the entire record is uniformly in the custody of the prothonotary of each court, and not in the keeping of the judges.(*k*) It is the duty of the plaintiff in error to see that the record is returned in due time. And if he makes default, the defendant in error may, after the return day, move for a rule upon him to return the record on or before a certain day, or *non-pros.* ; a reasonable time (usually four days) is allowed for this purpose. In order more effectually to expedite the decision of causes in the Supreme Court, the prothonotary is directed, by rule of March, 1833, to enter a *non-pros.*, according to the rule in all cases of writs of error where the record is not returned on or before the first return day of the second term after the *teste* of the writ : which *non-pros.* shall not be taken off by consent of parties. July is, however, not considered a term within this rule. When the writ is returned, but not before,(*l*) the plaintiff in error may move to amend, or the defendant in error to quash, or *non-pros.* the writ ; or it may abate, or be discontinued.(*m*)

Formerly, great certainty was required in making the writ agree with the record, nor could any defects therein be amended before the 5 Geo. I. c. 13, reported to be in force in Pennsylvania,(*n*) because, by the former statutes of amendment, the judges were only enabled to amend in affirmance of the judgment.(*o*) Upon this statute, it has become the practice to amend the writ of error, as a matter of course, without costs.(*p*) And it has been amended by striking out the name of one of the plaintiffs in error.(*q*) In the latter case, however, the recognizance of bail in error must also be amended.(*r*) But where a writ of error was returnable before the giving of the judgment on which it was brought, this was held to be such a fault as was not amendable under the statute.(*s*)

10. *Quashing writ.*

The general ground of quashing a writ of error is some fault or defect therein not amendable by the above statute. It would not be dismissed, because it was not returned to the term to which it was made returnable, because, by long-established practice, returns to writs of error have

ing that an execution is an entire indivisible thing, and perishable, or not, the goods may be delivered to the defendant. The true practical reason is that which demands of one who asks to delay a party having a regular judgment in his favor, the utmost diligence ; and if he delays so far that a seizure is made under the plaintiff's execution, it shall be carried on to perfection. Another reason is the costs. If the writ of error is a *supersedeas*, we have no power of imposing any terms as to costs ; and the case of an execution carried so far as this, is an item of some importance in the determination of the question. There

is no evidence before us in regard to want of notice of the levy and condemnation. R. D.

(*k*) 2 Bin. 439.
(*l*) 1 Caines's Rep. 251.
(*m*) If a plaintiff withdraws his writ, and has an entry of withdrawal made on the docket, is it not a *retraxit* which bars another writ? 1 Pa. R. 114.
(*n*) Rob. Dig. 48.
(*o*) 2 Bac. Abr. 463.
(*p*) Str. 863, 902.
(*q*) Ib. 683, 892 ; Cowp. 425.
(*r*) 2 W. Bl. 1067 ; see 5 Taunt. 86.
(*s*) Str. 807, 891 ; and see 1 Arch. Pr. 214, 215 ; 2 Dunl. Pr. 1142.

been received after the time to which they were returnable ;(*t*) and where it is returned in the usual form, the court will presume that it was presented during the sitting of the court to which it was directed, and by them properly returned.(*u*) We have seen,(*v*) that the writ will not be quashed, because, the oath that the writ was not intended for delay, was made *before* the trial, not because the recognizance of bail is irregular or void. After the defendant in error has pleaded *in nullo est erratum*, and issue joined, a motion to quash the writ is irregular ; still, the court would quash it of their own accord, if injustice were likely to be done.(*w*) Nor will the writ be quashed because a blank has been left in it for the month in which the court is to be held : it is a mere clerical error, which is amendable by the court.(*x*) But where the court below struck off an appeal from an award of arbitrators, and three days afterwards reinstated it, the writ was quashed, as it appeared that the action was depending in the Court of Common Pleas.(*y*) And where a plaintiff had received the amount of his judgment from the defendant, and afterwards took a writ of error, the writ was quashed.(*z*)

Where there is no jurisdiction, the writ will be quashed. Thus, the act of 20th March, 1810, declares, that judgment on *certiorari* to an alderman shall be final, and that no writ of error shall issue thereon, and a writ issued to any such judgment will be quashed.(*a*)

Where the record is legally removed, the proper course, where the writ has been taken out of time, is not to quash it, but to disregard the assignment of errors, and affirm the judgment.(*b*)

11. *Abatement of writ.*

The writ abates by the death of the plaintiff in error, or of any one of the plaintiffs, before errors assigned.(*c*) And the defendant may thereupon sue out a *scire facias quare executionem non*, to revive the judgment against the executors or administrators of the plaintiff in error ; but if the plaintiff die after errors assigned, it does not abate the writ. In such case, the defendant having joined in error, may proceed to get the judgment affirmed, if not erroneous ; but must then revive it against the representatives of the plaintiff in error.(*cc*) And in no case does the writ abate by the death of the defendant in error ; the action

(*t*) Res. *v.* Carmalt, 4 Y. 418.
(*u*) Ibid.
(*v*) *Ante*, 594, 605–6.
(*w*) Lessee of Todd *v.* Ockerman, 1 S. & R. 299.
(*x*) 5 S. & R. 352.
(*y*) Straub *v.* Smith, 2 S. & R. 382.
(*z*) Laughlin *v.* Peebles, 1 Pa. R. 114.
(*a*) Johnson *v.* Hibbard, 3 Wh. 12; see 4 Bin. 185 ; 2 S. & R. 112.
(*b*) Camp *v.* Welles, 1 J. 206.
(*c*) 3 S. & R. 271, referring to 2 Saund. 101, *n.*; 2 Tidd. 1097. Formerly, in England, the death of one of the plaintiffs in error abated the writ. But latterly it has been held under the statute 8 & 9 W. III. c. 11, ₰ 7, reported to be in force in Pennsylvania, Rob. Dig. 142, by which, on suggesting the death of a joint plaintiff or defendant, where the

cause of action survives, the writ or action shall not abate, but the action shall proceed, that on the death of one of several plaintiffs in error the writ of error does not abate : 1 Barn. & Ald. 586 ; and in a recent case, where the court below reversed the judgment obtained by husband and wife for slander of the wife, for which they sued out a writ of error, the Supreme Court abated the writ because she died after it issued. But if she had died after the judgment had been given for her husband and her, it would have been different. The judgment would then have survived to the husband. Eakin *v.* Raub, 12 S. & R. 76.
(*cc*) 2 Crompt. Pr. 401–2 ; 2 Barnes, 206 ; see 6 Wheaton, 260.

is proceeded in as if he were alive, till judgment be affirmed, which is then revived by *scire facias;* execution cannot, however, issue pending the writ of error.(*d*) The writ of *scire facias ad audiendum errores* not being in use in Pennsylvania, the plaintiff in error may proceed by rule on the defendant to plead to a general assignment of errors,(*e*) and hence it would seem, that the representatives of a deceased defendant might in the same mode be compelled to join in error.(*f*) If there are several defendants, one of whom dies, his death being suggested on the record, the writ proceeds against the survivors.(*g*) A writ of error may abate by the act of the party, as where it is brought by a feme sole, who afterwards marries, the writ abates *by her marriage,* and the court will give the defendant leave to take out execution, though she and her husband have brought a second writ of error.(*h*)

12. *Diminution of record.*

Where the whole of the record is not certified by the court below upon the writ of error, the plaintiff may *allege diminution* of the record, and pray a *certiorari* to the court below to bring up the part of the record which is wanting.(*i*) But it is a rule that a man cannot allege diminution contrary to the record which is certified.(*j*) The *certiorari* is a judicial writ issuing out of the court where the writ of error is depending, directed commonly to the judges of the court below, but may by consent be directed to the president alone.(*k*) The Supreme Court will not decide whether certain matters ought or ought not to be returned and certified as part of the record, but will leave it to the court below to determine whether the record contains the whole matter ;(*l*) and when it appears by their return that the whole record has been certified, a second *certiorari* upon a similar suggestion will not be granted.(*m*) No paper not attached to the record by the court below, shall be considered part of the record, even by consent; nor shall it, in any event, be used as such, except when certified by the court below, in pursuance of a writ of *certiorari.*(*n*) By the English practice, it is too late to allege a diminution or pray a *certiorari* after *in nullo est erratum* pleaded, without leave of the court.(*o*) With us the *certiorari* has been granted, upon the application of the plaintiff in error after issue joined and diminution alleged.(*p*) A *certiorari*, upon a suggestion of diminution in the record, may be made by the clerk, and need not be made by the judge of the court below.(*q*)

When any writ or return is lost, the docket-entry is the next best proof of its former existence, and, as far as it goes, of its contents; and after a former writ of error and decision on all points to which there was any objection, it will be assumed that the parts of the record then not objected to were regular and legal, and the Supreme Court will not reverse, when lost, on a supposition that they were defective.(*r*)

(*d*) Yelv. 112–13; Salk. 264,*pl.* 6; see 1 Arch. Pr. 216 ; see 6 Wheaton, 260.

(*e*) Comm. *v.* Emery, 2 Bin. 257.

(*f*) See Beard *v.* Deitz, 1 W. 309.

(*g*) 2 Saund. 100, *o.* ; 2 Dunl. Pr. 1144.

(*h*) 2 Str. 880, 1015 ; see 2 Saund. 101, *o.*

(*i*) 2 Bin. 436; 2 Bac. Abr. 468; see 8 S. & R. 10; 2 Tidd, 1109.

(*j*) 1 Rol. Abr. 764 ; 2 Tidd, 1104.

(*k*) See Comm. *v.* Cochran, 1 S. & R. 472.

(*l*) Ibid.

(*m*) Ibid.

(*n*) Rules S. C., March, 1828.

(*o*) 2 Crompt. Pr. 362.

(*p*) 2 Bin. 436.

(*q*) 9 Wheaton, 526.

(*r*) Jones *v.* Hartly, 3 W. 190.

13. *Assignment of error, and what may be assigned.*

If the writ of error be not quashed or abated, the plaintiff in error should, after the record is certified, forthwith proceed to assign his errors. The mode of obliging the plaintiff to assign errors is not, agreeably to the English practice, by issuing a *scire facias quare executionem non;* but, by a rule of the Supreme Court, his counsel is bound to make a written specification of the particular errors which he assigns, and on which he intends to rely, and to file the same in the prothonotary's office on or before the third day of the term to which the writ is returnable, and on the failure to do so the court may *non-pros.* the writ.(*s*) In strictness, the court cannot notice an error which has not been assigned, because its rule has not been complied with by such an omission. Nevertheless, the court always reserves to itself the right to correct an error which stares them in the face, when they think the justice of the case requires it.(*t*) If, from oversight, a material matter has been omitted in the specification, the court will permit it to be added to prevent injustice : but never on mere formal objections.(*u*)

An assignment of errors is in the nature of a declaration,(*v*) and is either of errors in fact, or errors in law. The former consist of matters of fact, not appearing on the face of the record, which, if true, prove the record to have been erroneous, as that the defendant in the original action being under age, appeared by attorney. A judgment (except in a real action) against an infant may be reversed after *full age,* and the fact must be tried *per pais,* and not by inspection.(*w*) And if *in nullo est erratum* is pleaded, the fact of infancy is thereby admitted.(*x*) The judgment is also erroneous if it appear that a feme plaintiff or defendant was under coverture at the time of commencing the action, or that a sole plaintiff or defendant died before verdict or interlocutory judgment.(*y*) By a late decision of the Supreme Court it would seem, however, that an exception, which depends on matter of fact, will not be recognized. They, therefore, refused to set aside an execution because it issued for illegal costs. The court below should be applied to in the first instance to tax the costs.(*z*)

Irregularities in the conduct of the jury in the court below being subjects entirely within its discretion, are not examinable upon a writ of error.(*a*) It cannot be assigned for error that the adverse party has renounced a matter agreed on for his own benefit;(*b*) and it is a general principle that a person shall not assign that for error, from which he has suffered no injury ;(*c*) nor is it error that the court below permitted evidence to be given in an early stage, which might properly have been reserved as rebutting evidence ;(*d*) nor that evidence was rejected by the court, not because it was incompetent, but because it was offered at an improper time ;(*e*) nor that a mistake was committed by the court during

---

(*s*) Rules, March 28, 1828.
(*t*) Anderson's Executors *v.* Long, 10 S. & R. 55; Berry *v.* Vantries, 12 Ibid. 89.
(*u*) Shenck *v.* Mingle, 13 S. & R. 32; Galbraith *v.* Green, 85; see Rules of Court, 6 S. & R. 600.
(*v*) 2 Bac. Ab. 485.
(*w*) Silver *v.* Shelbach, 1 D. 166.
(*x*) Moore *v.* McEwen, 5 S. & R. 373.

(*y*) Tidd, 1201.
(*z*) Shuman *v.* Pfruty, 1 Pa. R. 61.
(*a*) 1 Peters's Rep. 159.
(*b*) Prevost *v.* Nichols, 4 Y. 479.
(*c*) Allen *v.* Rostain, 11 S. & R. 373.
(*d*) Salmon *v.* Rance, 3 S. & R. 314; see Leagure *v.* Hillegas, 7 S. & R. 323.
(*e*) Irish *v.* Smith, 8 S. & R. 573; Frederick *v.* Gray, 10 S. & R. 182.

a preliminary and irrelevant examination of a witness on his *voire dire;*(*f*) so it is no cause for the reversal of a judgment that an error was committed in the trial of an immaterial part of an issue;(*g*) nor that incompetent testimony was admitted when the fact it was adduced to prove is afterwards established by other conclusive evidence;(*h*) nor that the court treated that as legal evidence which was illegal, but which was given without objection;(*i*) nor that material parts of the charge of the court below were dictated and drawn up by the counsel of one of the parties.(*j*) A judgment will not be reversed except for error apparent on the record, and if any presumption be admitted, it will rather be to support than reverse it.(*k*)

A party cannot, on error, complain of the court's opinion which is favorable to him;(*l*) or if a direction is given by the court as favorable to him as he had desired;(*m*) or of an answer to an abstract question.(*n*) If the party desire an answer as connected with the facts, he must embody them in his proposition, otherwise an abstract answer suffices.(*o*) It is the duty of the court to answer fully the points on which they are requested to charge, though not in the precise words of the proposition, nor to every repetition of it; one full answer is enough.(*p*) If the counsel ask a question of the court which is answered, they cannot afterwards complain that the court charged on matter of fact.(*q*) Nor will a judgment be reversed for an erroneous expression of the court's opinion on matter of fact, unless it appear clearly that the jury were thereby precluded from deciding for themselves.(*r*) Nor for an omission to instruct the jury on a point which the verdict has rendered immaterial.(*s*) Nor if illegal evidence be given without objection is it error for the court to consider it in their charge to the jury.(*t*) Whereever the admission of evidence is excepted to, the plaintiff in error must show, in his bill of exceptions, what the evidence was, otherwise the exceptions to it will be considered as waived.(*u*)

Errors in law are common or special. The common errors are, that the declaration is insufficient in law to maintain the action, and that judgment was given for the plaintiff instead of the defendant, or *vice versa.* Special errors are the want of an original writ, or warrant of attorney, or other matter appearing on the face of the record, which

---

(*f*) Brown *v.* Downing, 4 S. & R. 494.

(*g*) Edgar *v.* Boies, 11 S. & R. 445.

(*h*) Wolverton *v.* Com. 7 S. & R. 273.

(*i*) McCullough *v.* Wallace, 8 S. & R. 181.

(*j*) Selin *v.* Snyder, 11 S. & R. 324.

(*k*) Munderbach *v.* Lutz's Administrators, 14 S. & R. 220.

(*l*) Collins *v.* Rush, 7 S. & R. 147.

(*m*) Hubley *v.* Vanhorn, ibid. 185; Williams *v.* Carr, 1 Rawle, 420.

(*n*) Brown *v.* Caldwell, 10 S. & R. 114. The judge may refuse to declare the law to the jury on a mere abstract or hypothetical question propounded by the counsel, and not warranted by the evidence in the cause; yet, if he proceed to state the law upon such question, and states it erroneously, his opinion may be revised in the court above, and if it be such as may have had an influence on the jury, their verdict will be set aside. 11 Wheat. 59, 75. Where the party propounding the question is dissatisfied with the refusal of the court to answer it, he may except to the refusal, which exception will avail him, if he shows that the question was warranted by the testimony, and that the opinion he asked for ought to have been given. Id. ibid.

(*o*) Kleintobb *v.* Trescott, 4 W. 301.

(*p*) Geiger *v.* Welsh, 1 R. 349.

(*q*) McIlvaine *v.* McIlvaine, 6 S. & R. 559; Williams *v.* Carr, 1 R. 420.

(*r*) Riddle *v.* Murphy, 7 S. & R. 230.

(*s*) Munderbach *v.* Lutz's Administrators, 14 S. & R. 220.

(*t*) Scott *v.* Sheakly, 3 W. 50.

(*u*) Snowden *v.* Warder, 3 R. 101.

shows the judgment to have been erroneous.(v) The plaintiff may assign several errors in law, but only one error in fact;(w) and he cannot assign error in fact, and in law together, for these are distinct things, and require different trials; or anything which contradicts the record; or was for the advantage of the party assigning it;(x) or that was aided by appearance, or by not being taken advantage of in due time.(y) Thus the defendant cannot take advantage of the omission of the prothonotary's name to the process, if it is under seal, after appearing and pleading to issue.(z) This defect in process is also made good, by the act of 1806.(a) A plaintiff may assign for error the want of jurisdiction in a court of limited jurisdiction, to which he has chosen to resort.(b)

The plaintiff in error may show as a ground for reversing the judgment any substantial defect or error in the course of the proceedings, either not cured by the common law or by statute, or not waived by the party appearing on the record(c) or bill of exceptions annexed to it; as well as any incorrect decision of the court below on the mere right of the parties, as presented by the pleadings, special verdict, bill of exceptions, or opinion filed. Many defects in the proceedings, which are ground of error, have been noticed in the course of this work; but it would be impossible to enumerate the various other matters on which a writ of error may be founded, since there can be no question of law arising in a cause independent of the form and manner of proceeding, which may not be submitted to the appellate court after the decision of the inferior tribunal, if the party can in any way introduce it as part of the record.(d)

The death of a defendant between verdict and judgment, if not more than two terms intervene, cannot be assigned for error,(e) and where between the verdict and a motion for a new trial, the defendant having died, the motion for a new trial was overruled, and judgment entered after his death, but before its suggestion on record, it was *held* that this could not be assigned for error.(f)

An assignment of error that judgment is entered on all the counts, some of which are bad, is insufficient; the defective counts must be pointed out.(g)

At common law, the court will take notice of an error apparent on the face of the record, though no exception be taken in the subordinate tribunal.(h)

On a writ of error taken by the plaintiff, the court will not, on the application of the defendant, notice a collateral error, said to have been committed against the defendant, to which exception was not at the time taken.(i)

The court below having entered judgment for the plaintiff on the

(v) Tidd, 1202.
(w) F. N. B. 20.
(x) 2 Bac. Ab. 487–8–9, 490.
(y) Ibid. 492.
(z) Benjamin v. Armstrong, 2 S. & R. 392.
(a) 4 Sm. Laws, 329.
(b) 2 Cranch, 126.
(c) See Brac. L. M. 199, 530.

(d) 2 Dunl. Pr. 1150. *Vide supra*, 433, as to what cannot be alleged for error.
(e) Chase v. Hodges, 2 Barr, 48.
(f) M'Adam v. Stilwell, 1 H. 90.
(g) M'Kelvy v. Wilson, 9 Barr, 183.
(h) Meese v. Levis, 3 H. 386. BELL, J.
(i) Jackson v. Bank U. S. 10 Barr, 61.

plea of *nul tiel record*, the case went to trial on an issue of fact, on which there was a judgment for defendant. A writ of error being taken out by the plaintiff, it was *held*, that the defendant could not bring before the Supreme Court an alleged error by the court below, in entering the judgment on the plea of *nul tiel record*, for the plaintiff.(*j*)

The rule that the Supreme Court will reverse a judgment for the plaintiff, where it appears from the record that he has no cause of action, though the point may not have been taken below, or assigned for error, does not apply where, had the objection been taken at the proper time, the plaintiff might have been able to answer it.(*k*)

When the objection taken is general, error does not lie if the evidence or witness was admissible for any purpose.(*l*)

A court of error confines itself in the examination of evidence to the grounds of exception taken at the trial of the cause, as set forth in the bill of exceptions; therefore, where a question by counsel as to declarations of a person was objected to as irrelevant, the court will not inquire whether he was interested or dead.(*m*)

An assignment that the court erred in their charge to the jury generally, without any specification, will not be noticed in the Supreme Court.(*n*)

The Supreme Court will not permit an assignment of error in matters of substance, to be defeated by a mere want of formality; but will, if necessary, allow the party to amend.(*o*)

In considering exceptions to evidence, it is always to be taken into view for what purpose, and to prove what fact it was offered.(*p*) "The order of evidence," says Judge ROGERS, "is necessarily a matter resting in sound discretion. It is so peculiarly the province of the court which tries the issue, that we would not undertake to interfere with it, unless in an extreme case. They alone can determine when the justice of the case requires a relaxation of the general rules, by which the introduction of evidence is regulated."(*q*) As a general rule, therefore, a party must bring forward the several parts of his case in their order; and although the court has power to relax the rule in this respect, its refusal so to do is matter of legal discretion, not subject to a writ of error.(*r*)

When the question is as to the admissibility of secondary evidence, to supply the place of a lost writing, it is a matter of law, to be decided by the court, and unless such preliminary proof is given as authorizes its introduction, it is the duty of the court to reject it, and a refusal to do so is error.(*s*)

It is not error to receive evidence pertinent and relevant because it is not strictly *rebutting;* especially in a complicated case, and where the adverse party is not taken by surprise.(*t*)

Error assigned as to a declaration arising from its embracing only the general counts, and not being framed on a special contract proven

(*j*) Ibid.
(*k*) Paull *v.* Oliphant, 2 H. 342; see Clay *v.* Irwine, 4 W. & S. 233.
(*l*) County *v.* Leidy, 10 Barr, 45.
(*m*) Mills *v.* Buchanan, 2 H. 59.
(*n*) Zerbe *v.* Miller, 4 H. 488.
(*o*) Logan *v.* M'Ginnis, 2 J. 27.

(*p*) Eyrick *v.* Hetrick, 1 H. 491. BELL, J.
(*q*) Harden *v.* Hays, 2 H. 95.
(*r*) Columbia Bridge Co. *v.* Kline, Bright. R. 320.
(*s*) Porter *v.* Wilson, 1 H. 648. ROGERS, J.
(*t*) Sample *v.* Robb, 4 H. 305.

on the trial will not be noticed in the Supreme Court, if that exception had been taken on the trial.(*u*)

It is not error for the court to refuse to receive evidence of facts admitted by the opposite party.(*v*)

The admission or rejection of a deposition on account of the capacity of the witness to attend is ground for error.(*w*)

The Supreme Court will not reverse, because there was no preliminary notice of a special defence, when it does not appear from the record whether the notice was or was not given,(*x*) and it is now settled that objections to a special defence, on the ground that the requisite notice was not given, must be made on trial, otherwise they will not be heard by the court in bank.(*y*)

An objection to testimony, for want of notice of special matter, should appear to have been taken specially at the trial.(*z*)

Where in the trial of a cause, an error has been committed in the rejection of evidence, it was held, that the judgment must be reversed, although the facts of the case were undisputed, and though the parties had agreed that the court should direct such verdict as they thought proper upon the undisputed facts; the Supreme Court declining to say that the fact proposed to be proved by the evidence rejected might not have been disputed, or that the whole case might not then have been put to the jury.(*a*)

Though it is error to permit to be given to the jury, when objected to, a withdrawn declaration and a bill of particulars delivered under it, yet the court will not reverse when it appeared that no injury was really done thereby to the complaining party ;(*b*) and the same is the case where a witness *prima facie* interested on the face of his testimony has been admitted, where papers, which formed part of the offer in the court below, and which it is probable removed his interest, have been abstracted from the record.(*c*)   And so the answer of a witness to a question objected to, but which worked no injury, will not be examined in error.(*d*)

When evidence, competent and material at the time it was offered, becomes by a subsequent turn in the case incompetent and immaterial, and no request is made to the court to disregard it, it affords no ground for reversal.(*e*)

Judgment in ejectment will not be reversed because a deed, dated after suit brought, was read in evidence without objection on that account, where no injustice was done thereby.(*f*)

The admission of evidence which was irrelevant, but as to the effect of which the court charged rightly to the jury, is not ground for reversal on error,(*g*) and it will not be presumed that evidence admitted by the court below was irrelevant; it must be shown affirmatively and distinctly that a substantial error has been committed in this respect.(*h*)

(*u*) Wingate *v.* Mechanics' Bank, 10 Barr, 110.

(*v*) Harden *v.* Hays, 2 H. 91.
(*w*) Beitler *v.* Study, 10 Barr, 418.
See Pipher *v.* Lodge, 16 S. & R. 220.

(*x*) Basley *v.* Hoffman, 1 H. 603.
(*y*) Rearick *v.* Swinehart, 1 J. 233.
(*z*) Miller *v.* Stem, 2 J. 383.
(*a*) Hopkins *v.* Forsyth, 2 H. 34.

(*b*) Hall *v.* Rupley, 10 Barr, 231.
(*c*) Culberston *v.* Isete, 2 J. 199.
(*d*) Schoneman *v.* Fegeley, 2 H. 376.
(*e*) Atkins's Heirs *v.* Young, 2 J. 15.
(*f*) Uplinger *v.* Bryan, 2 J. 219.
(*g*) Stewart *v.* Walker, 2 H. 293.
(*h*) Garrigues *v.* Harris, Sup. Ct. 11 P. L. J.

Where the court below instructed the jury on the whole case to find a verdict for the defendant, though for an erroneous reason, the Supreme Court held, that the reason given formed no ground for error, the direction being in itself right,(i) and so where there is a misdirection in point of law where the verdict is on a distinct ground of fact to which the rule laid down is inapplicable, as where a judge erroneously charges that a plaintiff is not entitled to any interest, and the jury find a general verdict for the defendant, thus showing that no principal was due.(j)

Opinions expressed by the judge as to the weight of evidence, are not ground for error, unless delivered as of binding authority.(k)

Where the facts are recapitulated, and proper instructions given to the jury, an intimation by the court that there has been an abandonment of a settlement, is not error.(l)

It is error to direct the attention of the jury to a point on which there is no proof; as in an action on a note, to charge that the plaintiff is entitled to recover, unless "there be evidence in the cause to show that he obtained it by undue means," where, in fact, there is no such evidence;(m) and so of a charge which drew the attention of the jury from a conflict of testimony, as to the height of a dam, by referring a change in the height of the water, whereby plaintiff's lands were flooded, to causes which the Supreme Court considered inconsistent with the laws of hydrostatics, was held to be error.(n)

It seems that a mistake of a judge on the weight of testimony as to whether a witness is interested in the result of a suit, e.'g., as a partner, may be corrected on error.(o)

It is error in a court to leave to the jury the amount recoverable by a surety on a written assignment to him of a mortgage given to his principal, for a debt which he (the surety) has paid;(p) though this is not the case where the judge, in his charge to the jury, expresses his opinion of the hardship of the case, if this be justified by the circumstances.(q)

The Supreme Court will not reverse, on account of the rejection of proper evidence by the court below, when such evidence established a definite defence *pro tanto*, but will, where the defendant in error assents, modify the judgment by entering it for the amount of the judgment below, less the sum so proved.(r)

It is error to submit to the jury a question of fraudulent concealment and misrepresentation in the sale of land, of which there is, in fact, no evidence.(s)

An inaccuracy in the charge of the court, in directing the attention of the jury to a wrong period of time, is ground for reversal, and it is no answer to say, that the jury probably understood the court as having charged correctly.(t)

(i) Gast v. Porter, 1 H. 533.
(j) Brady v. Calhoun, 1 Pa. R. 140; Johnston v. Brackbill, id. 370.
(k) Sailor v. Hertzog, 10 Barr, 296; Schoneman v. Fegeley, 2 H. 376.
(l) Sample v. Robb, 4 H. 305.
(m) Snyder v. Wilt, 3 H. 59.
(n) Bovard v. Christy, 2 H. 267.

(o) Gordon v. Bowers, 4 H. 231.—Rogers, J.
(p) Knox v. Moatz, 3 H. 74.
(q) Grove v. Donaldson, 3 H. 138.
(r) Thomas v. Northern Liberties, 1 H. 117.
(s) Jones v. Wood, 4 H. 25.
(t) Brown v. Clark, 2 H. 469.

It is error to submit to the jury as an hypothesis, a state of facts of which there is no evidence, and which could not be inferred from a demurrer to evidence ;(*u*) but this is not so where the court, after answering a point submitted affirmatively, proceeds to qualify it, by stating, that if the facts were different from those assumed in the point, the law would be otherwise. The question always is, not whether a party is deprived of the advantage gained by an artful representation of a part of the case, but whether the court has laid down sound law for the decision of the whole.(*v*)

The court may omit a direction which, in one aspect of the case, would be useful to the party who omits to specifically ask for it; but this is no ground for reversal.(*w*)

Refusing to discharge a jury is not matter of error; the only remedy is motion for a new trial.(*x*) And so an error in refusing to withdraw a juror, will not be cause for reversal, when there was no fact in the case for a jury to decide.(*y*)

Where a court may quash or dissolve on extrinsic evidence, which cannot be put on the record, the presumption is, that everything was done rightly, and according to law.(*z*)

The ordering a cause for trial, or its continuance, is a matter within the discretion of the court below, and is not examinable on error.(*a*)

Where an issue was requested on the distribution of the proceeds of an execution, apparently to ascertain an immaterial fact, but it appeared from an entry by the court below, that the application was really made for another and allowable purpose, on which ground the court proceeded, the Supreme Court reversed for error, in refusing the issue for that purpose.(*b*)

The Supreme Court will not reverse, after a trial on the merits, under a statement in which the parties were correctly named, because an amendment of the transcript, which it was in the power of the court to make, was not formally entered on the record.(*c*)

The refusal to grant a new trial, is not the subject of a writ of error.(*d*)

14. *Pleas in error.*

On filing his assignment of errors, the plaintiff may rule the defendant to join in error within a reasonable time, which is usually four days.

The defendant may plead or demur to an assignment of errors. Pleas in error are common or special. The common plea or joinder is *in nullo est erratum*, or that there is no error in the record of proceedings, which is in the nature of a demurrer, and at once refers the matters of law arising thereon to the judgment of the court.(*e*) This plea is usually put in by the prothonotary, upon which the case is at issue, and is placed in its order on the argument-list. When a defendant in error demurs to an assignment of errors in fact, the court will allow him, after

(*u*) Haines *v.* Stouffer, 10 Barr, 363.
(*v*) Columbia Bridge Co. *v.* Kline, Bright. R. 320.
(*w*) Bitner *v.* Brough, 1 J. 127.
(*x*) Evans *v.* Mengil, 3 Barr, 239.
(*y*) Gearhart *v.* Jordan, 1 J. 325.
(*z*) Brown *v.* Ridgway, 10 Barr, 43 Per curiam.

(*a*) Porter *v.* Lee, 4 H. 412.
(*b*) Overholt's Appeal, 2 J. 224; see *ante*, 600.
(*c*) Eyster *v.* Rineman, 1 J. 147.
(*d*) Werkheiser *v.* Werkheiser, 6 W. & S. 184.
(*e*) Tidd, 1207.

judgment on the demurrer, to withdraw it, and rejoin to the assignment of errors.(f)

If the defendant in error would put in issue the truth of an error in fact assigned, he should traverse or deny it, and so join issue thereupon, and not plead *in nullo est erratum;* for, by so doing, he would acknowledge the fact alleged to be true.(g) If he would admit the fact, and yet insist that by law it is not error, he ought to rejoin *in nullo est erratum.* If an error in fact be assigned that is not assignable, or be ill assigned, *in nullo est erratum* is no confession of it, but shall be taken only for a demurrer.(h) If error be alleged in the body of the record, it is a good rejoinder; so, if error be alleged in a matter of record, not of the body of the record, but in a collateral thing, it is a good rejoinder.(i) But if errors in fact and in law are assigned, which we have seen cannot be assigned together, and the defendant plead *in nullo est erratum,* this is a confession of the error in fact, and the judgment must be reversed,(j) for he should have demurred for the duplicity.(k)

Special pleas to an assignment of errors contain matters in confession and avoidance, as a release of errors, or the statute of limitations, &c., to which the plaintiff in error may reply or demur, and proceed to trial or argument.(l)

The pleadings on an assignment of errors must be filed with the prothonotary of the Supreme Court, who, after issue joined, sets down the cause for argument. On an issue in fact, a record of *nisi prius* is made up, and the parties proceed to trial, as in common cases.(m)

By a rule of the Supreme Court,(n) " the prothonotary shall indorse on each writ of error or *certiorari* to remove proceedings hereafter issued, a rule to appear and plead at the return day of the writ; and on default of appearance when the cause is called for argument, and on proof of ten days' service on the defendant in error or his counsel below, the court will proceed *ex parte: And it is further ordered,* That the court proceed in like manner on proof of the like service of notice in appeal cases."

15. *Judgment in error, and herein of venire facias de novo.*

The judgment in error is to affirm, or recall, or reverse the former judgment; that the plaintiff be barred of his writ of error, or that a *venire facias de novo* be awarded. The common judgment for the defendant in error is, that the judgment be affirmed.(o) For error in fact that the judgment is recalled; for error in law it is reversed.(p)

Where a judgment is entire, it cannot be reversed in part, and affirmed for the residue.(q) So, when a judgment is entered jointly against two, which is erroneous as to one, it cannot be reversed as to one and affirmed as to the other.(r) So, where a verdict with entire damages was found for the plaintiff as to both charges in case for words spoken, and for causing him to be indicted, and it was afterwards held that the words were not actionable, the judgment was reversed *in toto.*(s) But if part

---

(f) 14 Johns. 417.
(g) 5 S. & R. 373; 9 Johns. 159; 15 Johns. 87.
(h) 2 Bac. Ab. 488; *vide* Tidd, 1208.
(i) 1 Ro. Ab. 763–4.
(j) 2 Bac. Ab. 487.
(k) 1 Str. 439.
(l) Tidd, 1210.

(m) Tidd, 1211.
(n) Dec. 14, 1837.
(o) Tidd, 1214.
(p) 2 Dunl. Pr. 1160.
(q) 14 Johns. 417; *sed vide* 6 Taunt. 654.
(r) Boaz *v.* Heister, 6 S. & R. 18.
(s) 2 Bac. Ab. 501.

of the words laid be not actionable, and several damages are given, it seems that the judgment shall be reversed in part only.(t)   It sometimes happens that a judgment may be reversed in part, and affirmed in part; as, where the judgment is good for the debt, but bad for the costs. Such were the cases of Cummins v. Sibley,(u) and Frederick v. Lookup.(v) And where a judgment is for two distinct matters, the one regular and the other erroneous, the court may reverse the distinct erroneous judgment, and affirm the distinct regular one.(w) But where the judgment in the court below, in an action against an executor, on the plea of *plene administravit*, was *de bonis testatoris*, &c., *et si non de bonis propriis*, the court refused to affirm the judgment in part, by retaining only the first words *de bonis testatoris*, and striking out the rest. Where there have been two judgments relating to the same matter, and the first judgment be reversed, the second, which is founded on it, must also be reversed; but the reversal of the last will not affect the first. As, if a judgment on an action of debt is against executors, and after a *scire facias* against them, judgment is given against them, to have execution of their proper goods, and error is brought on both judgments, in that case, if the first judgment be good and the last erroneous, the last only shall be reversed, and the first shall stand.(x) The law is settled that, where the writ of error is brought by the plaintiff, the Supreme Court may enter such judgment as ought to have been entered below; but where the defendant brings the writ of error, the court can only reverse the judgment.(y)

It has, indeed, been said generally that the power given to the Supreme Court, by the act of 1836, to modify as well as reverse the judgments of inferior courts, applies to civil as well as criminal cases. Thus, where it appears that a plaintiff in error has a definite defence, to a part of the claim, on which judgment has been entered against him below, the Supreme Court may, with the consent of the defendant in error, allow the judgment to stand for the residue.(z)

If the court below err in entering judgment with costs, it will be corrected by the Supreme Court without reversing for that.(a)

In a very recent case, a verdict was rendered in favor of the plaintiff, subject to the opinion of the court on a point reserved, on which the court afterwards entered judgment for the defendant. The Supreme Court, on error, reversed the judgment, and entered judgment for the plaintiff. It being afterwards suggested, that a motion on behalf *of the defendant*, for a new trial was undisposed of, and that the lower court had, notwithstanding its pendency, entered judgment for the *defendant*, the Supreme Court, on motion, permitted the reversal of the judgment to stand, but struck off the judgment entered for the *plaintiff*, and a *procedendo* was awarded.(b)

The object of the writ of *venire facias de novo* is to submit the same cause to the consideration of another jury, the Supreme Court

(t) Str. 188.
(u) 4 Burr. 2489.
(v) 4 Burr. 2018; Per TILGHMAN, C. J., Swearingen v. Pendleton, 4 S. & R. 396 ; see Clark v. McKisson, 6 S. & R. 87.
(w) Boaz v. Heister, 6 S. & R. 20.

(x) Ranek v. Becker, 12 S. & R. 426–7.
(y) Swearingen v. Pendleton, 4 S. & R. 396.
(z) Thomas v. Northern Liberties, 1 H. 120.
(a) Rentzheimer v. Bush, 2 Barr. 89.
(b) Harper v. Keely, 5 Harris, 234.

having corrected any error which may have taken place with respect to the former trial, as where there has been some irregularity in choosing or returning the jury, or where there has been some error in law in rejecting competent, or admitting incompetent evidence, or the jury have been misled by an erroneous opinion of the court with respect to the law, arising from the evidence.(c) And of late the same remedy has been extended to cases where entire damages have been assessed on several counts, some of which are bad, in order that the jury may have an opportunity of assessing the damages on each count severally.(d) Where there is a mere clerical error, there will be no difficulty in sending the record back, or in considering it as amended without sending it back.(e) But it will not be granted unless the error assigned has been committed in the course of the trial; therefore, it was refused, where it appeared from the plaintiff's own averment that there was no cause of action at the time the suit was commenced.(f) So where no sufficient consideration has been laid for the defendant's promise;(g) so where error in the course of the trial appeared, but the declaration was defective, and it besides appeared that the plaintiff could not in any event recover, the court would not award a *venire de novo*;(h) so if a judgment for a defendant be reversed, *a venire de novo* will not be awarded if it appear that the plaintiff's declaration contains no cause of action.(i) So, too, if it appear by the record that the plaintiff's claim does not constitute a cause of action, this court will reverse a judgment in his favor, although the point may not have been made in the court below, or assigned for error.(j) Neither will it be granted where the object of the defendant in error is to have another and quite a different cause submitted to the jury, as where his attempt is to expunge from a declaration drawn in slander of the husband and wife, a count for the slander of the husband, and to proceed to trial for the slander of the wife only; a practice like this would produce infinite confusion, expense, and delay. Error by a misjoinder of actions is not amended by the act of 1806,(k) which applies only to matters of *form* standing in the way of the *merits*, but it is by no means intended to alter the cause of action.(l) Nor can it be awarded unless there has been a *venire* actually issued, or the cause has been tried by a jury; therefore, where a cause was arbitrated, a *venire de novo* was refused after reversal upon error.(m) This case, however, is now provided for by the act of February, 1824,(n) which authorizes the Supreme Court in all cases in which a judgment or award of arbitrators may be reversed, to order the record to be remitted to the court from which it may have been removed, in order that such further proceedings may be had as the justice of the case may require.

Where the District Court sets aside a verdict for the plaintiff, and

(c) See Findlay *v.* Bear, 8 S. & R. 573. The power of the Supreme Court to award this process was first discussed and judicially recognized in the case of Sterret *v.* Bull, 1 Bin. 238, wherein it was said that it tends to the dispatch of justice as it prevents delay.

(d) Shaffer *v.* Kintzer, 1 Bin. 537.

(e) Langer *v.* Parish, 8 S. & R. 135.

(f) Miller *v.* Ralston, 1 S. & R. 309;

Reed *v.* Collins, 5 S. & R. 352; Langer *v.* Parish, 8 S. & R. 134.

(g) Whiteall *v.* Morse, 5 S. & R. 358.

(h) Wood *v.* Ludwig, 5 S. & R. 446.

(i) Griffith *v.* Eshelman, 4 W. 51.

(j) Hoffer *v.* Wightman, 5 W. 205.

(k) 4 Sm. Laws, 329.

(l) Ebersoll *v.* King, 5 Bin. 51.

(m) Ibid.

(n) Pamph. L. 27.

enters judgment of *nonsuit*, and the judgment is reversed on error, a *venire de novo* is granted of course.(*o*)   In such case, the defendant ought to have an opportunity, on a new trial of the cause, to obtain his bill of exceptions, which would be lost to him if the Supreme Court should, in such case, enter judgment for the plaintiff.(*p*)

Where a judgment for the plaintiff has been reversed for a want of jurisdiction appearing on the case, as left to the jury, he may, notwithstanding, have a *venire de novo*, if there were other facts in the cause withdrawn from the jury by the view taken by the court below, on which the jurisdiction might have been supported.(*q*)

Where a plaintiff has obtained the reversal of a judgment in his favor, and proceeds subsequently, by *venire de novo*, or *procedendo*, the effect is the same as though the reversed judgment had not been obtained, and the lien of a second judgment will not relate back.(*r*)

A judgment on a special verdict or case stated in the Supreme Court, reversing the court below is the judgment of the latter court, for all purposes and process of execution.(*s*)

The court will always support verdicts, where there have been trials on the merits, when they have it in their power; thus, where a judgment of the Common Pleas had been reversed on error, but before the record was remitted or a *venire facias de novo* awarded, the cause was again tried below; the Supreme Court, after error brought, ordered the record to be remitted and an award of a *venire de novo* to be entered, as of the term when the first judgment was reversed, inasmuch as they had power to do so originally, and the cause had been tried on its merits.(*t*) And by the act of 11th March, 1809, § 6, when the facts in any special verdict may be insufficiently or uncertainly found, the judges may remand the record and direct another trial, to ascertain the facts.

By the 11th section of the act of 1836,(*w*) as soon as the Supreme Court shall have rendered judgment, or made a final decree or decision, in any cause, action, or matter brought into the same by writ of error, *certiorari*, or appeal, such court shall order the records thereof, with their judgment or decree thereon written, and duly certified, to be remitted to the appropriate court, which judgment, decree, or decision, such court shall duly carry into execution and effect; or the said Supreme Court may, if they see cause, order execution thereof to be done by process issued out of the same, and thereupon order the record to be remitted, as aforesaid.

16. *Remittitur of record.*

When, therefore, judgment is given in the Supreme Court, or the writ of error abates, or is discontinued, the record is returned to the court whence it was removed, and the entry of this circumstance is termed a *remittitur*.   The party desirous of expediting the return of the record, usually advances the costs accrued upon the writ of error to the prothonotary, who makes out the *remittitur* or certificate of the decree of the Supreme Court, attaches it, with a bill of the costs paid, to the record, and immediately delivers it to the prothonotary of the court in which

(*o*) Wharton *v.* Williamson, 1 H. 273.
(*p*) Ibid. See Act of March 22, 1850, which secures this right.
(*q*) Seitzinger *v.* Steinberger, 2 J. 379.
(*r*) Lentz *v.* Lamplugh, 3 J. 346.

(*s*) Shaw *v.* Boyd, 2 J. 215.
(*t*) Albright *v.* McGinnis's Lessee, 4 Y. 518.
(*w*) Pamph. L. 787.

the case originated. The matter is then proceeded in by a *venire de novo*, execution, or *scire facias* against the bail in error, as the case may be, conformably to the judgment of the Supreme Court. If a *venire de novo* have been awarded, and on the next trial the opinion of the Supreme Court is read to the jury by one party, the other party may read the charge of the court below, to explain the opinion, though not as evidence of the law or fact.(*x*) We have already stated that the recognizance of bail is transmitted with the record, when taken before a judge of the Common Pleas. It therefore becomes a part of the record, and is on the affirmance of the judgment remitted to the court below. There is no distinction between the court of the Eastern District and the other districts of the Supreme Court in this particular; the record is remitted in all. The entire record, then, including the recognizance, being remitted to the court below, it is evident that the *scire facias* on the recognizance cannot issue from the Supreme Court, although taken there originally, but must be brought in that court where the record remains,(*y*) or elsewhere, if the defendant does not reside in such county.(*z*) It may be proper to observe that in the proceeding by *scire facias*, it is not necessary to sue out execution on the judgment in order to charge the bail, as a render of the body would not excuse the bail, nor anything but a release or satisfaction of the judgment satisfy the condition of the recognizance.(*a*)

17. *Costs in error.*(*aa*)

By the act of 1791, constituting the High Court of Errors and Appeals (which we have seen is now abolished), if the judgment was affirmed, or the plaintiff in error failed to prosecute his suit with effect, he was liable to double costs. But if the judgment was reversed, each party paid his own costs.(*b*) The practice relating to costs in error has already been given. The general rule is, that if the judgment be *affirmed*, the successful party is entitled to costs: but where the judgment of an inferior court is *reversed*, the costs in error are not *recovered* by the party who obtains the reversal,(*c*) and if levied by execution the court will order the different officers to refund them.(*d*) Neither is the party reversing the judgment liable for costs. In such cases the rule stated by the above act is adopted, by which each party is left to pay his own costs.(*e*)

Where a plaintiff, dissatisfied with a judgment, brings error unsuccessfully, none of the statutes on the subject entitle him to the costs in error.(*f*)

Where the Supreme Court reverses a judgment and orders a *venire facias de novo*, and the defendant in error pays the costs on such reversal, in order to take down the record to the Common Pleas, where he again obtains judgment, he may afterwards maintain *assumpsit* against the plaintiff in error, to recover back the costs so paid by him.(*g*) The general principle is that the law does not imply an *assumpsit*

(*x*) King *v.* Diehl, 9 S. & R. 409.
(*y*) Smith *v.* Ramsey, 6 S. & R. 573.
(*z*) See ¿ 7, Act of March, 1809, 5 Sm. Laws, 15.
(*a*) Smith *v.* Ramsey, 6 S. & R. 576.
(*aa*) See more fully *post*, "Costs."
(*b*) See 3 Sm. Laws, 33.

(*c*) Landis *v.* Shaeffer, 4 S. & R. 199.
(*d*) Wright *v.* Lessee of Small, 5 Bin. 204.
(*e*) Landis *v.* Shaeffer, 4 S. & R. 199.
(*f*) Cameron *v.* Paul, 1 J. 277.
(*g*) Hamilton *v.* Aslin, 3 W. 222.

for a voluntary service; but if the performance of it has been extorted by compulsion of law, a precedent request by the party served is unnecessary. And the principle holds, though there were no legal obligation binding the plaintiff's person, the instrument of compulsion being the jeopardy of his property or his rights, as where he pays rent for another, in order to release his own goods from a distress. How was it here? As each party is to pay his own costs on the reversal of a judgment, those paid by the plaintiff were incurred by the defendant on his writ of error. The prothonotary had a lien on the record for his costs; and without carrying it down, the plaintiff could not proceed to trial pursuant to the award of a *venire de novo*. What, then, was he to do? If he did not pay the costs himself, it is certain his antagonist would not pay them, as long as retention of the record in the Supreme Court should suspend a further prosecution of the action; and the plaintiff could not compel the prothonotary to sue for them, or to authorize a suit to be brought in his own name. He had no choice, therefore, but to pay himself and charge the defendant in a separate action.

With respect to the fees of the prothonotary of the Court of Error and his remedy to recover them, the following rules, laid down in a very recent decision of the Supreme Court,(h) must govern. "Where the defendant in the court below becomes plaintiff in error, and the judgment is affirmed, the prothonotary of the Supreme Court must look to the plaintiff in error for his fees, and cannot have recourse to plaintiff below, because the services were not done for him. So, where the plaintiff in the court below becomes plaintiff in error, and the judgment is affirmed, to him, and him only, must the prothonotary look for his fees. Where the plaintiff in error is subject to the costs in the Supreme Court by the affirmance of the judgment, and is insolvent, the prothonotary of the Supreme Court cannot have recourse to the securities in the recognizance entered into on the suing out of the writ of error, because he is no party to that recognizance. But where suit is brought on such recognizance, it is presumed that the judges of the court in which it is brought, on application by the officers to whom fees are due, will take care that the fees, so far as they are covered by the recognizance, shall be secured. When the judgment is reversed in the Supreme Court, and no *venire facias de novo* awarded, the prothonotary of the Supreme Court cannot recover his fees by directing the prothonotary of the inferior court to issue an execution therefor, because he has no judgment to warrant such execution. But his recourse must be to the plaintiff in error, for whom he performed the services on which the fees were due."(i) But "when this court reverses a judgment and orders a *venire de novo*, it has a right to impose terms as to costs. But where no terms are imposed, all the costs abide the final event of the suit. This practice has been uniform, and it is just, because the costs ought to fall on the party who is ultimately found to have been in the wrong. English authorities can have no weight in a case which depends on our own practice. It appears, however, that the Court of King's Bench and Common Pleas differ. In the latter, the costs abide the final

(h) Moore v. Porter, 13 S. & R. 100.
(i) Ibid. 201–2. As to the fees of officers of the courts generally, *vide ante*, *post*, "Costs."

event. In the former, they do not."(*j*) In Duncan *v.* Kirkpatrick,(*k*) it was held that *assumpsit* would not lie to recover back money collected by execution upon a judgment of the Court of Common Pleas of Franklin County, which had been reversed with an order that the money should be restored; but it was thought that such action might have been maintained had not an order of restitution accompanied the reversal of the judgment.(*l*)

18. *Restitution.*

After reversal of proceedings between landlord and tenant, a writ of restitution is not *ex debito justitiæ*, but depends on the grace of the court.(*m*) But upon reversal of an execution executed, it is generally a matter of course to award restitution of the money levied, and to transmit the record to the court below. The order of restitution should be made when the execution is reversed, but it may be made at a subsequent term, and the record remitted.(*n*) The court will not, however, proceed by attachment for disobeying an order of restitution ;(*o*) and *per curiam,* " the safest way is to send the record to the Court of Common Pleas, in order to have our judgment carried into effect, and this is the practice we will pursue in future."(*p*)

The rule, that in general restitution is a matter of course, applies mostly to cases in which an original judgment has been reversed, and not, for example, to a judgment on a *scire facias post annum et diem.* Thus, where the court reversed a judgment of the latter kind, on which the defendant's land was sold, and part of the money paid to other judgment creditors, and part to the plaintiff, the court refused to award restitution, but ordered the money received by the plaintiff to be brought into court, to await their further order ; and took no order as to that portion paid to the judgment creditors, as they were not before the court.(*q*) This went on the ground that the defendant was in insolvent circumstances. But where there is no suggestion that the plaintiff would be injured by the restitution, the court would not withhold it.(*r*) In the case of a reversal of an original judgment, " there is no room for presumption that there is anything due to the plaintiff."(*s*) It would seem, however, that if a judgment on a *scire facias* upon a mortgage should be reversed (which is an original judgment) for some defect in form, after the mortgaged property had been sold, the court would not award restitution to a defendant in insolvent circumstances, but would have the money brought into court, in order to abide the further proceedings of the plaintiff.(*t*) So where an original judgment is reversed, and the land was bound by judgments subsequent in date to it, the court will not award restitution to a defendant in insolvent circumstances, but will order the money to be brought into court, and apply it first to the discharge of all liens according to their priority, and the balance, if any, to the defendant himself.(*u*)

(*j*) Work *v.* Lessee of Maclay, 14 S. & R. 265, 267.
(*k*) 13 S. & R. 292.
(*l*) See Kennedy *v.* Hughey, 3 W. 267.
(*m*) Duncan *v.* Walker, 2 D. 205 ; Alden *v.* Lee, 1 Y. 160 ; ibid. 207.
(*n*) Cassel *v.* Duncan, 2 S. & R. 57.
(*o*) Duncan *v.* Findlay, 6 S. & R. 208.

(*p*) Ibid. Ranck *v.* Becker, 13 S. & R. 43.
(*q*) Kirk *v.* Eaton, 10 S. & R. 103.
(*r*) Id. 108.
(*s*) Ibid.
(*t*) See ibid.
(*u*) Frank *v.* Becker, 13 S. & R. 41.

On the reversal of a judgment, the Supreme Court will award restitution only of what the defendant in error has actually received. If, therefore, land has been sold by the sheriff, for a small sum, subject to the claim of the plaintiff, as ascertained by a verdict and judgment which has been removed to that court by writ of error, and the plaintiff purchases it of the sheriff's vendee, and obtains possession, the court will not order restitution of the amount subject to which the land was sold, as well as the price paid for it. Nor will they award a *scire facias*, to show cause why this should not be done; nor will they grant to the plaintiff in error such relief as to justice may appertain, where no specific relief is applied for.(v) By the 9th section of the act of 1705,(w) it is provided, that if any judgment, whereupon any lands, tenements, or hereditaments have been sold, shall be reversed for error, none of the said lands, &c., so as aforesaid taken or sold, nor any part thereof, shall be restored, nor the sheriff's sale or delivery thereof avoided, but restitution, in such cases only of the money or price for which such lands were sold. Where, however, the purchase is made under void process, this act will not prevent restitution of the land.(x) This act is said to be "strictly agreeable to the principles of the common law, in case of the sale of a term for years in England, in order that sales by sheriffs may not be defeated, *provided the sale has been to a stranger.*"(y) If, therefore, the sale has been made to the plaintiff in the execution, it would seem that restitution of the land itself might be had from him. So, if it were extended and delivered to him to pay in seven years, it shall be restored, and not merely the extended value.(z)

The Supreme Court, as we have seen above, will not interfere to enforce restitution, but will leave it to the court below, to whom they will remit the record with their order superscribed, for that purpose. There is a difference between the English practice and that which we pursue, in respect of restitution, which it may be relevant to point out in the present place, as it will show our course to be far more simple and less expensive. The English practice is thus stated: If execution on the former judgment have been actually executed, and the money paid over, the writ of restitution may issue without any previous *scire facias*; but if the money have not been paid over, a *scire facias quare executionem non*, suggesting the sum levied, &c., must previously issue.(a) But in our practice (although it would be a perfectly legal and proper course, if adopted), no writ of restitution is issued; but in lieu of it, an order for restitution is obtained, which, being disobeyed, the court may enforce by attachment; with regard to a *scire facias*, none is necessary, or ever issued. The writ of restitution, however, is in nature of an execution,(b) and in case the person of the plaintiff be out of the reach of an attachment, or it be inexpedient to proceed against his person in case of disobedience to an order, it would be advisable to issue this writ for the purpose of levying on his estate, real or personal, as it is apprehended, in this State,(c) and selling it to make the amount claimed.

(v) Cassel v. Cooke, 8 S. & R. 296.
(w) 1 Sm. Laws, 61.
(x) Burd v. Dansdale, 2 Bin. 80.
(y) Per YEATES, J., Lessee of Heister v. Fortner, ibid. 47.

(z) 1 Arch. Pr. 265.
(a) 2 Salk. 588; 1 Arch. Pr. 237.
(b) See Duncan v. Kirkpatrick, 13 S. & R. 294.
(c) See ibid. 293.

Where the defendant in the writ of restitution is an executor, it may be *de bonis testatoris si, et si non, de bonis propriis.* Where it is real estate which is claimed to be restored, and which has not been sold or passed out of the hands of the party, there appears to be nothing in the act which prevents the writ from operating upon it. Should this writ be levied upon real estate, it has not been decided whether an inquest should ensue to determine whether such estate will pay the claim in seven years.(*d*) Where a judgment is reversed *without* an order of restitution, *indebitatus assumpsit* will lie to recover back the amount obtained under the judgment, but not otherwise, unless the promise were made by a stranger on the consideration of a stay of execution.(*e*)

The question, whether a writ of restitution be a lien, and from what time, has lately been determined in our Supreme Court, in the case of Boal's Appeal.(*f*) The court said, that they would not consider the lien as commencing from the time of reversal, from the danger and almost certainty of affecting the rights of *bona fide* purchasers without notice, as this would be an unreasonable effect of the judgment of reversal. That it was not pretended it would bind lands through the whole district or in the county where the Supreme Court held its session, but in the county from whence the judgment came, and to which it must be remitted for execution, and this would expose it to the objection already mentioned. Therefore, it was the opinion of a majority of the court, that as the writ of restitution is strictly an execution, it comes within the same rule as other executions, and the lien commences on the goods from the time the writ goes into the hands of the sheriff; and on the lands, from the time of the levy, &c.(*g*) The opinion of the minority of the court, ROGERS and TODD, Js., was that the lien commences from the time of the remittance of the record, and docketing it in the county from which it was removed.

Restitution is not a matter of right, but rests in the exercise of a sound discretion, and the court will not order it, where the justice of the case does not call for it, or where the process is set aside for a mere slip, and there is danger that the plaintiff may lose his demand.(*h*)

19. *Limitation as to new suit.*

By the second section of the act of March 27, 1713,(*i*) it is enacted, that if in any of the suits which are enumerated in the first section, (which embrace personal actions only,) "judgment be given for the plaintiff, and the same be reversed by error, or a verdict pass for the plaintiff, and upon matter alleged in arrest of judgment, the judgment be given against the plaintiff, that he take nothing by his plaint, writ, or bill, then, and in every such case, the party plaintiff, his heirs, executors, or administrators, as the case may require, may commence a new action or suit, from time to time, within a year after such judgment reversed or given against the plaintiff as aforesaid, and not after."(*j*)

20. *Error coram vobis.*

Where an issue in fact has been decided, there is (as we have already seen) no appeal, in our law, from its decision, except in the way of mo-

---

- (*d*) See ibid. 294, as to the nature of this writ.
  (*e*) Ibid. 292.
  (*f*) 2 R. 37.
  (*g*) Ibid. 39, 40.

(*h*) Hargee *v.* The Commis. 2 J. 251.
(*i*) 1 Sm. Laws, 76.
(*j*) See Harris *v.* Dennis, 1 S. & R. 237.

tion for new trial; and its being wrongly decided is not error, in that technical sense to which a writ of error refers. So, if a matter of fact should exist which was not brought into issue, but which, if brought into issue, would have led to a different judgment, the existence of such fact does not, after judgment, amount to error in the proceedings. For example, if the defendant has a release, but does not plead it in bar, its existence cannot, after judgment, on the ground of error or otherwise, in any manner be brought forward.(*k*) But there are certain facts which affect the *validity and regularity of the legal proceeding itself;* such as the defendant having appeared in the suit while *under age,* by *attorney* and not by guardian;(*l*) but a defendant in ejectment cannot assign this for error.(*m*) So, where the plaintiff or defendant was a married woman at the commencement of the suit, or died before verdict or interlocutory judgment.(*n*) Such facts as these, however late discovered and alleged, are *errors in fact,* and sufficient to reverse the judgment upon writ of error. To such cases, the writ of error *coram vobis* applies; because the error in fact is not the error of the judges; and reversing it is not reversing their own judgment.(*o*) In the Court of King's Bench, in England, this proceeding is sometimes called error *coram vobis,* but it is said to be more correctly *coram nobis,* or *quæ coram nobis resident,* because the record and process on which it is founded are stated in the writ *to remain* in the court of our lord the king before the king himself.(*p*) But in Pennsylvania, the record and process being stated to remain before the judges of the court, a writ of this kind ought to be called a writ of error *coram vobis,* or *quæ coram vobis resident,* as in the Common Pleas of England.(*q*)

A writ of error of this description, that is, for error in fact, lies in the Court of Common Pleas, on a judgment in that court.(*r*) In Hill *v.* West,(*s*) it was said by the counsel for the plaintiff that they could find no precedent of a writ of error in Pennsylvania returnable *coram vobis.* That in Silver *v.* Shelback(*t*) a writ of error was brought to reverse a judgment in the Common Pleas of Philadelphia County, *wherein infancy was assigned for error,* the defendant below having appeared in his proper person, and the judgment was reversed. It has also been recently decided by the Supreme Court that the appearance of an infant by attorney, in the court below, is assignable for error in the former court.(*u*) In the State of New York, a writ of error for error in fact, on a judgment in a Court of Common Pleas, lies into the Supreme Court only, and not to the Court of Common Pleas, which cannot entertain a writ of error of any description.(*v*) In the case of Watson *et al. v.* Mercer,(*w*) which occurred at Lancaster, the Supreme Court held that a writ of error for error in fact could not be entertained by them when sitting out of the County of Philadelphia, as out of that county they could not call a jury to try any contested facts, the appropriate

---

(*k*) Steph. on Plead. 139, 140.
(*l*) Style, 406.
(*m*) 1 Str. 25.
(*n*) 2 Saund. 101, a.; see, further, 1 Arch. Pr. 212.
(*o*) 2 Tidd, 1033.
(*p*) 2 Saund. 131, a.
(*q*) See 2 Tidd. 1056, n.
(*r*) 1 Br. 75, 82, where see the subject

discussed, and the proceedings in error *coram vobis* set out at length; and see, further, as to the practice, 1 Arch. Pr. 243, 249.
(*s*) 4 Y. 385.
(*t*) 1 D. 165.
(*u*) Gilday *v.* Watson, 5 S. & R. 373.
(*v*) 14 Johns. 417; 20 Johns. 22.
(*w*) 17 S. & R. 343.

use of a writ of error *coram vobis* being to enable a court to correct its own errors; those errors which precede the rendition of the judgment. In practice, the same end is now generally attained by motion, sus- tained, if the case require it, by affidavits; and the latter mode has superseded the former in the British practice.(x)

Where defendant dies before judgment, a writ of error *coram vobis* is properly issued in the name of his administrator.(z)

21. *Proceedings on certiorari to aldermen and justices of the peace.*

We are now to take a view of the practice on writs of *certiorari* to justices of the peace, which, as was stated in the introductory part of this chapter, are in the nature of writs of error, as they lie only after the rendition of judgment by the magistrate, and abate for the same causes.(a)

Although the writ of *certiorari* is a writ of extensive application, and the Supreme Court has all the revisory powers of the King's Bench over inferior jurisdictions, yet when a special jurisdiction is created by statute, it cannot be taken from the magistrate, to whom it is given, to be exer- cised by that court. Its power, then, is purely correctional. Where a superior court has concurrent jurisdiction, it may issue its *certiorari* to remove an action, or an indictment, or other matter determinable by the course of the common law, and proceed in it as the inferior court would have done; but where a proceeding is according to a statute, a *certiorari* lies to remove it only after judgment and for revision as to its regularity.(aa)

The *writ of certiorari* is said to be a writ of error in every respect but form,(b) and is thus generally described by ROGERS, J. "A *certio- rari* is a writ where the court would be certified of a record in an- other, or sometimes in the same court, and he to whom it is directed ought to send the same record, or the tenor of it, as commanded by the writ, and if he fail to do so, then an *alias* is awarded; afterwards a *pluries*, with a clause of *vel causam nobis significas*, and then an at- tachment if good cause be not returned upon the *pluries*. It is a judi- cial writ, issuing out of the court to which the proceedings are to be

---

(x) 7 Peters's Rep. 144, 147–8.

(z) Devereux *v.* Roper, D. C. C. P. March 29, 1851. Why writ of error *coram nobis* should not be quashed. *Per curiam.* In this case, upon the sugges- tion that defendant died before the judg- ment was entered, a writ of *error coram nobis*, in the name of his administrator, has been allowed. That this is the pro- per proceeding, and rightly brought in the name of the administrator, is decided in Meggot *v.* Broughton, Cro. Eliz. 105, and by whom else than the administra- tor could it be brought? The idea that the entry of surety waived the error is certainly not tenable; for if he was dead at the time the surety was entered, how could a dead man be said to waive

anything? and it was not pretended that the surety was entered at the re- quest of the administrator after defend- ant's death was known.

As a matter of verbal criticism, I may be allowed to suggest that it is question- able whether (although this writ is call- ed in 1 Br. 76, a writ of *error coram no- bis*) the more proper appellation in Penn- sylvania be not *coram vobis*. The former name is applied to the King's Bench be- cause the king, in consideration of law, sits there himself, and the latter to the Court of Common Pleas.—R. D.

(a) Welker *v.* Welker, 3 Pa. R. 24.

(aa) Com. *v.* Nathans, 5 Barr, 124. See Carpenter's Case, 2 H. 486.

(b) Cooke *v.* Reinhart, 1 R. 321.

removed, directed to the judge or officer who has custody of the record.(c)

This writ, when required for the purpose referred to in this section, issues out of the Court of Common Pleas, is allowed by one of its judges, and directed to the alderman or justice of the peace by whom the judgment has been rendered, commanding him "to certify and send before them the plea with all things touching the same so full and entire as before him they remain, together with the writ itself; that they may further cause to be done thereupon that which of right and according to the laws and constitution of this commonwealth ought." The writ is tested as of the preceding term, and made returnable at the same time as other process.

The power of the Common Pleas to issue writs of *certiorari* is derived from the constitution of the State,(d) which declares that the judges of the Courts of Common Pleas shall within their respective counties have the like powers with the judges of the Supreme Court to issue writs of *certiorari* to justices of the peace. By the act of March 20 1810, § 24,(e) the power of the Supreme Court to remove proceedings had before a single justice of the peace by *certiorari* has been taken away.

The twenty-second section of the same act declares that in all cases either party shall have the privilege of removing the cause, by a writ of *certiorari*, from before any justice, whose duty it shall be to certify the whole proceeding had before him. The twenty-first section provides, "that no such writ shall be allowed by any judge within this commonwealth, until the party applying for it shall declare on oath or affirmation before such judge," (or, by the act of 1817,(f) before the prothonotary of the court,) "that it is not for the purpose of delay, but because, in the opinion of the party applying for the same, the cause of action was not cognizable before a justice, or that the proceedings proposed to be removed, are to the best of his knowledge unjust and illegal, and if not removed, will oblige him to pay more money, or to receive less from his opponent than is justly due; a copy of which affidavit shall be filed in the prothonotary's office." It is not necessary to pursue precisely the words of the act, but the affidavit should substantially set forth the reasons of removal; where, therefore, a party omitted to state in his affidavit, "that the proceedings, if not removed, would oblige him to pay more money than is justly due," the *certiorari* was quashed.(g) So in a *certiorari* to remove proceedings against the special bail, where the affidavit stated "that the proceedings, unless removed, would oblige the defendant to pay more money, *than he owed*,' the *certiorari* was dismissed.(h)

Previous to the issuing of the writ, the prothonotary takes a recognizance in the nature of bail in error, which is subscribed by the surety or bail upon the appearance-docket; it is conditioned that the party applying for the writ shall prosecute it with effect, and if the judgment of the justice be affirmed by the court that he shall pay the amount of the debt, interest, and costs, or else that the bail will pay it for him.

(c) Com. v. McAllister, 1 W. 307.
(d) Art. 5, § 1.
(e) 5 Sm. Laws, 171.
(f) 6 Re. Laws, 391.
(g) 1 Br. 217.
(h) Monell v. Phillips, C. P. Philad. June, 1825, MS.

It is only necessary for the like purposes, and in like cases as bail in error, being a mere extension, by the construction of the statutes requiring bail in error, to the case of *certiorari*.

By the second section of the act of March 27, 1833,(*i*) the agent or attorney of the party may make the required affidavit and recognizance.

The writ must be *specially allowed* before it can issue, and the omission of the *allocatur* or *allowance* will be fatal.(*j*) A *special allocatur*, however, was not held requisite in the case of a *certiorari* to remove proceedings of a justice to the Supreme Court :(*k*) "We know of no instance, wherein an application has been made to the court, or any judge in the vacation, for the allowance of a *certiorari*, to remove proceedings before justices of the peace in civil cases."(*l*) The practice is now for the president of the Common Pleas to allow a number of writs in blank, and leave them with the prothonotary, who fills them as occasion requires; but after a party has had the benefit of a hearing upon a *certiorari*, neither he nor his surety will be permitted to allege that the writ was not allowed; nor is it a defence in a *scire facias* upon the recognizance.(*m*)

After the writ has been allowed, it is issued under the seal of the court, and the signature of the prothonotary, returnable to the ensuing term like other process, and is delivered to the alderman or justice before whom the proceedings have been had, whose duty it is made by the act above mentioned, to certify the whole proceedings had before him, by sending the original precepts, a copy of the judgment, and execution or executions, if any be issued. Where this writ issues from a superior to an inferior court, the original record is to be returned. To return a mere transcript, would neither agree with the practice nor answer the exigence of the writ at the common law.(*n*) Where the entire record is not returned, the party may allege *diminution of record*, and the court will grant a rule upon the magistrate to send up that part of the record which is wanting.(*o*)

By the twenty-first section of the act of 1810, it is provided that no judgment shall be set aside on a *certiorari*, unless it is issued within twenty days after judgment rendered, and served within five days thereafter; and no execution shall be set aside, unless the *certiorari* is sued out and served within twenty days after the execution issued. Under this section, it has been determined that, after the expiration of twenty days from the rendition of the judgment, the court will not look into the judgment, although it be alleged that the defendant was not served with a summons, and that judgment was rendered without hearing, and by default, if it appear that the defendant had knowledge of the proceedings within the twenty days.(*p*)

By the ninth rule of the Common Pleas, "the particular exceptions intended to be insisted on, must be filed two days before the first argument day, and on default thereof, the judgment below shall be affirmed of course; the assignment of general errors is insufficient and void." This

(*i*) Pamph. L. p. 99.
(*j*) 1 Br. 217.
(*k*) Com. *v.* Turnpike Comp. 2 Bin. 257; Per TILGHMAN, C. J.
(*l*) Ibid.

(*m*) Patton *v.* Miller, 13 S. & R. 254.
(*n*) Torr's " Appeal," 1 R. 77.
(*o*) *Vide ante*, 611.
(*p*) 1 Ashm. 135.

provision has been held as applicable to civil actions exclusively.(q)   A former rule to the same effect was determined to be a valid one, and necessary for the dispatch of business.(r)   Although matters not excepted to will not be noticed by the court, where they relate merely to the regularity of the proceedings, yet they will reverse for want of jurisdiction in such case.(s)

It is the duty of the party excepting, to compel the return of the record in due time, by a rule which will be granted upon the magistrate by the court for that purpose.   The second section of the rule above cited, makes it the duty of the party suing out the writ, to cause the record to be returned two days before the first argument day, in default of which the writ will be dismissed.   Rules on magistrates to return them directed in due season, will be granted if applied for on the regular motion day. No other return than that of the record can be legally made.   The tribunal to which the *certiorari* issues, cannot inquire into the death of parties to the suit, and return such fact.   Such a return would be insufficient, and would subject them to an attachment.(t)   This rule, and the practice under it, are founded upon the concluding part of the twenty-fifth section of the act of 1810, which renders it the duty of the court to determine and decide thereon, at *the term* to which the proceedings of justices of the peace are *returnable* in pursuance of writs of *certiorari*.   After the record has been returned, it is settled that third persons cannot object to a misdirection of the writ, if the officer having the keeping of the record waive the objection and return it.   The death of the defendant in error, therefore, is no cause for quashing the writ, though it occurred before the writ issued.   It has never been the practice, in this State, to serve a copy of the writ on the attorney, as in England, nor is the writ accompanied by a citation, as in the federal courts.   But the Court of Review will take care that notice is given, and that proper parties are put on the record.   The mode is by ruling the administrator to appear and plead to the errors assigned.(u)   The attorneys for the respective parties shall each deliver a paper-book, setting forth the points to be discussed to each of the judges previous to the argument.   This rule also entitles *certioraris* to a preference on the argument-list.

It was formerly held that the court could not travel into the merits of the original question, but should take the case as stated upon the magistrate's return.(v)   But now, in order to prevent injustice, the court will make inquiry into the evidence given before the magistrate;(w) " this was going full as far, in my opinion, as any principle of law will warrant, and I think it would be inconvenient and illegal to go further."(x)   The magistrate is not required by any law to enter on his docket the evi-

---

(q) Caughey *v.* Mayor of Pittsburg, 12 S. & R. 53.

(r) Snyder *v.* Bauchman, 8 S. & R. 336; Simpson *v.* Wray, 7 Id. 336. A similar rule of another court in case of *certiorari* to remove the judgments of justices of the peace, was held applicable to the case of a proceeding before two justices and a jury, under the provision enabling purchasers at sheriff's

sales to obtain possession.   Simpson *v.* Wray, 7 S. & R. 336.

(s) 1 Ashm. 152.

(t) Com. *v.* McAllister, 1 W. 307.

(u) Ibid. 309.

(v) Overseers of Coventry *v.* Cummings, 2 D. 114.

(w) Buckmyer *v.* Dubs, 5 Bin. 30 ; and *per* TILGHMAN, C. J.

(x) Ibid.; Pray *v.* Reynolds, C. P. Phil. 1 Wh. Dig. "Justice," v. (a)

dence on which his judgment is founded. The court will presume that his judgment is rendered on legal proof.(y) He need only state the *demand* and the *kind* of evidence produced to support the plaintiff's claim, whether upon bond, note, penal or single bill, writing obligatory, book-debt, damages on assumption, or whatever it may be, so as to enable the court to discover the grounds of the controversy and his decision thereon ;(z) but if he does so enter it, and it is found insufficient to support the judgment, it will be reversed. Thus, where it appeared that judgment was rendered merely on the attestation of the party interested,(a) and the affidavit of the defendant, though not conclusive in establishing the error, will at least be sufficient to throw the *onus probandi* whether other evidence was produced upon his adversary.(b) So, where the proof before the magistrate was not the legal evidence which the law calls for, the court would probably set aside the proceedings, where the party had no appeal. But where he has an ample remedy by appeal, and, neglecting it, enters into a recognizance for stay of execution, the court will not interpose.(c)

Where it appears, on the face of the record, that the justice has exceeded his jurisdiction, by giving judgment and issuing execution for a greater sum than the act of assembly allows, the court will consider the whole as a nullity, and discharge a defendant committed under such judgment,(d) and the rule is that where an alderman or justice of the peace have no jurisdiction, the remedy is not by appeal, but by *certiorari*.(e) But where his jurisdiction evidently appears on the face of the record, the settled rule has been to form no presumption against the accuracy of the proceedings ;(f) and his judgment, though erroneous, is binding on the parties until reversed on *certiorari* or appeal.(g) As justices of the peace have not jurisdiction in *all* cases of contract, it ought to appear upon their proceedings what is the *nature* of the contract upon which the action is founded. If, therefore, it does not appear from the record that the justice has jurisdiction, the judgment will be reversed.(h) So, in an action for trespass to real estate, it should appear that the estate was situate in the county where the action was instituted, as well to prove the jurisdiction of the magistrate, as to enable the defendant to plead the recovery in bar to another action for the same trespass.(i) In an action on a bond before a justice, it is no objection to his jurisdiction that the penalty exceeds one hundred dollars, if the *real* debt does not.(j) This decision has been since sustained by the District Court of Philadelphia County, upon the converse of the proposition.(k) The court will call in the aid of affidavits to ascertain whether a justice has exceeded his jurisdiction, when it does not appear upon the record.(l) So, where there is reason to infer partiality or corrupt practice on the

(y) Buckmyer v. Dubs, 5 Bin. 31.
(z) 1 Br. 209 ; see ℥ 4, act of March, 1810, 5 Sm. Laws, 163 ; Addis. 27.
(a) Sharpe v. Thatcher, 2 D. 77.
(b) Vansciver v. Bolton, 2 D. 114.
(c) Morton v. Plowman, 1 Y. 251 ; Bradley v. Flowers, 4 Y. 436.
(d) Geyer v. Stoy, 1 D. 135.
(e) Overseers of St. Clair v. Overseers of Morn. 6 W. & S. 522. See 3 W. 363.
(f) Buckmyer v. Dubs, 5 Bin. 32 ;

Gibbs v. Alberti, 4 Y. 373 ; Bradley v. Flowers, id. 436.
(g) Emory v. Nelson, 9 S. & R. 12.
(h) 1 Br. 339.
(i) Ibid. 355.
(j) Per Hallowell, Pres't, Streeter v. Brown, C. P. Philad. March, 1825, MS. referring to 1 D. 308.
(k) Coates v. Cork, 1 M. 270.
(l) Burginhofen v. Martin, 3 Y. 479.

part of the justice in rendering judgment; as where he refuses to hear material testimony for either party, the court will permit the introduction of parol evidence.(*m*)   Or where he decides on the oath of the plaintiff alone.(*n*)   In such cases, parol evidence is necessarily admissible; and there may be cases in which the absence of jurisdiction can be established in no other way; as where one justice re-examines what has been already determined by another.(*o*)   So where it does not clearly appear whether the judgment is rendered against the defendant in his private or official capacity as a justice of the peace, who assigns for error an omission of the notice allowed by law to justices of the peace before suit instituted.(*p*)   But, in general, parol evidence is inadmissible if the proceedings appear on the face of the transcript to be regular, and the justice has acted within the sphere of his jurisdiction.(*q*)   The fact of his sending up the notes of parol evidence taken before him, will not alter the rule.(*r*)

Where an alderman convicted a defendant in a penalty under a by-law passed to give him jurisdiction for the purpose, but which was void: it was held that the remedy was by *certiorari*, and that the court did not err in quashing an appeal to such judgment, without quashing the proceedings.(*s*)

In an action of debt for a penalty for the violation of an ordinance, the magistrate should state on his record not only the substance of the ordinance, but what is alleged against the defendant, as to his acts, or omission of anything to be done, which exposes him to the penalty.(*t*)

The twenty-second section of the act of 1810, before mentioned, provides that the proceedings of a justice of the peace shall not be set aside or reversed for want of formality in the same, if it shall appear on the face thereof that the defendant confessed a judgment for any sum within the jurisdiction of the justice, or that a precept issued in the name of the commonwealth, requiring the defendant to appear before the justice, on some day certain, or directing the constable to bring the defendant forthwith before him, agreeably to the provisions of that act, and that the said constable having served the said precept, judgment was rendered, on the day fixed in the precept or on some other day, to which the cause was postponed by the justice with the knowledge of the parties; and no execution shall be set aside for informality, if it shall appear on the face of the same, that it issued in the name of the commonwealth, after the expiration of the proper period of time, and for the sum for which judgment had been rendered, together with interest thereon and costs, and a day mentioned on which return is to be made by the constable, and that the cause of action shall have been cognizable before a justice of the peace.

As regards the day of appearance and judgment, it is clear that it should be stated on the justice's docket: but if the day on which the parties appeared is mentioned, and then the docket-entry proceeds to state that the cause was examined, and judgment rendered, the court

---

(*m*) Worstall *v.* Meadowcroft, C. P. Phila. June, 1825, MS.
(*n*) 1 Ashm. 209.
(*o*) 1 Ashm. 215.
(*p*) Fitzsimmons *v.* Evans, C. P. Phila. June, 1825, MS.

(*q*) 1 Ashm. 51; ib. 64.
(*r*) Ib. 64.
(*s*) City of Pittsburg *v.* Young, 3 W. 363.
(*t*) Manayunk *v.* Davis, 2 Par. 289.

will presume that judgment was given on that day. The entry taken altogether will very well bear this meaning.(*u*) The opening or refusing to open a justice's judgment being matters of discretion, are not examinable on *certiorari;* and where from all the facts of the case a fair presumption arose that the justice refused to grant a continuance prayed for, because he believed the party to be guilty of laches, or because he believed it to be made merely for delay, the court refused to reverse the judgment.(*v*)

On a judgment by default, it must appear by the record, that the process was served as required by law, otherwise the judgment will be reversed on *certiorari.*(*w*)

The court will reverse a judgment rendered by default before a magistrate, unless it clearly appear on the face of the officer's return, that the summons has been served in the manner prescribed by law.(*x*)

On the affirmance or reversal of a judgment, the record is not remitted to the justice, as in cases of writs of error to inferior courts, but execution issues at once from the Common Pleas for the debt, interest, and costs in the former case, or for costs only in the latter, without referring the cause again to the justice.(*y*) The award of execution for the costs, is, upon reversal on a *certiorari*, as much a part of the judgment of reversal as is the reversal itself; and so inseparably is it connected with the execution which followed, that neither could be reversed without the other.(*z*) The party in whose favor the judgment has been affirmed, may also take a *scire facias* against the bail upon his recognizance, who, like the bail on a writ of error, is liable, without any previous process being had against the principal.(*a*) The judgment of the court upon a *certiorari* is final, and, as we have already stated,(*b*) no writ of error can issue thereon.(*c*)

On the hearing of a *certiorari* to the judgment of a justice, every reasonable presumption will be made in favor of his proceedings, consistent with the record.(*d*)

Where there are two penalties imposed by an ordinance, the judgment must be specific for which penalty it is rendered, and a judgment for too small a sum is as fatal as if for a larger sum than is given by the ordinance.(*e*)

Where it appeared by the record in a return to a *certiorari*, that the cause of action was "for a violation of the first section of an ordinance of the district aforesaid, passed the 1st July, 1820," nothing more being stated, the court reversed the proceeding for informality.(*f*)

In *certiorari*, the court will notice a substantial and fatal error in the proceedings, although the counsel have omitted to make it a special exception, when it is deemed essential for the purposes of justice.(*g*)

(*u*) Buckinger *v.* Dubs, 5 Bin. 29.
(*v*) 1 Ashm. 221.
(*w*) Fraily *v.* Sparks, 2 Par. 232.
(*x*) Buchanan *v.* Specht, C. C. P. P. C. 8 Leg. Int. 162.
(*y*) See Robbins *v.* Whitman, 1 D. 410; Welker *v.* Welker, 3 Pa. R. 24.
(*z*) Summerville *v.* Holliday, 1 W. 532.
(*a*) *Vide* Smith *v.* Ramsay, 6 S. & R. 573.
(*b*) *Ante*, 434.

(*c*) § 22, Act of March, 1810. Silvergood *v.* Storrick, 1 W. 532. It is otherwise; however, in the case of proceedings of two justices under the landlord and tenant law. Clark *v.* Yeat, 4 Bin. 185.
(*d*) Brown *v.* Quinton, C. P. Philadelphia County, 3 P. L. J. 425.
(*e*) Ibid. Manayunk *v.* Davis, 2 Par. 289.
(*f*) Fraily *v.* Sparks, 2 Par. 232.
(*g*) Com. *v.* Cane, 2 Par. 265.

In a summary conviction, the magistrate is bound to set forth the evidence at length on his record, for the proof must appear upon the record, to sustain every material charge. The magistrate must state the whole evidence on both sides, and not merely the result of it.(h)

Unless it appears upon the face of the proceedings, that the justice proceeded and rendered judgment upon the plaintiff's own oath, it must be so distinctly averred by way of exception, and shown by proof.(i)

The Common Pleas has no power to direct an issue to try disputed facts arising from a *certiorari* to a judgment of a justice.(j)

When the *certiorari* is *non-prossed*, the record must be remitted to the justice to be proceeded in; the defendant in error cannot have a *scire facias* in the Common Pleas. It never was the practice here or in England to treat a *non-pros.* as a final judgment, and in this respect there is no difference between a writ of error and a *certiorari*. The practice has been general, if not universal, to collect the debt in such case by an execution from the justice.(k)

The costs, in the event of a second action being brought and trial had, after a reversal of the prior judgment on a *certiorari*, are provided for by the twenty-fifth section of the act of 1810, already mentioned. It directs that when the plaintiff removes and reverses the justice's proceedings, and on a second trial before him or any other justice, if judgment shall not be obtained for a sum equal to or greater than the original judgment, the plaintiff shall pay all costs accrued on the second trial, as well as those which accrued at the court, including any fees not exceeding four dollars, which the defendant may have given his attorney in such trial, together with fifty cents per day to the defendant while attending court in defence of the proceedings; and where the defendant removes and reverses the judgment, and it shall appear that he attended the trial before the justice, or had legal notice to attend the same, and on a final trial being had as aforesaid, the plaintiff shall obtain judgment for a sum equal to or greater than the original judgment, the defendant shall pay all costs accrued on the second trial before the justice of the peace, as well as those which accrued at the court before whom the proceedings had been set aside, including any fees, which the plaintiff may have given to any attorney, not exceeding four dollars, to defend the proceedings of the justice, together with fifty cents per day while attending at court on the same; which costs shall be recovered before any justice of the peace, in the same manner as sums of a similar amount are recoverable.

The right to recover the costs on a writ of *certiorari*, depends on the relative amount recovered or abated by the subsequent judgment: therefore, upon the reversal, on *certiorari*, of an execution, on the ground that no judgment had been entered by the justice on an award of referees, and the judgment is subsequently entered and the money recovered, the costs of the *certiorari* cannot be recovered by the defendant in error from the plaintiff in error.(l)

(h) Ibid.
(i) Wilson v. Wilson, 5 P. L. J. 462.
BELL, P. J.

(j) Pool v. Morgan, 10 W. 53.
(k) Welker v. Welker, 3 Pa. R. 24.
(l) Atkinson v. Crossland, 4 W. 450.

CHAPTER XXVIII.

OF COSTS.

INCIDENT to the judgment are costs or allowances to a party for expenses incurred in conducting his suit, or for which he is responsible to the officers of the court for services rendered to him. They are called final, in contradistinction from interlocutory costs, or such as are awarded on interlocutory matters arising in the course of the suit, and which have already been considered whilst treating of the matters to which they relate. The former, or such as depend on the final event of the suit, will be the subject of the present chapter.

We shall proceed to consider the subject under the following heads:—

I. *Of the plaintiff's costs.*
   1. Of the plaintiff's right to costs generally, and in particular forms of action.
   2. Of the plaintiff's right to costs in actions within the jurisdiction of a justice of the peace, and where he recovers a sum less than that required by law to give the court jurisdiction.

II. *Of the defendant's costs.*
   1. Of the defendant's costs generally.
   2. Of costs where there are several defendants and one or more are acquitted by verdict.
   3. Of the defendant's right to costs as against an equitable plaintiff.
   4. Of security for costs.
   5. Of the costs of former actions.
   6. Of costs after tender and payment of money into court.

III. *Of costs on a writ of error.*

IV. *Of costs on appeal from aldermen and justices of the peace.*

V. *Of costs of reference and arbitration.*
   1. Voluntary.
   2. Compulsory.

VI. *Of costs in actions by and against particular persons.*

VII. *Of double and treble costs.*

VIII. *Of the taxation and recovery of costs.*

SECTION I.

OF THE PLAINTIFF'S COSTS.

1. *Of the plaintiff's right to costs generally, and in particular forms of action.*

At common law, neither the plaintiff nor the defendant was entitled to costs. In all actions, however, in which damages were recoverable, the plaintiff, if he had a verdict, was in effect allowed his costs; for the jury always computed them in damages. But the defendant was wholly without remedy for any expenses he had been put to, if he had a verdict, or the plaintiff were nonsuit; the amercement to which the plaintiff was subject in such a case, *pro falso clamore suo*, going entirely to the king. So that costs in their origin were rather a punishment of the party paying, than a recompense to the party receiving them.(*a*)

This was remedied, however, as to plaintiffs, by the statute of Gloucester, 6 Edw. I. c. 1,(*b*) by which it is provided "that the demandant may recover against the tenant the costs of his writ purchased, together with his damages aforesaid. And this act shall hold place in all cases where the party is to recover damages."

Though the statute only mentions the cost of the "writ purchased," the construction has been, that it extends to all the costs of the suit.(*c*) And it is now settled that the words, "in all cases," are general words, and that the plaintiff is entitled to costs in all actions in which damages are recoverable at the common law, or were given by the statute of Gloucester, and also where damages are given by any subsequent statute, although costs be not mentioned in the statute.(*d*)

Thus, in an action of debt upon a statute by a party aggrieved, for a certain penalty, the plaintiff shall recover costs of suit, although no costs are annexed by the act under which the action is brought.(*e*) But no costs are recoverable by a common informer or prosecutor *qui tam*, unless costs are expressly given by the act imposing the penalty.(*f*) The reason of the distinction being that, in an action by a party aggrieved for the penalty, a right vests in the plaintiff from the moment the offence is committed, for the detention which he is entitled to damages in debt; but in the case of a common informer or prosecutor *qui tam*, it is different, as he has no interest until judgment, and he is therefore not entitled to damages for the detention.(*g*) After the statute of Gloucester, the judges began to make it a rule, for the better execution of the statute, that the jury should tax the damages and costs separately; and when it was evident that the costs given by the jury were too little to answer the costs of the suit, the plaintiff prayed that the officer might

(*a*) Musser *v.* Good, 11 S. & R. 250.
(*b*) Rob. Dig. 107.
(*c*) 2 Inst. 288; Say. Costs, 4; 2 Wils. 91; Tappan *v.* The Columbia Bridge Co. 4 P. L. J. 224.
(*d*) 2 Wils. 91; Barnes, 151; S. C. J. 3 Burr. 1723; Say. Costs, 10; 1 T. R. 71; 6 T. R. 355; 7 T. R. 267.

(*e*) 1 H. Bl. 13; 7 T. R. 268; Norris *v.* Pilmore, 1 Y. 405; Ritchie *v.* Shannon, 2 R. 196.
(*f*) 1 Salk. 206; 1 Rol. Ab. 574; Buller's N. P. 33.
(*g*) Norris *v.* Pilmore, 1 Y. 405; Ritchie *v.* Shannon, 2 R. 196.

tax the costs inserted in the judgment; and this was the origin of costs *de incremento*.(*h*)   Thus, in giving their verdict in actions of debt or ejectment, the jury say they find for the plaintiff six cents damages and six cents costs, in order that the court may consistently add the increase of costs to the damages.   In cases where the verdict is for damages, they find so much damages and six cents costs.(*i*)   In ejectment, the plaintiff is entitled to costs if he obtain a verdict; and costs are awarded by the court on reports of referees, though they are, in Pennsylvania, seldom or never specified in ejectment causes.(*j*)   When the jury are *ex officio* bound to give costs, and omit to do so, the court may supply the deficiency.(*k*)   And if the jury assess costs in a case in which they are not recoverable, the judgment is to be entered without costs.(*l*)

The statute of Gloucester did not extend to cases in which no damages were recoverable by the common law.   Thus in partition, although the writ and count is *ad damnum*, yet as no damages were recoverable, the plaintiff was not entitled to costs.(*m*)   But by the third section of the act of 1835,(*n*) it is enacted that the costs in partition shall be paid by all the parties in proportion to their several interests; and this is held to include witness fees.(*o*)

So also in *scire facias* and actions of waste; the right to receive costs was given by the statute, 8 and 9 William III. chap. 11,(*p*) which enacted that "the plaintiff obtaining judgment or any award of execution after plea pleaded, or demurrer joined therein, shall likewise recover his costs of suit; and if the plaintiff shall become nonsuit, or suffer a discontinuance, or a verdict shall pass against him, the defendant shall recover his costs and have execution for the same in like manner as aforesaid."

Under this statute, a plaintiff in *scire facias* is entitled to costs only in the cases provided for by the statute, that is to say, where he obtains judgment after plea pleaded, or demurrer joined; and as costs are the creatures of the statute, and are in the nature of a penalty in the unsuccessful party, and the statutes imposing them are to be construed strictly,(*q*) it is held under this statute that, where the defendant in an action of *scire facias* suffers judgment by default, the plaintiff cannot recover costs, as the case is not within the statute.(*r*)   But costs are taxable in every proceeding by *scire facias*, whether an original suit or not; and where a terre tenant who was made party to a *scire facias* to revive a judgment pleaded to the suit, whereby costs were incurred, and judgment was entered for the plaintiff, the terre tenant was held to be liable personally for the costs.(*s*)

The commonwealth neither receives nor pays costs on her own prosecutions, whether civil or criminal, except where directed by act of assembly.   This exemption, whether it be called prerogative or privi-

---

(*h*) See Brightly on Costs, p. 14.
(*i*) *Vide* Brac. L. Mis. 196.
(*j*) Harvey *v.* Snow, 1 Y. 156.
(*k*) Zell *v.* Arnold, 2 Pa. R. 292; Bellas *v.* Levy, 2 R. 21; 1 Bingh. 182.
(*l*) 2 Saund. 257; Guier *v.* McFadden, 2 Bin. 587.
(*m*) Noy. 68; Stewart *v.* Baldwin, 1 Pa. R. 461.
(*n*) Act 11th of April; Dunlop, Dig. ed. 1849, p. 671.

(*o*) St. Peter's Church *v.* Zion Church, 4 P. L. J. 134.
(*p*) Rob. Dig. 140.
(*q*) Maus *v.* Maus, 10 W. 90; Com. *v.* Harkness, 4 Bin. 194; Ramsey *v.* Alexander, 5 S. & R. 344; Clemens *v.* Com. 7 W. 485; Salk. 206; 3 Burr. 1287.
(*r*) 1 Bing. 182; Arch. Pr. 289; 3 Bos. & Pul. 14.
(*s*) Haskins *v.* Low, 5 H: 64.

lege, is founded on the sovereign character of the State, amenable to no judicial tribunal, and subject to no process.(t)

In like manner, the United States are exempted from liability to the payment of costs.(u)

But this exemption of the State is not communicated nor communicable to those who sue in her name and for *their own exclusive benefit*, the action not being hers, nor under *her control*. Therefore, in actions on official bonds sued in the name of the commonwealth, for the use of parties aggrieved, or in actions brought by an assignee of the State, the court will look to the real party on the record, and compel him to pay the costs.(v) The act of March 1824,(w) forms, however, an exception to the rule above laid down. The second section directing the method of proceeding against retailers of foreign merchandise, for the duty thereon, provides, that "upon an appeal by a defendant in such action, the jury or arbitrators trying the cause shall decide whether the party appealing or the commonwealth shall pay the costs of suit; and when the decision is against the commonwealth, the costs shall be paid out of the county treasury; but in no case shall the commonwealth pay costs, except where the party appealing is not a retailer of foreign merchandise; or has not produced any other testimony on the appeal than was produced before the justice."

And the 12th section of the act of 14th June, 1836, in relation to writs of quo warranto,(x) provides, "that if the proceedings shall be instituted by the attorney-general at his own instance, it shall be lawful for the court, in their discretion, on giving judgment for the defendant, to order that the costs be paid by the county in which the matters complained of were alleged to have taken place." And in actions brought by the commonwealth upon the official bonds of prothonotaries, registers, and recorders, the 10th section of the act of 16th April, 1845,(y) directs judgment to be entered for the commonwealth with costs.

But the statute of Gloucester, giving costs to the plaintiff in all cases where he recovered damages, as above mentioned, was found to have the effect of encouraging suits for very trifling causes; and the legislature, therefore, were obliged to interfere, and have in some measure remedied the evil, by enacting that if the plaintiff, in certain cases, recover less than 40s. damages, he shall be entitled to no more costs than damages.

Thus in trespass, the general rule is that the plaintiff shall have costs, if he have a verdict, however trifling the damages may be. This rule, however, is considerably narrowed by the following statutes. By the statute 22 and 23 C. II. c. 9, which is in force in Pennsylvania, it is provided, that(z) in all actions of trespass, assault and battery, and other personal actions, wherein the judge at the trial shall not certify under his hand, upon the back of the record, that an assault and battery was sufficiently proved, or that the freehold or title of the land was chiefly in

(t) Com. v. Commissioners of County of Philadelphia, 8 S. & R. 151; Com. v. Johnson, 5 S. & R. 190. Irvin v. The Commissioners of Northumberland Co. 1 S. & R. 505; McKeehan v. The Commonwealth, 3 Barr, 153.

(u) U. S. v. Hooe, *et al.* 3 Cranch, 73; U. S. v. Barker, 2 Wheat. 395.

(v) Com. v. County Commissioners, 8 S. & R. 153; see also Stat. 24, H. VIII. c. 8; Rob. Dig. 123.

(w) Pamph. L. p. 32; Dunlop, Dig. ed. 1849, p. 426.

(x) Pamph. L. p. 622; Dunlop, Dig. ed. 1849, p. 767.

(y) Pamph. L. p. 534; Dunlop, Dig. ed. 1849, p. 1053.

(z) Rob. Dig. 138.

question, if the jury find damages under 40*s.* the plaintiff shall recover no more costs than damages.

Notwithstanding the generality of the words "other personal actions," this statute has always been confined to actions of assault and battery, and to such personal actions as relate to the freehold, or to things fixed to the freehold, that is, to cases where the freehold may by presumption come in question,(*a*) and the forty shillings damages in trespass, which entitle the plaintiff to recover full costs, are to be estimated in Pennsylvania currency, and are equal to $5.33.(*b*)

The plaintiff is not prevented from recovering full costs, although the damages do not amount to forty shillings, upon a writ of inquiry, as the statute does not extend to that case.(*c*) And to entitle the plaintiff to full costs in assault and battery, where the damages found by the jury are under forty shillings, the judge must certify that both the assault and the battery were proved.(*d*) And where the action is in form an action of assault and battery, yet if it is only maintainable in respect of special damages resulting from the offence, it is not within the statute ;(*e*) and the statute does not extend to an action of assault and battery, *per quod servitium amisit*, nor to trespass and assault upon, and criminal conversation with, the plaintiff's wife, nor to assault or false imprisonment.(*f*) But in an action for assault and battery, and tearing the plaintiff's clothes, if the plaintiff have a verdict for less than 40*s.* he shall have no more costs than damages, unless the judges certify; because the tearing of the clothes is a mere consequence of the battery, and not a substantive cause of action.(*g*) Even in cases clearly within the statute, however, if the defendant plead a justification, the plaintiff shall have full costs, although the verdict be for less than 40*s.* ;(*h*) and as under the plea of *non. cul.* with leave to give the special matter in evidence, the defendant may by our practice prove everything that amounts to a justification, it is unnecessary that the justification should appear from the record if the defendant actually justified.(*i*) But where the defendant only justifies the assault, the plaintiff cannot have full costs without a certificate.(*j*) And where there is a verdict for the defendant upon a plea of justification, and a verdict against him upon the plea of not guilty, the plaintiff is not entitled to full costs without a certificate.(*k*)

In trespass *quare clausum fregit*, the plaintiff is entitled to full costs, without a certificate, although the damages be under forty shillings, where it appears from the pleadings that the freehold, or title to the land, could not have come into question.(*l*) And so, also, where it appears on the face of the pleadings, or from the nature of the case, that the freehold or title to the land must have come into question, a certificate is not always necessary to entitle the plaintiff to full costs.(*m*) And

(*a*) Salk. 308 ; 3 Selwyn, 1134 ; Bul. N. P. 329 ; 1 Taunt. 357.
(*b*) Chapman *v.* Calder, 2 H. 357.
(*c*) 2 Bull. N. P. 329.
(*d*) 2 Lev. 102.
(*e*) 3 Keb. 184 ; 1 Salk, 208 ; 1 Stra. 192 ; 6 Dowl. 561.
(*f*) Str. 630–4, 504, 551, 645 ; 3 Wils. 319; and see 2 Arch. Pr. 1142; 2 Bl. 854.
(*g*) 5 T. R. 482 ; 1 H. Bl. 291.

(*h*) Fisher *v.* Johnson, 1 Br. 197 ; 1 East, 350 ; 3 Barn. & Ald. 443 ; 4 Taunt. 98.
(*i*) Fisher *v.* Johnson, 1 Br. 197 ; Wagner *v.* Day, D. C. Phil. 1827, MS.
(*j*) 3 T. R. 391.
(*k*) 1 Stra. 577.
(*l*) 1 Stra. 534 ; ibid. 551.
(*m*) Brightly on Costs, 36 ; 1 Freeman, 215 ; 2 Mod. 142 ; Gilb. H. C. P. 263.

where, in a declaration for trespass upon land, a count is added for injury to personal property, the plaintiff is entitled to full costs without a certificate.(n) And where, in an action of trespass, *quare clausum fregit*, and carrying away goods, a recovery of five dollars damages was had, the plaintiff was held to be entitled to full costs.(o) But where the further injury is laid by way of aggravation of the trespass on the land, the plaintiff is not entitled to costs without a certificate ;(p) and so, also, where the *asportavit* is only alleged by way of description of the manner in which the injury to land was committed.(q)

But by 8 and 9 W. III. c. 11,(r) if the judge certify that the trespass was wilful and malicious, the plaintiff shall have his full costs, although the verdict be for less than 40s.(s) Where the trespass has been committed after notice, the judge usually certifies under this act ;(t) but it is perfectly discretionary with him to do so, or not,(u) and he will not certify if it appear that the trespass was committed for the purpose of asserting a disputed right.(uu) The certificate in this case may, it seems, be granted out of court ; and the judge may certify at any time between verdict and final judgment.(v)

The plaintiff's general right to costs has been further restrained by the 4th section of our act of limitations, passed March 27, 1713,(w) copied from the 21st of James I. c. 16, which declares that in all actions upon the case for "slanderous words," if the damages found be under 40s., the plaintiff shall recover no more costs than damages. This statute, however, extends only to such words as are actionable of themselves ;(x) and it is settled that the statute does not extend to slander of title, for that is not so properly a slander as a cause of damage ;(y) and where the words are not actionable in themselves, but the special damage is the gist of the action, the plaintiff is entitled to full costs, although the damages may be under forty shillings ;(z) but where the words in themselves are actionable, but the special damage is laid by way of aggravation, and as the essential cause of action, the plaintiff is not entitled to more costs than damages.(a)

A plea of justification in slander will not take it out of the statute.(b) If damages under forty shillings be recovered in slander, and judgment entered for costs, on error brought by the defendant below, the judgment will be reversed *in toto*, and *venire facias de novo* awarded.(c)

Where a plaintiff appealed from an award of arbitrators in slander, allowing six cents damages, and the jury gave five dollars damages, it was held that though he could not recover more costs than damages, yet he was entitled to recover back the costs paid by him on the appeal from the award.(d)

(n) Say. Costs, 39 ; 1 Stra. 633.
(o) Williams v. Glenn, 2 Pa. R. 137 ; and see Chapman v. Calder, 2 H. 359.
(p) 3 Burr. 1282.
(q) 1 Doug. 780.
(r) Rob. Dig. 139.
(s) See Hullock, 94, 99.
(t) See 6 T. R. 11, 3 East, 495.
(u) 3 East, 495.
(uu) Ibid.
(v) 1 T. R. 636 ; 4 D. & R. 147 ; 2 B. & C. 580.
(w) 1 Sm. Laws, 77.

(x) 2 Bac. Abr. Costs, B, ; 2 Hullock, 27, 34.
(y) Cro. Car. 141 ; Str. 645 ; see Rob. Dig. 119.
(z) 1 Salk. 206 ; 7 Mod. 129 ; Barnes, 135 ; 2 W. Bl. 1062.
(a) 2 W. Bl. 1062 ; 1 Dowl. P. C. 406 ; 3 Burr. 1688 ; Barnes, 132.
(b) 2 Wilson, 258 ; 4 East, 567.
(c) Gailey v. Beard, 4 Y. 546 ; and see Allen v. Flock, 2 Pa. R. 159.
(d) Guy v. Wilkeson, 2 W. 133.

In all other actions on the case for torts, the plaintiff is entitled to his full costs of suit, however trifling the damages may be.

In England, the power of the judges is taken away by the statute as to giving costs *de incremento*, where the damages are under forty shillings, but although the court cannot increase the costs, the jury are not bound by the statute, and, therefore, they may give ten pounds costs, where they give but ten pence damages ; so where they give less than 40*s.* they may give full costs ;(*e*) and this rule has been adopted by the Supreme Court in construing our act of assembly.(*f*) The true reason why the court is bound while the jury are not, seems to be, that there being no measure of damages in those cases which fall within these statutes, the jury are not bound to give damages *eo nomine*, but may substantially do the same thing in another form, by increasing the costs to the amount of the damages intended to be given.(*g*) The construction of the statute always has been, that although the court cannot add the costs *de incremento*, yet the jury may find any sum in costs they please.(*h*) Thus, in trespass *quare clausum fregit*, the jury may give full costs, although they find damages under 40*s.*, and the judge does not certify that the freehold was in question.(*i*) This construction will not, however, be extended beyond adjudged cases, and the propriety of having extended it so far is reasonably doubted.(*j*)

But neither court nor jury can give costs if the legislature declare, in express terms, that they cannot be recovered.(*k*)

Where the jury or arbitrators find for the plaintiff with *full costs* or *costs of suit*, the plaintiff is entitled to have judgment entered for full costs.(*l*) It was held that where the verdict finds only *costs*, the plaintiff is only entitled to costs to the amount of damages ;(*m*) but a late case seems to have destroyed the distinction—as in an award in slander being for the plaintiff in " the sum of one dollar damages, and that the defendant pay the costs," the plaintiff was held entitled to the full costs of suit.(*n*)

In the District Court for the City and County of Philadelphia, it is provided by rule of court, that if the defendant makes an affidavit of defence as to part and the plaintiff will not accept judgment for the sum so admitted, but proceeds and recovers a sum no greater than such admitted amount, the plaintiff shall pay all costs accruing after such affidavit.(*o*) And a similar rule exists in the Court of Common Pleas.

Where there are several issues, and the substantial issue is found for the plaintiff, he is entitled to the general costs of the cause, with the exception of such parts of the costs of witnesses, papers, &c., as are applicable only to the issue on which the defendants have succeeded.(*p*) And this was decided to be the practice in Pennsylvania, in a case which occurred in the Common Pleas of Lancaster, in which the prothonotary

---

(*e*) 1 Salk. 207 ; Cornogg *v.* Abraham, 1 Y. 253.

(*f*) Stuart *v.* Harkins, 3 Bin. 321.

(*g*) Hinds *v.* Knox, 4 S. & R. 419.

(*h*) 6 Vin. Costs L. pl. 36.

(*i*) Hinds *v.* Knox, 4 S. & R. 417 ; Wilkinson *v.* Grey, 14 id. 345 ; Williams *v.* Glenn, 2 Pa. R. 137.

(*j*) *Vide* Stuart *v.* Harkins, 3 Bin. 323 ; Lewis *v.* England, 4 Bin. 5 ; Lentz *v.* Stroh, 6 S. & R. 39.

(*k*) Lewis *v.* England, 4 Bin. 5 ; Hinds *v.* Knox, 2 S. & R. 417 ; Fortune *v.* Tyler, 1 Ash. 11.

(*l*) Hinds *v.* Knox, 4 S. & R. 417 ; Wilkinson *v.* Grey, ibid. 345.

(*m*) Stuart *v.* Harkins, 3 Bin. 321.

(*n*) Moon *v.* Long, 2 J. 207.

(*o*) Rule iv.

(*p*) 3 Dowl. 687 ; 1 Dowl. 533.

was directed to strike out of the plaintiff's bill all costs not properly applicable to the count in which he recovered.(q)   And the general principle established by the cases is, that where there are several issues of fact upon several counts in the declaration, and a verdict passes for the plaintiff on any one of the issues, he is entitled to a general judgment for costs, and the defendant is not entitled to costs in the counts determined in his favor.(r)   This practice, however, in England, has been altered by rule giving the defendant costs on the issues on which he succeeds.(s)

When the defendant pays the debt after suit brought, the plaintiff is entitled to judgment for costs.(t)

And where payment was made after a summons has issued, and had been placed in the hands of the sheriff, but which had not been served, it was held that the plaintiff was entitled to receive the amount paid by him to the sheriff for the service of the writ.(u)

A plaintiff in ejectment, who has conveyed after action brought, cannot prosecute a pending ejectment to recover the costs already incurred.(v)

In proceedings for divorce under the act of 13th of March, 1815,(w) the court has power to award costs to the party in whose behalf the sentence or decree passes, or that each party shall pay his or her own costs, as to them shall appear reasonable and just.

In foreign attachment, the general rule is that no costs are allowed to either party.(x)   But in Pennsylvania, the plaintiff's right to costs, as against the defendant, is provided for by the 59th section of the act of 13th June, 1836 ;(y) and as against the garnishee refusing to answer by the 57th section of the same act.(z)

Where a feigned issue is directed by the Register's Court, to try the validity of a will, the costs of the Register's Court depend on the event of the verdict ; and where there had been a trial of a feigned issue, and the judgment was afterwards reversed, and a second trial took place, in which the same party was successful, the court refused to allow him the costs of the first trial.(a)

And so also where a feigned issue is ordered by a Court of Common Law,(b) and where a feigned issue is directed to try disputed facts arising on the distribution of the proceeds of a judicial sale of land, the costs are to be distributed among the several creditors, in proportion to the amounts to be received by each ;(c) and the costs of an issue *devisavit vel non* are to be borne by the parties to it, and not by the estate.(d)

2. *Of the plaintiff's right to costs in actions within the jurisdiction of a justice of the peace; and where he recovers a sum less than that required by law to give the court jurisdiction.*

The general rule, established by the statute of Gloucester, that the

---

(q) Northampton Bank v. Winder, 5 P. L. J. 94.

(r) 2 Doug. 677 ; 5 East, 261 ; 2 B. & P. 330 ; 6 T. R. 599 ; 2 Burr. 1232 ; 1 Brod. & Bingh. 224.

(s) Rule F. H. T. 2 W. 4, r. 74.

(t) Wagner v. Wagner, 9 Barr, 214.

(u) Drew v. Conrad, D. C. C. C. P. May 12, 1849, MS.

(v) Blackmore v. Gregg, 10 W. 226.

(w) Dunlop, Dig. ed. 1849, 321.

(x) Serjeant on Attachment, 130.

(y) Pamph. L. 582.

(z) As to the garnishee's right to costs, see *post,* "Defendant's Costs," 650–1.

(a) Harvard v. Davis, 1 Br. 334.

(b) Snyder v. Kunkleman, 2 W. 426.

(c) Cowden's Estate, 1 Barr, 283.

(d) Kopperhaffer v. Isaacs, 7 W. 170.

plaintiff is entitled to costs in all cases where he recovers damages, has been further restrained by the act of 20th March, 1810,(e) giving jurisdiction to justices of the peace in all causes of action arising in contract, with certain exceptions, where the sum demanded is not above one hundred dollars; and by the 26th section it is provided that any person who shall bring suit in court, for a debt or demand made cognizable by the justices, is debarred from costs, unless before the issuing of the original writ he files, in the office of the prothonotary, his oath or affirmation, that he verily believes "the debt due or damages sustained exceed the sum of one hundred dollars."

It is now settled, that where the amount recovered by the plaintiff in an action commenced in the Common Pleas, is reduced to a sum below one hundred dollars, by a set-off or cross demand, the plaintiff is entitled to costs without filing an affidavit, as required by the act of 1810,(f) and this whether the set-off or cross demand is of a liquidated or of an uncertain nature, although there appears, at first, to have been some doubt, where the set-off was of a certain nature and capable of calculation, whether the plaintiff was not bound to elect the proper tribunal at his peril, where due precaution would enable him to proceed with safety (g)   But in Grant v. Wallace,(h) the Supreme Court determined otherwise, GIBSON, C. J., dissenting for that reason.(i)   And this ruling has been followed in a later case, where, in a suit brought in the Common Pleas on a promissory note, in which the plaintiff recovered less than one hundred dollars, he was held to be entitled to costs, the note sued on being for more than one hundred dollars, and the claim having been reduced by an agreement that the price of a horse, and the amount of certain joint and separate claims of the defendants, which had been settled, should go off the note, which was proved on the trial.

As a justice of the peace has no jurisdiction in account render, a plaintiff suing his co-tenant in account render, and recovering a verdict under one hundred dollars, is entitled to costs.(j)

Where the plaintiff splits up into several suits before a justice an aggregate claim exceeding one hundred dollars, for which one suit might have been brought in court, the costs of one suit only can be recovered by him against the defendant.(k)

But it is to be noticed that there is a distinction to be drawn between the cases where the claim is reduced below one hundred dollars by a set-off and by a direct payment, as in the latter case the plaintiff will not be entitled to costs without filing a previous affidavit. This distinction, which was laid down in Cooper v. Coates,(l) a case which arose under an earlier act, limiting the jurisdiction of a justice of the peace

(e) 5 Sm. Laws, 161; Dunlop, Dig. ed. 1849, 280.

(f) Brailey v. Miller, 2 D. 74; Sadler v. Slobaugh, 3 S. & R. 388; Grant v. Wallace, 16 S. & R. 253; Spear v. Jamison, 2 S. & R. 531; Bartram v. McKee, 1 W. 39; Manning v. Eaton, 7 W. 346.

(g) Sadler v. Slobaugh, see 3 S. & R. 388.

(h) 16 S. & R. 253.

(i) It would appear from the opinion of the Chief Justice that the set-off was of an ascertained amount, although the report of the case does not mention its nature.

(j) Steffen v. Hartzell, 5 Wh. 448.

(k) Towanda Bank v. Ballard, 7 W. & S. 434.

(l) 1 D. 308.

to ten pounds, has been recognized and followed in cases which have arisen under the act of 1810.(m)

It is to be observed also that the 26th section is binding on arbitrators and juries as well as the court, and that they cannot by their finding compel the defendant to pay costs where the plaintiff under this act is not entitled to them;(n) and although the arbitrators award that each party shall pay his own costs, yet if the sum awarded carry costs, or if it has been reduced below one hundred dollars by a set-off, the plaintiff is entitled to costs.(o) Where the sum recovered is less than one hundred dollars, and the case is not within the jurisdiction of a justice of the peace, the plaintiff is, of course, entitled to costs without having previously filed an affidavit.(p)

Under the act of March 22, 1814, § 1,(q) the jurisdiction of justices of the peace of the several counties of the commonwealth and aldermen of the City of Philadelphia was extended to actions of trover and conversion and actions of trespass for injury done or committed on real or personal estate, where the value of the property claimed or the damages alleged to have been sustained, do not exceed one hundred dollars.

The 6th section provides, " That the said justices of the peace and aldermen shall have original jurisdiction of all cases of rent not exceeding one hundred dollars, *to be recovered as debts of similar amount are recoverable.*"

It has been held that the first section of this act does not deprive the Court of Common Pleas of jurisdiction; and, as there is no provision depriving a plaintiff of his costs, he will be entitled to full costs in actions of trespass and trover brought in the Common Pleas, although the amount of the claim and verdict recovered may be less than one hundred dollars.(r)

And by the act of the 13th of February, 1816,(s) it is provided that in all actions for the recovery of damages, for any trespass committed against real or personal estate before any justice or alderman, and referred agreeably to law, the referees shall be empowered, in addition to their report of the damages, to decide and report whether the plaintiff or defendant should pay the costs of such action, or in what proportion they should be paid by the plaintiff or defendant respectively.(t)

The 6th section of the act of 1814, conferring jurisdiction on aldermen and justices of the peace in cases of rent, provides for their recovery "as debts of a similar nature are recoverable."

There has been no decision as yet in the Supreme Court which determines whether, under the phraseology of this section, the provisions of the 26th section of the act of 1810, taking away the plaintiff's right to costs where suit is brought in the Common Pleas, are to be

(m) Stewart v. Mitchell, 13 S. & R. 287; Odell v. Culbert, 9 W. & S. 66; and in Barry v. Mervine, 4 Barr, 330.

(n) Heath v. Atkinson, 1 P. A. Br. 231; Grier v. McFadon, 1 Ash. 1; Sneively v. Weidman, 1 S. & R. 417; Lewis v. England, 4 Bin. 5.

(o) Spier v. Jamieson, 2 S. & R. 530.

(p) Zell v. Arnold, 2 Pa. R. 292;

Commonwealth v. Reynolds, 17 S. & R. 369; Shaw v. Levy, ibid. 102.

(q) 6 Sm. Laws, 182; Dunlap. Dig. ed. 1849, 305.

(r) Hinds v. Knox, 4 S. & R. 417; Clarkè v. McKisson, 6 S. & R. 87; Richards v. Gage, 1 Ash. 192.

(s) 6 Sm. Laws, 323.

(t) See Wilkinson v. Grey, 14 S. & R. 346.

considered as applying to cases of rent; in a late case, however, in the Court of Common Pleas of Philadelphia, in an action brought to recover arrears of ground-rent, the question being as to the plaintiff's right to costs, it was held by THOMPSON, P. J., that "if the plaintiff chooses to proceed under the act of April 8, 1840, in order to obtain judgment on two *nihils* in the Court of Common Pleas, he must pay his own costs. The act of April 8, 1840, does not restrict the jurisdiction of the Justice, nor extend that of the Court. The judgment, therefore, does not carry the costs."(u)

As the District Court for the City and County of Philadelphia has no jurisdiction, except where the amount in controversy exceeds one hundred dollars,(v) a plaintiff is never aided in the recovery of costs in the District Court by the previous filing of an affidavit; the rule being, that that court has no jurisdiction whatever, where the plaintiff could not recover costs, if he had sued in the Common Pleas, unless he filed a previous affidavit, before the erection of the District Court.(w)

In regard to the jurisdiction of the District Court,(x) it is only necessary here to remark that, where the plaintiff's demand is reduced by a set-off below one hundred dollars, the District Court has jurisdiction wherever the plaintiff would be entitled to costs in a similar case brought in the Common Pleas, without having made a previous affidavit of his belief that his claim exceeded that amount; and, in case of *tort*, the jurisdiction is determined by the amount demanded in the declaration.(y)

By the act of 29th March, 1810,(z) the original jurisdiction of the Supreme Court, in the City and County of Philadelphia, was restored in all civil actions wherein the matter in controversy is of the value of five hundred dollars and upwards; but there is no restriction as to costs. It follows, therefore, that in all cases where the court has jurisdiction, costs are of course. The act of September, 1786,(a) discouraged suits for small matters, by refusing costs where not more than fifty pounds were recovered. The act of March, 1810, did the same thing in a different but more effectual way; that is to say, by denying any jurisdiction in cases where *the value of the matter in controversy* was not at least five hundred dollars.(b) The act of September, 1786, § 5,(c) which first extended original jurisdiction to the Supreme Court in Philadelphia County, provided, that if any party should bring any suit therein and not recover more than fifty pounds, he should be allowed no costs of suit. A jury might, however, in addition to a penalty of fifty pounds, have given nominal damages in an action of debt by the party aggrieved, and in such case the plaintiff was entitled to full costs under the act of assembly.(d)

All disputes arising out of a policy and joined in the same action, are, therefore, considered the *matter in controversy*; and if the plaintiff, to a demand for a total loss exceeding five hundred dollars, join a count

(u) C. P. C. C. P. July 10, 1852; ix. Leg. Intel. 114.

(v) Act of March 30, 1811; 5 Sm. Laws, 223.

(w) Kline v. Wood, 9 S. & R. 300.

(x) See *ante*, 23.

(y) Rodman v. Hutchinson, 4 Wh.

242; Byrne v. Gordon, 2 P. A. Br. 271.

(z) 5 Sm. Laws, 158.

(a) 2 Sm. Laws, 392.

(b) *Per* TILGHMAN, C. J.; Wurts v. M'Fadden, 4 S. & R. 79.

(c) 2 Sm Laws, 392.

(d) Norris v. Pilmore, 1 Y. 405.

for money had and received, to recover back the premium, though the amount of such premium demanded be less than five hundred dollars, he is entitled to costs if he recover only on the count for money had and received.(e) So, where in trespass the case was arbitrated before declaration filed, and the award was two hundred and fifty dollars, and it was proved that the plaintiff's demand before the arbitrators exceeded five hundred dollars, it was held that he was entitled to costs.(f) In *tort*, the plaintiff having a right to estimate his damages at any sum, the amount stated in the declaration is the only criterion to be resorted to in settling the jurisdiction. If, therefore, the damages are laid at five hundred dollars, the plaintiff gets costs although he recovers a smaller sum.(g) In the case of an ejectment, the court would be obliged to receive affidavits as to the value of the controversy ; but in most cases it may be ascertained from the nature of the dispute and evidence in the cause.(h) All original jurisdiction being now taken from the Supreme Court, except as above stated, and continued by the act of 1836, as we have before seen, the decisions above quoted are useful so far only as they are connected with similar questions in the courts possessing such jurisdiction.

SECTION II.

DEFENDANT'S COSTS.

1. *Of the defendant's costs generally.*
By the statute, 4 Jac. 1, c. 13,(i) it is provided that, in all cases in which a plaintiff would be entitled to costs if he recovered, the defendant shall recover his costs if a verdict be found for him, or the plaintiff be nonsuit.

In the statute of Gloucester, no provision was made for the costs of a defendant in any case ; nor was any made, except in actions of replevin and writs of error, until the 23 H. VIII. c. 15,(j) which particularizes the actions wherein a defendant shall recover costs ; but the statute 4 Jac. 1, c, 13, reciting that the 23 H. VIII. c. 15, had been found a very beneficial law, extended the provisions of that statute to every action in which a plaintiff or demandant may recover costs.

By statute 18 Eliz. c. 5, in actions upon penal statutes by common informers, the defendant is entitled to his costs if he have a verdict, though the plaintiff would not be entitled even if he succeeded.(k)

The right of the defendant to costs where the plaintiff "shall not prosecute his suit with effect, but shall willingly suffer his suit to be delayed, or shall suffer the same to be discontinued, or be otherwise nonsuited therein," was given by the statute 8 Eliz. c. 2.(l)

A discontinuance is founded always upon the express or implied leave of the court ;(m) and a plaintiff cannot discontinue his suit except upon

(e) Wurts v. McFadden, 4 S. & R. 78.
(f) Bazin v. Barry, 3 S. & R. 461.
(g) Ib.; Hancock v. Barton, 1 S. & R. 269 ; M'Kissan v. Steel, 1 Y. 1.
(h) Per cur. Byrne v. Gordon, 2 Br. 274.
(i) Rob. Dig. 129.

(j) Rob. Dig. 129.
(k) 1 Salk. 30; Cowper, 366; 2 Strange, 1103 ; Hullock, 214, 220.
(l) Rob. Dig. 125.
(m) Schuylkill Bank v. Macalester, 6 W. & S. 147.

payment of costs; and until the payment of costs, there is no discontinuance;(n) and the entry of a *nol pros.* is a discontinuance within the statute.(o)

Where the judgment is arrested after verdict, each party pays his own costs.(p)

Where judgment is entered for the defendant on demurrer, he is entitled to costs by the statute 8 and 9 Will. III. c. 11; but the statute does not extend to the case where judgment is given for the defendant on a demurrer to a plea in abatement, because the statute speaks of suits which are vexatious, which does not appear to the court on pleas in abatement, but only on demurrers in bar.(q)

The plaintiff in replevin is entitled to costs by the statute of Gloucester; the defendant, or avowant, by statute 7 H. VIII. c. 4, which is declared in force, excepting those parts which relate to writs of *quare impedit* and avowsons.(r) By our act of assembly the defendant in replevin may avow for rent in arrear, and make cognizance generally, and if the plaintiff becomes nonsuit, discontinues his action, or has judgment given against him, the defendant, in such replevin, shall recover double costs of suit.(s) If the plaintiff be *non-prossed*, the defendant shall have his costs as in other cases.(t) If there be two defendants in replevin, one of whom is acquitted, he is not entitled to costs;(u) for replevin is not within the statute 8 and 9 W. III. c. 11.(v)

Replevin sureties by plaintiff to prosecute his suit with effect, are liable for costs to defendant, if plaintiff fails.(w)

Where the defendant in replevin avowed for rent in arrear, and there was an award of arbitrators in favor of avowant, the plaintiff is not compelled to pay double costs in order to obtain an appeal.(x)

The act of 3d April, 1779,(y) after providing that all writs of replevin granted or issued for any owner or owners of any goods or chattels levied, seized, or taken in execution, or by distress or otherwise, by any sheriff, naval officer, lieutenant, or sub-lieutenant of the City of Philadelphia, or of any county, constable, collector of the public taxes, or other officer, acting in their several offices under the authority of the State, are irregular, erroneous, and void—directs, that such writs may be quashed by the court to which they are made returnable, on motion, supported by affidavit; and the court *may and shall,* upon quashing the writ, award treble costs to the defendant. This act, however, does not apply to a writ of replevin brought by the owner of goods taken in execution against the sheriff's vendee;(z) nor to a writ issued against the defendant in the execution, by a third person, for goods which had been taken in execution for the debt of defendant.(a)

In actions of *scire facias,* the defendant is entitled to costs, by virtue of the 8 & 9 Will. III. c. 11,(b) which provides, that "if the plaintiff

(n) Arch. Prac. 1058.
(o) 3 T. R. 511.
(p) Cowp. 407; Gilbert, C. P. 272.
(q) 1 Salk. 194; S. C. 1 Ld. Raym. 336; 6 Mod. 88; 12, ibid. 195.
(r) Rob. Dig. 117; and see 4 J. I. c. 3, ib. 129.
(s) Act of March, 1772, 1 Sm. Laws, 372; see *post,* "Double and Treble Costs," 672.
(t) See 1 T. R. 372.

(u) 1 W. Bl. 355; 3 Burr. 1284,
(v) Rob. Dig. 139.
(w) Tibbal *v.* Cahoon, 10 W. 236.
(x) Hartley *v.* Bean, 1 M. 168.
(y) 1 Sm. Laws, 470; Dunl. Dig. ed. 1849, 122.
(z) Spearick *v.* Huber, 6 Bin. 2.
(a) English *v.* Dalbrow, 1 M. 160; Mulholm *v.* Cheney, Add. 301.
(b) Rob. Dig. 140.

become nonsuit, or suffer a discontinuance, or a verdict shall pass against him, the defendant shall recover costs.

The costs of a *scire facias* on a mechanic's lien are to be paid out of the fund raised by the sale of the building upon which the lien attached;(c) and where, during the pendency of a *scire facias*, the property was sold under an older lien, and the proceeds were absorbed by older lien creditors, the court will not aid either party in the recovery of costs, by permitting them to go on to trial.(d)

The defendant is not liable, personally, for costs on a *scire facias* on a mortgage, the judgment being exclusively *de terris;* nor does a tenant, applying by petition and permitted to defend, incur any personal liability for costs, unless there be a stipulation to that effect when his petition was granted ;(e) nor in a *scire facias* on a mechanic's lien is a contractor personally liable for costs.(f)

By the defalcation act of 1705,(g) if the jury find that the plaintiff is overpaid, they shall give their verdict for the defendant, and certify how much they find the plaintiff indebted to him over and above the sum demanded, which sum shall be recorded with the verdict, and be deemed as a debt of record ; and if the plaintiff refuse to pay the same, the defendant, for recovery thereof, shall have a *scire facias* against the plaintiff, and have execution for the same with the costs of that action. If, in the interim, the defendant have instituted a cross action, the plaintiff will be burdened with the costs of both suits—with those of the first, for having brought a vexatious action, and with those of the second, because the defendant shows a good cause of action. To suppose that, by virtue of this act, a man who is really a creditor shall not bring an action, because his debtor has already sued him, is pregnant with absurdity.(h)

The District Court has refused to allow cost to a defendant for his answer to a bill of discovery.(i)

With regard to the garnishee's right to costs in a *scire facias* in foreign attachment, if the plaintiff does not prove more in the hands of the garnishee than he admits by his plea, or his answers upon interrogatories, the plaintiff must pay costs ; but if more is proved, then the costs shall be paid by the garnishee.(j)

If a garnishee suffers judgment to go against himself, he is not liable for costs, because he has done nothing but pursue the path pointed out by law; but if he pleads a false plea, if he falsely denies that he has any effects in his hands, or there are effects exceeding those he admits, he is responsible for costs.(k) And a garnishee who has filed his answers to the interrogatories of the plaintiff, is entitled to recover his costs, if the plaintiff compels him to plead and prepare for trial, and then becomes nonsuit.(l)

It seems plain, from the tenor of the acts regulating attachment

---

(c) McLaughlin v. Smith, 2 Wh. 122.
(d) Matlack v. Deal, 1 M. 254.
(e) Wickersham v. Fetrow, 5 Barr, 260.
(f) Dickinson College v. Church, 1 W. & S. 465.
(g) 1 Sm. Laws, 49; Dunlop. Dig. ed. 1849, 45.
(h) Beache v. Bryan, and Bryan v. Beache, C. P. Sept. Term, 1767 ; MSS. Reports.
(i) Tenor v. Hutton, D. C. C. P. 7 Leg. Int. 50.
(j) Walker v. Dallas, 2 D. 113.
(k) Wood v. Lugwig, 5 S. & R. 446; Myers v. Urick, 1 Bin. 25.
(l) Hall v. Knapp, 1 Barr, 213.

executions, that the proceedings should be governed by the familiar rules in foreign attachments, when not otherwise directed. Hence the subject of costs to plaintiff and to garnishee are regulated by the old foreign attachment law; and a garnishee who answers interrogatories is entitled to costs, if the plaintiff proceeds to trial, and becomes non-suit.(m)

Where an attachment sur judgment was issued in each of three several cases, and several individuals and three corporations made garnishees, and an issue was joined with one of the corporations in each of the cases which were severally tried, and verdict and judgment entered for the garnishee, the prothonotary allowed the usual bill of costs as upon a suit in court, and on appeal the District Court affirmed the taxation.(n)

It is provided by the act of 1705, section 2,(o) that the garnishees shall be allowed, out of the effects attached, reasonable satisfaction for his attendance; this has always been held to include the expenses of counsel fee; and where a foreign attachment is laid for a smaller sum than is in the hands of the garnishee, he is not justified in withholding from his creditor more than sufficient to cover the debt claimed by the plaintiff in the attachment, the interest which would probably accumulate, costs, and a liberal allowance for expenses;(p) but the garnishee is not entitled to retain, as against the plaintiffs, the costs and expenses of subsequent writs of foreign attachment issued against the same defendants.(q)

In a sci. fa. in foreign attachment, the garnishees were held not to be entitled, upon judgment rendered for them, to the costs of an exemplification of an assignment which was produced by them on trial to prove their case.(r)

When there are several defendants who succeed in the action, the plaintiff may pay costs to which of them he pleases;(s) and if they fail, each of them is answerable for the whole costs.(t)

2. *Where there are several defendants, and one or more are acquitted by verdict.*

In trespass, assault, false imprisonment, or ejectment, if there be several defendants, and one of them is acquitted, he shall recover his costs in the like manner as if a verdict had been given against plaintiff, unless the judge shall immediately after the trial, in open court, certify upon the record that there was a reasonable cause for making such person a defendant.(u)

(m) Hall v. Knapp, 1 Barr, 213.

(n) Magruder v. Adams, D. C. C. C. P. Feb. 2, 1850. *Per curiam.* The 35th section of the act of June 16, 1836, relating to execution, provides that an attachment may issue in the case of a debt due the defendant; "but in such case a clause, in the nature of a *sci. fa.* against a garnishee in a foreign attachment, shall be inserted in such writ of attachment." It is clear, then, that the attachment occupies, in respect to the garnishee, the same place that a separate *scire facias* does against a garnishee in a foreign attachment, and it is not to be doubted that such a *scire facias* is a suit, costs in

which are recoverable as in the case of a suit commenced by original process. The question has been likened to a *sci. fa.* on a judgment against several *terre-tenants*, but there is no analogy. Appeal dismissed.

(o) 1 Sm. 46.

(p) Lickman v. Lapsley, 13 S. & R. 224.

(q) Warner v. Bancroft, 2 M. 75.

(r) Christmas v. Biddle, D. C. C. P. 7 Leg. Int. 66; see 1 H. 223.

(s) Str. 516, 1203.

(t) Bull. N. P. 335.

(u) 8 and 9 W. III. e. 11; Rob. Dig. 139.

When one of several defendants lets judgment go by default, and the other pleads a plea, which goes to the whole declaration, and shows that the plaintiff had no cause of action, if this plea be found for the defendant who pleaded it, he shall have costs ; and being an absolute bar, the other defendant shall have the benefit of it, and shall not pay costs to the plaintiff.(*v*) But when the plea goes merely to discharge the party pleading it, then the other party shall pay costs, though it be found against the plaintiff.(*w*)

This statute does not, however, extend to replevin ;(*x*) or to trespass on the case for a tort,(*y*) or trover ;(*yy*) and in all cases not within this statute, if the plaintiff proceed to trial against several defendants, and obtain a verdict against any one of them, the others will not be entitled to costs. But if some only of several defendants proceed to trial, the others having suffered judgment by default, and those who proceed to trial obtain a verdict, the defendants who obtain a verdict in such a case are entitled to their costs under the statute of 4 J. I. c. 3, although the plaintiff have his judgment and costs against the others who suffered judgment by default.(*z*)

The statute of 8 and 9 William III. c. 11, does not extend to an action of *scire facias*.

Thus, in a *scire facias* to revive a judgment against an administrator, with notice to several *terre-tenants*, a several issue was joined with each *terre-tenant*, and a verdict and judgment rendered against one tenant, and in favor of the others. It was held that the defendant in whose favor the verdict and judgment were given, were not entitled to recover their costs from the plaintiff.(*a*) But where there are several garnishees to a *scire facias* in proceeding in the nature of foreign attachment, it would seem that those obtaining judgment would be entitled to costs.(*b*)

3. *In the case of an equitable plaintiff.*

The act of April 23, 1829,(*c*) provides that "the equitable plaintiff, or person for whose use or benefit, and at whose instance any action has been, or may be presented, whether named on the record or not, shall be liable to execution on judgment against the legal plaintiff or plaintiffs : *Provided*, That where such equitable plaintiff or plaintiffs were not named on the record previous to judgment, his name shall be suggested on the record, supported by affidavit of his interest in the cause, before execution shall issue."

Where a suit has been carried on for the use of an assignee, the nominal plaintiff being insolvent, the court will permit the defendant, after verdict, to suggest upon the docket that the suit was for the use of the assignee, and will rule him to pay the costs.(*d*) So, in an action by the assignee of a bond irregularly assigned, brought in the name of the obligee for the former's use, the court will compel the assignee to pay the costs.(*e*) And where the assignee brings an action in the name of the assignor, without consulting or informing him of it (which is the

(*v*) 1 Lev. 63 ; 8 Mod. 217 ; 2 H. Bl. 28.
(*w*) Cro. Jac. 134 ; ca. 7 ; 3 T. R. 656.
(*x*) 3 Burr. 1284.
(*y*) 2 Str. 1005 ; 6 Bing. 530.
(*yy*) Barnes, 139.
(*z*) 2 H. Bl. 28 ; see 6 Taunt. 398.·
(*a*) Maus *v.* Maus, 10 W. 87.

(*b*) See Magruder *v.* Adams, *ante*, 651, note.
(*c*) Pamph. L. p. 335 ; Dunlop's Dig. ed. 1849.
(*d*) Canby *v.* Ridgeway, 1 Bin. 496 ; Hoak *v.* Hoak, 5 W. 80.
(*e*) Com. *v.* Co. Commissioners, 8 S. & R. 154.

experience of every day), the assignor is considered as out of the question, and the court would issue an attachment for costs against the person for whose use the suit is brought, in case of a judgment for the defendant.(f)   Any person who, at the commencement of suit, is entitled to a portion of the money claimed, is liable for costs.(g)   It is immaterial whether his name be in the record or not.(h)

The person for whose use an action has been brought, is liable in assumpsit, upon an express promise to pay to the defendant, in such action, the amount of costs incurred.(i)

He who procures the suit to be brought, though neither the legal nor equitable plaintiff, is liable for the costs, if there be no other from whom they can be recovered.(j)

In actions on official bonds, sued in the name of the commonwealth, for the use of parties aggrieved, or in action brought by an assignee of the State, the court will look to the real party on the record, and compel him to pay costs.(k)

4. *Security for costs.*

So necessary an appendage or incident to the judgment have costs now become, that the defendant may (under some circumstances) at an early period of the suit, call on the plaintiff to furnish security for the costs, or else to submit, in our practice, to a judgment of nonsuit or *nonpros.;* which security extends not only to costs already incurred, but also to prospective costs of the suit ;(l) and, therefore, the recognizance or obligation entered into by the plaintiff and his sureties, should be devised so as to bind them to the payment of costs in case the plaintiff should not prosecute his suit with effect.(m)   By a rule of the District Court of the City and County of Philadelphia, it is ordered, "That in cases where the plaintiff resides out of the State, in *qui tam* actions, in suits on administration or office bonds, or when the plaintiff, after suit brought, has taken the benefit of the insolvent laws, the defendant, on motion and affidavit of a just defence against the whole demand, may have a rule that the plaintiff give security for costs at or before some period to be appointed by the court; and, for want of such security, the court, on motion, may order judgment of nonsuit to be entered.(n)

Under this rule of court, the practice in that court is, that a rule on the plaintiff to give security for costs will not be granted, unless he is a non-resident of the State at the institution of the suit; and the affidavit of the party applying for such rule is defective unless it states such non-residence at the time of the institution of the suit.(o)

But, in the Supreme Court of Pennsylvania for the Eastern District, and the Court of Common Pleas of the County of Philadelphia, where similar rules prevail, the construction is different, and it is held that the rule requiring security for costs, applies as well to cases where the plaintiff has removed from the State *pendente lite,* as where he was a non-resi-

(f) Steele v. Phœnix Ins. Co. 3 Bin. 312; see Gallagher v. Milligan, 3 Pa. R. 178 ; Brewer v. Hayes, 2 W. 12.

(g) Gallagher v. Milligan, 3 Pa. R. 178.

(h) Ibid.

(i) Brewer v. Hayes, 2 W. 12.

(j) HUSTON, J., Utt v. Long, 6 W. & S. 178.

(k) Com. v. Co. Commissioners, 8 S. & R. 151.

(l) 1 Barn. & Ald. 331.

(m) See Bowne v. Arbuncle, Peters's C. C. R. 233 ; Ayres v. Sweigart, 6 W. 191.

(n) Rule lxxxvii.

(o) Searll v. Mann, 1 Miles, 321 ; Frost v. Earnest, D. C. C. C. P. Feb. 1836, MS.

dent at the commencement of the suit.   But application for the security must be made at the earliest possible time after the fact has come to his knowledge.   The court will not order it to be given where there has been an award by arbitrators in favor of the plaintiff, from which the defendant has not appealed.(*p*)

Security for costs will not be required where one of the plaintiffs resides within the State, although the others may reside out of it.(*q*) But where there are two plaintiffs, one of whom resides out of, and the other within the State, and the plaintiff within the State dies pending the suit, the defendant may have a rule for security for costs.(*r*)

Plaintiffs who live out of the jurisdiction of the court, may be compelled to give security for costs, although they sue in a representative character.(*s*)

It is no objection to the motion, that the defendant himself resides out of the State; and he will not be compelled to give security himself, in order to entitle him to it from the plaintiff,(*t*) except a defendant in replevin, residing out of the jurisdiction of the court, who cannot, it is said, be distinguished from any ordinary plaintiff, as to giving security for costs.(*u*)

In the practice of the English courts, it would be too late, after notice of trial given, to make this motion, if the defendant had an opportunity of making an earlier application.(*v*) But, in this State, it is never too late to grant a rule for security for costs, when it will not delay the trial.(*w*)

If not demanded in a reasonable time, the applicant cannot object to a trial because it has not been given;(*x*) and it is too late after an award of arbitrators, and an appeal by the defendant, for him to require security for costs.(*y*)

It cannot, however, be made in bailable actions, until after bail has been put in, and justified,(*z*) unless the defendant be in custody.(*a*) The rule of court above quoted, as far as regards insolvents, is applicable only to cases in which the beneficial interest in the action has passed to the assignee.   It cannot, therefore, be extended to a case in which damages are claimed for a personal *tort*.   Neither would it be a valid rule if it did expressly embrace such a case.(*b*)

As the case of infancy depends upon the common law, and not upon any written order of the English courts, it may, notwithstanding that the rule of the District Court does not include it, still be law in that court.

5. *Of the costs of former actions.*

The practice of the courts to stay proceedings in a second action, where the plaintiff has failed in a former action against the same defendant, for the same cause, until the costs of the former action are

(*p*) M'Garry *v.* Crispin, 4 P. L. J. 353; Sharp *v.* Buffington, 2 W. & S. 454.

(*q*) Zimmerman *v.* Mendenhall, 2 M. 402; 1 East, 431; 7 Taunt. 307.

(*r*) 2 Johns. Cas. 67.

(*s*) 1 Brod. & Bin. 277; 3 Moore, 602; 1 Dowl. 366.

(*t*) 6 Taunt. 379.

(*u*) 1 Brod. & Bin. 505.

(*v*) Arch. Pr. 1017.

(*w*) Shaw *v.* Wallace, 2 D. 179; ibid. 1 Y. 176.

(*x*) Hawkins *v.* Willbank, 4 Wash. C. C. R. 285.

(*y*) Cantelo *v.* Binns, 2 M. 86.

(*z*) Arch. Pr. 1017.

(*a*) Ibid.

(*b*) McFarland *v.* Brown, 11 S. & R. 121, 122.

paid, originated in the action of ejectment, and afterwards the practice was extended to other forms of action, but in all cases, as well in ejectment as others, *the vexation of the party* is the ground on which the court interposes in this way.(c) When the merits of the cause have been heard, and the plaintiff is either nonsuited or a verdict passes against him, the plaintiff will not be permitted to harass the defendant with a second suit on the same ground, until the costs of the first are discharged.(d) Therefore, where on the trial of an ejectment the plaintiff was nonsuited, the judge believing the form of action to have been mistaken, and the plaintiff brought a second action against the same defendant for the same cause, the court refused to stay proceedings until the costs of the former action were paid;(e) and where a plaintiff, who was the administrator of both husband and wife, brought trover as administrator of the wife, and suffered a nonsuit, and then brought suit for the same goods as the administrator of the husband, to whose estate the goods belonged; the court refused to stay proceedings until the costs of the former action were paid, on the ground that he did not unnecessarily vex the defendant.(f)

The practice of the courts to stay proceedings in a second suit until the costs of a former action for the same cause are paid, is a convenient and just mode of compelling the payment of costs due, as well to the officers of the court as to the party. And it will be adopted in the Supreme Court on the application of a proper party, though the first suit was in an inferior court and no bill of costs had been filed in it.(g)

If for the same cause of action, a variation in the names is immaterial.(h) And where an action was brought by A, assignee of B, the obligee in a bond, the court stayed proceedings until the costs of nonsuit in a previous action, instituted in the name of A, to the use of B, against the same defendant and on the same bond, were paid.(i)

Where the plaintiff in a former ejectment between the same parties, for the same land, was *non-prossed*, the court continued the cause until the costs of the former suit were paid.(j)

Proceedings in ejectment will be stayed until the costs of a former ejectment, in which the present plaintiff was one of the defendants, are paid.(k)

The rule that the court will stay proceedings in a second action until the costs of a former on the same cause of action are paid, applies in cases where no narr. has been filed in the second action; it being incumbent on the plaintiff to show the court, by affidavit or otherwise, that the cause of action is not the same.(l)

Proceedings in a suit will be stayed until the costs in a previous suit between the same parties, for the same cause of action, but different in form, are paid.(m)

(c) Cochran v. Perry, 4 P. L. J. 319; 4 Mod. 379; 2 T. R. 511; 3 Dowl. & Ryl. 58; 2 W. Bl. 741.

(d) Newton v. Bewley, 1 Br. 38.

(e) Cochran v. Perry, 4 P. L. J. 319:

(f) Cornelius v. Vanarsdallen, 3 Barr, 434.

(g) Flemming v. Penna. Ins. Co. 4 Barr, 475.

(h) Ibid.

(i) Newton v. Bewley, 1 Br. 38.

(j) Hurst's Lessee v. Jones, 4 D. 353.

(k) Altman v. Altman, 2 J. 246.

(l) Stiles v. Woodruff, D. C. C. P. 7 Leg. Int. 66.

(m) Koons v. Patterson, D. C. C. P. 9 Leg. Int. 11.

Application for a rule to stay proceedings until the costs of a former suit are paid, must be made to the court in bank.(n)

But the refusal of the court below to stay proceedings until the costs of a former suit are paid, is not the subject of a writ of error.(o)

Where the judgment is arrested on account of the insufficiency of the declaration, a new suit cannot be commenced for the same cause of action, until the costs are paid in the first suit, as in cases of verdict and judgment for defendant.(p)

6. *Of costs after tender and payment of money into court.*

By the act of 1705, sec. 2, it is provided that where a tender is made of the amount of the debt or demand, previously to the institution of suit, which the plaintiff refuses to accept, the plaintiff is not entitled to recover costs ;(q) but under this act, to entitle a defendant to recover costs from the plaintiff upon a plea of tender before suit brought, he must have pleaded a tender and paid the money into court.(r)

And it seems that payment must be made under a rule regularly obtained for that purpose, as a payment irregularly made cannot be recognized.(s)

And if the action was originally brought before a justice of the peace, the defendant must also have made the plea of tender before suit brought, and have offered the money to the plaintiff before the justice.(t) And this should appear on the alderman's record, in order to excuse the defendant from the payment of costs on appeal.(u)

Where the defendant has not made a tender before suit brought, he may tender afterwards the amount due, by paying it into court under a rule obtained for that purpose, together with the costs which have accrued up to that time ; and if the plaintiff proceeds to trial, he will be liable to pay the subsequently accruing costs to the defendant if he becomes nonsuit, or fails to recover a greater amount than the sum paid into court.(v) The plaintiff may at any time before the trial, if he chooses not to proceed further, obtain the costs up to the time of the defendant's paying money into court; but if the defendant has incurred any subsequent costs, he must be allowed them.(w)

Where the plaintiff becomes nonsuit, or the defendant obtains a verdict, after payment of money into court, the defendant is entitled to costs ;(x) and it would seem that in such cases the plaintiff is not entitled to the costs up to the time of the payment into court.(y)

And although after payment into court the defendant can never take it out, yet if the plaintiff becomes nonsuit, or fails in his action, the money, if not previously taken out, may be impounded to answer the defendant's costs.(z)

(n) Lessee of Plumsted v. Rudebagh, 1 Y. 502.

(o) Withers v. Haines, 2 Barr, 435.

(p) Act Aug. 2, 1842, sec. 12, Pamph. L. 460 ; Dunlap, Dig. ed. 1849, 986.

(q) 1 Sm. L. 49 ; Dunlap, Dig. ed. 1849, 48.

(r) Sheredine v. Gaul, 2 D. 190 ; Seibert v. Kline, 1 Barr, 38 ; Cornell v. Green, 10 S. & R. 14.

(s) Harvey v. Hackley, 6 W. 264.

(t) Seibert v. Kline, 1 Barr, 38.

(u) Dawson v. Collins, C. P. of P. Brightly on Costs, 281.

(v) 1 T. R. 629 ; ibid. 710 ; Arch. Pr. Lond. ed. 1840, 975 ; 2 Bos. & Pul. 56.

(w) 1 T. R. 629 ; ibid. 710.

(x) 4 T. R. 10 ; 1 T. R. 710 ; 2 M. 65.

(y) 3 T. R. 657 ; 4 T. R. 10 ; vide 1 T. R. 710, contra.

(z) Jenkins v. Cutchers, 2 M. 65 ; Barnes, 280.

If the defendant plead a tender without paying the money into court, the plea, as far as it respects the tender, is a mere nullity.

The following rule has been adopted in the Common Pleas of Philadelphia :—

A defendant may upon motion, and before he pleads, pay into court the amount which he admits to be due, together with costs up to that time. The plaintiff may receive the amount so paid, and either enter a discontinuance, or proceed to trial at his option. But in the latter case he shall pay all costs subsequently accruing, unless he recover judgment for a sum independently of that so admitted to be due and paid into court. § 1.(a)

SECTION III.

OF COSTS ON A WRIT OF ERROR.

No costs were recoverable on a writ of error by the statute of Gloucester, as no damages were recoverable therein. They were first given by statute 3 Henry VII., cap. 9,(b) against defendants who sue out a writ of error, afore execution had to reverse a judgment in favor of the plaintiffs, in case the judgment was affirmed, the writ of error discontinued, or the plaintiff in error became nonsuit. This statute gave costs only to the plaintiffs on the affirmance of a judgment in their favor on a writ of error sued out by the defendants to reverse it. The statute 13 Car. II. cap. 2, § 10,(c) gives double costs to the defendants in error, in a writ of error sued out by any person to reverse a judgment *given after verdict* in any court of record, where the judgment shall be affirmed.(d)

The statute 8 and 9 William III. cap. 11, § 10,(e) provides that after judgment for defendants, if the plaintiff or demandant sue out a writ of error, and the judgment should be affirmed, the writ discontinued, or the plaintiff become nonsuit, the defendant shall have judgment to recover his costs against the plaintiff or demandant.

It is to be observed that all these statutes give costs on the *affirmance* of the judgment only, and no costs, therefore, are recoverable on *the reversal* of a judgment on a writ of error.(f) And where the plaintiff sued out a writ of error on a judgment in his favor, and the Supreme Court affirmed the judgment below, the plaintiff in error was held not to be entitled to costs. As where a judgment is reversed, the Supreme Court gives no costs; if costs are levied by execution, they will order the money received by the different officers to be refunded.(g)

When the Supreme Court reverses a judgment and orders a *venire de novo*, it has a right to impose terms, as to costs; but where no terms are imposed the costs abide the final event of the suit.(h)

Where a judgment in favor of the plaintiff was reversed on a writ of

(a) Rule xxiv.
(b) Rob. Dig. 107.
(c) Rob. Dig. 138.
(d) This act is reported to be in force in Pennsylvania, see Rob. Dig. p. 138, but we are not aware that it is ever noticed in our practice. *Brightly on Costs,* 195. See Cameron *v.* Paul, 1 J. 277.

(e) Rob. Dig. 140.
(f) Landis *v.* Schaffer, 4 S. & R. 199; Work *v.* Lessee of Maclay, 14 S. & R. 265; Smith *v.* Sharp, 5 W. 292.
(g) Wright *v.* Small, 5 Bin. 204.
(h) Work *v.* Maclay, 14 S. & R. 295.

error sued out by the defendant below, the plaintiff having been obliged to pay the costs in error in order to take down the record to the Common Pleas, where a verdict and judgment was rendered in his favor, it was held that he was entitled to recover in *assumpsit* the costs incurred by the defendant in his writ of error, and which he was obliged to pay to remove the record.(*i*) But where the payment was not compulsory, the party paying them is not entitled to recover them; and, therefore, where a judgment entered upon an award was reversed by the Supreme Court, and the defendant in error paid the costs and brought the record down in order to get the award to enforce it otherwise, it was held, that the payment of the costs was voluntary, and that he could not recover the amount for the defendant.(*j*)

SECTION IV.

COSTS ON APPEAL FROM ALDERMEN AND JUSTICES OF THE PEACE.

The act of March 20, 1810,(*k*) provided that the party appellant shall be bound with surety in the nature of special bail, " if the plaintiff, in a sum sufficient to cover all the costs which have, or may accrue, with four dollars as counsel fee, and fifty cents per day for every day the appellee shall attend on such appeal, which the appellant shall be bound to pay if the judgment of the justice shall be affirmed by the court, or if he shall recover less than the amount of the judgment of the justice; if the defendant be the appellant, he shall be bound with surety as aforesaid, in a sum sufficient to cover the sum in controversy, all the costs, counsel fee, and daily pay as aforesaid, which he shall be bound to pay if the judgment of the justice shall be affirmed by the court, or if the plaintiff shall recover more than the amount of the judgment of the justice; but on the reversal or abatement of the amount of a judgment on an appeal, the defendant, if the appellant, shall be allowed his daily pay, counsel fee and costs only, in case he produces no evidence before the court other than that which he exhibited before the justice or referees."

There was no provision in this act as to costs when the plaintiff appealed from a judgment of a justice in favor of the defendant for a sum certain, which the plaintiff reduced on the appeal; but it was ruled that, in such cases, the plaintiff was not entitled to costs.(*l*) But in a case in which a plaintiff having appealed from the judgment of a justice of the peace against him, recovered a judgment in his favor in court, it was ruled that he was entitled to have a judgment for full costs.(*m*) The court held that the costs, not being *taken away* by the act, although not *given* by it, were recoverable under the statute of Gloucester.

By an appeal from the judgment of a justice, the plaintiff did not forfeit the costs accrued before the justice, though he did not recover on appeal more than he did before the justice.(*n*)

And upon a judgment by a justice for the plaintiff, an appeal to the Common Pleas by the defendant, a reference to arbitrators and award

(*i*) Hamilton *v.* Aslin, 3 W. 222.
(*j*) Richardson *v.* Cassilly, 5 W. 449.
(*k*) 5 Sm. Laws, 161, Dunlop's Dig. ed. of 1849, p. 270.

(*l*) Bowman *v.* Bean, 3 S. & R. 308.
(*m*) Adams *v.* M'Ilheney, 1 W. 53.
(*n*) Dearth *v.* Laughlin, 16 S. & R. 296.

for defendant, an appeal by plaintiff, and a verdict for the plaintiff for a sum less than the judgment of the justice, the judgment must be without costs since the appeal from the justice.(o)   And where, on an appeal from the judgment of a justice of the peace in favor of the plaintiff, the case was arbitrated, and an award made in favor of the plaintiff for the same sum, on which an appeal was entered, and on the trial the plaintiff was nonsuited, the defendant having given no evidence, the defendant was held entitled to costs.(p)   Again, in a suit before a justice, judgment was rendered for the plaintiff for forty dollars, from which the defendant appealed to the Common Pleas, where the cause was arbitrated, and an award rendered for the defendant, from which the plaintiff appealed. The cause was afterwards tried by jury, and a verdict and judgment given for the plaintiff for seventeen dollars, the defendant having produced new evidence: it was ruled that the defendant was liable to pay the costs which accrued before the justice, and to refund to the plaintiff the costs which he had paid on the appeal from the award of arbitrators, and that each party should pay his own costs which accrued subsequently to the award.(q)

The following is another illustration of the doctrine of costs under the two systems : Appeal by the defendant from the judgment of a justice in favor of the plaintiff for ninety-seven dollars : compulsory arbitration, and award for the plaintiff of one hundred dollars; appeal from the award by the defendant; trial in the Common Pleas, and verdict for the plaintiff for thirty-eight dollars : Held, that the plaintiff was not entitled to costs which accrued subsequently to the appeal.(r)

The plaintiff was entitled to costs, if, on an appeal by the defendant, the justice's judgment was *affirmed*, or if the plaintiff recovered *more*, whether new evidence was produced or not ; but where the defendant appealed, and obtained a reversal or abatement of the amount of the justice's judgment, he was entitled to his daily pay of fifty cents, counsel fee of four dollars and costs, provided he produced no evidence before the court other than that which he exhibited before the justice or referees.(s)   But if, when before the magistrate, he was refused time to prepare or produce his proof, or in case of judgment against him by default, the plaintiff refused his consent to a rehearing, the defendant was entitled to costs when he obtained a reversal or abatement of the amount of such judgment.(t)

On an appeal by a defendant from a justice of the peace, if the plaintiff recovered less in the Common Pleas than he did before the justice, and the defendant had produced evidence which he did not give before the justice, the plaintiff would recover his costs before the justice, but each party had to pay his own costs on the appeal.(u) A defendant who appealed from the judgment of a justice, and obtained a general verdict in his favor, might recover costs, though he produced new evidence to the jury, if that evidence had been offered before the justice, but had been rejected by him as incompetent.(v)   But where a judgment for costs was rendered for

(o) Wiseler v. Beaumont, 4 W. 29.
(p) Flick v. Boucher, 16 S. & R. 373.
(q) Ross v. Soles, 1 W. 43; see 1 Pa. R. 477.
(r) Boyer v. Amand, 2 ibid. 74.
(s) See Downs v. Lewis, 13 S. & R. 198.

(t) *Vide* 1 Br. 202.
(u) Kimball v. Saunders, 10 S. & R. 193; Tanner v. Cooke's Admin. 16. id. 167; and see, also, Franklin v. Wray, 1 W. 129; Grace v. Altemus, 15 S. & R. 133; Downs v. Lewis, 13 id. 198.
(v) McMillan v. Hall, 2 Pa. R. 73.

the plaintiff on an award for less than the justice's judgment, the Supreme Court refused to reverse it, because it did not appear on the record that no additional evidence was given to the arbitrators.(*w*)

The materiality of the new evidence adduced by the defendant, could not be inquired into on a question of costs; it was sufficient to preclude the defendant from recovering costs, that he produced new testimony.(*x*)

And the appellee was exonerated from the payment of costs, not only by the production of new facts, but also by the production of new evidence of the same facts; and, therefore, if witnesses were examined in court who were not produced before the justice, though to the same facts the appellant, if defendant, was not entitled to costs.(*y*)

The whole system of costs on appeals from the judgments of magistrates, was changed by the act of April 9, 1833,(*z*) which provides, "that the costs on appeals hereafter entered, from the judgments of justices of the peace and aldermen, shall abide the event of the suit, and be paid by the unsuccessful party as in other cases.

"*Provided*, That if the plaintiff be the appellant, he shall pay all costs which may accrue on the appeal, if in the event of the suit he shall not recover a greater sum, or a more favorable judgment than was rendered by the justice.

"*And provided, also*, That if the defendant, either on the trial of the cause before the justice or referees, or before an appeal is taken, shall offer to give the plaintiff a judgment for the amount which the defendant shall admit to be due, which offer it shall be the duty of the justice and of the referees to enter on the record; and if the said plaintiff, or his agent, shall not accept such offer, then, and in that case, if the defendant shall appeal, the plaintiff shall pay all the costs which shall accrue on the appeal, if he shall not, in the event of the suit, recover a greater amount than that for which the defendant offered to give a judgment; and in both cases the defendant's bill shall be taxed and paid by the plaintiff, in the same manner as if a judgment had been rendered in court for the defendant." § 1.

By this act, costs are made to abide the event of the suit without regard to the amount recovered, or whether the judgment be or be not more favorable to the party entering the appeal. Under it, a defendant who proceeds in his appeal, is not entitled to recover a counsel fee of four dollars, as under the act of 1810, and daily pay for his attendance on the appeal.(*a*)

And where defendant appeals and plaintiff obtains a verdict and judgment, he is entitled to full costs, although he finally recovers less than the alderman's judgment, and the report of arbitrators, from each of which the defendant appeals. The reasons given are, that costs are creatures of the statute; and where defendant is ultimately found indebted in any sum, which he neither paid nor offered to pay, or to confess judgment for, before appeal, he must pay all costs, not having brought himself within the exceptions.(*b*)

So, where the defendant appeals from a judgment of a justice of the

(*w*) Fitsimons *v.* Leckey, 3 id. 111.
(*x*) Feeny *v.* M'Farland, C. P. MS. Wh. Dig. "Justice," 385, 480.
(*y*) Tanner *v.* Cooke, 16 S. & R. 167.

(*z*) Pamph. L. 480, Dunlop's Dig. ed. 1849, 582.
(*a*) Shuey *v.* Bitner, 3 W. & S. 275.
(*b*) Lindsey *v.* Corah, 7 W. 235.

peace in his favor, for a sum certain, and on the trial there is a verdict and judgment for the defendant, for a sum less than the amount of the judgment of the justice, he is entitled to full costs.(c)

Where a defendant recovered a judgment, before a justice, for a certain sum, and the plaintiff appeals, and the arbitrators in the Common Pleas award "no cause of action," neither party shall have costs, as the case is not within the statute.(d)

It has been held, in a case which occurred in the Common Pleas of Bradford County, that on an appeal from the judgment of a justice, as well as when taken by plaintiff as by defendant, the court will, in some cases, for the purpose of justice and to determine the question of costs, ascertain by calculation whether the judgment obtained by the plaintiff in court, is for a greater sum or a more favorable judgment than was rendered by the justice. And where a plaintiff obtains before a justice all he asks, as the amount due to him upon a claim bearing interest if he appeal, and subsequently in court recovers no more than the amount rendered in his favor by the justice, with interest superadded from that time, in such case, he will be liable to pay the costs subsequent to the appeal.(e)

But this case would seem to be inconsistent with a decision of the Supreme Court, under the arbitration act, in which a plaintiff who appealed from an award in his favor, and recovered more than the sum awarded, but less than such amount, with interest, for the intermediate time, was allowed to recover full costs.(f)

The following decisions have been made as to what constitutes a sufficient tender to exempt the defendants from costs, under the act of 1833:—

A tender before a justice or referees, of a sum strictly equal to the debt sued for, is not equivalent to a tender of judgment; *although a tender of the debt and costs might be.* The defendant, therefore, is liable for the costs under the act of the 9th of April, 1833, although no more than the sum tendered be ultimately found due.(g)

But, in a late case, it was held, that it is not sufficient to relieve a defendant from the payment of costs accrued after appeal by him from a justice's judgment, that he has made a tender of the admitted sum, with the costs accrued. He must, also, have offered to give a judgment for such amount. The justice has authority to receive the money only on the foot of a judgment.(h)

After a verdict and judgment on an appeal from a justice, it is error in the court to receive depositions to prove that a tender had been made before the trial, under this act, so as to affect the question of costs.(i)

To exempt a defendant from, and to entitle him to costs, where the plaintiff is the successful party, the defendant must have offered, on the trial before the justice, or before appeal taken, to give the plaintiff judgment for a sum equal to or more than plaintiff eventually recovered. This offer the justice must enter on his record, as it cannot be proved by parol or other inferior evidence, and the justice is liable to the defend-

(c) Holman v. Fesler, 7 W. & S. 313; see McDowal v. Glass, 4 W. 389.
(d) Hoffman v. Hassan, 2 W. & S. 36.
(e) Davidson v. Smith, C. C. P. of Bradford, 3 P. L. J. 239.

(f) Haines v. Moorhead, 2 Barr, 65.
(g) McDowell v. Glass, 4 W. 389.
(h) Dickerson v. Anderson, 4 Wh. 78.
(i) McDowell v. Glass, 4 W. 389.

ant for any injury sustained by him through his omission so to enter it ;(j) and the offer is too late if made after appeal taken, though before the justice has made out his transcript.(k)

A certificate in the transcript of a justice, that the defendant offered to confess judgment for a certain amount, but of which there is no entry in the docket, is not sufficient to entitle the defendant to costs under the act of 1833; nor, *it seems*, would the oath of the justice be admitted to prove the fact.(l)

In a suit before a justice, the defendant after judgment against him, but before appeal, offered to confess judgment for a less amount, which the plaintiff declined to agree to. An appeal was then entered, on which the plaintiff placed on the docket of the justice an acceptance of the offer. An award of arbitrators for a less amount than the offer, was made in the Common Pleas, for the plaintiff. Held, that the plaintiff was not entitled to his costs, and that the defendant might deduct his from the judgment.(m)

When defendant entitles himself to costs by reducing the amount of the judgment appealed from, after an offer to confess a judgment for less, the court will set off the amount of the costs against the amount of the verdict.(mm)

The act of 20th of March, 1845,(n) provides " that the bail in cases of appeal from the judgments of aldermen and justices of the peace, and from the award of arbitrators, shall be bail absolute in double the probable amount of costs accrued, and likely to accrue in such cases, with one or more sufficient sureties, conditioned for the payment of all costs accrued, or that may be legally recovered in such cases, against the appellants." Although this act has been held to abolish the special requirements of the act of 1836, in reference to appeals from the awards of arbitrators,(nn) it does not appear in any manner to have affected the right to costs on appeals from judgments of aldermen and justices of the peace, as regulated by the act of 1833(o).

SECTION V.

COSTS OF REFERENCE AND ARBITRATION.

1. *Of costs of voluntary arbitration.*

The subject of costs in relation to awards, is to be considered, as previously intimated, first, on references under the English law, and under the act of 1836, which appears to supersede the acts of 1705 and 1806.

Where there is no cause in court, the award as to costs depends entirely upon the terms of the submission ; if the submission give the arbitrator no authority as to costs, he cannot award them. But where authority is given to him upon that subject, he may order either party to pay the costs, or each to pay a moiety, unless the submission

---

(j) Seibert v. Kline, 1 Barr, 38 ; Gardner v. Davis, 3 H. 41.
(k) Bogart v. Rathbone, 1 Barr, 188.
(l) Clemens v. Gilbert, 2 J. 255.
(m) Gardner v. Davis, 3 H. 41.
(mm) Magill v. Tomer, 6 W. 494.

(n) Pamph. L. p. 188 ; Dunlop, Dig. ed. 1849, p. 1035.
(nn) See *post*, 669.
(o) Clemens v. Gibbs, 2 J. 255 ; Gardner v. Davis, 3 H. 41.

require that the costs abide the event; or if the award be silent as to costs, each party must pay his own costs, and the costs of the reference equally.(*oo*)

Where there is a cause in court, the award, as to the costs of the *reference*, depends upon the terms of the rule or order under which the cause is referred, in the same manner as where there is no cause in court, as above mentioned; and if the rule or order give the arbitrator no authority as to costs, he cannot award them.(*p*) But if, by the rule or order of reference, the costs, generally, are to abide the event, this includes the costs of the reference as well as the costs of the cause, according to the practice of the King's Bench;(*pp*) although the rule is otherwise in the Court of Common Pleas.(*q*)

But as to the costs of the *action*, the arbitrator may order either party to pay them, without any express authority being given to him upon that subject by the rule or order of reference.(*r*) If by such rule or order, however, the costs are to abide the event, the arbitrator cannot exercise any discretion in the awarding of them; but the party who would have been entitled to costs if the action had proceeded shall be entitled to them under the award; and to the same amount, and under the same circumstances: and, therefore, where a plaintiff in trespass would be entitled only to as much costs as damages, he shall have no more under the award.(*s*) Where an award finds *costs*, without mentioning how much, it shall be intended such costs as are by law allowed in the case;(*t*) as if an award be given in slander for 40s. with costs, it shall be intended no more costs than damages. But it is otherwise where *full* costs are given,(*u*) or *costs of suit;(v)* since the statute of James I. restraining costs in slander, where the damages are under 40s., though binding on the court, is not so upon the jury.(*w*)

Referees under the act of 1705 cannot award costs of suit in the Common Pleas upon a sum which, by the laws giving jurisdiction to justices of the peace, will not carry costs, unless there is an agreement in the rule that they shall have power over the costs, or the plaintiff had made and filed an affidavit before the suit was brought, that he believed the debt was beyond the sum within a magistrate's jurisdiction.(*x*) So, under the act of assembly, which provided that a defendant who appealed from the judgment of a justice should not be subject to costs, where less was recovered against him on the appeal than the amount of the judgment or award appealed from, unless he produced new evidence, neither a jury nor arbitrator could give costs.(*y*) For these provisions as to the payment of costs in references, on certain events, may be considered as *restrictions*, which take away as effectually the power of arbitrators over costs, as those inserted in a submission to reference at common law.(*z*)

(*oo*) Arch. Pr. 1235.
(*p*) Ib. Wills, 64; Taunt. 213; see 1 Taunt. 165.
(*pp*) 9 East, 436.
(*q*) 1 B. & P. 34.
(*r*) Young *v.* Shook, 4 R. 299; 2 T. R. 644; 14 Johns, 161.
(*s*) 2 Arch. Pr. 288.
(*t*) Stuart *v.* Harkins, 3 Bin. 321.
(*u*) Ibid.

(*v*) Gower *v.* Clayton, 6 S. & R. 85.
(*w*) Stuart *v.* Harkins, 3 Bin. 321; Hinds *v.* Knox, 4 S. R. 417.
(*x*) Guier *v.* McFaden, 2 Bin. 587.; Lewis *v.* England, 4 Bin. 15.
(*y*) Lewis *v.* England, 4 Bin. 5; Guier *v.* McFaden, 1 Ash. 1.
(*z*) Ibid.; *sed vide*, Bedford *v.* Shilling, 4 S. & R. 409; Lentz *v.* Stroh, 6 S. & R. 39.

Costs are seldom or never specified in reports of referees in actions of ejectment, yet they will be allowed to the plaintiff, although the referees should award in his favor without finding costs. References in such cases are entered into to ascertain in whom the title is, and the costs are consequential thereon.(a)

Costs may be given under the statute of Gloucester, by the court to which a report of referees is made under the act of 1705, though not found by the referees.(b)

Where the arbitration fails to provide specifically for the payment of costs, the case is governed by the statutes regulating appeals from justices of the peace.(c)

Where there was an agreement to refer all matters in variance between the parties—there being no pending action or agreement to institute such action, and no rule of court was obtained, but the award was filed under the 1st section of the act of 21st March, 1806, and afterwards set aside on exceptions filed on account of the misconduct of one or more of the arbitrators—it was then agreed, upon the suggestion of the court, that the case should stand as a cause in court, as though upon an amicable action filed. The case was put at issue, tried, and a verdict rendered for plaintiff, the prothonotary having allowed the costs of the arbitration. The court, on appeal from his taxation, was of opinion that the agreement did not make the reference a part of the proceedings in court, and the costs of witness and arbitrators, and of depositions to sustain the award, were disallowed from the plaintiff's bill.(d)

Referees, under the act of 1806, are allowed each one dollar per day for their services, which sum is taxed with the other costs of suit; "but if either party do not appear on the day appointed for the referees to meet, the party neglecting to appear, either by himself, his agent, or attorney, shall be liable for all costs which may have accrued on that day in the action, unless it be made appear to the satisfaction of the referees that the absent party could not attend."(e)

By the third section of the same act, if the plaintiff file exceptions to an award under this act, " and the same is finally set aside, and he shall again prosecute his action, either in a court of justice or before other referees, and shall not recover a sum equal or greater than was first awarded, he shall not have judgment for costs, and shall pay the defendant seventy-five cents per day, while attending on the same; and if the defendant file such exceptions, and the award be set aside by the court, and the plaintiff by a new action shall recover a sum equal, or greater than the original award, then and in that case the plaintiff shall have judgment for all the costs accrued on such suit, together with seventy-five cents per day whilst attending the same."

2. *Of costs in compulsory arbitration.*

The arbitrators have no power to award costs when they find for the plaintiff in a sum below the jurisdiction of the court.(f) And although they award that each party shall pay his own costs, yet if the sum

(a) Harvey v. Snow, 1 Y. 159.
(b) Bellas v. Levy, 2 R. 21.
(c) Addison v. Hampson, 6 Barr, 463.
(d) Smith v. Farley, D. C. C. C. P. April 7, 1849. U. S.

(e) § 4, 4 Sm. Laws, 328; not re-enacted in the act of 1836.
(f) Lindenburger v. Unrum, 1 Br. 194; Heath v. Atkinson, 1 Br. 231; see, also, Lewis v. England, 4 Bin. 5.

awarded carry costs, or if it have been reduced below one hundred dollars by a set-off (the affidavit under the act of assembly being previously filed), the plaintiff is entitled to costs.(*g*)   Where an award was made in favor of the plaintiff for a sum within the jurisdiction of the court, and "that the plaintiff pay the costs," the court directed judgment to be entered for the plaintiff with costs.(*h*)   But it has been determined that a Court of Common Pleas has no authority to do this; for they have no power to alter an award of arbitrators, even if it be illegal on the face of it.(*k*)   If, therefore, arbitrators award costs to a party who is not entitled to them, the court cannot enter judgment on the award without costs; but the dissatisfied party must appeal to the Court of Common Pleas, or bring it before the Supreme Court, by writ of error.(*l*)   Every intendment, however, will be made in the latter court, in favor of the regularity of proceedings which are according to the course of the common law, and a judgment is consequently not to be reversed for anything but palpable error.   A judgment, therefore, by arbitrators, for a less sum than the magistrate awarded will not be reversed, unless it affirmatively appears on the record that no other evidence was given to the arbitrators than was heard by the magistrate.(*m*)

The 27th section of the act of 16th June, 1836,(*n*) provides that no appeal shall be allowed to either party from an award of arbitrators, until the appellant pay all the costs that may have accrued on such suit or action.   A subsequent section, however, authorizes an appeal by executors or administrators, or person suing, or being sued in a representative capacity, without a compliance with this rule, if such appellant shall not have taken out the rule of reference. § 31.

A municipal corporation has been held to be within the proviso contained in the 31st section of the act of 1836, allowing persons suing or being sued, in a representative capacity, to appeal without payment of costs.(*o*)   But where an action is brought on the transcript of a guardian's account, filed in the Common Pleas, which is arbitrated, the guardian, being sued as a defaulter, cannot appeal from the award, without the payment of costs.(*p*)

And the act of 15th March, 1847,(*q*) provides, that when any corporation (municipal corporations excepted), being sued, shall appeal or take a writ of error, the bail requisite in that case shall be taken absolute for the payment of debt, interest, and costs, on the affirmance of the judgment.

The appellant must also pay the costs of a former award which had been set aside by the court, when they impose no conditions as to the payment of the costs.   According to the usual practice, it is understood that they are to abide the final event of the suit; they are thrown into the general mass of costs, and it is as much incumbent on the appellant to pay them, as any other costs previous to the entry of an appeal.(*r*)

(*g*) Sp ar *v.* Jamieson, 2 S. & R. 530.
(*h*) Moffet *v.* Dorsey, 2 Br. 24.
(*k*) Post *v.* Sweet, 8 S. & R. 391. *But*
(*l*) Ibid. *ve 13. J. R. 198.*
(*m*) Fitzimmons *v.* Leckey, 3 Pa. R. 111. *That v. R. De Camp. 2. Rawle 149.*
(*n*) Pamph. L. 717; Dunlop Dig. ed. 1849, 793.

(*o*) Robinson *v.* Jefferson Co. 6 W. & S. 16.
(*p*) Royer *v.* Myers, 3 H. 87.
(*q*) Pamph. L. 361, Dunlop, Dig. ed. 1849, 1100.
(*r*) Per TILGHMAN, C. J.; Teely *v.* Barton, 5 S. &. R. 390.

But where the first rule of reference was not acted on, but was stricken off by order of the party who had entered it, it was held that the other party was not liable to the costs of such prior rule of reference, as he had done nothing to prevent its being carried into operation.(s) On an award in favor of a plaintiff in a *scire facias* to revive a judgment, the defendant on appealing from the award, is only bound to pay the costs of the action of *scire facias*, and not those of the original judgment.(t)

After payment of the costs taxed to the time of the appeal, the appeal cannot be dismissed because the appellant refuses paying other costs which had not been taxed at that time. But payment may be enforced by an order of court, and by attachment on non-compliance.(u) The costs to be paid by the appellant, shall nevertheless be taxed in the appellant's bill, and recovered of the adverse party in such cases only where, in the event of the suit, the appellant is entitled to recover costs agreeably to the provisions contained in the act.(v)

If the costs have been paid, the appeal is not affected by the appellant directing the prothonotary not to pay them over, which order is a mere nullity, and ought to be so treated.(w)

The payment of costs on the appeal was regulated by the 29th and 30th sections of the act which formed a complete system as to them. The 29th section directed that "if the plaintiff be the appellant, he shall by himself, his agent or attorney, with one or more sufficient sureties, be bound in recognizance with the prothonotary, the condition of which shall be, that if the said plaintiff shall not recover in the event of the suit, a sum greater, or a judgment more favorable than the report of the arbitrators, he shall pay all costs that shall accrue in consequence of said appeal, and one dollar per day for each and every day lost by the defendant in attending on such appeal.

And "if the defendant be the appellant, he shall by himself, his agent or attorney, produce one or more sufficient sureties, who shall enter into a recognizance with the prothonotary in the nature of special bail, the condition of which shall be, that if the plaintiff in the event of the suit shall obtain a judgment for a sum equal to, or greater, or a judgment as, or more favorable than the report of the arbitrators, the said defendant shall pay all costs that may accrue in consequence of said appeal, together with the sum or value of the property or thing awarded by the arbitrators, with one dollar per day for every day that shall be lost by the plaintiff in attending to such appeal, or in default thereof, shall surrender the defendant to the jail of the proper county. § 30.(x)

This recognizance bound the defendant to the payment of costs even where the plaintiff had forfeited his title to them by the infringement of some other act of assembly.(y) In a case where the plaintiff had commenced his action in the Common Pleas, which was arbitrated by the defendant, and an award for eighty dollars made, from which the defendant appealed, and the plaintiff afterwards obtained a verdict for eighty-six dollars; it was held that the defendant was subject to the payment of

(s) Fleetwood *v.* Vanatta, 1 Ash. 10.
(t) Hill *v.* Thomas, D. C. Philadelphia, May, 1827. MS.
(u) Fraley *v.* Nelson, 5 S. & R. 234; 1 Br. 150; Williams *v.* Haslep, 2 H. 157

(v) Act 16th June, 1836, § 32.
(w) Duffie *v.* Black, 1 Barr, 388.
(x) Act of 1836.
(y) Ilgenfritz *v.* Douglass, 6 Bin. 402.

all costs subsequent to the appeal, but not of any costs prior to the appeal. The reason was, that though the plaintiff forfeited costs by instituting an action in the Common Pleas which was within the jurisdiction of a justice, yet the defendant, by his appeal, bound himself to comply strictly with his recognizance, and to pay costs on failing in the appeal.

In order to entitle himself to this daily allowance, it seems that it was not necessary that the party should attend in proper person, on the appeal, inasmuch as his attorney in fact or his substitute can recover it; but it seems that the attorney at law is not so entitled.(z) Although there were several defendants entitled to the costs of an action, they could recover but for the daily attendance of one.(a)

On an appeal from the prothonotary's taxation of costs on award of arbitrators in which two cases had been tried together; held, 1. That the arbitrators were entitled to fees as for only one case; 2. That attorneys' fees were properly chargeable on the award; 3. That a reasonable charge for room-rent for the arbitration was correct, and sanctioned by ancient practice.(b)

Where there were several suits by several plaintiffs against the same defendants, and the causes were referred to arbitrators under the act of 1810, and an agreement made that one case should be tried before the arbitrators, and that they should return the same award in each of the other cases, and an award was made in each case for the defendant, from which the several plaintiffs appealed, and the cases were all set down for trial at the same term, and one case was tried and a verdict given for the defendant, after which the other plaintiffs discontinued; the defendant was held entitled to recover the per diem allowance given by the act of assembly, from each of the plaintiffs.(c)

In every action, whether of *tort* or contract, arbitrated under this law, either party had the right of appeal from an award in order to a trial by jury; and in the event of a jury not finding in his favor, as to the whole cause of action, but finding a verdict more favorable than the award, he was exempted from all costs which accrued on the appeal. In other words, a party appealing, if he succeeded in any degree, was not liable to the costs subsequent to the appeal. "The reason of this is most apparent; the party, by the verdict, is found to be aggrieved by the award; in seeking redress, costs are necessarily incurred, by the party persisting in the unjust award he has obtained; it is neither just nor reasonable that he should pay that party these costs; he should not be damnified by appealing for redress from an unjust sentence, which injustice is established by a verdict."(d) As the recognizance of the party appealing was to cover all the costs, that the other could recover; he was not liable to pay costs in any event, for which his recognizance was not a security.(e)

The governing principle in the system of costs resulting from the three sections before quoted from the act, was, that the appellant should pay costs, unless he succeeded, at least partially, in the appeal. "If the plaintiff appeals he pays costs, unless he recovers *more* than the

(z) Clay v. Karsher, 1 Br. 290.
(a) Shermer v. Rusling, 1 M. 415.
(b) Butcher v. Scott, C. P. C. C. P.
2 P. L. J. 287.

(c) Horner v. Harrington, 6 W. 331.
(d) Lentz v. Stroh, 6 S. & R. 34.
(e) Ibid.

arbitrators gave him. If the defendant appeals, he pays costs, unless he obtains an *abatement* of what the arbitrators gave the plaintiff, because in both these cases it must be presumed that there was no cause for the appeal. But although the party who succeeds but partially in his appeal, ought not to *pay* costs, yet it does not follow that he ought to *recover* costs; because, although the event has proved, that the award of the arbitrators was wrong; yet that may have been the fault of the arbitrators, and not of the party in whose favor the award was made. In such cases, therefore, each party is left to pay his own costs."(*f*) In such cases the adduction of new evidence on the trial did not affect the defendant's right of exemption from the costs after the appeal.(*g*)

Where a plaintiff who sued on a bond, appealed from the award of arbitrators finding the amount demanded for her as trustee, &c., and recovered the same amount in her own right, by a verdict and judgment. It was *held*, that this was a judgment more favorable than the award, in the sense of the words as used in the act relating to arbitration, and carried the costs since the appeal.(*h*)

A plaintiff appealing and recovering more than the award, though less than the awarded amount, with interest for the intermediate time, was entitled to full costs; the only practical criterion being the difference of amount finally recovered without reference to the elements of the verdict.(*i*) And if the plaintiff in ejectment obtained a verdict and judgment less favorable than the award of arbitrators appealed from by the defendant, the plaintiff was not entitled to costs subsequent to the appeal; nor could the defendant recover back the costs paid by him on the appeal.(*j*)

In the case, then, of an appeal by a defendant from an award of arbitrators, if the plaintiff obtained a verdict for a smaller sum than the award, the defendant was not entitled to a return of the costs paid on the appeal; and with respect to the costs accrued since the appeal, each party paid his own costs.(*k*) Nor as regards the costs, did it make any difference whether the cause was tried after the appeal by a jury, or referees under the act of 1705; in such case, therefore, referees could not award costs to the plaintiff.(*l*) This same principle prevails in the common law courts; for where a judgment of an inferior court is *reversed* on a writ of error, the costs in error are not recovered by the party who obtains the reversal. But, where the judgment is *affirmed*, costs are recovered. On an appeal from arbitrators, the law considered their report as *reversed*, where the judgment of the Court of Common Pleas is more favorable to the appellant than the report was.(*m*)

A plaintiff, nonsuited on appeal by defendant, must refund the costs paid on appealing, although the plaintiff may be administrator.(*n*)

But when the plaintiff appeals from an award of arbitrators in favor of the defendant and recovers, he is entitled to the costs which he paid on entering his appeal, as well as those costs which have accrued

(*f*) Landis *v.* Schaeffer, 4 S. & R. 196; Rankin *v.* Murry, 2 Pa. R. 74.

(*g*) Carney *v.* Kenney, 1 M. 9.

(*h*) Mosher *v.* Breniger, 4 P. L. J. 377.

(*i*) Haines *v.* Moorehead, 2 Barr, 65.

(*j*) Bellas *v.* Oyster, 7 W. 341.

(*k*) Pratt *v.* Naglee, 6 S. & R. 299; Holdship *v.* Alexander, 13 S. & R. 230.

(*l*) Ibid.; see Poke *v.* Kelley, 13 S. & R. 165.

(*m*) Landis *v.* Schaeffer, 4 S. & R. 196.

(*n*) Penrose *v.* Pawling, 8 W. & S. 379.

since.(o) So where the plaintiff appealed from an award in his own favor and obtained a verdict for a greater sum, because he was entitled to recover costs upon the award from which he appealed.(p) In such a case, it might be questionable whether the plaintiff could be obliged to pay, before he appealed, any more than the mere costs of the prothonotary. The last would seem to require payment only of such costs as *have* accrued, and, as the award is favorable to him, it seems clear that none have accrued for which *he* is liable. The Court of Common Pleas (Philadelphia) has, however, held otherwise; and the Supreme Court, in the last-cited case, sanctions impliedly that decision.(q) It presents a case for legislative interference; for, independently of its apparent injustice, the appellees are often irresponsible by the time they are called upon to return the costs.

If the defendant obtains a total reversal of the award, he is entitled to the costs which follow a final judgment. Such a case is not within the provisions of the act of 1810, as to costs ; they are given by the law as it existed before the passage of that act.(r)

Very material changes in the law of costs on appeal from awards of arbitrators were produced by the act of 12th of July, 1842,(rr) abolishing imprisonment for debt ; and by the act of March 20, 1845.(s) The latter act provides : " That in lieu of the bail heretofore required by law in the cases herein mentioned, the bail, in cases of appeal from the judgments of aldermen and justices of the peace, and from the award of arbitrators, shall be bail absolute in double the probable amount of costs accrued, and likely to accrue, in such cases, with one or more sufficient sureties, conditioned for the payment of all costs accrued, or that may be legally recovered in such cases against the appellants." § 1.

The effect of the act of 1842 was to abolish the recognizance of special bail on appeal from an award required by the 30th section of the act of 1836, as inconsistent with the design of that act.(t) And as, under the 1st section of the act of March 20, 1845, the special requirements of the act of 1836 are not revived, the costs follow the event of the suit ; and a plaintiff is entitled to costs incurred after an appeal by defendant from an award of arbitration, in which the plaintiff obtains a verdict less than the award.(u) The effect of that enactment is to supersede also the form of recognizance on appeal and a recognizance acknowledged by a plaintiff appellant, after the act of 1845, conditioned that the plaintiff would pay all costs " with one dollar for each and every day that should be lost by the defendant in such appeal," according to the provisions of the act of 1836, was held to be void.(v) The act of 20th March, 1845, however, does not interfere with the provision of the act of 1836, requiring payment on appeal of all costs due in the action up to that time.(w)

(o) Commonwealth v. Shannon, 13 S. & R. 109.

(p) Ibid.

(q) Copeland v. Hocker, C. P. MS. 1827.

(r) M'Lanahan v. Wyant, 1 Pa. R. 113.

(rr) Pamph. L. 339 ; Dunlop, Dig. ed. 1849, 971.

(s) Pamph. L. 188 ; Dunlop, Dig. ed. 1849, 1035.

(t) Beers v. West Branch Bk. 7 W. & S. 365 ; Remely v. Kuntz, 10 Barr, 180.

(u) Cameron v. Paul, 1 J. 277, affirming Remely v. Kuntz, 10 Barr, 180.

(v) Shuff v. Morgan, 7 Barr, 125.

(w) Merritt v. Smith, 2 Barr, 161. It has been thought proper to give the decisions under the act of 1836, although it will be perceived that its substantial provisions have been abolished by the

SECTION VI.

OF COSTS IN ACTIONS BY AND AGAINST PARTICULAR PERSONS.

In England, prior to a late statute,(x) in actions brought by executors or administrators, if the verdict were given for the defendant, the plaintiff in such case was not liable for costs,(y) unless the cause of action accrued after the testator's death,(z) and the plaintiff might have brought an action in his own name. Also, previously to that act, the plaintiff was not liable to the costs of a nonsuit unless the action were such that he might have brought it in his own name; nor to costs on judgments as in case of a nonsuit.(a) In an early case in Pennsylvania, the Supreme Court determined that the rule of the English law in this respect had been introduced into Pennsylvania, and that, consequently, on the discontinuance of a suit brought by an executor or administrator, although he was personally liable for the fees of the officers of the court, for services rendered to him, he was not liable *de bonis propriis*, for the costs of the defendant.(b) The ground of the distinction taken between fees and costs being, that costs are an allowance to a party for expenses incurred in conducting his suit; while fees are a compensation to an officer, for services rendered in the progress of the cause, which originally were in strictness demandable the instant at which the services were rendered.(c) But this decision, so far as it affects the defendant's costs, is now overruled, and an executor or administrator who fails in a suit instituted by himself is bound to pay costs, as well when he sues in his representative capacity, as when the cause of action arises after the death of the testator or intestate.(d)

Executors and administrators are liable for costs *de bonis propriis*, when, upon a plea of *plene administravit*, a verdict is found against them.(e) So when they have suffered a *non-pros.*(f) So when they plead a false plea.(g) In all other cases where an executor is liable for costs, they are to be levied *de bonis propriis*, if there be no goods sufficient of the testator to satisfy them.(h)

In actions by, as well as against executors or administrators, if they have a verdict, they are of course entitled to costs as in other cases.(i) So if one of several issues be found for them—as if they plead the general issue and *plene administravit*, and issues be taken on both, and the issue on *plene administravit* be found for, and the other issue against them—they are entitled to costs.(j)

---

act of 1845, as well for the purpose of tracing the history of the law on the subject, as because they may prove useful as decisions on cases arising under analagous branches of the law.

(x) 3 & 4 W. 4, c. 42, § 31.
(y) 1 Ld. Raym. 436; H. Bl. 528; 1 B. & P. 445.
(z) 7 T. R. 358; 10 East, 293; 5 T. R. 234.
(a) 2 Dowl. 388; 2 C. & M. 401; 2 H. Bl. 297; 4 Burr. 1928.
(b) Musser v. Good, 11 S. & R. 247.

(c) Ibid. 248.
(d) Muntorf v. Muntorf, 2 R. 180; Penrose v. Pawling, 8 W. & S. 380; Shaw v. Conway, 7 Barr, 136; Ewing v. Furness, 1 H. 531, overruling the case in 5 Pa. L. J. 505.
(e) Swearingen v. Pendleton, 4 S. & R. 396.
(f) Musser v. Good, 11 S. & R. 247.
(g) See 3 Burr. 1368; 1 W. Bl. 400.
(h) Arch. Pr. 881–2.
(i) Ibid.
(j) 1 Barn. & Ald. 254; and see 2 Arch. Pr. 133, 881.

Executors and administrators, whether plaintiffs or defendants, are exempt from the payment of costs on an appeal from an award against them, under the compulsory arbitration law of 1810, § 14.(k) The act provides that, where they are the party appellant, they shall have an appeal, as is by law allowed in other cases; that is, they may appeal without restrictions in the 11th, 12th, 13th, and 14th sections, which are unsuitable in the case of executors and administrators.(l) When the right of appeal was given as is by law allowed in other cases, the legislature must necessarily have meant other cases of appeal, as they stood independently of compulsory arbitration, wherein neither an affidavit, payment of costs, or giving a recognizance were made essential prerequisites to an appeal.(m) "This exemption with regard to executors or administrators is evidently just, because being merely trustees for the rights of others, and not supposed to be as well acquainted with the matter in contest as their testator or intestate, it would be hard to make them pay costs which in the event of the suit they might never recover again."

The same exemption is given by the 31st section of the arbitration act of 1836, if such appellant shall not have taken out the rule of reference,(n) and is extended also to minors. And the same exemption from the payment of costs on appeal from an award of arbitrators is contained in the 2d section of the act of 13th April, 1846.(o) Where executors, administrators, guardians, or trustees are appellants, they may also sue out a writ of error without security for costs,(p) so as to be a *supersedeas;* and they may appeal from a judgment of the Supreme Court at Nisi Prius to it in bank, without surety, under the provisions of the 6th section of the act of 26th July, 1842.(q)

In actions against executors for legacies, the justices of the courts respectively, upon consideration of the report of their account, shall, according to justice and equity, either award no costs, or costs out of the testators' estate, or in case they have been faulty, in delaying to pay the legacy demanded, or a proportional part thereof, without sufficient excuse, then out of the proper estate of the executors.(r)

The committee of a lunatic, in whose name suit was brought, is *prima facie* liable for costs.(s)

An infant defendant is liable for costs, although a guardian have been appointed.(t) In an action by an infant, if the defendant be entitled to costs, he may proceed for them by attachment against the *prochein amy* or guardian,(u) or it seems he may sue out execution, even a *ca. sa.* against the infant himself, whether he have sued by *prochein amy* or not.(v) But execution for the costs cannot be issued against a guardian, on a judgment for the defendant, in a suit brought in the minor's name by the guardian. The remedy is by attachment.(w)

(k) 5 Sm. Laws, 136.
(l) Ins. Co. of Pa. v. Hewes, 5 Bin. 510.
(m) Per YEATES, J., ibid. 511.
(n) Dunl. Dig. ed. 1849, 795.
(o) Pamph. L. 303; Dunl. Dig. ed. 1849, 1064.
(p) Act 16th June, 1836, § 8; Pamph. L. 763; Dunl. Dig. ed. 1849, 810.

(q) Pamph. L. 432; Dunl. Dig. ed. 1849, 979; Maule v. Shaffer, 2 Barr, 404.
(r) See § 5, act of 1772; 1 Sm. Laws, 383.
(s) Utt v. Long, 6 W. & S. 177.
(t) 2 Str. 1217; Dy. 104.
(u) 1 Str. 548; Barnes, 128.
(v) 2 Str. 1217; 13 East, 6.
(w) Bigger v. Westly, 13 S. & R. 347.

The guardian of a minor, in certain cases, may appeal from the judgment of a justice or from an award of arbitrators, without making the usual affidavit and without giving security or paying costs.(*x*)

SECTION VII.

OF DOUBLE AND TREBLE COSTS.

Where the plaintiff recovers single damages, he is only entitled to single costs, unless more be expressly given him by statute; but if double or treble damages are given by statute, the plaintiff is, in England, entitled to double or treble costs, although the statute contains no express direction to that effect.(*y*) The statute of Gloucester allowed only single costs, but double costs have since in some cases been given expressly by act of assembly. They are allowed to the avowant in replevin, as we have already seen,(*z*) but not upon an appeal by the plaintiff from an award of arbitrators in favor of the avowant. He can claim them only after final judgment;(*a*) and treble costs are awarded to the defendants in writs of replevin issued for any owners of goods taken in execution or by distress, by any sheriff, constable, &c., under the authority of the State; an action against any overseer of the poor or other person acting for him in his office, who fails in such action, discontinues or becomes nonsuit, is liable to double costs.(*b*) In an action against a justice of the peace under the act of 1772, § 6,(*c*) if the plaintiff obtains a verdict, and the justices certify on the back of the record, in open court, that the injury for which it was brought was wilfully and maliciously committed, he shall have double costs. Double costs is a relative term, and it has been settled that the plaintiff shall not recover double costs in the Supreme Court, when, in the court below, he could not be entitled to recover any.(*d*) By the act of 1772, § 2,(*e*) the plaintiff in a special action on the case for any pound breach or rescous of goods distrained, shall recover his treble damages and costs of suit against the offender, or the owner of the goods distrained, in case they be afterwards found to have come to his possession;(*f*) and double damages are expressly given to any person imprisoned or prosecuted without probable cause, to be recovered by action at common law against the informer or prosecutor.(*g*) So treble costs are allowed to the defendant in any action for acts done in pursuance of the militia law of April 2, 1822, where the jury acquit him, or the plaintiff is nonsuited or discontinues, &c. Double costs or charges are also given to any person sued by a retailer of liquors, for liquors or other expenses above twenty shillings; provided that the plaintiff, if the defendant be a servant, has been warned not to entertain him.(*h*)

Wherever, in England, a plaintiff is entitled to double or treble

x) Act of 27th March, 1833; Pamph. L. 99; Dunlop. Dig. ed. 1849, 566.

(*y*) Carth. 297; Ld. Raym. 19, S. C.; Salk. 205, pl. 2; and see 14 Johns. 328.

(*z*) *Ante,* 665.

(*a*) Hartley *v.* Bean, 1 M. 168.

(*b*) Act of March, 1771, § 33; 1 Sm. Laws, 345.

(*c*) Ibid. 365.

(*d*) Scott *v.* McKisson, 2 D. 184.

(*e*) 1 Sm. Laws, 370.

(*f*) *vide* § 3; ibid.

(*g*) Act of 1705; 1 Sm. Laws, 56.

(*h*) § 5, act of 26th August, 1721; 1 Sm. Laws, 126.

costs, the costs given by the court *de incremento*, are to be doubled or trebled, as well as those given by the jury.(*i*) According to the English practice (which seems to rest entirely on the table of costs *in principio*, and of which we know nothing here but the name), double or treble costs are not understood to mean twice or thrice the amount of single costs according to their literal import, but double costs consist of the single costs, and half of the single costs; and treble costs, of the single costs, half of the single costs, and half of that half.(*j*) In this State, it has been held that where an act of assembly gives treble costs, the English rule does not prevail, but the party is allowed three times the usual costs, with the exception that the fees of the officers are not to be trebled, where they are not regularly and usually payable by the defendant.(*k*)

SECTION VIII.

OF THE TAXATION AND RECOVERY OF COSTS.

The taxation of costs is a proceeding whereby the fees, disbursements, and expenses which the prevailing party is entitled to recover against his adversary, are settled and ascertained by a judge or other proper officer. Costs with us are uniformly taxed by the prothonotary, from whose taxation, however, an appeal may be had to the court.

After the final determination of a cause, the party entitled to costs files with the prothonotary a written specification of the fees and expenses which the law requires his adversary to pay; such as the witnesses' fees and mileage, daily pay, price of the subpœnas and service, the charges of commissioners for examining his witnesses out of the State, &c. This is called the plaintiff's or defendant's bill, and is inserted in the bill of costs taxed by the prothonotary. If objected to, it is taxed before the prothonotary upon notice to, or by agreement of the opposite party. Costs are sometimes ordered to be retained, by the prothonotary or sheriff, from a party, until the bill is taxed. In such cases, it is usual for the party claiming them to fix the time of taxation and notify his opponent. In other cases, the objecting party usually urges the taxation.

It is provided by rule, in the Court of Common Pleas of Philadelphia, and in the District Court for the City and County of Philadelphia, that any party intending to tax costs before the prothonotary, shall give him and the opposite party twenty-four hours' notice of such intention.— The time to be fixed for such taxation shall be from two to three o'clock P. M.

And in the District Court of Philadelphia, it is held to be the practice in that court, that an execution for costs may be issued without a previous taxation.(*l*)

(*i*) Cro. Eliz. 582, *ca.* 6; Carth. 294, 321; Str. 1048.

(*j*) 2 Arch. Pr. 1161; Hull. 483-4.

(*k*) Shoemaker *v.* Nesbit, 2 R. 201; Welsh *v.* Anthony, 4 H. 256.

(*l*) Hart *v.* Dickerson, D. C. C. P.

Sept. 16, 1848; Bright. Sup. 1849, 152. It is thought proper to add here the opinion of the court in full on this important point of practice, as the decision above quoted militates with the expression of opinion of the Supreme Court, in

I.—43

The amount of costs which may be demanded by the attorney and officers of the court, depends on the services that have been rendered; and the rate of compensation for those services is fixed by various acts, particularly by the act of 22d February, 1821,(m) denominated the fee-bill.(n) It is not intended to extract the particular provisions of the several acts relative to the rate of costs in all specified cases, since, in order to render the subject fully intelligible, it would be necessary to exhibit forms of bills of costs in a great variety of cases. Some few, however, of these provisions, it may be proper to notice.

5 W. 449. *Per curiam.* "This is a *fi. fa.* by defendant for costs, and the ground set up for setting it aside is, that it was issued without taxation or notice to plaintiff. The case of Richardson *v.* Cassidy (5 W. 449), is relied on as authority for the position that this is an irregularity. That case only decides, that the plaintiff's bill filed is not evidence in an action of assumpsit brought to recover the costs which had not been taxed. It is true that the court speak of the practice of issuing execution without taxation as a gross irregularity. That, however, is an extra-judicial *dictum*, and at all events, as it is a mere question of practice, can have no binding effect upon us. The practice of every court is within its own power, and not subject to review. The practice of this court to issue executions without a previous taxation of costs, is of very long standing, and we are not disposed to alter it. The right of the party against whom the writ has issued, to have the costs taxed upon very short notice to his opponent, effectually secures him against wrong, while at the same time, in a large majority of cases, as the amount of the costs is not disputed, an unnecessary form, accompanied with trouble and delay, is dispensed with. It would often happen that a defendant apprised by the plaintiff's notice of taxation, that an execution was about to issue, would seek to avoid it, either by removing or disposing of his goods, or delay it by an appeal from the taxation. Costs, in this State, have always been a very different affair from what they are in England. There is scarcely ever any dispute, except as to the mere costs, of evidence, depositions, commissions, and witnesses. The administration of justice, too, in Pennsylvania, is cheap to the parties. The legal costs of the heaviest trials form, generally, a very small percentage upon the sum in controversy." Rule dismissed.

(m) 7 Sm. L. 367, Dunlop Dig. ed. 1849, p. 362.

(n) "One main object of this law was to cut up by the roots the power which had been exercised by the courts, of allowing fees called *compensatory*, for services not specified in the several fee-bills. It is true that, in the last part of the 26th section of the act of 1814, still in force, the judges were prohibited to allow compensatory fees for any services not specified in that act, or *some other act of* assembly, but the words, *some other act of* assembly, seem intended to relate to acts which might afterwards be made." Kline *v.* Shannon, 7 S. & R. 378.

"It falls to the lot of almost every man to require the services of public officers. It is of very great importance, therefore, that every man should know what he has to pay; for if it is left to the parties to agree upon the compensation, a door is opened for perpetual litigation, and there is great danger of oppression to the lower and more ignorant people. It is for this reason that a table of fees has been established, which every officer is enjoined to exhibit to public view in his office. It is impossible for human wisdom to foresee every service which will arise. This must have been known to the legislature, and, therefore, in framing the table, they have taken care to allow, what on the whole will render offices sufficiently lucrative, although, for many services, there may be no compensation at all. In the sheriff's office, the commission on executions is the principal source of profit. It may happen that many hundred dollars may be earned in a few hours. If all services were paid for on the same scale, the burden on suitors would be intolerable. But that not being the case, the officer may be supposed, on the whole, to receive a reasonable payment for each service, although for many he receives nothing. It appears to me, therefore, that the fee-bill was intended to enumerate all the services for which the officer should be entitled to receive pay." Per TILGHMAN, C. J.; Irwin *v.* Commissioners of Northumberland Co. 1 S. & R. 506-7.

In the 5th section of the act of 21st March, 1806,(o) there is a provision that the plaintiff's attorney shall not be entitled to a judgment-fee, in any action of debt, whether judgment be confessed by the defendant, or rendered on the report of referees, or on the verdict of a jury. This provision, if it do away the judgment-fee in an action of debt prosecuted by an attorney,(p) is to be confined to the technical *action of debt*, and cannot be extended to any other form of suit.(q) And it was held not to deprive the attorney in such action of his fee, where the suit was ended, on discontinuance by the plaintiff, and payment of costs by the defendant, after the first term, and before judgment.(r)

And by the 26th section of the act of 1814, which constituted a prior fee-bill, if any officer shall take greater or other fees than are specified in the fee-bill, or shall charge or demand and take any of the fees ascertained in it, where the business for which such fees are chargeable shall not have been actually done, or shall charge or demand any fee for any services other than those expressly provided for by the fee-bill, such officer shall forfeit and pay to the party injured, fifty dollars, to be recovered as debts of the same amount are recoverable; and if the judges shall allow any officer any fees under the denominations of compensatory-fees, for any services not specified in this or some other act of assembly, it shall be considered a misdemeanor in office. By the 27th section, payment of fees may be refused to any officer who will not make out a bill of particulars, as prescribed by the fee-bill, signed by him, if required, and also a receipt, signed by him, of the fees paid. The fee-bill of 1821 continues these sections in force, and limits actions upon them to six months after the cause of action has accrued.

By the act of 11th April, 1825,(s) it is provided, "That in suits, on the same instrument, bond, or note, where several are bound; and in suits against the maker, indorser or indorsers, of any note; and in suits on any bill of exchange against the drawer, acceptor, or any indorser or indorsers thereof, there shall be a taxation and recovery of the attorney and counsel fees, taxable by law, in one of the said suits only, at the election of the party plaintiff, and no fees for attorney or counsel shall be allowed or taxed, in any suit or suits brought on the same instrument, bond, note, or bill of exchange, against the party or parties thereto, other than in one where the election is made as aforesaid."

This proviso being intended to prevent the multiplication of suits, is applicable to the plaintiff's attorney's fees only, and does not extend to the fees of the several defendants' attorneys, who, having no control in bringing the suits, are not deprived of their fees.(t)

An attorney's fee of three dollars is due upon an award of arbitrators, under the compulsory arbitration law.(u)

The act of 6th May, 1844, § 8,(v) provides, that no attorney or judgment fees shall be allowed or taxed on the entry of any judgment by confession, in any court in this commonwealth, where suit has not been

(o) 4 Sm. Laws, 328. Dunlop Dig. ed. 1849, p. 240.
(p) Del. Ins. Co. v. Gilpin, 1 Bin. 501.
(q) 2 Br. Appx. 24.
(r) Del. Ius. Co. v. Gilpin, 1 Bin. 501.
(s) Pamph. L. 225.

(t) Columbia Bank v. Halderman, 5 Pa. L. J. 28.
(u) Butcher v. Scott, 2 Pa. L. J. 287.
(v) Pamph. L. 564; Dunl. Dig. ed. 18.9, 1028.

previously commenced, and where the amount of said judgment shall not exceed the sum of one hundred dollars.

Where three members of the bar entered their appearance for a defendant, having been employed generally by him, but no warrant of attorney was given to either, it was *held* that the attorney's fee was equally to be divided between them ; though it was said that if the one first employed had received a warrant of attorney, he would have been exclusively entitled to the fee.(*w*)

No fees for witnesses can be taxed when the bill is disputed, without proof upon oath of the witness or some competent person acquainted with the facts of their attendance and travel.

On the taxation of costs, the plaintiff is competent to prove that he subpœnaed the witnesses, but not the fact of their attendance.(*x*) But it is not necessary that witnesses should attend before the prothonotary on the taxation of costs, to prove their attendance on the trial of the cause. The fact may be proved *aliunde.*(*y*)

In the taxation of witnesses' fees, the party is entitled to payment of fees for witnesses who have attended in good faith upon the trial at his instance, whether they have been subpœnaed or examined or not.(*z*) No general rule can be laid down as to the number or materiality of the witnesses for whom costs will be taxed, with safety to the suitors and the general practice—a party must come armed at all points, not knowing what will be conceded by his adversary or what all his witnesses will testify : upon such questions manifest oppression must be shown to justify the interposition of the court, and they will readily interfere in such instances ; but a design to oppress will never be presumed.(*a*) But a plaintiff can recover no more from the defendant for the fees of witnesses than he is liable to pay them himself. Therefore, where there are several actions depending, by the same plaintiff against different defendants, and the parties agree that the verdict and judgment in one case shall govern all, and the same witnesses are subpœnaed for each suit, the plaintiff is not entitled to recover from each defendant costs for the attendance of each witness.(*b*) Members of the bar are not entitled to witness-fees for attendance in a court in which they actually practice.(*c*) To entitle a party to the costs of his witnesses and of the service of subpœnas upon them, it is not necessary that their names should have been inserted in the subpœnas by the prothonotary, before delivering them to the party.(*d*) Nor is it necessary that witnesses should attend before the prothonotary on the taxation of costs, to prove their attendance on the trial of a cause. The fact may be proved *aliunde.*(*e*) Witnesses who attended before the prothonotary on the taxation of costs, to prove their attendance at the trial, are not entitled to fees for such attendance before the prothonotary.(*f*)

The charges for attendance of the witnesses before a commissioner,

(*w*) Hirst *v.* Dumell, 1 W. C. C. R. 438.

(*x*) Stokes *v.* Derringer, D. C. C. P. Oct. 2, 1847.

(*y*) McWilliams *v.* Hopkins, 1 Wh. 276.

(*z*) Ibid. 1 Wh. 276; De Benneville *v.* De Benneville, 1 Bin. 47.

(*a*) De Benneville *v.* De Benneville, 3 Y. 558.

(*b*) Curtis *v.* Buzzard, 15 S. & R. 21.

(*c*) McWilliams *v.* Hopkins, 1 Wh. 276.

(*d*) Id. ibid.

(*e*) Id. ibid.

(*f*) Id. ibid.

and the reasonable charges of the latter for swearing the witnesses and reducing their testimony to writing, are chargeable as costs against the party condemned in the action.(*g*)

A defendant, succeeding in several cases tried at the same term by several plaintiffs, cannot recover more than one *per diem* allowance and mileage of a witness who was subpœnaed in each case; but he may select any one of the plaintiffs to recover it from. If he has several witnesses, he may select of the plaintiffs, and recover part of the bill of costs of one, and part from another. He may, however, recover from each the service of subpœnas on the same witnesses in each case, but he can recover mileage in *one* case only. As to his own daily pay, if the attendance be on appeals from awards, he is entitled to it fully in each of such cases.(*h*)

In a controversy arising out of one and the same transaction between several and different plaintiffs, but the same defendant, who alone is liable for costs, a witness who is subpœnaed in the several suits by the respective plaintiffs, is entitled to single pay for each day's attendance, and no more, without regard to the number of suits in which he is called to testify.(*i*)

And where an individual appears in the double light of a witness for the prosecution in one cause, and for the defence in another cause, which are tried together, he is entitled to but one compensation, and must elect to whom he will recur for payment; and having so done, he is bound by his election.(*j*)

A witness residing in another State is not entitled to be paid his expenses in coming to the place of trial in Pennsylvania; he is entitled to mileage according to the fee-bill only from the line of this State, in the usual and ordinary route of travelling.(*k*)

Where the cause is made a *remanet*, that is, remains on the list untried for want of time, the costs incurred in bringing up witnesses, &c., are allowed to the party ultimately prevailing; and the same where a cause goes off upon any other occasion, without the fault or contrivance of the parties, and is afterwards brought to trial.(*l*)

A party is not entitled to an allowance in his bill of costs for the expense of office copies of deeds and other documents produced on the trial in support of his title.(*m*)

The expense of exemplifications of office papers were disallowed on taxation, where the papers were rejected on the trial.(*n*)

And the expenses attending a survey of the land in question are not taxable in the costs of an action of ejectment.(*o*) Neither are the costs of a bill to perpetuate testimony, although such testimony were used against the defendant.(*p*)

The District Court refused to allow costs to a defendant for his answer to a bill of discovery.(*q*) And in a *scire facias* in foreign attachment

(*g*) Tappan *v.* Columbia Bank and Bridge Co. 4 P. L. J. 224; see, also, Examiner's Costs, *ante*, 105. For costs of commissions generally, see 454.

(*h*) Horner *v.* Harrington, 6 W. 331.
(*i*) Batdorff *v.* Eckert, 3 Barr, 267.
(*j*) Com. *v.* Cozens, 1 Ash. 265.
(*k*) Leeds *v.* Loud, 2 M. 189.

(*l*) 5 Burr. 2693; see Work *v.* Lessee of Maclay, 14 S. & R. 265.
(*m*) Murphy *v.* Lloyd. 3 Wh. 356.
(*n*) Leeds *v.* Loud, 2 M. 189.
(*o*) 15 Johns. 238.
(*p*) McWilliams *v.* Hopkins, 1 Wh. 276.
(*q*) Tenor *v.* Hutton, D. C. C. P. 7 Leg. Int. 50.

the garnishees were held not to be entitled, upon judgment rendered for them, to the costs of an exemplification of an assignment which was produced by them on trial to prove their case.(r)

An appeal lies to the court by either party dissatisfied with the taxation, by motion and notice, as in ordinary cases, which, being placed in its order upon the argument-list, is heard at the period fixed for determining questions of law ; and the court will either correct the bill as to the erroneous items, refer the whole for retaxation, or dismiss the appeal, as the circumstances of the case may require.

Where the plaintiff has levied, by execution, costs to which he is not entitled, the court will compel him, by rule, to refund them, even after they have been distributed by the sheriff.(s)

At common law, error could not be assigned in a bill of costs. In England, where the terms of the judgment are set out at large, a gross sum is adjudged for the costs ; and a Court of Error cannot inquire into the constituent parts, because these cannot judicially be made to appear. Here, however, a different practice, long recognized, has made the costs so far a matter of record, as to enable the court to judge whether the constituent parts of the bill are such as the law allows. With us the judgment is never reduced to form, but signed in blank ; so that where parts of the costs are objectionable the remedy is not a reversal of the judgment *pro tanto*, unless there has been a special award of execution for those costs, but the execution is reversed so far as respects the objectionable matter, as having issued without a correspondent judgment to warrant it.(t)

The method of recovering costs between party and party, is by execution, or by attachment, which last is the only mode of recovering costs on an interlocutory rule or order, unless there has been an express promise to pay them.(u) If, under the former process, costs are levied, to which the party is not entitled, the court will compel him by rule to refund them even after they had been distributed by the sheriff.(v) Attachment for costs is rarely resorted to in Pennsylvania.

It would seem that the right of the State courts to compel payment of costs by attachment, is not impaired by the first section of the act of April, 1809.(w) They may make orders for payment of costs, and enforce their orders by attachment.(x) In proceeding by attachment a rule is first obtained upon the party to pay the costs, which must be served personally upon him ; a non-compliance with this rule amounts to a contempt, and comes within the spirit of the exceptions in the act. If the costs be not paid, the court, upon an affidavit of the circumstances, will grant an attachment, the rule for which is absolute in the first instance.(y)

Rules for payment of costs on judgments, are acts of the court which cannot be entered in vacation, but must be granted on motion in open court. In the court, and not in the party, is vested the power of fixing the time for payment of costs, under the penalty of judgment in case

(r) Christmas v. Biddle, D. C. C. P. 7 Leg. Int. 66.
(s) Harris v. Fortune, 1 Bin. 125.
(t) Barnet v. Ihrie, 1 R. 53.
(u) See 2 Dunl. Pr. 740; Fraley v. Nelson, 5 S. & R. 234.

(v) Harris v. Fortune, 1 Bin. 125.
(w) 5 Sm. Laws, 55 ; Terry v. Peterson, D. C. Phil.; 1 Wh. Dig. 139-140.
(x) Fraley v. Nelson, 5 S. & R. 234; Lyon v. McManus, 4 Bin. 171.
(y) See 2 Dunl. Pr. 740.

default be made.(z)   The party on whom the rule is granted is, of course, entitled to reasonable notice.(a)

To assist the parties in the recovery of costs, and to do justice between them, they are allowed to deduct, or set off the costs, or debt and costs, in one action, against those in another,(b) although the body of the defendant has been taken in execution, on the judgment which is offered as a set-off.(c)   "Judgments are set against each other not by force of statutes, but by the inherent power of the courts immemorially exercised, being almost the only equitable jurisdiction originally appertaining to them as courts of law.   An equitable right of setting off judgments, therefore, is permitted only where it will infringe on no other right of equal grade; consequently, it is not to affect an equitable assignee for value."(d)   Not being conferred by statute, it is not a legal power, nor is its exercise demandable of right.   Being discretionary, it is not the subject of a writ of error.(e)

In the English practice, where an application is made to set off costs and damages in one action against those recovered in a cross action, an attorney has a lien on the judgment obtained by his client against the opposite party, to the extent of his costs of that cause, and that only.(f) A judgment for costs obtained against an administrator plaintiff in one court, and assigned by the defendant to A, cannot be set off against a judgment for damages obtained by such administrator against A in another court.(g)

The setting off of one judgment against another has always been permitted, but they must be both in the *same right*.(h)   So, of a judgment against a demand not ascertained by judgment.(i)   Where the application is made by the party to whom the larger sum is due, the rule is for a stay of proceedings, on acknowledging satisfaction for a less sum ;(j) but where the less sum is due to the party applying, the rule is to have it deducted, and for a stay of proceedings on payment of the balance.(k)

One who is an active party in having a suit brought on, although his name does not appear upon the record, is liable to the witnesses for the plaintiff without an express promise to pay; and a witness may maintain an action against the party who has subpœnaed him and who has lost the cause, for his daily pay and expenses, without a previous demand of taxation of costs.(l)

The plaintiff in every civil action is eventually liable to the officers of the court for the fees prescribed by law, in case they cannot be procured from the defendant ; for in the contemplation of the law, he is supposed to have paid them as the action proceeded.(m)   Hence it is, that the award of execution is for all the costs to the plaintiff, "by him about his suit in that behalf expended."(n)   The general practice, both before

(z) Devinny v. Reeder, 1 Pa. R. 400.
(a) Ibid.
(b) 1 H. Bl. 217.
(c) 1 M. & S. 696.
(d) Ramsey's Appeal, 2 W. 230.
(e) Burns v. Thornbaugh, 3 Id. 78.
(f) 3 Barn. & Cress. 535.
(g) McWilliams v. Hopkins, 1 Wh. 275.
(h) *Vide* Dunkin v. Galbraith, 1 Br. 48; Hazlehurst v. Bayard, 3 Y. 152.

(i) Metzgar v. Metzgar, 1 R. 227.
(j) Bull. N. P. 336; 1 Taunt. 426.
(k) 4 T. R. 124.
(l) Utt v. Long, 6 W. & S. 174.
(m) Commonwealth v. County Commissioners, 8 S. & R. 153 ; Lyon v. McManus, 4 Bin. 172; Musser v. Good, 11 S. & R. 248; Banks v. Juniata Bank, 16 id. 155 ; see also 1 Peters's Rep. 233.
(n) Commonwealth v. County Commissioners, 8 S. & R. 153.

and since the Revolution, has been for the prothonotary to receive immediate payment for original writs, writs of removal, subpœnas, searches by the parties, copies of papers in the cause, and rules of court. But for other services, such as the entry of oyer and special imparlances, filing declarations, entries of pleas, and the like, the costs have been considered as abiding the event of the action.(*p*) So, that an action does not lie by the prothonotary to recover his fees in a cause which is still depending.(*q*) But, at the termination of the suit, he may recover them in an action in his own name, or he may include them in the execution issued by the successful party, as if they were a part of the latter's costs; and that where such party has himself nothing to receive; as in an execution against an executor on a discontinuance, who is liable to the officers for their fees for services rendered.(*r*)

Fees paid at the time of the services are necessarily taxed to the party as costs; but when not advanced, they are never included in his bill, but are indorsed on the execution as appertaining to the respective officers, and are collected by the sheriff to their use, and by him accounted for in his periodical settlements with them. Until their receipt by him, the party ordering the services is liable, but after that he is discharged, though the money be lost in the sheriff's hands. It is then the business of each officer to make him pay over his fees.(*s*)

The officers' fees are part of the plaintiff's costs, which he is supposed to have paid to them, and which he collects ostensibly for himself, but actually for them, by his execution. This has been the practice from the foundation of the State. Though the legal title to them is in the plaintiff, it is only as a trustee; and the officers may, consequently, sue out an execution for them in his own name.(*t*)

The prothonotary may maintain a suit for his fees against the party for whom the services are done, in the same manner as for other debts, and where the amount does not exceed one hundred dollars, he may sue before a magistrate. The fees are not chargeable to the attorney of the party for whom the services are done, unless he has become security for the costs.(*u*)

(*p*) Lyon *v*. McManus, 4 Bin. 172.
(*q*) Ibid. 167.
(*r*) Musser *v*. Good, 11 S. & R. 248.
(*s*) Beale *v*. The Com. 7 W. 186.

(*t*) Ranch *v*. Hill, 3 Barr, 423; see, however, Moore *v*. Porter, 13 S. & R. 100.

(*u*) Moore *v*. Porter, 13 S. & R. 100.

CHAPTER XXIX.

OF EXECUTION.

JUDGMENT having been perfected, the successful party may proceed to enforce satisfaction by issuing execution to the sheriff of the proper county, against the goods and chattels, lands and tenements of the debtor, which the sheriff is bound to seize and sell, and apply the proceeds to the discharge of the debt. The process used for selling goods and chattels, and levying on lands and tenements, is called a *fieri facias;* and, by a provision to be presently noticed, another process is given to the plaintiff in the nature of an attachment, upon which moneys, stock, and secret deposits, may be taken. The writ issued to effect a sale of real property after the levy, is called a *venditioni exponas.* But where the execution against the property has proved wholly or partially ineffectual, the plaintiff, in a certain class of cases, where the claim is on a tort, may proceed to coerce payment by arresting and imprisoning the debtor under a writ of execution, termed a *capias ad satisfaciendum;* which, though it may be taken at the same time with the *fieri facias,* can in no case be executed when the defendant has real or personal estate within the county sufficient to satisfy the judgment and costs; and if he has not sufficient, then it may be executed for the deficiency, and no more.(a) Thus imprisoned, he must be kept in close custody in jail, unless he can find sufficient security for his appearance at an ensuing insolvents' court. His most effectual means of procuring a total enlargement is by a surrender of his property, and a successful application for the benefit of the insolvent laws. The debt having been either voluntarily paid, or collected by execution, the judgment is then satisfied. In cases founded on contract, where a warrant of arrest is used upon due proof of fraud, the procedure, under the act of 1842, has been already pointed out.

The subject of execution, leaving out of consideration warrants of arrest and the remaining process afforded by the act of 1842, will be considered under the following heads:—

I. Of the nature and form of executions generally.
    1. Time of issuing writ.
    2. Executions against joint defendants.
    3. Executions upon bonds with penalty.
    4. Indorsement and form of writ.
    5. Return of writ and liability of sheriff thereon.

(a) §§ 27 and 28, act of 16th June, 1836, Pamph. L. 766.

6. Poundage and other charges.
7. Executions void or voidable.
8. Staying or setting aside executions by court.
II. Of the writ of *fieri facias,* and of the proceedings under it, as
    regards personal property.
  1. Nature of *fi. fa.*
  2. From what time its lien dates.
  3. Goods levied on, and herein of their seizure, removal, and of
    inventory.
  4. Staying writ, and its consequences, and herein of permitting
    goods to remain in defendant's custody.
  5. Exempted property.
  6. Levy on interest in lands as personalty,(*b*) and herein of fixtures.
  7. Levy on estate of corporations.(*c*)
  8. Levy on things pawned, and money.
  9. Sheriff's duty when goods are claimed by third party.
    (1). Enlarging time of writ.
    (2). Indemnity.
    (3). Interpleader.
 10. How far a levy is satisfaction of debt.
 11. Sale of property seized.
 12. Landlord's claims.
 13. Return to *fi. fa.*
 14. *Alias fi. fa.*
 15. *Venditioni exponas.*
 16. *Testatum fi. fa.,* and *fi. fa.* on judgments transferred under the
    act of April 16, 1840.
 17. Purchase of judgment by third party.
 18. Sale and payment of money by sheriff to attorney, and herein
    of payment to the sheriff.
 19. Distribution of proceeds.
III. Of equitable executions and proceedings to obtain a discovery
    under the act of 1836.
  1. Of bill of discovery.
  2. Of attachment in execution.
    (1). When an attachment lies.
    (2). What may be attached.
    (3). Practice.
  3. Proceedings to sell stock, &c.
IV. Of the writ of *fieri facias,* and the proceedings under it as regards
    lands and tenements, and herein of the writ of *liberari facias.*
  1. What interest in land may be levied on.
  2. How levy to be made.
  3. Levy on life estate.
  4. Inquisition.
  5. *Liberari facias.*
V. Of writs of *venditioni exponas* and *levari facias* on a mortgage, and
    proceedings under them.
  1. When a *venditioni exponas* issues.

(*b*) See *post,* section iv. (1st.)   (*c*) See, as to sequestration, section iv.
(3d.)

2. When a *levari facias* issues.
3. Notice and advertisements.
4. Manner of sale.
5. *Liberari facias* as to property unsold.
6. *Alias ven. ex.*
7. Setting aside sheriff's sale.
8. Sheriff's deed and its acknowledgment.
9. Application of proceeds.
    (1). Effect of sale on incumbrances.
    (2). Bringing money into court.
    (3). Practice in distribution of proceeds.
    (4). Appeal and *supersedeas.*
    (5). Application of surplus.
10. Reversal of judgment after sale.
11. Estate taken by purchaser.
12. Purchaser's remedy to obtain possession.
VI. Of the *capias ad satisfaciendum.*

SECTION I.

THE NATURE AND FORM OF EXECUTIONS GENERALLY.

1. *Time of issuing writ.*

Under the act of 1836, an execution of any judgment may be had at any time within a year and a day from the first day of the term at which it was rendered, provided that, if there be a stay of execution, the period shall be computed from the expiration of such stay.(*d*) Provided also, that there be no writ of error pending.(*e*) After the expiration of the period aforesaid, no execution could be issued upon any judgment, unless the party against whom it should have been rendered, his heirs, executors, or administrators, was first warned by a writ of *scire facias*, to show cause, if any he or they have, why an execution should not issue upon such judgment. § 2. But by the 4th section of the act of April 16, 1845, "Hereafter it shall not be deemed error to issue any writ of execution on a judgment, in any court, which has not been revived within a year and a day, if the same has been revived within five years." This act, it has been ruled, applies to executions as well on revived as on original judgments.(*f*)

The two sections of the act of 1836 are derived from the statute 13 Edw. I. c. 45;(*g*) the proviso to the first section being added in conformity with the decisions. Notwithstanding the language of the latter section, therefore, the old rule, even before the act of 1845, remained unchanged, that if a writ of execution be actually sued out within the year, and it be not executed so as to give the party the full benefit of his judgment, an *alias* execution may be sued out at any time afterwards without a *scire facias* to revive the judgment, though the

(*d*) § 1, Act of June 16, 1836 ; Pamph. L. 761.
(*e*) See Cas. Temp. Hardw. 53; 1 Mod. 20, *pl.* 53.

(*f*) Dailey *v.* Straus, 2 Barr, 401.
(*g*) Rob. Dig. 239.

first writ was not returned, if the continuances have been kept up by *vice comes non misit breve.*(*h*)   And it was not necessary that the last writ should be of the same species as the former, for a *ca. sa.*, for instance, may issue after the year, upon a *fi. fa.* regularly sued out before that time.(*i*)   Formerly, if a party died within the year and day after judgment obtained against him, a *fi. fa.* tested before his death could have been sued out against his goods in the hands of his executor or administrator,(*j*) or even if he died before judgment, but after the day in bank, judgment might have been signed as of the term in which he died, or if he died in vacation, then of the preceding term, and a *fi. fa.* tested the first day of such term might have been sued out and executed upon his goods in the hands of his executor, &c.(*k*)   But by the thirty-third section of the act of February 24, 1834,(*l*) it is now directed that no execution for the levy or sale of any real or personal estate of any decedent, shall be issued upon any judgment obtained against him in his lifetime, unless his personal representatives have been first warned, by a writ of *scire facias*, to show cause against the issuing thereof, notwithstanding the teste of such execution may bear date antecedently to his death.   To what extent the heirs and personal representatives of a decedent must be thus introduced as parties, and what is the form of the execution, will be fully considered in the next volume.(*m*)

Care must be taken not to sue out the writ before the judgment is actually signed.(*n*)

Execution may issue on a judgment confessed, on a judgment note, on the day it falls due, the maker not being entitled to the days of grace on it as on a negotiable note, although it has the usual words of such a note, with, however, an authority to an attorney to enter judgment, a release of errors, and a waiver of stay and inquisition.(*o*)

   2. Executions against joint defendants.

The execution must follow the judgment and be warranted by it.(*p*)   Hence, where there are a number of parties, it must be in the name of all the plaintiffs against all the defendants ;(*q*) and where judgment is entered against only one of two defendants, a joint execution is erroneous.(*r*)   A plaintiff who has recovered against several can have execution against the goods of the survivors only ; the goods of those who have died being discharged.(*s*)   But the judgment remains a lien upon the land of such deceased party, which may be rendered effective by a *soire facias* against the survivors and the representatives of him who is dead.(*t*)   In what cases execution is to be levied out of an executor's goods, will be treated hereafter.(*tt*)

Where several actions are brought against different parties for the same debt, as upon a promissory note, bail-bond, or bill of exchange, each party is liable to execution for the whole debt, and the costs of the

---

(*h*) Young *v.* Taylor, 2 Bin. 218; Lewis *v.* Smith, 2 S. & R. 142; Pennock *v.* Hart, 8 ibid. 378; and see 1 Arch. Pr. 255.
(*i*) Barnes, 213; 1 Saund. 219, *e.*
(*j*) 1 B. & P. 571; 2 Ld. Raym. 849.
(*k*) 7 T. R. 20.
(*l*) Pamph. L. 79.
(*m*) See vol. ii. "Executors, *Scire facias.*"

(*n*) 7 T. R. 21, *n.*; and see 2 Show. 494.
(*o*) Dunton *v.* Tyler, 3 Barr, 346.
(*p*) 2 Saund. 72, *h. k.*
(*q*) 5 Bac. Abr. 165 ; 6 T. R. 525.
(*r*) McPeake *v.* Hutchinson, 5 S. & R. 294.
(*s*) Comm. *v.* Miller's adm'rs, 8 S. & R. 457.
(*t*) Ibid.
(*tt*) Vol. ii. "Executor."

actions against himself; but neither of them is liable to the costs of the action against the other defendants.(u) But when the parties agree that the verdict and judgment in one case shall govern all, and the same witnesses are examined in each suit, the plaintiff is not entitled to recover from each defendant the costs for each witness.(v) The court will not stay proceedings upon payment of the debt and costs in an action against an acceptor of a bill, unless he also pay the costs of all the actions against the drawer and indorsers, he being the original defaulter.(w) And a creditor, who has judgment against the principal, against the indorsers, and against the absolute bail of the principal, and has issued execution and levied on the land of the principal, or of the absolute bail, may, nevertheless, have execution of the chattels of the indorsers. Nothing but actual satisfaction can prevent him.(x) And an execution issued on an absolute judgment, taken to indemnify the plaintiff as the surety of the defendant, for a debt not paid by the surety at the time of issuing the execution, is not erroneous or irregular; nor is it fraudulent by the statute of 18 Elizabeth. It is a measure to secure the surety by means intended to produce payment of the debt out of the effects of the principal by whom it is due.(y)

Under a joint-judgment the *fi. fa.* should be joint, as the execution must follow the nature of the judgment;(z) but this rule is technical, and has more of form than of substance in it; and the court out of which the process issues, will take care that it be not used so as to work injustice, and will protect a surety from an attempted disregard of a release to him by a creditor.(a)

By the act of April 11, 1825,(b) it is declared that the first section of an act passed the twenty-ninth day of March, one thousand eight hundred and nineteen, entitled, "An act regulating suits on promissory notes, and for taking stock in execution, is hereby repealed, excepting, nevertheless, the right of parties to any suits brought in conformity with the provisions of the said section, and now pending in any of the courts of this commonwealth, to continue and prosecute the same to final adjudication, in the same manner, and with the like effect, as if this act had not passed: *Provided*, That in suits on the same instrument, bond or note, where several are bound, and in suits against the maker, indorser, or indorsers of any note, and in suits on any bill of exchange against the drawer, acceptor, or any indorser or indorsers thereof, there shall be a taxation and recovery of the attorney and counsel fees, taxable by law, in one of the said suits only, at the election of the party plaintiff; and no fees for attorney or counsel shall be allowed, or taxed, in any suit or suits brought on the same instrument, bond, note, or bill of exchange, against the party or parties thereto, other than in one where the election is made as aforesaid.

3. *Executions upon bonds with penalty.*

In debt on bond for a penalty, the plaintiff cannot, by his execution, collect more than the sum mentioned in the condition of the bond, with

(u) Tidd. 1084.
(v) Curtis v. Buzzard, 15 S. & R. 21.
(w) Chitty on Bills, 473. *Vide* the act of 1825, *supra.*
(x) Gro v. Huntingdon Bank, 1 Pa. R. 425.

(y) Miller v. Howry, 3 Pa. R. 374.
(z) Shæffer v. Watkins, 7 W. & S. 219; Gibbs v. Atkinson, 3 P. L. J. 139.
(a) Mortland v. Himes, 8 Barr, 265.
(b) Pamph. L. 225, Troub. & H. Dig. 252.

interest and costs,(c) although the bond was given for a debt exceeding the amount of the condition.(d) But a judgment, by agreement of the parties, may be entered up for a debt then due, and also as a security for future advances to the defendant; and the plaintiff may collect, by execution, not only the sum actually due at the time the judgment was rendered, but the amount subsequently advanced to the defendant, provided the whole does not exceed the condition of the bond on which the judgment is given.(e) Where debt is brought to recover the interest due on bond, the principal of which is payable by instalments at distant days, judgment is entered for the penalty, with leave to take out execution in the first instance for the interest due at the commencement of the suit: and for the principal and interest subsequently accruing, the plaintiff must move the court for execution.(f)

4. *Indorsement and form of writ.*

The prothonotary indorses on the execution the amount of the actual debt, and the time from which interest is to be calculated, together with the costs of suit, as a direction to the sheriff for the sum which he is to levy; the sheriff adds to these his fees and poundage, and levies for the whole. If the defendant complains that injustice has been done him, immediate and liberal relief will be given, either by the court on motion, or by a judge at his chambers, upon laying before him a proper case, verified by oath.(g)

It is the sheriff's duty in levying to be governed by the amount indorsed on the *fi. fa.*, and not that contained in the body of the writ, which is often nominal. The indorsement is an official act, and must be taken to be correct until the contrary is shown.(h)

The writ bears *teste* in term time, and is made returnable on the several return days, in the same manner as original process, except that no time is limited between the issuing and return-day. If it is irregular, the defendant may move the court to set it aside. And this is the proper course, instead of going into the Supreme Court for relief on error.(i) An execution is good until reversed. It cannot be examined collaterally.(j) This writ is amendable.(k) Thus, an erroneous *teste* of a *fi. fa.* by the clerk was amended, although executed.(l) And the court will permit the *teste* and return-day of the *fi. fa.* to be amended by the *præcipe.*(m) So the *teste* and the return of an *alias venditioni exponas* were amended by the *præcipe.*(n) And the Supreme Court will, after error brought, issue a *certiorari* to bring up the *præcipe* to amend the writ by, from the earliest period,(o) the power of the court above, to amend, being asserted and exercised. " In matters arising from the mere *carelessness of the clerk in process*, it is to be observed, that those things which are amendable

---

(c) 12 Johns. 350. See *ante,* 356.
(d) 2 Caines's Rep. 256.
(e) 16 Johns. 165. *Sed vide* 4 Johns. Ch. R. 247.
(f) Sparks *v.* Garrigues, 1 Bin. 152; see Adams *v.* Bush, 5 W. 289.
To what extent the execution must conform to the debt really due, has been touched upon in a previous chapter. *Ante,* p. 356, and in the second volume it will be considered what form the execution in actions of debt should take.

(g) Lewis *v.* Smith, 2 S. & R. 155.
(h) Com. *v.* McCoy, 8 W. 155.
(i) Duncan *v.* Harris, 17 S. & R. 436.
(j) Stewart *v.* Stocken, 1 W. 135.
(k) See, generally, vol. ii. " Amendment."
(l) Baker *v.* Smith, 4 Y. 185.
(m) Berthon *v.* Keeley, 4 Y. 205.
(n) Shoemaker *v.* Knorr, 1 D. 197.
(o) Prevost *v.* Nichols, 4 Y. 483.

before error brought, are amendable afterwards, and if the inferior court doth not amend, then the superior court may amend them."(p) But the defendant in error must pay the costs of the amendment,(q) and executions.(r) So, where the judgment and *fi. fa.* differ, the latter may be amended by the former ;(s) and where a *fi. fa.* after levy, but before sale, was destroyed by accident, the court granted permission to make out a new *fi. fa.* to be delivered to the sheriff.(t) What property is embraced by the levy when the return is obscure, may be shown by parol evidence ;(u) and the *fi. fa.* was amended under the following circumstances, and the purchaser's title was held good. The writ had been correctly indorsed, but the body had relation to a different suit. The writ was executed and returned as if the contents corresponded with the indorsement. A *venditioni exponas* issued, on which the land levied on as the property of the defendant named by the indorsement, was sold.(v)

After many years, it will be presumed, in support of a title, that the lost *præcipe* contained a direction for a writ which would have authorized a sale ; and the court will amend the writ according to the levy, where it appears by the deed that all the land levied on was actually sold.(w)

5. *Return of writ, and liability of sheriff thereon.*

The sheriff is in strictness bound to return executed writs of execution. He may be ruled to do so by the plaintiff or defendant, and if he neglect to make his return before the expiration of the rule, the court upon motion will grant an attachment against him.(x) The several courts of the commonwealth, have power, by act of assembly, to issue attachments for enforcing the return of any writ for the payment of money received on any execution, and for the production of the body after a return of *cepi corpus*, or, in default thereof, for the payment of the debt and costs; and this power extends against former sheriffs and coroners.(y) If the property of the goods be in dispute, the court, upon this or any other reasonable cause, will enlarge the time for making the return until sufficient indemnity be given.(z) This indulgence will, however, be granted only in very special cases; it will be generally extended when the doubt arises from a point of law, and not mere matter of fact.(a) The sheriff ought not to wait until he has been ruled to return the writ, for the plaintiff, without proceeding by attachment, has an election to commence an action on the case in the first instance.(b) The return is made on the back of the writ, which is then filed with the prothonotary before, or on the day on which the rule to return it expires.

When the writ remains unreturned for years, the sheriff is presumed to have collected the amount; and he must rebut that presumption by proof that he did not, and why.(c)

The return can be made validly only by the sheriff himself. By the Stat. 12 Ed. II. c. 25, in force here, he is commanded to put his name to

(p) 8 Co. 162, a.
(q) Gilb. Hist. C. P. 167.
(r) Peddle v. Hollingshead, 9 S. & R. 284-5.
(s) Black v. Wistar, 4 D. 267.
(t) 3 Johns. 448.
(u) Scott v. Sheakly, 3 W. 50; see Burchard v. Rees, 1 Wh. 377.
(v) Owen v. Simpson, 3 W. 87.

(w) De Haas v. Bunn, 2 Barr, 339.
(x) 1 Arch. Pr. 262; *post*, 736.
(y) 7 Re. Laws, 496.
(z) Tidd, 917; and see 7 Taunt. 294; and see *post*, Sect. II. (9th.)
(a) See 1 Arch Pr. 262.
(b) See 2 Dunl. Pr. 775, and authorities there cited.
(c) Com. v. McKay, 8 W. 153.

it, that the court may know whose it is ; and therefore, a return by an
under sheriff is erroneous, though purporting to be in his name.   Still,
it may be ratified by the sheriff, so as to charge his sureties by delay to
move to set it aside.(d)

When an error or mistake is made by the sheriff, the proper course,
as will hereafter be fully seen,(e) is for him to ask leave to amend his
writ, which privilege, however, will be refused when intervening rights
will be thereby injured.(f)

The court cannot force the sheriff to amend, but will grant leave to
amend it.(g)

The sheriff can amend his return only by leave of the court, and no
further than its authority extends, which is to be measured by the extent of the affidavit to found it.   Beyond that, the amendment is void.
In contemplation of law, the amendment is made when allowed, the
affidavit being a sufficient material, when necessary, to reduce it to form.
No amendment should be allowed except for reasons expressly stated
and sworn to.(h)

The sheriff's return is as between the parties conclusive against him,
so that he cannot contradict it.(i)

A party may make an averment consistent with the sheriff's return,
or explanatory, of its legal bearing and effect, when the return is at
large.   But he cannot aver a matter directly at variance with the
facts stated in the return, contradictory to and falsifying it.(j)

"By his return, or what is equally efficacious, making a deed," says
Judge BELL, in a recent case, "the sheriff fixes himself for the price
bid.   That is a matter, thenceforth, between him and the purchaser."(k)

(d) Beale v. The Com. 7 W. 186.

(e) See vol. ii. "Amendments."

(f) Keyser v. Sutton, D. C. Oct. 6,
1849. Why sheriff should not have leave
to amend.   Per curiam.   The depositions show a plain mistake of the officer ;
and we see no reason why he should not
be permitted to amend.   While each
party is left to pursue his remedies
against the sheriff, the court will allow
him to make such a return as appears
supported by the facts of the case.
Though a levy was made under the last
writs subject to the first, it clearly appears there was no lien of the first writs,
and though the sale was made under all
the writs, it derived its force and effect
from the last writs only.—R. A.

Cadbury v. Duval.   June 30, 1849.
Why leave to sheriff to amend should
not be withdrawn.   Per curiam.   Upon
the 6th of March, 1848, the sheriff made
sale under a venditioni exponas to F. B.
Seybert, which he returned accordingly,
but that Mr. Seybert had failed to comply with the terms of said sale, and that
the premises remained in his hands unsold for want of buyers.   Upon the 19th
May, 1849, Mr. Seybert, through counsel, applied to the court and obtained

leave for the sheriff to amend his return,
the sheriff acquiescing.   It appears that
the purchaser, having at first declined,
is now willing to take the property.   A
motion has now been made in behalf of
other judgment creditors to the court to
rescind the leave thus given.   The granting or withholding leave to amend is a
matter within the sound discretion of
the court.   In reference to the sheriff, it
is exercised principally for his relief.
We do not think that this amendment
ought to have been granted, unless under
more special circumstances than have
been shown.   After the lapse of more
than a year to amend a sheriff's return,
not to correct an error or to relieve the
sheriff from liability on account thereof,
but to make that which was true speak
false for the accommodation of a purchaser who now sees that his bargain
was a good one, would not be, in our
opinion, the exercise of a sound discretion.—R. A.

(g) Mans v. Schermerhorn, 3 Wh. 13 ;
Boaz v. Updegrove, 5 Barr, 516.

(h) Lowry v. Coulter, 9 Barr, 353.

(i) Paxton v. Steckel, 2 Barr, 95.

(j) Knowles v. Lord, 4 Wh. 504.

(k) Hinds v. Scott, 1 J. 27.

But his omission to return an execution until after the return-day is not of itself such negligence as subjects him to an action."(l)

We have no statute requiring the old sheriff to turn over unexecuted writs to his successor, in writing; the practice is to hand them over to the successor whose duty it is to execute them. The duties of the old sheriff cease by mere tradition of the writs.(m)

Before return made courts always interpose to prevent injustice, but they cannot alter the effect of a return, although in a proper case they may enlarge the time for making it, or may grant leave to amend it. They will not countenance the introduction of parol evidence to control a return, except in an action against the sheriff for misconduct.(n)

By the sixty-third section of the act of April 15, 1834,(o) the sheriffs of the several counties are bound in a recognizance and bond with at least two sufficient sureties in sums proportioned to the extent of each county; the recognizance of the sheriff of Philadelphia County is in the sum of $80,000, and binds the estate of the obligors as effectually as a judgment. This lien is unlimited both in duration and extent.(p) The coroner in each county is also bound in a recognizance and bond with two sufficient sureties in one-fourth of the sum which is required of the sheriff of the same county. § 66.

A *scire facias* lies on the recognizance of the sheriff against him and his sureties, as well since the act of June 14, 1836, as before.(q)

A return of "money made" to a *venditioni*, discharges the debt, and fixes the right of the plaintiff and the liability of the sheriff in the same manner as such return to a *fi. fa.*(r)

Parol evidence is inadmissible to show that the return of a sheriff found in the office in the regular way, and purporting to have been made by him, was not in the sheriff's handwriting.(s)

The sheriff cannot contradict or avoid the legal effect of his return, either directly or indirectly; thus where the sheriff had attached a levy to a *fi. fa.*, but had appropriated the proceeds of the sale to a prior execution against the same goods, to which a levy, although actually made, had not been attached; it was held that he could not, in action against him for misappropriating the proceeds of sale, be allowed to show that a levy had been actually made under the first execution, by producing a paper purporting to be a levy, in connection with proof that it was the levy made, although it was not attached to the execution.(t)

It is not essential to the validity of the sheriff's return to an execution levied upon land, that it should set forth the deed or title under which the defendant holds.(u)

Although generally a sheriff's return is not evidence in his own favor, yet a return by *venditioni*, that he had sold land to A, is *prima facie*

(l) Com. v. Magee, 8 Barr, 248.
(m) Lesbey v. Gardner, 3 W. & S. 318.
(n) Per ROGERS, J., Mentz v. Hamman, 5 Wh. 155.
(o) Pamph. L. 537.
(p) 3 Pa. R. 286.
(q) Com. v. Lelar, 1 H. 23.

(r) Boaz v. Updegrove, 5 Barr, 516.
(s) Sample v. Coulson, 9 W. & S. 62.
(t) McClelland v. Slingluff, 7 W. & S. 134; Kintzing v. McElrath, 5 Barr, 466.
(u) Buckholder v. Sigler, 7 W. & S. 154.

evidence of the sale, &c., in an action by the sheriff against A, to recover the purchase-money.(v)

The sixth section of the act of June 14, 1836,(w) directs the mode of proceedings upon the official bonds of these officers, and will be more appropriately considered in our second volume under the head of *scire facias* on sheriff's bonds. It appears to have been the intention of the legislature to give the community security for redress against the sheriff in *all* cases of injury received by his official misconduct. His sureties are therefore liable in damages for the sheriff's trespass in seizing and selling the goods of B, under an execution against A.(x) The process against the sheriff's sureties in such action, or in any other actions, wherein any one of them happens to be defendant ought not to be intrusted to the sheriff. The exception to him is not confined to affinity, but if there is just cause of objection from his situation with regard to the party, the prothonotary upon this suggestion may direct the process to the coroner. The sheriff, however, being the proper officer for serving process, cannot be passed by without cause; but although no such cause exist, the writ is not void, and the coroner at his peril must execute all process directed to him by a court having jurisdiction. It is not for him to object that the direction is erroneous.(y)

6. *Poundage and other charges.*

On the execution of the writ, the sheriff is entitled to certain compensation termed poundage. The fee bill of February, 1821,(z) allows him for executing a *fi. fa.*, if the money is paid without levy or sale, one dollar; delivering lands or tenements to creditor (and no commission in such case to be taken), two dollars. Levying on lands or goods, and selling the same, for each dollar not exceeding three hundred dollars, two cents; for every dollar above three hundred dollars, and not exceeding one thousand, one cent; for every dollar above that sum, one half cent; and the same commission shall be allowed where the money is paid to him after levy made on personal property without sale; but none shall be allowed for more than the real debt, and then only for the sum actually received and paid over to the creditor. By an act of 1816,(a) a similar provision was made, which extends, however, to constables, as well as to sheriffs. The sheriff cannot charge the expenses of selling the goods by auction, because he is bound to sell them himself; yet if the auction be at the request of either party, that party must pay such expenses.(b) The charge of poundage where the defendant was discharged from a *ca. sa.* upon giving the plaintiff his promissory notes, was held improper, and was struck from the bill of costs.(c) But it is uniformly allowed upon payment of all judgments and mortgages prior to the judgment under which the sale was made.(d) The sheriff is entitled to poundage, on a *liberari facias*, but if the land be sold under a subsequent execution, before the expira-

---

(v) Hyskill *v.* Givin, 7 S. & R. 369; Cash *v.* Tozer, 1 W. & S. 519.

(w) Pamph. L. 637.

(x) Camack *v.* Com. 5 Bin. 184. The sheriff is answerable for the conduct of his deputy in taking such goods. Wilbur *v.* Strickland, 1 R. 458.

(y) Dalt. on Sheriffs, 104; Peal's Executors *v.* Com. 11 S. & R. 302.

(z) 7 Re. Laws, 368.

(a) 6 Sm. Laws, 372.

(b) 1 Arch. Pr. 263–4.

(c) 1 Br. 234.

(d) Petry *v.* Baubarlet, 1 Bin. 97.

tion of the term, he cannot charge poundage on the balance remaining due to the first creditor.(e)   On the same principle he is allowed it on the amount of liens paid, although they may have been *subsequent* to that under which the land was sold.(f)   The act of assembly of 1795, in giving poundage upon a *ca. sa.* confines it to cases where the money has been paid and received; and although hard upon the sheriff, the court cannot allow what the act refuses.(g)   After a levy on which an inquisition is held, land condemned, and a *venditioni exponas* issued, but countermanded by the plaintiff's attorney, he is entitled to the same commission, if plaintiff receives his debt and costs, as if the land had been sold.(h)   He may maintain an action for his poundage,(i) or he may retain it out of the money levied on the execution.   But he cannot refuse to execute a writ until his fees are paid.(j)

There is nothing in the fee bill of 1821 which allows the sheriff costs for employing a watchman to take charge of property.(k)

In an action against the sheriff to recover the penalty for taking fees for services not compensated by the act, it is sufficient to aver that the fees were taken for services other than those provided for by the act, without specifying for what services the fees were demanded.(l)

When he has received money by sale under an execution, but is tied up from paying it over by a rule of court, he is not liable for interest during such period; and this although purchasers have not paid him, and may be liable to him for interest.(m)

7. *Executions void or voidable.*

The sheriff is not allowed to disaffirm the right of the plaintiff to moneys made on an execution upon any allegation such as that his letters of administration are void, or that, being a trustee, he has not given the necessary security.   In such cases the court, however, will secure the creditors before the plaintiffs have leave to take the money out of court.(n)

If the writ be regular, the party may justify under it, though the judgment be erroneous, for this is the act of the court; and in justifying, the sheriff need only give the execution in evidence.(o)   This distinction exists between erroneous and irregular process; the latter is void from the beginning; under the first, a party may justify until it is

---

(e) Wall *v.* Lloyd's Executors, 1 S. & R. 320.

(f) 1 Br. 251.

(g) Milne *v.* Davis, 2 Bin. 137; see 5 T. R. 470.

(h) Middleson *v.* Summer, 3 S. & R. 549.

(i) 2 L. Raym. 1212; 1 Salk. 331; see 4 M. & S. 256.

(j) 1 Salk. 330, 331, 332.

(k) Patton's Estate, 2 Par. 103; Deal *v.* Hoover, D. C. Dec. 6, 1851. M. to take off a nonsuit. *Per curiam.* This is an action by the sheriff for watchman's fees, incurred under a *fi. fa.* in which defendant was plaintiff. It is admitted that defendant's attorney directed the plaintiff to put a watchman in charge. But that is by no means evidence from which a promise to pay for the watchman's services can be implied. Plaintiff was bound to keep the goods safely, and the direction of the plaintiff's attorney was simply a notice that he would be held responsible, if he suffered them to remain in the possession of the debtor defendant, and were lost. There was no consideration for the contract to pay the wages of a man hired by plaintiff to do what it was his duty to do; much less can one be implied from the mere request. Motion dismissed.

(l) Overholtzer *v.* McMichael, 10 Barr, 139.

(m) Stewart *v.* Stocker, 13 S. & R. 205.

(n) Dean *v.* Patton, 1 Pa. R. 438.

(o) 12 Johns. 395.

reversed, but not under an irregular process, because it was his own fault that it was irregular at first ;(p) and if the sheriff, or other officer in such case, join in the same plea with the party, he loses the benefit of his own defence. The sheriff, or other officer, however, may justify under an irregular judgment as well as an erroneous one, and, so as the writ be not void, it is a good justification, however erroneous, and the purchaser will gain a title under the sheriff.(q) An execution, issued before the stay of execution has expired, is irregular, and will be set aside by the court, or reversed on error. Still it is not void, but, like a judgment erroneously entered, is valid until reversed, nor can its validity be questioned by another execution creditor who sues the sheriff for the proceeds, or in any other case collaterally, except where there is collusion between the plaintiff and defendant in fraud of a third person.(r) And so a *fi. fa.* and sheriff's sale may be based on a judgment by default in an action of debt, and a like judgment on a *sci. fa.* to revive after plea pleaded, though there has been no assessment of damages, where the nominal and real debt has been indorsed on the execution.(s) When reversed for irregularity, after having been executed, it is a matter of course to award restitution of the money levied on the execution ; and to such an extent has the liberality of courts been carried of late years, that when executions have been irregularly issued or executed, the court, on mere motion, will set aside the proceedings, and order the money levied to be restored to the party.(t)

In case of plaintiff's death, the party who issues execution ought to substitute the personal representatives as a new party by *scire facias.* But the omission to do it does not *per se* make the execution void, or the party issuing it a trespasser, if he was entitled to collect the money upon it. Upon the authorities, such a proceeding is an erroneous and not an irregular and void one. It would be otherwise, however, if the party had no right : if, being a mere stranger, he interposed and set the officer on to do execution against one no longer liable. But even then, the party grieved ought to have the execution first set aside by a direct proceeding ; then he might have restitution, or recover damages in trespass ; but he cannot question it collaterally while the judgment and execution are in full force.(u)

8. *Staying or setting aside execution by court.*

The cases in which a court will open a judgment have been already fully considered ; and, of course, whenever the judgment is opened or set aside, the execution falls. But a rule to show cause why a judgment should not be opened, does not stay the proceedings without an order of the court to that effect; and the sheriff is liable for goods previously levied on under such judgment, which, by his neglect to sell, are levied on and sold under a subsequent execution, and the proceeds paid to the plaintiff in that suit.(v)

It may be considered as settled law that, independently of those cases where the execution is on its face irregular, where an execution,

(p) 3 Johns. 523.
(q) 1 Vez. 195 ; 1 M. & S. 425.
(r) Stewart v. Stocker, 13 S. & R. 203, 204.
(s) Gray v. Coulter, 4 Barr, 188.

(t) Per YEATES, J., Cassel v. Duncan, 2 S. & R. 58.
(u) Lay v. Sharp, 4 Wh. 340, *et seq.*, citing 3 Wils. 376; and see Darlington v. Speakman, 9 W. & S. 182.
(v) Spang v. Com. 2 J. 358.

has been issued without leave, and in violation of the agreement of the parties, the court has a power, which it is bound to exercise, to set it aside or stay proceedings until the plaintiff does justice by carrying into effect the terms and stipulations of an agreement. Thus, where land was purchased at a sheriff's sale for a part of the amount of the judgment, under an agreement that it was to be held as collateral security for the whole debt, and in violation of the agreement, an alias *fi. fa.* was taken out for the residue, it was held that the proper course was to set aside the writ, or stay proceedings upon it, though not to open the judgment to let the defendant into a defence on the merits.(*w*) And so, again, where it appears that the plaintiff had agreed that the debt sued for should only be levied out of a particular property, the court will control an execution so as to levy it out of such property.(*x*)

The authority exercised by a judge, at chambers, in a cause pending, is the authority of the court itself, and may be enforced by attachment, because disobedience of a judge's order is a contempt of court, and punishable as such. This jurisdiction is *ex necessitate rei*, to prevent oppression, and to facilitate the interlocutory proceedings of suits at law, and embraces a variety of important subjects.

The proper mode of proceeding in most cases, is by summons, in the nature of a rule *nisi*, fixing a day for a hearing, and served on the opposite party. Without this, the judge ought not to interfere, unless the order sought is of course. When the order is made, notice of it should be given to the party to be effected by it, otherwise he may disregard it. Notice is not always necessary, for an order may be, in some cases, without summons. Nor in any case is the omission fatal to the validity of the proceeding *ab initio.* Though indispensable to correct practice, a neglect to give it is but an irregularity furnishing ground to rescind the order made; yet it will not justify the officer's refusal to obey it. In this respect, the fiat at chambers is analogous to a writ which he is bound to execute, though irregular. He is not bound to give the plaintiff notice of the judge's order.(*y*) It is not cause for setting aside an execution that it was levied on land for which the defendant had no title, or that the lien of the judgment had been lost by lapse of time;(*z*) and hence, where, on application of assignees of real estate, the Court of Common Pleas stayed a *venditioni* issued on a judgment obtained after the assignment, the proceedings were reversed by the Supreme Court, who refused, at the same time, to inquire into the validity of the assignment, holding that the proper method of testing it would be in an ejectment between the sheriff's vendee and the assignees.(*a*)

The court will not, on motion to set aside a *fi. fa.*, inquire into the title of a third person, who claims the lands levied on, but will leave him to his ejectment; nor will the court, in such case, inquire into the existence of a lien on the land; though they would apply the proceeds to it, if valid, when the money is brought into court.(*b*)

Where a testator bequeathed to a certain legatee a legacy, payable in the event of the estate proving sufficient to pay prior legacies, the

(*w*) Harrison *v.* Soles, 6 Barr, 393.
(*x*) Irwin *v.* Shoemaker, 8 W. & S. 75.
(*y*) See Com. *v.* Magee, 8 Barr, 246, citing Bagley's Pr. 15, *et seq.*

(*z*) Seitzinger *v.* Fisher, 1 W. & S. 293.
(*a*) Neel *v.* Bank of Lewistown, 1 J. 16.
(*b*) Harrison *v.* Waln, 9 S. & R. 318.

court will not interfere to stay execution by the executors against the legatee on an antecedent debt, except where it is perfectly clear that the estate will be large enough to pay the legacy.(c)

SECTION II.

OF THE WRIT OF FIERI FACIAS, AND OF THE PROCEEDINGS UNDER IT, AS REGARDS PERSONAL PROPERTY.

1. *Nature of fi. fa.*

This writ, like all other writs of execution, must strictly pursue the judgment and be warranted by it.   In substance, it is a command to the sheriff or coroner, that of the goods and chattels of the party he cause to be made the sum recovered by the judgment (specifying it according to the form of action) and that he have the money and the writ before the judges of the court from which it issues, on the return-day thereof.(d)   Upon receiving the writ he is bound to indorse on it the day of the month, the year, and the hour of the day whereon he received it.(e)   And by section forty-one, if the defendant refuse or neglect to pay the debt and costs, the officer shall proceed to levy and sell so much of the defendant's personal estate as shall be sufficient, and make return of his proceedings according to the writ.   If the sheriff refuses to do so, an action may be supported against him on his official bond before the return of the writ.(f)   After a *fi. fa.* is executed upon the defendant's lands, the court will not set it aside, upon the ground that sufficient personal property has been found to satisfy the judgment since the inquisition ;(g) nor, after the debtor's goods have been taken in execution, can the creditor discharge them, and continue his judgment in force as to the land of the defendant.(h)

Executions issued by a justice on transcripts from another justice of the same county then in commission, are void, not being allowed by the act of assembly.(i)

Proceedings on a *fi. fa.* which has not been taken up with the writ of error, cannot be reviewed thereon.(j)

An attorney's *præcipe* for a *fi. fa.* on a transcript from a magistrate without a return of *nulla bona* by his constable, will not protect the prothonotary for such infraction of the act of assembly.(k)

Personal property only, not lands, can be levied on by execution from the Orphans' Court, under the 13th section of the act of March 29, 1832.

It is irregular to issue execution in an executor's name without suggesting the plaintiff's death, and substituting the executor's on the record; where, however, the money is levied on such execution, the Supreme Court on error will remit the record with directions to suggest the death, and substitute the executor's name, *nunc pro tunc.*(l)

(c) Dunn's Executors v. The American Philosophical Society, 2 Barr, 75.
   (d) 1 Arch. Pr. 265.
   (e) § 40, act of June 16, 1836.
   (f) Shannon v. Com. 8 S. & R. 450.
   (g) Hunt v. McClure, 2 Y. 387.
   (h) Hunt v. Breading, 12 S. & R. 37 ;

see Dean v. Patton, 13 Id. 342.
   (i) Hallowell v. Williams, 4 Barr, 339.
   (j) Nice v. Bowman, 6 W. 29.
   (k) Franklin v. Trimble, 5 Barr, 520.
   (l) Darlington v. Speakman, 9 W. & S. 182.   See *ante*, 692.

A writ of execution not levied until after the return-day is spent, and the writ, though retained by the officer beyond the return-day, is dead in his hands.(*m*)

2. *From what time its lien dates.*

By the common law, an execution had relation to the time when it was awarded, and, therefore, if the goods were purchased by a third person after the *teste*, although *bona fide*, and for a valuable consideration, they were nevertheless liable to be taken in execution in the hands of the purchaser. This has been so far altered in England by the statute of frauds, and in Pennsylvania by act of assembly, that chattels are now bound only from the delivery of the writ to the sheriff.(*n*) The thirty-ninth section of the act of June 16, 1836,(*o*) directs that " no writ of *fieri facias*, or other writ of execution, shall bind the property or the goods of the person against whom such writ of execution is sued forth, but from the time such writ shall be delivered to the sheriff, under sheriff, or coroner, to be executed." This provision is from the fourth section of the act of March, 1772. But there is a material difference between the case of *fi. fa.* in England and in Pennsylvania, arising from the doctrine of *market overt*. In England, if the defendant sells in *market overt*, even after delivery of the writ to the sheriff, it divests the goods of the lien; it is otherwise, however, in Pennsylvania, to which State the doctrine does not extend.(*p*) Under our act of assembly, then, no writ of *fi. fa.* or other writ of execution shall bind the goods of the defendant, but from the time of its delivery to the sheriff, which delivery may be effected by leaving it at his office or the house where he usually transacts his business;(*q*) thereupon the sheriff is directed to indorse on it the day of the month and year on which it was received.(*r*) The meaning of this provision is, that after the writ is so delivered, if the defendant make an assignment of his goods, the sheriff may take them in execution.(*s*) Thus, so far as relates to the party himself, and to all others, but purchasers for a valuable consideration, writs of execution bind the party's goods from the time of their *teste*.(*t*) So he may levy on goods which had been delivered by an agent of the defendant, who, however, had no authority to make such delivery, to a third person to whom the defendant was indebted, in payment of his debt.(*u*) If the writ lie dormant in the hands of the sheriff, without levy, for a considerable time, a *bona fide* sale will be valid.(*v*) It may be well to notice here the law as regards an execution issued by a justice of the peace. It differs from that issuing from a court in this, that, by express act of assembly, no such execution can be a lien on the property of the defendant before levy made thereon.(*w*)

Although the statute, being made in favor of purchasers, does not alter the law as between the parties, yet the lien of a *fi. fa.* does not relate back to the *teste* of the writ, so as to bind the property of goods

(*m*) Finn *v.* Com. 6 Barr, 460. See Lantz *v.* Worthington, 4 Barr, 103; Com. *v.* Magee, 8 Barr, 248.
(*n*) 8 S. & R. 509; see 2 S. & R. 157.
(*o*) Pamph. L. 768.
(*p*) Easton *v.* Worthington, 5 S. & R. 130.
(*q*) Mifflin *v.* Will, 2 Y. 177.
(*r*) *Vide* 1 Sm. Laws, 390, § 4, act of June, 1836, § 31, Pamph. L. 755.

(*s*) Tidd, 1037; 16 Johns. 287.
(*t*) 2 Saund. 219, *f*; 2 Vent. 218; Comb. 33, 145; 2 Show. 485; 1 Arch. Pr. 259.
(*u*) 18 Johns. 363.
(*v*) 9 Johns. 133.
(*w*) Act of March, 1820, 7 Re. Laws, 309; *vide ante*, 625–6, as to lien of writ of restitution.

as against the trustees in a voluntary assignment made by a debtor for the benefit of creditors, who may be considered as purchasers, claiming under a deed made to secure the honest antecedent debts of fair creditors.(x)

If the plaintiff die after a *fi. fa.* sued out, it may be executed notwithstanding, and the plaintiff's executor or administrator shall have the money; and should the defendant die, the execution may be served if it be issued in his lifetime.(y) When the plaintiff dies in vacation, the execution may be sued out by the executor or administrator, tested of the last term, and the court will not inquire when it was sued out.

Should two writs from different plaintiffs be delivered to the sheriff on the same day, or on different days, he ought to execute that first which was first delivered,(z) except it be fraudulent, when he ought to execute the other.(a) Should he, however, give preference to the last, the proceeding is not void; the property is bound by a sale so made, and the plaintiff in the first execution must take his remedy against the sheriff.(b)

Executions issued on the same day, and delivered to the sheriff at different periods of the day, must be paid out of the proceeds of the sale of personal property in the order, as to time, in which they came to the sheriff's hands.(c) "A case like the present," said Chief Justice GIBSON, delivering a "*per curiam,*" opinion, "could not occur in England, where the sheriff acts between conflicting execution creditors at his peril, and without the benefit of any other protection or guide than the mandate of his writ; consequently, if he happens to sell on the younger execution, the court, acting on his return as incontrovertible, awards the money to be paid over on it as if the sale were a rightful one, and leaves the disappointed creditor to his remedy by action. The extreme hazard of the sheriff's position has induced something like relaxation in his favor even there, when return of the execution is wanted to enable a party to charge him in an action; to enforce which, the favor of the court has sometimes been refused. Our own courts, however, have constantly interfered for beneficial purposes, before return made; and have awarded money in court to the creditor entitled to it by a strict performance of the sheriff's duty. This avoids delay and useless litigation, at the same time that justice between all parties is fully attained. At all events, the practice has received the confirmation of the legislature, who have added to it a trial by jury of contested facts, and the supervision of the court of the last resort. But though no such case in circumstances is found in the books, its principle has been involved in a contest for priority between an ordinary execution, and the statutory execution of a commission of bankruptcy, in respect to which it is held, that if the seizure of the goods is at an earlier period of the day than the act of bankruptcy, the execution is good.(d) Between conflicting judgments of the same day, contribution was decreed in Metzler v. Kilgore,(e) because the statute directs the actual date to be entered of record, with no greater particularity than to designate

---

(x) Lippincott v. Barker, 2 Bin. 187.
(y) 2 Ld. Raym. 1072; S. C. Salk.
322, pl. 10; see *ante*, 684.
(z) 2 Bac. Abr. 721.
(a) 4 East, 523.

(b) 12 Johns. 162; 18 Id. 311.
(c) Ulrick v. Dreyer, 2 W. 303.
(d) Watson's Law of Sheriff, 187.
(e) 3 Pa. R. 246.

the day, and being a matter of record it can be no further inquired of by evidence *in pais;* but a distinction was expressly recognized, in this respect, between the date of a judgment and the delivery of an execution. The court did right, therefore, to award the money to the executions according to priority of actual delivery."

If the leading features of the act of 1836, concerning executions, it was observed in a recent case, were fully carried out, regardless of former and sometimes conflicting decisions as to the priority of levies, the duties of sheriffs and the rights of parties, in conflicting executions, would be disentangled, and much litigation avoided. Each plaintiff ought to look to the sheriff for a faithful discharge of his duty, according to the writ and the statute, and if he disregarded them, then look to him alone. If, instead of this, he departs from the law, by permissive or collusive assent, or positive direction, so as to hinder or obstruct a subsequent execution, he ought to and will be postponed.(*f*) A *fi. fa.*, it was said in the same case, binds all the defendant's personal property in the bailiwick, from the time it is put in the sheriff's hands. But the object of the law is not to secure a continuing lien in favor of the execution creditor, but to enable him to obstruct fraudulent transfers by the debtor, and to secure his debt by a levy and sale of property fraudulently or illegally transferred to defeat the execution.(*g*)

It is settled, that the receipt of a second *fi. fa.* amounts, from the time it is indorsed by the sheriff, to a re-seizure of the goods on which a prior levy has been made, and thenceforth they are in his custody on all the writs.(*h*) The indorsement itself amounts to such re-seizure.(*i*)

The execution of a *fi. fa.* is one act and not divisible by points of time, *e. g.*, though a seizure be made before the giving a bond of indemnity to the sheriff, and a sale be made afterwards, the execution is considered as made under the writ *after* the giving of the bond.(*j*)

There is nothing in the act relating to the levy under a *fi. fa.*, which implies that the title of the creditors depends upon the time the goods were bound. The construction has uniformly been, that it depends on the time the writ was delivered to the sheriff, and by him indorsed thereon. Hence, the proceeds of sale, under three writs, must go to the two first, although the goods sold had been acquired by the debtor after they had been given to the sheriff, but before the third writ came to the sheriff's hands.(*k*)

Where an execution was levied on defendant's personal property, subject to former levies, and enumerating various articles of personal property (but not specifying any cord wood), "and all the defendant's personal property not exempted by law;" and a subsequent execution issued to the same term, which was returned, levied on certain personal property, naming it, subject to certain specified *fi. fa.'s*, and all former levies, remaining on said personal property of defendants, "and also a large quantity of cord-wood, and a small quantity of iron-ore;" it was held, that the proceeds of the sale of the wood and ore were applicable to the first execution, and that evidence was not admissible to show that the wood was acquired after the levy was made on the first

(*f*) Earl's Appeal, 1 H. 482.
(*g*) Earl's Appeal, 1 H. 485. COULTER, J.
(*h*) Watmough *v.* Francis, 7 W. 206.
(*i*) Watmough *v.* Francis, 7 Barr, 203.
(*j*) Watmough *v.* Francis, 7 Barr, 212.
(*k*) Shafner *v.* Gilmore, 3 W. & S. 439.

execution, if the same were acquired by defendant before the return-day of that execution.(*l*)

A creditor who has levied on the chattels of his debtor, will not after-wards be suffered to divert the levy, to the payment of a posterior judg-ment, in detriment of an intermediate lien; nor to keep afoot a judg-ment actually satisfied, so as in effect to give preference to an inferior security at the expense of a superior one.(*m*)

Where one constable levies on goods, another cannot, under a second execution, take the same goods out of his hands and sell them, though the first execution be on a fraudulent judgment. The right to the pro-ceeds must be determined by law.(*n*)

Where it does not appear when the goods were levied on by the sheriff, it will be presumed to have been prior to the return-day of the writ.(*o*)

The practice of indorsing the hour at which a writ of *fieri facias* is delivered to the sheriff, has prevailed so uninterruptedly, as, perhaps, to make the indorsement *prima facie* evidence of the hour; though the statute requires no more than the day to be stated.(*p*)

3. *Goods levied on, and herein of their seizure, removal, and of inventory.*

The holder of a *bona fide* valid judgment, is entitled to the fruits of execution, whether the property levied upon be personal or real, he taking the risks of sale under his process dependent on the fact of own-ership in the defendant at the time of judgment or execution. The most effectual and general mode of testing and defeating covinous trans-fers, is, by levy and sale of the property, and then by contesting the right with the person claiming title; and there is no difference as to the creditor's right to this course of proceeding, whether the property is in the debtor's possession, or that of the claimant of title. Hence, it is error to stay proceedings on execution, because an assignment for benefit of creditors has been made by the defendant.(*q*)

A bond or note cannot be levied on and sold as a chattel.(*r*)

Where the sheriff sold fixtures under a *fi. fa.*, with a verbal consent of the owner of the land, and the purchaser paid the price and took possession, his title is good against a subsequent vendee of the land, be-fore actual severance.(*s*)

When the judgment is on a note payable in the notes of a particular bank, the court will, under its equitable powers, so control the execution as to prevent injustice.(*t*) Thus, when the judgment is on bank notes, the court can so control the execution as to compel the delivering up of the notes.(*u*)

Before the act of 1836, goods pawned or gaged for a debt, or leased for years, could not be taken in execution for the debt of the pawnor or lessor; but the sheriff might sell them, subject to the rights of the pawnee

(*l*) Wilson's Appeal, 1 H. 426. Ro-gers, J.

(*m*) Cathcart's Appeal, 1 H. 422. See Hunt *v.* Breading, 12 S. & R. 37; Dean *v.* Patton, 13 S. & R. 341; and Wood *v.* Vanarsdale, 3 R. 40.

(*n*) Winegardner *v.* Hafer, 3 H. 144.

(*o*) Fetter *v.* Patton, 8 W. & S. 455.

(*p*) Metzler *v.* Kelgore, 3 P. R. 247.

(*q*) Neel *v.* Bank of Lewistown, 1 J. 18; see Stewart *v.* Coster, 1 J. 91.

(*r*) Rhoads *v.* Megonigal, 2 Barr, 40.

(*s*) Mitchell *v.* Freedly, 10 Barr, 198.

(*t*) Irvine *v.* Lumbermen's Bank, 2 W. & S. 210.

(*u*) Bk. United States *v.* Thayer, 2 W. & S. 448.

or lessee.(*v*) As will presently be seen, however, such interest may now be reached by an equitable execution.

The sheriff must designate the property seized under the execution, either in the body of his return, or by a reference to a schedule accompanying it, so that it may be known to posterior execution creditors, or dealers with the debtor, what property is affected by the lien. The sheriff may attach the levy to each execution, or may refer to the levy attached to another *fi. fa.* The omission to do either cannot be supplied by other proof. Hence, if he make a levy under a second execution, he must apply the money made to it, and not to a prior *fi. fa.* which he had returned without a levy, leaving the plaintiff on the first writ to his remedy against him for right.(*w*)

The sheriff must take property pointed out to him by the plaintiff in the execution, as belonging to the defendant, if it be his in fact, though it be doubtful then whether it be so or not, if the plaintiff offers to indemnify him. The sheriff takes the risk of a refusal, and is liable, should it appear that the property was in the defendant. But he is not liable at all events; and hence, an offer to indemnify him does not oblige him to sell the property of a third person.(*x*)

Under a levy on certain enumerated articles, and all the defendant's personal property, not exempted by law, the sheriff may sell all the defendant's property then possessed, or *afterwards* acquired, though not enumerated; and evidence will not be received, that part, after unenumerated goods sold, was acquired after the levy, if, in fact, they were acquired before the return-day of the writ. So, as to let in on the fund a second *fi. fa.* in the levy on which the sheriff specified those goods.(*y*)

It is not necessary for a sheriff or constable, who has several executions in his hands, and makes a levy on goods, to indorse a list of the goods levied upon, on each execution; by the practice he may make the indorsement on one execution, and refer to it in his return, on the others.(*z*)

Under the act of June 16, 1836, the sheriff is bound, 1st, to levy on as much of the defendant's estate as will satisfy debt, interest, and costs, in the discharge of which duty he is not bound to fractional exactness, but is entitled to a liberal latitude; 2d, to make out a schedule of the property levied on; and 3d, to sell after six days' public notice. The continuance of a lien, merely for the purpose of a lien, and the exclusion of other creditors, is unlawful, both for the execution plaintiff and the sheriff.(*a*)

When the sheriff levies on a specific article, or articles, naming them, without more, he will be confined to his levy; as, for example, where he levies on a horse, he will not be permitted to sell a cow, or other article of property. But not so when words are added which plainly indicate his intention to include other property, although not specifically named or enumerated.(*b*)

(*v*) Strodes *v.* Cavan, 3 W. 258; Lindsey *v.* Fuller, 10 W. 147.

(*w*) McClelland *v.* Slingluff, 7 W. & S. 135.

(*x*) Com. *v.* Watmough, 6 Wh. 140. As to indemnity, &c., see *post*, 719.

(*y*) Wilson's Appeal, 1 H. 426, citing 3 W. & S. 438, and explaining McClelland *v.* Slingluff, 7 W. & S. 134.

(*z*) McCormick *v.* Miller, 3 Pa. R. 230.

(*a*) Earl's Appeal, 1 H. 483.

(*b*) Wilson's Appeal, 1 H. 428. ROGERS, J.

In the execution of the writ of *fi. fa.* the sheriff cannot break open any outer door of the party's dwelling-house ;(c) unless in the case of a writ of *habere facias;* but having got entrance, he may in all cases break open an inner door, cupboards, trunks, &c., if necessary ;(e) and it has been held that he need not demand entrance at the inner doors, before they are broken open.(f)   The rule extends only to the party's dwelling-house, therefore the sheriff may break open the outer door of a barn or outhouse, or store or warehouse, standing separate from the dwelling-house, without a previous demand and refusal of admission ;(g) and goods may be taken through the windows if open.(h)   After demand and refusal of entrance, the sheriff may break open the outer door of a dwelling-house belonging to a third person, if the defendant or his goods be there ;(i) or if the defendant, after being arrested on a *capias*, escape into either his own or another's dwelling-house, the officer will be justified in breaking the outer door to retake him.(j)   Also, if after a peaceable entrance at the outer door of the party's dwelling-house, the sheriff or his officer be locked in, he may justify breaking open the outer door in order to get out; and the court will probably grant an attachment against the defendant.(k)   If the sheriff break an outer door, when he is not justified in doing so, this does not vitiate the execution, but merely renders the sheriff liable to an action of trespass.(l)   Where the sheriff enters the house of the defendant, his justification does not depend on his finding or not finding property.   But it is otherwise where he enters a stranger's house, in which case he is not justified, unless it turn out that the defendant had goods therein liable to execution.(m)   No settled rule appears to exist as to the length of time the sheriff should continue in the house of the defendant or a stranger upon a *fi. fa.;* he ought not, however, to remain there, unpermitted, longer than is necessary for the service of his process.(n)

A seizure of goods, in execution, to the value of the debt, whether they be sold or not, is a discharge of all responsibility on the part of the debtor, and, consequently, satisfies the judgment; further remedy being against the sheriff.   But this rule is inapplicable where the goods have been left in the continued possession of the defendant in the execution, and he has been permitted to use them as his own.(o)

The levying of an execution, operates to vest an interest in the sheriff, sufficient to enable him to pursue the goods levied in the hands of a trespasser; but, until sold, the property of the judgment debtor is not wholly divested; it remains in him, subject to the levy, and is at his disposal, burdened with the incumbrance.(p)

A levy is a seizure, and in England an actual one, though here the sheriff cannot be said to seize what is not within the range of his view.   The defendant may dispense with actual seizure, and thus give him a con-

---

(c) Cro. Eliz. 908 ; 2 Bac. Abr. Ex'n. N.
(e) 2 Show. 87 ; Cowp. 1.
(f) 4 Taunt. 619.
(g) 1 Sid. 189; 16 Johns. 287.
(h) Bing. on Ex. 244.
(i) 5 Co. 93, a; 1 Foster, 319.
(j) 6 Mod. 105.
(k) Cro. Jac. 555 ; Palm. 52.

(l) 1 Arch. Pr. 261.
(m) 5 Taunt. 769, 770.
(n) Tidd. 1049.
(o) Cathcart's Appeal, 1 H. 421. BELL, J.   Cummin's Appeal, 9 W. & S. 73 ; Davids v. Harris, 9 Barr, 501. See *post*, 702.
(p) Towar v. Barrington, Bright. R. 253.

structive possession against himself; but the agreement binds only themselves, not other creditors.(q) Hence, a return of levy on goods not within the sheriff's view, and not taken into custody, is no levy as to subsequent judgment creditors.(r)

Though an actual seizure is generally necessary to a valid levy of goods, yet it may be dispensed with for the defendant's accommodation, and as between him and the officer the levy is good. And so he may retain possession, for the officer becoming thereby *quoad hoc* his servant, and answerable to him in trespass *vi et armis*, should he retain or remove the goods after such levy and arrangement to hold for the officer.(s)

The sheriff need not take the property into actual custody. It is enough if it be forthcoming to answer the exigencies of the writ.(t)

The latest period for making the levy is the return-day of the writ.(u) Whilst it is in force, the sheriff is bound to make an actual levy on the goods, or on part of the goods in the name of the whole;(v) and he ought to designate them in the execution or schedule annexed, as it furnishes the means of ascertaining what goods were levied on.(w) To constitute a good levy, the sheriff should have the goods under his view and within his power, and merely proclaiming a levy on goods locked up in a store, and not in view, is not sufficient; the store should be broken open, the goods seized, and an inventory taken.(x) It is not necessary to make a list on each of several writs in the sheriff's hands at the time, one indorsement suffices, if referred to in his return to the others.(y) In executing the writ, the officer generally enters upon the premises in which the defendant's goods are, and leaves one of his assistants in possession of them.(z) Or, as is the practice here, the sheriff takes security for the forthcoming of the goods, but this is at his own risk. After levy made, it is sufficient as to a second *fi. fa.* given to the sheriff before sale, without a new levy.(a) By the seizure, he has such a property in the goods that he may maintain trespass or trover against the defendant or a third person for taking them away.(b) And this remedy is necessary for the protection of the sheriff; for he is answerable to the plaintiff for the value of the goods taken under the *fieri facias;* and the defendant is discharged from the judgment, and all further execution, if the sheriff has taken goods to the amount of the debt, although he does not satisfy the plaintiff.(c) The same sheriff who begins the execution must end it, although he go out of office before the sale.(d)

It is not necessary for the sheriff, in order to make his levy effectual, that he should first make out an inventory of the chattels; "nor is it necessary, perhaps, in all cases, that an inventory should be made out at any time. Neither is it necessary that the sheriff should remove the goods levied on immediately; nor that he put a person, in every case, immediately into the possession of them; a reasonable time must be allowed for this, which may be more or less, to be judged of according to attending circumstances. A levy, however, upon such property, can-

(q) Lowry v. Coulter, 9 Barr, 349.
(r) Ibid.
(s) Trovillo v. Tilford, 6 W. 468.
(t) Dorrance v. Com. 1 H. 160.
(u) Bing. on Ex. 242; *ante*, 688, 9.
(v) Lewis v. Smith, 2 S. & R. 144.
(w) 1 W. C. C. R. 29.
(x) 16 Johns. 287.

(y) McCormick v. Miller, 3 Pa. R. 230.
(z) See 1 M. & S. 711.
(a) 17 Johns. 16.
(b) 2 Saund. 47, ca. 5.
(c) 2 Saund. 47 ; 6 Mod. 292; Nagle v. Stroh, 4 W. 124.
(d) 1 Salk. 323.

not be made without the sheriff has it within his power and control, or at least within his view; and if having it so, he makes a levy upon it, it will be good if followed up afterwards within a reasonable time, by his taking possession in such manner as to apprise every body of the fact of its having been taken in execution."(e)

When the inventory is erroneous, the sheriff may have leave to amend it; or a party in interest may compel him to do so, or fix his liability, by filing exceptions to it.(f)

Interference by the plaintiff by which the execution of the writ is prevented, is a sufficient defence to the sheriff.(g)

4. *Staying writ, and its consequences, and herein of permitting goods to remain in defendant's custody.*

It is not the practice to remove goods levied on, provided the sheriff be secured as to their being produced when demanded; and the lien on the personal property has always been held to continue, though it has been removed on the *fi. fa.* unless fraud is proved.(h) But this lien is gone, as against a vendee or subsequent execution, if the sheriff take a bond from the defendant, conditioned for the return of the property.(i) So if suffering the goods to remain in the possession of the debtor, has given him a false credit, the creditor loses his lien.(j) And withdrawing the officer left in charge of the goods, suffering the debtor to go on in his business as usual, amounts to a relinquishment of the execution as against other execution creditors.(k) By the common law of England, a levy is held fraudulent where the goods are left in the hands of the defendant; and notwithstanding some decisions to the contrary, the only exception to this, as the law is understood here, is confined to household furniture. But even in this case the plaintiff must use reasonable diligence, for a levy will not protect furniture which has been suffered to remain in the defendant's possession several years, against a subsequent execution which has issued before the return of the first.(l) The latitude allowed by our law in the case of levies upon household furniture is not extended where merchandise or goods for sale have been taken in execution.(m) In the Circuit Court of the United States, it has been

(e) Wood v. Vanarsdale, 3 R. 405, 406.
(f) Parmentier v. Stewart, Leeds v. Stewart. D. C. Feb. 24, 1849. Why the sheriff should not be permitted to amend his inventory filed. *Per curiam.* The inventory filed is defective. It merely states a lot of lumber. In cases under this act of assembly, the operation of which is to relieve the sheriff from so heavy an amount of responsibility, it is the inclination of the court to require from the sheriff a particular inventory of his levy. It should be as detailed as possible—as much so as a merchant's account of stock. He ought not, however, to be permitted to extend his inventory to the prejudice of the surety by introducing other articles not strictly within the general terms he has employed at first. Sheriff allowed to amend by specifying the particulars of the lot of lumber mentioned in his inventory.

Lentz v. Witte. D. C. Feb. 24, 1849. Exceptions to sheriff's inventory. *Per curiam.* A very proper practice has been adopted in this case. The filing of exceptions in analogy to other cases will suspend the rule discharging the sheriff until he has filed a sufficient inventory, or procured a decision of the court upon the subject. In this case, the inventory is clearly insufficient. Exceptions sustained.

(g) Dorrance v. Com. 1 H. 160.
(h) 2 Y. 434, 524; 4 D. 167, 208, 213; see also 1 Br. 16; 2 id. 333; 5 Bin. 269; Keyser's Appeal, 1 H. 412.
(i) 1 Br. 366.
(j) Knox v. Summers, 4 Y. 477.
(k) Guardians of the Poor v. Lawrence, 4 Y. 194.
(l) Lewis v. Smith, 2 S. & R. 142; Cowden v. Brady, 8 S. & R. 510.
(m) Chancellor v. Phillips, 4 D. 213.

ruled generally that other executions will be preferred if on a *fi. fa.* the property be left with the debtor.(*n*)   In the same court, it was decided that where goods are levied on by virtue of a *fi. fa.* and left with the debtor *by order of the plaintiff*, the effect of the levy is suspended until a countermand; and a second execution levied on the same goods, before such countermand, and regularly proceeded in, will have a pre-ference.(*o*)   A suspension for one day is sufficient to give a preference to an intervening execution, and the length of time during which the levy is suspended is immaterial.(*p*)   It has even been said that the lien of an execution levied on goods may be lost by the slightest negligence in pursuing it.(*q*)

The cases ruling the levy to have been lost as to junior *fi. fas.*, by staying proceedings, are instances of indefinite stays, and where the executions appeared to be designed as covins, or to create liens separate from the possession; where, however, the sale is not *postponed*, but merely adjourned before the return-day, for a few days, a measure not inconsistent with making the money on the same writ, and creating no presumption that anything else was intended, the lien will not be lost. If adjourned until after the return-day, it would be equivalent to an indefinite postponement, and therefore fraudulent; but where the credi-tor really means to obtain his money under the writ, it would be unrea-sonable to interfere with his direction of it.(*r*)   Neither is the taking of a forthcoming bond by the sheriff for the delivery of the goods at the day of sale a dissolution of the levy, any more than is the taking a bond for stay of execution.   The creditor may press his lien, or his bond, or both, at the same time.(*s*)

Two creditors, A and B, on April 3, each issued executions against G, returnable on April 9.   On April 10, a third, C, issued an execu-tion, returnable to August term.   On all the writs was the indorse-ment, "levy at the risk of the plaintiff."   It was shown that A told the sheriff that the defendant's store was not to be closed, desiring that the clerk of the defendant's should attend the store, A to be paid out of the proceeds of the store.   The store continued open until about twelve days after the return-day of the first writ, the net amount of the sales in the mean time being paid to A.   The property levied on was sold under a fourth writ, which, however, was stayed.   It was held that A's execution was postponed to B's and C's.(*t*)

Orders to stay proceedings form a class of cases different from those relinquishing them altogether, as where a plaintiff directs him "not to proceed further on his writ," "to put no more costs upon it," &c., which will postpone him to a subsequent *fi. fa.*(*u*)

A *fi. fa.* placed in the plaintiff's hands and levied on personal pro-perty, with any other than a *bona fide* purpose of making the money under it, is fraudulent as against subsequent executions.   And any arrangement with the defendant, or other conduct of the plaintiff, evincing his intention not to have a sale of the goods, will postpone

(*n*) 1 W. C. C. R. 29; see also United States *v.* Conyngham, 4 D. 358.

(*o*) 3 W. C. C. R. 60.

(*p*) Ibid.   See a commentary on this decision in Brackenridge's L. M. p. 506.

(*q*) Cowden *v.* Brady, 8 S. & R. 510.

(*r*) Lantz *v.* Worthington, 4 Barr. 155.

(*s*) Ibid.

(*t*) Keyser's Appeal, 1 H. 409.

(*u*) Kauffett's Appeal, 9 W. 334.

his writ; notice to the sheriff to stay proceedings is not necessary to operate a postponement.(*v*)

A *fi. fa.* levied on personal property and stayed indefinitely by the plaintiff, loses its lien where the stay, long permitted, was made under an agreement which enabled the defendant to comply with a sale already made by him of the goods, and his vendees thus obtained credit, the fact of the levy being unknown to their creditors.(*w*)

At the instance of A, an execution creditor, the sheriff appointed a special deputy, who, with the defendants in the execution, made private sales of the goods at the store, as in the ordinary course of business. This course continued some days until other executions came in, upon which the store was closed, and a public sale had. The Supreme Court ruled that the prior execution was postponed.(*x*)

An order given by an execution creditor to the sheriff, to stay all further proceedings on his *fi. fa.* (which had been levied on the stock and produce of a farm) at his risk, until further directions, is a waiver of his priority, in favor of a second execution received by the sheriff during the continuance of the stay of the first.(*y*) And it was said by the judge who delivered the court's opinion : "All the cases cited (and I have examined them all) in Yeates's Reports, and in Johnson's and Cowen's Reports, and also the English cases, clearly establish the principle, that where the creditor interferes and directs a delay of sale, and leaves the goods with the debtor, in every such case, a second execution coming in, will have a preference."—"The evidence here(*z*) warrants the inference, that the plaintiff issued his *fieri facias*, not with an absolute intention of collecting his debt, but partly, at least, with a view to cover the property of the debtor for his use.(*a*)

If a plaintiff, after having levied an execution on personal property, directs the sheriff "to stay proceedings till further orders, the levy to remain," the lien of the execution is gone as respects third persons, whether purchasers or execution creditors, if the object of the arrangement were a security for the debt; and it is of no consequence whether the execution be returned or not, or whether or not third persons had notice of it, though it may be doubted whether, where an execution is levied upon all the goods and chattels of an innkeeper, consisting of a variety of household and kitchen furniture, and also of a quantity of liquors and bar furniture, which are suffered to remain in his possession between thirteen and fourteen months before any step is taken to effect a sale, it retains a lien.(*b*) "In *England*," said Rogers, J., "the practice is to remove the goods; and the fact that they are not removed, is a badge of fraud, so as to render them liable to a second execution, or to pass into the hands of a purchaser, discharged from the lien of the execution creditor. In this State, we have departed from the strictness of the English rule. It is not the practice to remove goods,

---

(*v*) Weir *v.* Hale, 3 W. & S. 285.

(*w*) McClure *v.* Ege, 7 W. 74, reviewing all the decisions, and showing the change of the law on this subject since Leidy *v.* Wallace, 4 D. 163, and citing Com. *v.* Strembeck, 3 R. 343.

(*x*) Bingham *v.* Young, 10 Barr, 395.
(*y*) Eberle *v.* Mayer, 1 R. 366.

(*z*) As in the case in 17 Johns. 276.
(*a*) And see also, to the same effect, Flick *v.* Troxsell, 7 W. & S. 65 ; Lowry *v.* Coulter, 9 Barr, 349 ; Eberle *v.* Mayer, 1 R. 366; Mentz *v.* Hamman, 5 Wh. 153.

(*b*) The Commonwealth *v.* Strembeck, 3 R. 341.

and the fact that they are not so, is not a badge of fraud. There is no certain rule how long they may, with safety to the execution creditor, be permitted to remain in the possession of the debtor. The cases have varied from one day to upwards of two years."(c) "We would not wish to be understood as attempting to impair the force of the earlier decisions, but it is necessary to inquire whether this be a case which comes within the reason of the exception. Here there was a levy on all the goods and chattels of an innkeeper, consisting of a variety of household and kitchen furniture, and also a quantity of liquors and bar furniture. There is no pretence to say, that part of the articles, on which the levy was made, came within the reason of the exemption of household goods. The beds on which he lodges his customers, with the liquor and food he supplies them, are the implements of his trade, the means by which he carries on his business, and no more entitled to protection on principles of humanity, or the peculiar necessities of the country, than the goods of the merchant, or the tools of the tradesman and mechanic. All the furniture of the house, except so much as may be necessary for the accommodation of the family, in a public inn, is intended for the same purpose. And how far and to what extent household furniture may be permitted to remain with the debtor, without the legal consequences which attend property of a different description, has not yet been decided. The principle has, heretofore, been laid down generally, that the act of suffering household goods to remain in the hands of the defendant after they are levied on, furnished no presumption of fraud here, as it did in England. Whether this extends to all a debtor's furniture, however valuable, without limitation, may, perhaps, some day, be worthy of serious investigation. The exemption of any species of property is to be regretted, as every day's experience shows that it tends to produce collusion and fraud. That there should be some limit, I think apparent, and what it may be, will be for the court to determine when the question arises."(d) The case of Eberle v. Mayer, is quoted by the learned judge as applicable, and that of Berry v. Smith,(e) as, "if possible, still nearer the point." In conclusion, he thus observes : "It has been seen that, in Pennsylvania, it is not necessary that the officer should remove the property, nor put a person in charge of the goods, nor sell them immediately, if this be done in a reasonable time. I would not, however, think it safe for creditors, at this day, when the condition of the country has so materially changed, to permit the levy to remain without sale of the goods, or some person having them in charge, so long a time as would seem to be authorized by the earlier cases."

If a *fieri facias* be issued, and returned, "levied as per inventory," &c., with an inventory annexed thereto, and immediately after its return, an *alias fieri facias* be issued on the same judgment, and put into the sheriff's hands, with instructions from the plaintiff's attorney to stay proceedings for the present, the object being merely to secure the debt due to his client, it must be postponed to a *fieri facias*, subsequently issued by another creditor, which has been duly acted upon.(f)

The Chief Justice, delivering the opinion of the court in the last case, said : "This case is said to have been ruled below on the authority of

(c) P. 342–4.
(d) P. 343.

(e) 3 Wash. C. C. Rep. 60.
(f) Hickman v. Caldwell, 4 R. 376.

I.—45

Howell *v.* Alkyn ;(*g*) and ruling it by the principles assumed by the judge to whom was assigned, in that case, the duty of pronouncing the judgment of the court, instead of ruling it by the point directly decided, the conclusion drawn by the president of the Common Pleas, could not well have been avoided. I feel bound to say, however, that those were not the principles of the cause as settled in consultation, the circumstances intended to have been made the test being the same that had been applied in Eberle *v.* Mayer,(*h*) and that has since been applied in the Commonwealth *v.* Strembeck,(*i*) to wit : the presence or the absence of a direction to stay proceedings on the levy. There was no such direction in Howell *v.* Alkyn ;(*j*) and the mere sufferance of procrastination by the officer, was held not to be fraudulent *per se.* Had the exact bearing and extent of the principles laid down in the opinion delivered been perceived at the time, the disclaimer would have been made then, which I feel it a duty to the profession and the court to make now. I am happy to have the authority of my brother ROGERS, the other survivor of the judges who then composed the court, for the entire accuracy of this statement, and for saying that the principles laid down by my brother HUSTON, were peculiar to him. Then, without intimating an opinion on the point made here, in relation to the supposed effect of the return on the rights of the parties, we will determine this case, as we have determined all others of a similar nature, by an application of the test just mentioned. The principle of this test is, that to levy with directions to proceed no further, can be referred to no object but the creation of a lien which the law does not tolerate."(*k*)

The plaintiff will not be considered as abandoning his levy on a *fi. fa.,* because he withdraws an *alias* before any proceedings had on the latter.(*l*) And, according to the cases by which the law has been definitely settled with us, an execution cannot be postponed, under any circumstances, for the default of the officer. In Hickman & Black *v.* Caldwell,(*m*) and the cases there cited, the rule appears to be that the sheriff's procrastination, even by sufferance of the execution creditor, is not fraudulent *per se;* and that the latter is to be postponed only where he has directed the sheriff not to proceed.(*n*)

(*g*) 2 R. 282.
(*h*) 1 R. 366.
(*i*) 3 R. 341.
(*j*) In that case a *levy was made* by the sheriff, and *on the next day*, the plaintiff ordered the sheriff to suffer the goods to *remain in the defendant's possession at the plaintiff's risk;* if this was not a " direction to stay proceedings on the levy," particularly where it operated for *ten weeks,* and until a second execution came in, we are at liberty to infer that this form of order to the sheriff would be a safe practice, and that it has the positive approbation of the Supreme Court, not only in the case in which it was upheld, but in the case above under consideration. It follows, that on giving such an order to the sheriff, nothing should be said that would lead him to judge that you wished to tie his hands. This doctrine is recognized and affirmed in

Keyser's Appeal, 1 H. 411–412. A *fieri facias* is not postponed by an indorsement by the plaintiff, "this levy at plaintiff's risk." It merely means that if the goods are not produced at time of sale, so far as regards the plaintiff, the sheriff is released, and an agreement to indemnify him for levy on goods of a stranger. But leaving the goods in store with defendant by arrangement, and authorizing his clerk to sell as usual, and selling until after the return-day—the proceeds going to the plaintiff, through the clerk, who was paid by him, is such an act as postpones the *fi. fa.* after executions.
(*k*) See Stewart *v.* Stocker, 13 S. & R. 204, 345 ; Corlies *v.* Stanbridge, 5 R. 286.
(*l*) Ingham *v.* Snyder, 1 Wh. 116.
(*m*) 4 R. 376.
(*n*) McCoy *v.* Reed, 5 W. 302.

If the sheriff be directed by the defendant acting for the plaintiff to proceed no further, the execution is fraudulent as to creditors.(o)

Although a seizure of goods on a *fi. fa.* to the value of the debt, whether they be sold or not, discharges the debt and satisfies the judgment, this rule is wholly inapplicable, where goods remain on defendant's hands, and are used by him, in which case it will not amount to satisfaction against other judgment creditors, however it may affect a surety. So the execution creditor may withdraw his writ without necessarily discharging his lien on the real estate as it respects other judgment creditors.(p) The reason is that no harm is thereby done to the latter, who may, if they choose to, proceed against the same goods, a prior withdrawing or sleeping execution interposing no hindrance to them.(q)

Where no intervening creditor's right is thereby affected, the priority of an execution creditor is revived by the failure of an arrangement made between him and a subsequent execution creditor, and upon which the stay was based. However liable for his default in the arrangement, the first creditor is not bound to lose his debt by parting with his priority without receiving the stipulated equivalent for it.(r)

Where, under the act of July 12, 1842, bond is given by a defendant for stay for one year after levy and appraisement of his goods, and return by the sheriff, that it would not bring two-thirds of the appraisement, the lien of the *fi. fa.* is not thereby divested; and a subsequent execution creditor selling the goods cannot take the proceeds against the creditor so stayed.(s)

Where a levy on personal property has been made on an execution, which is not returned, and, after the lapse of two years, the plaintiff assigns the balance on the judgment, and the assignee agrees, on receiving a revival of the judgment, that he will have the execution returned, but in fact does not direct the sheriff to return it; such an agreement will not postpone the claim of the assignee upon a mortgage, which secured the debt, for which the execution issued, in favor of one originally bound by the assigned judgment, but who, before execution issued, had sold to the other defendants in the judgment, his interest in the real estate in which they were interested, and which was bound by the mortgage and the original judgment.(t)

Where an execution was issued more than a month before the return-day, and levied on certain enumerated articles, "and all the rest of defendant's goods and chattels," and no further proceedings on the execution took place for two months, no inventory being returned, the defendant being permitted to carry on his business as usual, selling some of the goods, and acquiring others, and no direction given to the sheriff to proceed and sell: it was decided that the execution was postponed in favor of subsequent executions.(u)

An indorsement, "levy at the risk of the plaintiff," says ROGERS, J., in a case just cited, is understood to mean nothing more than that the property, until sale, may be left with the defendant, at the risk of the

(o) Lowry v. Coulter, 9 Barr, 349.
(p) Cathcart's Appeal, 1 H. 41.
(q) Ibid., citing 5 W. 300; 9 W. & S. 73; 1 Barr, 13. See also Earl's Appeal, 1 H. 483.

(r) Post v. Naglee, 1 Barr, 168.
(s) Sedgwick's Appeal, 7 W. & S. 260.
(t) Cathcart's Appeal, 1 H. 416.
(u) Earl's Appeal, 1 H. 483.

plaintiff, and not at the risk of the sheriff; that if the property is not produced on the day of sale, so far as regards the plaintiff, the sheriff is released; and further, perhaps, as an agreement to indemnify the sheriff for a levy on the goods of a stranger.(v)   But such an indorsement does not amount to a direct or implied stay of the proceedings, nor is it understood, without more, that the execution is put in the hands of the sheriff for security, and not for sale.(w)

The sheriff cannot deduct from the money made under a *fi. fa.* the expenses of additional watchmen whom he had employed at the defendant's request, in consequence of a delay in the sale at the instance of the latter.(x)

Where there are two several levies on the defendant's goods, an agreement by the first execution creditor with the defendant, to the effect that the levy of the former should be enforced only in case of a second execution coming in, together with other circumstances, on behalf of such creditor, evincing his intention not to have a sale of the property levied on, postpones his execution;(y) but such is not the case where there is a direction by the plaintiff to the sheriff, not so to push or proceed with his execution, if the sheriff refuse or neglect to comply, but proceeds without delay to levy or sell.(z)

Where, after a *fi. fa.* issued, A, who held collaterals in trust for the execution creditor, and was also assignee of the debtor, received money on account of the collaterals: It was held, that a subsequent execution creditor could not compel the application of that money to the debt thereby secured, but that the assignee might retain it for the general creditors, subject to the obligation to satisfy any deficiency under the execution.(a)

5. *Exempted property.*

By the act of 1836, which as will presently be seen is now superseded, the sheriff was authorized to seize and sell, as goods and chattels, everything of a tangible nature belonging to the defendant, except the following articles owned by, or in the possession of, the debtor, which by the 26th section of that act,(b) were exempt from sale on any execution for any debt contracted after the first day of September, one thousand eight hundred and twenty-eight, and also, for damages recovered since that day, except it be for damages done to real estate, to wit :—

I. Household utensils, not exceeding in value thirty dollars.

II. The necessary tools of a tradesman, not exceeding in value thirty dollars.

III. All wearing apparel of the defendant and his family.

IV. Four beds, and the necessary bedding.

V. A spinning wheel and reel.

VI. A stove, with the pipe of the same, and necessary fuel for three months.

(v) Keyser's Appeal, 1 H. 418; *ante*, 706.

(w) Ibid.

(x) Fitch's Appeal, 10 Barr, 461, 689, 690.

(y) Flick v. Troxsell, 7 W. & S. 65.

(z) Lancaster Sav. Inst. v. Weigand, *et al.* D. C. for C. C. of Lanc. 3 P. L. J. 523.

(a) Smith's Appeal, 2 Barr, 331.

(b) Pamph. L. 765.

VII. One cow, two hogs, also six sheep, with the wool thereof, or the yarn or cloth manufactured therefrom, and feed sufficient for the said cow, hogs, and sheep, from the first day of November until the last day of May.

VIII. Any quantity of meat not exceeding two hundred pounds, twenty bushels of potatoes, ten bushels of grain, or the meal made therefrom.

IX. Any quantity of flax not exceeding ten pounds, or the thread or linen made therefrom.

X. All Bibles and school-books in the use of the family.

The act of March 29, 1821(d) exempts one stove in the possession of any debtor from levy or sale on any execution or distress for rent, or other legal process for debts or rents.

And by the act of March 31, 1821,(f) every debtor is allowed to hold six sheep exempt from levy or sale in execution for any debt excepting for rent; and upon the decease of any poor inhabitant, the widow is allowed to retain for the comfort of herself and family, all goods and chattels that would have been exempted from execution during the life of such decedent. The uniform, arms, and accoutrements of every volunteer or person enrolled in the militia of this commonwealth, as well as the horse furniture of persons therein, entitled to use a horse, are exempted from execution by the act of April, 1822.(g) § 70.

By the act of 22d April, 1846,(h) the necessary tools of a tradesman shall be exempt from levy and sale by virtue of any warrant or execution. § 7.

"The following property, in addition to that already exempt from levy and sale, by virtue of any execution or distress for rent, shall, when owned by any person actually engaged in the science of agriculture, in like manner, be exempt from levy and sale, viz.: one horse, mare, or gelding, not exceeding in value fifty dollars; one set of horse gears and one plough, or, in lieu thereof, one yoke of oxen, with yoke and chain and one plough, at the option of the defendant." § 8.

But in 1849, the law in this respect underwent an entire change by the following legislation:—

Act of 9th April, 1849.(i) An act to exempt property to the value of three hundred dollars from levy and sale on execution, and distress for rents.

In lieu of the property now exempt by law from levy and sale on execution, issued upon any judgment obtained upon contract, and distress for rent, property to the value of three hundred dollars, exclusive of all wearing apparel of the defendant and his family, and all Bibles and school-books in use in the family (which shall remain exempted as heretofore) and no more owned by or in possession of any debtor shall be exempt from levy and sale on execution, or by distress for rent. § 1.

The sheriff, constable, or other officer charged with the execution

(d) 7 Re. Laws, 426.   (h) Pamph. L. 476.
(f) 7 Re. Laws, 445.   (i) Pamph L. 533.
(g) 7 Re. Laws, 646.

of any warrant issued by competent authority for the levying upon and selling the property either real or personal of any debtor, shall, if requested by the debtor, summon three disinterested and competent persons, who shall be sworn or affirmed to appraise the property which the said debtor may elect to retain under the provisions of this act, for which service the said appraiser shall be entitled to receive fifty cents each, to be claimed as part of the costs of the proceedings, and property thus chosen and appraised to the value of three hundred dollars, shall be exempt from levy and sale on the said execution or warrant, excepting warrants for the collection of taxes.   § 2.

In any case where the property levied upon, as aforesaid, shall consist of real estate of greater value than three hundred dollars, and the defendant in such [execution] shall elect to retain real estate, amounting in value to the whole sum of three hundred dollars, or any less sum, the appraisers aforesaid shall determine whether, in their opinion, the said real estate can be divided, without injury to or spoiling the whole; and if the said appraisers shall determine that the said real estate can be divided as aforesaid, then they shall proceed to set apart so much thereof as, in their opinion, shall be of sufficient [value] to answer the requirement of the defendant in such case, designating the same by proper metes and bounds; all of which proceedings shall be certified in writing by the said appraisers, or a majority of them, under their proper hands and seals, to the sheriff, under-sheriff, or coroner, charged with the execution of the writ in such case, who shall make return of the same to the proper court from which the writ issued, in connection with the said writ: Provided, that this section shall not be construed to affect or impair the liens of bonds or mortgages, or other contracts, for the purchase-money of the real estate of insolvent debtors.   § 3.

Upon return made of the writ aforesaid, with the proceedings thereon, the plaintiff in the case shall be entitled to have his writ of *venditioni exponas*, as in other cases, to sell the residue of the real estate included in the levy aforesaid, if the appraisers aforesaid shall have determined upon a division of the said real estate; but if the said appraisers shall determine against a division of said real estate, the plaintiff may have a writ of *venditioni exponas* to sell the whole of the real estate included in such levy; and it shall and may be lawful, in the latter case, for the defendant in the execution to receive from the sheriff or other officer of the proceeds of said sale so much as he would have received at the appraised value, had the said real estate been divided.   § 4.

The 26th section of the act entitled, " An act relating to executions," passed 16th June, 1836, and the 7th and 8th sections of an act entitled, "An act in regard to certain entries in ledgers, in the city of Pittsburg, and relating to the publishing of sheriff's sales, and for other purposes," passed 22d April, 1846, and all other acts inconsistent with this act be, and the same are, hereby repealed.   § 5.

The provisions of this act shall not take effect until the 4th day of July next, and shall apply only to debts contracted on and after that date.   § 6.

Act of 14th April, 1851.(*j*) It is hereby declared to be the true intent and meaning of the 5th section of the act passed the 9th day of April, 1849, entitled "An act to exempt property to the value of three hundred dollars from levy and sale on execution and distress for rent," that the 26th section of an act, entitled "An act relating to executions," passed the 16th day of June, Anno Domini 1836, and the 7th and 8th sections of an act, entitled "An act in regard to certain entries in ledgers, in the city of Pittsburgh, and relating to publishing sheriffs' sales, and for other purposes," passed the 22d day of April, 1846, are not repealed by said section of the act, so far as relates to all debts and contracts made and entered into prior to the 4th of July, 1849. § 17.

Act of May 4, 1852. That the sheriff of each county, in addition to his other fees, shall be allowed the sum of two dollars for the appraisement and return of property, retained by any debtor under the provisions of the act of 9th April, one thousand eight hundred and forty-nine, entitled "An act to exempt property to the value of three hundred dollars from levy and sale on execution, and distress for rent." § 3.

That the fees of each constable for the same service as that mentioned in the preceding, shall be one dollar. § 4.

Under these acts, the following decisions have been had:—

The omission of a debtor to give notice, before the sale of his real estate, of his claim to property to the value of three hundred dollars, under the act of 9th April, 1849, will be a bar to his claim to that amount of money out of the proceeds of the sale. The claim, as it respects real estate, should be made before inquisition. The act contemplates the debtor getting property at an appraisement as his exemption where practicable; and the right to demand the money out of proceeds of sale, is only in the last resort, when property does not admit of separation.(*k*)

The exemption is a privilege which the debtor may waive if he pleases. When he does waive it, in writing, he cannot afterwards claim it. The debtor failing to notify the officer having the execution, that he claims to have three hundred dollars' worth of property appraised after the levy is made, will be presumed to have waived the privilege which the law has given him.(*l*) It is clear, therefore, that the debtor cannot claim the money after the sheriff has made sale of the property. The law allows him to keep the property, but does not give a right to the money produced by the sale.(*m*) Where, therefore, a debtor signed an express waiver, in writing, after the levy was made, and the sheriff went on and sold the property, and after it was sold the debtor gave notice to the sheriff not to pay over the money to the plaintiff when it was paid in court, it was held that the debtor had lost his right to the exemption, and the money was ordered to be paid to the plaintiff in the execution.(*n*)

The act does not apply to a *levari facias* on a mortgage.(*o*)

(*j*) Pamph. L. 616.
(*k*) Miller's Appeal, 4 H. 301.
(*l*) Winchester *v.* Costello, 2 Par. 279.

(*m*) Ibid.
(*n*) Ibid.
(*o*) Morgan *v.* Noud, D. C. Nov. 8,

The court will refuse to grant a rule ordering a *venditioni exponas* in issue for the sale of property which the sheriff returns as claimed to be exempt by the defendant, but as to which the sheriff refuses to decide. The plaintiff must proceed without the interposition of the court.(*p*)

Very recently, it was ruled by the Supreme Court, that the defendant is entitled only, in respect to *personal* estate, to the articles selected, and not to their produce ; and his election must be made at the time of the levy, and under all circumstances before the sale.(*q*)   "Freese's

1851. Motion to take money out of court. *Per curiam.* The question presented on this motion is simply whether, in case of a sale on *levari facias* on a mortgage, the defendant is entitled to the benefit of the exemption of $300 provided by the act of April 9, 1849. The claim of the defendant does not fall within the words of the act. It is not a levy and sale upon judgment obtained upon contract. There is no levy; there is strictly no judgment obtained upon contract. By the 4th section it is provided, that where a defendant has elected to retain a part of the real estate divided and appraised by the sheriff's inquest, the plaintiff shall be entitled to have his writ of *venditioni exponas*, as in other cases to sell the residue of the real estate in other cases. This provision authoritatively fixes the kind of judgment and kind of proceeding upon which the exemption was intended to be allowed. It could be applied to this case no more than to proceedings upon a mechanic's lien. The proviso of the 3d section, that it shall not be construed to affect or impair the liens of bonds, mortgages, or other contracts for the purchase-money of the real estate of insolvent debtors, by excepting this species of mortgage, does not necessarily imply that the liens of all other mortgages are included. It is plainly a particular in a class, the whole of which, without regard to the form of the security, was for obvious reasons not intended to be embraced.

The reason and spirit of the act in excluding this class is in favor of the construction which also excludes mortgages. The mortgagee has a special lien, and he may enforce it in Pennsylvania by an ejectment against the mortgagor, in which proceeding it cannot be pretended that there could be any claim for the $300 exemption; and in case of a proceeding upon a mortgage against a terre tenant who had bought, subject to the mortgage, if the terre tenant could claim the exemption, it would be *that* much money taken out of the pockets of the mortgagor from whom he bought, and who would remain person-

ally liable; and it would not be pretended that the mortgagor, though nominally defendant, could set up any claim upon the proceeds of what had ceased to be his property.

In short, it is very plain that the legislature meant by judgments upon contracts judgments upon personal contracts, and that exemption can no more be claimed upon a *levari facias* upon a mortgage than it could be upon a *habere facias possessionem* in an ejectment.

R. A.

(*p*) Houston *v.* Smith, D. C. Sept. 13, 1851. Why *venditioni exponas* should not issue for property in sheriff's hands. *Per curiam.* The sheriff returns to the *fieri facias* that he has retained in his hands certain property claimed by defendant as exempt under the $300 exemption law, and he submits to the court to decide whether it is so or not. The plaintiff, with a view of obtaining the opinion of the court, asks for a special order for a *venditioni exponas* to the sheriff, commanding him to sell this property. If the property in question is exempt, the plaintiff will be liable to the defendant in an action for selling it under the *venditioni exponas,* and the order of this court will not protect him. If there is any property levied upon not delivered to defendant as exempt, plaintiff has a right to a *venditioni exponas* as a writ of course, without any special order. The opinion of this court at this period will stand the sheriff in no more stead than that of his counsel. It may be a case in which he would have a right to demand an indemnity from the plaintiff before proceeding; and the court, perhaps, would enlarge the time for making a return until a proper indemnity was given. We express no opinion upon that. We are clear, however, that the mode now suggested is not the proper mode, and we leave the plaintiff to his legal remedies. Rule dismissed without prejudice to plaintiff's right to issue a *venditioni exponas* if he sees fit.

(*q*) Hammer *v.* Fries, Pittsburg, Aug. 1852, reversing S. C. reported in 11 P. L. J.

personal property," said BLACK, C. J., "was levied on and sold. The proceeds amounted to $454 11. The defendant in the execution was present when the levy was made, but did not then claim that any of the goods were exempted by the act of 1849. About the commencement of the sale, however, he demanded the benefit of the statute. The sheriff sold the property, and paid the proceeds into court, and the court, on Freese's petition, ordered $300 of the money to be paid by him.

"We are of opinion that the debtor cannot, under any circumstances, entitle himself to three hundred dollars of the money for which personal property sells at sheriff's sale. The act speaks of property, not money. It requires him to select the goods he wishes to retain, and have them appraised, and property thus chosen and appraised, shall be exempt from levy and sale. This excludes the idea that he is to have his choice between retaining the property, and demanding money out of the proceeds. There are sound reasons why he should take the goods or take nothing. The law was made for the benefit of the families of debtors, rather than for the debtors themselves; and a family, stript of every comfort, might not be much the better of $300 in the pocket of a thriftless father. Property which appraisers would value at three hundred dollars, might not sell for the half of it; and if debtors had this choice, it would deprive the creditors of twice as much property as the law intended to take from them. A convenient friend could be got to buy it in at a price far below its value, and a *part* of the money awarded by the court would pay for it.

"The former laws on this subject specified the particular articles which might be retained. The act of 1849 gives the right of designating them to the debtor himself, fixes the quantity of them by their value, and points out the mode of ascertaining that value; but if he may be silent until after sale, he can virtually take property which he has not elected, to an amount far greater than the law allows him, and without applying the legal standard of its value. Such a construction is against the spirit as well as the letter of the statute.

"The debtor not being entitled to money, under any circumstances, would have no other remedy than an action against the officer, even if he had demanded his right, in a proper way, and béen refused; but he did not make the demand here in a manner which the sheriff was bound to notice. He did not point out the property he elected to retain, nor ask for an appraisement. He said nothing on the subject until it was too late. Regularly, a debtor who wishes to avail himself of this act, should make his election at the time of the levy; the legislature could have meant nothing else by saying that property so elected should be exempt from levy. But he may be in time if he demands it after it is seized, provided he does not wait so long that a compliance with his request would postpone the sale. His right is clearly gone, if he waits until the sale has begun.

"The decree of the Court of Common Pleas is reversed, and it is ordered that the fund in court be paid to the executing creditors in the order of their liens."

Where a defendant in execution was in the possession of two yoke of oxen, of one of which he was the owner, and of the other he had been the owner, but had sold them, and was left in possession by the vendee, for the purpose of breaking them, it was held, that though the sale was fraudulent as to creditors, yet it was good as between the vendor and vendee; and that the yoke of oxen still owned by defendant, was exempt from execution under the act of 22d April, 1846, the defendant electing to retain them.(r)

A defendant in an execution has no claim on the balance of a fund, arising from the sale of real estate remaining in the hands of an auditor for distribution, under the provisions of the act of 1849.(s)

In a judgment against a firm, a *fi. fa.* issued upon which the sheriff made a special return, that he levied upon the separate and joint effects of the parties; and that, in accordance with the recent act of assembly, he deducted $300 from their joint effects, leaving in his hands property to the value of $154 50, which he said the defendants claimed as exempt from execution. The court refused to make an order for a *venditioni.*(t)

Where there was no election by the debtor to retain real estate, and consequently no proceedings for the purpose of ascertaining whether it could be divided without injury to the whole, it is error to award to the debtor any part of the proceeds of sale.(u)

An order of court for a *vend. ex.* will not protect the sheriff in the sale of goods levied on under a *fi. fa.*, and claimed by the defendant as exempt under the $300 exemption law.(v)

An appraisement will be set aside by the court, where manifestly below the market price.(w) The court will interfere in such case upon depositions, before the return of the sheriff to the execution.(x)

The individual partners are not severally entitled under the act of 1849, to retain out of partnership effects levied on, specific articles to the value of $300.(y)

(r) Hetrick v. Campbell, 2 H. 263.

(s) Sennickson v. Fulton, D. C. C. P. 8 Leg. Int. 126.

(t) Ferguson v. Moore, D. C. C. P. 7 Leg. Int. 166.

(u) Weaver's Appeal, Sup. Ct. May, 1852.

(v) Houston v. Smith, D. C. C. P. *ante*, 712, note (p).

(w) Sleeper v. Nicholson, D. C. C. P. 9 Leg. Int. 54. Rule to set aside sheriff's appraisement. This is a case under the act of 9th April, 1849, the $300 exemption law. Upon the depositions submitted, we have no doubt that the appraisement is so much below the real market value of the property, that it would be highly unjust to the plaintiff to allow it to stand. We have held the subject under advisement, because this is the first case in which the interference of the court has been invoked to set aside the appraisement. Upon full reflection, we cannot doubt the power of the court to protect the rights of its suitors, and prevent them from being baffled in recovering the fruits of their judgment by a partial and unjust appraisement of goods elected by the defendant to be retained under the act.

All analogy is in favor of the exercise of such a power. Inquests of condemnation have always been subject to the supervision of the courts, and it would be too much to claim for the inquest of three men, exemption from the power exercised by the court over the verdict of twelve men in a trial publicly conducted under the superintendence of one of the members of the court. The only doubt suggested to our minds has been, whether the court could take cognizance of the appraisement until certified of the fact by the return of the sheriff. But, if we were obliged to wait for that, the goods appraised would, in many cases, be beyond our reach. The lien of the execution would be gone, and the wrong, in a majority of cases, would be irremediable. The court may interfere in cases somewhat similar, and on similar grounds, in setting aside sheriff's sales, in discharging on common bail, and other cases, before they are advised of the sheriff's proceedings by a formal return. Rule absolute.

(x) Ibid.

(y) Clegg v. Houston, D. C. Phil. 9 Leg. Int. 67.

6. Levy on interest in lands as personalty, and herein of fixtures.

The sheriff may sell leases or terms for years; the interest of a per-son in possession of land under a contract for the sale of it; *fructus industriales*, as corn growing;(z) and fixtures erected which may be removed by the tenant;(a) these different subjects being all regarded as personal property. Notes for the payment of money may also be taken under execution, but the sheriff must account for them at their full value if he sells them for less than was due thereon.(b) And where there are overplus moneys in the hands of the sheriff after satisfying the first execution, although they cannot, as it seems, be levied on by a second execution,(c) yet the court will direct the application of the sur-plus to the payment of subsequent judgment creditors according to their priority, to be determined when the proceeds arise from the sale of lands, by the date of the several judgments, or if from the sale of goods and chattels, by the delivery of their executions to the sheriff.(d)

The privilege which, for the benefit of trade, treats particular things as personalty, holds only between landlord and tenant, not between third persons and the owner of the ground.(e). Hence, a steam-engine, with its fixtures, for a bark-mill and tannery, erected by the defendant, the owner of the ground, when levied upon and sold with the ground, pass as real and not personal property.(f)

Leasehold property need not be sold by the sheriff on the premises.(g) On a sheriff's sale of a leasehold property, there is no necessity for a deed; his return to the execution is evidence of the sale of a chattel, whether real or personal.(h)

Under a *fi. fa.*, a set of rolls used in a mill, whether actually in place or detached to make room for such as were, cannot be levied upon against the mortgagor of the lot and rolling-mill with the apparatus at-tached thereto. The criterion of a fixture in a mansion-house or dwell-ing is actual and permanent fastening to the freehold; but this is not so as the criterion of a fixture in a manufactory or a mill, which, for the purposes of trade, must necessarily be different.(i) This decision is, however, confined to questions between vendor and vendee, heir and executor, debtor and execution creditor, and between co-tenants of the inheritance, and does not embrace those between tenant and landlord, or remainder-man.

A leasehold is the subject of levy and sale on a *fi. fa.* without inqui-sition and condemnation. A term of years is a chattel always held liable to sale on a common law execution, and our statute, which is an enabling one, left the writ of *fi. fa.*, as to chattels, exactly where it found it.(j)

7. Levy on estate of corporation.

The mode of proceeding on execution against corporations is so clearly stated in the act of June 16, 1836,(k) that we need only intro-duce here the several provisions in their order.

(z) 17 Johns. 128.
(a) Id. 116.
(b) Addis. 19.
(c) 1 Cranch, 117.
(d) 5 Johns. 163 ; 2 Bac. Abr. 715 ; 3 Caines's Rep. 84.
(e) Morgan v. Arthurs, 3 W. 140.
(f) Oves v. Ogelsby, 7 W. 106.

(g) Sowers v. Vie, 2 H. 99.
(h) Ibid.
(i) Voorhis v. Freeman, 2 W. & S. 116, overruling Chaffee v. Stewart and Gray v. Holdship, 17 S. & R. 415 ; see, also, Pyle v. Pennock, 2 W. & S. 390.
(j) Dalzell v. Lynch, 4 W. & S. 255.
(k) Pamph. L. 574.

All executions which shall be issued from any court of record, against any corporation, not being a county, township, or other public corporate body, shall command the sheriff, or other officer, to levy the sum recovered, together with the costs of suit, of the goods and chattels, lands and tenements of such corporation, and such execution shall be executed in the manner following, to wit:—

I. The officer charged with the execution of such writ shall go to the banking-house, or other principal office of such corporation, during the usual office hours, and demand of the president, or other chief officer, cashier, treasurer, secretary, chief clerk, or other officer having charge of such office, the amount of such execution, with legal costs.

II. If no person can be found on whom demand can be made, as aforesaid, or if the amount of such execution be not forthwith paid, in lawful money, after demand, as aforesaid, such officer shall seize personal property of said corporation, sufficient to satisfy the debt, interest, and costs, as aforesaid.

III. If the corporation against which such execution shall be issued be a banking company, and other sufficient personal property cannot be found, such officer shall take so much of any current coin, of gold, silver, or copper, which he may find, as shall be sufficient to satisfy the debt, interest, and costs, as aforesaid.

IV. If no sufficient personal property be found, as aforesaid, such officer shall levy such execution upon the real estate of such corporation, and thereupon proceed, in the manner provided in other cases, for the sale of land upon execution.   § 72.

In every case in which judgment shall have been obtained against such corporation, except as aforesaid; and an execution issued thereon shall have been returned unsatisfied, in part or in the whole, it shall be lawful for the court in which such judgment shall have been obtained, upon the bill or petition of the plaintiff in such judgment, to award a writ to sequester the goods, chattels, and credits, rents, issues, and profits, tolls, and receipts, from any road, canal, bridge, or other work, property, or estate of such corporation.   § 73.

The court shall, upon the awarding any such writ, appoint a sequestrator to execute the same, and to take charge of the property and funds taken or received by virtue of such writ, and to distribute the net proceeds thereof among all the creditors of such corporation, according to the rules established in the case of the insolvency of individuals; and such sequestrator shall have all the powers, and be subject to all the duties of trustees appointed under the law relating to insolvent debtors: *Provided,* That in the case of any work in the maintenance or repair of which the public may be interested, and which may from time to time require a portion of the revenue thereof, as aforesaid, to be expended thereon, the court which awards such writ shall make such allowances for such purpose, and otherwise take such order thereon as the public good shall require.   § 74.

The said court shall have power, at the time of awarding any such writ, or afterwards, to make such orders and decrees as may be necessary to carry the same into full and complete effect; and they may also make all such other orders and decrees in the premises, for the purpose of giving full and effectual relief to all the creditors of such corporation as shall be agreeable to equity, and they may enforce all such orders against all persons neglecting or refusing to comply therewith, or obstructing the execution thereof, or of such writ by attachment, or by a writ or writs to the sheriff or coroner, in aid of the sequestrator, or otherwise, as fully as a Court of Chancery might do.   § 75.

A sequestrator, says Judge BELL, in a recent case, is one who takes possession of property for a time, to satisfy a demand out of its rents and profits, without having any estate in the thing itself;(l) and though a sequestrator of an insolvent corporation, under the act relative to executions, is expressly clothed with all the powers, and made subject to all the duties of insolvent trustees, that provision of the insolvent acts, which vests the trustee with all the estate and property of the insolvent, and confers upon him the capacity to sue for and recover, in his own name, all such estates and property, and all debts, and things in action, belonging to the insolvent, seems to have been purposely omitted.   Though under our statutory execution a sequestrator may, under the order of the court, absolutely dispose of personal chattels sequestrated, his business with roads, canals, bridges, or other like property of a corporation, is merely to take the rents, issues, and profits, and distribute them, under the direction of the court, among the creditors; to enable him to perform this duty, he is authorized to take charge of the property and funds, but the legal title still remains in the corporation, to which, ultimately, the possession may again be united. And the same may be said of its issues and debts accruing, until finally disposed of.(m)   Originally, the object of sequestration was to punish a party in contempt, by taking possession of his lands and goods until he submitted to the decree of the court.   This is still the practice upon mesne process.(n)

Where a sequestrator has been appointed to a turnpike company, a suit for tolls accruing after his appointment should be brought in the name of the company, and not in that of the sequestrator.(o)

    8. *Levy on things pawned, and money.*

It is provided, by the act just cited, that goods or chattels pawned or pledged by a defendant as security for any debt, or liability, or demised, or in any manner delivered or bailed for a term, are liable to sale on execution, subject to all the rights and interests of the pawnee bailee, or lessee, to the possession or otherwise of such chattels by reason of such pledge, demise, or bailment.(p)   The section above quoted is one of the new features in the law of executions.(q)

By the twenty-fourth section of the act of June, 1836, the officer is authorized, "when he can find no real or other personal estate, to seize and take the amount to be levied by the writ of *fi. fa.*, of any current

(l) 2 H. 166.
(m) Ibid.
(n) Ibid.
(o) Beeler v. The Turnpike Co. 2 H. 162; see further, as to sequestration, *post*, Section iv. 1st; and generally as to proceedings against corporations, *post*, vol. ii. " Corporations."

(p) § 23; see 3 W. 258, citing W. on Sheriffs, 181; Tidd's Pr. 1042.
(q) The commissioners, in their remarks upon it, refer to Bro. Abr. tit. Execution, 107; Trespass, 92; 1 Arch. Pr. 268; 2 Bac. Abr. 715, 716, for the existing rules upon this subject.

gold, silver, or copper coin belonging to the defendant, or of any bank notes or current bills for the payment of money issued by any moneyed corporation at the par value of·such notes : *Provided,* that he shall not take them from the defendant's person, nor shall he retain or take any money levied by him on any other execution at defendant's suit, or instance." As a general provision the foregoing provision is new, but not so in relation to banks. Heretofore, the law was defective in respect to' all corporations, except banks, and then might be considered as supplemental to the act of March 22, 1817.(*r*) The method of attaching pawns in the hands of garnishees will be hereafter considered.(*s*)

 9. *Sheriff's duty when goods are claimed by third party.*
  (1.) *Enlarging time of writ.*

 The sheriff, under the writ of *fi. fa.*, is bound at his peril to take only the goods of the defendant. He is, therefore, a trespasser, if he take the goods of a third person, though the plaintiff assure him they are the defendant's property.(*t*) As the sheriff is bound to execute the writ at his peril, when the defendant becomes bankrupt, and his assignee claim the goods, or there be any doubt whether or not the goods are liable to be taken on a *fieri facias*, the sheriff should immediately apply to the court, from which the writ issues for protection, if one party will not give him a sufficient indemnity ; otherwise, by seizing the goods, or by returning *nulla bona*, he may subject himself to an action. And wherever the property, in goods seized on a *fieri facias*, is disputed, the court will, on the suggestion of a reasonable doubt, enlarge the time for the sheriff to make his return, until the right be tried between the contending parties, or until one of them has given a sufficient indemnity to the sheriff or his officers.(*u*) An inquest of office to ascertain the

---

(*r*) The subject is referred to in Ammant *v.* Turnpike Co. 13 S. & R. 212.
 (*s*) *Post,* 757.
 (*t*) 2 Bac. Abr. 715 ; 4 T. R. 633. As to the proper return, when part of the goods levied on are claimed by a third person, see Hunt *v.* Hunt; 2 P. L. J. 297.
 (*u*) Watson on Sheriffs, 137, 141; 4 W. 124; see 16 S. & R. 68, as to enlarging time of return until the sheriff is indemnified; and see also the following cases in the District Court of Philadelphia :—
 Keffer *v.* Britt. Saturday, February 19, 1848. Why the time for returning the writ should not be enlarged. *Per curiam.* In this case on the hearing, the rule was opposed on the ground of *laches* in the sheriff. The writ was returnable to the first Monday of November. The notice of an adverse claim was made to the sheriff, October 27, 1847. A rule by the plaintiff on the sheriff to return his writ was taken January 27th, and this rule by the sheriff on the following day, January 28th. This would present a case of *laches* on the part of the sheriff upon which the court would refuse to interfere for his relief by enlarg-

ing the time for his return. It is the duty of the sheriff where an adverse claim is made to personal property, promptly to give notice to the plaintiff's attorney of the fact. Since the hearing, the sheriff has handed to the court the affidavit of Samuel Halsell to prove the fact of immediate notice. As that is an *ex parte* affidavit, we cannot act upon it. We will enlarge this rule until Saturday next, for depositions on this point.
 As to the objection that the goods levied on were claimed under a bill of sale unaccompanied by possession, which is a fraud in law, we are in possession of no facts. It is enough that there is a claim presented to the sheriff, supported by affidavit, "of that kind which would reasonably raise a doubt or apprehension as to the title, or create a pause in the mind of a constant man," (Spangler *v.* The Commonwealth, 16 S. & R. 71.) And the plaintiff must make out a very strong case to justify him in requiring the sheriff to go on without an indemnity.
 Rule enlarged until Saturday, Feb. 26.

 Adams *v.* Hazlitt. D. C. Saturday, Feb. 26, 1848. Why the time for return

title cannot be held in Pennsylvania.(v) Neither will the court try the property in goods levied upon under a *fi. fa.*, unless in a very strong case; as it would deprive a party of his right to a jury trial.(w)

(2.) *Indemnity.*

It was formerly questioned whether a promise to indemnify a sheriff, if he made execution on such goods, were lawful. In several books it is said he ought to take notice of the goods of the party at his peril; but in other books it is said such promise is reasonable. This last opinion is to be preferred, and is the most consistent with modern practice.(x) And it has been held that if the goods be not in the defendant's possession, or if the owner's right be disputed, the officer may *require* indemnity of the plaintiff before seizure.(y) In a leading case in the Supreme Court,(z) it was held, that wherever there is a claim of property adverse to the defendant in the execution, of such a nature as would reasonably raise a doubt or apprehension as to the ownership, or create a pause in the mind of a constant man, the sheriff has a right to call on the plaintiff for a reasonable indemnity. In this case, which was well considered, the court said, that the inquest by the sheriff had never been introduced in this State, and would seem, from the decision in Weaver v. Lawrence,(a) not to be warranted; that in an action for a false return, the refusal to indemnify in a case where it might reasonably have been demanded by the sheriff, ought to be as complete a justification as an inquisition; and that this would be a fairer mode than to suffer the sheriff to hold his own inquisition for his own justification.(b)

The proper practice is, when indemnity is necessary, for the sheriff

of the writ of *fi. fa.* should not be enlarged.

Per curiam. In this case, the writ issued January 18th. The adverse claim was made January 21st. A bond of indemnity was given and accepted by the sheriff on January 31st; and the goods levied on were advertised to be sold on the 9th February. The surety in the bond of indemnity before that time, made a general assignment for the benefit of his creditors, and it is not pretended here that the indemnity is sufficient; but it is contended by the plaintiff that the sheriff having once accepted the indemnity as good, it is too late for him afterwards to refuse to proceed. He took the risk when he accepted the indemnity. We admit that this is too harsh a doctrine to apply to the case of the sheriff. He is obliged to incur great responsibilities at best, and we think when he discovers that insufficient sureties have been imposed upon him, he may at any time before the sale of the goods decline proceeding further, until the indemnity has been made good.

Another ground of objection to the making this rule absolute, is, that it is said parts of the goods levied on are claimed adversely. As long, however, as the plaintiff refuses to release the goods claimed from the operation of the levy, the sheriff is entitled to have the indulgence here asked for. If he sold the part unclaimed and returned no more, the plaintiff would have his action against him.

We repeat what we have already had occasion to say in more than one case lately, that a claim supported by affidavit is *prima facie* sufficient ground for the sheriff to pause and demand indemnity. And that it must be a strong case of want of title in the claimant and inability in the plaintiff to give indemnity, that would justify the court in refusing to enlarge the time for making the sheriff's return. If the plaintiff is a resident here, and a man of substance or character, the more groundless the claim, the easier will it be to procure indemnity; and if there is any risk at all, there is no reason, when he is liable, why he should throw it on the shoulders of the sheriff.

Rule absolute.

(v) Spangler v. Com. 16 S. & R. 68.
(w) Young v. Taylor, 2 Bin. 228.
(x) 1 Dane's Abr. 125, c. 1, a. 42, § 5.
(y) Ibid. § 6.
(z) Spangler v. Com. 16 S. & R. 68.
(a) 1 D. 156.
(b) Spangler v. Com. 16 S. & R. 70, 71.

to take a rule to stay proceedings until indemnity is given. This is not the case, however, with real estate.(c)

Where the sheriff has received, or is tendered, an indemnity, it is his duty to proceed, on pain of being attached or fixed for the debt.(d)

(3.) *Interpleader.*

Act of 10th. April, 1848.(e) Whereas, difficulties often arise in the execution of process against goods and chattels issued by or under the authority of the courts in the City and County of Philadelphia, and the County of Luzerne, by reason of claims made to such goods and chattels, by persons not being the parties against whom such process has issued, whereby sheriffs and other officers are exposed to the hazard and expense of actions; and it is reasonable to afford relief and protection in such cases to such sheriffs and other officers; therefore, when any such claim has been or shall be made to any goods or chattels taken, or entitled to be taken in execution under any such process, or to the proceeds of the value thereof, it shall and may be lawful to and for said courts from which such process issued, upon application of such sheriff or other officer, made before or after the return of such process, and as well before as after any action brought against such sheriff or other officer, to call before them, by rule of said court, as well the party issuing such process as the party making such claim, and thereupon to exercise for the adjustment of such claim, and the relief and protection of the sheriff or other officer, all the powers and authorities necessary, and make such rules and decisions as shall appear to be just, under the circumstances of the case; and the costs of all such proceedings shall be in the discretion of the court: *Provided*, it shall be lawful for the court to direct an issue for the trial of questions of fact, whenever the circumstances of the case require it.

The District Court in Philadelphia has made the following general rule to regulate proceedings under the act: "That whenever a rule taken by the sheriff, under the 9th section of the act of assembly passed April 10, 1848, entitled 'An act extending the chancery powers of, and to the jurisdiction and proceedings in, certain courts,' shall be made absolute by the court, without any special order or direction, a feigned issue shall be framed in such case, upon a wager, in the usual form, to determine whether the right of property in the goods levied on and claimed, or any part thereof, is in the defendant or in the claimant, in which issue the claimant shall be the plaintiff, and the plaintiff in the execution the defendant. That the declaration in such issue shall be filed by the claimant within fourteen days from the time such rule is made absolute; and within said time the claimant shall give bond to the plaintiff

---

(c) Meyer to use of Gault *v.* Riot, D. C. Monday, March 6, 1848. Motion by sheriff for rule to stay proceedings until indemnity. *Per curiam.* This is a *vend. exp.* levied upon real estate; and an adverse claimant, and, it is said, possessor of the premises levied on, has given the sheriff notice that he will hold him responsible for damages in levying upon, advertising, and selling his property. The sheriff, however, does not take possession of real estate as he does of goods and chattels, and deliver possession to the purchaser; all he does is, to sell the right, title, and interest of defendant. The practice of indemnifying the sheriff has never been extended to such a case, and we will not make the first precedent. Motion refused.

(d) Watmough *v.* Francis, 7 Barr, 215, ROGERS, J., though see Com. *v.* Watmough, 6 Wh. 150.

(e) Pamph. L. 450.

in such penal sum and with such security as shall be approved by one of the judges of this court, conditioned that the goods levied on and claimed shall be forthcoming upon the determination of the said issue to answer the execution of the plaintiff; if said issue shall be determined in favor of the said plaintiff, in the execution, or so many of them as shall be determined to belong to the defendant and to be subject to the execution of the said plaintiff. That when said declaration is filed and bond given, the sheriff do withdraw from the possession of such of the goods and chattels, seized by him under the execution, as are claimed by the claimant; that no action be brought against the said sheriff in respect of the said goods and chattels; and that the question of costs and all further questions be reserved until after the trial of the said issues.

XLVI. Ordered, that feigned issues be placed on the trial-list, according to the term and number of the execution under which they have been directed.

XLVII. That the prothonotary shall open and keep a docket, in which the proceedings in all feigned issues shall be entered, with a proper index.(*f*)

(*f*) The following opinions of the District Court of Philadelphia will be found of much importance in the construction of this act :—

Masser *v.* Auble, D. C. Saturday, May 6, 1848. Why the plaintiff and David Auble, Elizabeth Auble, Hiram Drake, L. R. Lockwood, should not maintain or relinquish their respective claims to the property levied on by the sheriff in this case. *Per curiam.* This is a rule taken by the sheriff under the provisions of the 9th section of an act of assembly, passed April 10, 1848, entitled "An act relating to the chancery powers of, and to the jurisdiction and proceedings in certain courts," in which, after reciting that "difficulties often arise in the execution of process against goods and chattels issued by or under the authority of the courts in the City and County of Philadelphia, and the County of Luzerne, by reason of claims made to such goods and chattels by persons not being the parties against whom such process has issued, whereby sheriffs and other officers are exposed to the hazard and expense of actions; and it is reasonable to afford relief and protection in such cases to such sheriffs and other officers," it enacts, that "when any such claim has been or shall be made to any goods or chattels taken, or entitled to be taken in execution, under any such process, or to the proceeds or value thereof, it shall and may be lawful to and for said courts from which such process issued, upon application of such sheriff or other officer, made before or after the return of such process, and as

well before as after any action brought against such sheriff or other officer to call before them, by rule of said court, as well the party issuing such process, as the party making such claim, and thereupon to exercise, for the adjustment of such claim and the relief and protection of the sheriff or other officer, all the powers and authorities necessary, and make such rules and decisions as shall appear to be just, under the circumstances of the case, and the cost of all such proceedings shall be in the discretion of the court: *Provided*, it shall be lawful for the court to direct an issue for the trial of questions of fact, whenever the circumstances of the case require it." This act is almost verbatim a copy of the British statute 1 & 2 Will. IV. c. 58, § 6. We have the advantage of the practice of the English courts in carrying it into operation, and this we have determined to adopt. The rule which was taken by the sheriff accords with that practice, and all the parties have appeared. The plaintiff has relinquished his claim as to the goods claimed by Lockwood; the other claimants still maintain their respective rights, and have laid before the court affidavits in support of them. The order made by the court in this case is as follows: That the sheriff file an inventory of the goods levied on. That the plaintiff, having, by his counsel, in open court, relinquished any claim upon the goods claimed by Lockwood, ordered that the sheriff withdraw from his possession of the goods claimed by Lockwood, and that plaintiff take no proceedings against him in respect of the goods so claimed. And ordered, that feigned issues are directed to be framed on or before the first Monday of June next, between the plaintiff and David Auble, Elizabeth Auble, and Hiram Drake, respectively, upon wagers in the usual form, to determine whether the right of property in the goods levied on, or any and what part thereof is in the defendant or in the claimant, respectively—in which issues the respective claimants shall be the plaintiffs, and the plaintiff in this suit defendant; and all proceedings on the said execution are hereby stayed until the further order of the court.

McCorn v. Esher, D. C. Saturday, May 13, 1848. Why the plaintiff and Jacob Esher should not maintain or relinquish. *Per curiam.* In this case, service of the rule has been accepted by the plaintiff's attorney, but he has not appeared to maintain his claim. The claimant has exhibited to the court on the other hand the evidence of his title.

Ordered, That the plaintiff not having appeared in obedience to the rule to maintain his claim, the sheriff withdraw from his possession of the goods levied on, and which are claimed by Jacob Esher, and that the plaintiff take no proceedings against him in respect of the goods so claimed.

Conkling v. Sayers, D. C. Saturday, Oct. 14, 1848. *Per curiam.* This was an application to the court to settle what are the proper terms of an issue under the general order made by the court in the case of rules to interplead for relief of the sheriff under the late act of assembly. The words of the order express the issue whether the right of property in the goods levied on be in the claimant or in the defendant in the execution. The claimant is in all cases to be the plaintiff, and the burden of the issue is upon him in the first instance. If he fails to make out his case, there must be a verdict for the defendant in the issue, and the jury need not in such a case go on to inquire whether the goods are the goods of the defendant, or whose goods they are. The claimant by the verdict is shown to be a stranger who has no right to intermeddle in what does not concern him. We are asked, however, in this case to go further, and make the particular title set up by the claimant a part of the issue. We ought not to do this. If he makes different and inconsistent claims at different times, that will be for the jury, and may be explained. To avoid the question whether evidence of a title different from that made to the

sheriff ought to be admitted in evidence on the trial, it will in all cases be the safest practice for the counsel of the claimant, if he means to vary from the title previously set up, to give distinct notice, a reasonable time before the trial of such his intention, to enable his adversary to come prepared to meet it. As the whole proceeding is under the control of the court, it is in our power to adopt such a practice as will best conduce to a fair trial upon the merits.

Bartram v. Ingram, D. C. Saturday, Oct. 21, 1848. This case properly falls *post,* section v. 9—(3). *Per curiam.* The 87th sec. of the act of June 16, 1836, provides that, "if any fact connected with the distribution of the proceeds of sheriff's sale shall be in dispute, the court shall, at the request in writing of any person interested, direct an issue to try the same." In Rigart's Appeal (7 W. & S. 267), the Supreme Court decided that the mandate to direct an issue, when facts are in contest, is peremptory, as the suitor's constitutional right of trial by jury cannot be infringed; though the application be not verified by affidavit. The act of 20th April, 1846 (Pamph. L. 411), entitled, " an act relative to lien creditors becoming purchasers at judicial sales, and for other purposes," after directing the sheriff to make a special return in such cases, and that if the right of the lien creditor is questioned, the court shall appoint an auditor who may report distribution or direct an issue, subjoins this *proviso. Provided,* that before an issue shall be directed upon the distribution of money arising from sales under execution or Orphans' Court sales, the applicant for such issue shall make affidavit that there are material facts in dispute, and shall set forth the nature and character thereof; upon which affidavit the court shall determine whether such issue shall be granted subject to a writ or appeal by such applicant if the issue be refused, in like manner as in other cases in which such writ now lies." It is evident from the introduction of the case of Orphans' Court sales, that this provision was not meant to be confined to the case of lien creditors becoming purchasers, which is the exclusive subject matter of the section to which it is attached, but to be general and applicable to all cases of applications for issues in the distribution of the proceeds of sheriff's sales. If so, it applies as well as does the 87th Sec. of the act of 1836, to the proceeds of personal as well as real estate. It has been the practice of the court, however, for some years past, not to order the proceeds of personal estate into court, except by cause shown by affidavit.

In the case before us, the affidavit substantially shows that the applicant is an execution creditor, having a lien on the fund; he avers his belief that plaintiff's judgment is fraudulent as against creditors; that is the fact in dispute. It may be that the reason is a fact, which in the form stated would not be admissible.

Still, we consider the plaintiff's admission enough in the present stage of the cause to justify us in directing an issue. The applicant may be able to adduce on the trial other competent evidence which will satisfy the jury, that at the time of the confession of this judgment, the defendant was not indebted to the plaintiff. Rule absolute.

Vandyke v. Bennett, D. C. Saturday, October 28, 1848. Why the plaintiff and Elijah Prentiss should not maintain or relinquish. *Per curiam.* This is the usual sheriff's rule to interplead, and the objection raised is, that no claim was made to the goods. This objection is made by the claimant, who produces his own affidavit, asserting that the goods levied on are exclusively his property, and he had actually brought an action of trespass against the sheriff for the same. It seems too plain for argument that such an action is sufficient claim to authorize us to make the rule. The act of assembly was intended for the protection of the sheriff in cases of this character. It is not for us to question its policy, but to carry out the intention of the legislators in good faith. It is plain that construction contended for by the claimant would make it a dead letter. Rule absolute.

Marriner v. Etting, D. C. Saturday, October 28, 1848. See also vol. ii. "Infants." Why Wm. Marriner, Sr., should not be released as next friend to plaintiff, and Thos. Rice substituted as next friend. *Per curiam.* The court undoubtedly has the power of substituting another person for the *prochein ami* who has commenced the suit, where his testimony becomes material, or for any other sufficient reason in their discretion. We must take care, however, not to word the order in such a manner as to release him from costs which have already accrued, which we have no power to do. Ordered that the name of Thomas Rice is substituted as next friend of the plaintiff in the place of Wm. Marriner, Sr.

Butterfield v. Hirst, December 4, 1849. Why claimant should not give bond without surety. *Per curiam.* We do not think that this is a case in which the claimant should be relieved from giving security. It appears that she made a conditional sale to the defendant, with a stipulation that she should retain the property until the purchase-money is paid. It depends upon the question whether possession was delivered to the vendee: if it was, the sale was fraudulent as to creditors. We have always refused to relieve a party claiming under a bill of sale from defendant, from giving security, merely on the allegation that possession had changed. It is a question for the jury, not for the court. This is a strictly analogous case. R. D.

Faulkner v. Voigt, D. C. No. 27, Saturday, November 4, 1848. Why sundry claimants should not give bond without surety. No. 28. Why the defendant should not give bond for Bergner, Sen. & Co. *Per curiam.* It appears that the defendant in this case is a commission merchant, and received the goods which have been levied on in that capacity from the claimants. They have never been the property of the defendant, nor do the claimants claim in any way through them. This is a case, then, in which we think they ought not to be required to give security beyond their own bonds. As to the case of the claimant who resides abroad, we do not think it would be proper to take the bond of the defendant, for whose debt they have been levied on. The court will extend the time for giving security in that case for a reasonable period; but if it cannot be obtained, the goods will have to be sold, and the proceeds paid into court to abide the determination of the issue. No. 27. Rule absolute. No. 28. Rule dismissed.

Baron v. McMackin, December 4, 1848. Why an attachment should not issue against the sheriff. *Per curiam.* This case grows out of a sheriff's rule of interpleader. It seems that on motion of the sheriff and filing of the usual affidavit of his deputy, that under a writ of *fi. fa.* he had taken possession of certain goods, &c., and that said goods still remain in the possession of the sheriff, the usual rule upon the plaintiff and claimant was granted. An inventory was filed, setting forth certain machinery, certain goods, and certain household furniture. The notice of the claimant was a general one—that he claimed the goods levied on. In answer to the rule, on May 22, 1848, the claimant filed an affidavit that, so far as he knew, there had been no actual levy, but that he had given the notice at the request of the sheriff's officer, and that nothing further being done, he supposed the levy abandoned, and proceeded, in the usual course of his business, to sell the dry goods. Another affidavit was filed June 6, in which, after referring to the former affidavit, he relinquishes his claim to the machinery, and maintained it only as to the dry goods. On the 12th of June, 1848, the court made the usual order, and "that all proceedings in said execution, so far as relates to the goods claimed, be stayed until the further order of the court." Under this order of court a feigned issue and bond was filed Nov. 24, 1848. Of course it only comprehends the household furniture. The plaintiff then took a rule upon the sheriff to return the writ, and, upon his default, the rule for an attachment now before us.

Nothing is clearer than, to entitle the sheriff to the benefit of a rule to interplead, he must have made an actual levy and taken actual possession. He is responsible, then, for the safe keeping of the property until the final order of the court is complied with, and the issue and bond approved and filed. He may, then, with safety, and not till then, abandon the possession. If he suffers the defendant, or claimant, or any one else, to eloign the goods, he becomes responsible if they are the goods of the defendant. If the claimant refuses to give bond, all that the court can do is to order the sheriff to proceed and sell. How can we say, as we have been asked to do in this case, you shall not give bond for part, unless you give bond for the whole of what you originally claimed? We can imagine how such a precedent would work.

It might, perhaps, be said, that the order of the court, staying proceedings, was necessarily to be referred to the goods, the claim of which was finally maintained on the hearing of the rule. Such is, undoubtedly, the interpretation to be placed upon the general order of the court. This was, however, an early case under the act of assembly, before the general order was made. We discharge this rule for an attachment, and make the following order:—

Ordered, That the sheriff do proceed with the execution in this case, so far as regards the goods levied on not mentioned in the feigned issue and bond of the claimant filed. R. D.

Vandyke *v.* Bennet; Chase *v.* Prentiss, Dec. 23, 1848. Sheriff's rule to interplead. Same rule. *Per curiam.* Two different plaintiffs in executions against different defendants, have directed the sheriff to levy upon the same goods. Under the first writ, he, of course, levied and took possession of the property as

the property of the first defendant. The goods being in the custody of the law, the second execution creditor has no right to require him to seize them manually under the second writ. Under the first writ, he must deliver possession to the purchaser; all that he can do under the second, is to sell the right, title, and interest of the defendant. In no event, if he pursues this course, can he be responsible to the plaintiff in either execution. Rules discharged.

Johnston *v.* Minor; Struthers *v.* Minor, June 4, 1849. Why the plaintiffs should not take the amount of their executions out of court. *Per curiam.* We have had considerable difficulty in arriving at our judgment in these cases. The point which arises is entirely new, and requires a very important principle to be settled upon the construction of the 9th section of the act of April 10, 1848, commonly known as the "sheriff's interpleader act." On June 27, 1848, Sayres levied an execution against Minor, "upon all the right, title, and interest of the defendant. in a certain establishment," &c. Conkling claimed to be the owner of this establishment. The sheriff took the usual rule, which was made absolute; a feigned issue was formed between Conkling as plaintiff, and Sayres as defendant, and a bond for the forthcoming of the property given by Conkling, with sureties; and, thereupon, the sheriff withdrew from the possession. The feigned issue is still pending and undetermined. On Sept. 18, 1848, another *fi. fa.* at the suit of Rankin against Minor, was levied upon the same property.

On Feb. 8, 1849, the plaintiffs in these two cases issued executions against the same defendant, to which the sheriff returns that he has levied upon the personal property of the defendant, subject to the two prior levies of Sayres and Rankin; and then goes on to state specially the fact of the issue, and bond, &c., and that he has sold the property for a certain sum. The money has been paid into court, and the question presented by this motion is, whether the property was discharged by the proceedings upon the sheriff's rule of interpleader, from the lien of Sayres's execution. As to Rankin's execution, he does not appear to be represented here; and were we about to make any order which could prejudice, we would delay it until such time as he could have an opportunity to be heard. We are of opinion, however, that the property has not been discharged by the proceedings upon the sheriff's sale of interpleader. The lien of an execution once attached upon personal property, continues until that property passes to another by a judicial sale, unless it should, in the mean time, be discharged by the laches of the party, or the sheriff. The law does no man wrong. A rule staying proceedings, being an act of the court, never affects the lien of the execution, however long it may be pending. The sheriff, under such a rule, continues answerable for the forthcoming of the property. The sheriff's rule of interpleader is, after all, nothing but a rule to stay proceedings until a certain question arising has been settled. To relieve the sheriff—to relieve the claimant, and restore him the use of his property—to relieve the plaintiff and defendant, that the goods may not be, in the mean time, eaten up by the costs and expenses—the court have adopted the practice of taking security from the claimant to the value of the goods, and then directing the sheriff to withdraw from the possession. If the goods in question should be eloigned, then, indeed, the plaintiff is turned over for his remedy to his bond; but if the identical goods can be followed and retaken, they may be reseized, and sold either upon the same writ of *fi. fa.*, or a *venditioni exponas*, grounded thereon, according to the circumstances. Why should the plaintiff be stripped of his security without his consent, further than is absolutely necessary for the administration of justice between the parties? He never agreed to substitute the bond for his lien, or to release the goods—it was the act of the court. He has been guilty of no laches. Nor are there any such overwhelming inconveniences as have been supposed. There are no market overts in Pennsylvania. The *bona fide* purchaser from a wrongful possessor acquires no title. A sale, by the claimant, of the goods left in his possession, will convey no title unless he is the owner. The man who buys, and pays his price, takes the goods with the implied warranty of title of the vendor, nothing more. It is upon that security our daily purchases are all made. Every loaf of bread, or yard of muslin we buy, for daily consumption, may be followed into our hands by the real owner. Such has been the law of Pennsylvania for more than a century and a half, and society has, nevertheless, got along very well. Occasional hard cases have been more than compensated by the security of property which the general principle has afforded.

In the case of Hogan *v.* Lucas (10 Peters, 400), where there was a proceeding, under a law of the State of Alabama,

precisely analogous to this, the Supreme Court of the United States held that the lien of the execution was not discharged by the giving of bond with security. Says Judge McLean, in delivering the opinion of the court: "On the giving of the bond the property is placed in the possession of the claimant. His custody is substituted for the custody of the sheriff. The property is not withdrawn from the custody of the law." In the hands of the claimant, under the bond for its delivery to the sheriff, the property is as free from the reach of other processes as it would have been in the hands of the sheriff. R. D.

Rump *v.* Williams, D. C. Saturday, October 21, 1848. Why the claimant should not be allowed to give bond without surety. Campbell *v.* Same. Same rule. *Per curiam.* In these cases, a sheriff's rule to interplead under the 9th section of the act of April 10, 1848, (Pamph. L. 450) has been made absolute. Under the general order of this court in such cases, it is the duty of the claimant to file a narr. in the feigned issue awarded within fourteen days, and to give bond, with sufficient security, to be approved by one of the judges of the court, that the goods levied on and claimed shall be forthcoming to answer the plaintiff's execution, in case the issue be determined against the plaintiff. If the claimant desires that the time for this purpose should be enlarged, he must make a special application to the court, which, upon reasonable cause shown, will enlarge the time. If he neither files his narr. nor gives the bond, the court, on motion of the sheriff or plaintiff in the execution, will make an order that the sheriff do proceed with the said execution, and that the claimant be barred of any action against the sheriff or any one acting by his authority, saving, however, his right of action against the plaintiff and all others. If he files the narr. but neglects to give the bond, the court, on motion, will order the sheriff to proceed and sell, and pay the proceeds of the sale into court, to abide the determination of the issue, and that the claimant be barred of any action against the sheriff and his officers in respect of such seizure and sale, saving his rights against the plaintiff and all others. Where, however, the case of the claimant is *prima facie* very clear, as where he avers that he does not derive title from or through defendant, and is in exclusive possession, or that his title is derived from a sale of defendant's goods under public authority, the claimant may obtain a rule on the plaintiff, in the execution, to show cause why he should not be permitted to give his bond without security. This is the rule which has been taken in this case. We are not satisfied, however, that a sufficient case has been made out. The execution of Campbell and Rump was for partnership debts, though on judgments against Bradley alone. Under that execution, as appears by the affidavit of the sheriff's officer, he took actual possession, as he had a right to do, of the partnership goods, on the 18th July, 1848. While the goods were thus in the actual possession of the sheriff, a levy was made by a constable, under an execution against Bradley alone, of all his interest in the goods, and a sale made to Martin Ryan. He says he is in exclusive possession. It is evident, however, that he shows no right against the sheriff under the prior execution. His possession, as far as appears, is a tortious one, as was that of the constable. If, however, the sheriff did not take actual possession, when he made the levy, then, perhaps, the plaintiff has lost his lien, and his recourse ought regularly to be against the sheriff. How far he may have lost that recourse by his submitting to the sheriff's rule to interplead being made absolute, it is not now for us to decide. Rule dismissed.

Peter v. Barron, Dec. 23, 1848. Why the claimant should not give bond without security. *Per curiam.* The claim is under a prior sheriff's sale of the same goods. The plaintiff might have controverted the fact, or shown circumstances to induce a suspicion that the sale was not conducted in the usual fair and open manner. He has not done so; but relies upon the simple fact that the claimant was the plaintiff in the prior execution, and the purchaser of all the goods levied on. We do not think that of itself ought to put the claimant to giving security. Rule absolute. Time extended to Dec. 30, 1848.

Guillou v. Healy, Saturday, March 13, 1852. Motion for a new trial. This was a feigned issue under the sheriff's interpleader act. The original debtor, as whose property the goods were levied on, was Isaac Rowe. It is objected that he was admitted as a witness for the plaintiff. However strong his bias may be in favor of the claimant, in most cases it is evident that his pecuniary interest is the other way, that the property should be applied to the payment of his debt. There was consideration and change of possession in favor of the claimant, and the only ground upon which his title was

attacked was actual fraud, intention on the part of Rowe, known to Guillou, to delay and defeat his creditors. This question was submitted to the jury, and it must be a strong case which would induce us to set aside a verdict in favor of honesty upon such an issue. The evidence, however, was by no means, in the opinion of the judge before whom it was tried, of so conclusive a character. Rule refused.

Jacobs v. Wells, Saturday, March 30, 1850. Why claimant's husband should not give bond. *Per curiam.* This is a case under the sheriff's interpleader act. The claimant is defendant's wife, who shows, indeed, that she does not derive title from her husband. Her own bond to restore would not bind her. She asks us to allow defendant's bond to be taken. We think, however, that we cannot do this, and that some person, not the defendant, must be found to answer for the forthcoming of the goods. Plaintiff has already the defendant for debt; defendant would not increase his present responsibility one iota by it. The payment of the debt, which he is already bound for, would discharge the debt bond. It may be unfortunate for a party like the claimant to be placed in this position, but we do not think we can relieve. If she cannot give security, the goods can be sold and the money paid into court to await the determination of the issue. R. D.

Belmont v. Norris, Saturday, April 27, 1850. Why plaintiff should not give security for damages. *Per curiam.* This is a case in which an interpleader has been awarded on motion of the sheriff. We see no reason for ordering the plaintiff in the execution to give security for damages. Unless the sheriff has been guilty of some outrage, there can be nothing but nominal damages; if he has, upon its being shown by deposition, the court would not relieve him by granting the interpleader.

The plaintiff being a non-resident, we order him to give security for the costs of the issue. In that respect, though in form defendant in the issue, the case is analogous to replevin, in which both parties are actors.

Security ordered in costs.

The following forms are in use in Philadelphia:—

CLAIMANT'S BOND.

Know all men by these presents, That —— held and firmly bound unto —— in the sum of —— lawful money of the

United States of America, to be paid to the said —— certain attorney, executors, administrators, or assigns: to which payment well and truly to be made, we and each of us, do bind ourselves and each of us, our and each of our heirs, executors, and administrators, firmly by these presents. Sealed with seal dated the —— day of —— in the year of our Lord one thousand eight hundred and ——

Whereas, the sheriff of Philadelphia County, by virtue of a certain writ of execution issued out of the —— commonly called a writ of *Fieri Facias* to —— Term, A. D. 184 No. —— at the suit of the said —— for the debt or sum of —— dollars and —— cents, together with interest and costs against the said —— has levied upon the goods and chattels mentioned in the schedule annexed and marked (A), which said goods and chattels are claimed by the said —— to be —— property ——

And whereas the said court, under the power granted by the Act of April 10, 1848, entitled, "An Act extending the chancery powers of, and to the said jurisdiction and proceedings in certain courts," have directed an issue to determine whether the right of property in the said goods levied upon and claimed, or any part thereof, is in the said claimant, and that the said claimant should give bond to the said —— in double the amount of his said judgment, and have approved of the said —— as such suret conditioned that the said goods so levied on and claimed as aforesaid, shall be forthcoming upon the determination of the said issue, to answer the said writ of execution of the said —— if the said issue shall be determined in favor, or that so many of them shall be so forthcoming as shall be determined not to belong to the said —— *Now the condition of this obligation is such*, That if the said goods so levied upon and claimed as aforesaid, shall be forthcoming upon the determination of the said issue to answer the said writ of execution, if the said issue shall be determined in favor of said ——, or if as many of them shall be forthcoming as shall be determined not to be the property of said ——, then this obligation to be null and void, otherwise to remain in full force and virtue.

Signed and sealed in the presence of

[SEAL]
[SEAL]

DECLARATION AND PLEA.

In the —— of —— Term in the year one thousand eight hundred and ——

City and County of Philadelphia, ss. —— complain of —— For that whereas heretofore, to wit: on the —— day of —— in the year of our Lord one thousand eight hundred and forty —— before the making of the promise and undertaking of the said defendant hereinafter mentioned, to wit: on the day and year aforesaid, at the city and county aforesaid, a certain discourse was had and moved by and between the said plaintiff and the said defendants, wherein a certain question then and there arose: that is to say, whether the right of property in certain goods and chattels, or any of them, viz.: —— which had been heretofore, to wit: on the —— day of —— in the year —— levied upon by the sheriff of Philadelphia County, under and by virtue of an execution or writ of *fieri facias* issued out of the said court to the term of —— eighteen hundred and —— at the suit of the said —— (defendant herein) against —— was in the said —— plaintiff herein at the time of the said levy; and in that discourse the said plaintiff then and there asserted and affirmed that the right of property in the said goods and chattels was in —— the said plaintiff at the time of the said levy thereupon; which said assertion and affirmation the said defendant then and there contradicted and denied, and then and there asserted the contrary thereof; and thereupon afterwards, to wit: on the day and year aforesaid, at the city and county aforesaid, in consideration that the said plaintiff at the special instance and request of the said defendant had then and there paid to the said defendant the sum of one hundred dollars, lawful money of the United States, he the said defendant undertook and then and there faithfully promised the said plaintiff to pay —— the sum of two hundred dollars of like lawful money, if the right of property in the said goods and chattels so as aforesaid levied upon, was at the time of the said levy thereon in the said plaintiff and the said plaintiff in fact say that the right of property in the said goods and chattels so as aforesaid levied upon, was at the time of the said levy thereon, in the said plaintiff to wit: at the city and county aforesaid, whereof the said defendant on the day and year aforesaid, at the city and county aforesaid, had notice: whereby he the said defendant then and there became liable to pay, and ought to have paid to the said plaintiff the said sum of two hundred dollars, yet the said defendant not regarding —— said promise and undertaking, but contriving, &c. intending, &c. hath not as yet paid the said

As under the act the claimant has the affirmation upon him, and must in all cases make out his claim to the satisfaction of the jury, although the defendant has no title, this is not enough for the claimant, unless he establish property in himself.(*g*) But where, under a feigned issue to determine the property to goods levied on by execution, the claimant set up a prior sheriff's sale of the goods to himself, under his own execution, but there was evidence to show that there was no bill of sale placed on the store; that the ringing of the bell was a mere sham; that the goods were sold in lumping lots, and brought but from one-fifth to one-eighth of their price, and that the same business was continued by the claimant with the same clerk; it was held, that in this case a verdict would not be disturbed which found such sale void under the statute of Elizabeth.(*h*)

The lien of the *fi. fa.* on a personal property is not discharged, although the claimant give bond for the forthcoming of the goods, and the sheriff be thereupon ordered to withdraw from the possession. On the giving of the bond, the property is placed in the possession of the claimant: his custody is substituted for the custody of the sheriff; the property is not withdrawn from the custody of the law. In the hands of the claimant, under the forthcoming bond, the property is as free from the reach of others, as it would have been in the hands of the sheriff.(*i*)

Where the issue is awarded to try the right of a non-resident plaintiffs to levy on goods said to belong to the defendant, the plaintiff must give security for costs, as in other cases.(*j*)

By the practice of the District Court, the order of court, under the sheriff's interpleader act, extends to absent claimants.(*k*)

10. *How far a levy is satisfaction of debt.*

By our practice, which in this respect differs from the English, a

sum of two hundred dollars or any part thereof, to the said plaintiff (although often thereunto requested), but to pay the same or any part thereof, has hitherto wholly neglected and refused, and still doth neglect and refuse, to the damage of the said plaintiff five hundred dollars, and therefore the plaintiff ha brought suit.

JOHN DOE, } Pledges, &c.
RICHARD ROE. }
Plaintiff's Attorney.

And the said —— by —— attorney, come and defend the wrong and injury when, &c., and say that the said plaintiff ought not to have and maintain —— aforesaid action thereof against the said defendant because he say that although true it is that the said discourse was had and moved by and between the said plaintiff and the said defendant, wherein the said question did arise as aforesaid, and that he the said defendant did undertake and promise in manner and form as the said plaintiff hath above in that behalf alleged: Nevertheless, for plea in this behalf the said defendant say that the

right of property in the said goods and chattels so as aforesaid levied upon, was not at the time of the said levy thereon in the said plaintiff in manner and form as the said plaintiff ha above in that behalf alleged, and of this the said defendant put sel upon the country.

Defendant's Attorney.

And the said plaintiff as to the plea of the said defendant above pleaded, and whereof the said plaintiff ha put sel upon the country, doth the like.

Plaintiff's Attorney.

(*g*) Conklin *v.* Sayer, D. C. C. P. Sept. 1848. *Ante*, 722.

(*h*) Van Reed *v.* Sorin, D. C. C. P. March, 1849. See Gilbert *v.* Hoffman, 2 W. 66; Wier *v.* Hale, 3 W. & S. 285; Smith's Appeal, 2 Barr, 331.

(*i*) Johnston *v.* Minor, D. C. C. P. June, 1849. *Ante*, 724. S. P. 10 Peters, 400; Bright. Sup. 1849, 150.

(*j*) Spicer *v.* Sellers, D. C. Dec. 9, 1848. Belmont *v.* Norris, *ante*, 726.

(*k*) Moore *v.* Lelar, D. C. C. P. 7 Leg. Int. 110.

general return of goods levied, whereby it does not clearly appear that they were insufficient to pay the debt and costs, does not discharge the defendant, and deprive the creditor of all remedy except as against the sheriff; and if the sheriff pay the fair amount of the sales to the plaintiff, it is all that is required of him, and the plaintiff may issue an *alias fi. fa.* or *ca. sa.* for the residue without application to the court. He is not responsible beyond the amount of the personal estate, which he either actually levied or might have levied upon the *fi. fa.*(*l*) Where, therefore, a *fi. fa.* was returned, levied on grain in the barn and in the ground, household furniture, &c. (described and left at the plaintiff's risk), it was held not to be evidence, that the judgment was completely satisfied, so as to make an *alias* for the residue void.(*m*) But a return to a *fi. fa.* levied on certain specified articles, with all the defendant's personal estate, is *prima facie* evidence of a levy to the value of the debt, and throws the burden of proving the value of the whole of the goods of the defendant in the execution upon the sheriff's security, when sued for the officer's refusal to sell the goods.(*n*)

The execution defendant's interest in the proceeds ceases on the return-day of the writ to the extent of the proceeds of sale. No matter how the plaintiff be delayed in obtaining the fund, provided the defendant has not aided in such delay, his debt is paid, and his liability to interest on the amount of such proceeds must cease.(*o*) But the mere seizure of personal property on execution is not *per se* a payment in law of so much, upon the judgment—it is so *sub modo* only: when the sale, however, is made and the money raised and appropriated, payment is considered as made.(*p*) In cases of levy and sale of real estate the rule is otherwise, and payment cannot be presumed until the actual receipt of the proceeds by the plaintiff has been permitted by the final order of the court.(*q*)

The principle is universal that in judicial sales there is no warranty; it is of course equally applicable to sales of personal, as to those of real estate. It results that a judgment is satisfied by a levy and sale of goods to its amount, under a *fi. fa.*, although the purchaser's title be defeated in an action of replevin, and it makes no difference that the plaintiff was the purchaser; he is concluded by the sheriff's return, and cannot renew his execution.(*r*)

But a levy on personal property is, *pro tanto*, a satisfaction if the levy be released by the plaintiff, and is lost to the defendant; though it is otherwise, where the release is at the request of the latter.(*s*)

11. *Sale of property seized.*

If the debt and costs are not paid, it becomes the sheriff's duty to make sale of the goods by public auction, a private sale being, in no case, justifiable.(*t*) Before sale, notice must be given thereof by the

(*l*) Taylor's Appeal, 1 Barr, 392, *post*, 736, 737.

(*m*) Little *v.* Lessee of Delancy, 5 Binn. 266, 272.

(*n*) Newlin *v.* Palmer, 11 S. & R. 99. See *post*, 736.

(*o*) Strohecker *v.* Farmers' Bank, 6 W. 100, 101.

(*p*) Lythe *v.* Mehaffy, 8 W. 247.

(*q*) Ibid.

(*r*) Freeman *v.* Caldwell, 10 W. 9; see Boas *v.* Updegrove, 5 Barr, 519, *post*, 732.

(*s*) Porter *v.* Boone, 1 W. & S. 251.

(*t*) Keyser's Appeal, 1 H. 411. See Lynch *v.* Com. 6 W. 495; Bingham *v.* Young, 10 Barr, 396.

officer during, at least, six days, by not fewer than six handbills, to be put up at such places as he shall deem best calculated to give information to the public of such sale.(*u*)   And where there is no bidder present but the plaintiff in the execution, and no bystanders, it is incumbent on the sheriff to inquire whether the requisite notice has been given, and a sale to him, made under such circumstances, no such notice of the sale having been given, is fraudulent and void.   "The mere fact," said Judge COULTER, in commenting on such a state of facts, "that there was no bidder but the plaintiff himself, and no bystanders, made the sale collusive and invalid.   Under such circumstances, it was the duty not only of the officer, but of the plaintiff, to have the sale adjourned.   For the principle that he who has the absolute control of the sale for his own benefit, cannot be a purchaser, is well established, unless there is a fair competition of bidders, or a lawful opportunity given for such competition; otherwise, the property of the debtor might be sacrificed.   And even the consent of the debtor would not cure the defect, for there is often collusion between him and a particular creditor.   The other creditors have an interest which must be protected.   Thus, it was ruled in 7 Watts, 365, "That an agreement between an execution creditor and the debtor, that personal property levied on should be sold on five days' notice by the sheriff, was fraudulent and void, against a subsequent execution, and that a sale under such circumstances to the execution creditor confers no title."   But a much stronger case is to be found in 3 Harris, 90.   It is more precisely apposite to the case in hand.   That was a sale, by a constable, of grain in the ground, where due notice had been given according to law.   The constable went to the fields where the grain was growing, which was the place appointed for the sale; the. plaintiff having instructed him to bid a certain sum for him.   The constable went into each field and made proclamation of the sale and bid, and no person appearing to bid more, went into the public road, which passed by the fields, and there proclaimed the sale and the bid, and knocked down the grain to the plaintiff.   The court below instructed the jury that the sale was fraudulent and invalid.   The *per curiam* opinion of the court is emphatic: "There can be no public sale without bidders or bystanders.   If there was one bidder, and he not the execution creditor, or the controller of the sale, it might make a case of difficulty, because, if the officer got a single bid, the property might be fairly struck down at its value, but not at a bid greatly below the value.   In such case, the officer ought to adjourn the sale.   If he did not, the inference of collusion between him and the bidder would be so strong that the least spark of evidence would invalidate.   But the case is infinitely worse when the execution creditor is both buyer and seller.   The presumption of collusion is then irresistible and conclusive."(*w*)   It is certain that the sheriff can disregard the highest bidder when the price is greatly inadequate, and adjourn the sale, or return that the goods remain unsold for want of bidders.(*x*) .The sheriff may, also, disregard a bid, conditioned that the money be applied to the bidder's execution, even though he was legally entitled to the proceeds of sale.(*y*)

(*u*) § 42, act of June 16, 1836.   This provision is taken from the act of March 21, 1806, § 11.

(*w*)See McMichael *v.* McDermott, 5 H. 353.

(*x*) 3 Campbl. 521.

(*y*) Faunce *v.* Sedgwick, 8 Barr, 407.

The sale should be made where the goods are. The articles must be pointed out and disposed of separately to an amount sufficient to satisfy the execution.(z) The goods cannot be delivered to the plaintiff in satisfaction of his debt; and if the sheriff levy, and pays him out of his own pocket, he cannot keep the goods to his own use. The plaintiff, however, may become the purchaser,(a) in which case he need not pay for the goods, unless the price exceed his demand, when he merely pays the surplus.(b)

The sheriff has a reasonable discretion in adjourning the sale.(c) He may sell the goods after the return-day, and even after he has gone out of office, without a *venditioni exponas.*(d)

The 42d section of the act of 1836 directs previous notice, by sufficient advertisements, of such sale. Secret or private sales are thus effectually prevented. And hence, where an execution creditor procured a special deputy to be appointed by the sheriff, and the goods levied on in a store were sold by him and the defendant, at private sale, until other *fi. fas.* were left with the sheriff, the prior execution was held to be postponed as fraudulent and collusive.(e) And the case is the same whether the sale be before or after the return-day of the writ, with or without notice.(f)

The notice of sale on execution, cannot be safely abridged by consent of parties, and a sale to the plaintiff would confer no title, as against a subsequent execution.(g)

It is not fraudulent in law to leave property purchased at sheriff's sale, in the possession of the former owner, for his use and consumption.(h) But if the debtor be in fact the real purchaser, and the nominal purchaser falsely alleges at the time of sale his intention of leaving the goods with the debtor as an act of benevolence, or of selling them again for the benefit of the creditors, by which the bystanders are induced not to bid, it is a fraud, and the property remains in the debtor, subject to execution. The declarations of the bystanders, at the time of the sale, are evidence as part of the *res gestæ.*(i)

Part owners of a vessel, who were not served with process, may consent that their shares shall be sold by the sheriff on an execution against other part owners, who had been served; and in such case, the parties consenting will be estopped from disputing the purchaser's title, and be entitled to come in upon the surplus proceeds of the sale.(j)

By the act of 10th April, 1849 :(k) "It shall and may be lawful for any court in the County of Philadelphia, from which any execution or order of sale shall issue for the sale of personal property, to inquire into the regularity and fairness of the sale at the instance of any party

(z) 8 Johns. 333.
(a) Ld. Raym. 251.
(b) 19 Johns. 84. With regard to real estate, see act of April 20, 1846, Purd. 466, *post,* sect. v. 4–9.
(c) 5 Johns. 345.
(d) Dorrance v. Com. 1 H. 163. Rogers, J. See Beale v. Com. 7 W. 186; Fitler v. Patten, 8 W. & S. 455; McMichael v. McDermott, 5 H. 353; 4

Wheat. 503; Salk. 323; 2 L. Raym. 1072.
(e) Bingham v. Young, 10 Barr, 396. Keyser's Appeal, 1 H. 411.
(f) Ibid.
(g) Gibbs v. Neely, 7 W. 305.
(h) Walter v. Gernant, 1 H. 515.
(i) Ibid.
(j) Hopkins v. Forsyth, 2 H. 34.
(k) Pamph. L. 597.

interested by execution, foreign or domestic attachment, or under a general assignment, upon affidavit of circumstances, before delivery of the goods; and if it appear that the sale shall have been so irregular or fraudulent, as, in the opinion of the court, to have produced a sacrifice of the property to the prejudice of any such party, it shall be competent for the court so set aside such sale, and the same property may be again exposed to sale, as if no such previous sale had been made; *Provided*, That it shall be lawful for the court to direct an issue for the trial of questions of fact, whenever the circumstances of the case shall require, and to order the sale in the mean time of all perishable or changeable goods, the proceeds to be held to abide the result of the trial."

In executing the writ, a sheriff is to be governed in the amount to be levied by the sum stated on the back of the writ, and not by that which is mentioned in the body of the writ; and this rule applies to the amount of costs indorsed, as well as to the ·debt to be levied, though the indorsement being a matter *in pais*, the sheriff may, in an action against him by the party in whose favor the execution issued, show that it was not the act of the proper officer, or that it was improperly made.(*l*)

The purchaser at sheriff's sale, who is the plaintiff in the first judgment and execution, is fixed under the principle of *caveat emptor*, for the amount of his bid, though his judgment, &c., is afterwards set aside, and he is bound to the sheriff for its payment.(*m*)

As has been already noticed, the principle that in judicial sales there is no warranty, applies equally to judicial sales of chattels and of land.(*n*)

Purchaser at sheriff's sale, who knows it is illegal, but only participates by buying the goods, is liable in replevin, but not in trespass.(*o*)

12. *Landlord's claim.*

The sheriff should take care, if the defendant be tenant of the premises on which the property is taken, that he complies with the provisions of the act of 16th June, 1836,(*p*) which directs that the goods and chattels being in or upon any messuage, lands, or tenements, which are or shall be demised for life or years, or otherwise taken by virtue of an execution, and liable to the distress of the landlord, shall be liable for the payment of any sums of money due for rent at the time of taking such goods in execution: *Provided*, That such rent shall not exceed one year's rent. § 83.

After the sale by the officers, of any goods or chattels as aforesaid, he shall first pay out of the proceeds of such sale the rent so due, and the surplus thereof, if any, he shall apply towards satisfying the judgment mentioned in such execution: *Provided*, That if the proceeds of the sale shall not be sufficient to pay the landlord, and the costs of the execution, the landlord shall be entitled to receive the proceeds, after deducting so much for costs, as he would be liable to pay in a case of a sale under distress. § 84.

Whenever any goods or chattels liable to the payment of rent as aforesaid, shall be seized in execution, the proceedings upon such ex-

(*l*) Com. *v.* McCoy, 8 W. 153.
(*m*) Piper *v.* Martin, 8 Barr, 211.
(*n*) Freeman *v.* Caldwell, 10 W. 10.

GIBSON, C. J. See Miller *v.* Fitch, 7 W. & S. 366, *ante*, 729.
(*o*) Ward *v.* Taylor, 1 Barr, 238.
(*p*) Pamph. L. 777.

ecution shall not be stayed by the plaintiff therein, without the consent of the person entitled to such rent, in writing, first had and obtained. § 85.

The former sections are from the act of March 21, 1772, § 4. The last section is new. The practice of staying proceedings on executions operated injuriously to landlords, as the rent is in practice computed only to the time of the levy.

The proviso to the eighty-fourth section was required to prevent the absorption of the whole proceeds in costs.(q)

The construction uniformly put upon the act is, that the growing rent may be apportioned, so that the landlord shall have it down to the time when the goods are taken in execution, and this although in the middle of a quarter; but he is not entitled to it to the time of sale;(r) and if the rent be reserved, without any deduction on account of taxes, which the tenant covenants to pay, the landlord cannot charge the goods taken in execution with any part of the sum due for taxes;(s) and this though no rent was actually due.(t)

But if the landlord had, previously to the levy and sale, distrained the property, and the tenant had replevied the same, he would not be entitled to have, out of the proceeds of the sale by the sheriff, any other amount of rent than that which accrued subsequently to the distress.(u)

A distinction may be here observed between our act and the English statute upon this subject; in Pennsylvania, the officer must pay the rent out of the proceeds of the sale; whereas, in England, it must be paid before the goods are removed. After a sale by the sheriff, the practice is to take a rule upon him to pay the amount of rent due out of the proceeds.(v) The existence of the rent due being a matter peculiarly within the landlord's knowledge, he is bound to give notice of it to the sheriff in time, to produce as little delay to the execution creditor as possible. Accordingly, he is bound to give notice of his claim before the execution is returned.(w) Whether he ought to give notice of it in time to enable the sheriff to extend his levy, seems to be undetermined, but the question might under some circumstances be decided against the landlord, and it will always, therefore, be safest for him to give the notice as early as possible. It may likewise under some circumstances become expedient for the execution creditor to ascertain from the landlord the amount of his claim for rent, and to notify the sheriff of it, so that he may regulate the extent of the levy and sale accordingly. He is in time, however, if the notice reaches the officer *subsequently* to a sale of a portion of the goods, but *before* the return.(x)

The rent which becomes due after sheriff's sale, passes to the purchaser, under the revised act of June, 1836, which does not change the law as it was under the act of April 6, 1802.

(q) Remarks of Commissioners.
(r) Binns v. Hudson, 5 Bin. 506; see West v. Sink, 2 Y. 274.
(s) Binns v. Hudson, 5 Bin. 506; Wayne v. Duke, 2 P. L. J. 297; Case v. Davis, 3 H. 80.
(t) Lichtenthaler v. Thompson, 13 S. & R. 158; see Wh. Dig. "Landlord," ii. (g)
(u) Lessee of Wilson v. Rhoads, 4 W. 39.
(v) West v. Sink, 2 Y. 274.
(w) Mitchell's Administrator v. Stewart, 13 S. & R. 295.
(x) Allen v. Lewis, 1 Ash. 184.

Where there has been an underletting, the immediate landlord of the defendant is alone entitled to claim rent not exceeding one year, under the 83d section of the act of 1836, out of goods sold by the sheriff under an execution.(*y*)

Goods in the custody of the law, under execution or attachment, cannot be distrained for rent.(*z*)

The landlord is entitled to the rent in arrear out of the proceeds of an execution levied by a constable.(*a*)

The provisions of the 83d and 84th sections of the act of 16th June, 1836, were intended to make amends to the landlord for taking away his power of distress by a judicial sale of the tenant's goods. But the act contemplates an existing tenancy at the sale. If there be no tenancy, there can be no right to distrain, and, consequently, no equivalent for it under this act. Thus, a surrender of the tenancy, after levy, but before sale on an execution, deprives the landlord of his claim for rent on the proceeds which, in such case, belong exclusively to the execution creditor.(*b*)

Where, by the terms of a lease, the tenant is to pay the taxes assessed upon the premises, the landlord is not entitled, out of the proceeds of sale of the tenant's goods, to the amount of taxes paid by him after the levy.(*c*)

In a feigned issue between a landlord and execution creditors to determine the amount of rent to be deducted from the proceeds of sale, after a set-off of a book account on the part of the tenant proved, to reduce the rent, the landlord cannot defalk from this rent falling due after the levy.(*d*).

The landlord is not confined to the current year, or the year immediately preceding the execution, in his claim for rent, but may claim for one year due previously.(*e*)

As arrears of ground-rent, being a lien, are to be paid out of the proceeds of sale of the land, the sheriff must see to their payment before he makes distribution amongst the other incumbrancers. He is personally responsible, and is not protected by his condition of sale, requiring the landlord's bill to be presented before he parts with the money.(*f*) His safety lies in paying the whole money into court, when ignorance or doubt exists, or controversy is threatened.(*g*)

The sheriff is bound, if it be possible, to give direct notice to the ground landlord, in case he undertakes to distribute the proceeds himself. A notice inserted in the conditions of sale, that "arrears of ground-rent will be paid out of the purchase-money, if the bills are presented to the sheriff, otherwise they will be paid by the purchaser," is not sufficient.(*h*)

Where there is a sale under two levies made at different dates, the landlord's claim is for rent down to the latest of the two levies.(*i*)

(*y*) Bromley *v.* Hopewell, 2 H. 400.

(*z*) Corbyn *v.* Bollman, 4 W. & S. 342.

(*a*) Seitzinger *v.* Steinberger, 2 J. 379; Morgan *v.* Moody, 6 W. & S. 333.

(*b*) Greider's Appeal, 5 Barr, 422, citing 5 Barn. & Cress. 88.

(*c*) Case *v.* Davis, 3 H. 80.

(*d*) Ibid.

(*e*) Richie *v.* McComley, 4 Barr, 475, citing 5 W. 140; see Parker's Appeal, 5 Barr, 390.

(*f*) Mather *v.* McMichael, 1 H. 301.

(*g*) Ibid.

(*h*) Mather *v.* McMichael, *ut sup.*

(*i*) Worley *v.* Merkley, D.C. Sept. 1852. Exceptions to auditor's report. *Per curi-*

13. *Return to fi. fa.*

The return to an execution is made in the sheriff's own name and also in that of his deputy, and, as has been seen, he will be allowed to make an addition to his return, if the omission has been accidental merely.(*j*) To a *fieri facias*, the returns usually made are, First, that he has caused to be made of the defendant's goods and chattels, the whole or part of the debt, &c., which he has ready to be paid to the plaintiff; but he need not specify the particular goods taken and sold.(*k*) Secondly, That he has taken goods to a certain amount, which remain in his hands unsold for want of buyers; or, Thirdly, "*nulla bona*," or that defendant has no goods and chattels, lands or tenements in his bailiwick, whereof he can cause to be made the sum directed or any part thereof. The return may be special, with the addition that defendant being an executor or administrator has wasted the goods of the tes-

am. Three executions were levied on the defendant's goods—one Jan. 27, 1852, for $266—the second, Feb. 11, 1852, for a sum more than sufficient to exhaust the proceeds of the goods which were sold under all the writs for $2811.63. It is immaterial to the question raised by the exception, and now to be determined by the court, what the date and amount of the third execution was.

That question is, whether the landlord is entitled to be paid his rent up to the date of the first or second levy.

After paying the rent up to the date of the first levy, and the full amount of the first execution, there was still a large sum to be appropriated to the second execution creditor, who claims now that the landlord should lose his rent between the date of the first and second execution.

The creditor admits the moral justice of the landlord's claim; but appears to think that, as the sale was made under all the executions, it was all one proceeding, and that it would lead to inconvenience to discriminate. It does not appear to us in the same light.

Had the sale been on the first execution alone, the sheriff would not have been justified in selling more than enough to satisfy the first execution, leaving the residue of the goods on the premises, the lawful security for the landlord's rent. Then if a sale had followed upon the second execution, the landlord's right would have been to be paid up to the levy of that execution. Ought it to make any difference, that the levy of the second execution was made pending the first? What inconvenience or uncertainty can result from holding that, so far as regards the landlord's claim, the sale was under each writ in succession to the extent of the proceeds

necessary to satisfy each writ? Had the defendant or landlord, after the sheriff had sold enough to satisfy the first execution, objected to his selling any more, the only answer he could have made to such an objection, would have been the production of the second writ. The act says: "The goods and chattels being in or upon any messuage, &c., taken by virtue of *an* execution, &c., shall be liable for the payment of any sums of money due for rent at the time of taking such goods in execution." Act 16th June, 1836, § 83. The article *an* seems to have been introduced in the legislature, but it would be too nice a verbal criticism to rely upon it, as showing that, so far as the landlord's claim is concerned, every execution stands by itself. It is enough that there is nothing in the words of the statute which militates against this construction.

Exception sustained, and ordered and decreed that Maria L. Tryon, or B. Newcomb, Esq., her attorney, be paid the sum of $228.25 of the fund in court, being for rent up to Feb. 11, 1852; and that Joseph Worley, or R. M. Logan, Esq., his attorney, be paid the sum of $2201.32 on account of his execution, and that in other respects the report of the auditor be confirmed and money distributed accordingly.

(*j*) Penna. Ins. Co. *v.* Ketland, 1 Bin. 499, *ante*, 687.

(*k*) Fitler *v.* Patton, 8 W. & S. 455; 6 Taunt. 576; but see Beale's Executors *v.* Com. 11 S. & R. 299, 304. It is enough to say: "I have levied and made of the goods and chattels of the within named C D, deceased, in the hands of A B, executor within mentioned, to the value of fifty dollars, which money I have ready. The answer of —— high sheriff." Fitler *v.* Patton, 8 W. & S. 455.

tator or intestate.(*l*) When the sheriff has returned *fieri feci*, a rule may be obtained upon him after the return-day to pay the money into court, and this rule may be enforced by attachment.(*m*) If he withholds payment an action of debt may be had on the return, or of *assumpsit* for money had and received.(*n*) The latter action lies also if he retain more money for fees, &c., than he is entitled to, at the suit of the creditor.(*o*)

When the sheriff seizes sufficient property of the defendant under an execution, he cannot make a second levy ;(*p*) the debtor is discharged from the judgment, and the plaintiff must look to the sheriff for his money ;(*q*) and the debtor may plead the discharge in bar to an action of debt, or *scire facias* upon the judgment,(*r*) being absolutely discharged to the extent of the levy, whether the sheriff ever sell the goods or return the writ or not ;(*s*) or even although they afterwards be rescued from him.(*t*) And if the sheriff returns that he has levied and left the goods in the hands of the debtor, the judgment must be treated as having been at one time actually satisfied. Whether it might be restored to its former incidents by agreement of the parties as between themselves is a question ; but it certainly could not be restored so as to deprive third persons of any advantage acquired by such return.(*u*) And after sale by writs of *venditioni exponas*, issued upon two judgments, the plaintiff cannot, even with the defendant's consent, have the proceeds of the goods (which had been originally levied on under the first judgment) applied to the satisfaction of the second judgment, so as to continue the lien of the first upon the defendant's land, to the exclusion of a mortgage recorded after the first judgment. Having made his election, and having, by his levy on the personal estate, the means of satisfaction in his hands, it would be against equity that he should relinquish it to the prejudice of another.(*v*) By the seizure of the goods the debt is discharged so far as the value.(*w*) But the possession of money by the sheriff arising from the sale of lands sufficient to satisfy a judgment earlier than that under which he sold, is not *per se* a satisfaction of an earlier judgment.(*x*)

The revocation of a levy on the goods of one of two sureties does not release his co-surety; as, between themselves, they are both principals, and the creditor is not bound to pursue his seizure of the goods of either for the benefit of the other.(*y*) And where two are jointly and severally bound, and execution is had against one of them, and his goods are seized but not sold, this cannot be pleaded in an action of debt against the other obligor, because it is no actual satisfaction.(*z*) How far a levy is satisfaction, has been already considered.(*a*)

The sheriff's return is conclusive evidence of the facts contained in

(*l*) Tidd, 1054; *vide ante*, 692.
(*m*) Act of 1822, 7 Re. Laws, 496; *vide ante*, 687.
(*n*) 3 Johns. 183.
(*o*) Starkie, 345.
(*p*) Hunt *v.* Breading, 12 S. & R. 41; 13 id. 344; 12 Johns. 207, *ante*, 728.
(*q*) 4 Johns. C. R. 228.
(*r*) 2 Bac. Abr. 720.
(*s*) 2 Mod. 214.
(*t*) 2 Saund. 343.

(*u*) Gratz *v.* Bayard, 11 S. & R. 41; Dean *v.* Patton, 13 id. 342, 343.
(*v*) Dean *v.* Patton, 13 S. & R. 341.
(*w*) Ibid. 346.
(*x*) Bank of Penna. *v.* Winger, 1 R. 295.
(*y*) Whitehill *v.* Wilson, 3 Pa. R. 405.
(*z*) Ld. Raym. 1072; Sicard *v.* Peterson, 3 S. & R. 468.
(*a*) *Ante*, 728.

it ;(*b*) and it is of no consequence on whose information he relies for the truth of such return.(*c*) But it will not excuse him, in an action for a false return, that he was misled either by the mistake or misrepresentation of his deputy ;(*d*) and it is no evidence of a levy, in a replevin by him for the goods.(*e*)

As has already been seen, where a plaintiff is deprived of the fruit of his levy on personal property by the act of the law, not by anything he did or would have avoided, he cannot be deprived of his lien on the defendant's land by the mere return of the sheriff, "levied." This return, whether true or false, is not conclusive evidence, as in England, of satisfaction, which discharges the judgment and fixes the sheriff. The return is open to explanation by evidence of subsequent circumstances, the proceeds of chattels being distributable according to priority of lien, like the proceeds of lands.(*f*)

A return of levied, to the value of the debt, even without a sale, *ipso facto*, discharges the judgment and throws the plaintiff on the responsibility of the sheriff and his sureties ; and the taking a bond for the money has the same effect.(*g*) Thus, a plaintiff, deprived of goods bought on his own execution by a replevin founded on an adverse title, cannot have another execution, because of the sheriff's return. The common law forms of execution show that every subsequent writ is based on the return of its predecessor ; and though professional indifference to scientific practice, and official inexperience perpetuated by official rotation, according to the views of GIBSON, C. J., has driven technical consistency from judicial proceedings, those forms may be profitably consulted as the unerring indices of the law.(*h*)

If an officer, on levying on goods, deliver them to a third person, on his giving a receipt to return them or pay the amount of the execution, he cannot afterwards take other goods of the defendant in execution ; and in such a case it is immaterial whether the property originally taken were sufficient to satisfy the execution or not, or that he had been unable to recover anything on the receipt.(*i*)

In some of the counties in this State, it is usual for the sheriffs to return "*debt and costs paid*," without stating the facts of levy or sale. Whether such would be considered a legal return, if made in proper time, is uncertain ; but after a delay of two years, it has been held to be unworthy of the name of a regular return, and inconclusive.(*j*)

The sheriff is not obliged, unless ruled to do so, to make a return to a *fi. fa.;* but when he does so, it is conclusive between other parties, and can be impeached only in an action against the sheriff. If it be false, or there be neglect of duty by him or his deputy, the sheriff alone is responsible to the injured party.(*k*) And should he go on to execution without resort to the safeguards of which he can avail himself,(*kk*) and return the writ so as to render the judgment extinct, and delay and

---

(*b*) Per ROGERS, J., Mentz *v.* Hamman, 5 Wh. 153.
(*c*) Ibid.
(*d*) Ibid.
(*e*) Snyder *v.* Beam, 1 Br. 366.
(*f*) Taylor's Appeal, 1 Barr, 392. See *ante*, 729.

(*g*) Boas *v.* Updegrove, 5. Barr, 519, citing 10 W. 9.
(*h*) Boas *v.* Updegrove 5 Barr, 519.
(*i*) 12 Johns. 207.
(*j*) Weidman *v.* Weitzel, 13 S. & R. 96.
(*k*) Per ROGERS, J., Mentz *v.* Hamman, 5 Wh. 154.
(*kk*) See *ante*, 718.

hinder its execution to the plaintiff's injury, he does so at his own peril, and will be accountable.(l)

When the property of the defendant, pointed out by the plaintiff, is sufficient to pay the debt, the sheriff is *prima facie* liable for the debt to the plaintiff, unless he proceeds to levy and sell before the return-day of the writ; though this liability ceases, if the execution be placed in the sheriff's hands without the *bona fide* intention of selling, or if the proceedings are stayed by the plaintiff, prior to a levy on an intervening execution; and the measure of damages is the injury sustained by the plaintiff; and when the injury is occasioned by his default, or his interference with the writ, in any stage of the proceedings under it, and where the injury is not solely chargeable on the sheriff, the damages may be nominal.(m)

A return that he has levied the debtor's goods, but without specifying the value, is *prima facie* evidence that they were of value sufficient to pay the plaintiff's debt.(n)

The return of the sheriff to a writ of *fi. fa.* that he paid over the surplus of the proceeds of the sale of a vessel, after satisfying the execution, to one of the owners, for himself, and as agent for the others, is not a legitimate part of the return, and the appropriate remedy of one of the part owners to recover his share, is in *assumpsit*, and not by an action for a false return.(o)

Proof of a levy is not inconsistent with a return of "stayed."(p)

14. *Alias fi. fa., and herein of second fi. fa. issued pending the first.*

If a part only of the money be levied, the plaintiff may have a *fi. fa.*(q) or a *ca. sa.* for the deficiency. The latter writ can in no case be executed when the defendant has property within the county sufficient to satisfy the judgment and costs. If he has not, then it may be executed for the deficiency and for no more.(r)

The first writ of *fi. fa.* should be previously returned, and recited in the second; where nothing has been levied on the first, the recital is unnecessary.(s) If the sheriff return that he has taken goods which remain in his hands unsold, for want of buyers, the plaintiff may have a *venditioni exponas* to compel a sale.(t) If goods are not taken to the value of the whole debt, he may have a *venditioni exponas* for the goods already taken, with a clause of *fi. fa.* for the residue of the debt: and, it is said, that if a sheriff seize goods to the value, and return it, he is bound to find buyers.(u)

An *alias* execution issued to the same term is irregular, and will be set aside.(v)

The issuing of an *alias fi. fa.* will not release the sheriff from liability incurred on the *fi. fa*, nor will the subsequent granting of a rule to show cause why the judgment should not be opened.(w)

(l) Miller v. Com. 5 Barr, 207.
(m) Dorrance v. Com. 1 H. 160.
(n) Beale v. The Com. 7 W. 187.
(o) Hopkins v. Forsyth, 2 H. 34.
(p) Farmers' and Drovers' Bank v. Fordyce, 1 Barr, 454.
(q) 2 Bac. Abr. 719; Bing. on Ex. 260.
(r) § 28, Act of June 16, 1836, *supra.*

(s) Tidd, 1056.
(t) Gibson v. Philad. Ins. Co. 1 Bin. 499.
(u) Cowp. 406; Bing. on Ex. 262.
(v) Shaffer v. Watkins, 7 W. & S. 229.
(w) Myers v. the Commonwealth, 2 W. & S. 60; see Evans v. Boggs, id. 229.

A *fi. fa.* cannot be issued upon a judgment revived by *scire facias*, while there is an outstanding *fi. fa.* upon the original judgment. 'The proper mode is to proceed on the original *fi. fa.* But where a creditor having two judgments, issue a *fi. fa.* upon the oldest of them, and levied it on the defendant's real estate which was extended, though the *liberari* was not executed, it was held, that this proceeding did not preclude him from having an execution upon the second judgment, although both judgments were laid before the inquest upon the first judgment.(*x*)

It seems, also, that a judgment creditor is not bound to follow out a levy on land, which has been found sufficient to pay, by its profits, the debt in seven years, but may bide his time, and come upon the proceeds of that or any other tract when sold upon any other execution.(*y*)

Where a plaintiff issues a *fi. fa.*, and levies on real estate to which the defendant has no title, and the defendant at the time disclaims all title to the same, and the plaintiff thereupon abandons further proceedings on the *fi. fa.*, and issues an *alias fi. fa.*, the latter will not be set aside on the application of the defendant, on the ground that the plaintiff was bound to pursue his levy and condemnation on the first *fi. fa.*(*z*)

A judgment having been obtained against several defendants, a *testatum fi. fa.* was issued, in pursuance of the 76th section of the act of 16th June, 1836, against one of them; two years afterwards a *fi. fa.* was issued against all, directed to the sheriff of the county where the judgment was obtained, the *testatum* being outstanding; it was held, that inasmuch as the *testatum* was unreturned, and that no execution had been issued against the other defendants within a year and a day after judgment, the second *fi. fa.* was irregular.(*a*)

It cannot be objected that two writs of execution were sued out on the same judgment to the same term, where the inquisition on which the first was founded was set aside and a new one held.(*b*)

An omission to recite in an *alias* or *pluries fi. fa.*, the proceedings under the first execution, although irregular, does not render such *alias* or *pluries* writ void.(*c*)

15. *Venditioni exponas.*

The sheriff may sell, and it is his duty to sell, in the case of a levy on personal property, without a *venditioni exponas.* This writ is only necessary to bring the sheriff into contempt, for not selling on the *fi. fa.*(*d*) If he has made the return of levied and unsold for want of buyers, there he is not liable, but a *venditioni exponas* must issue.(*e*)

Where a sheriff goes out of office, after returning that he has levied, but that the goods remain on his hands for want of buyers, instead of suing out a *venditioni exponas*, the plaintiff may sue out a *distringas nuper vice comitem*, directed to the present sheriff, commanding him to distrain the late sheriff to sell the goods.(*f*) The former sheriff must

---

(*x*) Gist *v.* Wilson, 2 W. 30.
(*y*) Taylor's Appeal, 1 Barr, 390.
(*z*) Coleman *v.* Mansfield, 1 M. 56. See Hunt *v.* Breading, 12 S. & R. 37; Morrison's Appeal, 1 Barr, 13.
(*a*) Gibbs *v.* Atkinson, D. C. C. P. 3 P. L. J. 139.

(*b*) Springer *v.* Brown, 9 Barr, 305.
(*c*) Coleman *v.* Mansfield, 1 M. 56.
(*d*) Beale's Executors *v.* Com. 11 S. & R. 304.
(*e*) Id. ibid.; Zane's Executors *v.* Com. D. 313.
(*f*) 2 Saund. 47, *l*; 1 Arch. Pr. 271.

thereupon sell the goods and pay over the money, otherwise he will forfeit issues to the amount of the debt.(*g*)

16. *Testatum fi. fa. and fi. fa. on judgments transferred under the act of April* 16, 1840.

The act of June 16, 1836, § 76,(*h*) provides, " If the defendant in any judgment for the recovery of money, shall have no real or personal estate in the county where such judgment may be obtained, it shall be lawful for the plaintiff, upon his own suggestion of that fact, verified by affidavit, without any previous writ, to have a *testatum* writ of *fieri facias*, directed to the sheriff or coroner of any other county where the defendant may have real or personal estate, which shall be made returnable into the court from which it shall issue. § 76.

If the estate of the defendant in the county in which a *testatum* writ of *fieri facias* shall first be issued, be insufficient to satisfy the judgment, it shall be lawful for the plaintiff to have in like manner an *alias* or *pluries* writs of *fieri facias*, in succession, into any other county in which the defendant may also have real or personal estate, until such judgment shall be fully satisfied. § 77.

It shall be the duty of every sheriff and coroner, on receiving a *testatum* writ of *fieri facias*, immediately to deliver the same to the prothonotary of the Court of Common Pleas of his proper county. § 78.

It shall be the duty of every prothonotary to whom any *testatum* writ of *fieri facias* shall be delivered, as aforesaid, forthwith to enter the same of record, in a docket to be provided for that purpose, and as of the preceding term, stating particularly the amount of the debt, or damages and costs, indorsed upon such writ ; and, thereupon, he shall redeliver the said writ to the sheriff or coroner, to be by him executed. § 79.

If any sheriff or coroner, to whom any *testatum* writ of execution shall be directed and delivered, as aforesaid, shall neglect or refuse to execute and return the same, according to the exigency thereof, he shall be amerced in the court where he ought to return it, and also be liable to the action of the party aggrieved. § 82.

The common law lien of a *testatum* execution, is an independent one only because the lien of the judgment is limited to lands in the same county ; but it is regulated by a separate act, and depends on considerations different from those which regulate liens of judgment.(*i*)

The act of 1823, relating to the lien of *testatum* executions, applies only where the execution created the lien, and not where it is used ' merely to effect a sale of the land.   Therefore, where a new county was established, and a *testatum* execution issued from the court of the old county to the new county in which the lands lay, to obtain a sale, it was held, that the lien of the judgment on the lands in the new county were

---

(*g*) 6 Mod. 295; see further, as to the distringas, *ante*, 299–300. Bing. on Ex'ns, 111, in Law Lib. vol. xiii.

(*h*) Pamph. L. 775.
(*i*) Jameson's Appeal, 6 Barr, 280.

not affected by the lapse of five years from the entry of the *testatum* execution.(*j*)

A sale of lands in Potter County, by the sheriff of Lycoming County, in 1840, after Potter County had been separated from Lycoming County, and organized into a separate county by virtue of the act of April 8, 1833, on process issued out of the Court of Common Pleas of Lycoming County, though on a judgment remaining in Lycoming County, not transferred by any acts of assembly on the subject, was held to be irregular and void, and that the proper method was by a *testatum fi. fa.* directed to the sheriff of Potter County.(*k*)

Where a *testatum fi. fa.* from the District Court of Philadelphia County was executed by the sheriff of Crawford County, who indorsed his return on it, and placed it in the post-office, directed to the prothonotary of the District Court, but it was not received; the District Court ordered a duplicate writ to issue *nunc pro tunc.*(*l*)

Where a *fi. fa.* has been issued and returned *nulla bona*, it is not necessary to file a suggestion according to the 76th section of the act of 1836.(*m*)

Testatum executions are now almost entirely superseded by process issued under the following acts:—

Act of April 16, 1840.(*n*) In addition to the remedies now provided by law, hereafter any judgments, in any District Court, or Court of Common Pleas in Pennsylvania, may be transferred from the court in which they are entered, to any other District Court, or Court of Common Pleas in this commonwealth, by filing of record in said other court, a certified copy of the whole record in the case; and any prothonotary receiving such certified copy of record, in any case in which judgment has been entered by another court, or in another court, by transcript from justices of the peace, shall file the same, and forthwith transcribe the docket-entry thereof into his own docket, and the case may then be proceeded in, and the judgments and costs collected by executions, bill of discovery, or attachment, as prescribed by the act, entitled "An act relating to executions," passed the sixteenth day of June, one thousand eight hundred and thirty-six; and as to lien, revivals, executions, and so forth, it shall have the same force and effect, and no other, as if the judgment had been entered, or the transcript been originally filed in the same court to which it may thus be transferred. § 1.

Act of April 2, 1841,(*o*) The provisions of the first section of the act of sixteenth of April, one thousand eight hundred and forty, entitled "An act relating to executions, and for other purposes," shall be extended to judgments rendered in the City and County of Philadelphia, in the Supreme Court for the Eastern District of Pennsylvania; and said judgments may be transferred to any District Court or Court of Common Pleas of the commonwealth, under the provisions of said act. § 11.

(*j*) West's Appeal, 5 W. 87. See King *v.* Carter. 1 Barr, 154.
(*k*) King *v.* Carter, 1 Barr, 147.
(*l*) Clark *v.* Field, 1 M. 244.
(*m*) Boyer *v.* Kimber, 2 M. 393.
(*n*) Pamph. L. 410. See, as to construction of this act, *ante*, 581.
(*o*) Ibid. 139.

Act of April 4, 1843.(*p*)   The first section of the act of the sixteenth April, eighteen hundred and forty, entitled "An act relating to executions, and for other purposes," shall not be so construed as to destroy or impair the validity of the lien of any judgment in the county in which the same was originally entered, or to which the same may be transferred under the provisions of said section.   § 7.

Act of April 6, 1845.   It is hereby declared to be the same intent, meaning, and construction of the first section of the act, entitled "An act relating to executions and for other purposes," approved April sixteenth, eighteen hundred and forty, that any record therein mentioned, where any party to the judgment may, at any time, have died, might be transmitted and filed in any court in any county, either before or after the substitution of the legal representatives of any deceased party, and the substitution be made after filing such record; and that in all cases in which any such record should be transferred, and filed before any such substitution, the court into which the record might be removed, should, after substitution of parties, proceed thereon as if the judgment had been originally entered in said court; and no judgment or record, so transmitted and filed before such substitution, shall be set aside, stricken off, or in any way affected or invalidated, by reason of there being no substitution of parties, before such transmission and filing thereof, and all records and judgments which may have been set aside, or stricken off, shall be, and the same are hereby restored to all intents and purposes: *Provided*, This section shall not interfere with, or affect any case which may have been adjudicated by the Supreme Court, or settled by the parties in interest: *Provided also*, That this section shall not affect any interest of any person who may have entered any judgment, subsequent to such setting aside, or striking off, and before such restoration.

The resolution of April 16, 1845,(*q*) correcting errors in certain acts, declares the following proviso, added to the eleventh section of the bill entitled, "An act concerning certain sheriffs' and coroners' sales, and for other purposes," to be taken and considered as part of said section: *Provided also*, That this section shall not affect any interest of any person who may have entered any judgment subsequent to such setting aside and striking off, and before such restoration: *And provided*, That nothing in the act, entitled "An act supplementary to an act, entitled 'An act to preserve and perfect the validity of judgments entered upon the continuance and appearance dockets of the courts and for other purposes,'" shall be construed so as to affect or prejudice the rights or interests of any mortgage or judgment creditor acquired before the passage of the said act and supplement thereto.

Act of January 24, 1849.(*r*)   The eleventh section of the act, entitled "An act concerning certain sheriffs' and coroners' sales, and for other purposes," approved the 16th day of April, 1845, so far as the same may affect any judgment, mortgage, or other lien duly entered, recorded, or filed, or any right or interest of either of the parties to the

(*p*) Pamph. L. 131.   (*r*) Ibid. 676.
(*q*) Ibid. 558.

judgment transferred, or of any other person or persons, duly vested or accrued prior to the passage of the said act, be and the same is hereby repealed. § 1.

Under the act of the 16th April, 1840, a valid and subsisting judgment may be transferred, after the death of the plaintiff therein, from the court of the county in which it was originally obtained and entered, to the court of another county; and the suggestion of the death of the party, and the substitution of administrators, may be made before the transfer, in the court of the county in which it was originally obtained and entered, or after the transfer, in the court of the county in which it may have been transferred, for the purpose of proceeding to execution; and such transfer, where there is no administrator, may be made by a creditor to secure assets; and so it seems, it may be made by an heir, under similar circumstances.(s)

A certificate of a prothonotary, that "the foregoing docket-entry is as full and complete as the same now remains of record in said court," is not sufficient to authorize a copy of the docket-entry in a cause to be filed under the act of April 16, 1840, for the purpose of transferring the judgment from one county to another. The whole record should be certified.(t) The transcript of a judgment in the Common Pleas, entered in another county in pursuance of the act of April 16, 1840, is not an actual judgment of the court of the county in which it is entered, but a quasi judgment for limited purposes; it is evidence of a judgment in the court in which it was originally obtained;(u) and where the original judgment was set aside at the instance of the defendant, for irregularity, and the execution in the second county stayed; held, that the judgment on the transcript fell with it, and that the plaintiff having obtained a new judgment, but no transcript of it having been entered, this last judgment has no lien in the county in which the transcript had been first entered.(v)

17. *Purchase of judgment by third party.*

For a variety of reasons, which it would be irrelevant to enumerate here, it may be deemed proper by a third person, not a party on record, where the execution has failed of its object, to purchase the judgment, and to take an assignment of it from the plaintiff.(vv) When this is done, the plaintiff becomes a trustee to his use, and he may enforce the judgment, or not, at his pleasure. Such assignments are liberally supported by the court, particularly where the purchaser has taken one in consequence of, or to protect himself from the *mala fides* of the defendant. As, for example, where the bail has purchased a judgment, his principal keeping without the reach of a bail-piece.(w) Where an execution was issued against several defendants, and the assignee in trust for the creditors of one paid the amount thereof to the sheriff, who marked the execution satisfied, it was ruled, that if such payment were a purchase of the judgment, the sheriff might correct the indorsement, and proceed on the writ.(x)

(s) Walt v. Swinehart, 8 Barr, 97.
(t) Updegraff v. Perry, 4 Barr, 291; see Bank of Chester County v. Olwine, 6 P. L. J. 154.
(u) Brandt's Appeal, 4 H. 343.
(v) Ibid.
(vv) See *ante*, 580.
(w) See Ketland v. Medford, 1 Bin. 497.
(x) Kuhn v. North, 10 S. & R. 399;

18. *Payment of money by sheriff to attorney, &c., and herein of payment to the sheriff.*

This topic was the subject of examination by GIBSON, C. J., in Irwin v. Workman.(y) "In Miles v. Richwine,"(z) he said, "a constable was not suffered to apply an execution in his hands to his own debt. It is certainly neither politic nor just to put impediments in the way of execution creditors, or suffer an officer to obstruct them by a pretence of title to their moneys in his hands. An attorney has not a lien on money in the hands of another; and the transfer of a security for his fee, gives the sheriff no better right to retain it than he had before; for it is not to be endured that an executive agent of the law shall set off a debt even previously due him, much less purchase a title to money in his hands by the subsequent procurement of a cross-demand, which could not have been procured for purposes of defalcation by the original debtor. To relax the direct responsibility of the officer, in a case like this, would let in a flood of vexation and oppression. The defendant, therefore, could not protect himself by becoming the holder of the plaintiff's note. Neither can he protect himself by payment over to the plaintiff's attorney, with notice of the revocation of his authority. Where an authority is not coupled with an interest in the thing to be recovered, the right to revoke, with or without cause, is as indisputable in relation to its existence between an attorney and his client, as it is in any other case of delegated power. It is not for a sheriff to interpose further than to ascertain whether the authority incidental to the relation has been restricted or revoked. As regards receiving, it was certainly restricted, in this instance, by an explicit direction to pay but to the special order of the client, and subsequently revoked by a dismissal of the attorney. With notice of this, the sheriff could avoid the consequences of a mispayment but by showing that the attorney had acquired an independent ownership of the money paid to him, and that he himself stood in the attitude of a stakeholder."(a)

The sheriff's acceptance of payment in bank notes discharges the obligation; he takes the notes as cash, and however worthless they may prove, he must account for them as cash.(b)

A payment, by the sheriff, of money made on an execution to one of the several plaintiffs, discharges the sheriff, unless notified not to pay; and he cannot maintain a suit subsequently against the one to whom he has so paid, for the use of the others.(c)

It is text-law that a sheriff may sell the goods on a *fi. fa.* after the return of his writ, and hence a payment to him is good after its return, because he has power to sell them notwithstanding, and the debtor has a right to redeem them by payment, without waiting for a *venditioni exponas.* The sheriff's sureties are therefore chargeable, and the debtor is discharged by such a payment.(d)

---

see Wood v. Vanarsdale, 3 R. 401; Mehaffy v. Share, 2 Pa. R. 361; Fleming v. Beaver, 2 R. 128. For a more full consideration of the law respecting assignments of judgments, the reader is referred to a former chapter.
(y) 3 R. 199.

(z) 2 R. 199.
(a) See Newbaker v. Alricks, 5 W. 183.
(b) Harper v. Fox, 7. W. & S. 142.
(c) Lazarus v. Follmer, 4 W. & S. 9.
(d) Beale v. The Com. 7 W. 185.

19. *Distribution of proceeds.*

This subject will hereafter be fully considered, when the proceeds of real estate are considered; and it has already been treated of, so far as concerns the landlord's priority. The following act, however, may be properly here introduced :—

Act of April 2, 1849, § 3.(e)—In all cases of executions, landlords' warrants, attachments, and writs of a similar nature, hereafter to be issued against any person or persons, or chartered company engaged in the operations before mentioned, it shall be lawful for such miners, laborers, and mechanics, to give notice of their claim or claims, and the amount thereof, to the officer executing either of such writs, at any time before the actual sale of property levied on ; and such officers shall pay to such miners, mechanics, or laborers, out of the proceeds of sale, the amount each is justly and legally entitled to receive, not exceeding fifty dollars, in like manner as rents are now paying in such cases : *Provided*, That the provisions of this act shall only extend to Schuylkill, Berks, Washington, Centre, Somerset, Westmoreland, and Carbon Counties.

SECTION III.

OF EQUITABLE EXECUTIONS, AND PROCEEDINGS TO OBTAIN A DISCOVERY UNDER THE ACT OF 1836.

Before the passage of the act of 1836, the debtor's deposits of money, debts due to, and goods pawned by him, stocks and other property, real or personal, held under secret trusts for him, or fraudulently incumbered, were inaccessible by process or otherwise, except, perhaps, by the tardy and usually unprofitable scrutiny of the insolvent laws. The act sought to diminish this evil, by enabling the judgment creditor to levy immediately on the stock or moneys of the defendant under the ordinary writ of *fieri facias*, where it is not screened by any fictitious incumbrance or transfer ; and also by giving a new adaptation of the old process in foreign attachment to the purpose of an execution upon which all such property may be attached or taken in satisfaction of the judgment. Under it, the defendant, and all persons holding his effects, may be compelled to disclose the requisite information relating thereto upon a bill of discovery, or interrogatories, to be framed according to the rules and practice in Courts of Equity. Adequate power is given to the Courts of Common Pleas for these purposes ; thus, to guard against the absconding or departure of any of the parties in the bill, they are empowered to direct a clause of *capias* in the *scire facias* against them, under the rules relating to the garnishees in foreign attachments, and they are authorized to regulate the payment of costs, at their discretion, according to the rules in equity.

The act itself appears to furnish a complete view of the principles and practice to be observed in pursuing it, and the precedents or forms in foreign attachments, if not precisely adapted to the provisions of the ensuing portions of it, are at least sufficiently analogous to render more

(e) Pamph. L. 337.

than a reference to them, in Mr. Sergeant's treatise on the law of foreign attachment, superfluous.

The subject will be examined under the following heads :—

I. Of the proceedings to discover the defendant's effects.

II. Of the proceedings to levy deposits and debts due to the defendant.

III. Of the proceedings to sell stock, &c.

1. *Of the proceedings to discover the defendant's effects.*

It shall be lawful for the plaintiff in any judgment, for the recovery of money obtained in any court of this commonwealth, to have a bill for the discovery of the real and personal estate of the defendant in such judgment.　§ 9.

Such bill may be filed against the defendant in the judgment, and against any person having possession of such real or personal estate, or who may owe or be accountable for the same, or may have knowledge of the same, and shall be filed in the Court of Common Pleas of the county in which such judgment may be ; or if the person of whom discovery may be sought shall reside out of such county, such bill may be filed in the Court of Common Pleas of the county where such person shall reside.　§ 10.

Every such bill shall set forth—

I. The recovery of a judgment, as aforesaid, and the amount actually due thereon.

II. That there is reason to believe that the defendant in such judgment has real or personal estate, wherewith the same may be satisfied.

III. That such real estate has been conveyed, transferred, or incumbered, or that such personal estate has been removed, transferred, or concealed, or that, by reason of concealment, or fraudulent transfer, or incumbrance thereof, the complainant is prevented from having execution of his judgment.

IV. If such bill shall be filed against any person other than the defendant in such judgment, it shall set forth, also, that such person has possession or knowledge of such real or personal estate, or that he can make discovery of such facts as will enable the plaintiff to have satisfaction of his judgment.　§ 11.

But no such bill shall be filed, unless the complainant therein shall make oath or affirmation, to be filed therewith, that he verily believes the facts set forth therein to be true.　§ 12.

The complainant in such bills may also, either in the said bill, or by interrogatories to be filed therewith, propound to the defendants therein named such questions touching the subject-matter thereof as may be necessary or proper for the purposes thereof, and as may be according to the rules and practice of Courts of Equity.　§ 13.

Upon the filing of such bill, it shall be lawful for the court, or any judge thereof, in vacation, to award a writ of *scire facias* to the sheriff, requiring him to make known to the defendants therein named, that they be and appear, at a certain time to be appointed by the said court, to answer the said bill, and all such interrogatories as shall be propounded to them, or show cause why they should not, and abide the judgment of the court in the premises. § 14.

But no such defendant shall be compelled to answer such bill or interrogatories, at the time so appointed, unless a copy of such bill and interrogatories shall have been served upon him, at least ten days previously thereto. § 15.

It shall be lawful for the court or judge, at the time of answering such writ of *scire facias* to order that a clause of *capias* be inserted in such writ, against the defendants, or any one or more of them, under the rules and regulations provided in the case of a garnishee in a foreign attachment.(*f*) § 16.

From the time of the service of any *scire facias* as aforesaid, upon any person other than the defendant in the judgment, the personal property of the defendant in the hands of such person, shall be bound thereby, and shall be liable to be taken in execution, at the instance of the plaintiff in such judgment, in like manner as goods or effects in the hands of the garnishee in a foreign attachment; and if such person shall transfer such personal property to any other person, after such service, he shall be liable to pay the value thereof to the complainant, out of his own proper goods and chattels. § 17.

The costs of all proceedings as aforesaid, shall be within the discretion of the court, in which such bill shall be filed, who shall have power to direct payment of the same, by either of the parties, to such bill, according to the rules of equity and justice. § 18.

The subject of discovery generally has been already considered.(*g*) It remains to notice a few practical points connected with this particular head.

Under the ninth and tenth sections just quoted, it has been decided by the Court of Common Pleas, of Philadelphia County, that, though they have full power to compel a discovery of a defendant's effects upon the prayer of a plaintiff having a judgment in *another* court, yet that they cannot award execution of it against the effects after such discovery in the Common Pleas. Their power to issue executions is confined to judgments rendered by their own court, and resort in such case must be had, under the thirty-fifth section, to that in which the judgment is.(*h*)

Act of April 24, 1848, § 2. The oath required by the twelfth section of the said act may be made by the agent, attorney, or any disinterested person on behalf of the complainant in any bill of discovery.

It was formerly thought by the Common Pleas, in Philadelphia, that their power to issue execution against personal property after discovery on a *scire facias*, under the thirty-fifth section, does not extend to the case of a judgment on a transcript from an alderman filed

(*f*) See Serg. on Att. 16.
(*g*) *Ante*, 77.

(*h*) Platt *v.* Bridges, C. P. Phil. 1837, MS.

therein.(*i*) But the law now seems to be that a transcript is a judgment which ·can be used for the purpose of equitable as well as of other executions.(*ii*)

A bill of discovery lies to discover *debts* due a defendant ;(*j*) and the court will sustain a bill for the discovery of the real estate in aid of judgment against him, in all cases where the knowledge of such real estate is contained in the mind alone of the defendant, as where property is held in trust for him, either through conveyance, in which he is named as *cestui que trusts*, or where the trust is entirely secret and concealed; but where the defendant's property, and every interest belonging to him, is spread out in the public records, so that all necessary information can be obtained there, by search made by the complainant, the court will not compel the defendant to exhibit the same in his answers.(*k*)

A bill lies against a corporation under the act. But such a bill can only be filed by a sequestrator appointed under the provisions of that act.(*l*)

Leaving a copy of a bill of discovery and interrogatories at the dwelling-house of the defendant, in the presence of one or more of the adult members of his family, is a good service under the 15th section of the act.(*m*)

The proceedings in a *scire facias* upon the bill are substantially the same as those in a *scire facias* in foreign attachment, and therefore, where the defendant and garnishee in a bill of discovery have waived their privilege of trial by jury, by omitting to plead to the *scire facias*, and have submitted their case upon their answers to the interrogatories, the court may render a joint judgment against them both for the amount of plaintiff's debt.(*n*)

The defendant in a bill to compel discovery of effects liable to execution, is bound to answer, although ten days did not intervene between the service and return of the *scire facias*, though he is not bound to answer until ten days from the service of a copy of the bill and interrogatories. But the objection that sufficient time did not intervene, cannot be taken advantage of by demurrer to the bill. The proper course is to move to quash the process for irregularity.(*o*)

Though it is not the practice to compel a discovery of the defendant's personal property in aid of an execution at law until a *fi. fa.* has issued, and been returned *nulla bona*, yet discovery will be compelled of real estate without such previous execution, and a plaintiff is entitled to the bill of discovery, although he has made a levy on goods alleged to be of the defendant, if the sheriff has been prevented from proceeding by an allegation that the property has been transferred to another.(*p*)

The District Court has no jurisdiction under the act.(*q*)

2. *Of attachment in execution.*

The act of 1836 in this respect is as follows :—

In the case of stock, if it shall be held in another name than that of

(*i*) Perot *v.* Spicer, C. P. Phila. 1837, MS.

(*ii*) Hitchcock *v.* Long, 2 W. & S. 169.

(*j*) Bevans *v.* Turnpike, 10 Barr, 174.

(*k*) Rose *v.* Lloyd, 2 P. L. J. 321; KING, P. J. See *ante*, 77, &c.

(*l*) Bevans *v.* The Turnpike, 10 Barr, 174; see 10 Barr, 281.

(*m*) Gouldey *v.* Gillespie, 4 P. L. J. 510.

(*n*) Shaffer *v.* Watkins, 7 W. & S. 219.

(*o*) Large *v.* Bristol Transportation Co. 2 Ash. 394.

(*p*) Ibid. See *ante*, 77, &c.

(*q*) Gouldey *v.* Gillespie, 4 P. L. J. 91.

the real owner thereof, the plaintiff shall file in the office of the prothonotary of the court an affidavit stating that he verily believes such
stock to be really the property of the defendant, and shall enter into
recognizance, with two sufficient sureties, conditioned for the payment
of such damages as the court may adjudge, to the party to whom such
stock shall really belong, in case such stock should not be the property
of the defendant. § 32.(r)

Upon the filing of such affidavit and recognizance, it shall be lawful
for the prothonotary to issue process, in the nature of an attachment,
against such stock, with a clause of summons to the person in whose
name the same may be held, in the nature of a writ of *scire facias*
against garnishees in a foreign attachment, and thereupon the plaintiff
may proceed to judgment, execution, and sale of the said stock in the
manner allowed in cases of foreign attachment against personal estate.
§ 33.

The following is the form of writ used in Philadelphia County under
this section:—
City and County of Philadelphia, *ss.*
The Commonwealth of Pennsylvania to the sheriff of Philadelphia
County, greeting:
We command you, that you attach A B, late of your county, by all
and singular his goods and chattels, rights and credits, in whose hands
or possession soever the same may be found, in your bailiwick, so that
he be and appear before our judges, at Philadelphia, at our District
Court, for the City and County of Philadelphia, there to be held the
first Monday of ——— next, to answer C D; and also that, by honest
and lawful men of your bailiwick, you make known to E F, late of your
county, that he be and appear before our said court on the said first
Monday of ——— next, to show if anything they the said A B and
E F, have, or has, or know to say why a certain judgment obtained in
our said court on the ——— day of ———, by the said C D, in the sum
of ———, besides costs of suit, shall not be levied of the effects of the
said A B, in his the said E F's hands.

The like proceedings may be had against stock owned by a defendant,
and held in his own name, without the affidavit and recognizance aforesaid; and if any person shall claim to be the owner of such stock, he
may, upon filing an affidavit that the stock is really his property, and
entering into a recognizance with two sufficient sureties, conditioned for
the payment of such damages as the court may adjudge to the plaintiff,
if such stock should really belong to the defendant, the court shall admit
him to become a party upon the record, and take defence, in like manner as if he were made garnishee in the writ. § 34.(s)

(r) The basis of the foregoing section
is the act of 29th March, 1819, Pamph.
L. 217, which is confined to the case
of stock, whilst this law embraces also
debts due to the defendant and deposits
of money belonging to him. The principle upon which this extension was
proposed will be found stated in the
report of the commissioners to revise
the civil code of January 9, 1835. The
provisions appear to be fully adapted to
effect the purposes contemplated.
(s) See Serg. on Att. p. 22.

In the case of a debt due to the defendant, or of a deposit of money made by him, or of goods or chattels pawned, pledged, or demised, as aforesaid, the same may be attached and levied in satisfaction of the judgment, in the manner allowed in the case of a foreign attachment; but in such case, a clause, in the nature of a *scire facias* against a garnishée in foreign attachment, shall be inserted in such writ of attachment, requiring such debtor, depository, bailee, pawnee, or person holding by demise as aforesaid, to appear at the next term of the court, or at such other time as the court from which such process may issue shall appoint, and show cause why such judgment shall not be levied of the effects of the defendant in his hands.   § 35.

It shall be the duty of the officer charged with the execution of such writ, to serve a copy thereof, upon the defendant in such judgment, and upon every person and corporation within his proper county, named in the said writ of attachment, in the manner provided for the service of a writ of summons in a personal action.   § 36.

From and after the service of such writ, all stock belonging to the defendant in the corporation, upon which service shall be so made, and all debts, and all deposits of money, and all other effects belonging or due to defendant, by the person or corporation upon which service shall be so made, shall remain attached in the hands of such corporation or person, in the manner heretofore practised and allowed in the case of foreign attachment.   § 37.(*t*)

If judgment shall be given for the plaintiff in such attachment, it shall be lawful for him to have execution thereof as follows to wit:—

I. If the property attached be stock in a corporation, as aforesaid, the execution shall be by a writ of *fieri facias* against the original defendant, by virtue of which such stock, or so much thereof as shall be necessary to satisfy the judgment and costs may be sold by the sheriff, as in other cases.

II. If the property attached be a deposit in money, or a debt due, as aforesaid, execution shall be had in the manner allowed in the case of effects in the hands of a garnishee in a foreign attachment.   § 38.(*u*)

The subject of attachment in execution will be considered under the following heads:—

    (1). Where an attachment lies.
    (2). What may be attached.
    (3). Practice.

After which will be considered the practice in proceedings to sell stock, &c.

    (1). *Where an attachment lies.*

That portion of the act which prescribes the writ has been given

---

(*t*) See Serg. on Att. 15.
(*u*) See Serg. on Att. 26, *et seq.* The practice under this head will be considered presently, after the subject of attachment is considered.

above. Since its passage, its provisions have been extended by the act of March 20, 1845, sect. iv., which is as follows:—

So much of the act of assembly, passed 16th day of June, 1836, entitled, "An act relating to executions," as provides for the levy and recovery of stock, deposits and debts due to defendants by process of attachment and *scire facias*, is hereby extended to all cases of attachments to be issued upon judgments against corporations (other than municipal corporations); and from and after the passage of this act, all such process, which hereafter may be issued, may be proceeded into final judgment and execution, in the same manner and under the same rules and regulations as are directed against corporations, by the provisions of the act of 16th June, 1836, relating to executions;(v) and that so much of the 36th section of the act of 16th June, 1836, as requires service of the attachment on any defendant, be and the same is hereby repealed, except where the defendant is a resident of the county in which the attachment issued.

That this act shall take effect on the 1st day of June next, and so much of the existing laws as are hereby altered or supplied, be and the same are hereby repealed. § 5.

An attachment in execution, it is now well settled, is in substance, if not in form, an execution, differing from a *fi. fa.* only in that it reaches effects which the latter cannot. Hence it is subject to the rules governing executions, and cannot issue on an award until final judgment.(x)

A transcript of a justice's judgment, filed in the Common Pleas, is such a judgment of that court that a *fi. fa.* may issue on it against either personal or real property of the defendant, and consequently an attachment of execution may also be issued on it.(y)

An attachment can issue after the lapse of five years from the rendition of the original judgment, without the intervention of a *sci. fa.* to revive.(z) Where the judgment was prior to the act of 1836, it was at first thought this could not be done,(a) while it was admitted this could be cured by a revival.(b) It is now settled, however, that judgments prior to the act of 1836 stand on the same footing as judgments subsequent to that act.(c)

A prior return of "*nulla bona*" is essential to the validity of an attachment issued on a justice's transcript filed in the Common Pleas.(d)

(2.) *What may be attached.*

The act applies to debts in suit and unsatisfied judgments;(e) to a note deposited in pawn, the pawnee being made garnishee;(f) to the wages· of the apprentices of a debtor, a party with whom they were working under an agreement with the debtor, being made garnishee;(g) to money

(v) See Ridge, T. C. v. Peddie, 4 Barr, 490.

(x) Wray v. Tammany, 1 H. 394.

(y) Hitchcock v. Long, 2 W. & S. 169.

(z) Gemmil v. Butler, 4 Barr, 232; Hubner v. Chave, 5 Barr, 115; see Ogilsby v. Lee, 7 W. & S. 379.

(a) Burnham v. Justus, 2 M. 420.

(b) Hall v. Geiger, 2 M. 321.

(c) Bank v. Ralston, 7 Barr, 482.

(d) Clevenstone v. Law, 5 P. L. J. 459; BELL, J., see Moore v. Risdon, ibid. 429; Guerin v. Guest, 4 P. L. J. 471; Hitchcok v. Long, 2 W. & S. 170.

(e) Crabb v. Jones, 2 M. 130; Sweeney v. Allen, 1 Barr, 380.

(f) Rhoads v. McGonigal, 2 Barr, 39.

(g) Faunce v. Lesley, 6 Barr, 121.

in the hands of an attorney-at-law belonging to his client ;(*h*) to a claim on a loss from fire, which had been ascertained by arbitration ;(*i*) to funds in the hands of assignees under a void assignment ;(*j*) and to a debt which, though uncertain at the attachment, becomes fixed and definite at the time of answer.(*k*)

An attachment, however, does not lie upon fees due a juror ;(*l*) nor upon money in the hands of a public officer due a subordinate ;(*m*) nor upon money in a constable's hands, being the excess of proceeds of an execution ;(*n*) nor generally upon money raised by process of law in the hands of a sheriff ;(*o*) or a justice of the peace.(*p*)

The 5th sec. of the act of 15th April, 1845, provides that the wages of any laborer shall not be attached in his employer's hands. This act was intended to secure to the actual laborer what was earned by his own hands, not to protect the contracts of those who profit by the labor of others.(*q*)

Under the act of 1836, an attachment execution did not lie against a corporation. The legislature, as has been seen, have since changed the law in this respect.(*r*) Under that act, the property of an insolvent corporation could not be seized for the benefit of a particular creditor.(*s*)

A creditor will not be permitted, by means of an attachment in execution, to attach the unpaid purchase-money of land, to the prejudice of prior judgment creditors of the vendor.(*t*)

Money in hands of a treasurer of school directors cannot be attached any more than in the hands of a sheriff, prothonotary, State, or county treasurer, or other fiscal officer of the State, or of municipal bodies.(*u*)

Where the land in which a husband has a curtesy is bound as to his interest by a judgment against him, the proceeds of sale of the land are also bound, and the husband's release to the purchaser cannot divest his creditors' interest in it, which was fixed by the judgment. That interest may be attached in execution in the funds of the purchaser as garnishee. The plaintiff in such case is entitled to the possession of the fund, and to take the produce of it during his life, giving such security for the ultimate restoration of it to the wife, or her representatives, at his death, as the court may direct. It is, however, not such a life estate as comes within the sixth section of the act of 1840, authorizing a sequestrator to be appointed; that act does not extend to land already converted into money.(*v*)

Whether debts due to a defendant in the attachment, in his character of executor, he being also interested in the estate as legatee, are attachable, is a point which the court ought not to decide summarily, on a

(*h*) Riley *v.* Hirst, 2 Barr, 346.
(*i*) Boyle *v.* Franklin Ins. Co. 7 W. & S. 76.
'(*j*) Stewart *v.* McMinn, 5 W. & S. 100 ; Seal *v.* Duffy, 4 Barr, 274.
(*k*) Franklin Fire Ins. Co. *v.* West, 8 W. & S. 350.
(*l*) Simons *v.* Whartenby, 4 P. L. J. 226.
(*m*) Bulkley *v.* Eckert, 3 Barr, 368; Pierson *v.* McCormick, 2 P. L. J. 201.

(*n*) Crossen *v.* McAllister, 2 P. L. J. 199.
(*o*) Fretz *v.* Heller, 2 W. & S. 400.
(*p*) Corbyn *v.* Bollman, 4 W. & S. 342.
(*q*) Heebner *v.* Chave, 5 Barr, 115.
(*r*) Ridge, T. C. *v.* Peddle, 4 Barr, 490.
(*s*) Ibid.
(*t*) Stewart *v.* Coder, 1 J. 91.
(*u*) Bulkley *v.* Eckert, 3 Barr, 369.
(*v*) Lancaster Bank *v.* Stauffer, 10 Barr, 398.

motion to quash the attachment. The defendant has a right to appear and plead, and try the issue by jury, whether the debt was due to the estate or belonged to the executor himself.(w)

By the act of April 13, 1843, § 10,(x) all legacies given and lands devised to any person or persons, and any interest which any person or persons may have in real or personal estate of any decedent, by will or otherwise, which are subject to foreign attachment by the act of 27th July, 1842, entitled "An act to enable creditors to attach legacies and property in the hands of executors and administrators, and for other purposes," shall be subject to be attached and levied upon in satisfaction of any judgment in the same manner as debts due are made subject to execution by the 22d section of the act of 16th June, 1836, entitled "An act relating to executions." *Provided*, That the plaintiff in said judgment shall tender to the garnishee or garnishees, if he or they be executors or administrators, a bond with sufficient security, as is provided by 2d section of said act of 27th of July, 1842, and the same rights, in all respects, which the debtor may have, and no greater in any respect whatever are hereby placed within the power of the attaching creditor.

The Supreme Court having held that under this act an attachment did not lie against a distributive share, until it be ascertained, on a settlement of the administration account,(y) the legislature, on April 10, 1849, passed the following act: "The 10th section of the act of April 13, 1843, entitled 'An act to convey certain real estate, and for other purposes,' providing that all legacies given, and lands devised to any person or persons, and any interest which any person or persons may have in the real or personal estate of any decedent, by will or otherwise, which are subject to foreign attachment by the act of the 27th of July, A. D. 1842, entitled 'An act to enable creditors to attach legacies and property in the hands of executors and administrators, and for other purposes,' shall be subject to be attached and levied upon in satisfaction of any judgment, in the same manner as debts due are made subject to execution by the 22d section of the act of 16th, June, A. D. 1836, entitled "An act relative to executions," shall be deemed to authorize the issuing and service of process in the nature of attachment, at any time after the interest which any person or persons may have in the real or personal estate of any decedent, shall have accrued by reason of the death of such decedent: *Provided*, That a sale of the aforesaid interest of the defendant in the proceeding by attachment, authorized by the aforesaid 10th section of [the act of] 13th April, A. D. 1843, shall not be compelled by any process of execution, until a year shall have elapsed from the time when the interest aforesaid vested in the defendant, unless the executors or administrators of the decedent shall have sooner filed their account. In all cases when executors, administrators, or trustees of the estate of decedents shall have been made garnishees in the process, in the nature of attachment, authorized by the 10th section of the act of 13th April, A. D. 1843, entitled 'An act to convey certain real estate, and for other pur-

(w) Pleasants *v.* Cowden, 7 W. & S. 379.

(x) Pend. 463.

(y) McCreary *v.* Topper, 10 Barr, 419, BELL, J., dissenting: S. P. Bank of Chester *v.* Ralston, 7 Barr, 482.

I.—48

poses,' they shall be entitled to their costs, as well as the expenses necessarily incurred by them in attending to the proceeding in which they may have been garnishees."

In a case decided by the Supreme Court at Sunbury, in July, 1849, on an issue arising, of course, before the passage of the above act, it appears that after lands sold by an administrator, the purchase-money of which was unpaid, an administration account was settled by the administrator, upon which a balance remained for distribution. An attachment in execution was held to lie against the administrator, as garnishee upon a judgment in which a legatee was defendant; it appearing that there were no debts, and it not being disputed that there was a large sum to be distributed among the legatees.(z) The distinction between this case and Bank of Chester v. Ralston(a) has been thought to be, that in the latter there were outstanding debts, and no administration account had been settled; in the former there were no debts, and there was a balance for distribution remaining.

In a case occurring shortly afterwards, it appeared that the testator had directed certain real estate to be sold at the death of his wife, and the proceeds distributed among his children. After the lapse of more than thirty years after his death, an administration account was filed, accounting for a part of the purchase-money of the real estate, which had been sold in the interval. The amount thereby admitted to be due by the administrator, together with the proceeds of other land subsequently sold on proceedings in partition, were sufficient to pay all the record debts of the testator. It was held, that the share of one of the children in the residue of the purchase-money aforesaid, was subject to attachment-execution in the hands of the purchaser.(b)

Under the act of 1843, a legacy may be attached in execution in whosesoever hands it may be: therefore, where a testator directed certain lands to be sold after the death of his wife, and the proceeds distributed among his children, it was held, that a creditor of one of these might attach his distributive share of the purchase-money remaining due in the hands of the purchaser after such sale.(c)

An attachment in execution lies on a judgment against a husband, to bind the valuation-money of lands in which the wife was an heir, which lands, in proceedings in partition, have been accepted by other heirs; but on the sci. fa. against the garnishee, a sequestrator cannot be appointed. The wife's share is to be paid to the creditor for the husband's life, on giving security to restore it on his death to the wife or her representatives.(d)

While proceeds of an estate, and uncollected debts transferred by assignment rendered void for want of being recorded, may be attached by creditors not coming in under the assignment, as they are considered debts due to the assignor within the 35th section of the act of 16th June, 1836,(e) it is clear now that such proceeds of sales cannot be attached, where the debtor's interest has been previously levied on by the plaintiff in the attachment, and released on bond given by the assignees, which has been forfeited and paid, nor where, by a second assignment,

(z) Brady v. Grant, 1 J. 361.
(a) 7 Barr, 482.
(b) Baldy v. Brady, 3 H. 103.
(c) Ibid.

(d) Lancaster Bank v. Stouffer, 10 Barr, 398.
(e) Stewart v. McMinn, 5 W. & S. 102.

after the assignee's sale, the debtor has passed all claim prior to the attachment.(*f*) In a recent case, it appeared that a voluntary assignee, under an assignment void as to creditors, his accounts having been audited in the Common Pleas, was directed to pay over the proceeds to certain creditors. A check for a dividend having been sent to an attorney of a particular creditor, was returned by the latter. It was held that the money so returned remained liable to attachment in the hands of the voluntary assignee.(*g*)

Debts due *in præsenti*, but payable *in futuro*, may be attached ;(*h*) though it seems the District Court will refuse to enter a special judgment against the garnishee in such case.(*i*) That court, however, has always held that an overdue note may be attached in the hands of the maker for the debt of the holder of it.(*j*)

(*f*) Taylor *v.* Hulme, 4 W. & S. 407.
(*g*) Mitchell *v.* Stiles, 1 H. 306.
(*h*) Fulweiler *v.* Hughes, 5 H. 440.
(*i*) Kent *v.* Schuylkill Navigation Company, D. C. Saturday, June 19, 1852. Attachment sur judgment. *Per curiam.* It has been decided by the Supreme Court that an attachment of execution is available as a process to attach debts not due at the time it is served. The words of the act of assembly are, "debts due to the defendant," and upon the natural construction of these words this court has uniformly held that debts not due could not be attached. In this very case we refused to give a judgment on this ground, when application was formerly made for this purpose. We are bound to yield to the decision of the Supreme Court, though as yet we are uninformed as to the reasons of it. The debt, in this case, is not yet due, and will not be due until 1st Jan. 1856. In foreign attachment, a debt growing due upon bond or contract may be attached before it is due and payable, and judgment may be against the garnishee, but execution shall not issue till the time of payment. The act of assembly in regard to attachment of execution, provides how execution shall be issued against the garnishee in case of a judgment for a debt due, and evidently contemplates that, whenever the plaintiff is entitled to judgment, he shall have execution. We decline, then, entering the special judgment asked for in this case. The attachment itself gives him all that such a judgment could give him against the garnishee—a lien upon the debt and its accruing interest. We are not at present prepared to say what is the proper practice to adopt under the new aspect presented by the recent decision of the Supreme Court. All that we do at present is to refuse to enter the special judgment now prayed for. Rule dismissed.

(*j*) Wetmore *v.* Price, D. C. Saturday, April 8, 1848. Rule for a new trial. *Per curiam.* We are of opinion that a negotiable note may, after it is due, be attached in the hands of the maker for the debt of the then holder of it. An attachment is payment to the defendant, or, what is in effect the same thing, it is an appropriation of the fund made by the law exercising the power of the defendant to the attaching creditor. The case of Hughes *v.* Large, 2 Barr, 103, then, does not apply. It is there decided that a debt due to the maker from the payee cannot be set off against the indorsee of a note overdue; but it is not decided there, or anywhere else, that a direct payment made by the maker to the payee will not avail the former. We think, however, that Anthony was a competent witness, and should have been admitted. It was alleged that at the time the attachment was laid, the defendant had passed the note for value to Anthony, and he was offered as a witness to prove this. As the matter then appeared, he could not have been affected by the result of the verdict, nor could it have been given in evidence for or against him in a suit by him against the maker. If a garnishee suffers the goods of A to be condemned in his hands as the goods of B, the condemnation will not protect him against an action by A. EYRE, C.J., in Phillips *v.* Hunter, 2 H. Bl. 410. If, indeed, it had appeared either *aliundo* or by the examination of Anthony upon his *voire dire*, that he had been notified to take defence in this suit, the case would then have been different. He would then have been concluded by the result, and the verdict and judgment would have been evidence against him. But this is not to be inferred without evidence, and the mere fact that he knew of the suit, is not enough, unless he has tendered to him the right to intervene

While the attachment does not *per se* affect the negotiable character of an attached note, it seems that where a note, not yet matured, is attached, the court will grant an injunction to restrain the holder from negotiating it.(*k*)

Goods deposited by the defendant in the garnishee's store, are not liable to attachment.(*l*)

and defend in the name of the garnishee. Coates *v.* Roberts, 4 R. 100. Rule absolute.

(*k*) Kieffer *v.* Ehler, S. C. Aug. 52. Lowrie, J.—Care is to be taken that laws of general, shall not be regarded as of universal application; and this caution is required in relation to the laws for attaching debts in execution, and declaring that " all debts" so attached shall remain in the hands of the garnishee to answer the debt. In acts of assembly, as well as in common parlance, the word " all" is a general, rather than a universal term, and is to be understood in one sense or the other, according to the demands of sound reason.

It is certainly broad enough to include debts due by bills of exchange and promissory notes, and there is nothing in their nature that excludes them from its operation. But they have a legal quality that renders the hold of an attachment upon them very uncertain.

Unlike all other property, they carry their whole evidence of title on their face, and the law assures the right of him who obtains them for valuable consideration, by regular indorsement and without actual notice of any adverse claim, or of such suspicious circumstances as should lead to inquiry. To hold that an attachment prevents a subsequent *bona fide* indorser for value from acquiring a good title, would be almost a destruction of one of the essential characteristics of negotiable paper. It would be a great injury to persons in embarrassed circumstances holding such paper; for no one could buy it from them with any confidence in the title. Moreover, it would present the strange result, that the more hands such paper had passed through, and the more indorsers there were on it, the less it would be worth in the money market, for it would be subject to the more risks of attachment. Under such views it has always been held, that an attachment is unavailable against a *bona fide* holder for value of negotiable paper who obtains it after attachment, before maturity and without notice. Ludlow *v.* Bingham, 4 D. 47; Maine Ins. Co. *v.* Weeks, 7 Mass. 439; Eves *v.* Tuttle, 3 Conn. 27; Huff *v.* Mil-

ler, 7 Yerger, 42; Hindsdill *v.* Stafford, 11 Verm. 309; Little *v.* Hale, id. 482; Eunson *v.* Healy, 2 Mass. 32; Grant *v.* Shaw, 16 id. 344; Cushman *v.* Haynes, 20 Pick. 132.

The doctrine of implied notice by *lis pendens* is totally inapplicable to such cases, and is everywhere weakened in its operation, even where it is admitted to exist. In a case of bankruptcy, notice may be implied; because that refers to the general circumstances of a previous holder into which a purchaser is expected to inquire, and not to a special fact, like an attachment, which may have its origin in any magistrate's office in any county in the State.

Certainly, the negotiation of such paper by a defendant, after he has had notice of the attachment, is a fraud upon the law; and we think that the court from which the attachment issues has power to prevent this by requiring the instrument to be placed in such custody as will prevent it from being misapplied, taking care that it shall be demanded at maturity, and that proper notice be given to indorsers, if necessary, and that the money, if paid, shall stand in place of the note or bill to abide the event.

Judgment reversed, and judgment for defendant below.

(*l*) Good *v.* Abertauffer, D. C. P. Jan. 6, 1849. Motion for judgment against garnishee. *Per curiam.* This is an attachment of execution. The property in the hands of the garnishee, as appears by his answer, consists of goods. They were deposited by the defendant in the garnishee's store. They may be liable to a charge for storage, though the garnishee does not set that up. Admitting the lien to exist, they are, notwithstanding, " not goods pawned or pledged by him (defendant) as security for any debt or liability, or which have been demised, or in any manner delivered or bailed for a term." Referring back the words of the 35th section of the act of 16th June, 1836 (Purd. 446), to the 23d section, the words " pawned, pledged, or demised, as aforesaid," have this meaning. It can only mean an actual pawn or pledge for any debt or liability by defendant, not merely a lien arising

When it appears that the garnishees hold goods pawned or pledged to them by the defendant, the court, on judgment being taken against them, will award a *fi. fa.* to sell all the right, title, and interest of the defendant in the specific goods.(*m*)

A municipal corporation cannot be made garnishee.(*n*)

(3). *Practice.*

It seems that the legislature intended to make the proceedings under the act of 16th June, 1836, relating to attachment executions, substantially the same as in foreign attachment, with certain differences, such as the employment of a bill of discovery and interrogatories instead of mere interrogatories, and that the bill may be filed against the defendant in the judgment and the garnishee or person having possession of the estate, &c., and must set forth certain grounds for the complaint specified in the act.(*o*) It would seem also that the proceedings in foreign attachment on a *scire facias* against the garnishee, are to be followed in the *scire facias*, that the defendant may plead to it and take issue, and have any disputed fact tried by jury;(*p*) and that the court may render a judgment thereon, either on the verdict of the jury or otherwise, in the same manner as in foreign attachment. If so, then, by the foreign attachment act of 13th June, 1836, §§ 58, 59, if issue be taken, and a trial be had on the *scire facias*, the jury are to find

by implication of law. This, therefore, is not a case for attachment of execution. Motion refused. (See for *fi. fa.* *ante*, 717.)

(*m*) Lamb *v.* Vansciver, D. C. Dec. 22, 1849. Rule for judgment against garnishees. *Per curiam.* It appears by the answers of the garnishees, that they hold certain articles of personal property belonging to defendants as a pawn, pledge, or security for debts, advances, or liabilities. The act of assembly of 16th June, 1836, relating to executions, is not very clear in its provisions in regard to goods pawned or pledged. The 23d section provides, that "goods or chattels of the defendant in any writ of *fieri facias*, which shall have been pawned or pledged by him as security for any debt or liability, or which have been demised, or in any manner delivered or bailed for a term, shall be liable to sale upon execution as aforesaid, subject, nevertheless, to all and singular the rights and interests of the pawnee, bailee, or lessee, to the possession or otherwise, of such chattels or goods, by reason of such pledge, demise, or bailment." The 35th section, however, extends the attachment execution to "goods or chattels pawned, pledged, or demised, as aforesaid;" but in the 38th section, which sets out with professing to give the proper execution in all cases of judgment against the garnishees in the process of attachment execution, no notice whatever is taken of the case of

goods pawned, pledged, or demised. It appears to us, however, that we must construe the whole act together, so as to give effect to all its parts, and, therefore, that whenever it appears upon the answers of the garnishees filed, that they have in their possession goods or chattels, pledged, &c., we must award a writ of *fi. fa.*, under the 23d section, to sell all the right, title, and interest of the defendants in the specific goods.

Judgment against defendant for the amount admitted, and *fi. fa.* awarded as to the balance, against the goods admitted to be held by both garnishees.

(*n*) Keeley *v.* Murray, D. C. Nov. 22, 1851. *Per curiam.* We are satisfied that, upon the principle established in Buckley *v.* Eckert *et al.* (3 Barr, 368), a municipal corporation cannot be made garnishees in an attachment of execution. The situation of the defendants does not appear to us to be distinguished from that of a sheriff or prothonotary, who has money in his hands as a public officer; and it has been determined that these are not liable to the process of attachment. Great public inconvenience must follow, if these corporations are compelled to answer to the claims of creditors of all the persons with whom they have business or to whom money is payable by them.   R. A.

(*o*) See Keeler *v.* Knapp, 1 Barr, 23.

(*p*) See Pleasants *v.* Cowden, 7 W. & S. 374.

what goods or effects, if any, were in the garnishee's hands at the time of the attachment executed or afterwards, and the value thereof; and after verdict for plaintiff, he may have execution of his judgment to be levied of the goods so found, and also execution against the garnishee, as of his proper debt, if he neglect to produce the goods or pay the debt. But this is the only case in which it is required that the specific goods be levied on in the first instance, and it is after issue and verdict of a jury.

By § 57, when the judgment is rendered by the court for neglect or refusal to appear and answer interrogatories, it is against the garnishee and his estate for the amount of the plaintiff's demand. No provision is made for the case that occurs where both the defendants answer the interrogatories denying their liability, and judgment is rendered thereon by the court without any pleading to the *scire facias* or trial. But by analogy to the case provided for in section 57, and from the inference that the defendants have waived the privilege given by the 58th and 59th sections by omitting to plead, and instead of a trial submitting to the court's decision on their defence without application for a different course ; the judgment on the answers may be rendered by the 57th section against the 60th, the defendants and their estate for the amount of the plaintiff's debt. The act authorizes the joinder of the original defendant and other persons in the *scire facias*, and the judgment, of course, may be joint, especially if they do not plead at all, or do not sever in their pleas. The *fi. fa.* also should, in such case, be joint.(*q*)

The answers are primary evidence for the defendant when read to the jury, not requiring of him further proof to support them.(*r*)

A judgment against a garnishee, who is a justice of the peace, for not answering interrogatories as to the number, amount, and time of entry of judgments on his docket in favor of the defendant in the attachment, and the names of the defendants therein, is erroneous; as the interrogatories must concern the estate or effects of the defendant in his hands, or debts due by him to the defendant.(*s*) A judgment, however, was sustained for not answering interrogatories ; " that he has in his possession goods and effects of the defendant to an amount to satisfy the demand of the plaintiff, together with all legal costs and charges."(*t*)

Judgments will not be entered against garnishees on their answers, unless such answers contain a distinct admission of funds in possession, or of such facts as leave the possession of such funds a mere inference of law.(*u*)

(*q*) Shaffer *v.* Watkins, 7 W. & S. 226; *ante*, 684.

(*r*) Erskine *v.* Sangston, 7 W. 150.

(*s*) Corbyn *v.* Bollman, 4 W. & S. 342.

(*t*) Ibid.

(*u*) Mercer *v.* Whitaker, D. C. Dec. 9, 1848. Rule for judgment against garnishees. *Per curiam.* It is a rule of practice of the court, intended for the protection of garnishees against the claims of those whose funds or effects they have in hand, never to render a judgment against them upon answers filed, unless those answers contain either a distinct admission of funds in possession, or of such facts as leave the possession of such funds a mere inference of law. In this case, so far as any point has been pressed upon us, the answers of the garnishee show these facts : The defendants, in the judgment upon which the attachment of execution in this case issued, on the 19th of November, 1847, executed to the garnishee two assignments of their estate in Delaware and Maryland, for the benefit of their credi-

˙ The garnishee is not necessarily obliged to annex to his answers copies of the correspondence between him and the defendant ; and, in general, the court will relieve him from so doing.(v)

Where the defendant dies after attachment laid, but before interrogatories tendered to the garnishee, the court, upon a proper case shown,

tors. These assignments were not recorded in Philadelphia, where the assignors resided, and we may assume that they were void as to the creditors, according to Weber v. Samuel (7 Barr, 499). Yet, it is clear that they were good between the parties, and passed the legal title to the assignee (Seal v. Duffy, 4 Barr, 274). Under these assignments the garnishee has received certain assets. Before the attachment in this case was laid, however, he had incurred certain liabilities to the creditors of the defendants, under the authority of their assignments, to the amount of $6,816. This is more than sufficient to cover all the money at present in his hands. It is distinctly averred that these liabilities were incurred in execution of the assignment being in effect, as we understand it, in payment of debts of assignors, in anticipation of the receipt of funds under the assignment by the garnishee's own paper, received by the creditor in satisfaction. We are not prepared, as a point of law, to say, that the garnishee cannot protect himself by funds afterwards received. It will be a question for a jury, as we are at present advised, whether these acts of the garnishee were honestly in the execution of his trust.

As to the securities, or policies of insurance, which he recovered—the balance, after paying his advances, whatever it may be—has passed, under an assignment made by him, to James W. Harriss, on the 26th of February, 1848, before the attachment was laid, in trust for the creditors of the defendants, Adams & Co. It may be that this transfer has not cured the fault in the non-recording of the original assignment; and it may be that the garnishee could not thus relieve himself from the responsibility of the trust which he assumed. It may be that he will continue liable for the acts and precepts of the new trustee; but has not the title passed by this assignment, and is not James W. Harriss the proper garnishee, who will be entitled to collect and receive the assets? The contrary was not pressed; but it was urged that the liabilities incurred, and advances made by the garnishee, could not be considered, in law, as under and in execution of the assignment, which, we

think, as has been stated, to be a question of fact. R. D.

Fithian v. Brooks. Dec. 6, 1851. Rule for judgment against garnishees. *Per curiam.* The established practice of the court is not to give judgment against garnishees, unless upon an express admission of assets, or, at least, the admission of such facts, that the possession of assets necessarily results as a question of law. If the answers are not "full and direct," judgment may be rendered against them on that account, but that is a different proceeding, and on different grounds from that pursued here. The answers here clearly set up that the garnishees purchased of the defendants, upon an agreement, or undertaking of both parties, as to the acts of third persons, in which they were disappointed ; and that, upon discovery, the terms were modified so that the garnishees were to pay the defendant as soon as it was convenient. Now, however improbable such a story, though it may have the appearance of fraud on the creditors—though, therefore, the goods, or their proceeds, may be subject to the execution, or attachment of the creditors, it is impossible for us to say that the plaintiffs here are entitled to judgment against the garnishees as for a debt admitted to be due. R. D.

Roberts v. Steiner, D. C. Saturday, Nov. 11, 1848. Rule for judgment against garnishees. *Per curiam.* It is a settled practice with the court not to give a judgment against garnishees upon their answers, unless they contain a clear and unqualified admission of funds in hand belonging to defendant, or of facts which make the existence of such funds an inference of law. In this case, it appears that the defendants are a foreign commission-house, of whom the garnishee bought goods, and they have been notified, by a firm in England, that they will hold them responsible for the price. Surely, the garnishees do not mean to admit the funds out of their hands in the face of this notice. We will not look into the letters of the alleged claimants to see whether their claim is consistent with the facts sworn to by the garnishees, for, after all, those letters are mere evidence, not admissions *in judicio.* R. D.

(v) Duffield v. Morris, 4 P. L. J. 79.

will enter judgment against the garnishee without requiring the executors of the defendant to be made parties.(*w*)

Where the answers are indirect or evasive, the court will compel a supplemental answer, or else give judgment.(*x*)

The exhibition of interrogatories in attachment is a measure to charge, and not to discharge the garnishee. It is in the nature of a bill of discovery, and if he confess nothing, the parties are where they started. If he disclose a case for plaintiff, there is judgment on his confession at once. If he denies the facts charged, the plaintiff is no more bound by it than by a denial in an answer to a bill in chancery; the interrogatories have failed, but he may go to a jury to make out his case *aliunde*. Hence no judgment can be entered for the garnishee on his answer; the court can only refuse judgment for the plaintiff.(*y*)

The garnishee is not bound to answer interrogatories which do not concern estate or effects of the defendant in the garnishee's hands or a debt due by him. Thus, he is not bound to answer how many judgments stand on his docket as a justice in the defendant's favor;(*z*) and it would seem that, by analogy to the cases of prothonotaries and sheriffs, justices of the peace cannot be made garnishees as to moneys collected on judgment before them.(*a*)

No provision is made in the act as to the nature of the judgment against the garnishee making default in appearance after *sci. fa.* served. The only cases provided are: 1. Where he neglects or refuses to answer interrogatories; then, by the 57th section, he is to be adjudged to have in his possession goods and effects of defendant to the amount of the demand, and execution is to issue as on a judgment for his proper debt. 2.

(*w*) Etting *v.* Moses, Saturday, Sept. 28, 1852. Rule for judgment against garnishees. The award of the auditor in the Orphans' Court, which, confirmed, became the decree of that court, ascertained, conclusively, that the fund in the hands of the garnishees was due and payable to the original defendant, and precludes inquiry as to that question here.

This attachment was sued out, and served in the defendant's lifetime. It is supposed that the defendant having died pending the attachment, the proceeding must be revived by *scire facias* against his legal representatives, before judgment can be finally entered against the garnishee. The attachment is, in substance, an execution, as it was levied in the defendant's lifetime; analogy is opposed to the doctrine that the personal representative must be warned. As, in the other case, if there is equitable ground, they will be let in to take defence. Rule absolute.

(*x*) Jones *v.* Hacker, D. C. Sept. 22, 1849. Rule for judgment against garnishees. *Per curiam.* This was a rule to show cause why judgment should not be entered against garnishee for want of "full, direct, and true" answers. The answers are objected to as not being sufficiently full and direct. It appears upon the whole answer taken together, that the original defendant being indebted to the garnishee had placed in his hands certain securities as absolute payment of the debt, which were received as such, and the defendant discharged. The plaintiff asks what these securities were. This the garnishee has avoided, or refused to answer. We think the plaintiff has a right to a full and direct answer to the interrogations, so as to be informed of the true nature of the transaction between the debtor and garnishee. It may be that the garnishee is thus compelled to discover effects now exclusively his own, and in which the debtor has no interest, but they were once the property of the debtor, and to say that the garnishee is excused in such a case from answering, is to afford the means of a very convenient cover and concealment to the grossest frauds upon creditors.

Supplemental answer allowed.

(*y*) Hess *v.* Shorb, 7 Barr, 232.

(*z*) Corbyn *v.* Bollman, 4 W. & S. 343. See *ante*, 752.

(*a*) Ibid.

Where there is a verdict against the garnishee; then, by § 58, the jury find what goods are in his hands, and their value, and execution, is twofold: 1, by § 59, of the goods and effects so found in his hands, or so much as may satisfy the demand; and 2, by § 60, against him as of his proper debt, if he refuses to produce the goods and effects; and this seems to be the proper mode in judgments by default. A default to appear, is tantamount to a confession that he has the attached goods in hand.(b) The judgment to be taken under such circumstances is not to be general, but that the plaintiff have execution of so much of the debt, &c., due by the garnishee to the defendant, and attached in his hands, as may satisfy the judgment of the plaintiff, with interest and costs; and if the garnishee refuse or neglect on demand by the sheriff to pay the same, then the same to be levied of his, the garnishee's goods, lands, and person according to law, as in the case of a judgment against him for his proper debt; and that the garnishee be thereupon discharged as against the defendant of the sum so attached and levied.(c)

On the same day in which an attachment in execution was served upon the garnishees, the latter purchased a judgment against the defendant, of an amount greater than their indebtedness to him. It was held, that the burden was on the garnishees to show that the judgment was acquired by them prior to the service of the attachment, and that failing in this, the set-off was not admissible, as between the garnishees and the execution plaintiff.(d)

The garnishee is bound to make every just and legal defence which other parties interested in the fund in his hands could make, or he will be answerable to them therefor.(e) He "is bound to contest every foot of the ground; and payment before judgment against him would be no defence" to an action for the debt attached.(f)

A voluntary payment into court by the garnishee execution which is applied by the prothonotary to the payment of other debts than that of the plaintiff, will not discharge the former.(g)

Where the amount of a judgment has been attached in the hands of defendant by a creditor of the plaintiff, proceedings in the original action will be stayed.(h)

(b) Layman v. Beam, 6 Wh. 185.
(c) Layman v. Beam, 6 Wh. 181.
(d) Pennell v. Grubb, 1 H. 552.
(e) Baldy v. Brady, 3 H. 103. COULTER, J.
(f) Stoner v. Com. 4 H. 392.
(g) Baldy v. Beady, supra.
(h) Paxson v. Sanderson, D. C. C. P. 8 Leg. Int. 54. Daly v. Derringer, Monday, March 1, 1852. Why proceedings should not be stayed. The ground upon which this application is based is, that since the judgment, the debt has been attached in the hands of the defendant by a judgment creditor of the plaintiff. It is plausible to say that in such case the money may be made upon the execution, and paid into court, but there would be found to be practical difficulties in the way of such proceeding; with-

out adverting to other difficulties, a voluntary payment by the defendant to the sheriff, or into court, would be in effect the same as a payment to the plaintiff. The attachment is no lien upon any particular money or property. It is clear that the defendant is entitled to an audita querela, and it is expedient to give relief summarily on motion, rather than to put the parties to that writ. If the money were paid into court, it would in general, be necessary to refer it to an auditor, and the delay and expense would be much greater than for the defendant to appear, answer, and submit to a judgment on the attachment; the plaintiff being a party to that proceeding, can intervene to expedite it. Should there be questions arising out of assignments, &c., so much the more reason for leaving

Satisfaction on attachment in execution, as in all other cases, is effected only by a levy on goods sufficient to pay the debt, or by actual payment; and a judgment by an attachment creditor against the garnishee is no satisfaction *per se* of the judgment against the original debtor.(*i*) The plaintiff can only have one satisfaction, but he is entitled to all process necessary to obtain that; hence, he may take out an attachment of execution pending a *fi. fa.*, if no levy has been made on it.(*j*) But where, while an attachment is pending, the plaintiff issues a *fi. fa.*, the defendant may have either the attachment or the *fi. fa.* set aside at his election.(*k*)

The law exempting property to the value of $300, does not apply to cases of attachment execution.(*l*)

It is not necessary to suggest in the writ the nature of the property to be attached; the act prescribes the writ in general terms.(*m*)

The clause of *scire facias* should not embrace the defendant's name, but merely the garnishee's; though if added it is not error, but merely surplusage.(*n*)

The officer attaching ought to set out specifically in his return that he attached the note or debt.(*o*)

Where third parties claim a fund which had been attached under an attachment in execution, as the property of the defendant, the garnishees may be treated as stakeholders, and the claimants admitted to interplead.(*p*)

---

such questions to be decided in the regular course, rather than upon a question of distribution, in which it would be very doubtful what the effect would be upon the several claims. Rule absolute.

(*i*) Baldwin's Executors, 4 Barr, 248.

(*j*) Tams *v.* Wardle, 5 W. & S. 221. See Wray *v.* Tammany, 1 H. 379.

(*k*) Myers *v.* Riot, D. C. March 25, 1848. Why the execution should not be set aside. *Per curiam.* An attachment of execution issued upon this judgment, April 1, 1847. It was duly served, and Anthony G. Querville garnisheed. Interrogatories were exhibited and answers filed. A rule to plead was entered, and upon the 3d July, 1847, *nulla bona* was pleaded and the cause at issue. After this, upon the 29th Jan., 1848, an alias *fi. fa.* was issued, upon which an inquisition has been held; property condemned, and a *vend. exp.* sued out.

These last proceedings certainly have placed it in the power of the defendant to elect which writ he would have set aside, the *fi. fa.* or the attachment. Though he might have purchased both, he could not use both, and having procured one of them to be served, he must first dispose of that before he can proceed to execute the other. (Miller *v.* Parnell, 6 Taunt. 370; Davies *v.* Scott, 2 M. 52; Tams *v.* Wardle, 5 W. & S. 222.) The defendant has accordingly asked us to set aside the alias *fi. fa.* and the proceedings based thereon; which is accordingly done. Rule absolute.

(*l*) Vezia *v.* Viench, D. C. C. P. 8 Leg. Int. 54.

(*m*) Layman *v.* Beam, 6 Wh. 184.

(*n*) Ibid.

(*o*) Rhoads *v.* McGonigal, 2 Barr, 39.

(*p*) Brady *v.* Grant, 1 J. 361; Snyder *v.* Wetherly, D. C. March 1, 1852. Rule for interpleader. This is a case of attachment execution. The defendant being garnished by a creditor of the plaintiff with an attachment execution, and this suit appearing to have been marked to the use of a third person, asks to pay the money into court under the interpleader act, and that the attachment creditor and the assignee may interplead. We are of opinion that this is not a case within the provisions of the interpleader act. An attachment execution is not a suit in the sense of that act. The act certainly contemplates a claim of property, a right thereto claimed by, or supposed to belong to, some other person not party to the suit. There might be a great many attachment executions in precisely the same right, against the same defendant in suit; they must all be brought in as parties. This is one of the many practical inconveniences which might be mentioned. Rule discharged.

The issue on *nulla bona* is, whether the garnishee had effects in his hands or not, and the verdict should respond to it. But if it does not, the court may mould it into shape after it is rendered.(*q*)

Under the plea of *nulla bona*, the jury should be sworn as to the garnishee alone, for it is clear that, under such a state of facts, the proceedings against the garnishee and defendant are distinct and hostile; and though there be a plea of payment by the defendant, the disposal of the issue is not a prerequisite to the trial of that between the plaintiff and garnishee.(*s*)

The garnishee, says GIBSON, C. J., may plead anything against the plaintiff in the *scire facias* that he can plead against his own original creditor, except that the debt is not presently demandable; and even that may be pleaded by him in stay of execution. In no other respects does the attaching creditor stand on other ground than that of the creditor for whom he is substituted. The judgment in the attachment suit against the defendant establishes no more than the existence of the debt claimed by the attaching creditor from his immediate creditor by assignment when the attachment was laid; or in case of foreign attachment, that the attachment was dissolved by his death before final judgment.(*t*)

The attachment process is only auxiliary to the old mode of execution, to aid in the enforcement, and not to extinguish the effect of judgment. Hence, an attachment laid cannot be pleaded in abatement by the defendant until satisfaction by payment, or a levy on goods sufficient to pay the debt. The garnishee may plead it in abatement when sued on the debt attached,(*u*) or it may be pleaded in bar by the garnishee to an action on the original debt;(*v*) and the court, it seems, under proper circumstances, will compel the plaintiff to proceed in the attachment.(*w*)

The garnishee is not entitled to a stay of execution on entering secu-

---

(*q*) Flanagin *v.* Wetherell, 5 Wh. 286.

(*s*) McCormack *v.* Hancock, 2 Barr, 310.

(*t*) Farmers' and Mechanics' Bank *v.* Little, 8 W. & S. 206,

(*u*) Fitzsimmons's App. 4 Barr, 248; Wray *v.* Tammany, 1 H. 394.

(*v*) Maynard *v.* Nekervis, 9 Barr, 81.

(*w*) Pretz *v.* Northampton Bank; Anspack *v.* Northampton Bank, D. C. Dec. 4, 1849. Why plaintiff should not proceed, or the attachment be dissolved. *Per curiam.* These are cases of attachment of execution which have been pending many years. One of the garnishees being sued, not by the defendant in the attachment, but by a third person claiming the debt attached adversely in the Supreme Court, he put in an affidavit of defence, alleging, it is said, the pendency of this attachment; whereupon that court gave judgment, but stayed the execution. If the affidavit in that case contained an allegation that the note in suit was claimed to be the property of another, as whose it had been attached, this court would have considered the affidavit sufficient, and either sent the case to a jury to determine the question to whom the note or debt belonged, or, upon the money being brought into court, awarded an interpleader between the claimants. It has been held, in the Supreme Court, that an attachment execution is pleadable in bar. Maynard *v.* Nekervis, 9 Barr, 81. And if a debtor is threatened with contradictory claims to the same thing, whether attempted to be enforced by suit or attachment, he is surely entitled to relief. It is not, however, our intention to examine whether the course adopted in the Supreme Court, or that which we have indicated, is the most consonant to sound practice. All that we decide at present is against the application now made, on the ground that sufficient evidence of the interest of the party now applying has not been laid before us. R. D.

rity, under the 3d and 4th sections of the act of 16th June, 1836, relating to executions.(x)

As early as 1842, the Supreme Court decided that under the act the defendant must be served with a copy of the attachment execution, as in cases of summons, and that a return of *non est inventus* as to him would not sustain a judgment against the garnishee;(y) and in 1844, SERJEANT, J., said that as a copy of the attachment is to be served on the defendant as well as on the garnishee, as in personal actions, to which he appeared and pleaded as on a *scire facias*, a revival was unnecessary previous to issuing an attachment execution, such a revival being only required for ordinary executions, where there is no summons of the defendant, nor day in court given.(z)

Shortly afterwards, it was ruled that although the 36th section of the act renders it necessary to serve the defendant with a copy of the writ, if he can be found, yet it is not necessary or proper that the jury in the issue against the garnishees should be sworn as to him. His interest is adverse to the plaintiff's, and also to the garnishees, and he may be a witness for the latter.(a)

To obviate the difficulties of obtaining service, the following legislation was had :—

Act of 29th April, 1844, § 1.(b)   In proceedings under the thirty-fifth and thirty-sixth sections of the act, entitled "An act relating to executions," passed the 16th day of June, Anno Domini one thousand eight hundred and thirty-six, the same shall be considered valid, except in cases where the service thereof has already been set aside by the court, without a service thereof on the defendant in the judgment, in case he resides, or did reside, when the process issued out of the county, or in case such service cannot be, or could not have been made upon such defendant by the officer within his bailiwick : *Provided*, That when service in any process, as aforesaid, heretofore issued, has been made upon the defendant or defendants, the lien of said process shall be prior to all other process, where service has not been made upon the defendant or defendants, and which service is rendered valid by this act.

Act of 15th March, 1847; § 3.(c)   *Whereas*, by the thirty-sixth section of the act, entitled "An act relating to executions," passed the 16th day of June, Anno Domini 1836, it is made the duty of the officer charged with the execution of a writ to attach debts in the hands of a garnishee, to serve a copy of said writ upon the defendant against whom the proceeding is had : *And whereas*, the Supreme Court decided, that without the said service being made upon the original defendant, the attachment was invalid and of no effect : *And whereas*, the general assembly of this commonwealth, by an act passed the 29th day of April, 1844, declared that said proceedings in attachments should be valid without said service in certain cases : *And whereas*, said last mentioned act may operate great injustice in cases where persons, relying

(x) Woolston v. Adler, D. C. C. P. 9 Leg. Int. 2.

(y) Corbyn v. Bollman, 4 W. & S. 343.

(z) Ogilsby v. Lee, 7 W. & S. 444.

(a) McCormac v. Hancock, 2 Barr, 310.

(b) Pamph. L. 512.

(c) Pamph. L. 397.

upon the law as it stood before the passage of said act, have paid the moneys due to the defendant in the attachment, or in cases where the property or moneys attached may have been *bona fide* assigned or transferred to third persons ; for remedy of which,

Be it enacted, That all cases of proceedings to attach debts, rights, credits, or property of any description had prior to the passage of said act of 29th April, 1844, where the writ was not served on the original defendant, and where, before the passage of said act, the garnishee had paid to the original defendant the moneys due, or had returned to him the goods, rights, and credits in his possession, as well as where *bona fide* assignments had been made to third persons, without notice of the original attachment, in all such cases it is hereby declared that said attachments, so executed, as aforesaid, shall not be held valid; anything in said act of 29th day of April, Anno Domini 1844, to the contrary notwithstanding: *Provided*, That this act shall only apply to proceedings now pending where final judgments have not been rendered.(*d*)

The court will not go into evidence to prove the falsity of the return of *nihil* against the defendant, unless where the defendant comes and shows a defence on the merits.(*e*) § 4.

Where a debt in suit is attached, the person who acquires title to it may prosecute it to execution by marking the action to his use.(*f*) The attachment carries with it, also, the right to use all the securities, incidents, or guarantees of the debt.(*g*)

(*d*) See, also, act of March 2, 1845.

(*e*) Murphey *v.* Burke, D. C. Saturday, March 30, 1850. Why attachment execution should not be set aside. *Per curiam.* This attachment was issued Nov, 10, 1849, and on the same day was served on the garnishee. On Nov. 12, 1849, the defendant died. As to him, the sheriff returned *nihil habet.* We have recently had occasion to examine the question of the form of the sheriff's return. The court will not go into oral evidence to prove its falsity, unless, indeed, in a single case, where a defendant comes in, and, showing a defence on the merits, asks to be let in. Now, here the only question is the true meaning of *nihil habet.* Does it mean "that service cannot be, or could not have been, made upon such defendant by the officer within his bailiwick ?" We think it is equivalent to that, and that it is not necessary that the sheriff should, in his return, specially negative the fact of residence. R. D.

Bencke *v.* Frick, D. C. Saturday, June 10, 1848. Why the attachment should not be set aside. *Per curiam.* In this case, an attachment of execution was issued, to which the sheriff returned as to the defendant, *nihil habet.* The garnishee appeared, and, upon his answers, a judgment in favor of the plaintiff was duly rendered. This is a motion by the defendant to set aside the attachment on the ground that there was no service upon him, and that, in point of fact, at the time the writ issued and judgment was entered, he was resident of the County of Philadelphia, being an inmate of the Blockley almshouse. Much ingenuity has been displayed on the point whether the defendant had a legal residence within the county. We do not deem it necessary to consider that question. The sheriff's return is conclusive that defendant is not a resident. It is true we are in the practice, in the exercise of a legal discretion, of relieving parties from the consequences of a false return, where they are really injured. Thus, in the common case of a summons returned " served," and a judgment by default, upon proof that the defendant in fact had no notice, made timely application for relief, and has a defence, we invariably open the judgment, and let the defendant into a defence. Here, it is not alleged that the defendant has any defence; no injury has been done; a portion of his property, in the hands of his garnishee, will be applied in discharge of a just debt. There is nothing, therefore, in the case, which calls for the exercise of our discretionary powers, and the proceedings on their face are regular. Rule dismissed.

(*f*) Sweeny *v.* Allen, 1 Barr, 380.

(*g*) Baldwin's Estate, 4 Barr, 248 ; see Fox *v.* Foster, 4 Barr, 119.

Where an attachment is laid upon a debt, it operates to restrain the garnishee from paying over the money, either to his individual creditor, or to the attaching creditor, until the attachment is disposed of, and then only according to the result of such disposal.(h)

How far the negotiation of a note may be restrained has been already considered.(hh)

The court will not grant a rule on application of the defendant requiring the garnishee to plead.(i)

It is clear that the plaintiff may, at any time, withdraw his attachment and issue a fresh one.(j)

It is error in the court to quash an attachment in execution issued on a judgment recovered more than five years before by the plaintiff's testatrix, and which was served on the garnishee on the 27th of March, 1845, and returned *nihil* as to the defendant in the judgment on which it issued.(k)

Where a defendant has entered an appearance *de bene esse* to an attachment in execution, and moved to open the original judgment, he cannot complain of want of notice, for without an appearance he could not have been heard on his motion.(l)

The practice of opening judgments by default when the defendant comes in promptly, makes excuse for his default, and shows a good defence, is extended with peculiar liberality to garnishees.(m)

(h) Ege v. Koontz, 3 Barr, 109.

(hh) See *ante*, 756.

(i) Wood v. Miller, Sept. 1, 1851. Why garnishee should not plead. *Per curiam.* This is an application by the defendant in the attachment execution calling upon the garnishee to plead. It is certainly a novelty in practice, but that would not be an insuperable objection to it if the ends of justice could not be otherwise attained. We see, however, no difficulty in the way of the defendant prosecuting his claim against the garnishee. Should this attachment be pleaded in bar, he can raise any question which may be raised on the attachment, particularly as it will be an answer to show that the claim was not subject to the attachment. It is true the attaching creditor, perhaps, would not be bound by that judgment, but that is of no consequence to the defendant, though it is to the garnishee. It would seem, therefore, to be the interest of the garnishee to have the attachment expedited and brought to a decision; because in that both his creditor and the plaintiff are parties, and all would be concluded by the result. That is a matter, however, for his consideration exclusively. R. D.

(j) Tradesman's Bank v. Nelson, D. C. Oct. 4, 1851. Why attachment should not be dissolved. *Per curiam.* We see nothing to hinder a plaintiff from withdrawing or abandoning an attachment of execution and issuing another. It is

not like the discontinuance of an action, but may be assimilated to the withdrawal of a levy, or the stay of proceedings upon a *fi. fa.*, which, certainly, was never considered to interfere with his right to take out another execution. R.D.

(k) Gemmil v. Butler, 4 Barr, 232.

(l) Skidmore v. Bradford, 4 Barr, 296.

(m) Carlin v. Cavenaugh, D. C. Saturday, March 18, 1848. Why execution should not be set aside, judgment opened, and garnishee let into a defence. *Per curiam.* This was an attachment of execution, which, upon the 24th Dec. 1847, was served on the Franklin Fire Ins. Co. No appearance was entered, and upon the 28th Feb. 1848, a judgment was rendered against the garnishee for want of appearance. The affidavit shows a defence by the garnishees, and the application by them to open the judgment is in time. It is barely possible that the plaintiff, by waiving interrogatories, could have had a trial at Dec. term; but it is not the ordinary course. Besides, the court will exercise more liberality in favor of a garnishee (who is a stranger, and involved in a litigation between the defendant and his creditors, without any default on his part) than of an original party. Rule absolute.

Small v. Hurlbut, defendant—Todd, garnishee, March 10, 1849. Why judgment should not be opened. *Per curiam.* This was an attachment of execution, and judgment by default was entered

An office rule may be entered upon the garnishee to answer on twenty days' notice, conformably to the 41st rule of court relating to foreign attachments.(*n*)

Where bank stock owned by a defendant, but held in another's name, is levied on by attachment in execution, the proceeding must be brought in the county where the garnishee resides.(*o*)

Where a plaintiff in attachment in execution, who has filed interroga_tories, and obtained answers, is not content to abide by the answers, but compels the garnishee to plead, and then suffers a nonsuit, the gar_nishee is entitled to his costs.(*p*)

It seems, however, that the plaintiff would recover his costs, if he proved more in the hands of the garnishee than was admitted in his answers.(*q*) But a garnishee who suffers judgment to go against him is not liable for costs, because he has done nothing but pursue the course pointed out by the law. But if he pleads a false plea, or if he falsely deny that he has goods in his hands, he is responsible for costs.(*r*)

---

against the garnishee for want of appearance. It is the practice of the court, in all cases of judgment by default, to open them where the defendant comes in promptly, makes some excuse for his default, and shows a good defence. The court is even more liberal in regard to garnishees than other defendants; for they are strangers to the controversy, and made parties to a lawsuit, from the mere fact that they happen to have, or the plaintiff supposes they have, money which belongs to the defendant, and which, if they have, they may be ready and willing to pay on demand. Here the garnishee says, he knew neither of the parties, had no knowledge of defendant, and, of course, no knowledge of any money belonging to him in his hand. In point of fact, the allegation is, that he is the maker of a promissory note of which the defendant is the holder, which might very well be without garnishee knowing it. The excuse for not appearing is indeed a very slight one—perhaps badly expressed, viz., that it was more from inadvertence, than any other cause, that he did not appear. But we are never very strict in these cases; the neglect or inadvertence of counsel has, time and again, been admitted as an excuse, and we see not why the same privilege should not be allowed to the party, where, as here, he is not sued for a debt or tort of his own, but dragged into a controversy between other persons. R. A.

Wray *v.* Winner, Saturday, March 13, 1852. Rule to set aside judgment and *fi. fa.* The court has always dealt with liberality towards garnishees against whom a judgment by default may be

entered. The garnishee has sworn.to a defence, and it is plain upon the depositions that his appearance was not entered in due time, owing to a mistake by the person employed by him to enter his appearance. Rule absolute.

(*n*) Wiener *v.* Davis, D. C. C. C. P. 6 P. L. J. 567.

(*o*) Cowden *v.* West Branch Bank, 7 W. & S. 432.

(*p*) Keeler *v.* Knapp, 1 Barr, 213.

(*q*) Ibid.

(*r*) Fogle *v.* Coyle. D. C. March 29, 1851. Why plaintiff should not take the money out of court. *Per curiam*. This was an attachment of execution. Two defendants were garnisheed, as to one of whom on the trial, the plaintiff was nonsuited, as to the other obtained a verdict. The one against whom the verdict was obtained has paid the money into court, and the garnishee as to whom the nonsuit was entered now opposes this rule, and asks that we should retain enough to pay his costs. But these are separate issues, and we cannot see upon what principle there can be any lien on this money. As well might a defendant, in an entirely different suit, come in and ask to have his costs, due to him by the plaintiff, paid out of it. Again, the defendant who has paid the money in, opposes the rule, and asks that we should impose upon the plaintiff, as a term or condition, that we should enter satisfaction. In other words, he takes the position that he is not liable for costs. The law is very well settled to the contrary. If the garnishee suffers judgment to go against him, in that case he is not liable to costs, because he has done nothing but pursue the path pointed out by the

3. *Proceedings to sell stock, &c.*

That portion of the act of 1836, relating to deposits and debts, has been already given.(*rr*) The twenty-second section provides, that the stock owned by any defendant in any body corporate, also deposits of money in any bank, or with any person or body corporate or politic, belonging to him, and debts due to him, shall be liable to execution like other chattels, subject, however, to all lawful claims thereon, of such body corporate or person.

The proceedings in the nature of attachment against stock or other effects held for the defendant, have been just noticed.

By the provisions of the act of 29th March, 1819,(*s*) stocks are liable to execution only for the debts of the *real* owners thereof. But when held in the name of *another*, process in the nature of a foreign attachment must first issue against the stock, and the person in whose name it is held be summoned as garnishee. Hence, although stock has not been transferred on the books pursuant to the bank rules, after a sale, it cannot be taken in execution, but the creditor must resort to his process of attachment. The rule which obliges exclusive possession of chattels to be taken by the buyer to secure them against execution as against the vendor, does not apply to transfers of stock.(*t*)

Where stock, belonging to defendant, is held in another name, the act of assembly is express, that there shall be a clause of summons to the person in whose name it is held, in the nature of a *fi. fa.* against garnishees in a foreign attachment. Such person must, therefore, be made garnishee, and the suit is properly brought in the county where he lives.(*u*)

The second section of the act of 29th March, 1819, authorizing stock held in corporations by individuals, in their own names, to be taken in execution, and sold in the same manner as goods and chattels, subject to any debt due by the holder to the corporation, is not repealed by the act of 16th June, 1836, relating to executions.(*v*) This section, it was ruled by Judge WOODWARD, applies only to stock held in the name of the real owner.(*w*)

SECTION IV.

OF THE WRIT OF FIERI FACIAS, AND THE PROCEEDINGS UNDER IT AS REGARDS LANDS AND TENEMENTS; AND HEREIN OF THE WRIT OF LIBERARI FACIAS.

1. *What interest in lands may be levied on.*

When sufficient personal property cannot be found by the officer on the writs just mentioned, the defendant's lands, tenements, and hereditaments, which, with certain modifications in this State, are considered

---

law. But if he pleads a false plea, if he falsely denies that he has any effects in his hands, or there are effects exceeding those he admits, he is responsible for costs. Keeler *v.* Knapp, 1 Barr, 213, and cases there cited. R. A.

(*rr*) *Ante,* 750.

(*s*) 7 Sm. Laws, 217.
(*t*) Com. *v.* Watmough, 6 Wh. 138.
(*u*) Cowden *v.* West Br. Bank, 7 W. & S. 433.
(*v*) Lex *v.* Potters, 4 Il. 295.
(*w*) Ibid.

as chattels for payment of debts,(x) are, by the act of June 16, 1836,(y) liable to be seized and sold upon judgment and execution. At common law, an equitable estate is not bound by a judgment, or subject to an execution, though the creditors may have relief in chancery. We have no Court of Chancery, and have, therefore, from necessity, established it as a principle, that both judgments and executions have an immediate operation on equitable estates. Upon this principle, therefore, it has been determined that the judgment creditors of a vendee of land, who has paid part of the purchase-money and has possession of the land, but has received no deed, may sell the equitable title of such vendee under execution, and that they are entitled to the proceeds of sale in prefer- ence to the vendor.(z)

How far a judgment binds real estate it would be out of place here to consider.(a) To what extent interest in realty may be sold as person- alty, has been examined in a previous section.(b) It remains now merely to give a general sketch of the real interests which may be taken in executions in a Pennsylvania court.

The words of the act of 1705(c) embrace all possible titles, contin- gent or otherwise, where there is a real interest, such as the interest of a tenant by the *curtesy initiate* of his wife's land,(d) or a vested re- mainder in tail, both which may be taken in execution;(e) or a rent- charge, or any other legal or equitable interest in lands;(f) but not such an interest as that of an heir apparent;(g) nor the interest of a mortgagee in lands.(h)

A judgment binds the legal estate of a vendor in lands, after the exe- cution of an article of agreement, but before the execution of a deed; and on a sale under such judgment, the sheriff's vendee stands precisely in the place of the original vendor, and is entitled to the unpaid pur- chase-money; payment of which he may enforce by ejectment against the terre-tenant.(i) Judgments against vendor and vendee, respectively, by their different creditors, bind the right of each in the land whether legal or equitable.(j)

A devise to grandchildren, "provided" that their father "have the privilege of living on the place with his children during his life," gives but a license, not liable to judgment and execution.(k)

Lands of deceased persons are also considered as assets for the pay- ment of debts, and although they do not actually go into the hands of the executor or administrator as assets in the ordinary way, yet the former practice was that they might be taken and sold under execution for payment of debts on a judgment against the executor or admi- nistrator, for it was thought unnecessary, as well as unusual, to bring

---

(x) Andrew's Lessee v. Fleming, 2 D. 94; Cowden v. Brady, 8 S. & R. 508; Himes v. Jacobs, 1 Pa. R. 158.
(y) Pamph. L. 769, § 43.
(z) Auwerter v. Mathiott, 9 S. & R. 397; and see, particularly, vol. i. 66–67.
(a) See Wh. Dig. "Judgment."
(b) See *ante*, 715.
(c) 1 Sm. Laws, 57.
(d) Burd v. Lessee of Dansdale, 2 Bin. 91.
(e) Lessee of Humphreys v. Hum-

phreys, 1 Y. 429; 2 id. 24; Fuller v. McCall, 2 D. 223.
(f) Shaupe v. Shaupe, 12 S. & R. 12; 1 R. 162, 329.
(g) Lessee of Humphreys v. Hum- phreys, 1 Y. 429.
(h) Rickard v. Madeira, 1 R. 325.
(i) Allen v. Reesor, 16 S. & R. 10.
(j) Ib. 425.
(k) Calhoun v. Jester, 1 J. 474.

the action against the heir;(*l*) and GIBSON, J., took an early opportunity to lament the consequences of a procedure where the representative only can be sued, and after judgment the lands may be levied
upon in the hands of the heir.(*ll*)   Lands could be seized on a judgment
against the executor, who need do no more than discharge himself of
eventual liability in respect to the personal assets; and it became common to pray judgment of the land after the executor had discharged
himself on a *plene administravit.*(*m*)   Lands could, therefore, be taken
in execution for debt in the hands of a purchaser from the heir or devisee;
and as to lands thus taken in execution after the death of the debtor, the
widow was barred of her dower under our acts of assembly.(*n*) Since these
decisions, however, the act of February 24, 1834, § 34,(*o*) directed, that
in all actions against executors or administrators of a decedent who shall
have left real estate, where the plaintiff intends to charge such real estate
with the payment of his debt, the widow and heirs, or devisees, and the
guardians of such as are minors, shall be made parties thereto; and in
case such widow and heirs, or devisees, and their guardians, reside out
of the county, it shall be competent for the court to direct notice of the
writ issued therein, to be served by publication or otherwise, as such
court may determine by rule of court; and if notice of such writ shall
not be served on such widow and heirs, or devisees, and their guardians,
the judgment obtained in such action shall not be levied or paid out of
the real estate of such widow, heirs, or devisees, as shall not have been
served with notice of such writ.(*p*)

What is the proper practice for the purpose of thus charging land
with the decedent's debts will be considered in the next volume.

By the third section of the act of March, 1817,(*q*) re-enacted by the
act of June, 1836, § 72, before mentioned, the lands and tenements of
any corporation are also made liable to executions in default of personal
property.

As has been seen, all possible contingent interests in land, whether
legal or equitable, are the subject of levy;(*r*) as, for instance, an executory devise;(*s*) tenancy by the curtesy;(*t*) and a leasehold interest.(*u*)
Nor does it matter that the land is in the possession of a stranger, even
holding under an adverse title;(*v*) and therefore, land in the hands of
a voluntary assignee may be sold for the assignor's debts, the question
of title subsequently arising between the sheriff's vendee and the
assignee.(*w*) But by a doctrine applied with great liberality in this
State, a testator or grantor may so settle real estate as to secure it to
the object of his bounty free from execution.   In the first case in
which this question arose, a testator directed his executors to purchase
a tract of land, to be conveyed to them in trust for his son, who was to
have the rents, issues, and profits thereof; but the same not to be
liable for any debts contracted, or which may be contracted, by him;

(*l*) See Guier *v.* Kelly, 2 Bin. 298;
Cowden *v.* Brady, 8 S. & R. 508, 457.
(*ll*) Fritz *v.* Evans, 13 S. & R. 14.
(*m*) Himes *v.* Jacobs, 1 Pa. R. 158.
(*n*) Lyle *v.* Forenan, 1 D. 483–4.
(*o*) Pamph. L. 80.
(*p*) Nass *v.* Vanswearingen, 7 S.&R. 195.
(*q*) 6 Re. Laws, 439.

(*r*) Rickert *v.* Madeira, 1 R. 329; De
Haas *v.* Bunn, 2 Barr, 337.
(*s*) De Haas *v.* Bunn, 2 Barr, 337.
(*t*) Burd *v.* Dansdale, 2 Bin. 80; see
post, 772.
(*u*) Dalzell *v.* Lynch, 4 W. & S. 255.
(*v*) Jarrett *v.* Tomlinson, 3 W. & S. 114.
(*w*) Neal *v.* Bank, 1 J. 18.

and at his death, the land to vest in the heirs of his body in fee ; and if he should die without heirs of his body, then the land to vest in the right heirs of the testator ; and the executors purchased land, which was settled according to the trusts of the will. It was held, that the son had not such an interest in the land as could be taken in execution, and sold for his debts.(x) And so in a subsequent case, a testator devised certain lots of ground to his son in fee, and in the last clause of the will gave the same to trustees in fee, in trust, during the son's natural life, to pay the rents arising therefrom to the son or his appointees, and to transfer the same at the son's death to his appointees by will, or, in default of such appointment, to his heirs under the intestate act, with power to sell and reinvest the proceeds, or to convey to the son, provided he should be relieved from embarrassment ; it was held, that the son had no estate in the land liable to execution under a *fi. fa.*(y)

We have seen before that lands purchased after the judgment, and aliened *bona fide* previously to the execution, are not, however, included in the property mentioned in the act, and that they are not liable to be levied upon under this process. But if, after acquired lands are found in the hands of the debtor, unaliened at the delivery of the execution to the sheriff, they are bound by the execution, and may be sold under it.(yy) If the defendant aliens his land after judgment, but before execution, the plaintiff may, nevertheless, proceed against it in the hands of the alienee, without resorting to a *scire facias* against the terre-tenants ; neither the act of 1705, nor the practice which has obtained under it, demands such process.(z)

2. *How levy is to be made.*

The forty-third section of the act of June 16, 1836, above quoted, directs, "that if sufficient personal estate cannot be found by the officer, he shall proceed to levy upon the defendant's real estate, or such part thereof as he may deem sufficient to pay the sum to be levied, as aforesaid, but not less than a whole tract shall be levied on." The first step, therefore, towards the execution of this writ is the levy, to constitute which no actual entry upon or seizure of the lands and tenements need be made by the sheriff, who does not in the case of land, as he does in the case of chattels, take the thing levied out of the defendant's possession.(zz) The act is silent as to the manner of its performance ; and gives no directions as to notice to the defendant. The return of the levy would seem to be sufficient notice ; but by the forty-sixth section of the act of 1836, the defendant is entitled to be notified of the subsequent inquisition, and if there be no notice in fact, either of the levy or the inquest, the proceedings cannot be supported.(a) Generally, the levy controls all the subsequent proceedings : therefore, if a levy be on a rent-charge, and the *venditioni exponas* command the sheriff to sell it, but he advertises the *lot* on which it is charged, and makes a deed to the purchaser, purporting to convey the lot, and no application be made

(x) Fisher *v.* Taylor, 2 R. 33, Todd, J., dissenting ; see Eyrick *v.* Hetrick, 1 H. 491 ; and see also Ashurst *v.* Given, 5 W. & S. 323, which were cases where the debts were prior to the deed.

(y) Vaux *v.* Parke, 7 W. & S. 19 ; see Norris *v.* Johnston, 5 Barr, 289.

(yy) 3 Griffith's L. R. 250.

(z) Young *v.* Taylor, 2 Bin. 228.

(zz) Cowden *v.* Brady, 8 S. & R. 509.

(a) Heydrick *v.* Eaton, 2 Bin. 217 ; *vide post,* 777.

to set aside the sale at the proper time, the rent-charge passes to the purchaser.(b) A difference between the sheriff's deed and the levy *venditioni exponas* and conditions of sale, in stating the number of acres in a tract sold by him, is unimportant.(c)

It is necessary, when it is intended to levy on real estate, to furnish the sheriff with a description of the property by metes and bounds, as set forth in the defendant's title-papers on record, and to attend before the jury of inquiry with a statement and evidence of the nature and amount of the incumbrances which may exist upon it in the shape of mortgages, judgments, taxes, ground-rents, &c., in order to effect a condemnation.

In levies on real estate, more laxity of description is allowed than in deeds, because the title-papers are not always accessible to the plaintiff. It is enough if the levy shows what was intended to be levied on ; and where doubtful expressions are used, the construction should be favorable to the recovery of the debt by the plaintiff.(d)

A levy ought not to be construed beyond the natural meaning of its words where there is nothing else to explain them. The description of real estate in a levy is usually furnished by the plaintiff, who may embrace in it whatever he chooses ; and if he use limited and restrained language, the purchaser claiming under the plaintiff's levy and sale must take according to the description ; thus, if the levy be on half of a tract, he takes no more at the sale, although the defendant may then be owner of the whole.(e)

The sheriff is not bound to levy on all the defendant's lands in his bailiwick : neither can he cut up and divide particular tracts, a levy upon a part of a tract being illegal and prohibited by the act ; nor can an administrator agree to such a levy.(f) But he is bound to follow the directions of the plaintiff as to seizing on a specific tract, and this is constantly done.(g) So, if there be a general judgment affecting different estates, or distinct tracts, the judgment creditor may direct a levy to be made on one only ; although if the estate levied on has been sold or conveyed by the defendant subsequently to the judgment, and the remaining lands are sufficient to satisfy all the liens, court will interfere.(h) A party is not restricted in his levy to premises which have been mortgaged, where suit has been brought upon a bond which accompanies the mortgage. But if there be any dispute as to the distribution of the proceeds, the court will decide how the money shall be disposed of, when it is paid into court.(i) When the levy is set aside, the plaintiff cannot proceed to sell without a fresh levy; and a sale made under a *venditioni exponas* issued without such fresh levy, would be void.(j)

3. *Levy on life estate.*

The levy having been made, the sheriff could formerly have proceeded and sold without an inquest, if the estate was one of uncertain duration, as an estate for life, or a reversion or remainder dependent on

(b) Streaper v. Fisher, 1 R. 155, 162.
(c) Arnold v. Gorr, 1 R. 223.
(d) Inman v. Kutz, 10 W. 100.
(e) McCormick v. Harvey, 9 W. 482.
(f) Snyder v. Castor, 4 Y. 443.
(g) Maybury v. Jones, ib. 21.
(h) Mevey's App. 4 Barr, 80. Cow-

den's Est. 1 Barr, 279. Nailer v. Stanley, 10 S. & R. 450, *post*, 792, 796, 822; though see 1 Journ. Jurisp. 92.
(i) Morris' ex'rs v. McConaughey's ex'rs, 1 Y. 9, 12.
(j) Burd v. Lessee of Dansdale, 2 Bin. 80.

life estates, as it was deemed uncertain whether the former would last seven years, or the latter come into possession within that period, and as the only use of an inquisition was to ascertain whether the rents and profits of the land would discharge the judgment in that time.(*k*) In such case, an inquest held on an estate for life, was considered irregular, and was quashed.(*l*) So, if the property consisted of a vacant lot in a town, or of mere woodlands unimproved, an inquest was unnecessary;(*m*) and where it was evident that the debt and costs could not be satisfied within seven years, out of the annual rents and profits, the want of an inquisition did not vitiate the sale.(*n*) But the law has recently been changed, so far as regards estates for life in improved lands yielding rents; and, indeed, so fluctuating and uncertain has been the legislation in this respect, that it is necessary, for its proper understanding, to insert the several acts of assembly in full, in chronological order.

By the 68th section of the act of June, 1836, it is directed that whenever an estate for life, in any improved lands or tenements, yielding rents, issues, or profits, shall be seized in execution, it shall be the duty of the sheriff to ascertain, by an inquest, in the manner usually practised, the clear profits yearly of such real estate, making reasonable allowances for taxes, necessary repairs, and all reprises; and he shall make return of such inquisition to the court, with his writ.

Upon the return of such writ, it shall be lawful for the plaintiff to have such estate extended, and deliver to him, by a writ of *liberari facias*, according to the valuation of the inquest aforesaid, in the manner, and according to the rules hereinbefore provided in the case of other real estate; or, at his election, the court shall award a writ to sequester the rents, issues, and profits of such estate, and appoint a sequestrator to carry the same into effect. § 69.

The sequestrator appointed as aforesaid, shall have power, according to the direction of the court, to rent or sell such lands or tenements, for such term, during the life of the person upon whom such estate therein shall depend, as shall be sufficient to satisfy all the liens against the same, together with all charges for taxes, repairs, and expenses, which shall be incurred during the said term; and he shall apply the proceeds thereof, under the direction of the court, in the payment of such liens according to their priority. § 70.

The court shall have power to require from such sequestrator a bond, with sufficient surety, for the faithful execution of his trust, and to compel him to account, from time to time, as they shall think necessary; and they may make all such orders, allowances, and decrees, in the premises, and enforce the same, in like manner, and as fully and effectually as a Court of Chancery might do in the like case. § 71.

(*k*) Burd *v.* Lessee of Dansdale, 2 Bin. 91; Roe *v.* Humphreys, 1 Y. 427.
(*l*) Howell *v.* Woolfort, 2 D. 75.
(*m*) Lessee of Duncan *v.* Robinson, 2 Y. 455.
(*n*) Lessee of Grant *v.* Eddy, 2 Y. 150.

Act of October 13, 1840.(*p*) Whenever an estate for life, in any improved lands or tenements, yielding rents, issues, or profits, shall hereafter be taken in execution, the court shall, upon the application of a lien creditor, award a writ to sequester the rents, issues, and profits of such estate, and appoint a sequestrator to carry the same into effect. § 6.

The sequestrator, so appointed, shall have power, according to the direction of the court, to rent or sell such lands or tenements, for such term during the life of the persons upon whom such estate therein shall depend, as shall be sufficient to satisfy all the liens against the same, together with all charges for taxes, repairs, and expenses, which shall be incurred during said term, and he shall apply the proceeds thereof under the direction of the court in the payment of such liens according to their priority. § 7.

The court shall have power, if they deem it necessary, to require from such sequestrator a bond with sufficient security for the faithful execution of his trust, and to compel him to account, from time to time, as they shall think necessary ; and they may make all such orders, allowances, and decrees in the premises, and enforce the same in like manner, and as fully and effectually, as a Court of Chancery might do in the like case. § 8.

The fifty-second, fifty-third, fifty-fourth, fifty-fifth, fifty-sixth, fifty-seventh, sixty-fifth, sixty-seventh, sixty-eighth, sixty-ninth, seventieth, and seventy-first sections of the act last recited, are hereby repealed ; except in such cases as may have already occurred, and so far as the same may be necessary to complete a proceeding commenced under the same. § 9.

Act of 24th January, 1849.(*q*) It is hereby declared to be the true intent and meaning of the sixth section of the "Act relating to Orphans' Courts, and for other purposes," passed the 13th day of October, A. D. 1840, that sales under executions of life estates, yielding rents, issues, or profits, may be made in the manner provided by law in the case of estates of inheritance, in all cases where some lien creditor shall not, on or before the return-day of the first writ of *venditioni exponas* whereon a sale shall be advertised, have procured a sequestrator to be appointed ; and all such sales heretofore made, are hereby declared good and valid, except in such cases where the contrary has been finally determined by the Supreme Court, or by any Court of Common Pleas, and no writ of error to such decision has been taken. § 3.

From and after the first day of July next, it shall be the duty of every sheriff or coroner holding inquisitions on lands yielding rents, issues, or profits, taken in execution, wherein the defendant has only a life estate, where the same shall be condemned, upon request made, and notice given to the plaintiff in the writ, his agent or attorney, at least

(*p*) Pamph. L. 1.   (*q*) Ibid. 676.

three days before the holding of such inquisition, by the defendant, his agent or attorney, or the occupant of the land, to cause the inquest to make an appraisement of the yearly value of such lands, and to return the same with or as part of the inquisition and condemnation, and thereupon, before any writ of *venditioni exponas* shall issue, the plaintiff shall wait thirty days from the date of such inquisition, for the defendant, his agent, attorney, or occupant of the land, to elect, by notice in writing to the sheriff or coroner, to pay the plaintiff the annual valuation in half yearly payments; and on failure of the defendant so to elect to pay, or on neglect or failure to pay, for thirty days after any half yearly payment shall be due and payable, the like proceedings may be had as are now directed by law in cases wherein estates of inheritance taken in execution are extended on a sheriff's inquest: *Provided*, That nothing herein contained shall prevent the appointment of a sequestrator on application of any lien creditor under the provisions of the third section of this act, and of the act therein referred to : *Provided, further*, That the writ of *venditioni exponas*, as authorized by the third section, shall not be issued in any case wherein the annual rent, found by the jury aforesaid, shall be sufficient to pay the interest on the debts entered of record : *And provided also*, That no such writ shall be issued unless by the direction of the proper court; and on the application of any lien creditor for a writ of *venditioni exponas*, the tenant for life shall have at least ten days' notice of the application for such writ. § 4.

It shall be the duty of every sheriff, or coroner acting as sheriff, in all cases, where a sequestrator of rents, issues, and profits of a life estate in lands has been or hereafter shall be appointed, upon requisition upon him in writing for that purpose made by such sequestrator with the sanction of any one of the judges of the courts of the county, and as often as so required, to put and keep such sequestrator, his vendees or lessees, in full and undisturbed possession of the lands and tenements, with the appurtenances levied on ; and in such cases the sheriff or coroner shall have the same powers and privileges, and be entitled to the same fees, as in executing writs of *habere facias possessionem* and of *estrepement ;* and if any tenant for life, defendant in any such execution, or any other person or persons, shall unlawfully disturb the possession of such sequestrator, his vendee or lessee, or shall obstruct or molest the sheriff or coroner in the execution of the duties enjoined by this section of this act, he or they shall, for every such offence, be subject to prosecution by indictment, and upon conviction thereof, shall be sentenced to pay a fine not exceeding one hundred dollars, the costs of prosecution, and imprisonment in the county jail for a term not exceeding six calender months; and shall also be liable to such damages as such sequestrator, his vendee or lessee, or the plaintiff in such executions shall have sustained, to be recovered by actions of trespass, as damages in actions of trespass are now by law recoverable ; and the courts, or any judge or justice of the peace or alderman may, upon cause shown, require of all such offenders surety of the peace, for the prevention or against the repetition of such offences. § 5.

Act of April 14, 1851, § 2.(*s*)   The third section of the act, entitled "An act relating to judgments and the acknowledgment of deeds, and sequestration of life estates, and relative to the high constable of the borough of Wilkesbarre," being No. 419 of Pamphlet Laws of 1849, shall not be construed to extend to any cases of sales of life estates where sales have been made, and ejectment and other possessory actions may have been brought by the purchaser or purchasers previously to the passage of the said act.

Under the act of 16th June, 1836, a life estate in land is not the subject of levy or sale on execution.   The first execution creditor proceeding against it and obtaining a delivery to him of a *liberari*, is entitled to receive the rents and profits in justification of his judgment, to the exclusion even of an older judgment creditor, but whose execution is junior.(*t*)

The same construction was given to the act of 1840, under which it was expressly decided that a life estate was not the subject of levy and execution.(*u*)   The legislature, however, by the act of January 24, 1849, already given, declared it "to be the true intent and meaning of the act of 1840, that sales under execution of life estates, yielding rents, issues, and profits, may be made in the manner provided by law in the case of estates of inheritance, in all cases where some lien creditor shall not, on or before the return-day of the first writ of *venditioni exponas*, whereon a sale shall be advertised, procure a sequestrator to be appointed."

The act of 13th October, 1840, it was said by the court, in an earlier case, is carefully guarded, highly remedial, and calculated to protect the owner, as well as lien creditors, from the sacrifices resulting from sales by the sheriff under the old law.   The act imperatively directs that the court shall, on the application of lien creditors, award a writ to sequester the rents of the property.   It makes no distinction as to the kind of creditor who may apply, and the Supreme Court refused to make an exemption in favor of a *levari facias* on a mechanic's lien, which was declared to be an execution within the words and spirit of the act.   The application for a sequestrator may be made at any time before sale of the estate under execution.   The sequestrator has ample power to do justice to all the creditors according to their priority, and the court can compel him to do his duty.(*v*)

The sixth section of the act of 1840, authorizes an appointment of a sequestrator only, where an unconverted life estate is taken into execution, in order to make the debt out of the rents and profits, without a sale ; but neither the letter nor the spirit of the enactment extends to land already turned into money.(*w*)

In estimating the value of a life estate, the rule generally adopted in England is to put it at one-third of the price or value of the fee simple estate, including the life estate ; and this rule is adopted in Pennsylvania.(*x*)

(*s*) Pamph. L. 616.
(*t*) Mar *v.* Watts, 8 W. 319.
(*u*) Eyrick *v.* Hetrick, 1 H. 488 ; affirming Dennison's Appeal, 1 Barr, 201 ; Ponget *v.* Stombaugh, 2 Barr, 485.

(*v*) Rutland *v.* Kelly, 6 W. & S. 484.
(*w*) Lancaster County Bank *v.* Stauffer, 10 Barr, 401, GIBSON, C. J.
(*x*) Dennison's Appeal, 1 Barr, 201.

4. *Inquisition.*

By the 44th section of the act of June, 1836, whenever real estate shall be taken in execution, as aforesaid, by any sheriff, it shall be his duty to summon an inquest, for the purpose of ascertaining whether the rents and profits of such estate, beyond all reprises, will be sufficient to satisfy, within seven years, the judgment upon which such execution was issued, with the interest and costs of suit, and he shall make a return, in due form of law, of the inquisition so taken, to the court, with the writ.

Provided, That the defendant in any execution, being at the time of issuing thereof the owner of such real estate, or the person owning such estate by title from him, may, by writing, filed in the proper court, dispense with and waive an inquisition, as aforesaid, and in such case the sheriff may, after giving notice, in the manner hereinafter provided, proceed to sell such real estate, upon the writ of *fieri facias,* before the return-day thereof, without any other writ. § 45.

This section is derived from the act of March 6, 1820, § 1, with the addition of the clauses authorizing a sale to be made on the *fi. fa.* when the inquest is waived, and enabling the owners of the property, since the lien attached, to waive the inquest.

The sheriff shall give at least five days' notice of the time and place of the holding of such inquisition, to the defendant in the execution, or, if he be not found within the county, to his attorney or agent, and if the attorney or agent be not known to him, he shall give such notice by a handbill, to be fixed upon the premises. § 46.

Every such inquisition shall be held on the premises taken in execution, as aforesaid, if required by the defendant, or his agent, and notice of such requisition be given to the sheriff, or other officer, executing such writ. § 47.

The latter sections are derived from the act of March 21, 1806, § 11.(*y*)

The day on which the inquisition is taken, is not a matter of record, but a matter *in pais ;* when a blank for the date is left in it, the time may be shown by parol evidence, but not by the sheriff's docket.(*z*)

Act of 13th June, 1840, § 12.(*a*) When any part of any lands or real estate, which lie in one or more adjoining tracts, in different counties, has been or shall be taken in execution, under any writ of *fieri facias,* or writ of *levari facias,* issued out of any court in either county, it shall be the duty of the sheriff to summon an inquest, for the purpose of ascertaining whether that part of said land which has been taken in execution, can be sold separately and apart from the other part of said land lying in the adjoining county or counties, without prejudice to the whole, or to the interest of the defendant or defendants, or any of his, her, or their lien creditors, or other person, who may be interested in

(*y*) See Heydrick *v.* Eaton, 2 Bin. 215.   (*a*) Pamph. L. 689.
(*z*) Thomas *v.* Wright, 9 S. & R. 87.

the proceeds thereof; and also how much, and what part of said lands in such adjoining county or counties, ought to be so sold with that part taken in execution as aforesaid, describing the same by metes and bounds; and he shall make a return in due form of law, of the inquisition taken with the writ, and if the said inquest shall find that the part of said lands taken in execution, cannot be sold separately from the other part lying in the adjoining counties, or a portion of the same, without prejudice as aforesaid, and the inquisition shall be approved by the court, the plaintiff may have a writ of *venditioni exponas*, or writ of *levari facias*, as the case may require (or a writ of *alias* or *pluries venditioni exponas*, or *alias* or *pluries levari facias*, as the same may be necessary), to sell said lands and real estate, taken in execution; and other part in such inquisition mentioned and described by virtue thereof, the said lands and real estate shall be exposed to sale—sold and conveyed as in other cases; and the person or persons to whom the said lands and real estate may be sold, shall and may take, hold, and enjoy the same, as if the same were situate wholly in the county in which such writ issued: *Provided,* That, upon the return of the said inquisition, the plaintiff shall cause a copy of the docket-entry and the whole proceeding connected with the said writ, to be filed in the office of the prothonotary of the said adjoining county or counties in which any of the lands mentioned in said inquisition are situate, which shall be entered on the records of such office; and from the date of said entry the judgment on which said writs issued shall be a lien on the lands within the county in which the said proceedings shall be entered, and copies of all subsequent proceedings in said case, shall, in like manner, be filed and entered in the office of such prothonotary, immediately after the sheriff shall make a return of the sale of said premises: *And provided also,* That notice of the sale shall be given in each county in which the lands to be sold lie, as is now required to be given in cases of sheriff's sales. And in all cases of a tract or adjoining tracts of lands situate in different counties as aforesaid, in which any writs of execution have been issued, and no sale under the same has been made, it shall be lawful for the plaintiff to issue an *alias* or *pluries fieri facias*, or *alias* or *pluries levari facias*, as may be proper; and the like proceedings shall be had thereon as above provided. In case there should be any liens on the parts of said lands lying in the adjoining county or counties, in which the above-mentioned proceedings are directed to be filed and entered, existing previous to filing and entering such proceedings, the court shall, after the return of the sale, ascertain and determine, in such manner as they may think proper, what proportion of the proceeds of such sale shall be applied in satisfaction of such previous liens.(*b*)

Act of October 13, 1840.(*c*)—Upon the return of a writ of *fieri facias*, levied upon real estate of the defendant, with the inquisition, assessing the value of the yearly rents or profits thereof, the plaintiff may, at his election, instead of suing out a writ of *liberari facias*, for the purpose of having the said real estate delivered to him at the valuation and appraisement, permit the defendant, or defendants, or any other person, or persons, claiming under him, or them, by demise, or title, subsequent

(*b*) 5 P. L. J. 74; *post*, 784.   (*c*) Pamph. L. 1.

to the judgment upon which the said *fieri facias* issued, to retain the possession of the said real estate at the annual valuation and appraisement so as aforesaid, made by the inquest. And the said plaintiff, or his attorney, shall signify his election, so to permit the said defendants, or other person so claiming, to the sheriff, who may have the said writ of *fieri facias* in his hands for execution, within [ten] days after holding of the inquisition ; and it shall be the duty of the said sheriff to notify the said defendant, or other person so claiming thereof, within ten days after said notice shall be given to him by the plaintiff. And it shall be the duty of the said defendant, or other person so claiming, within ten days thereafter, to notify the said sheriff of his willingness to retain the said real estate at the annual valuation and appraisement so as aforesaid, made in pursuance of the act, entitled " An act relating to executions," passed the sixteenth day of June, one thousand eight hundred and thirty-six ; and upon his neglect or refusal so to do, the plaintiff may have a writ of *venditioni exponas* to sell the said real estate for the payment of his debt. All which notices, required by this act, shall be in writing, signed by the parties or their attorneys ; and shall be served by delivering a copy to the party, plaintiff, or defendant, or to the person in possession of the real estate, or leaving the same at his residence with an adult member of his family ; and of all which the said sheriff shall make return according to law, and be entitled to mileage as in other cases. § 2.

If the said defendant, or defendants, or other person claiming the said real estate as aforesaid, shall signify his or their willingness to retain the same at the valuation and appraisement, in pursuance of the first section of this act, he or they shall thereby become liable to pay to the plaintiff the amount of the said annual valuations and appraisement in half yearly instalments, until the debt, interest, and cost of the said *fieri facias* be fully paid ; the first of said instalments to be paid in six months from the day the defendant, or person claiming as aforesaid, shall deliver notice to the sheriff, declaring his or their willingness to retain said real estate, which date the sheriff is hereby required to indorse on said notice, and on failure to make payment for a period of thirty days after any half yearly instalment shall become due, it shall be lawful for the plaintiff, his agent, or attorney, upon making affidavit thereof, and filing the same in the prothonotary's office, to issue a writ of *venditioni exponas* for the sale of said real estate, as fully, and with like effect, as though a condemnation thereof had taken place. § 3.

On the return, by the sheriff, of the notices and proceedings prescribed by the second and third sections of this act, it shall be lawful for the court out of which the *fieri facias* issued, on the application of any creditor, to make an order directing the manner in which the money arising from such half yearly instalments, shall be distributed among the different lien creditors, according to the priority of their liens, in the same manner and with like effect as in case of distribution of money arising from sheriff's sales ; and it shall be the duty of the defendant, or person in possession of said estate, to pay said instalments to the plaintiff or party entitled to receive the same under such decree, or to his or their agent or attorney, or to the sheriff of the proper county, where such plaintiff or person, his or their agent or attorney, reside out of said county. § 4.

Where real estate has heretofore been extended on a writ of *fieri facias*, and no writ of *liberari facias* issued to take possession thereof, it shall be lawful for the plaintiff to either issue out his writ of *liberari facias*, or give the defendant thirty days' notice of his election, to permit the defendant to retain possession of the same ; and the defendant shall, within twenty days thereafter, notify the plaintiff whether he will retain the same or deliver over said premises to the plaintiff at the annual valuation, and on failure so to do, or on failure to pay said valuation half yearly, like proceedings shall be had for the sale of said premises as is prescribed by the second and third sections of this act. The notices to be served and returns thereof made in the manner before prescribed.(*d*)   § 5.

Act of April 16, 1845, § 3. In all cases where real estate has heretofore been extended, and the plaintiff has failed to signify within ten days after the inquisition, his election, to permit the defendant to retain the possession at the appraisement, it shall be lawful for any such plaintiff to signify such election within sixty days from the passage of this act, and to proceed therein, in all other respects, as to the acceptance or refusal of the defendant, or other person claiming under him, and as to sale of the premises as is directed in other cases.

Act of February 10, 1846.(*e*) So much of the act, entitled "An act relating to Orphans' Courts, and for other purposes," passed the thirteenth of October, one thousand eight hundred and forty, as requires the plaintiff in any writ of *fieri facias*, or his attorney, to give notice to the sheriff signifying his election, to permit the defendant or defendants, or persons claiming under him, or them, to retain the possession of real estate, at its valuation and appraisement, within ten days after holding inquisition, be and the same is hereby repealed ; and it shall be lawful for any plaintiff, or his attorney, to give the notice to the sheriff as is required by said act, at any time after holding inquisition; and in cases where any plaintiff, or his attorney, has heretofore failed to signify such election to the sheriff within the space of ten days after inquisition, it shall be lawful to do so at any time prior to the first day of October next, and to proceed therein, in all other respects, as to the acceptance or refusal of the defendant, or other persons claiming under him, and as to sale of the premises, as is directed by existing laws : *Provided*, That this act shall not be construed to authorize a notice in any case wherein a writ of *liberari facias* has been or may be executed.(*f*)   § 1.

The notice required to be given by the provisions of the act referred to in the first section of this act, from the defendant or defendants, or other person or persons claiming under him or them, to the sheriff, of his or their willingness to retain possession under the valuation of the inquest, may be given at any time within thirty days from the time of the reception by him, or them, of the notice of plaintiff's election, to

---

(*d*) See Shields *v.* Miltenberger, 2 H.   (*e*) Pamph. L. 37.
77.   (*f*) See Shields *v.* Miltenberger, 2 H.
                                                  77.

allow him so to retain the same; and in cases where the defendant or defendants, or other person or persons so claiming, have neglected to give such notice within the time allowed, it shall be lawful for him or them to give the same, on or before the first day of October next: *Provided*, That no such notice shall be given in cases where writs of *venditioni exponas* have been, or may be issued, on account of the said notice not having been given according to law. § 2.

Act of May 4, 1852, § 3. That in all cases of real estate mainly valuable as developed mineral lands, levied upon by virtue of a writ of *fieri facias*, and an inquest shall be held thereon in pursuance of the provisions of the forty-fourth section of the act of the sixteenth of June, 1836, entitled "An act relating to executions," it shall be the duty of the inquest, in ascertaining the yearly rents and profits of such real estate, to take into consideration the amount of rent or mineral leave paid, and which said real estate may produce from the iron ore, coal, or other minerals mined from such estate, and which its capacity, as developed mineral land may or shall produce, and said inquest shall estimate the rent or mineral leave aforesaid, with the other rents and profits of the same for the next succeeding seven years, and in case such rent, mineral leave and profits shall be sufficient to satisfy the judgment upon which said execution was issued, with interest and costs of suit beyond all reprises within said seven years, it shall be the duty of the inquest to extend said real estate and determine the amount of rental to be paid, in each of the next succeeding seven years, respectively.

The jury of inquiry must consist of at least twelve men, who together with the sheriff, compose what is denominated a court of inquiry, usually held on the Friday preceding the return-day of the process. There is, however, nothing in the act of assembly which precludes the sheriff from holding an inquest after the return of the *fi. fa.*, and such has always been the practice when found necessary. Therefore, when the inquest has been quashed for irregularity, he may proceed to hold a new one without a new *fi. fa.(g)* The jury cannot enlarge the sheriff's levy as returned.(*h*)

In forming their judgment, the jury are bound to take into consideration mortgages against the estate in execution, which are clearly included in the term "reprises," mentioned in the statute of 4th Anne; and the instalments of a mortgage becoming due within the seven years next after inquisition, ought to be regarded by them in their judgment.(*i*) But the practice has been universal ever since the act of 1705, to require a condemnation of land, notwithstanding they are subject to mortgage.(*j*) To enable the jury to decide upon the sufficiency of lands, it is the uniform practice to calculate the interest on judgments for the seven years.(*k*) The court has a control over the conduct of their officers before whom an inquest of office has been executed. They may set aside an inquisition on the ground of misconduct in the jurors, or where it clearly appears that the sum affixed is extravagantly high. And where the court below assigned an insufficient reason for setting aside

(*g*) Weaver *v.* Lawrence, 1 D. 379.
(*h*) Lessee of Rodgers *v.* Gibson, 4 Y. 477.
111.
(*i*) Pulaski *v.* King, 1 Y. 477.
(*j*) Ibid.; Naples *v.* Minier, 3 Pa. R. 477.
(*k*) 1 Sm. Laws, 63, *n.*

an inquisition and extent, the Supreme Court being of opinion that the court below were convinced that the jury had valued the land too highly, refused to reverse the judgment.(*l*) Where the plaintiff produced an affidavit, which showed that the lands could not possibly pay the debt by extent, the court quashed the execution at the costs of the plaintiff, who was desirous that it should be set aside in order that he might pursue another course.(*m*) But after a *fi. fa.* executed and lands extended, it is not a sufficient reason for setting it aside, that, since the inquisition, sufficient personal property has been found.(*n*)

In making their valuation, the usual mode is for the jurors to make separate estimates, and, after adding them together, return the medium value as their valuation. The propriety of this course has been recognized where it is resorted to, not as a decision of the question, but as an approximation to unanimity by the inquest.(*o*)

If land be extended under one inquisition, the plaintiff will not be precluded from issuing an execution on another coexistent judgment, levying on the same land, and having another inquisition, even though both judgments were brought into the view of the first jury.(*p*) A *fi. fa.* having been issued and levied on real estate, and the judgment being subsequently revived, by *scire facias*, another *fi. fa.* ought not to be issued on the revived judgment, but an inquest should be held under the first execution.(*q*)

It has not been the practice to obtain a formal approval of the inquisition, before suing out a *ven. ex.* It seems, that the issuing of the latter writ being in contemplation of law the act of the court, is a sufficient approval to satisfy the act 1836, at least as to strangers.(*r*)

An inquest finding lands sufficient to pay in seven years is not equivalent to satisfaction; the *fi. fa.* may be discontinued on leave of court, and an *alias* had against other property, or plaintiff may await the sale of the original subject of levy on a subsequent execution, and then come in on the proceeds. Even part satisfaction by rents under an extent does not deprive him of his lien for the residue when divested of his term by such a sale; *a fortiori*, he is not deprived, by any of these, of his remedy on a mortgage given to secure the same debt.(*s*)

It matters not whether the waiver of inquisition be filed before or after the sale. It is enough if the plaintiff has the written authority before he proceeds on the *fi. fa.*, and it is returned with his proceedings.(*t*)

There is nothing, says Judge ROGERS, in the statute, enabling a defendant to dispense with an inquisition, which makes it compulsory to pursue the method pointed out; and as it is for the benefit of the debtor, there is nothing in the way to prevent him from consenting in some other mode, as by writing merely, by acceptance of the purchase-money, or in other ways, that may estop him in equity from asserting title to the estate.(*u*)

As the heir, before the act of 1834,(*uu*) was not known as a party on the record, the personal representative of a deceased defendant might

(*l*) Miller *v.* Milford, 2 S. & R. 35, 38.
(*m*) Hunt *v.* McClure, 2 Y. 387.
(*n*) Ibid.
(*o*) White *v.* White, 5 R. 61.
(*p*) Gist *v.* Wilson, 2 W. 30.
(*q*) Id. ib.
(*r*) Crawford *v.* Boyer, 2 H. 380.

(*s*) Gro. *v.* Huntingdon Bank, 1 Pa. R. 426; Lyons *v.* Ott, 6 Wh. 165.
(*t*) Overton *v.* Tozer, 7 W. 333.
(*u*) Mitchell *v.* Freedly, 10 Barr, 209. ROGERS, J.
(*uu*) *Ante*, 770.

formerly have waived the condemnation of land levied on a judgment against him.(*v*)

The 45th section of the revised act of 1836 directs that, on a written waiver of an inquisition by a defendant, the plaintiff shall proceed to see such estate on the *fi. fa.* before the return-day without any further writ. It has been the sanctioned practice to see after the return-day on writs of *venditioni exponas* whilst they remained in the sheriff's hands; but the supposed advantages of this practice, even in the absence of the express words of this statute, would not induce the court again to sanction a practice so anomalous, were it a matter of the first impression; when, therefore, no evidence of defendant's assent existed to a sale on a *fi. fa.* after the return-day, the sale was held void, though the sheriff returned that he had advertised and offered the property for sale on the return-day, and adjourned it *by consent* to the day of actual sale, and although the sheriff's deed had been long previously acknowledged after exceptions thereto.(*w*)

By the statutory enactments, as they now exist, when the defendants refuse to accept under the provisions of the law of 1840, the plaintiff is thrown upon his remedy, to take the lands at the appraisement.(*x*)

Inquisitions are not contemplated where the estates levied on are of uncertain duration, as where the defendant is seized in fee, liable, however, to be defeated by his dying and leaving children.(*y*)

It is the duty of the jury to fix the annual clear value beyond all reprises, which include expenses of repairs, taxes, costs, trouble, &c.(*z*) "In all the counties where I was acquainted with the practice," says Judge COULTER, "they add seventeen per cent. interest to the liens, and then add all the costs, fix the net annual rent beyond repairs and taxes, and payable at the commencement of the year; and if this will pay the debt and interest of all the liens, with the interest and costs, the land is extended, and either the defendant or plaintiff must take at that valuation."(*a*)

Since the act of 1836, the rightful owner of the estate, whether in or out of possession, is the only person who may dispense with the inquisition.(*b*) And an insolvent assignor, after a voluntary assignment, is not such a person.(*c*)

The 1st section of the act of 6th March, 1820, and the 45th section of the act of 16th June, 1826, were only declaratory of the existing practice. There is no form of waiver prescribed. Where it is contained in the warrant of attorney to confess judgment of which a memorandum is made on the record, it is sufficient, although the warrant itself was not on file.(*d*)

The want of an inquisition and condemnation or waiver thereof is not cured by the acknowledgment of the sheriff's deed.(*e*) The sale is absolutely void.(*f*)

The defendant alone can take advantage of the want of approval by the court of the inquisition of condemnation of real estate levied on under a *fi. fa.*, and that only within a reasonable time.(*g*)

(*v*) Hunt *v.* Develing, 8 W. 405. See Crawford *v.* Boyer, *post*, note (*g*).
(*w*) Cash *v.* Tozer, 1 W. & S. 526.
(*x*) Mellon *v.* Campbell, 1 J. 416.
(*y*) Stewart *v.* Kenower, 7 W. & S. 293. See *ante*, 773.
(*z*) Mellon *v.* Campbell, 1 J. 416.

(*a*) 1 J. 416.
(*b*) McLaughlin *v.* Shields, 2 J. 283.
(*c*) Pepper *v.* Copeland, 2 M. 419.
(*d*) Kimball *v.* Kelsey, 1 Barr, 183.
(*e*) Shoemaker *v.* Ballard, 3 H. 92.
(*f*) Baird *v.* Lent, 8 W. 422.
(*g*) Crawford *v.* Boyer, 2 H. 380.

The second section of the act of October, 1840, gives a *venditioni exponas* for the sale of extended lands, when the execution creditor, within ten days after inquisition found, signifies his election to permit the defendant to retain the premises levied at the ascertained yearly rental, and the latter neglects or refuses, for ten days thereafter, to notify his acceptance of the offer. And by the act of February, 1846, this notice may be given at any time before a *levari facias.*(h)

Where lands are taken by the defendant in the execution at an annual valuation fixed by the inquest, a mortgage creditor whose lien would not have been discharged by a sale of the lands under such execution is not entitled to the fund.(i)

Under the act of 13th of June, 1840, which allows real estate lying in one or more adjoining tracts in different counties to be taken in execution, the court require, that, to entitle the inquisition to the approbation of the court, notice shall be given to the defendant of the time and place of holding the same, according to the 46th section of the act of 16th June, 1836, and an affidavit filed. If the defendant demand it, the inquisition must be held on the premises, according to the 47th section of the same act; and the motion to approve the inquisition cannot be made before the Saturday succeeding the return-day of the writ, when the inquisition, if in other respects regular, will be approved, unless exceptions have been filed. The inquest is not to ascertain whether that part of the tract which lies beyond the sheriff's bailiwick can be sold separately from that within it, without prejudice to the whole, but whether the part taken in execution situate within the sheriff's bailiwick can be sold separately.(j)

5. *Liberari facias.*

If the clear profits of the real estate of any such defendant will, in the opinion of the inquest, be sufficient to pay the debt or damages to be levied as aforesaid, together with the costs, the sheriff or other officer shall proceed, by the inquest as aforesaid, to assess the value of the yearly rents or profits of such lands beyond all reprises, and make return thereof to the court, with his writ, as aforesaid. § 48.(k)

Upon the return of such writ, with the inquisition assessing the value of the yearly rents or profits, as aforesaid, the plaintiff may have a writ of *liberari facias*, to deliver the said real estate, with the appurtenances, to

(h) Shields v. Miltenberger, 2 H. 77. BELL, J. See *ante*, 778.

(i) Bank v. Patterson, 9 Barr, 311.

(j) Worthington v. Worthington, 5 P. L. J. 74. SHARSWOOD, J.

(k) These sections are derived from the act of 1705, § 2. In practice, it has been usual to call a second inquest, and cases have occurred in which the inquest have assessed the rents, &c., at a value which would not be sufficient to pay the debt, &c., in seven years. In such cases, both inquests (that held on the *fi. fa.* and the *liberari*) have been set aside. It appears that two inquisitions are not necessary. If the inquest summoned on the *fi. fa.* find the rents, &c., sufficient to pay, it would be more convenient to require that they should proceed to assess precisely their value, so that the lands may be delivered by the sheriff at their valuation, if a *liberari* should be sued out. From subsequent provisions, it appears that neither party is bound by the assessed value whether it be too much or too little. Upon a *scire facias ad computandum*, the plaintiff may be required to account for what he shall have received, and to allow so much and no more. The reference in the text to the writs of *elegit*, in England, is expunged.—*Remarks of Commissioners.*

him at the valuation and appraisement aforesaid, to be holden by him, his executors, administrators, and assigns, until such debt or damages, with lawful interest thereon, from the day of the judgment rendered, be fully levied thereout, and make return thereof, under his hand and seal, to the court. § 49.

On the execution of a writ of *liberari facias* as aforesaid, where the defendant, or any person claiming under him by demise or title, subse_ quent to the judgment, is in possession of premises to be extended, the sheriff shall deliver the actual possession thereof to the plaintiff or his agent. § 50.

Lands or tenements shall be extended as aforesaid upon execution, according to the priority of the judgments, in all cases where two or more writs of *liberari facias*, issued thereon, shall be in the hands of the sheriff or other officer at the same time, for execution; but whenever any real estate shall be extended in satisfaction of any judgment as aforesaid, such extent shall not be distributed or discharged by virtue of any writ of *liberari facias*, issued upon any other judgment, whether previously or subsequently obtained. § 51.

It shall be lawful for the defendant, at the expiration of the time or term for which his real estate shall be delivered as aforesaid, to require the plaintiff, by a writ of *scire facias*, to settle an account of the rents, issues, and profits of such real estate, during his possession as aforesaid, and show cause why the defendant should not have his land again. § 52.

It shall also be lawful for the defendant to have a writ of *scire facias*, for the purpose aforesaid, at any time during the said term, on making affidavit, to be filed of record, that he verily believes that the plaintiff has been fully satisfied for his judgment, interests, and costs. § 53.

If it shall appear upon the accounting as aforesaid, that the plaintiff has been fully satisfied for the amount of his judgment, with interest and costs, after deducting for his reasonable expenses and labors, the court shall give judgment of restitution to the defendant, and shall award thereupon a writ to deliver the premises to him. § 54.

If it shall appear upon the accounting aforesaid, that the plaintiff has received more than the amount of his judgment, interest, and costs, after deducting for his reasonable labors and expenses as aforesaid, the court shall adjudge him to pay the surplus to the defendant, and enforce the payment by execution. § 55.

If it shall appear upon the accounting as aforesaid, or in any other proceeding instituted by the defendant in the execution to obtain pos- session, that the plaintiff has not received the amount of his judgment, interest, and costs as aforesaid, and that he has used reasonable skill and diligence in the management of such real estate, during the time of his occupancy as aforesaid, it shall be lawful for him to retain the pos- session of such real estate, until he be fully paid and satisfied out of the same as aforesaid, unless the defendant, his heirs or assigns, shall forthwith pay him the residue of the sum to be levied as aforesaid. § 56.

It shall also be lawful for the plaintiff, whenever he shall be fully paid and satisfied for his judgment, and before the expiration of the time or term aforesaid, to settle his account in court, after notice given the defendant, and surrender to him his estate. § 57.

If, before the expiration of an extent made as aforesaid, any other debt or damages shall be recovered against the same defendant, his heirs, executors, or administrators, which, with what remains due upon such extent, cannot all be satisfied out of the yearly profits of the real estate so extended, within seven years from such recovery, and execution be issued therefor, the sheriff or other officer shall certify the same, by inquisition as aforesaid, upon the return of such writ, and thereupon the court may award a writ of *venditioni exponas*, to sell such real estate. § 58.

If, before the expiration of an extent as aforesaid, the estate extended should be sold by virtue of any other execution, the plaintiff to whom such real estate shall be delivered, shall justly and equitably account for the rents, issues, and profits actually received by him during his occupancy, and the residue of his judgment, with the interest and costs, shall be paid out of the proceeds of the sale as in other cases. § 59.(*l*)

If any real estate delivered to any person by virtue of any *liberari facias*, as aforesaid, shall, upon any lawful title or cause, and without any fraud, collusion, or other default, be recovered, or lawfully taken from the possession of such person, his executors, administrators, or assigns, before he or they shall have levied and recovered the whole debt or damages for which real estate was delivered in execution, as aforesaid, it shall be lawful for him, his executors or administrators, to have a writ of *scire facias* upon such judgment, against the defendant therein, his executors or administrators, to show cause why the plaintiff should not have execution for the residue of the judgment and costs. § 60.

In following the manner and method of delivering lands upon writs of *elegit* in England, it was formerly conceived that the sheriff, on a *liberari facias*, could only deliver the legal possession to the plaintiff, but could not turn the defendant out of the *actual* possession, and that recourse should be had to an action of ejectment to obtain the benefit of this process.(*m*) To remedy this mischief, it was provided by the act of

---

(*l*) These seven latter sections relate to the writ of *scire facias* to account. They are new as positive provisions, and alter, to some extent, the law. The act of 1705 refers to the practice upon writs of *elegit* in England; we have adopted in these sections what we conceived to be the rule of justice. In England, it seems, courts of law are bound by the inquest, but Courts of Equity grant relief, and order an account, according to the actual profits, Wall *v.* Lloyd's Executors, 1 S. & R. 323; 2 Saund. 72; n. & w. The provision in section fifty-nine, applies to the case where the estate extended shall be sold during the extent. It is adopted from the case of Wall *v.* Lloyd's Executors, 1 S. & R. 323. *Remarks of Commissioners.*

(*m*) 1 Sm. Laws, 63, n.

April, 1807, § 6,(*n*) which is supplied by the act just cited, "that on the execution of a *liberari facias*, where the defendant or his tenant is in possession of the premises to be extended, the sheriff shall deliver the actual possession thereof to the plaintiff or his agent."(*o*) The mere return to the *liberari* by the sheriff, that he had delivered possession to the plaintiff, does not vest the title in such plaintiff; it is only an authority to enter, and he must obtain the *actual* possession, or bring an ejectment, before it can be considered, in an ejectment between others, as a subsisting title in him.(*p*) When, under the old law, possession was delivered on a *liberari facias* by the sheriff, or taken by the consent of the parties, it was held to operate as a satisfaction of the debt.(*q*) A recital in the body of the inquisition, that the sheriff had delivered the premises in satisfaction of the debt, was held inoperative, as being no part of the return till made so by reference from the indorsement on the writ, which, for that purpose, ought to be in these or similar words: "The execution of this writ appears in a certain schedule hereunto annexed."(*r*)

After an inquest has returned, that the rents and profits will pay the debt in seven years, the plaintiff cannot discontinue his *fi. fa.* and take out a new one, without leave of the court. This has been the practice and understanding of the courts of *nisi prius*, and great inconveniences might ensue from a contrary practice; because the plaintiff might set aside the proceedings, and levy again on the same land repeatedly, until he got a jury to condemn it, which would be taking away from the defendant the benefit of the act of assembly on this subject.(*s*) But where land was extended on a *fi. fa.*, and upon motion the inquisition and extent were set aside, and some time afterwards the plaintiff took out an *alias fi. fa.* whereon the same land was levied upon and sold, it being objected that as only the inquisition under the first *fi. fa.* was set aside, the writ and levy remained, which made the second *fi. fa.* erroneous; it was held that the first *fi. fa.* was in form relinquished, though not in substance; and as it was the cause of no hardship to the defendant, who would be protected against unnecessary costs, the court upheld the second *fi. fa.*(*t*) In the former case, the plaintiff attempted to relinquish his inquisition after the property was found sufficient to pay in seven years, but here the inquest was set aside; the matter rested solely on the levy, which may be relinquished, provided the defendant be protected against unnecessary costs.(*u*)

Where a plaintiff levies on real estate to which the defendant had no title, and actually disclaims title, the levy may be abandoned, and an *alias fi. fa.* issued. The plaintiff in such case is not bound to pursue his proceedings on the first writ;(*v*) nor, so far as the defendant is concerned, is the return of "levied and condemned" a satisfaction of the execution.(*w*) But where there is an outstanding *fi. fa.* on the original judgment, a *fi. fa.* cannot be issued on the judgment upon a *scire facias*

(*n*) 4 Ibid. 477.
(*o*) *Vide* 9 S. & R. 92.
(*p*) Ibid. 87.
(*q*) Barnet *v.* Washebaugh, 16 S. & R. 410.
(*r*) Shewell *v.* Meredith, 3 Pa. R. 17.
(*s*) McCullough *v.* Guetner, 1 Bin.

215; and see Miller *v.* Milford, 2 S. & R. 37; Wilson *v.* Hewson, 2 J. 115, *post*, 788.
(*t*) Ibid.
(*u*) Ibid.
(*v*) Coleman *v.* Mansfield, 1 M. 56.
(*w*) Ibid.

to revive such original.   The proper mode is to proceed on the first
fi. fa.(*x*)

Upon the extending of the land, the sheriff is entitled to poundage on
the whole debt, under a former act of assembly.   But poundage cannot
be again charged on the balance due the plaintiff on the *liberari facias*,
and which the sheriff receives when the land is sold under the act just
mentioned.(*y*)   The sheriff cannot charge for attendance : and the jury
being entitled to no more than the compensation given by law for their
attendance, must bear their own expenses ; a charge of this kind will,
on application, be stricken off.(*z*)   See further, as to the writ of *liberari*,
under the act of 1836, where the plaintiff is unable to sell on a *venditioni exponas.*(*a*)

By the sixty-first section of the act of June, 1836, it is directed that
if the inquest shall find that the clear profits of any real estate levied as
aforesaid, will not be sufficient to satisfy, within seven years, the debt
or damages in such execution, and the same shall be approved of by the
court, the plaintiff in such writ may have a writ of *venditioni exponas*,
to sell such real estate, for and towards the satisfaction of his judgment.
The proceedings upon this writ will be more fully considered in the
ensuing section.

An inquisition having been held and the land condemned, the object
of the law is obtained, and it is unnecessary that other judgment creditors should go to the expense of new inquisitions : where, therefore, an
inquest and condemnation had been obtained upon a *fi. fa.*, it was held
that another judgment creditor might take out a *venditioni exponas*
without another inquisition.(*b*)   When these proceedings have been had,
the plaintiff cannot abandon them, and take out a *ca. sa.*, without the
leave of the court, although he finds the property so covered with older
judgments as to render his levy wholly unavailable.(*c*)

If the premises are occupied under an existing lease, given by the
defendant prior to the judgment, the sheriff should so return it specially,
because the plaintiff would be entitled to receive and compel payment
of the arrearages of the rent in liquidation of the debt.   A return that
he had delivered possession, without more, renders him liable for a false
return.(*d*)

Where land has been extended on a *fi. fa.*, an *alias* writ may be
granted by the court, where other debts have been contracted in the
mean time, which the property would not pay in seven years ;(*e*) and it
seems, that where land extended on a *fi. fa.* is levied on and condemned
under an *alias*, issued without leave of the court, the defendant may
have it set aside before the acknowledgment of the sheriff's deed.(*f*)

The act of 1836, § 39, as has just been seen, provides, that the lands shall
be delivered to the plaintiff, his heirs, &c., at the appraisement, until
the debt and damages, with lawful interest thereon, be fully levied
thereon.   The 52d and 57th sections of the act of 1836, are expressly

(*x*) Gist *v.* Wilson, 2 W. 30.
(*y*) Wall *v.* Lloyd's ex'rs, 1 S. & R.
320.
(*z*) Ibid.
(*a*) *Post,* § 5.
(*b*) McCormick *v.* Mason, 1 S. & R.
98.

(*c*) Bank of Pa. *v.* Latshaw, 9 S. &
R. 9.
(*d*) McMichael *v.* McKeon, 10 Barr,
143.
(*e*) Wilson *v.* Hewser, 2 J. 115; see
ante, 787.
(*f*) Ibid. 109.

repealed by the act of 13th October, 1840; so that now, when a defendant refuses to accept under the provisions of that act, the plaintiff must take the land at the appraisement, until he is satisfied fully. There is no hardship in this, because the jury are bound to fix the clear yearly value, beyond all reprises, which include repairs, taxes, costs, trouble, &c. The mode of fixing the rent varies in the different counties, but in all the practice is to add 17 per cent. interest to the liens, and then add all costs, fix the net annual rent, beyond repairs and taxes, payable at the commencement of the year; and if this will pay the debt and interest of all the liens, with the interest and costs, the land is extended, and either the defendant or plaintiff must take at that valuation. The plaintiff cannot, under any of the statutes, charge commission for receiving the rents, by himself or his agent.(g)

Under the act of 1705, and certain sections of that of 1836, if plaintiff held over, defendant might have resorted, as he still may, perhaps, to the *sci. fa. ad computandum.* But there is no necessity for that writ now, under the existing act.(h)

If the jury act improperly, as by refusing to hear evidence of the yearly value of the premises, or otherwise, the defendant's mode of redress is by a timely application to the court from whence the process issues, to quash the inquisition : it is too late to raise such objection in an ejectment instituted for the property after the condemnation and sheriff's sale.(i)

As has already been noticed, the bare seizing of land in execution to the value of the debt is not satisfaction. The rents and profits being found sufficient to produce satisfaction in seven years, the creditor may proceed to an extent or not, at his election; and having declined to take satisfaction out of the profits, it is clear the debt remains.(j)

We have already seen,(k) that where it is suggested and verified by the party's affidavit that the defendant has no lands or tenements in the county, the plaintiff may have a *testatum,* without any previous writ, directed to the sheriff of the county where the defendant may have real or personal estate. The proceedings and consequences of the officer's neglect thereon have been also stated. By the 80th section of the same act, every *testatum* shall be a lien on the real estate of the defendants within the county where it shall be entered of record during five years from such entry, unless the debt and costs be sooner paid.

SECTION V.

OF THE WRITS OF VENDITIONI EXPONAS AND LEVARI FACIAS ON A MORTGAGE.

1. *When a venditioni exponas issues.*

We have seen that, by the 61st section of the act of 1836, the writ of *venditioni exponas* issues for the sale of lands or tenements, when the sheriff has duly certified upon his return to the *fi. fa.* that the profits

(g) Mellon v. Campbell, 1 J. 417.
(h) Ibid.
(i) Lessee of Murphy v. McCleary, 3 Y. 405.

(j) Gro v. Huntingdon Bank, 1 Pa. R. 426; Lyons v. Ott, 6 Wh. 165.
(k) *Ante,* 740.

thereof are not sufficient to satisfy the amount within seven years. Without a previous *fi. fa.* the *venditioni* would be irregular, and a sheriff's sale under it would be set aside on motion, although the land have been levied on and condemned by a *fi. fa.* on another judgment against the same defendant.(*l*)   The levy under the *fi. fa.* controls all the subsequent proceedings, and governs where a variance exists between them.(*m*) It has also been seen that, by the 58th section, if the lands have been extended, and other executions have been subsequently obtained, the amount of which, with what remains due on such extent, cannot all be satisfied out of the yearly profits within seven years, the sheriff shall certify the same by inquisition, as aforesaid, upon the return of such writ of execution, and thereupon a writ or writs of *venditioni exponas* shall issue to sell such real estate.   Without this process, a sheriff's sale of lands, levied upon and condemned, is, in this State, invalid,(*n*) except in the case of a *scire facias* on a mortgage, when no *venditioni exponas* is necessary.(*o*)   A mere clerical error in the writ, such as a mistake in a party's name, or the omission of the prothonotary's signature (the seal of the court being attached), is amendable at any time by the court from which it issues, and even if error were brought, the Supreme Court would order an amendment.(*p*)

After a levy on personal property of the debtor, the execution creditor, on whose execution the levy has been made, may withdraw the execution without discharging thereby the lien of his judgment on the real estate of the defendant, as it respects other judgment creditors.(*q*)

A sale of real estate on a *ven. ex.*, without condemnation by inquest or a waiver of the inquisition is void, nor is it cured by the acknowledgment of the sheriff's deed.(*r*)

A writ of *venditioni exponas* is directed generally to the sheriff of the county; and if the sheriff who receives the writ goes out of office before it is executed, his successor may proceed upon it to sell the property, and make a deed to the purchaser.(*s*)

It has not been the practice to obtain a formal approval of the inquisition before suing out a *ven. ex.*   It seems that the issuing of the latter writ, being in contemplation of law the act of the court, is a sufficient approval to satisfy the act of 1336, at least as to strangers.(*t*)

2. *When a levari facias issues.*

By the fourth section of the act of 1705,(*u*) it is declared lawful for the sheriff or other officer, by a writ of *levari facias*, to seize and take all other lands, tenements, and hereditaments, in execution, and thereupon with all convenient speed, either with or without any writ of *venditioni exponas*, to make public sale thereof for the most they will yield, and pay the price or value of the same to the party, towards satisfaction of his debt, damages, and costs. . In practice, this portion of the act was pursued only in proceedings upon a mortgage, wherein the form

---

(*l*) Lippincott *v.* Tanner, 1 M. 286.
(*m*) Grubb *v.* Guilford, 4 W. 244; see Owen *v.* Simpson, 3 W. 87.
(*n*) Lessee of Porter *v* Neelan, 4 Y. 108; Lessee of Glancy *v.* Jones, id. 212; and see Cowden *v.* Brady, 8 S. & R. 507.
(*o*) Lessee of Glancy *v.* Jones, 4 Y. 213.
(*p*) Cluggage *v.* Lessee of Duncan, 4

S. & R. 120; McCormick *v.* Mason, 97; Peddle *v.* Hollingshead, 9 S. & R. 284-5.
(*q*) Cathcart's Appeal, 1 H. 416.
(*r*) Shoemaker *v.* Ballard, 3 H. 92; Baird *v.* Lent, 8 W. 422; *ante*, 783.
(*s*) Leshey *v.* Gardner, 3 W. & S. 314.
(*t*) Crawford *v.* Boyer, 2 H. 380.
(*u*) 1 Sm. Laws, 59.

of notice and sale is similar to that heretofore observed upon other executions. And as the act of 1836 supplies a complete system of process
of executions in all cases except mortgages, the former is now introduced with reference only to proceedings upon those instruments.

The sixth section of the act of 1705, provides that the plaintiff in
the *scire facias* on a mortgage shall have execution by *levari facias*
directed to the proper officer, by virtue whereof the mortgaged premises
shall be taken in execution and exposed to sale in the manner indicated
by the fourth section of the act; and, upon sale, conveyed to the buyer,
and the price of the same rendered to the mortgagee. But for want of
buyers, to be delivered to the mortgagee in the manner previously
directed in the same section concerning other lands to be sold or delivered upon executions for other debts; and when so sold or delivered,
the person to whom they are so sold or delivered shall hold them for
such estates as they were sold or delivered, freed from all equity of
redemption and other incumbrances made or suffered by the mortgagor.

The fourth section directs that, in case the premises cannot be sold
upon the *levari facias*, the officer shall "make return upon the writ
that he exposed them to sale, and that the same remain in his hands
unsold for want of buyers; which return shall not make the officer liable
to answer the amount contained in the writ, but a writ, called a *liberari
facias* shall forthwith be awarded and directed to the officer, commanding him to deliver to the party such part or parts of the lands, tenements, and hereditaments, as shall satisfy his debt, damages, and interest,
from the time of the judgment given, with costs of suit, according to the
valuation of twelve men, to hold to him as his free tenement, in satisfaction of his debt, damages, and costs, or so much thereof as those
lands, by the valuation thereof as aforesaid, shall amount unto, and if it
fall short, the party may have execution for the residue against the
defendant's body, lands, or goods, as the laws of this province shall
direct and appoint from time to time concerning other executions."
Although the act directs a *liberari facias* to issue when the sheriff
returns on the *levari facias* that the premises remain unsold for want
of buyers, yet the ancient construction and practice have been that the
plaintiff is not obliged to proceed by *liberari facias*, but may have an
alias levari facias, if he thinks proper.(v) The writ of *liberari facias*
does not appear to have been resorted to very frequently under this
section; probably because on an *alias levari facias* the party could usually
effect a sale to others, or become the purchaser himself, thus avoiding
the expense, trouble, and loss of time attending an inquest upon the
other process. Where it is executed, however, by actual delivery of
possession, it is a satisfaction of the debt.(w) If the property can be
sold under the *levari facias*, the sheriff proceeds as upon other executions. If the sheriff does not receive the money on an effectual sale,
there is nothing to prevent the plaintiff from going on to complete his
execution. If the sheriff return to a *levari facias* "struck off for a certain sum, and that he cannot make title, therefore remains unsold," the
plaintiff may issue a new execution. So, if he returns the premises unsold.(x) An omission in the writ of the command to levy the debt is

(v) Topper *v.* Taylor, 6 S. & R. 174.　　　(x) Peddle *v.* Hollingshead, 9 S. & R.
(w) Barnet *v.* Washebaugh, 16 S. &　277.
R. 410.

a clerical mistake, which, like similar ones in other writs of execution, is amendable by the court above, after error brought. But the defendant in error must pay the costs of the amendment and execution.(y) Under this writ, the sheriff cannot sell grain growing on the mortgaged premises.(z)

The *levari facias* given to mechanics and material men by the 21st section of the act of 16th June, 1836, is an execution, and comes within the provisions of the act of 13th October, 1840, relating to the sequestration of life estates.(a)

Where the mortgage included several parcels of real estate, it was held, that a *levari*, directing the sale of only one, was erroneous and irregular, in not following the judgment.(b)

Where a mortgagor has sold a part of the mortgaged premises, the mortgagee, upon suing out the mortgage, is bound to proceed first against that part of the land remaining in the mortgagor's hands, and will not be permitted to come upon the portion sold until he has exhausted such portion so remaining: and where the mortgagor has sold the whole in two parts, at two successive periods, the mortgagee must, in the first instance, come upon the part last sold, before attacking the other.(c)

An error in the writ is amendable which recites only the amount of the debt, and interest on the mortgage from the time it was due, instead of interest to the date of judgment, and interest thereafter on the aggregate. The plaintiff is entitled to such latter interest to the time of sale and confirmation.(d)

The first part of the fourth section directs, that " before the sale be made, the sheriff, or other officer, shall cause so many writings to be made upon parchment, or good paper, as the debtor or defendant shall reasonably desire or request, or so many, without such request, as may be sufficient to signify and give notice of such sales or vendues, and of the day and hour when, and of the place where the same will be, and what lands or tenements are to be sold, and where they lie, which notice shall be given to the defendant, and the said parchments or papers shall be fixed by the sheriff or other officer, in the most public places of the county or city, at least ten days before the sale." The defendant is, therefore, under this act, entitled to ten days' notice from the sheriff, but it has been decided that such notice need not be a written or printed one.(e)

It is not necessary that the required notice of sale should appear upon the sheriff's return to a *levari facias*, and upon the trial of an ejectment, the fact of notice is not necessary to be proved by the party insisting on the validity of the sale, unless evidence be given to raise a presumption, that such notice had not been given. In such cases it is presumed that the sheriff has performed his duty unless the reverse appears.(f) The notice is, in practice, seldom in fact given to the defendant, but an

---

(y) Peddle v. Hollingshead, 9 S. & R. 284–5.

(z) Myers v. White, 1 R. 353.
(a) Pentland v. Kelly, 6 W. & S. 483.
(b) Stuckert v. Ellis, 2 M. 433.
(c) Mevey's Appeal, 4 Barr, 80; Cowden's Estate, 1 Barr, 279, affirming Nailer v. Stanly, 10 S. & R. 450, which was shaken by Corporation v. Wallace, 5 R. 109; and see Bank of Pennsylvania v. Winger, 1 R. 303; Fluck v. Replogle, 1 H. 405; see *ante*, 772, *post*, 796, 822.
(d) Mohn v. Heister, 6 W. 53, citing Mason's Executors, 5 W. 464.
(e) 1 Br. 320; C. P. Philad.
(f) Topper v. Taylor, 6 S. & R. 173.

advertisement is usually posted by the sheriff on the premises advertised for sale.(*g*)

Although the act is not clearly expressed, it has been the invariable usage for the sheriff to sell to the mortgagee as well as to a stranger, provided he be the highest bidder, no matter whether for a sum less than the debt and costs, and to make a deed to him, sanctioned by an acknowledgment in open court.(*h*) This procedure upon a mortgage cannot be resorted to after a sale of the mortgaged premises has been already effected under a judgment upon an accompanying bond and warrant. Should the creditor fail in obtaining his debt after such a sale, his only remedy is an action of ejectment to recover possession of the premises.(*i*)

3. *Notice and advertisements.*

The sixty-second section of the act of June, 1836, directs that before any sale of real estate shall be made as aforesaid, the officer shall cause so many written or printed handbills to be made, upon parchment or good paper, as the debtor or defendant shall reasonably request, or so many, without such request, as may be sufficient to give notice of such sale, and of the day and hour when, and the place where the same will be, and what lands or tenements are to be sold, and the place where they lie, which notice shall be given to the defendant, and one of the said papers or parchments shall be fixed by the sheriff, or other officer, upon the premises, and the others of them in the most public places of the county or city, at least ten days before such sale.(*ii*)

The officer shall also give notice of every such sale, by advertisement, describing the real estate to be sold, and the time and place of sale as aforesaid, in at least two newspapers, one in the English, and the other (except in the City and County of Philadelphia) in the German language, if such there are printed in the county where such real estate may be, or if there be no newspaper printed in such county, then in the newspaper printed nearest thereto, once a week, during three successive weeks previous to such sale, under penalty of fifty dollars to the party aggrieved by any such neglect, to be recovered as debts of like amount are recovered : *Provided*, That nothing herein shall debar any party aggrieved from recovering the damages which he may actually sustain by reason of such neglect. § 63.

By the act of 22d April, 1846, § 2 :(*j*) " From and after the passage of this act, it shall not be lawful for the sheriffs and coroners of the several counties of this commonwealth, to publish the sales of real estate, as required by the sixty-third section of the act of the sixteenth of June, A. D. eighteen hundred and thirty-six, in any two newspapers published in any one office, or in any two newspapers published by any one man, or any one company of men."

It has been a practice of long standing, for the sheriff to advertise a sale of lands on a *venditioni exponas* before the return-day, and to adjourn and complete the sale afterwards.(*k*) This practice, in the country,

---

(*g*) On the next page, the general features of sheriff's notices will be considered at large.
(*h*) Blythe *v.* Richards, 10 S. & R. 261.
(*i*) McCall *v.* Lenox, 9 S. & R. 304–5; *vide* Scott *v.* Israel, 2 Bin. 146.

(*ii*) *Post*, 805–7, &c.
(*j*) Pamph. L. 476.
(*k*) McCormick *v.* Meason, 1 S. & R. 92 ; Gordon *v.* Kennedy, 2 Bin. 291; Blythe *v.* Richards, 10 S. & R. 261.

tends much to the advantage of the debtor. The writ being always returnable the first day of the term, the land is duly advertised for sale on a day previous to the return-day, or on that day, and is then not uncommonly adjourned to some more public day during the court week, when, from the attendance of a large number of citizens, a better price may be reasonably expected from the competition of bidders. But in such cases it is usual in many counties to issue another *venditioni*, tested on the first day of the term, for greater caution.(*l*)

In a case, however, where the sheriff advertised the sale on a day *subsequent* to the return-day, the sale was held to be good, and parol evidence of a long-continued practice, in a particular county, to make sales in this manner, was ruled to be admissible.(*m*)

Precision is required in describing the property and its appurtenances, calculated to promote an advantageous sale. Where, therefore, a house and kitchen erected on a lot, were omitted by the sheriff in the advertisement, the sale was set aside. And it is not enough that the buildings are proclaimed at the time of sale, because by the omission many persons may have been prevented from attending.(*n*) So, where the sheriff advertises mortgaged property as subject to a higher ground-rent than it really is, and it is sold at an under value, the sale will be set aside, although the mistake be previously rectified.(*o*)

To promote fairness in such sales, the District Court of the City and County of Philadelphia have decided that the advertisements of the sheriff should be posted in the most conspicuous situations, and that negative testimony would be received of a non-compliance with this rule; as, that the witness had not seen the advertisements in such places, and that, if there, he must have seen them; and also, that the names of the defendants whose property is to be sold should be inserted in the handbills and papers. And in a late case, the court intimated that the sheriff should, at the time of the sale, read the names of the party whose property has been seized, as well as the description, in order that the agents of those concerned might know when the sale is commenced, from the one circumstance, if not from the other. In this case, the sale was set aside on another ground: namely, that in consequence of the sickness of the plaintiff's attorney, who was unable to attend the sale, and who had sent an agent to bid up to a certain price, the property had brought but one-fifth of what the agent had been instructed to bid for it, the agent only knowing the property from the defendant's name, and having been prevented from bidding by the sheriff's omitting to read it; and also because the sum obtained was much below the value of the premises. And the court said that where, through the attorney's sickness, a loss had accrued to his client by a sale, it should be set aside upon a stipulation to pay the costs of the sale, and that the property should bring, on a second sale, as much as the affidavits alleged it ought to have brought.(*p*) And in a more recent case, where it appeared that the sheriff had omitted to fix one of the handbills on the premises ten clear days before the day of sale, pursuant to the 62d section of the act of 1836, the court set aside the sale.(*q*)

(*l*) 1 Sm. Laws, 66, n.
(*m*) Blythe *v.* Richards, 10 S. & R. 261.
(*n*) 1 Br. 320.
(*o*) Wells *v.* Pfeiffer, 4 Y. 203.

(*p*) Garret *v.* Shaw, D. C. Philadelphia, Vend. Exp. June T. 1830.
(*q*) Rinehart *v.* Tiernan, D. C. Dec. 1836, MS. To what extent deficiency in

W_here a small piece of land is purchased by the owner of a tract adjoining it for the purpose of uniting it therewith, and of using, improving, and occupying the whole as one tract and it is so used and occupied, it becomes united to the larger tract; and it is sufficient, in order to include both in a levy, for the sheriff to describe them generally as one tract, without any particular description of the lesser tract, or specification of the title under which it is held.(r)·

Omission in the advertisement of the irredeemability of a ground-rent, where there is a reference to the deed in which the ground-rent is fully described, is not fatal to the sale; nor that the ordinary appendages, such as kitchen, and privy, &c., are not set out.(s)

Under the sixty-third section of the act of 1836, there need not be three weeks between the first advertisement and the day of sale. It is sufficient that the sale is advertised once in every week of three weeks preceding the day of sale.(t)

4. *Manner of sale.*

Upon a sheriff's sale of real property, the general rule prescribed by public utility is, that different lots of ground, houses, and parcels of land, should be sold separately; as many persons might purchase *one*, who could not buy *several* houses; and bidders, by selling all together, would be discouraged, to the public injury. It is essential to the protection of unfortunate debtors, that lumping sales should be disallowed where distinct ones can be effected. Thus, if there be a lot of ground, out of which an entire ground-rent is payable, with three tenements on it, but so divided that a portion of it is used with each tenement, it must be sold in three distinct parcels, otherwise the sale will be set aside. So, in all cases in violation of this general rule, unless the sheriff satisfies the court that they form clear exceptions to it.(u) This rule will not obtain, however, where the property is from its nature incapable of partition; but only where distinct pieces can conveniently be sold separately. Thus, a sale of two undivided third parts of three contiguous houses on one lot was confirmed, as few persons would choose to purchase an undivided interest in a house incapable of division.(v) So, distinct tenements on one entire farm, occupied by different persons, must follow the principal estate, and be sold as parcel of it. So if, after judgment, the defendant sells part of the land and separates the tract by an ideal line, the sheriff may sell the whole.(w) The sheriff ought not to sell more of the property than will probably satisfy the execution, and which can conveniently and reasonably be sold separately;(x) and he cannot sell more than he has actually levied upon.(y)

The sheriff is not bound to sell in a lump all the land described in the mortgage. He may and ought to sell in *parcels* as the property is occupied and enjoyed; and the court will so direct him to sell, and in

notice will be ground for setting aside a sale, will be hereafter noticed; *post*, 803, 4, 5, 6, 7.

(r) Buckholder v. Sigler, 7 W. & S. 154.

(s) Steinmetz v. Stokes, D. C. C. P. *post*, 806; Gilbert v. Jackson, *post*, 808.

(t) Williams v. Moore, *post*, 807; overruling Francis v. Norris, 2 M. 150.

(u) Ryerson v. Nicholson, 2 Y. 517; Vastine v. Fury, 2 S. & R. 434; Rowley v. Brown, 1 Bin. 62; *post*, 803, 4, 5, 808-9.

(v) Prior v. Britton, 2 Y. 550.

(w) Dickey's Case, C. P. 1 Journ. Jurisp. 91.

(x) 8 Johns. 333.

(y) 4 Y. 111.

such order as will produce most, and so protect the terre-tenant's rights and equities.(z)

Where the owner of two several lots of ground, subject to a judgment, conveys one of them to a third party, and afterwards has another judgment obtained against him, the vendee of the first-mentioned lot has an equity so far superior to the second judgment creditor, that the latter cannot compel the first judgment creditor to come first upon the lot thus conveyed, so as to leave the residue of the defendant's estate as satisfaction for the second judgment.(a)

If there be two judgment creditors, and one have a lien on two tracts, and the other on one only, and the proceeds of a sheriff's sale to be brought into court, the former will be required to exhaust the proceeds of that upon which the latter has no lien, before he will be allowed to apply the proceeds of the other tract to the payment of his judgment.(b)

A owned two lots, and mortgaged them to B, and then sold lot 1 to C, and agreed with him that lot 2 should pay the mortgage to B. C mortgaged lot 1 to A for the purchase-money, which mortgage came into the hands of D. B having taken both lots into execution on his mortgage, and sold them, the court set aside the sale on application of C, and ordered B to proceed to sell lot 2, and then, only in case it did not bring enough to cover debt, interest, and costs, to sell lot 1.(c)

Where there are several tracts, the sheriff has no right to sell more than will extinguish the liens. Thus, where plaintiff held a mortgage against five adjoining houses, which were described as three parcels, Nos. 1, 2, and 3, on a writ of *levari facias*, the sheriff sold the property in that order, No. 1 bringing a price sufficient to pay in full the debt, interest, and costs, there being no other liens enforceable against the premises, it was held that the sale of Nos. 2 and 3 was irregular, and as to them the sale was set aside.(d)

Where a subdivision of property about to be sold at sheriff's sale is necessary, the proper course, in case the parties cannot agree among themselves as to a plan, is for an application to be made to the court whence the execution issues, which, on sufficient cause being shown, will order the manner in which the property is to be divided ;(e) but notice of an intended subdivision of land, to be sold at sheriff's sale, should be given in the handbills, and should not be reserved until the time of sale. Where a bid has been made at a sheriff's sale by auction, and the sale adjourned, the bid is withdrawn by implication.(f)

It is not a fraud in the plaintiff intending to purchase at the sale, if he does not make known to the bidders the amount of mortgages or incumbrances against it, or whether it is sold subject to, or clear of, them. Nor is it a part of the sheriff's duty to examine and know the state of any incumbrances besides that under which he sells. Whether or not it

---

(z) Mevey's Appeal, 4 Barr, 80, and *ante,* 792, *note* (c); *post,* 822.

(a) Bruner's Appeal, 7 W. & S. 269; see Zeigler v. Long, 2 W. 206; see Cowden's Estate, 1 Barr, 267; see *ante,* 772.

(b) Hastings's Case, 10 W. 304; see Lea v. Hopkins, 7 Barr, 492; Bruner's Appeal, 7 W. & S. 269.

(c) Winberg v. Reiff, D. C. C. P. 4 Barr, 88, note (a) ; see Mevey's Appeal, 4 Barr, 80.

(d) Richards v. Brittin, D. C. C. C. P. 5 P. L. J. 73.

(e) Newman v. Callahan, D. C. C. P. April, 1848 ; *post,* 804–809.

(f) Donaldson v. Kerr, 6 Barr, 486.

will discharge the property from other liens, the rule *caveat emptor* fully applies to all such sales.(*g*)

As the law prescribes the conditions of sale, a departure from them by the sheriff is invalid, and hence he cannot ordinarily stipulate the continuance of a lien which the law decrees to be divested by the sale, and an attempt to do so will not, usually, bind the parties in interest.(*h*) And so, where the owner of a mortgage which was a prior lien, purchases the property at sheriff's sale under a prior incumbrance, he is not entitled, in the absence of stipulations inserted in the conditions of sale, to a deed from the sheriff, on offering to credit the amount of his bid in satisfaction of the mortgage.(*i*)

Under the writ of *venditioni exponas*, the sheriff must sell, not merely to the *highest* but the *best* bidder; therefore, if the highest bidder is unable to pay, the sheriff may make an offer to the next highest bidder. If the property is not paid for after a sale, the return should be that "the premises were knocked down to A B for so much; and the said A B has not paid the purchase-money, and that, therefore, the premises remain unsold."(*j*) If a purchaser forfeit his pretensions as the highest bidder, the sheriff may refuse giving him a deed, at his own risk, and the merits of the purchaser's case may be ascertained in an action by him against the sheriff.(*k*)

The principle stated in Reigle *v.* Sieger,(*l*) that the sheriff is bound by the statute to sell the debtor's interest, whatever it may be, without terms or conditions, affecting the title, is enforced in a later case,(*m*) where the court rebuked the sheriff for selling land subject to the widow's dower, as one of the conditions, as if the law were incompetent to protect her interests without his aid.

Where defendant's estate is a fee-simple, nothing less than a fee can be legally sold on execution, without his consent; and hence a levy and sale of the estate of A, as tenant by the curtesy, passes no title, if he had the fee.(*n*)

In Philadelphia County, the sheriff is liable to be imposed upon by persons unknown to him, who occasionally contract to purchase at his sales, with no other intent than to get time for the defendant, or to speculate on the property by selling their contract within the ten days. Frequent defeats of sheriff's sales are thus produced, and to guard against them he now requires, in such cases, an advance of a certain portion of the purchase-money, as earnest. If it be refused, he puts up the property again, or offers it to the next highest bidder.

The purchase of lands on behalf of a client, is not within the trust confided to an attorney, and he is not entitled to a deed from the sheriff without paying the purchase-money, or giving a receipt on behalf of his principal. A receipt, provided there were no collusion, would justify the sheriff in giving a deed. But if the plaintiff himself should apply to the

---

(*g*) Carson's sale, 6 W. 140.
(*h*) Mather *v.* McMichael, 1 H. 305, per BELL, J. See Reigle *v.* Seiger, 2 Pa. R. 340; Mode's Appeal, 6 W. & S. 280; Randolph's Appeal, 5 Barr, 242; Wood *v.* Lewis, 2 H. 92.
(*i*) Crawford *v.* Boyer, 2 H. 380.
(*j*) Zahtzinger *v.* Pole, 1 D. 419.

(*k*) Vastine *v.* Fury, 2 S. & R. 435; see Auwerter *v.* Mathiot, 9 S. & R. 397; Weidler *v.* Farmer's Bank of Lancaster, 11 S. & R. 134.
(*l*) 2 Pa. R.
(*m*) Aulenbaugh *v.* Umbehauer, 8 W. 49, 50.
(*n*) McLaughlin *v.* Shields, 2 J. 283.

court, before the deed is acknowledged, and insist on payment of the money, the court would suspend the acknowledgment, until the money was paid, or set aside the sale if it were not paid in a short time.(*o*) An attorney cannot purchase the land for his own benefit, to the prejudice of his client, for a less sum than the amount of the claim upon which it was being sold. And if there be two plaintiffs in the execution, he cannot purchase for the benefit of one, without the consent of the other, for a less sum than the whole amount of the claim. And if he do so purchase, and the sheriff make a deed to one of the plaintiffs, under such circumstances, there is a resulting trust for both.(*oo*)

Lien creditors may purchase jointly at sheriff's sale, if all be open and fair, and if their combination tend to raise and not to depress.(*p*)

Where there is an agreement between the plaintiff in an execution and a third party, before the sale, that the latter, in case the land is bought in by the plaintiff, shall take from him at a certain fixed price, and the agreement is carried into effect, the amount which is to be applied to the discharge of the judgment, and to be credited to the defendant, is the price agreed to be paid, and not that bid at the sale; and this must also be considered the price of the land, not only between the plaintiff and defendant, but as regards all parties interested in the price.(*r*)

It is a settled principle, that as between the debtor or his representatives, and the sheriff, a purchase by the sheriff, or by any one in trust for him, without the debtor's consent, is void. From principles of the soundest policy, the law will not endure that the same person should be both the seller and the purchaser. But if the debtor consents, his representatives cannot impeach it; or, if he does not know or consent, the sale will not be disturbed to the prejudice of a subsequent *bona fide* purchaser, without notice.(*s*) The plaintiff has a right to suspend the sale where it may eventuate in a sacrifice, or where a little indulgence may render a sale unnecessary; and during these proceedings on a *testatum execution*, he retains his lien, provided he continues his process in such a manner as to give public notice that he means to hold the land. This may be done by issuing writs of *venditioni exponas*, from term to term, and delivering them to the sheriff.(*t*)

It is laid down in one of our cases, that the sale is always for money, to be paid down, unless the conditions make other provisions. The purchaser, on the property being struck down to him, is immediately answerable to the sheriff, who is not bound to wait until the return of the writ; for if the purchaser do not pay, he may immediately put it up again and return it to the first bidder, or may sue for the amount of purchase-money, and that without tendering a deed acknowledged.(*u*) But in a more recent case, this doctrine is said to be in contradiction with the case of Vastine *v.* Fury.(*v*) The propositions deduced by the reporters from the latter case are these: "In ordinary cases, there is no reason

(*o*) Pearson *v.* Morrison, 2 S. & R. 21.
(*oo*) *Ante*, 219, 220.
(*p*) Small *v.* Jones, 1 W. & S. 136; 6 W. & S. 122.
(*r*) Young *v.* Stone, 4 W. & S. 45.
(*s*) Lessee of Lazarus *v.* Bryson, 3 Bin. 58.

(*t*) Cowden *v.* Brady, 8 S. & R. 507.
(*u*) Negley *v.* Stewart, 10 S. & R. 207; Scott *v.* Greenough, 7 S. & R. 197.
(*v*) 2 S. & R. 426. See Holdship *v.* Doran, 2 Pa. R. 17.

to justify a sheriff in demanding the money, on a sale of lands, before he can give a title, or the purchaser can get possession. Unless a bidder is notoriously insolvent, the sheriff cannot, long before the return-day of his writ, make a return, that the purchaser has not paid, and therefore unsold for want of buyers: and when he does so, and has made no demand, and has no evidence to justify him in so doing, the bidder is not liable for a difference in price." "A sheriff may, after the return-day of his writ, sustain an action against a bidder at his sale, to recover from him the amount of his bid, without having first tendered him a deed." "An action against a bidder at a sheriff's sale, for the difference between the amount of his bid and that at which the land was struck down at a subsequent sale, must be brought either in the name of the sheriff, on the privity of contract, or in that of some one who was injured." As the opinion of the court in this case contains a concise review of the decisions on this subject, the inquirer is particularly referred to it. And as the decisions and dicta, with reference to the powers and duties of the sheriff, and of the highest bidder at his sale of lands, are said by the learned judge who delivered the court's opinion, not to agree exactly with each other, he proceeds to notice them, and to apply them to the different practice that obtains in different counties upon sheriff's sales.

A sheriff is bound to sell a debtor's whole interest in the land, and can lawfully reserve nothing for him, either in the land or the price of it.(w)

Leasehold property need not be sold by the sheriff on the premises.(x)

By the act of 16th April, 1845,(y) all sales of real property within this commonwealth, made since the passage of the act to which this is a supplement, by sheriffs or coroners, after the return-day of their several writs of *levari facias, fieri facias, venditioni exponas*, or other writ of execution shall not, on any account of such irregularity in such proceedings, be set aside, invalidated, or in any manner affected, and such sales so made shall be held as good and valid to all intents and purposes as if such sales had been made on or before the return-day of such writs respectively; but this section shall not affect any sale heretofore adjudged to be illegal by any court. § 1.

After the first day of July next, all sales of real estate by sheriffs or coroners, shall be made on or before the return-day of the writs respectively, or within six days thereafter. § 2.

Prior to this act, a sale held under execution *after* the return-day, was void—and even with consent of the defendant, it was void against a subsequent purchaser at sheriff's sale, under an incumbrance which would have been discharged by the first sale, had it been valid. As to such a sale held prior to the act of 1845, the latter act has been decided to be unconstitutional.(z)

When one has a judgment on distinct pieces of land, he may select which to proceed against first, if one be insufficient; but when money is

(w) Aulenbaugh v. Umbehauer, 8 W. 50, S. C. 3 W. & S. 259; Reigle v. Seiger, 2 P. R. 340; Fretz v. Heller, 2 W. & S. 399.

(x) Sowers v. Vie, 2 H. 99.
(y) Pamph. L. 538.
(z) Dale v. Metcalf, 9 Barr, 108.

brought into court, and there are contending claimants, it will be distributed according to equity.(a)

When a creditor has two funds for payment, he may be compelled by another creditor who has but one of them, to apply the proceeds of sale by execution, so as to leave to the latter a resort for payment of his debt to the only fund in his power.(b)

5. *Liberari facias as to property unsold.*

It is directed by the sixty-fourth section of the act of June, 1836, that in case the said real estate, so to be exposed, cannot be sold, then the officer shall make return upon his writ, that he exposed such real estate to sale, and the same remained in his hands unsold, for want of buyers, and such return shall not make the officer liable to answer the debt or damages mentioned in such writ.

It shall be lawful for the plaintiff in such writ, whenever the officer shall return upon the same that such real estate remains in his hands unsold as aforesaid, to have the same valued as aforesaid, or so much thereof as shall satisfy his judgment, with the interest from the day on which it was rendered, and costs; thereupon, he may have a writ of *liberari facias* awarded and directed to such officer, commanding him to deliver to the plaintiff such part or parts of such real estate as shall satisfy his debt of damages and interest, from the time of the judgment given, with costs of suit, according to the valuation aforesaid, to hold to him and his heirs, forever, as his free tenement, in satisfaction of his debt, damages, and costs, or of so much thereof as such real estate, by the valuation aforesaid, shall amount to; or, at his election, such plaintiff may have another writ or writs of *venditioni exponas* awarded as aforesaid, for the sale of the same real estate. § 65.

All real estate which shall be sold or delivered as aforesaid, by any sheriff or other officer, with the appurtenances, shall be quietly and peaceably held and enjoyed by the person to whom the same shall be sold or delivered, and by the heirs, successors, or assigns of such person, as fully and amply, and for such estate and estates, and under the same rents and services, as he or they for whose debt or duty the same shall be sold or delivered, might, could, or ought to do, at or before the taking thereof in execution. § 66.

In case the plaintiff to whom land shall be delivered in satisfaction of his debt as aforesaid shall be evicted, upon any lawful title, without any fraud, collusion, or other default, he may, upon settling an account of such sums and profits as he has received from such estate, and may be entitled to retain, deducting for his reasonable expenses and labors, have a writ of *scire facias* upon such judgment, against the defendant, his executors or administrators, to show cause why he should not have execution for the residue of his judgment, with costs; and if no sufficient cause be shown, execution may issue, notwithstanding the delivery of such real estate to him, in satisfaction of his judgment, as aforesaid.(c) § 67.

(a) Hastings's Case, 10 Watts, 303.
(b) Ibid.
(c) This section is derived from the statute 32 H. VIII. c. 5; Rob. Dig. 241. It extends the provision of this statute to the case of lands delivered in satisfac-

Upon a *liberari facias*, the sheriff is bound to deliver actual possession of the premises to the plaintiff, where the defendant or his tenant is in possession ; and where a sheriff had returned to a *liberari facias*, " executed as within commanded," it was held that the plaintiff could not take out an *alias* writ, although evidence was given to prove that actual possession had not been delivered.(*e*)

A sheriff, who, under a *liberari*, delivers possession of premises held under a lease for years, should return that fact specially. And should he return that he had given possession, without more, he becomes liable for a false return.(*f*)

6. Alias venditioni exponas.

The plaintiff, instead of resorting to the writ of *liberari facias* above described, may take out an *alias venditioni exponas*, and upon it again endeavor to make a sale of the premises. If successful, the sale will not be set aside for mere inadequacy of price ;(*g*) although an offer be made with security that the property, if again set up, shall bring a large advance, the court having no power to open the biddings in such a case. Neither will it be set aside on the application of a purchaser for a defect of title, where there has been no fraud in the sale.(*h*) But upon any appearance of fraud, the inadequacy of price, though not conclusive of itself to avoid a sale, affords an argument of great weight against a purchaser to whom such fraud is imputed. And if the purchaser possess a knowledge of facts unknown to others attending the sale, and which if known, would have had an influence upon the sale, the court would not permit a deed to him to be acknowledged, but will set the sale aside.(*i*) So if puffers be employed at the sale to raise the price against the real bidders, which is a fraud upon them, or if any other fraud or unfair practices have existed, such sale will be held void.(*j*) The court will not willingly listen to a motion to quash a *venditioni*, on the ground that other property in the hands of purchasers from the defendant, after the judgment, and liable to contribute, might have been levied on.(*k*) It would seem reasonable in such case that the moving party should have notified the plaintiff of the existence of such lands, so that he might have included them in his levy.(*l*)

7. Setting aside sheriff's sale.

The subject of setting aside sheriffs' sales. for inadequacy of price received the particular consideration of a part of the Supreme Court in a leading case.(*m*) It was said by Ross, J., the Chief Justice concurring,

tion of the debt. The statute was designed for cases of extent. In section sixty, the provision has a similar application. This section furnishes an inducement for the use of the writ of *lib. fa.*, after *venditioni*, and no sufficient price offered. Lands are frequently sold at a great sacrifice, still, the purchaser must look to the title, for he acquires only the defendant's right. This section reverses the rule as it respects the plaintiff, who receives upon this writ the lands of his debtor in satisfaction of the debt. The plaintiff, after eviction, should be allowed a recourse to his judgment for the residue.—*Remarks of Commissioners.*

(*e*) Sawyer *v.* Curtis, 2 Ash. 127.
(*f*) McMichael *v.* Keon, 10 Barr, 143.
(*g*) McLaughlin's Lessee *v.* Dawson, 4 D. 221 ; Lessee of Murphy *v.* McCleary, 3 Y. 405 ; Simon *v.* Simon, 1 M. 406 ; see Young's Appeal, 2 Pa. R. 380 ; 1 Journ. Jurisp. 92.
(*h*) Juniata Bank *v.* Brown, 5 S. & R. 226.
(*i*) 1 Br. 187.
(*j*) Ib. 346 ; 1 Journ. Jurisp. 91.
(*k*) 1 Peters's Rep. 140.
(*l*) Ib.
(*m*) Young's Appeal, 2 Pa. R. 380.

that " the *bona fide* purchaser at a public sale of land, the moment it is knocked off to him, if he complies in all respects with the conditions of sale, instantly acquires a vested right to the property sold. Such a purchaser would be bound by his bargain thus made, although his bid greatly exceeded its value: And if he purchase at a *bona fide* sale greatly below the value, the vendor would be bound by the sale. Equality, in this case at least, is equity. The vendee certainly should have the advantage of a purchase at a price below the value, when he is bound by a purchase at a price greatly exceeding the true value.(*n*) In order to set aside a sheriff's sale, there must be satisfactory evidence of fraud, or abuse of power in the sheriff.(*o*) A collusion between a purchaser and strangers by unfair means to procure the sale, and the purchase to be made below what it would have brought if such means had not been resorted to, would also be sufficient to set aside a sale.(*p*) These general observations are made with the hope that any practice in opposition to these principles, which may have arisen in some of the courts as to sheriffs' sales, may be corrected. It is not a sound exercise of the discretionary power of a court to destroy the vested rights of a fair purchaser, either from feelings of sympathy for the defendant in the execution, or because the court may not see any peculiar hardship in the *bona fide* purchaser's being arbitrarily deprived of his just and equitable right."—"A motion has been made to dismiss the appeal in this case, because an appeal does not lie at common law, and it is not given by the act of April 16, 1827, under which act, this appeal has been entered. In the opinion of the court, this act is limited in its operation to cases where there may be disputes about the distribution of moneys, arising from sales made by sheriffs or coroners. This is not a dispute about the distribution of money, but about the power of a court to set aside a sheriff's sale, for the reasons assigned in the opinion of the court below. It is, therefore, not within the provisions of the act, and the appeal must be dismissed."—"Whether the purchaser is left without a remedy, is a question not at this time regularly before the court. Whether a writ of error will lie or whether the purchaser can, by refusing to take back his money, sustain an ejectment for the land, are questions, which may merit consideration when they come regularly before this court." The other three judges concurred in dismissing the appeal, but as the other question had not been argued, they would not express any opinion upon it.

The remedy of a purchaser, who has bid at sheriff's sale under a misapprehension as to his rights, is by application to the court to set aside the sale.(*q*)

The following decisions of the District Courts of Philadelphia and Alleghany will be found important in practice :—

Even after acknowledgment of sheriff's deed, the sale may be set aside, where the plaintiff in the execution being the highest bidder had the sale adjourned, and then purchased the property at a lower rate.(*s*)

Though it is irregular for the court to set aside a sheriff's sale, unless

---

(*n*) 2 Conn. Rep. 821, 835.
(*o*) Wood *v.* Monell, *et al.* 1 Johns. Ch. Rep. 502.
(*p*) See 4 Johns. Ch. Rep. 254.

(*q*) Crawford *v.* Boyer, 2 H. 380.
(*s*) Vanneman *v.* Cooper, D. C. All. 9 P. L. J. 266.

notice is given to all the parties interested, yet where a sale was set aside without notice to a defendant, who thereupon suffered the second sale to proceed, without calling, at the time, the attention of the court to the irregularity, the court afterwards refused relief.(t)

A sale will be set aside, where, by plaintiff's direction, it was made subject to prior liens.(u)

It is a general rule that, where the sheriff sells different parcels of houses together, the sale will be set aside; and it is not necessary in such case, that it should appear that the price was inadequate ;(v) and neither a common disadvantage, nor a common benefit, as where houses are situated on different sides of the same court, and possess a common right of way and privies, or are connected by a common vault extending from one to another, will justify the lumping of them together on a sheriff's sale ; and where such is the case, the sale will be set aside,(w) though where lots of ground in a cemetery are sold in the lump instead of separately, the court will not, on that ground alone, interfere to set aside the sheriff's sale.(x)

A sale will not be set aside, if the land be sufficiently described in the advertisement, though not in the levy.(y)

A mortgage creditor, who has bid in property improperly described at a sheriff's sale, and failed to comply with the terms of sale, is not thereby estopped from objecting to a second sale, under the same erroneous description.(z)

Inadequacy of price is not, of itself, a sufficient reason for setting aside a sheriff's sale ;(a) and where an offer was made with security that the property, if again set up for sale, should bring a large advance, the court declared that they had not power to open the biddings, and refused to set aside the sale.(b) But whenever there is an appearance of fraud at a sheriff's sale, the inadequacy of price—though not conclusive in itself to avoid a sale—affords an argument of great weight against a purchaser to whom the fraud is imputed.(c)

Where the inadequacy is very gross, the court will take advantage of any irregularity in the proceedings, however slight. Where there is an inadequacy, but not very gross, security is required that a greater sum will be offered at the second sale. But in neither case can the sale be set aside where the proceedings are strictly regular ;(d) and it is not enough to establish inadequacy of price, on a motion to set aside a sheriff's sale, that it be shown that a third person, who was not himself

---

(t) Ingersoll v. Sherry, D. C. C. P. post, 808.

(u) Dunlap v. Gray, D. C. All. Lowrie, J.

(v) Connell v. Hughes, D. C. C. P. 8 Leg. Int. 130. See ante, 795; post, 805.

(w) Tate v. Carberry, D. C. C. P. post, 809.

(x) Cemetery Co. v. Potts, D. C. C. P. 8 Leg. Int. 158.

(y) Dunlap v. Gra , D. C. All. Lowrie, J. ante, 794; see also post, 806.

(z) Connell v. Hughes, D. C. C. P. 8 Leg. Int. 130.

(a) Weitzell v. Fry, 4 D. 221 ; Dickey's Case, Common Pleas, April,1820, 1 Journal Jurisprudence, 92 ; Murphy v. McCleary, 3 Y. 405 ; Cooper v. Galbraith, 3 W. C. C. R. 546 ; Carson's Sale, 6 W. 140 ; Simon v. Simon, 1 M. 404 ; post, 805.

(b) Dickey's Case, ut supra ; Percival v. Bryant, 7 P. L. J. 196; Whitacre v. Pratt, post, 805-6.

(c) Ibid. ; Weitzell v. Fry, 4 D. 221.

(d) Whitacre v. Pratt, D. C. C. P. post, 805 ; see Vanneman v. Cooper, 8 P. L. J. 190.

called and examined under oath, had stated that he would give a greater sum, if the property was put up again.(e)

As to its own proceedings, the District Court may properly grant the same relief on motion that was formerly granted under the old practice by *audita querela*, writ of error *coram nobis*, or bill in equity.(f) Where a judgment, on which a sheriff's sale is founded, is set aside, the setting aside of a sale of land thereunder follows, as, of course, on the ground of restitution.(g)

It is no objection to the setting aside a sheriff's sale, where the deed is still in the sheriff's hands, that a term has elapsed since the acknowledgment of the deed.(h)

Long delay, not accounted for, in an application to set aside a sheriff's sale, though before the acknowledgment of the deed, will be ground for the court to refuse it.(i)

Where the sheriff establishes a rule on the sale of real estate, at auction, as in selling according to the alphabetical order of the names of counsel, a departure from it will be a ground of setting aside a sale.(j)

(e) Steinmetz v. Stokes, D. C. C. P. Oct. 1848; *post*, 806.

(f) Stephens v. Stephens, D. C. All. 7 Leg. Int. 183.

(g) Ibid.

(h) Ibid.

(i) George v. Graham, D. C. C. P. 7 Leg. Int. 98; Young v. Walls, *post*, 808.

(j) Sergeant v. Goslin, C. C. Philad. 9 Leg. Int. 34. The following opinions of Judge SHARSWOOD have mostly been noticed in the text. They are, however, here given in full, not only from their authoritativeness, but from the terse and lucid manner in which they explain the practice on a branch of law of much difficulty and importance:—

Newman v. Callaghan, D. C. Saturday, April 22, 1848. Why sheriff's sale should be set aside. *Per curiam.* Whenever a lot is sold, in separate parcels, we think, the subdivisions in which it is to be sold should appear in the handbills and advertisements, in order that bidders may have the opportunity to examine and decide beforehand what sum to offer for each parcel. Cautious men would hesitate to make up their minds during the hurry of the sale; and, probably, decline bidding altogether.

No doubt, a creditor has no right to cut up an entire lot according to his own pleasure. If there are the marks of an actual division on the ground, he should follow that. In this case there were three distinct tenements, though two of them were dilapidated and uninhabitable. Yet the lot was sold in two parts of very unequal size. The brick building was sold by itself, not including a passage and watercourse by the side of it in actual use with it. In practice, it is the safer course, where there is any doubt, to notify the defendant, or terre-tenants, of the subdivision intended to be made, and if they refuse to furnish any other as more satisfactory, it must be a very strong and peculiar case in which the court would interfere to set aside the sale. Rule absolute.

Biddle v. Rudolph, D. C. April 29, 1848. Why sheriff's sale should not be set aside. *Per curiam.* The sole ground alleged in support of this motion is that the two properties described in the handbill acquired at different times, subject to unequal ground-rents, have been sold together. It is very evident, however, that the two lots in question have been improved and used for one single purpose; that of a livery stable with the usual appurtenances for such a purpose. It is clear also that the sale of it in two separate lots would destroy its use and value for the purpose to which it is now appropriated. It may be that a division would be better, with a view to its future improvement, in a different way. But is a plaintiff to enter into these calculations and conjectures? It is the settled principle upon which the court acts in cases of this kind, that the plaintiff is to look at the actual state of the premises, and no further. Who can doubt that, if the sale had been in separate parcels, and the value of the present improvements had thus been destroyed, the proceeding, if the result had been unsatisfactory to any party, except the plaintiff, would have been set aside?

Creditors are entitled to receive their debts, without unnecessary delay; and if they have done nothing, but what was clearly right and the proceedings have been perfectly regular, on what principle can the court interfere? As to the fact that the titles of the two lots were different and the ground-rents unequal, that can make no difference. We have often decided that separate lots, though derived from the same common source of title and subject to one paramount ground-rent, more than the value of each particular lot and its improvement must still be sold separately; thus throwing upon the purchaser the risk and trouble, after being obliged to pay the whole paramount ground-rent, of seeking contribution from the owners of the other parcels. This is a much stronger case than its converse, which is now before us. Our discretion in cases of this kind is a legal discretion, not to be exercised at random, according to mere whim or caprice, but according to settled principles and rules. Rule dismissed.

Barrow *v.* Rhoads, D. C. Saturday, April 29, 1848. Why sheriff's sale should not be set aside. *Per curiam.* This was a *levari facias* upon a judgment by confession in a *sci. fa.* on a mechanic's claim. The house against which the claim was filed is built on the rear end of a lot 20 feet front on Somerset street, in the district of Richmond, by 100 feet to Hewson street, and one lot was conveyed to defendant by that description. Somerset street is a principal street in Richmond, 60 feet wide; Hewson street, in the rear end of the lot, is 30 feet wide. The house stands on the rear of the lot, a short distance back of Hewson street, is about 16 feet front, and the entire lot, 100 feet deep, is fenced off across the centre, leaving the house in the rear with 50 feet of the lot before and behind it inclosed. By the 4th, 5th, 6th, and 7th sections of the act of 16th June, 1836 (Purd. 799), provisions are made for the designation of the boundaries of the lot or curtilage appurtenant to buildings subject to liens according to that act. By the 8th section it is provided, that " if execution shall be awarded for the levy and sale of any lot or piece of ground, upon which a building shall be erected as aforesaid, before the boundaries of the lot or curtilage which ought to be appurtenant thereto shall be designated, it shall be lawful for the court, upon application, to stay such execution until such designation shall be made, and

thereupon order the sale to proceed in such manner and for such part or parts, and in such parcels, as shall be most convenient for the administration of equity among all persons interested." It will be seen that it was the duty of the defendant to have interposed before the sale; and if the plaintiff were not also in fault we would not now interfere. But the description advertised, and according to which the sale was made—following in this respect the description in the claim—does not designate the boundaries of the lot. The only words are " the lot or piece of ground, and curtilage appurtenant to said building." This is altogether too vague. Rule absolute.

Evans *v.* Miller, D. C. Saturday, June 10, 1848. Why sheriff's sale should not be set aside. *Per curiam.* Sheriff's sales are never set aside merely for inadequacy of price, though in cases where it is very gross the court will take advantage of an irregularity in the proceedings, which, under other circumstances, they might be disposed to overlook. Here it is by no means clear that there has been any such gross inadequacy as to bring the case within the category here referred to. Without that consideration, the mistake of an inch or two in the breadth or depth of the lot, and which evidently had no influence on the sale, is too trifling to justify our interposition. Especially would our interference be unwarrantable where, as here, the sale is upon a fourth *pluries levari facias*, the same description having been inserted and continued in this long series of writs and advertisements without objection by the defendant. Rule dismissed.

Whitacre *v.* Pratt, D. C. Saturday, Sept. 16, 1848. Rule to set aside a sheriff's sale. *Per curiam.* We think the description in this case defective. The fact that the premises were an established tavern-stand, and the house and out-houses calculated for a house of public entertainment, ought to have been stated, although we do not mean to say that, if the description is in other respects sufficiently certain, we would set aside a sale on that ground alone, unless indeed accompanied with gross inadequacy of price. Here, however, the premises were situated in a village, the names of the streets in which were given, but not the name of the village; so that a knowledge of the situation of the premises would necessarily be confined to those readers of the description who knew that there were streets of that name in the village of Bridesburg, and none other such in the large district incorporated or unincorporated, popularly and legally perhaps called the Northern Liberties. We are to look at substance in matters of this kind, and not make our judgment to depend on questions of legal nicety, such as whether the village of Bridesburg, not being incorporated, has any legal existence, or whether the rest of the Northern Liberties, except that which is an incorporated district, is properly to be called the unincorporated Northern Liberties, or simply the Northern Liberties. As to the defendant's having acquiesced in the first advertisement, that argument might avail in the mouth of the plaintiff, who has been delayed, and it may be injured, but the purchaser is in the same situation as if this were the first sale.

We take occasion to say that the court has never changed the principle upon which it acts in cases in which there appears to be inadequacy of price. It is not of itself any ground; but where it is very gross the court will take advantage of any irregularity in the proceedings, however slight, to set the sale aside. Where there is inadequacy, but not very gross, the court requires security that advance will be bid at a second sale. In other words, where a doubt may be suggested as to the inadequacy, the offer of security that the property will bring a certain, much larger sum, will have decisive weight with the court in determining the question. We say this in explanation of the case of Perceval v. Bryant (7 Law Journ. 196), the circumstances of which are not remembered, but by the affidavit on which the rule in that case was granted several irregularities are alleged, and certainly the court did not mean to hold that mere inadequacy of price, where the proceedings have been all strictly regular, is of itself a sufficient ground to set aside a sale, even when a higher bid is offered to be secured. Rule absolute.

Hall v. Mayer, D. C. Saturday, Sept. 30, 1848. Why sheriff's sale should not be set aside. *Per curiam.* This was a sale under a *levari facias,* upon proceedings upon a mortgage, and one ground upon which the sale is asked to be set aside is that no notice was given to the defendant, as required by the fourth sect. of the act of 1705 (Purd. 291, note). That is the only act of assembly in force regulating executions upon judgments on mortgages, and it certainly expressly provides for notice to the defendant. The sheriff, however, is presumed to have done his duty, and without mean-

ing to decide anything in regard to the point of notice in this case, as there is another sufficient reason for setting the sale aside, we may be permitted to remark that we have before us no affidavit of defendant, that he did not receive notice which would at least seem to be essential to authorize the court to set aside the sale on this ground.

It appears, however, that the premises had been fitted up at a very considerable expense as a tavern. We think this was an improvement, which ought to have been stated. Rule absolute.

Steinmetz v. Stokes, D.C. Saturday, Oct. 14, 1848. Why sheriff's sale should not be set aside. *Per curiam.* It is objected that the sheriff's bill did not describe the back buildings—that is, not independent improvements on the rear of the lot, but the usual necessary offices of every dwelling, as kitchen, bath-house, privy, &c. Such particularity has never been required.

Again, it is said, that the bill does not state that the ground-rent, to which the property is subject, is redeemable. It gives the date of the ground-rent deed, however; and this was enough to put every one upon inquiry, as to the nature and character of the charge.

And, lastly, we are by no means satisfied, by the evidence, that there is any inadequacy of price. We have no evidence as to the value. To prove that somebody had offered to give a certain sum without producing that person, is manifestly nothing but that person's declaration, not under oath, of his opinion as to its value. The remark has no application to this case from anything that appears; but it is clear to be seen how easy such evidence could be manufactured; and this is the only evidence we have before us. Rule dismissed.

Campbell v. Ruddack, Dec. 23, 1848. Why sheriff's sale should not be set aside. *Per curiam.* Inadequacy of price is, of itself, no reason for setting aside a sale. Here the circumstance relied on to take the case out of the general rule, is, that the sale on this occasion commenced half an hour earlier than the previous sale of the sheriff. The change of hour, however, was duly notified in the bills and advertisements; and it is notorious that the hour for commencing such sales varies with the different seasons of the year. This, therefore, is no ground whatever for our interference. Nor can we perceive any reason for making any difference in these cases when the purchaser is a member of the bar. Rule discharged.

Fisher v. Stokes, May 12, 1849. Why

sheriff's sale as to second described property should not be set aside. *Per curiam.* The misdescription in this case is very palpable; and though if it appeared that defendant had acquiesced, with a view to the property being bought in' by a friend, we would not interfere, we cannot act upon such a surmise without notice. To conclude, a defendant, in case of misdescription, should have distinct notice of the intended description before the advertisement within a reasonable time, so that he may have the opportunity of having it amended. R. A.

Williams *v.* Moore, May 26, 1849. Why sheriff's sale should not be set aside. *Per curiam.* If the proceedings have been regular, we do not think that there has been any such inadequacy of price established as would justify us in interfering to set aside this sale.

It is objected, however, that the law has not been complied with in regard to the advertisement of the sale. The 62d section of the act of June 16, 1836 (Purd. 449), provides, that before any sale of real estate shall be made, the officer shall cause so many handbills to be made, &c., "which notice shall be given to the defendant, and one of the said papers or parchments shall be fixed by the sheriff or other officer upon the premises; and the others of them in the most public places of the county or city, *at least ten days before such sale.*" The 63d section then provides, that "the officer shall also give notice of every such sale by advertisement, describing the real estate to be sold, and the time and place of sale as aforesaid, in at least two newspapers, one in the English, and the other (except in the City and County of Philadelphia), in the German language, if such there are printed in the county where such real estate may be; or if there be no newspaper printed in such county, then in the newspaper printed nearest thereto, *once a week, during three successive weeks previous to such sale,* under penalty of fifty dollars to the party aggrieved by any such neglect, &c." In the case before us, as the one of the newspaper, and as the organ of publication, the first advertisement was inserted on Saturday, April 21; the second on Monday, April 23; the third on Monday, April 30; and a fourth on Monday, May 7, which was the day on which the sale took place. It is said that the law requires that three full weeks should elapse from the date of the first advertisement to the day of sale; here, however, there were but seventeen days, both inclusive.

It is evident that the 62d section was that which was intended to provide for the extent of the notice, "at least ten days before such sale." The provision therein made for "so many written or printed handbills, upon parchment or good paper, as the debtor or defendant shall reasonably request; or so many, without such request, as may be sufficient to give notice of such sale," was by the 4th section of the act of 1705, and so continued as to this city and county (see act of March 27, 1824, Pamph. L. 119), up to the passage of the act of 16, 1836. The 63d section of that act superseded the provision in regard to advertisement; and it is plain, from the old provision in regard to notice to the defendant, "at least ten days before such sale" having been suffered to remain, that the only object of that section was to provide further publicity, and not to extend the time of notice. It enacts, then, under a penalty, that the sale shall be advertised *once a week, during three successive weeks, previous to such sale.* It is not pretended that this requires that the successive advertisements should be at the distance of a week from each other. A week is a definite period of time, commencing on Sunday and ending on Saturday (Ronkendorff *v.* Taylor, Lessee, 4 Peters, 361). In the case before us the law has been literally complied with. There was an advertisement on some day of the three weeks which preceded the sale. It is difficult to perceive any warrant in the words or spirit of the act, for the idea that "the advertisement, 'once a week,' has relation to the full expiration of the whole week, from the date of the first advertisement, and so as to the remaining three weeks."

It is only necessary to advert to the fact, that in many, if not most of the counties, there are two or more newspapers published weekly on different days; and as the argument, if good, at all, must hold good as to each of the newspapers in which the publication takes place, the result is, that more than three weeks must often elapse before the terms of the law could be complied with. If, for example, in the case before us, the newspaper used had been published on Saturdays and Mondays, and the first publication had been made on April 21, the sale could not have taken place before Monday, May 14, twenty-four days from the first publication; and cases might be supposed in which a still longer period must elapse.

It has been decided in Stoever's Appeal (3 W. & S. 157), that the advertisement provided by law to be made by an executor or administrator, for successive weeks, need be made only in so many consecutive weeks.

The case of Bachelor *v.* Bachelor (1 Mass. 256), is a case in point. There an order was made by the court that a certain notice should be published in a newspaper specified, *"three weeks successively."* The notice was inserted in the paper pointed out (it happened to be a paper which was issued from the press twice weekly), first in the paper of Saturday, June 30; secondly, Saturday, July 7 ; and thirdly, Wednesday, July 11. And it was held that the order had been substantially complied with.

The case of Francis *v.* Norris, heretofore decided by this court, and reported 2 M. 150, is, undoubtedly, opposite to this conclusion. It is within the recollection of one of this court, and who was also a member of the court at the time that decision was made, that it was decided, in the course of the current business of a Saturday, by two only of the court. Although unwilling to overrule precedents, yet, we are of opinion, that in cases of this nature, whether sound interpretation of the statute, as well as the policy of affording greater facility to the collection of debts are concurrent, that a hasty decision of this nature, which only regulates the practice, without any effect upon titles, ought not to outweigh such considerations as have been presented. R. D.

Hough *v.* Lorentz, November 17, 1849. Rule to set aside sheriff's sale. *Per curiam.* *Caveat emptor* is the rule which rigidly applies to sheriffs' sales, as far as title and incumbrances are concerned. It might easily be made to appear that the inconveniences of allowing a bidder at a public judicial sale to come in and be relieved from his bid, on the ground that the defendant had no title, or an imperfect one, would far outweigh the occasional hardship of a case, where an ignorant or ill-advised purchaser may lose his money without an equivalent, or be involved in a lawsuit. In this instance, however, ignorance cannot be properly allowed as an excuse, even though it may have existed ; for clear and distinct notice that the title of the purchaser would be controverted was made at the sale. That the purchaser was deaf, and did not hear so as to understand the import of the notice which was made, does not make the case any better. He should act in such matters through the agency of others. The objections which have been urged to the advertisement are mere typographical errors, by which

a vigilant man, who had made the necessary searches, could not have been misled. R. D.

Ulrich *v.* McCann, Saturday, April 27, 1850. Rule to set aside sheriff's sale. *Per curiam.* Wherever the price is inadequate, the court will lay hold of any circumstance of irregularity to set aside the sale. In this case, however, it is unnecessary to invoke this principle. It appears upon the evidence before us that the lot No. 2 has a common right to an alley not mentioned in the advertisement, an important circumstance, which would weigh in setting aside any sale. R. A.

Young *v.* Walls, Saturday, June 8, 1850. Rule to set aside sheriff's sale. *Per curiam.* Good faith requires that the application to set aside a sheriff's sale should be made at the earliest possible period. It is true, that if made at any time before the acknowledgment of the sheriff's deed, it may be entertained, but it does not follow that a party may sleep upon his rights, while a purchaser, at expense and inconvenience, which cannot in all cases be compensated, has prepared himself to consummate the title. That is the case here. The sale was on the 6th of May, and motion not made till 26th of May. The delay has not been accounted for, and it would be impossible for us now to make such a decision as would place the purchaser completely in *statu quo.* We decline, therefore, to interfere. R. D.

Ingersoll *v.* Sherry, Saturday, April 20, 1850. Rule to set aside sheriff's sale. *Per curiam.* It was undoubtedly irregular to set aside the first sheriff's sale without notice to defendant. The court acted on the assurance that all parties had notice.

In all cases hereafter the court will require an affidavit of service upon all parties (to wit: plaintiff, defendant, purchaser, and sheriff) who may not have appeared at the taking of the depositions, or upon the hearing of the rule. The defendant here, however, suffered the second sale to go on without coming in and asking the court to rescind its order, and calling their attention to this irregularity. It affords no ground, therefore, to regard his application to set aside the second sale favorably. Apart from this we see no ground to interfere. R. D.

Gilbert *v.* Jackson, Saturday, Sept. 7, 1850. Rule to set aside sheriff's sale. *Per curiam.* This is an application to set aside a sheriff's sale on the ground of misdescription. The alleged error is

It is not a sufficient reason for setting aside a sale that the plaintiff's counsel did not receive special notice of the intended sale, according to an alleged practice, in consequence of which neglect, the price was inadequate.(*k*)

The court refused to set aside a sale, on the ground that one of the defendants was the purchaser; he being the husband of another defendant, who with her trustee had executed a mortgage of her separate estate, which by the terms of the trust deed might have been executed without him.(*l*)

The general practice of the District Court for the City and County of Philadelphia is, on motions to set aside proceedings at sheriff's sale of land, not to determine questions of title; and this rule is based on the fact that, in ordinary cases, the possession of real property is not necessarily changed—a purchaser being obliged to bring ejectment, when the title he has acquired is disputed. When, however, the process of the court is used to produce a summary transfer of the posses-

in not particularly describing the kitchen and back buildings attached to the dwelling-house and used with it. Although all material improvements must be set forth, the sheriff ought not to go into a full description of them like in an auctioneer's puff. It is enough that the buildings and improvements are mentioned. Bidders can inquire and ascertain their extent and character. We have always decided that it was not necessary particularly to mention and describe kitchens. They are a part of the dwelling-house which here is mentioned. R. D.

Tait *v.* Carberry, Saturday, Dec. 14, 1850. Rule to set aside sheriff's sale. *Per curiam.* We must be very clearly satisfied before we will confirm what is termed a *lumping* sale of several houses. In general, a sale of several houses comes so much more within the means of purchasers that slight inconveniences ought not to be suffered to change the rule. Where it is manifestly for the interest of all parties, there will rarely be difficulty in procuring their assent, which of course obviates all objections. It is always a reasonable precaution to call upon the defendant or terre-tenant before the sale, and ask him to propose a plan for selling the houses otherwise than together. It has been frequently held, that a common incumbrance, a lien upon all and each of the properties, formed no decisive reason for selling them together. Why, then, should a common privilege? Here the houses were situated on both sides of a court, in which they possessed a common right of way, with a privy or privies in common. It is said, also, that the space

under the court was occupied by vaults, and that each two houses facing each other in the court had the vault extending from the one to the other in common between them. This might have been a reason for considering the two houses thus situated as one house, but no reason for lumping the whole ten together in one sale. R. A.

Shields *v.* Kuhn, Dec. 1, 1851. Rule to set aside sheriff's sale. *Per curiam.* It is not pretended but there was a flagrant misdescription, affording ample ground for making this rule absolute. But it is alleged that Thomas Sowerman —who makes this application—has no interest, he being a creditor by a judgment, the lien of which has been discharged by a judicial sale. Whether his lien be discharged or not depends, not only upon a question of law of great nicety and importance, which certainly has never been decided in the Supreme Court, but in a certain aspect of the case may depend upon the *bona fides* of a certain deed, which it is alleged by the purchaser who opposes this application to have been fraudulent and void as to creditors; and he has offered to establish this point by depositions. We are clear, however, that upon such a question as this we ought not to assume the decision of such a controversy in a collateral proceeding like this. It is enough to show a *prima facie* case of interest, though it may be controverted, to let in a party to set aside a sheriff's sale; otherwise, indeed, his most important rights and property might be immediately sacrificed. R. A.

(*k*) Kern *v.* Murphy, 2 M. 157.
(*l*) Ibid.

sion, as in the case of an extent, the reason of the rule fails, and the rule fails with it.(*m*)

The fact that premises to be sold at sheriff's sale had been fitted up as a tavern, at considerable expense, should be stated in the advertisements; and the omission of such statement is ground for setting aside the sale ;(*n*) and a sheriff's sale of a tavern in Bridesburg was set aside, where the advertisement stated the names of the streets, but not the name of the village ; the court saying, that though no mere inadequacy of price was cause for setting aside, yet where such inadequacy existed, advantage would be taken of other defects, if it was made satisfactory that the property would bring a larger price at the next sale, and that, where that was doubtful, security would be required.(*o*)

The continuance of the sale to past ten o'clock in the night, accompanied with a precipitate sale at a low price, whereby the plaintiff in the execution was prevented from buying it, when he then desired the property to be set up again, which was refused, was held by Judge SERGEANT ground to set aside the sale.(*p*)

A defendant, who has recently been discharged as a bankrupt, is not entitled to ask that the sale should be set aside ;(*q*) but judgment creditors are entitled to be heard in opposition to the confirmation of the sale.(*r*)

8. Sheriff's deed, and its acknowledgment.

A seizure of land by the sheriff under a *fi. fa.* does not divest the estate of the debtor ; nor does a sale at auction by the sheriff, unless the purchase-money is paid and a deed delivered.(*s*)   The deed should describe the lands conveyed with reasonable certainty, and unless so described, no estate passes to the grantee,(*t*) and a special return upon the execution seems not to be sufficient.(*u*)   The validity of the deed is not affected by an incorrect recital of the execution thereon, or by the entire omission of such recital, so long as the sheriff possessed a sufficient authority to warrant the sale.(*v*)

By the act of 1836, § 94, the officer making sale of any real estate under execution, shall make return thereof, indorsed or annexed to such writ, and give the buyer a deed, duly executed and acknowledged in court, for what is sold : in the manner hitherto practised in case of the sale of lands by sheriffs, upon execution.

The next section prescribes the recitals of the proceedings in the deed as follows :—

It shall be lawful for the purchaser of any real estate at a sheriff's sale, to cause the judgment, and all and singular, the process issued thereon, under which such estate may have been seized and sold, together with all and singular the returns of such process, made by the officer executing the same, to be recited and set forth fully and at large,

---

(*m*) Pray *v.* Brock, 2 P. L. J. 341. See *ante*, 809.

(*n*) Hall *v.* Mayer, D. C. C. P. Sept. 1848; *ante*, 806.

(*o*) Whittaker *v.* Pratt, D. C. C. P. July, 1848; *ante*, 805.

(*p*) Greenwood *v.* Lehigh Coal Company, 3 P. L. J. 22.

(*q*) Laird *v.* Laird, D. C. Lanc. 3 P. L. J. 474.

(*r*) Cash *v.* Tozer, 1 W. & S. 528. See Watson *v.* Willard, 9 Barr, 75 ; Shields *v.* Kuhn, *ante*, 809.

(*s*) 8 Johns. 520.

(*t*) 11 Johns. 365 ; 13 Johns. 537.

(*u*) 13 Johns. 471.

(*v*) 10 Johns. 381.

in the deed to be executed by him therefor, by the sheriff, as aforesaid; and if the prothonotary or clerk of the said court shall, by order thereof, certify and attest, under the seal of the said court, that such judgment and process are recited and contained in the said deed, truly, fully, and entire, as the same remain in his office, such deed shall be good evidence of such judgment and process upon any trial at law, wherein the said real estate may be in controversy, in the same manner as the original records would be, if produced and offered in evidence. § 95.

This section introduced a new practice. Hitherto, on the trial of title depending on sheriff's sales, it was necessary to produce the judgment and executions on which the sheriff's deed was grounded. In the words of the commissioners, this alteration of the practice is safe, convenient to purchasers, and conducive to expedition in trials.

A sale, and the consummation of that sale by deed, are acts which the sheriff may do by deputy,(w) but it is our practice to have the deeds executed by the sheriff. Upon sales of real estate, the fourth section of the act of 1705, directs him to give the buyer a deed duly executed and acknowledged in court for what is sold; as the sheriff is not bound and cannot be ruled to return the writ before the return-day thereof, and as exceptions to sheriff's sales cannot be made before, the acknowledgment cannot be taken prior to the return-day: and a premature acknowledgment is a nullity.(x) The acknowledgment cannot be dispensed with, and can be made nowhere but in court; it is often necessary to set the sale aside and order a new one, and where cause of complaint exists, the party applies to the court before the deed is acknowledged, and the acknowledgment is then suspended until the matter is decided.(y) This rule would seem to be subject to exceptions, judging from an early case,(z) where the court say: "The usage of acknowledging sheriffs' deeds of lands in the term succeeding the sales is certainly attended with many conveniences, and ought to be followed; it gives debtors and creditors an opportunity of making their complaints on a day certain, which are soon heard and determined, and much time and great expense are saved thereby. The words of the act, however, are only directory, and do not invalidate a sheriff's deed for want of an acknowledgment in court, which does not appear to be indispensably requisite in all given cases, as after a great lapse of time and no objection made by the debtor. But in its operation it is subject to every exception which may be had against the sheriff's deed on its acknowledgment being tendered in court." The court in which the deed is to be acknowledged is that from which the *venditioni* issues and to which it is to be returned.(a) From this it may be gathered that, generally speaking, the deed is not complete, and cannot be recorded or given in evidence, until it is acknowledged;(b) and to give the purchasers the right to notify the tenant to remove, under the act of 1802, the acknowledgment was essential.(c) But when acknowledged, it relates

---

(w) 10 Johns. 223.

(x) Lessee of Murphy v. McCleary, 3 Y. 406; Lessee of Glancy v. Jones, 4 Y. 214.

(y) Woods v. Lane, 2 S. & R. 55.

(z) Lessee of Morehead v. Pearce, 2 Y. 458.

(a) McCormick v. Meason, 1 S. & R. 99.

(b) Hawk v. Stouch, 5 S. & R. 161.

(c) Ibid. Hall v. Benner, 1 Pa. R. 402.

back to the time of its execution, and the legal title vests in the grantee from that time, and the equitable title from the time of sale if he paid his money according to the terms of sale.(d)   Previously to the act of 1836 just cited, as to returns of writs, it was necessary, by a rule of one of our courts, that the process under which the sale has been made shall be duly returned and filed with the prothonotary, before the acknowledgment of any deed executed by him can be taken.(e)   And in a case determined before the act of 1836, it was held to be no objection to the title of a purchaser at a sheriff's sale, that the *venditioni exponas* was not returned until long after the acknowledgment of the sheriff's deed, and long after the sheriff, who made the sale, had gone out of office.(f) But the court said, that such neglect in sheriffs was much to be censured.

The ninety-sixth section of the act of 1836, prescribes the manner in which acknowledgments of deeds of real estate by the sheriff shall be made:—

I. In the case of executions from the Supreme Court, the acknowledgment shall be made by the officer who executed the deed before the said court, in bank, sitting within the respective district, or before one of the judges of the said court, sitting at *nisi prius*, within the county in which such real estate may be, or before the Court of Common Pleas of the county, or the District Court of the city and county in which such real estate may be.

II. In case of *testatum* writs of execution, the acknowledgment may be made as aforesaid, in the Court of Common Pleas of the county, or District Court of the city and county, in which such real estate may be.

III. In all other cases, the acknowledgment as aforesaid shall be made in the court from which the execution issued.

But no such acknowledgment shall be allowed, unless the same shall be made upon public proclamation, in open court, at a time appointed by the court for the purpose, or notice shall have been previously affixed in the office of the prothonotary, specifying the names of the parties to the execution, and the name of the purchaser of such real estate, and the time at which the acknowledgment is intended to be made, at least one week after the return-day of the writ of execution, nor in case of acknowledgment made in any court, except that from which the execution issued, unless notice shall appear to have been given to the parties to the execution, in the manner provided for the service of a writ of summons in a personal action.(g)   § 97.

Whenever the acknowledgment shall be made as aforesaid, in any other court than that from which the process shall have issued, the same shall be good, notwithstanding the same may have been made before the return-day of the execution.   § 98.

It shall be the duty of the sheriff acknowledging any deed as aforesaid, in any other court than that from which the process issued upon

(d) 3 Griff. L. R. 251.
(e) Rules Dist. Ct. Phil. January, 1822.
(f) Smull v. Mickley, 1 R. 95.

(g) As will presently be seen, the practice, under this and the succeeding acts *in pari materia*, is fully defined in Philadelphia, by rule, *post*, 818.

which the sale shall have been made, immediately thereafter to return the same into the office of the prothonotary or clerk of the court from which the same shall have been issued. § 99.

When application shall have been made to any court, to take the acknowledgment of a deed for real estate, sold upon the process issued by any other court, the court to which such application shall be made, shall have power to examine the regularity and validity of such sale, and set the same aside, if there be cause; and if the proceeds of such sale shall be paid into the said court, they may order the distribution thereof, in like manner as if such sale had been made by virtue of process issued from such court. § 100.

It is believed that the foregoing revised sections comprise all the previous laws and decisions on the subject of acknowledgment of deeds.(h)

The one hundred and first section of the act of 1836 provides for the case of the sheriff's dying or resigning before sale, as follows :—

If the officer by whom any real estate shall have been taken in execution, shall die, resign, be removed from office, or if his term of office shall expire before sale thereof, the proceedings upon such execution shall be continued and completed by his successor in office, and all other necessary and proper writs and process in such case shall be directed to such successor, and be executed by him, and a deed be made and acknowledged by him, in like manner and with like effect as such acts might have been done by the former officer if he had continued in office.

The next section provides for a similar occurrence after sale, but before deed executed, viz. :—

Whenever any real estate shall be sold under any execution as aforesaid, and the officer who shall make the sale shall die, resign, or be removed from office, or if the term of his office shall expire before any deed shall be executed and acknowledged by him, in due form of law, the Supreme Court, or the court in which the judgment was obtained, shall have power, upon the petition of the plaintiff in such judgment, or the purchaser of such real estate, setting forth specially the facts of the case, by an order, to be entered upon their records, to direct the sheriff for the time being to execute a deed of such real estate to the purchaser thereof. § 102.

It shall be the duty of the sheriff or other officer, to whom any such order shall be directed in pursuance thereof, and after the payment of the purchase-money of such real estate, with such costs and charges, if any, as may remain unpaid, to the former sheriff or officer, to execute, deliver, and acknowledge such deed or deeds, and perform and do such other matters and things as the sheriff or officer who made such sale, might, could, or ought to have done, in and about the premises; which deed, so executed, shall be as effectual in law, as if the title had been completed by the former officer. § 103.

(h) Remarks of Commissioners.

The several courts aforesaid shall have like power to compel the sheriff or coroner, making sale as aforesaid, to perfect the title of purchasers, in cases of defective or informal execution of sheriffs' or coroners' deeds, and they may grant relief in the manner, and upon the terms and conditions aforesaid, and with like effect. § 104.

In the case of a deed executed, but not acknowledged by the old sheriff, the proper course under the act of 1764, § 2,(*i*) was held to be to apply for an order to have a new deed executed and acknowledged by the sheriff for the time being, as he cannot acknowledge the former deed, which was not in fact his own act. There would seem, however, to be no objection under it, to the acknowledgment by one who has been sheriff, of a deed which he had executed while in office, and this has been the common practice.(*j*) The practice under these decisions has been recognized on argument by the District Court of Philadelphia County, in the case of Stanley, *et al.*,(*k*) where it was decided that the word "removed," in the act of 1764, alludes to a removal by the expiration of his term, as well as for misconduct in office. So, a deed defectively acknowledged may be reacknowledged by the old sheriff after he is out of office.(*l*)

By the first section of the act of May 3, 1832,(*m*) all the provisions of the second section of an act passed the twenty-third day of March, seventeen hundred and sixty-four, and of the first section of an act passed the second day of April, eighteen hundred and three, are extended to cases where sheriffs' or coroners' deeds for lands and tenements, sold on execution, are or hereafter may be defectively executed or acknowledged, and the several courts of this commonwealth are empowered to grant the same relief, and perfect the title of purchasers in cases of defective and informal execution or acknowledgment of sheriffs' or coroners' deeds, in the same manner and on the same terms and conditions as in cases provided for by the said sections of the several acts of assembly above recited.

The sheriff is not bound to acknowledge his deed before he demands the money, because it may be that the purchaser will not pay, and in that case the sheriff has a right to put up the land to sale again, or to return that it remains unsold. The purchaser runs no risk in paying the money and accepting the deed before its acknowledgment, because the court will compel the sheriff to make the acknowledgment.(*n*) In a suit, therefore, against the purchaser for the purchase-money, it is not necessary to aver a tender of a deed acknowledged. Unless other conditions are specified, it is a cash sale, and the delivery of the deed is an act subsequent to the payment of the money.(*o*) The purchaser after accepting a deed acknowledged, and keeping possession of it without objection, cannot resist payment of the purchase-money on the ground of a defect therein.(*p*) Neither can he object to receive the deed on the ground of a defect of title, where the sale was fairly made: he buys on

(*i*) 1 Sm. Laws, 263.
(*j*) Woods *v.* Lane, 2 S. & R. 55.
(*k*) November, 1826, MS.
(*l*) Adams *v.* Thomas, 6 Bin. 254.
(*m*) Pamph. L. 404.

(*n*) Scott *v.* Greenough, 7 S. & R. 199.
(*o*) Negley *v.* Stewart, 10 S. & R. 207.
(*p*) Scott *v.* Greenough, 7 S. & R. 199.
Vide supra, 795, 6, &c.

his own knowledge and judgment, and the maxim *caveat emptor* applies with all its force to him. Lands are frequently sold greatly below their value, because the usual understanding is, that the purchaser takes his chance of the title.(*q*) But it would seem that such purchaser takes the legal estate of the defendant discharged from secret trusts, of which no notice is given until after the deed is acknowledged.(*r*)

The title of a purchaser other than the plaintiff cannot be affected by an irregularity in the proceedings, of which he had not notice.(*s*) For " it is the interest of all parties, creditors and debtors, to encourage and protect *bona fide* purchasers at sheriffs' sales: and this is the policy of the law. No wise man would buy at sheriff's sale, and give anything like the value, if he was to be affected by notice of adverse claims, not publicly communicated at the time of the sale to the bidders, though made known to the sheriff; notice to him is not sufficient, he not being considered the agent of such purchaser."(*t*) After deed executed, the defendant cannot call on the purchaser to give up the sale on the ground that part of the land sold was not included in the levy, though he tender sufficient to cover the expenses. By the defendant's representation at the sale, that certain land is included in the levy, the land passes in equity to the purchaser, though it was not actually included in the levy, provided the purchaser was acting innocently.(*u*)

In order that advantage of any irregularity in the sale or proceedings may be effectually taken, the party complaining should make his exception previously to the approval of the deed by the sheriff, which takes place as a matter of course, at the term to which the process is returnable, unless good ground be shown against it; and upon the trial of an ejectment instituted by the sheriff's vendee, the court will not inquire into the formality of the proceedings on which the sale was founded.(*v*) If a sale has been made under void or irregular process, the court will not permit the sheriff to acknowledge the deed.(*w*) A *levari facias* issued several years after judgment without a *scire facias* to revive it, is voidable, but not void; the court issuing it may set it aside, or it may be avoided by a writ of error. But the sheriff is authorized to make sale under it, and no other court can question the validity of the execution in an action of ejectment.(*x*) If the sheriff has behaved improperly, the remedy of the party injured is confined to the sheriff, after the deed has received the sanction of the court.(*y*) But questions of title, as will presently be seen, will not here be litigated, and the court will not, on a motion for an order that the sheriff perfect the title to lands sold to the plaintiff in the suit by the former sheriff on a *venditioni exponas*, inquire into the fairness of the original judgment, because those who complain against it have it in their power to try it in an ejectment.(*z*)

The sheriff cannot be *compelled* to alter his return as to matter of

(*q*) Smith *v.* Painter, 5 S. & R. 225.
(*r*) Ibid.
(*s*) Stahle *v.* Spohn, 8 S. & R. 327.
(*t*) Per DUNCAN, J., ibid. *vide* Smith *v.* Painter, 5 S. & R. 225, 257; Lessee of Lazarus *v.* Bryson, 3 Bin. 59.
(*u*) Harker *v.* Conrad, 12 S. & R. 304.

(*v*) Young *v.* Taylor, 2 Bin. 227.
(*w*) Ibid. 2 Bin. 218.
(*x*) Vastine *v.* Fury, 2 S. & R. 430.
(*y*) McCulloch's Case, 1 Y. 40, S. P.; 1 Br. 218.
(*z*) Field *v.* Earle, 4 S. & R. 82.

fact, but *may* do so on leave given by the court.(*zz*)   And this leave is important to him, as he may be liable to an action by the purchaser in case of a false return.   If on a *levari* he sells lands, but at the instance of the plaintiff's attorney returns them unsold for want of buyers, on account of the purchaser's delaying payment, and upon a second *levari* sells them to the plaintiff, the court may, before the deed is acknowledged, confirm the first, and set aside the second sale; they do not exceed their powers in making an order for the amendment of the sheriff's return to the first writ and confirming the original sale.(*a*)

Where the sheriff, through a clerical mistake, returned to a writ of *levari facias*, that he had sold the property to *John L.*, and the deed was made and acknowledged accordingly, when the real name of the purchaser was *Joseph L.*, the court, on being satisfied of the fact, permitted the return and deed to be amended according to the truth, and directed the sheriff to reacknowledge the deed;(*b*) and so where there has been an entry on the deed, it would be competent for the court to amend the record by making a registry of the acknowledgment, though this would in no case be permitted without saving the rights of third persons.(*c*)

Judgment creditors are entitled to be heard in opposition to the confirmation of a sheriff's sale; and they are consequently privies.(*d*)

Where a sheriff's deed has been duly acknowledged, the court refused to interfere on the application of a second mortgagee, although the acknowledgment had been made before the return of the writ, and the ten days' notice required by law had not been given.(*e*)

Where, after a sale of lands, under a *test. fi. fa.*, of which the writ was not entered in the prothonotary's office, a sale was made to the plaintiff, and the defendant moved to set aside the sale, upon which the record ended, and nothing was done for twenty years, the court, at the end of that period, refused to direct a deed to be acknowledged by the sheriff; there being no proof of the payment of the purchase-money, and there being intermediate terre-tenants for value without notice.(*f*)

The acknowledgment of a sheriff's deed in open court, and registering it in the prothonotary's office, are equivalent to recording it in the office of the recorder of deeds as notice to a subsequent purchaser from the defendant in the execution.(*g*)

The acknowledgment proved only by the certificate of the prothonotary indorsed upon the deed, and not under the seal of office, is made evidence by the act of 5th April, 1842, and the act of April 4, 1844 ;(*h*) and by the act of April 24, 1846, copies of the deed as recorded in the recorder's office are evidence.

The provisions of the act on this subject are directory, and after acknowledgment and delivery of the deed to the purchaser, it is to be presumed that they have been complied with.(*i*)   Even were such deed inoperative, the defendant would be precluded from alleging it, by the

---

(*zz*) *Ante*, 688.
(*a*) Vastine *v.* Fury, 2 S. & R. 426.
(*b*) Rapin *v.* Dealy, 1 M. 339.
(*c*) Bellas *v.* McCarty, 10 W. 31. Rogers, J.
(*d*) Cash *v.* Tozer, 1 W. & S. 528.

See Watson *v.* Willard, 9 Barr, 95, and *ante*, 810.
(*e*) Solomon *v.* Parnell, 2 M. 264.
(*f*) Richards *v.* Dutot, 7 Barr, 431.
(*g*) Naglee *v.* Albright, 4 Wh. 291.
(*h*) See Wilson *v.* Howson, 2 J. 109.
(*i*) Stroble *v.* Smith, 8 W. 280.

principle settled in Adlum v. Yard,(*j*) where he takes the balance of the proceeds of sale out of court.(*k*)

The court will not order a succeeding sheriff to execute a deed where the transaction is stale, as where, more than twenty years after a sale under execution, no proof of payment of the purchase-money or perfection of the sale appears, and there are terre-tenants purchasers for value without notice of the proceedings.(*l*) The proper practice is, for the old sheriff to hand over to his successor, without deed, the unexecuted process, whose duty it is to execute it; and where a *venditioni exponas* was directed to a sheriff who was going out of office, and it appeared that both the old and new sheriff were present at the sale, and the deed which was made by the latter created a sale by the former sheriff, and the writ, which had never been returned, was found among the papers of the old sheriff, it was held, that the deed was not void, though, under some circumstances, voidable; and in this case the purchase-money having been paid, and the debtor having accepted a lease of the premises for the purchaser, it was held, that he was estopped from making the objections.(*m*)

It is immaterial that the wrong year is indorsed on a petition that a sheriff may acknowledge a deed made by his predecessor, where entries on the docket and the recitals in the deed correspond and are regular.(*n*)

The acknowledgment of the deed by the sheriff is a judicial act of the court, which can be established only by the record of it;(*o*) though the certificate of the prothonotary, as has just been seen, is admissible for this purpose.(*p*) Until it is acknowledged, the legal title does not pass; the vendee cannot demand the rents, or recover the possession.(*q*)

A sheriff's deed must be acknowledged in open court, to render it valid against a *bona fide* purchaser, without notice either actual or constructive. The acknowledgment is a judicial act, which must appear of record, and cannot be proved by parol evidence in a collateral proceeding, whether by witnesses present in court at the time of the acknowledgment, by witnesses who saw the entry of the acknowledgment on the deed, or by the production of the deed itself, with an acknowledgment on the back, where no registry has been made of it in court.(*r*)

Where lands situate in Dauphin County had been sold by virtue of an execution upon a judgment obtained in 1797, in the Supreme Court in Philadelphia, on a *scire facias* upon a mortgage, it was held, that the acknowledgment of the sheriff's deed could not, under the act of 1836, be made before the Supreme Court in the Eastern District, but must, if made in that court, be made at its session in the Middle District.(*s*)

The absence of authority, or the presence of fraud, utterly frustrates the operation of a sheriff's sale, as a means of transmission of title, and may be insisted on after acknowledgment. But mere irregularities of

(*j*) 1 R. 171.
(*k*) Ibid. See Hinds *v.* Scott, 1 J. 26.
(*l*) Richards *v.* Dretot, 7 Barr, 430.
(*m*) Leshey *v.* Gardner, 3 W. & S. 314.
   Woods *v.* Halsey, 9 Barr, 144.
(*n*) Patterson *v.* Stewart, 10 W. 472.
(*o*) Ibid. *ante*, 810.
(*q*) Bellas *v.* McCarty, 10 W. 13.

(*r*) See the learned opinions of Justices ROGERS and KENNEDY, in relation to acknowledgment of sheriffs' deeds. Bellas *v.* McCarty, 10 W. 13, 30, 31. (HUSTON, J. and KENNEDY, J. dissenting.) Patterson *v.* Stewart, id. 472; Robb *v.* Ankeney, 4 W. & S. 128.

(*s*) Chambers *v.* Carson, 2 Wh. 437.

omission, or commission, are cured by the tacit acquiescence of those who ought to object before acknowledgment.(*t*)

Where a judgment was entered on September 24, 1829, a *fi. fa.* issued to November term, 1829, and levied on land, which was afterwards condemned by an inquisition, held on December 4, 1834, on which an execution was issued, and the land sold on January 9, 1835, it was held, that a sheriff's deed, under such levy,·conveyed a good title as against the judgment defendant, the want of a previous *sci. fa. qu. ex non* being cured by the acknowledgment.(*u*)

Where land extended on a *fi. fa.* is levied on, and condemned on an alias *fi. fa.*, issued without leave on the same judgment, the defendant may have it set aside. But if he omits to do this, he waives his right against the sheriff's vendee, in whose favor every intendment must be made.(*v*)

Where there has been a *fi. fa.*, levy and condemnation, and *ven. ex.*, the want of a return to the writ is cured by the acknowledgment of the sheriff's deed, for the land levied on.(*w*)

By the act of 21st April, 1846, § 1,(*x*) "In all cases where any real estate hath been heretofore sold, or shall hereafter be sold, under any execution issued out of any of the Courts of Record in this commonwealth, and the sheriff, or other officer making such sale, shall have made, or hereafter may make a defective or informal return of his proceedings upon such execution, it shall be lawful for the purchaser at such sale, or other person or persons interested therein, to apply by bill or petition, to the court out of which such execution issued, setting forth the facts of the case; and after due notice, to be given in such manner as the court may direct, to such purchaser or defendant in the execution, as whose property the same may have been sold, or to the executors, or administrators and heirs of such purchaser or defendant, or devisee of such estate, and to all other persons interested therein, to appear in such court, on a day certain to be fixed by said court, and answer such bill or petition; and thereupon, the said court shall have power to examine into the facts of the case, and make such order and decree therein as justice and equity may require, either by dismissing such bill or petition, or by correcting and amending such return to the execution, according to the truth of the case, and directing the sheriff, for the time being, to execute a deed of such real estate to the purchaser thereof, or to such other person or persons, for the use of such as may be entitled thereto, under such sale, upon such terms and conditions as the said court may determine, and justice and equity require; which deed so executed and acknowledged, as sheriffs' deeds are usually acknowledged, shall be as effectual in law as if the proper return had been made, and the title had been completed according to law."

The rules of the District Court of Philadelphia, in reference to the acknowledgment of sheriffs' deeds, are as follows:—

XCV. 1. Returns by the sheriff upon process issued by this court for the sale of real estate, made in pursuance of the act of assembly, entitled "An act relative to lien creditors becoming purchasers at judicial sales

(*t*) Shields *v.* Miltenberger, 2 H. 76.   (*w*) Hinds *v.* Scott, 1 J. 26.
(*u*) Hinds *v.* Scott, 1 J. 27.   (*x*) Pamph. L. 430.
(*v*) Wilson *v.* Howser, 2 J. 109.

and for other purposes," passed the twenty-eighth day of April, eighteen hundred and forty-six, shall be read in open court on the Saturday next following the day on which sheriff's return shall be made.

2. Any person interested in the proceeds of any real estate returned sold as aforesaid, may file exceptions to the right of the purchaser mentioned in the return to the same or to any part thereof, but such exceptions must be founded upon material facts in dispute, the nature and character of which must be set forth and verified by affidavit or upon some matter of law appearing of record.

3. Exceptions to the right of the purchaser to the proceeds of any sale as aforesaid, may be filed in the office of the prothonotary of this court on or before the Wednesday next following the day on which the return of sale shall have been read as aforesaid, but not otherwise.

4. The party filing exceptions as aforesaid, may enter thereupon of course in the office of the prothonotary a rule upon the purchaser to show cause why the sale should not be set aside, which rule shall be made returnable on the Saturday next following the day upon which the exceptions shall be filed as aforesaid, of which rule he shall forthwith give notice to the purchaser or to his attorney.

5. On the return of the rule entered as aforesaid, the court will appoint an auditor to make a distribution of the proceeds of the sale and make report thereof to the court, or direct an issue to determine the validity of the lien of the purchaser if the case shall require it, and thereupon stay all further proceedings under such rule until the report of the auditor shall be made and approved by the court, or the issue directed as aforesaid shall be determined. If the exceptions are insufficient the court will dismiss the same and discharge the rule.

6. The report of auditors appointed as aforesaid, shall be subject to the rules applicable to the reports of auditors, distributing the proceeds of sheriffs' sales in other cases. And the party in whose favor the verdict on an issue directed as aforesaid shall have been rendered, shall be entitled to enter judgment thereon according to the rules applicable to verdicts in other cases.

7. If it shall appear by the report of the auditor appointed as aforesaid, or by the verdict of the jury, that the purchaser is not entitled to receive the proceeds of sale or a part thereof, the rule entered as aforesaid shall become absolute of course unless the purchaser shall, within ten days after the report of the auditor shall be approved as aforesaid, or the party prevailing in the issue shall be entitled to judgment, pay or cause to be paid to the sheriff who made the sale, the whole of the purchase-money, or so much of it as it shall be adjudged he is not entitled to retain.

8. If no exceptions shall be made and filed as aforesaid, or if the exceptions filed shall be dismissed by the court, the sheriff will be allowed to acknowledge his deed for the estate sold as aforesaid, and deliver the same to the purchaser thereof on the Saturday next following the day upon which his return shall have been read as aforesaid, or on any other subsequent day appointed by the court for the acknowledgment of sheriffs' deeds, unless a motion shall be pending to set aside the sale for irregularity of the proceedings or for some other cause.(*y*)

(*y*) Sept. 19, 1846.

When, under the 96th section of the act of June 16, 1836, acknowledgment of a sheriff's deed is to be made in one court, under an execution issued from another court, the proper practice is for the sheriff to apply to the former court by petition, informing them of the fact of the sale under the execution of the other court, and praying for leave to acknowledge, on a certain day, so far in advance, that he may be able to give the notice required by the act.(z)

9. Application of proceeds.

(1). Effect of sale on incumbrances.

When the sheriff sells land by virtue of an execution, it has been a practice of long standing—independently of the act of 1830, and its corollaries, which will be presently noticed—to sell it for its *full value* without regard to the lien of judgments, and to apply the purchase-money to the discharge of those liens, according to their order.(a)   The diffi-

---

(z) Wrigand v. Matthews, Oct. 27, 1849. Why application, made by the purchaser, for leave to have a sheriff's deed acknowledged to him, should not be rescinded. *Per curiam.* This is the case of an execution issuing out of the Supreme Court. It is provided by the 96th section of the act of June 16, 1836, relating to executions, that "in the case of executions from the Supreme Court, the acknowledgment shall be made by the officer, who executed the deed, before the said court, in bank, sitting within the respective district, or before one of the judges of the said court, sitting at Nisi Prius within the county in which such real estate may be, or before the Court of Common Pleas, or the District Court of the city and county, such real estate may be." The 97th section provides, that "in case of acknowledgment made in any court, except that from which the execution issued," notice must be given to the parties to the execution in the manner provided for the service of a writ of summons in a personal action. And then by the 100th section, "Where application shall have been made to any court to take the acknowledgment of a deed for real estate sold upon the process issued by any other court, the court, to which such application shall be made, shall have power to examine the regularity and validity of such sale, and set the same aside." In strictness of practice, the proper time to move for a rule to set aside the sheriff's sale, is when the sheriff has returned the writ, and thus put the court officially in possession of the fact, that a sale for a certain price, to a certain individual, had taken place, and is in court, with deed ready to be acknowledged, and proclamation thereupon made according to law. A practice, probably coeval with the administration of justice in the Pro-

vince of Pennsylvania, grounded upon the convenience of suitors, has allowed such motions to be made at any time after the sale and before the return of writ. It is plain, however, that in cases under the 100th section, something must be done with the case of an execution issuing out of the Supreme Court, before it can be settled what court shall have jurisdiction. It is impossible for this court to assume the power to inquire into the regularity and validity of the sale, until it is first settled that in this court the acknowledgment is to take place as often as we had set aside the sale; the deed might still be acknowledged in either of the other courts mentioned in the 96th section. It is plain from reason, and the express words of 100th section, that "application to the court to take the acknowledgment" is a condition precedent to the vesting of any power in the court "other than that from which the execution issued." The only question is by whom the application is to be made, and evidently it must be by the sheriff. He is the officer who executes the deed and by whom it is to be acknowledged, and he alone has a right to elect in what court to make the acknowledgment.

The proper practice in these cases, therefore, is for the sheriff to apply to the court by petition, informing them of the fact of the sale under the execution of the Supreme Court, and praying for leave to acknowledge, on a certain day, so far in advance, that he may be able to "give notice to the parties to the execution in the manner provided for the service of a writ of summons in a personal action."

In this case, the application was made by the purchaser, and was, therefore, irregular. R. A.

(a) See McCall v. Lenox, 9 S. & R.

culty formerly encountered by him in discharging those liens, and the injury sustained by judgment creditors who were compelled to wait for their money in the interim, were obviated by the act of 1798,(b) which provides that "no judgment shall continue a lien on real estate during a longer term than five years, unless revived by *scire facias.*"(c) When a legacy is charged on lands, the sheriff's vendee takes it discharged from the lien of the legacy. And a purchaser of land sold by order of the Orphans' Court is in the same situation as the sheriff's vendee.(d) The lien creditors must look to the application of the fund at their peril, everything which a due attention to their interest would have entitled them to receive being considered as paid by operation of law, as regards the debtor.(e) But a prior judgment creditor may waive his priority in favor of a subsequent one without extinguishing his judgment, which may be satisfied out of any other lands bound by it. And if the subsequent judgment creditor become the assignee of the first judgments, he succeeds to all the rights of the assignor.(f) On a sale by a prior judgment creditor, a mortgagee is entitled to take the residue of the proceeds after payment of the judgments. And although he give notice of his mortgage by advertisement at the time of sale, this does not estop him from claiming the proceeds on the ground that he thereby injured the sale.(g)

It is settled that, on a sheriff's sale of land, all the liens on it *due at the time of sale*, when they can be reduced to a certainty, are entitled to payment out of the proceeds.(h) But to this rule there are several exceptions, one of which is that of a recognizance of a sheriff and his sureties, under the act of 13th April, 1834. It is a lien expressly created for a great public object, which cannot be impaired by any judicial sale.(i) And so of liens expressly created by acts of assembly, such as the interest of the widow in one-third of the valuation of land taken by an heir at the appraisement, and the lien or interest of the heirs for that third, at the death of the widow.(j)

Under the general rule, fall arrears of ground-rent,(k) a legacy charged on the land, and arrears of annuity payable to a widow; but the future arrears are excepted, because of the impossibility of computing their amount. As to them, the purchaser takes the land subject thereto, but free of arrears due and payable.(l)

Ground-rent under deed, with clause of re-entry, is payable out of a sheriff's sale of the property, under a judgment by a stranger in preference to such judgment.(m)

The date of the sheriff's sale is the point of time to which all liens

306, 314; Harrison *v.* Waln, id. 318; Auwerter *v.* Mathiot, id. 403.

(b) 3 Sm. Laws, 331.

(c) 3 Bin. 358.

(d) McLanahan *v.* Wyant, 1 Pa. R. 112; Barnet *v.* Washebaugh, 16 S. & R. 410.

(e) Finney's Administrators *v.* Com. 1 Pa. R. 240; Bank of Penna. *v.* Winger, 1 R. 295.

(f) Bank of Penna. *v.* Winger, 1 R. 295.

(g) Lindle *v.* Neville, 13 S. & R. 227.

(h) Mohlin's Appeal, 5 Barr, 420; see 3 W. & S. 28.

(i) Re. McKenzie's, 3 Barr, 159.

(j) Moor *v.* Shultz, 1 H. 103. Coulter, J.

(k) Ter Hoven *v.* Kerns, 2 Barr, 96. See Bantleon *v.* Smith, 2 Bin. 146; Sands *v.* Smith, 3 W. & S. 12; Pancoast's Appeal, 8 W. & S. 381; Creigh *v.* Shatto, 9 W. & S. 84; Western Bank *v.* Willetts, 2 P. L. J. 45.

(l) Reed *v.* Reed, 1 W. & S. 239.

(m) Pancoast's Appeal, 8 W. & S. 381.

entitled to payment out of the proceeds are to be computed. Ground-rents are on no better footing in this respect than judgments, and for subsequently accruing rent the purchaser must be resorted to, although he may not have received his deed for a long time afterwards, owing to a motion to set aside the sale.(n)

In a late case in the Supreme Court, it appeared that D, after giving his wife a life-estate in the residue of his lands, devised the remainder to trustees in fee, in trust to sell and apply the proceeds to the payment of any debts "to which the same may be subject, and is not otherwise provided for." D died in 1842, and a few months afterwards the trustees conveyed part of the land to the widow in fee, no money passing at the sale, shortly after which the widow mortgaged the land so conveyed bona fide to C. The land being afterwards sold under the mortgage, it was held that C was entitled to priority in the distribution of the proceeds over creditors of the testator who obtained judgment within five years after the latter's death.(o)

On the distribution of sales of real estate by the sheriff, a lien for the balance of the purchase-money, subject to which the land was sold to the defendant, is entitled to priority over subsequent creditors.(p) But a grantee who claims the land by conveyance from the defendant in the execution anterior to the judgments against him, is not entitled to the proceeds of sale in preference to the judgment creditors. If his claim be valid, it may be set up against the purchaser at sheriff's sale.(q)

Where land subject to a mortgage was divided into two portions, one of which was sold to A, and the other subsequently to B, it was held that the tract sold to B was first to be exhausted before coming upon that sold to A.(r)

Under an execution by a third party, a sheriff's sale took place, of lands, on which, at the time of the sale, certain arrearages of ground-rent were due, which the sheriff neglected to pay, distributing the fund among subsequent liens: It was held that he thereby became personally liable for the same; nor was his liability affected by the fact that one of the conditions of sale was that arrears of ground-rent were to be paid out of the purchase-money, if the bills were presented to the sheriff, otherwise they were to be paid by the purchaser.(s)

A sheriff has no right to impose any conditions, or to exact a promise to refund on the payment over of money raised on execution, to a judgment creditor, so long as the judgment remains a lien.(t)

Where a first lien is good as against a second, and the second is good as against a third, the first lien will be entitled to priority in payment, although from peculiar circumstances it may be inferior to the third.(u)

A very important alteration in the law, as originally held, was effected by the act of April 6, 1830. Before the passage of that act, the law, as has already been observed, was settled that the purchaser of land

(n) Walton v. West, 4 Wh. 221.
(o) Cadbury v. Duval, 10 Barr, 265.
(p) Barnitz v. Smith, 1 W. & S. 142.
(q) Helffich's Appeal, 3 H. 382.
(r) Fluck v. Replogle, 1 H. 405; affirming Mevey's Appeal, 4 Barr, 80; Cowden's Est. 1 Barr, 479; Nailer v. Stanley, 10 S. & R. 450. See "Mortgage;" and ante, 772, 792, 796.

(s) Mather v. McMichael, 1 H. 301.
(t) Lewis v. Rodgers, 4 H. 18.
(u) Wilcocks v. Waln, 10 S. & R. 380; Moore's Appeal, 7 W. & S. 298; Manufacturers' Bank v. Bank of Pennsylvania, 7 W. & S. 335; Tomb's Appeal, 9 Barr, 61.

at the sheriff's sale, took it clear of incumbrances, and the purchase-money went to the lien creditors, according to their legal priority; but, even then, a levy, subject to a specific lien and advertisement, sale and deed subject to it, did not pass the land free from that lien; but the purchaser took subject to it, because all the parties to a transaction can modify the terms as they please, provided they do not contravene express written law, or public policy.(v) That act is as follows:—

From the passage of this act, where a lien of a mortgage upon real estate is, or shall be, prior to all other liens upon the same property, except other mortgages, ground-rents, and the purchase-money due to the commonwealth, the lien of such mortgage shall not be destroyed, or in any way affected, by any sale made by virtue or authority of any writ of *venditioni exponas.* § 1.

No sale, made by virtue or authority of any writ of *levari facias,* issued upon a judgment in a suit upon a mortgage, shall destroy, or in any way affect the prior lien of any other such mortgage as aforesaid. § 2.

By the act of April 11, 1835,(w) § 2, "no lien, created by virtue of the act of assembly, passed the third day of February, 1824, entitled 'An act relating to taxes on certain real estate in the City of Philadelphia,' should be construed to be within the meaning of the act of assembly of April 6, 1830, entitled 'A supplement to an act, entitled "An act for taking lands in execution for the payment of debts,"'" passed in 1705."

By the act of April 16, 1845,(x) the "provisions contained in the first section of the act to which this is a supplement shall extend, and shall always be deemed and taken to extend, to all cases of sales made by virtue or authority of any writ of execution." § 1.

The lien of a mortgage upon any real estate situate in the City or County of Philadelphia, shall not be destroyed, or in any way affected by any sale of the mortgaged premises under a subsequent judgment (other than one entered upon a claim, which was a lien on the premises, prior to the recording of such mortgage), by reason of the prior lien of any tax, charge, or assessment whatsoever; but the same shall continue as if such prior lien did not exist, where, by existing laws, the lien of such mortgage would otherwise continue: *Provided,* That the continuance of the lien of such mortgage shall not prevent the discharge of such prior liens for taxes, charges, or assessments by such sale, or the satisfaction thereof, out of the proceeds of such sale. § 4.

The entering of any judgment for the same debt, secured by any mortgage, shall not cause a sheriff's sale of the mortgaged premises to destroy, or in any way affect the lien of such mortgage; nor shall the plaintiff in such judgment be entitled to any part of the proceeds of

(v) Shultze v. Diehl, 2 Pa. R. 277; see Luce v. Snively, 4 W. 397.

(w) Pamph. L. 190.
(x) Ibid. 488.

such sale : *Provided, always,* That such sale has not been made under or by virtue of such judgment. § 5.

By the act of April 20, 1846, § 4, the provisions of the first section of the act of April 16, 1845, entitled " An act concerning sheriffs' and coroners' sales, and for other purposes," be, and the same is hereby extended to all sales made by any sheriff or coroner, and for which deeds have been acknowledged, prior to the passage of this act, so far as to correct the error in making such sales, after the expiration of six days subsequent to the return-day of the execution.

By the act of January 23, 1849, § 4,(*y*) the lien of a mortgage upon any real estate situate in the City or County of Philadelphia, shall not be destroyed, or in any way affected by the sale of the mortgaged premises, under or by virtue of any process to enforce the payment of any tax, claim, or assessment whatsoever, which, by existing laws, may be a lien on said real estate, unless said sale shall be made under a judgment obtained upon a claim which was duly registered in the proper office, prior to the recording of such mortgage.

The following points have been decided under the last-recited acts :—
The act of April 6, 1830, directs that the lien shall not be divested when it is prior to all other liens on the same property; and since this act, a subsequent judgment creditor can sell only the equity of redemption.(*z*)
It is the time of the commencement of the lien, and not the registration of the mortgage, that regulates the subsequent sale by writ.(*a*)
A mortgage, though prior in date to a judgment, is postponed to the judgment when the mortgagee neglects to record the mortgage in time, under the act of March 28, 1820 ; and it is of no importance in such case, that the judgment creditor had notice of the mortgage. The doctrine of notice, whether arising from actual possession of the mortgage or express notice, does not apply to a creditor, but to purchasers only. The date of the respective entries on record, determines the priority, with the single exception in the act in favor of mortgagees for the purchase-money, where they are allowed sixty days to record the mortgage ; creditors, as regards liens, are placed on the same footing.(*b*)
The entering up of the bond accompanying the mortgage, does not affect the lien of the latter ; nor does the issuing a *fi. fa.* on the judgment, which is returned *nulla bona,* amount to satisfaction of the judgment or mortgage. The mortgage is a pledge of the real estate to secure the amount of the bond, and vests the freehold in the mortgagee, subject to the equity of redemption ; and the warrant of attorney accompanying the bond, authorizes the entry of the bond of record, without affecting the lien of the mortgage. Hence, a purchaser at sheriff's sale, under a judgment subsequent to the recording of the mortgage (a first incumbrance), but prior to the entry of the warrant accompanying it,

(*y*) Pamph. L. 686.
(*z*) Pierce *v.* Potter, 7 W. 475 ; Boyer *v.* Heister, 6 Wh. 210 ; Bratton's Appeal, 8 Barr, 167.

(*a*) Bratton's Appeal, 8 Barr, 169.
(*b*) Hulings *v.* Guthrie, 4 Barr, 124.

must pay the amount of his bid, and take it subject to the mortgage debt, pursuant to the act of April 6, 1830.(c)

The lien of a mortgage is discharged by a sale under execution on a judgment on a bond which accompanied the mortgage, and was entered up subsequently to the mortgage.

The object of the act of 1830 was, professedly, to guard the prior mortgage creditor from disturbance by those who should come after him, and who were entitled only to what should be left, when he should have been satisfied; but it was not meant to guard his priority against another priority under his own control, even for debts arising out of a different transaction, as he is not a *subsequent* creditor within the act. He may, if he chooses, free only the equity of redemption; but if he does not propose the estate expressly subject to the mortgage, he will be taken to free the fee, as he would have been before the statute.(d)

As the lien of a mortgage, when prior to all others, is unaffected by a sale on a judgment, it follows that it is also unaffected by an *extent* of the time under an inquest upon such judgment; and the fund arising therefrom, must accordingly go to the latter.(e)

When there are several distinct parcels of land, bound by the same incumbrance, even a judicial sale of one of them will not necessarily divest the incumbrance as to the others, unless there exist an equity, calling imperatively on the creditor to look to the fund raised by the sale, and he refuses to do so, after notice.(f)

A sale of the mortgaged premises on a younger judgment for the same debt, divests the lien of the mortgage, and transfers the whole estate, legal and equitable, to the purchaser;(g) and where it appeared that a judgment had been entered against a mortgagor for interest due on a mortgage, the principal of which was payable *in futuro*, and not yet due, it was held that a sheriff's sale under such judgment divested the lien of the mortgage; and that the proceeds were payable to the mortgagee in preference to judgment creditors, whose liens intervened between the mortgage and the judgment for interest.(h)   The act of 1845, applies only where the sale is not made under the judgment entered for the original consideration, and hence a sale under such judgment carries the fee and discharges the lien of the mortgage.(hh)

Lands were mortgaged to A to secure bonds payable *in futuro*, subsequently to which mortgages were given to B to secure other debts. The interest on A's bonds not being paid, judgment was obtained on the same before the time due for the payment of the principal, and the land was sold on a *venditioni* issued under the same.   It was held, that the mortgages of both A and B, as well as all other subsequent incumbrances, were divested.(i)

The date of the sheriff's sale is the time by which to test the priority of a mortgage to other incumbrances, under the act of 1830.(j)

(c) Kuhn's Appeal, 2 Barr, 264; *ante,* 824.

(d) Berg r v. Hiester, 6 Wh. 214.

(e) Banke v. Patterson, 9 Barr, 311.

(f) Konigmaker v. Brown, 2 H. 274. BELL, J.

(g) Bank v. Chester, 1 J. 287. Wood-

ward, P. J. See Clarke v. Stanley, 10 Barr, 478.

(h) Id, 283.

(hh) Ibid. See Pierce v. Potter, 7 W. 475; Harts v. Woods, 8 Barr, 471.

(i) Clarke v. Stanley, 10 Barr, 472.

(j) Ibid.

The act of 1830 was not intended to effect any alteration in the nature or lien of a prior mortgage, except protection against a sale on a junior incumbrance.(k)

The fifth section of the act of 1845 applies to all cases where a mortgage and a judgment are taken for the same debt, whether the judgment be entered before or after the mortgage. The act is retrospective, and applies to mortgages given before its passage.(l)

A first mortgagee who buys in the land at sheriff's sale, is not entitled to have his bid applied to the discharge of his mortgage, to the exclusion of subsequent lien creditors.(m)

The lien of a mortgage in the County of Philadelphia, recorded in 1836, is not destroyed by a sheriff's sale, made by virtue of a *levari facias*, founded on a judgment recovered for taxes assessed in 1842, and subsequently; there being no other incumbrance on the land sold prior to the mortgage.(n)

Lands bound by a sheriff's recognizance are discharged from its lien by a sheriff's sale under a prior mortgage.(o)

A mortgage given on land on which there was a prior judgment entered against a former owner, is discharged by a sheriff's sale under a judgment against the mortgagor subsequent to the mortgage.(p)

A sale prior to the act of 6th April, 1830, under a judgment confessed for interest on a bond secured by mortgage, discharged the lien of the mortgage, although the defendant had aliened before the judgment, because it related back to the date of the mortgage.(r)

The act of 1824 gave to taxes, rates, and levies thereafter imposed for any purpose on real estate in Philadelphia, a lien thereon prior to "any recognizance, mortgage, judgment, debt, obligation, or responsibility which said real estate may become chargeable with or liable to" after the passing of the acts. Down to 1830, a judicial sale would have divested a municipal claim and all other liens. But the act of 6th April, 1830, directed that thereafter, where a mortgage was the first lien, a sale by a younger lien should not divest the lien of the mortgage. But by the then law, municipal taxes, &c., irrespective of date of assessment, took precedence of even first mortgages within the city and county; hence a sale under a junior judgment destroyed the hold of a first mortgage whenever any sum was due to the municipal corporations for taxes. Then for remedy came the act of 1835, which provided that the existence of a municipal lien shall not work such effect. But it left that kind of lien to stand for every other purpose where it stood before the act last mentioned. Hence a sale under a later lien will not affect a prior mortgage, though legally it be subordinate to the prior lien of a municipal charge. It followed that, prior to the act of 1845, the prior municipal lien was necessarily preserved by the intervening mortgage.(s)

(k) Id. 475. BELL, J.
(l) Callender's Appeal, Sup. Ct. May, 1852.
(m) Crawford v. Boyer, 2 H. 382.
(n) Perry v. Brinton, 1 H. 205.
(o) Spang v. Com. 2 J. 358.
(p) Byers v. Hoch, 1 J. 258.
(r) Hartz v. Woods, 8 Barr, 471.
(s) North. Libs. v. Swaim, 1 H. 113,

117. See Perry v. Brinton, Id. 202, which decides that the lien of a mortgage (a first incumbrance except taxes) is not destroyed by a sheriff's sale under a judgment for taxes *subsequently* assessed. The lien is preserved by the acts of 6th April, 1830, and the 11th April, 1835.

By the act of 1849, just given, the same principle is extended to all liens for taxes.

District claims are liens only on the lots in front, though there are several adjoining owned by the same party.(*t*)

(2). *Bringing money into court.*

If the officer's return is that he has sold the property mentioned in the writ, and received money, &c., the party applies to him for payment, and the sheriff is immediately responsible to him for the amount.(*u*) If he refuses, the mode is to rule him to pay the money into court; which being done, an order will be given to the prothonotary to pay it over, if no objection exists.

The practice is not to order the money into court except upon application of a lien creditor, who shows some reasonable ground to dispute the right of the execution plaintiff. A party whose execution comes in after the sale has no such right.(*v*)

Although the officer is directed to bring the money into court, and in strictness ought to do so, yet he may, and usually does, pay it to the plaintiff, and this would be a sufficient return to the writ. If the sheriff by mistake pays money, made by him on an execution, to a plaintiff in a junior execution, when he ought to have paid it to a senior, he cannot recover it back, although he has thus made himself liable to pay it likewise to the senior execution creditor;(*w*) nor is the party receiving it liable to the senior execution creditor.(*x*) If he has any doubt as to the right of the plaintiff to receive the money, he pays it into court and thereby discharges himself from responsibility; or if a third person claims a right to the money, he may rule him to pay it into court, and when this is ordered, such person may assert his right to the money or any part of it, and the court will, in its discretion, determine these contested claims upon a rule to show cause.(*y*) The proceeds of land and of grain

(*t*) Stiles *v.* Brock & Co. 1 Barr, 217.

(*u*) 7 S. & R. 200.

(*v*) Stinson *v.* McEwen, D. C. Saturday, April 8, 1848. Motion for a rule on the sheriff to pay money into court. *Per curiam.* The money in the hands of the sheriff is the proceeds of personal property. It is our practice in such cases never to order the money into court unless upon the application of some one who has a lien upon it, and who shows some reasonable ground to dispute the right of the plaintiff upon whose process it was made. The applicant here is an execution creditor, but his execution was not placed in the hands of the sheriff until after the sale. The counsel for the applicant supposes that, by virtue of his execution, the sheriff could take any current coin or bank notes in his possession belonging to defendant, and that he, therefore, stands in the position of a party having a lien. (Act of June 16, 1836, sec. 24, 25, Purd. 445.) However, the money in the sheriff's hands in no case specifically belongs to any party, so as to be subject to execution. The plaintiff in an execution, or the defendant as to any surplus has no property in the particular coin or bank notes the sheriff may have received on the sale of the goods. (Turner *v.* Fendall, 1 Cranch, 134.) By the proviso to the 24th sec. of the act of 16th June, 1836, the sheriff is prohibited from taking or retaining "any money which shall have been levied by him, at the suit or instance of the defendant, upon any other execution." The same reason applies to money belonging to the defendant in his hands made upon an execution against him. Such money has been often held not to be subject to an attachment. (Ross *v.* Clarke, 1 D. 355; Fretz *v.* Keller, 2 W. & S. 397; Riley *v.* Hirst, 2 Barr, 347.)

Motion refused.

(*w*) Durie *v.* Johnson, 3 Pa. R. 221.

(*x*) Diechman *v.* Northampton Bank, 1 R. 54.

(*y*) See Harrison *v.* Waln, 9 S. & R. 318. And see *ante*, "Payment of Money into Court," 374.

growing upon it, when sold on the same execution, may go to different creditors. In a case where grain had not been sown when a *fi. fa.* levied on the land was returned, but was sown after, and then levied on by another creditor under another execution, and then came a *venditioni exponas* to sell the land, the purchaser cannot claim the proceeds of the grain, but they belong to the second execution creditor.(z)

(3). *Practice in distribution of proceeds.*

By the act of June 16, 1836, relating to executions, it is provided that, in all cases of sale upon execution as aforesaid, where there shall be disputes concerning the distribution of the money arising therefrom, the court from which the execution shall have issued shall have power, after reasonable notice given, either personally or by advertisement, to hear and determine the same, according to law and equity.

If any fact connected with such distribution shall be in dispute, the court shall, at the request, in writing, of any person interested, direct an issue to try the same, and the judgment upon such issue shall be subject to a writ of error, in like manner as other cases wherein writs of error now lie.   § 87.

Upon a writ of error issued as aforesaid, the whole record shall be returned, and it shall be competent for any person aggrieved by the decree of distribution, to take exceptions thereto, if the judgment upon such issue should be affirmed.   § 88.

Any person aggrieved by the decree of the court in any case of distribution made, without the intervention of a jury, may, at any time within twenty days thereafter, appeal from the same to the Supreme Court.   § 89.

Provided, That if a writ of error or an appeal shall not be taken within twenty days from the decree of distribution, the court may order the money to be paid, according to such decree.   § 90.

Every person who shall sue out a writ of error, or shall appeal to the Supreme Court, upon any proceeding as aforesaid, shall make oath or affirmation, that his writ of error or appeal is not intended for delay; and he shall, to make it a *supersedeas,* also give security, by recognizance, with sufficient surety, in the court in which the proceeding was had, or before one of the judges thereof, to prosecute his appeal, or writ of error, with effect, and to pay all costs that shall be adjudged against him.   § 91.

It shall be lawful for the court into which any money arising from a sheriff's sale shall be paid, in case of a writ of error, or appeal from any decree as aforesaid, to order the investment of the fund in the debt of this commonwealth, or of the United States, or upon real security, or it shall be lawful for such court to order the payment of the money according to the decree of distribution, if the distributees shall give sufficient real security to refund the same, with the interest thereon, or so much thereof as shall be required by the court, if such

---

(z) Stambough *v.* Teale, 2 R. 161.

decree shall be reversed, or altered, and in such case the order of restitution may be enforced by a writ of *fieri facias*, or otherwise. § 92.

By the act of April 13, 1843, § 9,(*a*) in all cases where sheriffs' sales of any debtor's real estate have been or shall be made in several counties, and one or more liens shall be claimed to exist against the real estate so situate and sold in several counties, the Court of Common Pleas of the county in which the first sale was or shall be made, or in case a special court shall be necessary, then the president judge of any district adjoining the same shall have jurisdiction to decree distribution of the whole of the funds so raised by the said sales: provided, that in case of a special court, as aforesaid, the said judge holding the same, before making the final decree of distribution, shall try all the necessary issues in fact in the proper county where the said issues may be formed.

By the act of 20th April, 1846.(*b*) From and after the passage of this act, whenever the purchaser or purchasers of real estate, at Orphans' Court or sheriffs' sale, shall appear from the proper record to be entitled, as a lien creditor, to receive the whole or any portion of the proceeds of said sale, it shall be the duty of the sheriff, administrator, executor, or other person making such sale, to receive the receipt of such purchaser or purchasers, for the amount which he or they would appear, from the record as aforesaid, to be entitled to receive: *Provided*, That this section shall not be so construed as to prevent the right of said sheriff, administrator, executor, or other person aforesaid, to demand and receive, at the time of sale, a sum sufficient to cover all legal costs entitled to be paid out of the proceeds of said sale: *And provided further*, That before any purchaser or purchasers shall receive the benefit of this section, he or they shall produce to the sheriff, or other person so making said sale, a duly certified statement from the proper records, under the hand and official seal of the proper officer, showing that he is a lien creditor, entitled to receive any part of the proceeds of sale as aforesaid. § 1.

It shall be the duty of the said sheriff, executor, administrator, or other person making sale as aforesaid, in all cases when he or they shall receive the receipt of the purchaser as aforesaid, to state the fact in the return of the proceedings of said sale, and attach thereto a list of the liens upon the property sold, which said return shall be read in open court, on some day during the term, to be fixed by the order of court; and if the right of said purchaser or purchasers, to the money mentioned in said return, shall be questioned or disputed by any person interested, the court shall, thereupon, appoint an auditor, who, after due notice given to the persons interested, in such manner as the court may direct, shall make a report, distributing the proceeds of such sale, with the facts and reasons upon which such distribution is made, to be approved by the court; or to direct an issue to determine the validity of said lien, and all further proceedings shall be stayed, until the said issue shall be decided; and in case it shall be determined that the said purchaser or purchasers were not entitled to receive said money, it shall be the duty of

(*a*) Pamph. L. 233.   (*b*) Pamph. L. 411.

the proper court to set aside the sale, and direct the real estate to be re-sold, unless the money is paid to the sheriff, or other person making the sale, within ten days thereafter: *Provided*, That nothing in this act shall be so construed as to prevent the purchaser or purchasers, in case the said real estate, upon the second or subsequent sale, does not bring a sum equal to the amount bid by him or them, from being liable for such deficiency: *Provided*, That before an issue shall be directed upon the distribution of money arising from sales under execution, or Orphans' Court sales, the applicant for such issue shall make affidavit that there are material facts in dispute therein, and shall set forth the nature and character thereof; upon which affidavit the court shall determine whether such issue shall be granted, subject to a writ of error or appeal by such applicant, if the issue be refused, in like manner as in other cases in which such writ now lies.   § 2.(*c*)

Upon granting any such issue, it shall be discretionary with the court, so soon as the money arising from such sale shall have been paid into court, upon the application of the party or parties appearing, by the record *prima facie* entitled to the said fund, to order the same to be invested *pendente lite*, in the debt of the United States, or some other sufficient security, subject to the decree of the court.   § 3.

The only evidence of judgment liens the sheriff is bound to regard, in the absence of all other proof, is the judgment-docket; and if a prior judgment entered only on the appearance-docket is thus overlooked by the prothonotary in making his search, the creditor may look to him for the loss sustained by his omission to enter it on the judgment-docket.(*d*) A purchaser or judgment creditor is not bound to look beyond the judgment-docket, but he may go to correct a mistaken entry.(*e*)

It is settled that a sheriff, of his own authority merely, distributing proceeds of an execution before the return-day, does so at his own risk.(*f*)

(*c*) Lippincott *v.* Lippincott, D. C. Saturday, Sept. 25, 1852. Exceptions to sheriff's return. *Per curiam.* This is a case, under the act of 1846, relating to lien creditors becoming purchasers at judicial sales. The trustees of the bank of the U. S., in whose favor a decree of the Court of C. P., in equity, has passed for a large sum of money, and whose interest is not questioned, have filed exceptions to the sheriff's return, that he has taken plaintiff's receipt for the purchase-money. The affidavit, which includes a demand for an issue, states, very distinctly, that the mortgage, upon which the plaintiff claims the proceeds of the sale, "was given without any consideration whatever, and with the intention of hindering and delaying the exceptants, and other just creditors, of the defendant, and preventing the payment of his debts and liabilities." The facts stated in the affidavit, as sustaining this allegation, may not amount to sufficient proof; they may be inconclusive, or susceptible of explanation, by reference to the state of the stock market, and the general fall of the value of all securities at the period referred to; but surely the question is one of fact, which it is the province of a jury to decide, and if the exceptants have complied with the terms of the law by setting out material facts to be in dispute, and stating their nature and character, we have no power to deny them the constitutional right to appeal to the proper tribunal. Issue awarded. See also further, as to issue, *post*, 838, and to receipts, *ante*, 819.

(*d*) Mann's Appeal, 1 Barr, 24. See Mehaffy's Appeal, 7 W. & S. 201; Bear *v.* Patterson, 3 W. & S. 323.

(*e*) Hance's Appeal, 1 Barr, 408. See Act of April 3, 1843, ¿ 1; and Act of April 16, 1849, ¿ 5, Purd. 997, 1353.

(*f*) 1 Pet. C. C. R. 243.

In practice, he usually takes that risk, and where there are no conflicting claims, it is very well to avoid the delay and expense of paying the money into court. But this will not excuse him if he commit a blunder, however unintentional. All the cases agree, that where he has several writs against the same defendant, he cannot safely pay one plaintiff before the return-day, and, perhaps, some days after, except on notice to and with the assent of the others. The junior has, until then, to contest the right of the senior to the fund, and the sheriff has no right to prefer his antagonist. When the sheriff has notice, he cannot safely discharge it, even after the return-day, but should pay into court or force the plaintiffs to rule him to do so.(g)

The sheriff, where he makes the sale, is bound to appropriate the avails, in discharge of recorded liens. He may, if he will, pay the money into court according to the command of his writs; and where ignorance or doubt exists, or controversy is threatened, his safety lies in this course. Because of the expense and delay attendant upon it, this ought not to be done where the officer sees his way clear; yet if he choose to undertake distribution, it is unquestionably on his own responsibility.(h) But where there are several executions levied upon goods, says Judge KENNEDY, it is the duty of the sheriff generally to apply the money according to the order of time in which they came into his hands; though cases may occur perhaps where the court would take charge of the money, and direct the appropriation of it; as for instance where collusion is alleged between the defendant and the plaintiff in an execution for the purpose of defrauding other execution creditors.(i)

The Court of Common Pleas having made a mistake in the distribution of the proceeds of a sheriff's sale, a mortgage creditor aggrieved, petitioned the court at the next term after the decree, but after the twenty days allowed by law for an appeal had expired, the fund still remaining in court: it was held, that the court had the power to review its decision and grant relief.(j)

When the proceeds of land sold by the sheriff are in court for distribution, it has an equitable jurisdiction to set-off one judgment against another, independently of the defalcation act.(k) Such set-offs, however, cannot be allowed unless there are judgments.(l)

In a recent case in the District Court of Philadelphia, it appeared that on a fi. fa. by A against B, the sheriff returned, "levied and sold part of the property." On a subsequent fi. fa. by C against B, he returned that he sold the other part for another sum, and the levy was on personal property. It was held, that A was entitled to the whole fund raised on both executions, it being no more than sufficient to pay his debts and costs.(m)

The practice of making orders for distribution of money not paid into court is erroneous, and ought not to be pursued except where sanctioned by statute. Without the actual grasp of the fund, the court are power-

---

(g) See the cases collected in Williams's Appeal, 9 Barr, 267.

(h) Mather v. McMichael, 1 H. 303; per BELL, J. See Waterman v. Conyngham, 1 P. C. C. 2.

(i) Lytle v. Mehaffey, 8 W. 275, 276.

(j) Beck's Appeal, 3 H. 406.

(k) Coate's Appeal, 7 W. & S. 99.

(l) Cornwell's Appeal, 7 W. & S. 305.

(m) McCahen v. Bennett, D. C. C. P. 7 Leg. Int. 7.

less for its distribution.(n)   Such a decree will afford no protection to the sheriff paying under it.(o)

Although a lien creditor be entitled to receive payment from the fund, yet if he omits to appeal from an auditor's report against him, he can have no redress in the Supreme Court, on an appeal therefrom by another creditor. Each exceptant must appeal from himself or be precluded from relief.(p)

After execution levied on the interest of one of two partners for an individual debt, the other partner made a cash payment to the sheriff on account of the debt, and by promising to pay the balance, induced the sheriff to suspend proceedings. Before a sale took place, an execution was placed in the sheriff's hands against both partners, on a judgment entered on a joint bond, under which execution the sheriff levied on the partnership effects, which effects he afterwards sold under both writs. It was held, that the execution first in time was entitled to the fund, there being no evidence that the judgment on which the second issued was for a partnership debt, and the mere fact of there being a joint bond signed by the two partners not establishing that fact.(q)

Where a separate execution against one partner was left with the sheriff, and on the same day an execution against the firm was placed in his hands, and three days after another execution against the firm was left with him, and the sheriff returned on all the writs that he had sold the property of A & B (the partners) for, &c., it was held, that the return showed that the entire partnership property was sold, at one operation, under all the writs, and that the separate execution creditor could not come upon the fund until the joint creditors are paid.(r)

As under the 86th section of the act of 1836, the distribution of the proceeds of sheriffs' sales is to be determined according to law and *equity;* an auditor to whom is referred a fund arising from the sale of partnership property on separate executions, may settle the partnership accounts, in order to ascertain the share of each partner, and the rights of their creditors;(rr) and, as will be seen more fully hereafter,(s) when the sheriff, after selling the firm's assets, returns that he has done so, first, under an execution against a single partner individually, and secondly, under executions against the firm, the auditor is bound to go behind the returns, and inquire whether the money belonged to the individual or the firm.(t)   Between equitable claimants, generally, the court will be governed by the principles of equity.(u)

Where a sheriff under several executions against one defendant sells his property, and brings the whole fund into court without discrimination of amount, an auditor would be right in refusing to take jurisdiction of the case, but where he does, and all parties appear, there is no ground for exception.(v)

A party is entitled to demand an issue on matters of fact, although he may have delayed it until all the evidence has been heard, and the case argued before the court.(w)

(n) Williams's Appeal, 9 Barr, 267.
(o) Ibid.
(p) Cash's Appeal, 1 Barr, 166.
(q) Snodgrass's Appeal, 1 H. 471.
(r) King's Appeal, 9 Barr, 124.
(rr) Kelly's Appeal, 4 H. 59.

(s) *Post,* vol. ii. "Partnership."
(t) Vandike's Appeal, 5 H. 271.
(u) Kohl v. Harting, 8 W. 464.
(v) Flanagan v. McAffee, D. C. C. P. 7 Leg. Int. 114.
(w) Trimble's Appeal, 6 W. 133.

Before making distribution of money arising from a sheriff's sale, it is the duty of the court to cause notice to be given to all persons inte. rested, either personally or by such advertisements as they may deem proper; and on an appeal, the Supreme Court will take such order on a proper application, as to prevent the rights of persons being affected who have no opportunity of being heard.(x)

The fund should be in the actual possession of the court at the time of such decree. The practice of ordering distribution of money not paid in is erroneous, and ought not to be pursued, except where sanc. tioned by act of assembly.(y)

A subsequent execution creditor cannot, after sale by the sheriff and return made by him, object to the plaintiff in the prior execution taking the amount of his execution, either on the ground that it was made re- turnable to a wrong return-day, or that the same plaintiff had afterwards issued an attachment in execution.(z)

The claimant must establish his priority over other creditors at the time the proceeds of sale of the land are before the court for distribu- tion. If he does not do so, but permits a distribution to be made, and the residue, after the payment of liens on the land, be decreed to volun- tary assignees of the debtor for distribution according to the deed of trust, his claim will then come too late. Such decree is a final disposi- tion of the whole matter which passes *in rem judicatam*, and being un- appealed from binds him here, no less than it bound him in the court below.(zz)

In an appeal from a decree distributing a fund arising from the judi- cial sale of land, the court will not take notice of the rejected claims of a third party who neglects to appeal from the decree, although such party is clearly entitled to the money in court.(a)

Where there are three executions against the same defendant in the hands of the sheriff, and the property levied on was claimed by a third person, and the plaintiff in the last execution only indemnified the sheriff, upon which he proceeded to sell, it was held, that the last execution creditor was not entitled to any preference by reason of the indemnity, but that the executions were to be paid according to the priority of lien.(b)

A party cannot be permitted to receive a benefit from a judgment who could not have been prejudiced by it. Thus where a lien creditor of a fund in court for distribution had, in pursuance of an agreement with other lien creditors, singly petitioned for an issue to try the validity of a prior judgment, and a verdict was given in his favor, it was held, that the other lien creditors who had remained quiescent, could- derive no benefit from that verdict, and that the petitioner and respondent were the only parties to the proceeding.(c)

If the facts involved in a question as to the alleged fraudulency of a judgment as to creditors are clear of doubt or difficulty, the judge of the court having jurisdiction, sitting as chancellor, may and ought to decide upon them without the intervention of a jury. Such a reference is only

(x) Boal's Appeal, 2 R. 37.
(y) Williams's Appeal, 9 Barr, 267.
(z) Philadelphia Loan Co. *v.* Amies, 2 M. 292.
(zz) Finney's Appeal, 3 Barr, 312.

(a) Cash's Appeal, 1 Barr, 166.
(b) Girard Bank *v.* Norristown Rail- road Co. 2 M. 447.
(c) Shultz's Appeal, 1 Barr, 251.

made in equity to satisfy the conscience of the court concerning doubts as to the facts, and is, therefore, discretionary.(*d*)

Distribution will be made, not among the *cestuis que trust* individually, but to the trustee as their representative.(*e*)

The Rules of the District Court of Philadelphia in respect to the practice of auditors are as follows :—

XIII. Auditors hereafter to be appointed, shall be members of the bar, who have been admitted to practice at least two years.

XIV. In all cases where the proceeds of any sheriff's sale shall be brought into court for distribution, and the claims upon the said fund shall be referred to an auditor for adjustment, public notice of the time and place of hearing shall be given by the auditor by advertisement, made twice successively in the *Legal Intelligencer*, published in Philadelphia, and also for ten successive days (Sundays excepted) in one daily newspaper of the City of Philadelphia. A written or printed notice of the time and place of hearing shall also be posted by the auditor in the office of the prothonotary of this court, at least six days before the hearing. In the notices aforesaid, all persons shall be required to make their claims before such auditor, or be debarred from coming in upon said fund.

XV. In cases referred as aforesaid to an auditor, it shall be the duty of any person, desiring an issue to be formed under the 87th section of the act of assembly relating to executions, passed the 16th June, 1836, to reduce his request to writing, particularly stating therein any fact which he disputes, and to present the same to the auditor within forty-eight hours after the hearing by the auditor has been concluded ; and it shall be the duty of the auditor forthwith to make report to the court of the presentation of such written requests to him, annexing said paper to such report.(*f*)

XVI. Reports of auditors distributing the proceeds of sheriff's sales, shall, upon motion in open court, be confirmed *nisi* when filed ; and unless exceptions shall be made thereto in writing, and filed within eight days after the confirmation *nisi* as aforesaid, the said reports shall be deemed to be confirmed absolutely : *Provided,* That notice shall be given by the auditor to the parties who appeared before him, or their attorneys, of the time and place of making his report as aforesaid, and that proof of such notice be filed of record.

In a recent case decided at Sunbury,(*g*) the practice in reference to auditors is laid down by Judge LOWRIE with remarkable fulness and precision. Although the question arose on an appeal from the Orphans' Court, the points adjudicated are of equal interest in all cases of chancery reference. As stated by the learned judge, they are as follows :—

1. The purpose for which an auditor is appointed should be distinctively stated in the order of reference, the usual purpose being to state an account, to report facts ; and to report facts with his opinion thereon, and these purposes indicate the duty to be performed by him.

2. The court that appoints him may review his report on exceptions

(*d*) Baker *v.* Williamson, 2 Barr, 119 ; Johns *v.* Erb, 5 Barr, 232.

(*e*) Yarnal *v.* Tyson's Appeal, 3 Barr, 363.

(*f*) 1 M. 353.

(*g*) Menga's Appeal, opinion filed July 27, 1852.

filed thereto, and cannot properly set aside or modify it, except for errors of fact, or law specifically excepted to in proper time.(*h*)

3. For reasons that would justify the granting of a new trial by jury, the court should remand the case for rehearing and report to the same auditor; and if the rehearing be for reasons personal to the auditor, then another may be substituted in his place. The court will itself correct such palpable errors as arise from mere mistake of computation.

4. In general it is his duty, when requested, to report all the facts and inferences of facts, that are necessary to sustain the conclusion at which he arrives. Except when appointed to report the evidence, he does not perform his duty by returning the testimony taken by him, and the court does not look at the evidence, unless the report is excepted to for some facts specifically alleged to be untruly found by the auditor.

5. Where evidence is offered and objected to, and he is desired by a party to note it for the opinion of the court, he should distinctively state the offer and its purpose, and the objection thereto and his ruling thereon. In some cases he can also state how the report should be in case the evidence has been erroneously admitted or reported by him. And it may be very proper in some cases to report the question of evidence to the court for decision and suspend the proceedings, until it is decided.(*j*)

6. In stating an account, he is not obliged to state the facts upon which he finds the several items to be correct, unless he be specifically requested so to do by the party objecting to the item; and no general request as to all or several items should be regarded.

7. The Supreme Court inquires only into errors actually committed by the court below, and does not look at the report but for the purpose of ascertaining what exceptions were taken to it below, and how they were decided. No new matter can be assigned for error there, otherwise they might reverse the court for matter never decided by them, which is not the province of a court of error. The errors assigned should distinctly allege error in the court below in deciding upon certain specified exceptions taken to the report.

8. Where facts have been found by the auditors, and approved by the court below, the case must manifest most flagrant error, in order to justify the Supreme Court in interfering with the report. Even on appeal as distinguished from a writ of error, they cannot properly be called upon to try questions of fact.

9. Where facts have been found and are thus excepted to, the court, if they cannot approve the report, may, at the request of either party, order a jury trial, and then the very facts upon which the legal conclusion depends, should be distinctively and severally stated in the issue, so that there can be no dispute as to what is to be found. But the court may itself correct the report.

10. It is very proper for the auditor to aid the court by giving the

(*h*) In matters of fact the error should be plain, and the burden is on the exceptant. Stehman's Appeal, 5 Barr, 413; Ludlam's Est. 1 H. 190; Haines *v.* Barr, D. C. 7 Leg. Int. 521; Yardley *v.* Holby, *post*, 836.

(*j*) The same view is taken by the District Court in Philad., Haines *v.* Barr, 7 Leg. Int. 521. Though see Woelper's Appeal, 2 Barr, 71; Rossiter's Appeal, 2 Barr, 471.

reason for his judgment, but when he does so, it is more regular to annex his opinion to, than to embody it in his report.

11. He should take sufficient notes of all testimony taken before him, and annex the same to his report; unless where the practice of the court requires him to return the same for the inspection of the court, in case his report of facts be excepted to.

12. Every exception to a report should point specifically to the very error complained of, otherwise it cannot properly be noticed. General exceptions display a want of skill, and also imply that no particular error has been discovered.

13. An excellent rule for securing a careful and well-considered report, and preventing frivolous exceptions, is the usual chancery rule adopted by the Supreme Court and by some of the subordinate courts, which is, that the auditors shall give the several parties ten days' notice that his report is ready for signing, that they may have an opportunity of excepting to it before him. If it be thus excepted to, he reconsiders, and, if necessary, amends his report before filing it, and no exceptions are noticed in court that were not filed before the auditor. Thus no report can be set aside, except on points to which the auditor's attention has been directed, and then the same point is distinctly presented to the court below, and reviewed by them. "We think," says LOWRIE, J., "the rule is of sufficient value to recommend itself for general adoption."

The same view, as to the power of an auditor over the facts, is taken by the District Court of Philadelphia.(k)

When lands are sold under judgment against their different parties, the auditor and court in distribution must decide on their respective titles, and whether one is entitled by purchase of the whole, or whether there is a resulting trust for the others.(l)

The auditor's fees come out of the fund in court;(m) though by the analogies drawn from Orphans' Court practice, the costs incurred in adjudicating frivolous exceptions may be put on the exceptant.(n)

A lien creditor is not excluded from a fund by reason of having neglected to present his claim to the auditor before his report is filed, if application be made before final judgment or decree; and even afterwards, the court may, in order to avoid injustice, open such judgment or decree.(o)

(k) Yardley v. Holby, Saturday, June 26, 1852. Exceptions to auditor's report. *Per curiam.* The decision of an auditor upon the facts of a case is conclusive. The party had a right to demand an issue, and not having exercised that right, must be taken to have acquiesced in the submission of the matter to the judgment of the auditor. Of the competency of the witness Cromwell there can be no doubt. He was the assignor of one of the claims, and was called by the other lien creditors to prove that the claim was paid by the defendant before he assigned. The ground of objection was, that one dollar, of the consideration of the assignment, remained unpaid, as came out in the course of his testimony. But that was no claim on the fund; a personal claim only against the assignee. We think, therefore, the witness was rightly admitted.

As to the question presented under the exemption law, we also agree with the auditor, that the claim of the defendant in the case of real estate must be made under the *fi. fa.*, and before a *venditioni exponas*; otherwise it is waived. Exceptions dismissed.

(l) *In re* Brown's Est. Myer's Appeal, 2 Barr, 464.

(m) *In re* Baldwin's Est. Fitzsimons's Appeal, 4 Barr, 248.

(n) Wh. Dig. "Courts," xvii. "Executors," xiv.

(o) Ross's Estate, 9 Barr, 17.

To what extent an auditor distributing funds under an execution is competent to consider the validity of a lien on the fund, is a subject of much interest, which has been already partially considered.(*p*) It is clear that he may, on motion of subsequent incumbrancer, adjudicate upon the validity of a prior mechanic's claim ;(*q*) and even where there is a judg-ment on a *scire facias* on a mechanic's lien, it seems that it is within the jurisdiction of an auditor distributing a fund produced by sale of real estate, to examine into the regularity and validity of the lien, when the question arises between parties other than those who were parties or privies to the judgment.(*r*)　It is clear, also, that he cannot, on the de-

---

(*p*) See *ante*, 569, &c.

(*q*) Knobb's Appeal, 10 Barr, 186; Thomas *v.* James, 7 W. & S. 381.

(*r*) Cadwalader *v.* Montgomery, D. C. Sept. 11, 1852. Exceptions to auditor's report. *Per curiam.* Upon a rule to set aside the *levari facias* in this case, and let a terre-tenant into defence, the opinion of the court was fully expressed upon the validity of this mortgage, and upon the sufficiency of the record of it to make it available against lien creditors and others. As other parties now appear who did not take part then, we have heard these questions argued at length, and with ability; but it has not resulted in producing any change in our opinion.

As this dispenses of the whole case, it is unnecessary to examine the other questions discussed as to the validity of the liens and the demand of an issue thereon. As, however, one point—the right of the auditor, where there has been a judgment on a *scire facias* on a mechanic's lien, to inquire and decide as to the regularity and validity of the lien when the question arises between parties other than those who were parties and privies to the judgment—is one of considerable frequency and importance in practice, we think it proper to add that we are against the exceptants also on that point.

A judgment may be attacked collaterally before an auditor for fraud or collusion, and if an issue is demanded, he is bound to report such issue; but if no issue is demanded, he may decide that it is fraudulent as to the party impeaching, and exclude it from the distribution, or postpone it.

It is not competent, however, for any third person to attach a judgment on the ground of error or irregularity, which can only be taken advantage of by a party or privy on writ of error.

Where, however, a creditor has a lien prior to the date of the judgment, and it is claimed that the judgment takes priority of him, because rendered upon a debt which was a lien prior to the judgment, there it is competent to the creditor holding a lien prior to the date of the judgment, to dispute the validity of the prior lien.

A simple case will illustrate this position. A judgment has lost its lien by the lapse of five years, then another lien is entered, and afterwards upon a *scire facias* to revive the first judgment, a judgment of revival is entered. The intervening judgment creditor, purchaser, or mortgagee may undoubtedly show that the lien of the revived judgment was gone, notwithstanding the judgment of revivor.

It does not appear in Lauman's Appeal (8 Barr, 473), whether judgments upon the liens were obtained prior or subsequent to the entry of the judgments which are called in the report *subsequent*. If they were subsequent, the decision in that case is entirely consistent with the opinion here expressed. We cannot think that the Supreme Court meant to decide that if a mechanic's claim was not a valid lien from the want of compliance with the requisites of the act of assembly, if it was uncertain as to description, failed in specifying the date, character, and amount of the claim, if it had not been filed in time ; these defects could all be cured as against an intervening creditor, mortgagee, or purchaser, by a judgment of which he had no notice, and to which he was no party.

There may be reason for holding, and that is all we can suppose the Supreme Court meant to decide, that a man who lends or pays his money after the judgment, takes subject to the lien of the judgment, *qua* judgment, which may have, with great appearance of justice, the effect given to it of a general judgment, though its lien may from the nature of its proceedings be merely specific. Thus a judgment on a *scire facias* on an unrecorded mortgage may be a lien from its date *qua* judgment, but surely a party who had advanced his money before upon the faith that there was no record, or that the record was insufficient and void, is not concluded by the subsequent judg-

fendant's motion, take cognizance of any fraud or irregularity,(s) though it is said he may adjourn the audit to enable a party to apply to the court to open the judgment, or he may take testimony to show payment since its rendition.(t) But the inclination of opinion now is, that while third parties may attack a judgment before an auditor for fraud or collusion,(u) only the defendant or his representatives can object to the erroneous entry of judgment or issuing of execution; neither can the latter do so collaterally, or otherwise than by writ of error or application to the court below.(v)

Under the 87th section of the act of June 16, 1836, relating to executions, where one of the claimants on the fund for distribution arising from a sheriff's sale, makes an allegation of a fact pertinent to the inquiry before the court, the truth of which is disputed by another claimant, and an issue is claimed, such issue must be restricted specially to the ascertainment of the particular matter in dispute. The whole subject of the distribution is not to be comprised within the issue. The application to the court must be in writing, stating distinctly the matter in dispute, to ascertain which the party desires an issue or issues. The issues may be as numerous as the subjects of disagreement; but each issue may be limited to a single inquiry; and all the issues, with the leave of the court, may be tried by the same jury.(w)

By the present practice, under the act of April 20, 1846, it is necessary, in order to enable an issue to be demanded, for the applicant to make affidavit that there are material facts in dispute, setting forth the nature and character thereof; and upon this affidavit it is for the court to determine whether such issue shall be granted, subject to a writ of error.(x)

ment, upon the *scire facias* to which he was neither party nor privy. A judgment is conclusive evidence to all the world, that there is such a judgment; a debt of record with a lien. No mere stranger can object that it is erroneous. But beyond its legal effects as a judgment, as evidence that the debt recovered was due ten days or ten years before— that the debt had a particular quality or anything else, though as between the parties this enters into the very vitality of the judgment, it is not even evidence as against strangers, much less conclusive of their rights. Exceptions dismissed.

(s) See *ante*, 569, &c.
(t) Dyott's case, 2 W. & S. 567; see Lowber's Appeal, 8 W. & S. 387.
(u) *Ante*, 569, 571; Cadwalader *v.* Montgomery, *supra*.
(v) Lowber's Appeal, 8 W. & S. 387.
(w) McDaniel *v.* Haly, 1 M. 353.
(x) Biddle *v.* King, D. C. Sept. 11, 1852. Why demand for issue should not be allowed. *Per curiam.* The proviso to the second section of the act of 20th April, 1846, is not the only instance

in modern legislation of a general law enacted and incorporated in the shape of a proviso to some particular and limited statute. The act of 20th April, 1846, § 2, is undoubtedly confined to the case of proceedings upon lien creditors becoming purchasers at judicial sales, but the proviso reads: "*Provided*, That before an issue shall be directed upon the distribution of money arising *from sales under execution* or Orphans' Court sales, the applicant for such issue shall make affidavit that there are material facts in dispute therein, and shall set forth the nature and character thereof; upon which affidavit the court shall determine whether such issue shall be granted, subject to a writ of error or appeal by such applicant, if the issue be refused, in like manner as in other cases in which such writ now lies." If this language was separated from its context, and stood as an independent section, no doubt could be entertained on the subject. The reason of the law is the life of the law. No reason can be assigned for such a proviso in the case of purchasers claiming

The results of the issues as to facts are to be received implicitly and incorporated with such other facts as the parties in interest may consent to, or as the court, when the parties do not expressly agree, shall itself ascertain. All controversy, as to the facts, must terminate with the finding of the issues.(*y*)

The vendee of the sheriff's vendee, when there is a question whether a particular incumbrance is discharged or no, is "a party interested," who may demand an issue, and is consequently concluded by a decree of distribution regularly made, though it appear he had no notice of the proceedings in the same.(*z*)

The court, by whom an issue to try the right to money brought in by the sheriff is directed, may and ought to mould the issue into the form calculated to answer the end proposed; and if it is found that this has not been done, may arrest the proceedings and begin anew.(*a*)

To the issue, only the excepting creditors are parties.(*b*)

The trial of the issue is subject to all the rules in relation to jury trials.(*c*)

The Supreme Court will not reverse for a refusal to direct an issue, where there are no facts to submit, or their determination would not affect the result.(*d*)

An issue was directed by the court to try the right to certain moneys in the hands of the sheriff, arising from a sale of real estate, and the sheriff was made defendant in the issue, without any specific direction as to the costs; a verdict having been given for the plaintiff, the Court of Common Pleas entered judgment thereon, with costs, which the Supreme Court affirmed.(*e*)

After a petition to the court to award an issue, or to appoint auditors

the benefit of the act as lien creditors, which does not apply with equal force to every other case. In truth, such a general provision was imperatively required. Under the 87th section of the act of 16th June, 1836, and the construction of that act in Reigart's Appeal (7 W. & S. 267), any one interested in the distribution of the proceeds of a sheriff's sale, by a mere allegation that there were facts connected with such distribution in dispute, had a right to an issue; and thus to tie up the fund for a considerable time; and as the court has no power to order an investment during the pendency of such issue, a serious injury was thus done to the rights of parties, and that without showing a *prima facie* case for the delay. Thus an unjust power was placed in the hands of persons which, as they would not be losers, and might be gainers, would be, and was, used for the purpose of forcing unjust compromises. The act of 1840 has remedied the evil, by requiring the applicant to set forth the nature and the character of the facts which he alleges to be in dispute, and giving the court power to judge of them materially, subject to a writ of error or appeal. By the

third section it provides that the court may order the fund to be invested during the pendency of the issue; and by the 92d section of the act of 16th June, 1836, the court are clothed with a similar power of investing the fund pending a writ of error or appeal. Thus something like a rational system has been established, which there is no reason, either in the words or spirit of the statute, to say shall be confined to the single case of lien creditors becoming purchasers at judicial sales. As the demand for an issue in this case is unaccompanied by an affidavit, as required by the act, this rule must be made absolute. See also Bartram *v.* Ingram, *ante,* 722; and also *ante,* 830.

(*y*) McDaniel *v.* Haly, 1 M. 353.
(*z*) Towers *v.* Tuscarora Academy, 8 Barr, 297.
(*a*) Stewart *v.* Stocker, 1 W. 135.
(*b*) Steel *v.* Bridenback, 7 W. & S. 150; Tombs's Appeal, 9 Barr, 61.
(*c*) McDaniel *v.* Haly, 1 M. 353.
(*d*) Dougherty's Estate, 9 W. & S. 192; Dickerson's Appeal, 7 Barr, 250; Overholt's Appeal, 2 J. 224; ROGERS, J.
(*e*) Hipple *v.* Hoffman, 2 W. 85.

to investigate the facts, on a dispute arising as to the proceeds of a sheriff's sale, the fact that the court takes the latter alternative and not the former, cannot afterwards be complained of as error.(*f*)

The costs incurred in several feigned issues framed for the purpose of trying the rights of several creditors to a fund arising from a judicial sale, must be paid severally out of the money awarded to pay each particular debt; though it seems, generally, expenses incident to the whole procedure are to be apportioned among the several creditors in proportion to the amount coming to and received by each.(*g*)

Under the 88th section of the act of 1836, upon a writ of error to the judgment on the issue, should the Supreme Court affirm the same, that court will then entertain exceptions as to the decree of distribution made by the court below, upon the whole case, and order distribution accordingly. But should the Supreme Court reverse the judgment on the issue, *it seems* that they would remit the record to the court below for a trial thereon.(*h*)

Where an issue is outstanding, arising on the distribution of a fund, the court will not permit even an undisputed dividend to be taken out of court until the issue is decided.(*i*)

Where the first judgment creditor succeeds on a feigned issue directed with the second to determine the validity of his judgment, but, on the trial of an issue directed with the third judgment creditor, the first is found to be fraudulent, he is, nevertheless, entitled to so much of the proceeds of the sheriff's sale as between the second and third judgment creditor would have gone to the second, for his judgment being valid against the second, he is entitled to use the priority of the second over subsequent judgment creditors.(*j*)

A defendant in an execution, the proceeds of whose property is in court for appropriation, may be examined as a witness on the trial of a feigned issue, to ascertain facts in relation to such appropriation, where his interest is equally balanced.(*k*)

The practice in feigned issues under the sheriff's interpleader act has been already considered.(*kk*)

(4.) *Appeal and supersedeas.*

It is necessary, in order to make an appeal a supersedeas, that it should be perfected within twenty days from the decree of distribution, by the oath and security provided by the 91st section of the act of 16th June, 1836 ; and it is expressly provided by the 90th section, that if an appeal shall not be taken within twenty days from the decree of distribution, the court may order the money to be paid according to such decree.(*l*)

(5.) *Application of surplus.*

By the ninety-third section of the act of 1836, whenever the proceeds of a sale upon execution as aforesaid shall be more than sufficient to satisfy the liens upon the property sold, the officer making such sale or receiving such proceeds, shall pay the surplus to the debtor, unless

---

(*f*) Dickerson's Appeal, 7 Barr, 257.
(*g*) Cowden's Estate, 1 Barr, 267.
(*h*) McDaniel *v.* Haly, 1 M. 353.
(*i*) Pepper *v.* Bavington, D. C. C. P. Sept. 1848 ; see McDaniel *v.* Haly, 1 M. 353.

(*j*) Tombs's Appeal, 9 Barr, 61.
(*k*) Stewart *v.* Stocker, 1 W. 135 ; Guillon *v.* Healy, *ante*, 726.
(*kk*) *Ante*, 720, &c.
(*l*) Thorp *v.* Thorp, D. C. P. May 6, 1848.

the fund shall have been paid into court, and then, and not before, such officer shall be discharged thereof, upon record in the court to which he shall make return of his proceedings concerning such execution.

In the case of a sale of lands of a decedent, the practice before the act of 1834 was to pay the surplus to his executor, in whose hands it is assets for payment of other debts, and not to the heir or devisee, because, should other debts appear, there would be a necessity for new suits and executions for the purpose of selling other lands, whereby the estate would be subjected to heavy costs. Exceptions to this rule were allowed where it appeared that there were no other debts outstanding, or that the executor was insolvent, in which cases the court would order the surplus to be paid to the heir or devisee.(m) But by the thirty-third section of the last-mentioned act 1834,(n) § 33, it is provided that the surplus shall be paid to the executor or administrator for distribution, upon his giving bond, to the satisfaction of the court, for the legal distribution thereof; provided that it be distributed as the real estate of which it is the proceeds would have been.(o)

The return of the sheriff to a writ of *fi. fa.*, that he paid over the surplus of the proceeds of the sale of a vessel, after satisfying the execution, to one of the owners, for himself, and as agent for the others, is not a legitimate part of the return, and the appropriate remedy of one of the part owners to recover his share, is in *assumpsit*, and not by an action for a false return.(p)

Where A had devised land to his widow, B, for life, remainder to his two children, C and D, and B joined in a mortgage of the land for the proper debt of C and D, and the land was sold under a *levari facias;* B was allowed to take the surplus moneys out of court, in preference to the judgment creditors of C and D, on giving security for the payment of the principal sum after her death.(q)

Where money is made on a *fi. fa.* the sheriff cannot set up any claim on the surplus proceeds, by reason of a debt due him by the defendant, nor for the expenses incurred in taking care of goods, where the sale was deferred at the instance of defendant, and on his promise to pay the expense.(r)

Where a debtor sold his real estate voluntarily, after judgments obtained against him, and it was afterwards sold at sheriff's sale, on executions on two of those judgments, and on one which was not obtained till after the voluntary sale, and it was purchased by the first purchaser, it was held that the latter was entitled to the balance of the purchase money which remained after discharging the judgments to which it was subject at the time of the voluntary sale, in preference to the plaintiff in the judgment obtained *after* such sale.(s)

10. *Reversal of judgment after sale.*

By the ninth section of the act of 1805,(t) the purchaser is protected in the event of a reversal of the judgment under which the sale took

(m) Per TILGHMAN, C. J., Guier v. Kelly, 2 Bin. 298–9.
(n) Pamph. L. 70.
(o) Morrison's Case, 9 W. & S. 116.
(p) Hopkins v. Forsyth, 2 H. 34.
(q) Bloomfield v. Budden, 2 D. 183;

S. C. 1 Y. 187; Mollison v. Bowman, 5 P. L. J. 181.
(r) Fitch's Appeal, 10 Barr, 461.
(s) Bitting and Waterman's Appeal, 5 Harris, 211.
(t) Sm. Laws, 60.

place, but not where the sale was made under void process. In case
of reversal, the act provides that none of the lands, tenements, or hereditaments shall be restored, nor the sale or delivery thereof avoided,
but restitution only shall be made of the money or price for which the
same shall be sold.(u)   This act applies as well to cases of judgments
reversed for errors of fact as well as of law.(v)

11. *Estate taken by purchaser.*

The purchaser takes the same estate as the debtor, and in the case
of a sale under a mortgage, nothing further goes to the purchaser than
the property sold shall appear to be mortgaged for.   If the defendant
were a tenant, the purchaser will be a tenant also, and in an action of
ejectment by the landlord cannot dispute his title.(w)   So, on sale of
an equitable interest held on articles of agreement, the purchaser holds
the possession subject to the payment of the purchase-money.(x)   The
purchaser, under a mortgage, holds the estate clearly discharged and
freed from all equity and benefit of redemption, and all other incumbrances made or suffered by the mortgagor, his heirs or assigns,(y) nor
does he take the land subject to a previous judgment against a former
owner, unless sold expressly subject to such prior judgment.   Where,
therefore, money is in the sheriff's hands from a sale of land under a
judgment against the present owner, creditors who have liens upon
the land by virtue of judgments against the former owner, are entitled
to payment out of this fund ; and if the sheriff, instead of satisfying
such liens, pays over the balance of the purchase-money to the defendant in the execution, the previous judgment creditors may recover from
him the amount of their respective liens.(z)   So a purchaser of land
under a *fi. fa.* and *venditioni exponas* issued on a judgment entered up
by virtue of a warrant of attorney, given with a bond and mortgage,
holds it clear of a lease made by the mortgagor, after the mortgage,
but before the entry of the judgment on the bond.(zz)

A party who gives notice of a particular claim of title at a sheriff's
sale of real estate, will afterwards, as against a purchaser at such sale,
be restricted to the particular title thus given out.(a)

The quantity of land which passes by a sheriff's sale to a purchaser
is to be ascertained by the return to the levy, which, in the absence of
reasonable doubt, is to be construed by the court alone ; but where, by
reason of uncertainty, or looseness of description, evidence *aliunde* is
resorted to, to ascertain the quantity, and define the boundaries of the
land included in the levy, the whole of the evidence is to be referred
to the jury.(aa)

Though a less estate may pass under a misdescription in the levy, a
greater cannot.(b)

A purchase by a ministerial officer, such as a deputy sheriff, at a judicial sale, where there is no actual fraud, is voidable, and not void, and

(u) Heister *v.* Foster, 2 Bin. 46 ; Burd
v. Dinsdale, ib. 80.
(v) Warder *v.* Tainter, 4 W. 286.
(w) 3 Caines's Rep. 188 ; Stahle *v.*
Spohn, 8 S. & R. 325.
(x) Ibid.
(y) § 6, act of 1705, 1 Sm. Laws, 59.
(z) Com. *v.* Alexander, 14 S. & R. 257.

(zz) McCall *v.* Lenox, 9 S. & R. 302.
(a) Eshbock *v.* Zimmerman, 2 Barr,
313 ; Brown *v.* Bank of Chambersburg,
3 Barr, 187 ; Randal *v.* Silverthorn, 4
Barr, 177.
(aa) Hoffman *v.* Danner, 2 H. 25.
(b) M'Laughlin *v.* Shields, 2 J. 287.
ROGERS, J.

the legal title passes to the purchaser, until set aside by a competent tribunal, which will only be done by reimbursing the purchaser his outlay.(*bb*)

In the exercise of a reasonable discretion, the courts have not been rigid in the application of the maxim of *caveat emptor* to judicial sales, but have always liberally interfered for the protection of an erring purchaser untainted by fraud.(*c*)

There are two cardinal points of difference between execution of land under our acts of 1700 and 1705, and execution of it under the stat. Westmin. 2. In England, for execution purposes a judgment binds the land as a specific thing; but with us, the debtor's title or estate in it is bound without regard to whether he was seized or disseized at the time of the rendition.

Again, land is taken in execution, under the English statute, and delivered specifically to the creditor to make satisfaction by its profits without regard to the debtor's title to it: under our statutes, the sheriff sells, not the land, as the incontestable property of the debtor, but his estate in it or title to it as a chattel, and at the purchaser's risk.(*d*)

Conveyances of land to a trustee for the benefit of an insolvent *cestui que trust*, "are favored and sustained by the law, as suggested by the best feelings of our nature, and doing harm to no one;" and land thus conveyed was held not to be liable to execution and sale at the suit of a creditor of the *cestui que trust*, whose debt was prior to the conveyance.(*e*)

The land of a judgment debtor was sold by the sheriff, and deed made to the purchaser, while the grain was growing thereon. After the acknowledgment of the deed, an execution creditor of the debtor levied on the grain and sold it, and the purchaser brought suit against the tenant of the purchaser of the land for cutting and removing the grain. It was held, that the grain passed by the sheriff's sale of the land, and that the purchaser of the grain could not recover.(*f*) The test as to whether grain growing passes to the purchaser of the land at sheriff's sale, is whether there has, or has not, been a previous severance, either actually or by private or judicial sale.(*g*)

After the execution and recording of a mortgage, but before the issuing of a *scire facias* thereon, the mortgagor leased a portion of the mortgaged premises for a year to a cropper, who paid the rent in advance and sowed grain upon it. Before the grain was cut, the land was sold at sheriff's sale, under proceedings on the mortgage, commenced after the making of the lease. It was held that the grantee of the purchaser of the land was entitled to recover damages from the cropper for cutting and removing the grain.(*h*)

By the act of 1836, as well as on general principles, the purchaser is entitled to rent only from the acknowledgment of the deed; before which time he is not entitled to possession or profits of the land, and

---

(*bb*) Jackson *v.* McGinnis, 2 H. 331.
(*c*) BELL, J., Crawford *v.* Boyer, 2 H. 380.
(*d*) Mitchell *v.* Hamilton, 8 Barr, 488; citing Jefferson *v.* Morton, 2 Saund. 6.
(*e*) Eyrick *v.* Hetrick, 1 H. 491; BELL, J., citing Ashhurst *v.* Given, 5 W. & S.

323; Fisher *v.* Taylor, 2 R. 33; and see Vaux *v.* Park, 7 W. & S. 19, and *ante*, 770.
(*f*) Bear *v.* Bitzer, 4 H. 175.
(*g*) Bear *v.* Bitzer, 4 H. 175; Groff *v.* Levan, id. 179.
(*h*) Groff *v.* Levan, 4 H. 179.

consequently not liable personally for ground-rent accruing between the day of sale and the date of his deed. "And the reason is," says ROGERS, J., "that although the title may for many purposes be referred to the sale, yet the purchaser acquires no title except an imperfect one, until the sale receives the sanction of the court."(*i*)

The purchaser may affirm or disaffirm an existing lease of the premises.(*j*) By affirming it, he may claim the rent payable under it; but if he disaffirms it, as by notifying tenant to quit, he can claim no rent under the lease. If by the contract the rent is payable in advance, a purchaser, in the middle of a year, is not entitled to the rent payable by the tenant at the beginning of it, for that was due before the acknowledgment of the deed.(*k*) The object of the 119th section of the act of June 16, 1836, was to avoid the fraud and collusion arising from payment of rents in advance, where they were not by the terms of the lease due, and thus deprive the purchaser of so much. If, therefore, the tenant anticipate his payments after the rendition of the judgment, he does it at the risk of liability, under the act, to pay over again to the purchaser.(*l*)

Where, by the terms of the lease, the tenant is to retain the rent, and apply it to the payment of a debt for which he has become surety for the lessor, the purchaser is entitled to nothing.(*m*)

It is not correct to say the purchaser at sheriff's sale has no better title than the debtor had at the time of the sale. His title dates, in many respects, from the lien of the judgment. He holds discharged of latent trusts, and of intervening conveyances, leases, and incumbrances made by the debtor. If it were not so, the debtor might dispose of the land, and thus defeat the judgment creditors; whereas, the general rule is that the sale on the judgment overreaches the *mesne* acts of the debtor, and passes the title discharged from them. The acts of assembly of 1802 and 1814 give relief only to persons claiming against the sheriff's deed by title paramount to the defendant's title, or by title derived from the defendant prior to the judgment. Any other person in possession must surrender it to the purchaser, or may be ejected by summary process. "No contract," says Mr. Justice DUNCAN, in Lennox *v.* McCall,(*n*) " between the lessee and the debtor can deprive or delay the creditor of the benefit of his judgment, or the purchaser, at sheriff's sale, of the benefit of his purchase. A lease can no more deprive them of their rights than a conveyance in fee simple. A debtor might give a lease for any number of years, receive the whole rent in advance, and thus deprive the purchaser of all benefit from his purchase till after the expiration of his lease." The same may be said of all other modes of transferring the land, or impairing its enjoyment.(*o*) When the plaintiff buys, and refuses to comply with the terms of sale, he will be liable to a subsequent judgment creditor for the loss on a resale, and cannot set up the defective description in the levy as a defence.(*p*)

12. *Purchaser's remedy to obtain possession.*

(*i*) Thomas *v.* Connell, 5 Barr, 13.
(*j*) Groff *v.* Levan, 4 H. 179.
(*k*) F. and M. Bank *v.* Ege, 9 W. 437.
(*l*) Bank *v.* Ege, 7 W. 436; Fullerton *v.* Shauffer, 2 J. 221.
(*m*) Fullerton *v.* Shauffer, 2 J. 221.

(*n*) 3 S. & R. 97.
(*o*) Per SERGEANT, J., delivering the opinion of the court in McCormick *v.* McMurtrie, 4 Watts, 195.
(*p*) Spang *v.* Schneider, 10 Barr, 193.

By the sale and conveyance, the defendant becomes *quasi* a tenant at will to the purchaser, and his possession is not deemed adverse.(*q*) The defendant will not be suffered to set up an adverse title, and as between him and the purchaser in an action of ejectment, the latter can recover on the strength of the sale and sheriff's deed without showing other title. From the time of the levy, the *jus possessionis* is in the sheriff's vendee where the debtor is in possession at the time of the levy, and the debtor cannot, with a view to defeat the creditor, treacherously deliver possession even to the real owner, who must pursue his remedy against the purchaser.(*r*)

By the one hundred and nineteenth section of the act of 1836, if the property is at the time of sale, or afterwards, held by a tenant or lessee, or person holding, or claiming to hold, the same under the defendant in such execution, the purchaser of such lands or tenements shall, upon receiving a deed for the same, as aforesaid, be deemed the landlord of such tenant, lessee, or other person, and shall have the like remedies to recover any rents or sums accruing subsequently to the acknowledgment of a deed to him, as aforesaid, whether such accruing rent may have been paid in advance or not, if paid after the rendition of the judgment on which sale was made, as such defendant might have had, if no such sale had been made. § 119.

If, after notice shall be given of such sale, as aforesaid, such tenant, lessee, or other person shall pay any rent or sum accruing subsequently to the acknowledgment of such deed, notice given him, as aforesaid, to such defendant, such tenant, lessee, or other person so paying, shall, nevertheless, be liable to pay the same to the purchaser. § 120.

These sections are derived from the act of April 6, 1802, § 3, altered so as to give the purchaser at sheriff's sale the rights of a landlord subsequently to the acknowledgment of a deed to him.(*s*)

By the return of the sheriff of a sale of land, and the acknowledgment of the deed, the title to the land is vested in the purchaser, and the sheriff becomes fixed for the amount bid.(*t*) The acknowledgment of the sheriff's deed is not conclusive evidence of delivery, but taken in connection with the fact of possession of the land being taken by the vendee, and continued, it is a strong proof of it.(*u*)

After the sheriff's deed is duly acknowledged, should the purchaser be unable to obtain quiet possession, he may then, but not before,(*v*) resort to the mode directed by the act of June, 1836, the provisions of which we will here introduce at length.

Whenever any lands or tenements shall be sold by virtue of execution, as aforesaid, the purchaser of such estate may, after the acknowledgment of a deed therefor to him, by the sheriff, give notice to the defendant, as whose property the same shall have been sold, or to the persons in possession of such estate under him, by title derived from him subsequently to the judgment under which the same were sold, and require

---

(*q*) 1 Johns. Ca. 153 ; Stahle *v.* Spohn, 8 S. & R. 326.
(*r*) Ibid.
(*s*) See Schearer *v.* Stanly, 2 R. 278 ; Remarks of Commissioners.
(*t*) 2 Pa. R. 223.
(*u*) Id. ibid.
(*v*) Hawk *v.* Stouch, 5 S. & R. 161.

him, or them, to surrender the possession thereof to him, within three months from the date of such notice. § 105.

If the defendant, or any person in possession under him, as aforesaid, shall refuse, or neglect to comply with the notice and requisition of the purchaser, as aforesaid, such purchaser, or his heirs, or assigns, may apply, by petition, to any two justices of the peace, or aldermen, of the city, town, or county where such real estate may be, setting forth:—

I. That he purchased the premises at a sheriff's or coroner's sale.

II. That the person in possession at the time of such application is the defendant, as whose property such real estate was sold, or that he came into possession thereof under him.

III. That such person in possession had notice, as aforesaid, of such sale, and was required to give up such estate three months previously to such application. § 106.

If the application, as aforesaid, shall be verified by the oath or affirmation of the petitioner, or if probable cause to believe the facts therein set forth be otherwise shown, the said justices are hereby enjoined and required forthwith to issue their warrant, in the nature of a summons, directed to the sheriff of the county, commanding him to summon a jury of twelve men of his bailiwick, to appear before the said justices, at a time and place to be specified, within four days next after the issuing thereof, and also to summon the defendant, or person in possession, as aforesaid, at the same time to appear before them and the said jury, to show cause, if any he has, why delivery of the possession of such lands or tenements should not be forthwith given to the petitioner. § 107.

If, at the time and place appointed for the hearing of the parties, the defendant, or person in possession, as aforesaid, shall fail to appear, the said justices shall require proof, by oath or affirmation, of the due service of such warrant upon him, and of the manner of such service : *Provided*, That such service shall have been made three days before the return. § 108.

If the defendant, or other person in possession under him, as aforesaid, shall be duly summoned, as aforesaid, or if he shall appear, the said justices and jury shall proceed to inquire—

I. Whether the petitioner, or those under whom he claims, has or have, become the purchaser of such real estate, at a sheriff's or coroner's sale, as aforesaid, and a sheriff's or coroner's deed for the same, duly acknowledged and certified, shall be full and conclusive evidence of that fact, before such justices and jury.

II. Whether the person in possession of such real estate was the defendant in the execution under which such real estate was sold, or came into the possession thereof under him, as aforesaid.

III. Whether the person so in possession has had three months' notice of such sale, previous to such application. § 109.

Upon the finding of the facts, as aforesaid, the justices shall make a record thereof, and thereupon they shall award the possession of such real estate to the petitioner. § 110.

In case of a finding for the petitioner, as aforesaid, the jury shall assess such damages as they shall think right, against such defendant, or person in possession, for the unjust detention of the premises, and thereupon the said justices shall enter judgment for the damages assessed, and reasonable costs, and such judgment shall be final and conclusive to the parties. § 111.

The said justices shall thereupon issue their warrant, directed to the sheriff, commanding him forthwith to deliver to the petitioner, his heirs or assigns, full possession of such lands or tenements, and to levy the costs taxed by the said justices, and the damages assessed by the jury, as aforesaid. § 112.

No *certiorari*, which may be issued to remove such proceedings, shall be a *supersedeas*, or have any effect to prevent or delay the execution aforesaid, or the delivery of the possession, agreeably thereto. § 113.

If the person in possession of the premises shall make oath or affirmation before the justices—

I. That he has not come into possession, and does not claim to hold the same under the defendant in the execution, but in his own right, or

II. That he has not come into possession under title derived to him from the said defendant, before the judgment under which the execution and sale took place, and shall become bound in a recognizance, with one or more sufficient sureties, in the manner hereinafter provided, the said justices shall forbear to give the judgment aforesaid. § 114.

If the person in possession of the premises shall make oath or affirmation, before the justices, that he does not hold the same under said defendant, but under some other person whom he shall name, the said justices shall forthwith issue a summons to such person, requiring him to appear before them, at a certain time therein named, not exceeding thirty days thence following, and if at such time the said person shall appear, and make oath or affirmation that he verily believes that he is legally entitled to the premises in dispute, and that he does not claim under the said defendant, but by a different title, or that he claims under the said defendant by title derived before the judgment aforesaid, and shall enter into a recognizance, with sureties, as aforesaid, in such case also, the justices shall forbear to give judgment. § 115.

The oath or affirmation which shall be administered to such claimant, shall be in the following form, to wit:—

I do (swear or affirm) that I verily believe that I am legally entitled to hold the premises in dispute, against the petitioner—that I do not claim the same by, from, or under the defendant, as whose property the same were sold (as the case may be)—that I do not claim the same by, from, or under the defendant, as whose property the same were sold, by title derived to me subsequently to the rendition of the judgment under which the same were sold, but by a different title, &c.   § 116.

The recognizance aforesaid shall be taken in a sum fully sufficient to cover and secure, as well the value of the rents and mesne profits of such lands or tenements, which may have accrued, and which may be expected to accrue, before the final decision of the said claim, as all costs and damages, with condition that he shall appear at the next Court of Common Pleas, or District Court, having jurisdiction, and then and there plead to any declaration in ejectment, which may be filed against him, and thereupon proceed to trial, in due course of practice, and in case he shall fail therein, that he will deliver up the said premises to the purchaser, and to pay him the full value of the rents or mesne profits of the premises, accrued from the time of the purchase. § 117.

If such recognizance shall be forfeited, the justices aforesaid shall proceed to give judgment, and cause such real estate to be delivered up to the petitioner, in the manner hereinbefore enjoined and directed. § 118.(w)

" The sheriff's deed is conclusive evidence of the right and possession against the defendant in the execution, and all claiming under him after the judgment.   If there are matters of defence accruing subsequent to a judgment, and prior to a sale, such as payment and satisfaction, or release, the defendant may obtain relief by motion to the court to stay proceedings, or to set aside the process, or, perhaps, to stop the acknowledgment of the sheriff's deed ; but these matters cannot be set up to defeat the purchaser's right to possession under the deed."(x)   And the defendant will not be permitted to show, that the judgment on which the land was sold, had been paid, although the purchaser who was seeking to obtain the possession were the plaintiff in that judgment.(y)

The proceedings in a case of this description, may be removed by writ of *certiorari* to the Supreme Court or Common Pleas, at the party's election, for although the power of the former court to remove proceedings had before a justice of the peace has been taken away by an act of assembly, it has been decided, that this relates to cases before a single justice, and not to proceedings before two justices for the recovery of the possession of houses or land.(z)

The statute giving the right to transfer the suit to the Common Pleas, authorizes the person in possession of land sold by the sheriff, to make oath that " he does not claim the land through or under the defendant, as where property is the same that was sold by title derived subsequently to the rendition of the judgment under which it was sold, but by a different title ;" and he thus becomes the actor in court, and must establish

---

(w) The decisions under the old law on this subject may be traced in Lenox v. McCall, 3 S. & R. 95, 101 ; Hawk v. Skuch, 5 S. & R. 159; Snyder v. Bauchman, 8 S. & R. 340 ; Clark v. Yeat, 4 Bin. 185 ; Simpson v. Jack, 13 S. & R. 278 ; Hale v. Henrie, 2 W. 147.

(x) Hale v. Henrie, 2 W. 147.
(y) Ibid. 143.
(z) Lenox v. McCall, 3 S. & R. 101; vide 4 Bin. 185 ; 8 S. & R. 340 ; Cooke v. Reinhart, 1 R. 317.

that he claims under a title which governs and overrides the one sold by the sheriff, or else he fails; and therefore the judgment, execution, and sale are admitted, and are, in fact, part of the process, and the sheriff's deed is properly admissible in evidence, even though the acknowledgment was taken after the sheriff's term had expired, and the deed was not delivered to the purchaser until some time after the acknowledgment. The record of the justice is part of the *res gestæ* of the whole case, and may be exhibited in evidence for the purpose of showing when the proceedings were commenced. In the proceeding commenced before the justices, evidence that "the acknowledgment was taken after the expiration of the sheriff's term of office," and "that the deed had not been delivered by the sheriff to the purchaser, until some time after the acknowledgment," is inadmissible.(*a*)

It is for the jury, and not for the justices, to assess the damages, and error for the justices so to do; and to a *sci. fa. sur recog.* on damages so assessed, the plea of *nul tiel record* is sufficient.(*b*)

In a very late case, the evidence was that a tenant for years of a devisee purchased the land under a judgment against the devisor, the estate of the devisee having been previously sold under a judgment against him. The tenant purchasing under the judgment against the devisor, was said to hold by a title paramount to his lessor, and to be within the provisions of the 114th section of the act of 1836, and hence not liable to summary proceedings to obtain possession on the part of the purchaser of the estate of his landlord.(*c*)

After the usual recognizance is entered into to appear at the next term of the court, and plead to any action of ejectment, &c., it is not necessary that the plaintiff should go on and prosecute the proceedings before the alderman to an issue, but it is a sufficient satisfaction of the terms of the recognizance for him to proceed at the next term of the proper court with an ejectment; and upon a verdict thereupon for mesne profits and costs, and a return of *nulla bona*, the bail in the recognizance becomes liable thereupon.(*d*)

The sheriff's or coroner's deed, duly acknowledged and certified, is made by the act full and conclusive evidence of the purchase before such justices and jury. In such case, the only question submitted to the justices and jury is, whether there is a sheriff's or coroner's deed, in fact and form, duly acknowledged in open court, and duly certified under the seal of the court: it was never intended by the act to make such tribunal a court of error to examine the regularity of the proceedings in court as to the judgment, process of sale, and execution of deed.(*e*)

An amicable action of ejectment commenced at the third term succeeding the date of the recognizance, entered into by the defendant with his sureties, and a recovery therein, is not evidence against the surety, to charge him according to the condition of the recognizance, the bond being for the appearance, &c., of the defendant at the next term.(*f*)

(*a*) Dean *v.* Connelly, 6 Barr, 239.

(*b*) Hull *v.* Russell (C. P. Wyoming), 10 P. L. J. 131.

(*c*) Elliott *v.* Ackla, 9 Barr, 42; see Newell *v.* Gibbs, 1 W. & S. 496.

(*d*) Tenbrooke *v.* Bell, D. C. C. P. Dec. 1848.

(*e*) Dean *v.* Connelly, 6 Barr, 239.

(*f*) Hibbs *v.* Rue, 4 Barr, 348.

I.—54

Evidence offered by a party inconsistent with the affidavit and claim of title made by him in proceedings before two justices, to recover possession of land sold at sheriff's sale, is inadmissible.(*g*)

SECTION V.

OF THE CAPIAS AD SATISFACIENDUM.

Before the act of June 16, 1836, a *fieri facias* and a *capias ad satisfaciendum* might have been had at the same time against the goods and body of the defendant, but both could not have been served ;(*h*) and should the plaintiff have levied his *fi. fa.* on defendant's lands, and then taken him upon a *ca. sa.*, the defendant might, at his option, have set aside either of the writs.(*i*) It was a very general practice to issue both writs at the same time, where it was uncertain that the defendant had property, and finding none, the sheriff was then enabled, by an immediate service of the *ca. sa.*, to obtain the only remaining security for the plaintiff's claim—the debtor's body. By the 27th section of the act of 1836, this practice has been recognized. It enables the plaintiff to take both writs at the same time.

But if the *fi. fa.* be in operation, he cannot legally proceed against the body of the defendant; and when a *fi. fa.* is returned "levied subject to prior executions," it is incumbent on the plaintiff, before he can issue a *ca. sa.*, to compel a sale of the property levied on, in order to put a judicial termination to the first writ ;(*j*) and although he finds the property altogether worthless as a means of satisfaction, he cannot abandon a levy upon real property condemned, and take out a *ca. sa.* without the leave of the court.(*k*) Should the defendant submit to a *ca. sa.*, and obtain his discharge under the insolvent law, after a levy upon his lands by the same plaintiff, then the *fi. fa.* and all proceedings under it are gone, and upon a sale under a *venditioni exponas* after such discharge, the sheriff will not be allowed to acknowledge a deed to the purchaser, upon the principle that the *ca. sa.* having been submitted to, the *fi. fa.* becomes irregular.(*l*)

In delivering the opinion of the court in the case last referred to, it was said by YEATES, J., that it seemed highly questionable, whether a plaintiff, after the defendant had been arrested and discharged on giving bond to apply for the benefit of the insolvent laws, could withdraw his *ca. sa.* and issue a *fi. fa.* without the leave of the court. This implies, that he thought such a withdrawal might be allowed by the court. But in a subsequent case, it was said by GIBSON, J., that he presumed the doubt of the above-mentioned judge arose from considering the arrest as *satisfaction* till the defendant should be finally discharged ; and if it were, the assent of the court would perhaps not be a sufficient sanction for the issuing of a new writ.(*m*)

If personal property be levied on by the sheriff, and returned under a *fi. fa.*, and the plaintiff releases the levy, this is an extinguishment of

(*g*) Kimball *v.* Kelsey, 1 Barr, 183.
(*h*) 2 Br. 144.
(*i*) Tiffin *v.* Tiffin, 2 Bin. 230.
(*j*) *Per curiam*, 2 Br. 144.

(*k*) Pa. Bank *v.* Latshaw, 9 S. & R. 9.
(*l*) 2 Bin. 218.
(*m*) Bank of Pa. *v.* Latshaw, 9 S. & R. 10.

the debt as respects third persons; but as between the plaintiff and defendant, it does not operate as a satisfaction, if the judgment remains unpaid.(n)

The 27th section of the act of 1836, being taken from that of April, 1807, the decisions under the latter are here introduced.

Notwithstanding the act of 1807, § 5,(o) which provides that no writ of *capias ad satisfaciendum* shall issue in any case when defendant may have real or personal estate to satisfy the plaintiff's demand, or if the whole cannot be satisfied thereby, then only for the residue thereof, the plaintiff may at his peril issue a *ca. sa.* in the first instance.(p) There is no warrant in the law for the position that the plaintiff must *first* issue a *fi. fa.*, for if the defendant confesses he has no property, the plaintiff undoubtedly may take a *ca. sa.* in the first instance at his peril.(q) But he must be careful not to execute the *ca. sa.* until it is ascertained that the defendant has not property to satisfy the judgment, and this he may do by calling on him to show his property. There may be cases in which the immediate use of this writ may be absolutely necessary to secure a debt, but then the safe course is to let it be accompanied with a *fi. fa.*, with directions to the officer to execute the *capias* only in case the defendant refuses to show property. If the plaintiff will not take this precaution, he subjects himself to an action of trespass *vi et armis*,(r) if it appear that the defendant had sufficient property to satisfy the judgment. In such case, the *ca. sa.* being not merely irregular, but *void*, will on motion be quashed by the court.(s) But the writ, though void, is nevertheless a justification to the officer who executed it.(t) After the defendant has been legally discharged from, and retaken upon the same execution, it is too late to offer to show property: the offer should be made previous to the original arrest.(u) If *nulla bona* be returned to a *fi. fa.* or *non est inventus* to a *ca. sa.*, the party may afterwards sue out an *alias* writ of the same species, or if part only can be levied on a *fi. fa.* he may have a new writ for the remainder.(v)

The writ of *capias ad satisfaciendum*—which, it should be observed, is still of use in all cases of tort—commands the sheriff to take the defendant, and him safely keep, so that he may have his body in court on the return-day, to satisfy the plaintiff. If the defendant be already in custody in the suit, he cannot compel the plaintiff to charge him in execution, or submit to be superseded, as in the English practice, but may obtain relief under the insolvent laws.

The writ of *capias ad satisfaciendum* lies after judgment in most instances in which the defendant was subject to a *capias ad respondendum* before, and plaintiffs are subject to it, where judgment has been given against them for costs. But it does not lie against members of Congress and of the legislature, *eundo, morando, et redeundo*, to, at, and from the places of the sitting of Congress, or of the legislature; nor against ambassadors, and other public ministers, or their domestic servants;(w) and the *charge d'affaires* of a foreign government, who was delayed in

---

(n) Duncan v. Harris, 17 S. & R. 436.
(o) 4 Sm. Laws, 477.
(p) Young v. Taylor, 2 Bin. 218.
(q) Per TILGHMAN, C. J., Hecker v. Jarret, 3 Bin. 407; see Allison v. Rheam, 3 S. & R. 143.

(r) Berry v. Hamill, 12 S. & R. 210.
(s) Allison v. Rheam, 3 S. & R. 139.
(t) Ibid.
(u) Hecker v. Jarret, 3 Bin. 404.
(v) 4 Johns. 407.
(w) Ante, 177.

this country by circumstances, after his official functions had ceased, was held not to be liable to process in a civil suit.(x)   Neither does it lie against members of corporations aggregate for any matter relating to their corporate concerns;(y) nor against an heir on a special judgment for the debt of his ancestor, to be levied of the lands descended; nor against executors or administrators, unless a *devastavit* be returned.(z) An infant is liable to this process ;(a) and it may be issued against bail.(b) Women are privileged from arrest by the twenty-ninth section of the act of June, 1836, *supra*, which provides that no female shall be arrested or imprisoned on a *ca. sa.* for any debt contracted since the eighth day of February, 1819, nor for any damages recovered for the breach of a contract entered into after the passing of said act.   They remain liable to arrest in actions founded upon tort, or claims arising otherwise than *ex contractu.*

By the thirtieth section of the act of June, 1836, no citizen of this commonwealth shall be arrested or imprisoned on such writ for any sum less than five dollars and thirty-four cents, on any contract made since July the 4th, 1833 ; and by the act of 1842, this privilege is extended to all cases of contract whatsoever.

A *capias ad satisfaciendum* cannot be executed upon suitors, or their witnesses, coming to, or attending upon, or returning from courts of justice.(c)   Nor can it be executed at a time or place, when, or where the defendant is privileged from arrest; and the order of a court of competent jurisdiction, discharging a defendant from arrest upon this ground, must be a conclusive justification in an action against the sheriff for an escape.(d)   This privilege, as regards suitors, was denied in two cases,(e) which, although never expressly overruled, have been often doubted.(f)   The privilege of a witness does not, however, extend throughout the term at which the cause was marked for trial, nor will it protect him while he is transacting his private business after he has been discharged from the obligation of the subpœna.(g)   The doctrine of privilege will not be extended to the injury of honest creditors ; therefore, where applications were made by a defendant who alleged that he had come to Philadelphia to obtain from the executive council the commissions of some officers of the militia within his department, as lieutenants of Berks County ; and, by another, on the ground of his being a sheriff elect of the same county, who came to solicit his commission and give the usual security, the court refused their discharge from arrest, observing that they had not been required to attend by the executive council, and had evidently come upon their own private business.(h) The court will not interfere in a summary way, and relieve a defendant from an execution, unless his case is made out entirely to their satisfaction ; where his equity is not clear, they will leave him to his action.(i)

(x) Garwood v. Dennis, 4 D. 321.
(y) *Ante*, 177.
(z) Bingh. on Executions, 106.
(a) 2 Str. 1227.
(b) 6 Johns. 97 ; Starkie, 502.
(c) Bingh. on Executions, 105 ; Hurst's Case, 4 D. 387–8 ; Broome v. Hurst, 4 Y. 124. n.; United States v. Edme, 9 S. & R. 147, and see this case ; *contra*, Hannum v. Askew, 1 Y. 25.

(d) Per Washington, J., 4 D. 388.
(e) Starrett's Case, 1 D. 356 ; Hannum v. Askew, 1 Y. 25.
(f) *Vide* Hurst's Case, 4 D. 388, in note ; Miles v. McCullough, 1 Bin. 77.
(g) Smythe v. Banks, 4 D. 329.
(h) Morgan v. Eckert, Morgan v. Bower, 1 D. 295.
(i) Pearce v. Afflick, 4 Bin. 344.

All officers and privates of militia are privileged from execution or other process, when called into actual service; nor can it issue until thirty days after the return of such officer or private to his usual place of abode, or until forty days after his discharge. Process other-wise issued, will be quashed at the cost of the party who has applied therefor.(*j*)

In point of form, this process must pursue the judgment;(*k*) there-fore, on a joint judgment against several defendants, it must include them all.(*l*) If it be informal, it may be amended, in like manner as the *fieri facias*.(*m*) In matters arising from the mere carelessness of the clerk, in process, amendments are allowed even after error brought.(*n*)

When the sheriff has arrested and committed the debtor to jail, his return to the writ is, " *C. C. & C.*," that is, *Cepi corpus et committitur*. If the defendant cannot be found in his bailiwick, he returns the writ, " *N. E. I.*," that is, *Non est inventus*. When the debtor has given bond for his appearance under the insolvent law, the sheriff adds to his return, after stating the arrest, that the defendant was discharged by order of the court, or of the judge subscribing such discharge. After this, and before final discharge by the Insolvent Court, a *fi. fa.* would be irregular.(*o*) On the return of *non est inventus*, the plaintiff may sue out an *alias capias* into the same, or a *testatum capias* into a different county.(*p*) The eighty-first section of the act of June 16, 1836,(*q*) directs, that " if the defendant in any judgment, as aforesaid, shall have no real or personal estate within the commonwealth, and if the defend-ant cannot be found within the county where such judgment may be, it shall be lawful for the plaintiff, if he shall make affidavit of the fact, to the best of his knowledge and belief, to have, upon his own suggestion, and without any previous writ, a *testatum* writ, or, at the same time, several *testatum* writs of *capias ad satisfaciendum*, into any county or counties, which writs shall be made returnable to the court from which they shall issue : *Provided*, That the plaintiff shall not be allowed the costs of more than one of several such writs, unless the court shall be satisfied that the plaintiff had sufficient cause for issuing the same." This provision was deemed necessary, with the restriction stated, in order to reach absconding debtors.(*s*) If the sheriff cannot serve the writ on account of some privilege enjoyed by the defendant, he returns the writ specially. The truth of these returns may be contested in an action for a false return.(*t*) The return to this writ, as well as the pro-duction of the debtor's body, after a return of *cepi corpus*, may be en-forced by attachment ; to obtain which, application must be made whilst the sheriff is in office, or within two years after its termination.(*u*)

There is no rule more clearly laid down, or more firmly established, than that the plaintiff who has delivered process to the sheriff to be exe-cuted, has nothing to do with the official misconduct or mismanagement

(*j*) Act of April, 1822, § 70, 7 Re. Laws, 646.
(*k*) Tidd, 1064.
(*l*) 6 T. R. 526–7.
(*m*) Barnes, 10; 3 Wils. 58; 4 Taunt. 322.
(*n*) *Vide* Peddle *v.* Hollingshead, 9 S. & R. 284–5; *ante,* 686, *post,* vol. ii.

' Amendments."
(*o*) 1 M. 397.
(*p*) Bingh. on Executions, 225.
(*q*) Pamph. L. 775.
(*s*) Remarks of Commissioners.
(*t*) 1 Arch. Pr. 278.
(*u*) *Vide* 7 Re. Laws, 496.

of the under sheriff; and that where, by the arrest of an under sheriff or bailiff, the prisoner is in legal estimation in the custody of the high sheriff, the latter is exclusively liable: that a prisoner in actual custody on one writ is, by operation of law, in custody on every other writ lodged against him in the sheriff's office, and that, if he escape, the plaintiff may declare that he was arrested by virtue of such other writ, is equally clear.(v) Upon this principle, therefore, it has been recently decided that the sheriff is liable for an escape, where he has returned *non est inventus* to a *ca. sa.* which had been delivered to him, if, prior to the return-day, his deputy had the defendant in custody under another *ca. sa.* and discharged him; though it do not appear that the sheriff knew of the latter writ, or that the deputy knew of the former.(w)

Whether the judgment or execution be avoidable, is a point which the sheriff is never permitted to raise; and having arrested the party, he is bound to keep him till he is discharged by due course of law.(x)

Upon being arrested under a *capias ad satisfaciendum*, the defendant has three alternatives; either to satisfy the plaintiff's claim, give bond for his appearance at the next insolvents' court, or else to continue in close custody. And so strict was the law on the subject of the sheriff's duty, as to the custody of the debtor's body, that it was long before it was settled that payment to the sheriff on a *capias ad satisfaciendum*, was a good payment.(y) Upon receiving the money, the sheriff is bound to pay it over to the real, and not to the nominal plaintiff, where the writ is indorsed to the use of the former. If he does not, he is liable to an attachment.(z) His commission on receiving and paying over money to the creditor under this process is the same as that allowed under other executions, and subject to the same restriction.

An officer cannot apply this writ, in his hands, to the satisfaction of his own debt;(a) the coroner having a *ca. sa.* against the sheriff to whom he was indebted, gave him a receipt in full, and engaged to settle the amount with the plaintiff, but failed to do so; it was held, that this did not discharge the execution, actual payment alone being competent to produce that effect. So, in the Bank of Orange v. Wakeman,(b) where the sheriff's deputy took the defendant's negotiable note, gave a receipt and returned the execution satisfied, it was determined that the defendant was still liable. So, two officers cannot set off executions in their hands against each other, as such an arrangement would substitute the officer for the defendant, and if one of them were insolvent and the other not, the set-off would effect an injurious change of liability.(c) To avoid this and other mischiefs, the law will not endure the mingling of private transactions with official duties.

The sheriff cannot release the defendant from the execution, upon his giving security for payment of the debt, and such security is void.(d)

(v) 5 Co. 89; Ro. Abr. 94; Salk, 273, pl. 6.

(w) Wheeler v. Hambright, 9 S. & R. 390.

(x) 16 Johns. 155; Com. v. Leckey, 1 W. 67.

(y) Per Duncan, J., Sharpe v. Speckenagle, 3 S. & R. 467.

(z) Zantzinger v. Old, 2 D. 265.

(a) Miles v. Richwine, 2 R. 200. In Codwin v. Field, 9 Johns. 263.

(b) 1 Cowen, 46.

(c) Miles v. Richwine, 2 R. 199.

(d) 13 Johns. 366; 8 Johns. 98; Dowdel v. Hamm, 2 W. 63.

So, in *qui tam* actions, the plaintiff having no right to discharge the judgment, or compound with the defendant, without leave of the court or payment of the judgment, the defendant's discharge, so far as relates to the moiety of the penalty belonging to the commonwealth is void, and cannot excuse an escape.(*e*) So, where a single judge discharges a defendant from execution upon a *habeas corpus*, without notice to the plaintiff, the proceeding is void, and here the defendant may be retaken in execution;(*f*) nor can the Supreme Court discharge from a *ca. sa.* issued out of the Court of Common Pleas.(*g*) But if the plaintiff, having the defendant in execution, consent to his discharge, though it be on terms which are not subsequently fulfilled, or upon giving fresh security, which afterwards becomes ineffectual, the debt is extinguished;(*h*) and the plaintiff cannot resort to the judgment again, or charge the defendant's person in execution, although discharged upon an express agreement that he should be liable to be retaken, in case of non-compliance with the terms.(*i*)

If the plaintiff in the *ca. sa.* or his assignee, trustee, or agent, direct the sheriff to execute it in a particular way, and the sheriff obey, as he is bound to do, he will be relieved from all responsibility in case of loss or escape, and the former must take the consequences.(*j*) The attorney at law of the plaintiff is empowered to discharge the defendant, and the sheriff must obey his instructions.(*k*) But if in an action against the sheriff for an escape, it appears that the order was given after the escape, it will not relieve the sheriff.(*l*)

If two persons are bound in an obligation jointly and severally, and sued severally, each may be taken in execution, or one may be taken on a *capias ad satisfaciendum*, and the property of the other levied on by a *fieri facias*, which could not be, if the debt was *satisfied* by taking one in execution ; for there can be but *one satisfaction for one debt*, although one hundred persons are bound for it; but if *one* makes *actual satisfaction by payment of the money*, all the rest are discharged. There is a difference, therefore, between an actual satisfaction and that kind of legal satisfaction arising from the arrest on a *capias ad satisfaciendum*. When the body of the defendant has been taken in execution, this, during the confinement, amounts to a discharge of the debt, and the plaintiff can never have against him, while in jail, any other execution. But the arrest on a *capias ad satisfaciendum* is, in itself, no satisfaction of the debt ;(*m*) nor does a discharge by the insolvent act discharge the debtor from the debt, but only from imprisonment, unless the plaintiff consented to the discharge; then, indeed, the debt is gone.(*n*) Neither does a discharge of a defendant, under the insolvent law, after arrest upon a *ca. sa.* discharge his surety for a stay of execution.(*o*) If the plaintiff discharge one of several defendants taken on a joint *capias*, he cannot afterwards retake such defendant or take any of

---

(*e*) 11 Johns. 476.
(*f*) Hecker *v.* Jarret, 3 Bin. 411.
(*g*) Com. *v.* Leckey, 1 W. 66.
(*h*) Sharpe *v.* Speckenagle, 3 S. & R. 464; Heisse *v.* Markland, 2 R. 274; Barnes, 205 ; 11 Johns. 476 ; 2 Bac. Ab. 719; 6 T. R. 527; 1 Barn. & Ald. 297.
(*i*) 5 Johns. 364; 2 East, 243 ; Bingh. on Ex'ns, 266.

(*j*) Dowdel *v.* Hamm, 2 W. 61, 63.
(*k*) Scott *v.* Seiler, 5 W. 235.
(*l*) Ibid.
(*m*) *Vide* Hunt *v.* McClure, 2 Y. 387.
(*n*) Sharpe *v.* Speckenagle, 3 S. & R. 464.
(*o*) Ibid.

the others.(*p*)   But if one is discharged as an insolvent debtor, this, being the act of the law, will not discharge the other.(*q*)   And where separate suits were brought against two joint obligors, judgments recovered, and both the obligors taken in execution, the one for the debt and the other for the costs, it was held that the plaintiff, by discharging the defendant in execution for the costs only, did not discharge the other defendant, and it was not a satisfaction of the debt for which he was imprisoned.(*r*)   Where a plaintiff takes the defendant's body in execution, he relinquishes his lien on the defendant's lands; and if other creditors sell them in execution, and then the defendant is discharged by the insolvent act, the plaintiff cannot resort to the land, nor has he any claim to any part of the purchase-money.(*s*)

Although a defendant be taken in execution, yet the debt may still become the subject of a set-off, in a cross-action ;(*t*) for, under the defalcation act of Pennsylvania, though silent on the subject, the setting off of one judgment against another has always been permitted, under the idea of their being debts.(*u*)

By the common law, where a person died in jail, the plaintiff had no further remedy ;(*v*) but by the statute 21 J. I. c. 24,(*w*) if the defendant dies while charged in execution under this writ, he may sue out afterwards a new execution against his lands, goods, or chattels.(*x*)   And by the thirty-first section of the act of June 16, 1836,(*y*) a judgment shall [not](*z*) be deemed satisfied by the arrest or imprisonment of the defendant on a *ca. sa.* if he die in prison or escape, or be discharged by reason of privilege, or at his own request; but the plaintiff may have such remedies at law for the recovery of the judgment, as he would have been entitled to if the writ had not issued; saving, nevertheless, all rights and interests which may have accrued to others between the issuing of the writ, and the death or escape of the party.   This section is derived from the statute of 1 Jac. I. c. 13; 21 Jac. I. c. 4, and 8 and 9 Wm. III. c. 27.(*a*)   If a party escape or be rescued from arrest on a *ca. sa.*, though the sheriff is thereby liable, because he ought to have taken the *posse comitatus,* yet the plaintiff may retake such prisoner on a new *ca. sa.* or sue out another kind of execution on the judgment, and shall not be compelled to take his remedy against the sheriff, who may be dead or insolvent.(*b*)   He may proceed against the sheriff for the escape, who cannot take advantage of a want of a *scire facias* to ground the *ca. sa.* upon, which had issued *post annum et diem.*(*c*)   In an action of debt for an escape from a *ca. sa.*, the jury must find the whole debt and costs, the plaintiff being entitled to recover them, in the same manner as he could have done against the debtor ;(*d*) for the insolvency of the debtor

(*p*) 6 T. R. 526.
(*q*) 2 Bac. Ab. 719 ; Bingh. on Ex'ns, 266.
(*r*) 8 Johns. 339.
(*s*) Freeman *v.* Ruston, 4 D. 217 ; *vide* Sharpe *v.* Speckenagle, 3 S. & R. 466.
(*t*) 1 M. & S. 696.
(*u*) 1 Br. 48 ; Ferett *v.* Melly, 3 Y. 153 ; *ante,* 409.
(*v*) Hob. 52 ; 6 T. R. 526.
(*w*) Rob. Dig. 246.
(*x*) Sharpe *v.* Speckenagle, 3 S. & R. 465–6.

(*y*) *Supra.*
(*z*) By a clerical error this word has been omitted in the original draft of the act.
(*a*) See Rob. Dig. 247. See *post,* 858.
(*b*) 2 Bac. Ab. 719 ; Bingh. on Ex'ns, 256 ; see Sharpe *v.* Speckenagle, 3 S. & R. 464.
(*c*) 1 Salk. 273 ; cited 2 Burr. 1188.
(*d*) Duncan *v.* Klinefelter, 5 W. 141 ; Shewel *v.* Fell, 3 Y. 17; ibid. 4 id. 47; Wolverton *v.* Com. 7 S. & R. 273 ; 8 Mass. 373.

could not be given in evidence as it could if the escape had been on mesne process.(e) It is held, however, that where the action is case, the measure of damages is open to the investigation and discretion of the jury.(f) He may, at the same time, take out a *fieri facias* against the property of the defendant, for the remedies are not inconsistent with each other.(g) After an escape the sheriff may himself retake the defendant, unless the escape were with his permission;(h) but in the latter case he cannot arrest or detain him without new process.(i)

When a debtor is arrested in execution, he may apply by petition to any one of the judges of the Court of Common Pleas for the county in which he is so taken, and upon giving bond, with security, for the plaintiff, in double the amount of the debt, conditioned for his appearance at the next term of the said court, and then and there to present his petition for the benefit of the insolvent laws of this commonwealth, and comply with all the requisitions of the said law, and abide all the orders of the said court in that behalf, or in default thereof, and if he fail in obtaining his discharge as an insolvent debtor, that he shall surrender himself to the jail of the said county, then an order is given to the sheriff, jailer or keeper, to discharge him upon payment of jail fees.(j) By the fourth section of the same act, the prothonotary, as well as the judge, may approve the security and make the order for the debtor's discharge. Upon making a return of this order upon the process, the sheriff is entirely exonerated. When this is done, should the defendant not apply for or obtain the benefit of the insolvent law, and forfeit his bond, a second execution may be issued against him. But if, when he is in custody under the second execution, the plaintiff discharges him from prison, without the assent of the surety, the debt is satisfied, and no action can be maintained against the surety upon the bond.(k) This decision is founded on the principle that the debt was extinguished by the discharge.

Another mode of obtaining a discharge from imprisonment is afforded by the nineteenth section of the act of 1814,(l) commonly called "The Bread Act," to which, having before had occasion to quote it at length, we shall here simply refer.

A discharge, by the Common Pleas, of a person as a poor insolvent debtor, under the Bread Act, cannot be impeached in a collateral way, by proof that, at the time of his discharge, he was in possession of a sufficient sum of money to pay the debt for which he was confined.(m)

These acts are, however, confined in their operation to a discharge of the debtor's person from the particular debt for which he may have been arrested. In order, therefore, to secure himself from arrest upon any other process, his most effectual method is by a successful application for the benefit of the several acts of assembly for the relief of insolvent debtors, after surrendering all his property for the benefit of his creditors. These acts, the judicial decisions, and the system of pro-

(e) Ibid.
(f) Duncan v. Klinefelter, 5 W. 141; 6 Johns. 270; 5 Mass. 310.
(g) 8 Johns. 361.
(h) Barnes, 373; 2 T. R. 25.
(i) 2 Johns. Ca. 3.

(j) Vide act of June 11, 1836, § 6, Pamph. L. 729.
(k) Palethorpe v. Lesher, 2 R. 272.
(l) 6 Sm. Laws, 195.
(m) McKinney v. Crawford, 8 S. & R. 351.

cedure observed under them in the Insolvent's Court, are fully collated and explained in Mr. Ingraham's Treatise on the Law of Insolvency.

The sheriff will be permitted to amend his return upon application being made in a reasonable time, and showing clearly that it was made under a mistake of fact which, from its nature, might not be within his knowledge; as where he arrests a man of the same name as the real defendant, and returns the arrest of the latter. But not where the application to amend is delayed until after suit brought against him for an escape.(n)

The plaintiff's affidavit to hold to bail, under the act of 13th June, 1836, is insufficient, if it does not comply with the requisitions of the act, and the *capias* will be quashed, although a full affidavit be filed at the same time by another person in plaintiff's employ, who is not such an agent as the act contemplates.(o)   What particularity is requisite in affidavits, and when the defendant will be discharged on common bail, has been already considered.(oo)

A voluntary surrender by one who has given bond to take benefit will not relieve his bail from the obligation of his bond that the defendant shall present his petition and abide the orders of the court, &c.(p)

It is the duty of the sheriff arresting a defendant in his own bailiwick, upon a *testatum ca. sa.*, to commit him to the jail thereof, and not of the county whence the writ issued, which latter would, it seems, amount to an escape.(q)

Prior to the act of 16th June, 1836, a defendant's discharge from arrest on a *ca. sa.* by the plaintiff, extinguished not only the judgment and all remedy on any promise, but that which formed the immediate consideration of his discharge : a subsequent promise is *nudum pactum*.(r)   The section above mentioned has changed the law, and in such case the remedy remains on the judgment as if no *ca. sa.* had issued.

The lien of a judgment is not discharged by an agreement to release defendant from arrest on a *ca. sa.* on the judgment, on payment of costs and jail fees, without prejudice to his future liability for the judgment unimpaired.(s)

Though at the time a debt was contracted neither defendant was a subject of arrest, yet there is no reason why the consequences of joinder in responsibility should not extend to prospective as well as to present disfranchisement, and why, therefore, a *capias* should not issue against both.(t)

(n) Scott v. Seily, 5 W. 235 ; *ante*, 856.
(o) Bromly v. Joseph, 3 Wh. 10.   See *ante*, 856.
(oo) *Ante*, 288.
(p) Wolfram v. Strickhouser, 1 W. & S. 381.

(q) Avery v. Leely, 3 W. & S. 494.
(r) Snevily v. Rind, 9 W. 396.
(s) Jackson v. Knight, 4 W. & S. 412.
(t) Ex parte Overich, 3 Wh. 175.

CHAPTER XXX.

OF MOTIONS AND AUDITA QUERELA.

1. *Motions.*

HAVING in the preceding chapters traced the progress of the cause from its commencement, by the issuing of the original process, to the award of the judicial consequence of either party's success, and the modes of enforcing it by execution, we shall close this volume with a few additional notes on the subject of motions and their incidents, with a view to the introduction of some decisions and rules of court hitherto unnoticed. We do not pretend to give an enumeration of the various motions which are or may be made in our courts, as is done in the English books of common law practice, because, from the liberality of our practice, and the absence of a Court of Chancery in the State, a much more extensive use is made of motions than would be allowable in the courts of law in England. We may, therefore, quote, in the present place, the language of an English writer, who wished to excuse himself from entering into a detail of the practice in chancery, as suitable to express the reasons which prevent us from undertaking an account of all the exigencies which may be met through the medium of motions in our courts: " The minutiæ of practical business can only be taught by practice; yet, in the common law proceedings, the books are generally very accurate, and will, on reference, furnish the necessary information. But it is not so in chancery practice. This is not carried on with that exactness and precision with which the practice of other courts must be conducted; *when any difficulty arises, motions are generally resorted to,* the result of which depends on the circumstances which come before the court; and with the acquaintance of only one party's case, it is not easy to determine what that will be, till the contents of affidavits, the state of facts, and other proceedings, are known."(a)

A motion is an application to a court by a party or his counsel, and the order made by a court on any motion, when drawn into form, is called a rule. A motion is either for a rule absolute, in the first instance; or, it is only for a rule to show cause; or, as it is frequently called, a rule *nisi*, which is afterwards discharged or made absolute by the court, on argument. By the general practice, all motions made by counsel must be put in writing, and delivered to the prothonotary, to be entered on the minutes and filed, the time of delivery to be indorsed by the prothonotary. Motions are of a civil or criminal nature. Rules for attach-

(a) Advice on the Study of Law, pp. 85–6. Am ed. 1811.

ments are the only criminal rules granted which have any relation to a civil suit.(b)

On a motion for a rule to show cause, depositions on the adverse side will not be received; when the rule applied for is granted, upon proper grounds, shown, the adverse party, with his depositions, will be fully heard on the argument.(c) The affidavit of a party is sufficient to lay a ground for a rule to show cause.(d)

When a rule, whether absolute, or to show cause, has been obtained, a copy of the rule must be served on the opposite party or his attorney. If there be any irregularity in the service of a rule *nisi*, it will be waived by the party's afterwards appearing and showing cause against the rule.(e) The rule thus granted, requires the opposite party to show cause upon some day certain in term, at the discretion of the court. When a rule is entered, and no day of hearing is fixed, it is returnable to the next term, or in the District Court, on the succeeding Saturday.(f) If the rule be to set aside proceedings for irregularity, and to stay proceedings in the mean time, it suspends them all, for all purposes, until the rule is discharged;(g) and if any proceedings, directly or collaterally, be had in the cause, in the mean time, the court, upon application, will set them aside.(h) A decision, by which proceedings are set aside, disposes of all subsequent motions respecting the proceeding so treated.(i)

Upon the day appointed by the rule, the opposite party must show cause against it, unless by consent, or by the order of the court, it stand over until another day in the same term. Either party, however, if not prepared to support, or show cause against the rule, may move that it be enlarged to a future day in the same or next term. But it is not, by any means, of course, that the court should thus enlarge a rule; sufficient grounds must be stated to induce them to do so.(j) If the application be made by the party who obtained the rule, the court usually grant it where it is in his own delay; but not where it would have the effect of detaining the opposite party in custody, nor in other cases, without consent or some evident necessity: if moved for by the opposite party, the court will frequently enlarge it upon terms; or if the rule were not served in time to give the party an opportunity of showing cause against it, he may demand that the rule be enlarged as a matter of right.(k) If it be enlarged to a subsequent term, it is called on in its order upon the motion or argument list; but if it be enlarged, or stand over to another day in the same term, either party may bring it on, upon the day so appointed, by moving to discharge the rule, or to make it absolute.(l)

Upon the day appointed for showing cause, or when the rule is reached on the list, cause is to be shown; but not, as in England, by the counsel against the rule, but by him who has taken it; except in rules to show cause of action, when the plaintiff's counsel, before the defendant's counsel proceeds, reads his affidavit, which (independently

(b) 2 Arch. Pr. 266.
(c) Snyder *v.* Castor, 4 Y. 443.
(d) Hoar *v.* Mulvey, 1 Bin. 145.
(e) Tidd's Pr. 445.
(f) 1 Br. 220. See *ante*, 692, where motions to stay executions are treated in full.

(g) 4 T. R. 176.
(h) 2 Arch. Pr. 267.
(i) Etter *v.* Edwards, 4 W. 63.
(j) 2 Arch. Pr. 267-8.
(k) Ibid. Tidd's Pr. 447-8; and see 1 Smith's Rep. K. B. 199.
(l) 2 Arch. Pr. 268.

of the rules of the District Court, which will be examined presently), is said to be the uniform practice of Pennsylvania.(*m*) If no cause be shown, when the rule is called by the court for argument, the court, on affidavit of service (though, perhaps, hearing the counsel in support of the rule first), will, in their discretion, make it absolute. A copy of the rule, thus granted, should be served on the opposite party or his attorney. If counsel on neither side attend, when the cause is called on, it loses its place, and the court will not return to it, until they have gone through the list, and, beginning it anew, come to it a second time.

It may be proper to repeat here, that causes are put down for argument on the list, according to the respective terms and numbers of the actions, and not according to the dates of the motions and rules.(*n*)

Rules by consent of parties, or their attorneys, are rules of course, and are entered by the prothonotary on filing them. All agreements of attorneys, touching the business of the courts, shall be in writing, otherwise they will be considered of no validity, and the court will pay no regard to them.(*o*) An agreement of attorneys or counsel to abide by the opinion of a professional gentleman, will be supported and enforced by the court.(*p*)

The general practice is, that on all motions or rules to show cause, on the hearing of which facts are to be investigated, the testimony of the witnesses are to be taken by depositions in writing, before a judge, justice of the peace, alderman, or an examiner, appointed by the court, upon reasonable notice in writing to the opposite party, or his attorney; and no witnesses will be examined at the bar, but by a special and previous order of the court.

A rule to take depositions is always implied in a rule to show cause, as in case of a rule to show cause why an attachment should not be quashed, the facts, if disputed, are to be ascertained by affidavits.(*q*)

The affidavit of a party, though it may lay a ground for a rule to show cause, cannot be heard on the argument of that rule; but proof must be produced from a different quarter, and throughout the State.(*r*) On the hearing of any motion or application, after a rule to show cause has been granted, no affidavit will be read, unless notice has been given to the opposite party, that an opportunity may be afforded to cross-examine.

The general rule is, that all notices, where the party has a known attorney, may be given to that attorney or his agent;(*t*) but where a rule of court requires notice to be given to the opposite party, notice to his attorney is not sufficient,(*u*) unless there be an express recognition of the notice on the part of the attorney. It was also held, that service of notice on the attorney, under such a rule, is sufficient in the case of depositions, unless the attorney object at the time of service, and that his silence is equivalent to an agreement which will bind his client.(*v*) Why this construction should be confined to the case of depositions is

---

(*m*) 2 Br. 40.
(*n*) 1 B. 214.
(*o*) R. 10, D. Ct. Philada.; R. 24, C. P. Philada. 1824; Shippen's Lessee *v.* Bush, 1 D. 251.
(*p*) Cahill *v.* Benn, 6 Bin. 99; see Galbreath *v.* Colt, 4 Y. 551.

(*q*) 1 Br. 256.
(*r*) Hoar *v.* Mulvey, 1 Bin. 145; S. P. Coxe *v.* Nicholls, 2 Y. 546.
(*t*) 1 Br. 15. See *ante*, 226, 7.
(*u*) Nash *v.* Gilkeson, 5 S. & R. 352.
(*v*) *Ante*, 435, 6.

not very apparent; for, if we examine the reason which dictated it, namely, that the exemption of the attorney is a personal privilege, which he may waive at pleasure, we shall find it applicable to every case in which the transmission of notice by an attorney to his client involves any trouble or responsibility.(w) But though there has been considerable oscillation of judicial sentiment on the subject, the old rule may be now considered to be virtually reaffirmed, that even where a rule of court directs notice to be served on a party, service on the attorney is sufficient, where the attorney, on receiving notice, makes no objection.(x)

In some cases the court will interfere, or grant relief on motion, without laying a party under the necessity of proceeding in other more circuitous and expensive modes peculiar to the English practice. Of some of these, mention having already been made, we will here only refer to them, in order to avoid repetition.(y)

The rules of the District Court in this respect are as follows:—

LXI. Upon rules to show cause of action, or to dissolve foreign attachments, the party who is to show cause is to begin and conclude; in all other cases, the party who obtains the rule to show cause is to begin and conclude.

LXII. Unless otherwise specially directed by rule of court, two counsel, but not more, may be heard on each side of a cause or matter on the motion or argument list. The counsel of the party having, according to the practice of the court, the right to begin, shall state the grounds relied upon, and cite all the authorities intended to be adduced in their support. The counsel of the opposite party shall then be fully heard; if two, they shall follow each other in order of seniority. The counsel who began, if alone, shall reply: if two are concerned on that side, this duty shall devolve upon his colleague. The reply is to be confined to an examination of the points made by the opposite counsel.

LIX. Upon every rule to show cause why judgment should not be entered for want of a sufficient affidavit of defence, the plaintiff shall furnish to the court before the hearing of the rule a copy of the bill, note, bond, book entries, claim, or other instrument of writing, or the affidavit of loan filed by the plaintiff, and also a copy of the affidavit of defence filed by the defendant. *And whenever the copies are not furnished as aforesaid, the rule shall be discharged.*

LX. In motions and rules for new trials, the party who obtains the same, shall furnish to each of the judges a copy of the reasons filed; and on application to amend the pleadings, the party making the application shall furnish for the use of the court one copy of the pleadings on file, and of the proposed amendments.

LXI. In all arguments on the reports of referees, copies of the report, and of the exceptions thereto, if any be filed, shall be furnished to each of the judges before the commencement of the argument. If exceptions be filed by the defendant, this duty shall devolve on him; otherwise on the plaintiff.

LXII. In all law arguments on demurrers, reserved points, special verdicts, motions in arrest of judgment, cases stated for the opinion of the court, and exceptions to auditor's reports, the party who is entitled

(w) See Newlin v. Newlin, 8 S. & R. 41.   (y) *Vide ante*, 226, 7, 436, 7, 8, &c.,
(x) See *ante*, 436.   625, &c.

to begin and conclude the argument shall furnish to each of the judges a paper-book containing a full and distinct statement of all facts conducive to a ready comprehension of the matter to be argued. And this rule shall extend to every cause or matter (not otherwise specifically provided for) entitled to be placed on either the argument or motion list.

Where a suitor or witness privileged from arrest, has been taken on a *capias*, the court, of which the arrest is a contempt, will discharge him, though the court from which the process issues have refused to discharge. It is the privilege of the court, for the protection of the party to whom the common law gave a writ of privilege in that case, in lieu of which, summary relief on motion is now substituted, and this cannot be denied, on proper grounds shown.(*x*)

Another case, in which relief would be granted in a summary manner on motion, is, where a party, having recovered in ejectment the whole land for which the action was brought, uses no means whatever to enforce the judgment, but brings a second ejectment; here, if the defendant were willing to surrender the land, the court would interfere on motion to protect him from the costs of a new ejectment.(*y*)

2. *Audita querela.*

The writ of *audita querela*, which is the commencement of an action somewhat in the nature of a bill in equity, to be relieved against some oppression of the plaintiff, states that the *complaint of the defendant has been heard*, and setting forth the matter of the complaint commands the court to call the parties before them, and after having heard, to do justice between them, *e. g.*, in case of an execution awarded or likely to be awarded against the party upon some ground of injustice pointed out to the court.(*z*) The liberality of the courts in granting relief upon motion, and the greater frequency of applications to the Courts of Equity, have, in England, almost superseded the use of the writ of *audita querela;* as it is there held that relief may be granted upon motion in cases proper for an *audita querela*, where it is not granted upon some foreign matter, as a release; but where the ground of relief is a release, when there is some doubt about the execution, or some matter of fact which cannot be clearly ascertained by affidavit, and therefore proper to be tried, the courts there have driven the defendant to his *audita querela.*(*a*) But it is probable from the language of Mr. Justice DUNCAN, in delivering the opinion of the Supreme Court in a recent case,(*b*) that no distinction of a similar nature would be observed in Pennsylvania. For he says, that "wherever the writ of *audita querela* would lie, the court would grant relief on motion," and, that "so universal is the course of granting summary relief, that it has driven out of use, and rendered obsolete, the writ of *audita querela;*"(*c*) and further, that in a case wherein *audita querela* would lie,

(*x*) United States *v.* Edme, 9 S. & R. 149.

(*y*) Rambler *v.* Tryon, 7 S. & R. 90. As to motions to obtain equitable relief in our courts, either through their immediate decree, or the medium of feigned issues, *vide supra*, 67, 243, 244. As to motions to open judgments, *supra*, 422 –424.

(*z*) Sherid. Pr. 609.

(*a*) 2 Saund. 148, c.

(*b*) Share *v.* Becker, 8 S. & R. 239.

(*c*) Ibid. 242.

but in which the court had interposed on motion, if they doubted the proof, they would direct an issue to try the fact.(*d*) But the writ is not obsolete ;(*dd*) and very recently it was decided, in the District Court in Philadelphia, that it might issue in Pennsylvania, and this even after the refusal of summary relief by the court on motion upon the same grounds.(*e*) But the writ will not be allowed where the petition does not set forth the grounds of relief with such certainty as would be subsequently held good on demurrer.(*f*) It was intimated that the writ should not issue upon matters which constitute a mere equitable defence, such as would not be cognizable at law.(*g*)

With regard to this writ, however, there is a peculiarity worthy of notice, which involves an advantage that does not appear to attend on the remedy by motions in lieu of it. In England, an *audita querela* is a commission to the judges to examine the cause, and is *in nature of trespass ;* and *damages* are given if the execution be without right.(*h*) Now in the case of a motion for relief, it is very clear that the judges would not award damages to the defendant, however, they might protect him from the plaintiff's unjust oppression, and it is equally clear, that if an issue were directed to try the matter of fact, the jury could not assess damages, but would be confined to passing upon the fact ;(*i*) but in *audita querela*, if the issue be to the contrary, damages may be assessed.

When the court will interfere on such a motion, it will stay the execution until justice can be done, and an issue being directed, on the plea of payment with leave, &c., it is thus put in the power of the court to try and decide *equitably* on the matter arising subsequent to the judgment, the same as if it were invested with chancery jurisdiction.(*k*) The jury, however, cannot find anything to be due to the defendant, and a verdict awarding a balance in his favor would be erroneous.(*l*) The utmost a defendant can ask on such an application for relief is, that he should be discharged from the judgment.(*m*) " In no case is the defendant entitled to a judgment for a sum of money, except where he has given matter of *defalcation* in evidence, and a balance is found in his favor."(*n*) The case from which the preceding rules have been extracted,(*o*) furnishes an example of an occasion in which an *audita querela* might have been resorted to with advantage; for the defendant might in that equitable proceeding have secured, in the shape of damages, the balance of money which upon a motion and issue was erroneously awarded him. The objections to such proceeding appear to be, its dilatoriness and expense. The first is incident to all legal transactions, but can be materially obviated by the assistance of the court, in framing judicious rules; but even where an issue is ordered after motion for summary relief, the issue must take the chance of delay which every other cause on the trial-list is exposed to, before it can be

(*d*) Ibid.
(*dd*) Witherow *v.* Keller, 11 S. & R. 274.
(*e*) Schott *v.* McFarland, D. C. C. P. *post,* 58.
(*f*) Ibid.
(*g*) Ibid. Where an *audita querela* will lie in general, see Stephens *v.* Stephens, D. C. All. *post.*

(*h*) 2 Saund. 148, b.
(*i*) *Vide supra.*
(*k*) Harper *v.* Kean, 11 S. & R. 290 ; Beale's Executors *v.* Com. id. 299.
(*l*) Id. 280.
(*m*) Id. 292.
(*n*) Per TILGHMAN, C. J., ibid.
(*o*) Harper, *et al. v.* Kean.

brought on for trial. The second objection, however it may avail in England, can hardly be admitted in this State, when the moderateness of its fee bill is considered. With regard to the execution, it is difficult to see a reason why the court should not stay it in this proceeding as in any other, without putting the party to the necessity of suing out a *supersedeas.*

Audita querela lies only in the court where the judgment is given, they having the best knowledge of all the proceedings in the same cause.(*p*)

(*p*) 2 Bulst. 10; Beale's Executors *v.* Com. 11 S. & R. 299.

Judge LOWRIE has favored the editor with the following full report of a very interesting case, on this head, decided by him in Pittsburg, in 1848.

E. W. Stephens *v.* A. C. Stephens, and the administrator of his wife. Where the court sets aside or opens a judgment, they will also set aside a sale of land made under it, though the sheriff's deed has been acknowledged, if it be still in the hands of the sheriff.

It is no objection to the setting aside a sheriff's sale, where the deed is still in the sheriff's hands, that a term has elapsed since the acknowledgment of the deed.

As to its own proceedings, this court may properly grant the same relief on *motion*, that was formerly granted under the old practice, by *audita querela, writ of error coram nobis, and bill in equity.*

The cases in which relief may be granted in these procedures.

When a judgment, on which a sheriff's sale is founded, is set aside, the setting aside of the sale follows as of course on the ground of *restitution.*

On petition and affidavit of W. C. Nelson, one of the heirs of Cornelia Stephens, late Cornelia Nelson, rule to show cause why the judgment should not be opened and the heirs permitted to take defence, and why the sale on the *lev. fa.* and the acknowledgment of the sheriff's deed should not be set aside.

The material facts of the case are, that this is a *sci. fa.* on a mortgage given by Allen C. Stephens, and Cornelia his wife, on the 18th of January, 1843, for $3000 on the land of the wife, descended from her father. The wife was a minor when the mortgage was executed. She was dead when the suit was brought, and at that time her heirs were the brother and sisters of her father. The writ was served on her administrator, but he did not appear to make any defence— two *nihils* were returned as to A. C. Stephens. No notice was given to the heirs

of the wife, and they were residing out of the State and did not hear of the proceedings until very recently. Judgment by default was entered for the amount due, execution issued, and the land sold to the plaintiff for $2000. The sheriff's deed was acknowledged May 20, 1848, in April Term, but remained in the sheriff's hands until September 11, 1848, in July Term, when, on the petition of W. C. Nelson, for the heirs and affidavit of the above facts, the presiding judge made an order at Chambers on the sheriff to withhold the delivery of the deed until the further order of the court. Allen C. Stephens died since the sale.

Messrs. Kuhn and Williams, for the rule, cite Veneman *v.* Cooper, decided in this court, and Jackson *v.* Sternlerg, 20 Johns. 49.

Mr. Dunlop, *contra,* cites 4 Penn. St. Rep. 80; 1 W. 491; 1 Y. 40; 9 S. & R. 395; 10 W. 22; 12 Pet. 488; 1 Wh. 21.

OPINION OF THE COURT.

LOWRIE, J.—The motion in this case is objected to on account of want of interest on the part of these heirs, or because their interests are not affected by the judgment—the plaintiff not having chosen to make them parties to the proceeding, 1 W. 491. The plaintiff, then, would seem to say, we did not buy the interest of Mrs. Stephens, because the deed is void as to her for non-age; we did not affect the title of her heirs by the judgment, for we did not make her heirs parties; we did not charge her personal representative, though we did make him a party, for this is a proceeding *in rem* for real property; we charged only the curtesy estate of A. C. Stephens, and that is all we got for our bid of $2000, and now he is dead and that estate is ended; yet we insist on having our deed and paying our money. However singular this may seem, I think it is all the plaintiff could get by this deed.

But it is not very clear that the judgment has *no* effect as against the heirs. It is sufficient to justify their interference if the judgment would be but *prima facie* evidence that this is the deed of Mrs. Stephens. And as, in all controversies concerning land, the heirs have a right to a writ of error or *audita querela* on a judgment against their ancestor, so they have a right to be heard in this form. And it may be of great importance to save the parties from having another knot added to the warp of their entangled web.

But it is further objected that the parties come too late in asking the interference of the court, because a term has passed both since the judgment and since the acknowledgment or confirmation of the deed. We do not think so. I cannot help thinking that the assertion so often made, that no court can reverse or amend its own final judgments for errors of fact or law, after the term at which they were entered, is, so far as our practice is concerned, little else than a humbug, useful only to frighten ignorance and rashness from meddling with matters too great for their comprehension.

It was applied in England to prevent alteration of the records after enrolment. But here they are never enrolled, and we have given the rule but little application. The fact is we amend, open, and set aside judgments not only after a term, but after years, governed only by the facts and equity of the case and by wise cautions of the Supreme Court as to the rights of third persons. Even in England, in what is properly called amendments, the rule is beginning to be regarded as one rather of caution than of binding obligation. See Richardson *v.* Mellish, 11 E. C. L. Rep. 127; 3 T. R. 349; 4 Maule & S. 94.—Even as to errors in process and in the judgment, though formerly they were heard only on *audita querela* or on writ of error in the same court (*coram nobis* or *vobis*), or by the illiberal disposition of the courts of law, making the machinery of justice more important than justice itself, thrown into Chancery. These are now heard or remedied on motion, if the material facts be not doubtful, or the ground of relief doubtful in point of law. In the latter event, the court may still put the parties to their independent or collateral remedies.

But these forms of remedies can scarcely be said to be in use with us, though they are recognized as still existing, 1 W. & S. 438; 1 Br. 82; 17 S. & R. 344; 1 M. 46; 11 S. & R. 274, 290. Yet we arrive at the same results on motion, 8 S. & R. 235, and it is no just ground of complaint on the part of the plaintiff, at least, that the opening or setting aside of judgments is mere matter of discretion, and is not a subject of error, for neither would the granting of *audita querela*, and a stay of proceedings thereon, be a subject of error, though a judgment under that process would be so, and so is our action subsequent to opening or setting aside judgments. Defendants might complain of an unjust refusal to open a judgment and let in a defence, if they could not still use the *audita querela*, or writ of error in the same court. But I do not know why these may not still be used, though their use is very uncommon, owing to the liberal use of our much simpler practice of granting the relief on motion. 11 S. & R. 290; 1 R. 323.

Chancery grants relief by injunction to stay proceedings where it is shown that a judgment is satisfied or was procured by fraud; or where it is used to enforce payment of a penalty; or where it is tainted with anything contrary to public policy, if the defendant had no chance of making his defence at law; or wherever, by fraud, accident, mistake, or otherwise, the plaintiff has an unfair advantage which would make the court an instrument of injustice; and in these cases, *we* grant relief much more simply and beautifully on motion, by "the court laying its hands upon the action," (9 W. 94,) and preventing its execution, if in equity the party is entitled to relief.

The writ of error in the same court (*coram nobis* or *vobis*), lies to correct errors of fact, as that the party was under age, or coverture; or was dead at the time of the verdict or judgment; or for clerical errors in process; or errors in the execution of process. For all these cases we grant relief on motion.

The writ of *audita querela* lies for release, payment, or other discharge after verdict or judgment; where the sheriff or bail is made liable by judgment, and the principal debt is afterwards satisfied, or judgment reversed; where there are several judgments for the same claim and one is satisfied; where judgment is entered against a minor after two *nihils;* where a party has not been served with process; where no execution is issued on a forged statute merchant or staple (the judgment bond takes their place with us), or on a statute tainted with usury, or other matter contrary to public policy; or one that is connected with a satisfied defeasance; where payment is improperly obtained; to release from execution a discharged bankrupt; where a judgment is obtained in fraud of an existing agreement as to the conduct of the suit; where execution is improperly issued or erroneously executed, and where one whose lands are equally liable with the lands of another wishes to obtain contribution.—This is the English and American practice on *audita querela,* though it is now the almost universal practice to grant the same relief on motion. With us it is the only mode in use.

It must, therefore, be apparent that this is such a case as would be relieved anywhere in some form, and here it must be done on motion. I take pleasure in giving credit to the counsel for the heirs in this case, for having prosecuted their claims for relief by petition, and in a manner more than usually direct and lucid.

Then as to the acknowledgment of the sheriff's deed. In the case of Vaneman *v.* Cooper, this court decided that the mere fact of the acknowledgment of the deed without delivery, is not of itself sufficient to take away the power of the court to arrest an unjust use of its process; that the deed is still in the power of the court while it is in the hands of its officer; and I know not why the confirmation of a sale is not as open to subsequent objection before it is completely executed as other judgments. It is more summary than most of them. What has been said as to the opening and setting aside of judgments is sufficient to show that the fact of a term having passed is no valid objection.

But the parties are entitled to have the sale set aside on the doctrine of restitution alone. This arises whenever a party has lost anything by the process of the court, and that process is afterwards reversed or set aside. The rule is, that whenever it is in the power of the court to restore the specific thing lost, it will do it. If it cannot do this, it will do the best in its power. 2 S. & R. 58; Yelv. 179.

ORDER.—On hearing of the parties by their respective counsel, it is ordered, for the reasons appearing in the petition on which this proceeding is founded, that the judgment in this case be opened, on the heirs of Cornelia Stephens having their appearance entered by counsel, and that the sale of the land on the *lev. fa.* be set aside, the acknowledgment of the sheriff's deed rescinded, and the deed cancelled.

Note.—In order to obtain the sheriff's deed, E. W. Stephens afterwards filed a bill in equity to compel the sheriff to deliver the deed, on the ground that the court had no power to order its cancellation.—This bill was dismissed by the court, and the decree thereon was affirmed by the Supreme Court.

Equally interesting is the following case in the District Court of Philadelphia:—

Schott *v.* McFarland. Sur rule to show cause why execution should not be set aside, judgment opened, and defendants let into a defence.

Defendants asked to open a judgment entered on a bond given for the purchase-money of land in Mercer County sold to them in 1845, by deed, with general warranty from plaintiff's assignor, and gave in evidence that one Morrison, the original owner had in 1808 laid out a town upon the property, and sold 60 or 70 lots to purchasers, whose deeds were recorded. They also proved that parts of the property had been sold for taxes, as the property of these purchasers in 1848, when defendants had bought in many of the lots.

Mr. W. H. RAWLE, for the rule. 1. An outstanding title in third persons being a good defence in Pennsylvania to an action for the purchase-money (Withers *v.* Atkinson, 1 W. 248; Ludwig *v.* Huntzinger, 5 W. & S. 58), defendants are entitled to relief if they can here show what would constitute such a defence. They need not prove eviction. Hart *v.* Porter, 5 S. & R. 204; Share *v.* Anderson, 7 S. & R. 42, 61. As to the actual claim under the outstanding title, possession follows title in unseated lands as these are shown to be by the tax sales. Mather *v.* Trinity Church, 3 S. & R. 514; 8 Johns. 263; 9 Johns. 377; and the purchasers under provision are to be deemed in possession.

Defendants should not here be driven to this action on the warranty. Cresson *v.* Miller, 2 W. 272. The distinction between general and special warranty will not avail plaintiff. Lucas *v.* Wolbert, 10 Barr, 73.

Mr. PORTER, *contra.* There is no evidence of any one *actually claiming* title under Morrison's deed, and the authorities are express. Ludwig *v.* Huntzinger, 5 W. & S. 51; Bradford *v.* Potts, 9 Barr, 37; Lighty *v.* Sharb, 3 Pa. R. Defendants are actually in possession of the property, and how can they set up a legal presumptive possession in other persons? Besides, the record of the deeds to Morrison, was constructive notice to defendants.

Per curiam.—This is a judgment on bond and warrant, originally given by defendant to the Rev. Dr. Engles, as the consideration in part of a tract of land in Mercer County in this State. The defendant asks to be let into a defence on the ground of failure of consideration, that the title of the vendor to a part of the tract was not good.

It appears that one Joseph Morrison, who conveyed to Dr. Engles in 1845, had laid out, as early as 1808, a town, to be called *Shenango*, on a part of the premises, and made divers conveyances to persons of lots in the said town. The project fell through, no claim has ever been made by any of these persons, and indeed a large part of their title, good or bad, has been extinguished by the defendants suffering the ground to be sold for taxes accrued since the conveyance to them, thus vesting in them a paramount indisputable title. It was held in Ludwick v. Huntzinger (5 W. & S. 51), that, to rebut the presumption arising from acceptance of a deed and giving bond, it must be shown to constitute a defence to an action for the purchase-money, that the title is positively bad by proving a superior and indisputable title in another person *asserting such title.* The same law has been distinctly recognized in the later case of Bradford v. Potts (9 Barr, 37). Indeed, substituting the constructive notice in the present case by the recording of Morrison's deeds for the town lots, for the actual notice in Bradford v. Potts, the two cases are identical, for here the defendants had the precaution to require a covenant of general warranty. We may say, therefore, with the judge in Bradford v. Potts: "Here there was no covenant broken. The defendants accepted the title, and took their warranty with full knowledge of the alleged adverse title. They shall not detain the purchase-money when their possession has not been disturbed." Rule discharged.

After the above opinion was delivered, defendants' counsel presented a petition from them setting forth the above facts, and that there were "divers persons actually claiming title" to the property, and that defendants had been put to great expense in the purchase of some of these titles, and that others remained still outstanding in actual claimants, and asked for an *audita querela.*—*Per*

curiam. "Is not the writ said to be obsolete in 6 Barr? And can a party have it after application for summary relief on motion? But take the rule." Recognizance was entered to prosecute with effect.

March 23.—Mr. W. H. RAWLE, for the rule. In Curtis v. Slosson, 6 Barr, 267, the court, in saying that the writ of *audita querela* is not in use, meant no more than did TILGHMAN, C. J., in Harper v. Kean, 11 S. & R. 290, viz.: that it was not frequently resorted to. In the case preceding, he observed, that "if issued he presumed no lawyer would question its legality." The writ is more used now in England than it has been for many years prior to the present century. Though always recognized (Lord Porchester v. Petrie, reported in note to 2 Wms. Saund. 148), and as "a proper method and the most unexceptionable one," (4 Burr. 2287,) it had been seldom used, owing to the growing practice of giving relief on motion, 1 Lord Raym. 439; 2 Strange, 1075, &c., though even then, if the relief were questionable, the party was still turned to his *audita querela,* 1 Lord Raym. 439; 12 Mod. 584, 340. Of late, it has been more used. Giles v. Nathans, 5 Taunt. 558; Lister v. Mundell, 1 B. & P. 269; 2 Marsh, 37; Baker v. Ridgway, 2 Bing. 41, and 9 Moore, 114.

And one has been issued in 1847, in Giles v. Hutt, 1 Excheq. R. (Meeson, Welsby & Hurlstone), 59, 701.

The writ has been recognized and employed in

New York.—Wardell v. Eden, Coleman's Cases, 157; same case, 2 Johns. Cases, 258; Baker v. Judges of Ulster, 4 John. R. 191; Bowne v. Joy, 9 John. R. 221; Brooks v. Hunt, 17 John. R. 484; U. S. Bank v. Jenkins, 18 John. 305, &c.

Massachusetts.—Lovejoy v. Webber, 10 Mass. 103; Little v. The Bank, 14 Mass. 448; Bracket v. Winslow, 17 Mass. 159, &c.

Connecticut.—Lothrop v. Bennet, Kirby, 187; Luddington v. Peck, 2 Conn. 700; Hall v. Fitch, 1 Root. 151, &c.

Maine.—Byant v. Johnson, 24 Maine, 304.

Virginia.—Smock v. Dade, 5 Rand. 639.

South Carolina.—Longworth v. Screven, 2 Hill, 298.

Mississippi.—Hicks v. Murphy, Walk. 66; 7 How. Miss. 103.

In the *United States* Courts, Wilson v. Watson, Peters's C. C. R. 269, and in

Vermont, the Revised Statutes of 1839, cap. 37, expressly provide for it.

That the writ is *matter of right* is shown by all the authorities. See particularly Coleman's Cases, 157, per KENT, J., 1 M. W. & H. Exch. R. 701, &c.

An *audita querela* issued from this court in 1842. Another in 1845, and another in 1847.

(*Per curiam*.—We cannot consider this an open question, having issued such a writ from this court.)

The object of the writ, then, being to give the defendant a day in court, he cannot be deprived of that unless by laches. 2 Saund. 148, note. Granting relief on motion has grown into practice as *matter of convenience* to the defendant. An *audita querela* is as much matter of right at common law, as a bill of exceptions by statute, yet a part would never (in the absence of a previous rule of court such as formerly existed) be deemed to waive the latter by applying for a rule for a new trial.

The court may make a rule that they will not hear a motion to open a judgment unless a party waive his *audita querela*, but they cannot do so in a case before them. In the last case of *audita querela* here, a rule to open the judgment had been discharged.

Mr. PORTER, *contra*. Defendants' petition does not set forth the names of those now claiming title, nor how much is claimed, nor the amount of expenses incurred by defendants in purchasing the other outstanding titles. A *supersedeas* does not necessarily follow an *audita querela*, but is discretionary with the court, 1 Bac. Abr. 513. Nor should the writ be granted after a party has applied for summary relief on motion, Giles *v.* Nathans, Lister *v.* Mundell, Smock *v.* Dede, Longworth *v.* Screven, Wilson *v.* Watson, all cited on the other side.

Reply. The petition comprises everything required in Ludwig *v.* Huntzinger. By entering recognizance, a party is entitled to a *supersedeas*, Fitzh. Nat. Brev. 238. It is on a second *audita querela* after nonsuit of the first that there shall be no *supersedeas*. Com. Dig. Aud. Qu.

April 6. *Per curiam*.—The District Court which preceded the present organization of this court decided (though not, as we are informed, without great hesitation), that the writ of *audita querela* might be used in Pennsylvania, and also that it might be resorted to after an unsuccessful effort to obtain the summary interposition of the court on motion.

Were the question any longer *res integra*, we would now decide the latter point in the negative. Every consideration of equity and expediency requires, in our opinion, that the party should abide by his election. At least that where he has applied and been unsuccessful, he should not be entitled to a *supersedeas*. There is not wanting authority, or at least strong analogy for such a course even by the strict common law practice in *audita querela*. If the *audita querela* be founded on a deed, that deed must be proved in court before a *supersedeas* shall be granted. Langston *v.* Grant, 1 Salk. 92; 12 Mod. 105. So, the writ shall not be allowed, nor a *supersedeas* thereupon, unless the release, &c., upon which it is founded be proved by the witnesses present in court, 1 Sid. 351. And indeed it is laid down in a book of authority (Com. Dig. Aud. Qu. E. 5), that there shall be no *supersedeas* unless the *audita querela* be founded in writing. There is nothing inconsistent in refusing the *supersedeas*, for *audita querela* is an action in the nature of trespass; damages are given if the execution be without right (Com. Dig. Aud. Qu. A.) If the plaintiff in *audita querela* has judgment, he shall be restored to what he has lost. Brown *v.* Burnett, (1 Sid. 74), Anon.; 12 Mod. 598. But there can be no restitution, unless the money remains in the sheriff's hands (1 Kilb. 260, pl. 39). This court has followed, however, in the footsteps of their predecessors, and it is too late now to retrace. It is to be hoped that the Supreme Court will soon have the opportunity afforded them of deciding between conflicting opinions, and settle judiciously the law and practice upon this interesting subject.

There is one point, however, not heretofore decided except it may be *sub silentio*, and upon which, as it was not raised or argued in the case before us, we will not now express any opinion: that is, how far a mere equitable defence, such as would not be at all cognizable at law, as an answer to the cause of action, even if it arose before judgment, can be made the ground of an *audita querela*. There may be sound reasons for holding that this antiquated proceeding shall not be used for other causes than is strictly allowable in the English courts; and it is certain that, for such a ground as is set forth in the case before us, the party would be driven in England into chancery for relief.

We decide this case, however, upon the ground that the complaint is not sufficiently certain. It would be useless to issue the writ which must follow the complaint, if upon demurrer it would be held bad. In *audita querela*, on a defeasance of covenants in an indenture, the declarations should set out the covenants and show performance specially. Puttenham *v.* Puttenham, 3 Dy. 297, pl. 25. Now it seems to us that the complaint in this case does not set forth with sufficient certainty the alleged equitable ground for the writ. It does not state any one person in particular who claims the land in question, nor does it specify with certainty what part is so claimed. These are matters which lie in the complainant's knowledge, and he ought to state them. Rule discharged.

The petition in this case, which is drawn with great care, is annexed as a precedent.

In the District Court for the City and County of Philadelphia. The suggestion, petition, and grievous complaint of James M'Farland and John S. King showeth and giveth the court here to understand, that on the tenth day of January, A. D. 1845, William M. Engles and Charlotte S. his wife, by indenture of that date, conveyed to said James M'Farland and John S. King, a certain tract of land in the County of Mercer, and State of Pennsylvania, therein particularly described, containing five hundred acres with the usual allowance, &c., for the consideration of the sum of five thousand dollars; that said James M'Farland and John S. King, on the day and year aforesaid, executed their certain bond (accompanied with a mortgage on said premises), in the penal sum of ten thousand dollars, conditioned for the payment of one thousand dollars at the time of the execution thereof, and the residue of four thousand dollars with interest thereon, in four years from the date thereof, and that the said James M'Farland and John S. King paid the said sum of one thousand dollars. That before and at the time of the execution of said indenture and bond and mortgage, the said James M'Farland and John S. King were given by said Engles to understand and believe, and verily did understand and believe, that said Engles was seized in his demesne as of fee, of all the premises described in said indenture. That the said James M'Farland and John S. King, since the execution of said indenture and bond and mortgage, have discovered that there was at the time of the execution thereof a superior

and indisputable outstanding title to a large and valuable part of said premises so purported to be conveyed as aforesaid, then subsisting in divers persons actually claiming title thereto, to wit, by virtue of divers deeds executed to them by Joseph Morrison, the owner of said premises, prior to the alleged vesting of said pretended title in said Engles; and that the said James M'Farland and John S. King have since been put to great expense in the purchase of some of said outstanding titles, and that other of said titles are still in divers persons actually claiming under them. That said Engles did commence proceedings by writ of *scire facias* on said mortgage in Mercer County, against the said James M'Farland and John S. King; but on learning the nature and extent of the defence thereto, said proceedings have been discontinued.

That judgment has been entered on a warrant of attorney accompanying said bond, against said James M'Farland and John S. King, in the said District Court to March Term, 1849, and a writ of *fieri facias* issued thereon, and a *testatum* writ of *fieri facias* issued to Mercer County. And although by virtue of the premises, the said James M'Farland and John S. King were entitled to require the further execution of said writ of *fieri facias* to be stayed, and that no further proceeding should be had thereon, as the said James M'Farland and John S. King are by proper ways and means ready to make manifest, nevertheless one William Schott, purporting to be assignee of said Engles (which said Schott had caused judgment to be entered and execution issued as aforesaid), not regarding the premises aforesaid, but continuing unjustly to oppress the said James M'Farland and John S. King by reason of the judgment aforesaid, as aforesaid entered, hath directed the sheriff of Mercer County to proceed under color and pretence of said writ of *testatum fieri facias*, and levy upon the premises aforesaid, and make of said lands and tenements the amount for which judgment has been entered as aforesaid, with interest and costs of suit, refuses to cause proceedings to be stayed upon said suit, and endeavors unjustly to cause the premises aforesaid to be sold by color and pretence thereof, to the great and manifest damage and grievance of the said James M'Farland and John S. King; wherefore they humbly implore this honorable court to grant them proper remedy in this behalf, by allowing them to have a writ of *audita querela* upon the premises against the said Schott, assignee of said Engles. And the said James M'Farland and John S. King are willing, and hereby offer to give and justify good and sufficient bail by two sureties according to law in this behalf. And they pray your honorable court that their complaint in this behalf being heard, the said Schott, assignee aforesaid, may be called before you, and the reasons of the parties being heard that you may cause full and speedy justice to be done to the said James M'Farland and John S. King, as of right and according to the laws and custom of the commonwealth shall be proper and just to be done.

And the said James M'Farland and John S. King, as in duty bound, will ever pray. JAMES M'FARLAND, JOHN S. KING.

END OF VOL. I.